T0180727

Lecture Notes of the Institute for Computer Sciences, Social Informatics and Telecommunications Engineering 419

More information about this series at https://link.springer.com/bookseries/8197

Takahiro Hara · Hirozumi Yamaguchi (Eds.)

Mobile and Ubiquitous Systems: Computing, Networking and Services

18th EAI International Conference, MobiQuitous 2021
Virtual Event, November 8–11, 2021
Proceedings

 Springer

Editors
Takahiro Hara
Osaka University
Osaka, Japan

Hirozumi Yamaguchi ⓘ
Osaka University
Osaka, Japan

ISSN 1867-8211   ISSN 1867-822X   (electronic)
Lecture Notes of the Institute for Computer Sciences, Social Informatics
and Telecommunications Engineering
ISBN 978-3-030-94821-4   ISBN 978-3-030-94822-1   (eBook)
https://doi.org/10.1007/978-3-030-94822-1

This Springer imprint is published by the registered company Springer Nature Switzerland AG
The registered company address is: Gewerbestrasse 11, 6330 Cham, Switzerland

Preface

We are delighted to introduce the proceedings of the eighteenth edition of the European Alliance for Innovation (EAI) International Conference on Mobile and Ubiquitous Systems: Computing, Networking and Services (MobiQuitous 2021). Despite the considerable research effort in the area of mobile and ubiquitous computing over nearly two decades, and the maturity of some of its base technologies, many challenges persist. The goal of this conference series is to provide a forum for presenting and discussing high-quality research in the field, involving international practitioners and researchers from diverse backgrounds. Areas addressed by MobiQuitous include systems, applications, social networks, middleware, networking, sensing, data management, data processing, and services, all with special focus on mobile and ubiquitous computing.

The technical program of Mobiquitous 2021 consisted of 26 full papers, selected from 79 submitted papers, in oral presentation sessions at the main conference track. The acceptance rate was 33%. Aside from the high-quality technical paper presentations, the technical program also featured two keynote speeches, one industrial session, one poster and demo session, and four technical workshops. The two keynote speeches were given by Chieko Asakawa (IBM Fellow/Chief Executive Director of the National Museum of Emerging Science and Innovation (Miraikan, Japan) and Claudio Bettini (University of Milan, Italy). The industrial session included two invited speeches by Chihiro Ono (KDDI Research, Inc., Japan) and Kota Tsubouchi (Yahoo! Japan Corporation, Japan). The poster and demo session consisted of 11 presentations.

The four workshops organized were the First Workshop on Ubiquitous and Multi-domain User Modeling (UMUM 2021), the First International Workshop on Smart Society Technologies (IWSST 2021), the Fourth International Workshop on Mobile Ubiquitous Systems, Infrastructures, Communications and AppLications (MUSICAL 2021 Fall) and the Workshop on Innovative Technologies for the Healthcare Empowerment (InnovTech4Health). The UMUM 2021 workshop aimed to address how to build ubiquitous and multi-domain user models and increase their applicability in real-world contexts. The IWSST 2021 workshop aimed to discuss technologies and applications that solve relevant problems in modern society. The MUSICAL 2021 Fall workshop aimed to discuss technologies related to future mobile ubiquitous systems. The InnovTech4Health workshop focused on the development of information and communication technologies for wellbeing.

Coordination with the steering chair, Imrich Chlamtac, was essential for the success of the conference. We sincerely appreciate his constant support and guidance. It was also a great pleasure to work with such an excellent organizing committee team for their hard work in organizing and supporting the conference. In particular, we are grateful to the Technical Program Committee who completed the peer-review process for technical papers and helped to put together a high-quality technical program. We are also grateful to the conference manager, Karolina Marcinova, for her support and all the authors who submitted their papers to the MobiQuitous 2021 conference and workshops.

We strongly believe that MobiQuitous provides a good forum for all researchers, developers, and practitioners to discuss current and future research directions of mobile and ubiquitous computing. We also expect that the future MobiQuitous conferences will be as successful and stimulating as this year's, as indicated by the contributions presented in this volume.

November 2021

Takahiro Hara
Hirozumi Yamaguchi
Takuya Maekawa
Stephan Sigg
Vaskar Raychoudhury

Conference Organization

Steering Committee

Imrich Chlamtac   University of Trento, Italy

Organizing Committee

General Chairs

Takahiro Hara   Osaka University, Japan
Hirozumi Yamaguchi   Osaka University, Japan

Technical Program Committee Chairs

Takuya Maekawa   Osaka University, Japan
Stephan Sigg   Aalto University, Finland
Vaskar Raychoudhury   Miami University, USA

Local Chairs

Shigemi Ishida   Kyushu University, Japan
Tetsuya Shigeyasu   Prefectural University of Hiroshima, Japan

Sponsorship and Exhibits Chair

Susumu Ishihara   Shizuoka University, Japan

Workshops Chairs

Takuya Yoshihiro   Wakayama University, Japan
Janick Edinger   University of Mannheim, Germany
Md Osman Gani   Miami University, USA

Publicity and Social Media Chairs

Keiichi Yasumoto   NAIST, Japan
Stephan Haller   Bern University of Applied Sciences, Switzerland

Publications Chair

Akira Uchiyama   Osaka University, Japan

Web Chair

Hiroki Yoshikawa   Osaka University, Japan

Posters and Demos Chairs

Yutaka Arakawa   Kyushu University, Japan
JeongGil Ko   Yonsei University, Japan

Industry Track Chair

Atsushi Tagami   KDDI Research, Japan

Financial Chair

Akimitsu Kanzaki   Shimane University, Japan

Award Committee Chair

Hiroshi Shigeno   Keio University, Japan

Student Volunteer Chair

Teruhiro Mizumoto   Osaka University, Japan

Technical Program Committee

Michele Albano   Aalborg University, Finland
Kenichi Arai   Nagasaki University, Japan
Yutaka Arakawa   Kyushu University, Japan
Christian Becker   University of Mannheim, Germany
Michael Beigl   Karlsruhe Institute of Technology, Germany
Paolo Bellavista   University of Bologna, Germany
Saadi Boudjit   Paris University 13, France
Beenish Chaudhry   University of Louisiana at Lafayette, USA
Jingyuan Cheng   University of Science and Technology of China, China
Gabriele Civitarese   University of Milan, Italy
Luca Davoli   University of Parma, Italy
Pari Delir Haghighi   Monash University, Australia
Shi Dianxi   National University of Defense Technology, China
Andrzej Duda   Grenoble Institute of Technology, France
Yu Enokibori   Nagoya University, Japan

Viktor Erdelyi	Osaka University, Japan
Paulo Ferreira	University of Oslo, Norway
Stefan Fischer	University of Lübeck, Germany
Kary Främling	Aalto University, Finland
Chris Gniady	University of Arizona, USA
Bin Guo	Northwestern Polytechnical University, China
Alireza Hassani	Deakin University, Australia
Peizhao Hu	Rochester Institute of Technology, USA
Sozo Inoue	Kyushu Institute of Technology, Japan
Shigemi Ishida	Future University Hakodate, Japan
Susumu Ishihara	Shizuoka University, Japan
Naoya Isoyama	Kobe University, Japan
Beihong Jin	Institute of Software, Chinese Academy of Sciences, China
Akimitsu Kanzaki	Shimane University, Japan
Nobuo Kawaguchi	Nagoya University, Japan
Fahim Khan	University of Tokyo, Japan
Yasue Kishino	NTT, Japan
Yoji Kiyota	LIFULL Co., Ltd., Japan
Quan Kong	Hitachi, Ltd., Japan
Matthias Kranz	University of Passau, Germany
Satoshi Kurihara	Keio University, Japan
Brent Lagesse	University of Washington Bothell, USA
Philippe Lalanda	Joseph Fourier University, France
Spyros Lalis	University of Thessaly, Greece
Guohao Lan	Duke University, USA
Dongman Lee	KAIST, South Korea
Uichin Lee	KAIST, South Korea
Seng Loke	Deakin University, Australia
Takuya Maekawa	Osaka University, Japan
A. K. M. Jahangir Majumder	University of South Carolina Upstate, USA
Gustavo Marfia	University of Bologna, Italy
Chulhong Min	Nokia Bell Labs, USA
Sajib Mistry	Curtin University, Perth, Australia
Teruhiro Mizumoto	Osaka University, Japan
Kazuya Murao	Ritsumeikan University, Japan
Kazuya Ohara	NTT Communication Science Laboratories, Japan
Ren Ohmura	Toyohashi University of Technology, Japan
Tadashi Okoshi	Keio University, Japan
Santi Phithakkitnukoon	Chiang Mai University, Thailand
Vaskar Raychoudhury	Miami University, USA
Hamada Rizk	Osaka University, Japan/Tanta University, Egypt
Kay Roemer	TU Graz, Austria
George Roussos	Birkbeck, University of London, UK
Navrati Saxena	San Jose State University, USA

Bastian Schäfermeier	University of Kassel, Germany
Sougata Sen	BITS Pilani, Goa, India
Arash Shaghaghi	UNSW Sydney, Australia
Hiroshi Shigeno	Keio University, Japan
Tetsuya Shigeyasu	Prefectural University of Hiroshima, Japan
Atsushi Shimada	Kyushu University, Japan
Stephan Sigg	Aalto University, Finland
Witawas Srisa-an	University of Nebraska-Lincoln, USA
Yasuyuki Sumi	Future University Hakodate, Japan
Chiu Tan	Temple University, Japan
Akihito Taya	Aoyama Gakuin University, Japan
Tsutomu Terada	Kobe University, Japan
Akira Uchiyama	Osaka University, Japan
Hiroki Watanabe	Hokkaido University, Japan
Lars Wolf	TU Braunschweig, Germany
Weitao Xu	City University of Hong Kong, Hong Kong
Keiichi Yasumoto	Nara Institute of Science and Technology, Japan
Hiroyuki Yomo	Kansai University, Japan
Kristina Yordanova	University of Rostock, Germany
Takuya Yoshihiro	Wakayama University, Japan
Yanmin Zhu	Shanghai Jiao Tong University, China

Contents

**The First Workshop on Ubiquitous and Multi-domain
User Modeling (UMUM2021)**

**The First International Workshop on Smart Society
Technologies (IWSST2021)**

**The Fourth International Workshop on Mobile Ubiquitous Systems,
Infrastructures, Communications and AppLications
(MUSICAL 2021 Fall)**

**Innovative Technologies for the Healthcare Empowerment
(InnovTech4Health)**

Short Papers

MobiQuitous 2021

Event Detection and Event-Relevant Tweet Extraction with Human Mobility

Naoto Takeda[✉], Daisuke Kamisaka, Roberto Legaspi, Yutaro Mishima, and Atsunori Minamikawa

KDDI Research, Inc., Fujimino-shi, Saitama 356-8502, Japan
{no-takeda,da-kamisaka,ro-legaspi,yu-mishima,
at-minamikawa}@kddi-research.jp

Abstract. Event detection has been proved important in various applications, such as route selection to avoid the congestion an event causes or deciding whether to join an event that one is interested in. While geotagged tweets are popular sources of information for event detection, they are usually insufficient for accurate detection when scarce. On the other hand, non-geotagged tweets are more abundant, but include much noise that also deters accurate event detection. In this work, we aimed to enhance detection performance by combining aggregated smartphone GPS data and non-geotagged tweets. We propose a novel method to detect events based on deviations from inferred normal human mobility, selecting event-related topics that correlated with human mobility, and extracting event-relevant tweets by scoring each tweet according to its relevance to an event. The relevance of each tweet is gauged from the tweet's meaning and posting time. We conducted empirical evaluations using data that include multiple events, such as baseball game and airport congestion. Our proposed method detected 9 out of 10 events regardless of the type and scale of the events, which attests improvement over the geotag-based method. We also confirmed that our model was able to extract the essential event-relevant tweets with an average accuracy of over 90%.

Keywords: Event detection · Congestion detection · Topic extraction · Tweet extraction · Human mobility

1 Introduction

Event detection leverages changes in crowd density in a given location to detect crowd events [8,18,30]. An event is defined as "something that happens at specific time and place with consequence" [3], e.g., a festival or a train accident. These events have the potential to cause congestion, i.e., high crowd density, [14] (hereafter, "events" are limited to those that cause congestion). With event detection, it is important to grasp what is occurring [33] independent of event type, i.e., scheduled or unscheduled, as well as event scale, i.e., large or small,

T. Hara and H. Yamaguchi (Eds.): MobiQuitous 2021, LNICST 419, pp. 3–23, 2022.
https://doi.org/10.1007/978-3-030-94822-1_1

for people to act efficiently and appropriately, such as to avoid congestion or participate if they are interested. For instance, if a person notices that there is a congestion of people at a certain station due to a train accident (unscheduled event), he will take another station. Or, if somebody is sightseeing and notices congestion in the vicinity due to a festival (scheduled event), she might decide to join the festivities. Currently more compelling is during the COVID-19 pandemic in which there is increasing demand to detect an event that is accompanied by increasing crowd size to prevent a potential superspreader event from growing.

Research on event detection has garnered wide interest in recent years, especially at this age where social media have become ubiquitous. Twitter is one of the most frequently used data sources for event detection due to its immediacy. Most studies relied on geotagged tweets to identify locations [16,31,37,38] and to extract tweets that helped people understand the events in detail (i.e., event-relevant tweets). However, the number of geotagged tweets is usually very small (0.9% of all tweets [7,23]), which is decreasing even further in recent years [17]. On the other hand, while non-geotagged tweets are abundant in number, they also pose a challenge since they are accompanied by considerable noise, i.e., event-irrelevant tweets. As alternative, human mobility data aggregated from smartphone GPS readings is often used to detect congestion occurring in cities. Several studies that used human mobility data identified locations where congestion is occurring in a city by focusing on anomalies, i.e., abnormal concentration of population density in grid cells [14,27]. Human mobility can be represented as time series data indicative of the increase or decrease in population per grid cell for each timeslot by computing the unique users from GPS readings [14,27,28]. Utilizing these GPS-based methods is one solution to detecting the event that caused congestion. However, such human mobility data does not include information on the cause of events, such as traffic accidents, daily rush hours, or population concentration caused by a major festival. Lastly, supervised and unsupervised approaches in machine learning have been proposed, albeit both present significant limitations. Notably, while supervised approaches demand a lot of manual annotations [4,9,15], unsupervised approaches require manual inspection to discover the event-relevant tweets [1].

To address the challenges above, we propose an unsupervised event detection approach that is agnostic to event type and scale, and employs human mobility data aggregated from smart phone GPS readings. Further, we also propose an accompanying event-relevant tweet extraction method using non-geotagged tweets. The details are as follows.

(1) **Event detection:** To detect events, we infer normal human mobility pattern for each grid cell using past human mobility data, and we compute an anomaly score that represents the difference between the inferred normal mobility and the present mobility per grid cell. Our method detects an event when the anomaly score exceeds a predefined threshold that is indicative of the intensity of congestion.

(2) **Event-relevant tweet extraction:** Also in this study, event-relevant tweets are extracted as information for understanding an occurring event. Our

method extracts event-relevant tweets from noisy non-geotagged tweets in three steps. First, our method collects tweets only if they include the POI (point of interest) name that is associated to the grid cell in which the event is detected. Second, our method vectorizes the each tweet and clusters tweets with similar topics, and then selects the event-related cluster based on the correlation between human mobility and topic transitions of the cluster. Finally, our method extracts event-relevant tweets based on three scores, which focus on (a) the topic of the tweet, (b) coupling of the tweet's posting time and human mobility, and (c) coupling of the tweet's posting time and event-related topic transitions.

By tracking human mobility, our method can anticipate crowd congestion. To our knowledge, there has yet to be a method for detecting a congestion event while at the same time providing related information about such event. Our contributions are threefold:

- a framework for detecting an event and extracting event-relevant tweets that were not geotagged;
- an unsupervised event-relevant tweet extraction method from non-geotagged and unannotated tweets based on correlations between topic transitions in the tweets and human mobility transitions; and
- use of real-world datasets to evaluate and validate our method above that can detect events independent of event type and scale, as well as extract essential tweets related to the events.

2   Related Work

In this research, we tackle the problem of event detection from smartphone GPS readings, and the extraction of informative event-relevant tweets that can help people understand an event. We first describe in this section the existing, pertinent event detection research works. Afterwards, we describe existing research on event-relevant tweet extraction.

2.1   Event Detection

A simple and intuitive approach to detecting events is to use installed monitoring hardware. For instance, several studies have used surveillance cameras to detect congestion [22, 39]. However, in general, not all facilities and streets are equipped with cameras, only some of the relatively lager facilities. Therefore, such an approach cannot detect events in as many places as possible, especially those small but perhaps crucial events that may happen in small facilities. Other event detection methods related to commuting and transportation have been proposed using railroad smart card history [35] and bus trajectories [21]. These methods can capture unscheduled events such as train delays and road accidents. However, they also rely heavily on specific domain data. For example, with a railroad smart card history [35], only train station (domain) related data, e.g., sudden increase in the number of people in a station (due to train accident), can be detected as an event. Thus, there is a limit to the types of events that can be captured. Our aim is to detect events occurring in a city independent of domain, event type (scheduled or unscheduled) and scale. Hence, less constraining data sources and methods are needed.

Twitter, one of the most popular social networking platforms today, is a promising source of data for detecting various types of events in varying scale. Many studies on event detection have focused on the burst, i.e., drastic increase in volume, of event-related keywords in the Twitter stream [5,10,11,25,32]. However, keyword burst may not always be indicative of a congestion. Tweets also burst when, say, a well-known celebrity dies or a grave disaster occurs in another country, which are instances where observers of the event do not necessarily concentrate physically in the same place. These methods therefore may not shed light on whether an event is causing real-world congestion. Some event detection studies have leveraged geotagged tweets, which include location data of where the tweets were posted, to identify the location of an event where there is concentration of people [16,31,37,38]. However, only 0.9% of all tweets are geotagged [7,23]. Moreover, the number of geotagged tweets decreased since June 2019 when geotagging options were removed [17]. Obviously, geotag-based methods could no longer detect events when no geotagged tweets are posted.

Smartphone GPS is a city-level and situation-agnostic (no information about the situation is provided) data source that has also recently garnered attention. Smartphone GPS data are often collected via applications installed with user permission [34], and it is possible to capture human mobility as an increase or decrease in population by counting the number of unique users per grid cell in each timeslot. Coinciding with this development is anomaly detection using human mobility that is also getting the attention of the research community [14,27,28]. For instance, Neumann et al. [28] proposed a method that uses a day's data of human mobility as a feature to classify whether the day is special (e.g., December 24 or long weekends) or not by computing how much human mobility on that day deviated from normal. However, a day's worth of data (24 h) is needed before classification can be achieved, which makes real-time event detection difficult. The research works of Fuse et al. [14] and Mishima et al. [27] are similar in that they detect anomalies emerging from grid cells in real time. Fuse et al. [14] classified whether an anomaly occurred or not using a sticky hierarchical Dirichlet process - hidden Markov model (sHDP-HMM). Fuse et al.'s approach learns the latent state and hyperparameters of the training data that represent the normal state, and the sHDP-HMM infers the latent state of the test data with the learned hyperparameters. It compares the normal state and the latent state of the test data, and detects an anomaly if they are unequal. Mishima et al. [27] computed for an anomaly score that indicates the difference from normal human mobility volume per grid cell, where this normalcy is inferred using past human mobility data. An anomaly is detected when the anomaly score exceeds a predefined threshold value. Both approaches, Fuse et al. and Mishima et al., albeit promising for detecting events that have caused congestion, only tested in their experiments train accidents, typhoons, and New

Year's holidays, and there is no sufficient verification regarding event type and scale. In addition, Fuse et al.'s approach was necessary to manually define one day of normal human mobility as training data per grid cell, while Mishima et al.'s approach automatically estimates normal human mobility from multiple days. To avoid overfitting of training data and to automatically estimate normal human mobility for a large number of grid cells, we applied Mishima et al.'s approach to event detection for a variety of event types and scales, and verified its limitations.

Note that since GPS-based event detection does not provide information to people on what kind of event is occurring, we need to extract such missing information from event-relevant tweets (see below).

2.2   Understanding Events with Event-Relevant Tweets

To understand an event in detail, one solution is to extract tweets that provide a lot of information describing the event (e.g., posts by users who are enjoying a festival or news about a train accident), hence, the event-relevant tweets. In recent years, several studies have been conducted to extract event-relevant tweets. There are those that have used supervised learning, with labeled tweets as training data, to classify whether each tweet is event-relevant or not [4,9,15]. For example, Chen et al. [9] used the CBOW model to embed tweets and classified them into traffic-relevant and traffic-irrelevant tweets using CNN and LSTM. These studies require manual annotations of the collected tweets, which is expensive and not scalable. It becomes insurmountable for this methods to detect all events while being non-cognizant of event type or scale since with more types and varying sizes of events are more annotated training data needed.

There are also research works on event-relevant tweet extraction using unsupervised learning. Ahmed et al. [1], for example, extracted event-relevant tweets by clustering tweets that contained event-related words (e.g., for traffic events, "traffic" and "accident"). Specifically, tweets were vectorized using TF-IDF and k-means. The event-related clusters were manually discovered from among clusters, and tweets that belonged to these clusters were considered event-relevant tweets. However, manual cluster discovery, manual setting of event-related words, and manual setting of an appropriate number of clusters are required, are nontrivial, and needless to say, laborious.

Our work, on the other hand, focuses on the correlation between human mobility and tweet topic transition. Our method automatically selects topics and their essential tweets relevant to the event without necessitating manual annotation and geotagged tweets. We elucidate our method in the next section.

3   Proposed Method

We now describe our approach for detecting events and extracting event-relevant tweets. Figure 1 shows the framework of our approach. First, our method detects an event in a grid cell, which indicates a higher than normal concentration of

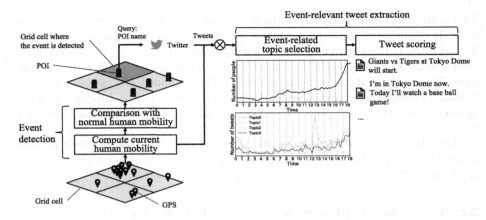

Fig. 1. Framework of our approach

human mobility in that location, by calculating from GPS data the number of unique users in a grid cell. Next, our method extracts event-relevant tweets useful for understanding what is occurring in the event using the POI names associated to grid cell where the event is detected. To extract event-relevant tweets regardless of event types and scales, event-related topics that correlate with human mobility are selected and three scores are computed for each tweet considering the tweet's meaning and the posting time. We detail these below.

3.1 Event Detection from Smartphone GPS Data

We adopted the approach of Mishima and colleagues [27] for event detection. We use smartphone GPS data that consists of a timestamp, latitude and longitude to compute for human mobility. The basic idea is to infer what a *normal* human mobility per grid cell is using past human mobility data, and then to compute an anomaly score based on how the magnitude of the current human mobility deviates from the inferred normal human mobility. Our method detects an event for each timeslot (i.e., a unit of time in which the population in a grid cell is aggregated using GPS) when the anomaly score exceeds a predefined threshold value.

The method of Mishima et al. [27] infers normal human mobility for each grid cell, as well as day-group, i.e., the characteristics of each day (e.g., weekday, weekend/holiday, or first day of a consecutive holiday) because human mobility trends are different between weekdays and weekends. First, the method divides the smartphone GPS data to each grid cell and day-group according to latitude, longitude, and timestamp, and computes human mobility transitions, where human mobility is the number of unique users in a grid cell. Hereafter, event detection for a single grid cell c is described and the same process is applied to all grid cells. The human mobility dataset V is the number of unique users per each day-group and per each timeslot, and is represented as: $V \in \mathbb{R}^{N_g, N_t}$, where

N_g is the number of day-groups defined, N_t is the number of timeslots per day (e.g., 96 if the time interval is 15 min). It then clusters the human mobility data for each day-group and computes the average of human mobility for each cluster. The clustering is performed for each combination of day-group g to obtain clusters $\boldsymbol{CL}_g$, represented as: $\boldsymbol{CL}_g = \{\boldsymbol{cl}_{g,i} \mid i = 1, 2, \ldots, K\} = \text{kmeans}(\boldsymbol{v}_g \in \boldsymbol{V}, K)$, where $\boldsymbol{cl}_{g,i}$ is the i-th cluster, $\boldsymbol{v}_g$ is N_t-dimensional human mobility and K is a parameter indicating the number of clusters. The cluster with high human mobility is not suited to indicate normal human mobility because it may contain days when anomalies occurred. Thus, the average of each timeslot of human mobility is computed for each cluster, and the cluster with the smallest sum of these values is selected as the normalcy baseline in each grid cell. The cluster which represents the normal human mobility $\boldsymbol{cl}_{g,i^*}$ is selected as the minimum sum of all N_t-dimensional volumes (i.e., the number of unique users for each time slot) as follows:

$$cl_{g,i^*} = \underset{i \in \{1,\ldots,K\}}{\arg \min} \sum_{t=1}^{N_t} \mu_{i,t}, \tag{1}$$

where μ_i is the mean vector of human mobility in cluster $\boldsymbol{cl}_{g,i}$. The normal human mobility is defined as the mean and standard deviation of $\boldsymbol{cl}_{g,i^*}$, i.e., $\boldsymbol{\mu}_{g,i^*} = \{\mu_{g,i^*,t} \mid t = 1, 2, \ldots, N_t\}$, $\boldsymbol{\sigma}_{g,i^*} = \{\sigma_{g,i^*,t} \mid t = 1, 2, \ldots, N_t\}$. From here we derive the anomaly score $A_{g,t}$ for current state of human mobility $v_{g,t}$ as the z-score, that is,

$$A_{g,t} = \frac{v_{g,t} - \mu_{g,i^*,t}}{\sigma_{g,i^*,t}}. \tag{2}$$

The following then becomes the function for detecting an event:

$$\text{IsEvent}(A_{g,t}) = \begin{cases} \text{true,} & \text{if } A_{g,t} > \phi \\ \text{false,} & \text{otherwise.} \end{cases} \tag{3}$$

where ϕ is the predefined threshold value. As an example, with the process above, event detection is performed every 15 min across the 250 m × 250 m grid cells throughout the city.

3.2   Event-Relevant Tweet Extraction

Our method extracts event-relevant tweets in three steps: tweet collection with POI names, event-related topic selection, and tweet scoring. First, it collects tweets containing POI names related to grid cells triggered by the event detection. We constructed in advance a grid cell-POI database that directly associates the grid cells to the POI names they contain. This database is automatically created from an open dataset containing the POI names, latitudes, and longitudes. For example, the open dataset includes POI names for sports facilities such as "Tokyo Dome (a stadium in Japan)", train stations such as "Shibuya Station (a train station in Japan)", theaters, parks, airports, and schools. We represent the grid cell-POI database as P, where P_c denotes the multiple POI names contained in grid cell c. When an anomaly is detected in grid cell c at time slot t_e, tweets that include POI names from that cell are extracted, i.e., $TW_c = \{tw_t \mid p_c \in P_c, 1 \leq t \leq t_e\}$. Tweets tw_t are tweets posted at timeslot t. Obviously, here, tweets posted only before the event detection time are used. Note, however, that even if we collect tweets that include the POI names, they could still include considerable amount of tweets that are not event-relevant. Hereafter, we omit the subscript c to describe the event-relevant tweet extraction for a single grid cell c.

Next, our method performs clustering on TW based on semantics, i.e., feature vectors to select a cluster that has the highest relevance to the event, i.e., event-related topic. Each tweet is vectorized with a pretrained BERT (Bidirectional Encoder Representations from Transformers) model [12] to learn the representation of semantic distance between tweets. BERT is a Transformer-based language representation model that can vectorize sentences in a context-aware manner. BERT encodes TW into feature vectors $F = \{f_i \mid i = 1, 2, \ldots, N\}$, where f_i is the average feature vector of all words included in a tweet and represents the meaning of tw_i, i.e., $f_i = \frac{1}{M} \sum_{j=1}^{M} \text{BERT}(w_j \in W)$, where $W = \{w_j \mid w_j \in tw_i, j = 1, 2, \ldots, M\}$ and M is the number of words in tw_i. Afterwards, we apply k-means clustering to segregate the tweets into some topics towards extracting an event-related topic. Tweet topics TP are extracted by k-means using $TP = \{tp_i \mid i = 1, 2, \ldots, L\} = \text{kmeans}(F, L)$. There are efforts to vectorize documents (or words) with BERT and cluster similar meanings with k-means, and the effectiveness of these efforts have been verified [19, 26]. However, methods for automatically determining the number of clusters have not been sufficiently explored. Thus, in our study, to discover the optimal number of clusters L^*, we increment L in sequence and evaluate the clustering result for each L based on the correlation of time series changes between human mobility and topic transitions. A topic transition is a time series of the number of tweets in each topic for each timeslot (Fig. 2(a)). Topic transition for a tp_i is represented as $TV_i = \{|tw_t| \mid tw_t \in TW, 1 \leq t \leq t_e\}$. Considering that topics appearing in tweets are mostly independent, only event-related topics are expected to be highly correlated with human mobility (Fig. 2(b)). When human mobility data is $V = \{v_t \in V \mid 1 \leq t \leq t_e\}$ and event-related topic is $(tp_o \in TP)$, our assumption is $TV_o \propto V$. We compute the correlation and independence score (CI) for each L. CI_L is computed using the following:

$$CI_L = \frac{\max_{1 \leq i \leq L} \left\{ \dfrac{\text{cov}\,(TV_i, V)}{\sigma\,(TV_i)\,\sigma\,(V)} \right\}}{\max_{i \neq j} \left\{ \dfrac{\text{cov}\,(TV_i, TV_j)}{\sigma\,(TV_i)\,\sigma\,(TV_j)} \right\}}, \tag{4}$$

$$L^* = \arg \max_{L} CI_L, \tag{5}$$

where $\sigma(TV_i)$ is the standard deviation of TV_i, and $\text{cov}(TV_i, TV_j)$ is the covariance of TV_i and TV_j. The denominator in Eq. (4) indicates the highest correla-

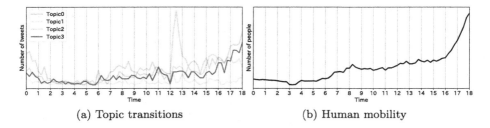

(a) Topic transitions (b) Human mobility

Fig. 2. Topic transitions and human mobility in a grid cell with an anomaly caused at 18:00. Topic 3 is selected as event-related topic because of its high correlation with human mobility.

tion value between topics (a low value indicates that the topics are independent of each other), and the numerator indicates the highest correlation value between human mobility transition and each topic transition (a high value indicates that the topic correlated with human mobility is included). Thus, if the CI_L is high, the clustering result indicates that the topics are independent of each other and contain topics that are highly correlated with human mobility transition. Ultimately, we adopt the value of L that maximizes CI_L as the optimal value L^*. We select the topic tp_o that has the maximum correlation with human mobility as an event-related topic containing the event-relevant tweets when the number of clusters is L^*. Figure 2(a) shows an example of extracted topics, with $L^* = 4$, from a grid cell with a detected event. The correlations between human mobility (Fig. 2(b)) and Topic 0 to 3 were 0.64, 0.37, 0.77, and 0.86, respectively. Thus, our approach selected Topic 3 (red line in Fig. 2(a)) as an event-related topic tp_o. Although there is a burst of tweets in Topic 0 (blue line in Fig. 2(a)) at 12:30 due to an announcement of a future event, our approach successfully identified it as the topic that was not related to the event. Our method can therefore eliminate such noisy topic.

Finally, we scored each tweet to extract those that are especially relevant to the event from the plethora of tweets that belong to tp_o. The top scoring tweets allow the user to understand what is occurring in the grid cell where the event is detected. To extract the event-relevant tweets, we focus not only on the meaning of the tweets, but also tweet posting time because such tweets are frequently posted at relevant times, such as during or just before the event. We consider the time when event-relevant tweets are likely to be posted depends on the event type. For example, during a festival, tweets from people enjoying the festival are posted while the festival is on-going, i.e., when the human mobility volume is high. On the other hand, during a live concert, people do not tweet while watching, instead, so many tweets are posted just before the concert starts i.e., when event-related topics are frequently posted (they are posted after the event as well, but we need to extract tweets at the event detection time, such as before the event starts or during the event). Thus, to extract event-relevant tweets, we defined three different weighting schemes based on three hypotheses.

I. Event-relevant tweets are located close in the feature space to the average feature vector of tweets belonging to event-related topic.
II. Event-relevant tweets are more likely to be posted during times when there are more event participants.
III. Event-relevant tweets are more likely to be posted during the times when the event-related topics appear more frequently.

We start by defining the *D-Score* based on H-I (H, henceforth, stands for hypothesis). We consider the tweets that are representative of a topic are distributed close to the average feature vector of tweets with the event-related topic, inspired by existing document representative phrase extraction method [6]. We obtained the topic vector by averaging vectors in the event-related topic, i.e., $t\text{-}vec = \mu_{tp_o}$. The *D-Score* reflects the distance from the *t-vec* to each tweet in the feature space. A tweet with a higher *D-Score* indicates that it is semantically similar to the *t-vec*. The *D-Score* in the tweet $tw \in tp_o$ is computed using the following equations, normalized by the z-score:

$$
D\text{-}Score_{tw} = \frac{\cos(tw, t\text{-}vec) - \frac{1}{N}\sum_i^N \cos(tw_i, t\text{-}vec)}{\sqrt{\frac{1}{N}\sum_i^N (\cos(tw_i, t\text{-}vec) - \frac{1}{N}\sum_i^N \cos(tw_i, t\text{-}vec))^2}}, \tag{6}
$$

where $\cos(tw, t\text{-}vec)$ is the cosine similarity between tw and *t-vec*, N is the number of tweets belonging to tp_o, i.e., $N = |tp_o|$.

Second, we defined the *HV-Score* based on H-II. Even if the tweets are about an event-related topics, they may contain event-irrelevant tweets. Thus, we consider that during high human mobility, event participants and people caught in the crowds post numerous event-relevant tweets, and assume that the more likely a tweet is posted at a time human mobility volume is high, the more likely also it will be an event-relevant tweet. We therefore focus on weighting tweets based on human mobility. The *HV-Score* indicates the relative human mobility transition per timeslot, and can be computed in the posting timeslot t as

$$
HV\text{-}Score_t = \frac{v_t - \mu_V}{\sigma_V}, \tag{7}
$$

where μ_V and σ_V are the mean and standard deviation, respectively, of the human mobility transition.

Third, we defined the *PT-Score* based on H-III. Our method weights each tweet based on the number of tweets on the event-related topic. For events such as live concerts and stage performances, the number of tweets decreases during the event because people participating in the event refrain from posting tweets. Instead, users post numerous tweets about their expectations of participating in the event just before the event starts. Thus, for such events, weight should be given to tweets posted when there are many posts about an event-related topic.

The *PT-Score* indicates the number of posted tweets regarding the event-related topic in each timeslot, and is computed in the posting timeslot t as

$$PT\text{-}Score_t = \frac{|\boldsymbol{tw}_t| - \mu_{TV_o}}{\sigma_{TV_o}}, \tag{8}$$

where μ_{TV_o} and σ_{TV_o} are the mean and standard deviation, respectively, of the number of posted tweets about the event-related topics.

Note that we normalized each score above using z-score so that these different scores can be added together. In the succeeding section, we show how we combined these three scores to come up with four different scoring schemes and then compare how they contribute to our method's performance.

4 Experiments

We evaluated our method in two experiments. We first describe here in detail the datasets we used, and then describe our experiment set-up to evaluate the detection capability of our method compared to geotag-based method, given both scheduled and unscheduled events at different scales (**Experiment-I**). Finally, we describe our event-relevant tweet extraction experiment to evaluate whether users can understand what is occurring in the event (i.e., the cause and time of the event) by referring to the extracted tweets (**Experiment-II**).

4.1 Datasets

We created datasets for each experiment[1] because there are no open datasets with human mobility data attached to a tweet dataset. Our target events include nine scheduled events and five unscheduled events as shown in Table 1. We selected events that can elicit behavior responses from people, such as those that affect urban traffic flow and stimulate users to consider avoiding traffic congestion (e.g., due to baseball game or train delay) or draw people in to participate (e.g., festival, live concert). We also considered these events to have had hundreds to hundreds of thousands of participants in order for us to examine the effect of differences in scale. For the human mobility data, we aggregated the smartphone GPS data of users who agreed to provide their location data, which were collected by an application made by a Japanese mobile carrier. The minimum time interval for each GPS data instance was two minutes, with the sampling rate depending on the smartphone's model and signal conditions. We utilized GPS readings that were collected between May 1, 2019 and Sept. 30, 2020 from several million people. The human mobility data were computed every 15 min (i.e., $N_t = 96$) in 250 m × 250 m grid cells in Japan's Tokyo and Aichi prefectures.

---

[1] We cannot disclose the number of tweets and the number of people in each experiment due to the agreed terms of use.

Table 1. Details of the target events. If the number of participants in an event was not officially announced (e.g., unscheduled events), the maximum capacity of the venue is provided instead. The times of the events are the officially announced times of their occurrence.

Event type	ID	POI name	Event name	Event date and time	No. of participants
Scheduled events	A	Meiji Jingu Stadium (large scale stadiums)	Baseball game	July 29, 2020 18:00 ~	4,982
	B	TOHO CINEMAS Ikebukuro (movie theatre)	Opening a branch	July 03, 2020 9:00 ~	Up to 1,735
	C	Shinjuku BLAZE (small concert venue)	Live concert	July 11, 2020 12:30 ~	Up to 800
	D	Shinjuku LOFT (small concert venue)	Live concert	Sep. 27, 2020 17:15 ~	Up to 550
	E	Shibuya Eggman (small concert venue)	Live concert	Sep. 09, 2020 19:45 ~	Up to 350
	F	Tokyo Dome (large scale stadiums)	Baseball game	July 26, 2019 18:00 ~	45,817
	G	Tokyo Big Sight (convention center)	Sales exhibition	July 14, 2019 11:00 ~	Approx. 48,000[a]
	H	Nagoya Dome (large scale stadiums)	Live concert	May 26, 2019 16:00 ~	49,692
	I	Port of Nagoya	Fireworks festival	July 15, 2019 19:00 ~	Approx. 360,000 (total for one day)
Unscheduled events	J	Ikebukuro Station	Train delay	June 29, 2020 08:30 ~	Approx. 560,000 (total for one day)
	K	Sugamo Station	Unannounced street speech by a politician	July 03, 2020 12:00 ~	Approx. 76,000 (total for one day)
	L	Tokyo International Airport	Heavy congestion	Sep. 19, 2020[b]	Approx. 200,000 (total for one day)
	M	Shibuya Station	Train delay	June 29, 2020 08:30 ~	Approx. 360,000 (total for one day)
	N	Oizumi-gakuen Station	Train delay	Sep. 03, 2020 17:40 ~	Approx. 87,000 (total for one day)

[a] Calculate the average number of participants per event based on the number of participants and the number of events per year.
[b] The time is not described because it is not clear what time the congestion occurred.

As for the tweet datasets, we used both geotagged and non-geotagged tweets containing POI names. The tweet datasets were sampled from 10% of all tweets posted within Japan. In Exp-I, we used geotagged tweets as baseline by aggregating the time series of hourly geotagged tweet volumes on a per grid-cell basis in the month in which the target event occurred. For Exp-II, we used tweets containing the grid cell-associated POI names. We created the grid cell-POI database by processing an open dataset[2] that contains the latitude and longitude of major and local POIs within Japan. BERT for vectorizing each tweet is pretrained on Wikipedia[3], and this model is often used to vectorize Japanese tweets [2, 36].

---

[2] https://nlftp.mlit.go.jp/ksj/index.html.
[3] https://github.com/cl-tohoku/bert-japanese.

4.2   Experiment-I: Event Detection Experiment

Our method and comparative methods were evaluated on whether each target event was detected in the grid cell where it occurred. The event-detection time was also evaluated because if the target event could be anticipated early or detected quickly, relevant information could be delivered before people are caught in a congestion or before the event is over.

We defined the number of day groups $N_g = 8$ (i.e., $2 \times 2 \times 2$) according to whether the day, previous day, and next day are either weekday or week-end/holiday considering that human mobility vary depending on the day of the week as well as the type of the previous or succeeding day (e.g., even on the same weekday, Wednesdays and Fridays should be different day groups.). We computed for normal human mobility using data within the past two months before a target event occurred. We performed k-means clustering to compute the normal human mobility in each grid cell, searched for the parameters that would optimally detect the correct events, and set the number of clusters $K = 2$ and the threshold $\phi = 3$. We explain below the technical details.

The most common conventional event detection approach is a geotag-based method. However, it will not be able to accurately detect events because the number of geotagged tweets is very small now (e.g., only 17 geotagged tweets were posted throughout the day in event L). We benchmarked two comparative methods (henceforth, CM) using the SR approach [29], a state-of-the-art unsupervised anomaly detection method. We denoted as **CM-1** the SR-based approach that uses the transition of the number of geotagged tweets per hour, **CM-2** the SR-based approach that uses human mobility data, and we denote our proposed method as **PM**. SR approach can detect anomalies using a saliency map even if similar patterns have not appeared in the past. For both human mobility data and changes in tweet volume, the shape of the time series differs greatly depending on the event type, e.g., the amount of data increases rapidly in the case of train accidents, but on the other hand, gradually increases before the start of the event in the case of concert events. The SR method is suitable as a comparison method because it has been verified to be robust to various shapes of time series data [29]. As SR hyperparameters, the threshold τ is set to 3, the number of estimated points ρ is set to 5, and the sliding window size ω is set to 30, respectively, based on the search for the best parameters for event detection. Note that non-geotagged tweets cannot be used for Exp-I because it is impossible to identify the location in small grid cell units.

Table 2 shows the results of Exp-I. PM detected 9 out of 10 events, contrast with CM-1 that detected only 3 events and CM-2 with just 4 events. PM detected events B, D, J, K, M, and N that were not detected by CM-1. In these events, no geotagged tweets were posted around the time of the event. CM-1 detected events A, C, and L, but only a very small number of geotagged tweets were posted at that time (up to three tweets for event L), so if a few geotagged tweets are posted in a grid cell, the event may be falsely detected. Also, PM detected events B, C, D, K, and M that were not detected by CM-2. We confirmed that human mobility in these events was different from the normal human mobility, although the magnitude of the peaks themselves was not large. Therefore, it is considered that PM could detect these events.

Table 2. Results of Exp-I. The number in parentheses indicates the difference between event detection time and event occurrence time.

Event type	ID	POI name	Event date and time	PM	CM-1	CM-2
Scheduled events	A	Meiji Jingu Stadium	July 29, 2020 18:00~	−75	±0	+60
	B	TOHO CINEMAS Ikebukuro	July 03, 2020 09:00~	−15	×	×
	C	Shinjuku BLAZE	July 11, 2020 12:30~	−15	−30	×
	D	Shinjuku LOFT	Sep. 27, 2020 17:15~	−30	×	×
	E	Shibuya Eggman	Sep. 09, 2020 19:45~	×	×	×
Unscheduled events	J	Ikebukuro Station	June 29, 2020 08:30 ~	+15	×	+60
	K	Sugamo Station	July 03, 2020 12:00 ~	+30	×	×
	L	Tokyo International Airport	Sep. 19, 2020	−15[a]	±0	+105
	M	Shibuya Station	June 29, 2020 08:30 ~	+30	×	×
	N	Oizumi-gakuen Station	Sep. 03, 2020 17:40 ~	+5	×	+15

[a] The difference between the detection time of the proposed method and CM-1.

Let us take for instance the ones in Fig. 3, which compares human mobility during normal days and the day-event for events A (baseball game) and K (unannounced street speech). CM-1 and CM-2 detected event A that have significant increase in human mobility (i.e., Fig. 3(a)), but did not detect the event K that have relatively small increases (i.e., Figure 3(b)). PM was able to detect even small increases in human mobility because it looks at the difference to the normal human mobility transitions (difference between blue and orange lines in Fig. 3(b)), whereas CM-2 did not because it only considers current transitions in human mobility (orange line in Fig. 3(b)). Even if we set the threshold τ of CM-2 to a smaller value, we may find event K, but at the same time, we will find many false positives. Although PM was able to detect 9 out of 10 events of different scales (ranging from 550 to 560,000 participants), a small-scale live concert with up to 350 participants (i.e., event E) was not detected. This result is due to the large number of people outside the venue, albeit within the grid cell, as well as the relatively low impact of this small event (in case the number of participants in the event is very small compared to $v_{g,t,c}$). The detection of such relatively small-scale events may be achieved by setting an adjustable grid cell, e.g., define the rectangular polygon data for concert venue individually.

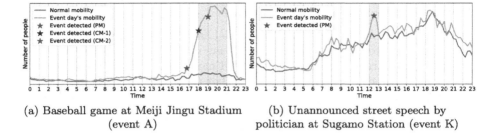

(a) Baseball game at Meiji Jingu Stadium   (b) Unannounced street speech by
(event A)   politician at Sugamo Station (event K)

Fig. 3. Comparison of human mobility between normal days and the day-event. The highlighted blocks indicate the duration of the event.

PM detected on average 22 and 77.5 min earlier than CM-1 (for events A, C, and L), and CM-2 (for events A, J, L, and N) respectively. For the scheduled events, we assumed that people gradually gathered for the start-time of the event, which caused congestion even before the event started. In Fig. 3(a), in fact, we confirmed that people gradually gathered from approximately 16:00, two hours before the event started at 18:00. PM detected the event at 16:45 (75 mins earlier), while CM-1 detected it at 18:00 ($\pm$0 min), and CM-2 detected it at 19:00 (60 mins later). Thus, PM detected these events even before they started. Further, we considered that the unscheduled events J, M, N (train delays), and K (unannounced street speech), people gathered in the grid cell immediately after the event starts, resulting in a sudden concentration of people in a short period of time compared to scheduled events. In Fig. 3(b), we can see that people gathered between 12:00 and 13:00 for event K, and PM was able to detect this event in real time while congestion was occurring within that short duration. The unscheduled event L (heavy congestion at an airport) does not have a clear event occurrence time, but PM detected congestion at 6:00 in the morning, 15 min earlier than CM-1 and 120 min earlier than CM-2. CM-1 and CM-2 did not detect the events until the time when people had clearly formed a crowd, since it detects the events characterized by significant increase in human mobility. What these results suggest is that PM can deliver information even before an event congestion ends (i.e., with a maximum delay of 30 min, and a minimum of 75 min before the event starts), given different event types and scales.

4.3 Experiment-II: Event-Relevant Tweet Extraction Experiment

We now discuss our qualitatively evaluation of the extracted tweets, i.e., whether they are relevant to the event or not. Annotators manually evaluated whether the extracted tweets are effective for understanding the target events. We compared among four scores, i.e., each with different strategies using variant combinations of equations (6)–(8). Tweet extraction based solely on the D-$Score$ is denoted as **M-1**, D-$Score + HV$-$Score$ as **M-2**, D-$Score + PT$-$Score$ as **M-3**, and lastly, D-$Score + HV$-$Score + PT$-$Score$ as **M-4**. The optimal number of clusters L^* for each event is automatically determined by our method (see Sect. 3.2). We compared these four methods to two baselines:

- **B-1:** The most intuitive and simple method assumes that tweets with a posting time closer to the event-detection time are more likely to be event-relevant tweets. The extracted tweets included POI names and ordered from the time they were posted until close to the time that the event was detected.
- **B-2:** To verify the effectiveness of our method to select the event-related topic, we extracted tweets that included POI names and ordered them based on their distance to the centroid of all the tweets in the feature space without topic clustering, i.e., the score of a tweet tw is computed as follows: B-2-$Score_{tw} = \cos(tw, \mu_{TW})$. This method is similar to techniques used in existing document summarization tasks [6].

Using an existing study [24] as our reference, we manually evaluated the relevance of the extracted tweets to the event in question. Each method scored the tweets' relevance to the event, and then the 10 tweets with the highest scores were extracted as event-relevant tweets. Three annotators graded the value of each tweet (420 tweets in total, since there are 6 methods and 7 events) on a 3-point scale. A grade of 2 means that the annotator can identify what event is occurring (i.e., the cause and time of the event) by referring to the tweet. A grade of 1 means one can identify what event, but other interpretations are also possible. A grade of 0 means one cannot identify the event just by referring to the tweet. Each method was evaluated by the percentage of tweets that were given a grade of 2 by at least two annotators. Lastly here, we computed for Fleiss' κ to measure the inter-rater agreement [13]. κ was 0.976 (an almost perfect agreement) on all tweet grades provided by our three annotators. This suggests that each tweet grade is highly reliable.

Table 3 shows the evaluation results we obtained, which demonstrate that M-4 performs well on these datasets. In 5 out of 7 events, all 10 tweets that were extracted are event-relevant. In particular, the M-4 score for the baseball game at the Tokyo Dome (event F) is a significant improvement from B-2's (i.e., 0.70 and 0.20, respectively). The tweets extracted using B-1 and B-2 gave out incorrect topics on events that were held at the same place. In event F for instance, a popular singer announced during a baseball game via Twitter a future live concert event at the Tokyo Dome, and many Twitter users simultaneously posted tweets about that future event. Consequently, B-1 and B-2 incorrectly extracted the tweets that were about the upcoming live concert instead of the tweets about the ongoing baseball game. This is because B-1 and B-2 were not able to select the event-related topic. However, M-4 incorrectly extracted a few tweets that were not relevant to the event, specifically, 5 tweets at events F and L out of all the 70 extracted tweets. These tweets coincidentally slipped into the relevant topics at the time the event occurred. For instance, the irrelevant tweets at Tokyo Dome (event F) included contents about baseball video games and baseball games at the Tokyo Dome the following day. It is difficult to filter these tweets because they are also tweets about baseball. To eliminate such tweets, setting the appropriate stop words (e.g., "video") or extracting the current tweets by considering the tense of the tweet content would be effective. Further, our method scored 0.80 on the heavy congestion at Tokyo International Airport (event L), while B-2 scored 0.90 (however, one of the two irrelevant tweets was given a grade of 2 by one annotator and 1 by two annotators). The 6 out of 10 tweets extracted using B-2 were short statements of user's thoughts, citing the same breaking news about the event (i.e., airport congestion). We found that when many similar event-relevant tweets are posted at the same time and no other topics are posted (i.e., less diversity in the semantics of the tweets), they can be correctly extracted regardless of the topic. This suggest that it is possible to not cluster the tweets if they are not widely distributed in the feature space because such distribution indicates lack of semantic diversity among tweets.

Table 3. Results of the evaluation of each method

Event type	ID	POI name	B-1	B-2	M-1	M-2	M-3	M-4
Scheduled events	F	Tokyo Dome	0.30	0.20	0.60	**0.70**	0.60	**0.70**
	G	Tokyo Big Sight	0.20	0.90	0.80	0.90	**1.00**	**1.00**
	H	Nagoya Dome	0.70	0.70	0.90	0.70	**1.00**	**1.00**
	I	Port of Nagoya	0.60	0.60	0.70	**1.00**	0.80	**1.00**
Unscheduled events	L	Tokyo International Airport	0.40	**0.90**	0.50	0.60	0.80	0.80
	M	Shibuya Station	0.50	0.90	**1.00**	**1.00**	**1.00**	**1.00**
	N	Oizumi-gakuen Station	0.90	**1.00**	**1.00**	**1.00**	**1.00**	**1.00**
Total average			0.51	0.74	0.79	0.84	0.89	**0.93**

Table 3 also shows the improvement in score with the addition of the HV-$Score$ (M-2 and M-4) for the fireworks festival at the Port of Nagoya (event I). We confirmed that the event-relevant tweets about the festival were mostly posted during the event. We can obtain a higher score by focusing on the times when people are concentrating (HV-$Score$) rather than focusing on the times when there are many tweets (PT-$Score$). However, for the live concert at Nagoya Dome (event H), the score was improved by adding the PT-$Score$ (M-3). We can observe in Fig. 4 that the number of tweets drastically decreased during the live concert because people participating in the event refrained from posting tweets. In this case, the PT-$Score$ is effective because it focuses on the time when there are many tweets (i.e., 15:00). This suggests that it is important to focus on both the human mobility transition and the number of tweets when selecting the topics to extract for determining the event-relevant tweets.

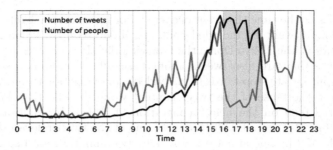

Fig. 4. Number of tweets and human mobility transitions at the Nagoya Dome (event H). The highlighted block indicates the duration of the event.

Table 4 shows sample tweets that were extracted using M-4 and are given a grade of 2. We can identify what event is occurring at the POI by referring to tweets like the one in Table 4. For example, in event I, users can understand that congestion is occurring in a particular grid cell and that the cause of the congestion is a festival, and if they are intrigued by the tweets, they might consider participating. Also, in event M, users may consider changing their route to avoid the congestion due to the train delay. In summary, our method that considers these characteristics, $D\text{-}Score + HV\text{-}Score + PT\text{-}Score$, i.e., M-4, was the most robust of the six methods independent to the type of event.

Table 4. Examples of extracted tweets using Method 4

ID	POI name	Event name	Examples of extracted tweets
F	Tokyo Dome	Baseball game	"Giants vs Tigers[a] at Tokyo Dome. Solate's first appearance at the Tokyo Dome."
G	Tokyo Big Sight	Sales exhibition	"I'm here to help my friends move around Tokyo Big Sight for Comitia[b]. I'm at P41A on the upper floor."
H	Nagoya Dome	Live concert	"16:00 starts. Mr. children[c] Tour "Against All GRAVITY" at Nagoya Dome will start soon!"
I	Port of Nagoya	Fireworks festival	"I noticed there are a lot of people in yukata, but then I realized the fireworks display will start at the Port of Nagoya."
M	Shibuya Station	Train delay	"Accident at Shibuya Station on the Yamanote Line: Broken windshield."

[a] Japanese professional baseball team
[b] Sales exhibition of self-published works
[c] Japanese rock band

5   Conclusion and Future Work

Focusing on the correlation between topic transitions in tweets and human mobility transitions, we proposed an unsupervised method to detect events with high crowd density (congestion) and to extract event-relevant tweets that were not geotagged nor annotated. Our method extracts the relevant tweets by scoring each tweet's relevance to an event based on its topic and posting time.

We conducted evaluations using real-world multiple events (such as baseball games and airport congestion) datasets. In our event detection experiment, we confirmed that our method outperformed the state-of-the-art anomaly detection method regarding the number of events detected and event detection time, regardless of the type (i.e., scheduled or unscheduled) and scale of the events. In our event-relevant tweet extraction experiment, we confirmed that our method can extract event-relevant tweets compared to other baseline methods. We also showed that focusing on temporal data of human mobility transition is effective for events during which users post tweets (e.g., festival), and focusing on the temporal data of tweet volumes is effective for events in which people refrain from posting tweets during the event (e.g., live concert). Based on the results we obtained, our next step includes automatically weighting each score according to event type and scale to improve the accuracy of event-relevant tweet extraction. (e.g., for festival events, weight the HV-$Score$).

Although many GPS-based applications and privacy protection methods have been proposed in recent years [20], further investigation is needed to determine whether our method is effective using more sparse alternative location data, e.g., CDR.

References

1. Ahmed, M.F., Vanajakshi, L., Suriyanarayanan, R.: Real-time traffic congestion information from tweets using supervised and unsupervised machine learning techniques. Transp. Dev. Econ. **5**(2), 1–11 (2019). https://doi.org/10.1007/s40890-019-0088-2
2. Akahori, T., Dohsaka, K., Ishii, M., Ito, H.: Efficient creation of Japanese tweet emotion dataset using sentence-final expressions. In: 2021 IEEE 3rd Global Conference on Life Sciences and Technologies, pp. 501–505 (2021)
3. Allan, J.: Introduction to Topic detection and Tracking. In: Allan, J. (eds) Topic Detection and Tracking. The Information Retrieval Series, vol. 12, pp. 1–16. Springer, Boston, (2002). https://doi.org/10.1007/978-1-4615-0933-2_1
4. Alsaedi, N., Burnap, P., Rana, O.: Can we predict a riot? disruptive event detection using twitter. ACM Trans. Internet Technol. **17**(2), 1–26 (2017)
5. Bhuvaneswari, A., Valliyammai, C.: Identifying event bursts using log-normal distribution of tweet arrival rate in twitter stream. In: Proceedings of the 10th International Conference on Advanced Computing, pp. 339–343 (2018)
6. Bennani-Smires, K., Musat, C., Hossmann, A., Baeriswyl, M., Jaggi, M.: Simple unsupervised keyphrase extraction using sentence embeddings. In: Proceedings of the 22nd Conference on Computational Natural Language Learning, pp. 221–229 (2018)

7. de Bruijn, J.A., de Moel, H., Jongman, B., Wagemaker, J., Aerts, J.C.J.H.: TAGGS: grouping tweets to improve global geoparsing for disaster response. J. Geovisualization Spat. Anal. **2**(1), 1–14 (2017). https://doi.org/10.1007/s41651-017-0010-6

8. Calabrese, F., Ferrari, L., Blondel, V.D.: Urban sensing using mobile phone network data: a survey of research. ACM Comput. Surv. **47**(2), 25-1-25-20 (2014)

9. Chen, Y., Lv, Y., Wang, X., Li, L., Wang, F.Y.: Detecting traffic information from social media texts with deep learning approaches. IEEE Trans. Intell. Transp. Syst. **20**(8), 3049–3058 (2019)

10. Comito, C., Forestiero, A., Pizzuti, C.: Bursty event detection in twitter streams. ACM Trans. Knowl. Discov. Data **13**(4), 1–28 (2019)

11. Cordeiro, M.: Twitter event detection: combining wavelet analysis and topic inference summarization. In: Proceedings of the 7th Doctoral Symposium in Informatics Engineering, pp. 123–138 (2012)

12. Devlin, J., Chang, M.W., Lee, K., Toutanova, K.: BERT: pre-training of deep bidirectional transformers for language understanding. In: Proceedings of the 2019 Conference of the North American Chapter of the Association for Computational Linguistics: Human Language Technologies, vol. 1, pp. 4171–4186 (2019)

13. Fleiss, J.L.: Measuring nominal scale agreement among many raters. Psychol. Bull. **76**(5), 378–382 (1971)

14. Fuse, T., Kamiya, K.: Statistical anomaly detection in human dynamics monitoring using a hierarchical dirichlet process hidden markov model. IEEE Trans. Intell. Transp. Syst. **18**(11), 3083–3092 (2017)

15. Gutiérrez, C., Figuerias, P., Oliveira, P., Costa, R., Jardim-Goncalves, R.: Twitter mining for traffic events detection. In: Proceedings of the 2015 Science and Information Conference, pp. 371–378 (2015)

16. Han, Y., Karunasekera, S., Leckie, C., Harwood, A.: Multi-spatial scale event detection from geo-tagged tweet streams via power-law verification. In: Proceedings of the 2019 IEEE International Conference on Big Data, pp. 1131–1136 (2019)

17. Hu, Y., Wang, R.Q.: Understanding the removal of precise geotagging in tweets. Nat. Human Behav. **4**, 1219–1221 (2020)

18. Kaiser, M.S., et al.: Advances in crowd analysis for urban applications through urban event detection. IEEE Trans. Intell. Transp. Syst. **19**(10), 3092–3112 (2018)

19. Kaviani, M., Rahmani, H.: EmHash: hashtag recommendation using neural network based on BERT embedding. In: 2020 6th International Conference on Web Research, pp. 113–118 (2020)

20. Kong, X., et al.: Big trajectory data: a survey of applications and services. IEEE Access **6**, 58295–58306 (2018)

21. Kong, X., Song, X., Xia, F., Guo, H., Wang, J., Tolba, A.: LoTAD: long-term traffic anomaly detection based on crowdsourced bus trajectory data. World Wide Web **21**(3), 825–847 (2018)

22. Lam, C.T., Gao, H., Ng, B.: A real-time traffic congestion detection system using on-line images. In: Proceedings of the 2017 IEEE 17th International Conference on Communication Technology, pp. 1548–1552 (2017)

23. Lee, K., Ganti, R., Srivatsa, M., Mohapatra, P.: Spatio-temporal provenance: identifying location information from unstructured text. In: Proceedings of the 2013 IEEE International Conference on Pervasive Computing and Communications Workshops, pp. 499–504 (2013)

24. Mele, I., Crestani, F.: A Multi-source collection of event-labeled news documents. In: Proceedings of the 2019 ACM SIGIR International Conference on Theory of Information Retrieval, pp. 205–208 (2019)

25. Metzler, D., Cai, C., Hovy, E.: Structured event retrieval over microblog archives. In: Proceedings of the 2012 Conference of the North American Chapter of the Association for Computational Linguistics: Human Language Technologies, pp. 646–655 (2012)
26. Miller, D.: Leveraging BERT for extractive text summarization on lectures. arXiv preprint, arXiv:1906.04165 (2019)
27. Mishima, Y., Minamikawa, A.: Anomaly detection of urban dynamics in an extreme weather with mobile GPS data. In: Proceedings of NetMob 2019 (2019)
28. Neumann, J., Zao, M., Karatzoglou, A., Oliver, N.: Event detection in communication and transportation data. In: Pattern Recognition and Image Analysis, pp. 827–838 (2013)
29. Ren, H., et al.: Time-series anomaly detection service at Microsoft. In: Proceedings of the 25th ACM SIGKDD International Conference on Knowledge Discovery and Data Mining, pp. 3009–3017 (2019)
30. Silveira Jacques Junior, J.C., Musse, S.R., Jung, C.R.: Crowd analysis using computer vision techniques. IEEE Sig. Process. Mag. **27**(5), 66–77 (2010)
31. Wei, H., Zhou, H., Sankaranarayanan, J., Sengupta, S., Samet, H.: Detecting latest local events from geotagged tweet streams. In: Proceedings of the 26th ACM SIGSPATIAL International Conference on Advances in Geographic Information Systems, pp. 520–523 (2018)
32. Weng, J., Lee, B.S.: Event detection in twitter. In: Proceedings of the 5th International AAAI Conference on Weblogs and Social Media (2011)
33. Xu, Z., et al.: Crowdsourcing based description of urban emergency events using social media big data. IEEE Trans. Cloud Comput. **8**(2), 387–397 (2020)
34. Yabe, T., Tsubouchi, K., Sudo, A.: A framework for evacuation hotspot detection after large scale disasters using location data from smartphones: case study of Kumamoto earthquake. In: Proceedings of the 24th ACM SIGSPATIAL International Conference on Advances in Geographic Information Systems, pp. 1–10 (2016)
35. Yamaki, S., Lin, S.D., Kameyama, W.: Detection of anomaly state caused by unexpected accident using data of smart card for public transportation. In: Proceedings of the 2019 IEEE International Conference on Big Data, pp. 1693–1698 (2019)
36. Yamamoto, K., Shimada, K.: Acquisition of periodic events with person attributes. In: 2020 International Conference on Asian Language Processing, pp. 229–234 (2020)
37. Zhang, C., et al.: TrioVecEvent: embedding-based online local event detection in geo-tagged tweet streams. In: Proceedings of the 23rd ACM SIGKDD International Conference on Knowledge Discovery and Data Mining, pp. 595–604 (2017)
38. Zhang, C., et al.: GeoBurst: real-time local event detection in geo-tagged tweet streams. In: Proceedings 39th International ACM SIGIR Conference on Research and Development in Information Retrieval, pp. 513–522 (2016)
39. Zhang, Q., Chan, A.B.: Wide-area crowd counting via ground-plane density maps and multi-view fusion CNNs. In: Proceedings of the 2019 IEEE/CVF Conference on Computer Vision and Pattern Recognition, pp. 8289–8298 (2019)

Design of Room-Layout Estimator Using Smart Speaker

Tomoki Joya[1][(✉)], Shigemi Ishida[2], Yudai Mitsukude[1], and Yutaka Arakawa[1]

[1] ISEE, Kyushu University, Fukuoka 819-0395, Japan
joya.tomoki@arakawa-lab.com, mitsukude@f.ait.kyushu-u.ac.jp,
arakawa@ait.kyushu-u.ac.jp
[2] Future University Hakodate, Hokkaido 041-8655, Japan
ish@fun.ac.jp

Abstract. In this study, we propose a room-layout-based appliance control for voice user interfaces (VUIs), such as smart speakers. VUI-based appliance control requires a control command including *which device* to *do what*. However, we often experience an ambiguous target problem: the control target device in a control command is ambiguous because an ambiguous room name and demonstrative words are frequently used to specify the target device. To address this problem, we utilized a room layout to estimate the control target. A user implicitly aims to control devices in a room where they are. Therefore, we estimate the room where the user is now based on the room layout, which is estimated on a smart speaker, to determine the control target. In this study, we present the design of a room-layout estimator as the first step toward room-layout-based appliance control. The experimental evaluations conducted in our 1-bedroom smart house revealed that our room-layout estimator estimates room directions and room types with accuracies of 0.850 and 0.714, respectively.

Keywords: Voice User Interface (VUI) · Acoustic sensing · Room direction and type estimation

1 Introduction

Currently, smart home appliances are becoming prevalent owing to recent advances in wireless communication and Internet of Things (IoT)-related technologies. Using smart speakers working as a voice user interface (VUI), such as Google Home and Amazon Alexa, we can control smart home appliances using our voice.

For VUI-based control, we need to specify *which device* to *do what*. For example, we can turn on the lights by ordering a smart speaker to *turn on the light in the living room*. In this example, we need to explicitly specify the light in

This work was supported in part by the Japan Society for the Promotion of Science (JSPS) KAKENHI Grant Numbers JP21K11847, JP20KK0258, and JP19KT0020 as well as the Cooperative Research Project Program of RIEC, Tohoku University.

T. Hara and H. Yamaguchi (Eds.): MobiQuitous 2021, LNICST 419, pp. 24–39, 2022.
https://doi.org/10.1007/978-3-030-94822-1_2

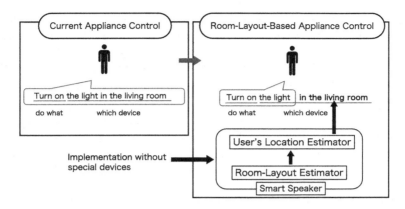

Fig. 1. Concept of room-layout-based appliance control for smart speakers

the *living room* because there are lights in every room. To uniquely specify the target device, we often use room names that are configured to a smart speaker before using the smart speaker.

However, smart speakers often experience ambiguous target problems. We often forget to specify a room name because we implicitly aim to control devices in the room where we are in. A target device specified by demonstrative words, such as *this light* also causes a similar ambiguity.

Another cause of the ambiguous target problem is the ambiguity in the room names. Different names are often used to specify rooms. For example, we might attempt to turn on the light in the living room by ordering *turn on the light in the drawing room* or *turn on the light in the front room.*

To address the ambiguous target problem, context-aware decision-making has been proposed [2,3]. In context-aware decision-making approaches, the control target is estimated based on the user's context. However, user context estimation requires sensors and a machine-learning model pre-trained with the user's previous behaviors.

In this study, we propose a new approach, room-layout-based appliance control, as shown in Fig. 1. In practical situations, ambiguous control commands are often used, such as *turn on the light.* When a user makes an ambiguous command, such as *turn on the light*, we assume that the user aims to order *turn on the light in the room they are in.* A smart speaker, therefore, estimates the room where the user is located using a user's location estimator. The room layout, which comprises room directions and types, such as a living room and bedroom, is also estimated by a smart speaker using a room-layout estimator to determine the room name where the control target is located.

As a first step toward this goal, in this study, we present the design of a room-layout estimator for smart speakers. Our assumption here is that smart speakers are equipped with a couple of microphones to estimate the user location. Analyzing the sound source direction, the room-layout estimator first estimates the direction of the rooms. The type of the rooms is then estimated based on the activity sound, such as faucet sound, dish sound, and TV sounds, derived from the room direction. Although smart speakers on the market have a single microphone, we believe that in the near future, smart speakers will be equipped with multiple microphones to improve robustness to noise and to improve users' voice separation performance.

Our main contributions are as follows:

- We propose a room-layout-based appliance control method for smart speakers. To the best of our knowledge, this is the first attempt to utilize the layout of rooms estimated on smart speakers to determine the control target appliance.
- We present the design of a room-layout estimator for smart speakers equipped with multiple microphones. In contrast to existing sound source localization technologies, our approach for the room-layout estimation utilizes the room-specific characteristics of the reflected sound to distinguish different rooms.
- We show the basic performance of our room-layout estimator through experimental evaluations. We collected the home activity sound data from two different houses. The experimental evaluations demonstrated that the room-direction estimation accuracy and room-type estimation accuracy were 0.850 and 0.714, respectively.

The remainder of this paper is organized as follows. Section 2 describes related work on sound source localization in indoor environments. In Sect. 3, we present the design of our room-layout estimator that utilizes multiple microphones on a smart speaker, followed by experimental evaluations in Sect. 4. Finally, the paper is concluded in Sect. 5.

2   Related Work

To the best of our knowledge, this is the first attempt to estimate a room layout using a microphone array rather than sound sources.

Sound source localization, which estimates the location of sound sources using a microphone array, has been widely studied and includes time delay estimation, beamforming, and subspace-based methods. Typical time delay estimators are cross-correlation-based methods where sound sources' locations are estimated by calculating the cross-correlations between microphones [7,12,15]. The beamforming methods are represented by delay-and-sum beamformers, which combine sound signals on multiple microphones with phase compensation [14,16]. The representative subspace-based method is the MUSIC method that utilizes the orthogonality of signal and noise components in the spatial correlation matrix of microphone array signals to estimate the location of sound sources [4,11].

Numerous studies on sound source localization have attempted to reduce the influence of reflected sound signals in indoor environments, where the sound localization performance degrades because of reverberation.

Suzuki et al. presented a sub-band peak hold process, which considers the amplitude of a direct sound signal, the sound signal that first reaches the microphones, and masks the reflected sound signals that reach subsequent to the direct

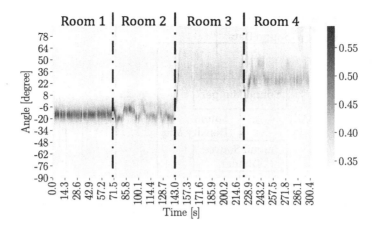

Fig. 2. Example of a sound density map with a single sound source moving in 4 rooms

sound [13]. Okamoto et al. applies a spatial averaging method to a 3-dimensional space model by dividing a microphone array into multiple sub-arrays and averaging the spatial matrices of each subarray [8].

Ishi et al. estimates the locations of multiple sound sources using a spatial model and a ceiling-mounted microphone array comprising 16 microphones [5]. A 3-dimensional space model is utilized to estimate the influence of the reflected sound signals. Ribeiro et al. also reported a sound source localization robust to reflected signals relying on an actual 3-dimensional space model [10].

However, these methods require a large number of microphones, for example, 16 microphones. 3-dimensional space modeling is a novel approach, where high computational resources or considerable human effort are required to construct the space model. The estimation of the room layout using a resource-limited smart speaker with a limited number of microphones is associated with numerous unsolved problems.

3   Room-Layout Estimator for Smart Speaker

3.1   Approach

Our primary approach to estimating the room layout is to extract the reverberation features using a *sound density map* (a map of the sound power distribution as a function of time for each angle). We found that the sound signals from different rooms have different reverberation features because of the differences in size, wall locations, and diffraction objects. The difference in reverberation features appears as a difference in the *band* on the sound density map. Therefore, we distinguish sound signals from different rooms based on the features of bands on a sound density map using unsupervised learning algorithms.

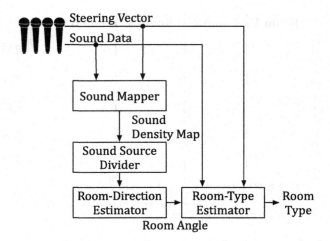

Fig. 3. Overview of room-layout estimator for smart speaker

Figure 2 shows an example of a sound density map with a single sound source, this is, a vacuum cleaner, moving in four rooms. We installed a microphone array in a room of a 1-bedroom smart house and collected sound signals to draw a sound density map using the MUSIC method [11]. In Fig. 2, the moving sound source moves from one room to the next room at the time indicated by the dashed lines. We can confirm that the width and fluctuation of the band appearing on the sound density map are dependent on the location of the sound source.

There are multiple sound sources in a practical environment, resulting in multiple bands corresponding to the sound sources on a sound density map. We first divide the sound sources and then group them by estimating the room where the sound source was located, by unsupervised learning with features extracted from a sound density map.

3.2   Assumptions

We assume that our method, that is, the room-layout estimator for a smart speaker, is used in a residential environment, such as a 2-bedroom house where multiple rooms are on the same floor and are located adjacent to each other with doors separating them. A smart speaker with a microphone array was installed in one of the rooms. Our goal is to estimate the room layout of rooms connected via a door to a room where the smart speaker is installed. In these rooms, multiple people live together. They might make living noises at different locations simultaneously. The number of rooms next to the room where the smart speaker is installed is given before the room-layout estimation.

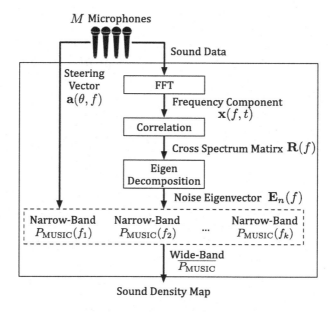

Fig. 4. Overview of sound mapper

3.3 Design Overview

Figure 3 shows an overview of the room-layout estimator for a smart speaker. The room-layout estimator comprises a sound mapper, sound source divider, room-direction estimator, and room-type estimator. The sound mapper retrieves sound data using a microphone array and calculates the sound power distribution at each angle using the MUSIC method to draw a sound density map. The sound source divider groups sound density map points into sound sources, which are more grouped into rooms where the sound source is located in the room-direction estimator to estimate the room direction. The room type is finally estimated by the room-type estimator using supervised learning with features extracted from the sound signals of each room.

The following sections describe the details of each component.

3.4 Sound Mapper

The sound mapper performs the MUSIC to draw a sound density map, which is a map of the sound power distribution for each angle as a function of time. The MUSIC method has a high angle estimation resolution and is useful for extracting reverberation features as fluctuations in the sound arrival direction.

Figure 4 shows an overview of the sound mapper. As shown in Fig. 4, the sound mapper collects sound data using a microphone array. A steering vector, a vector describing the phase differences of sound signals on each microphone, was also calculated from the physical arrangement of the microphone array.

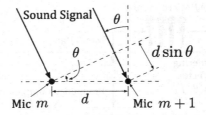

Fig. 5. Difference in sound traveling distance between two linearly aligned microphones

The collected sound signals are segmented using a fixed time-length window for the fast Fourier transform (FFT). Let $\mathbf{x}(f, t)$ be an M-dimensional column vector of sound frequency components of frequency f at time t, where M is the number of microphones in the microphone array. The sound mapper calculates the cross-spectrum matrix $\mathbf{R}(f)$ as follows:

$$\mathbf{R}(f) = E\left[\mathbf{x}^H(f, t)\, \mathbf{x}(f, t)\right], \tag{1}$$

where $\mathbf{z}^H$ denotes the Hermitian transpose of a vector $\mathbf{z}$, and $E[\ ]$ denotes an averaging process. We then calculated the eigenvalues and eigenvectors of the cross-spectrum matrix $\mathbf{R}(f)$. The number of signal and noise components was estimated based on the distribution of the magnitudes of the eigenvalues over multiple windows. Assuming that we have $N(< M)$ signal components, we obtain the noise eigenvectors $\mathbf{E}_n(f)$ corresponding to the remaining $M - N$ eigenvalues.

The steering vector was calculated from the physical arrangement of the microphone array. As shown in Fig. 5, the difference in the sound traveling distance between two linearly aligned microphones separated by distance d is $d \sin \theta$, where θ is the sound arrival angle. $d \sin \theta$ corresponds to a phase difference of $2\pi f d \sin \theta / c$, where c is the speed of sound in air. The steering vector $\mathbf{a}(\theta, f)$ of M linearly aligned microphones is calculated as

$$\mathbf{a}(\theta, f) = \left[\, 1\ e^{-j\phi}\ e^{-j2\phi} \cdots e^{-j(M-1)\phi}\,\right]^T \tag{2}$$

where $\phi = 2\pi f d \sin \theta / c$, and ^{T} denotes the transpose operation. Although we used an example of linearly aligned microphones, the same idea can be used to calculate the steering vector for a different microphone setup.

Using the eigenvectors $\mathbf{E}_n(f)$ and the steering vector $\mathbf{a}(\theta, f)$, we derive the narrow-band sound power distribution $P_{\mathrm{MUSIC}}(\theta, f)$ as

$$P_{\mathrm{MUSIC}}(\theta, f) = \frac{1}{\mathbf{a}^H(\theta, f)\, \mathbf{E}_n(f)\, \mathbf{E}_n{}^H(f)\, \mathbf{a}(\theta, f)}. \tag{3}$$

We finally derive the wide-band sound power distribution $\overline{P_{\mathrm{MUSIC}}}$ as

$$\overline{P_{\mathrm{MUSIC}}} = \frac{1}{k} \sum_f P_{\mathrm{MUSIC}}(\theta, f). \tag{4}$$

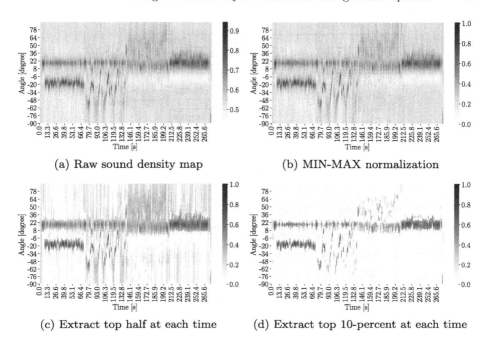

(a) Raw sound density map   (b) MIN-MAX normalization

(c) Extract top half at each time   (d) Extract top 10-percent at each time

Fig. 6. Overview of filtering on sound density map

Here, we assume that there are k frequency components in the FFT results. $\overline{P_{\text{MUSIC}}}$ has peaks at the angles corresponding to the sound sources. We drew $\overline{P_{\text{MUSIC}}}$ as a function of angle and time to derive a *sound density map*.

We apply a filtering process to the sound density map because the raw sound density map includes sound power information corresponding to the noise components. Figure 6 shows an overview of the filtering process. We first apply a MIN-MAX normalization process (Fig. 6b) and extract the top half points at each time t (Fig. 6c). The top 10% points were finally extracted at each time t (Fig. 6d).

3.5 Sound Source Divider

The sound source divider groups the points on a sound density map into sound sources. A sound source does not move quickly, resulting in a continuous band on the sound density map. Multiple bands can be observed on a sound density map when there are multiple sound sources. We apply DBSCAN, a density-based clustering method, to a sound density map to group points on a sound density map into sound sources.

Figure 7 presents an overview of the sound source divider. The clustering process comprises two steps.

In the first step, we extract sound density map points corresponding to sound sources in the room where the smart speaker, that is, the microphone array, is

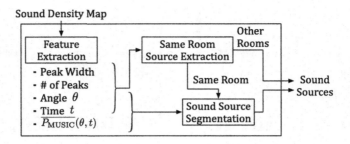

Fig. 7. Overview of sound source divider

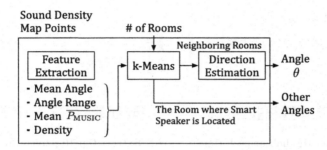

Fig. 8. Overview of room-direction estimator

installed. We perform DBSCAN clustering with four features: peak width at time t, the number of peaks at time t, angle θ, and time t. Each cluster is a set of sound density map points corresponding to a single sound source.

In the second step, the extracted sound density map points, corresponding to sound signals from the room where the smart speaker is installed, are more grouped into sound sources. Sound signals from sound sources in the same room as a smart speaker show specific features. The second step utilizes the DBSCAN clustering with three features, different from the first step: angle θ, time t, and wide-band sound power information $\overline{P_{\mathrm{MUSIC}}}(\theta, t)$. Sound sources in the same room as the smart speaker were estimated based on the angle variance of points in clusters divided in the first step. The cluster that has the largest angle variance is estimated as the sound source in the same room as the smart speaker because the sound signal can arrive from any direction in the room.

Finally, all the clustering results are merged to complete the sound source segmentation.

3.6 Room-Direction Estimator

Figure 8 shows an overview of the room-direction estimator, which first groups sound sources into rooms where the sound source is located using k-means clustering. The k-means clustering utilizes four types of features calculated for each sound source: mean angle, the range of angle, mean sound power $\overline{P_{\mathrm{MUSIC}}}(\theta, t)$,

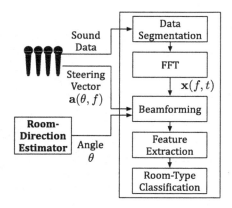

Fig. 9. Overview of room-type estimator

and the density of the sound density map points. The density is the ratio of the number of sound density map points to the area size of the rectangle where the sound density map points are located; k is set as the number of rooms, as is assumed to be given.

The room-direction estimator then calculates the most frequent sound arrival angle in each cluster, estimating the room direction. The room where the smart speaker is located is excluded from the room-direction estimation because the room direction cannot be defined there. The smart speaker co-located room was easily estimated based on the angle variance.

3.7   Room-Type Estimator

Figure 9 shows an overview of the room-type estimator, which synthesizes the sound signals in the same room and estimates the room-type using supervised learning. The room-type estimator first calculates the frequency components $\mathbf{x}(f, t)$, which is the same process as in the sound mapper. The synthesized sound signal was then calculated as follows:

$$y(f, t) = \mathbf{a}^{T}(\theta, f)\,\mathbf{x}(f, t), \tag{5}$$

where $\mathbf{a}(\theta, f)$ is the steering vector given in Sect. 3.4.

The synthesized sound signal $y(f, t)$ is divided by a fixed time-length window to extract features for supervised learning. We calculated the basic statistics (i.e., mean, maximum, minimum, and variance) of six types of 25 metrics below in each window as features, referring to [1], resulting in a 100-dimensional feature vector.

1. MFCCs: 20 Mel frequency cepstrum coefficients (MFCCs)
2. Zero crossing rate: the rate at which the positive and negative amplitudes are switched in the time-domain waveform

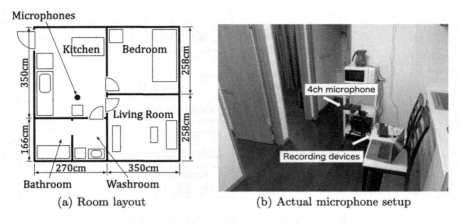

(a) Room layout   (b) Actual microphone setup

Fig. 10. Experiment setup

3. RMS: root mean square of sound signals
4. Spectral flatness: a measure of noise-like sounds noise-like [6,9]
5. Spectral centroid: barycenter of the spectrum [9]
6. Spectral roll-off: frequency such that the major components of the sound energy are contained below this frequency [9]

The room-type estimator finally classifies the room type of each room using the 100-dimensional feature vectors. We did not limit the classifier algorithm. We used a random forest classifier in this study as an example. The classifier model is trained in advance using sound data collected in a typical residential environment and is not limited to the actual smart speaker location.

4   Evaluation

We conducted initial evaluations using sound data collected in our 1-bedroom smart house. We also collected sound data of specific daily activities in a normal house, which is used for training the room-type estimator. We separately evaluated two tasks in our room-layout estimation: room-direction and room-type estimations.

4.1   Experiment Setup

Figure 10 shows the room layout and the actual microphone setup in our smart house. A 4-channel microphone array, that is, four AZDEN SGM-990 microphones separated by 50 mm, was installed in the living room on a tripod 1 m away from the walls at a height of 0.7 m, as shown in Fig. 10a. Sound data were collected using a Behringer UMC404HD USB audio interface connected to a laptop at a sampling rate of 44.1 kHz with a code length of 16 bits.

Table 1. Dataset used for evaluation of room-direction estimation

Dataset (40 s × 20)	Sound source 1 (Subject A voice)	Sound source 2 (Subject B voice)
Bedroom DS	Bedroom	Bedroom (10 s)
Kitchen DS	Kitchen	→ kitchen (10 s)
Washroom DS	Washroom	→ washroom (10 s)
Living DS	Living room	→ living (10 s)

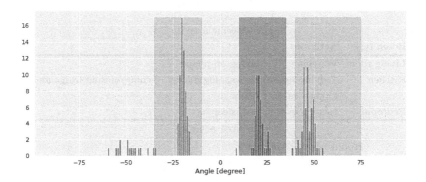

Fig. 11. Histogram of room-direction estimation results

4.2 Room-Direction Estimation Performance

To evaluate the room-direction estimation performance, we collected sound data while two subjects, A and B, were talking and walking in our smart house, creating four datasets, as shown in Table 1. Each dataset comprised 20 40-s recordings. Each recording was sound data collected while the subject A was freely walking in a room, as indicated in Table 1. Subject B was freely walking in a room for 10 s and moved to another room, as indicated in Table 1.

Room-direction estimation performance was evaluated with respect to two aspects: the room-based sound source clustering performance and room direction accuracy. The room-based sound source clustering performance was evaluated using the adjusted Rand index (ARI), which is a commonly used metric for evaluation of clustering performance. Room direction accuracy was evaluated using the rate of the number of trials that correctly estimated the room direction. As shown in Fig. 10, the microphone array was installed in the kitchen, which was next to the living room, bedroom, and bathroom; k in the room-direction estimator, that is, the number of clusters for the k-means, was therefore set to 4.

Figure 11 shows a histogram of the room-direction estimation results. The red, green, and yellow rectangles represent the correct room directions of the bedroom, living room, and washroom, respectively. The mean ARI was 0.725. The direction estimation accuracy, that is, the rate of the number of trials in the red, green, and yellow rectangles in Fig. 11, was 0.850. We can confirm that

Table 2. Room-direction estimation performance for each dataset

Dataset	Mean ARI	Direction estimation accuracy
Bedroom DS	0.897	0.783
Kitchen DS	0.327	0.683
Washroom DS	0.746	0.967
Living DS	0.925	0.967

Table 3. Activities used in room-type estimation evaluation

(a) Specific activity

Room type	Activities
Living room	Watching TV, talking on phone
Kitchen	Tidying up dishes, washing dishes, opening/closing fridge and kitchen cabinet doors
Bedroom	turning over in bed, sleeping

(b)Free activity

Room type	Activities
Living room	Watching TV
Kitchen	Washing dishes, eating, using microwave
Bedroom	Using smartphone on a bed, sleeping

our room-direction estimator successfully estimated the room direction with no training data.

For reference, the direction estimation accuracy was increased to 0.875 when the trials with ARI were greater than 0.9. Room-direction estimation performance relies heavily on the accuracy of sound source clustering in rooms.

We also compared the performance of room-direction estimation for each dataset. Table 2 shows the mean ARI and direction estimation accuracies for each dataset. From the table, we can observe that the performance with the kitchen dataset was significantly lower than that with other datasets. As shown in Table 1, the kitchen dataset includes the sound signals of subject A in the kitchen, where microphones were installed. Because the sound signals from the room where the microphones were installed can reach the microphones from any direction, the sound source segmentation described in Sect. 3.5 was highly unsuccessful, resulting in s significant degradation in performance.

4.3   Room-Type Estimation Performance

To evaluate the room-type estimation performance, we collected sound data in our smart house while the subject stayed in each room. We installed a microphone at the same height and location, as indicated in Fig. 10, and collected sound data for activity in each room. The sound data were collected both in a

Table 4. Activities for training of room-type estimator

Room type	Activities
Living room	Watching TV, talking
Kitchen	Cutting, frying, eating, washing dishes, using microwave
Bedroom	Sleeping

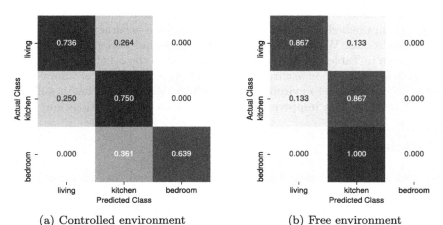

(a) Controlled environment   (b) Free environment

Fig. 12. Confusion matrices of room-type estimation results

controlled environment where the subject performed a specific activity and in a free environment where the subject stayed in a specific room doing activities freely. In the controlled environment, the sound data of each activity shown in Table 3a were collected for 120 s. In the free environment, we collected sound data for 30 min in each room. We emphasize that we gave no instructions for activity during the stay in the free environment. The actual activities during the 30 min are shown in Table 3b.

We also collected training data for room-type estimation because the room-type estimator uses supervised learning. The training data were collected in a normal house, while one subject performed the activity shown in Table 4. We used a Sony PCM-D100 recorder with an embedded microphone to evaluate the influence of the microphone and environmental differences. Each activity sound was recorded for 120 s.

We evaluated the room-type classification accuracy both in the controlled and in the free environments using the room-type estimation model trained with the data collected in the normal house. We divided the sound data with 10-s windows and calculated the features using the windowed data, which were used as input to the room-type estimator. Note that we did not perform the sound signal synthesis described in Sect. 3.7 as an initial evaluation in this study, evaluating the raw room-type estimation performance to validate the feasibility of our proposal.

Figure 12 shows the confusion matrices of the room-type estimation results. Figures 12a and 12b show the confusion matrices for the controlled and free environments, respectively. The mean accuracies in the controlled and free environments of the room-type estimation were 0.714 and 0.536, respectively. Even though the room type was estimated using the model trained with the data collected in a different environment, we derived a high estimation accuracy. We can conclude that the room-type estimation can be realized using the estimation model trained in advance with data collected in a normal house environment.

However, in the bedroom, the room-type estimation accuracy was lower than that in other rooms. We can easily guess that the sound power of the bedroom activity shown in Table 3 is relatively low compared to the other room activities, resulting in low estimation accuracy. The room-type estimation accuracy in the bedroom in a controlled environment was 0.639. We believe that a sufficient amount of training data improves the accuracy of room-type estimation.

5   Conclusion

In this study, we presented the design of a room-layout estimator for smart speakers. The room layout, that is, the direction and type of the adjacent rooms, is estimated using reverberation features that are extracted from a sound density map, which is a map of sound power distribution as a function of time. The sound sources were grouped into rooms where the sound source was located by unsupervised learning to estimate the room direction. The room type was finally estimated by supervised learning using a pre-trained model. We conducted experimental evaluations and demonstrated that our room-type estimator successfully estimated room directions and room types with accuracies of 0.850 and 0.714, respectively. In our future work, we plan to improve the accuracy of room-type estimation in the bedroom by introducing novel features. We also plan to study the influence of the location of large objects, such as furniture, and verify our method for different room layouts.

References

1. Bountourakis, V., Vrysis, L., Papanikolaou, G.: Machine learning algorithms for environmental sound recognition: towards soundscape semantics. In: Proceedings of the Audio Mostly 2015 on Interaction With Sound. AM '15, Association for Computing Machinery, pp. 1–7. New York, NY, USA (2015). https://doi.org/10.1145/2814895.2814905
2. Chahuara, P., Portet, F., Vacher, M.: Making context aware decision from uncertain information in a smart home: a Markov logic network approach. In: Ambient Intelligence, vol. 8309, pp. 78–93. Springer International Publishing, Cham (2013). https://doi.org/10.1007/978-3-319-03647-2_6
3. Chahuara, P., Portet, F., Vacher, M.: Context-aware decision making under uncertainty for voice-based control of smart home. Expert Syst. Appl. **75**, 63–79 (2017). https://doi.org/10.1016/j.eswa.2017.01.014

4. Danès, P., Bonnal, J.: Information-theoretic detection of broadband sources in a coherent beamspace MUSIC scheme. In: 2010 IEEE/RSJ International Conference on Intelligent Robots and Systems, pp. 1976–1981. IEEE, Taipei (2010). https://doi.org/10.1109/IROS.2010.5651249

5. Ishi, C.T., Even, J., Hagita, N.: Using multiple microphone arrays and reflections for 3D localization of sound sources. In: 2013 IEEE/RSJ International Conference on Intelligent Robots and Systems, pp. 3937–3942 (2013). https://doi.org/10.1109/IROS.2013.6696919

6. Johnston, J.D.: Transform coding of audio signals using perceptual noise criteria. IEEE J. Selected Areas Commun. **6**(2) (1988). https://doi.org/10.1109/49.608

7. Knapp, C., Carter, G.: The generalized correlation method for estimation of time delay. IEEE Trans. Acoustics Speech Signal Process. **24**(4), 320–327 (1976). https://doi.org/10.1109/TASSP.1976.1162830

8. Okamoto, T., Nishimura, R., Iwaya, Y.: Estimation of sound source positions using a surrounding microphone array. Acoustical Sci. Technol. **28**(3), 181–189 (2007). https://doi.org/10.1250/ast.28.181

9. Peeters, G.: A large set of audio features for sound description (similarity and classification) in the CUIDADO project (2004). recherche.ircam.fr/equipes/analyse/synthese/peeters/ARTICLES/Peeters/2003/cuidadoaudiofeatures.pdf

10. Ribeiro, F., Zhang, C., Florencio, D.A., Ba, D.E.: Using reverberation to improve range and elevation discrimination for small array sound source localization. IEEE Trans. Audio Speech Lang. Proc. **18**(7), 1781–1792 (2010). https://doi.org/10.1109/TASL.2010.2052250

11. Schmidt, R.: Multiple emitter location and signal parameter estimation. IEEE Trans. Antennas Propagation **34**(3), 276–280 (1986). https://doi.org/10.1109/TAP.1986.1143830

12. Silverman, H.F.: An algorithm for determining talker location using a linear microphone array and optimal hyperbolic fit. In: Proceedings of the Workshop on Speech and Natural Language. HLT '90, Association for Computational Linguistics, pp. 151–156. USA (1990). https://doi.org/10.3115/116580.116632

13. Suzuki, T., Kaneda, Y.: Improving the robustness of multiple signal classification (MUSIC) method to reflected sounds by sub-band peak-hold processing. Acoust. Sci. Tech. **30**(5), 387–389 (2009). https://doi.org/10.1250/ast.30.387

14. Tanaka, M., Kaneda, Y.: Performance of sound source direction estimation methods under reverberant conditions. J. Acoust. Society Japan (E) **14**(4), 291–292 (1993). https://doi.org/10.1250/ast.14.291

15. Wang, H., Chu, P.: Voice source localization for automatic camera pointing system in videoconferencing. In: 1997 IEEE International Conference on Acoustics, Speech, and Signal Processing. vol. 1, pp. 187–190 (1997). https://doi.org/10.1109/ICASSP.1997.599595

16. Warsitz, E., Haeb-Umbach, R.: Blind acoustic beamforming based on generalized eigenvalue decomposition. IEEE Trans. Audio Speech Lang. Process. **15**(5), 1529–1539 (2007). https://doi.org/10.1109/TASL.2007.898454

Dynamic Taxi Ride-Sharing Through Adaptive Request Propagation Using Regional Taxi Demand and Supply

Haoxiang Yu[1]([✉])(iD), Vaskar Raychoudhury[2](iD), and Snehanshu Saha[3](iD)

[1] Department of Electrical and Computer Engineering,
The University of Texas at Austin, Austin, TX, USA
hxyu@utexas.edu
[2] Departmen of CSE, Miami University, Oxford, OH, USA
raychov@miamioh.edu
[3] Department of CS&IS and APPCAIR, BITS Pilani Goa Campus, Goa, India

Abstract. Taxi ride-sharing is an emerging public transportation model that provides several benefits in terms of cost, environmental impact, and road congestion. It is further popularized through market available app-based systems, such as Uber, Lyft, Didi, etc. However, those systems are limited due to their centralized architecture, high cost sharing with the driver, and proprietary business model. Distributed ride-sharing, on the other hand, involves only passengers and drivers and operates in a peer-to-peer manner. But, distributed ride-sharing systems often suffer due to Spatio-temporal constraints associated with taxi demand and supply as well as broadcast message storms. While we have observed dynamic and distributed ride-sharing systems which address the Spatio-temporal issues, there is hardly any effort to reduce their message overhead. In this paper, we present a hybrid model of ride-sharing where a central server adaptively calculates transmission range for passenger request propagation using Spatio-temporal information of ride-sharing success rate for the past 30-minute. Passengers use the adaptive transmission range to find the best shared-ride using a distributed manner. Our extensive empirical evaluation shows that our proposed approach increases the overall ride-sharing success rate and taxi utilization while significantly reducing the communication overhead, request processing time, and passenger waiting time.

Keywords: Dynamic ride sharing · Adaptive transmission range · Distributed algorithm · Spatio-temporal constraints

1 Introduction

United Nations has recently forecasted that by 2050, 68% of the world's population is going to live in cities in order to avail a decent livelihood and better

T. Hara and H. Yamaguchi (Eds.): MobiQuitous 2021, LNICST 419, pp. 40–56, 2022.
https://doi.org/10.1007/978-3-030-94822-1_3

infrastructures [12]. This "could add another 2.5 billion people to urban areas by 2050". Needless to say that this will stretch the infrastructure and public facilities available in the cities as they hardly grow at the same level as the population. Gradual expansion of urban boundaries force people to take up residences farther away from the centre and commute to work on a daily basis. Multitude of individual vehicles lead to traffic congestion and the resulting revenue loss and environmental impact. In order to address the problem ride-sharing is coming up as an efficient solution which can transport multiple commuters sharing part or whole of their commute. Taxicabs and other online app-based taxi services, such as *UberPool*[1], *Lyft*[2] and *DiDi*[3] can do miracles in this domain. We have seen huge growth of such services in recent year. However, most of the market available ride-sharing service are proprietary and have a centralized system model which is non-scalable and failure-prone.

In order to address the challenges associated with the centralized ride-sharing systems, researchers have proposed various alternate distributed ride-sharing systems which work by peer-to-peer coordination of passengers and taxi drivers [6,15]. However, distributed ride-sharing problem is non-trivial as it heavily depends on the various user and application related parameters. The spatiotemporal co-location of passengers are crucial to combining individual rides and assigning them into a shared taxicab. While this is feasible for static ride-sharing environment where a group of passengers share the same start and end points or take a cab operating on a fixed route (e.g., from Airport to the downtown), it is not the same for dynamic ride-sharing situations. In dynamic ride-sharing, a passenger request can arrive at anytime and a taxi might need to calculate in real-time, the feasibility of a detour from the current route (while carrying one or more passengers) in order to accommodate the new request. Research shows that dynamic ride matching is a NP-hard problem [10] in itself. Moreover, distributed ride-sharing aims to propagate passenger requests to a larger area in order to reach more taxis, which increases the chance of successfully finding a matching ride. However, this approach is sure to increase the number of messages and the overall processing and response time of the system even though the success rate improves.

An in-depth analysis of large-scale taxi demand and supply information for the Chicago metropolitan region [1,2] shows that passenger and taxi distribution over an urban area is unbalanced. Figure 1 shows the spatial distribution of passenger requests per hour across the community areas of Chicago. We can notice three distinct zones with different levels of passenger density - significantly high (dense zone), significantly low (sparse zone), and the areas which are in between the two extremes (target zone). We can create an intervention in the target zone in terms of adaptive transmission range control and can achieve the desired impact. Adaptive transmission control strategy will reduce transmission range in areas with a high success rate of ride-sharing, so that, fewer taxis receive

---

[1] Uber: https://www.uber.com/.

[2] Lyft: https://www.lyft.com/.

[3] DiDi: https://www.didiglobal.com/.

new passenger requests while maintaining the current success rate. Alternately, the transmission range will be increased for areas with a lower success rate of ride-sharing, in order to reach more taxis and to improve the success rate.

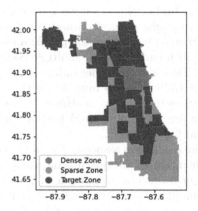

Fig. 1. Spatial Distribution of Ride-share Requests across Chicago Metropolitan Region

In this paper, we have proposed a hybrid ride-sharing system that uses peer-to-peer communication between passengers and taxi drivers to book shared rides. A server is deployed to analyze real-time passenger and taxi distribution in Chicago metropolitan area (see Fig. 1) based on a historical trend analysis (of the past 30-minute) of ride-sharing success rate. The server then provides a suitable transmission range to a querying passenger based on their spatio-temporal requirements. The server also prepares itself to serve better by using predictive analysis of passenger demand across the Chicago metropolitan region using the Prophet forecasting model [11]. Extensive empirical evaluation shows that our proposed ride-sharing system with an adaptive transmission range can improve the ride-sharing success rate for different community areas with various traffic demands while reducing the message overhead and passenger waiting time. Our system also enhances taxi occupancy and utilization by efficiently implementing ride-sharing algorithms through adaptive transmission range control.

In summary, this paper makes the following novel and unique contributions.

- We analyze the ride requests to understand the spatio-temporal distribution of passenger demand and taxi supply throughout the Chicago metropolitan area. To adapt to the constantly changing passenger demand and taxi supply, we propose a novel adaptive transmission range control system for request propagation.
- We develop a hybrid taxi ride-sharing system that includes passenger feedback to dynamically fine-tune transmission range to achieve a higher success rate for ride-sharing while reducing computation and communication overhead. Our taxi ride-sharing algorithm works in a purely distributed manner.

- Simulation studies using the Chicago taxi dataset show that adaptive transmission range can successfully control message propagation and corresponding processing overhead of taxi ride-sharing. Also, our system reduces passenger waiting time while improving taxi utilization.

2   Related Work

Taxi ride-sharing is coming up at a fast pace as a transportation solution for the next generation. It originated as a Dial-a-Ride Problem (DARP) [14] which is basically a static ride-sharing problem much like Carpooling (trips pre-coordinated between a set of passengers for a fixed set of destinations, like home to office) [4]. Psaraftis, et al. [10] have shown that the DARP is NP-hard with possible multi-objective extensions. Given the intricacies of the problem, taxi ride-sharing has attracted many researchers throughout the last decade [5,8,9,13]. Agatz, et al. [3] have provided a thorough analysis of the various aspects of both static and dynamic ride-sharing problems. However, the Spatio-temporal challenges posed by the recent on-demand dynamic and distributed taxi ride-sharing systems have not been paid enough attention. The first known distributed taxi-ride-sharing algorithm was proposed by D'Orey, et al. [7] but without significant empirical evaluation. Bathla, et al. [6] proposed the first properly evaluated and significantly efficient distributed Taxi Ride Sharing (TRS) algorithm was tested using large-scale continuous GPS traces of 4,000 taxis in Shanghai, China. An extension of this work with better results was presented by Yu, et al. [15]. However, their results are simulated using single trip taxi data in Chicago metropolitan region [1]. We, on the other hand, proposed a distributed and dynamic taxi ride-sharing system with a partly hybrid architecture to control the request propagation range. We are using a server which has a global view of the taxi demand and ride sharing success rate only through passenger communicated messages. We have also used a voluminous set of actual ride-sharing data [2] made available by Chicago Transport Authority.

3   System Model and Assumptions

Figure 2 shows the overall architecture of our proposed ride-sharing system which works in a hybrid manner. Passengers query the T_x-server to find out the best transmission range for propagating their requests. The operation of the T_x-server is further explained in Sect. 3.1. Once the adaptive transmission range is obtained from the T_x-server, the rest of the operation (finding shared rides) is performed in a purely distributed fashion involving the passengers and the taxi drivers. Request messages for ride-sharing are sent to all the taxis within the transmission range (T_x) in a single or multi-hop manner.

Our algorithm uses a variety of variables and data structures (see Table 1) and a set of seven (7) different types of messages (see Table 2) required to facilitate the adaptive ride-sharing operations.

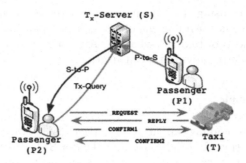

Fig. 2. System architecture

Table 1. Variables used

Variable	Significance
P_{id}	Unique integer identifier of a Passenger P
S_p	Pick-up location (latitude, longitude) of P
D_p	Drop off location (latitude, longitude) of P
t	Time at which P made a ride-sharing request
$time_d$	Time (in units) estimated by T to reach D_p from S_p (considering current state of Q_t and real road network topology)
Δ	Maximum Time (in mins.) up to which the time d can be exceeded from the actual time of trip (aka. detour tolerance)
T_{id}	Unique integer identifier of a Taxi T
T_{loc}	Current location (latitude, longitude) of T
P_{nbr}	All taxi within neighborhood of P_{id}
N_{vac}	Number of available seats (in integer) in T
e	Pick-up (e_{pick}) or drop-off (e_{drop}) event
Q_e	Temporary queue of e at T_{id}
Q_t	Temporary queue of $REQUEST$ at T_{id}
L_{con}	Permanent list of confirmed passengers at T_{id}
L_e	List of e associated with L_{con}
$time(T_{loc}, D_p)$	Time (in units) estimated by at T_{id} to reach D_p from T_{loc}
L_{reply}	Sorted list of $REPLY$ messages stored at P_{id}
T_{nbr}	All taxi within neighborhood of T_{id}
τ_p	Timer at at P_{id}
S_f	Success Flag which records if the trip request is successful or not
L	Spatial region (community areas of Chicago)
N	Number of available Taxicabs for the whole city (across all the L)
$T_x^{C_L}$	The adaptive transmission range for area L at current time instant

Table 2. Messages used in algorithm

Messages	Significance
$P\text{-}to\text{-}S$ (L, S_f)	P reports to T_x-Server current values of L and S_f.
$T_x Query$ (P_{id}, L)	T_x value query message from P to T_x-Server
$S\text{-}to\text{-}P$ (T_x^{Now})	Reply from T_x-Server to P with the new T_x
$REQUEST$ $(P_{id}, S_p, D_p, t, \Delta)$	Request for ride-sharing sent by P
$REPLY$ $(T_{id}, time_p, time_d)$	Reply from T to P with estimated pick-up time, drop off time and cost for ride
$CONFIRM\ 1$ (P_{id})	Acceptance / Rejection status sent by P to T
$CONFIRM\ 2$ (T_{id})	Acceptance / Rejection status sent by T to P

3.1 Generating Adaptive Transmission Range

Figure 2 shows the presence of the T_x-server for generating an adaptive transmission range for passenger request propagation. T_x is adaptively determined based on historical data about the ride-sharing success rate of all the passengers from a particular area and for the previous 30-minute-time span. Passengers query the T_x-server to find out the best transmission range and the server provides the same calculation using the historical data of ride-sharing success rate based on Spatio-temporal parameters.

The Eq. 1 shows the formula for calculating the current transmission range $(T_x^{C_L})$ for area L based on historical values of localized success rates.

$$T_x^{C_L} = \begin{cases} T_x^{C_L - t} * \kappa^+, \ if \ (Succ_{rs}^{(L)} < \Gamma_{low}) \\ T_x^{C_L - t} * \kappa^-, \ if \ (Succ_{rs}^{(L)} > \Gamma_{high}) \end{cases} \tag{1}$$

Where, $t = 30$ minutes, so $C_L - t$ signifies time which is 30 min prior to the current time (C). κ $(\kappa^+ >= 1, \kappa^- <= 1)$ is a parameter depending on the localized success rate of ride-sharing $(Succ_{rs}^{(L)})$ (see Sect. 6.2) which is again upper bounded by Γ_{high} and lower-bounded by Γ_{low}. We have varied κ and Γ to empirically find best values for these parameters.

3.2 Practical Assumptions

We make the following assumptions for our proposed ride-sharing system:

- For any passenger, drop-off time should be after the pickup time.
- Wireless communication between taxis and passengers may incur message loss and transmission delays. So, we use timers at passenger and taxi-end to handle lost messages.
- Taxis are mobile entities and they can change position significantly during the time a passenger sends out a ride-sharing request and by the time the request is confirmed. We have incorporated measures in our algorithms to handle the overall system dynamics.
- Each ride-sharing request is considered separately and for a single passenger.
- Taxi drivers must address the detour tolerance (Δ) specified by a passenger.

4   Algorithm for Taxi Ride-Sharing Using Adaptive Transmission Range

In this Section, we describe the functioning of our ride-sharing algorithm which contains a passenger to T_x-server communication and a separate passenger to Taxi communication algorithm. So, we have divided the algorithm into passenger-end (Algorithm 1), T_x-Server-end (Algorithm 2) and taxi-end (Algorithm 3).

4.1   Algorithm at Passenger-End

Ride-share scheduling starts by a passenger P_{id} when s/he broadcasts a *REQUEST* message and initializes a timer (τ_p). In order to prevent any broadcast storm, a transmission range (T_x) is provided for first hop message distribution. E.g., if $T_x = 100$ then the REQUEST message will be received by all the taxi drivers within 100 m from the passenger. If none of the taxis are available to serve the passenger, then they distribute the REQUEST to their 1-hop neighborhood and propagate it in this way until a maximum request distribution range is reached. The passenger receives zero (0) or more *REPLY* messages from taxi drivers until the timer (τ_p) expires. S/he then chooses the taxi which can complete the trip in minimum amount of time (or we can select some other parameter, like cost), acknowledges with a *CONFIRM 1* message and re-starts the timer (τ_p). The passenger must wait for a *CONFIRM 2* message from the same taxi before the trip can be finally confirmed. The *CONFIRM 2* message has been introduced to account for the highly dynamic nature of the environment as a taxi can move or confirm some other passenger before the current passenger receives a confirmation. So, we can say that our system is resilient to system dynamics resulting from node mobility, message loss and delay. In case no *CONFIRM 2* message is received by the time τ_p expires, the passenger can resend the REQUEST message up to two more times. Once a ride-sharing request is confirmed or not after a total of three attempts, the passenger sends a *P-to-S* message to the T_x-server carrying information about his local community area and the status of finding the shared-ride (successful or not).

4.2   Algorithm at T_x-Server-end

The T_x-Server receives *P-to-S* messages from passengers across the complete region. The messages are then stored in a queue in the temporal order of arrival. Every 30 min, messages are de-queued and used to calculate success rate of ride sharing for a particular community area L. The server then calculates the adaptive transmission range for a particular area L following Eq. (1). When a passenger sends out the T_xQuery for their current location, the server sends the $T_x^{C_L}$ through a *S-to-P* message.

Algorithm 1: Algorithm at Passenger P_{id} Side

---

1 Broadcast $REQUEST$ to all $T_{id} \in P_{nbr}$
   //Collect incoming REPLY messages until τ_p expires
2 $L.append$ ($REPLY$ message)
3 Sort L based on $time_d$
4 Send $CONFIRM\ 1$ to the taxi with minimum $time_d$ and start τ_p
5 Wait for $CONFIRM\ 2$ from T until τ_p expires
6 **if** $CONFIRM\ 2$ *received* **then**
7 | Send P-to-S to the T_x-Server with L and $S_f = True$
8 **else if** τ_p *expired* **then**
9 | Send P-to-S to the T_x-Server with L and $S_f = False$

4.3 Algorithm at Taxi-End

Passenger requests for ride-sharing are received by taxi and stored locally in a temporally ordered message queue. As long as a taxi has vacant seats (we assume that a taxi can carry at most 4 passengers at a time) and pending requests, it will execute the *RouteValidation()* function. This function actually generates all possible route permutations considering the confirmed events and the temporary events in the queues (Q_e and Q_{con}) and finds the best route for the passenger in terms of the minimum detour delay. The route selected must abide by the practical assumptions listed for our system in Section III. B.

After a taxi determines a passenger whom it can pickup, a *REPLY* message is sent. Taxis sequentially process requests and can send multiple REPLY for one vacant seat. As discussed in Section IV.A, passengers can choose the best offer and send a *CONFIRM 1* message. When a taxi receives the first *CONFIRM 1* message from a passenger for an ongoing booking negotiation, it re-calculates the *RouteValidation()* function to make sure that the passenger can still be accepted given its current status. This step helps us to cope with the extremely dynamic nature of this distributed system. If the route re-validation is successful, a *CONFIRM 2* message is sent to the passenger confirming the booking. The passenger record is then added to L_{con} and the corresponding pickup and dropoff events (e_{pick} and e_{drop}) are added to the taxi schedule (L_e). The taxi will keep checking all of the incoming *CONFIRM 1* messages until there is no remaining vacant seat.

5 Spatio-Temporal Passenger Demand and Taxi Supply Analysis

Our T_x-Server calculates the adaptive transmission range based on the historical data and also predicts the future passenger demand in an area based on the historical trend. It takes into account periodic and non-periodic trends into consideration following the Prophet model that we discuss in this Section. Prophet model [11] is a time series data forecasting model to capture non-linear trends

---

Algorithm 2: Algorithm at T_x-Server Side

//On receiving a P-to-S message
1 *Enqueue* P-to-S(L, S_f) in L_s and add the current time stamp - T_c
   //Keep processing the messages in L_s in FIFO order
2 *Dequeue* P-to-S(L, S_f) from L_s
3 $M_s \leftarrow (L, S_f, T_c)$
   //For all the M_s received at time T_c, where $T_c = T_{curr} - 30$ (minutes)
4 Calculate ride-sharing success rate for area L
5 Calculate $T_x^{C_L}$
   //On receiving a $T_x Query$ message from P_{id} in area L
6 Send $T_x^{C_L}$ to P_{id} via S-to-P message

---

along with seasonal effects which varies in a daily, weekly, and yearly manner as well as during holidays. It works best with time series that have strong seasonal effects and several seasons of historical data. Prophet can robustly handle seasonal variation time series data and can efficiently deal with outliers. Prophet forecasting model is composed of several linear and non-linear time series functions and can be represented using the Eq. (2):

$$y(t) = g(t) + s(t) + h(t) + \epsilon(t) \tag{2}$$

where, y(t) signifies the predicted value; g(t) captures the non-periodic changes through a linear or a logistic function; s(t) represents the period or seasonal changes in terms of yearly, monthly, weekly, daily or any other patterns; h(t) shows the irregular or holiday patterns for 1 or more days and finally, $\epsilon(t)$ will capture any other types of changes not captured by the rest of the parameters. So, in summary, the model can be represented as a combination of various regular and irregular trends:

Forecasted Value = Non-periodic segment-wise time series trend + seasonal time series trend + holiday / festival impacts + errors / noise

Prophet model can be declared either as a linear or as a logistic model. While in linear models, there is no pre-specified maximum or minimum limit; for logistic models, the highest and lowest values are pre-set. If the data contains parameters which can attain saturation, like processing power, etc., then we should use a logistic function for that saturating growth model. Otherwise, the default linear model with constant growth rate can be used. In this study, we used the linear model in which the various outliers in the dataset are normalized to have a more homogeneous data pool. The linear trend model is shown in Eq. (3):

$$g(t) = (k + a(t)^T \delta)t + (m + a(t)^T \gamma) \tag{3}$$

Here k represents the growth rate, δ captures the rate adjustments, and m is the offset parameter. In order to make the function a continuous one, the parameter γ_j is set to: $-s_j \delta_j$.

Algorithm 3: Algorithm at Taxi T_{id}

//On receiving a REQUEST message

1   *Enqueue* REQUEST in temporally ordered Q_t

   //Keep processing REQUEST messages from (Q_t) in FIFO order

2   $r = (P_{id}, S_p, D_p, t) \leftarrow Dequeue(Q_t)$

3   $Q_e \leftarrow Enqueue(r.e_{drop})$

4   $Q_e \leftarrow Enqueue(r.e_{pick})$

5   **if** $Q_t \neq \emptyset$ *AND* $N_{vac} \neq 0$ **then**

6   **if** *Route Validation*$(Q_e, L_e) \neq \emptyset$ **then**

7   Send *REPLY* to P_{id}

8   **else**

9   **Forward** r to all $T_{id} \in T_{nbr}$

10 **else if** $N_{vac} = 0$ **then**

11   **Forward** r to all $T_{id} \in T_{nbr}$

  // On receiving a *CONFIRM 1* message

12 **if** $N_{vac} \neq 0$ **then**

13   **if** *Route Validation*$(Q_e, L_e) \neq \emptyset$ **then**

14   Send *CONFIRMATION 2* to P_{id} (for r)

15          $L_{con} \leftarrow r$

16          $L_e \leftarrow r.e_{pick}$

17          $L_e \leftarrow r.e_{drop}$

  Route Validation(Q_e, L_e)

18 **for** $Q_e.length$ **do**

19   **for** $L_e.length$ **do**

20   Routes[k] = $Q_e \times L_e$

           //Generate all possible permutations of events

21 **foreach** *route* $\in Routes[k]$ **do**

22   **foreach** $P_{id} \in L_{con}$ **do**

23   **if** $((time(T_{loc}, D_p) > ((time_d + \Delta) - $ *time already travelled*$))$ **then**

24   The route is NOT valid drop it

25 **if** $Routes[k] \neq \emptyset$ **then**

26   We choose the route with the minimum detour time for P_{id}

27   **return** *route*

Rate adjustments are parameters associated with trend changes that can occur in the growth model and are represented as *changepoints*. If there are S changepoints at times $S_j = 1, 2, 3, ..., S$, then rate adjustment parameter δ can be defined as

$$\delta \in \mathbb{R}^{\mathbb{S}} \tag{4}$$

where, δ_j denotes the rate change occurring at time s_j. $a(t)$ in Eq. (3) can be expressed as a vector

$$a(t) \in \{0, 1\}^S \tag{5}$$

whose values can vary as follows:

$$a_j(t) = \begin{cases} 1, & \text{if } t \geq s_j, \\ 0, & \text{otherwise} \end{cases} \tag{6}$$

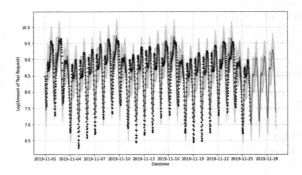

Fig. 3. Result of Prophet Forecast Model for Chicago Community Area 8

So, the growth rate at time t will be $k + a(t)^T \delta$, where k is the base rate and the remaining terms signify required adjustments up to the time t. At the time of the adjustment of base rate k, the offset parameter m must be adjusted as well, in order to connect the endpoints of the segments. In Fig. 3, we present an example graph showing prediction results of the number of passenger requests in Chicago community area 8, depending on the pre-trained model, date-time, and historical 3-hour-data. While the black dots in the figure show real data points from the dataset, the blue lines show the predicted result.

The demand prediction model described above, helps the T_x server to calculate the adaptive transmission range more accurately depending on the spatio-temporal variation.

6   Performance Evaluation

We have resorted to simulation-based experimentation and testing for evaluating our proposed algorithms as it was not possible to consider a dynamic deployment using a number of real taxis due to various practical and possibly legal restrictions. In this section, we discuss in detail the platform, metrics, and results of our simulation experiments.

6.1   Simulation Setup

In the simulation of our algorithm, we use the Chicago taxi ride-share dataset [2] which is open, recent (2018–2021), and voluminous. We have tested with a subset of the total records and our data contains 259351 records from 06–19–2019 covering all the 77 community areas in the Chicago metropolitan area. The dataset obfuscates the actual pickup and drop-off location and time of passengers in order to maintain their privacy. We have also simulated using data for longer periods (up to 1 month) and the trends of the results are observed to be similar. More details of the dataset and other simulation parameters are presented in Table 3. We would like to mention that after experimenting with different values of κ and Γ, we settled for the values shown in the table. We found that the current values can achieve stability of adaptive transmission range and not create race conditions.

Table 3. Simulation Parameters

Parameters	Value
Initial transmission range $T_x(init)$	100, 800 (in mtr.)
Max. transmission range (T_{max})	2 KMs
Simulation period	06–19–2019 00:00 - 23:59
Number of taxis (N)	200, 400, 2000
Capacity of each Taxi (N)	4
Message delay (δ)	1 - 5 Millisecond(s)
Detour tolerance / Δ	5 min
τ_p	3 min
κ^+ (See Eq. 1)	1.2
κ^- (See Eq. 1)	0.8
Γ_{high} (See Eq. 1)	0.9
Γ_{low} (See Eq. 1)	0.5

Our simulation framework is built over Java and makes use of an Intel(R) Xeon (TM) Gold 6126 (2.6 GHz 12 Cores/24 Threads) processor with 96 GB memory for the experiment.

6.2 Performance Metrics

We evaluate our algorithms with respect to the following four performance metrics.

1. **Localized Success Rate** ($SUCC_{rs}^{(L)}$): For a particular community area L in Chicago, where $L \in \{1, 2, ..., 77\}$, *localized success rate* is measured as the ratio of the number of confirmed shared-ride requests to the total number of requests originating from area L.

2. **Taxi Activation Ratio** (Act_r): What percentage of taxicabs are really being used (carried one or more passengers) during the simulation period.
3. **Average Occupancy Period (per Taxi)** $(Occu_{avg})$: Ratio of the time a taxi had two or more passenger(s) to the total time the taxi travelled on road. We take the average of all the taxis that were actually used.
4. **Average Waiting Time to Pickup** $(Waiting_p^{avg})$: It is the average waiting time between the instant at which a passenger sent out the first *REQUEST* message and the instant s/he got picked up by a taxi (for all the successful ride-sharing requests).

6.3   Area Types

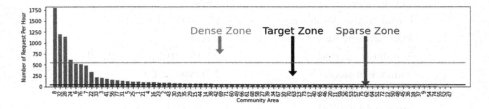

Fig. 4. Sorted list of community areas in Chicago in the order of passenger density

Based on the average number passenger requests originating from different community areas (77) in Chicago, we separate Chicago metropolitan region into three different types of zones as discussed below (see Fig. 4). Those three different zones are:

1. **Dense Zone:** Community areas with significantly high number of passenger requests ($\geq$ 545 requests per hour) are considered as dense. For the dense zone, our goal is to reduce the M_{avg}^L and R_{avg}^L while maintaining high $SUCC_{rs}^{(L)}$ by auto adjusting the T_x.
2. **Sparse Zone:** Sparse zone are those which generates significantly low number of passenger requests ($\leq$ 46 requests per hour). Our experiments show that sparse zones does not show any noticeable improvement $SUCC_{rs}^{(L)}$ by adaptively changing the T_x.
3. **Target Zone:** Except the dense and sparse zones, the remaining community areas are our target zones which generates considerable number of passenger requests ($\geq$ 46 and $\leq$ 545). We call this as our target zone, since we noticed maximum improvement in $SUCC_{rs}^{(L)}$ takes place by auto adjusting the T_x.

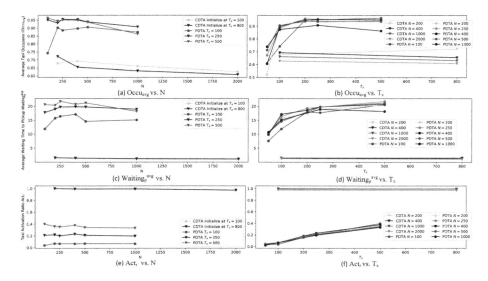

Fig. 5. Performance results

6.4 Evaluation Results and Analysis

In this section we present our results along with in-depth analysis and explanation. Our empirical results have been compared with a previous distributed ride-sharing system [15] which we call 'PDTA' for the sake of convenience. Similarly, we call the currently proposed ride-sharing solution as 'CDTA'.

Figure 5 (a) and (b) shows the variation of average taxi occupancy $Occu_{avg}$ of our system with respect to changing values of total number of taxis (N) and the variable transmission range (T_x). Similarly, Fig. (c) and (d) are plotting the average passenger waiting time to pick up $(Waiting_p^{avg})$ and the Fig. (e) and (f) are depicting how much of the available taxis in the system are being used for ride-sharing (Act_r).

Figure 5 (e) and (f) shows that the adaptive T_x significantly increase the Act_r over PDTA and reaches as high as 100%. For the CDTA, T_x values of 100 and 800 hardly has any effect on the final result. Similar result can be seen in Fig. 5 (b) and (d) for $Occu_{avg}$ and $Waiting_p^{avg}$. As a result of achieving high Act_r, our system (CDTA) improves average taxi utilization $Occu_{avg}$ (see Fig. 5 (a)) compared to PDTA. Since, the adaptive T_x increases overall ride-sharing success rate, the passenger waiting time is reduced as shown in Fig. 5 (c). We can notice that $Waiting_p^{avg}$ for CDTA is reduced by at least 10 times while compared to the PDTA.

While analyzing physical significance of the results, we notice the following trends. Act_r in Fig. 5 (e) is very high because our adaptive T_x control strategy can improve T_x in sparse zones and thereby achieve better taxi utilization and high rate of ride-sharing success. Also, we can see in Fig. 5 (c), the overall passenger waiting time before pickup is reduced. We believe that our adaptive T_x method

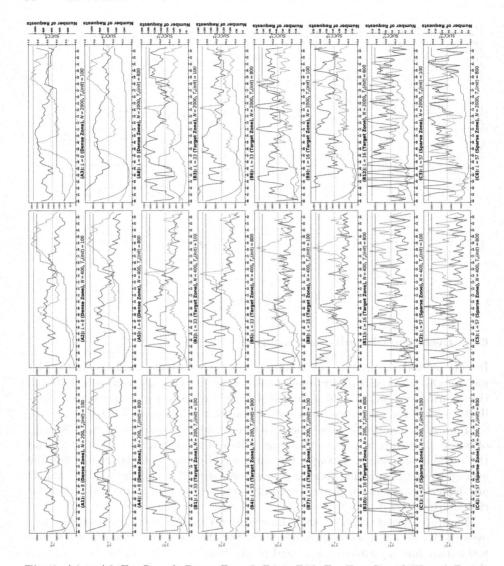

Fig. 6. A1 to A6: For Sample Dense Zone 8, B1 to B12: For Two Sample Target Zones 33 and 16, C1 to C6: For Sparse Zone 57

reduce request propagation in dense zones which reduces average response time and leads to faster taxi response. Since, the bulk of the request originate from the dense zone, reducing processing overhead for those brings down the overall processing time and endures less waiting time before passenger pickup.

Figure 6 represents variation of adaptive T_x with respect to changing values of taxi numbers (N) and initial transmission range ($T_x(init)$) for the three types of zones - *dense*, *sparse* and *target*. We observe that for same community area (L)

and same N, adaptive T_x always stabilizes to the similar range even the $T_x(init)$ varies from anywhere between 100 to 800 m (Fig. 6 (A1)). On the other hand, if we vary N, while keeping $T_x(init)$ constant, the adaptive T_x will change until it reaches the maximum request propagation range (T_{max}). We must clarify that with less value of N, T_x keeps increasing until it reaches T_{max} in order to find matching rides for the user. Clearly, with higher value of N, ride sharing success rate can stay high even at a lower value of T_x which reduces communication and processing overhead (Fig. 6 (B4, B5)). Evidently, with fixed N and $T_x(init)$, the dense zones require lower value of T_x than the target and sparse zones (Fig. 6 (A1, B1, and C1)).

7 Conclusion and Future Work

In this paper, we have proposed a novel ride-sharing system and algorithm which works by peer-to-peer interaction between the major participants - passengers and taxi drivers. In order to ensure a high success rate of ride-sharing and to reduce communication and processing overhead, we have introduced a server that takes passenger feedback on the success or failure of their ride-sharing attempt. This information is used to generate historical analysis of the Spatio-temporal distribution of ride-sharing success rates across the Chicago metropolitan area. Based on that, the server recommends different transmission range for ride-share request propagation to different users depending on their current location and time. Our approach has been evaluated to improve the ride-sharing success rate while reducing the message overhead and overall response time. In the future, we would like to apply our technique to other metropolitan regions of the world where traffic data is made available. We also plan to experiment with parameters such as κ and Γ to study their effects on the system performance in more detail.

Acknowledgments. This work was supported by Dr. Jens Mueller, Director, High-Performance Computing Services at Miami University through the use of the Redhawk cluster.

References

1. Chicago data: taxi trips. data.cityofchicago.org/Transportation/Taxi-Trips/wrvz-psew/. Accessed Jan 2020
2. Chicago data: transportation network providers. data.cityofchicago.org/Transportation-Network-Providers-Trips/m6dm-c72p/. Accessed Jan 2020
3. Agatz, N., Erera, A., Savelsbergh, M., Wang, X.: Optimization for dynamic ridesharing: a review. European J. Oper. Res. **223**(2), 295–303 (2012)
4. Baldacci, R., Maniezzo, V., Mingozzi, A.: An exact method for the car pooling problem based on lagrangean column generation. Oper. Res. **52**(3), 422–439 (2004)
5. Barann, B., Beverungen, D., Müller, O.: An open-data approach for quantifying the potential of taxi ridesharing. Decision Support Syst. **99**, 86–95 (2017)
6. Bathla, K., Raychoudhury, V., Saxena, D., Kshemkalyani, A.D.: Real-time distributed taxi ride sharing. In: 2018 21st International Conference on Intelligent Transportation Systems (ITSC), pp. 2044–2051. IEEE (2018)

7. d'Orey, P.M., Fernandes, R., Ferreira, M.: Empirical evaluation of a dynamic and distributed taxi-sharing system. In: 2012 15th International IEEE Conference on Intelligent Transportation Systems, pp. 140–146. IEEE (2012)
8. Ma, S., Zheng, Y., Wolfson, O.: T-share: a large-scale dynamic taxi ridesharing service. In: 2013 IEEE 29th International Conference on Data Engineering (ICDE), pp. 410–421 (2013). https://doi.org/10.1109/ICDE.2013.6544843
9. Ma, S., Zheng, Y., Wolfson, O.: Real-time city-scale taxi ridesharing. IEEE Trans. Knowl. Data Eng. **27**(7), 1782–1795 (2014)
10. Psaraftis, H.N.: A dynamic programming solution to the single vehicle many-to-many immediate request dial-a-ride problem. Transp. Sci. **14**(2), 130–154 (1980)
11. team, F.C.D.S.: Prophet: Automatic forecasting procedure (2021). github.com/facebook/prophet
12. UN: UN Report (2018). www.un.org/development/desa/en/news/population/2018-revision-of-world-urbanization-prospects.html. Accessed 29 Apr 2021
13. Wang, Y., Zheng, B., Lim, E.P.: Understanding the effects of taxi ride-sharing-a case study of singapore. Comput. Environ. Urban Syst. **69**, 124–132 (2018)
14. Xiang, Z., Chu, C., Chen, H.: A fast heuristic for solving a large-scale static dial-a-ride problem under complex constraints. European J. Oper. Res. **174**(2), 1117–1139 (2006)
15. Yu, H., Raychoudhury, V., Silwal, S.: Dynamic taxi ride sharing using localized communication. In: Proceedings of the 21st International Conference on Distributed Computing and Networking, pp. 1–10 (2020)

Exploring the Challenges of Using Food Journaling Apps: A Case-study with Young Adults

Tejal Lalitkumar Karnavat, Jaskaran Singh Bhatia, Surjya Ghosh, and Sougata Sen[✉]

Department of Computer Science and Information Systems,
BITS Pilani Goa Campus, Goa, India
{h20200044,f20180230,surjyag,sougatas}@goa.bits-pilani.ac.in

Abstract. Food journaling applications enable tracking food consumption, physical activities, and overall self-consciousness and Quality of Life (QoL). Although these apps can improve self-consciousness, there are several challenges that prevent widespread usage of these apps in the long term. In this paper, we investigate the major challenges faced by young adult users while using these apps. To identify these challenges, we performed two user studies. In the first study, we performed a large-scale online crowd-sourced survey involving more than 150 participants who use, or have used at least one food journaling app. This study highlighted the major challenges faced by the users of these apps. We performed a follow-up study to validate these findings in a more realistic setting. The second study involved 31 participants (in the age range of 22 to 27 years), who used the MyFitnessPal app continuously for 10 d to record their caloric input and output. We performed a thematic analysis on the qualitative data of the exit interview, which highlighted a few themes, corroborating with the major challenges faced by the users in UI, search options (for food), serving size, and reminders while using these apps. We reflect on these findings to discuss a set of plausible avenues to increase the long term and widespread usage of these applications.

Keywords: Food journaling · Digital health monitoring · Personal health informatics

1 Introduction

Food diaries and activity logs have traditionally been a pen and paper based, where individuals manually noted down their activities and food habits. These diaries and logs played an important role in increasing self-awareness and self-monitoring that was intended towards improving one's lifestyle; they also allowed individuals to monitor the (im)balance in food consumption-based caloric intake and physical activity-based caloric output [67]. Researchers, historically, have

The original version of this chapter was revised: a DOI was added to reference number 15 and a name was corrected in Sect. 2.2. The correction to this chapter is available at https://doi.org/10.1007/978-3-030-94822-1_58

T. Hara and H. Yamaguchi (Eds.): MobiQuitous 2021, LNICST 419, pp. 57–83, 2022.
https://doi.org/10.1007/978-3-030-94822-1_4

relied on these diaries for understanding exercise and intake patterns [35], and used this information in applications such as understanding causes and effects of obesity [40], food-related allergies and symptom triggers [39], and mental health and well being [31]. With the ubiquity of smartphones and wearable devices, recently, many applications have emerged that enable digital diaries for tracking food consumption, monitoring physical activities performed, and providing insights to make necessary adjustments to improve the Quality of Life (QoL) [14, 24].

Currently, several apps like MyFitnessPal, Cronometer, EasyDietDiary, Noom Weight Loss Coach, Calorie Counter PRO, My Plate Calorie Tracker LITE, HealthifyMe, and Value Diary Plus are available that enable daily food and fitness tracking [38]. We use the term *digital health monitoring* apps to collectively refer to this category of apps. Although these digital health monitoring apps have several advantages over the 'pen and paper'-based diary approach, monitoring food consumption and tracking activity using these apps have several challenges. First, most of these apps *still* require the users to manually log their food consumption details (such as food name, serving amount). This requires significant user engagement and often disengages the participants from using the apps in the long-run [21, 59]. Imagine the burden such a manually logging approach can have on a user who has to log their food and activity details day in, day out! Second, manually logging food items introduces recall and other similar biases [28]. Sometimes such recall biases are intentional to avoid social stigma. Third, users find it challenging to make entries due to the absence of geography-specific food database. For example, food items commonly consumed in North America can be significantly different than those consumed in Asia or European countries. As a result, having a generic food database poses the challenges of searching desired food item and estimating portion sizes. Fourth, the user interfaces of these applications are often not very intuitive; sometimes even the regular app users struggle during food logging, searching, and checking caloric breakdown [13]. All of these challenges together often limit the widespread and continuous usage of these digital health monitoring applications. To address these challenges, several researchers have worked towards automatic tracking of food consumption by using food images [21, 68], and sensor-based gesture capturing [3, 62, 65]. However, automated food tracking is often impeded by the large variety of food items (and it's combination), and the challenge of automatically inferring the portion sizes [38]. Until these automated food tracking approaches reach a self-sustainable state of maturity, we must ensure that the digital health monitoring apps that require manual input ensure user engagement by being easy to use and help users meet their desired goals.

We, in this paper, answer the following question, "what are the major challenges that digital health monitoring application users (specifically young adults) face while using these apps?" We concentrated on *young adult* because they are underrepresented in life-style related trials as compared to other adult population [42], but they have more exposure in using smartphone-based apps and in adopting new technologies [1]. Therefore, the insights provided by these apps can add value to the life-style of this group of population. To understand the challenges faced by this population, we performed an web-based survey (using a crowd-sourcing platform[1]), recruiting over 150 participants across the globe (see Sect. 3 for details). These participants have experience of using at least one food tracking application. The major findings from this survey indicates that the users have difficulties in – (a) navigating through the UI for recording (and finding) specific details, (b) searching food items (especially region-specific items), (c) recording portion size and/or estimating calorie count. Motivated by these findings, we performed a follow-up study involving 31 participants (see Sect. 4 for details). In this study, the participants used the MyFitnessPal application[2] for 10 d to record their caloric consumption; we also conducted a post-study survey with all participants and performed (a) a system usability study of the app (see Sect. 4.2 for details), (b) compliance pattern during the study (see Sect. 4.3 for details), and (c) a thematic analysis of the qualitative data (Details in Sect. 4.4). Overall, the key contributions of this work are as follows,

– An online crowd-sourced survey involving more than 150 participants, which reveals that complicated UI, difficult navigation path, difficulty in serving size estimation are a few of the major challenges encountered by the participants to track caloric input and output in these digital diet & activity tracking applications.
– Thematic analysis of a followup study that was carried out using the MyFitnessPal application involving 31 participants revealed that improving UI, improving food database & adopting efficient search strategies, making the reminder service efficient, estimating serving size & nutrient values, and tracking physical activities in intelligent manner should be considered for widespread adoption and usage of digital health monitoring apps.

2   Background and Related Work

Noting down meals consumed or activities performed has several benefits such as it enables self-reflection [29,47], helps in symptom tracking [39], or even correlating with external triggers [10]. Even before computers became popular, individuals would use pen and paper to make notes of items that they consumed. However, with the advent of personal computers and more recently mobile devices, one can use these devices to make a digital note of the food items consumed or exercises performed. To simplify the process, several entities have developed apps that can be used for food monitoring [13,36]. These apps also help in automatically noting down user activities. However, challenges such as the effort needed to add a food item to the app reduces its usability [16]. Next, We discuss several tracking methodologies, motivation and use cases of existing digital health monitoring apps, especially related to food logging. We subsequently discuss two approaches of food logging – (i) self-reporting and (ii) automated food journaling.

---

[1]   https://www.microworkers.com/.
[2]   https://www.myfitnesspal.com/.

2.1 Digital Health Monitor: Key Functionalities

Digital health monitors allow tracking of one's food consumption patterns, including monitoring micro-nutrient consumption. These digital health monitors have varied functionalities and individuals use it for purposes such as losing weight, developing healthier eating habits, and understanding causes of certain symptoms [19, 22]. Indeed, several studies have shown that these food journaling apps help individuals maintain their goals [37]. Oyibo et al. have shown that goal-setting and self-monitoring are drivers of fitness in users from individualist cultures, and social support is the driver among collectivist users [55]. Chung et al. have demonstrated that enabling people to self-track their diet can help them collect relevant data for their health goals, and can enable their nutritionists and healthcare experts better understand their eating habits and symptoms related to eating disorders [20]. This assists them in preparing personalized plans and strategies, and saves consultation time because patients find it easier to recall and review their diet history by using the diet-trackers. Moreover, several studies have shown that such journaling benefits individuals with eating disorders such as bulimia nervosa [66]. In addition to achieving the stated goals, these apps also help an individual's mental health and well being, an added advantage of these journaling apps [4]. However, factors such as complex navigation in the app, difficulty of searching or adding food items, and providing too much information often discourage individuals from using these apps [22]. Thus, needed are digital health monitoring apps that people will continue using consistently so that the apps can serve their purpose and help individuals achieve their goals.

2.2 Self-reporting Based Tracking Approaches

Clinicians have historically relied on self-reporting to determine an individual's eating behavior [25]. An individual self-reports by either manually noting down details about the meal and their hunger or fullness levels [8], or by performing an end-of-day recall [8]. Alternately, self-reports can be created by a trained dietitian who contacts the user and collects their 24 h dietary recall [5]. However, it is well known that self-reports can be biased and individuals often under-report or over-report their caloric intake [32, 60]. Additionally, it is infeasible for clinicians to continuously monitor a patient's eating habits outside the laboratory setting. To keep users engaged, researchers have experimented with various alternate food logging techniques. Prior studies have also shown that users tend to gravitate towards other non-conventional methods like social media to track their diets. Chung et al. noted that users prefer clicking photos of their food and sharing them on Instagram, as compared to performing the logging using a lesser visually-stimulating MyFitnessPal app [19]. Immediate feedback and support from the community help users stay motivated towards their healthy eating goals. For example, Goyal et al. allowed users to capture images of the food item that was subsequently sent to dietitians [30]. These works indicate that there is a gap between the diet trackers that are available and the user's expectation from these trackers.

One major challenge with food journaling apps is the process of adding food items to the journal (further described in Sect. 4). Indeed, there is a large variance in the manner in which the journal users report their food consumption, as noted by Silva et al. [48]. In a limited user study, the authors observed that experienced digital health monitoring app users often described their food consumption details in manners that could lead to ambiguity. One reason for this variance could be attributed to the challenge in searching and adding food items to the journal. Users get accustomed to a particular journaling style. To ease the searching process, Jung et al. designed a new mobile food logger, Eat and Track(EaT) [38]. The Search-accelerator of EaT consisted of two elements; namely, the Search-accelerator pink buttons and the history. The pink buttons were used to refine the search; to arrive at the target item faster when the list of items appearing for a search was huge. The history consisted of previously logged items. EaT enabled participants to search for food items easily. However, database and search errors still occurred that need to be further addressed to improvise the process of food logging. Beenish Chaudhry reviewed a popular diet tracking app, *Fooducate* to understand if mobile apps are effective to help users follow a healthy diet [15]. The author found that *Fooducate* improved individual's food choices, increased awareness, weight loss, and personalized care; whereas users disliked the time required to verify new food items added to the database, the inaccurate nutritional content displayed for home-cooked meals, limited personalization, and non-optimal interaction design. Another key challenge encountered by the users while reporting the food consumption is the difficulty to accurately estimate the serving size, which needs to be considered.

2.3 Automated Tracking Approaches

To bridge the gap between what is consumed by individuals and what is reported, researchers have explored various automatic dietary monitoring techniques [36]. Both, commercial and custom wearable devices have shown tremendous promise in identifying and monitoring eating behaviors and general well-being in free-living conditions [52,57]. In automated food journaling approaches, such as smartwatch based [61], or custom device based [11,69] approaches, it is necessary to allow users to report whether they were actually consuming a meal; sometimes users even need to mention what they were eating. Such automated journaling research work often requires manual entry of items for validation purpose. Thus, even automated food journaling research can benefit from a user friendly food journal that individuals use continuously. Wearable cameras, with their ability to visually confirm events, are becoming common approach for food journaling. Work such as usage of SenseCam and other similar cameras laying the ground work for automated image based journaling [33,58]. Recent advances in image processing can enable identifying food items present in images. Kiyoharu Aizawa et al. developed *FoodLog*, a tool for recording food-related images and texts of items that an individual consumed [2]. They developed an image processing technique to identify food images and their result showed that users preferred the image-assisted input mode.

Although promising, these automatic approaches have some limitations in terms of estimating portion size, micro-nutrient details, and user-friendliness. All of these can significantly hinder the usage of this technology. Our work focuses on understanding such challenges and finding avenues so that the digital health monitoring apps can be widely used.

3 Study I: Web-Based Survey

To collect user's understanding of a digital health monitoring app, we conducted *Study I*, a web-based survey. The objectives of the study were two-folds: (1) to understand the motivation and engagement of using either a digital health monitoring app or a food journaling app, and (2) to find the major challenges faced by the users while using these apps. It must be noted that it may be possible for different users to have different motivations for using these apps. However, in this preliminary survey, we concentrated on the macro-level findings, i.e. the overall set of challenges faced and a high-level understanding of motivation for a user to use these apps. To ensure generalizability, we launched the survey on a web-based crowdsourcing platform so that it could reach to the participants with varied profile (nationality, gender, level of education etc.). Next, we discuss the survey design, study procedure, and the key findings.

3.1 Survey Design

We designed the web-based survey consisting of questions to collect user demographics, motivation to use a digital health monitoring app (& user engagement), user experience, and the challenges faced while using the digital health monitoring apps. We present the categories of the survey questionnaires in Table 1. Questions asking users about their motivation for using a fitness tracker app, challenges that they faced, advantages of using a fitness tracking application and missing features were open-ended, while other questions were based on a 7-point Likert scale. In Table 1, we have underlined the the open-ended questions.

Table 1. Category of the survey questionnaires used in the web-based study. Underlined items are open-ended.

Question category	Items
Demographic	Age, gender, country
Familiarity with apps	Name of the app, usage duration
Motivation	Motivation, influence on eating habit, lifestyle, ability to diligently record the details, other motivation
User experience	Satisfaction, UI experience, tracking experience, feedback, reminder, key missing features
Challenges	UI related, food search related, serving size related, other challenges

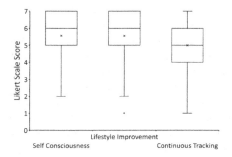 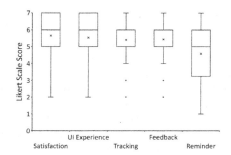

(a) Scores in different motivational aspects

(b) Scores in user experience aspects

Fig. 1. Score distribution for different motivational and user experience aspects based on the web-based survey - (a) scores in different motivational aspects of using the apps, (b) scores in terms of different user experience parameters of these apps

3.2 Study Procedure

We launched the survey on the microWorkers platform,[3] a web-based crowd-sourcing platform. The survey's inclusion criteria were– (a) the age of the participant should be in the range of 18 to 40 years, and (b) the participant should have at least 1 month usage experience of any diet or fitness tracking application. We anticipated that the survey would take around 10 min to complete and we compensated each participant with USD 1.00 via the portal once they had satisfactorily completed the survey, i.e., they answered every question. We also adopted the following steps to increase the authenticity of the responses – (a) we discarded all responses that were filled within 2 min (as completing the entire survey in less than 2 min is unlikely) (b) we discarded all responses that have same score for all the questions.

Since we wanted a generalized response for the questions, we did not impose any restriction on the nationality of the participants, gender, and eating habits. We received a total of 163 responses, out of which 11 were discarded based on the above-mentioned elimination criteria. We used responses from 152 participants (115 male, 37 female), residing in 13 different countries for our evaluation.

3.3 Findings

We next discuss the findings from the web-based survey. Specifically, we discuss – motivation and user engagement, user experience, and challenges faced by the users in these apps.

Motivation and User Engagement: We validated the respondent's motivation and engagement while using these apps by asking questions such as effect of

---

[3] https://www.microworkers.com/.

logging on lifestyle, and eating habits, in addition to directly asking about the user's motivation to use the app. Most of the participants indicated that their primary motivation of using these apps were to track the food consumption and weight tracking that would help them lead a healthier life-style. A majority of the participants agreed that their eating habits (60% of the respondents) and overall lifestyle (55% of respondents) had improved to some extent after they started tracking their diet and physical activities via these apps (as presented in Fig. 1a). *Self Consciousness* and *Lifestyle Improvement* plots respectively have a comparatively high score; score 7 corresponds to participants strongly agreeing to the improvement. However, participants also agreed that they often failed (evident from comparatively lower score of the *Continuous Tracking* plot) to diligently track caloric intake and output using the app. It is interesting to note that the variance is large for the *Continuous Tracking* plot.

User Experience: We designed the survey questions to capture the users' experience while using these apps. Specifically, we asked if they were satisfied with the app in general, with the app's UI, and if there were places where the app could be improved. We present the distribution of score for the questions related to user experience in Fig. 1b. From the figure we observe that the users were somewhat satisfied with the app (*Satisfaction* plot) and the UI experience (*UI Experience* plot) of using these apps (score 7 corresponding to extremely satisfied). The users also indicated the scope of improvement in terms of tracking food items (*Tracking* plot), and the feedback or insights (*Feedback*) that the app provided. Interestingly, the score for reminder services (*Reminder* plot) was lower, while there was a large variation in the responses – as evident from the large inter-quartile range, indicating that respondents did not very commonly use (or understand how to use) the reminder service that these apps provide.

Challenges: Next, we collected responses regarding the challenges faced by the respondents, and divided the challenges in the following categories - UI related, food search related, and serving size related challenges. We present the five-number score summary related to these categories in Fig. 2a, 2b, and 2c respectively. In terms of the UI related challenges, participants indicated their displeasure of making lots of text entry to complete a diary (*Text Entry*; high score indicates that they felt that significant text entry effort is required), difficulty in navigating to suitable pages in the app easily (*Option Finding*; high score indicates that app is easy to navigate through) and lack of a concise home page (*Home Page*) as depicted in Fig. 2a. Overall, the participants were satisfied with the food items present in the database of the app that they used – Higher values in *Food Option* indicates that the database had most items present that users were looking for. However, participants mentioned that the searching process was tiresome, as evident from the variation in *Tiresome Search* plot (higher means more tiresome) of Fig. 2b. Additionally, we observed that several participants did not explore alternate searching approaches (e.g., image based or voice-based) and were not sure if such alternate approaches would be

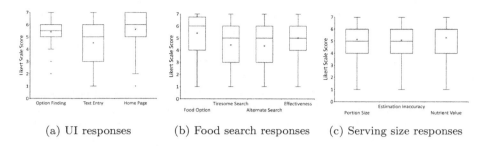

(a) UI responses   (b) Food search responses   (c) Serving size responses

Fig. 2. Score distribution related to different set of challenges experience by the users - (a) UI related responses (b) Food search related responses (c) Serving size related responses

effective (*Effectiveness*) in improving the searching experience. Participants also indicated challenges related to serving size estimation, inaccuracies in the estimated size and nutrient values as observed from score summary in Fig. 2c. For *Portion Size*, a high score indicated that users could easily record the serving sizes. However, the recorded serving size could be inaccurate. Indeed, this was captured in the *Estimation Inaccuracy*, where a high score indicated that users believe inaccuracies were introduced while entering serving sizes. For *Nutrient Values*, a high score indicates users agreed with the nutrient values displayed by the app. Overall, we see that participants were particularly worried about the estimation inaccuracy.

3.4   Lessons Learnt (Key Takeaways)

The major takeaways from this survey were:

- It was interesting to note that participants were highly motivated to use these apps. They mostly agreed that they observed some changes in their life-style after longitudinally using these apps. However, they indicated the lack of discipline in continuous usage of these apps for a long period of time. They also highlighted a number of challenges and missing features in these applications which limited realizing the full potential of tracking life-style using these applications.
- Participants agreed that presentation-related factors such as complicated UI, complex navigation path, large amount of text entry, difficulty in estimating serving size, clarity in nutrient values could be improved to better engage the application users.

Guided by these findings, we further investigated the challenges encountered by the users after using a specific application for a time period. To identify those challenges, we performed a follow-up study with participants in one geographic location, which is discussed next.

4   Study II: Case Study with MyFitnessPal Application

In Sect. 3, we identified the issues commonly faced by users of digital health monitoring apps. As Study I was done using a platform that was available globally, and the respondents indicated using various types of apps, the findings were generic. To ensure that the findings of the survey translated similarly for participants who were in the same geographic location, and used the same app, we conducted a more focused user study. Similar to the survey, the objective of this study was to find the challenges faced by users while using a specific digital health monitoring app on a regular basis. Additionally, we aimed to understand the perspective of users about a calorie monitoring and activity logging application.

4.1   Methods

For the study – Study II – we recruited 31 participants (9 males, 22 females, all aged between 22 and 27 years of age) using a word of mouth approach. At the start of the study, participants completed a pre-study questionnaire, details of which are summarised in Table 2. Participants were instructed to use the MyFitnessPal application continuously, for 10 d [13]. We selected this app because it is one of the most popular digital health monitoring app [46] and has been used by the researchers in earlier studies (e.g., by Jung et al. [38]).

Table 2. Details of questions asked to participants at the start of the study to capture user information.

Category of question	Questions
Demographics related	Age range, BMI, occupation, residence type
General	Prior experience of using digital health monitoring apps, and fitness trackers
Lifestyle related	Health monitoring approach and frequency, smartphone usage duration,
	Meal consumption pattern and frequency, exercise pattern and frequency
Occupation related	Whether working/studying from home, role, duration of study (student only)

We asked participants to install the MyFitnessPal app on their personal smartphone and log their nutrition and activeness level during the study period of 10 d. We specifically instructed participants to log their meals and activities at least twice a day. At the end of the 10 d, we observed that 3 participants did not comply with the instructions and thus we removed their data from the analysis, leaving us with 28 participants' (9 males, 19 females) data to analyse. Based on our pre-study interview, we learnt that 18 participants had never used a digital health monitoring app before, while 10 either regularly use it or had used it in the past. We also found via self-report that the participants were regular smartphone users, with an average of 4.32 h (s = 2.51 h) of usage per day. All (but one) participants with BMI above 25 kgs/m^2 indicated the motivation of using the app was tracking food quality or monitoring weight, whereas a few participants with BMI below 25 kg/m^2 did not have a motivation to use the digital health monitoring app. This can be intuitively explained that participants with higher BMI might be more interested in monitoring their eating habit and weight. We have summarised participant details in Table 3. For the 28 participants, we collected the user's response for the system usability scale (SUS) [12] survey at the end of the study. SUS is a standard well-known survey conducted using a 10-question survey for testing the usability of web and mobile applications. We also collected the user experience by asking them to fill survey questionnaires (at the end of the study) as summarised in Table 4. We moderated the response collection process for one third of the participants (randomly selected), where one member of the research team observed the participants filling out the survey. Such moderation, although labor-intensive, ensures that participants responded sincerely.

Analysis Approach: We performed three types of analysis. First, we wanted to understand the usability of MyFitnessPal, as reported by the participants. To this end, we analysed the SUS using an approach described by Liang et al. [45]. Second, we aimed to investigate if users continuously used the MyFitnessPal app over the 10 d of the study. To this end, we quantitatively analysed the number of meals that were reported over the period of 10 d. Third, we wanted to understand users' feedback about the digital health monitoring app that they used. For this understanding, we adopted a mixed method approach [23] to analyse the qualitative data collected at the end of the study. In summary, we used the usability responses, survey questionnaire as well as feedback from participants to answer the following questions,

- *How* do users perceive the digital health monitoring apps (e.g., MyFitnessPal app in this study)? We explore this in Sect. 4.2.
- *When* do users log their data in the digital health monitoring apps? We obtain the results of this in Sect. 4.3.
- *What* are the user perspectives of these apps? We answer this question in Sect. 4.4.

4.2   Understanding the Usability of the Digital Health Monitoring App

We carry out this usability study based on the collected SUS scores. An approach to interpret the SUS score is by normalizing the scores of each question and converting the 40 point response for the 10 questions (respondent scores each question between 0 and 4) into a 100 point scale by multiplying the score with 2.5 [45]. A score below 68 is considered as a below average score, i.e., the respondent did not find the application usable.

Table 3. Demographic details of the participants in our study, including details about usage of digital health monitoring apps. BMI range: $<18.5\,\mathrm{kg/m^2}$: Underweight (Uw); 18.5 to $24.9\,\mathrm{kg/m^2}$: Normal (N); 25 to $29.9\,\mathrm{kg/m^2}$: Overweight (Ow); $>=30\,\mathrm{kg/m^2}$: Obese (Ob). Occupation: S–Student; WP–Working professional.

User id	Age range	BMI range	Occupation	Food logging app usage experience	Diet and exercise monitoring frequency	Motivation to use
P01	25-27	N	S	No	-	Other/No
P02	25-27	Uw	WP	No	Don't monitor	Other/No
P03	25-27	N	S	No	Once a week	Weight watch Food quality
P04	25-27	N	WP	No	Don't monitor	Food quality
P05	22-24	N	S	Yes MyFitnessPal, HealthifyMe	A few times a week	Weight watch
P06	22-24	Uw	S	No	Don't monitor	Weight watch, Food quality
P07	25-27	Ow	S	No	A few times a week	Other/No
P08	25-27	N	S	No	A few times a week	Food quality
P09	25-27	N	WP	No	Once a week	Others/No
P10	25-27	N	S	Yes HealthifyMe	A few times a week	Weight watch, Food quality
P11	22-24	N	S	No	A few times a week	Others/No
P12	22-24	Uw	S	No	Don't monitor	Other/No
P13	22-24	N	S	Yes MyNetDiary	Daily	Weight watch, Food quality
P14	22-24	Ow	WP, S	No	A few times a week	Weight watch
P15	22-24	N	S	No	A few times a week	Other/No
P17	22-24	N	S	No	A few times a week	Weight watch
P19	22-24	Ob	WP	Yes HealthifyMe	Once a week	Weight watch, Food quality
P20	25-27	N	S	Yes HealthifyMe	A few times a week	Weight watch, Food quality
P21	25-27	N	WP	No	Once a week	Weight watch
P22	25-27	Ow	WP	No	A few times a week	Weight watch
P23	22-24	N	S	No	A few times a week	Weight watch
P24	25-27	N	S	No	A few times a week	Other/No
P25	25-27	Ow	S	Yes HealthifyMe	A few times a week	Weight watch, Food quality
P26	25-27	N	WP	No	A few times a week	Food quality
P27	22-24	N	S	Yes HealthifyMe	A few times a week	Other/No
P28	25-27	N	S	No	Don't monitor	Weight watch, Food quality
P29	25-27	N	S	Yes Don't remember	A few times a week	Weight watch
P31	25-27	N	WP	Yes Samsung Health	A few times a week	Other/No

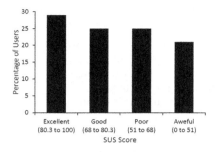

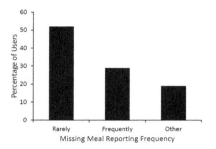

Fig. 3. Users response to the usability of the digital health tracking application (MyFitnessPal). We observe that almost 50% of respondents are not satisfied with the application.

Fig. 4. Users response to how often they missed to log details during the study

Based on the responses of the 28 participants, we observed that 53.6% of users rated the app above 68 (i.e., good) and 46.4% of the respondents considered the digital health monitoring app as not usable. 21.4% of the respondents considered the app to be awful (score below 51) and 25% of the participants marked it as poor (score 51 to 68). Only 28.6% of the users considered the app to be excellent. Based on this findings, one can claim that digital health monitoring apps are unlikely to achieve their goal for almost 50% of users, if not more, which also corroborates with earlier findings [56]. We present the distribution of SUS scores in Fig. 3.

4.3   Data Logging Frequency

We next analyze the users' data logging frequency in the MyFitnesssPal app during the study. This will allow us to understand whether there is a need to nudge specific participants based on their data logging pattern. Specifically, analysing the data logging frequency will allow measuring the engagement of the participants with the app. To understand the logging frequency, we asked participants "how frequently they missed recording their diet or exercise details?" Interestingly, 53.57% of the participants responded that they rarely missed to record their daily-log. We also found that 28.57% of the participants responded that they missed out to record the details frequently, while the remaining participants did not provide an answer. We show the distribution of missing out logging in Fig. 4.

To further confirm the participants self-reported data logging pattern, we randomly selected 18 participants (9 males, 9 females) from the pool of 28 users and asked them to share their eating and exercise pattern log. From this log, we observed that participants reported 19.22 meals on average over the period of 10 d with a standard deviation of 10.58. 17 of the participants had at least one day where no meal entry was logged, while 11 participants had at least 3 d

Table 4. Questionnaire to capture user's experience in using a digital health monitoring application

Category	Question summary
General	Motivation of using the app, lifestyle changes observed since using the app, features participants used, features that they would have liked to use
Reminder related	Usage of reminder, usefulness of reminders
Logging experience	general opinion, difficulties encountered, food item searching related, Food item quantity related, frequency of logging, reasons for not logging, approach to filling the journal, guided nutrition tracking related, goal related, features they want to see in future

where no meal or exercise was recorded. This reveals that there is a growing need to build systems that can automatically log these details (or improve the data logging frequency) for an individual. However, that is beyond the scope of this paper; several researchers have explored that research direction [52, 61].

4.4 Thematic Analysis of Qualitative Data

We performed a thematic analysis of the qualitative data collected through the survey questionnaire (Table 4). Our analysis included a mix of both inductive and deductive approaches. Three coders first created an individual code book based on the responses of the participants. The coders subsequently discussed among themselves, and used an affinity diagram-based approach to identify and organize common themes that emerged from each coder's interpretation. In case of any disagreements between interpretation of responses, the three coders discussed among themselves to resolve any conflict that arose.

The themes and codebook generated based on the interview data is presented in Tables 5 and 6. Specifically, we concentrated on the following aspects — motivation for using the digital health monitoring apps, behavioral changes participants noticed at the end of the study, the missing features (or functionalities) that participants observed in the app and overall experience in using these apps.

Motivation of Using Digital Health Monitoring Apps: Our respondents used the digital fitness monitoring app with two major motivation – keeping track of their weight (44.74% of codes) and monitoring the quality of food that they were consuming (28.95% of codes). We labeled these two motivations as – *weight watching* and *food quality* – the primary themes that emerged for the app usage.

Weight Watching: For the weight watch theme, we found that respondents primarily used these apps for weight-related purposes (28.95% of all codes).

Table 5. Mapping different codes to themes based on the thematic analysis of the *qualitative data for motivation and behavioral change aspects.* The last column indicate the frequency of the code for a given aspect.

Aspect	Theme	Code	Code frequency (%)
Motivation	Weight watch	Weight related	28.95
		Activity/Workout related	5.26
		Fitness related	10.53
	Food quality, nutrient	Calorie/Tracking related	15.79
		Eating healthy/nutrition related	13.16
	Other/None	Other/None	26.32
Behavioral change (after using the app)	Weight / activity related	Better logging/tracking	9.37
		Exercising regularly	3.12
	Food related	Calorie conscious	25
		Food conscious	18.75
		Improved water intake	6.25
		Eating at right time	3.12
	Other/No change	Other/No change	34.37

This included losing, maintaining or gaining weight – e.g., *"To gain weight and have proper calorie intake"*– (P06). Participants also commonly used the app for fitness tracking (10.53% of all codes). The responses for the codes were not mutually exclusive, i.e., some participants mentioned more than one code – *"Weight Loss, Fitness"* – (P22). A third code that emerged was the use of these apps for activity and workout monitoring. Surprisingly, this code was substantially less common as compared to other themes. It might be attributed to participants relying on a digital health monitoring app predominantly for food journaling purpose, rather than fitness tracking.

Food Quality: For the food quality theme, participants' concerns were primarily regarding calorie tracking (15.79% of all codes) and eating healthy (13.16% of all codes). Although this theme has a relationship with weight, however, since the participants explicitly did not mention that they were interested in watching their weight, we segregated this theme from weight watching. For example, P20 mentioned *"My goal is to track my meals and see how much calorie intake I have on a regular basis"*, while P25 responded *"Follow a healthy diet with a basic workout"*. Since food quality monitoring is used for purposes such as symptom tracking or investigating correlations [20,39,51], and we did not observe any relation between these responses with weight watching, we segregated them into a separate theme.

Participant's Perspective About Behavior Changes After Using the App: As 64.28% of the participants in our study had never used a digital health monitoring app previously, we wanted to understand if the participants observed change in behavior after using the app for some time. We asked all participants (including ones who had used any digital health monitoring app previously) about the behavior change they observed at the end of the study. Similar to the motivation at the start of the study, we primarily observed that two themes emerged – themes that were weight related and food related. However, unlike the initial motivation of using digital health apps, in this case, we observe that 53.12% of the codes were related to food consumption, whereas 12.5% of the codes were related to weight (or activity). This implies that although participants started using the app with the motivation of weight tracking, however, mostly their food consumption behavior changed at the end of the study (albeit both of these are correlated).

In this (post-study behavioral change) aspect, *calorie conscious* (25%) and *food conscious* (18.75%) codes were most frequently observed for food related theme – *"I became more cautious about the calories I'm consuming"*– (P21), and *"Yes, I started being more aware of how much junk I could eat. It helped me analyze my dietary habits and pushed me to eating more healthy food."* – (P20) were two responses that we obtained in this regard. The usage of the app also motivated *"Eating at the right times"* – (P08), and helped them become *".. more self conscious of what I eat due to logging it in. Keeping track of calories quantifies the whole process so it is better planned."* – (P03).

Missing Functionalities: Participants indicated that there were several short-comings and missing functionalities in the digital health monitoring app that they used. We categorized these functionalities into the following themes – UI improvement, Improved food database, Serving size estimation, Efficient reminder service, and Intelligent activity tracking.

User Interface (UI) Improvement: 27.59% of the codes corresponding to the user response indicated that the UI of the app reduced its usability. Respondents specifically mentioned two components in the UI – 24.14% of the codes indicated that the overall UI presentation was cluttered, making it difficult to navigate and use the app, while another 3.45% of the codes indicated specifically that the UI affected their ability to easily log food items. Specifically, P4 mentioned *"The UI can be more simplified"*, while P7 mentioned that *"UI should be more interactive and attractive. Ease of use and navigating the app can be a little cumbersome sometimes"*. P14 had similar comments too. One of the respondents suggested that there should be *"A feature for logging in monotonous eating routine instead of individually logging it for every meal. Like if I eat'A' in bfast,'B' in lunch and'C' in dinner. Then it should just ask for a prompt at the end of the day like:"Did you follow the plan"? And it'd be done with a simple yes/no instead of logging in for the whole day"* – (P03).

Table 6. Mapping different codes to themes based on the thematic analysis of the *qualitative data for missing functionalities and overall experience aspects.* The last column indicate the frequency of the code for a given aspect.

Aspect	Theme	Code	Code frequency (%)
Missing feature	UI improvement	Easy food logging	3.45
		UI/presentation	24.14
	Improved food database	region-specific food items	3.45
		Veg, non-veg separation	3.45
	Serving size estimation	portion size	6.9
		Micronutrient in free version	3.45
	Efficient reminder service	Water drinking reminder	3.45
	Intelligent activity tracking	Goal-based activity tracker	3.45
		Activity tracker for other sports	3.45
		Integration with other apps	3.45
	Other/Nothing	Other/Nothing	41.38
Overall experience (Positive)	Food database	Food options	13.63
		Accuracy	4.54
	Tracker	Calorie Tracker	22.72
		Logging	9.09
		Exercise Tracker	9.09
	UI/ presentation	Food analysis	4.54
		UI	4.54
		Meal Division	4.54
	Features	Add meals	9.09
		Reminders	4.54
		Recipes	9.09
		Some useful features	4.54
Overall experience (Negative)	Food database	Food options	23.07
		Varying calories	3.84
	Tracker	Logging	19.23
		Exercise tracker	3.84
		Search	7.69
	UI/ presentation	UI	11.53
		Serving sizes	15.38
	Advertisements	Ads	3.84
	Feature	Not region specific	7.69
		Other features	3.84

Improved Food Database and Serving Size Estimation: The next two themes that emerged based on the challenges that the participants faced due to missing functionalities were improved food database and serving size estimation.

For the improved food database theme, participants indicated that there were several instances where region specific food items were not present in the food database (3.45% of the codes). One take away for future digital health application developers is to "...*sort recipes according to a geographical location...Show recommendations according to the country or state a person is residing in.*" – (P31), and have "*Different sections for Vegetarians and non Vegetarians*" – (P12).

Many participants mentioned that tracking the portion size and estimating micro-nutrient content in a serving is one of the most challenging tasks in the food logging process. It is easier to use "*Measurement metrics as 100 gm as default instead of cups/ lbs for some food items.*" – (P13). Alternately, providing "*Images of portion sizes could be nice*" – (P26). P26 further mentioned that sometimes they would "*select a value and it would turn out to be lot less*" than the amount that they consumed. P20 also noted the absence of micro-nutrient details in the basic version of the app – "*Could add the tracking of micro-nutrients in the free version.*". From the feedback, it is evident that end-users expect an easy measuring technique to quantify not only food items consumed, but also their micro-nutrients.

Efficient Reminder Service and Intelligent Activity Tracking: Other challenges that emerged were related to activity tracking and reminder, which correspond to intelligent activity tracking and efficient reminder service theme respectively. We investigated the possible reasons for missing out on logging details (activity and diet data) during the study and learnt that forgetfulness (18.75% of codes), and work-schedule (15.62% of codes) are the top two reasons for missing out recording the details. A recent study by Chung et al. also noted that users forget to log because of their busy schedule [20]. In the current study , participants indicated that reminders could help prevent the issue of *logging forgetfulness*. For example, P25 suggested "*water drinking reminder*" may be useful as available in some other fitness apps (e.g., HealthifyMe). Participants also noted that it would be helpful for having the ability to automatically track the intake and output calories.

Overall Experience: Finally, we asked participants about their overall experience of using the digital health monitoring app; including the features they liked and the challenges they faced. Interestingly, the response was a mix of completely positive, completely negative or an in-between response. Figure 5 shows the percentage of responses that were either positive, negative, or a mix of both. We divided the responses into themes as noted in Table 6 and discuss them next.

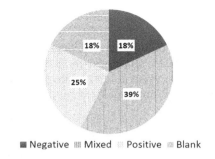

■ Negative ▥ Mixed ▦ Positive ▨ Blank

Fig. 5. Overall experience of participants of in using the MyFitnessPal digital health monitoring application.

Positive Experience: With respect to the positive experience, key advantages pointed out by the users were related to tracker and food database theme. The codes (e.g., calories tracker, exercise tracker) related to tracker theme constitute 40.9% of the codes. For example, "*...maintaining the diary was fun...*" – (P21). Similarly, codes related to food database theme constitute 18.17% and evident from sample responses like "*I was happy about the food options that were available...*" – (P14). A few codes (e.g., custom meals, recipes and reminders) constitute to 27.27% leading to other features theme.

Negative Experience: In case of negative experience also, tracker and food database theme are found to be very important. For example, "*The challenge I faced while using this app was not getting the correct option for my food logging. I had to find close substitutes for the food I had to log in.*" – (P23) and 26.91% of the codes correspond to food database theme. Another 30.77% of the codes pointed out that tracking the food items as well as exercise logs day in, day out was a major challenge as captured within the tracker theme. UI (or presentation) is also appeared to be a key theme as more than 26% codes (e.g., UI, serving size) correspond to this theme. For example, "*I found it difficult to log in everyday, maybe because of the unattractive interface*" – (P14), and "*Adding items to list was a tedious task also the UI of the app is not very appealing*" – (P06) were some of the responses that were recorded. 7.69% of the codes mentioned that the app was not *region specific*, and this was a major disadvantage leading to required features theme.

4.5 Lessons Learnt (Key Takeaways)

The key takeaways from Study II were:

1. Majority of the participants were able to track their caloric input and output during the study. The primary motivation of using these digital health apps were weight and food tracking and most of the participants mentioned in the post-study survey that they had become more self-conscious in terms of food and activity tracking. Although, this demonstrates the role of these apps in

improving the life-style, there are several challenges shared by the users in these apps.
2. The participants primarily mentioned challenges that we mapped to different themes - UI improvement, improved food database, estimating serving size, improving reminder services, and tracking activities in intelligent way. Improving (or adding) these functionalities can increase the user engagement further in these applications.

5   Discussion

We observed a set of challenges that users encountered while using food journaling apps. While the studies reinforce the major motivation of using these apps is to increase self-consciousness and self-monitoring in terms of healthy life-style (e.g., food consumption, activity tracking), they also highlight a set of challenges to realize the full potential of these applications. Thus, the current studies have implications in terms of development of a standardized measurement of calorie-counting and fitness tracking. Next, we discuss the key themes around the challenges faced by the users and the possible strategies to overcome those.

5.1   Improving User Interface

One of the major challenges that we observed with participants in our studies is related to the interface and the navigation path in these applications. In our studies, we observed multiple challenges mentioned by the users in terms of user interaction – (a) lot of information presented in the home screen that makes it challenging to filter the most essential ones, (b) difficulty in navigating through the application for efficiently locating different options for tracking, logging, and report generation, and (c) often a significant amount of text needs to be entered for searching and logging purposes.

Different applications used in earlier studies tried to improve user experience by considering these challenges [26]. However, as we observed in our studies, users prefer to see only relevant details on the home page. To achieve this, it may be useful to implement personalized and configurable pages so that users can select only the relevant information based on their preference. Similarly, while food logging, it may be useful to automatically copy over previous day's (or same day of the previous week or by adopting some other approach) food items (and then allow to edit as appropriate) to reduce the text logging effort.

5.2   Improving Food Database and Searching Strategy

In our studies, we observed that users mentioned challenges related to searching food items. These primarily stemmed from two sources – (a) the search is not efficient due to lot of text entry (and correction to find the relevant items from the list), (b) missing regional or location-specific food items.

To counter these issues, different approaches can be considered such as improving the food database considering user geographic location. While some earlier works performed studies based on a region specific food items [38], designing a dynamic range of food database based on user location can refine the search experience. But, revealing user location might raise privacy concerns. Thus, future digital health monitoring apps should make the food database more localized only if the user consents to providing their location. Similarly, to improve the searching strategy, these apps can implement simple segregation techniques based on user's food preference (vegan, vegetarian, and non-vegetarian). Moreover, the search screen can be designed by monitoring user's food habits so that the frequently consumed food items can be searched more efficiently rather than searching in a large database.

5.3 Estimating Serving Size and Nutrient Values

Another key challenge that we identified was automatically inferring portion size and nutrient values from the food items. Users have expressed concerns that the automatically inferred nutrient values may be inaccurate because they were unsure if they had indicated the correct quantity of food consumed. The estimated quantity based on the mixture of different food ingredients can be inaccurate as well.

Although advancements have been made in image-based [21,54], bar-code based [17,41], voice memo-based [49,63] and gesture-based [6,7] monitoring of the eating activity, however, there is still no fully automated food journaling app that exists. Creating an automated food journaling app is challenging because any of the above mentioned modalities can track only specific activities during eating episode such as when a person is eating or how a person is eating; they cannot log all details that humans can manually log. Thus it is necessary to make strides in both automated food journaling as well as manual journaling apps. The manual food journaling apps can provide ground truth for future automated digital health monitoring apps.

5.4 Improving Reminder Service and User Engagement

Our findings (as well as similar finding by other researchers) reveal that one of the key reasons for not logging the food consumption details is due to one's forgetful nature [40]. Although we observed the compliance rate in our study was high, however, a few of the studies mentioned that compliance rate can degrade over time [38]. As a result, effective strategies to improve user engagement are essential to collect data over long duration.

In our study, we also observed that participants mentioned that it would be useful to add 'drinking water reminders' in the MyFitnessPal application. Prior studies have identified that to improve the engagement in completing tasks, ambient reminders may be useful [9,43,53]. Similarly, some Quantified Self (QS) studies have identified that approaches like rewarding (e.g., leaderboard, badges) [34,44], gamification [27,64], self-reflection [18,29,39] may be useful in calorie tracking applications as well to improve user engagement and data logging, an important consideration for future digital health monitoring applications.

5.5   Efficient Activity Tracking

Another source of inconvenience for the users in our studies was the lack of the functionality to automatically infer physical activities (e.g., walking) that they performed. A few users also expressed challenges in terms of integrating physical activity data from the wearable devices in the health tracking applications.

We perceive the digital health tracking applications to be a single source to monitor and provide insights to improve the overall quality of life (QoL). To achieve this, seamless integration of different physical activity and sleep tracking devices with food journaling apps is essential. We also envision the ability of inferring mental health (emotion) in these applications can make them a true companion as there is close relationship between eating habits and emotional conditions [50].

5.6   Limitations

We acknowledge several limitations in our current work. First, the number of participants in the study is relatively small. Therefore, increasing the number of participants from diverse profile can aid to find other insights. Second, the duration of the study was only 10 d. Therefore, it may be possible that during the study, the usage behavior changes (with time) have not been noticed. These behavioral changes need to be further investigated by running a long-term user study. Finally, in this study, we primarily concentrated on identifying the first-hand challenges encountered by the young adults while using the digital health tracking apps. But we did not consider the challenges associated after applying some interventions, e.g., we did not consider the implications of any nudge (e.g., reminder) after detecting any change in the continued usage pattern. However, these set of challenges can be explored in the future studies.

6   Conclusion

In this paper, we investigate the major challenges faced by the young adult groups while using a smartphone-based food and activity tracking application. Towards the objective, we performed two user studies– the first study was performed in the form of a web-based crowdsource survey in which 150+ participants responded and expressed the key challenges they encounter while using these applications. The key takeaways from this survey were that the participants face major challenges in navigating through the application screens, searching food items, recording serving sizes, and inferring nutrient values in a food item. Guided by these findings, we performed a followup study involving 31 young adults, who used MyFitnessPal application to track their diets and physical activities for 10 d followed by an exit interview. We carried out thematic analysis on the qualitative data of the interview, which revealed several themes like UI improvement, food database & search strategy improvement, efficient activity tracking, and serving size & nutrient value estimation. All these themes corroborate with the major challenges encountered by the users in these apps that need to be addressed for widespread usage of these apps. We also discuss possible approaches (e.g., presence of a configurable, personalized home screen highlighting key parameters, improving search based on food preference, provision for automating monotonous entries, personalized reminder services) that future digital health monitoring application developers can adopt to counter these challenges to increase user engagement in the long-term.

References

1. Abi-Jaoude, E., Naylor, K.T., Pignatiello, A.: Smartphones, social media use and youth mental health. Cmaj **192**(6), E136–E141 (2020)
2. Aizawa, K., Ogawa, M.: Foodlog: multimedia tool for healthcare applications. IEEE MultiMed. **22**(2), 4–8 (2015). https://doi.org/10.1109/MMUL.2015.39
3. Amft, O., Tröster, G.: On-body sensing solutions for automatic dietary monitoring. IEEE Pervasive Comput. **8**(2), 62–70 (2009)
4. Ayobi, A., Marshall, P., Cox, A.L., Chen, Y.: Quantifying the body and caring for the mind: self-tracking in multiple sclerosis. Association for Computing Machinery, pp. 6889–6901. New York, NY, USA (2017). https://doi.org/10.1145/3025453.3025869
5. Baranowski, T.: 24-hour recall and diet record methods. Nutrit. Epidemiol. **40**, 49–69 (2012)
6. Bedri, A., et al.: EarBit: using wearable sensors to detect eating episodes in unconstrained environments. Proceed. ACM Interact. Mobile Wearable Ubiquitous Technol. **1**(3), 1–20 (2017). https://doi.org/10.1145/3130902
7. Bedri, A., Li, D., Khurana, R., Bhuwalka, K., Goel, M.: Fitbyte: automatic diet monitoring in unconstrained situations using multimodal sensing on eyeglasses. In: Conference on Human Factors in Computing Systems. CHI '20, pp. 1–12. ACM (2020)
8. Bellisle, F., Dalix, A.M., De Castro, J.: Eating patterns in french subjects studied by the "weekly food diary" method. Appetite **32**(1), 46–52 (1999)
9. Bentley, F., Tollmar, K.: The power of mobile notifications to increase wellbeing logging behavior. In: Proceedings of the SIGCHI Conference on Human Factors in Computing Systems, pp. 1095–1098 (2013)
10. Bi, S., et al.: Measuring children's eating behavior with a wearable device. In: IEEE International Conference on Healthcare Informatics (ICHI), pp. 1–11. IEEE (2020)
11. Bi, S., et al.: Auracle: detecting eating episodes with an ear-mounted sensor. Proceed. ACM Interact. Mobile Wearab. Ubiquit. Technol. **2**(3), 92 (2018)
12. Brooke, J.: SUS-A quick and dirty usability scale. CRC Press (1996)
13. Centers for Disease Control and Prevention: Designing an improved myfitnesspal experience. uxdesign.cc/ui-ux-case-study-designing-an-improved-myfitnesspal-experience-3492bbe4923c. Accessed 6 Jun 2021
14. Chai, W., Nigg, C.R., Pagano, I.S., Motl, R.W., Horwath, C., Dishman, R.K.: Associations of quality of life with physical activity, fruit and vegetable consumption, and physical inactivity in a free living, multiethnic population in hawaii: a longitudinal study. Int. J. Behav. Nutrition Physic. Activity **7**(1), 1–6 (2010)

15. Chaudhry, B.M.: Food for thought. mHealth **5**(20) (2019). https://doi.org/10.21037/mhealth.2019.06.02

16. Chen, J., Berkman, W., Bardouh, M., Ng, C.Y.K., Allman-Farinelli, M.: The use of a food logging app in the naturalistic setting fails to provide accurate measurements of nutrients and poses usability challenges. Nutrition **57**, 208–216 (2019)

17. Chen, Y.S., Wong, J.E., Ayob, A.F., Othman, N.E., Poh, B.K.: Can malaysian young adults report dietary intake using a food diary mobile application? a pilot study on acceptability and compliance. Nutrients **9**(1), 62 (2017)

18. Choe, E.K., Lee, B., Zhu, H., Riche, N.H., Baur, D.: Understanding self-reflection: how people reflect on personal data through visual data exploration. In: Proceedings of the 11th EAI International Conference on Pervasive Computing Technologies for Healthcare, pp. 173–182 (2017)

19. Chung, C.F., Agapie, E., Schroeder, J., Mishra, S., Fogarty, J., Munson, S.A.: When personal tracking becomes social: Examining the use of instagram for healthy eating. In: Conference on Human Factors in Computing Systems - Proceedings. Association for Computing Machinery. vol. 2017, pp. 1674–1687 (2017). https://doi.org/10.1145/3025453.3025747

20. Chung, C.F., et al.: Identifying and planning for individualized change: patient-provider collaboration using lightweight food diaries in healthy eating and irritable bowel syndrome. Proc. ACM Interact. Mob. Wearable Ubiquitous Technol. **3**(1) (2019). https://doi.org/10.1145/3314394

21. Cordeiro, F., Bales, E., Cherry, E., Fogarty, J.: Rethinking the mobile food journal: exploring opportunities for lightweight photo-based capture. In: Conference on Human Factors in Computing Systems - Proceedings. Association for Computing Machinery. vol. 2015, pp. 3207–3216 (2015). https://doi.org/10.1145/2702123.2702154

22. Cordeiro, F., et al.: Barriers and negative nudges: exploring challenges in food journaling. In: Proceedings of the 33rd Annual ACM Conference on Human Factors in Computing Systems, pp. 1159–1162. ACM (2015)

23. Creswell, J.W.: Mixed-method research: introduction and application. In: Handbook of educational policy, pp. 455–472. Elsevier (1999)

24. Drewnowski, A., Evans, W.J.: Nutrition, physical activity, and quality of life in older adults: summary. J. Gerontol. Series A Biol. Sci. Med. Sci **56**(2), 89–94 (2001)

25. Fairburn, C.G., Beglin, S.J.: Assessment of eating disorders: interview or self-report questionnaire? Int. J. Eating Disorders **16**(4), 363–370 (1994)

26. Ferrara, G., Kim, J., Lin, S., Hua, J., Seto, E., et al.: A focused review of smartphone diet-tracking apps: usability, functionality, coherence with behavior change theory, and comparative validity of nutrient intake and energy estimates. JMIR mHealth uHealth **7**(5), e9232 (2019)

27. Fitz-Walter, Z., Tjondronegoro, D., Wyeth, P.: Orientation passport: using gamification to engage university students. In: Proceedings of the 23rd Australian Computer-Human Interaction Conference, pp. 122–125 (2011)

28. Friedenreich, C.M., Howe, G.R., Miller, A.B.: An investigation of recall bias in the reporting of past food intake among breast cancer cases and controls. Ann. Epidemiol. **1**(5), 439–453 (1991)

29. Ghosh, S., Mitra, B., De, P.: Towards improving emotion self-report collection using self-reflection. In: Extended Abstracts of the 2020 CHI Conference on Human Factors in Computing Systems, pp. 1–8 (2020)

30. Goyal, S., Liu, Q., Tajul-Arifin, K., Awan, W., Wadhwa, B., Liu, Z.: I ate this: a photo-based food journaling system with expert feedback. arXiv preprint arXiv:1702.05957 (2017)
31. Hardy, S., Gray, R.: The secret food diary of a person diagnosed with schizophrenia. J. Psychiat. Mental Health Nursing **19**(7), 603–609 (2012)
32. Heitmann, B.L., Lissner, L.: Dietary underreporting by obese individuals-is it specific or non-specific? BMJ (Clinical research ed.) **311**(7011), 986–9 (1995). https://doi.org/10.1136/bmj.311.7011.986 www.ncbi.nlm.nih.gov/pubmed/7580640 www.pubmedcentral.nih.gov/articlerender.fcgi?artid=PMC2550989
33. Hodges, S., et al.: A retrospective memory aid. In: International Conference on Ubiquitous Computing, pp. 177–193. Springer (2006)
34. Hosio, S., Goncalves, J., Lehdonvirta, V., Ferreira, D., Kostakos, V.: Situated crowdsourcing using a market model. In: Proceedings of the 27th Annual ACM Symposium on User Interface Software and Technology, pp. 55–64 (2014)
35. Houser, H.B., Sorensen, A., Littell, A., Vandervort, J., et al.: Dietary intake of non-hospitalized persons with multiple sclerosis. 1. food diary and coding methods. J. Am. Diet. Assoc. **54**, 391–397 (1969)
36. Illner, A., Freisling, H., Boeing, H., Huybrechts, I., Crispim, S., Slimani, N.: Review and evaluation of innovative technologies for measuring diet in nutritional epidemiology. Int. J. Epidemiol. **41**(4), 1187–1203 (2012)
37. Johnson, F., Wardle, J.: The association between weight loss and engagement with a web-based food and exercise diary in a commercial weight loss programme: a retrospective analysis. Int. J. Behav. Nutrition Phys. Activity **8**(1), 1–7 (2011)
38. Jung, J., et al.: Foundations for systematic evaluation and benchmarking of a mobile food logger in a large-scale nutrition study. Proceed. ACM Interact. Mobile Wearable Ubiquitous Technol. **4**(2), 1–25 (2020)
39. Karkar, R., et al: Tummytrials: a feasibility study of using self-experimentation to detect individualized food triggers. In: Proceedings of the 2017 CHI Conference on Human Factors in Computing Systems. CHI '17, Association for Computing Machinery, pp. 6850–6863. New York, NY, USA (2017). https://doi.org/10.1145/3025453.3025480
40. Kim, Y., Ji, S., Lee, H., Kim, J.W., Yoo, S., Lee, J.: "My doctor is keeping an eye on me!" exploring the clinical applicability of a mobile food logger. In: Proceedings of the 2016 CHI Conference on Human Factors in Computing Systems, pp. 5620–5631 (2016)
41. Kumar, N., Lopez, C., Caldeira, C.M., Pethe, S., Si, B., Kobsa, A.: Calnag: effortless multiuser calorie tracking. In: 2016 IEEE International Conference on Pervasive Computing and Communication Workshops (PerCom Workshops), pp. 1–4. IEEE (2016)
42. Lanoye, A., Gorin, A.A., LaRose, J.G.: Young adults' attitudes and perceptions of obesity and weight management: implications for treatment development. Current Obesity Reports **5**(1), 14–22 (2016)
43. Lee, M.L., Dey, A.K.: Real-time feedback for improving medication taking. In: Proceedings of the SIGCHI Conference on Human Factors in Computing Systems, pp. 2259–2268 (2014)
44. Li, I., Dey, A.K., Forlizzi, J.: Understanding my data, myself: supporting self-reflection with ubicomp technologies. In: Proceedings of the 13th International Conference on Ubiquitous Computing, pp. 405–414 (2011)
45. Liang, J., et al.: Usability study of mainstream wearable fitness devices: feature analysis and system usability scale evaluation. JMIR mHealth uHealth **6**(11), e11066 (2018)

46. Lifewire: Adult obesity facts. www.lifewire.com/best-food-tracker-apps-4172287. Accessed 6 Jun 2021
47. Lupton, D.: The quantified self. John Wiley and Sons (2016)
48. M. Silva, L., A. Epstein, D.: Investigating preferred food description practices in digital food journaling. In: DIS '21, Association for Computing Machinery, pp. 589–605. New York, NY, USA (2021). https://doi.org/10.1145/3461778.3462145
49. Mamykina, L., Mynatt, E., Davidson, P., Greenblatt, D.: Mahi: investigation of social scaffolding for reflective thinking in diabetes management. In: Proceedings of the SIGCHI Conference on Human Factors in Computing Systems, pp. 477–486 (2008)
50. McCaig, D., Elliott, M.T., Prnjak, K., Walasek, L., Meyer, C.: Engagement with myfitnesspal in eating disorders: qualitative insights from online forums. Int. J. Eating Disorders 53(3), 404–411 (2020)
51. Miles, S., Frewer, L.J.: Investigating specific concerns about different food hazards. Food Qual. Preference 12(1), 47–61 (2001)
52. Mirtchouk, M., Lustig, D., Smith, A., Ching, I., Zheng, M., Kleinberg, S.: Recognizing eating from body-worn sensors. Proceed. ACM Interact. Mobile Wearable Ubiquitous Technol. 1(3), 1–20 (2017). https://doi.org/10.1145/3131894
53. Muller, H., Kazakova, A., Pielot, M., Heuten, W., Boll, S.: Ambient timer-unobtrusively reminding users of upcoming tasks with ambient light. In: Kotze, P., Marsden, G., Lindgaard, G., Wesson, J., Winckler, M. (eds.) Human-Computer Interaction. LNCS, vol. 8117. Springer, Heidelberg (2013). https://doi.org/10.1007/978-3-642-40483-2_15
54. Noronha, J., Hysen, E., Zhang, H., Gajos, K.Z.: PlateMate: Crowdsourcing nutrition analysis from food photographs. In: Proceedings of the Annual ACM Symposium on User Interface Software and Technology (UIST'11), pp. 1–11 (2011). https://doi.org/10.1145/2047196.2047198
55. Oyibo, K., Olagunju, A.H., Olabenjo, B., Adaji, I., Deters, R., Vassileva, J.: Ben'fit: Design, implementation and evaluation of a culture-tailored fitness app. In: Adjunct Publication of the 27th Conference on User Modeling, Adaptation and Personalization. UMAP'19 Adjunct, Association for Computing Machinery, pp. 161–166. New York, NY, USA (2019). https://doi.org/10.1145/3314183.3323854
56. Powell, T.: Web design. McGraw-Hill Professional Publishing (2002)
57. Rahman, T., et al.: BodyBeat: a mobile system for sensing non-speech body sounds. In: Proceedings of the Annual International Conference on Mobile Systems, Applications, and Services (Mobisys'14). Association for Computing Machinery (2014). https://doi.org/10.1145/2594368.2594386
58. Reddy, S., Parker, A., Hyman, J., Burke, J., Estrin, D., Hansen, M.: Image browsing, processing, and clustering for participatory sensing: lessons from a DietSense prototype. In: Proceedings of the 4th Workshop on Embedded Networked Sensors, EmNets 2007, pp. 13–17 (2007). https://doi.org/10.1145/1278972.1278975
59. Rowland, M.K., et al.: Field testing of the use of intake24-an online 24-hour dietary recall system. Nutrients 10(11), 1690 (2018)
60. Schoeller, D.A.: Limitations in the assessment of dietary energy intake by self-report. Metabolism 44(2), 18–22 (1995). https://doi.org/10.1016/0026-04959590204-X
61. Sen, S., Subbaraju, V., Misra, A., Balan, R., Lee, Y.: Annapurna: an automated smartwatch-based eating detection and food journaling system. Pervasive Mobile Comput. 68, 101259 (2020)

62. Sen, S., Subbaraju, V., Misra, A., Balan, R.K., Lee, Y.: The case for smartwatch-based diet monitoring. In: IEEE International Conference on Pervasive Computing and Communication Workshops, PerCom Workshops 2015. Institute of Electrical and Electronics Engineers Inc. (2015). https://doi.org/10.1109/PERCOMW.2015.7134103
63. Siek, K.A., Connelly, K.H., Rogers, Y., Rohwer, P., Lambert, D., Welch, J.L.: When do we eat? an evaluation of food items input into an electronic food monitoring application. In: 2006 Pervasive Health Conference and Workshops, pp. 1–10. IEEE (2006)
64. Van Berkel, N., Goncalves, J., Hosio, S., Kostakos, V.: Gamification of mobile experience sampling improves data quality and quantity. Proceed. ACM Interact. Mobile Wearable Ubiquitous Technol. 1(3) (2017)
65. Vu, T., Lin, F., Alshurafa, N., Xu, W.: Wearable food intake monitoring technologies: a comprehensive review. Computers 6(1), 4 (2017)
66. Wasson, D.H., Jackson, M.: An analysis of the role of overeaters anonymous in women's recovery from bulimia nervosa. Eating Disorders 12(4), 337–356 (2004)
67. Woteki, C.E., Thomas, P.R.: Eat for life. the food and nutrition board's guide to reducing your risk of chronic disease. Clin. Nutrition Insight 19(3), 7 (1993)
68. Zepeda, L., Deal, D.: Think before you eat: photographic food diaries as intervention tools to change dietary decision making and attitudes. Int. J. Consumer Stud. 32(6), 692–698 (2008)
69. Zhang, S., et al.: Necksense: a multi-sensor necklace for detecting eating activities in free-living conditions. Proceed ACM Interact. Mobile Wearable Ubiquitous Technol. 4(2), 1–26 (2020)

Fine-Grained Respiration Monitoring During Overnight Sleep Using IR-UWB Radar

Siheng Li[1,2], Zhi Wang[1,2], Fusang Zhang[1,2,3], and Beihong Jin[1,2(✉)]

[1] State Key Laboratory of Computer Science, Institute of Software,
Chinese Academy of Sciences, Beijing 100190, China
{lisiheng19,wangzhi20,zhangfusang,jbh}@otcaix.iscas.ac.cn
[2] University of Chinese Academy of Sciences, Beijing 100190, China
[3] State Key Laboratory for Novel Software Technology, Nanjing University,
Nanjing 210093, China

Abstract. Recently, vital sign and sleep monitoring using wireless signals has made great progress. However, overnight respiration monitoring remains a challenge due to human unconscious and uncontrollable movements during sleep. In the paper, we explore the potential of an IR-UWB radar and implement a fine-grained overnight respiration monitoring prototype. Particularly, we exploit the complementarity between amplitude and phase of the radar signal to eliminate blind spots, thus improving the detection rate of overnight respiration monitoring. Moreover, we propose a circle fitting based phase restoration algorithm to correct the respiration depth distortion, and further recognize four respiration patterns (i.e., apnea pattern, Tachypnea pattern, Kussmaul pattern and rapid change pattern of respiration rate), thus enabling fine-grained respiration monitoring during overnight sleep. The experimental results show that our prototype achieves high respiration detection rates and accurate respiration rates, outperforming the two existing approaches. In addition, our prototype has captured the apnea pattern many times in the real sleep scenarios.

Keywords: Contactless sensing · Vital sign monitoring · IR-UWB Radar

1 Introduction

Respiration during sleep is an important indicator of human health, which can reflect the progression of some diseases and decline in health. At the very least, respiration disorders during sleep affect the quality of sleep and cause fatigue during the day. Furthermore, chronic lack of high-quality sleep might lead to obesity [15]. What is worse, severe sleep disorders such as Sleep Apnea Syndrome (SAS) [5] can increase the risk of sudden death in adults. Therefore, it is

© ICST Institute for Computer Sciences, Social Informatics and Telecommunications Engineering 2022
Published by Springer Nature Switzerland AG 2022. All Rights Reserved
T. Hara and H. Yamaguchi (Eds.): MobiQuitous 2021, LNICST 419, pp. 84–101, 2022.
https://doi.org/10.1007/978-3-030-94822-1_5

important to monitor human respiration throughout the night, which is beneficial for diagnosis and treatment of sleep disorders.

In clinical settings, traditional methods for continuous respiration monitoring are capnography [4] and thoracic impedance pneumography [11]. These methods are intrusive and require the subject to stay in hospital or sleep laboratory for a long period of time, which prevents them from wide deployment and in-home use.

Recently, wearable devices such as Flow chest straps [1] have been developed to detect the respiration state but they make users feel uncomfortable while wearing them overnight. The alternative solution is the contactless sensing [2, 18, 19], which is non-intrusive and easy to deploy at home. However, the existing work on respiration monitoring often requires the subject to sit in chair or lie in bed still, limiting the changes in distance and orientation between the subject and the device. Such settings do not match reality. In real scenarios, the subject is completely unconscious and uncontrollable during sleep. Movements of different body parts will cause changes in distance and orientation between the subject and the device. Therefore, overnight respiration monitoring is still a challenge.

In the paper, for overnight respiration monitoring, we explore the ability of the Impulse-Radio Ultra-Wideband (IR-UWB) radar. However, the results of preliminary respiration monitoring experiments are not good enough. We find that, when signal amplitude or phase is used individually for overnight respiration sensing, there exists different blind spots (namely locations where respiration detection experiences poor performance) which are observed for the first time in radar sensing but has been observed in Wi-Fi sensing [22], making it hard to achieve full-time respiration monitoring. Additionally, the human respiration depth estimated from the radar signals has a wide range of variation or even becomes invalid values, which we define as the respiration depth distortion.

We carefully examine the blind spots and the respiration depth distortion, and then offer the solutions and implement a fine-grained overnight respiration monitoring prototype. The main contributions of the paper are as follows.

- We exploit the complementarity between amplitude and phase of received radar signal to eliminate the blind spots and enhance the detectable rate of respiration during overnight sleep, thus enabling overnight respiration monitoring.
- We propose a circle fitting based phase restoration algorithm to restore the signal phase and estimate the real respiration depth, thus solving the respiration depth distortion.
- We combine the respiration rate and respiration depth to identify four respiration patterns that may occur during sleep, including apnea pattern, Tachypnea pattern, Kussmaul pattern and rapid change pattern of respiration rate, thus enabling fine-grained respiration monitoring.
- We conduct extensive experiments to evaluate the performance of our prototype under realistic settings. The experimental results show that our prototype outperforms the two existing approaches and achieves a median error in respiration rate estimation of 0.27 bpm and 100% recognition accuracy for four respiration patterns during sleep.

2 Preliminary Study: Analyzing IR-UWB Signals for Sensing Respiration

As we know, an IR-UWB radar continuously transmits the pulse signals at a certain interval (i.e., Pulse Repetition Interval, PRI) and collects the signals reflected by subjects in the environment. The received signals are down-converted to obtain the I and Q baseband signals, which are recorded in a 2D complex matrix (as shown in Fig. 1), where the row is defined as the "fast time" dimension and the column is defined as the "slow time" dimension. Fast time dimension contains reflective pulse responses with different time delays during a PRI, denoting different distance bins, and slow time dimension updates every PRI [24]. Therefore, when a subject is stationary at a certain position, we can find the fast time bin corresponding to the subject and take a slice along the slow time dimension from the 2D matrix of received signals, getting a 1D time series which is an estimation of the signal reflecting the tiny changes in distance between the subject and the device over time. Visualizing the 1D slice in the IQ domain, we can obtain a series of scattered signal samples, which form an arc-shaped trajectory centered at a certain point. For each signal sample H, its amplitude (i.e., $|H|$, denoted by A) and phase (i.e., the angle between H and the I-axis, denoted by θ) can be obtained, the corresponding waveforms are shown in Fig. 2.

In principle, when a subject breathes at rest, the periodic changes in the distance between the subject's chest and the radar will result in the periodic changes in amplitude and phase of the received signal. In other words, the amplitude or phase waveform of the received signal corresponds to the subject's respiration waveform. However, is the principle described above always true? In real sleep scenarios, a subject will move and change his/her sleeping posture and position, which is recorded in the reflected signal. Then, what is the motion-sleep ratio and how does the motion affect the overnight respiration sensing? On the other hand, when a subject faces the radar and breathes, the amplitude increase and decrease of the received signal correspond to the inhalation and exhalation of the body part (e.g., chest), which can reflect the respiration depth theoretically. However, affected by the environment, the magnitude of the signals attenuates nonlinearly as propagating. Therefore, the amplitude difference can only roughly reflect the respiration depth, not precisely correspond to the respiration depth. Different from amplitude, the phase of the received signals is not affected by the environment, and only related to the distance between the human and the radar. That is to say, we can estimate the respiration depth by $\Delta d = -\frac{\lambda}{4\pi}\Delta\Phi$ [3], where λ is the wavelength of the signals, Δd is the change in distance between the human body and the radar over a period of time, and $\Delta\Phi$ is the phase change in the same period of time. However, is this respiration depth estimation method feasible in real sleep scenarios?

We collect the signals of a COTS IR-UWB radar in a real sleep scenario (3 nights of 3 subjects), and analyze the amplitude and phase waveforms of the signals, respectively. The observations we get are as follows.

Observation 1: Respiration is not detectable in all the locations when amplitude or phase of the received signals is used individually.

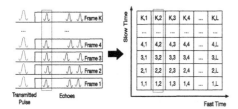

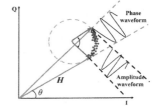

Fig. 1. Received signal matrix.

Fig. 2. Signal change patterns of amplitude and phase.

In contrast with the ground truth, we find that about 78% of the amplitude waveforms of the received signals are relatively regular, corresponding to states when the subjects breathe steadily. These waveforms can be regarded as respiration waveforms. Meanwhile, about 10% of the amplitude waveforms correspond to the movements of the subjects which result in more significant changes in the waveform than normal respiration. The amplitude waveforms left are disordered. A similar phenomenon is also observed from the phase waveforms of the signals.

Particularly, we observe that the waveforms differ in different locations and orientations between the subject and the radar. Two examples are shown in Fig. 3. (i) When the subject is lying on the back with his/her sideways chest facing the radar 0.72 m away, the amplitude waveform is disordered while the phase waveform is regular, as shown in Fig. 3(a). (ii) When the subject is lying on one side with his/her chest facing the radar 0.62 m away, the amplitude waveform is regular while the phase waveform is disordered, as shown in Fig. 3(b).

The above results illustrate three points. (i) When a subject breathes normally, whether the amplitude or phase waveform can reflect his/her respiration waveform depends on the distance and orientation between the subject and the radar. (ii) When amplitude or phase of the received signal is used individually, there are locations where the waveforms are disordered and respiration cannot be detected there. We call it the blind spot problem. (iii) The amplitude and phase of the received signal may be complementary to each other, i.e., their blind spots may not overlap. This observation can be used to improve the detection rate of respiration.

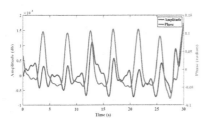

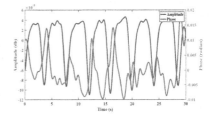

(a) Posture: lying on the back, distance from device: 0.72m.

(b) Posture: lying on one side, distance from device: 0.62m.

Fig. 3. Amplitude and phase of two 30 s windows (from a certain subject).

Observation 2: Distortion exists in estimated respiration depth during overnight sleep.

We choose the phase waveform when the subject breathes steadily, calculate the phase changes between all neighboring pairs of peak and valley, and then estimate the respiration depth by $\Delta d = -\frac{\lambda}{4\pi}\Delta\Phi$. We find that the estimated respiration depth has the minimum of 0.01 cm and the maximum of 0.70 cm. However, the depth of 0.01 cm is not a valid respiration depth according to our common sense. By analyzing the estimated method, we know that the distortion of the estimated respiration depth is derived from the distortion of the phase change. That is, the received signals are affected by the multipath phenomenon in the environment. The distance and orientation between a subject and a radar vary during the night, so does his/her sleeping posture. Therefore, the phase we calculate is in fact one distorted by the superposition of these factors. We should eliminate effects of these factors to get more realistic respiration depths.

3   Our Respiration Monitoring Prototype

3.1   Overview

Our respiration monitoring prototype, as shown in Fig. 4, consists of five modules: Signal Preprocessing, Signal Waveform Classification, Respiration Rate Measurement, Respiration Depth Estimation and Respiration Pattern Recognition.

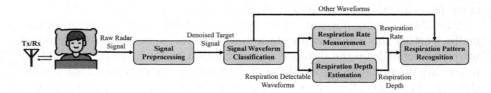

Fig. 4. System architecture of our prototype.

Signal Preprocessing. Signal preprocessing is divided into three steps: background subtraction, human identification and noise reduction. (i) We adopt a 30 s sliding window with none overlay to segment the received radar signals. Then, we apply the background subtraction method in [21] to remove clutter from the original received signals, which is caused by all static reflectors in the background environment, and retain the reflected signal from human body. (ii) Human identification is to identify the signal from human body from the received signal matrix. Here, we use amplitude of the signal for human identification. In detail, given each background-subtracted signal matrix over the 30 s sliding window, we perform FFT along the slow time dimension to obtain a Doppler map. As we know, when the amplitude peak of a column on the Doppler map is within a frequency range of 0.1 Hz to 0.85 Hz, the fast-time index of the largest amplitude peak among all the columns corresponds to the location of human. Therefore, we take a slice from the 2D original received signal matrix by the fast-time index, and get a 1D time series as an estimation of reflected signal from human body. (iii) We employ the Savitzky-Golay polynomial least squares filter (SG Filter) [10] to remove the high-frequency noise from the signal while preserving the steep changes and remaining the positions of the peaks and valleys [8]. Finally, we perform a detrend operation on the denoised signal to remove the polynomial trend of the time series.

Signal Waveform Classification. After obtaining the reflected signal from human body, we can get the amplitude and phase waveforms of the reflected signal. Then we divide the signal waveforms into three categories: body movement waveforms, respiration detectable waveforms and other waveforms.

We propose a window depth-based method to detect whether the waveform corresponds to a body motion. Specifically, we calculate the phase difference between the maximum and minimum phase values within each 30 s window, and then calculate the relative displacement of human body during each 30 s window, referred to as the window depth. Considering that the window depth is close to the human respiration depth in terms of physical meaning, we set the threshold of window depth to the maximum normal human respiration depth (i.e., 1 cm). If the window depth exceeds this threshold, then we believe a body movement occurs in the current window.

Subsequently, for all the windows without body movements, we apply autocorrelation [23] on both amplitude waveforms and phase waveforms to identify respiration detectable waveforms. The details are described in Sect. 3.2.

After eliminating body movement waveforms and respiration detectable waveforms, the remaining waveforms are referred to as other waveforms, which are generally disordered. However, they might reflect some abnormal information of the human body, so we send them to the Respiration Pattern Recognition module for further processing.

Respiration Rate Measurement. We utilize autocorrelation to measure the respiration rates given respiration detectable waveforms. Figure 5 shows a respiration waveform and its autocorrelation result. We get the lag (shift) of the maximum peak (i.e., N in Fig. 5), and then measure the respiration rate by $\frac{60}{N/f_s}$, where f_s is the radar sampling frequency.

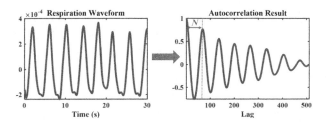

Fig. 5. Applying autocorrelation on respiration waveform.

Respiration Depth Estimation. We estimate the respiration depth given the respiration detectable waveform. We propose a circle fitting based phase restoration algorithm to restore signal phase and estimate the real respiration depth of human, thus solving the respiration depth distortion problem described in Sect. 2. The details of respiration depth estimation are described in Sect. 3.3.

Respiration Pattern Recognition. We combine the respiration rate and respiration depth to recognize four respiration patterns during sleep. The details are in Sect. 3.4.

3.2   Identifying Respiration Detectable Waveform

We identify respiration detectable waveforms by applying autocorrelation on signal waveforms. The autocorrelation function describes the similarity of a signal to a shifted version of itself, and the maximum peak value in the autocorrelation result represents the periodicity of the signal. That is, if the peak value exceeds a certain threshold, then the signal has a regular waveform (i.e., strong periodicity). Further, the lag (shift) of the maximum peak (i.e., N in Fig. 5) can be used to calculate the signal cycle by N/f_s. Normally, a respiration waveform of the detected subject is periodic. Therefore, the maximum peak value in its autocorrelation result should be high, and the signal cycle N/f_s is also the respiration cycle of humans. Since the normal human respiration cycle lasts 2–10 s, we limit the range of the lag from $2 \cdot f_s$ to $10 \cdot f_s$, further obtaining the maximum peak value among this range, which is denoted by respiration autocorrelation value hereafter. Thus, given the threshold of the respiration autocorrelation value, we can determine whether a signal waveform is highly periodic and the cycle is within the range of the normal respiration cycle of humans by analyzing the autocorrelation result of signal amplitude or phase waveform, further classifying whether the signal waveform is a respiration detectable waveform.

However, due to existence of the blind spots observed in Sect. 2, we cannot identify all the respiration detectable waveforms using amplitude or phase waveform individually. Therefore, if we can prove the complementarity of respiration detectable portions between signal amplitude and phase waveforms, then we can utilize the complementarity to identify a respiration detectable waveform. We first show that amplitude and phase are complementary to each other theoretically.

The received radar signal H is the superposition of all the path components in the same distance bin as human, and can be divided into two components: the static component H_s and the dynamic component H_d. H_s consists of reflection paths from different stationary body parts (e.g., head and legs) and static objects in the same distance as human in the environment, while H_d is mainly determined by the reflection path from dynamic body part (i.e., chest while breathing). H rotates synchronously with H_d. Supposing that H_d rotates 360° clockwise from point A in Fig. 6(a), the corresponding amplitude and phase waveforms are plotted in Fig. 6(b).

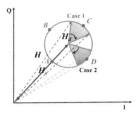

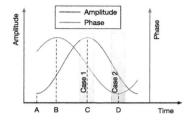

(a) Two arc cases of sig-
nals in IQ domain.

(b) Amplitude and phase waveform fragments in two cases.

Fig. 6. Complementarity between amplitude and phase.

However, H_d does not rotate 360° as human breathes (e.g., Fig. 2), but move
back and forth along a circular arc. Different arcs in Fig. 6(a) result in different
fragments of amplitude and phase waveforms in Fig. 6(b) (e.g., Case 1 and Case
2 in Fig. 6). We find that a bad position for amplitude waveform turns out to be
a good position for phase waveform, and vice versa. However, are there any positions where both amplitude and phase change slightly and non-monotonically
(i.e., both in bad location) during normal respiration? Some research for Wi-Fi
signals [17,22] find that human's normal respiration tends to cause H_d to rotate
about 60°. In Fig. 6(b), a window corresponding to 60° cannot find a situation in
which both amplitude and phase change slightly and non-monotonically, no matter how much the window slides. Thus we prove the complementarity between
amplitude and phase.

Further, we propose that if the respiration autocorrelation value of either
amplitude waveform or phase waveform of the signal in current window exceeds
the threshold, the signal waveform will be identified as a respiration detectable
waveform, and the one with higher respiration autocorrelation value between
amplitude and phase waveform will be used to measure respiration rate. If neither of them exceeds the threshold, it reveals that the waveform in current window
has poor regularity, and we classify such waveform as other waveform. Figure 7
presents three examples of signal waveforms, where respiration autocorrelation
value exceeding threshold is in green, and value not exceeding threshold is in red.

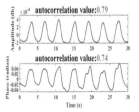

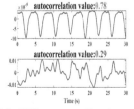

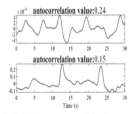

(a) Both amplitude and
phase are over the threshold
(respiration detectable).

(b) Either amplitude or
phase is over the threshold
(respiration detectable).

(c) Neither amplitude nor
phase is over the threshold
(respiration undetectable).

Fig. 7. Signal waveform examples of different respiration autocorrelation values. (Color
figure online)

3.3   Estimating Respiration Depth

For the respiration depth distortion (i.e., phase distortion) problem observed in Sect. 2, we analyze it here by projecting the signal onto the complex plane (i.e., IQ domain). As shown in Fig. 8, the decomposition of the signal can be expressed as $H = H_s + H_d$. When the detected subject breathes, H_d rotates along a circular arc, resulting in rotating of H synchronously. Using the phase change $\Delta\Phi$ (i.e., θ_i in Fig. 8) during rotating of received signal H, the respiration depth can be estimated by $\Delta d = -\frac{\lambda}{4\pi}\Delta\Phi$. However, the phase change $\Delta\Phi$ is not the real phase change caused by the subject (i.e., θ_c in Fig. 8) due to the effect of H_s. Therefore, we need to restore the phase change from θ_i to θ_c so as to estimate the real respiration depth.

In this subsection, we propose a circle fitting based phase restoration algorithm to estimate real human respiration depth during sleep. As described above, the respiration depth distortion problem we observe originates from the phase change distortion. Therefore, we fit a circle based on the signal samples in IQ domain. Then the static component H_s can be eliminated by translating the circle center to the origin of coordinates [7]. As a result, $H = H_d$, $\theta_i = \theta_c$ and the phase change is proportional to the displacement of humans. Details are as follows.

Let $X = \{x_i\}_N$, $x_i \in R^2$ denote the signal samples in IQ domain, $c \in R^2$ denote the fitted circle center, and r denote the radius of the fitted circle. We formalize the following optimization problem to solve c^* and r^*:

$$c^*, r^* = \arg\min_{c,r} \sum_{x_i \in X} (\|x_i - c\| - r)^2 \tag{1}$$

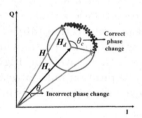

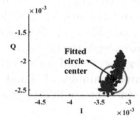

Fig. 8. Signal decomposition in IQ domain.

Fig. 9. Example of simple circle fitting result.

It is a nonlinear least squares optimization problem which can be solved using the least squares method in [6]. However, this simple circle fitting method fails to obtain the correct circle when signal samples distribute dispersedly or have low signal quality (such as low signal-to-noise ratio (SNR)), as shown in Fig. 9. Therefore, rather than using all signal samples, we select part of signal samples which can form a regular circular arc as representative samples, and fit a circle based on these samples. The entire algorithm procedure is as follows.

- Firstly, for each respiration detectable waveform, we choose the one with higher respiration autocorrelation value from its amplitude and phase waveform as the final respiration waveform.
- Secondly, we find all peaks and valleys of the final respiration waveform. To remove the fake peaks and valleys, we add two constraints to the peak/valley identification. (i) We set the minimum distance between two neighboring peaks or valleys to $60 \cdot f_s / br_{max}$, where f_s is the radar sampling frequency and br_{max} is human's maximum possible respiration rate (30 bpm in this paper). (ii) We compare each peak or valley to the samples within a window of length $60/br_{max}$ centered at itself. The peak or valley should be the maximum or minimum one within the specified window. Otherwise, it is identified as a fake peak or valley and removed.
- Thirdly, we treat all neighboring peak-to-valley and valley-to-peak waveforms as candidate waveforms. Then, we fit the circle using the least squares method, based on the signal samples selected from all samples by the index range of each candidate waveform. Supposing that there are K candidate waveforms in a 30 s window, we get K candidate circle centers c_j and K candidate radii r_j at last, where $j \in [1, K]$. We calculate the fitting error e_j for each candidate:

$$e_j = \frac{1}{N} \sum_{i=1}^{N} (\|x_i - c_j\| - r_j)^2, j \in [1, K] \tag{2}$$

- Lastly, we choose the circle center with the lowest fitting error as the final circle center, as shown in Fig. 10. We can see that our method solves the problem in Fig. 9.

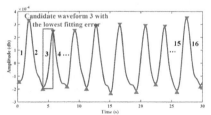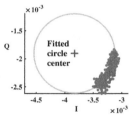

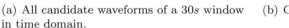

(a) All candidate waveforms of a 30s window in time domain.   (b) Circle fitting result.

Fig. 10. Example of circle fitting result using our method.

After obtaining the final circle center, we eliminate the static component H_s from the signal and calculate its phase waveform. Then, we locate all peaks and valleys within current 30 s window, and obtain phase changes between all pairs of neighboring peak and valley. Finally, the respiration depths are estimated by $\Delta d = -\frac{\lambda}{4\pi} \Delta \Phi$.

3.4 Capturing Respiration Patterns

Table 1 shows four respiration patterns which are clinically significant. If these respiration patterns are detected to occur frequently during sleep, then the detected subject may suffer from the corresponding respiration-related disease.

From Table 1, we can see that Tachypnea pattern and Kussmaul pattern can be identified by setting thresholds on respiration rate and respiration depth, respectively. Rapid change pattern of respiration rate can be identified by setting the threshold on the respiration rate. We adopt a 30 s sliding window with 1 s sliding step to recognize these three respiration patterns from the respiration detectable waveforms.

The apnea pattern is identified from the other waveforms. We use a 10 s sliding window with 1 s sliding step to scan the waveforms, and calculate the variance of the waveform in each window. If the variance of the current window drops by α percent compared to the previous normal window, and is less than a pre-defined threshold β (α, β are set to 0.8 and 8.3×10^{-5}, respectively), we consider apnea occurs in the current window, where β is used to avoid our algorithm identifying the respiration depth change as apnea. By recording the starting time of the first apnea window and the ending time of the last apnea window, we can obtain the duration of the apnea pattern.

Table 1. Four respiration patterns.

Respiration pattern	Definition	Clinical significance
Apnea	Breathing stops for at least 10 s	Frequent apnea relates to SAS
Tachypnea	Breathing is fast but shallow with respiration rate over 24 bpm	Seen in respiratory muscle paralysis, severe bullae and pulmonary diseases such as pneumonia, pleurisy and pneumothorax
Kussmaul	Breathing is slow but deep	Seen in severe metabolic acidosis, such as diabetic ketoacidosis and uremic acidosis
Rapid change of respiration rate	Respiration rate rapidly change from fast to slow or from slow to fast	Slowed respiration is commonly associated with shock and apparent intracranial pressure increase. Increased respiration is commonly associated with fever, anemia, hyperthyroidism, pneumonia and pleurisy

4   Evaluation

4.1   Experimental Setup

Prototype Implementation. We employ a COTS IR-UWB radar XETHRU model X4M05 to collect signals. The radar has the center frequency of 7.3 GHz, the bandwidth of 1.4 GHz, and the sampling frequency of 23.328 GHz. Considering the effect of human's respiration frequency and SNR, we set the frame per second to 17. The radar is connected to a Raspberry Pi via a Dupont line, and all of them are packaged as a compact device, whose appearance and internal structure are shown in Fig. 11. We implement the prototype in Matlab. The demo video is provided at https://youtu.be/lEmYbo8kydA.

Data Collection. Our experimental scenario is shown in Fig. 12. Our device is placed at the bedside of the bedroom and orientates towards the sleeper. We recruit 7 volunteers aged from 22 to 34 years old and collect the data of 17 nights (108 h in total).[1]

Ground Truth. We adopt a 3-lead sleep monitor i.e., Heal Force PC-3000 as shown in Fig. 12, to record respiration rates which are treated as the ground truth. A high-definition camera (i.e., an ONTOP FHD camera) is employed to record real-time waveforms displayed on the sleep monitor. Meanwhile, we use an infrared camera (i.e., EZVIZ C6CN camera) to record the sleep scenes overnight, which is used as the ground truth of human movements.

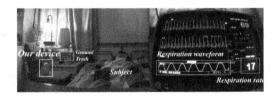

Fig. 11. Appearance and internal structure of our device.

Fig. 12. Experimental setting and ground truth device.

4.2   Overnight Respiration Detection Performance

Respiration Rate Estimation Evaluation. The estimation error of respiration rate is defined as the absolute value of the difference between the estimated respiration rate R_E and the ground truth R_G, i.e., $|R_E - R_G|$. For evaluating the

---

[1] The data collection procedure was approved by the Institutional Review Board (IRB). Each volunteer is required to sign an informed consent form before the experiments.

estimation errors of our system, two algorithms presented by Raheel et al. [13] and Liu et al. [9] respectively are chosen as competitors. Here, Raheel et al. employ a UWB radar to estimate human respiration rates and heart rates when humans are still. Liu et al. employ a Wi-Fi device to monitor vital signs during overnight sleep. We implement their algorithms and migrate them to our UWB radar. Using our sleep data as input, we execute all three algorithms and get the experimental results as shown in Fig. 13 and Fig. 14.

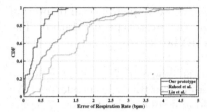

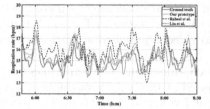

Fig. 13. CDFs of respiration rate estimation errors.

Fig. 14. Respiration rate curves of a certain interval of one night.

Firstly, as a case study, Fig. 14 shows the respiration rate curves of the same subject within the same interval under different algorithms, which shows that our curve fits the ground truth curve best. Secondly, Fig. 13 shows the cumulative distribution functions (CDFs) of the respiration rate estimation errors of three algorithms. We can see that our system achieves a median error of 0.27 bpm and a maximum error of 1.27 bpm, while the median and maximum error of Raheel et al. are 1.27 bpm and 3.94 bpm, respectively, and the median and maximum error of Liu et al. are 0.66 bpm and 4.80 bpm, respectively. In brief, our system achieves the lowest respiration rate estimation errors.

Respiration Detection Rate Evaluation. The respiration detection rate is defined as the ratio of the duration where respiration is detectable over the duration of the entire night's sleep. We derive two variants from our algorithm, one using amplitude alone and another using phase alone. Figure 15 and Fig. 16 show the average respiration detection rates and respiration rate estimation errors of three algorithms. We can see that our algorithm achieves a respiration detection rate of 82.99% and a median estimation error of respiration rate of 0.27 bpm. As a comparison, the respiration detection rate and median respiration rate estimation error are 78.43% and 0.34 bpm for the amplitude variant and 78.05% and 0.27 bpm for the phase variant, respectively. Experimental results demonstrate that our algorithm not only finds more respiration detectable waveforms, but also reduces the estimation error of respiration rate.

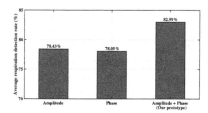

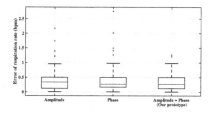

Fig. 15. Respiration detection rate.

Fig. 16. Respiration rate estimation error.

4.3   Fine-Grained Respiration Detection Performance

Respiration Depth Detection Evaluation. We evaluate the respiration depth restoration performance of the proposed circle fitting based algorithm under different respiration depths and positions by the following experiments. Firstly, the subjects with chest facing the radar are asked to perform normal respiration for 30 s, then deep respiration for 30 s and then gradually return to

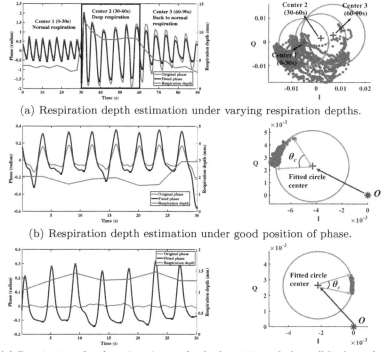

(a) Respiration depth estimation under varying respiration depths.

(b) Respiration depth estimation under good position of phase.

(c) Respiration depth estimation under bad position of phase (blind spot).

Fig. 17. Respiration depth evaluation.

normal respiration in the last 30 s. By this way, we simulate a respiration pattern whose phase varies largely over time. The experimental results are shown in Fig. 17(a), where our algorithm fits a new circle center every 30 s, and is able to restore more realistic change in respiration depth. Secondly, the subjects are required to adjust the orientation of their chests towards the radar so that the phase waveforms generated by their reflections are regular (subjects in a good position for phase to detect respiration) or disordered (subjects in a bad position for phase to detect respiration). The experimental results demonstrate that our algorithm can successfully restore the respiration depth regardless of whether the subjects are in a good position (Fig. 17(b)) or a bad position (Fig. 17(c)) for phase to detect respiration.

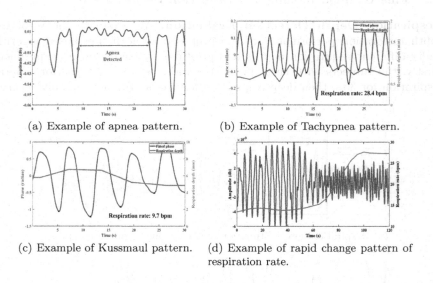

(a) Example of apnea pattern.   (b) Example of Tachypnea pattern.

(c) Example of Kussmaul pattern.   (d) Example of rapid change pattern of respiration rate.

Fig. 18. Different respiration patterns.

Respiration Pattern Detection Evaluation. We detect four respiration patterns, including apnea pattern, Tachypnea pattern, Kussmaul pattern and rapid change pattern of respiration rate, from overnight sleep signals.

- **Apnea pattern.** We perform the apnea detection on the sleep data of 17 nights, and find apnea appears five times. We compare them with the respiration waveforms provided by the sleep monitor, and the results show that our algorithm achieves 100% detection accuracy in detecting apnea during sleep. Figure 18(a) shows an example of apnea waveform at a certain night. It can be seen that the respiration waveform between 9 and 23 s becomes flat, and the whole apnea duration lasts for 14 s.

- **Tachypnea pattern and Kussmaul pattern.** Since our overnight data do not contain these patterns, we require the subjects to lie in bed with chest facing the device, and then simulate the patterns for 30 s, respectively. The experimental results show that our algorithm is able to detect these simulated respiration patterns, as shown in Figs. 18(b) and Fig. 18(c).
- **Rapid change pattern of respiration rate.** Since the rapid change pattern of respiration rate did not occur in our overnight sleep data, we require the subjects to perform normal respiration for 60 s, and then rapid respiration for 60 s. The experimental results show that our algorithm is able to detect this simulated respiration pattern, as shown in Fig. 18(d).

5   Related Work

With the development of wireless sensing technology, a number of wireless signal based solutions on vital sign and sleep monitoring have been proposed. Some solutions [12,16] exploit FMCW acoustic signals, and some solutions [2,8,22] exploit Wi-Fi signals. However, acoustic and Wi-Fi signals are sensitive to interference from the environment, thus leading to unstable sensing performance. On the other hand, although the quality of RFID signals is relatively stable, RFID-based solutions have to face the high deployment costs, which causes the difficulty in large scale deployment.

Compared with acoustic, RFID and Wi-Fi signals, radar signals are highly resistant to interference and have strong penetration capability, which make it popular with applications such as ranging, tracking and imaging. Some work has employed radars for vital sign sensing. For example, DoppleSleep [14] employs a commercial 24 GHz short-range Doppler continuous wave radar to continuously track human vital signs, enabling real-time and efficient sleep monitoring. Vital-Radio [3] exploits a FMCW radar to monitor respiration and heart rates, which also supports through-wall and multi-subject sensing. mmVital [20] uses a millimeter wave radar to monitor vital signs. It enables indoor multi-person detection and through-wall detection by introducing directional beamforming methods on the received signal strength information of the 60 GHz millimeter wave. In particular, Raheel et al. [13] use an IR-UWB radar to monitor human respiration and heart rates. Zheng et al. [24] also use an IR-UWB radar to perform in-vehicle vital sign monitoring.

We find existing solutions on respiration and sleep monitoring mainly focus on normal conditions (e.g., subject in a sober state sits in chair or lies in bed), which is not applicable to the overnight sleep scenario. By contrast, our work provides overnight respiration monitoring and can capture four respiration patterns such as apnea, which operates well in real sleep scenarios.

6   Conclusion

In this paper, we implement a prototype which is capable of overnight and fine-grained respiration monitoring. By exploiting IR-UWB radar as the front-end for data collection, our prototype is contact-free, of high-precision, and easy to deploy. Moreover, our prototype can provide both high detection rates and low estimation errors of respiration rates. Furthermore, it can also recognize four respiration patterns.

In the near future, real clinical experiments are expected to be conducted to evaluate the performance on patient's respiration monitoring. Further, we will extend our work to overnight heartbeat monitoring and sleep stage classification.

Acknowledgments. This work was supported by the National Natural Science Foundation of China under Grants No. 61802373 and No. 62072450.

References

1. Flow chest straps (2018). https://www.wareable.com/wearable-tech/sweetzpot-flow-breathing-chest-strap-2018
2. Abdelnasser, H., Harras, K.A., Youssef, M.: UbiBreathe: a ubiquitous non-invasive WiFi-based breathing estimator. In: Proceedings of the 16th ACM International Symposium on Mobile Ad Hoc Networking and Computing, pp. 277–286 (2015)
3. Adib, F., Mao, H., Kabelac, Z., Katabi, D., Miller, R.C.: Smart homes that monitor breathing and heart rate. In: Proceedings of the 33rd Annual ACM Conference on Human Factors in Computing Systems, pp. 837–846 (2015)
4. Anderson, J.A., Vann, W.F.: Respiratory monitoring during pediatric sedation: pulse oximetry and capnography. Pediatr. Dent. **10**(2), 94–101 (1988)
5. Azagra-Calero, E., Espinar-Escalona, E., Barrera-Mora, J.M., Llamas-Carreras, J.M., Solano-Reina, E.: Obstructive sleep apnea syndrome (OSAS). Review of the literature. Medicina Oral, Patologia Oral y Cirugia Bucal **17**(6), e925 (2012)
6. Chernov, N., Lesort, C.: Least squares fitting of circles. J. Math. Imaging Vis. **23**(3), 239–252 (2005)
7. Jiang, C., Guo, J., He, Y., Jin, M., Li, S., Liu, Y.: mmVib: micrometer-level vibration measurement with mmwave radar. In: Proceedings of the 26th Annual International Conference on Mobile Computing and Networking, pp. 1–13 (2020)
8. Khamis, A., Kusy, B., Chou, C.T., Hu, W.: WiRelax: towards real-time respiratory biofeedback during meditation using WiFi. Ad Hoc Netw. **107**, 102226 (2020)
9. Liu, J., Chen, Y., Wang, Y., Chen, X., Cheng, J., Yang, J.: Monitoring vital signs and postures during sleep using WiFi signals. IEEE Internet Things J. **5**(3), 2071–2084 (2018)
10. Luo, J., Ying, K., Bai, J.: Savitzky-Golay smoothing and differentiation filter for even number data. Signal Process. **85**(7), 1429–1434 (2005)
11. Młyńczak, M., Cybulski, G.: Improvement of body posture changes detection during ambulatory respiratory measurements using impedance pneumography signals. In: Kyriacou, E., Christofides, S., Pattichis, C.S. (eds.) XIV Mediterranean Conference on Medical and Biological Engineering and Computing 2016. IP, vol. 57, pp. 167–171. Springer, Cham (2016). https://doi.org/10.1007/978-3-319-32703-7_34
12. Nandakumar, R., Gollakota, S., Watson, N.: Contactless sleep apnea detection on smartphones. In: Proceedings of the 13th Annual International Conference on Mobile Systems, Applications, and Services, pp. 45–57 (2015)
13. Raheel, M.S., et al.: Breathing and heartrate monitoring system using IR-UWB radar. In: 2019 13th International Conference on Signal Processing and Communication Systems (ICSPCS), pp. 1–5. IEEE (2019)

14. Rahman, T., et al.: DoppleSleep: a contactless unobtrusive sleep sensing system using short-range doppler radar. In: Proceedings of the 2015 ACM International Joint Conference on Pervasive and Ubiquitous Computing, pp. 39–50 (2015)
15. Vorona, R.D., Winn, M.P., Babineau, T.W., Eng, B.P., Feldman, H.R., Ware, J.C.: Overweight and obese patients in a primary care population report less sleep than patients with a normal body mass index. Arch. Intern. Med. **165**(1), 25–30 (2005)
16. Wang, A., Sunshine, J.E., Gollakota, S.: Contactless infant monitoring using white noise. In: The 25th Annual International Conference on Mobile Computing and Networking, pp. 1–16 (2019)
17. Wang, H., et al.: Human respiration detection with commodity WiFi devices: do user location and body orientation matter? In: Proceedings of the 2016 ACM International Joint Conference on Pervasive and Ubiquitous Computing, pp. 25–36 (2016)
18. Wang, T., Zhang, D., Zheng, Y., Gu, T., Zhou, X., Dorizzi, B.: C-FMCW based contactless respiration detection using acoustic signal. In: Proceedings of the ACM on Interactive, Mobile, Wearable and Ubiquitous Technologies, vol. 1, no. 4, pp. 1–20 (2018)
19. Wang, Y., Zheng, Y.: TagBreathe: monitor breathing with commodity RFID systems. IEEE Trans. Mob. Comput. **19**(4), 969–981 (2019)
20. Yang, Z., Pathak, P.H., Zeng, Y., Liran, X., Mohapatra, P.: Monitoring vital signs using millimeter wave. In: Proceedings of the 17th ACM International Symposium on Mobile Ad Hoc Networking and Computing, pp. 211–220 (2016)
21. Yim, D.H., Cho, S.H.: An equidistance multi-human detection algorithm based on noise level using mono-static IR-UWB radar system. In: Future Communication, Information and Computer Science: Proceedings of the 2014 International Conference on Future Communication, Information and Computer Science (FCICS 2014), Beijing, China, 22–23 May 2014, p. 131. CRC Press (2015)
22. Zeng, Y., Wu, D., Gao, R., Gu, T., Zhang, D.: FullBreathe: full human respiration detection exploiting complementarity of CSI phase and amplitude of WiFi signals. In: Proceedings of the ACM on Interactive, Mobile, Wearable and Ubiquitous Technologies, vol. 2, no. 3, pp. 1–19 (2018)
23. Zeng, Y., Wu, D., Xiong, J., Yi, E., Gao, R., Zhang, D.: FarSense: pushing the range limit of WiFi-based respiration sensing with CSI ratio of two antennas. In: Proceedings of the ACM on Interactive, Mobile, Wearable and Ubiquitous Technologies, vol. 3, no. 3, pp. 1–26 (2019)
24. Zheng, T., Chen, Z., Cai, C., Luo, J., Zhang, X.: V2iFi: in-vehicle vital sign monitoring via compact RF sensing. In: Proceedings of the ACM on Interactive, Mobile, Wearable and Ubiquitous Technologies, vol. 4, no. 2, pp. 1–27 (2020)

Teledrive: A *Multi-master* Hybrid Mobile Telerobotics System with Federated *Avatar* Control

Ashis Sau[✉], Abhijan Bhattacharyya, and Madhurima Ganguly

TCS Research, Tata Consultancy Services, Kolkata, India
{ashis.sau,abhijan.bhattacharyya,ganguly.madhurima}@tcs.com

Abstract. This paper addresses the issue of inherent delay in cloud-centric architecture a scenario where multiple remote human users join a tele-presence/tele-operation session with a robot such that any one of the users may take exclusive control of the robot and remotely maneuver it as the Avatar of the current Master. It presents a novel WebRTC based signaling protocol which allows a hybrid topology for the multi-user session. While the audio/video conferencing happens over cloud, each Master can create an on-demand peer-to-peer channel with the Avatar for the desired duration of maneuvering the Avatar. Thus, it allows low-latency delivery of command resulting in better experience for the end-user. The system is deployed in public cloud and is operational. The efficacy of the system is established through benchmarking against cloud-centric architecture in real-life field trials.

Keywords: Telepresence · Cloud-robotics · P2P · WebRTC

1 Introduction

1.1 Motivation

The prevalent pandemic situation requires the human civilization to continue 'social' cooperation while maintaining physical 'distancing'. Hence, the unprecedented hindrances in traveling, physical assembling, etc. has reinforced the need for mobile telerobotics based applications. In mobile telerobotics a human Master interacts with a remote environment through a robot. The robot in the remote environment acts like an Avatar of the human Master. In the simplest form, the Master establishes a real-time audio-video chat with the Avatar over the Internet and, based on the visual feedback from the Avatar, the Master sends control commands to remotely maneuver the Avatar in real-time. In a Telepresence scenario the maneuvering is limited to moving the robot around the remote environment as desired by the Master. The off-the-shelve telerobotics systems are mostly one-to-one. A single Master connects to an Avatar remotely and maneuvers it while having audio/video exchange with the remote environment.

© ICST Institute for Computer Sciences, Social Informatics and Telecommunications Engineering 2022
Published by Springer Nature Switzerland AG 2022. All Rights Reserved
T. Hara and H. Yamaguchi (Eds.): MobiQuitous 2021, LNICST 419, pp. 102–114, 2022.
https://doi.org/10.1007/978-3-030-94822-1_6

However, in a practical collaborative situation, it may be required that multiple human users need to connect to the robot simultaneously in a session to perform a composite task through the robot. While having a real-time multiparty A/V conference, each user may need to perform a part of the task. Thus, each user needs to act as a Master for a certain duration with exclusive access to the robot and the robot acts as the Avatar of that particular user for the stipulated period. Once, the task is completed, current Master may relinquish the control. Another user may take control and elevates as a Master. However, irrespective of which user is the current Master, all the users are able to continue participating in the A/V chat and receive visual feedback from the Avatar as well as other users. For example, in a telemedicine scenario (Fig. 1), a medical assistant and a specialist doctor may join a session with a telerobot from two distant locations to provide consultation to a patient in isolation ward. In the beginning the medical assistant, who is aware of the geography of the patient's premise, remotely maneuvers the robot to navigate near the patient. After this she relinquishes the control and the specialist doctor takes control and becomes the Master to pursue further interactions with the patient. The medical assistant continues in the A/V conference to follow the doctor's instructions.

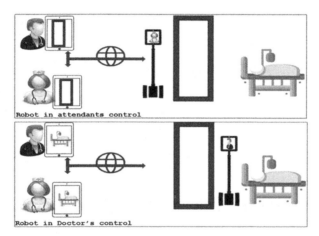

Fig. 1. The telemedicine application with users collaborating with the robot.

1.2   WebRTC in Telerobotics

WebRTC [1] is the dominant technology for real-time telerobotics applications like [2]. It is primarily designed to use the Internet browser as the user interface (UI) for multimedia conferencing. The audio/video is exchanged over the media channel on SRTP [1] and any other data is exchanged over a reliable data-channel on SCTP. The main reason of WebRTC's popularity is its inherent capability to establish low-latency end-to-end (E2E) channel through peer-to-peer (P2P) connection between the browsers of the participating Master and Avatar (Fig. 2a) [3]. However, the P2P connection may have to pass through a TURN (Traversal Using Relays around NAT) server when a direct P2P is not possible for nodes behind restricted NATs (Fig. 2b) [4, 5]. Most telerobotics solutions work in a P2P setting with only one Master connecting the Avatar. However, in a multiuser scenario all the participating parties, including the robot, would require to connect through a conferencing server in cloud in a star-like topology. This would break the true P2P paradigm. The cloud centricity causes delay in both transfer of control commands as well as in sharing the visual feedback which is critical for the end-user Quality of Experience (QoE) for telerobotics.

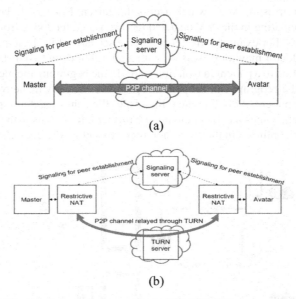

Fig. 2. a) WebRTC with direct P2P connection. b) WebRTC P2P connection via TURN server.

1.3   Salient Contribution and Organization of the Paper

This paper primarily addresses the latency issue of such cloud-centric multi-user telerobotics system. The key contribution of this paper is, *Teledrive*, a practical production-grade deployment of the telerobotics architecture such that, while remaining cloud-centric, the delay-critical control commands can be transferred over a P2P data-channel between the robot and the current Master on demand. Thus, *Teledrive* enables a dynamic configuration with hybrid topology where the media is exchanged over the server in the cloud and the control is transferred over the on-the-fly P2P connection. Thereby *Teledrive* aims to improve the latency in maneuvering the Avatar. Such an architecture is unique to best of our knowledge.

Furthermore, since multiuser telepresence system, as described, is not available, we modified *Teledrive* to a completely cloud-based system where the control is also transferred through the cloud server. We compare the performance of the cloud version and hybrid version of teledrive in both Quality of Service (QoS) and QoE measures in a practical deployment with distant users connecting to a custom robotic base and prove the efficacy of the hybrid *Teledrive*. QoE measures are performed based on user experience on completion of a task by the Avatar. Also, since the media always travels through the cloud, we compare the impact of reduced delay in the control path against the video latency as revealed in the QoE experiments.

Even further, we check the performance of hybrid *Teledrive* in two different P2P settings: with TURN and without TURN. We show that the performance of the hybrid version is further improved when the P2P is established without TURN.

To best of our knowledge, such an extensive practical deployment based benchmarking and architectural innovation is not present in the existing literatures. We hope that this work would open up new research directions towards delay compensation in cloud-centric telerobotics.

The rest of the paper is organized as follow. The next section describes the detail architecture of *Teledrive* for both cloud centric and hybrid versions. Section 3 describes the S/W and H/W deployment of the system for the required testbed. Section 4 describes the experiment methods for QoS and QoE aspects and the results with relevant analysis. Section 5 presents description of the related state-of-the-art. Finally the paper concludes with future research directions.

2 System Architecture

2.1 Generic Architecture

The multi-user connectivity is established through a special node called *broadcaster* (Fig. 3a). The *broadcaster* maintains separate P2P relationship with each human user nodes and the robot. Thus the 'star' is formed. The *broadcaster* receives A/V feedback from all the individual nodes over the P2P media channel and shares the composite A/V combining all the feeds all the other users connected to the *broadcaster* over the individual P2P channel. The *broadcaster* maintains the states of all the peers in each P2P channel and a *media-manager* inside the *broadcaster* is responsible for combining the video in a customized manner for each peer. The *state-register* maintains the state for each peer's connection state, especially the state of the robot. Figure 3b depicts the state transition between different robot states. The state also contains which user is the current Master (as discussed next). The *signaling server* helps establish the peering of the broadcaster with each peer. The *signaling server* and the *broadcaster* both are in public cloud. The Master users and the Avatar can be behind different types of NATs or contain public IPs. The P2P connections may traverse through a TURN server or be direct depending on whether the respective peer is behind restrictive NAT.

We have used a custom messaging for signaling. The basic application message structure in JSON format is:

```
{"connection-type":< >, "room-id":< >, "message-type":< >,
"message":< >}.
```

Interpretation of each parameter is given in Table 1. The individual message semantics are given in Fig. 3c. Each node has to specify its intended roleplay, i.e., Master (*peer type 'M'*) or Avatar (*peer type 'A'*). Type *'B'* is dedicated for the *Broadcaster*. Based on that it is decided whether the control interfaces are going appear for the user or not. The i-th Master would have the control interfaces enabled only when it is able to establish a control channel with the robot successfully.

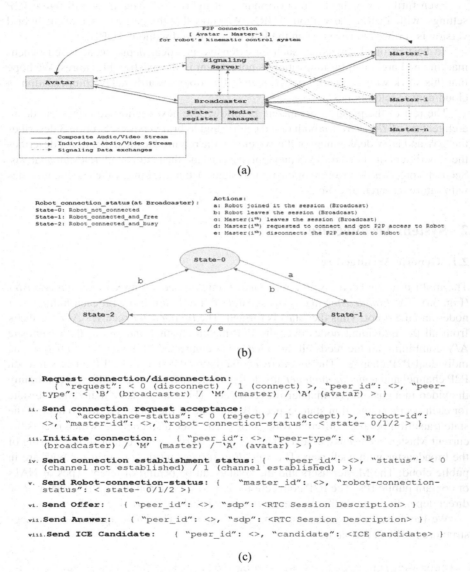

(a)

(b)

i. **Request connection/disconnection:**
   { "request": < 0 (disconnect) / 1 (connect) >, "peer_id": <>, "peer-type": < 'B' (broadcaster) / 'M' (master) / 'A' (avatar) > }

ii. **Send connection request acceptance:**
   { "acceptance-status": < 0 (reject) / 1 (accept) >, "robot-id": <>, "master-id": <>, "robot-connection-status": < state- 0/1/2 > }

iii. **Initiate connection:**   { "peer_id": <>, "peer-type": < 'B' (broadcaster) / 'M' (master) / 'A' (avatar) > }

iv. **Send connection establishment status:** {   "peer_id": <>, "status": < 0 (channel not established) / 1 (channel established) >}

v. **Send Robot-connection-status:** {   "master_id": <>, "robot-connection-status": < state- 0/1/2 >}

vi. **Send Offer:**   { "peer_id": <>, "sdp": <RTC Session Description> }

vii. **Send Answer:**   { "peer_id": <>, "sdp": <RTC Session Description> }

viii. **Send ICE Candidate:**   { "peer_id": <>, "candidate": <ICE Candidate> }

(c)

Fig. 3. (a) The generic WebRTC based architecture for Teledrive; (b) the robot state machine maintained at the broadcaster; (c) the semantics of individual message types exchanged.

In the general cloud-only configuration, each potential Master willing to control the Avatar sends a data channel request to the broadcaster through the signaling server. The broadcaster always maintains a data channel connection to the Avatar. If the broadcaster finds the status of the Avatar as 'free', it intimates connected status to the ith user and the user is elevated as Master. The Avatar state is changed to 'busy' and all other peers are notified the same. Henceforth, until disconnection, the ith Master sends all the control commands to the broadcaster peer, which in turn relays it to the Avatar. The execution status is likewise relayed back to the Master. Thus, both the A/V information and control information are relayed through the broadcaster in the cloud.

Table 1. Description of parameters in Teledrive message formats.

Parameter	Interpretation
Connection-type	0: Connection for broadcaster 1: Connection for any other peer
Room-id	<any string>: The meeting room ID for the session
Message-type	000: Request connection/disconnection 001: Send connection request acceptance 010: Initiate connection 011: Send connection establishment status 100: Send Robot-connection-status 101: Send Offer 110: Send Answer 111: Send ICE Candidate
Message	Type-specific message in JSON format (Ref. Fig. 3c)

2.2 Protocol for the Hybrid Topology

For the hybrid configuration, which is the key architectural contribution of this paper, the *broadcaster* involves a few more signaling to facilitate a P2P connection between the ith *Master* and the *Avatar* (Fig. 4a). In this case, when the ith *Master* wants to connect to the *Avatar*, *signaling server* that to the *broadcaster* which maintains all the states of connected peers. In response, the *broadcaster* notifies the ICE ID [1] and current state of the *Avatar* to the *signaling server* and it relays that to the ith user. The *signaling server* also requests the *Avatar* to offer a peer connection to the ICE candidate corresponding to the ith user. Once the ICE candidate states are exchanged between the Master and the Avatar, the *signaling server* notifies the same to the *broadcaster* and a P2P data channel is established between the ith *Master* and the *Avatar*. Thus, while the A/V is still exchanged via the *broadcaster* through star topology, the control is transferred over a P2P connection to ensure low-latency as will be proven in the next sections.

Once the ith *Master* disconnects the control (Fig. 4b), the *signaling server* ceases the P2P *data channel* and intimates the same to the *broadcaster*. The *broadcaster* marks the *Avatar* as *free* and notifies all the other users. Figure 4c illustrates the protocol to decline the P2P control connection request when the Robot is altogether disconnected from the ongoing session or is acquired by any other *Master*.

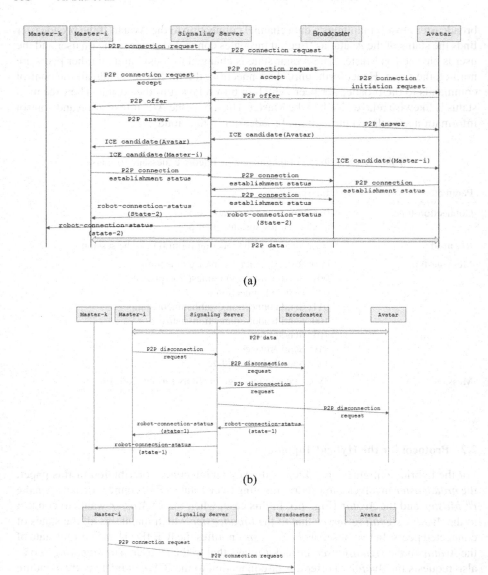

Fig. 4. The timing diagram of the protocol to (a) establish P2P control channel between the ith Master and the Avatar when the Avatar is in free state; (b) decline a connection attempt when the robot is busy, (c) decline a connection request when the robot is not in the ongoing session or already acquired by other *Master*.

3   Deployment and Test-Bed

We have created a custom built WebRTC stack using the standard WebRTC APIs using
Java Script and HTML 5. The *signaling server* runs on node.js. The nodes acting as
Master/Avatar uses Chrome or Mozilla browsers for the user interface. The *broadcaster*
uses a headless chrome implementation called *puppeteer* [6]. The media manager within
the *broadcaster* is built using the *video stream merger* APIs from *NPM registry* [7]. The
Avatar is an Intel Core i5 laptop running Ubuntu 16.04. The *Avatar* laptop is fixed
on a custom-built robotic base created using "Arduino Uno R3" microcontroller. The
microcontroller is connected to the laptop through USB port. The microcontroller is
augmented with L293D motor driver shield, 4 gear motors running 4 wheels in front,
rear, left and right directions. The system is powered by a 2200 mAh battery. The Avatar
machine is installed with Python 3.9. The interfacing between the controller and the
Avatar machine is done through serial port using *PySerial* library APIs. All commands
are passed through this. The connection between the *Avatar* browser and the Python
module is done through a WebSocket within the scope of the local host. The browser
code runs a WebSocket client which connects to local Python WebSocket server on
the *Avatar* laptop. The WebSocket server houses the *PySerial* APIs. Thus all the control
commands received by the *Avatar* browser are transferred to the microcontroller through
the WebSocket connection. This way the ith *Master* can use the browser UI to remotely
maneuver the Avatar.

The broadcaster and the signaling servers are hosted in AWS cloud on two EC2
t3.xlarge instances. The TURN server is built using COTURN [8] on one of the instances.
The cloud instances are located in the *US-EAST region*.

Figure 5(a) and (b) show the user interfaces for the active *Master* user and the
Avatar respectively in a real-life experiment with three potential *Master* users and the
Avatar joining from different locations around the city of *Kolkata, India* and the distance
between the Avatar and other users range between *50 to 100 km*.

4   Experiments, Results and Analysis

4.1   On Network Aspects

We first compare the latency performance in terms of the closed loop response time in
terms of:

$$RTT = t2 - t1,$$

where, t1 = time recorded at the Master browser when a command button is pressed
and t2 = time recorded when an acknowledgement is received at the Master browser.

The Java Script is modified to report *RTT* on the *Master* browser after every command. We note the values for 3 different users from three different locations as specified
above at four different segments of the day. The segments are *morning (7–7:30 am),
afternoon (2–2:30 pm), evening (6–6:30 pm), night (9–9:30 pm)*. The five-day average
of *RTT* for all the users for each segment of the day and the overall average is shown
for both cloud-only configuration and the hybrid configuration in Fig. 6. The *Avatar* is

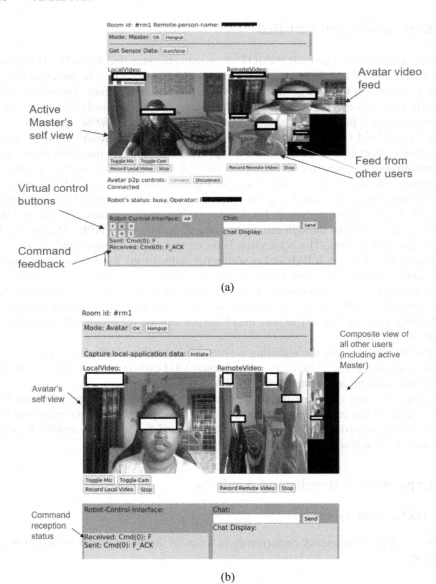

Fig. 5. (a) UI of the active Master; (b) UI of the Avatar.

connected to an ISP via WiFi AP such that the ISP forces *server reflexive address* [4] for all nodes connected to it. Thus, all the WebRTC peering are over the TURN server. It is observed that in India most of WiFi service provider ISPs force the use of NAT.

From the result we see that in the hybrid mode the command response is received much faster than the cloud-only mode. This is because, in hybrid mode, the control commands pass through the P2P channel, rather than through the *broadcaster* cloud. Although it passes through the TURN relay, still we get a reduction in the order of several hundreds of milliseconds.

We repeat the above experiment with all users and the *Avatar* connecting using 4G SIM from smartphones, rather than WiFi APs. In this case TURN relay is not required. We compare the command response for hybrid-mode with the situation where P2P is established through TURN server. The result is shown in Fig. 7. We observe that there is a further reduction by hundreds of milliseconds in the latency when the TURN relay is not used. One of the reasons of such a huge reduction is that the TURN server's location is in US, while P2P is formed within India. It is also to be seen that in the peak hours the difference in RTT for the two configurations minimizes. This also due to the load in the long backhaul during the peak usage in India and US respectively. Relocating the TURN server in India might have reduced the delay in TURN. Also, the effect of time axis is not significant for direct P2P. Hence, the results strongly establish the efficacy of hybrid Teledrive.

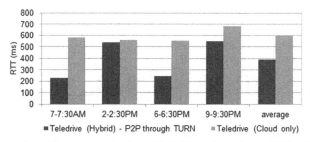

Fig. 6. RTT comparison between cloud only and hybrid configurations of Teledrive when the P2P command control channel passes through TURN server.

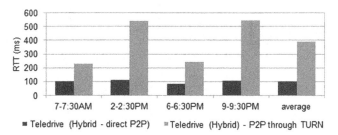

Fig. 7. RTT comparison between two different types of P2P command control channel for the same hybrid configuration: One passes through TURN server and the other is direct.

4.2 On Visual Aspects

For application user's paramount importance for QoE would be when the user sees the desired visual feedback from the Avatar after pressing a command button. To accomplish this, we create a set up as shown in Fig. 8. We place a blue bottle in camera-front at the original position of the Avatar and put a red bottle at a perpendicular position such that the Avatar faces this bottle when it rotates left by ninety degrees. We use the H/W platform described in Sect. 3. We repeat the similar exercise as described above. However, every Master presses only the L (rotate left) button. We developed a time calculation tool for this by enhancing Java Script code running at the Master browser. Whenever the user presses L a timer starts on the browser. As soon as the Master sees the complete view of the red bottle on the console, he/she presses a stop button and the timer stops. We call this time *Response time* defined as:

$$Execution\ time = t2 - t1,$$

where, t1 = time recorded at the Master browser when L command button is pressed and t2 = time recorded when Master presses stop button.

The results of this exercise are shown in Fig. 9 as average in time buckets and the overall average. We see a faster average response for the hybrid configuration. This is because the execution starts much earlier in case of hybrid configuration since the desired command is communicated to the *Avatar* much faster due to the P2P between the *Master* and *Avatar*.

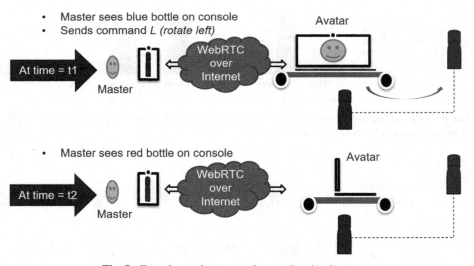

Fig. 8. Experimental setup to observe the visual aspects

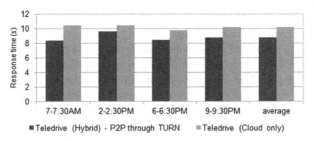

Fig. 9. Result of experiments on visual aspects

5   Analysis on the State-of-the-Art

To best of our knowledge we have not encountered any multiuser federated Telerobot controlling architecture as specified in this paper. [9] discloses an application which would allow doctors and nurses to join a telemedicine session with robot. However, this primarily deal with GUI design for the solution and does not disclose any Internet based real-time architecture as *Teledrive*. [10] proposes a multiuser robot control, but they deal with modelling the human behaviour when both user controls the robot simultaneous to access the different sensors of the robot to perform parts of a task collaboratively. It also does not deal with any Internet based architecture for federated Tele-presence or Tele-operation with a hybrid topology as *Teledrive*.

There are many literatures like [11] which have dealt with delay compensation in cloud robotics. But they deal with AI based solutions in specific environments.

WebRTC has been widely used in commercial Telepresence systems as [2] but those do not support a multiparty system. Literatures like [3] emphasize the importance of WebRTC in futuristic haptic communication and propose standardization of haptic data exchange, but it does not deal with any multi-user federated control scenario. Even literatures like [12, 13] also deal with the simple peer-to-peer scenario.

6   Conclusion

Teledrive consists of a unique Telerobotics communication architecture with custom signaling protocol built using WebRTC APIs. The hybrid topology allows multiple human users join a session along with a telerobot. While the users may continue A/V conferencing through a cloud infrastructure, any one of the human users may acquire exclusive control on the robot and make it his/her Avatar. The commands to control the Avatar would no longer travel through the cloud, rather, in the interest of reduced latency in remote execution, would be transmitted over an on demand P2P channel created between the active *Master* and the *Avatar*. The practical on-field deployment of the architecture is proven to have better performance compared to cloud centric architecture. To best of our knowledge, there are no off-the-shelve solution available that allow such multi-user federated fast maneuvering of a telerobot.

We look forward to deploy this on a standard platform as [2]. The future plan is to extend this hybrid topology to multirobot systems. Also, it remains to be seen whether the latency saving in sending the command is reciprocated by the visual feedback which still travels through the cloud. We would need to observe the time taken by the video to reach the *Master* after the execution has finished at the *Avatar* side. The resulting investigations may reveal new dimensions of research in compensating the delay in the video to reciprocate the low-latency command path. We will explore this in our next publication.

References

1. Alvestrand, H.: RFC 8825, Overview: Real-Time Protocols for Browser-Based Applications, IETF (2021)
2. Double Robotics - Telepresence Robot for the Hybrid Office. https://www.doublerobotics.com/. Accessed 18 July 2021
3. Iiyoshi, K., et al.: Towards standardization of haptic handshake for tactile internet: a WebRTC-based implementation. In: 2019 IEEE International Symposium on Haptic, Audio and Visual Environments and Games (HAVE), Malaysia (2019)
4. Keranen, A., Holmberg, C., Rosenberg, J.: RFC 8445, Interactive Connectivity Establishment (ICE): A Protocol for Network Address Translator (NAT) Traversal, IETF (2018)
5. Ford, B., Srisuresh, P., Kegel, D.: Peer-to-peer communication across network address translators. In: Proceedings of the Annual Conference on USENIX Annual Technical Conference, ACM, USA (2005)
6. Puppeteer. https://github.com/puppeteer/puppeteer. Accessed 18 July 2021
7. Video-Stream-Merger – npm. https://www.npmjs.com/package/video-stream-merger. Accessed 18 July 2021
8. Coturn. https://github.com/coturn/coturn. Accessed 18 July 2021
9. Wang, Y., Jordan, C. S., Pinter, M.: Tele-presence robot system with multi-cast facility, United States Patent No. US 984219B2 (2017)
10. Lee, D.G., et al.: Human-centered evaluation of multi-user teleoperation for mobile manipulator in unmanned offshore plants. In: 3 IEEE/RSJ International Conference on Intelligent Robots and Systems (IROS), Japan (2013)
11. Tian, N., Tanwani, A.K., Goldberg, K., Sojoudi, S.: Mitigating Network Latency in Cloud-Based Teleoperation Using Motion Segmentation and Synthesis, International Symposium on Robotics Research, Vietnam (2019)
12. Melendez-Fernandez, F., Galindo, C., Gonzalez-Jimenez, J.: A web-based solution for robotic telepresence. Int. J. Adv. Robot. Syst., SAGE (2017)
13. Tan, Q., et al.: Toward a telepresence robot empowered smart lab. Smart Learn. Environ. 6(1), 1–19 (2019). https://doi.org/10.1186/s40561-019-0084-3

Is This IoT Device Likely to Be Secure? Risk Score Prediction for IoT Devices Using Gradient Boosting Machines

Carlos A. Rivera A.[1]([✉]), Arash Shaghaghi[1,2], David D. Nguyen[1], and Salil S. Kanhere[1]

[1] The University of New South Wales (UNSW), Sydney, Australia
{c.riveraalvarez,d.d.nguyen,salil.kanhere}@unsw.edu.au
[2] RMIT University, Melbourne, Australia
arash.shaghaghi@rmit.edu.au

Abstract. Security risk assessment and prediction are critical for organisations deploying Internet of Things (IoT) devices. An absolute minimum requirement for enterprises is to verify the security risk of IoT devices for the reported vulnerabilities in the National Vulnerability Database (NVD). This paper proposes a novel risk prediction for IoT devices based on publicly available information about them. Our solution provides an easy and cost-efficient solution for enterprises of all sizes to predict the security risk of deploying new IoT devices. After an extensive analysis of the NVD records over the past eight years, we have created a unique, systematic, and balanced dataset for vulnerable IoT devices, including key technical features complemented with functional and descriptive features available from public resources. We then use machine learning classification models such as Gradient Boosting Decision Trees (GBDT) over this dataset and achieve 71% prediction accuracy in classifying the severity of device vulnerability score.

Keywords: IoT Security Risk Prediction · National Vulnerability Database (NVD) · CVE · IoT security · Machine learning

1 Introduction

Internet of Things (IoT) devices facilitate advancements and financial benefits for organisations and continue to transform and impact organisational processes and structures. Nonetheless, they expand the plethora of attacks already aimed at organisations. IoT devices present unique challenges that cannot be adequately managed using conventional approaches. Traditional security mechanisms and risk assessment frameworks deployed in organisations fall short when it comes to IoT devices [13]. Moreover, decision-makers and technical staff responsible have been reported to overlook the security risks imposed by IoT devices due to their limited knowledge about them [13].

© ICST Institute for Computer Sciences, Social Informatics and Telecommunications Engineering 2022
Published by Springer Nature Switzerland AG 2022. All Rights Reserved
T. Hara and H. Yamaguchi (Eds.): MobiQuitous 2021, LNICST 419, pp. 115–127, 2022.
https://doi.org/10.1007/978-3-030-94822-1_7

Typically, IoT devices are produced by manufacturers and sold 'as is' [9]. The lack of standards and legal frameworks leave the security of devices as an option to manufacturers who are predominantly focused on issues such as cost, size, usability, and time-to-market. Vulnerability assessment of IoT devices is also costly for enterprises, given the exponential growth in numbers, variety, and configurations. Moreover, ongoing advancements in IoT devices limit the support period by manufacturers providing security patches [14]. As a result, IoT devices become 'orphans' much earlier than traditional computing devices. Nonetheless, these vulnerable IoT have been reported to remain connected to networks leading to massive global security threats such as Mirai [2]. In another example, a recent report by CyberCX confirmed that password-less IoT devices are still affecting various organisations [1].

This paper provides a risk score prediction solution for enterprises, allowing system administrators to carry out an easy and cost-efficient risk prediction based on an IoT device's publicly available information. We studied the National Vulnerability Database (NVD)[1] records and analysed 1153 vulnerable IoT devices reported within the past eight years. We then created a dataset of these vulnerable devices and collected a set of twenty-seven features for each device (e.g., manufacturer, device type, price, and authentication capability). Thereafter, a set of eleven features were shortlisted that allowed creating a balanced dataset. Using Gradient Boosting Decision Trees (GBDT) machine learning model over this dataset, we achieve 71% accuracy in predicting the device vulnerability risk. Our solution is complementary to the vulnerability analysis of IoT devices (e.g., [10,11,21]), which is an expensive and time-consuming process requiring in-depth analysis of devices (e.g., white-box analysis). In other words, our risk prediction solution allows filtering out high-risk IoT devices and reducing vulnerability analysis related costs. Risk prediction is also complementary to other IoT threat detection and prevention solutions actively explored in the IoT security literature (e.g., [6,8,15,17,18,20]).

The rest of this paper is structured as follows: we review the relevant literature in Sect. 2. In Sect. 3, we discuss in detail our research methodology, adversary model, assumptions, data transformation, the IoT vulnerability database created, and machine learning classification model used. In Sect. 4, we present our evaluation results and conclude the paper with a discussion and conclusions in Sect. 5.

2   Related Work

Automatic analysis and classification of vulnerability databases has been the subject of prior research (not specific to IoT). For instance, authors in [12], used Topic Models to analyse security trends in CVE databases with no expert knowledge. In [11,19], Bayesian Networks were used to categorise vulnerabilities from CVE databases according to their security types. To the best of our knowledge,

---

[1] https://nvd.nist.gov.

however, risk prediction for IoT devices using their publicly accessible features is novel in the related literature.

We believe the solution proposed by authors in [3] is the closest work to ours, where authors aim to predict the category of a vulnerable IoT device. Authors in [3] propose a classification of device-related vulnerability data for IoT and IIoT equipment. Authors divided Common Vulnerabilities and Exposures (CVE) records from NVD's public dataset into seven categories: home equipment, SCADA, etc. They then used the support vector machine (SVM) classifier on the device and vulnerability data to predict 'new vulnerabilities' categories. To narrow the data universe, they opted only to obtain data flagged with the value h (hardware).

In our proposal, we combine features from NVD with publicly accessible information about devices to create a new balanced (i.e., without missing data) dataset of vulnerable IoT devices. In other words, we noticed data imbalance based on information available in the paper. Specifically, this issue can be observed in one of the results presented, where the training data contained vulnerabilities from the years 2014 to 2017 and test data from the year 2018. Here, the classification model returned zero percentage in Recall and Precision for one of the classes and poor (below 55%) percentages in precision in five other classes, leaving one class with results over 60%. Whereas for Recall, only two classes had results above 60%, leaving the rest with values below 45%. These results indicate that the model used in [3] struggled to differentiate some of the classes. In our solution, we performed several processes to our dataset to determine the level of imbalance which was later leveraged over the model. We verified the effect of these corrective actions over the evaluation metrics and verified that the class imbalance was indeed lesser. Also, we confirm that the model increased the level of confidence predicting all the classes.

Authors in [3] performed analysis over models rather than over the data. Whereas in our implementation, we analysed the data thoroughly to identify the adequate machine learning model. Although authors in [3] aim to predict the category of vulnerable IoT/IIOT devices, they used the entire dataset since the NVD dataset records contain poor references to their target type of devices. In our proposal, however, we narrow the analysis to only IoT devices, and we ensured that all the other features were directly related to the target devices. We also create a unique IoT vulnerability dataset with information about each device that could be re-used in future research. Finally, authors in [3] aimed to use data from previous years, e.g. 2015, as training data to predict new vulnerabilities from the year 2016 (as test data). Our model, however, contains records from the years 2013 to 2021 (up to 17th of June), and we split the data using the whole dataset rather than per each year.

3   Inception of Risk Score Prediction Through Ensemble Models

3.1   Dataset, Data Transformation, Models and Evaluation Metrics

In this paper, we propose a classification model to predict the risk score (CVSS-based) of IoT devices. For this, we use create a unique IoT vulnerability inclusive of key technical features complemented with functional and descriptive features extracted from public resources. In the following sub-sections, we explain the structure of the dataset, collection method, transformation, models and evaluation metrics.

We make the following assumptions for the data to be of use:

I. We selected the NVD as the primary source of information about vulnerabilities related to IoT devices as well as different Internet sources to complement the records related to specific devices.
II. The NVD database contains information about vulnerabilities and risk on many systems, however, we narrowed our scope of study to IoT devices in part of the following categories: Home security, Home Telecommunications, Small Office Telecommunication, Medical Smart Devices, Wearable Technology and Other. This last classification is used to describe devices such as Toys, Tracking devices, Accessories and Smart Storage. This classification is flexible so it can host a device that cannot be put in any other.
III. We acknowledge the existence of other types of IoT devices such as industrial controls, modules, controllers, telecommunications for middle or big organisations, mobile phones, tablets, and energy transmission. Though, none of them is included in the study. We, however, recognise the intention of the study is flexible and can be re-directed or extended.
IV. The aim of the study does not require experimentation over any physical or virtual device(s).
V. The information obtained from the NVD contains records of IoT devices from the year 2013 and up to the current year, updated to the June version.

Dataset. To prove the effectiveness and novel approach of our theory, we searched for datasets with content related to vulnerabilities and other information related to IoT devices. For it, we used the vulnerabilities database (NVD) of NIST (National Institute of Standards and Technology). This database is constructed from the CVE database and complemented with the vulnerability score (CVSS), the technical specification of the affected software or hardware (Common Platform Enumeration - CPE), and a list of weaknesses related to the vulnerability disclosed (Common Weakness Enumeration - CWE). Note the CVE database contains the description of the vulnerability and affected product, a record id, references to web pages with detailed information of the vulnerability, and Date of record creation. We analysed the NVD and extracted information from the different elements to conform to an initial set of features. From this process and after processing several records we encounter several inconsistencies, for instance, the features expecting to receive information of devices had inconsistencies or were difficult to standardise. Because of these limitations, we concluded that using the NVD as the sole information provider was not ideal and decided to design a new dataset. This new dataset would use different sources, thus new features. This would resolve the limitations presented before. Note that the NVD would serve as the basis of our dataset but also have added information about IoT devices (affected by vulnerabilities disclosed at the NVD).

Table 1. Description of dataset features

Feature name	Data type	Unique values	Details
Brand	Categorical	129	Name of the device reported on the CVE
Product type	Categorical	71	Phrase describing the product
Category	Categorical	5	SmartHome, Medical, Wearable, Telecomm, and Other
Price	Continuous	Inf	Reported in US Dollars
Protocols	Categorical	8	Protocols used in Communication Capability
Data storage	Binary	2	Location of data Locally or Remotely
Personal information	Binary	2	Personal information data used: Yes or No
Location track	Binary	2	Tracks physical location: Yes or No
Communication capability	Categorical	31	Communication technology
Authorisation encryption	Categorical	4	Encryption used: Symmetric, Asymmetric, None, or Both
Risk score	Categorical	4	From CVSS V3: Low, Medium, High, or Critical

We carried a thorough analysis and justification of use to select a final set of features for the new dataset. For instance, the feature 'Brand', can be used to identify brands of vulnerable products or rate brands by the number of vulnerable products. We also realised that the combination of this feature with others like 'Type of Product' can help with the identification of the most vulnerable products amongst brands. We assessed all the twenty-seven initial features, agreeing on accepting only nine. Being these, Brand, Product Type, Category, Price, Protocol, Data Storage, Personal Information, Location Management, Communication Capability, Authorisation Encryption and Risk Score. Note Risk Score is used as the output feature. The full description of the dataset features is shown in Table 1. The records added from the NVD range from the year 2013 to the year 2021. And, to keep the dataset updated with the latest records, carried a sweep to the NVD over the year 2021 up to June. Noteworthy to mention that as a part of our measurement mechanism on the behaviour of the models in the different classes, we added eight synthetic records, one record per classification belonging to two specific products (A smart speaker and a smart camera). We report 1,153 as the final number of records collected, in Table 2 we disclose the distribution among classes.

Table 2. Distribution of dataset classes

Classification	Counts	Distribution %
Low	176	15%
Medium	138	12%
High	183	16%
Critical	656	57%

Data Imbalance. The dataset is assessed to look for data imbalance. Note that whenever a dataset has a class imbalance, there exist strategies to reduce the imbalance and thus obtain better results. In the case of our dataset, we already know it contains imbalanced classes (Table 2), however, we still need to carry a cross-validation test to re-balance the parts of the dataset. The common approach to carry the cross-validation cannot be used in our dataset as it is known that this method is not recommended for a dataset with imbalance (It just splits the data into k folds). Rather we used the Repeated Stratified K-Fold Cross Validation (RSCV). The principal advantage of this approach is the method used to split the data in a distributed manner, where each fold contains the same percentage of samples per class, hence, reducing the class imbalance.

Data Transformation. We applied the Label Encoding technique that assigns a vector to each unique value, for each categorical feature. Later we applied the Normalised Text Frequency technique to convert the numbers into frequencies. To this point, the data on each feature has a representation in frequency. We found from this that the values are very sparse in some of the features.

The sparseness of the data can be reduced through the application of a function. We tested four scaler functions and compared the data afterwards. We found the scaler that uses the Standard function as adequate to our data. This scaler reduced the gap of the peak values between classes. Note that leaving the data without being scaled harms the model (Comparative Results in Sect. 4).

Although the data seems ready for the models, we applied another refinement function. This time, to organise the data into clusters (Utilises data similarity). For this, we used the K-means function in combination with another function that reduces the dimensionality (K-means does not perform well with high dimensional data). We compared two popular methods to carry this task are the PCA (Principal Component Analysis) and t-SNE (T-Distributed Stochastic Neighbour

Embedding). The former generates clusters while also reduces dimensions by centring the data and measuring the distances from each point to the y-axis and x-axis, then the average distance for both axes is obtained, the data is centred through the obtained averages. The latter reduces the dimensionality of data with non-linear relationships, which is indeed the case with our data. T-SNE, unlike PCA, calculates a similarity measure, which is obtained by calculating the distance between points, finally, all the points with proportional similarities are clustered. The effect of applying the t-SNE function into the data is that it clusters better the data, this due to its function that utilises similarity distance between points. However, this function demonstrated that rather than improving the model metrics, which affected contrarily, so we concluded to not using it. We show in Table 4 the results of utilising the models with and without the t-SNE function.

Machine Learning Classification Models. We found it appropriate for our selected output label, based on the CVSS Severity, to use Classification Models. For this, we found that classification models work in individual format or an aggregated manner (ensemble mode) and that the latter has emerged as being better to tackle classification problems [7]. Hence, we chose Ensemble models.

Ensemble models are designed to combine predictions from several built-in models, which in comparison to single models, can take advantage of the array capability of several sub-models to increase the prediction. Also, these models can improve the output. And lastly, their inner loss function helps to reduce the error and resolving bias problems from individual models.

From the various ensemble models for classification, we chose Gradient Boosting Decision Trees (GBDT) over AdaBoost Classification (ABC), Random Forest Classifier (RFC), Extra Tree Classifier (ETC), and Voting Classifier (VC). Note that in general, the listed models tend to manage differently their capability to reduce the prediction error. In particular, each model manages different approaches to improve the prediction. For instance, the ABC model manages the base models through weights and prediction repetition over the training dataset and returns the prediction with the least error rate, the RFC model builds a group of random decision trees containing random subsets of attributes. Here all the trees provide a predicted class value, and utilising the common voting approach they select the class with the majority of votes, the VC model is the simplest, which hosts multiple base models and the final output is the result of a majority voting process, and lastly, the GBC model combines several weak sum-models into a strong one, trains the base models in a sequence manner and assigns weights to every training record. The boosting process focuses on those records hard to classify by over-representing (assigning higher weights) them in the training set of the next iteration. Every new iteration on the model will focus on those records considered hard to classify. Furthermore, the results are combined from all the base learners through a majority voting approach.

We find the GBDT model with superior capabilities than the other models. One of the advantages of this model is the weight management strategy, which results in a better predictive approach (known as hard-to-classify). Furthermore, its sequential approach to order the internal models improves the final prediction. Thirdly, its built-in approach to managing class weights resolves imbalance problems. On the other hand, the most representative weaknesses we have with the voting approach (based on a simple majority of votes) is that it is not efficient in managing neutral cases [4]. Added to this, the tuning process makes it difficult to find the best parameters and requires large searches. Finally, the process to reduce the loss may lead to overfitting outlier samples. Despite the intricacies of using the GBDT model we find it the best option amongst the selected models. Thus, we select GBDT as the primary model to use and for benchmark the RFC and VC. Note that we are discarding the ABC and ETC because in previous tests, these models returned the lowest performance metrics.

Evaluation Metrics. The approaches we used to evaluate the selected classification models are through the application of the RSCV and the execution of the model after splitting the dataset into Training and Test. The results from the former approach will measure the accuracy from each model and based on the number of repetitions and k folds specified (2 repetitions and 5 folds in our case). For the latter approach, we will use the metrics Precision, Recall, F-1 and Accuracy. By itself, each metric provides part of the story, but together they help to confirm the correctness of the results from the selected model. Note that in multi-class prediction, Precision, Recall and F-1 have a variation in the calculation due to the classes [5], this is known at the Micro and Macro levels.

- **Micro Level**, computes the average of all samples without using class weights. This value is equal to the accuracy of the model.
- **Macro Level**, computes the overall mean of all classes, here the class weights are included.

Note that the Macro level approach for the metrics is recommended for datasets with imbalanced classes, which is the case of our dataset. Henceforth, the measurement of metrics will be focused on all the classes equally.

4   Experiments and Results

4.1   Experimental Setup

The validated dataset was uploaded to the Google Colab platform used for evaluations. Here, the resources are allocated as a default configuration with variable amounts such as 0.8–25 GB in RAM and 38–107 GB in Hard Drive space. The environment works under Python version 3.0 with the libraries Sklearn, Pandas, Numpy, Matplotlib, Seaborn, Pydrive, Phik, and Plotly.

To tune the models' parameters, we used the tool 'GridSearchCV' (from Scikit-learn[2]) that carries a tuning process of the parameters with the most influence on the prediction, for each selected model. For instance, the tool provided that the adequate parameters for the GBC (Gradient Boosting Classifier)

---

[2] https://scikit-learn.org/stable/.

should be set with 10,000 as the number of estimators (number of boosting stages to perform), a learning rate of 0.01 (shrinks the contribution of each tree), as the maximum depth of 500 (of the individual regression estimators), and a minimum of impurity decrease value of 1e−2 (A node will be split based on this parameter). For the RFC, the tuning function recommended setting the parameter of class weight on 'balanced' (To re-balance the classes by applying weights) and leaving the rest of the parameters with their default values. And, in the case of the VC (Voting Classifier) model, it receives the sub-classifier models AbC, GBC, ETC and RFC (each with the tuned parameters) and 'type of voting' is set on 'soft'. Note that all the parameters not mentioned, are left with their default values because of the models perform better with that configuration. In the next section, we will discuss the results from each model and carry a complete evaluation process.

4.2   Evaluation Results

We show the results (Table 3) from running the selected models(GBC, RFC, and VC) through the RSCV and from not-applying/applying t-SNE clustering or PCA. The comparison is intended to show the negative effects in the accuracy metric. For better appreciation, the values equally or over 70% are in bold.

Table 3. Accuracy results from applying RSCV (5 folds, 2 repeats) over the selected models. Run-A refers to the results from the models without applying t-SNE clustering or PCA, Run-B refers to the results from the models after applying t-SNE clustering, and Run-C refers to the results from the models after applying PCA. The columns label represent the number of Run(1, 2) next to the number of fold(1-5), All the values are in % format.

	R1-F1	R1-F2	R1-F3	R1-F4	R1-F5	R2-F1	R2-F2	R2-F3	R2-F4	R2-F5
Run-A										
GBC	67.1	69.7	69.3	**70.9**	**72.2**	**73.6**	66.2	66.7	**70.9**	67.8
VC	64.1	65.8	67.5	67.8	63.9	**70.6**	67.1	65.8	67.0	65.2
RFC	65.4	68.0	67.1	**71.3**	65.7	68.0	66.7	67.5	67.8	69.6
Run-B										
GBC	58.4	61.9	66.2	67.8	64.3	66.2	67.5	67.1	64.8	67.8
VC	60.2	61.9	66.7	67.0	63.9	65.4	68.8	64.9	64.3	64.8
RFC	61.9	67.5	69.7	69.6	67.4	67.5	68.0	**71.0**	67.0	**72.6**
Run-C										
GBC	62.0	62.7	66.4	64.1	63.3	64.6	65.3	66.0	61.9	60.9
VC	62.3	63.6	63.2	66.1	59.6	66.7	67.1	62.3	61.3	63.0
RFC	63.2	66.7	63.6	64.8	60.0	65.8	65.4	64.5	60.4	67.0

In a second comparison we analysed the negative impact of using t-SNE clustering or PCA versus not using them. For this, we used the metrics Precision,

Recall, and F-1, obtained from the testing results. In this analysis, we only show the results from the main model GBC. In Table 4 we show the results of the comparison. Our quantitative benchmarks demonstrate that dimensionality reduction methods (PCS and t-SNE) reduce the performance of the selected models, with only three trials registering an average score above 70% (shown in bold).

Table 4. Precision, Recall and F-1, from applying GBC model. The section labelled WO/DR (without dimensionality reduction) shows the results from using the dataset without t-SNE clustering or PCA. The section W/t-SNE (With T-SNE clustering applied) shows the results from using the dataset after applying t-SNE clustering. And the section W/PCA (With PCA applied) shows the results of using the dataset after applying PCA. The column labels represent the data classes Low, Medium, High, Critical, Macro (Macro Average Result) and Micro/ACC (Micro Average Result or Accuracy). All the values are in % format.

WO/DR	Low	Medium	High	Critical	Macro	Micro/ACC
Precision	**75.0**	50.0	56.7	**76.6**	64.6	**71.0**
Recall	63.2	42.9	53.1	**83.5**	60.6	**71.0**
F-1	68.6	46.2	54.8	**79.9**	62.4	**71.0**
W/t-SNE	Low	Medium	High	Critical	Macro	Micro/ACC
Precision	50.0	59.1	61.3	**74.0**	61.1	67.5
Recall	45.7	46.4	51.4	**82.4**	56.5	67.5
F-1	47.8	52.0	55.9	**78.0**	58.4	67.5
W/PCA	Low	Medium	High	Critical	Macro	Micro/ACC
Precision	69.2	50.0	59.4	**73.8**	63.1	68.8
Recall	51.4	42.9	51.4	**84.0**	57.4	68.8
F-1	59.0	46.2	55.1	**78.6**	59.7	68.8

5   Discussion and Conclusion

5.1   Discussion

From the dataset transformation process, we argue that our dataset features provided the models with the minimum features through which carried the prediction. To confirm this assumption, we used the correlation plot (see Fig. 1). Through the plot, we confirmed the correlation between pairs of features was not so high amongst most of the pair of classes, except for a couple of pairs that had values over 80%. This means that one of the features may not be necessary to be included. For this, we applied a dimensionality reduction process where we drop those unnecessary features and check for variations in the metrics from the primary model. The results obtained allowed us to confirm that

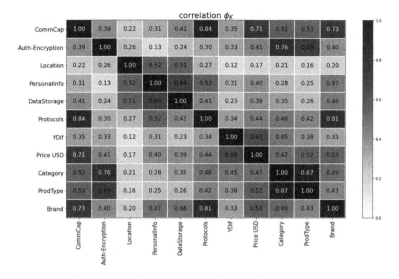

Fig. 1. Correlation plot for all the features in the dataset.

the dropped features are needed as every time one of those features were eliminated, the effect in the metrics was noticeable in a decrease of the values. We argue then that all the features from which we constructed our dataset are the minimum required for the model to provide decent prediction metrics. Another approaches to carry dimensionality reduction are t-SNE clustering and PCA. We applied both approaches with the purpose of improving the results for each model. For this, we tuned the relevant parameters and in some cases the data was clustered as a result. We observed in some other cases that these algorithms struggled to completely segregate points from the different classes. This could be responsible for lower model performance in comparison to the trials without the application of any dimensionality reduction. While this approach is effective with some problems, it was not effective with our risk prediction dataset. This was also the case when applied the PCA approach.

5.2   Conclusion and Future Work

We have proposed a novel approach to predict the risk score in IoT devices. Our solution is complementary to IoT security threat detection and prevention mechanisms (e.g., [16]) and risk management frameworks. Our proposed risk score calculation solution enables enterprises to perform an easy and cost-efficient analysis of IoT devices to filter out the high-risk categories just by relying on their publicly accessible information. As part of this work, we created the first balanced vulnerability dataset for IoT devices with 1153 records accessible to future researchers in the field. The dataset was used to feed and train the GBDT machine learning model for the prediction of a risk score for

IoT devices, which achieved 71% prediction accuracy. In the future, we plan to extend this analysis and use the dataset to provide more specific predictions on the type of vulnerability of devices and suggest a set of recommended actions to the system administrators to protect their networks.

References

1. CyberCX security report, November 2020. https://cybercx.com.au/cyber-security-resources/cybercx-security-report-november-2020
2. Antonakakis, M., et al.: Understanding the Mirai botnet. In: 26th USENIX Security Symposium USENIX Security 17, pp. 1093–1110 (2017)
3. Blinowski, G.J., Piotrowski, P.: CVE based classification of vulnerable IoT systems. In: Zamojski, W., Mazurkiewicz, J., Sugier, J., Walkowiak, T., Kacprzyk, J. (eds.) DepCoS-RELCOMEX 2020. AISC, vol. 1173, pp. 82–93. Springer, Cham (2020). https://doi.org/10.1007/978-3-030-48256-5_9
4. Cranor, L.F.: Declared-Strategy Voting: An Instrument for Group Decision-Making. Washington University in St. Louis (1996)
5. Grandini, M., Bagli, E., Visani, G.: Metrics for multi-class classification: an overview. arXiv preprint arXiv:2008.05756 (2020)
6. Hasan, M., Islam, M.M., Zarif, M.I.I., Hashem, M.: Attack and anomaly detection in IoT sensors in IoT sites using machine learning approaches. Internet Things 7, 100059 (2019)
7. Kotu, V., Deshpande, B.: Predictive Analytics and Data Mining: Concepts and Practice with RapidMiner. Morgan Kaufmann, Burlington (2014)
8. Kumar, A., Lim, T.J.: EDIMA: early detection of IoT malware network activity using machine learning techniques. In: 2019 IEEE 5th World Forum on Internet of Things (WF-IoT), pp. 289–294. IEEE (2019)
9. Maroof, U., Shaghaghi, A., Jha, S.: PLAR: towards a pluggable software architecture for securing IoT devices. In: Proceedings of the 2nd International ACM Workshop on Security and Privacy for the Internet-of-Things, pp. 50–57 (2019)
10. Meidan, Y., Sachidananda, V., Peng, H., Sagron, R., Elovici, Y., Shabtai, A.: A novel approach for detecting vulnerable IoT devices connected behind a home NAT. Comput. Secur. 97, 101968 (2020)
11. Na, S., Kim, T., Kim, H.: A study on the classification of common vulnerabilities and exposures using Naïve Bayes. In: BWCCA 2016. LNDECT, vol. 2, pp. 657–662. Springer, Cham (2017). https://doi.org/10.1007/978-3-319-49106-6_65
12. Neuhaus, S., Zimmermann, T.: Security trend analysis with CVE topic models. In: 2010 IEEE 21st International Symposium on Software Reliability Engineering, pp. 111–120. IEEE (2010)
13. Nurse, J.R., Creese, S., De Roure, D.: Security risk assessment in Internet of Things systems. IT Prof. 19(5), 20–26 (2017)
14. Puggioni, E., Shaghaghi, A., Doss, R., Kanhere, S.S.: Towards decentralized IoT updates delivery leveraging blockchain and zero-knowledge proofs. In: 2020 IEEE 19th International Symposium on Network Computing and Applications (NCA), pp. 1–10. IEEE (2020)
15. Saha, T., Aaraj, N., Ajjarapu, N., Jha, N.K.: SHARKS: Smart Hacking Approaches for RisK Scanning in Internet-of-Things and cyber-physical systems based on machine learning. IEEE Trans. Emerging Top. Comput. (2021)

16. Shaghaghi, A., Kanhere, S.S., et al.: Towards a distributed defence mechanism against IoT-based bots. In: 2020 IEEE 45th Conference on Local Computer Networks (LCN), pp. 449–452. IEEE (2020)
17. Skowron, M., Janicki, A., Mazurczyk, W.: Traffic fingerprinting attacks on Internet of Things using machine learning. IEEE Access **8**, 20386–20400 (2020)
18. Tien, C.W., Chen, S.W., Ban, T., Kuo, S.Y.: Machine learning framework to analyze IoT malware using elf and opcode features. Digital Threats: Res. Pract. **1**(1), 1–19 (2020)
19. Wang, J.A., Guo, M.: Vulnerability categorization using Bayesian networks. In: Proceedings of the Sixth Annual Workshop on Cyber Security and Information Intelligence Research, pp. 1–4 (2010)
20. Zeadally, S., Tsikerdekis, M.: Securing internet of things (IoT) with machine learning. In. J. Commun. Syst. **33**(1), e4169 (2020)
21. Zhang, Y.J., Liao, P., Huang, K.Z., Liu, Y.l.: An automatic approach for scoring vulnerabilities in risk assessment. In: 2nd International Conference on Electrical and Electronic Engineering (EEE 2019), pp. 256–261. Atlantis Press (2019)

Optimizing Unlicensed Coexistence Network Performance Through Data Learning

Srikant Manas Kala[1]($\boxtimes$), Vanlin Sathya[2], Kunal Dahiya[3], Teruo Higashino[1], and Hirozumi Yamaguchi[1]

[1] Mobile Computing Laboratory, Osaka University, Osaka, Japan
{manas_kala,higashino,h-yamagu}@ist.osaka-u.ac.jp
[2] The University of Chicago, Chicago, IL, USA
vanlin@chicago.edu
[3] Indian Institute of Technology Delhi, Delhi, India

Abstract. Unlicensed LTE-WiFi coexistence networks are undergoing consistent densification to meet the rising mobile data demands. With the increase in coexistence network complexity, it is important to study network feature relationships (NFRs) and utilize them to optimize dense coexistence network performance. This work studies NFRs in unlicensed LTE-WiFi (LTE-U and LTE-LAA) networks through supervised learning of network data collected from real-world experiments. Different 802.11 standards and varying channel bandwidths are considered in the experiments and the learning model selection policy is precisely outlined. Thereafter, a comparative analysis of different LTE-WiFi network configurations is performed through learning model parameters such as R-sq, residual error, outliers, choice of predictor, *etc.* Further, a Network Feature Relationship based Optimization (NeFRO) framework is proposed. NeFRO improves upon the conventional optimization formulations by utilizing the feature-relationship equations learned from network data. It is demonstrated to be highly suitable for time-critical dense coexistence networks through two optimization objectives, *viz.*, network capacity and signal strength. NeFRO is validated against four recent works on network optimization. NeFRO is successfully able to reduce optimization convergence time by as much as 24% while maintaining accuracy as high as 97.16%, on average.

Keywords: LTE-WiFi coexistence · Network optimization · Machine learning

1 Introduction

Cellular networks are a vital component of a truly mobile augmented reality (AR) system/application such as "Pokemon Go," as they offer the widest coverage to the end-users. With the rising demand for immersive AR experience, the AR

T. Hara and H. Yamaguchi (Eds.): MobiQuitous 2021, LNICST 419, pp. 128–149, 2022.
https://doi.org/10.1007/978-3-030-94822-1_8

market is set to cross $100 Billion and the total mobile network traffic is expected to exceed 300 Exabytes per month in 2026 [10].

However, mobile AR traffic is latency-critical, uplink-heavy, and bursty in nature and the current LTE/LTE-A (Long Term Evolution/Long Term Evolution-Advanced) networks lack the capability to offer a seamless mobile AR experience [2]. Consequently, cellular operators have taken several measures such as dense deployment of small-cells (SCs) and access points (APs) and utilization of the unlicensed spectrum through LTE-WiFi coexistence.

The prospect of effectively utilizing the unlicensed spectrum through *LTE in unlicensed spectrum* (LTE-U) and *LTE license assisted access* (LTE-LAA) appeals to the mobile operators. Hence, there is a rapid deployment of both LTE small-cells and Wi-Fi APs in the 5 GHz band where 500 MHz of the unlicensed spectrum is shared by both LTE and Wi-Fi networks [19, 25].

This work focuses on two aspects of LTE-WiFi coexistence *viz.*, coexistence network performance analysis and time-critical optimization. To that end, a comparative performance analysis of unlicensed LTE standards (LTE-U/LAA) is done through network feature relationship parameters learned from network data. Thereafter, the learned feature relationships are utilized to reduce the time-cost of performance optimization in a dense coexistence network.

1.1 Motivation

With the proliferation of unlicensed coexistence networks, there has been a significant debate on the comparison of LTE-U and LAA standards and their performance. While cellular operators such as AT&T and Verizon have opted in favor of LAA deployments [25], recent works claim that LTE-U may offer better coexistence with Wi-Fi under specific conditions [7].

The existing comparative studies of LTE unlicensed standards are lacking in three respects. First, they primarily rely on simulations and make several assumptions [7, 8]. Secondly, the offered comparative analysis is based only on *measurements*, *i.e.*, by simply comparing several network performance evaluation metrics such as throughput, latency, number of re-transmissions, *etc.* In contrast, *feature relationship analysis* looks for patterns in network data that can reveal relationships between network variables such as dependence, correlation, causation, *etc.* Finally, the variation in performance of LTE unlicensed variant with the variation in coexisting Wi-Fi standard is often overlooked. In addition, the impact of factors such as bandwidth allocation and signaling data is rarely studied.

With the increase in the deployment of small-cells and access points, dense networks (DNs) with inter-site distance ≤ 10 m, and ultra-dense networks (UDNs) with inter-site distance ≤ 5 m, have proliferated in most urban centers [14]. Thus, performance optimization of the rapidly growing dense coexistence networks is a major challenge. This becomes particularly important when time-critical mobile AR services/applications need to be supported by coexistence networks. However, the literature currently lacks network feature relationship (NFR) analysis from the perspective of dense LTE-WiFi coexistence networks. Further, to the best of our knowledge no existing study makes use of network feature relationships in dense coexistence network optimization.

1.2 Contributions

In this work, we address these concerns through the following contributions

- Study network feature relationship in dense coexistence networks such as SINR-Capacity relationship, through machine learning algorithms.
- Analyze the impact of factors such as the choice of LTE unlicensed standard, coexisting Wi-Fi standard, and bandwidth allocation on NFRs in coexistence networks.
- Compare LTE-LAA/LTE-U and Wi-Fi 802.11n/ac coexistence performance based on NFR parameters such as the choice of predictor variable, R-sq (model validity), residual error (absolute and normalized), outliers, *etc.*
- Utilize NFRs to optimize dense coexistence network performance through network capacity and signal strength optimization.

The comparative analysis in this work is distinct from the state-of-the-art studies [7, 8] in that it is not limited to measuring and analyzing individual network variables. It involves data-learning to discover feature relationship patterns which determine network performance. Further, the data is gathered through real-time experiments instead of simulations. For the experiments, dense and ultra-dense co-existence networks were implemented with the help of USRP NI-SDRs and WiFi APs. The *learning model selection policy* considered for feature relationship analysis is also explicitly described for replication and validation.

2 A Review of Related Works

2.1 Network Feature Relationships in Dense Networks

In the recent past, several state-of-the-art studies have used regression algorithms, decision trees, and other machine learning techniques for NFR analysis [1, 6, 17, 19]. Some of these works leverage the learned NFRs to improve network performance. For example, learning 802.11n feature relationships can facilitate improved configuration selection and enhanced rate adaption [1]. Yet, the current literature lacks a robust analysis of NFRs, such as the capacity-interference relationship (CIR) in unlicensed coexistence networks.

Further, as shown in Fig. 1, densification of LTE-WiFi coexistence systems will exacerbate the adverse impact of interference and pose additional challenges. While densification may lead to an initial gain in LTE-WiFi coexistence system capacity, network performance eventually deteriorates with rise in density [28]. Moreover, the impact of factors *e.g.,* unlicensed LTE variant, Wi-Fi standard, bandwidth allocated, and signaling data, *etc.,* on dense coexistence CIR also remains unexplored. For example, the analysis presented in [18] is limited to demonstrating how the SINR-Capacity relationship differs in regular and dense/ultra-dense networks, and fails to explore the impact of the factors listed above.

Therefore, this work focuses on various aspects of the relationship between interference and network performance in a dense coexistence network.

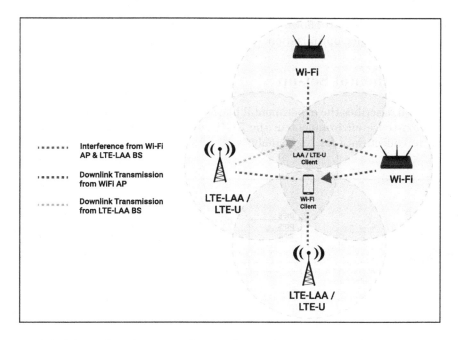

Fig. 1. Interference in dense unlicensed coexistence networks

2.2   Optimization Challenges in Dense Networks

The need for low association times and fast-handovers in a dense environment makes network optimization **time-critical**. However, consistent densification significantly increases network scale and complexity which leads to high convergence times and computational overhead to arrive at optimal solutions [14]. This is a major challenge for ultra-low-latency AR applications as already the LTE/LTE-A deployments account for almost 30% of the end-to-end AR latency [2]. With densification, the latency problem will exacerbate and diminish the gains in throughput.

Thus, it is important not only to study the impact of densification on NFRs but also ascertain how these feature relationships can be used to accelerate optimization in dense coexistence networks by making it computationally less expensive [13]. Broadly speaking, wireless network performance can be optimized through three major frameworks *viz.*, optimization, machine learning, and a hybrid approach that involves machine learning based optimization [13,21].

This work paves the way for an empirical and practical approach to *network feature relationship based optimization* (NeFRO). NeFRO adopts the hybrid model wherein feature relationships learned from network data serve as a constraint in network optimization formulations. By using the feature relationship equation for performance optimization, NeFRO accounts for the ambient network environment and is free from theoretical pre-suppositions. Due to

these factors, NeFRO is shown to significantly reduce the time-costs in dense
network performance optimization.

3   Experimental Set-up

This section describes the experimental platform designed to create a dense LTE-
WiFi coexistence environment in the 5 GHz unlicensed spectrum. The testbed
is used to collect data for NFR analysis.

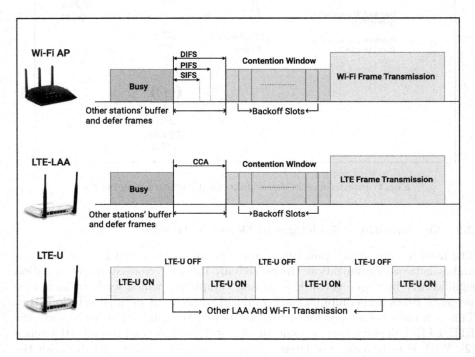

Fig. 2. Wi-Fi, LTE-LAA, and LTE-U: Channel Access Mechanisms

3.1   Testbed Design

Two variants of LTE unlicensed operation have been standardized and released,
viz., LTE-U and LTE-LAA, albeit with starkly different medium sensing and
access mechanisms. LTE-U relies on a load-dependent duty-cycle mechanism
based on Carrier Sense Adaptive Transmission (CSAT). On the other hand,
LTE-LAA depends on a Listen-Before-Talk (LBT) mechanism which is similar
to the CSMA/CD MAC protocol of Wi-Fi, making it relatively easier for LAA
to coexist with IEEE 802.11 WLANs. The medium access mechanisms of the
two LTE unlicensed variants and Wi-Fi are juxtaposed in Fig. 2.

LAA-LTE/LTE-U Platform. The National Instruments *NI RIO* testing-platform is used as the LAA/LTE-U testbed as shown in Fig. 3 (a). The PHY on the NI Labview system is the standard PHY implementation as prescribed in the LTE-A 3GPP release. More technical details on the testbed are presented in Table 1. The system offers high operational flexibility through advanced user-defined configuration of signal transmission and reception. Several network parameters can be configured, such as the sub-carrier modulation scheme, resource block allocation, LAA transmission opportunity (TXOP), Energy Detection (ED) threshold, LBT category option, LTE-U duty cylce ON & OFF, transmission power, OFDM parameters (*e.g.*, 1 to 3 control channels), carrier frequency offset, and timing offset estimation.

Wi-Fi Platform. Netgear wireless routers are used to design the Wi-Fi testbed. The off-the-shelf Wi-Fi routers, supporting both 802.11n and 802.11ac in the 5 GHz band serve as the typical Wi-Fi nodes. The Wi-Fi testbed supports easy modification and monitoring of parameters and functions in both the MAC and PHY layers of Wi-Fi such as DIFS, CWmin, CWmax, channel bandwidth, and transmission power.

3.2   Experiment Design

All experiments are carried out in the typical setting of an indoor office at the University of Chicago campus. This work focuses mainly on gathering SNR and throughput data for NFR analysis. Other network parameters such as contention window size, request to send (RTS), clear to send (CTS), inter-beacon interval time, power range, channel assignment (static or dynamic), and bandwidth in the PHY layer are also configured as required. In the experiments, the LAA transmitter always uses LBT protocol to sense if the channel is available and the maximum TXOP is 8 ms, which is similar to the transmission of LTE-A in licensed bands. The Power Spectral Density (PSD) of LAA transmissions is controlled so as to ensure that the power of the interference from LAA is below Clear Channel Assessment (CCA) threshold of Wi-Fi communications. Several experiments were designed to explore dense unlicensed coexistence performance by creating combinations of LAA/LTE-U, 802.11n/802.11ac, and different bandwidths (5/10/15/20 MHz). LAA and LTE-U use the same underlying mechanism of Dynamic Bandwidth Adaptation (DBA) for spectral efficiency as LTE-A. Therefore, while Wi-Fi APs generally operate in a bandwidth of 20 MHz, LAA and LTE-U possess the capability to support multiple bandwidths (1.4/3/5/10/15/20 MHz). Bandwidth is an important factor that may influence capacity interference relationship due to cross-talk interference. Therefore, this work considers bandwidth to be an important parameter for CIR analysis. Further, dense random topologies are considered where LAA/LTE-U/Wi-Fi nodes are placed at inter-nodal distances of 5 m to 10 m. A representative illustration is presented in Fig. 3 (b). Apart from a small inter-nodal distance, a dense coexistence scenario in an indoor setting is also interesting due to the prevalence of

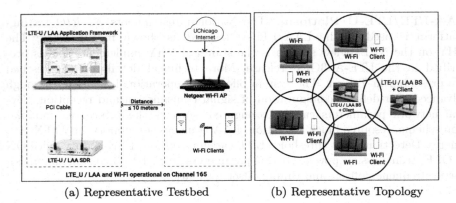

(a) Representative Testbed   (b) Representative Topology

Fig. 3. Experimental set-up

significant multi-path fading and presence of obstacles such as walls, furniture, objects, etc.

Table 1. Experiment parameters

Parameter	Value
Number of nodes	6
Transmission power	23 dBm
Operating frequency	5 GHz
LTE-U/LAA RF transmission	Loopback
LTE transmission channel	PDSCH, PDCCH
Data traffic	Full buffer
Wi-Fi channel access protocol	CSMA
LAA channel access protocol	LBT

*PDSCH - Physical Downlink Shared Channel

4   Network Feature Relationship Analysis Methodology

Regression is a popular machine learning paradigm used to determine the relationship between network parameters in continuous space [1,6,17,19]. Regression algorithms not only offer reliable feature relationships, but also provide insights into the relationship in terms of model validity, outliers, residual error *etc.* Thus CIR is modeled as a bi-directional regression problem where the goal is to estimate or predict network capacity through SINR feature points, and vice versa.

4.1   Learning Algorithms for Relationship Analysis

Let N represent the number of training points and let dimensionality of the feature vector be denoted by D. Then, the coexistence network data can be represented as $\{\mathbf{x}_i, y_i\}_{i=1}^{N}$, where $\mathbf{x}_i \in \mathbb{R}^D$ is the feature vector and $y_i \in \mathbb{R}$ is the ground truth value for i^{th} training point. The goal is to learn a mapping $f : \mathbf{x}_i \to y_i$ where x_i is the predictor (SINR or Capacity) and y_i is the response (Capacity or SINR). This work considers the following basket of learning algorithms for the regression analysis:

- **Linear Regression.** This group of algorithms learns a linear relationship by solving $\arg\min_{\mathbf{w},b} \sum_{i=1}^{N} ||(\mathbf{w}^\top \mathbf{x}_i + b) - y_i||_2^2 + \alpha \mathbf{w}^\top \mathbf{w}$ [24]. Here, the weight vector is denoted by $\mathbf{w} \in \mathbb{R}^D$ and the bias term is $b \in \mathbb{R}$. Further, the weightage (importance) of the l_2-regularization term is controlled by the hyper-parameter denoted by α, which is set to zero for Ordinary Least Squares Linear Regression (OLS). However, for Ridge Regression (RR), α is set through k-fold cross validation (kCV).
- **Kernel Ridge Regression.** A non-linear mapping is expected to be more suitable for the SINR-Capacity relationship [16]. Therefore, we make use of the Kernel Ridge Regression [24] that employs non-linear transformations such as Polynomial and Radial Basis Function (RBF). Its goal is to solve $\arg\min_{\mathbf{w},b} \sum_{i=1}^{N} ||K(\mathbf{w}, \mathbf{x}_i) + b - y_i||_2^2 + \alpha \mathbf{w}^\top \mathbf{w}$. Here, $\mathbf{w} \in \mathbb{R}^D$ is the weight vector, $b \in \mathbb{R}$ is the bias term, and α is a hyper-parameter defined above. Finally, $K(a, b)$ is a kernel function which allows to compute dot product in an arbitrary large space without the need to explicitly project features in high dimensional space. Varying the kernel function as RBF and Polynomial leads to Kernel RBF Regression (RBF) and Multi-variate Polynomial Regression (MPR), respectively.

4.2   Selection of Regression Models

Regression Model selection depends upon objective criteria such as R-sq, higher-order terms, *etc.*, and some subjective value-judgments, *e.g.*, selecting a model with a higher R-sq even if the higher-order terms are not significant. However, studies often discuss network feature relationships and existence of correlation without going into the details of the underlying regression models [6]. Failure to highlight such details poses a challenge while replicating these studies. To avoid this problem, the model selection policy considered in this work is described below.

Regression Model Selection Policy. The regression algorithms are subjected to *k-Fold Cross-validation (kCV)* averaged over 30 runs (for $k = 5$). Feature relationship models are evaluated based on their R-sq or *Regression Model Validity* (RMV). A high RMV value signifies the *goodness* of the fit. Also, outlier detection and removal is performed using the Local Outlier Factor (LOF) algorithm.

First, CIR models with 1–3 degree polynomials are learned and to avoid over-fitting of feature point data, the higher-order terms considered are limited to statistically significant cubic terms. Further, the optimal model is chosen on the basis of RMV via kCV as it best explains the feature relationship [23]. For example, between a CIR model learned from the baseline data-set and the model learned from the data-set processed through LOF outlier removal, the model and feature relationship with the higher RMV is considered. This work focuses primarily on quadratic CIR models for the following reasons. First, the % difference in average RMVs of linear & quadratic and quadratic & cubic models is 3.63% and 0.98% respectively. Thus, as compared to quadratic models, the linear models exhibit a relatively weak CIR and the RMV gain in cubic models is very low. Second, CIR in wireless networks is expected to be quadratic [12]. Finally, low convergence time is a primary constraint in dense network optimization. Whatever little gain the higher RMV of a cubic model might offer in performance optimization, will be irrelevant compared to the increase in the computational overhead of a third-degree polynomial constraint.

4.3 Analytical Methodology

To study the impact of dense network configuration on NFRs, it is necessary to isolate individual network parameters and observe the consequent variation in the feature relationship.

Comparative Themes. The analysis seeks to draw a comparison between the performance of LTE unlicensed variants (LTE-U and LTE-LAA) in coexistence with the Wi-Fi variants (802.11n/ac). We also study the impact of bandwidth allocation and the choice of predictor variable on CIR in these network configurations. Thus, a total of 32 Test Scenarios are considered (denoted by TS_i, where $i \in \{1 \ldots 32\}$). Each TS_i indicates a unique unlicensed coexistence network scenario based on the LTE unlicensed variant (LTE-U/LTE-LAA), coexisting Wi-Fi standard (802.11n/ac), bandwidth allocated (5/10/15/20 MHz), and predictor variable (SINR/Capacity). For each TS_i, the CIR model is selected through the regression model selection policy outlined earlier.

Comparison Parameters. The performance of different LTE-WiFi network configurations is evaluated through analysis of learning parameters such as model validity, standard deviation in RMV, residual standard deviation (RSD), outliers, *etc.* Trends of average network values observed in the experiments are used as well. For each of these parameters, two types of comparisons are carried out, *viz.* scenario-specific comparison and component-specific comparison for LTE-WiFi-Predictor configurations. The former is aimed at a comparative analysis of individual network scenarios (*e.g.,* LTE-U, 802.11n, at 5 MHz vs. LTE-LAA, 802.11n, at 5 MHz) while the second is aimed at capturing component level trends (*e.g.,* SINR as a predictor vs. Capacity as a predictor). Reliable inferences are drawn only if the findings are consistent at both levels of comparative analysis. Wherever possible, plausible explanations are offered.

5   CIR in Dense Unlicensed Coexistence Networks

CIR model parameters are analyzed, and the results are presented for scenario-specific comparisons in Fig. 4, and configuration-level trends in Fig. 5. Please note that only for Fig. 5 (b), a logarithmic scale is used to show "% Difference" due to a high variation in values. Based on these results, various aspects of unlicensed coexistence network performance are discussed ahead. Some results, such as those related to outliers, are mentioned during the course of the discussion itself.

5.1   Unlicensed LTE: LTE-U vs LAA

We begin with measurement based observations on average network capacity, as most comparative studies primarily focus on this metric [7]. In 75% of the test-scenarios, LTE-LAA outperforms LTE-U in coexistence with corresponding Wi-Fi variant (n/ac). Likewise, in 87.5% scenarios, 802.11ac outperforms 802.11n in coexistence with corresponding LTE variant (LTE-U/LAA). Further, LTE-LAA in coexistence with 802.11n/ac offers a higher SINR on average than LTE-U in all scenarios save one.

The LBT mechanism of LAA is quite similar to the CSMA channel access protocol of Wi-Fi and leads to a higher network capacity on average in LTE-LAA. Further, LAA nodes sense the energy level on the medium (-72 dBm) prior to transmission which mitigates co-channel interference from Wi-Fi and other LAA APs, ensuring higher SINR on average than LTE-U. On the contrary LTE-U has a duty-cycle based channel access mechanism which leads to inefficient transmissions and packet-collisions in both, the LTE-U and Wi-Fi components of the coexistence system.

Regression Model Validity (RMV). LAA and LTE-U models fare equally well, in a scenario specific comparison with $\leq 5\%$ difference in RMVs in 13/16 comparisons (26/32 scenarios). CIR in LAA seems to be only slightly better as it outperforms LTE-U in the remaining 3 scenarios. In terms of average RMVs across all 32 scenarios, LAA and LTE-U are comparable, although LAA has a slight edge ($<1\%$). Likewise, in LAA-WiFi-Predictor configuration combinations, LAA has a slight edge (0–2%). Prima facie, based on RMV alone, CIR does not seem to be impacted by the unlicensed LTE variant. However, RMV can not be considered to be the sole goodness-of-fit measure for feature relationships. Higher RMV is an indicator of the variation in dependent variable explained by the model, but it does not indicate how far the data-points lie from the regression line. Further, the standard deviation of RMV with kCV for a specific scenario must also be low. The analysis ahead explores these dimensions.

Residual Standard Deviation (RSD). The capability of a feature relationship model to make accurate predictions is highly desirable for the model to be deployed in real-world network performance management. Thus, residual error or RSD is a measure of precision of the model's predictions and should ideally be low for a robust CIR.

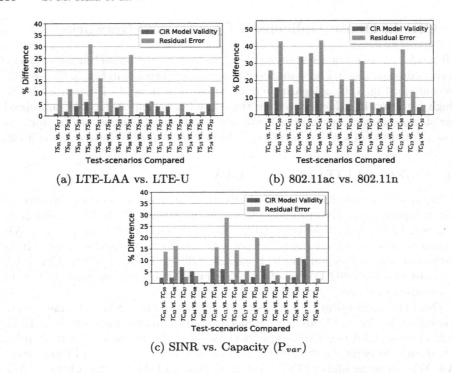

(a) LTE-LAA vs. LTE-U

(b) 802.11ac vs. 802.11n

(c) SINR vs. Capacity (P_{var})

Fig. 4. Test-scenario specific comparative analysis

Higher residual error is observed in twice as many LTE-U scenarios as compared to LAA scenarios (5% margin of error). On average, LTE-U scenarios have a 6% higher RSD than LAA. Further, average residual error in all LTE-WiFi-Predictor network-configurations is lower for LAA when compared to LTE-U. Thus, LAA models seem to be more precise in their ability to predict coexistence network performance, regardless of the response variable (Capacity or SINR).

Gain and Standard Deviation in RMV. It is important to notice the standard deviation (SD) in CIR model validities when subjected to kCV, especially after LOF outlier removal. While outlier reduction yields higher RMVs, the Gain in RMV should be accompanied with low SD in RMV, averaged across all kCV runs. Thus, we consider high Gain and low SD as a characteristic for stable CIR models.

LTE-U fares much worse than LAA in terms of both Gain and SD. LAA outperforms LTE-U by 47.67% in Gain and registers a 24.5% lower SD, averaged across all scenarios. A similar trend can be observed in LTE-WiFi-Predictor combinations as well. Thus, LAA has a higher Gain post-outlier-removal along with a lower SD, which demonstrates robustness of the LAA CIR models.

Outliers. For a network system, the outlier % may be considered to be a good indicator of the degree of fluctuation in network performance, and consequently

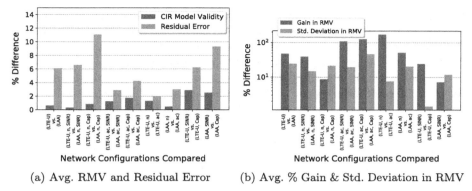

(a) Avg. RMV and Residual Error   (b) Avg. % Gain & Std. Deviation in RMV

Fig. 5. Configuration-level comparative analysis

the ability of a network to deliver the promised Quality of Service (QoS). However, the selection of outlier detection algorithm is a subjective choice. While this work steers clear of making inferences based on outliers, we compare the outliers in LTE-U and LAA data detected by LOF algorithm with the outliers detected by "Minitab," a standard tool for data-analysis [22]. Minitab's outlier detection algorithm labels samples with extreme "leverage points" and "large residuals" as outliers. As expected the percentage of data-points labeled as outliers is different in LOF and Minitab. However, LTE-U has higher a fraction of outliers as compared to LAA in both LOF (by 9.11%) and Minitab (by 5.14%).

The reason for high fluctuation in LTE-U can be attributed to greater susceptibility of an LTE-U node to the unpredictable interference from Wi-Fi APs in its proximity. This primarily happens during the LTE-U ON state as there are no energy detection thresholds in LTE-U. Unlike LTE-U, Wi-Fi considers the energy threshold as -62 dBm and preamble detection threshold as -82 dBm. Similar to Wi-Fi, the LBT mechanism in LAA has an energy threshold of -72 dBm, making it less vulnerable to interference from Wi-Fi APs, and ensuring fewer extreme network performance fluctuations. Thus, LAA seems to offer a more reliable performance from the perspective of end-user QoS experience.

LTE-LAA vs LTE-U: A Feature Relationship Perspective. A clear pattern emerges after the analysis of various learning model parameters. Residual error, standard deviation in RMV, and outlier % in LTE-U is higher than LAA, while post-outlier-removal Gain in RMV is lower. This is true for the majority of test-scenarios regardless of the choice of Wi-Fi variant, predictor variable, and bandwidth allocated. Thus, CIR in LTE-LAA networks is qualitatively better in terms of the spread of data along the expected curve fit. This implies that LAA offers greater consistency in networks performance and lower fluctuations in system variables such as the signal strength or the throughput at the end-user device. This finding has a strong correlation with the industry trends. The Global Mobile Suppliers Association (GMSA) report states that 38 operators in

21 countries have made investments in LAA as compared to only 11 operators investing in LTE-U. In terms of global deployments, 30 operators are planning to deploy or are actively deploying LAA networks in 18 countries, in contrast to LTE-U which is being deployed in only 3 countries. Further, LTE-U deployments are designed with an upgrade path to LAA and eLAA [3]. Clearly, LAA is the preferred choice of industry for LTE unlicensed networks. From a data-learning perspective, this appears to be reasonable as LAA offers a more robust network performance than LTE-U.

5.2   Wi-Fi: 802.11n vs 802.11ac

Measurement Based Analysis. 802.11ac outperforms 802.11n in 87.5% scenarios in terms of average network capacity. This is expected as 802.11ac supports 80 MHz channels (with optional support up to 160 MHz), higher modulation schemes (256 QAM), and 8 × 8 Multi-user Multiple-input Multiple-output (MU-MIMO), among other features.

Feature Relationship Analysis. 802.11ac is slightly better than 802.11n in scenario-specific RMV comparison, while in terms of component-specific average RMV, the two are comparable. The post-outlier-removal Gain in 802.11n is much higher, even though the average RMVs are comparable. However, 802.11ac has a lower deviation in model validities, which implies more reliable CIR models than 802.11n. In terms of residual error, 802.11ac registers lower error in 33% more models as compared to 802.11n. This signifies more accurate predictive modeling in 802.11ac.

802.11ac vs 802.11n: A Feature Relationship Perspective. The CIR analysis reveals only a marginal advantage in coexistence performance for 802.11ac as compared to 802.11n. The trends are underwhelming because the 802.11ac standard supports compressed *beamforming* which along with channel state information (CSI) is quite efficient in mitigating link-conflicts [5]. Hence, a stronger relationship between network capacity and SINR was expected.

However, the observations can be reasonably explained through two facts. First, in an LTE-WiFi coexistence system, the unlicensed LTE (LTE-U/LAA) subsystem has a greater impact on the performance of the Wi-Fi subsystem than the latter has on the former. Thus, the unlicensed LTE subsystem is the primary determinant of the overall system performance. Second, the adverse impact of LTE-U on coexisting Wi-Fi (n/ac) performance is much worse than that of LAA on Wi-Fi [7]. The duty cycling mechanism of LTE-U combined with the LTE-U's transmission at energy threshold's lower than those prescribed by Wi-Fi cause interference to Wi-Fi transmissions [15]. LAA's LBT avoids collisions with Wi-Fi transmissions, and leads to a better coexistence system performance. This is observed in the LTE-WiFi-Predictor combination analysis as well.

Thus, from a data analysis perspective, the unlicensed LTE is the dominant subsystem in the coexistence paradigm, and determines the overall system performance. Further, the feature relationship analysis of network-data also supports the findings from measurement based studies that LTE-U has a higher adverse impact on Wi-Fi performance as compared to LAA [7]. Another major takeaway is that it seems more appropriate to study the Wi-Fi (n/ac/ax) subsystems performance only in conjugation with the coexisting unlicensed LTE (LTE-U/LAA) or 5G NR-U subsystem.

5.3 Choice of Network Predictor Variable

A bidirectional regression analysis reveals the impact that the choice of predictor variable *e.g.,* SINR (P_{SINR}) or Capacity (P_{Cap}), has on network feature relationships. We find that network capacity is a much better predictor of SINR than SINR is of network capacity. This is a pattern that can be clearly and consistently seen across all CIR model parameters and all comparative themes without any ambiguity. In scenario-specific comparison, RMV of P_{SINR} models is always either comparable to, or lower than P_{Cap} models. RMV of P_{Cap} models is higher on average for both LTE-U and LAA components when compared to RMV of corresponding P_{SINR} models. P_{Cap} models also exhibit a significantly higher post-outlier-removal Gain and lower average standard deviation in RMV. Finally, the residual error is higher in P_{SINR} on average, and in twice as many scenarios, when compared to P_{Cap}.

It may seem counter-intuitive that it is more accurate to predict the expected values of SINR for given values of network capacity, than the reverse. However, recent analysis of operator data gathered from public LAA deployments shows that high SINR doesn't always guarantee high throughput in coexistence deployments, as end-user QoS depends on other factors such as resource block allocation [19]. On the other hand, for high throughput a high SINR is a necessary, if not a sufficient condition.

Thus, the direction of NFR analysis and the choice of predictor has a clear effect on the learned network model, regardless of the unlicensed LTE and Wi-Fi variants considered. Further, this also indicates that other variables may also be relevant to the unlicensed coexistence NFR analysis such as resource block allocation, physical cell-id, *etc.*

5.4 Impact of Bandwidth

From Fig. 6 (a), prima facie it appears that when throughput is the response variable, the residual error of the models increases consistently with bandwidth. This pattern seems consistent for both LTE-U and LAA models. This would make sense as well, because with higher bandwidth allocation there is a greater possibility of fluctuation in network capacity values in real-world systems due to poor resource allocation and temporal variation in factors such as interference.

To confirm this pattern, we normalized the coexistence data and learned the feature relationships and associated parameters again. The data was normalized as $\hat{\mathbf{z}} = \frac{\mathbf{z} - \mu}{\sigma}$, where μ, σ are the mean and the standard deviation of the data. As a result, the processed data is zero mean and unit variance, and thus more suited to evaluate the impact of bandwidth. Prior to normalization, in 11 out of 12 scenario-specific comparisons the RSD had increased with an increase in bandwidth. However, after normalization, in almost half the scenarios there is no increase in residual error with increase in bandwidth and the earlier trend is non-existent.

This finding has serious implications for QoS promised to the end-user. Cellular operators attempt to satisfy the guaranteed user demand according to the data plan. Had higher bandwidth allocation exhibited an association (if not causation) with greater fluctuation in network performance, it would be worrisome. However, this does not seem to be the case.

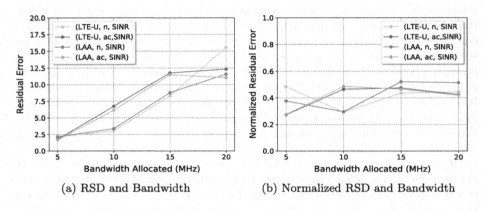

(a) RSD and Bandwidth   (b) Normalized RSD and Bandwidth

Fig. 6. Impact of bandwidth

6   NFRs and Dense Network Optimization

The feature relationships learned from network-data can be further utilized in improving dense network performance.

6.1   Network Feature Relationship Based Optimization (NeFRO)

To facilitate the use of NFRs in network performance enhancement, this work proposes the **Network Feature Relationship based Optimization** (NeFRO) framework. The high-level schema of the NeFRO framework is outlined in Fig. 7. First, data is collected for a network deployment periodically. In each epoch, network feature relationship analysis is performed using machine learning algorithms. Strong NFRs are identified and selected for possible utilization in network performance optimization. These NFRs are fed to a *constraint selector module* that selects relevant constraints for the optimization model/formulation. The module compares an NFR learned from network data for a network feature-point set $\{f_1, f_2, \ldots, f_n\}$ with available theoretical constraints relevant to the feature point set. While the NFR is more "suitable," as it is derived from actual network data, it still has to be tested for *convergence time viability*. Thus the

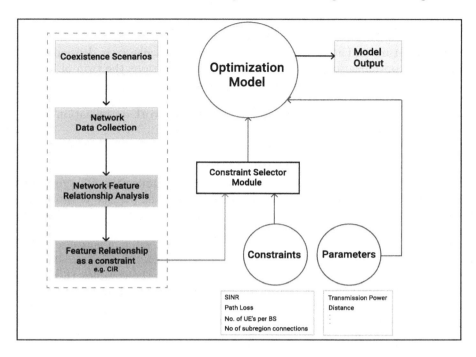

Fig. 7. Network feature relationship based optimization

constraint selector module compares the NFR with the theoretical constraint for complexity, and selects the more viable constraint for network optimization. Although the illustration highlights the process-flow for a coexistence network, the NeFRO approach will apply similarly to network optimization in all wireless networks, with minor modifications, if required.

Benefits of the NeFRO Approach. There are several advantages of the proposed NeFRO framework over conventional network optimization. First, since the learned NFRs are grounded in empirical data, they reflect the ambient network conditions. Therefore, it is more practical to use them in network performance optimization than theoretical constraints involving similar network variables. Second, NFRs can be used "as is" in optimization without making any assumptions, unlike theoretical constraints which need to be justified through assumptions. Finally, if the learned NFRs are less complex than the theoretical constraints, it automatically solves the problem of arbitrary or forced relaxation of constraints. Even if the NFRs are of a comparable complexity and require similar computational overhead, they have the advantage of reflecting the actual network parameter dynamics, which facilitates a more informed network optimization.

6.2   Implementation and Validation of NeFRO

Convergence time and accuracy trade-off is a primary challenge in dense network performance optimization [20]. Therefore, NeFRO envisions the twin objectives of *convergence time reduction*, while maintaining high *accuracy*, vis-à-vis the baseline optimization model. The validation of NeFRO is done by implementing it on recent state-of-the-art studies on coexistence network optimization.

Validation Methodology. The validation methodology involves the following steps. First, works with two optimization objectives are considered, *viz.* network signal strength optimization and network capacity optimization. The proposed optimization models are implemented on GAMS [11], as per the network configuration and specifications of the testbed/experiments. Second, the baseline optimization models are implemented for the test-scenarios considered in this work. Further, two values are observed, (a) the optimal value of network performance metric (SINR or Capacity), and (b) the *convergence time* required by the formulation to arrive at the optimal value. Thereafter, the complex theoretical SINR-Capacity constraint in each of the proposed optimization formulation is replaced with the second-degree polynomial CIR equation derived from feature relationship analysis in this work. Please note that the baseline models that optimize network capacity are considered for test-scenarios with SINR as the predictor, and vice-versa.

Evaluation of NeFRO. Two yardsticks are considered to carry out the performance evaluation of NeFRO. First, is the closeness of the "NeFRO Optimal" value generated by the NeFRO model, to the optimal value generated by the baseline literature model. This is referred to as the **Accuracy** of the NeFRO model. Accuracy can be defined as, the *"% difference in the optimal value generated by the baseline model and the NeFRO-optimal value."* Second, is the reduction in the time taken by the NeFRO model to arrive at the optimal value. This is defined as **Convergence Time Fraction** (CTF). CTF indicates *"what fraction (%) of the baseline model's convergence time is NeFRO's convergence time."* [1]

Thus, NeFRO is evaluated on its ability to offer a *low CTF* while maintaining *high Accuracy*, with respect to the baseline optimization model. Please note that the state-of-the-art optimization models are implemented for the small-scale dense unlicensed coexistence scenarios implemented on the experimental testbed. We expect that in a real-world network of a much higher scale and density, the benefits of NeFRO will be far more pronounced.

Baseline Optimization Models Considered. Four recent works are considered that propose formulations to optimize coexistence network performance.

---

[1] For example, if baseline model takes 10 ms to converge at the optimal solution, and NeFRO requires 9 ms to arrive at the NeFRO-optimal value, then CTF is 90%.

Two of these works aim at optimizing network capacity, while the other two optimize signal strength available to the UEs. A brief description is presented, starting with the capacity optimization works. An optimal resource allocation scheme aimed at maximizing LTE-LAA capacity in a LTE-WiFi coexistence network is proposed in [9]. Another study proposes an LBT-compliant channel access approach for both LTE-U/LAA in the 5 GHz band that seeks to maximize system throughput, while also mitigating the impact of interference from the unlicensed LTE on the Wi-Fi subsystems capacity [27]. Further, [26] seeks to enhance and optimize network signal strength for LTE-U/LAA coexistence networks through strategic optimal placement of nodes. Finally, the model proposed in [4], aims to optimize network performance by taking into account the spectrum usage of Wi-Fi APs in addition to the optimal placement of nodes. Henceforth, the capacity optimization models *viz.*, [9] and [27], are referred to as COM$_1$ and COM$_2$, respectively. Likewise, signal-strength optimization models *viz.*, [4] and [26], are referred to as SOM$_1$ and SOM$_2$, respectively.

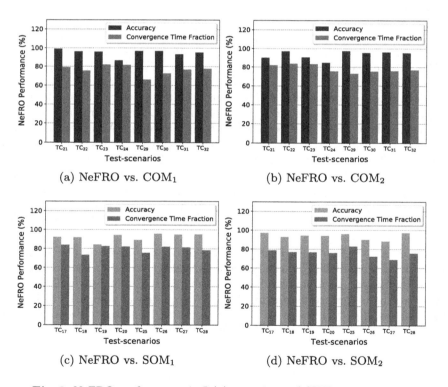

(a) NeFRO vs. COM$_1$ (b) NeFRO vs. COM$_2$

(c) NeFRO vs. SOM$_1$ (d) NeFRO vs. SOM$_2$

Fig. 8. NeFRO performance in LAA capacity and SINR optimization

6.3   Optimization Results and Performance Evaluation

The results of the optimization simulations run on GAMS are presented in Fig. 8 and Fig. 9, for LAA and LTE-U test-scenarios, respectively. Further, Figs. 8 (a), 8 (b), 9 (a), and 9 (b), present results for test-scenarios where the objective is to optimize network capacity. The remaining figures show results for signal-strength optimization test-scenarios.

It can be discerned that NeFRO performs remarkably well by reducing the required convergence times while delivering NeFRO-optimal values very close to the optimal results of the respective models. A scenario-specific evaluation of NeFRO can be performed by observing the difference in the length of bars of Accuracy and CTF for a particular test-scenario. The greater the difference in their height, the lower is the trade-off, and the better is the NeFRO performance. Two points are noteworthy. First, in LAA scenarios NeFRO offers a significant reduction in convergence time, while in LTE-U scenarios, the CTF is somewhat subdued. Network optimization in LTE-U is inherently more challenging due to its channel access mechanism. Hence, it is more computationally intensive, and requires a longer convergence time. Second, for LAA scenarios the difference in NeFRO performance for capacity optimization and SINR optimization is negligible. However, in LTE-U, there appears to be a difference in NeFRO performance for these two objectives. Particularly, the CTF for SINR optimization in LTE-U is rather low.

The average performance of NeFRO across all test-scenarios for the four optimization models is presented in Table 2. On average, when compared to SOM_1 and SOM_2, the CTF of NeFRO is lower than its average Accuracy, showing a marginal gain. However, Fig. 9 (d) shows that for two scenarios there seems to be no overall gain from NeFRO as compared to SOM_2. Thus one dimension that needs to be further investigated is the variation in accuracy and convergence time-trade off with application of NeFRO. It is possible that the correlation or association between the RMV of the learned model and the network performance metric which is the objective of the optimization (SINR or Capacity), may explain this variation.

In general, NeFRO outperforms the baseline model across all test-scenarios, and both unlicensed LTE variants, by significantly reducing the convergence time. The average Accuracy, as shown in Table 2, is very high as well. Further, NeFRO seems to perform better in LTE-LAA scenarios as compared to LTE-U, which can be expected based on the discussion and findings presented in this work. Thus, the NeFRO framework stands validated.

Table 2. Performance trends in test-scenarios

NeFRO parameter	LTE-LAA scenarios (%)				LTE-U scenarios (%)			
	COM_1	COM_2	SOM_1	SOM_2	COM_1	COM_2	SOM_1	SOM_2
CTF	76.46	78.25	79.89	76.02	90.10	89.05	94.17	93.60
Accuracy	95.04	93.31	92.28	93.82	94.97	96.12	96.38	97.16

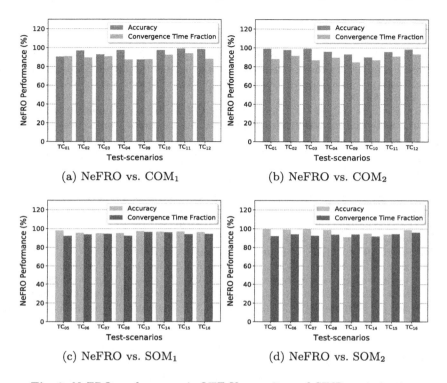

(a) NeFRO vs. COM_1 (b) NeFRO vs. COM_2

(c) NeFRO vs. SOM_1 (d) NeFRO vs. SOM_2

Fig. 9. NeFRO performance in LTE-U capacity and SINR optimization

7 Conclusion and Future Direction

This work presented a comparative study of unlicensed coexistence networks through network feature relationship analysis. Network-data was collected through comprehensive real-world experiments and then analyzed through a family of regression algorithms. The relevance of network feature relationships was highlighted by analyzing LTE-WiFi networks on a variety of regression model parameters such a R-sq, residual error, *etc.* Several insightful inferences were made on aspects such as the impact of bandwidth, residual error, and outliers on coexistence network performance. Further, NeFRO, a feature relationship based optimization framework was proposed and validated through signal strength and capacity optimization. NeFRO offered reduced convergence times by as much as 24% and offered accuracy as high as 97.16% on average.

In the future, we will investigate convergence time and accuracy trade-off by considering feature relationships of varying degrees. Further, studying the association between the R-sq of the learned models and the network performance metrics is also a relevant topic. The impact of control/signaling data on network feature relationships will be explored as well. Most importantly, we intend to implement an AR system on a simulator and employ NeFRO to reduce latency.

References

1. Abedi, A., Brecht, T.: Examining relationships between 802.11n physical layer transmission feature combinations. In: Proceedings of the 19th ACM International Conference on Modeling, Analysis and Simulation of Wireless and Mobile Systems, pp. 229–238 (2016)
2. Apicharttrisorn, K., et al.: Characterization of multi-user augmented reality over cellular networks. In: 2020 17th Annual IEEE International Conference on Sensing, Communication, and Networking (SECON), pp. 1–9. IEEE (2020)
3. Association, G.M.S.: LTE Unlicensed Reports (2020). https://gsacom.com/technology/lte-unlicensed/
4. Baswade, A.M., Shashi, K.M., Tamma, B.R., Antony, F.A.: On placement of LAA/LTE-U base stations in heterogeneous wireless networks. In: Proceedings of the 19th International Conference on Distributed Computing and Networking (ICDCN), Varanasi, India, 4–7 January 2018 (2018)
5. Bejarano, O., Knightly, E.W., Park, M.: IEEE 802.11 ac: from channelization to multi-user MIMO. IEEE Commun. Mag. **51**(10), 84–90 (2013)
6. Biswas, S., Bicket, J., Wong, E., Musaloiu-e, R., Bhartia, A., Aguayo, D.: Large-scale measurements of wireless network behavior. In: Proceedings of the 2015 ACM Conference on Special Interest Group on Data Communication, pp. 153–165 (2015)
7. Bojović, B., Giupponi, L., Ali, Z., Miozzo, M.: Evaluating unlicensed LTE technologies: LAA vs LTE-U. IEEE Access **7**, 89714–89751 (2019)
8. Cavalcante, A.M., et al.: Performance evaluation of LTE and Wi-Fi coexistence in unlicensed bands. In: 2013 IEEE 77th Vehicular Technology Conference (VTC Spring), pp. 1–6. IEEE (2013)
9. Chen, Q., Yu, G., Ding, Z.: Enhanced LAA for unlicensed LTE deployment based on TXOP contention. IEEE Trans. Commun. **67**(1), 417–429 (2019)
10. Ericcson: Ericcson mobility report, 2021. Update (2021). www.ericsson.com/en/mobility-report/reports/june-2021
11. GAMS: General Algebraic Modeling System. http://www.gams.com. Accessed March 2019
12. Gupta, P., Kumar, P.R.: The capacity of wireless networks. IEEE Trans. Inf. Theory **46**(2), 388–404 (2000)
13. Hirzallah, M.A.: Protocols and algorithms for harmonious coexistence over unlicensed bands in next-generation wireless networks. Ph.D. thesis, The University of Arizona (2020)
14. Ho, L., Gacanin, H.: Design principles for ultra-dense Wi-Fi deployments. In: Proceedings of the IEEE Wireless Communications and Networking Conference (WCNC), Barcelona, Spain, 15–18 April 2018, pp. 1–6 (2018)
15. Jindal, N., Breslin, D., Norman, A.: LTE-U and Wi-Fi: a coexistence study by google, Wi-Fi LTE-U coexistence test workshop (2015)
16. Kala, S.M., Reddy, M.P.K., Musham, R., Tamma, B.R.: Interference mitigation in wireless mesh networks through radio co-location aware conflict graphs. Wirel. Netw. **22**(2), 679–702 (2015). https://doi.org/10.1007/s11276-015-1002-4
17. Kala, S.M., Sathya, V., Seah Winston K.G., Tamma, B.R.: CIRNO: leveraging capacity interference relationship for dense networks optimization. In: 2020 IEEE Wireless Communications and Networking Conference (WCNC), pp. 1–6. IEEE (2020)

18. Kala, S.M., Sathya, V., Seah, W.K., Yamaguchi, H., Higashino, T.: Evaluation of theoretical interference estimation metrics for dense Wi-Fi networks. In: 2021 International Conference on COMmunication Systems & NETworkS (COMSNETS), pp. 351–359. IEEE (2021)
19. Kala, S.M., Sathya, V., Yamatsuta, E., Yamaguchi, H., Higashino, T.: Operator data driven cell-selection in LTE-LAA coexistence networks. In: International Conference on Distributed Computing and Networking 2021, pp. 206–214 (2021)
20. Kamel, M., Hamouda, W., Youssef, A.: Ultra-dense networks: a survey. IEEE Commun. Surv. Tutor. **18**(4), 2522–2545 (2016)
21. Mao, Q., Hu, F., Hao, Q.: Deep learning for intelligent wireless networks: a comprehensive survey. IEEE Commun. Surv. Tutor. **20**(4), 2595–2621 (2018)
22. Minitab, I.: Minitab Release 17: Statistical Software for Windows. Minitab Inc., State College (2014)
23. Montgomery, D.C., Peck, E.A., Vining, G.G.: Introduction to Linear Regression Analysis, vol. 821. Wiley, Hoboken (2012)
24. Murphy, K.P.: Machine Learning: A Probabilistic Perspective. The MIT Press, Cambridge (2012)
25. Sathya, V., Kala, S.M., Rochman, M.I., Ghosh, M., Roy, S.: Standardization advances for cellular and Wi-Fi coexistence in the unlicensed 5 and 6 GHz bands. GetMobile: Mob. Comput. Commun. **24**(1), 5–15 (2020)
26. Sathya, V., Ramamurthy, A., Tamma, B.R.: On placement and dynamic power control of femtocells in LTE HetNets. In: Proceedings of IEEE Globecom, Austin, TX, USA, 8–12 December 2014, pp. 4394–4399 (2014)
27. Valls, V., Garcia-Saavedra, A., Costa, X., Leith, D.J.: Maximizing LTE capacity in unlicensed bands (LTE-U/LAA) while fairly coexisting with 802.11 WLANs. IEEE Commun. Lett. **20**(6), 1219–1222 (2016)
28. Zhang, H., Chu, X., Guo, W., Wang, S.: Coexistence of Wi-Fi and heterogeneous small cell networks sharing unlicensed spectrum. IEEE Commun. Mag. **53**(3), 158–164 (2015)

One-Shot Wayfinding Method for Blind People via OCR and Arrow Analysis with a 360-Degree Smartphone Camera

Yutaro Yamanaka[1]([✉]), Seita Kayukawa[2], Hironobu Takagi[3], Yuichi Nagaoka[4], Yoshimune Hiratsuka[5], and Satoshi Kurihara[1]

[1] Graduate School of Science and Technology, Keio University, Kanagawa, Japan
`yutaroyamanaka@keio.jp`
[2] Waseda University, Tokyo, Japan
[3] IBM Research - Tokyo, Tokyo, Japan
[4] Tokyo Independent Living Support Center for the Visually Impaired, Tokyo, Japan
[5] Department of Ophthalmology, Juntendo University School of Medicine, Tokyo, Japan

Abstract. We present a wayfinding method that assists blind people in determining the correct direction to a destination by taking a *one-shot* image. Signage is standard in public buildings and used to help visitors, but has little benefit for blind people. Our *one-shot wayfinding method* recognizes surrounding signage in all directions from an equirectangular image captured using a 360-degree smartphone camera. The method analyzes the relationship between detected text and arrows on signage and estimates the correct direction toward the user's destination. In other words, the method enables wayfinding for the blind without requiring either environmental modifications (*e.g.* Bluetooth beacons) or preparation of map data. In a user study, we compared our method with a baseline method: a signage reader using a smartphone camera with a standard field of view. We found that our method enabled the participants to decide directions more efficiently than with the baseline method.

Keywords: Visual impairment · Signage · OCR · Arrow detection

1 Introduction

Signage is standard in public buildings and shows directions toward points of interest to help visitors find their way [14], but it has little benefit for blind people. Recent studies have proposed assistive technologies that can recognize signage information (*e.g.* text or pictograms on signage) by combining a smartphone camera and computer vision technologies such as optical character recognition (OCR) [2,29]. One difficulty for blind people in using such signage recognition systems is taking pictures with the appropriate framing and aiming the camera toward a sign quickly and accurately [15,24]. Thus, blind users sometimes cannot obtain required information from these systems. In this situation, it can be

T. Hara and H. Yamaguchi (Eds.): MobiQuitous 2021, LNICST 419, pp. 150–168, 2022.
https://doi.org/10.1007/978-3-030-94822-1_9

difficult for them to distinguish whether the reason is a lack of signage in the environment or incorrect camera framing.

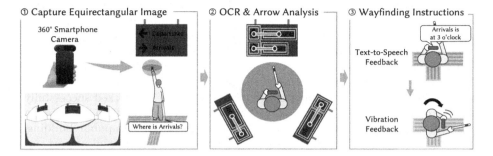

Fig. 1. Overview of our *one-shot wayfinding* method for blind people. 1) When approaching an intersection in a public building, a blind user takes a picture with a 360-degree camera attached to a smartphone. 2) The method detects text and arrows on surrounding signage and links them to estimate the direction to a destination. 3) The method provides wayfinding instructions for the estimated direction via text-to-speech and vibration feedback.

To overcome this limitation, we developed a *one-shot wayfinding* method, which uses a 360-degree smartphone camera that captures all signage around a user in only one shot without having to adjust the camera aim. To decide the correct direction to a destination, blind people need to understand the directions of arrows on signs. For example, as shown in Fig. 1, a sign with a right arrow indicates to turn right at the intersection. Therefore, our wayfinding method was developed to recognize not only text but also arrows that point in the direction to a destination. The method recognizes text, arrows, and text-arrow associations on surrounding signage, and it converts the direction of each arrow into an egocentric direction (*i.e.* a direction relative to the user's body). Then, it verbalizes the egocentric direction in terms of a clock position, which is a standard way of presenting directions to blind people. In other words, our approach enables a wayfinding method for blind people that does not require either environmental modifications, such as markers, Bluetooth Low Energy (BLE) beacons, and Wi-Fi beacons, or preparation of data, such as maps and points-of-interest datasets.

The proposed method first detects text and arrows from a captured equirectangular image by using an OCR system and a convolutional neural network (CNN) object detector. It then links detected text to each detected arrow via a minimum spanning tree (MST). We set the edge weights to link text and arrows by considering the relationship between them (*e.g.* text above an arrow tends to have a weaker correspondence with the arrow than text below the arrow). For example, in Fig. 1 (2), the method links "Departures" and "Arrivals" to the left and right arrows, respectively. It then estimates the directions to the destinations in egocentric coordinates relative to the user's current orientation. For instance, when a sign in front of the user shows "Arrivals" and this is linked to a right arrow, the smartphone says, *"'Arrivals' is at 3 o'clock."* To further convey the estimated direction, the smartphone gives vibration alerts when the user faces the correct direction (Fig. 1 (3)).

To evaluate the usability of our method, we performed a user study with eight blind people. To provide a baseline system, we implemented a simple signage reader system that uses the RGB camera built into a smartphone (not a 360-degree camera). We asked the participants to find the correct direction to a destination by using either the proposed system or the baseline system. To evaluate the effectiveness of each system's interface, we designed a Wizard-of-Oz-style [17] study using images for which our algorithm worked successfully. Because of the COVID-19 outbreak, we conducted the user study in a laboratory space that reproduced wayfinding decision-making situations in public buildings by using pre-captured images from places such as an international airport and a railway station. We observed that the proposed system enabled the participants to determine directions with a smaller amount of rotation than with the baseline system. The participants' feedback also supported our hypothesis that the proposed system is useful for wayfinding tasks in public buildings. On the basis of our findings, we discuss future directions to develop a more flexible and comfortable wayfinding system for public buildings.

2   Related Work

2.1   Indoor Navigation and Wayfinding System for Blind People

Navigating large and unfamiliar public buildings (*e.g.* international airports, railway stations, and shopping centers) is a challenging task for blind people [12,13]. Thus, researchers have proposed various types of indoor navigation systems for blind people. Most of these systems provide turn-by-turn navigation instructions by using localization technologies (*e.g.* Bluetooth Low Energy (BLE) beacons [3,30], ultra-wide band (UWB) [4], and Wi-Fi [10]) or environment databases (*e.g.* images [32] and maps [22]). While these navigation or wayfinding systems can provide accurate wayfinding instructions, they require installing sensors or code in the environment or constructing a database of the environment.

To implement a wayfinding or navigation system that does not require additional sensors or databases, recent research using computer vision has enabled systems that can recognize useful information for wayfinding (*e.g.* doors [8], flat floors [11], pictograms and text on signage [29,35]). However, sign locations do not always correspond to the route to a destination. For example, a sign with a right arrow indicates that the destination is to the right, not at the sign's location. To overcome this limitation, we propose a wayfinding method that can recognize not only text but also arrows that show the direction to a destination. By analyzing the relationship between detected text and arrows, the method gives blind users egocentric directions toward their destinations.

2.2   Environment Recognition via Smartphone Camera

With the expansion of smartphone usage in the blind people community [25], various smartphone camera-based recognition systems have been proposed to help blind users obtain information on their surroundings (*e.g.* object [1,2,6,18, 29,38], text [1,2,6,38], and signage [29,31]). However, it is still challenging for blind users to capture an entire target object with a smartphone camera [15,24]. While capture-assistance systems using audio [15,21,33,37] or vibration [21] have been proposed, standard smartphone cameras require blind users to rotate them and face them toward objects. Having blind people change their orientation may cause them to lose their way and become disoriented [16]. We thus use a 360-degree smartphone camera, which can capture all surrounding signage in one shot, for wayfinding tasks; we call this *one-shot wayfinding*.

3   Design: One-Shot Wayfinding Method

Here, we describe our wayfinding method design specifically for the following typical situation: Blind pedestrians walk through a public building such as an airport, railway station, or shopping center. They walk along the tactile pavings in the building but is unfamiliar with the route. Thus, when they approach a tactile paving intersection, they cannot decide which direction to take.

3.1   One-Shot Wayfinding Method with 360-Degree Camera

While there are smartphone-based assistive technologies that can recognize information on the surroundings via a smartphone camera [1,2,6,18,29,31,37,38], it is challenging for blind users to point a camera toward a target and capture its entirety [15,24]. When blind users cannot obtain required information with such technologies, it can be difficult for them to distinguish whether the reason is a lack of signage in the environment or incorrect camera framing.

Therefore, we attach a 360-degree camera to a smartphone. Compared with built-in smartphone cameras with a standard field of view (FoV), 360-degree cameras have three advantages: (1) they can capture all surrounding signage (including directly behind) in one shot, (2) they can capture the whole of each sign (*i.e.* no text is cut off), and (3) they do not require aiming. This is why we call our method a *one-shot wayfinding*. In other words, it can distinguish whether there is signage around a user with only one camera shot.

3.2   Wayfinding Instructions via OCR and Arrow Analysis

The combination of a 360-degree camera and OCR can recognize text appearing around a user, including non-signage text (*e.g.* posters and signboards). However, reading out all text can cognitively overwhelm the user [26]. In addition, sign locations do not always correspond to the route to a destination. For example, when a user approaches an intersection and a sign with a right arrow is in front of the user, it indicates that the destination is to the right, not at the sign location (Fig. 1). In this situation, the system should tell the user to turn right.

To overcome these limitations, we designed our wayfinding method to detect not only text but also arrows on signage. The method then links detected text to each detected arrow by considering their spatial relationship, through a process we call *arrow analysis*. By using the linking results, the method recognizes only signage text and estimates the egocentric direction to each destination (Sect. 4). It then instructs the user on the correct direction to the destination.

4   Implementation

Our one-shot wayfinding method consists of two components: (1) a **web API** that performs equirectangular image preprocessing, arrow detection, OCR, and arrow analysis; and (2) a **smartphone interface** that estimates egocentric directions to destinations and provides wayfinding instructions. For our user study with blind people, we attached an Insta360 ONE,[1] which can capture 7K (6912 × 3456 pixels) equirectangular images, to an iPhone6.[2] Captured images are horizontally corrected by the camera's built-in gyroscope. As a result, blind users can capture equirectangular images horizontally without concern for the smartphone's angle and rotation. After capturing an image, the method sends it to the web API on our server.

4.1   Equirectangular Image Preprocessing

Because equirectangular images are spatially distorted and unsuitable for arrow detection, the method first converts a captured image into cubemap images (1728 × 1728 pixels). The method converts the equirectangular image into five cubemap images having 18-degree horizontal overlaps. The method uses the five cubemap images for arrow detection, and the original equirectangular image and the back cubemap image for OCR.

4.2   Arrow Detection and OCR

The method detects arrows by using the YOLOv3 object detector [28]. To train the arrow detection model, we collected 1140 arrow images taken in public spaces from Open Images Dataset [20] and Flicker API[3] (only Creative-Commons-licensed images). We annotated the collected images with bounding boxes and four types of arrow labels (straight, down, right, or left). The method detects bounding boxes of arrows from the five cubemap images and obtains their positions in the equirectangular image coordinate system. Because of the cubemap images' overlaps, the method may detect the same arrow twice from different

---

[1] https://www.insta360.com/product/insta360-one/.

[2] https://support.apple.com/kb/sp705.

[3] https://www.flickr.com/services/api/.

a) Definition of Edge Weights

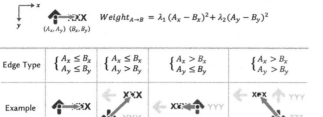

b) Edge Design

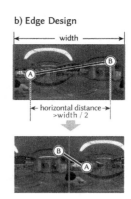

Edge Type	$\begin{cases} A_x \leq B_x \\ A_y \leq B_y \end{cases}$	$\begin{cases} A_x \leq B_x \\ A_y > B_y \end{cases}$	$\begin{cases} A_x > B_x \\ A_y \leq B_y \end{cases}$	$\begin{cases} A_x > B_x \\ A_y > B_y \end{cases}$
Example				
(λ_1, λ_2)	$(1, 1)$	$(1, 50)$	$(4, 1)$	$(4, 50)$

Fig. 2. a) Edge weights are defined according to the related positions of two nodes. b) If the horizontal distance between two nodes is more than half the width of the equirectangular image, the distance is recalculated by shifting the image $180°$.

cubemap images. In that case, it picks the bounding box with the higher confidence value.

The method detects text on the captured equirectangular image by using an OCR package from Google Cloud Vision API.[4] As each end of the equirectangular image may contain separated text from behind the user, the method also uses the back cubemap image for OCR. Then, the method obtains the center positions of detected text in the equirectangular image coordinate system.

4.3 Arrow Analysis

Next, the method connects detected text to each detected arrow by using a minimum spanning tree (MST) [9]. It constructs a directed graph with two types of nodes: (1) arrow nodes representing the center positions of the detected arrow bounding boxes, and (2) text nodes representing the center positions of the detected text. In the graph, edges connect among text nodes and between text and arrow nodes, but not among arrow nodes.

As shown in Fig. 2a, the method defines edge weights according to the related positions of two nodes and the lengths of edges. A signage design guideline [14] reported that left-aligned signage (text to the right of arrows) makes recognition more comfortable for those whose language is read from left to right. Thus, the method sets the edge weight higher when a node connects to the left or above nodes. Following our observations, we set the edge weight values (λ_1, λ_2) as illustrated in Fig. 2a. The horizontal distance of an edge may be more than half the width of the equirectangular image (blue edge in Fig. 2b). In that case, the method horizontally shifts the equirectangular image $180°$ and then calculates the edge weight (red edge in Fig. 2b).

---

[4] https://cloud.google.com/vision/docs/ocr/.

The method adds a new node that links to each arrow node with a zero-weight edge and applies the MST algorithm [9] from the new node. Then, it removes edges whose weight is zero or more than 5000. As a result, it obtains trees with an arrow node as the root node and text nodes as the child nodes (Fig. 4a). We assumed that each root (arrow) node's label (*i.e.* right, left, straight, or down) indicates the direction toward a destination provided by the child (text) nodes.

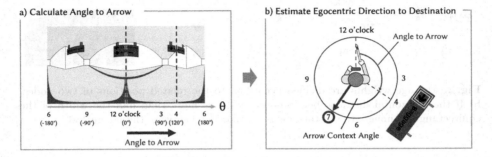

Fig. 3. Direction estimation. a) The method calculates the *angle to arrow*, which is the angle between the center positions of an arrow and the equirectangular image. b) The method estimates the egocentric direction to a destination by adding the *arrow context angle* to the *angle to arrow*.

4.4   Direction Estimation

From the arrow analysis results, the method estimates the angle to the destination indicated by the text on a sign. As illustrated in Fig. 3a, it first calculates the angle between an arrow's center position and the center of the equirectangular image (*angle to arrow*). It then estimates the angle to the destination on the basis of the predicted arrow label (Fig. 3b). We assumed that a straight or down arrow indicates that the destination is in the same directions as a sign and that a right or left arrow indicates that the destination is 90° to the right or left of a sign. Concretely, we define an *arrow context angle* on the basis of four types of arrow labels: straight/down arrows are 0°, left is −90°, and right is 90°. The method obtains the egocentric direction to the destination by adding the *arrow context angle* to the *angle to arrow* (Fig. 3b).

4.5   Process Evaluation

We evaluated the OCR and arrow analysis processes by using equirectangular images captured in public buildings. As there are no open datasets of equirectangular images capturing signage in public buildings, we constructed our own dataset. It consists of 104 images captured at tactile paving intersections in an international airport (43 images) and a railway station (61 images). We also used these images in our user evaluation (Sect. 5). For the process evaluation, we annotated 255 arrows and 330 text instances on signage that are useful for wayfinding at intersections, the area of a sign covered by each arrow, and the directions of the tactile paving branches indicated by each arrow on a sign.

Table 1 shows each process's accuracy. We obtained the arrow analysis accuracy by calculating the algorithm's success rate in linking the annotated arrows and text. For the direction estimation accuracy, we calculated the success rate in recognizing the correct tactile paving branch as the closest branch to the direction estimated by the method for each annotated arrow. Two diagonal arrows were also included in the failed cases of the arrow detection. The table also lists the method's overall performance as defined by the success rate in linking the text and the correct tactile paving branch. Figure 4 shows examples of the OCR and arrow analysis results. In Fig. 4a, the method linked text on sign to the appropriate arrow. On the other hand, we observed many failure cases. One cause of failure was incorrect arrow and text detection. The detection performance, especially for OCR, was worse for small text and arrows. Another cause was signage design: the arrow analysis accuracy decreased when there was a narrow space between arrows (Fig. 4b) or a wide space separating text (Fig. 4c). We will discuss possible solutions to improve each process's accuracy in Sect. 7.2.

Table 1. Summary of process evaluation results.

	Arrow detection (%)	OCR (%)	Arrow analysis (%)	Direction estimation (%)	Overall performance (%)
International airport	88.0	55.2	90.0	83.6	45.7
Railway station	85.7	58.4	60.0	85.0	41.1
Total	86.7	57.3	70.9	84.5	42.7

a) Success Case   b) Failure Case 1   c) Failure Case 2

Fig. 4. a) Success case: all text linked to the appropriate arrow. b) Failure case 1: narrow space between arrows, 9 of 104 images. c) Failure case 2: wide space separating text, 33 of 104 images.

4.6   User Interface

Wayfinding Instructions. The method provides wayfinding instructions to the user via text-to-speech and vibration feedback. After estimating the direction of text, the smartphone first reads out instructions in terms of clock positions. For example, suppose the user inputs "Arrivals" to the smartphone, and the estimated direction to "Arrivals" is 120° to the right of the user's current orientation. In this case, the smartphone calculates the clock position of the estimated direction and says, *"Arrivals is at 4 o'clock."* Loomis *et al.* showed that instructions given with clock positions can help blind people navigate to a specific destinations [23].

While text-to-speech feedback can provide clear information for blind people, it is difficult for them to slightly adjust their orientation [30]. Accordingly, we designed an interface combining audio and vibration alerts. The smartphone gives vibration alerts when the user is facing the expected direction. The current orientation is obtained with the smartphone's built-in gyroscope.

Smartphone Interface. The smartphone interface has three buttons: (1) Record button located at the top pf the smartphone screen: Used to register destination-related keywords via speech input. (2) Capture button located in the bottom left: Used to capture an equirectangular image while holding the camera overhead. (3) All button located in the bottom right: Used to hear readout of all text linked to arrows. The user can push this button when the smartphone does not read out any audio instructions related to the registered keywords. On the basis of audio feedback, the user can register new keywords or conclude that there is no useful signage around the user.

5   User Study

To evaluate the effectiveness of our wayfinding method interface, we performed a user study with eight blind participants: five legally blind people and three totally blind people (P3. P5, and P6), as listed in Table 2. They all considered themselves to have good orientation and mobility skills. Seven participants (P1–P4, P6–P8) regularly used a white cane, and P5 as their navigation aids and P5 owned a guide dog. In this study, we compared our one-shot wayfinding system against a baseline system: a signage reader using a smartphone camera with a standard field of view (FoV).

5.1   Experimental Setup

User Study in Laboratory Space. We performed our study in a laboratory space rather than public buildings given the restriction under the COVID-19 pandemic situation. We used equirectangular images pre-captured at tactile paving intersections in public buildings (Sect. 4.5). For each captured image, we laid tactile paving on the laboratory floor to reproduce the real intersections captured at those points. To focus on evaluating the effectiveness of each interface for signage-recognition-based wayfinding, we designed a Wizard-of-Oz-style study [17] using equirectangular images for which our algorithm worked successfully (Sect. 5.1).

Proposed System. When a user pushed the "capture button" (Sect. 4.6), the system obtained the smartphone's orientation relative to the tactile paving via the smartphone's gyroscope. Using this orientation, the system shifted the equirectangular image to match the direction and the center of the image. We argue that this process reproduced the scenario of a user capturing an equirectangular image at a tactile paving intersection in a public building. Next, the system sent the shifted image to the web API to get wayfinding instructions.

Baseline System. Inspired by smartphone camera-based recognition applications for visually impaired people [2, 18, 29, 31], we implemented a simple signage reader system using a smartphone camera with a standard FoV as the baseline system. To operate in the laboratory space, the baseline system used pre-captured equirectangular images and the pre-obtained results of arrow detection and the OCR for these images. During the wayfinding task, the system obtained the smartphone's current orientation via its gyroscope sensor. It then read out the registered text and all arrow labels within the pre-defined FoV (horizontal FoV: 100°; vertical FoV: 80°) around the smartphone's direction. When more than one arrow label was within the FoV, the system read out the labels in order from top left to bottom right.

Table 2. Demographic information of our participants, task accuracy, and SUS score for each system.

Demographic information			Task accuracy (%)		SUS score	
ID	Eyesight	Age	Proposed	Baseline	Proposed	Baseline
P1	Legally blind	43	100	50	60	**80**
P2	Legally blind	46	100	50	**90**	65
P3	Totally blind	48	87.5	87.5	**72.5**	62.5
P4	Legally blind	52	100	75	62.5	**85**
P5	Totally blind	41	87.5	62.5	**75**	30
P6	Totally blind	47	87.5	87.5	**95**	82.5
P7	Legally blind	55	100	87.5	**90**	82.5
P8	Legally blind	39	87.5	100	**82.5**	20
Mean		46.4	93.8	75.0	78.4	63.4
SD		5.4	6.7	18.9	13.1	25.3

Dataset. For the Wizard-of-Oz-style study, we picked eight pairs of equirectangular images for which our algorithm worked successfully from the dataset used for the process evaluation (Sect. 4.5) and asked participants to perform wayfinding tasks with either the proposed or baseline system for each pair of images. We chose pairs with (1) the same building (an airport or a station), (2) the same direction on the target sign (right, left, forward, or backward from the participant's orientation during image capture), and (3) the same number of tactile paving branches at the intersection (three or four). The participants were divided into two groups, X and Y, and the dataset was divided into two groups of images, A and B. Group X completed the wayfinding tasks for image group A with the proposed system and image group B with the baseline, while group Y used the opposite system for each of A and B. The order of the systems and images was randomized for each participant.

5.2 Task

We asked the participants to choose the pre-defined correct direction from the tactile paving branches on the floor with either the proposed or baseline system. The participants held the smartphone with one hand and their white cane with the other. At the beginning of each task, the experimenter registered the destination and gave the phone to the participants. We asked them to find the correct tactile paving branch to the destination (*e.g.* "Please select the tactile paving branch to 'Arrivals.'"). The participants used each system to decide the correct direction and reported verbally that they had completed the task if they found the correct branch.

To provide egocentric clock-position-based instructions correctly, we instructed the participants to capture images while keeping the camera's horizontal direction with the user's face direction. The proposed system could continuously obtain the smartphone's current angle relative to the initial angle when the user captured the image by using the smartphone's gyroscope. Therefore, the vibration feedback can correctly convey the estimated direction to users even if the smartphone's direction and the face direction are misaligned.

5.3 Procedure

After obtaining informed consent (IRB approved) from the participants, we first administered a questionnaire on demographics and navigation habits. Next, we described the two systems (proposed and baseline) and conducted a short training session (15–20 min) to familiarize the participants with each system. Then, we asked the participants to perform wayfinding tasks with either the proposed or baseline system. As they performed the tasks, the interfaces and the dataset (dataset A and B described in Sect. 5.1) were changed in a counter-balanced order. After all tasks were completed, we interviewed the participants. The task process took around 20 min, while the whole experiment took approximately 90 min per participant.

5.4 Metrics

Task Accuracy and Task Completion Time. We defined the rate of success in deciding the correct tactile paving branch as the *task accuracy*. In addition, during the main session, we measured the *task completion time* for each task.

Note that the proposed system estimated the correct direction by using the web API for every task, but the baseline system used pre-obtained results for arrow detection and OCR and thus required no processing time to read signage. One of the study's main goals was to evaluate the effectiveness of each system's interface. Therefore, in measuring the task completion time with the proposed system, we both included and excluded the processing time.

Rotation Efficiency. We measured the amount of rotation (yaw angle) of each system during each task with the smartphone's gyroscope. We then obtained the *rotation efficiency* by calculating the absolute difference between the participant's rotation and the angle between the participant's initial orientation and the correct tactile paving branch. Lower rotation efficiency values mean that participants could decide the correct direction without extra rotation. Because the rotation efficiency became too large when the participants chose the wrong direction, we only calculated it for cases of success.

Interview. After completing all the tasks, we asked participants to rate four sentences by using a 7-point Likert scale ranging from "1: strongly disagree" to "7: strongly agree", with 4 denoting "neutral."

Q1: *"I decided the direction confidently with the proposed/baseline/no system."*[5]
Q2: *"The proposed/baseline system helped me in wayfinding."*
Q3: *"The proposed/baseline system was easy to use."*
Q4: *"I felt comfortable with the proposed/baseline system."*

We also asked the participants to rate each item on the system usability scale (SUS) [7]. Finally, we asked open-ended questions about the advantages and disadvantages of each system, and we asked for suggestions to improve each system.

6 Results

6.1 Overall Performance

Task Accuracy. Table 2 lists the task accuracy of each interface for each participant. Five of the eight participants had a higher task accuracy with the proposed system than with the baseline system. Though the average task accuracy of the proposed system (93.8%; 60/64) was higher than that of the baseline (75%; 48/64), we found no significant differences between them ($p = 0.057$).

---

[5] All communication with the participants was in their native language. In this paper, we describe any translated content in the form of *"translated content"*.

Task Completion Time. Figure 5 shows the average task completion time of each system for each condition (target sign direction: left, front, right, and back) and for all conditions. Figure 5 also shows the average task completion time for the proposed system excluding the processing time Here, we report the mean and SD of the processing time: the communication time was 1.01 ± 0.62 s, the web API processing time was 6.91 ± 0.78 s (Intel Xeon E5-2698 v4, 2.20 GHz, NVIDIA GTX Station), and the total processing time was 7.92 ± 0.88 s. Our statistical analysis by using a Wilcoxon signed-rank test revealed that the proposed system (**excluding** the processing time) enabled the participants to complete the tasks significantly quicker than with the baseline system ($p < 0.0001$). This was also the case when the participants tried to read signage behind them ($p = 0.004$ for the task completion time **including** the processing time).

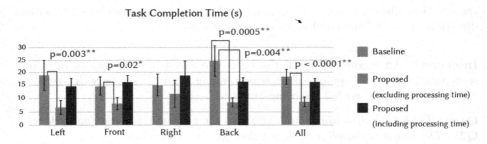

Fig. 5. Task completion time, with bars showing 95% confidence intervals and p-values for a Wilcoxon signed-rank test on the task completion time. ** and * indicate 0.005 and 0.05 levels of significance, respectively.

Rotation Efficiency. The mean, SD, and 95% confidence interval of the rotation efficiency for each system were as follows: mean $= 66.6$, SD $= 94.3$, and 95% confidence interval $= 40.1$–93.1 for the proposed system; mean $= 110.1$, SD $= 98.3$, and 95% confidence interval $= 81.6$–138.7 for the baseline system. When we compared each system's results by using a Mann-Whitney test, we observed a significant difference ($p = 0.00095$) in the rotation efficiency. This result showed that participants using the proposed system found the correct direction without extra rotation as compared with the baseline system.

Video Observation. The video recordings enabled us to analyze the participants' behavior when they chose the wrong tactile paving branch. Four participants using the proposed system (P3, P5, P6, and P8) sometimes selected the wrong branch when the system estimated that the correct direction was between two branches (4 failure cases /64 total trials). On the other hand, six participants using the baseline system (P2–P7) sometimes chose the wrong branch when the system read out multiple arrow labels.

System Ratings. Table 2 lists the SUS scores for each participant. Six of the eight participants gave a higher SUS score to the proposed system than to the baseline system. Figure 6 summarizes the results for the Likert scale questions. For all questions, the proposed system received positive ratings (*i. e.* the median rating was more than four). Participants who valued the baseline system more on Q4 (comfort) mainly pointed out the weight of the proposed system. We describe the detailed comments on the usability of each system in a later section.

6.2 Qualitative System Feedback

Six of the eight participants (P3–P8) agreed that our signage reader systems (both proposed and baseline) can be useful in wayfinding decision-making situations: A1: *"I am not confident in walking alone in public spaces, so I would like to use a system that reads signage to tell me the direction to my destination."* (P3); and A2: *"It would be easier to move with confidence if the system read the signage in unfamiliar places."* (P4).

Fig. 6. Summary of Likert scale responses (1: strongly disagree to 7: strongly agree).

Six participants (P2, P3, P5–P8) gave positive feedback on our one-shot wayfinding system because it does not require users to change their orientation and scan surrounding signage: A3: *"Rotating on the spot with the second (baseline) system destroyed my mental map. I appreciated the first (proposed) system because it did not require me to turn my body in various directions."* (P5); and A4: *"The 360-degree camera made it possible to determine directions without moving and rotating, and I thought it could be used in buildings I have never visited."* (P8) However, P4 preferred to face his camera toward surrounding signage: A5: *"I found the first (baseline) system natural and easy to use because it read the signage in the direction I was facing."* (P4).

Six participants (P2, P3, P5–P8) appreciated the proposed system's wayfinding instructions with integrated clock-position-based audio feedback and vibration feedback: A6: *"The second (proposed) system allowed me to intuitively and accurately understand the direction. On the other hand, with the first (baseline) system, I took more time to think about the direction to the destination after facing the sign direction."* (P2); A7: *"The vibration feedback of the first (proposed) system gave me confidence that I was facing the correct direction. The directional feedback of the second (baseline) system was vague, and I was not confident in my direction after rotating."* (P7); and A8: *"The directional instructions using the clock position instantly gave me a clear vision of the direction I needed to face. I thought the vibration feedback would be useful for determining the direction even where there are no landmarks such as tactile paving."* (P6).

Five participants (P3–P7) gave negative feedback on the baseline because it sometimes read out multiple arrow labels: A9: *"When the first (baseline) system read out multiple arrow labels, I had to figure out which one was the true direction to the destination."* (P4) In contrast, P1 preferred the baseline system's simple audio instructions ("turn right/left") to the proposed system's clock-position instructions: A10: *"It was difficult for me to understand the clock-position directions of the first (proposed) system, while the second (baseline) system's directional instructions were easy to understand intuitively."* (P1).

Regarding suggestions to improve our systems for use in public buildings, we obtained the following comments: A11: *"I want to check the direction when I walk along a road and reach an intersection."* (P3); and A12: *"I want to check my direction when I lose confidence while walking on tactile paving."* (P6).

Half the participants (P2, P4–P6) mentioned that the proposed system with the 360-degree camera was heavy: A13: *"The camera was so heavy that walking with it all the time was a burden."* (P4) Finally, one participant mentioned the limitation of the user study in a laboratory space as compared with real-world use: A14: *"It was difficult to get a true feel for the usability of both systems without using them in a real environment."* (P3).

7   Discussion

7.1   Effectiveness of One-Shot Wayfinding Method

The results showed that the task accuracy of the proposed system (93.8%) was higher than that of the baseline (75%), with $p = 0.057$. In addition, the proposed system significantly reduced the extra rotation as compared with the baseline system (Sect. 6.1). The participants also agreed that the proposed system had an advantage in not requiring users to change their orientation and scan surrounding signage [A3–A4]. Participants' feedback on the interface also supported the proposed system's effectiveness [A6–A8].

Regarding the rotation effectiveness, users with the baseline system had to decide correct positions on the basis of arrow reading results, but the proposed system directly provides the correct direction from arrow analysis results. We argue that this accounted for the difference in the task completion time. Excluding the processing time, the proposed system's task completion time (Fig. 5) was significantly shorter than that of the baseline system. Moreover, when the target sign was located behind the participant's initial position, the proposed system's task completion time, including the processing time, was significantly shorter than that of the baseline (Fig. 5).

7.2   Toward More Accurate Wayfinding Systems

For the Wizard-of-Oz-style study, we used equirectangular images for which our algorithm worked successfully from the dataset. However, through the process evaluation (Sect. 4.5), We observed that our algorithm can be improved for real-world usage, and further evaluation in various environments is needed. The arrow detection and OCR performance was a bottleneck for the wayfinding method's accuracy. Specifically, the accuracy, particularly for OCR, decreased when signage was far away from the user. To improve the detection accuracy, we will consider designing an interface that guides the user close to a sign by using arrow or signage detection [34,35] results and then allows them to retake the equirectangular image at a place close to the target sign.

As listed in Table 1, while our graph-theory-based arrow analysis method achieved relatively high accuracy at an international airport (90.0%), its accuracy at an railway station was only 60.0%. The method analyzes arrows by considering only the relative positions of arrows and text. To improve the arrow analysis, we will consider using signage boundaries or CNN-based computer vision techniques such as document layout analysis [5].

While our direction estimation process achieved 84.5% task accuracy, the estimation accuracy decreased when a sign did not directly face the 360-degree camera. To increase direction estimation accuracy, one possible solution would be to detect surrounding cues such as the directions of tactile paving branches from the captured images [36] and use these results for direction estimation.

7.3   Future System Design

Processing Time Reduction. We found no significant differences in the overall task completion time between the proposed system (**including** the processing time) and the baseline system (Fig. 5). Regarding the processing time, we expect to exploit the ever-improving processing power of CPUs and GPUs and the ever-increasing communication bandwidth. We will also design faster algorithms and find a better edge-cloud balance to reduce the processing time.

User Interface Design. While the proposed system's overall performance was positive, we also found opportunities to improve the user interface. Six participants preferred the proposed system, which automatically estimates the correct direction [A3–A4], but P4 gave the baseline system a higher SUS score because it allows users to estimate the correct direction from arrow detection results [A5]. While many participants commented positively on the proposed system's clock-position-based instructions [A6 and A8], P1 found them difficult to understand [A10]. We argue that the requirements for a wayfinding system depend on the user's orientation and mobility (O&M) skills, familiarity with the target public building, and individual preferences. We aim to further explore various types of interface options, including sonification method [27], 3D spatialized audio [23], vibration patterns [16,19], and shape-changing devices [16], to provide more suitable wayfinding instructions to users.

7.4   Limitation of Laboratory-Based User Study

As P3 commented [A14], we agree that there are many differences between our study in a laboratory space and a real-world study in public buildings. First, in a public building, the user would have to stop at a tactile paving intersection to capture images. The lab-based study, which used pre-captured images, did not reproduce this procedure. Second, in complex buildings that repeatedly require wayfinding tasks, users may choose the wrong direction. The lab-based study missed an opportunity to understand how users recover from errors in wayfinding tasks. Third, the acoustic environment in public buildings is hardly reproducible in a laboratory study, which prevents the use of techniques such as echolocation (*e.g.* the direction of wide-open spaces) and sound landmarks (*e.g.* escalators). Thus, we need to confirm the system's practical usability in public buildings that facilitate echolocation and other senses. To explore more suitable interfaces and algorithms in a real-world setting, we will conduct a study in which blind participants are asked to approach a specific goal turn-by-turn in a public space by recognizing signage with our method.

8   Conclusion

We proposed a *one-shot wayfinding* method that uses a 360-degree smartphone camera to recognize all signage around a blind user. The method analyzes the relationship between detected text and arrows on signage and estimates the egocentric direction to a destination. It provides text-to-speech feedback of the estimated direction on the basis of clock positions and gives vibration alerts when the user faces the indicated direction. A user study with eight blind participants in a laboratory revealed that the proposed system enabled them to choose the correct tactile paving branch to a destination more efficiently than with a baseline system. The proposed system significantly reduced the extra rotation, and the task completion time excluding the processing time was significantly shorter than that of the baseline system. While the participants' feedback supported our hypothesis that the proposed method is useful for wayfinding tasks, we also recognized the need for a real-world user study in public buildings. The proposed method has the possibility of assisting users in unknown places without requiring either environmental modifications like distributed beacons or preparation of maps or points-of-interest datasets. We hope to explore this possibility further and make the technology practical to help blind people with daily activities.

Acknowledgments. We would like to thank all participants who took part in our user study. We would also thank Japan Airport Terminal Co., Ltd. and East Japan Railway Company. This work was supported by AMED (JP20dk0310108, JP21dk0310108h0002), JSPS KAKENHI (JP20J23018), and Grant-in-Aid for Young Scientists (Early Bird, Waseda Research Institute for Science and Engineering, BD070Z003100).

References

1. BeSpecular (2016). https://www.bespecular.com
2. Seeing AI (2017). https://www.microsoft.com/en-us/seeing-ai
3. Ahmetovic, D., Gleason, C., Ruan, C., Kitani, K., Takagi, H., Asakawa, C.: NavCog: a navigational cognitive assistant for the blind. In: MobileHCI (2016)
4. Alnafessah, A., Al-Ammar, M.A., Alhadhrami, S., Al-Salman, A., Al-Khalifa, H.S.: Developing an ultra wideband indoor navigation system for visually impaired people. IJDSN **12**, 403–416 (2016)
5. Augusto Borges Oliveira, D., Palhares Viana, M.: Fast CNN-based document layout analysis. In: ICCVW (2017)
6. Bigham, J.P., et al.: VizWiz: nearly real-time answers to visual questions. In: UIST (2010)
7. Brooke, J.: SUS: a 'quick and dirty' usability. In: Usability Evaluation in Industry, p. 189 (1996)
8. Fiannaca, A., Apostolopoulous, I., Folmer, E.: HEADLOCK: a wearable navigation aid that helps blind cane users traverse large open spaces. In: ASSETS (2014)
9. Gabow, H.N., Galil, Z., Spencer, T., Tarjan, R.E.: Efficient algorithms for finding minimum spanning trees in undirected and directed graphs. Combinatorica **6**(2), 109–122 (1986). https://doi.org/10.1007/BF02579168
10. Gallagher, T., Wise, E., Li, B., Dempster, A.G., Rizos, C., Ramsey-Stewart, E.: Indoor positioning system based on sensor fusion for the blind and visually impaired. In: IPIN (2012)
11. Garcia, G., Nahapetian, A.: Wearable computing for image-based indoor navigation of the visually impaired. In: WH. A (2015)
12. Guentert, M.: Improving public transit accessibility for blind riders: a train station navigation assistant. In: ASSETS (2011)
13. Guerreiro, J.A., Ahmetovic, D., Sato, D., Kitani, K., Asakawa, C.: Airport accessibility and navigation assistance for people with visual impairments. In: CHI (2019)
14. Guidelines, I.H.F.: Wayfinding Guidelines International Health Facility Guidelines (2016). http://www.healthfacilityguidelines.com/GuidelineIndex/Index/Wayfinding-Guidelines
15. Jayant, C., Ji, H., White, S., Bigham, J.P.: Supporting blind photography. In: ASSETS (2011)
16. Kayukawa, S., Tatsuya, I., Takagi, H., Morishima, S., Asakawa, C.: Guiding blind pedestrians in public spaces by understanding walking behavior of nearby pedestrians. IMWUT **4**(3), 1–22 (2020)
17. Kelley, J.F.: An iterative design methodology for user-friendly natural language office information applications. TOIS **2**(1), 26–41 (1984)
18. Ko, E., Ju, J.S., Kim, E.Y.: Situation-based indoor wayfinding system for the visually impaired. In: ASSETS (2011)
19. Kuribayashi, M., Kayukawa, S., Takagi, H., Asakawa, C., Morishima, S.: LineChaser: a smartphone-based navigation system for blind people to stand in line. In: CHI (2021)
20. Kuznetsova, A., et al.: The open images dataset v4: unified image classification, object detection, and visual relationship detection at scale. IJCV **128**(7), 1956–1981 (2020)
21. Lee, K., Hong, J., Pimento, S., Jarjue, E., Kacorri, H.: Revisiting blind photography in the context of teachable object recognizers. In: ASSETS (2019)

22. Li, B., Muñoz, J.P., Rong, X., Xiao, J., Tian, Y., Arditi, A.: ISANA: wearable context-aware indoor assistive navigation with obstacle avoidance for the blind. In: ECCVW (2016)
23. Loomis, J.M., Lippa, Y., Klatzky, R.L., Golledge, R.G.: Spatial updating of locations specified by 3-D sound and spatial language. JEP:LMC **28**(2), 335 (2002)
24. Manduchi, R., Coughlan, J.M.: The last meter: blind visual guidance to a target. In: CHI (2014)
25. Pal, J., Viswanathan, A., Song, J.H.: Smartphone adoption drivers and challenges in urban living: cases from Seoul and Bangalore. In: IHCI (2016)
26. Panëels, S.A., Olmos, A., Blum, J.R., Cooperstock, J.R.: Listen to it yourself! Evaluating usability of what's around me? For the blind. In: CHI (2013)
27. Presti, G., et al.: WatchOut: obstacle sonification for people with visual impairment or blindness. In: ASSETS (2019)
28. Redmon, J., Farhadi, A.: YOLOv3: an incremental improvement. arXiv (2018)
29. Saha, M., Fiannaca, A.J., Kneisel, M., Cutrell, E., Morris, M.R.: Closing the gap: designing for the last-few-meters wayfinding problem for people with visual impairments. In: ASSETS (2019)
30. Sato, D., Oh, U., Naito, K., Takagi, H., Kitani, K., Asakawa, C.: NavCog3: an evaluation of a smartphone-based blind indoor navigation assistant with semantic features in a large-scale environment. In: ASSETS (2017)
31. Shen, H., Coughlan, J.M.: Towards a real-time system for finding and reading signs for visually impaired users. In: Miesenberger, K., Karshmer, A., Penaz, P., Zagler, W. (eds.) ICCHP 2012. LNCS, vol. 7383, pp. 41–47. Springer, Heidelberg (2012). https://doi.org/10.1007/978-3-642-31534-3_7
32. Treuillet, S., Royer, E.: Outdoor/indoor vision based localization for blind pedestrian navigation assistance. IJIG **10**, 481–496 (2010)
33. Vázquez, M., Steinfeld, A.: Helping visually impaired users properly aim a camera. In: ASSETS (2012)
34. Wang, S., Tian, Y.: Indoor signage detection based on saliency map and bipartite graph matching. In: ICBBW (2011)
35. Wang, S., Tian, Y.: Camera-based signage detection and recognition for blind persons. In: Miesenberger, K., Karshmer, A., Penaz, P., Zagler, W. (eds.) ICCHP 2012. LNCS, vol. 7383, pp. 17–24. Springer, Heidelberg (2012). https://doi.org/10.1007/978-3-642-31534-3_3
36. Yamanaka, Y., Takaya, E., Kurihara, S.: Tactile tile detection integrated with ground detection using an RGB-depth sensor. In: ICAART (2020)
37. Zhao, Y., Wu, S., Reynolds, L., Azenkot, S.: A face recognition application for people with visual impairments: understanding use beyond the lab. In: CHI (2018)
38. Zhong, Y., Lasecki, W.S., Brady, E., Bigham, J.P.: RegionSpeak: quick comprehensive spatial descriptions of complex images for blind users. In: CHI (2015)

WiFi-Based Multi-task Sensing

Xie Zhang, Chengpei Tang$^{(\boxtimes)}$, Yasong An, and Kang Yin

Sun Yat-Sen University, Guangzhou 510006, China
tchengp@mail.sysu.edu.cn

Abstract. WiFi-based sensing has aroused immense attention over recent years. The rationale is that the signal fluctuations caused by humans carry the information of human behavior which can be extracted from the channel state information of WiFi. Still, the prior studies mainly focus on single-task sensing (STS), e.g., gesture recognition, indoor localization, user identification. Since the fluctuations caused by gestures are highly coupling with body features and the user's location, we propose a WiFi-based multi-task sensing model (Wimuse) to perform gesture recognition, indoor localization, and user identification tasks simultaneously. However, these tasks have different difficulty levels (i.e., imbalance issue) and need task-specific information (i.e., discrepancy issue). To address these issues, the knowledge distillation technique and task-specific residual adaptor are adopted in Wimuse. We first train the STS model for each task. Then, for solving the imbalance issue, the extracted common feature in Wimuse is encouraged to get close to the counterpart features of the STS models. Further, for each task, a task-specific residual adaptor is applied to extract the task-specific compensation feature which is fused with the common feature to address the discrepancy issue. We conduct comprehensive experiments on three public datasets and evaluation suggests that Wimuse achieves state-of-the-art performance with the average accuracy of 85.20%, 98.39%, and 98.725% on the joint task of gesture recognition, indoor localization, and user identification, respectively.

Keywords: Channel state information · Gesture recognition · Human identification · Knowledge distillation · Localization · Multi-task learning · WiFi-based sensing

1 Introduction

WiFi-based sensing has drawn considerable interest over recent years due to its pervasive availability, non-intrusiveness, and low-cost deployment. Numerous studies [1–3] have shown that WiFi-based human sensing can be regarded as a promising candidate to promote human-computer interaction in the Internet of Things (IoT) era. The basic principle of WiFi-based sensing is that some of the signals are absorbed, reflected, or scattered by humans on the propagation, leading to the signal fluctuations which carry the information of human behavior. Further, the signal fluctuations are described by the channel state information (CSI) of WiFi, which can be captured from commercial WiFi devices [4, 5].

© ICST Institute for Computer Sciences, Social Informatics and Telecommunications Engineering 2022
Published by Springer Nature Switzerland AG 2022. All Rights Reserved
T. Hara and H. Yamaguchi (Eds.): MobiQuitous 2021, LNICST 419, pp. 169–189, 2022.
https://doi.org/10.1007/978-3-030-94822-1_10

Despite significant advances in the field of WiFi-based sensing, various pioneering approaches are limited to single-task sensing (STS), such as human activity recognition [6], indoor localization [7], gait identification [8], breath detection [9]. There are some studies on WiFi-based multi-user gesture recognition [10, 11]. However, to our best knowledge, ARIL [1] and WiHF [12] are the only two works on WiFi-based multi-task sensing (MTS). Specifically, ARIL aims to perform the joint task of activity recognition and indoor localization, constructed on the universal software radio peripheral devices, not the commercial WiFi devices, which decreased the practicability. WiHF focuses on simultaneously enabling cross-domain gesture recognition and user identification, which can only deal with the joint gesture recognition and user identification task.

Based on the observation that the signal fluctuations are related to human gestures, body features, and indoor locations, we propose a WiFi-based multi-task sensing model (Wimuse) to perform gesture recognition, user identification, and indoor localization simultaneously. The exploitation of WiFi-based MTS will provide more users' information than STS, which will promote many IoT applications. For example, in the smart home application, Wimuse can provide the information of 'who does what and where?' that will facilitate the smart home system precisely responds to the user. More specifically, we can use 'hand up' to increase the television volume in front of the user and turn on the light with the same gesture in the bathroom. In addition, to ensure safety, adults can use 'draw circle' to turn on the stove, while children cannot use the same gesture to open it.

However, there are two issues in MTS. i) The difficulty levels of these tasks are different, leading to the imbalance issue [13]. Specifically, the gesture recognition task is more difficult than both the indoor localization and the user identification tasks, which may cause two types of undesirable situations in the training phase: the performance of the indoor localization and the user identification tasks are far superior to that of the gesture recognition task. In another case, the gesture recognition task performed well, while the other two tasks are overfitting. ii) Different tasks need task-specific information, namely, the task discrepancy issue. For example, the gesture recognition task needs more detailed pose information than the indoor localization task. However, the detailed pose information is redundant information for the indoor localization task, while this task requires more information about the spatial distribution of objects. Even worse, the useful information of one task may be others' noise [14].

To address these issues, we adopt the knowledge distillation technique [15] and task-specific residual adaptor [16] in Wimuse. Concretely, inspired by the knowledge-distillation-based method [13], we first train the STS model for each task which provides the task-specific feature. Then, in the training phase, we encourage the extracted common feature of Wimuse to get close to all the task-specific features after a linear transform under the Euclidean distance. In this way, the common feature will prevent being dominated by a particular task. For the discrepancy issue, a task-specific residual adaptor is added to extract the task-specific compensation feature for each task which concatenates with the common feature to form the feature of each task in Wimuse. In addition, the predictive logits for each task in Wimuse are encouraged to be similar to that produced by the corresponding trained STS model, which will transfer their generalization ability to Wimuse.

We conduct comprehensive experiments on three public datasets: ARIL dataset [1], CSIDA dataset [17], and Widar3.0 dataset [18]. The experimental results show that Wimuse achieves state-of-art performance on the joint gesture recognition, localization, and user identification task. In summary, our contributions are listed as follows.

i.   To our best knowledge, Wimuse is the first approach of WiFi-based MTS involving more than two tasks and achieve promising performance.
ii. We reveal the imbalance and discrepancy issues in WiFi-based MTS and novelly adopt the knowledge distillation technique and task-specific residual adaptor to address these issues.
iii. We evaluate Wimuse on three public datasets, the results show that Wimuse achieves the average accuracy of 85.20%, 98.39%, and 98.725% for the joint gesture recognition, indoor localization, and user identification tasks.

2   Related Work

In this section, we first introduce the WiFi-based sensing approaches. Then, some studies on multi-task learning and knowledge distillation are briefly presented.

2.1   WiFi-Based Sensing

Numerous studies of WiFi-based sensing have been proposed on many applications, including gesture recognition, indoor localization, and human identification, etc.

In [3], the authors proposed SignFi, based on a convolutional neural network (CNN), to recognize gestures. The experimental results showed the average accuracy is 86.66% by using the CSI as input, which shown the effectiveness of CNN for extracting the features from CSI samples. To promote the practicability of WiFi-based sensing, [19] proposed a WiFi-based gesture recognition system for smartphones. In addition, due to the environmental sensitivity of WiFi signals, [20] adopted adversarial learning to train environment-invariant feature extractors to construct a robust WiFi-based gesture recognition system. It is worth noting that [10] and [11] accomplished gesture recognition systems that can recognize multiple users' gestures simultaneously.

WiFi-based indoor localization approaches can be summarized into two categories: **i) Physical approaches** try to estimate physical factors of WiFi signal, such as Angle of Arrival (AOA), Time of Flight (TOF), and Doppler Frequency Shift (DFS). Then, the target position is calculated through physical and geometric models based on the estimated physical factors. For example, [21] proposed an indoor localization system, named Phaser, based on the estimation of AOA. In addition, K. Wu et al. [22] proposed a fine-grand indoor localization method FILA to directly estimate the distance between the object and the three fixed access points. **ii) Pattern-based approaches** are dedicated to finding the location-discriminate representation of CSI to perform the localization task. Fingerprint-based localization is the most commonly used pattern-based approach, the main idea of which is to collect CSI samples of all possible locations in the area of interest to build a fingerprint database. Next, two methods are applied to perform the localization using the fingerprints. One is to match the unknown fingerprints with those in the database and return the location of the best-fitted fingerprint [7]. The other is to train a deep learning model to map the fingerprints to their location labels using the fingerprint database as a training dataset, then return the location label of the trained model with the unknown fingerprint as input [1, 23, 24]. Note that, in this work, we adopt the latter method for the indoor localization task.

User identification is the process of associating a user with a predefined identity. WiHF [12] performed user identification and gesture recognition using CSI in a real-time manner based on the difference between the personal user performing styles and the unique gesture characteristics. In [25], the authors conducted a feasibility study for user identification using the CSI of the user's in-air handwritten signatures. In this work, the user identification is performed based on the observation that the CSI is different with different users even at the same position and performing the same gesture.

2.2 Multi-task Learning

Multi-task learning is a subfield of machine learning that is dedicated to constructing one model to perform multiple tasks simultaneously. Multi-task learning has been studied in various research fields, including computer vision [26], natural language processing [27], speech recognition [28], etc. However, according to existing works, two challenges hinder the better performance and efficiency to be improved.

The first one is called task-imbalance that the multi-task learning model is dominated by a particular task leading to unacceptable performances of the other tasks. Some previous studies addressed this issue with balanced loss weighting and parameter updating strategies [29, 30]. In [31], the authors explicitly cast multi-task learning as multi-objective optimization, with the overall objective of finding a Pareto optimal solution. Wei-Hong Li et al. [13] constructed a novel idea combining the knowledge distillation method to solve the task imbalance issue. Based on this idea, a more in-depth study is conducted and some new solutions are proposed in this paper.

The other is task-discrepancy for different tasks may require different task-specific information. The lack of task-specific information may degrade the performance of the multi-task learning model. Even worse, the task-specific information of different tasks may contract with each other, which means that one's useful information may others' noise [14]. In this work, we adopt the residual adaptor blocks [16] to extract the task-specific compensation information to address this issue.

2.3 Knowledge Distillation

Knowledge distillation (KD), proposed by Hinton et al. [15], is dedicated to transforming the learned knowledge in an ensemble of models into a single model and is adopted in model compression [32], transfer learning [33], domain adaptation [34], and multimodal learning [35], etc.

In addition to success in single-task learning, knowledge distillation has also been proved to be efficient in multi-task learning. Dan Xu et al. [36] proposed a novel multi-task guided prediction-and-distillation network to perform the joint tasks for depth estimation and scene parsing. Sahil Chelaramani et al. [37] proposed the use of multi-task learning and knowledge distillation to improve fine-grained recognition of eye diseases using a small labeled dataset of fundus images.

In this work, we adopt the knowledge distillation technique to address the task-imbalance issue, which is inspired by the knowledge distillation-based method [13]. In addition, to sufficiently exploit the trained STS model, we add a new loss in Wimuse to encourage the predictive logits for each task to get closer to that produced by the corresponding trained STS model. The experimental results conduct that this trick can promote the performance of Wimuse.

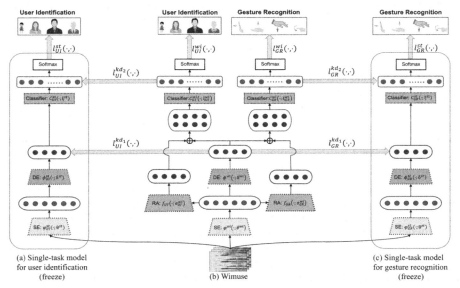

Fig. 1. The framework of Wiumuse (an example in the two-task condition, i.e. user identification and gesture recognition). We first train the task-specific STS model for each task (i.e. (a) and (c)). Then, freezing the learned parameters of the STS models. In the training phase of Wimuse, we optimize the parameters by minimizing the losses.

3 Methodology

In this section, we present the framework of Wimuse as shown in Fig. 1. Concretely, we first introduce the input and four basic modules (i.e., shallow encoder, deep encoder, task-specific residual adaptor, and classifier). Then, we will discuss the STS model and the naïve MTS model. Finally, Wimuse is proposed.

3.1 Overview

As illustrated in Fig. 1, we adopt the CSI sample as input to implement the sensing tasks. Specifically, CSI reflects multipath fluctuations of WiFi signal on all subcarriers. For each subcarrier, we can model the channel impulse response as:

$$h(t) = \sum_{i=0}^{I-1} a_i \delta(t - \tau_i) e^{-j2\pi f_i} \tag{1}$$

where I denotes the number of signal paths. a_i, $2\pi f_i$, and τ_i are the attenuation factor, phase shift, and time delay of the signal on the i-th path, respectively. In addition, f_i represents the frequency of subcarrier, $\delta(t)$ is the Dirac delta function.

Further, the orthogonal frequency division multiplexing receiver can sample the CIR in all subcarriers to construct a complex matrix, i.e., a CSI matrix. Hence that, CSI can be denoted as:

$$H = \|H\| e^{j \angle H} \tag{2}$$

where H denotes the CSI measurement on all subcarriers. $\|H\|$ and $\angle H$ represent the amplitude and phase, respectively.

In this work, we adopt $\|H\| \in R^{L \times S \times T}$ as input, where L is the number of links, namely, $L = RX \times TX$, RX and TX is the number of antennas of the receiver and the transmitter. S denotes the number of subcarriers. P represents the length of sampling, which is determined by the sampling rate r of the CSI capture tool and the gesture execution time t (i.e., $P = r \times t$). hence that, the input $\|H\| \in R^{L \times S \times P}$ can be regarded as the reflection of signal fluctuations on three dimensions, i.e., spatial, frequency, and time.

In addition, we provide four basic modules to construct the STS model, the naïve MTS model, and Wimuse. Note that the implementation details of these modules are presented in Sect. 4, while a brief introduction is as follows.

i.   **shallow encoder (SE)**: For extracting the features on links of input $\|H\| \in R^{L \times S \times P}$, the shallow encoder, denoted as $\varphi(\cdot)$, contains a grouping convolutional layer and a max-pooling layer, where the number of groups equals the number of links L.

ii. **deep encoder (DE)**: By using the low-level features extracted by the Shallow Encoder as input, a deeper convolutional subnetwork $\phi(\cdot)$ is adopted to fusion the features of different links and extract high-level features. In addition, this module is constructed based on the structure of ResNet [38].

iii. **task-specific residual adaptor (RA)**: To deal with the task discrepancy issue, a Task-specific residual adaptor $f(\cdot)$, which contains only one convolutional layer, is adopted in the Wimuse to gain the task-specific compensation feature from the low-level features.

iv. **classifier**: For each classification task, a classifier $C(\cdot)$, which contains a convolutional layer and a fully connected layer, is adopted to output the logits. Then, by using the softmax function on the predictive logits, the probability over categories is produced.

Note that, all the convolutional layers in the above modules adopt one-dimensional convolution along the time dimension of CSI. We using superscripts *st*, *mt*, and *wi* to denote the modules in the STS model, the naïve MTS model, and the Wimuse model, respectively. In addition, the subscript of the above modules' symbols represents the task, i.e., *UI* denotes user identification, *GR* is the gesture recognition, and *IL* presents indoor localization. For example, $C_{UI}^{st}(\cdot)$ presents the Classifier module of an STS model at the user identification task.

3.2 Single-Task Sensing Model

Consider that we have a dataset D that contains N training CSI samples H_n and their labels $y_n \in \{1, 2, \ldots, M\}$, for $n \in \{1, 2, \ldots, N\}$, where M is the number of categories. In this case, the STS model is composed of three parts: **i)** a shallow encoder $\varphi^{st}(\cdot; \theta^{st})$, where θ^{st} are the learned parameters. Given a CSI sample H_n as input, the output of $\varphi^{st}(\cdot; \theta^{st})$ is the low-level features on all links, i.e. $F_n^{st,low} = \varphi^{st}(H_n; \theta^{st})$. **ii)** a deep encoder $\phi^{st}(\cdot; \delta^{st})$ is adopted to fusion the low-level features across links and map to high-level features $F^{st,high}$, where δ^{st} denotes the learned parameters. Hence, the output of the Deep Encoder is $F_n^{st,high} = \phi^{st}(\cdot; \delta^{st}) \circ \varphi^{st}(H_n; \theta^{st})$. **iii)** To output the predictive probability distribution over categories, a classifier $C(\cdot; \xi^{st})$ is used to output the predictive logits $\mathbf{Z}^{st} \in R^M$, where ξ^{st} presents the learned parameters. Particularly, the predictive logits of H_n is $\mathbf{Z}_n^{st} = C(\cdot; \xi^{st}) \circ \phi^{st}(\cdot; \delta^{st}) \circ \varphi^{st}(H_n; \theta^{st})$. Then, the predictive probability distribution p_n of H_n over categories is produced by using the softmax function as follows:

$$p_n(\widehat{y_n} = m|H_n) = \sigma(\mathbf{Z}_n^{st})_m \tag{3}$$

where $\widehat{y_n}$ is the predicted label of H_n and $m \in \{1, 2, \ldots, M\}$. $\sigma(\cdot)_m$ is the softmax function, defined as:

$$\sigma(\mathbf{Z})_m = \frac{e^{Z_m}}{\sum_{k=1}^{M} e^{Z_k}}, \quad for \ \mathbf{Z} \in \mathbf{R}^M, m \in \{1, 2, \ldots, M\} \tag{4}$$

To optimize the parameters of the STS model, a loss function $l^{st}(\cdot, \cdot)$ based on cross-entropy is adopted. The loss for H_n is as follows:

$$l^{st}(p_n, y_n) = -\sum_{m=1}^{M} (1|y_n = m) \log(p_n(\widehat{y_n} = m|H_n)) \tag{5}$$

where $(1|y_n = m)$ means if $y_n = m$ is true, $(1|y_n = m)$ equals 1, otherwise, 0.

The goal is to minimize the sum of losses overall training samples.

$$\left(\theta_{opt}^{st}, \delta_{opt}^{st}, \xi_{opt}^{st}\right) = arg \min_{\theta^{st}, \delta^{st}, \xi^{st}} \sum_{n=1}^{N} l^{st}(p_n, y_n) \tag{6}$$

3.3 Naïve Multi-task Sensing Model

The naïve MTS model is based on the classic multi-task learning model proposed in [26]. Specifically, the naïve MTS model has only one difference from the STS model. Consider that we are given a dataset D containing N training CSI samples H_n and their labels y_n where $n \in \{1, 2, \ldots, N\}$. Note that, there are T tasks to performance, i.e. $y_n \in R^T$. The element $y_{t,n} \in \{1, 2, \ldots, M_t\}$ is the label of H_n on the t − th task, where M_t is the number of categories on the t-th task.

The naïve MTS model has the same encoder structure as the above STS model. Then the high-level features $F_n^{mt,high}$ of H_n is $\phi^{mt}(\cdot; \delta^{mt}) \circ \varphi^{mt}(H_n; \theta^{mt})$. Compared with the STS model, there are T classifiers in the naïve MTS model, e.g. $C_t^{mt}(\cdot; \xi^{mt})$ is the classifier of the t-th task. Further, the predictive logits of H_n on the t-th task is $Z_{t,n}^{mt} = C_t^{mt}(\cdot; \xi_t^{mt}) \circ \phi^{mt}(\cdot; \delta_t^{mt}) \circ \varphi^{mt}(H_n; \theta^{mt}) \in R^M$. Finally, the predictive probability distribution of H_n over category on the t-th task is:

$$p_{t,n}(\widehat{y_{t,n}} = m_t | H_n) = \sigma(Z_{t,n}^{mt})_{m_t}, \quad for \ \ m_t \in \{1, 2, \ldots, M_t\} \tag{7}$$

where $\widehat{y_{t,n}}$ is the predicted label of H_n on the t-th task, $m_t \in \{1, 2, \ldots, M_t\}$. $\sigma(\cdot)_{m_t}$ is the softmax function as (4).

The loss function for the t-th task $l_t^{mt}(\cdot, \cdot)$ in naïve MTS model is the same as that in STS model, i.e. $l_t^{mt}(p_{t,n}, y_{t,n}) = l^{st}(p_{t,n}, y_{t,n})$. Then the linear combination of all the task-specific loss constructs the final loss of the naïve MTS model, namely,

$$l^{mt}(p_n, y_n) = \sum_{t=1}^{T} \omega_t l_t^{mt}(p_{t,n}, y_{t,n}) \tag{8}$$

where ω_t is a hyperparameter for the t-th task, $p_n = \{p_{1,n}, p_{2,n}, \cdots, p_{T,n}\}$ is the set of predictive probability distributions of the sample of all tasks.

Finally, the naïve MTS model can be learned by optimizing the following loss:

$$\left(\theta^{mt}, \delta^{mt}, \xi_1^{mt}, \xi_2^{mt}, \cdots, \xi_T^{mt}\right)_{opt} = arg \min_{\theta^{mt}, \delta^{mt}, \xi_1^{mt}, \xi_2^{mt}, \cdots, \xi_T^{mt}} \sum_{n=1}^{N} \sum_{t=1}^{T} \omega_t l_t^{mt}(p_{t,n}, y_{t,n}) \tag{9}$$

3.4 Wimuse Model

The Wimuse model is based on the naïve MTS model while introducing the knowledge distillation method and task-specific residual adaptor to address the task imbalance and discrepancy issues.

Given the same dataset D as the above MTS model. In this case, the Wimuse model is composed as following parts:

i)   We first adopt a shallow encoder, denoted as $\varphi^{wi}(\cdot; \theta^{wi})$, to extract the low-level features on all links, θ^{wi} is the learned parameters. For example, the low-level features of the sample H_n is $F_n^{wi,low} = \varphi^{wi}(H_n; \theta^{wi})$.

ii) To address the task discrepancy issue, we adopt a task-specific residual adaptor $f(\cdot; \sigma^{wi})$ for each task to extract the task-specific compensation feature, denoted as $F^{wi,comp}$. For example, the task-specific compensation feature of H_n at the t − th task is $F_{t,n}^{wi,comp} = f_t(\cdot; \sigma_t^{wi}) \circ \varphi^{wi}(H_n; \theta^{wi})$.

iii) The common feature $F_n^{wi,comm}$ of sample H_n for all tasks are extracted by a deep encoder $\phi^{wi}(\cdot; \delta^{wi})$ using $F_n^{wi,low}$ as input, i.e. $F_n^{wi,comm} = \phi^{wi}(F_n^{wi,low}; \delta^{wi})$.

iv) Similar to the MTS model, Wimuse also have T classifiers, e.g. for the t − th task, the classifier is $C_t^{wi}(\cdot; \xi_t^{wi})$. Note that, the input for each classifier is the composition of the corresponding task-specific compensation feature and the common features. For example, the input for $C_t^{wi}(\cdot; \xi_t^{wi})$ of the sample H_n is $F_{t,n}^{wi,comp} \oplus F_n^{wi,comm}$, where $\oplus$ presents the concatenate operation. In addition, the output of $C_t^{wi}(\cdot; \xi_t^{wi})$, for the sample H_n, is the predictive logits of the t-th task, i.e.

$$Z_{t,n}^{wi} = C_t^{wi}\left(F_{t,n}^{wi,comp} \oplus F_n^{wi,comm}; \xi_t^{wi}\right) \tag{10}$$

For the task imbalance issue, a knowledge-distillation-based method [13] is adopted in Wimuse. Concretely, for each task, we first train an STS model, e.g. for the t-th task, we train an STS model $M_t^{st}(\cdot; \theta^{st}, \delta^{st}, \xi^{st})$. Then we freeze the learned parameters of this model. Further, with an input H_n, M_t^{st} can provide the high-level features $F_{t,n}^{st,high}$ and the logits $Z_{t,n}^{st}$ for the t-th task. Then, at the training phase of Wimuse, we construct a loss function $l_t^{kd_1}(\cdot, \cdot)$ to encourage the common feature $F_n^{wi,comm}$, extracted by Wimuse, to get close to all of the high-level features produced by the trained STL models after a linear transform under the Euclidean distance. For example, for the t-th task on the sample H_n, the loss $l_{t,n}^{kd_1}$ is as follows:

$$l_{t,n}^{kd_1} = \left\| \frac{LT_t\left(F_n^{wi,comm}\right)}{\left\|LT_t\left(F_n^{wi,comm}\right)\right\|_2} - \frac{F_{t,n}^{st,high}}{\left\|F_{t,n}^{st,high}\right\|_2} \right\|_2 \tag{11}$$

where $LT_t(\cdot)$ is the linear transform for the t-th task, which is implemented as a $1 \times 1 \times C \times C$ convolution, where C is the depth (number of channels) of $F_n^{wi,comm}$.

Furthermore, to sufficiently exploit the trained STS models, we also encourage the predictive logits $Z_{t,n}^{wi}$ to be similar with the logits $Z_{t,n}^{st}$ for sample H_n on the t-th task, which leads to another loss:

$$l_{t,n}^{kd_2} = - \sum_{m_t=1}^{M_t} \left(P_{1,m_t} \cdot \log\left(P_{2,m_t}\right)\right) \tag{12}$$

Where P_{1,m_t} and P_{2,m_t} is the predictive probability distribution based on $Z_{t,n}^{wi}$ and $Z_{t,n}^{st}$, calculated as follows:

$$P_{1,m_t} = \sigma\left(\frac{Z_{t,n}^{wi}}{\tau}\right)_{m_t} \tag{13}$$

$$P_{2,m_t} = \sigma\left(\frac{Z_{t,n}^{st}}{\tau}\right)_{m_t} \tag{14}$$

Where $\sigma(\cdot)_{m_t}$ is the softmax function as (4). And τ is a hyperparameter to adjust the intensity of distillation [15].

The final output of Wimuse for input sample H_n is a set of the probability distribution $P_n = \{p_{1,n}, p_{2,n}, \cdots, p_{T,n}\}$ of all T tasks. The element is defined as follows:

$$p_{t,n}\left(\widehat{y_{t,n}} = m_t | H_n\right) = \sigma\left(Z_{t,n}^{wi}\right)_{m_t} \tag{15}$$

where $\widehat{y_{t,n}}$ is the predicted label of H_n on the t-th task, and $m_t \in \{1, 2, \ldots, M_t\}$. $\sigma(\cdot)_{m_t}$ is the softmax function as (4).

The loss function for the final prediction is as follows,

$$l^{wi}\left(p_n, y_n\right) = \sum_{t=1}^{T} \omega_t l_t^{wi}\left(p_{t,n}, y_{t,n}\right) \tag{16}$$

where ω_t is a hyperparameter for the t-th task and $l_t^{wi}(\cdot, \cdot)$ is identical with $l^{st}(\cdot, \cdot)$ (refer to (5)).

The parameters of Wimuse can be learned by minimizing the following loss:

$$l(\text{D}) = \sum_{n=1}^{N} \sum_{t=1}^{T} \left(\omega_t l_t^{wi}\left(p_{t,n}, y_{t,n}\right) + \lambda l_{t,n}^{kd_1} + l_{t,n}^{kd_2}\right) \tag{17}$$

where D is the training set and λ is the weight of the loss $l_t^{kd_1}$.

Algorithm 1: Episode-based training for Wimuse

$\varphi_t^{st}(\cdot)$: the pre-trained shallow encoder of single task model (STM) for t-th task.
$\phi_t^{st}(\cdot)$: the pre-trained deep encoder of STM for t-th task.
$C_t^{st}(\cdot)$: the pre-trained classifier of STM for t-th task.
$\varphi^{wi}(\cdot)$: the shallow encoder of Wimuse.
$\phi^{wi}(\cdot)$: the deep encoder of Wimuse.
$C_t^{wi}(\cdot)$: the classifier of the t-th task in Wimuse.
$f_t(\cdot)$: the task-specific residual adaptor of Wimuse for the t-th task.

Input: Training set P= $\{(x_i, y_{t,i})\}_{i=1}^N$, where $y_{t,i} \in \{1,2,...,M_t\}$ is the label of sample x_i on the $t - $th task, and where M_t is the number of categories on the t-th task.

Output: The loss J of a randomly generated episode.

Beginning:
   Give a sample $(x_i, y_{t,i})$ from P randomly.
   $F^{wi,comm} = \phi^{wi}(\cdot) \circ \varphi^{wi}(x_i)$.
   // calculate the common feature in Wimuse
   $F_{t,i}^{wi,comp} = f_t(\cdot) \circ \varphi^{wi}(x_i)$
   // calculate the compensation feature of the t-th task in Wimuse
   for t in $\{1,2,...T\}$ do
      $Z_t^{wi} = C_t^{wi}(F_{t,n}^{wi,comp} \oplus F_n^{wi,comm})$
      // calculate the predictive logits of the t-th task in Wimuse
      $F_t^{st,high} = \phi_t^{st}(\cdot) \circ \varphi_t^{st}(x_i)$
      // calculate the high-level feature of the t-th task in pre-trained STM.
      $Z_t^{st} = C_t^{st}(\cdot) \circ \phi_t^{st}(\cdot) \circ \varphi_t^{st}(x_i)$.
      // calculate the predictive logits of the t-th task in pre-trained STM.
      Calculate $l_{t,i}^{kd1}$ (where the kd1 loss of the t-th task) by using (11).
      Calculate $l_{t,i}^{kd2}$ (i.e., the kd2 loss of the t-th task) by using (12).
      Calculate $l_{t,i}^{wi}$ (i.e., the final loss of the t-th task) by using (16).
   End for
   $L \leftarrow 0$ // Initialize loss.
   $L \leftarrow \sum_{t=1}^T (\omega_t l_t^{wi}(p_{t,n}, y_{t,n}) + \lambda l_{t,n}^{kd1} + l_{t,n}^{kd2})$ // Update loss.
End

---

4 Experiment

In this section, we evaluate Wimuse on three public datasets under two-task and three-task sensing scenarios through using the amplitude data. As for the whole dataset, we divide 80% of them for training and 20% for testing.

CSI measured on commercial WiFi devices is well-known to contain phase offsets, including carrier frequency offset (CFO), sampling frequency offset (SFO), and symbol timing offset (STO). These phase offsets are strongly relevant to the CSI capture device, which means the phase data of various public datasets has different phase offsets and we can not use the same methods to eliminate them. In addition, we are inclined to have a more general model. Therefore, we give up the phase data of these public datasets and just use the amplitude data of them.

The pseudocode of the training scheme of Wimuse is in Algorithm 1, and the python code of Wimuse is available at https://github.com/Zhang-xie/Wimuse.

4.1 Datasets

ARIL Dataset. ARIL dataset is proposed in [1] for the joint task of activity recognition and indoor location. Specifically, it contains the CSI samples of six gestures (i.e., up, down, left, right, circle, and cross.) in 16 locations of one room by one volunteer. In addition, the CSI samples were collected by using a pair of universal software radio peripherals (USRPs) and the total number of samples is 1440. Each sample has the shape of $1 \times 52 \times 192$, i.e. one link, 52 subcarriers, and 192 packets for one sample.

CSIDA Dataset. CSIDA dataset [17] contains CSI samples of six gestures (i.e., hand left, hand right, lift, press, draw circle, and draw zigzag) in five different locations by five users. The samples are captured from laptops (i.e., one transmitter and one receiver) equipped with the Atheros CSI tool [39]. In addition, devices are set to work at monitor mode at 5 GHz to capture information of 114 subcarriers. The transmitter and receiver activate one and three antennas, respectively. Further, the sampling rate is 1000 packets per s and the gesture execution time is 1.8 s. There are 1500 samples with the shape $3 \times 114 \times 1800$.

Widar3.0 Dataset. Widar3.0 [18] contains two sub-datasets: Dataset1 contains 12000 CSI samples collected from 16 users performing six gestures (push & pull, sweep, clap, slide, draw a circle and draw zigzag) in five different locations at three different environments, i.e., a classroom, an office, and a hall. Dataset2 holds 5,000 instances of two volunteers (one male and one female) drawing numbers 0–9 in a horizontal plane. In addition, each CSI sample in the Widar3.0 dataset is collected by six receivers and one transmitter all with three antennas. Due to the use of the 802.11n CSI tool [5], there are 30 subcarriers for each link, and send 1000 package per s. The CSI sample of one receiver has the shape of $3 \times 30 \times P$, where P represents the length of sampling from 1300 to 2200. In this work, we only adopt the samples from one receiver and Dataset1 to evaluate gesture recognition, user identification, and localization tasks.

4.2 Baselines

In this work, we compare our method Wimuse with four baselines. Note that, these baselines are constructed for CSI samples with the proposed basic modules keeping the original framework. The architecture details of the basic modules are illustrated in Table 1.

Table 1. The architectures of the basic modules

Module	Layers	Input (No. channel × length)	Kernel size	stride
Shallow encoder	1D-Convolution	$(L * S) \times P$	7×1	2
	1D-BatchNorm	$(128 * L) \times (P/2)$	–	–
	1D-Max-pooling	$(128 * L) \times (P/2)$	3×1	2
Deep encoder	1D-Convolution	$(128 * L) \times (P/4)$	3×1	1
	1D-BatchNorm	$(128 * L) \times (P/4)$	–	–
	1D-Convolution	$(128 * L) \times (P/4)$	3×1	1
	1D-BatchNorm	$(128 * L) \times (P/4)$	–	–
	1D-Convolution	$(128 * L) \times (P/4)$	3×1	2
	1D-BatchNorm	$(128 * L) \times (P/8)$	–	–
	1D-Convolution	$(128 * L) \times (P/8)$	3×1	1
	1D-BatchNorm	$(128 * L) \times (P/8)$	–	–
	1D-Convolution	$(128 * L) \times (P/8)$	3×1	2
	1D-BatchNorm	$(128 * L) \times (P/8)$	–	–
	1D-Convolution	$(128 * L) \times (P/8)$	3×1	1
	1D-BatchNorm	$(128 * L) \times (P/8)$	–	–
Classifier	1D-Convolution	$(128 * L) \times (P/8)$	3×1	1
	1D-BatchNorm	$(128*L*2) \times 10$	–	–
	1D-AadAvgPool	$(128*L*2) \times 10$	–	–
	Linear	$(128*L*2) \times 1$	–	–
Residual adaptor	1D-Convolution	$(128 * L) \times (P/4)$	3×1	2
	1D-BatchNorm	$(128 * L) \times (P/8)$	–	–

S denotes the number of CSI subcarriers. P represents the time length of the CSI sample. L is the number of links. 1D is the abbreviation of one-dimensional. AadAvgPool is the adaptive average pooling layer.

- The **STS** model for each task.
- **NMTS**: The naïve MTS model learned by minimizing the loss in (9) with the hyperparameters $\omega_t = 1$ for all tasks.
- **UMTS**: The naïve MTS model is enhanced by a principled approach [29] which weighs multiple loss functions by considering the homoscedastic uncertainty of each task to address the task unbalanced issue.
- **KDMTS**: This approach [13] addresses the unbalanced issue based on knowledge distillation. Since this method is published for joint image segmentation and depth estimation tasks, we implement this method with the abovementioned basic modules keeping the original framework.

4.3 Comparison

We compare our method to the baselines. Besides, on the ARIL dataset, we also compared it with the ARIL method [1]. We use the mean accuracy as an evaluation standard.

Table 2. Performance of various methods on ARIL dataset (Accuracy: %)

Type	Method	Two-task Sensing		Average
		GR	IL	
STS	–	88.77	98.69	93.73
MTS	NMTS	93.19	98.45	95.82
	ARIL	88.13	95.68	91.91
	UMTS	94.15	98.80	96.48
	KDMTS	93.79	98.45	96.12
	Wimuse (ours)	**95.70**	**99.16**	**97.43**

GR, IL are the abbreviations of gesture recognition and indoor localization, respectively.

Results on ARIL. Firstly, we evaluate all methods on the ARIL dataset. We set the minibatch size as eight and use Adam [40] for optimizing the models. The initial learning rate is set to 0.001 and we train all methods for 500 epochs in total where we scaled the learning rate by 0.5 every 100 epochs until the 350th epoch. In Wimuse, weights of task-specific residual adaptor losses (i.e. Eq. (11)) and logits losses (i.e. Eq. (12)) are set uniformly. After the hyperparameter (λ) search, it is set 4.0 for KDMTS, and 8.0 for Wimuse. In addition, another hyperparameter (τ) to adjust the intensity of distillation is also set to 8.0 in Wimuse.

As shown in Table 2, except for the ARIL method, the MTS methods obtain better overall performance than STS, which proves that MTS models can learn more informative features than the STS model. Furthermore, ARIL obtains worse overall performance because of its deep neural network and negligence of the abovementioned task-imbalance even task-discrepancy problem. In contrast, our method achieves significantly better performance than any other MTS method, i.e. our method achieves an accuracy of 95.70% for gesture recognition and 99.16% for indoor localization, which results from our solutions of the task-imbalance and task-discrepancy problem.

Results on Widar3.0 Dataset. Different from the experimental setup on ARIL, we performed two groups of experiments on the Widar3.0 dataset. 1) the two-task sensing including the joint gesture recognition and indoor localization task, the joint gesture recognition and user identification task, and the joint indoor localization and user identification task. 2) The three-task sensing is the joint of gesture recognition, IL, and user identification tasks. Corresponding to the four experiments, we set the hyperparameter λ and τ to the same value 2.0. Beyond this, the other experimental setups are the same as those in experiments on the ARIL dataset.

Table 3. Performance of various methods on Widar3.0 (Accuracy: %)

Type	Method	Two-task Sensing		Two-task Sensing		Two-task Sensing		Three-task Sensing		
		GR	IL	GR	UI	IL	UI	GR	IL	UI
STS	–	–	–	–	–	–	–	80.42	**96.96**	97.19
MTS	NMTS	81.79	96.15	81.63	97.29	96.24	97.17	81.74	96.38	96.78
	UMTS	80.7	96.19	82.09	97.45	95.36	97.26	81.70	96.38	96.78
	KDMTS	82.53	96.24	81.44	97.17	96.20	97.52	83.65	96.92	97.01
	Wimuse (ours)	**85.27**	**96.84**	**82.46**	**97.59**	**96.46**	**97.91**	**83.79**	96.73	**98.05**

GR, IL, and UI are the abbreviations of gesture recognition, indoor localization, and user identification.

From the results shown in Table 3, we can see that it is possible to tackle multiple sensing tasks within a network and achieve performance improvement on some tasks, e.g. compared with STS on the three-task sensing experiment, the NMTS model achieves better performance on gesture recognition though it causes indoor localization and user identification to a tiny drop. Though the effectivities of using NMTS, it is also clear that the task-imbalance even task-discrepancy problem exists for the recognition accuracy of gesture recognition is lower a lot than both of that in indoor localization and user identification tasks. Then we apply existing methods for solving the task-imbalance problem. From the results of using UMTS and KDMTS, UMTS performs as well as KDMTS obtains better overall performance than NMTS. However, they perform solely better on gesture recognition but worse on indoor localization and user identification in the comparison with the STS model.

In comparison with these methods, our method obtains significant overall performance and achieves better results than other MTS models and STS, which strongly verifies the effectiveness of our proposed strategies for feature-logits distillation and compensation of the task-specific features.

Results on CSIDA. Similar to Widar 3.0, we set the hyperparameter λ and τ to the same value for four different experiments, respectively $\lambda = 2.0$ and $\tau = 2.0$, as well.

As shown in Table 4, except for UMTS, the MTS models obtain better performance on gesture recognition tasks than the STS model and almost as excellent performance on indoor localization and user identification as the STS model. We assume that the UMTS may merely fit for applications in computer vision because its performance worse than NMTS. In addition, KDMTS performs slightly worse than NMTS, and our method remains outstanding performance among these methods.

Table 4. Performance of various methods on CSIDA (Accuracy: %)

Type	Method	Two-task Sensing		Two-task Sensing		Two-task Sensing		Three-task Sensing		
		GR	IL	GR	UI	IL	UI	GR	IL	UI
STS	–	–	–	–	–	–	–	80.26	99.64	99.82
MTS	NMTS	82.31	99.76	83.24	99.88	99.82	**99.97**	84.30	99.82	99.40
	UMTS	70.12	99.94	80.02	**99.98**	99.88	99.88	78.38	99.76	99.82
	KDMTS	81.78	99.94	83.13	99.88	99.92	99.76	82.72	99.88	99.94
	Wimuse (ours)	**83.07**	**99.94**	**83.48**	99.24	**99.92**	99.82	**84.53**	**99.94**	**99.97**

GR, IL, and UI are the abbreviations of gesture recognition, indoor localization, and user identification.

4.4 Discussion

To better analyze the effect of the task-specific residual adaptor and the logits distillation, we conduct an ablation study on three datasets.

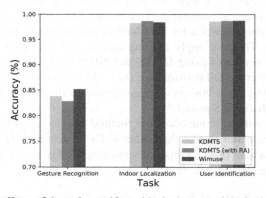

Fig. 2. The effects of the task-specific residual adaptor and the logits distillation

Analysis of Task-Specific Residual Adaptor. As mentioned in Sect. 3, we proposed the residual adaptor (RA), which can extract the task-specific compensation feature from the low-level features, to deal with the discrepancy issue.

From the result shown in Fig. 2, adding the task-specific RA in the KDMTS model obtains better performance on indoor localization and user identification than that it. However, it does not boost the performance of gesture recognition. As for this, we think the reason is that there is a lack of supervised information to train the RA. Since the loss of KDMTS is only related to the common feature extraction and the final predicted labels, we introduce the logits distillation to supply enough information for training.

Analysis of Logits Distillation. As mentioned above, we considered that the supervised information is not enough to train an excellent RA. Then we add logits distillation to sufficiently exploit the trained STS models and enrich the supervised information for Wimuse, which is proved to be extremely efficient.

As presented in Fig. 2, it is clear that Wimuse, adding the logits distillation, achieves a significantly better overall performance. As we expected, the logits distillation brought more information from the trained STS models to Wimuse for better performance.

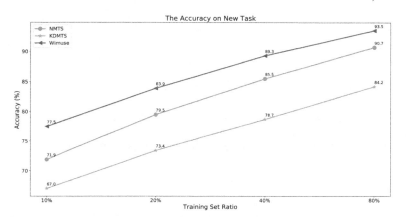

Fig. 3. The effects of the task-specific residual adaptor and the logits distillation

Analysis of Task Scalability. We conduct experiments on CSIDA and Widar3.0 datasets to evaluate the task scalability of Wimuse. Specifically, we construct the three-task version model by adding some modules to the pre-trained two-task version model. Then, we trained the added parts of the three-task version with the new task.

As shown in Fig. 3, the accuracies of NMTS, KDMTS, and Wimuse increase steadily along with the growth of the training set ratio. Further, Wimuse achieves higher accuracy than the other two models, which shows that Wimuse has better task scalability than other models. And the learned common features are more general than those in other models.

Analysis of Model Complexity and Computational Cost. We also compare the model complexity, memory consumption, and runtime under the joint task of gesture recognition and indoor localization on the ARIL dataset. The input size is 52×192 with batch size as 16. As Table 5 demonstrated, the MTS methods (except the ARIL method) have fewer parameters, operations, memory consumption, and runtime. It proves that MTS methods consume less, but is more efficient. In addition, compare with other MTS methods, KDMTS (with RA) and Wimuse increased the computational cost and model complexity. But it is still better than ARIL on computational cost and model complexity.

Table 5. The comparison of different methods.

Type	Method	No. parameters	No. Mult-adds (Million)	Memory (MB)	Time (ms)
STS	For GR task	674,566	285.56	16.18	46.243
	For IL task	677,136	285.60	16.19	45.776
MTS	ARIL	3,490,246	480.82	29.02	50.714
	NMTS	563,222	298.20	16.00	46.767
	UMTS	563,222	298.20	16.00	46.811
	KDMTS	563,222	298.20	16.00	45.831
	KDMTS (with RA)	662,038	411.45	21.12	46.243
	Wimuse (ours)	662,038	411.45	21.12	46.243

'No. parameters' denotes the number of the trainable parameters. 'No. Multi-adds' represents the number of multiplexes and addition operations in labeling a new sample. 'Memory' and 'Time' are the storage memory and time needed in labeling a new sample, respectively.

5   Conclusion

In this paper, we propose a WiFi-based multi-task sensing model (Wimuse) to perform gesture recognition, user identification, and indoor localization simultaneously. First, We reveal the imbalance and discrepancy issues in WiFi-based MTS. Then, we adopt the knowledge distillation technique and task-specific residual adaptor to address these issues. Next, we conduct comprehensive experiments on three public datasets (i.e., the ARIL dataset, the CSIDA dataset, and the Widar3.0 dataset). The evaluation suggests that Wimuse achieves state-of-the-art performance with the average accuracy of 85.20%, 98.39%, and 98.725% on the joint task of gesture recognition, indoor localization, and user identification task respectively.

Though we get satisfying results on Wimuse, there exists still two aspects for improvement, which are that we make no use of the phase data of CSI and we just achieve three tasks simultaneously. There are several fruitful directions for future investigation. i) Wimuse adopt CNN to extract features from the CSI samples. The CSI is time-series data while CNN is not suitable for sequence data. We need to adjust Wimuse to adapt the streaming data. ii) There are other more tasks that we need to exploit for the WiFi-based MTS, such as breath detection, user orientation estimation, fall detection. iii) Since the CSI can be captured from a commercial WiFi device, we can try to deploy Wimuse into the WiFi device. And this requires a lightweight design of Wimuse to satisfy the limitations of memory, computing power in WiFi devices. iv) We can try to utilize the phase data of CSI by developing a general phase denoise method to achieve better performance.

References

1. Wang, F., Feng, J., Zhao, Y., Zhang, X., Zhang, S., Han, J.: Joint activity recognition and indoor localization with WiFi fingerprints. IEEE Access 7, 80058–80068 (2019). https://doi.org/10.1109/ACCESS.2019.2923743
2. Jiang, H., Cai, C., Ma, X., Yang, Y., Liu, J.: Smart home based on WiFi sensing: a survey. IEEE Access 6, 13317–13325 (2018)
3. Ma, Y., Zhou, G., Wang, S., Zhao, H., Jung, W.: SignFi: sign language recognition using WiFi. Proc. ACM Interact. Mob. Wearable Ubiquitous Technol. 2(1), 23:1–23:21 (2018). https://doi.org/10.1145/3191755
4. Atif, M., Muralidharan, S., Ko, H., Yoo, B.: Wi-ESP—a tool for CSI-based device-free Wi-Fi sensing (DFWS). J. Comput. Design Eng. 7(5), 644–656 (2020). https://doi.org/10.1093/jcde/qwaa048
5. Halperin, D., Wenjun, H., Sheth, A., Wetherall, D.: Tool release: gathering 802.11n traces with channel state information. ACM SIGCOMM Comput. Commun. Rev. 41(1), 53–53 (2011). https://doi.org/10.1145/1925861.1925870
6. Jiang, W., et al.: Towards environment independent device free human activity recognition. In: Proceedings of the 24th Annual International Conference on Mobile Computing and Networking, New York, October 2018, pp. 289–304. https://doi.org/10.1145/3241539.3241548
7. Yang, Z., Zhou, Z., Liu, Y.: From RSSI to CSI: indoor localization via channel response. ACM Comput. Surv. 46(2), 1–32 (2013). https://doi.org/10.1145/2543581.2543592
8. Zhang, Y., Zheng, Y., Zhang, G., Qian, K., Qian, C., Yang, Z.: GaitID: robust Wi-Fi based gait recognition. In: Yu, D., Dressler, F., Yu, J. (eds.) WASA 2020. LNCS, vol. 12384, pp. 730–742. Springer, Cham (2020). https://doi.org/10.1007/978-3-030-59016-1_60
9. Zhang, D., Hu, Y., Chen, Y., Zeng, B.: BreathTrack: tracking indoor human breath status via commodity WiFi. IEEE Internet Things J. 6(2), 3899–3911 (2019)
10. Tan, S., Zhang, L., Wang, Z., Yang, J.: MultiTrack: multi-user tracking and activity recognition using commodity WiFi. In: Proceedings of the 2019 CHI Conference on Human Factors in Computing Systems, New York, May 2019, pp. 1–12. https://doi.org/10.1145/3290605.3300766
11. Venkatnarayan, R.H., Mahmood, S., Shahzad, M.: WiFi based multi-user gesture recognition. IEEE Trans. Mobile Comput. 20(3), 1242–1256 (2019)
12. Li, C., Liu, M., Cao, Z.: WiHF: enable user identified gesture recognition with WiFi, pp. 586–595 (2020)
13. Li, W.-H., Bilen, H.: Knowledge distillation for multi-task learning. In: Bartoli, A., Fusiello, A. (eds.) ECCV 2020. LNCS, vol. 12540, pp. 163–176. Springer, Cham (2020). https://doi.org/10.1007/978-3-030-65414-6_13
14. Maninis, K.-K., Radosavovic, I., Kokkinos, I.: Attentive single-tasking of multiple tasks. In: Proceedings of the IEEE/CVF Conference on Computer Vision and Pattern Recognition, pp. 1851–1860 (2019)
15. Hinton, G., Vinyals, O., Dean, J.: Distilling the knowledge in a neural network (2015). http://arxiv.org/abs/1503.02531. Accessed 02 May 2021
16. Rebuffi, S.-A., Bilen, H., Vedaldi, A.: Efficient Parametrization of Multi-Domain Deep Neural Networks, pp. 8119–8127 (2018). https://openaccess.thecvf.com/content_cvpr_2018/html/Rebuffi_Efficient_Parametrization_of_CVPR_2018_paper.html. Accessed 21 May 2021
17. Pengli, H., Tang, C., Yin, K., Zhang, X.: WiGR: a practical Wi-Fi-based gesture recognition system with a lightweight few-shot network. Appl. Sci. 11(8), 3329 (2021). https://doi.org/10.3390/app11083329

18. Zheng, Y., et al.: Zero-effort cross-domain gesture recognition with Wi-Fi. In: Proceedings of the 17th Annual International Conference on Mobile Systems, Applications, and Services, New York, June 2019, pp. 313–325 (2019). https://doi.org/10.1145/3307334.3326081
19. Li, T., Shi, C., Li, P., Chen, P.: A novel gesture recognition system based on CSI extracted from a smartphone with nexmon firmware. Sensors **21**(1), 222 (2021)
20. Zou, H., Yang, J., Zhou, Y., Xie, L., Spanos, C.J.: Robust WiFi-enabled device-free gesture recognition via unsupervised adversarial domain adaptation. In: 2018 27th International Conference on Computer Communication and Networks (ICCCN), July 2018, pp. 1–8. https://doi.org/10.1109/ICCCN.2018.8487345
21. Gjengset, J., Xiong, J., McPhillips, G., Jamieson, K.: Phaser: enabling phased array signal processing on commodity WiFi access points. In: Proceedings of the 20th Annual International Conference on Mobile Computing and Networking, pp. 153–164 (2014)
22. Wu, K., Xiao, J., Yi, Y., Gao, M., Ni, L.M.: FILA: fine-grained indoor localization. In: 2012 Proceedings IEEE INFOCOM, March 2012, pp. 2210–2218 (2012). https://doi.org/10.1109/INFCOM.2012.6195606
23. Liu, W., Chen, H., Deng, Z., Zheng, X., Fu, X., Cheng, Q.: LC-DNN: local connection based deep neural network for Indoor localization with CSI. IEEE Access **8**, 108720–108730 (2020). https://doi.org/10.1109/ACCESS.2020.3000927
24. Zhang, Y., Wang, W., Xu, C., Qin, J., Yu, S., Zhang, Y.: SICD: novel single-access-point indoor localization based on CSI-MIMO with dimensionality reduction. Sensors **21**(4), 1325 (2021). https://doi.org/10.3390/s21041325
25. Jung, J., Moon, H.-C., Kim, J., Kim, D., Toh, K.-A.: Wi-Fi based user identification using in-air handwritten signature. IEEE Access **9**, 53548–53565 (2021). https://doi.org/10.1109/ACCESS.2021.3071228
26. Zhang, Z., Luo, P., Loy, C.C., Tang, X.: Facial landmark detection by deep multi-task learning. In: Fleet, D., Pajdla, T., Schiele, B., Tuytelaars, T. (eds.) ECCV 2014. LNCS, vol. 8694, pp. 94–108. Springer, Cham (2014). https://doi.org/10.1007/978-3-319-10599-4_7
27. Wang, A., Singh, A., Michael, J., Hill, F., Levy, O., Bowman, S.R.: GLUE: A Multi-Task Benchmark and Analysis Platform for Natural Language Understanding (2019). http://arxiv.org/abs/1804.07461. Accessed 28 May 2021
28. Deng, L., Hinton, G., Kingsbury, B.: New types of deep neural network learning for speech recognition and related applications: an overview. In: 2013 IEEE International Conference on Acoustics, Speech and Signal Processing, May 2013, pp. 8599–8603 (2013). https://doi.org/10.1109/ICASSP.2013.6639344
29. Kendall, A., Gal, Y., Cipolla, R.: Multi-task learning using uncertainty to weigh losses for scene geometry and semantics. In: Proceedings of the IEEE Conference on Computer Vision and Pattern Recognition, 2018, pp. 7482–7491 (2018)
30. Guo, M., Haque, A., Huang, D.-A., Yeung, S., Fei-Fei, L.: Dynamic Task Prioritization for Multitask Learning, 2018, pp. 270–287 (2018). https://openaccess.thecvf.com/content_ECCV_2018/html/Michelle_Guo_Focus_on_the_ECCV_2018_paper.html. Accessed 28 May 2021
31. Sener, O., Koltun, V.: Multi-Task Learning as Multi-Objective Optimization (2019). http://arxiv.org/abs/1810.04650. Accessed 28 May 2021
32. Sun, S., Cheng, Y., Gan, Z., Liu, J.: Patient Knowledge Distillation for Bert Model Compressions (2019). https://arxiv.org/abs/1908.09355
33. Yim, J., Joo, D., Bae, J., Kim, J.: A gift from knowledge distillation: fast optimization, network minimization and transfer learning. In: Proceedings of the IEEE Conference on Computer Vision and Pattern Recognition, 2017, pp. 4133–4141 (2017)

34. Orbes-Arteainst, M., et al.: Knowledge distillation for semi-supervised domain adaptation. In: Zhou, L., et al. (eds.) OR 2.0 Context-Aware Operating Theaters and Machine Learning in Clinical Neuroimaging, pp. 68–76. Springer International Publishing, Cham (2019). https://doi.org/10.1007/978-3-030-32695-1_8

35. Kumar, S., Banerjee, B., Chaudhuri, S.: Online Sensor Hallucination via Knowledge Distillation for Multimodal Image Classification (2019). https://arxiv.org/abs/1908.10559

36. Xu, D., Ouyang, W., Wang, X., Sebe, N.: Pad-net: multi-tasks guided prediction-and-distillation network for simultaneous depth estimation and scene parsing. In: Proceedings of the IEEE Conference on Computer Vision and Pattern Recognition, 2018, pp. 675–684 (2018)

37. Chelaramani, S., Gupta, M., Agarwal, V., Gupta, P., Habash, R.: Multi-task Knowledge Distillation for Eye Disease Prediction, 2021, pp. 3983–3993 (2021). https://openaccess.thecvf.com/content/WACV2021/html/Chelaramani_Multi-Task_Knowledge_Distillation_for_Eye_Disease_Prediction_WACV_2021_paper.html. Accessed 28 May 2021

38. He, K., Zhang, X., Ren, S., Sun, J.: Deep Residual Learning for Image Recognition, 2016, pp. 770–778 (2016). https://openaccess.thecvf.com/content_cvpr_2016/html/He_Deep_Residual_Learning_CVPR_2016_paper.html. Accessed 23 Oct 2020

39. Xie, Y., Li, Z., Li, M.: Precise power delay profiling with commodity Wi-Fi. IEEE Trans. Mob. Comput. **18**(6), 1342–1355 (2019). https://doi.org/10.1109/TMC.2018.2860991

40. Kingma, D.P., Ba, J.: Adam: A Method for Stochastic Optimization (2014). https://arxiv.org/abs/1412.6980

A User-Centric Privacy-Preserving Approach to Control Data Collection, Storage, and Disclosure in Own Smart Home Environments

Chathurangi Ishara Wickramasinghe$^{(\boxtimes)}$ and Delphine Reinhardt

University of Göttingen, Göttingen, Germany
c.wickramasinghe@stud.uni-goettingen.de, reinhardt@cs.uni-goettingen.de

Abstract. The smart environments around us collect a vast amount of data and disclose those data to third parties, thus potentially endangering our privacy. Research works and the European General Data Protection Regulation (GDPR) call for more user involvement in the privacy-preserving process. Existing privacy-preserving solutions do not present a solution for the entire data collection and disclosure process, while fully putting the users in the center. Therefore, in this paper, we address four main weaknesses of the existing solutions. This led us to derive a user-centric privacy-preserving approach, which allows the end users to control the entire data collection, storage, and disclosure process in smart home environments. Our approach includes: (1) applying different minimization and aggregation levels to control the data collection, (2) mechanisms helping users to assess the sensitivity level of the collected data types, (3) a model balancing privacy risks with benefits allows users to make decisions by considering their attitude towards data collection and sharing, and (4) an approach presenting privacy risks and advantages arising from sharing collected context-data allows users to make context-dependent data sharing decisions. Our paper also outlines how the proposed privacy-preserving approach can be implemented in the existing IoT system architecture in the future.

Keywords: Internet of Things · IoT · Social IoT and privacy · Usability · Data protection · Data collection · Smart objects · Smart home · Smart environments

1 Introduction

Technological progress has contributed to the fact that pervasive systems with their services have become an essential part of our everyday life. The main goal of pervasive computing systems is to enhance the quality of the end users' life without requiring extensive technical knowledge from the end users [24]. Smart environments, such as smart home, smart city, smart office, etc. are one of the

T. Hara and H. Yamaguchi (Eds.): MobiQuitous 2021, LNICST 419, pp. 190–206, 2022.
https://doi.org/10.1007/978-3-030-94822-1_11

parts of the technological development in the context of pervasive computing systems. In this paper, we concentrate on smart home environments, in which the end users are interacting with various smart objects, such as smart bulbs, smart door locks, smart fridges, smart heater systems, etc. [8]. While those smart objects improve our lives in different areas, they also collect sensor-based data of their owners as well as their environment and disclose those data towards third parties [31,32]. To meet the arising privacy issues in this context, several privacy-preserving solutions have been proposed, such as [1,3,6,9,11,12,19,20]. Note that most of them do not involve the end users in their design in order to improve the acceptance of those solutions and do not allow end users to control the entire data collection and disclosure process.

Laws, such as the European law on data protection and privacy, GDPR, still call for more user involvement in the privacy protection process [21]. Additionally, the GDPR with different rights such as "Right for Access" and "Right to be Forgotten" [Art. 5, 12, 15, 17 and 19], also calls for designing privacy-preserving approaches for smart environments, which allow users to have more transparency and more control on the protection of the personal data processing [14,21,27]. Therefore, in a previous work, a questionnaire-based study was carried out, in which six **User-Centric-Control-Points** (UCCPs) were identified as requirements for user-centric privacy-preserving solutions for smart home environments [29]. The UCCPs allow end users to have more transparency and to control (a) which information is collected in which granularity, (b) what is disclosed to whom and (c) for which purpose, while considering the associated context-based privacy risks and (social or personal) advantages [29]. The six derived UCCPs from [29] are:

- **Data Object Tagging**: Allowing users to tag the smart objects as sensitive or non-sensitive according to their perception,
- **Data Minimization**: Allowing users to limit the data collection by the smart objects,
- **Data Granularity**: Allowing users to set the data collected granularity for their review,
- **Data Sharing**: Allowing users to balance the associated risks and social or personal advantages arising from sharing the collected context-data,
- **Data Disclosure Limitation**: Allowing users to control the data sharing with the options to share or to delete the collected data,
- **Data Access Limitations**: Allowing users to limit the data access and used purposes.

In this paper, we use these UCCPs in order to address the four main weaknesses of the existing privacy-preserving solutions and to derive a user-centric privacy-preserving approach for smart home environments. Addressing those four weaknesses helps end users to (1) apply different minimization and aggregation levels in order to control the data collection [21], (2) to assess the sensitivity level of the collected data types in order to make a conscious decision regarding data disclosure [14], (3) to balance privacy risks with benefits in order to make data sharing decisions by considering their own attitude towards data collection and

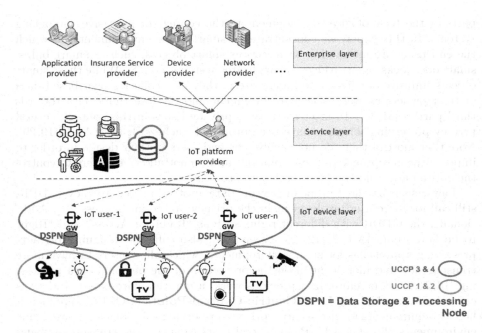

Fig. 1. Our user-centric privacy-preserving solution integrated in the IoT system architecture from [10]

sharing, and (4) to make data sharing decisions after considering the context-based privacy risks and advantages [14] arising from the different collected data types from all the smart objects in their own smart home environment at one point in time.

Our derived user-centric privacy-preserving approach can be implemented in already existing IoT system architectures. IoT system architectures include three layers: IoT device-, service- and enterprise layer [10]. While the IoT device layer consists of smart objects, gateways and Internet connection, the service layer includes the services of the IoT platform providers, such as data flow, processing, storage, and sharing tools, etc. [10]. The third layer, the enterprise layer, comprises business applications and service management technologies [10]. There are mainly two options on how to implement a user-centric privacy-preserving solution in such an IoT architecture. The options are (1) integrating a **Data Storage and Processing Node**, ($DSPN$), in the IoT device layer [2] and (2) supplying end users with a private cloud solution by an IoT platform provider [1] in the service layer. While the first option offers a storage node in their smart home environment (at the device layer), which collects and releases the collected context-data to the service layer according to users' setting in the user-centric privacy-preserving solution [2], the second option provides a data storage option in the service layer of the provider, which saves collected context-data of the smart home owners outside of their smart home environment. We recommend to implement our proposed privacy-preserving solution including four UCCPs, as described in Sect. 2, in the IoT device layer in order to give end users the opportunity to control the entire data collection, storage, and disclosure process in their smart home environments, as illustrated in Fig. 1. Such integration would allow to meet the demanded requirements by the GDPR [21]. Note that the implementation of our approach is however out of scope of this manuscript.

To sum up, in comparison to previous works, our derived user-centric approach has the added value, that it enables the end users to use pervasive computing systems, in this case composed as intelligent objects in smart home environments, with having more transparency and control over the entire data collection and disclosure process without explicit awareness of the underlying communications and computing technologies. Additionally, our approach can be implemented in IoT system architectures in the future and will enable end users to control the entire data collection, storage, and disclosure process.

The remaining of this paper is structured as follows. We first present our user-centric privacy-preserving solution for smart home environments considering the above mentioned four weaknesses in Sect. 2 and its qualitative evaluation in Sect. 3. In Sect. 4, we discuss our proposed model. Related work and closing remarks conclude this paper in Sect. 5 and in Sect. 6, respectively.

2 Our Proposed User-Centric Privacy-Preserving Approach

2.1 Overview of the Entire Privacy-Preserving Model with UCCPs

Figure 2 presents our user-centric privacy-preserving approach including four UCCPs and their interrelationships. In the following, the functions of UCCPs are described in detail.

Our model proposes recommendations regarding data disclosure while considering the users' attitude related to data collection and sharing. While the user settings of the four UCCPs allow end users to control the entire data collection and disclosure process in their smart home environments, the integration of the proposed privacy-preserving solution in the IoT architecture allows end users to control the entire data storage until the data are released or deleted by the smart home owner. Table 1 summarizes the four user settings from UCCPs 1 to 4 with the time of their execution.

The time of execution includes three stages: Registration (R, comprises the first time users start setting up the smart object and initial utilization), Update (U, comprises the point of time when the smart object has been updated) and Aggregation Period (P, comprises the period set by the users for the review of the collected data). The details regarding each users' settings are presented in the corresponding UCCPs. In order to address the mentioned four weaknesses in Sect. 1 and to allow end users to control the entire data collection and disclosure process, our approach includes the following components. While UCCP 1 and 3 include mechanisms helping users to assess the sensitivity level of the collected

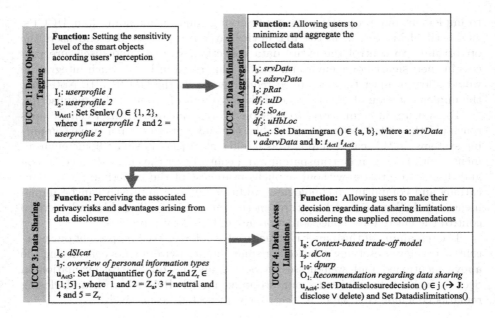

Fig. 2. Four UCCPs and their interrelationships

data, UCCP 2 includes different minimization and aggregation levels for different types of the collected data. Furthermore, UCCP 4 contains a model balancing privacy risks with personal and social benefits by considering the users' attitude regarding data collection and disclosure as well as the function helping end users to make context-based privacy-preserving data sharing decisions.

2.2   UCCPs for Controlling the Data Collection Process

UCCP 1, named as Data Object Tagging, and UCCP 2, named as Data Minimization and Aggregation, allow end users to control the data collection process. End users are asked to set the settings regarding these two UCCPs during the **registration process** of the smart objects. In order to capture users' attitude regarding data collection and privacy-preserving, end users are asked in the user setting u_{Act1}: *Set Senlev()* $\in \{1,2\}$ of UCCP 1, to assign themselves to one of the two profiles described in this model, $(uprofile_1, uprofile_2)$[1]. If the users assign themselves to the $uprofile_1$, then the sensitivity level for the objects in smart

---

[1] **User profile one** ($uprofile_1$): Martha does not care which kind of data are collected by her smart objects and is ready to disclose all the data, including the personal data according to the definition of the Article 4 of the GDPR [21] (information directly or indirectly linkable to Martha), to different data consumers for different purposes.
   User profile two ($uprofile_2$): Martha wants to know which data types are collected by her smart objects in order to supply the smart objects' services and which additional data types are collected. If these collected data include personal data according to the definition of the Article 4 of the GDPR [21] (information directly or indirectly linkable to Martha), then she likes to tag the smart objects as *sensitive* and otherwise she will tag the smart objects as *non sensitive*.

Table 1. Summary of the user actions of the approach *(X means user must set and (X) means user can set)*

User action	Registration (R)	Update (U)	Aggregation Period (P)
UCCP 1: *Set Senlev()*: Setting the sensitivity level	X	(X)	
UCCP 2: *Set Datamingran()*: Minimizing and aggregating the data	X	(X)	(X)
UCCP 3: *Set Dataquantifier()*: Weighting between privacy risks and advantages			X
UCCP 4: *Set Datadisclosuredecision ()* and *Set Datadislimitations ()*: Setting the data consumer and purposes by data sharing			X

home is set to the value 1 with the label *non sensitive* and if the users choose $uprofile_2$, then the sensitivity level for the objects in smart home is set to the value 2 with the label *sensitive*. By default or if, users feel in-between the given profiles, then the sensitivity level for the objects in smart home is also set to the value 2 with the label *sensitive*.

Complementary to UCCP 1, UCCP 2 allows end users to minimize and aggregate the data collected. With the user setting, u_{Act2}: *Set Datamingran()* ϵ {a,b} in UCCP 2, where **a**: *srvData* ν *adsrvData* and **b**: t_{Act1} ν t_{Act2}, end users are asked to set the minimization and aggregation options in order to control the data collection and data aggregation for data sharing. While *srvData* includes data collected to provide the objects' service, *adsrvData* includes additional data collected by smart objects' sensors. The setting options regarding data aggregation allow end users to choose between two options. The two options are (1) exact time of each action of the smart object for daily review (t_{Act1}) or (2) time period users want to aggregate and review the collected data by their smart objects (t_{Act2}), for example weekly, monthly, etc.[2]. In order to supply end users with more background information concerning the smart object providers the privacy ratings of the providers (*pRat*) is presented. The *pRat* is presented based on the approach in [34], which includes a 5-star-based rating system with the icon "i" next to it giving more explanation regarding the rating, for instance the data of your smart home environment are directly saved in the providers' cloud and you cannot be sure who can get access to your data and for which

---

[2] An example for t_{Act1} could be that the smart object owner is absent at 07:30 am on 5th of February and present again at 8 pm in the living room. He gets up at 06:30 am and switches on his smart bulbs in two rooms, namely bathroom and sleeping room. In contrast to this, an example for t_{Act2} could be that the smart object owner is available at home at various times per month and switches on his smart bulbs 200 times per month.

purpose [34][3]. In case, the user setting is missing, the default settings regarding *Set Datamingran()* are: a is assigned to $srvData$ and b is assigned to t_{Act2} including *monthly* as the aggregation period.

In order to simplify the applicability of our approach for end users, the UCCP 2 also includes three default settings regarding the variables, uID including detail information about users' personal identity, So_{Act} including setting the data aggregation layer, and $uHbLoc$ including the recording of users' availability at home and exact home-based location, for instance the user is present in the living room. The default settings are presented to the end users and if they like they are allowed to change these default settings. The default settings for uID is assigned to $status1$ including approximate and general information about the person and default settings for So_{Act} is assigned to So_{Act1}, which means that the granularity of the data is set at the layer of sensors. The default settings regarding $uHbLoc$ is assigned to $status1$, which ensures that no data regarding home-based location is collected. In case of updates, the end users get a push notification, which asks them, whether they want to adjust the settings in UCCP 2 regarding minimizing and aggregating the data collected by their smart objects. In addition, the users also can adjust the settings regarding the aggregation period (t_{Act1} ν t_{Act2}) during the review at the end of the previous aggregation period.

2.3   UCCPs for Controlling the Data Disclosure Process

UCCPs 3, named as Data Sharing, and UCCPs 4, named as Data Access Limitations, allow end users to control the data disclosure process. End users are asked to set the settings regarding these two UCCPs during the **aggregation period** of the smart objects, which users set in the UCCP 2 with t_{Act1} ν t_{Act2}. In order to capture users' sense for associated privacy risks and advantages arising from data sharing, end users are asked in the user setting *Set Dataquantifier ()* of UCCP 3 to set their personal quantifier between their own risk sensitivity (Z_r) and their own sense of advantage (Z_a). If the sense of advantages (Z_a) is higher than the risk sensitivity (Z_r), then the quantifier can be assigned to values 1 or 2, if the risk sensitivity is higher, then the quantifier can be assigned to values 4 or 5 and if the sense of advantages and risk sensitivity are equal, then the quantifier can be assigned to value 3 (neutral). In order to allow end users to perceive the associated privacy risks and advantages and to assess the sensitivity of different information types in the context of data disclosure, end users are provided with data sharing information categories ($dSIcat$) in Table 2 and an overview of personal information types in Table 3 by smart object providers. While $dSIcat$ present the associated privacy risks and (personal and social) advantages arising from disclosing the collected data, the overview of personal information types including different information in various context assigned to types of the $dSIcat$ (from Table 2) helps end users to assess the sensitivity of the information types.

---

[3]   The approach from Zimmermann et al. [34] is a 5-star-based rating system. This system is similar to a star-based product rating we know for example on Amazon. The 5-star-ratings of each provider result from the given information by each provider and user experiences with the corresponding smart object.

Our approach includes the presented categories in *dSIcat*, because those represent the privacy risks and advantages arising from data disclosure in smart home environments and the former papers, such as [5,6,12,16,33,34], also classify the categories from *dSIcat* as relevant categories in this context. Additionally, as in the other contexts [16,22], different types of personal data are also collected in smart home environments and our approach considers the relevant personal information types summarized in Table 2 in this context. The *dSIcat* and overview of personal information types must be supplied and updated at the latest by the time, when the end users start reviewing the collected data at the end of each pre-defined aggregation period. Furthermore, end users are also allowed to add categories to *dSIcat* during the review at the end of previous aggregation period after learning over a certain period. The default setting regarding UCCP 3 includes that the quantifier is set to the value 5, which means that the risk sensitivity (Z_a) is higher than the sense of advantage.

In addition to UCCP 3, UCCP 4 allows end users to make their decision regarding data sharing and limit the data access after considering the recommendations supplied by our context-based trade-off decision model. While the user setting u_{Act4}: *Set Datadisclosuredecision () ϵ j* (where j can be assigned to disclose ν delete) allows the end users to choose between the two options ("disclose" or "delete"), the user setting *Set Datadislimitations ()* allows end users to limit the data consumers $(dCon)^4$ and usage purposes $(dPurp)^5$ in case of data sharing. *dCon* get a rating based on the 5-star-rating approach[6], which is based on the approach from [34]. In case, the user settings are missing, the default setting for *Set Datadisclosuredecision ()* is set to *delete*. The inputs regarding *dCon* and *dPurp* must be provided and updated from smart object providers at the latest by the start of end user reviewing at the end of each pre-defined aggregation period.

In order to support end users in their data disclosure decision making process, our approach supplies recommendations based on our context-based trade-off decision model, which considers the user settings of the previous UCCPs, 1, 2 and 3. The formula of our model bases on the Markowitz's risk-return model from [17]. The Markowitz's risk-return model is rated as one of the most popular risk models in finance [17]. The formula of the Markowitz's risk-return model is:

$$U(x) = E(x) - O \times Var(x) \tag{1}$$

---

[4] *dCon* include third parties getting access to disclosed data, such as doctors, insurance company, government agencies, etc.

[5] *dPurp* informs end users for which purpose, such as personal health plan, statistical purposes, etc., the shared data are used by the *dCon*.

[6] Each *dCon* has to answer several questions, for instance, where the data are saved, for which purpose the data are used, with which other companies/associations the data are shared, etc. Based on the answers of the *dCon*, they get a rating based on the 5-star-rating approach.

The original Markowitz's risk-return model formula[7], presented under formula 1, was adjusted for our approach. In the following the balancing formula of our proposed approach is explained briefly. In the formula of our approach, we use the following two additional abbreviations: So for *smart object* and b for *behaviour*. The operation $E(x)$ includes the following equation in our approach[8]. It considers the default and user settings from UCCP 2 and UCCP 3 regarding uID, $uHbLoc$ and quantifier between Z_a and Z_r.

$$E(x) = Z_a \times (uID \times uHbLoc \times So_{ia}) \tag{2}$$

Else it is:

$$E(x) = (uID \times uHbLoc \times So_{ia}) \tag{3}$$

The operation $O \times Var(x)$ includes the following equation in our approach[9]. It considers the default and user settings from UCCP 2 and UCCP 3 regarding uID, $uHbLoc$ and quantifier between Z_a and Z_r.

$$O \times Var(x) = Z_r \times (uID \times uHbLoc \times So_{ip}) \tag{4}$$

Else it is:

$$O \times Var(x) = (uID \times uHbLoc \times So_{ip}) \tag{5}$$

The output of this UCCP O_1 results from the following $if-clause$: $O_1 = if\ (U(x) = E(x) - O \times Var(x) > 0)$, then "Disclose the collected data of $f(b)$", else "Do not disclose the collected data of $f(b)$". This $if - clause$ means that the context-based trade-off model of our approach suggests end users to disclose the collected data, concluded in the formula $f(b)$, if the associated advantages are weighted higher by the end users in comparison to the arising privacy risks $(U(x) > 0)$. Otherwise, the end users are suggested not to disclose the collected data summarized in $f(b)$. As mentioned above, the formula $f(b)$ summarizes the collected data in the interaction of all existing smart objects So in users' smart home environment according to the users' settings regarding the UCCPs 1 to 3. If the users set *Set Datamingran(b)* is assigned to t_{Act1} in UCCP 2, then all the smart objects' actions with their exact time of execution are summarized for the users' daily review:

---

[7] $U(x)$: Trade-off between expected payoff with main focus on the pure profit and the variability of the payoff (risk) of an investment x;
$E(x)$: Expected payoff with main focus on the pure profit of an investment x;
O: Risk attitude of the decision maker, O assigned to 0 means risk-neutral; $O > 0$ means risk averse and $O < 0$ means risk-seeking;
$Var(x)$: Variability of the payoff (risk) of an investment x.

[8] Summary of the **associated advantages** ia_x from $dSIcat$ regarding all the So the user owns in his/her smart home environment: $So_{ia} = (So_{1ia1} + So_{1ia2} + So_{2ia1} + So_{2ia2} + ... + So_{nia1} + So_{nia2})$.

[9] Summary of the **associated privacy risks** ip_x from $dSIcat$ regarding all the So the user owns in his smart home environment. At this point, the sensitivity level $SetSenlev()$ regarding the So, which users set in UCCP 1, is also considered: So_ip = Set Senlev $(So_{all}) \times [(So_{1ip1} + So_{1ip2} + ...) + (So_{2ip1} + So_{2ip2} + ...) + ... + (So_{nip1} + So_{nip2} + ...)]$

Table 2. I_6: Overview of the data sharing information categories ($dSIcat$) [5,6,12,16, 33,34]

Abbreviation of category	Category name	Category description
ip_1: Associated privacy risks 1	Discrimination and Manipulation	Using to create special contract and discriminate the users, for example, manipulating the device owners with contracts
ip_2: Associated privacy risks 2	Burglaries and Misuse	Using the data to harm the users, for instance, breaking in after analysing data about home availability and smart door lock
ip_3: Associated privacy risks 3	Profiling	Using the data to track the users and manipulate the users and steal the users' identity
ip_4: Associated privacy risks 4	Carrier risks	Using the data to find out characteristics of the users, for example, analysing and disclosing such information can result in risks for future employers
ip_5: Associated privacy risks 5	Damaging	Using the data to damage the device owners, for instance identity theft based on the disclosed sensor data
ip_6: Associated privacy risks 6	Personal Exposure	Using the data to publish things users are doing, for example, data disclosure could result in being exposed because they had done something they did not want their friends and family to know about, maybe also to carry out Propaganda, etc.
i_{a1}: Associated social advantage 1	Personal Advantages	Using the data to provide the user specific contracts and users can earn money
i_{a2}: Associated social advantage 2	Social Advantages	Using for statistical aims, for example, using data for research works, market analysis

Table 3. I_7 - Extract from the overview of the personal information types and their associated $dSIcat$ [16,22]

Information type	Directly	Linkable	dSIcat					
			ip_1	ip_2	ip_3	ip_4	ip_5	ip_6
Body size	–	x	x	x	–	–	–	–
Voice print	–	x	x	–	–	–	–	–
Body and facial images	x	–	x	x	–	–	–	–
Biological characteristics/Biometrics	x	–	x	x	–	x	–	–
Recording of using health equipment	–	x	x	x	x	–	x	x

$$f(b) = \sum_{b_{t1\ Act1}}^{b_{tn\ Act1}} = [b_{t1\ Act1} + b_{t2\ Act1} + ... + b_{tn\ Act1}] \tag{6}$$

$$b_{t1\ Act1} = t_{1\ Act1} \times (So_{1\ Act1} + So_{2\ Act1} + ... + So_{n\ Act1}) \tag{7}$$

$$b_{tn\ Act1} = t_{n\ Act1} \times (So_{1\ Act1} + So_{2\ Act1} + ... + So_{n\ Act1}) \tag{8}$$

If the users assigned *Set Datamingran(b)* to t_{Act2} with weekly in UCCP 2, then all the smart objects' actions with rough information are aggregated for the users' review period, in this case weekly base:

$$f(b) = b_{Act2}; b_{Act2} = t_{Act2} \times (So_{1\ Act2} + So_{2\ Act2} + ... + So_{n\ Act2}) \tag{9}$$

To sum up, our approach also allows the end users to adopt the settings of the previous review period regarding the four UCCPs in the upcoming aggregation periods.

3   Evaluation

The proposed user-centric privacy-preserving model addresses weaknesses of the already existing privacy-preserving solutions in IoT, as mentioned in Sect. 1. In this section, we evaluate our proposed model qualitatively. In order to outline the added value of our model, we evaluate our approach with already existing approaches, [1,3,6,12]. The existing approaches from [1,3,6,12] are relevant works in this area and provide the basis for our approach. While [6] presents a reference architecture including a trade-off decision component, [12] proposes a Role Based Access Control framework, which can be applied in the context of data sharing in smart home environments. However, the detailed and qualitative evaluation of these approaches shows that both approaches do not allow the users to control the entire data collection, storage, and disclosure process. Furthermore, the papers [1,3] present a security and privacy-preserving solution as well as privacy negotiation mechanisms for IoT environments. Although these approaches provide the basis for our proposed approach, they do not give sufficient options for the user to control the privacy-preserving data collection, storage, and disclosure.

The evaluation metrics are organized in two categories: (1) Privacy-preserving functionalities of the proposed solutions and (2) the rights of the smart object owners. The qualitative evaluation metrics for each category are derived from [15,18,21,29]. Table 4 outlines the results of this qualitative evaluation. Each evaluation category contains five metrics, which are evaluated by using the following rating scale: ○ = no possibility; ◑ = partially possible; and ● = possible.

4   Discussion and Limitations

4.1   Discussion

With our proposed privacy-preserving approach, we (1) address four weaknesses of the previous approaches, as mentioned in Sect. 1, (2) empower end users

Table 4. Results of the qualitative evaluation

Evaluation category	Metrics	Our model	Model 2 [6]	Model 3 [12]	Model 4 [1]	Model 5 [3]
Privacy-preserving functionalities	Data minimization [18]	●	○	○	○	○
	Limited data processing for specific purposes (smart object service) [18]	●	○	○	◐	○
	Data aggregation [18]	●	○	○	◐	○
	Privacy-preserving data storage [18,21]	●	◐	○	◐	●
	Transparent processing of collected personal data	●	●	○	○	◐
Rights of the smart object owners	End users to limit the data collection [21,29]	●	○	○	○	○
	End users to limit the data access [21,29] by limiting the data consumers and usage purposes [29]	●	◐	◐	◐	●
	End users to assess the sensitivity level of the collected data types [29]	●	◐	○	○	◐
	End users to have transparency about data processing [15,21], for instance, arising privacy risks by disclosing	●	◐	○	○	○
	End users to evaluate the context-data before data disclosing [29]	●	○	○	○	◐

to control the entire data collection, storage, and disclosure process, and (3) help end users to make context-based privacy-preserving data sharing decisions. By proposing a user-centric privacy-preserving approach, which can be implemented in the future in existing IoT architectures, we address the demands from the GDPR [21], especially rights such as "Right for Access" and "Right to be Forgotten" (Art. 5, 12, 15, 17 and 19). Addressing the mentioned weaknesses from [6,14] and therefore including minimization and aggregation levels in our proposed approach for smart home environment allows end users to control the entire data collection process. Additionally, the related work with already proposed privacy-preserving solutions in this context, mentioned in Sect. 5, outlines that those solutions do not include mechanisms enabling end users to assess the sensitivity level of the collected data. Those mechanisms help to increase the transparency in this context, which is also required by the GDPR [21]. There are few privacy-preserving approaches including context-based permission systems [13], security frameworks for smart objects [23,25], and privacy risk trade-off/negotiation models [1,3,5,6,12], but they still include weaknesses, which we address in our approach as outlined in Table 4, for instance presenting the associated privacy risks and advantages arising from sharing the collected data types from all the smart objects in smart home environments at one point in time and giving end users the opportunity to make the data disclosure decision consciously after assessing the sensitivity level of the context-based collected data.

As mentioned above, the included context-based trade-off decision model in our proposed approach provides end users with recommendations regarding the data disclosure based on their attitude regarding data collection and disclosure. However, it must be investigated in the future, whether end users are willing to have such trade-off decision-making model based recommendations. Moreover, they are asked to make settings considering their attitude towards data collection and disclosure. Therefore, they get several information as inputs in our approach, such as $pRat$, $dSIcat$, $dCon$, $dPurp$, etc. These inputs must be tested with end users within a user study to find out whether they want to have the pre-defined inputs and/or whether they are willing to have more information than the existing inputs of the proposed approach in order to consider those information in their data-disclosure decision-making process. It should be emphasised, that it is essential to give end users the opportunity to assess the sensitivity level of their collected data in order to avoid inappropriate decisions regarding data disclosure. The derived data sharing information categories ($dSIcat$) in Table 2, the overview of the personal information types in Table 3, and their classification to $dSIcat$ in our model may help end users to assess the sensitivity level of the collected data. These input information are based on a literature review and must be quantified with the help of an online questionnaire, which we will address in our future research work. In this context, it would be interesting to find out whether such overviews with personal information types assigned to categories, such as $dSIcat$, help the end users to assess the sensitivity level of their own personal data.

4.2 Limitations

Finally, our work has few limitations. The findings are mainly based on a literature review and on the results of a previously carried out questionnaire-based survey [29]. The derived model in Sect. 2 must be validated with a user questionnaire and studies, which we target to address in the near future.

5 Related Work

In previous works, different approaches have been proposed regarding privacy-preserving solutions for IoT, such as [5,6,12]. While [12] presents a Role Based Access Control (RBAC) framework including k-anonymity mechanisms, in [5,6] Barhamgi et al. present a reference data sharing architecture for privacy engineering in environments with smart health care devices. The proposed architecture includes trade-off data sharing decision components, which allow the smart object owners to make pragmatic data sharing decision balancing privacy risks and potential benefits. Both solutions aim at giving the opportunity to users to manage the data disclosure of their smart health care device. Moreover, [1] and [3] propose further privacy-preserving solutions. While [1] presents a security and privacy-preserving IoT architecture for smart home environments, [3] proposes privacy negotiation mechanism for IoT environments. Both solutions address the privacy-preserving issues in IoT environments, specially in the context of smart homes, for instance, ensuring privacy-preserving data storage, allowing end users to limit the data access, etc. However, these approaches [1,3,5,6,12] include few limitations, such as (1) the end users cannot control the entire data collection, storage, and disclosure process in their smart home environment, (2) users cannot make context-based data-disclosure decisions considering all the data collected by the smart objects in a smart home environment, (3) users have no possibilities to control the data collection process, and (4) users do not have the possibility to apply data minimization and aggregation strategies as well as data usage limitations. Furthermore, in [34] a smart home configurator is introduced, which supports the end users' decision-making process regarding smart home technologies when buying the smart objects. This configurator depicts the smart home data processes and informs end users about the implications regarding privacy and security in order to increase transparency and reduce the lack of clarity in the decision-making process during the purchase process. This approach [34] does not allow the end users to control the entire data collection, storage, and disclosure process while using those smart objects in their own smart home environment. Moreover, few user studies are carried out, such as [31,33], in order to analyse users' mental and threat models of privacy consequences and obstacles for the privacy protection. These user studies deliver valuable hints regarding user-centric privacy-preserving solutions, such as giving users the transparency about privacy consequences in an understandable way and limiting data recipients, etc., but do not present a general user-centric privacy-preserving approach regarding the disclosure of context-based data in smart home environments with different smart objects. Moreover, some prior works, such as [4,7,13,26,28,30], present further privacy-preserving standalone solutions including context-based permission systems, privacy-preserving policies, authentication protocols and data encryption methods in order to protect the collected sensor data by smart objects. Additionally, there are few works, such as [16,22], which propose information sensitivity typologies. In their survey results, they summarize different information types from various contexts to derived sensitivity levels in an understandable way [16,22].

In comparison to all the above-mentioned previous work, our approach concentrates on user-centric control points integrated privacy-preserving approach closing four main weaknesses of existing approaches, such as data minimization and aggregation levels, evaluation mechanisms for data sensitivity level, context-based trade-off decision model supplying data sharing recommendations while considering end users' settings regarding their attitude towards data collection and disclosure as well as balancing privacy risks and personal and social advantages.

6   Conclusions and Future Work

Within the scope of this paper, we have derived a user-centric privacy-preserving approach considering user-centric-control-points, called UCCPs. To sum up, it allows the end users to control the entire data collection, storage, and disclosure process by considering different minimization and aggregation levels, applying mechanisms helping users to assess the sensitivity level of the collected data types, by balancing the arising privacy risks and (social and personal) advantages and applying functions helping end users to make context-based privacy-preserving data sharing decisions. With this approach we address the existing weaknesses of the previous proposed solutions and empower end users to have more control over the processing of their personal data in the smart home environment.

In future work, we plan (1) to implement the proposed approach in a smart home environment and to carry out (2) user studies to investigate its performance as well as users' acceptance and derive further requirements regarding the proposed approach in this paper. Furthermore, we also plan (3) to conduct questionnaire-based studies in order to find out whether the overview of personal information types assigned to $dSIcat$ categories helps end users to assess the sensitivity level of their collected personal data.

Acknowledgments. We thank the anonymous reviewers for their feedback and Alexander Richter for his support. Furthermore, we would like to thank Daniel Franke and Birgit Schuhbauer for proofreading.

References

1. Abu-Tair, M., et al.: Towards secure and privacy-preserving IoT enabled smart home: architecture and experimental study. Sensors **20**(21), 1–14 (2020)
2. Aïvodji, U.M., Gambs, S., Martin, A.: IOTFLA: a secured and privacy-preserving smart home architecture implementing federated learning: a secured and privacy-preserving smart home architecture implementing federated learning. In: Proceedings of 2019 IEEE Security and Privacy Workshops (SPW), pp. 175–180 (2019)
3. Alanezi, K., Mishra, S.: Incorporating individual and group privacy preferences in the Internet of Things. J. Ambient Intell. Humanized Comput. 1–16 (2021). https://doi.org/10.1007/s12652-021-02959-7
4. Alcaide, A., Palomar, E., Montero-Castillo, J., Ribagorda, A.: Anonymous authentication for privacy-preserving IoT target-driven applications. Comput. Secur. **37**, 111–123 (2013)
5. Barhamgi, M., et al.: POSTER: Enabling end-users to protect their privacy, pp. 905–907 (2017)
6. Barhamgi, M., et al.: Enabling end-users to protect their privacy. In: Proceedings of the 2017 ACM on Asia Conference on Computer and Communications Security, pp. 905–907. ACM (2017)
7. Cao, J., Carminati, B., Ferrari, E., Tan, K.L.: Castle: continuously anonymizing data streams. IEEE Trans. Dependable Secure Comput. **8**(3), 337–352 (2010)
8. Carretero, J., García, J.D.: The Internet of Things: connecting the world. Pers. Ubiquit. Comput. **18**(2), 445–447 (2014)

9. Chakravorty, A., Wlodarczyk, T., Rong, C.: Privacy preserving data analytics for smart homes. In: Proceedings of 2013 IEEE Security and Privacy Workshops, pp. 23–27 (2013)
10. Firoozjaei, M.D., Lu, R., Ghorbani, A.A.: An evaluation framework for privacy-preserving solutions applicable for blockchain-based Internet-of-Things platforms. Secur. Priv. **3**(6), 1–28 (2020)
11. Huang, X., Craig, P., Lin, H., Yan, Z.: SecIoT: a security framework for the Internet of Things. Secur. Commun. Netw. **9**(16), 3083–3094 (2016)
12. Huang, X., Fu, R., Chen, B., Zhang, T., Roscoe, A.: User interactive Internet of Things privacy preserved access control. In: International Conference for Internet Technology and Secured Transactions, pp. 597–602 (2012)
13. Jia, Y.J., et al.: ContexloT: towards providing contextual integrity to applied IoT platforms. In: Network and Distributed System Security Symposium (NDSS), pp. 1–15 (2017)
14. Kounoudes, A.D., Kapitsaki, G.M.: A mapping of IoT user-centric privacy preserving approaches to the GDPR. Internet Things **11**, 100179 (2020)
15. Lin, J., Yu, W., Zhang, N., Yang, X., Zhang, H., Zhao, W.: A survey on Internet of Things: architecture, enabling technologies, security and privacy, and applications. IEEE Internet Things J. **4**(5), 1125–1142 (2017)
16. Milne, G., Pettinico, G., Hajjat, F., Markos, E.: Information sensitivity typology: mapping the degree and type of risk consumers perceive in personal data sharing. J. Consum. Aff. **51**(1), 133–161 (2016)
17. Nagengast, A.J., Braun, D.A., Wolpert, D.M.: Risk-sensitivity and the mean-variance trade-off: decision making in sensorimotor control. Proc. Roy. Soc. B Biol. Sci. **278**, 2325–2332 (2011)
18. Oetzel, M.C., Spiekermann, S.: A systematic methodology for privacy impact assessments: a design science approach. Eur. J. Inf. Syst. **23**(2), 126–150 (2014)
19. Ouaddah, A., Abou Elkalam, A., Ait Ouahman, A.: FairAccess: a new blockchain-based access control framework for the Internet of Things. Secur. Commun. Netw. **9**(18), 5943–5964 (2016)
20. Perera, C., McCormick, C., Bandara, A.K., Price, B.A., Nuseibeh, B.: Privacy-by-design framework for assessing Internet of Things applications and platforms. In: Proceedings of the 6th International Conference on the Internet of Things, pp. 83–92. ACM (2016)
21. Regulation (EU): 2016/679 of the European Parliament and of the Council of 27 April 2016 on the Protection of Natural Persons with Regard to the Processing of Personal Data and on the Free Movement of Such Data, and Repealing Directive 95/46/EC (General Data Protection Regulation). Official Journal of the European Union L119/1, pp. 1–88 (2016)
22. Rumbold, J., Pierscionek, B.: What are data? A categorization of the data sensitivity spectrum. Big Data Res. **12**, 49–59 (2018)
23. Sachidananda, V., Siboni, S., Shabtai, A., Toh, J., Bhairav, S., Elovici, Y.: Let the cat out of the bag: a holistic approach towards security analysis of the Internet of Things. In: Proceedings of the 3rd ACM International Workshop on IoT Privacy, Trust, and Security (IoTPTS), pp. 3–10 (2017)
24. Satyanarayanan, M.: Pervasive computing: vision and challenges. IEEE Pers. Commun. **8**(4), 10–17 (2001)
25. Siboni, S., Shabtai, A., Tippenhauer, N.O., Lee, J., Elovici, Y.: Advanced security testbed framework for wearable IoT devices. ACM Trans. Internet Technol. **16**(4), 1–25 (2016)

26. Su, J., Cao, D., Zhao, B., Wang, X., You, I.: ePASS: an expressive attribute-based signature scheme with privacy and an unforgeability guarantee for the Internet of Things. Futur. Gener. Comput. Syst. **33**, 11–18 (2014)
27. Tabassum, M., Kosinski, T., Lipford, H.R.: 'I don't own the data': end user perceptions of smart home device data practices and risks. In: Proceedings of SOUPS 2015, Symposium on Usable Privacy and Security, pp. 435–450 (2019)
28. Wang, X., Zhang, J., Schooler, E.M., Ion, M.: Performance evaluation of attribute-based encryption: toward data privacy in the IoT. In: 2014 IEEE International Conference on Communications (ICC), pp. 725–730 (2014)
29. Wickramasinghe, C.I., Reinhardt, D.: A survey-based exploration of users' awareness and their willingness to protect their data with smart objects. In: Friedewald, M., Önen, M., Lievens, E., Krenn, S., Fricker, S. (eds.) Privacy and Identity 2019. IAICT, vol. 576, pp. 427–446. Springer, Cham (2020). https://doi.org/10.1007/978-3-030-42504-3_27
30. Yang, J.C., Fang, B.X.: Security model and key technologies for the Internet of Things. J. Chin. Univ. Posts Telecommun. **18**, 109–112 (2011)
31. Zeng, E., Mare, S., Roesner, F.: End user security and privacy concerns with smart homes. In: Proceedings of SOUPS 2013, Symposium on Usable Privacy and Security, pp. 65–80 (2017)
32. Zhou, W., Jia, Y., Peng, A., Zhang, Y., Liu, P.: The effect of IoT new features on security and privacy: new threats, existing solutions, and challenges yet to be solved. IEEE Internet Things J. **6**(2), 1606–1616 (2019)
33. Zimmermann, V., Bennighof, M., Edel, M., Hoffmann, O., Jung, J., Wick, M.: 'Home, smart home' - exploring end users' mental models of smart homes. In: Mensch und Computer 2018-Workshop Band, pp. 401–417 (2018)
34. Zimmermann, V., Dickhaut, E., Gerber, P., Vogt, J.: Vision: shining light on smart homes - supporting informed decision-making of end users. In: Proceedings of 2019 IEEE European Symposium on Security and Privacy Workshops (EuroS PW), pp. 149–153 (2019)

Q-Learning-Based Spatial Reuse Method Considering Throughput Fairness by Negative Reward for High Throughput

Mirai Takematsu[1]([✉]) [iD], Shota Sakai[1] [iD], Masashi Kunibe[1] [iD],
and Hiroshi Shigeno[2] [iD]

[1] Graduate School of Science and Technology, Keio University, Yokohama,
Kanagawa 223-8522, Japan
{takematsu,sakai,kunibe}@mos.ics.keio.ac.jp
[2] Keio University, Yokohama, Kanagawa 223-8522, Japan
shigeno@mos.ics.keio.ac.jp

Abstract. In this paper, we propose a Q-learning-based spatial reuse method considering throughput fairness in Wireless LANs (WLANs). In Spatial Reuse (SR) methods, wireless nodes try to use wireless resources efficiently by controlling both the Transmission Power (TP) and Carrier Sense Threshold (CST). When wireless nodes are densely deployed, the SR methods have difficulty to achieve both the high aggregate throughput and throughput fairness because the mutual interference among the wireless nodes becomes severe. The proposed method removes the difficulty by utilizing Q-learning where wireless nodes can learn the adequate CST and TP by themselves. The proposed method motivates nodes to use wireless resources actively by rewards, while it suppresses nodes with high throughput using the resources by negative rewards. As a result, the wireless resources are distributed among nodes with low throughput, and the proposed method achieves both the high aggregate throughput and throughput fairness. Simulation results show that the proposed method improves the aggregate throughput with keeping throughput fairness.

Keywords: Dense Wireless LAN · Spatial reuse · Q-learning

1 Introduction

With the increase of wireless nodes such as smartphones and Access Points (APs), the efficient wireless resource utilization has been paid attention in Wireless Local Area Networks (WLANs). In WLANs, the wireless nodes send packets avoiding packet collisions for utilizing the wireless resources efficiently. The simultaneous packet transmissions on the same channel will be results in packet collisions and the involved packets will be lost. The IEEE 802.11 standard implements Carrier Sense Multiple Access with Collision Avoidance (CSMA/CA) to avoid the packet collisions [1]. In CSMA/CA, nodes perform carrier sense before

T. Hara and H. Yamaguchi (Eds.): MobiQuitous 2021, LNICST 419, pp. 207–219, 2022.
https://doi.org/10.1007/978-3-030-94822-1_12

transmitting packets to detect transmissions from the other nodes. Specifically, the nodes detect the transmission if the received signal power exceeds Carrier Sense Threshold (CST). However, when the nodes are densely deployed in WLANs, they have difficulty to utilize wireless resources efficiently even by CSMA/CA. Specifically, they suffer from the following two problems in dense environments: the hidden node problem and the exposed node problem [2]. In the hidden node problem, packets of different nodes frequently collide at receiving nodes because they cannot recognize with each other by carrier sense due to the high CST of them or low Transmission Power (TP). In the exposed node problem, nodes rarely send packets because they perform carrier sense excessively due to the low CST of them or high TP of others.

To mitigate the hidden node problem and exposed node problem, spatial reuse methods have been paid attention as the methods allow nodes to conduct adequate carrier sense using Dynamic Sensitivity Control (DSC) and Transmit Power Control (TPC). Specifically, DSC allows nodes to change their CST, and TPC allows nodes to change their TP. On the other hand, the spatial reuse methods have difficulty to conduct adequate DSC and TPC in dense environments because the mutual interference among nodes becomes complex. To solve the difficulty, the spatial reuse methods using Machine Learning (ML), such as Neural Network (NN) and Q-learning, have been paid attention. By utilizing ML, the nodes can learn adequate DSC and TPC autonomously without a lot of knowledge of the complex interference among them. In NN-based methods, nodes learn their controls by training data, and the methods have to create the data based on the positions of nodes previously [3,4]. In contrast, the nodes learn their controls only by rewards in Q-learning-based methods. Therefore, Q-learning-based methods are more flexible than NN-based methods for learning DSC and TPC.

One of the challenges of Q-learning-based methods is to determine rewards for both the high aggregate throughput and throughput fairness. F. Wilhelmi et al. introduced the throughput of each node as the reward to achieve the high aggregate throughput [5]. Since the nodes try to obtain high rewards, the aggregate throughput of them also becomes high. However, the reward has a possibility to allocate wireless resources to nodes unfairly for the high aggregate throughput. To achieve throughput fairness, F. Wilhelmi et al. also introduced the minimum throughput of nodes in networks as the reward [5]. Since the nodes try to obtain high rewards, the minimum throughput in the network also increases. As a result, the difference between the minimum throughput and the maximum throughput in the network decreases, and throughput fairness is achieved. On the other hands, the reward has a possibility to suppress the aggregate throughput because it is determined based on the minimum throughput.

In this paper, we propose a Q-learning-based spatial reuse method considering throughput fairness for high throughput. The goal of the proposed method is that wireless nodes learn the adequate CST and TP for both the high aggregate throughput and throughput fairness by rewards of Q-learning. To achieve the high aggregate throughput, we utilize the throughput of nodes as rewards of them. As a result, they seek the CST and TP that improve the throughput of them to obtain high rewards. In contrast, to prevent some nodes from monopolizing wireless resources, we give the negative rewards to the nodes with the high throughput. As a result, they learn to suppress wireless resources by DSC and TPC. The wireless resources of the nodes with the high throughput are distributed among the nodes with the low throughput, and they finally learn CST and TP that achieve throughput fairness among them.

The contribution of this paper is as follows:

- To achieve both the high aggregate throughput and throughput fairness, we propose the Q-learning-based spatial reuse method using the negative reward for the high throughput.
- Simulation results show that the proposed method improves the aggregate throughput with keeping throughput fairness in the comparison with the previous methods.

The remainder of this paper is organized as follows: Sect. 2 explains related work. Section 3 presents the proposed method. Section 4 shows the evaluation results. Section 5 concludes this paper.

2   Related Work

For achieving the efficient wireless resource utilization, spatial reuse methods have been paid attention. The challenging task of the spatial reuse methods is to achieve both the high aggregate throughput and throughput fairness by using DSC and TPC in dense environments. Since DSC and TPC of nodes influence on the those of the other nodes, it becomes difficult for them to conduct DSC and TPC considering the mutual influence on the others in dense environments [5]. To remove the difficulty from DSC and TPC, ML-based spatial reuse methods, such as NN-based methods [3,4] and Q-learning-based methods, have been paid attention. In ML, nodes can learn the optimal CST and TP autonomously without much knowledge of the mutual influence. Specifically in NN-based methods, the nodes learn their controls based on training data. On the other hands, the data depends on the positions of nodes. In contrast, the nodes can learn their controls only by rewards for the controls in Q-learning methods. Therefore, Q-learning-based-methods can easily be implemented rather than NN-based-methods.

First, we explain details of Q-learning in Sect. 2.1. Then, we explain Q-learning-based spatial reuse methods in Sect. 2.2. Finally, we explain the motivation of this paper in Sect. 2.3.

2.1   Q-Learning

Q-learning [6] is one of RL methods, and the purpose of Q-learning is that agents learn optimal actions by updating expected rewards in Q-tables. Q-tables are composed of expected rewards, states, and actions. Specifically, the expected rewards are allocated to pairs of states and actions in Q-tables. At each time step, agents select actions for states from their Q-tables. Then, Q-learning gives rewards for the actions. By using the rewards, the agents update the expected rewards for the actions and states. Specifically, when agent i gets reward $r_{i,t}$ for action a_t and state s_t at time t, it updates Q-table $\hat{Q}(s_t, a_t)$ for the action and state as follows:

$$\hat{Q}(s_t, a_t) \leftarrow (1 - \alpha_t)\hat{Q}(s_t, a_t) + \alpha_t(r_{i,t} + \gamma(\max_{a'} \hat{Q}(s_{t+1}, a'))), \qquad (1)$$

where α_t and $\max_{a'} \hat{Q}(s_{t+1}, a')$ denote a learning rate at time t and a maximum expected reward for next state s_{t+1}, respectively, and γ is a discount factor parameter. On the other hands, Eq. (1) cannot be applied with the case that agents cannot observe their states completely. Especially, WLANs belong to the case because wireless nodes cannot observe all the other nodes. To apply Q-learning with the case, stateless Q-learning was proposed [7]. The stateless Q-learning can be applied with the case that there is one state and one optimal action for the state. Q-tables are composed of the expected rewards and the actions. Specifically, when agent i gets reward $r_{i,t}$ for action a_t at time t, it updates Q-table $\hat{Q}(a_t)$ for the action as follows:

$$\hat{Q}(a_t) \leftarrow (1 - \alpha_t)\hat{Q}(a_t) + \alpha_t(r_{i,t} + \gamma(\max_{a'} \hat{Q}(a'))). \qquad (2)$$

In Q-learning, agents have the possibility to learn suboptimal actions when they continuously select actions with the highest expected rewards among all the actions in Q-tables at every time step. To decrease the possibility, ε-greedy strategy was proposed [8]. In ε-greedy strategy, the agents select their actions randomly from their Q-tables with probability ε. In contrast, with probability $1 - \varepsilon$, they select the actions with the highest expected rewards among all the actions in Q-tables.

2.2 Q-Learning-Based Spatial Reuse Methods

The goal of Q-learning-based spatial reuse methods is to define adequate rewards for achieving both the high aggregate throughput and throughput fairness. By defining the rewards, nodes can learn adequate CST and TP by themselves.

F. Wilhelmi et al. introduced the throughput of nodes as the selfish reward for achieving the high aggregate throughput [5]. Specifically, reward $r_{i,t}$ for node i at time t is expressed as:

$$r_{i,t} = \frac{\Gamma_{i,t}}{\Gamma_i^*}, \qquad (3)$$

where $\Gamma_{i,t}$ and Γ_i^* denote the throughput of node i at time t and the maximum achievable throughput of node i, respectively. The reward motivates node i to learn CST and TP that improve $\Gamma_{i,t}$. As a result, the aggregate throughput is also improved by the reward. Furthermore, to achieve throughput fairness, F. Wilhelmi et al. proposed environment-aware reward considering the minimum throughput in networks [5]. Specifically, reward $r_{\mathscr{O},t}$ for the nodes in network $\mathscr{O}$ at time t is expressed as:

$$r_{\mathscr{O},t} = \frac{\min_{i \in \mathscr{O}} \Gamma_{i,t}}{\Gamma^*_{\mathscr{O},t}}, \qquad (4)$$

where $\min_{i \in \mathscr{O}} \Gamma_{i,t}$ and $\Gamma^*_{\mathscr{O},t}$ denote the minimum throughput and the maximum throughput in network $\mathscr{O}$ at time t, respectively. The reward motivates the nodes to learn CST and TP that improve the minimum throughput in the network. As a result, the difference between the minimum throughput and maximum throughput gradually decreases, and throughput fairness is achieved.

2.3 Motivation

Although the selfish reward-based method improves the aggregate throughput, the method does not consider throughput fairness. As a result, the method allocates wireless resources to nodes unfairly. Although the environment-aware reward-based method can allocate the wireless resources to the nodes fairly, the method has the limitation to improve the aggregate throughput because the reward is determined based on the minimum throughput in networks. Motivated by the above, we argue that there is a room to improve the aggregate throughput with keeping throughput fairness among the nodes.

3 Proposal

In this paper, we propose the Q-learning-based spatial reuse method considering throughput fairness by negative reward for high throughput. In the proposed method, wireless nodes learn the adequate CST and TP for the high aggregate throughput and throughput fairness by rewards of Q-learning. The main idea of the proposed method is that it distributes wireless resources of nodes with the high throughput among nodes with the low throughput. To distribute the wireless resources, the proposed method gives negative rewards to the nodes with the high throughput. As a result, the nodes with the high throughput learn to suppress the wireless resource utilization by DSC and TPC. In contrast, the proposed method gives rewards to the nodes with low throughput for motivating them to use the wireless resources actively. As a result, the nodes with the low throughput learn to obtain the wireless resources from the nodes with the high throughput by TPC and DSC, and they achieve both the high aggregate throughput and throughput fairness.

First, we explain the system model of the proposed method in Sect. 3.1. Then, we show the flowchart of the proposed method in Sect. 3.2. Finally, we explain the algorithm of the proposed method in Sect. 3.3.

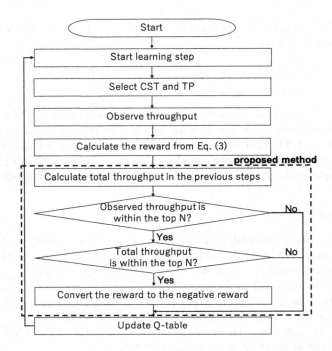

Fig. 1. Flowchart of the proposed method

3.1 System Model

We assume that wireless nodes are composed of wireless Stations (STAs) and
APs. The Q-learning-based methods including the proposed method are implemented in the STAs. We assume that the STAs can estimate the throughput of
all the STAs and APs by observing channels. The STAs conduct carrier sense
using DSC and TPC and send packets to neighbor nodes. The APs only receive
the packets. At each time step, STAs estimate the throughput of the others and
calculate their rewards based on the throughput. After the calculation, the STAs
determine CST and TP based on their rewards.

3.2 Flowchart of the Proposed Method

Figure 1 shows the flowchart of the proposed method. The proposed method is
implemented in STAs. First, the STAs select the CST and TP based on their
Q-tables. After that, they observe the throughput of them. By using the throughput, they calculate their rewards based on Eq. (3). In the proposed method, if the
throughput of them is higher than that of other STAs, the proposed method converts their rewards to negative rewards. Specifically, the proposed method gives
the negative reward to STA i if throughuput $\Gamma_{i,t}$ of STA i at time t satisfies with
the following two conditions:

Algorithm 1. Algorithm for Determing Action of STA i

Input: $\mathcal{A}$: set of possible action, $|A| = K$

   Initialize : timestep $t = 0$, $\varepsilon_0 = 1.0$, $\hat{Q}(a_k) = 0$, $a_k \in \mathcal{A}$

   while true **do**

      Action selection

$$a_t = \begin{cases} \arg\max_{1,\ldots,K} \hat{Q}(a_k) & \text{with probabikity } 1 - \varepsilon \\ \text{Randomly select from } \hat{Q} & \text{with probability } \varepsilon. \end{cases}$$

      Reward calculation

$$r_{i,t} = \begin{cases} -\frac{\Gamma_{i,t}}{\Gamma_i^*} & \text{if throughput } \Gamma_{i,t} \text{ satisfies conditions (5) and (6)}, \\ \frac{\Gamma_{i,t}}{\Gamma_i^*} & \text{otherwise.} \end{cases}$$

      Q-table updation

      $\hat{Q}(a_t) \leftarrow (1 - \alpha_t)\hat{Q}(a_t) + \alpha_t(r_{i,t} + \gamma(\max_{a'} \hat{Q}(a')))$

      $\varepsilon_t \leftarrow \frac{\varepsilon_0}{\sqrt{t}}, t \leftarrow t + 1$

   end while

$$|\{j \mid \Gamma_{i,t} \leq \Gamma_{j,t}, 1 \leq j \leq n\}| \leq N, \tag{5}$$

$$|\{j \mid \Gamma_{i,sum} \leq \Gamma_{j,sum}, 1 \leq j \leq n\}| \leq N, \quad \Gamma_{i,sum} = \sum_{t=1}^{T} \Gamma_{i,t}, \tag{6}$$

where n and T denote the number of the STAs in the network and a current timestep, respectively. Equation (5) means that STA i is in the top N STAs with the highest throughput among all the STAs. Equation (6) means that STA i is in the top N STAs with the highest total throughput among all the STAs. If STAs satisfy with conditions (5) and (6), they convert their rewards by multiplying the rewards by -1. Finally, they update their Q-tables based on Eq. (2).

3.3 Algorithm for Determining CST and TP

In the proposed method, STAs select the CST and TP with high rewards from Q-tables and update their Q-tables with rewards. The algorithm of the proposed method is shown in Algorithm 1. The algorithm is composed of action selection, reward calculation, and Q-table updation.

In the action selection, STAs select their actions based on their Q-tables. The actions are the pairs of CST and TP. The STAs select their actions from their Q-tables with ε-greedy strategy [8]. Specifically, with probability ε, they randomly select their actions from their Q-tables. In contrast, with probability $1 - \varepsilon$, they select their actions with the highest rewards among all the actions in their Q-tables. The proposed algorithm decreases the value of ε as time passes because the STAs do not need to explore for adequate actions as Q-learning progresses. In the reward calculation, they calculate their rewards using the throughput of them. Specifically, throughput $\Gamma_{i,t}$ of STA i at time t is calculated as:

$$\Gamma_{i,t} = \frac{\beta^i_{(t,t-T_{observe})}}{T_{observe}}, \tag{7}$$

Table 1. Simulation parameters

Wi-Fi standard	IEEE802.11ac
Frequency band (GHz)	5
Channel number	38
Channel bandwidth (MHz)	20
MCS	7
Propagation loss	Residential path loss model [9]
Fading/Shadowing	None
Mobility model	Static
Traffic model	CBR
Traffic load	Full buffer (uplink)
Max Aggregation	64
RTS/CTS	None
Antenna gain (dBi)	0
Noise figure (dBm)	7
TP (dBm)	AP: 20, STA: {3, 5, 8, 11, 14, 17, 20, 23}
CST (dBm)	AP: −76, STA: {−82, −79, −76, −73, −70, −67, −64, −62}
Simulation time (s)	10000
Timestep (s)	0.5
ε_0	1.0
α_t	0.5
γ	0.9
$T_{observe}$ (s)	0.5

where $T_{observe}$ and $\beta^i_{(t,t-T_{observe})}$ denote the observation time for the throughput and the number of successfully received bits of the STA i between $t - T_{observe}$ and t, respectively. We assume that the STAs can observe the throughput of the other STAs by observing channels. By using the throughput, they calculate their rewards based on Eq. (3). If the throughput of them satisfies with the conditions (5) and (6), they convert their rewards by multiplying the rewards by -1. Finally, in the Q-table updation, they update their Q-tables by their rewards based on Eq. (2).

4   Evaluation

We assume the scenario as one floor of 10×2 apartments. The size of one apartment is $10\,\text{m} \times 10\,\text{m} \times 3\,\text{m}$. We deployed one STA and one AP to each apartment, and the STAs and APs were randomly placed in the apartments. The height of all the STAs and APs was fixed to $1.5\,\text{m}$. In this scenario, the STAs created packets based on the Wi-Fi standard at regular interval, and the

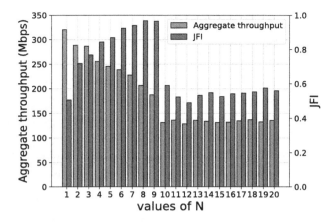

Fig. 2. Aggregate throughput and JFI with changing N in the proposed method.

APs only received the packets. We used ns-3.30.1 as a network simulator [10]. The propagation loss was calculated using the residential path model [9]. The simulation parameters are shown in Table 1.

We compare the proposed reward (Proposal) with the selfish reward (Selfish) and environment-aware reward (Env) in terms of the aggregate throughput and throughput fairness in Sect. 4.2. The selfish reward and environment-aware reward are calculated by Eqs. (3) and (4). To evaluate throughput fairness, we utilized Jain's Fairness Index (JFI) [11] that is calculated as:

$$\mathcal{J}(x_1, x_2, ..., x_n) = \frac{(\sum_{i=1}^{n} x_i)^2}{n \sum_{i=1}^{n} x_i^2}, \qquad (8)$$

where x_i and n denote the experienced throughput by STA i and the total number of STAs, respectively.

First, we evaluate the influence of the variable N for negative rewards in Sect. 4.1. Then, we compare the proposed reward with the selfish reward and environment-aware reward in terms of the aggregate throughput and throughput fairness in Sect. 4.2.

4.1   Influence of the Variable N for Negative Rewards

Figure 2 shows the aggregate throughput and JFI with changing N in the proposed method. As shown in Fig. 2, the value of JFI increases as the value of N increases from 1 to 9. This is because the throughputs of N STAs are distributed among the other STAs with the low throughput. As the value of N increases, the more the STAs with the low throughput can obtain the throughput from STAs with the high throughput. As a result, the proposed method improves throughput fairness among all the STAs by increasing the value of N. In contrast with JFI, the aggregate throughput decreases as the value of N increases from 1 to

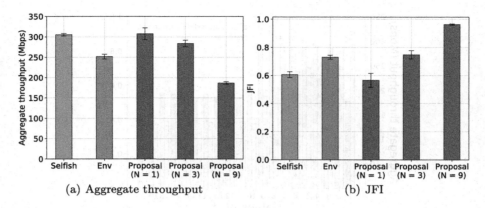

(a) Aggregate throughput   (b) JFI

Fig. 3. Comparison among the proposed reward, selfish reward, and environment-aware reward in terms of the aggregate throughput and JFI.

9. This is because the proposed method gives the negative rewards to the N STAs for their high throughput. As a result, the aggregate throughput decreases as the number of N increases. These results indicate that there is the trade-off between the aggregate throughput and throughput fairness.

When the value of N is between 10 and 20, the values of the aggregate throughput and JFI become low. This is because the penalty excessively suppresses the throughput of the STAs. As a result, the aggregate throughput decreases. Moreover, in the case where N is more than half of the learning STAs, the STAs with the low throughput are suppressed as much as the STAs with the high throughput. As a result, throughput fairness decreases.

In Fig. 2, when the values of N are 1, 3, and 9, the proposed method achieves the highest aggregate throughput, balance between the aggregate throughput and throughput fairness, and high throughput fairness, respectively. Therefore, we use 1, 3, and 9 as the value of N to compare the proposed method with the other methods in the next subsection.

4.2   Comparison with Previous Methods

Figure 3 shows the comparison among the proposed reward, selfish reward, and environment-aware reward in terms of the aggregate throughput and JFI. As shown in Fig. 3, the proposed method with $N = 3$ improves the aggregate throughput and JFI by 12.7% and 2.3% compared with the environment-aware reward-based method, respectively. Furthermore, in comparison with the selfish reward-based method, the proposed method with $N = 3$ improves JFI by 23.4% with slightly decreasing the aggregate throughput. These results indicate that the proposed method can achieve both the high aggregate throughput and throughput fairness effectively compared with the other methods by setting the adequate value to N. When the value of N is 9, the proposed method improves JFI by 31.7% compared with the environment-aware reward-based method. In

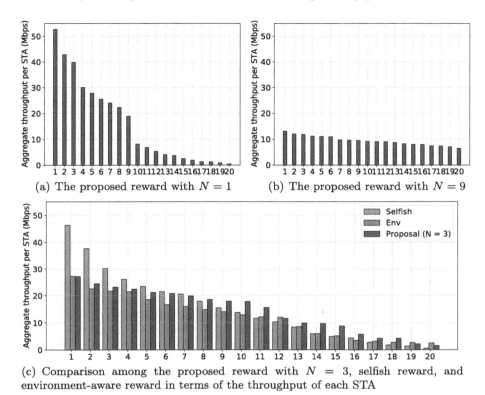

(a) The proposed reward with $N = 1$

(b) The proposed reward with $N = 9$

(c) Comparison among the proposed reward with $N = 3$, selfish reward, and environment-aware reward in terms of the throughput of each STA

Fig. 4. Aggregate throughput of each STA.

the proposed method, a lot of STAs receive negative rewards as the value of N increases. Therefore, throughput fairness increases as the value of N increases. In the environment-aware reward-based method, the minimum throughput in the network is given to all the STAs. On the other hands, all the STAs do not influence on the minimum throughput. Therefore, the reward contributes to throughput fairness to some extent.

To analyze the aggregate throughput and throughput fairness in details, we evaluated the aggregate throughput of each STA in Fig. 4. As shown in Fig. 4-(a), the STAs 1–9 get almost all the aggregate throughput in the network. This result indicates that the proposed method with $N = 1$ has the tendency to allocate wireless resources to STAs unfairly for achieving the high aggregate throughput in the network. The similar tendency can be seen in the selfish reward-based method in Fig. 4-(c). In contrast with these methods, as shown in Fig. 4-(b), all the STAs get the aggregate throughput fairly, and the aggregate throughput of them is low, however. This is because the mutual interference among the STAs becomes severe as the wireless resources are allocated to them fairly. As a result, the STAs suppress the other STAs to get the wireless resources.

As shown in Fig. 4-(c), the proposed method with $N = 3$ improves the aggregate throughput of almost all the STAs compared with the environment-aware reward-based method. By giving positive and negative rewards to the STAs with the low throughput and those with the high throughput respectively, the proposed method improves the aggregate throughput of the STAs with keeping throughput fairness. In contrast, the environment-aware reward-based method gives the minimum throughput in the network to the STAs for achieving throughput fairness. As a result, the method has the limitation to improve the aggregate throughput of STAs.

5   Conclusions

In this paper, we proposed the Q-learning-based spatial reuse method considering throughput fairness by negative reward for high throughput. The proposed method motivates nodes with the low throughput to use wireless resources by the rewards, while it suppresses the nodes with the high throughput to use the wireless resources by negative rewards. In simulation results, we have confirmed that the proposed method with $N = 3$ improved throughput fairness and the aggregate throughput by 12.7% and 2.3% compared with environment-aware reward-based method, respectively. Furthermore, the proposed method with $N = 3$ improved throughput fairness by 23.4% compared with the selfish reward-based method with keeping the aggregate throughput.

References

1. IEEE Standard for Information technology—telecommunications and information exchange between systems Local and metropolitan area networks—Specific requirements - Part 11: Wireless LAN Medium Access Control (MAC) and Physical Layer (PHY) Specifications. IEEE STD 802.11-2016 (Revision of IEEE STD 802.11-2012), pp. 1–3534 (2016)
2. Nishide, K., Kubo, H., Shinkuma, R., Takahashi, T.: Detecting hidden and exposed terminal problems in densely deployed wireless networks. IEEE Trans. Wireless Commun. 11(11), 3841–3849 (2012)
3. Jamil, I., Cariou, L., Hélard, J.-F.: Novel learning-based spatial reuse optimization in dense WLAN deployments. EURASIP J. Wirel. Commun. Netw. 2016(1), 1–19 (2016). https://doi.org/10.1186/s13638-016-0632-2
4. Ak, E., Canberk, B.: FSC: two-scale AI-driven fair sensitivity control for 802.11ax networks. In: GLOBECOM 2020–2020 IEEE Global Communications Conference, pp. 1–6 (2020)
5. Wilhelmi, F., Barrachina-Muñoz, S., Bellalta, B., Cano, C., Jonsson, A., Neu, G.: Potential and pitfalls of multi-armed bandits for decentralized spatial reuse in WLANs. J. Netw. Comput. Appl. 127, 26–42 (2019)
6. Watkins, C., Dayan, P.: Q-learning. Mach. Learn. 8, 279–292 (1992)
7. Morozs, N., Clarke, T., Grace, D.: Cognitive spectrum management in dynamic cellular environments: a case-based Q-learning approach. Eng. Appl. Artif. Intell. 55, 239–249 (2016)

8. Sutton, R.S., Barto, A.G.: Reinforcement Learning: An Introduction. A Bradford Book. The MIT Press, Cambridge (2018)
9. TGax simulation scenarios. https://mentor.ieee.org/802.11/dcn/14/11-14-0980-16-00ax-simulation-scenarios.docx. Accessed 19 July 2021
10. ns-3 (online). https://www.nsnam.org/. Accessed 19 July 2021
11. Jain, R., Chiu, D., Hawe, W.: A quantitative measure of fairness and discrimination for resource allocation in shared computer systems. CoRR cs.NI/9809099 (1998)

System Architecture for Autonomous Drone-Based Remote Sensing

Manos Koutsoubelias[✉], Nasos Grigoropoulos, Giorgos Polychronis,
Giannis Badakis, and Spyros Lalis

Electrical and Computer Engineering Department,
University of Thessaly, Volos, Greece
{emkouts,athgrigo,gpolychronis,badakis,lalis}@uth.gr

Abstract. Thanks to modern autopilot hardware and software, multi-rotor drones can fly and perform different maneuvers in a precise way, guided merely by high-level commands. This, in turn, opens the way towards fully automated drone-based systems whose operation can be driven by a computer program, without any human intervention. In this work, we present a modular architecture for such a system, which integrates a drone, a hangar, battery charger and a weather station with the necessary software components so as to provide an autonomous remote sensing service, which can operate at the edge while being interfaced as needed with external systems and applications. The proposed system architecture is described in detail, focusing on the core software components and the interaction between them. We also discuss the drone and ground station that is used to test our implementation in the field as well as a simulation environment which allows us to perform a wide range of experiments in a flexible and controlled way.

Keywords: System architecture · Software design · Drones ·
Automation · Remote monitoring · Edge computing

1 Introduction

Remote monitoring has long been used to gather data about geographical regions of interest. For many years this was done through advanced satellite technology. However, this comes at a very high cost and in numerous cases data for the area of interest is available only during specific times of the day depending on the location and field of view of the satellite carrying the required sensing equipment. For this reason, a large number of on-demand sensing tasks were conducted using manned aircraft equipped with the proper sensors.

This research has been co-finance by the European Union and Greek national funds through the Operational Program Competitiveness, Entrepreneurship and Innovation, under the call RESEARCH - CREATE - INNOVATE, project PV-Auto-Scout, code T1EDK-02435.

T. Hara and H. Yamaguchi (Eds.): MobiQuitous 2021, LNICST 419, pp. 220–242, 2022.
https://doi.org/10.1007/978-3-030-94822-1_13

During the recent years, a far cheaper and more flexible approach is to use unmanned aerial vehicles, also referred to as drones. Indeed, drones have become very popular and are now being used in an increasing number of applications, such as agriculture, structural health monitoring and surveillance. What drives this widespread use is the fact that modern drones can practically fly on their own, thanks to advanced embedded autopilot subsystems which continuously gather data from various on-board sensors, process them in real-time, and take all the steering decisions necessary to keep the vehicle steady during flight. In particular, multi-rotor drones (polycopters) can perform very precise maneuvers and even hold completely still, hovering in their current position. As a result, these drones can be flown via simple high-level commands, even by laymen who have little or no piloting experience.

In the same manner, such drones can be flown by computer programs too. There are several efforts to provide suitable tools and programming abstractions that simplify the development of computer-driven missions. Moreover, using available precision landing sensor technologies, the drone can accurately land even on small target areas, such as the landing pad of a hangar that can provide shelter when the drone is not being used and serve as a battery recharging (or battery switching) station during missions.

By combining these technologies, it becomes possible to fully automate the entire cycle of drone operation, thereby opening the way to a new class of drone-based remote sensing systems. This is particularly attractive if the drone routinely needs to perform the same sensing tasks over an area of interest, as this is typically the case in several monitoring and surveillance applications.

In this paper, we present a complete architecture for such a system, which integrates a drone, its hangar and battery charging subsystem, a local weather station and all the software components that are needed in order to provide a complete and fully autonomous remote sensing service. The main contributions of the paper are: (i) We propose a modular architecture for autonomous drone-based remote sensing systems, which can operate at the edge in a standalone way or as part of a more complex ecosystem. (ii) We describe the proposed design in detail, focusing on the software components that are responsible for the core system operation and mission execution. (iii) We discuss the drone and ground station setup we use in our field tests as well as a simulation environment used to test the functionality of our system in the lab for a wide range of scenarios.

We wish to note that our work focuses on outdoor sensing scenarios, using drones with autonomous flight, navigation and landing capability – many such platforms exist, and nowadays it is also relatively straightforward to even have custom designs, such as the drone we use in our tests. While some elements of the proposed system could be potentially reused to support indoor scenarios, this direction is beyond the scope of this work.

The rest of the paper is structured as follows. Section 2 presents the high-level system architecture. Section 3 discusses the main management logic, while Sect. 4 focuses on the aspect of mission execution. Section 5 describes the hardware-based and simulation-based setup used to test our implementation. Section 6 gives an overview of related work. Finally, Sect. 7 concludes the paper and provides some directions for future work.

2   System Concept and Architecture

We assume a geographical area or specific points of interest where certain sensing tasks can be performed using a drone. On the one hand, there can be standard sensing tasks that have to be conducted on a periodic basis, without any explicit request. On the other hand, certain sensing tasks may be introduced on demand, triggered by requests coming from external systems, e.g., end-user applications.

To support such a remote sensing capability, we propose a system that can manage the full cycle of operation—not just the flight of the drone during a mission, but also all the take-off and landing, storage and battery charging procedures—with little or no human intervention. Of course, the sensing equipment that needs to be mounted on the drone, the data collected via these sensors and the processing that needs to be performed on this data, all depend on the application. Nevertheless, having a general system design and implementation, which properly addresses all the application-neutral aspects of such a drone-based remote sensing system, is of big value as it is then possible to support any specific application with minimal customization and debugging effort.

In the spirit of edge computing, we envision such a system to run on a ground station close to the area of operation. This way one can have a direct and low-latency communication with the drone via WiFi or long-range RF technology, enabling autonomous and robust operation without relying on fast and stable connectivity with the cloud—even in the era of 5G, good Internet connectivity is by no means guaranteed if the system needs to operate in remote areas. The basic system infrastructure includes a suitably designed hangar where the drone can land autonomously, a battery charging subsystem (inside the hangar) and a local weather station, with which the ground station can communicate over dedicated serial links or a local area network. We assume that standard GPS accuracy is sufficient for the navigation and sensing tasks of the drone. To support applications with higher accuracy requirements, the system infrastructure and the drone need to be equipped with more advanced positioning subsystems, such as GPS RTK and/or visual positioning systems (VPS), but this does not affect the proposed system design. Finally, we assume that the drone can land on the hangar with high accuracy, supported by an appropriate precision landing mechanism, and dock on the battery charging system without manual intervention.

From a software perspective, the proposed system is built in a modular way, being composed of micro-services which are combined to provide the overall functionality. The top-level system architecture is shown in Fig. 1. Some components play the role of high-level drivers and provide access to the physical parts of the system, while others are responsible for purely software-based functions. Next, we outline the role of each component.

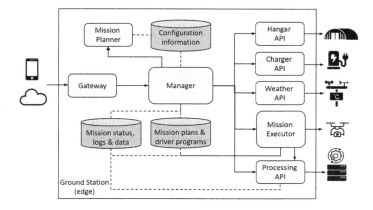

Fig. 1. Top-level system architecture.

The Gateway provides a technology-neutral interface towards external systems, including the end-user application through which the system can be managed remotely. Its role is to convey incoming requests to the Manager and send back the corresponding replies. Note that the interaction with external systems is not crucial for the core system operation; the system can execute monitoring tasks in an autonomous manner, even when having unstable/bad connectivity to external systems. Of course, access to the Gateway needs to be properly secured in order to avoid unauthorized access. This can be achieved using well-established technologies, such as VPNs in combination with more refined access control mechanisms (which is not the focus of this work).

The heart of the system is the Manager, which is responsible for the automation of the entire cycle of operation. Briefly, the Manager picks the mission plan for the sensing task at hand, makes the initial preparations and starts the execution of the plan. During execution, it monitors progress and updates the mission state. When the mission is completed, the Manager performs the necessary finalization actions so that the system becomes ready for the next sensing task. Section 3 describes the Manager in more detail.

The mission plans for the sensing tasks can be predefined or generated in a dynamic way. The former typically applies to standard tasks with fixed operational parameters. The latter is needed for tasks with open parameters that are determined at launch time (e.g., the specific points of interest are supplied as part of an on-demand sensing request), or to support replanning in case a sensing task is aborted. In these cases, the Mission Planner is invoked in order to produce a suitable plan. If the application does not have such requirements, the Mission Planner component becomes superfluous and is not included in the system configuration.

The Mission Executor is responsible for the actual execution of the mission plans. This is done using a so-called driver program, which parses the plan and performs the required interactions with the drone. It is important to note that the system may support various types/formats of sensing missions, and each mission type typically comes with its own driver program. The internal operation of the Mission Executor is described in Sect. 4.

The rest of the components serve as front-ends for different peripheral subsystems. The Hangar API supports the interaction with the hangar where the drone is stored, while the Charger API is used to access the battery charging subsystem. Information about the current weather conditions can be retrieved via the Weather API that communicates with a local station near the area of operation. Finally, the Processing API is used to process the data collected by the drone by employing suitable services, which may run locally on the ground station or be deployed in more powerful nearby edge infrastructure. Data processing may take place during the mission or once the mission completes, depending on the application and system configuration. Of course, the Processing API is not needed for pure data collection applications.

Further, the system keeps certain information on persistent storage. This includes specific points of interest, no-fly zones and drone characteristics, e.g., estimated flight time as a function of average flight speed, which may need to be taken into account when generating a new mission plan. Also, the system stores the available (predefined or auto-generated) mission plans and the driver program(s) for their execution. Last but not least, it keeps a log for each sensing task and corresponding mission execution, including its status and the data that was collected (and possibly processed) in this context. The different system components create/access this information via a shared repository, e.g., using a database for structured information in conjunction with a file system for unstructured data. This information can also be inspected and updated by authorized external systems and end-user applications via the Gateway.

3   Manager

The Manager oversees the different phases of a full monitoring cycle, in a similar way this would be done by a human operator. Namely, it invokes other components to perform the necessary actions and decides when to move the system to the next state of operation.

The internal organization of the Manager is shown in Fig. 2. It includes an RPC Server that is invoked by the Gateway when external requests arrive, an event-driven finite state machine (FSM) that implements the coordination of the operation cycle, and a set of observers that monitor different processes or subsystems and issue an event when certain conditions apply. These entities are independent threads running concurrently to each other. Sensing tasks are kept in a queue, sorted according to the scheduled start times. The events generated by the observers are kept in a separate FIFO queue, from where they are retrieved and handled by the FSM in a sequential manner. The operation of the FSM and the observers is described in more detail in the following subsections.

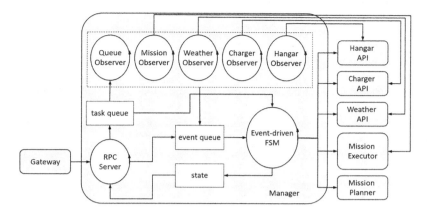

Fig. 2. Internal organization of the Manager.

3.1 Finite State Machine

The FSM runs in a loop. In each iteration, the next event is removed from the queue and the respective handler is invoked, which performs a state transition along with some actions. An event is dropped if it is not compatible with the current state or the last processed event was of the same type. If the queue is empty, the FSM blocks until an event is added to the queue.

The FSM has six states, representing the key phases of the operation cycle. The state diagram and the respective transitions are given in Fig. 3. The events that trigger the state transitions are indicated by the capitalized labels over the edges while the sources of each event are given in brackets. Figure 4 shows the core logic of the event handlers, where the dashed arrows denote the logical flow between handler invocations resulting as a side-effect of event generation.

Initially, the Manager is in the READY state where the drone is fully charged and can be used for the next sensing task. A new cycle is triggered via the START event, generated by the Queue Observer when it is time to start the next sensing task. As a result, the Manager invokes the Mission Planner to generate the mission plan for the task at hand, if such a plan is not already available. It also confirms, via the Weather API, that the weather conditions are good (else the task is postponed for a later point in time and the state remains READY). Then, the hangar is instructed to open its hatch via a call to the respective API. Since this operation may take some time, it is tracked by the Hangar Observer while the system moves in the OPENING state. When the hangar opens, the Hangar Observer generates an OPENED event. As a result, the Manager invokes the Mission Executor to start the execution of the mission plan, and moves to the RUNNING state.

Once the mission completes and the drone has properly landed, the Mission Observer generates the DONE event. The Manager then checks the mission status, and if the mission was aborted it may reschedule the remainder of the task (discussed in more detail in the sequel). In any case, the Manager instructs

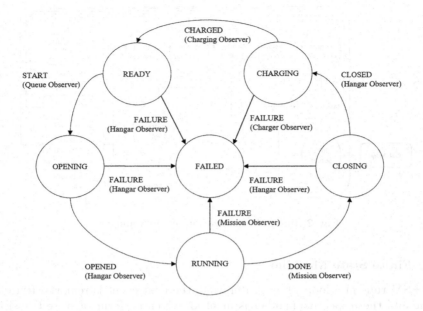

Fig. 3. State diagram of the FSM.

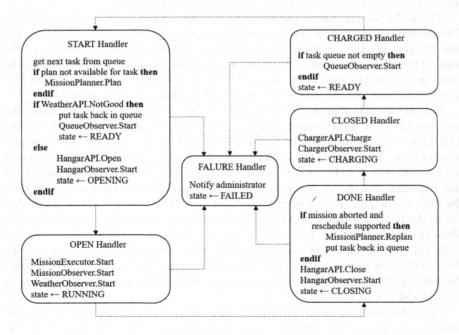

Fig. 4. Event handling logic of the FSM.

the hangar to close its hatch and moves to the CLOSING state, and when the Hangar Observer generates the CLOSED event the Manager starts charging the drone's batteries via the Charger API and enters the CHARGING state. Finally, when the Charger Observer generates a CHARGED event, the Manager starts the Queue Observer, if the task queue is not empty, and makes the transition back to the READY state from where the system can repeat the same procedure for the next sensing task. If there are no pending scheduled tasks, the system remains idle until a new task is submitted via the Gateway, in which case the RPC Server adds it in the queue and starts the Queue Observer.

During the above cycle of operation, some hard failures may occur which cannot be handled by the Manager in a graceful manner so that the system can continue its operation. More specifically, in the OPENING state, the hangar may not open; in the RUNNING state, the drone may not respond to critical commands or fail to land properly; in the CLOSING state, the hangar may not close; also, in the CHARGING state, the charger may not be able to properly charge the drone's batteries. In all these cases, a FAILURE event is generated by the respective observer. In turn, the Manager notifies the administrator and makes the transition to the FAILED state. The system remains in this state until it is reset manually; in some cases, it may be possible for the administrator to inspect and correct the problem remotely, via the Gateway, while other problems may require physical intervention. We note that a mission abort is not considered a hard failure. Even if a sensing task is stopped prematurely, it may be perfectly possible to reschedule it or proceed with the next task in the queue.

3.2 Observers

The observers are started on a need-to basis by the event handlers of the FSM, as indicated in Fig. 4. An observer is automatically stopped when it generates an event or the FSM makes a state transition.

The Queue Observer is responsible for triggering the execution of the next sensing task. To this end, it checks the task queue, determines when the next task needs to start and sets a timer accordingly in order to issue the START event. If a task is postponed or rescheduled, it is put back at the head of the queue so that its execution starts as early as possible.

The Hangar Observer uses the Hangar API to receive information about the position of its door/hatch. When this is fully opened or closed, it generates the OPENED and CLOSED event, respectively. If a problem occurs when trying to open/close the hatch, the FAILURE event is generated.

The Charger Observer uses the Charger API to check the progress of battery charging. When the drone's batteries are fully charged, it issues the CHARGED event. If charging does not work properly, it issues the FAILURE event.

The Weather Observer uses the Weather API to receive information about the weather conditions from the local station. If weather conditions deteriorate while a mission is already in progress, the Mission Executor is invoked to abort the mission. Note that the Weather Observer does not abort the mission itself nor does it generate an FSM event; if the Mission Executor indeed aborts the mission, the corresponding DONE event will be generated by the Mission Observer, discussed next.

The Mission Observer periodically polls the Mission Executor in order to receive information about the mission execution status. If the mission was terminated in a graceful manner, either because it was completed or because it was aborted, the Mission Observer generates the DONE event. If the mission status indicates abnormal termination due to a hard problem, the observer generates a FAILURE event.

3.3 Task Rescheduling and Data Processing

As was mentioned above, if a sensing task is aborted, the Manager can reschedule it so that it is completed as planned. To this end, the driver program needs to record in the system repository additional information regarding the degree of mission completion. In turn, the Manager can pass this information to the Mission Planner in order to produce a new plan for the remaining part of the task. Furthermore, to reduce the number of take-offs and landings that are performed by the drone, the Mission Planner can be asked to combine the rescheduled task with the next one in the queue, provided both have the same type. Note, however, that it may not be possible to support such an automated rescheduling and replanning for all sensing tasks and mission types. If an aborted task cannot be rescheduled, it keeps this status so that the administrator can take further action as needed, e.g., by manually submitting a suitable follow-up sensing task.

The data that is collected by the drone is stored by the driver program in the system repository from where it can be inspected/retrieved via the Gateway. Moreover, in some application scenarios, this data may need to be processed before making it available to external systems. This can be performed through an independent process running in parallel to the core mission control loop, in order to retrieve the data from the repository, invoke the corresponding data processing services via the Processing API, and store back the results. We do not elaborate about this aspect here, as this is does not affect the core operation of the system. Finally, we note that the mission itself can be data-driven, in which case some data processing will be performed by the driver program, without involving the Manager; we discuss this aspect at the end of the next section.

3.4 System Failures

As mentioned above, if any subsystem fails (Hangar, Battery Charger, Mission Executor), the Manager will enter the FAILED state, and the user (system administrator) will be notified in order to take action. If the Manager itself fails (e.g., the host machine crashes), this will be detected by the user when attempting to interact with it through the Gateway. Upon restart after an abrupt crash, the Manager enters the FAILED state and the user is notified as usual.

Of course, a system failure may also occur during the execution of a sensing task. In this case, the wireless connection between the Manager and the drone will break, and the drone will return and land autonomously, without requiring any external guidance. In principle, the Manager can resume such tasks, practically in the same way this is done for tasks that are aborted: by checking the logs and invoking the Mission Planner to produce a new plan for the part of the task that was not completed due to the system crash. In this particular case, however, we adopt a more conservative approach: the Manager does not attempt to automatically resume operation after a failure, and it has to be reset manually.

Finally, we note that it is possible to make the Manager fault-tolerant by adopting replication techniques, such as [16] or [24], so that system operation continues smoothly as long as at least one of the replicas remains operational. This discussion, however, is beyond the scope of this paper.

4   Mission Executor

The Mission Executor component is responsible for actually running a sensing task according to its specific mission plan, while communicating with the drone as needed. The interaction with the Manager takes places through an RPC Server, while the core functionality of mission execution is implemented in a separate environment that is invoked by the RPC Server, via a suitable front-end that hides technology-specific details. In our current prototype, the mission execution environment is implemented using the TeCoLa platform [23], as shown in Fig. 5. TeCoLa supports a flexible, service-oriented interaction with the drone in Python, and can work over different wireless technologies, including WiFi and long-range RF.

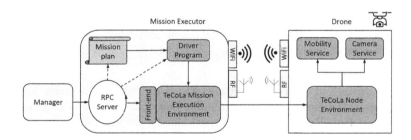

Fig. 5. Mission execution approach.

In a nutshell, the Mission Executor takes as input a mission plan and the driver program that will parse and execute the plan by invoking the drone's service as needed. The driver program runs on top of the Mission Execution Environment, which takes care of the underlying communication with the drone over a wireless link. The drone, in turn, runs the Node Environment, which processes the requests of the Mission Execution Environment, calls the corresponding local services and sends back the replies. In the basic system configuration used to test our system, the drone provides two services: the mobility service for the navigation-related functions of the autopilot, and the camera service for taking pictures via the onboard camera.

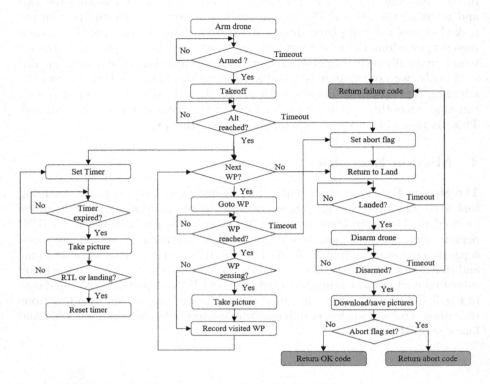

Fig. 6. Main logic of a driver program for taking aerial images over a target area following a waypoint-based mission plan.

As an example of a driver program, Fig. 6 illustrates the main logic of a program that is designed to execute waypoint-based mission plans while using the camera as a sensor. Pictures are taken periodically during the entire mission as the drone moves between the waypoints, as well as at certain waypoints specified in the plan. Initially, the program arms the drone and instructs it to take-off. It also starts a timer in order to perform periodic sensing, shown in the figure as an independent thread. Concurrently, in a loop, the program instructs the drone to move to the next waypoint. If a focused sensing action is required at that point, the drone is instructed to take a picture before moving to the next waypoint. When the drone successfully visits all waypoints, it is instructed to return and land. Finally, the drone is disarmed, the recorded pictures are downloaded from the drone and saved in the system repository, and the program returns a success code, leading to the generation of the DONE event by the Mission Observer.

If the drone does not reach the take-off altitude or a waypoint within a reasonable amount of time, this is considered as an indication of very localized adverse weather conditions that are not detectable by the weather station. To be safe, the driver program decides to abort the mission, and instructs the drone to return to the hangar and land immediately. Similar checks can be performed for other things, such as the drone's battery level in order to abort the mission if this drops below a safety margin (not shown in Fig. 6 to avoid clutter). In any case, the fact that the plan was not carried out to full completion is reflected in the return code of the program and the mission completion status reported by the Mission Executor to the Manager, so that the latter can identify and reschedule aborted tasks. Also, in the above example, the driver program explicitly records each waypoint that is successfully visited by the drone. This information can be passed (along with the original plan) to the Mission Planner to produce a plan for the rest of the sensing task. Recall that even if the mission completion status indicates an abort rather than full completion, the Mission Observer will still generate a DONE event as the system can continue its operation.

If the drone fails to arm/disarm or does not land properly, is not possible for the system to continue operation without manual inspection and perhaps even hands-on maintenance. In these cases, the driver program terminates immediately with a failure code, which leads to the generation of a FAILURE event by the Mission Observer. Several additional safety checks, e.g., for smooth motor operation and lack of vibrations, can be performed along the same lines, in order to put the system in the FAILED state whenever human intervention is required (to focus on the essence, the example in Fig. 6 does not include such checks).

At any point in time during execution, the Manager may ask the Mission Executor to pause, continue or abort the mission, due to a corresponding external request received via the Gateway. Also, the Weather Observer may request an abort if it detects deteriorating weather conditions. In these cases, the Mission Executor up-calls special handlers of the driver program, which take the necessary actions. More specifically, on pause, the last command that was sent to the drone is recorded and the drone is instructed to hover in its current position, while the driver program is suspended. When requested to continue execution, the last command is re-sent to the drone and the driver program is resumed. Finally, a requested abort leads to the same behavior as when the driver program takes this decision by itself. The event handling logic of the driver program is not shown in Fig. 6 for brevity.

We wish to stress that the format of the mission plans as well as the driver program used for their execution can both be customized according to the application's requirements. It is also straightforward to introduce additional drone sensor (and actuator) services, provided the drone features the corresponding hardware. Furthermore, the system can employ different types of missions and corresponding driver programs, which may rely on platforms other than TeCoLa; one merely needs to a add a corresponding mission execution environment and front-end. This flexibility is important for sensing applications where there is no single size that fits all needs. In particular, it is possible to support dynamic data-driven missions. This can be done using a suitable driver program, which receives data from the drone during the mission (e.g., at specific waypoints), processes this data and guides the drone based on the results. To minimize delays, heavyweight data transfers between the drone and the driver program on the ground station would need to be performed over sufficiently fast wireless links. The driver program can perform the required data processing by invoking in a direct way the appropriate services via the Processing API, without involving the Manager. Depending on the system configuration and available computing resources, the data processing services can run locally on the ground station or at a powerful edge infrastructure with good connectivity to the ground station.

5   Functional Testing

We have implemented a complete system prototype, where all the software components discussed in the previous sections are separate microservices, packaged as Docker containers in order to support a managed deployment on the ground station. The mission plans used to test our implementation are waypoint-based, and the logic of the driver program that executes such plans is similar to that in Fig. 6, with several additional checks that may lead to an abort or failure depending on the gravity of the detected issue. We have performed a wide range of tests using a custom drone and ground-station but also a suitable simulation environment. We describe the two setups in more detail below.

5.1   Field Setup

The setup used to perform tests in the field is shown in Fig. 7. The drone is a custom hexacopter with a CUAV V5 nano autopilot board [10], which provides all flight-related sensors and runs the popular ArduPilot [1] autopilot software for multicopters. The drone features as a separate companion board a Raspberry Pi 3 Model B [8] (RPi) with a quad-core ARM Cortex A53 processor at 1.2 GHz and 1 GB of RAM, running the Debian-based Raspberry Pi OS Buster, the officially supported Linux distribution for the RPi. The RPi is connected to the autopilot board over serial and runs the TeCoLa Node Environment. The mobility service employs the DroneKit library [3], which communicates with the autopilot through MAVProxy [6]. The camera service accesses an onboard 8 MP RPi Camera Module v2 [9] via the picamera library [7].

For the ground station we use an Intel NUC mini PC running a Ubuntu 16.0 LTS Linux distribution, powered via an external car battery. Since the field tests focus on the operation of the core system components, this configuration does not include a weather station, a hangar or battery charger subsystem. Instead, the Weather API is hardwired to report good weather conditions, the Hangar API produces open/close events right after receiving the corresponding commands, and the battery charging status reported by the Charger API is set manually when the drone is equipped with fresh batteries. Also, to have full control on the missions that are performed in the field, we do not use a Mission Planner component. All tests are based on manually prepared mission plans and no rescheduling takes place in case of an abort.

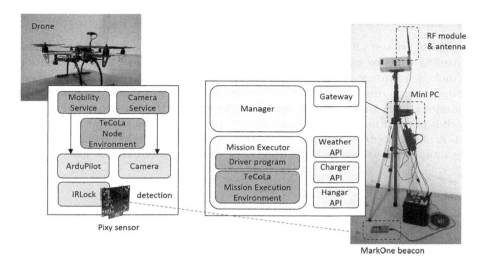

Fig. 7. System setup used in the field tests.

Precision landing is supported in the same way as this would be the case in a real deployment. More specifically, we use the IRLock mechanism [5], which is already supported by the off-the-shelf ArduPilot distribution. IRLock relies on the onboard Pixy camera sensor to track an IR beacon. To achieve robust tracking, we use the MarkOne beacon, which can be detected from a height of up to 15 m. The beacon is powered by the same external battery as the mini PC, using a long cable so that it can be placed at the desired landing position.

The communication between the ground station and the drone can be configured to go over WiFi or RF telemetry. Both the drone and the embedded computer have corresponding interfaces; the latter has an integrated WiFi antenna, while the RF module is externally connected to it via USB and is mounted on a pole for better coverage. The system can be configured to use only one of these interfaces, or both of them concurrently with the option of service-based binding. For instance, the RF which has a longer range can be used for the more critical mobility service, whereas the WiFi which can support higher throughput can be used for the camera service.

While field trials are important to verify the desired system operation under real conditions, they also come with several limitations, primarily due to safety rules and regulations in drone operation. Field trials are also very time consuming since they require extensive preparation and travel. For these reasons, a large number of more complex experiments are performed using a simulated setup described in the sequel.

5.2 Simulated Setup

To thoroughly test all system functions and several corner cases in a flexible and controlled way, we use a modular setup, which integrates different simulation technologies through virtual machine (VM) and container technology in order to support experimentation with different virtual unmanned vehicles and virtual ground stations. In this particular setup, we employ the Gazebo simulator [4], which is popular in the robotics community and has built-in support for the simulation of polycopters, and ns3 [27] for the simulation of wireless communication. The setup is illustrated in Fig. 8 and is described in more detail below.

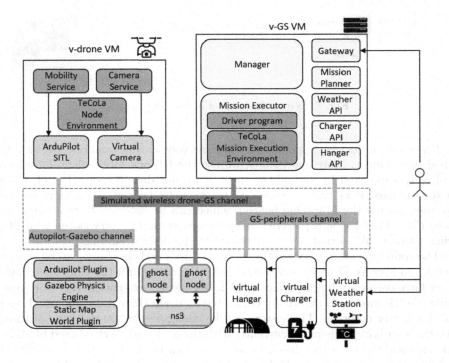

Fig. 8. System setup using the Gazebo simulator and ns3.

The drone functions are implemented within a virtual machine (v-drone VM), mimicking a drone configuration where the flight controller and the companion computer coexist on the same board. The autopilot software and the TeCoLa Node Environment with the mobility and the camera services run as containers within the v-drone VM. In this setup, we employ the official software-in-the-loop (SITL) configuration of Ardupilot [2], coupled to the physics engine of Gazebo that models the behavior of a typical quadcopter with high fidelity. Gazebo itself runs in a separate container, outside the v-drone VM, and communicates with the SITL ArduPilot via the Ardupilot plugin over a dedicated communication channel of the simulation environment. In addition, Gazebo is configured to use the static map world plugin, which provides a ground plane with satellite imagery used to feed real images to a virtual camera. The mobility service in the v-drone VM communicates with the autopilot via Dronekit, in the same way this is done in the real drone. The camera service is modified to access a virtual camera container, which communicates with Gazebo to return images based on the drone's current position in the virtual world.

The ground station is also a virtual machine (v-GS VM) that includes the entire management system. The communication between the v-drone and the v-GS occurs over a virtual WiFi network. This is simulated using ns3, which is configured to operate according to the 802.11b standard, and is accessed by the VMs via proper (virtual) wireless interfaces that map into corresponding so-called ghost nodes in ns3. We note that the WiFi simulation also takes into account the distance between the ground station and the drone. The position of the ground station is fixed at startup, while the position of the drone is updated at runtime based on the reports of the autopilot that are sent to ns3 via a side channel (not shown in the figure to avoid clutter).

In this configuration, we use a simple Mission Planner component, which takes as input a sequence of waypoints and produces a plan in the format that is expected by the driver program. The plans are produced taking into account the drone's operational autonomy (battery capacity vs energy needed for the drone to fly at a certain speed). If a sensing task is too large, the planner will produce several smaller plans, which the Manager schedules in sequence via the task queue. The planner can also combine smaller plans into larger ones. This feature is used when the Manager reschedules a task after an abort, in order to merge it with the next one in the task queue (if any).

For the weather station, the hangar and the battery charger, we use mockups which run as independent containers and are accessed by the corresponding API components over a separate communication channel. These mockups can be pre-configured as well as interactively controlled by the user during the simulation to behave according to the test scenario. More specifically, the weather station can report different conditions, while the hangar can open/close its hatch and the charger appear to charge the drone's battery with a configurable delay or exhibit a malfunction.

5.3   User Interface

In our prototype, all system entities can be accessed and monitored via command-line tools and different logs. Furthermore, as an indicative interactive user interface, we have developed a simple GUI, shown in Fig. 9.

Through this GUI, the user can start, pause, continue and abort missions as well as view the current drone position on top of a google map along with some basic status information. There is also a panel, next to the map view and above the control buttons, for displaying the most recent photo taken by the drone (as soon as this is stored in the system repository).

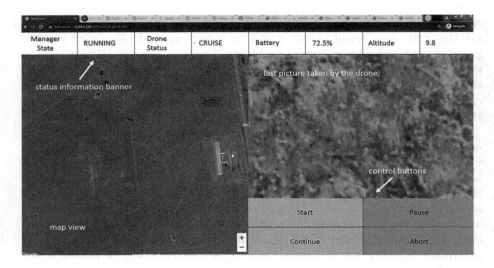

Fig. 9. Snapshot of user interface during system operation.

We note that the GUI is designed as an independent (web-based) application, which communicates with our system via the Gateway. It can be used to interact with the real ground station in field tests as well as with the virtual ground station when performing simulated tests.

5.4   Indicative Test Scenario

Using the simulated setup, we have tested our implementation extensively for a wide range of scenarios regarding different cases of user intervention (mission pause, continue and abort), dynamically changing weather conditions, failures of the hangar/chargers and disconnections between the ground station and the drone. To give an indicative example, assume the administrator has added a periodic sensing task for scanning a target area of 300×300 m through several passes at an altitude of 10 m. The desired path of the task is defined via a sequence of waypoints with a "horizontal" distance of 300 m and a "vertical" distance of 20 m, depicted in Fig. 10a by the gray bullets.

The total flight distance that needs to be covered is about 5 Km without taking into account take-off and landing, at a specified flying speed of 4 m/s. However, at that speed, the drone has an autonomy of only about 3.5 Km. As a consequence, this task is mapped to two smaller mission plans, illustrated in Fig. 10a in orange and blue color, respectively. Since this is a periodic task, these plans are produced offline and are stored in the system repository from where they are retrieved by the Manager when the task is started.

During the execution of the first plan (orange), the weather station is set to report bad conditions. As a result, the mission is aborted at the point marked in Fig. 10b and the drone returns back to base and lands. The remaining part of the first plan is rescheduled and merged with the second plan (blue), thereby producing a new ad-hoc plan (green) that is executed as soon as the drone's batteries are fully charged.

Figure 11a shows the sequence of system events that are generated for/during the execution of this sensing task, in line with what was described in Sect. 3. To

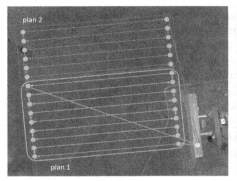
(a) Initial offline plans.

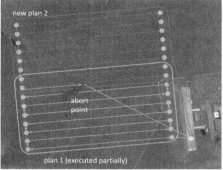
(b) Modified ad-hoc second plan.

Fig. 10. Original and adapted plan due to abort. (Color figure online)

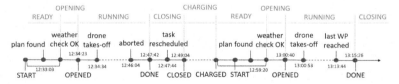
(a) Sequence of system events, actions and states (timeline not in scale).

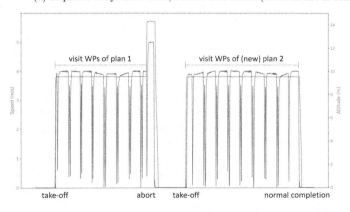
(b) Flight speed and altitude of the drone.

Fig. 11. System events and drone flight data. (Color figure online)

display events that occur at widely different time scales, the timeline is not in scale but merely illustrates the logical sequence of events with their timestamps (given that granularity is in seconds, some events have the same timestamp; also, larger time periods are denoted by a dashed line). The state of the FSM at the various time intervals is indicated above the timeline (in blue). As can be seen by observing the event timestamps, the simulation environment is configured so that the time needed for the hangar to fully open/close its hatch is to 80 s, while the delay for charging the drone's batteries is set to 10 min (of course, the actual recharging time for the batteries of the real drone is much larger).

Figure 11b depicts the drone's speed and flight altitude relative to the home position, which are recorded during the experiment in the system logs (as done during real flight tests). Once the drone takes off and starts the mission according to the first plan, its altitude remains constant at about 10 m, while its speed is roughly 4 m/s except when the drone slows down in order to turn at the specified waypoints. When the sensing task is aborted, the mission driver program activates the return-to-land behavior. As a result, the drone immediately rises to a default altitude of 15 m and then moves with a default speed of 5 m/s to the home position where it lands. The same basic pattern is repeated during the execution of the second plan. The difference is that, in this case, the entire mission is completed successfully, thus the drone follows the planned path back to home without changing the specified flight altitude or speed.

6   Related Work

There is a growing body of work on supporting the development of autonomous drone-based monitoring and tracking applications. Below, we briefly discuss indicative efforts. A modular system for object-tracking applications is presented in [28], consisting of a drone with an onboard computer, a camera and positioning sensors like GPS. The camera images and sensor data are processed on the onboard computer in order to detect the target object and infer the drone's position. The results fed in a mission planning module, also running on the onboard unit, which sends suitable control commands to the drone's flight controller so as to follow and approach the target object. [18] describes a drone-based system for structural health monitoring. The drone is equipped with a camera and an onboard computer that processes the camera images to detect special AR tags, which are used to mark the desired points (structural elements) of interest. It also features a separate stereo vision subsystem with two special (CCD point-grey) cameras. The drone flies autonomously to the points of interest where it takes stereoscopic images. After the flight, these images are transferred to a high-performance computer in order to perform the required data processing. The goal of the system presented in [29] is to pursuit intruder drones based on external alerts. When an intruder drone enters the area, another drone is used to detect, track and jam the intruder. The drone is equipped with a camera, an onboard unit that processes the camera images in order to detect the intruder drone and guide the drone by sending signals to the flight controller, and a software-defined radio used to jam the intruder as well as for self localization. The authors in [11] propose a system for precision agriculture using UAVs and an edge server. The photos taken by the UAVs are processed on an edge server to extract relevant features for the crop in question, and to decide if more samples are needed, in which case the next flight plan for the UAVs is produced. The above efforts focus on the autonomous operation and flight control of the drone, in some cases with the help of edge computing infrastructure. Our work is complementary to such efforts, with the goal to automate the full operation cycle of drone-based sensing systems, including storage, battery-charging, weather checking, mission planning, mission execution and data processing, without any human intervention. The proposed design can be flexibly customized to support different specific application scenarios, including the ones outline above.

There are several efforts on supporting the coordinated usage of multiple robots or drones. TeCoLa [23] abstracts autonomous robots as nodes providing different services that can be accessed remotely via method calls with at-most-once semantics. Mobility is modelled as a special service. The application program can transparently discover and invoke the available nodes as needed, while there is also support for the dynamic formation and grouped invocation of smaller teams. Resh [12] is a domain-specific language and orchestration system for multi-robot systems. Each robot has an agent that communicates with a centralized runtime in order to advertise its capabilities/status and translate the Resh protocol to the local robot-specific API. Dolphin [26] also follows a centralized approach for task execution using a static team of autonomous vehicles, where the platform's runtime system is responsible for polling the vehicles, sending tasks to them and managing platform-specific operations. In [13], the ScaFi programming language is used to let a multi-agent system achieve a collective goal in a distributed fashion. An iterative protocol is followed, whereby each agent evaluates its local state, checks for any messages coming from its neighbors, runs an aggregation program based on the current context, performs corresponding actions, updates its state and notifies its neighbors. Maple-Swarm [21] allows the developer to submit partial high-level plans. These plans are used as input to generate specific tasks for one or more robots, based on their capabilities and the current state of the system. Our work is largely orthogonal to the problem of coordinated task execution. In terms of design, the proposed system architecture can be extended to support sensing tasks with more than one drones. In a nutshell, the Manager would need to handle multiple hangar and battery charging subsystems in order to keep track of the drones that are ready to be used for sensing tasks, the Planner would need to produce individual mission plans while ensuring the necessary safety boundaries between the drones that will be used at the same time, and the driver program would have to be written accordingly in order to execute these mission plans in a coordinated way. Our current implementation uses TeCoLa for mission execution, which already provides support for team-level operations that could be used to support sensing tasks with multiple drones. However, in principle, any other platform could be used to write the driver program for executing such sensing tasks.

Some researchers investigate the remote usage of UAVs following cloud-based approaches. In [32], UAVs appear as cloud services managed by a central coordinator, which takes care of the underlying communication and maintains the sessions between UAVs and their users. [14] proposes a cloud service through which users can interactively request missions using an Android application. The service plans the path, picks the best available UAV and sends the mission to the UAV's autopilot, while the user can monitor the mission by receiving live status data and video streaming. Dronemap Planner [22] virtualizes UAVs by offering suitable control and data retrieval web services, which run in the cloud and can be invoked by third-party applications via standard web-service protocols. All these approaches are definitely interesting if ones wishes for UAVs to become a shared resource that can be used by different users possibly even at the same time. Our work goes in the opposite direction, focusing on the automation of remote sensing systems that employ their own (possibly highly customized) drones and ground infrastructure in an exclusive way. Also, both control and data processing take place at the edge, making it possible for the system to operate with full autonomy even when having poor connectivity with the cloud. If needed, the proposed system can also work in the cloud, using a 5G link for the communication with the drone, provided the latency and bandwidth are sufficient for the application in question.

Our work has some common goals with the concept of autonomic computing [19]. The benefits of an abstract architectural approach for autonomic computing systems are stressed in [25], where the authors motivate their model inspired by the domain of robotics. Most work in this area of research focuses on resource/service monitoring and provisioning in cloud environments so as to maintain QoS and satisfy SLA requirements [15,17,30], while several self-* properties have also been studied in the context of flying ad-hoc networks [20,31]. In contrast, the approach proposed in this paper tackles the self-management of drone-based remote sensing systems, by monitoring key parameters of system operation and taking corrective or preventive actions as needed.

7 Conclusion

We have presented a complete architecture for edge-based remote sensing systems that rely on drones. The system is designed to support the full cycle of operation in an automated way, without requiring good connectivity to the cloud or any human intervention (except when serious, non-recoverable failures occur). We have implemented all software components of the proposed architecture and have tested their functionality using both a real drone and ground station as well as a suitable simulation environment. Thanks to its modular design, the system can be flexibly customized according to application requirements, in terms of both the drone and the mission types/driver programs that will be used to support the desired sensing tasks. Also, data processing can be performed during the execution or after the completion of a sensing task, as needed.

As a next step, we intend to investigate the support of sensing tasks via multiple drones in more depth. Apart from writing suitable driver programs that perform the necessary coordination, which is already feasible in our current prototype, an additional challenge is to address the management of multiple hangars and battery chargers as well as to perform a dynamic replanning when a drone, hangar or battery charger fails so that the task is performed by the drones that remain fully operational.

References

1. ArduPilot autopilot. http://ardupilot.org
2. ArduPilot SITL. http://ardupilot.org/dev/docs/sitl-simulator-software-in-the-loop.html
3. DroneKit. http://dronekit.io/
4. Gazebo simulator. http://gazebosim.org/
5. IRLock tracking system. https://irlock.com
6. MAVProxy software. http://ardupilot.github.io/MAVProxy/html/index.html
7. Picamera interface. https://github.com/waveform80/picamera
8. Raspberry Pi 3. https://www.raspberrypi.org/products/raspberry-pi-3-model-b/
9. Raspberry Pi camera. https://www.raspberrypi.org/products/camera-module-v2/
10. V5 Nano. http://doc.cuav.net/flight-controller/v5-autopilot/en/v5-nano.html
11. Boubin, J., Chumley, J., Stewart, C., Khanal, S.: Autonomic computing challenges in fully autonomous precision agriculture. In: IEEE International Conference on Autonomic Computing (ICAC), pp. 11–17 (2019)
12. Carroll, M., Namjoshi, K.S., Segall, I.: The Resh programming language for multirobot orchestration. arXiv preprint arXiv:2103.13921 (2021)
13. Casadei, R., Aguzzi, G., Viroli, M.: A programming approach to collective autonomy. J. Sens. Actuator Netw. **10**(2), 27 (2021)
14. Ermacora, G., Rosa, S., Toma, A.: Fly4smartcity: a cloud robotics service for smart city applications. J. Ambient Intell. Smart Environ. **8**(3), 347–358 (2016)
15. Ferrer, A.J., Becker, S., Schmidt, F., Thamsen, L., Kao, O.: Towards a cognitive compute continuum: an architecture for ad-hoc self-managed swarms. arXiv preprint arXiv:2103.06026 (2021)
16. Gerkey, B., Mataric, M.: Pusher-watcher: an approach to fault-tolerant tightly-coupled robot coordination. In: IEEE International Conference on Robotics and Automation, vol. 1, pp. 464–469 (2002)
17. Gill, S.S., Chana, I., Singh, M., Buyya, R.: Radar: self-configuring and self-healing in resource management for enhancing quality of cloud services. Concurrency Comput. Pract. Experience **31**(1), e4834 (2019)
18. Kalaitzakis, M., Kattil, S.R., Vitzilaios, N., Rizos, D., Sutton, M.: Dynamic structural health monitoring using a DIC-enabled drone. In: International Conference on Unmanned Aircraft Systems (ICUAS), pp. 321–327 (2019)
19. Kephart, J.O., Chess, D.M.: The vision of autonomic computing. Computer **36**(1), 41–50 (2003)
20. Kim, G.H., Nam, J.C., Mahmud, I., Cho, Y.Z.: Multi-drone control and network self-recovery for flying ad hoc networks. In: International Conference on Ubiquitous and Future Networks (ICUFN), pp. 148–150 (2016)
21. Kosak, O., Huhn, L., Bohn, F., Wanninger, C., Hoffmann, A., Reif, W.: Maple-swarm: programming collective behavior for ensembles by extending HTN-planning. In: International Symposium on Leveraging Applications of Formal Methods, pp. 507–524 (2020)

22. Koubâa, A., et al.: Dronemap planner: a service-oriented cloud-based management system for the internet-of-drones. Ad Hoc Netw. **86**(1), 46–62 (2019)
23. Koutsoubelias, M., Lalis, S.: TeCoLa: a programming framework for dynamic and heterogeneous robotic teams. In: International Conference on Mobile and Ubiquitous Systems: Computing, Networking and Services (Mobiquitous), pp. 115–124 (2016)
24. Koutsoubelias, M., Lalis, S.: Fault-tolerance support for mobile robotic applications. In: IEEE International Symposium on Industrial Embedded Systems (SIES), pp. 1–10 (2018)
25. Kramer, J., Magee, J.: Self-managed systems: an architectural challenge. In: Future of Software Engineering (FOSE), pp. 259–268 (2007)
26. Lima, K., Marques, E.R., Pinto, J., Sousa, J.B.: Dolphin: a task orchestration language for autonomous vehicle networks. In: IEEE/RSJ International Conference on Intelligent Robots and Systems (IROS), pp. 603–610 (2018)
27. Riley, G.F., Henderson, T.R.: The ns-3 network simulator. In: Wehrle, K., Güneş, M., Gross, J. (eds.) Modeling and Tools for Network Simulation, pp. 15–34. Springer, Heidelberg (2010). https://doi.org/10.1007/978-3-642-12331-3_2
28. Smyczyński, P., Starzec, Ł., Granosik, G.: Autonomous drone control system for object tracking: flexible system design with implementation example. In: IEEE International Conference on Methods and Models in Automation and Robotics (MMAR), pp. 734–738 (2017)
29. Souli, N., et al.: Horizonblock: implementation of an autonomous counter-drone system. In: International Conference on Unmanned Aircraft Systems (ICUAS), pp. 398–404 (2020)
30. Toffetti, G., Brunner, S., Blöchlinger, M., Dudouet, F., Edmonds, A.: An architecture for self-managing microservices. In: International Workshop on Automated Incident Management in Cloud, pp. 19–24 (2015)
31. Yang, T., Foh, C.H., Heliot, F., Leow, C.Y., Chatzimisios, P.: Self-organization drone-based unmanned aerial vehicles (UAV) networks. In: IEEE International Conference on Communications (ICC), pp. 1–6 (2019)
32. Yapp, J., Seker, R., Babiceanu, R.: UAV as a service: enabling on-demand access and on-the-fly re-tasking of multi-tenant UAVs using cloud services. In: IEEE/AIAA Digital Avionics Systems Conference (DASC), pp. 1–8 (2016)

Adaptive Replica Selection in Mobile Edge Environments

João Dias, João A. Silva, and Hervé Paulino$^{(\boxtimes)}$

NOVA Laboratory for Computer Science and Informatics (NOVA LINCS),
Department of Computer Science, NOVA School of Science and Technology,
NOVA University Lisbon, Caparica, Portugal
{jpm.dias,jaa.silva}@campus.fct.unl.pt, herve.paulino@fct.unl.pt

Abstract. Mobile Edge Computing (MEC) is a paradigm that aims to bring cloud services closer to mobile clients, effectively reducing latency and saving backbone bandwidth. As in cloud environments, many applications make use of replication to enhance their quality of service. However, here, data generated by the mobile devices is usually kept near its source, and can have multiple replicas scattered through the network (e.g., on the mobile devices or on edge servers). When requesting data, replica selection can have a significant impact in multiple aspects of a system, e.g., load balancing, throughput, or energy efficiency. Thus, the possible herd behavior combined with the unreliable wireless communication channels can cause systems to under-perform. In this paper, we propose MECERRA, a replica ranking algorithm tailored for the characteristics of MEC environments. Additionally, we detail WASABI, a flexible replica ranking framework that also handles the management of system metrics. We implement MECERRA in WASABI, and integrate it into a data storage system for edge networks, building an adaptive replica selection scheme. We use the resulting system to evaluate our proposal and compare it against related work. Results show that MECERRA is able to greatly increase the probability of finding the best replica, and WASABI provides low overhead.

Keywords: Replica selection · Replica ranking · Mobile edge computing · Replication

1 Introduction

Mobile Edge Computing (MEC) [1] brings cloud services closer to the mobile clients, i.e., to the *edge* of the network, by leveraging on the storage and computing resources of small servers deployed in base stations. By being closer to

This work was partially supported by *Fundação para a Ciência e a Tecnologia* through project *DeDuCe* (PTDC/CCI-COM/32166/2017) and the *NOVA LINCS* research center (UIDB/04516/2020).

T. Hara and H. Yamaguchi (Eds.): MobiQuitous 2021, LNICST 419, pp. 243–263, 2022.
https://doi.org/10.1007/978-3-030-94822-1_14

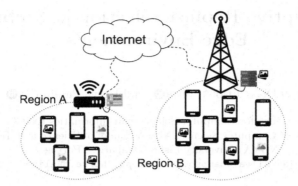

Fig. 1. Example MEC scenario. The two different pictures depicted in the phones represent replicas of two data items. Hence, both items have two replicas on region A, and one of them has four replicas on region B (including one on the edge server) while the other item has only one.

the data sources, MEC servers effectively reduce end-to-end delays and save backbone bandwidth for those cases that strictly require remote cloud infrastructures. This paradigm promotes the reduction of network bottlenecks, and allows the support of new applications with strict latency requirements. Additionally, by residing at the network edge, MEC servers are capable of collecting real-time network data, like congestion rates or subscriber mobility [2]. Furthermore, there is also the proposal of using the mobile devices themselves as actual edge nodes, harnessing their resources [13].

Both in MEC and cloud environments, many applications and services use data replication as a way to improve performance and overall quality of service. With replication, data items can have multiple replicas scattered among several nodes of the system, depending on the used replica management strategy. Consider the scenario of Fig. 1, on which a data sharing MEC application leverages on the publish-subscribe interaction pattern to enable data sharing (such as photos) among co-located users. As times evolves, the shared data items are downloaded by the users, spawning new replicas (on the mobile devices), and may also be cached by the MEC servers. In this context, when a node is notified that a new data item (matching one of its subscriptions) has been published, it is faced with the decision of selecting from which replica to download the item from. This decision can have a significant impact in multiple aspects of a system—such as load balancing, throughput, or energy efficiency—both on the server and client-sides. Aspects that can be even more exacerbated when referring to mobile devices and MEC scenarios. Thus, the question arises as how to decide which replica to contact for each data item request.

Replica ranking and selection has been addressed in cloud environments [3, 15,16], but these solutions do not take into account the idiosyncrasies of MEC systems, such as the high churn or energy constraints of mobile devices. In turn, data storage systems for MEC environments do not employ adaptive replica selection mechanisms. Also, most of the solutions do not take into account the evolution of the system, using static strategies [10,13,14]. To the best of our knowledge, the only exception is MobiTribe [17], which centralizes that decision on a proxy server that has the knowledge of the entire system (and of the ongoing requests)—a solution that is not very resilient and difficult to apply in the decentralized MEC scenarios that we target.

In this paper, we propose MECERRA, a replica ranking algorithm specifically tailored for MEC environments, that addresses the challenges raised in these environments, namely churn, dynamic replica set, energy constraints, and metric freshness. Additionally, we detail WASABI, a flexible replica ranking framework, that handles both the management of system metrics and replica ranking according to those metrics. WASABI forms a continuous feedback loop between clients and servers in order to grant clients with a fresh (albeit usually partial) view of the system. Using server-emitted, as well as client-observed metrics as parameters to the underlying replica ranking algorithm, clients are able to sort the available replicas for a given request. We implement MECERRA in WASABI, and build an adaptive replica selection scheme, by integrating this into a data storage and dissemination system for edge networks [13]. We use the resulting system to evaluate our proposal and compare it against other algorithms in related work. Experimental results through simulation show that MECERRA finds the best replica much often than the alternatives, and WASABI provides low overhead (that can be further configured).

In sum, the contributions of this paper are the following: 1) MECERRA, a replica ranking algorithm tailored for MEC environments (Sect. 3); 2) WASABI, a flexible replica ranking framework (Sect. 4); and 3) the evaluation of our prototype in simulation, comparing it with other replica ranking algorithms (Sect. 5).

2   Related Work

Nowadays, data is usually replicated and distributed across servers for availability, performance and scalability. Consequently, several replica servers might be available to answer a given request. In this context, the overall performance of a system that employs replication techniques is greatly dependant of two challenges: replica *placement* and *selection*. Replica placement is the problem of placing duplicate copies of a data item in the most appropriate nodes. In turn, replica selection is the problem of selecting the best replica of a required data item, at a given instant in time. In this paper our focus is directed to the replica selection problem in the context of MEC systems.

2.1   Replica Management in MEC Systems

Replicated storage is one of the building blocks of edge computing systems. Replication in this context might happen at the level of the edge server, at the mobile client level, or even at both. However, replica selection research in the field [5–7,11] has focused almost exclusively on choosing the most appropriate edge server, among several that cache a given replicated data item, primarily stored in some cloud storage system.

We are addressing a different problem. We are considering systems that preferably keep the data on the edge, allowing for replicas to exist both on edge servers and on the mobile devices. In this context, some proposals employ *full replication* (e.g., TOTA [8]), but the majority use *partial replication*. TOTA and GHT [10] rely solely on their *active replication* policy to get data across the system. However, systems like EPHESUS [14] or THYME GARDENBED [13] have an *active replication* policy for new data, but then use other nodes requesting the content as *passive* replicas. Then, in order to select a replica for data retrieval, systems like GHT and EPHESUS delegate to the Distributed Hash Table (DHT) logic. In turn, THYME GARDENBED always prefers the edge server when available, otherwise falls back to the DHT.

As far as we know, MobiTribe [17] is the only system with a dynamic strategy for this, but is achieved by centralizing all the decision power onto the (edge) server which acts as a proxy to redirect data requests.

In the end, none of these systems employ a sophisticated replica selection mechanism that takes into account network, load, or device-specific metrics to make an isolated informed decision of which replica should be contacted.

2.2 Replica Selection in Cloud Environments

Replica ranking algorithms for cloud environments can be classified into three categories [3]. **Information-agnostic** algorithms pick a replica in an uninformed way, not taking into account any extra information or external metrics (e.g., random or round-robin strategies). Next, **client-independent** algorithms take into account metrics independently measured by the client, without any aid from the servers. Lastly, **feedback** algorithms build on top of *client-independent* algorithms by adding *piggybacked* information with the returned values from the server, which means that both clients and servers form a feedback system.

C3 [16] is a *feedback* algorithm that combines two mechanisms in order to carefully manage tail latencies in a distributed system: (i) a load-balancing, replica ranking scheme that is informed by a continuous stream of in-band feedback about a server's load, and (ii) a distributed rate control and back-pressure mechanism. With replica ranking, clients individually rank servers according to a scoring function, with the scores serving as a proxy for the latency to expect from the corresponding server. Servers piggyback information about their queue size and approximate service time on each response to a client, and clients maintain a weighted moving average of these metrics. There is also a *concurrency compensation* that is calculated to account for both the existence of other clients in the system and the number of requests that are potentially in flight. If the *concurrency compensation* is not taken into account for the estimation of each server's queue-size, replica selection gets prone to herd behaviors. The number of requests that a client has pending over a given server also weights on the server's score. It was also decided to penalize scores over queue sizes using a non-linear function. This is because for a given server A with a service time n times faster than server B, such server would be able to get the same score as server B while holding a queue n times longer. If the service time of A then increases due to an unpredictable event such as a garbage collection pause, all requests in its queue would incur higher waiting times.

The purpose of the rate control and back-pressure module is to ensure that the combined demand of all clients on a single server remains within that server's capacity. Although such component might have a positive impact on data-center environments [16], where all nodes are continuously engaged in high throughput/high bandwidth operations, for systems composed of energy-constrained nodes that will not be the case. Here, we argue that it might even hurt latencies if a low *sending rate* threshold was to be configured where we could easily hit the quota on all replicas and incur in unnecessary waiting times imposed by the client itself. For these reasons, we decided to discard the rate control and back-pressure component.

L2 [3] is a *client-independent* algorithm which is simpler than *C3* but can achieve a similar performance in terms of tail latency. It gives consideration to both the selection of the fastest replica server and the load balance among replica servers. Thus, the authors conclude that the intricate rate control mechanism of C3 itself is not helpful to reduce the tail latency. Even though it can achieve a similar performance comparatively to C3 in cloud environments, MEC environments are in contrast more volatile, and present additional challenges. Here, communication channels are less reliable and the available replicas are constantly varying. Therefore, we argue that it is best to use a *feedback* algorithm which provides extra contextual information on the replicas to support their decisions.

NetRS [15] tries to overcome the pitfalls of other replica ranking algorithms, where each client is responsible for picking a replica on its own, by centralizing the selection power on programmable network devices. By doing this, it can achieve a more accurate load distribution of requests and completely avoid herd behaviour. Although this might make sense in a cloud-based environment, it is not suitable for MEC environments.

Other works have built upon C3. Of these we highlight On-Off [4] and TAP [19] that address replica selection under poor timeliness conditions. On-Off improves C3's rate control by replacing the latter's cubic-function-based approach by one that associates two states to replicas: ON, by default, and OFF, for a short period of time whenever the replica is considered bad. In turn, TAP replaces C3's use of Exponentially Weighted Moving Averages (EWMAs) in queue-size estimation by a prediction algorithm that takes into consideration the trend of the servers' queue-size variation over time.

3   Replica Ranking in MEC Environments

From our analysis of existing replica ranking algorithms, C3 [16] presents itself as the most well-suited solution for MEC environments. It provides enough information for understanding the servers' resource occupation, and the network conditions, while also providing intrinsic load-balancing and the ability to avoid herd behavior. However, there are critical MEC-related challenges that are not addressed, namely churn, energy efficiency, metric freshness and the volatility of the replica set (i.e., the number of replicas is not known a priori and may vary in time, due to churn). In this section, we elaborate on how these challenges may be addressed in the MEC context, and present the foundations of an algorithm that handles them: MECERRA.

Churn. Contrarily to cloud systems, MEC systems are deployed in highly volatile environments, where nodes often experience movement, effectively shifting their physical location, and use a wireless communication medium that might degrade with physical distance and obstacles (and other external interferences). With mobility, two outcomes are possible: i) the nodes move within range of the beacon for the wireless medium (e.g. the Access Point (AP)), or ii) they cross the range boundary, effectively leaving or rejoining the system. Regarding i), C3 provides the means to detect node movement since a server's network latency should be directly influenced by their distance to the connected network device. This means that the clients' perceived response time will increase or decrease when the server gets closer or further to the beacon, respectively and directly impacting the computed score.

However, this might not be enough to cope with ii). When a node leaves the system, the outgoing requests targeting it will be left hanging. To react to such situation, we can leverage the error conditions, and make use of predefined reply timeout values. On a timeout, we can simply stop tracking the request and use the timeout's value as the perceived response time, which will penalize the replica's score as intended. An alternative is to use the *outgoing requests count* to that node, which will potentially never decrease, and hence reduce the chances of the node being picked again as a designated replica. Without extra bookkeeping and logic, this penalty would, however, be perpetual and keep penalizing the node if it ever rejoins the system. Given this, we advocate for the timeout alternative (maybe with some dynamic setting policy). It is thus important for MEC systems to have a request timeout policy in place to react and adapt to node churn.

Dynamic Replica Set. Due to churn and node movement, more often than usual, a client might be faced with the situation where it has unknown nodes within a list of replicas to rank. In such case, several approaches are possible: i) be pessimistic and always consider these replicas last; ii) be optimistic and favour them over the remainder; iii) or try to be impartial and prefer them over *bad* replicas, but only after the *good* ones.

To define the quality of a replica, we require scores to be values in a closed interval, and classify as *bad* and *good* the replicas whose score is, respectively, lower or higher than the interval's medium value, referred to as the *neutral score*.

Energy Awareness. Mobile devices are limited by their battery capacity, which may differ considerably among devices. It is also common for nodes to join the system with only part of their total battery capacity and the remaining capacity be shared by several applications. Being of the system's interest to keep the maximum number of nodes online for as long as possible, the replica ranking algorithm should take this metric into account and score replicas according to their current battery capacity. Furthermore, it is important to observe the battery's evolution over time [9,18]. Batteries drop at different rates and some might even be increasing (e.g., when connected to some power source, like a powerbank).

Metric Freshness. Freshness (or timeliness) relates to the time elapsed from the instant a value is last registered (for a given metric) and its use in the ranking algorithm. It is directly bound to the ability of a node to perceive the system's actual state. Hence, the older the value, the less trustworthy it likely is.

The impact of freshness is higher on the server-side metrics, as these report a server's state at a given instant in time. Although some server metrics, such a battery state, may be accurately modelled from the client-side, others, such as *pending request queue size*, cannot. The same holds for the client-side metrics, e.g. a client always knows the exact value of the *outstanding requests* on a given server, but the perceived end-to-end latency (i.e., *response time*) depends of external conditions that cannot be accurately estimated beforehand. Thus, we see freshness as a concern that must be individually evaluated for each metric. This allows for a better fine-tuning of the replica ranking process and accommodates the possible asynchronous reading or computing of the metrics (resulting in some metrics being older than others).

To better represent the values of discrete metrics, a simple but effective approach (also used by C3) are EWMAs. Concerning continuous metrics that can be estimated on the client-side, we make use of decay functions.

3.1 The MECERRA Ranking Algorithm

Having discussed the challenges raised by MEC, we now move to the presentation of our proposal: the MECERRA algorithm.

Building on C3, we evaluate a replica considering its internal state (*queue size* and *service time*), on how much demand we already have over that server (*outstanding requests*), and on the *response time*. We additionally consider the replicas' *battery capacity*. The outstanding requests and last reported battery value are registered as absolute values, while the remainder metrics are stored as averages (i.e., EWMAs).

To rank a set of replicas, we need to compute their individual score. For that purpose, the set of metrics stored about a node is retrieved and passed to function REPLICASCORE of Algorithm 1. If any metric essential to compute a score is missing, the replica cannot be (yet) classified and, hence, the function falls back to the neutral score (line 24). Otherwise, the expected latency is computed in a way similar to C3 (lines 13 to 15) by computing the value for the following formula:

$$lat = (rt - st) + \hat{qs} \cdot st$$

Algorithm 1. MEC Enhanced Replica Ranking Algorithm.

1: MAX_LATENCY   ▷ Maximum latency assumed for communication
2: BATTERY_WEIGHT   ▷ Weight of the battery metric wrt the remainder
3: PENALTY_PERCENTAGE   ▷ Penalty assigned to nodes when communication fails
4: numberNodes   ▷ Estimate of the number of nodes currently in the system

5: **function** REPLICASCORE(*metrics*, *penalty*)
6:     **if** HASESSENTIALMETRICS(*metrics*) **then**
7:         $qs \leftarrow metrics.$GET('queueSize')
8:         $st \leftarrow metrics.$GET('serviceTime')
9:         $or \leftarrow metrics.$GET('outstandingRequests')
10:        $rt \leftarrow metrics.$GET('responseTime')
11:        $(bat^{rec}, ts^{rec}) \leftarrow metrics.$GET('battery')
12:        $\hat{bat} \leftarrow$ BATEST(bat^{rec}, ts^{rec}) ▷ battery capacity estimate
13:        $cc \leftarrow or \times$ numberNodes   ▷ concurrency compensation
14:        $\hat{qs} \leftarrow (1 + cc + qs)^3$ ▷ queue size estimate
15:        $lat \leftarrow (rt - st) + (\hat{qs} \times st)$ ▷ expected latency
16:        $ls \leftarrow ($MAX_LATENCY$ - lat) \times \frac{100}{\text{MAX_LATENCY}}$ ▷ latency score
17:        $wls \leftarrow (1 -$ BATTERY_WEIGHT$) \times ls$ ▷ weighted latency score
18:        $s \leftarrow$ BATTERY_WEIGHT$ \times bat^{rec} + wls$ ▷ score with recorded data
19:        $\hat{s} \leftarrow$ BATTERY_WEIGHT$ \times \hat{bat} + wls$ ▷ score with battery estimate
20:        **if** $\hat{s} >$ NEUTRAL_SCORE $\wedge$ $s <$ NEUTRAL_SCORE **then**
21:            **return** NEUTRAL_SCORE $\times$ *penalty*
22:        **else**
23:            **return** $\hat{s} \times$ *penalty*
24:    **return** NEUTRAL_SCORE $\times$ *penalty*

25: **procedure** ONTIMEOUT(*node*, *requestId*, *timeout_value*)
26:     $requests \leftarrow requestMap[node]$
27:     $requests \leftarrow requests \setminus \{requestId\}$
28:     RECORDRESPONSETIME(*node*, *timeout_value*)
29:     $penaltyMap[node] \leftarrow$ PENALTY_PERCENTAGE

---

where rt, st and $\hat{qs}$ are, respectively, the replica's observed response time, service time and queue-size estimation.

Due to the volatility of the environment, the concurrency compensation factor (cc in line 13) takes into consideration an estimate of the number of nodes currently in the system. This value may change in-between but never during a replica raking process, otherwise it would render scores non-comparable.

The REPLICASCORE function also takes into consideration the last recorded battery value (bat^{rec}) and an estimate of its current value ($\hat{bat}$), obtained in line 12 by calling function BATEST (defined ahead). From these two values, two scores are computed, s and $\hat{s}$, each calculated from the expected latency and correspondent battery value, converted to the same scale and weighted according to a previously defined relative importance (lines 16 to 19). The score computed from the estimated value is considered whenever both scores are above or below the neutral score. Otherwise, if the prediction causes the replica to cross the *good*-to-*bad* replica boundary, the neutral score is used instead (lines 20 to 22). This approach guarantees that replicas from which nothing is known won't be chosen over replicas previously considered *good*, but now estimated to have become *bad*.

The final score may be subjected to a *penalty* factor that penalizes replicas to which the latest communication attempt failed. This penalty is set on timeouts (procedure ONTIMEOUT of Algorithm 1), along with the removal of the request from the outstanding request list and the record of the response time, which will trigger the computing of the associated EWMA (lines 28 and 29). Note that the penalty is also applied in the neutral score branch to avoid repeatedly choosing yet unknown replicas to which communication is failing.

Battery Capacity Estimation. Being the battery a resource that is continuously being consumed, a battery value bat^{rec} recorded at instant ts^{rec} may not represent battery's value at the current instant ts^{now}. To estimate the current capacity of a battery when it is draining (the last recorded value is lower than the previous) we use the following decay function:

$$\text{BATEST}(bat^{rec}, ts^{rec}) = bat^{rec} - (ts^{now} - ts^{rec}) \cdot \frac{\theta}{\epsilon} \cdot \nu \cdot \beta$$

where ϵ denotes the time elapsed since the first message exchanged between the client and the target node, θ denotes how many bytes have been transferred between the target node and the client (upstream and downstream) since they first connected, ν represents an estimate of how many nodes are currently in the system, and β is a pre-defined value for the cost of battery consumption for every byte sent or received.

To the measured value, the function subtracts an estimate of the energy spent from ts^{rec} until now. To that end, we multiply the measurement's age by the *byte per millisecond* rate (θ/ϵ), to represent a rough estimation of how many bytes have been transferred, in average, between the target nodes and the remainder. The result is then multiplied by the number of nodes to account for the remainder nodes in the system and obtain some sort of *concurrency compensation*. The final factor (β) accounts for the average energy needed to communicate a byte in the used communication medium.

3.2 Handling Popularity Bursts on Under-Replicated Data

In some situations, there may be the case of a sudden demand for content that still has not been replicated across the system. An example of such scenario is when someone publishes something to an over-subscribed topic on a publish/subscribe system (i.e., a very popular topic). Because that item has just been published, there are no replicas. However, as the system sends out notifications for all subscribers, the publishing party will be flooded with all the data requests.

Unfortunately, replica ranking algorithms are not the solution here since there are no replicas to select from. To solve this problem, we came up with a redirection mechanism to leverage the emerging replicas from this initial request.

The problem with having a single entity serving all data requests is that: i) some of these requests will incur in long waiting queues, potentially resulting on a timeout on the client side; and ii) if we are serving the contents from mobile nodes, then these will have their battery drained faster.

Our solution consists of having server nodes register which data items they have served to whom recently, allowing for them to present a list of alternative replicas to any request that would otherwise have to wait for others to finish. By taking this *fail fast* approach, we avoid making the client wait for something that might not arrive. On its end, the client can decide whether to take one of the suggested alternatives or pick some other replica it already knows. If there are no alternatives, however, we still put the request on a queue. With this, servers are capable of better distributing their load with other emerging replicas, potentially preserving both their battery life and the system's liveness.

4   The WASABI Framework

In order for a client to make an informed decision on which is the best server (or replica) to contact when requesting a data item, it needs to collect information about the existing servers in the system. Thus, we present WASABI, a modular and extensible replica ranking framework. It handles the collection and management of system metrics, as well as replica ranking according to the collected metrics.

To allow the implementation of a wide range of replica ranking algorithms, WASABI enables the collection of metrics from both the client and server sides. It is also parametric, allowing the configuration and implementation of the majority of its components.

4.1   Overview

Figure 2 depicts a general overview of the WASABI framework. To be flexible, and cover scenarios both with functionally symmetric or asymmetric systems, the framework is divided into independent server and client modules, each of which can coexist in any node of the system (i.e., any node can be a server, a client, or both at the same time).

WASABI can be seen as a middleware that is embedded in an application and sits above its network communication layer. Overall, the server module collects system metrics, and aggregates them into Metrics bundles on demand. Thus, when a message is about to be sent on the server side, the application queries the server module for a Metrics bundle and piggybacks it in the message, before sending it. When a message is received on the client side, the application extracts the piggybacked metrics from the message, before sending it up the stack. At this moment, the client can also take the opportunity to measure some pertinent

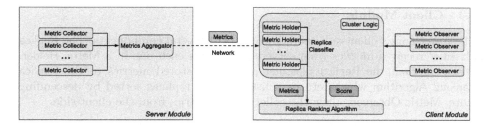

Fig. 2. WASABI architecture overview.

metric. Then, both the extracted and the measured metrics are recorded by the client module, associating them with the corresponding server. In turn, when a client is about to send a request for a data item, it first contacts the client module asking for a list of replicas ordered from best to worst, and then decides which to contact. The client module makes use of the previously collected metrics to sort a known set of replicas according to a predefined ranking algorithm.

In the framework, a Metric is represented by a double-precision floating point value, identified by a system-wide generic label (e.g., a string). Meanwhile, a Metrics bundle is simply a set of metrics concerning a server, represented as a map of labels to metric values.

4.2   Server Module

The framework's server-side module consists of only two different components: one *Metric Collector* for each metric the application wants to keep track, which in turn are registered in the *Metrics Aggregator*.

Metric Collector. This component contains the necessary logic to read and/or compute a system metric. It employs a *pull-based* strategy, whereby it needs to be registered in the framework, which in turn polls this component for metric values. Typically, it is a *functional* component, i.e., it performs stateless computations to produce a value. Thus, it suffices to implement its interface, which contains a single method: `collect(): double`. For other scenarios where stateful computations might be required, we provide a *Sample Metric Collector*, that stores metric samples and returns a value based on those samples when queried. As an example of a typical use case, we provide the *Average Metric Collector* that computes the average of the stored metric samples.

Metrics Aggregator. To be able to aggregate their values, collectors have to register in the *Metrics Aggregator*, mapping collectors to their labels. Thus, the main function of this component is to aggregate the registered *Metric Collectors*, for producing Metrics bundle on demand. When queried, through method `getMetrics(): Metrics`, this component polls all the registered collectors for their values, and returns a bundle to be sent to the client.

4.3   Client Module

The framework's client-side module consists of several components. The Replica Classifier receives metrics from servers, and keeps each one in a Metric Holder. When queried, the Replica Classifier passes the stored metrics to the Replica Ranking Algorithm which returns a list with the replicas sorted by descending score. Metric Observers allow the collection of metrics from the client-side.

Metric Observer. It works similarly to a Metric Collector on the server-side, by encapsulating the logic for reading and/or computing a system metric. However, while collectors are pull-based, observers employ a *push-based* strategy, not requiring to register within the framework. Instead, they push their readings into the Replica Classifier. This push model is required to update the stored information regarding a given replica on system events, such as network activity. A typical example is the measurement of the server response time, for which we record the request identifier with a timestamp, and when the response is received, measure the elapsed time. Additionally to this Response Time Observer, we also provide the Outstanding Requests Observer, to track how many outstanding requests there are to a server.

Replica Ranking Algorithm. This component encapsulates the ranking algorithm, i.e., it computes a score given a set of metrics over a replica. It requires the implementation of the method `score(m: Metrics): double`, which is also responsible for handling missing metrics.

Metric Holder. This is simply a container for a metric's current value, allowing to set a different retention policy for each metric registered on the Replica Classifier, i.e., we can keep just a discrete value, or something more complex such as a moving average. We offer a variety of Metric Holders, namely a record, a counter, and an exponential moving average.

Replica Classifier. This is the central component of the client module, responsible for classifying the available replicas for a given request. It does so by taking a set of replicas and sorting them by descending order of the score given by the Replica Ranking Algorithm. Naturally, the accuracy of that ordering is proportional to the amount of collected metrics over that set of replicas and of its freshness. All metrics required by the Replica Ranking Algorithm should be registered in the classifier at bootstrap time. However, the Replica Classifier does not hold metrics directly, but rather stores them within Metric Holders, indexed by server. As metrics are received and stored in their corresponding containers, unrecognized metrics are ignored. Metrics can also be registered together with a decay function. When scoring a replica, this decay function considers the elapsed time since the last recorded value for the given metric and updates the value accordingly.

Cluster Logic. Because some systems might have the need to tell apart clusters of nodes from individual nodes (e.g., cluster-based DHTs), we introduce the (optional) Cluster Logic component. It requires the implementation of two methods: a predicate which determines whether a given replica represents a cluster or not; and a method which retrieves the cluster replicas from the known replica set on the Replica Classifier. When classifying, a cluster gets the average score of all its composing (known) replicas.

5   Experimental Results

In order to evaluate our solution we integrated it with THYME GARDENBED [12, 13], a time-aware reactive data storage and dissemination system for MEC environments that offers a time-aware topic-based publish/subscribe interaction model. Mobile devices may publish content and subscribe to their topics of interest. Subscriptions are bound to time intervals that may encompass the past, the present, and the future, matching with all publications (to the same topic) performed in the subscribed time interval. A successful match triggers notifications to the interested devices (also referred to as *nodes*). The notification does not carry the data item itself, but a rather small description (such as a photo thumbnail) and the list of known replicas to where download the item from, among other information. If a node chooses to download the item, it then becomes itself a new replica, in a *passive* replication mechanism. Moreover, edge servers (one per region) periodically inspect the region and retrieve the region's most popular data items, according to a pre-defined popularity-based ranking algorithm. Thus, among other things, the edge servers also cache replicas of some of the items published in their region (see Fig. 1). Lastly, the system may also be configured to actively replicate data items. This configuration may be set on a per-item granularity and the replicas are stored in the mobile devices organized in a cluster-based DHT. In sum, when a node receives a list of replicas, this list may contain passive and active replicas hosted by mobile devices, as well as a replica cached by the edge server.

In this context, our evaluation seeks to answer the following questions: 1) how good is our replica ranking algorithm? 2) how much overhead does the underlying feedback system introduces and does it pose as a decent trade-off? and 3) does the redirection mechanism presented in Sect. 3.2 helps in improving the load balance in some extreme cases?

5.1   Experimental Setup

To evaluate our solution we resort to the emulation of the mobile devices. This emulation environment allows us to perform experiments with a large number of devices, as well as better control the operations performed by each device, without having to develop a new implementation of WASABI. The code running on the experiments is exactly the same that runs of the Android devices.

The emulator is built on a trace-based framework that accepts a trace file containing the operations we want each node to perform and when. The framework runs on a single process, emulating each mobile device in a separate thread (and from here, each device can use as many threads as necessary). Furthermore, the emulator replaces the Network Layer to support logical dissemination of messages between any number of virtual nodes. This allows us to simulate network conditions and control communication in a predictive manner. Each operation within the trace maps to an *action*: the logical representation of the operation. Each kind of action has a mapped *behavior* that represents the effect the action should cause in the system.

To support our simulated scenario, we made use of a computational cluster. We ran the mobile device emulator in one node and a (non-simulated) edge server in a second one. The communication between emulator and edge server was made through the network connection link, while the communication between nodes was made through the logical layer provided by the emulator.

5.2   Replica Selection

To assess whether or not we consistently pick the best replica, we need to know two things for each download (i.e., data request): the chosen replica and the actual best replica. To know which replica was chosen is just a matter of recording it. However, to know which would have otherwise been the best choice requires a bit more effort. For this, we use an *oracle*.

The *oracle* is an external component that needs to be fed with the whole system information to be able to answer any question with the highest degree of certainty. It is composed of two parts: i) an extra persistent logging component that is enabled within the system nodes to record their state and downloads information; and ii) a post-processing script which computes metrics (e.g., how good was the replica selection on each specific download) from the data previously collected at runtime.

Using the recorded system snapshots, which contain the most up-to-date metrics of each node and their stored contents at each moment, we can use the *oracle* to compute the optimal replica system-wide for each node's decision. With this, we can now answer our first question: *how good is our replica ranking algorithm?*

For this test, we defined the following baselines: **Random Selection** - the client sorts the available replicas in an arbitrary fashion; **Edge First** - the client always picks the edge server whenever it is available; **C3** - the cloud envisioned implementation of C3; and **Mecerra** - our proposed replica ranking algorithm.

To properly evaluate the effects of our solution, we decided to create a scenario with lots of subscriptions and publications. Our trace is divided in four parts: 1) spawn 64 nodes and let them join the system (only after all the nodes are online and ready do we proceed); 2) all nodes have a 50% chance of subscribing to each of the available topics. This will cause some topics to be more subscribed than others, which will cause some published items to be popular later on; 3) after all the subscriptions comes a barrage of publications. As before, each node

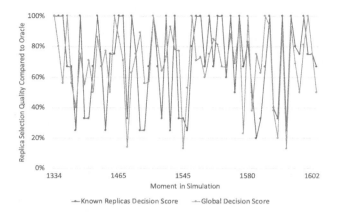

Fig. 3. Replica selection benchmark (Random Selection).

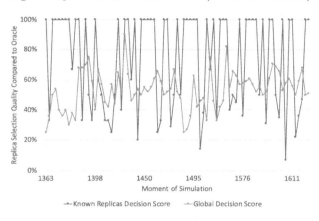

Fig. 4. Replica selection benchmark (Edge First).

has a 50% chance of making a publication on each topic. This will trigger several notifications on each publication, which in turn will trigger the same number of downloads; 4) all nodes have a 70% chance to subscribe to the topics they have not subscribed before. These subscriptions, however, are spanning to the past, meaning that each of them will pick all the items published to the same topic on the previous step. In this phase we will continuously have a high volume of downloads in the system which means that smart replica ranking and selection might play a big part in load balancing and resource management. We use the same trace to run simulations for each of the previously outlined baselines.

Random Selection is the most inconsistent baseline. Figure 3 shows its replica selection quality, having the blue plot represent how good the selection was for a given download considering the available metrics on the client at that moment (this can also be seen as a direct comparison to MECERRA); and the orange plot represents how good the selection was considering the actual state of the

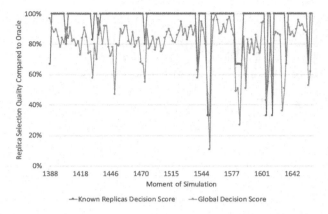

Fig. 5. Replica selection benchmark (C3).

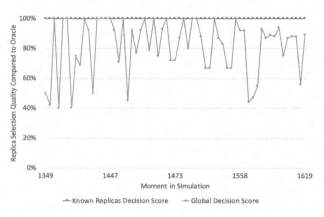

Fig. 6. Replica selection benchmark (MECERRA).

whole system at the same moment, as provided by the *oracle*. Here, the average selection quality is 69% and 68%, respectively. This is only because this has no logical selection criteria and is thus not affected by the asynchrony between stored metrics and actual system state. We can argue that it is not a bad result and that it even takes the best available replica for some of the downloads. But the fact is that these were all scenarios where the edge server was an option and was picked by chance. In fact, most downloads only consider a tiny part of all the existing replicas–40% on average–which is about 3.6 known replicas for each download. Given that we only considered downloads with 3 or more available replicas at the client, there was a high number of downloads where the client only had 3 options, amongst them being the edge server which was the actual best option most of the times. Other than that, we rarely see any download with a selection score over 80% and there are more below 40% than on any other baseline. It is also worth noting that the trace executions for the

Random Selection always yielded less total downloads than any of the others, meaning that some download requests incurred in big waiting queues.

Edge First was the previous strategy of THYME GARDENBED, and consists of always preferring the edge server when it's available, otherwise falling back to *Random Selection*. Just like *Random Selection*, it is not making use of any metrics available on the client, but as we can see from Fig. 4 the selected replica frequently matches the best option the client could compute using the available information (blue plot). This is because even though our underlying framework does not distinguish between edge and mobile servers, the edge server is always reporting 100% battery and the expected latencies are very reasonable. However, considering the actual state of the system on each download, we can see that from our sample, the edge server was **never** the best option. This is because most nodes were concurrently downloading files from it, creating a hot-spot which, in the face of edge server delays or network congestion, can compromise system liveness. The average selection quality is 73% and 53%, respectively. The 20% gap between how good the selected replica was according to the available metrics of the client versus how good it was considering the actual snapshot of the system at that given moment is explained by the fact that each client only had a partial view of the system (on average only 40% of the existing replicas were known) and some of the available metrics were not the freshest.

C3 was our highlighted cloud algorithm. From Fig. 5 we see a positive increase in the replica selection quality compared to the previous baselines, scoring an average of around 90% when considering the clients' local metrics and 80% considering the global system state. Although it is a cloud algorithm, we can see the benefit of an adaptive ranking scheme fed by a feedback loop between servers and clients. In spite of the improvement, there were still some less optimal selections, namely the ones below 40% quality. These are explained by the fact that *C3* does not cover the several challenges that arise from transitioning from the cloud to the MEC environment, such as considering servers' battery levels or ranking replicas it has not seen before, even preferring replicas it knows perform badly over new ones.

MECERRA was made specifically for MEC environments, building on top of our findings from the cloud and covering all the new concerns. Looking at Fig. 6 we can see clear improvements from any other baseline. First, we look at the selection quality from the clients' local metrics which is consistently at 100%. This simply means that the ranking algorithm is correct since it is always producing the same result as the oracle, considering the exact same set of replica metrics. The most interesting part is indeed the selection quality considering the global system state. Here, we had many more 100% selections than any other baseline. Moreover, most selections stayed around 80% to 100% while the remaining choices did not drop below 40%. On average, the replica selection quality was 82%. The average increase is not as steep as it was from *Edge First* to *C3*, which can be attributed to the few selections that still scored below 60%. This, however, can only be increased if we can improve the feedback system since the worst selections were caused by the fact that, like on the other benchmarks,

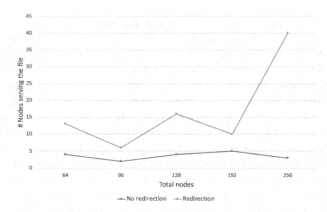

Fig. 7. How many nodes served the file.

we only knew around 40% of the available replicas on each download and on some cases some of the metrics stored on the client side did not accurately reflect the target replica state anymore.

The bottom-line is that with a feedback system the quality of the selected replicas is directly proportional to the amount and freshness of the available information.

5.3   Framework Overhead

We now evaluate the increase in byte count introduced by adding metrics the each system message. To do this, we ran a similar trace to the previous and registered all the bytes sent by each node. After, we aggregate all these values to have a total amount of bytes transferred during the simulation. We ran the simulation for our version of THYME GARDENBED and then repeated the process with a version without WASABI. In the end, we compared the two values.

With this comparison, we observed an increase of about $10\% \times w_r$, where w_r denotes the ratio of messages carrying WASABI information. On average, each metric payload increased the size of each message by about 50 bytes. At this size, the metrics payload was smaller than any system message. So, in the case of THYME GARDENBED, adding WASABI with MECERRA yields much greater improvements (around 29% increase) than the maximum overhead (10% more bytes transferred for $w_r = 1$). This is a considerable improvement which will reflect in the system's resource management and liveness.

5.4   Redirection Mechanism

To evaluate the redirection mechanism presented in Sect. 3.2, we designed a trace where all nodes subscribe to a topic and then one of them publishes a (big) file to that topic, causing all others to download the file. Each node sends its download request with 1 s distance from the previous one and each download operation

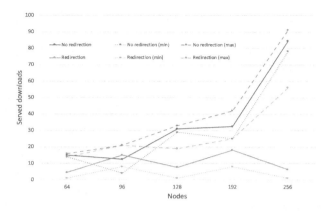

Fig. 8. Downloads served by serving nodes.

takes 5 s to finish. We also configured 8 s timeouts. We have then created 5 variants of this trace with 64, 96, 128, 192 and 256 nodes and ran each variant with and without the redirection mechanism, to understand the difference in load distribution. Also, because THYME GARDENBED groups the mobile nodes on clusters, we tried to guarantee a 1:4 ratio of clusters to nodes which means that, on average, a cluster should be comprised of 4 nodes.

Indeed, from Fig. 7 we can see that the redirection mechanism effectively enables more nodes to serve the file that is on demand, decentralizing the load from the publishing party. When no redirection was in place, the maximum number of nodes participating in distributing the requested file were at most 5, which is the approximate number of nodes in a cluster. If redirection was enabled though, this number increased on every experiment, showing a considerable growth on the 256 nodes mark.

Additionally, Fig. 8 shows the average downloads each serving node served on each simulation. Here we confirm that each serving node serves a lot more requests when there is no redirection than with the alternative. With redirection, the average of downloads served by a single node never crossed 20 whereas without redirection it went over 80. Both the maximum and minimum plots followed the average plot on both scenarios, with the exception of the maximum number of downloads registered for the simulation with 256 nodes and redirection enabled, where a single node served 56 downloads. This, however, is still considerably less than the 91 registered for its counterpart.

Regarding timeouts, there was only a negligible amount in the simulations with no redirections and higher node counts.

6   Conclusion

In this paper, we presented MECERRA, a replica ranking algorithm that directly addresses the inherent challenges of MEC environments, which, to our knowledge, no other replica ranking or replica selection algorithm does. We also detailed WASABI, a flexible and lightweight replica ranking framework on top of which we implement MECERRA. Finally, we integrate this ensemble into a data storage and dissemination system for edge networks, building an adaptive replica selection scheme.

To validate our solution we resorted to simulation. From our experimental results, we can see that MECERRA is able to outperform *C3* in MEC environments, ranking the best available replica as #1 eight times more often. It also provides a less volatile replica selection quality, not dropping below 40%. Still, the less satisfying selections were only due to lack of available information on the client, which, on average, only knew 40% of the existing replicas. We have also measured the increase in network traffic caused by the feedback system, reaching a small overhead of roughly 10%. Finally, the redirection mechanism allows the system to take earlier advantage of newly emerging replicas, effectively sharing the load with those. With 256 nodes, there were eight times more nodes answering requests, when comparing with the system without redirection mechanism. In turn, each serving node ended up serving eighth times less requests with the redirection mechanism.

As future work, we would consider alternative communication channels. There is a wide range of wireless mediums we can leverage to circumvent problems that arise on the current one (e.g., congestion in the AP when using Wi-Fi) and ultimately provide a better quality of service.

References

1. Abbas, N., Zhang, Y., Taherkordi, A., Skeie, T.: Mobile edge computing: a survey. IEEE Internet Things J. **5**(1), 450–465 (2018). https://doi.org/10.1109/JIOT.2017. 2750180
2. Beck, M.T., Werner, M., Feld, S., Schimper, T.: Mobile edge computing: a taxonomy. In: AFIN 2014: The Sixth International Conference on Advances in Future Internet, pp. 48–54. IARIA (2014)
3. Jiang, W., Xie, H., Zhou, X., Fang, L., Wang, J.: Performance analysis and improvement of replica selection algorithms for key-value stores. In: Fox, G.C. (ed.) 2017 IEEE 10th International Conference on Cloud Computing (CLOUD), Honolulu, HI, USA, 25–30 June 2017, pp. 786–789. IEEE Computer Society (2017). https:// doi.org/10.1109/CLOUD.2017.115
4. Jiang, W., Xie, H., Zhou, X., Fang, L., Wang, J.: Haste makes waste: the on-off algorithm for replica selection in key-value stores. J. Parallel Distrib. Comput. **130**, 80–90 (2019). https://doi.org/10.1016/j.jpdc.2019.03.017
5. Li, C., Tang, J., Luo, Y.: Scalable replica selection based on node service capability for improving data access performance in edge computing environment. J. Supercomput. **75**(11), 7209–7243 (2019). https://doi.org/10.1007/s11227-019-02930-6
6. Li, C., Song, M., Zhang, M., Luo, Y.: Effective replica management for improving reliability and availability in edge-cloud computing environment. J. Parallel Distrib. Comput. **143**, 107–128 (2020). https://doi.org/10.1016/j.jpdc.2020.04.012
7. Li, C., Wang, Y., Tang, H., Luo, Y.: Dynamic multi-objective optimized replica placement and migration strategies for SaaS applications in edge cloud. Future Gener. Comput. Syst. **100**, 921–937 (2019). https://doi.org/10.1016/j.future.2019. 05.003

8. Mamei, M., Zambonelli, F.: Programming pervasive and mobile computing applications with the TOTA middleware. In: Proceedings of the Second IEEE International Conference on Pervasive Computing and Communications (PerCom 2004), 14–17 March 2004, Orlando, FL, USA, pp. 263–276. IEEE Computer Society (2004). https://doi.org/10.1109/PERCOM.2004.1276864

9. Metri, G., Agrawal, A., Peri, R., Shi, W.: What is eating up battery life on my smartphone: a case study. In: International Conference on Energy Aware Computing, ICEAC 2012, Guzelyurt, Cyprus, 3–5 December 2012, pp. 1–6. IEEE (2012). https://doi.org/10.1109/ICEAC.2012.6471003

10. Ratnasamy, S., et al.: GHT: a geographic hash table for data-centric storage. In: Raghavendra, C.S., Sivalingam, K.M. (eds.) Proceedings of the First ACM International Workshop on Wireless Sensor Networks and Applications, WSNA 2002, Atlanta, Georgia, USA, 28 September 2002, pp. 78–87. ACM (2002). https://doi.org/10.1145/570738.570750

11. Shao, Z., Huang, C., Li, H.: Replica selection and placement techniques on the IoT and edge computing: a deep study. Wirel. Networks 27(7), 5039–5055 (2021). https://doi.org/10.1007/s11276-021-02793-x

12. Silva, J.A., Cerqueira, F., Paulino, H., Lourenço, J.M., Leitão, J., Preguiça, N.M.: It's about thyme: on the design and implementation of a time-aware reactive storage system for pervasive edge computing environments. Future Gener. Comput. Syst. 118, 14–36 (2021). https://doi.org/10.1016/j.future.2020.12.008

13. Silva, J.A., Vieira, P., Paulino, H.: Data storage and sharing for mobile devices in multi-region edge networks. In: 21st IEEE International Symposium on "A World of Wireless, Mobile and Multimedia Networks", WoWMoM 2020, Cork, Ireland, 31 August–3 September 2020, pp. 40–49. IEEE (2020). https://doi.org/10.1109/WoWMoM49955.2020.00021

14. Silva, J.A., Monteiro, R., Paulino, H., Lourenço, J.M.: Ephemeral data storage for networks of hand-held devices. In: IEEE Trustcom/BigDataSE/ISPA, pp. 1106–1113. IEEE (2016). https://doi.org/10.1109/TrustCom.2016.0182

15. Su, Y., Feng, D., Hua, Y., Shi, Z., Zhu, T.: NetRS: cutting response latency in distributed key-value stores with in-network replica selection. In: 38th IEEE International Conference on Distributed Computing Systems, ICDCS 2018, Vienna, Austria, 2–6 July 2018, pp. 143–153. IEEE Computer Society (2018). https://doi.org/10.1109/ICDCS.2018.00024

16. Suresh, P.L., Canini, M., Schmid, S., Feldmann, A.: C3: cutting tail latency in cloud data stores via adaptive replica selection. In: 12th USENIX Symposium on Networked Systems Design and Implementation, NSDI 2015, Oakland, CA, USA, 4–6 May 2015, pp. 513–527. USENIX Association (2015). https://www.usenix.org/conference/nsdi15/technical-sessions/presentation/suresh

17. Thilakarathna, K., Petander, H., Mestre, J., Seneviratne, A.: MobiTribe: cost efficient distributed user generated content sharing on smartphones. IEEE Trans. Mob. Comput. 13(9), 2058–2070 (2014). https://doi.org/10.1109/TMC.2013.89

18. Vallina-Rodriguez, N., Hui, P., Crowcroft, J., Rice, A.C.: Exhausting battery statistics: understanding the energy demands on mobile handsets. In: Cox, L.P., Wolman, A. (eds.) Proceedings of the 2ndt ACM SIGCOMM Workshop on Networking, Systems, and Applications for Mobile Handhelds, MobiHeld 2010, New Delhi, India, 30 August 2010, pp. 9–14. ACM (2010). https://doi.org/10.1145/1851322.1851327

19. Zhou, X., Fang, L., Xie, H., Jiang, W.: TAP: timeliness-aware predication-based replica selection algorithm for key-value stores. Concurr. Comput. Pract. Exp. 31(17) (2019). https://doi.org/10.1002/cpe.5171

Generalizing Wireless Ad Hoc Routing for Future Edge Applications

André Rosa[✉], Pedro Ákos Costa, and João Leitão

NOVA LINCS and DI/Nova School of Science and Technology, UNL,
Almada, Portugal
{af.rosa,pah.costa}@campus.fct.unl,
jc.leitao@fct.unl.pt

Abstract. Wireless *ad hoc* networks are becoming increasingly relevant due to their suitability for Internet-of-Things (IoT) applications. These networks are comprised of devices that communicate directly with each other through the wireless medium. In applications deployed over a large area, each device is unable to directly contact all others, and thus they must cooperate to achieve multi-hop communication. The essential service for this is *Routing*, which is crucial for most applications and services in multi-hop *ad hoc* networks. Although many wireless routing protocols have been proposed, no single protocol is deemed the most suitable for all scenarios. Therefore, it is crucial to identify the key differences and similarities between protocols to better compare, combine, or dynamically elect which one to use in different settings and conditions. However, identifying such key similarities and distinctions is challenging due to highly heterogeneous specifications and assumptions. In this paper, we propose a conceptual framework for specifying routing protocols for wireless *ad hoc* networks, which abstracts their common elements and that can be parameterized to capture the behavior of particular instances of existing protocols. Furthermore, since many wireless *ad hoc* routing protocols lack systematic experimental evaluation on real networks, we leverage an implementation of our framework to conduct an experimental evaluation of several representative protocols using commodity devices.

Keywords: Routing · Wireless Ad Hoc · Framework · IoT

1 Introduction

In recent times, we have been witnessing the emergence of the *Internet-of-Things (IoT)*: ubiquitous networks of interconnected everyday objects (e.g., vehicles, buildings, household appliances) capable of performing computations and exchanging data with other devices [1,31]. A vast amount of IoT applications depends on Cloud services, and their deployments rely on infrastructure-based

This work was partially supported by NOVA LINCS (FC&T grant UIDB/04516/2020) and NG-STORAGE (FC&T grant PTDC/CCI-INF/32038/2017).

T. Hara and H. Yamaguchi (Eds.): MobiQuitous 2021, LNICST 419, pp. 264–279, 2022.
https://doi.org/10.1007/978-3-030-94822-1_15

wireless networks [41]. This architecture, however, is becoming unsuitable for several IoT scenarios due to its inherent limitations. On the one hand, the ever-increasing amounts of data produced and consumed by IoT devices are rendering the Cloud unable to collect, process, and reply promptly as well as increasing the operational costs [11]. On the other hand, while infrastructure-based wireless networks provide fairly reliable, high-speed, and high-bandwidth links, they also inhibit the flexibility of applications since they constrain the mobility of devices and require attention to their deployment, configuration, and relocation.

The demand to offload computations from the Cloud motivates a paradigm shift towards Edge Computing [25], which exploits the computational capabilities of peripheral network devices that are located near end-users. In this sense, *wireless ad hoc networks*, i.e., decentralized set of devices that communicate directly through the wireless medium without relying on any pre-existent infrastructure, emerge as a more flexible and robust platform than infrastructure-based wireless networks for materializing Edge Computing in the context of IoT. These networks are suitable for situations with inadequate, inexistent, unavailable, or debilitated network infrastructures [1,31], such as: rescue/support on natural disasters; environmental monitoring; autonomous vehicles; and smart cities or homes. As such, IoT has been inducing the contemporary reemergence of wireless *ad hoc* networks.

On these networks, the devices, also called nodes, are typically scattered through a wide area, being unable to communicate directly with all the others, forming a multi-hop network. Consequently, they must cooperate, by retransmitting messages on behalf of other nodes, so that communication can be achieved among all devices. This essential service is named *Routing*, enabling point-to-point communication by message forwarding among nodes. A plethora of routing protocols for wireless *ad hoc* networks have been already proposed over the years, exploring and combining different techniques. Nonetheless, due to these networks' highly dynamic and heterogeneous nature, no single protocol is deemed the most suitable for all scenarios. Therefore, it is crucial to identify how the different protocols relate to each other to better compare, combine, or dynamically select them. However, uncovering the relations among them is rather challenging due to heterogeneous specifications and assumptions. This observation motivated us to devise a framework for specifying routing protocols for these networks, which abstracts their common elements while offering parameters to materialize particular instances.

In addition, the vast majority of routing protocols have only been evaluated through simulations [3,9,10], since they provide an accessible, inexpensive, and controlled evaluation environment. Nonetheless, even the most detailed simulations are unable to capture the particular characteristics of real wireless *ad hoc* environments [2,5], usually employing inaccurate models, not considering hardware limitations of wireless interfaces, or ignoring external sources of interference in the wireless medium. Although real testbeds have been employed in the past to evaluate some protocols [20,22], they generally resort to grid topologies with equidistant nodes and without external interference, which is highly unrealistic;

or consist of few nodes (less than 10), which are not enough to derive significant conclusions. Therefore, leveraging an implementation of our routing framework, we conducted an experimental evaluation of five representative routing protocols on a real wireless *ad hoc* network formed by commodity devices.

The remainder of this paper is structured as follows: Sect. 2 analyzes routing in wireless *ad hoc* networks; Sect. 3 delves into our framework; Sect. 4 presents the details of our experimental evaluation; Sect. 5 briefly discusses the related work; and Sect. 6 concludes the paper with some final remarks.

2   Routing in Wireless Ad Hoc

A plethora of routing protocols has been proposed throughout the years, exploring different techniques to increase the robustness and efficiency of network-wide communications. These protocols are categorized mainly by their route provision strategy as proactive [6,7,27], reactive [18,29,40], or hybrid [16,28,30]. However, in this paper, we make an effort to better characterize these protocols down to their fundamental operation, going beyond the employed route provision strategy. In this sense, the operation of routing protocols can be divided into two complementary parts, the *route computation* and the *message forwarding*.

2.1   Route Computation

Computing routes is the main concern of routing protocols and hence encompass a variety of essential components, which include *discover* a node's *neighbors* (i.e., nodes with whom the local node can directly exchange messages), *identify* the *cost* of direct communication, apply *distributed strategies* to actually *compute routes*, and *disseminate information* to inform other nodes of existing routes.

At the basis of any routing protocol is *neighbor discovery*, essential for computing routes as it provides each node with information about the other nodes which can be directly reachable by itself. However, routing protocols must ensure some Quality of Service (QoS), thus neighbor discovery must obtain properties of the wireless links between neighboring nodes. One of such properties is the bidirectionality of communication [6,7], i.e., both nodes can send and receive messages from each other, as it is often crucial to ensure two-way communication.

In addition, routing protocols require *cost* metrics to select the best routes, as in general there might be multiple available routes from each node to each destination. The cost of a route is a function of its constituent link's costs, usually the sum [6]. However, other functions can be employed [27,40]. These metrics can be in their simplest form the number of hops towards the destination, or incorporate properties of the links, such as the link's expected number of transmissions to deliver a message (ETX) [19,23], the link's expected transmission time (ETT) [12], the link's stability [13,27,40], the congestion of the nodes [24], or the energy spent using the link [37]. In this sense, routing protocols resort to a *cost function* that evaluates the local links and is used to qualify each route.

The process of actually computing routes requires the distributed cooperation of nodes and leverages each node's local neighborhood information. In this sense, there are three main *computation strategies* to distributively construct routes: *i*) *distance-vector* [6,17,18,29], where each node announces the cost of its best route towards a given destination, allowing the other nodes to assign as next-hop the neighbor which provides the best route; *ii*) *link-state* [7,15,39], where nodes gather, through collaborative dissemination, the complete, or a connected sub-set, of the network topology, and locally compute the best routes to all reachable destinations; and *iii*) *link-reversal* [14,28,30], where the nodes distributively construct a directed acyclic graph (DAG) over the network topology for each destination, with each directed path in the DAG corresponding to a route to the destination. Note that these high-level strategies can be further specialized to better fit specific routing protocols, which we discuss in more detail in the next section. Since routes are computed in a distributed way, each node does not have to be aware of the complete routes, only their next-hops. This information is typically encoded by the routing strategies in a conceptual data structure, local to each node, called the *routing table* [7,17]. In some protocols, these tables may contain additional information [18] or even not be used at all [21].

Finally, routing protocols need to propagate control messages throughout the network to enable the computation of routes through the use of some computation strategy. Across the literature, routing protocols employ several *dissemination strategies*, even within the same protocol, which can be grouped into specific communication patterns according to the nature and intended destinations of such messages into: *network-wide* [7,27,29] or *limited-hop broadcast* [6,16], to inform all or a sub-set of the nodes; *bordercast* [16], to inform a specific sub-set of the nodes; or (*network-wide*) *unicast* [18,29] to inform a single node.

2.2   Message Forwarding

Besides route computation, routing protocols are also responsible for leveraging the computed routes to forward applicational messages. To this end, routing protocols employ different *forwarding strategies* that provide different trade-offs across reliability and communication overhead.

The simplest strategy is to forward to the next-hop contained in the routing table. However, other strategies can be found in the literature. For instance, *multipath* protocols [26] leverage several routes to the same destination to increase the chances of delivering messages. Alternatively, *opportunistic* protocols [4,35] employ coordination mechanisms to dynamically elect, from a set of candidate next-hops, the one which will proceed with the forwarding of each message. As another option, *geographic* protocols [21,32] use the nodes' coordinates to base their forwarding decisions. Furthermore, *source* routing protocols [18] do not require each route's intermediary nodes to maintain information regarding the route. Instead, the nodes which originate messages maintain the complete routes, which are then carried within the messages to allow the intermediary nodes to retrieve their next-hop to whom they will forward it. Finally, some protocols [6,29,40] rely on the explicit or implicit *acknowledgment* and retransmission of messages to increase the reliability of their forwarding strategies.

3   Routing Framework for Wireless Ad Hoc Networks

In this section, we present our conceptual routing framework, which captures a broad spectrum of existing routing protocols for wireless *ad hoc* networks. The framework's design follows directly from the observations made in Sect. 2. In the following, we present an overview of the workflow of events in a generic routing protocol, which lies at the core of our framework. In addition, we also present the notation used to specify routing protocols using our framework and illustrate this using a representative set of existing routing protocols.

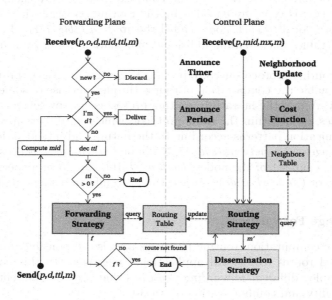

Fig. 1. Routing framework execution flow.

3.1   Overview

Figure 1 illustrates the execution flow captured by our framework, which is divided into two parts: the *control plane*, responsible for computing routes, and the *forwarding plane*, responsible for forwarding applicational messages.

Control Plane. The control plane is responsible for processing internal events to manage the routing strategy. There are three main entry points in this plane: a *neighborhood update*, that is processed by the **cost function**; the set off of an *announce timer*, that is processed by the **announce period**; and the reception of a *control message*, that is directly processed by the **routing strategy**.

Neighborhood updates are assumed to be provided by an external discovery protocol that is outside the scope of this paper. However, a neighborhood update must encode either the discovery, suspicion of failure, or an update to the state of a communication link with a neighboring node. This update is processed by the **cost function**, which assigns a cost metric to that neighbor. Next, the framework updates its internal neighborhood table containing essential information for each neighbor, such as the link cost and bidirectionality and the neighbor's address, which is leveraged by the **routing strategy** to compute routes.

The announce timer is a periodic timer that informs the **routing strategy** to disseminate a new control message, and is employed by protocols following a proactive or hybrid routing strategy. When the announce timer is triggered, it is first processed by the **announce period** which is responsible to reset it. This enables the usage of dynamic periods for announcements [33].

The reception of a control message is immediately processed by the **routing strategy**. A control message is composed of four parts: (p, mid, mx, m), respectively, the identifier of the node that generated the control message, the message's unique identifier, metadata obtained from the message's propagation and which is associated with a specific dissemination strategy, and the message payload that encodes data specific to the routing strategy.

These three events flow into the main component of the control plane: the **routing strategy**. The routing strategy evaluates these events, which may lead into an update on the routing table and/or the dissemination of a new control message. On either case, the routing strategy may query the framework's internal neighborhood table to obtain cost metrics and bidirectionality information to compute or update a new or existing route. Finally, in the case a new control message is to be disseminated, the framework delivers the message to the **dissemination strategy** that is responsible to send it to all intended destinations.

Forwarding Plane. The forwarding plane is responsible for handling the flow of applicational messages and applying a **forwarding strategy**, which can be triggered by two events: a *request to send* a message to an arbitrary destination, or the *reception* of a forwarded message from a neighboring node.

To request the forwarding of a message, the application must provide the following parameters: (p, d, ttl, m), respectively, the local node's identifier, the identifier of the destination node, a time-to-live, and the message payload. Upon receiving such request, the framework first generates a message identifier (mid) to uniquely identify the message in the network. Then, the message enters the flow of received messages in the forwarding plane.

Upon the reception of a message, the framework verifies if the message was already processed, discarding it if so. Next, if the destination of the message is the local node, it is delivered to the application, continuing otherwise to the next processing stage, where the *ttl* is decremented and verified. If the *ttl* has expired, the forwarding of the message ends, otherwise the message is delegated to the *forwarding strategy* which will obtain the next-hop, potentially consulting the framework's routing table, and send the message to it. If no next-hop was found or the message could not be successfully forwarded, the routing strategy in the control plane is notified, possibly requesting the dissemination of a new control message, such as a route request in reactive protocols [18, 29]. Otherwise, the workflow for that message ends.

3.2 Framework Parameters

Our framework represents a generic (or meta) routing protocol that can be parameterized to express a multitude of different protocols with different properties and strategies. To specify a routing protocol in our framework, one only has to define five parameters: (FS, AP, CF, RS, DS), where FS is the forwarding strategy, AP is the announce period, CF the cost function, RS the routing strategy, and DS is the dissemination strategy. In the following we discuss some alternatives of possible values for these parameters, being that they can also assume a value of $\perp$ to encode not employing a specific parameter.

Forwarding Strategies are responsible for selecting the next-hop, and forwarding to it, any applicational message. These strategies can be SIMPLE, where it simply retrieves the first next-hop contained in the routing table; MULTI-PATH, where instead multiple next-hops are retrieved from the routing table and one is selected according to some criteria; SOURCE, where the complete route is retrieved and piggybacked in the message, allowing intermediary nodes to become aware of their next-hops; ACKED(s), that extends a strategy s with explicit acknowledgments and retransmissions of forwarded messages; OPPORTUNISTIC, where the next-hop is dynamically selected; and GEOGRAPHIC where the next-hop is chosen as the neighbor geographically closer to the destination.

Announce Period is a natural number t that represents the interval between periodic announcements of control messages. This value can be the result of a function when the protocol employs dynamic periods.

Cost Functions assign cost metrics to links to qualify the routes, and include: HOPS, which is always 1 so that the routes' cost is their number of hops; ETX, which estimates the expected number of retransmissions for a successful forwarding; ETT, which estimates the expected time for a successful forwarding; AGE, where the time elapsed since the neighbor was detected is used to estimate the cost, with older neighbors representing better links (i.e., more stable); DIST, which uses the geographic distance between the local node and the neighbor, with higher costs representing better links (i.e., closer to the destination); and MCX, where the number of control messages received from different sources and neighbors is considered, with higher counts representing better links.

Routing Strategies are responsible for computing routes, and include: LINKSTATE, that periodically disseminates a small sub-set of the known topology, allowing all nodes to gather the global topology which is used to locally compute routes to all reachable destinations. MULTIDISTVEC, which disseminates a portion of the local routing table containing all known destinations and associated costs, allowing each node to select the best routes to each destination. SINGLEDISTVEC(m), which disseminates the local node's identify across the network, with the m parameter controling if this dissemination is proactive (pro) or reactive (re), and uses information regarding the path taken by the control messages to calculate routes to the origin node. LINKREVERSAL(m), that distributively constructs a DAG directed to the local node, with the m parameter encoding if the DAG's construction is triggered proactively (pro) or reactively (re). And ZONE(i, o, r), where a proactive routing strategy i is employed within routing zones with a limited scope of r hops, and a reactive strategy o is employed to compute routes towards nodes outside of these zones.

Table 1. Specification of routing protocols.

Label	Ref	FS	AP	CF	RS	DS
OLSR	[7]	SIMPLE	5	ETX	LINKSTATE	BCAST(∞)
FSR	[15]	SIMPLE	5	ETX	LINKSTATE	BCAST(1)
BABEL	[6]	SIMPLE	5	ETX	MULTIDISTVEC	BCAST(1) ∪ BCAST(∞)
BATMAN	[27]	SIMPLE	5	MCX	SINGLEDISTVEC(pro)	BCAST(∞)
JOKER	[35]	OPPORTUNISTIC	5	MCX	SINGLEDISTVEC(pro)	BCAST(∞)
AODV	[29]	SIMPLE	⊥	ETX	SINGLEDISTVEC(re)	BCAST(∞) ∪ UCAST
DSR	[18]	SOURCE	⊥	ETX	SINGLEDISTVEC(re)	BCAST(∞) ∪ UCAST
ABR	[40]	SIMPLE	⊥	AGE	SINGLEDISTVEC(re)	BCAST(∞) ∪ UCAST
ZRP	[16]	SIMPLE	5	ETX	ZONE(i, o, r)	BCAST(r) ∪ BORDERCAST ∪ UCAST
TORA	[28]	SIMPLE	⊥	⊥	LINKREVERSAL(m)	BCAST(∞) ∪ BCAST(1)
GPSR	[21]	GEOGRAPHIC	⊥	DIST	⊥	⊥

Dissemination Strategies are responsible for disseminating control messages to their intended destinations. These can be: BCAST(h), where control messages are broadcast throughout the entire network if h is ∞, or up to limited number of hops h, otherwise. BORDERCAST, where messages are disseminated to the nodes at the border of routing zones. And UCAST, where messages are sent to a single destination, leveraging previously discovered routes.

With these parameters, we can define a large number of protocols found in the literature. Table 1 contains an illustrative set of examples. The values of the AP column are in seconds. In the next section, we present our experimental evaluation resorting to some of these protocols.

4   Experimental Evaluation

In this section, we present our evaluation work resorting to an experimental assessment of representative routing protocols found in the literature, and implemented using a prototype of our proposed framework, that follows the execution flow previously presented in Fig. 1. In the following we detail our experimental setting, followed by the presentation of the experimental results.

4.1 Experimental Setting

The framework, all its modules, and the companion discovery and broadcast protocols were implemented in the C programming language resorting to the Yggdrasil framework [8]. Our framework operates over WiFi (802.11b/g/n standard at 2.4 GHz), without any MAC or PHY changes. We selected the five most well-known representative routing protocols to evaluate: OLSR, BABEL, BATMAN, AODV, and DSR, which were configured as indicated in Table 1. The first three protocols are proactive, employing different routing strategies, and the other two are reactive, employing distinct forwarding strategies. Due to lack of space, we omit further descriptions of these protocols. The interval of the periodic announcements of the companion discovery protocol were configured with a value of 5 s, to minimize the contention and collisions in the wireless medium.

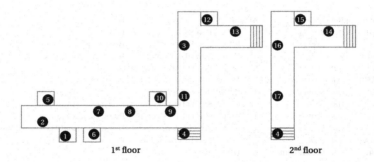

Fig. 2. Network deployment.

The experimental evaluation was conducted in a wireless *ad hoc* network composed of 17 Raspberry Pi 3 - model B, that were dispersed through the rooms and hallways (with approximately 30 m) of our department building across two floors, as schematically illustrated in Fig. 2.

Each node executed one of the routing protocols, a companion discovery protocol, a companion broadcast protocol, and a simple ping application for a period of 10 min, including grace periods of 2 min at the beginning and end. The ping application, at every second, requests to the routing protocol to send a message to a randomly selected destination (other than the local node), which upon the reception replies with the same message to the source node. This behavior allows to evaluate the selected routes in both directions.

For each routing protocol, we measured its *reliability*, as the ratio of messages that were successfully received back; its *latency*, as the average round-trip-time (RTT) of each message; and its *communication overhead*, as the total number of transmissions incurred by the dissemination of control messages by the routing protocol and all companion protocols.

We evaluated each protocol in four scenarios: one without node faults and three with deterministic node faults of the first two nodes, five nodes, and nine nodes from the sequence 3, 12, 7, 9, 11, 2, 5, 10, 14. In the experiments with faults, these were introduced simultaneously at the middle point of the experiment (5 min). Furthermore, the nodes configured to fail were never selected to be the destination of messages as to not affect reliability measurements. Each experiment was executed three times, in a random order, and the results show the average of all runs. Next, we present and discuss the experimental results.

4.2   Experimental Results

Figure 3 presents in each plot the results for the reliability, represented in the y axis, discriminated by node and on average (the last set of columns) represented in the x axis. Overall, all protocols achieved a reliability above 85% in all scenarios, with the proactive protocols (OLSR, BABEL, and BATMAN) achieving higher reliability than the reactive ones. This is explained by the nodes dropping requested messages while route computation is being performed and routes being constantly broken and re-computed due to unstable neighbors, whose impact is

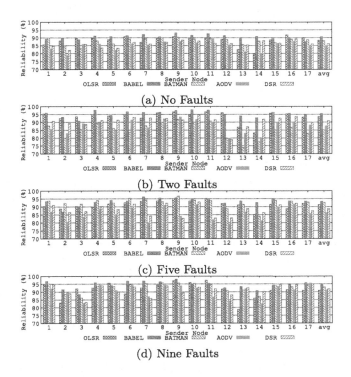

Fig. 3. Reliability of routing protocols.

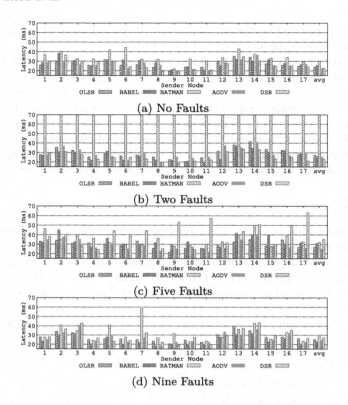

Fig. 4. Average latency of routing protocols.

mitigated in proactive solutions since routes are continuously updated. BABEL
was the protocol that achieved higher reliability on average, in all scenarios. The
reason for this behavior is that, among the proactive protocols, BABEL was the
one with the lowest overhead (discussed further ahead) and, as such, this lead
to less interferences in the wireless medium causing less message losses.

Among the reactive protocols, DSR achieved a slightly higher reliability than
AODV in all scenarios. We suspect this behavior was caused by unstable neighborhood relations that induced the routes to break, leading the intermediary
nodes in AODV to remove the routes from their routing tables. This instability
impacted DSR less since the full routes are carried within the messages.

We note that, as the number of failures increases so does the reliability of
the protocols. This is due to the fact that the resulting network after the faults
had more stable paths, had less unstable redundant paths, and less interference
between the nodes. Furthermore, in the scenario with two faults (Fig. 3b), we
note that BATMAN had significantly lower reliability when compared to the
other scenarios. This was caused by the emergence of a high number of short-
lived routing loops. These loops emerge since BATMAN's routing strategy has
no loop prevention mechanism and the combination of BATMAN's cost function

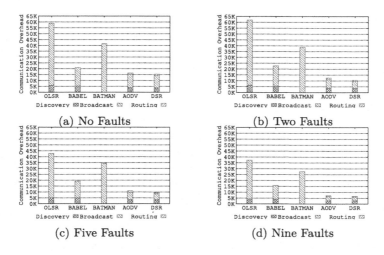

(a) No Faults

(b) Two Faults

(c) Five Faults

(d) Nine Faults

Fig. 5. Total communication overhead per routing protocol.

and dissemination strategy, allied with unstable neighborhoods, cause the nodes to frequently change their selected next-hops.

Figure 4 presents in each plot the average latency in milliseconds (ms) in the y axis, across all nodes and on average (the last set of columns), represented in the x axis. Overall, all protocols achieved a latency below 35 ms in all scenarios, with approximately the same average latency per scenario. The reason behind these results is that all the protocols converged to the same routes being selected (with approximately 2.1 hops on average) since almost all protocols used the same cost metric and the diversity of available routes to compute in our network deployment was small. The exception was BATMAN, consistently being the protocol with the highest latency, due to the formation of short-lived routing loops that were observed during the experiment across all scenarios.

Figure 5 presents in each plot the results of the total communication overhead, represented in the y axis, for each protocol, represented in the x axis. The overhead is discriminated into three types: the *discovery overhead*, as the number of transmissions incurred by the discovery protocol, the *broadcast overhead*, as the number of transmissions incurred by the broadcast protocol, and the *routing overhead*, as the number of transmissions incurred to disseminate control messages with unicast. We begin to note that, as the number of failures increases, the overhead decreases as fewer nodes disseminate control messages. Overall, OLSR presented the highest overhead since its routing strategy triggered the dissemination of unscheduled control messages whenever the selected sub-set of the topology to disseminate (with broadcast) changed, which frequently happened due to unstable neighborhood relations.

The reactive routing protocols, AODV and DSR, presented the lowest overhead across all scenarios. This is the result of caching eavesdropped routes destined to other nodes which allows less route requests to be disseminated.

The BATMAN protocol has the second highest overhead, which is fundamentally caused by the constant periodic broadcasting of a node's identity. In addition, BATMAN's neighbor discovery process is merged with the dissemination of such control messages, allowing to have no additional discovery overhead.

5   Related Work

In this section, we discuss the related work on systematizing routing protocols for wireless *ad hoc* networks. Throughout the literature, not many authors have attempted to perform such task. Nonetheless, a few exceptions can be found.

The Independent Zone Routing (IZR) [34] framework enables the hybridization of proactive and reactive protocols while allowing to dynamically adapt the amount of proactive and reactive behavior. However, although IZR allows combining practically any proactive and reactive solutions, it considers them as "black boxes" and does not attempt to decompose them into their fundamental constituents to properly analyze each routing solution, as we do in this paper.

The Relay Node Set (RNS) [38] in contrast, is an analytical framework for comparing the communication overhead of routing protocols. RNS views each protocol as a handler of sets of nodes that retransmit control messages, being that each protocol may manage more than one of these sets at a time. In this sense, this framework dissects each protocol from an evaluation standpoint and not according to their internal operation, as our framework does.

Finally, the Multi-Mode Routing Protocol (MMRP) [36] framework independently selects the most suitable protocol for a given region of the network according to its local characteristics, allowing the coexistence of multiple protocols within the same network (called multi-mode routing). However, MMRP is not flexible enough to specify the majority of the existing protocols since it heavily relies on a single and specific architectural pattern, only suitable for a restricted set of solutions, unlike our framework which is much more generic.

6   Final Remarks

In this paper, we presented a conceptual framework to specify routing protocols for wireless *ad hoc* networks that abstracts the protocols' common aspects, a task that is not trivial due to their nature, and exposes parameters that capture the behavior of particular solutions. Leveraging a prototype of our framework, we implemented a representative set of existing routing protocols and evaluated their performance in a real wireless *ad hoc* network formed by commodity devices. The results showed interesting observations that have not been explored and discussed before in the context of routing protocols in wireless *ad hoc* networks. BATMAN, which is considered in the literature as one of the best protocols, was not only never the best regarding the reliability in any scenario but also was the worst regarding the latency in all scenarios. Furthermore, reactive protocols presented similar reliability to proactive ones despite the unstable neighborhoods and node faults, due to the usage of route caching, while having much lower overhead. However, these results cannot be extrapolated to other topologies, and more exhaustive evaluations should be carried out.

References

1. Al-Fuqaha, A., Guizani, M., Mohammadi, M., Aledhari, M., Ayyash, M.: Internet of things: a survey on enabling technologies, protocols, and applications. IEEE Commun. Surv. Tutor. **17**(4), 2347–2376 (2015)
2. Andel, T.R., Yasinsac, A.: On the credibility of manet simulations. Computer **39**(7), 48–54 (2006)
3. Baraković, S., Baraković, J.: Comparative performance evaluation of mobile ad hoc routing protocols. In: The 33rd International Convention MIPRO, pp. 518–523 (2010)
4. Boukerche, A., Darehshoorzadeh, A.: Opportunistic routing in wireless networks: models, algorithms, and classifications. ACM Comput. Surv. **47**(2), 1–36 (2014)
5. Cavin, D., Sasson, Y., Schiper, A.: On the accuracy of manet simulators. In: Proceedings of the Second ACM International Workshop on Principles of Mobile Computing, POMC 2002, pp. 38–43. Association for Computing Machinery (2002)
6. Chroboczek, J., Schinazi, D.: The Babel Routing Protocol. Technical report, January 2021
7. Clausen, T.H., Dearlove, C., Jacquet, P., Herberg, U.: The Optimized Link State Routing Protocol Version 2. Technical report, April 2014
8. Costa, P.A., Rosa, A., Leitão, J.A.: Enabling wireless ad hoc edge systems with Yggdrasil. In: Proceedings of the 35th Annual ACM Symposium on Applied Computing, SAC 2020, pp. 2129–2136. Association for Computing Machinery, New York (2020)
9. Das, S.R., Castaneda, R., Yan, J., Sengupta, R.: Comparative performance evaluation of routing protocols for mobile, ad hoc networks. In: Proceedings 7th International Conference on Computer Communications and Networks (Cat. No. 98EX226), pp. 153–161 (1998)
10. Das, S.R., Castañeda, R., Yan, J.: Simulation-based performance evaluation of routing protocols for mobile ad hoc networks. Mobi. Netw. Appl. **5**(3), 179–189 (2000). https://doi.org/10.1023/A:1019108612308
11. Dillon, T., Wu, C., Chang, E.: Cloud computing: issues and challenges. In: 2010 24th IEEE International Conference on Advanced Information Networking and Applications, pp. 27–33 (2010)
12. Draves, R., Padhye, J., Zill, B.: Routing in multi-radio, multi-hop wireless mesh networks. In: Proceedings of the 10th Annual International Conference on Mobile Computing and Networking, MobiCom 2004, pp. 114–128. Association for Computing Machinery (2004)
13. Dube, R., Rais, C.D., Wang, K.-Y., Tripathi, S.K.: Signal stability-based adaptive routing (SSA) for ad hoc mobile networks. IEEE Pers. Commun. **4**(1), 36–45 (1997)
14. Gafni, E., Bertsekas, D.: Distributed algorithms for generating loop-free routes in networks with frequently changing topology. IEEE Trans. Commun. **29**(1), 11–18 (1981)
15. Gerla, M.: Fisheye State Routing Protocol (FSR) for Ad Hoc Networks. Internet-Draft draft-ietf-manet-fsr-03. Internet Engineering Task Force, June 2002
16. Haas, Z.J.: A new routing protocol for the reconfigurable wireless networks. In: Proceedings of ICUPC 97–6th International Conference on Universal Personal Communications, vol. 2, pp. 562–566, October 1997

17. He, G.: Destination-sequenced distance vector (DSDV) protocol, pp. 1–9. Networking Laboratory. Helsinki University of Technology (2002)

18. Hu, Y.C., Maltz, D.A., Johnson, D.B.: The Dynamic Source Routing Protocol (DSR) for Mobile Ad Hoc Networks for IPv4. Technical report 4728, February 2007

19. Javaid, N., Javaid, A., Khan, I.A., Djouani, K.: Performance study of ETX based wireless routing metrics. In: 2009 2nd International Conference on Computer, Control and Communication, pp. 1–7 (2009)

20. Johnson, D., Hancke, G.: Comparison of two routing metrics in OLSR on a grid based mesh network. Ad Hoc Netw. **7**(2), 374–387 (2009)

21. Karp, B., Kung, H.T.: GPSR: greedy perimeter stateless routing for wireless networks. In: Proceedings of the 6th Annual International Conference on Mobile Computing and Networking, MobiCom 2000, pp. 243–254. Association for Computing Machinery (2000)

22. Kiess, W., Mauve, M.: A survey on real-world implementations of mobile ad-hoc networks. Ad Hoc Netw. **5**(3), 324–339 (2007)

23. Kim, K.H., Shin, K.G.: On accurate measurement of link quality in multi-hop wireless mesh networks. In: Proceedings of the 12th Annual International Conference on Mobile Computing and Networking, MobiCom 2006, pp. 38–49. Association for Computing Machinery (2006)

24. Lee, S., Gerla, M.: Dynamic load-aware routing in ad hoc networks. In: ICC 2001. IEEE International Conference on Communications. Conference Record (Cat. No. 01CH37240), vol. 10, pp. 3206–3210 (2001)

25. Leitão, J., Costa, P.Á., Gomes, M.C., Preguiça, N.M.: Towards enabling novel edge-enabled applications. Technical report, Faculdade de Ciências e Tecnologia da Universidade Nova de Lisboa (2018). https://dblp.org/rec/bib/journals/corr/abs-1805-06989

26. Mueller, S., Tsang, R.P., Ghosal, D.: Multipath routing in mobile ad hoc networks: issues and challenges. In: Calzarossa, M.C., Gelenbe, E. (eds.) MASCOTS 2003. LNCS, vol. 2965, pp. 209–234. Springer, Heidelberg (2004). https://doi.org/10.1007/978-3-540-24663-3_10

27. Neumann, A., Aichele, C., Lindner, M., Wunderlich, S.: Better Approach to Mobile Ad-hoc Networking (BATMAN). Internet-Draft draft-wunderlich-openmesh-manet-routing-00, Internet Engineering Task Force, April 2008

28. Park, V.D., Corson, D.S.M.: Temporally-Ordered Routing Algorithm (TORA) Version 1 Functional Specification. Internet-Draft draft-ietf-manet-tora-spec-04, Internet Engineering Task Force, July 2001

29. Perkins, C.E., Ratliff, S., Dowdell, J., Steenbrink, L., Pritchard, V.: Ad Hoc On-demand Distance Vector Version 2 (AODVv2) Routing. Internet-Draft draft-perkins-manet-aodvv2-03, Internet Engineering Task Force, February 2019

30. Ramasubramanian, V., Haas, Z.J., Sirer, E.G.: Sharp: a hybrid adaptive routing protocol for mobile ad hoc networks. In: Proceedings of the 4th ACM International Symposium on Mobile Ad Hoc Networking and Computing, MobiHoc 2003, pp. 303–314. Association for Computing Machinery (2003)D

31. Reina, D.G., Toral, S.L., Barrero, F., Bessis, N., Asimakopoulou, E.: The role of ad hoc networks in the internet of things: a case scenario for smart environments. In: Internet of Things and Inter-cooperative Computational Technologies for Collective Intelligence. Studies in Computational Intelligence, 460th edn., pp. 89–113. Springer, Heidelberg (2013). https://doi.org/10.1007/978-3-642-34952-2_4

32. Ruehrup, S.: Theory and practice of geographic routing. In: Liu, H., Yiu-Wing Leung, X.C. (ed.) Ad hoc and Sensor Wireless Networks: Architectures, Algorithms and Protocols, vol. 69, chap. 5, pp. 69–88. Bentham Science (2009)
33. Samar, P., Haas, Z.: Strategies for broadcasting updates by proactive routing protocols in mobile ad hoc networks. In: MILCOM 2002, Proceedings, vol. 2, pp. 873–878 (2002)
34. Samar, P., Pearlman, M.R., Haas, Z.J.: Independent zone routing: an adaptive hybrid routing framework for ad hoc wireless networks. IEEE/ACM Trans. Netw. **12**(4), 595–608 (2004)
35. Sanchez-Iborra, R., Cano, M.: Joker: a novel opportunistic routing protocol. IEEE J. Sel. Areas Commun. **34**(5), 1690–1703 (2016). https://doi.org/10.1109/JSAC. 2016.2545439
36. Santivanez, C.A., Stavrakakis, I.: Towards adaptable Ad Hoc networks: the routing experience. In: Smirnov, M. (ed.) WAC 2004. LNCS, vol. 3457, pp. 229–244. Springer, Heidelberg (2005). https://doi.org/10.1007/11520184_18
37. Shah, R.C., Rabaey, J.M.: Energy aware routing for low energy ad hoc sensor networks. In: 2002 IEEE Wireless Communications and Networking Conference Record. WCNC 2002 (Cat. No. 02TH8609), vol. 1, pp. 350–355 (2002)
38. Lin, T., Midkiff, S.F., Park, J.S.: A framework for wireless ad hoc routing protocols. In: 2003 IEEE Wireless Communications and Networking, WCNC 2003, vol. 2, pp. 1162–1167 (2003)
39. Templin, F.L., Ogier, R., Lewis, M.S.: Topology Dissemination Based on Reverse-Path Forwarding (TBRPF). Technical report, February 2004
40. Toh, C.K.: Long-lived Ad Hoc Routing based on the Concept of Associativity. Internet-Draft draft-ietf-manet-longlived-adhoc-routing-00, Internet Engineering Task Force, March 1999
41. Xu, L.D., He, W., Li, S.: Internet of things in industries: a survey. IEEE Trans. Industr. Inf. **10**(4), 2233–2243 (2014)

Longitudinal Compliance Analysis of Android Applications with Privacy Policies

Saad Sajid Hashmi[1]([✉]), Nazar Waheed[2], Gioacchino Tangari[1],
Muhammad Ikram[1], and Stephen Smith[1]

[1] Macquarie University, Sydney, Australia
saad.hashmi@hdr.mq.edu.au
{gioacchino.tangari,muhammad.ikram,stephen.smith}@mq.edu.au
[2] University of Technology Sydney, Sydney, Australia
nazar.waheed@student.uts.edu.au

Abstract. Contemporary mobile applications (apps) are designed to track, use, and share users' data, often without their consent, which results in potential privacy and transparency issues. To investigate whether mobile apps have always been (non-)transparent regarding how they collect information about users, we perform a longitudinal analysis of the historical versions of 268 Android apps. These apps comprise 5,240 app releases or versions between 2008 and 2016. We detect inconsistencies between apps' behaviors and the stated use of data collection in privacy policies to reveal compliance issues. We utilize machine learning techniques to classify the privacy policy text and identify the purported practices that collect and/or share users' personal information, such as phone numbers and email addresses. We then uncover the data leaks of an app through static and dynamic analysis. Over time, our results show a steady increase in the number of apps' data collection practices that are undisclosed in the privacy policies. This behavior is particularly troubling since privacy policy is the primary tool for describing the app's privacy protection practices. We find that newer versions of the apps are likely to be more non-compliant than their preceding versions. The discrepancies between the purported and the actual data practices show that privacy policies are often incoherent with the apps' behaviors, thus defying the 'notice and choice' principle when users install apps.

Keywords: Data privacy · Mobile applications · Privacy policy · Static analysis · Dynamic analysis

1 Introduction

"Privacy is the claim of individuals, groups, or institutions to determine for themselves when, how, and to what extent information about them is communi-

© ICST Institute for Computer Sciences, Social Informatics and Telecommunications Engineering 2022
Published by Springer Nature Switzerland AG 2022. All Rights Reserved
T. Hara and H. Yamaguchi (Eds.): MobiQuitous 2021, LNICST 419, pp. 280–305, 2022.
https://doi.org/10.1007/978-3-030-94822-1_16

cated to others."[1] Between October 2012 and February 2013, Snapchat's privacy policy said, "We do not ask for, track, or access any location-specific information from your device at any time while you are using the Snapchat application" [1]. However, Snapchat did the opposite by collecting and sharing users' geo-location information (Wi-Fi and cell-based location data) to its analytics tracking service provider. Federal Trade Commission (FTC) of the United States initiated an investigation, and in December 2014 ordered Snapchat to implement a comprehensive privacy program addressing risks to users' privacy [2].

In February 2019, FTC fined TikTok 5.7 million USD for illegally collecting children's personal data [3]. Between 2019-20, in the United States, several federal lawsuits against TikTok were filed citing the harvesting of users' (including children's) personal data without consent. In July 2020, these lawsuits were incorporated into a single class-action lawsuit. In February 2021, a settlement was reached where TikTok agreed to pay 92 million USD and stop the collection of users' bio-metric and location data [4]. Currently, TikTok is facing a privacy lawsuit in the United Kingdom for violating child privacy laws in the collection of personal information and sharing it with third-parties [5].

The examples of Snapchat, TikTok, and various other apps [6] highlight that online service providers frequently do not comply with their privacy policies, despite the presence of regulations related to the disclosure of privacy practices. These regulations include the California Online Privacy Protection Act (CalOPPA) [7], California Consumer Privacy Act (CCPA) [8], and Children's Online Privacy Protection Act (COPPA) [9] in the US, General Data Protection Regulation (GDPR) in the EU [10], Data Protection Act in the UK [11], and the Privacy Act in Australia [12]. Although there are limitations to privacy policies (such as they are not often read [13], take a long time to read [14], and are hard to comprehend [15]), privacy policies remain the legally recognized standard of protecting privacy based on the "notice and choice" principle [16]. This principle gives users a notice of the data practices performed by the app (or service) before that data is collected. The users then have the choice to *opt-in* (i.e., give permission) or *opt-out* (i.e., decline permission) of giving access to their details.

Several studies have shown the behavior of contemporary apps to be non-compliant with the stated disclosures in their privacy policies [17–23]. Given that the compliance landscape is continuously evolving, we aim to determine whether the non-compliant behavior has changed with time. In this study, we investigate the compliance of Android apps with their privacy policies over time, ranging from 2008 and 2016. We detect and analyze the personally identifiable information (PII) leaked by an app, disregarding the practices made public by the publisher in the app's privacy policy. We leverage machine learning (ML) techniques to classify the text of apps' privacy policies and identify the purported practices that collect and/or share data (e.g., phone number). We then uncover the actual data leaks of an app through static analysis (*examining the app code*) and dynamic analysis (*inspecting the network traffic generated by the app*). While relying on existing techniques, this study is, to our knowledge, the first effort to

---

[1] Alan Westin, Privacy and Freedom, 1967.

integrate app and privacy policy text analysis to measure how the apps' privacy conducts have evolved.

The main contributions of this paper are as follows:

- We identify the data collection practices (*privacy practices*) disclosed in 3,151 privacy policies (obtained from 2012 to 2019) of 405[2] apps using machine learning classifiers. We find that 2,422 privacy policies from 327 different apps disclose at least one of these practices, with an average of 7.86 per policy (Sect. 3.1).
- We analyze historical versions of popular apps from 2008 to 2016, based on the union of leaks observed via static and dynamic analysis. The results show an increase in the average number of leaks per app version over time. Surprisingly, the average number of leaks to third-parties rose from 2.7 in 2011 to 4.43 in 2016 (Sect. 3.2).
- Our analysis reveals that the compliance of apps with their privacy policy is steadily decreasing from 33.16% in 2011 to 10.76% in 2016. Also, newer versions of the apps are performing more privacy policy violations than their immediately preceding version. For instance, 9.2% of the app versions released in 2016 show an increase in first-party violations compared to their preceding version, whereas only 2.5% show a decrease (Sect. 3.3).

The rest of the paper is organized as follows: In Sect. 2, we describe our data collection approach and present our analysis methodology. In Sect. 3, we discuss the findings of our analysis. Section 6 reviews the related work, and we conclude and discuss future research directions in Sect. 7.

2   Dataset and Methodology

Figure 1 depicts our methodology. In the following, we explain the steps involved in our data collection and analysis.

2.1   Dataset

Mobile Apps. We select Android apps that are *(i)* popular, *(ii)* have multiple versions, *(iii)* are susceptible to network traffic interception, and *(iv)* have privacy policy in the app's home-page on Google Play. The popular apps we selected were either in the top 600 free apps based on the Google Play Store ranking, or in the top 50 in each app category, as of 10 Jan 2017. We discard apps with less than four versions and apps for which we can not intercept TLS (Transport Layer Security) traffic (e.g., apps with non-native Android TLS libraries such as Twitter, Dropbox). We also discard apps that do not contain privacy policy on their home-page at Google Play. For the compliance analysis, we collect 5,240 unique APKs that correspond to 268 apps.

We download the selected apps and their previous versions from an unofficial Google Play API [24] that requires the package name and version code to

---

[2] *see* Sect. A for clarification on different number of apps reported.

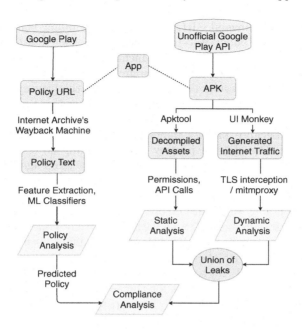

Fig. 1. Overview of our approach. We perform compliance analysis after taking the union of personal identifiable information (PII) leaks detected in both the static and dynamic analysis.

download an APK. We infer the release date of the package from the last modification time of the files inside the APK (such as `AndroidManifest.xml` and `META-INF/MANIFEST.MF`). If the date is incorrect (e.g., before 2008), we refer to third-party services (appcensus.io, apkpure.com) for inferring the release dates.

Privacy Policies. Google requires Android app developers to disclose the collection and sharing of users' data [25]. Accordingly, on Google Play Store, each application must provide a link to the privacy policy on its home-page.

For the most updated version of each app, first, we access the URL of the privacy policy from the app's home-page (https://play.google.com/store/apps/details?id=[pname] followed by the package name, i.e., *pname*), and then scrape privacy policy link to extract the privacy policy text.

To obtain the privacy policies of the previous versions of the same app, we leverage the Internet Archive's Wayback Machine [26], which gives us access to previous snapshots of the app's privacy policy page. Since 1996, the Wayback Machine has archived full websites, including JavaScript codes, style sheets, and any multimedia resources that it can identify statically from the website's content. We refer to the single capture of a web-page as a *snapshot*. Wayback Machine mirrors past snapshots of these websites on its servers. Note that we cannot extract the privacy policy content if the URL obtained from the app's home-page refers to an invalid URL, or if the privacy policy is not found on that URL, or if the privacy policy web-page contains another link that refers to the privacy policy text. Also, the Wayback Machine poses some challenges (such as web-page redirect or varied frequency of archived snapshots) in capturing a specific web-page [27]. This results in a miss to capture the privacy policy snapshot in that three-month window, and we move to the next three-month window.

There are instances where a single privacy policy is mapped to multiple app versions. This is because privacy policies only became mandatory on Google Play in 2018 [28]. Therefore, a privacy policy residing on a given URL today may not have been residing on the same URL a few years ago. If the Wayback Machine does not archive a policy's web-page, then the current policy's web-page (obtained in 2019) is mapped to all the app releases. Furthermore, we are unable to obtain policy web-pages before 2012. Therefore, the app releases prior to 2012 have a high difference in time with the privacy policy date. It may also be possible that the source code of an app is modified when releasing a new version however comes with the old privacy policy.

We use Memento API [29] to capture snapshots at intervals of three months and obtain multiple privacy policies for the same app. Memento API provides the nearest time-stamp for the archived snapshot of a website from the date provided. By comparing the app version's release date with the snapshot dates of the privacy policy web-page, we obtain the snapshot immediately after the app version's release date. For example, if an app released versions in Feb'16, Aug'16 and Dec'16, and the app's privacy policy snapshots are from Jan'16, Jul'16, and Jan'17, then the Feb'16 app version will be assigned the Jul'16 privacy policy. Similarly, Aug'16 and Dec'16 app versions will be assigned the Jan'17 privacy policy snapshot.

2.2 Privacy Policy Analysis

We characterize the identification of privacy practices (i.e., app behaviors that leak PII) from the app's privacy policy as a supervised classification problem. We initially pre-process the privacy policy text and then apply machine-learning classifiers to predict the privacy practices.

Data Pre-processing: From the privacy policy URL, we obtain the text of the privacy policy by scraping the *<body>* tag of the HTML page. Within the *<body>* tag, we discard unnecessary content nested in other tags (such as *<script>*, *<style>*, *<meta>*, and *<noscript>*). Some archived pages in Wayback Machine have text in a particular format (for example, beginning with "success" and ending with "TIMESTAMPS") prefixed to the original text. We discard all prefix text prior to the analysis of privacy policy text.

Next, we convert the privacy policy text into segments (or paragraphs) by ensuring that a single paragraph does not contain less than fifty characters, except if it is the last paragraph of the privacy policy. Previous work has shown that practices are better captured from the policy text if the text is broken down into segments [30,31]. If a text segment (other than the last segment) has less than fifty characters, it is likely to be the heading of the next paragraph; therefore, we merge it with the next text segment. We also combine two adjacent text segments if their combined length is less than 250 characters. After converting the text into segments, we lowercase all segments, and normalize whitespaces and apostrophes (for example, we change words like *haven't* and *don't* to *have not* and *do not* respectively). We finally discard non-alpha and non-ASCII characters and also remove single-character words from the text segments.

Finally, we extract vectors for the segment text by taking the union of TF-IDF [32] vector and a vector of hand-crafted features obtained from [33]. We choose TF-IDF because it is the most popular weighting scheme in the domain of text mining and information retrieval [34,35]. We create the TF-IDF vector using `TfidfVectorizer` [36] with English stop words from the Natural Language Toolkit (NLTK) corpus. The vector of hand-crafted features comprises boolean values corresponding to the presence or absence of custom strings in the training dataset. For example, we use the strings `cookie`, `web beacon`, and `tracking pixel` to indicate the disclosure of `Identifier_Cookie` practice.

Training Data: To build a training dataset, we leverage the work of Zimmeck et al. [22] where they created a privacy policy corpus of 350 most popular mobile apps (APP-350 corpus [37]). All the 350 apps selected have more than 5 million downloads. Legal experts annotated the privacy policies to identify the privacy practices mentioned in the policy text. The annotated label on a privacy policy comprises three parts (or tiers): *(i)* a general or specific practice (twenty-eight unique practices in total), *(ii)* whether that practice has been performed or not, and *(iii)* whether that practice is associated with first or third-party. In first-party practice, the PII is accessed by the code of the app itself, and in third-party practice, the PII is accessed by third-party libraries (such as analytics, advertisements, or social networks). The annotation labels are assigned to the segments (or paragraphs) rather than the whole policy text. The union of labels for the segments provides the disclosure in the whole policy text. We randomly split the APP-350 corpus into training data (n = 250) and test data (n = 100).

Classification Problem: For a given privacy policy, we aim to detect the disclosure of privacy practices. A privacy practice comprises three components: *(i)* type of PII (e.g., `Contact`), *(ii)* negation or approval of the practice being performed (`Performed` or `Not Performed`), and *(iii)* party (`1stParty` or `3rdParty`). We characterize this task as a multi-label text classification problem.

We sub-divide the classification task to identify: *(i)* PII type, *(ii)* procedure i.e., practice has been performed or not, and *(iii)* first-party or third-party. If we make classifier for each unique combination, we will require 112 classifiers for each combination of PII type, perform/not perform, and first/third-party. The limitation of this approach is that the training samples for most of these combinations are limited (less than 100). Therefore, after sub-dividing the classification problem, we only require thirty-two classifiers (twenty-eight for unique PII types, two for procedure (`Performed` or `Not Performed`), and two for *parties*). For example, `Contact_Email_Address Performed 3rdParty` will be assigned to a text segment for which `Contact_Email_Address`, `Performed`, and `3rdParty` classifiers all return a positive value for that text segment. We consider a policy text discloses a privacy practice if at least one segment in the text returns positive values for at least one PII type classifier, `Performed` classifier, and `1stParty` and/or `3rdParty` classifiers.

We utilize One-vs-the-rest (OvR) [38] classification strategy and test our approach with the Multinomial Naive Bayes [39], Logistic Regression [40], and Linear Support Vector Classifiers (SVC) [41]. We select Linear SVC as our classifier for unseen policies' text due to its superior performance on the test dataset (n = 100). In particular, the average F1 score (%) for all classifiers with Multinomial Naive Bayes and Logistic Regression is 17.37% and 67.54%, respectively, while for Linear SVC, we obtain an average F1 score of 73.75%. Table 7 shows the performance of our classifiers. Our approach achieves high accuracy, ranging from 91.16% to 100% for all the classifiers.

2.3   Static Analysis

Resources of an app that are required to run it on a device are bundled together in an Android Package Kit (APK). In the static analysis of mobile apps, after downloading the APK, we decompile it using Apktool [42]. Decompiling APK yields the assets (including byte-code in the DEX format) and metadata (in the XML format). After disassembling .dex files into smali format, we extract the API calls. We also extract the app permissions from the `AndroidManifest.xml` file. If an app needs access to a resource outside its sandbox, then it will request the appropriate permission in the `AndroidManifest.xml` file. API calls that do not have the required permissions are not executed, for example, the API `android.telephony.TelephonyManager.getImei` requires READ_PRIVILEGED_PHONE_STATE permission to retrieve the IMEI (International Mobile Equipment Identity). In particular, we utilize the Android APIs from [22] and obtain their required permissions from Android API reference [43]. If we observe an API call for a particular privacy practice in the source code, we check if the required permissions are also requested in the app manifest file. We identify that practice is being performed (for a given privacy practice) if both the relevant API call(s) and the required permission(s) exist.

We distinguish the API *function* calls into system calls, first-party calls, and third-party calls. Calls made by the Android class are classified as system calls. We differentiate between first and third-party calls by comparing the classes based on Java's reversed internet domain naming convention [44]. The .`smali` file's package name is matched with the app's package name. If *(i)* both top and second-level domains match , or *(ii)* the .`smali` file's package looks obfuscated (e.g., `b/a/y.smali`), we classify the API call as first-party. Otherwise, it is classified as a third-party call. In our analysis, we only consider the API calls made by first or third-parties.

Besides obtaining the third-party "domains" invoking the API calls, we need to extract the corresponding company names in order to check if these appear in the privacy policy text or not. Since a company can acquire multiple domains, we leverage the previous work of Binns et al. [45] in the domain-company ownership. For example, if the API call is from `adsense.com` then we check for the existence of terms "adsense", "google" and "alphabet" in the privacy policy text. If we find any of the terms in the policy text, we consider the third-party domain as disclosed.

2.4 Dynamic Analysis

A limitation of static analysis is its inability to capture dynamically loaded code and analyze obfuscated function calls [46]. To overcome this limitation, following the work by Ren et al. [47], we complement our approach with the dynamic analysis of apps. We employ ReCon [48], a transparency control tool that relies on the machine-learning classification to identify leaks of privacy-related information in the mobile-app traffic [49]. In particular, using a public dataset of annotated traffic flows [50], we train a machine-learning classifier (C4.5 decision tree) to predict whether traffic flow is leaking PII. As a feature set, the classifier takes a concatenation of the text of URI, Referrer, postData text, and all other HTTP headers in the flow. The validation accuracy of the classifier is 97.2% (AUC = 0.987), with 97.8% precision and 96.6% recall. For those flows predicted to leak (any) PII, we extract the performed privacy practices by matching the feature set against a predefined set of keywords and regular expressions from ReCon [51].

The gold standard for identifying privacy leaks is by manually logging into the apps and interacting with them. However, this approach is impractical at scale. To automate the analysis, we rely on Android's UI/Application Exerciser Monkey [52], a command-line tool that generates pseudo-random user events such as swipes, clicks, or touches. While running an app, we use mitmproxy [53] (a TLS-capable interception proxy) to capture all app-generated traffic (HTTP and HTTPS) on a dual-stack [54] WiFi in our testbed. Prior work showed that synthetic usage patterns could lead to underestimating the number of privacy leaks compared to manual (human) interactions [49] since random streams of Monkey events may miss some function calls. While this is a common drawback of automation approaches, Android's Monkey exhibits the best code coverage among existing automation tools [55].

In our effort to capture most—if not all—the privacy leaks produced by an app, we take the union of leaks from static and dynamic analysis. Since labels are different in the two cases, we map dynamic leak labels onto the static ones. To this end, we compare the descriptions of static leak labels (*see* Table 6) with the ones of dynamic leak labels in [47]. Table 1 lists the conversion between the leak labels. We keep the static leak labels as our final ones since they match the labels in the privacy policy text, making them convenient for the following subsection.

Table 1. Label mapping between PII leaks from static analysis (*static* leaks) and leaks from dynamic analysis (*dynamic* leaks).

Static leaks	Dynamic leaks
Contact	firstName, lastName
Contact E Mail Address	email (+ hash)
Contact Password	password (+ hash)
Contact Phone Number	phone number
Demographics Gender	gender
Identifier	hardware serial (+ hash)
Identifier {Ad ID, Cookie}	gsf id, advertiser id (+ hash)
Identifier Device ID	android id (+ hash)
Identifier IMEI	imei (+ hash)
Identifier {IMSI, Mobile Carrier, SIM Serial}	sim id
Identifier MAC	mac addr (+ hash)
Location {Bluetooth, Cell Tower, GPS, IP Address, WiFi}	location

2.5   Compliance Analysis

In the compliance analysis, we compare the leak labels with the privacy policy labels. We consider a compliance violation to have occurred if there is a positive value for a leak label and non-positive value(s) for the corresponding policy text label(s). For some dynamic leaks labels in Table 1, a positive value for a leak label is mapped to multiple labels in static leaks. For example, a positive value for gsf id will result in mapping of positive values for both Identifier Ad ID and Identifier Cookie. Therefore, if we compare individual combined leak labels only, then we may come across unintended violations. For example, if there are positive values for Identifier Ad ID and Identifier Cookie in the leak labels, but only a positive value for Identifier Cookie in the policy text labels, then our system would be flagging Identifier Ad ID as a violation. Thus, to avoid these unintended violations caused by our mapping table, we consider a violation to have occurred if the policy labels do not return a positive value for any of the similar labels (both Identifier Ad ID and Identifier Cookie in this example).

For APKs that leak PII to third-parties, we also check for the existence of those third-party domains in the APK's privacy policy text. We examine the domains that are not frequently mentioned in the privacy policies. Note that the mention of the domain in privacy policy does not necessarily imply that the policy text is indicating the sharing of PII with that domain, but the absence of the domain from the policy text definitely implies that the company or domain of the organization with which the app shares PII is not disclosed. Furthermore, by distinguishing apps according to their categories, we identify the most transparent categories (complying with the privacy policies) and categories that have the most compliance issues.

3   Analysis and Results

In this section, we discuss our analysis of apps' privacy policies and then present leakages observed via our methodology. Finally, we present an analysis of apps compliance with their privacy policies.

3.1   Privacy Policy Analysis

We obtain 3,151 unique privacy policies (P.P.) from the Internet Archive and map them to 7,998 different app versions of 405 apps. We term an app's privacy policy as unique if it is obtained on a different date for an app. For example, if we collect two privacy policies of an app from Internet Archive on two separate dates, we term that two P.P. as unique, even if the contents of both the policies are identical.

To map the P.P. to the different app versions, we bind each APK to the app's privacy policy immediately after the APK release date. We note that 42.6% of the analyzed APKs have a time difference of fewer than 12 months between the APK release date and the P.P. date (*see* Sect. B).

The collected privacy policies contain 143,783 policy segments (or paragraphs) in total. We restrict this set by considering only those segments that return positive values on *(i)* at least one of the twenty-eight practice classifiers (e.g., Contact), *(ii)* procedure (i.e., the practice described in the segment is being performed or not performed), and *(iii)* parties (i.e., 1st Party or 3rd party). Out of a total of 143,783 policy segments, 19,371 segments return a positive value for the above three categories. We term these segments as *valid segments*. The valid segments span across 2,455 privacy policies mapped to 329 apps. We will rely on this subset (valid segments) to measure privacy policy violations in the remainder of the analysis.

Figure 2a shows the distribution of the valid policy segments by the procedure. A vast majority (97.48%) of valid policy segments have a positive value for the Performed classifier. These segments (n = 18,882) span across 2,422 P.P. mapped to 327 apps. This also includes the segments that return positive values for both Performed and Not Performed classifiers. A segment is not contradictory if it has positive values for both Performed and Not Performed. For example, the segment *"we will only store your email and will not collect your location"* can have positive values returned by both the classifiers. In such cases however, our classifiers are unable to distinguish between Performed PII type(s) and Not Performed type(s). Therefore, to overcome this limitation and prevent falsely flagging a policy for a violation, we assign all flagged PII types as Performed. Similarly, for the segments that return positive values for both the parties (n = 2,944), we consider the flagged PII types(s) to be Performed by both the parties. Among the segments that return positive value for the Performed classifier (n = 18,882), most have at least one practice being performed by the first-party (88.14%).

The segments that return a positive value for the Not Performed classifier only (n = 489) span across the P.P. of 89 apps and 382 APKs. Among them, 33

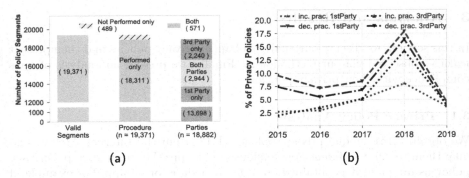

Fig. 2. (a) Breakdown of valid segments (n = 19,371) into Procedure (Performed / Not Performed). Valid segments for which Performed classifier returns a positive value (n = 18,882; Performed + Both) are broken down further into parties (1st / 3rd). (b) Percent of P.P. versions in the given year showing an increase/decrease in the number of practices disclosed. Among the newer versions of P.P. each year, more number of them continue to disclose less PII.

APKs comprising eight apps have segments that only return a positive value for the `Not Performed` classifier, i.e., these APKs' P.P. only state that PII-revealing practices are not performed. The three most common practices disclosed in the P.P. are `Identifier Cookie`, `Identifier IP Address`, and `Contact E Mail Address`. We empirically observe that the number of practices disclosed in the analyzed P.P. is 19,038. This number implies an average of 7.86 per APK, or 7.75 if we also include the APKs whose policy segments only return a positive value for the `Not Performed` classifier.

For a given year, a P.P. of an app can have multiple versions (based on the date the P.P. was obtained). Among all the P.P. that disclose the collection of PII to 1st party, 86.5% comprise multiple versions in the same year (86.1% for 3rd party, respectively). Among these multiple versions, we compare the P.P. of an app to their preceding version to identify if they are disclosing the collection of more or less PII. Figure 2b shows the annual disclosure trend of P.P. obtained in the years 2015–2019. We do not consider P.P. before 2015 due to fewer versions available (<10 annually). We observe the prevalence of P.P. with fewer PII disclosures compared to their preceding version. In particular, 17.9% of P.P. in 2018 show decreasing numbers of 3rd party disclosures (respectively, 16.4% 1st party disclosures), whereas only 8% of P.P. are found with more 3rd party disclosures (respectively, 14.2% 1st party disclosures). For apps whose behavior (leaks) remain uniform, the drop in the number of disclosures in P.P. can have potential compliance issues.

3.2 Analyzing Leakages

Static Analysis: We analyze 7,741 different APKs (or app versions) of 350 different apps, from which we extract the PII-sensitive API calls. Among these

Table 2. Number of unique apps (and versions i.e., APKs) with at least one PII leak. We report the leaks revealed by static and dynamic analysis. We also enumerate the apps (and APKs), which are common to both the analysis. We only consider the apps with retrieved privacy policy.

Year	(A) Static		(B) Dynamic		(A ∩ **B**)	
	#Apps	#APKs	#Apps	#APKs	#Apps	#APKs
2008	3	33	5	44	2	30
2009	6	32	6	18	3	4
2010	24	102	17	34	13	20
2011	47	253	39	119	26	69
2012	87	550	66	197	53	171
2013	136	868	81	334	66	299
2014	173	1302	110	525	95	476
2015	272	2035	208	1018	178	847
2016	301	2485	235	1492	197	1242

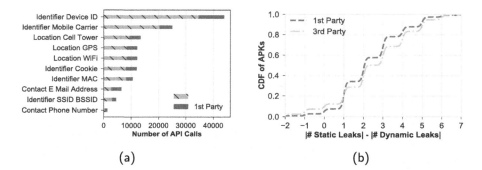

(a)   (b)

Fig. 3. (a) Number of sensitive API calls observed in the static analysis. (b) Difference in number of static leaks and dynamic leaks. At least 85% of analyzed APKs have more leaks discovered in the static analysis than in the dynamic analysis.

calls, 24.2% (n = 28,001) are made by the first-party whereas 75.8% calls (n = 87,497) are initiated by third-party services or domains.

Figure 3a shows the distribution of these API calls to different types of PII. `Identifier Device ID` and `Identifier Mobile Carrier` are the top two PII that API calls (from both first and third-parties) are collecting.

Contrasting Static and Dynamic Leaks: Table 2 shows the annual distribution of apps and versions (APKs) that report PII leak(s) through static analysis, dynamic analysis, and both.

We observe significant differences in the sets of PII-leaks found by static analysis and dynamic analysis, with the former revealing more leaks than the latter in the majority of cases (>85% of analyzed APKs) as shown in

292   S. S. Hashmi et al.

Table 3. Summary of PII Leaks from analyzed apps. In columns 2, 3, and 6, the numbers in parenthesis i.e., () represent the number of versions of apps (APKs).

Year	#Apps (#APKs)	Leaks to 1st party			Leaks to 3rd party		
		# Apps (#APKs)	#Leaks	#Leaks per APK	#Apps (#APKs)	#Leaks	#Leaks per APK
2008	6 (47)	4 (34)	116	3.41	5 (34)	0	0
2009	9 (46)	6 (29)	116	4.00	6 (21)	12	0.57
2010	28 (116)	20 (84)	252	3.00	21 (63)	187	2.97
2011	59 (303)	39 (169)	558	3.30	53 (269)	726	2.70
2012	99 (576)	67 (354)	1127	3.18	94 (525)	1531	2.92
2013	149 (903)	99 (637)	2217	3.48	141 (835)	3202	3.83
2014	188 (1351)	132 (940)	3289	3.50	182 (1306)	5780	4.43
2015	302 (2206)	207 (1485)	5475	3.69	300 (2155)	9228	4.28
2016	339 (2735)	234 (1841)	7184	3.90	336 (2707)	11998	4.43

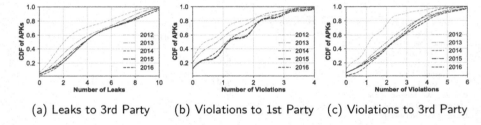

(a) Leaks to 3rd Party   (b) Violations to 1st Party   (c) Violations to 3rd Party

Fig. 4. Cumulative Distribution Functions (CDFs) of leaks for (a) 3rd party. Annual CDF of violations for (b) 1st party, and (c) 3rd party. Over time, the total number of leaks from APKs and PII violations are increasing.

Fig. 3b. For example, com.ace.cleaner version 6.0 leaked Identifier Device ID, Contact E Mail Address, Identifier MAC, and Identifier Mobile Carrier to third-parties in the static analysis whereas only advertiser id, and location were leaked to third-parties in the dynamic analysis. Part of the PII leaks is missed by dynamic analysis due to limitations of Android's UI/Application Exerciser Monkey in triggering all PII-related API calls. At the same time, we observe that static analysis could not detect some PII leaks (user's ad ID, cookie ID, location data sharing) as these appeared in dynamically loaded code or obfuscated function calls. The limitations of both static and dynamic analysis demonstrate that only the union set of leaks from the static and dynamic analysis can allow for effective or useful profiling of the privacy-related behavior of an app.

Besides, we examine the prevalence of detection from either static or dynamic analysis for different PII leaks in the period 2012–2016 – we do not analyze the years before 2012 due to insufficient data (<350 APKs). We empirically

Table 4. Summary of contradictions or violations of analyzed apps with their privacy policies. In column 2, the numbers in parenthesis i.e., () represent the number of app versions (APKs).

Year	#Apps (#APKs) with ≥ 1 valid seg.	#(%) APKs comply. with P.P.	#Leaks total	#Leaks viol. P.P.	#Leaks per APK viol. P.P.	#Leaks to 1st P. viol. P.P.	#Leaks to 3rd P. viol. P.P.
2008	3 (11)	11 (100)	8	0	0	0	0
2009	5 (24)	18 (75)	57	9	0.38	0.38	0
2010	18 (80)	37 (46.25)	313	71	0.89	0.56	0.32
2011	37 (187)	62 (33.16)	820	240	1.28	0.70	0.59
2012	69 (364)	117 (32.14)	1622	556	1.53	0.65	0.88
2013	96 (584)	104 (17.81)	3473	1264	2.16	0.77	1.39
2014	126 (860)	79 (9.19)	5332	2160	2.51	1.00	1.51
2015	195 (1381)	149 (10.79)	8640	3909	2.83	1.10	1.73
2016	225 (1748)	188 (10.76)	11338	5210	2.98	1.04	1.94

observe that the most commonly accessed PII is the `Identifier Device ID` by first-parties and `Identifier Mobile Carrier` and `Identifier Device ID` by third-parties.

Trend of Leaks: We then take the union of PII leaks observed in static and dynamic leaks using the mapping table (*see* Table 1). The summary of combined leaks, shown in Table 3, suggest that the average number of PII leaks per APK has risen consistently since 2012, from an average of 3.18 to first-parties (respectively, 2.92 to third-parties) in 2012 to 3.9 (respectively, 4.43 to third-parties) in 2016. Another interesting takeaway is the rise of leaks to third-parties in comparison to the first-parties. Till 2012, apps leaked PII mostly to the first-parties, and since then, they have been leaking mostly to third-parties. We can also observe this trend in Fig. 4, which shows a more significant increase over time for the third-party leaks (Fig. 4a) compared to the case of first-party leaks . For instance, 62.9% of the APKs exhibit less than three leaks to third-parties in 2012, compared to 27.3% in 2016. Similarly, 21.7% of the APKs exhibit more than five leaks to third-parties in 2012, which increased to 31.1% in 2016. This trend can be attributed to the increasing embedding of ad and tracking libraries in the apps [56,57].

3.3   Compliance Analysis

Disclosure of Practices Performed: In the compliance analysis, we compare the combined (static and dynamic) leaks of an APK with the practices reported in the privacy policy. A privacy policy violation occurs if a leak observed in static/dynamic analysis is not mentioned in the privacy policy. For example, our analysis finds that the app `com.fitbit.FitbitMobile` [58] with the version code 2182996 (APK release date: 22 Jun 2016) has privacy policy (dated: 16 Sep 2016) violations for `Identifier Device ID`, and `Identifier Mobile/Sim` practices being performed by the third-parties. On manually inspecting the privacy policy text, we do not find the disclosure of the practices mentioned above for third-parties. For disclosing data to third-parties, the app's policy states: *"Data*

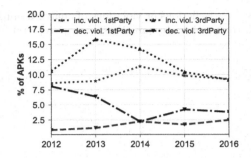

Fig. 5. Percent of APKs released in the given year showing an increase/decrease in the number of violations compared to their preceding version (APK). Newer versions of apps continue to leak more PII that violate privacy policy.

That Could Identify You Personally Identifiable Information (PII) is data that includes a personal identifier like your name, email or address, or data that could reasonably be linked back to you. We will only share this data under extremely limited circumstances". This generic clause may seem to be allowing the app developers to share the user's data, but Android's policy on user data states that the developers must describe the data being collected and explain their usage [25]. This means that the PII sharing from the Fitbit app does not comply with the declared public privacy policy of the app.

Table 4 lists the annual summary of violations observed in APKs. These violations only refer to those APKs whose privacy policy contains at least one valid segment i.e., a segment that returns positive values on *(i)* at least one of the twenty-eight practice classifiers (e.g., Identifier Cookie), *(ii)* procedure (i.e., the practice being described in the segment is being performed or not performed), and *(iii)* parties (i.e., 1st Party or 3rd party). Most of the policy text segments (124,412/143,783) that we classified did not return positive values for the above three categories (*see* Sect. 3.1). For these cases, our machine-learning classifier could not determine whether the policy text presents a practice as "performed" or "not performed" by the parties. From Table 4, we can observe that the compliance of APKs with their P.P. has decreased considerably from 33.16% in 2011 to 10.76% in 2016. The average number of leaks per APK that is not disclosed in the P.P. is also steadily increasing. We can observe this trend in Fig. 4b and c, showing that the number of P.P. violations is consistently increasing overtime for a significant fraction of APKs.

We empirically note that `Identifier Mobile/Sim` (grouping of `Identifier IMSI`, `Identifier Mobile Carrier`, and `Identifier SIM Serial` based on the mappings in Table 1) annually contributes to more than 25% of first-party and more than 30% of third-party violations. `Identifier Device ID` is next, comprising more than 20% of annual violations. This suggests that privacy policy violations are often due to apps *fingerprinting* users' mobile devices without revealing it.

Table 5. Breakdown of privacy policies based on the disclosure of 3rd party domains with which their APKs share PII.

% (#) of APKs with Privacy Policies (P.P.) mentioning		
ALL 3rd party domains	NONE 3rd party domains	PARTIAL 3rd party domains
17.8% (1,419)	23.85% (1,901)	58.35% (4,651)

Compliance of an App Across Newer Versions: For a newer version (APK) of an app released, it can have *(i)* equal number, *(ii)* higher number, or *(iii)* smaller number of privacy policy violations compared to the preceding version of the given app. Figure 5 shows the annual compliance trend of APKs released in the years 2012-16 compared to their preceding version. For example, if an app released versions in Oct'15, Dec'15, Feb'16, Jul'16, and Nov'16, then for the year 2016, the number of violations of APK released in Nov'16 will be compared with Jul'16, Jul'16 will be compared with Feb'16, and Feb'16 will be compared with Dec'15. For the set of app versions released in 2012–2016, we observe the prevalence of apps with more privacy policy violations compared to their preceding version. In particular, 9.1% of APKs from 2016 show increasing numbers of third-party violations (respectively, 9.2% first-party violations), whereas only 3.8% of APKs are found with fewer third-party violations (respectively, 2.5% first-party violations).

Disclosure of 3rd Party Domains: Given the set of PII leaks to third-party domains, we verify whether those domains are mentioned in the P.P. text. Table 5

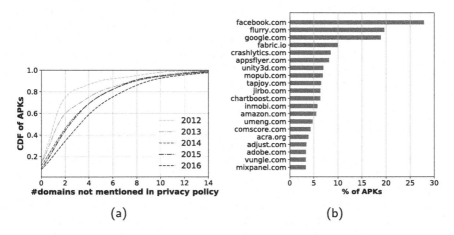

(a)   (b)

Fig. 6. (a) CDFs of number of domains not mentioned in the privacy policy of APKs. Each subsequent year, APKs share PII to more 3rd party domains that are not disclosed in their privacy policy. (b) Prevalence of undisclosed domains among the privacy policies of APKs.

shows the distribution of P.P. based on the disclosure of third-party domains. We note that a vast majority of P.P. (82.2%) do not mention at least one domain with which they share PII.

Figure 6a shows the annual distribution of the number of domains that are not mentioned in the P.P. We observe a significant increase in the number of third-party domains that app publishers do not disclose despite being involved in PII sharing. In particular, while in 2012, almost 70% of the released APKs had no more than one 3rd party domain "missed" by their privacy policies; in 2016, this percentage dropped to less than 30%. Figure 6b shows the twenty most recurrent domains that are not disclosed in the privacy policies. Overall, these twenty domains account for 49.5% of the total instances where third-party domains are not disclosed. Each of these domains provides a library for analytical services, advertisements, social networking, or utility/developer tools to the app. The most frequently not mentioned domain in the privacy policies by app publishers is facebook.com, accounting for more than a quarter (27.8%) of the analyzed APKs. It is followed by flurry.com (19.7%) and google.com (18.9%).

4   Discussion

The increase in the number of violations over time is concerning. The causes of increased violations can be that *(i)* the P.P. has shrunk, i.e., newer versions of P.P. of an app are disclosing the collection (or sharing) of less number of PII, *(ii)* the behavior of app has changed, i.e., newer versions of an app are leaking more PII, *(iii)* or both. We observe in Fig. 2b that among the newer versions of P.P., the number of P.P. that had a decrease in the number of disclosed practices compared to the preceding version were in greater proportion than those that had an increased disclosure of PII. Furthermore, as evident from Table 3, the number of leaks has also been on the rise, particularly to third-party domains. With the rise of third-party advertisements and analytics services, this comes as no surprise. The increase in the concealment of third-party domains (most recurring domains being advertisement and analytics) from the P.P. text (*see* Fig. 6a) lends further support to this argument.

5   Limitations

Despite our best efforts to longitudinally analyze apps' compliance, there are still some limitations to our work.

To scale up the study and cope with a large number of apps/versions, we leveraged automated analysis tools and machine learning classification. While this may result in "false positive" detection of privacy violations, the risk of false positives is, in fact, limited: static app analysis techniques are deterministic (they rely on pattern matching), and dynamic privacy leak detection has high validation accuracy (above 97%).

The use of machine learning and natural language processing for analyzing the privacy policy texts has some limitations. Privacy policies with generic statements or subjectively redundant words are arduous to interpret without human intervention. The use of subjective verbiage in handling users' data is also not recommended by Android [25].

In this study, the level of severity of privacy leaks is a fixed assumption. For example, some users may find the location a more intrusive leak than email id and vice-versa. Furthermore, the gap between the app version release date and the P.P. date (policy snapshot that matches the release date) can be several months. This gap is because the Wayback Machine could not find a P.P. snapshot closer to the release date. Therefore, it may be possible that the policy under consideration is significantly different from the irretrievable one and thus may not be accurately reflecting the app version's data practices.

6 Related Work

In recent years, there have been many research studies on the privacy implications of web tracking, and privacy protection [59–63]. In privacy policies, apps' developers must declare all the permissions an app will require to perform the tasks; however, previous study has shown that websites rarely disclose "Do Not Track" DNT in their privacy policies, and most websites do not comply with DNT even after disclosing it [64].

Zimmeck et al. [22], Slavin et al. [17], and Wang et al. [18] employed static analysis for analyzing privacy policy violations in Android apps. Zimmeck et al. [22] and Slavin et al. [17] used Android API calls to identify the collection of users' PII from mobile devices. Using native code, Wang et al. [18] check data transparency for data provided by users via GUI components. Han et al. [21] used static and dynamic analysis to compare free and paid versions of the apps for data leaks, embedded third-party libraries, and sensitive permissions. Reyes et al. [19], Okoyomon et al. [20], and Andow et al. [23] leveraged dynamic analysis for identifying contradictions in the behavior of apps with the privacy policies or regulations.

Perhaps, a much closer work to our's is by Ren et al. [47], where they monitored the network traffic to detect PII leaks of 512 Android apps across different versions. They show that apps leak PII to more third-party domains over time. We build on this work by conducting a compliance analysis of apps across different versions by taking the union of leaks detected in static and dynamic analysis and then comparing those leaks with the disclosure of PII in privacy policies.

The above studies have significantly contributed to the understanding of privacy leaks in Android apps by performing a *static* or *dynamic* analysis of apps. However, these studies have been conducted at a snapshot and have not been comprehensively evaluated over time. Given that the mobile ecosystem is continuously evolving, measurement studies longitudinally starting in the present may not comprehensively illuminate privacy policy violation trends to improve compliance. To fill this research gap, our study incorporates a longitudinal analysis spanning eight years. Furthermore, static analysis alone cannot deal with dynamically loaded code and obfuscated function calls, while dynamic analysis is prone to miss part of the function calls in the app. Our methodology raises the bar in the analysis of privacy leaks by combining static and dynamic analysis to capture most–if not all–of the leaks in Android apps. To our knowledge, the comprehensive longitudinal view on the Android app compliance with privacy policies has not been explored yet.

7   Concluding Remarks

In this paper, we analyzed the 5,240 historical versions, from 2008 to 2016, of 268 popular Android apps and investigated their compliance with the app privacy policies (P.P.). Our study found that most apps follow practices that contravene what is declared in their privacy policy. Our results also showed that apps are becoming more prone to violating their privacy policy than before, as we observed that the percentage of released app versions that comply with their privacy policy is steadily declining over time. In particular, the newer app versions disclose fewer PII collections in their P.P. and share more of a user's private information through practices not mentioned in the P.P. This trend is of primary concern to users, especially considering that P.P. remains the cornerstone for protecting online privacy.

As future work, we aim to extend our study to recent years to evaluate the change in the data disclosure and collection (or sharing) practices caused by the GDPR. We also plan to study the similarity between the privacy policy of non-compliant apps to determine if third-party privacy policy generators have created their privacy policy. In this manner, app developers can be notified of the breach since app developers are often not experts in policy compliance and privacy laws.

8   Appendix

A   Apps Selection

For the privacy policy analysis, we obtain 3,151 privacy policies and map them to 405 apps (comprising 7,998 APKs). Among the 3,151 privacy policies, 2,455 contain at least one *valid* segment and are mapped to 329 apps. From the 405 apps, we successfully download and analyze (static + dynamic) 350 apps comprising 7,741 APKs (or app versions) from the unofficial Google Play API. For each APK, we obtain its release date and assign a privacy policy based on the closest timestamp after the release date. For the compliance analysis, we only consider the APKs with at least one valid segment in their assigned privacy policy. Among the 7,741 APKs (spanning 350 apps) that we analyzed, 5,240 APKs (spanning 268 apps) satisfy the criterion and are considered for compliance analysis. It is possible for a given app to appear in privacy policy analysis and leaks analysis but not in compliance analysis. For example, an app has four versions (v1.1, v1.2, v1.3, and v1.4) and three unique privacy policies (pp1, pp2, and pp3). Suppose that pp1 is assigned to v1.1 and v1.2, and pp3 is assigned to v1.3 and v1.4. If pp2 contains valid segment(s), but pp1 and pp3 do not contain any valid segment, then the given app will not feature in the compliance analysis.

B   Date difference

Figure 7 shows the time difference in months between the date when the privacy policy was crawled by the Wayback Machine and the release date of the app. 42.6% APKs have a time difference of fewer than 12 months with their mapped privacy policy date.

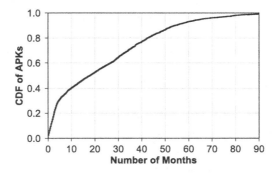

Fig. 7. Difference in months between the privacy policy date and APK release date.

C   Label Descriptions and Classifiers Performance

Table 6 describes the various PII labels used in our privacy policy classification. Table 7 shows the performance of various machine learning classification algorithms on the test data-set of APP-350 corpus [37].

Table 6. Descriptions of PII disclosures in the privacy policies that are collected/shared.

Data type (PII)	Description
Contact	Unspecified contact data
Contact_Address_Book	Contact data from a user's address book on the phone
Contact_City	User's city
Contact_E_Mail_Address	User's e-mail
Contact_Password	User's password
Contact_Phone_Number	User's phone number
Contact_Postal_Address	User's postal address
Contact_ZIP	User's ZIP code
Demographic	User's unspecified demographic data
Demographic_Age	User's age (including birth date and age range)
Demographic_Gender	User's gender
Identifier	User's unspecified identifiers
Identifier_Ad_ID	User's ad ID (such as the Google Ad ID)
Identifier_Cookie	User's HTTP cookies, flash cookies, pixel tags, or similar identifiers
Identifier_Device_ID	User's device ID (such as the Android ID)
Identifier_IMEI	User's IMEI (International Mobile Equipment Identity)
Identifier_IMSI	User's IMSI (International Mobile Subscriber Identity)
Identifier_IP_Address	User's IP address
Identifier_MAC	User's MAC address
Identifier_Mobile_Carrier	User's mobile carrier name or other mobile carrier identifier
Identifier_SIM_Serial	User's SIM serial number
Identifier_SSID_BSSID	User's SSID or BSSID
Location	User's unspecified location data
Location_Bluetooth	User's Bluetooth location data
Location_Cell_Tower	User's cell tower location data
Location_GPS	User's GPS location data
Location_IP_Address	User's IP location data
Location_WiFi	User's WiFi location data

Table 7. Performance of different classifiers. Multinomial Naive Bayes (MNB), Logistic Regression (LReg), and Linear Support Vector Classifier (SVC). The accuracy scores for SVC range from 91.16% to 100%.

Classifiers	Accuracy (%)			Precision (%)		
	MNB	LReg	SVC	MNB	LReg	SVC
Contact	98.6	98.7	98.8	0	77.8	65.4
Contact_Address_Book	98.8	99.3	99.4	0	79.5	80.5
Contact_City	99.6	99.8	99.8	0	81.8	73.3
Contact_E_Mail_Address	95.9	97.3	97.2	84.8	84.8	83
Contact_Password	98.8	99.2	99.4	0	70.7	78.6
Contact_Phone_Number	97	98.8	98.8	9.1	86.7	83.6
Contact_Postal_Address	98	98.6	99	0	68.5	80.3
Contact_ZIP	99.4	99.8	99.8	0	94.1	94.4
Demographic	98.7	99.6	99.6	25	79.2	78.9
Demographic_Age	98.3	99.3	99.4	16.7	89.3	90
Demographic_Gender	98.9	99.6	99.6	16.7	79.3	79.3
Identifier	99.1	99.1	99.1	0	0	66.7
Identifier_Ad_ID	98.8	99.7	99.8	0	97.7	97.8
Identifier_Cookie	95.4	98.7	98.5	90.3	88	88.6
Identifier_Device_ID	97.9	99	99	73.6	86.7	83.7
Identifier_IMEI	99.4	99.8	99.9	50	92.6	93.1
Identifier_IMSI	99.9	99.9	99.9	0	100	100
Identifier_IP_Address	99.1	99.4	99.4	90.1	94.1	94.8
Identifier_MAC	99.3	99.9	99.9	0	92.6	96.3
Identifier_Mobile_Carrier	99.4	99.7	99.7	0	100	85.7
Identifier_SIM_Serial	99.8	99.8	99.8	0	44.4	56.3
Identifier_SSID_BSSID	99.8	99.8	99.9	0	0	100
Location	96.7	98.8	98.8	80.9	86.5	87
Location_Bluetooth	99.4	99.8	99.8	0	80	81
Location_Cell_Tower	99.5	99.9	99.9	25	79.2	81.8
Location_GPS	99	99.7	99.7	64.7	90.2	88.7
Location_IP_Address	99.3	99.6	99.6	0	85.7	78.3
Location_WiFi	99.6	99.8	99.8	70	77.8	83.3
Performed	90.5	91.7	91.2	91.7	90.9	86.3
Not_Performed	98.6	98.9	98.7	3.2	34.2	30.5
1stParty	91	92.5	92.3	81	85	82.7
3rdParty	94.9	96.7	96.7	53.3	73.8	71.6
Average	98.06	98.82	98.82	28.94	77.22	81.92

References

1. Complaint In the Matter of Snapchat, Inc., December 2014. https://www.ftc.gov/system/files/documents/cases/141231snapchatcmpt.pdf,. Accessed 15 Oct 2021
2. Decision and Order In the Matter of Snapchat, Inc., December 2014. https://www.ftc.gov/system/files/documents/cases/141231snapchatdo.pdf. Accessed 15 Oct 2021
3. Video Social Networking App Musical.ly Agrees to Settle FTC Allegations That it Violated Children's Privacy Law (2019). https://www.ftc.gov/news-events/press-releases/2019/02/video-social-networking-app-musically-agrees-settle-ftc. Accessed 15 Oct 2021
4. TikTok To Pay $92 Million To Settle Class-Action Suit Over 'Theft' Of Personal Data (2021). https://www.npr.org/2021/02/25/971460327. Accessed 15 Oct 2021
5. TikTok Child Privacy Lawsuit Alleges Misuse of Personal Data of Millions of Minors (2021). https://www.cpomagazine.com/data-protection/tiktok-child-privacy-lawsuit-alleges-misuse-of-personal-data-of-millions-of-minors. Accessed 15 Oct 2021
6. 1 in 5 children's Google Play Apps breach Children's Online Privacy Protection Act rules'(2021). https://www.comparitech.com/blog/vpn-privacy/app-coppa-study. Accessed 15 Oct 2021
7. California Legislative Information - Internet Privacy Requirements (2003). https://leginfo.legislature.ca.gov/faces/codes_displaySection.html. Accessed 15 Oct 2021
8. California Legislative Information - AB-375 Privacy: personal information: businesses (2018). https://leginfo.legislature.ca.gov/faces/billTextClient.xhtml. Accessed 15 Oct 2021
9. Children's Online Privacy Protection Act of 1998 (COPPA) (1998). https://www.govtrack.us/congress/bills/105/hr4328. Accessed 15 Oct 2021
10. EU Regulation - protection of natural persons with regard to the processing of personal data and on the free movement of such data (2016). https://eur-lex.europa.eu/eli/reg/2016/679/oj. Accessed 15 Oct 2021
11. Data Protection Act 2018 (2018). https://www.legislation.gov.uk/ukpga/2018/12/contents. Accessed 15 Oct 2021
12. The Privacy Act - OAIC (1988). https://www.oaic.gov.au/privacy/the-privacy-act. Accessed: 15 Oct 2021
13. Jensen, C., Potts, C., Jensen, C.: Privacy practices of internet users: self-reports versus observed behavior. Int. J. Hum. Comput. Stud. **63**(1–2), 203–227 (2005)
14. McDonald, A.M., Cranor, L.F.: The cost of reading privacy policies. I/S J. Law Policy Inf. Soc. (Isjlp) **4**, 543–568 (2008)
15. Jensen, C., Potts, C.: Privacy Policies as Decision-Making Tools: An Evaluation of Online Privacy Notices. Association for Computing Machinery, New York (2004)
16. Cranor, L.F.: Necessary but not sufficient: standardized mechanisms for privacy notice and choice. J. Telecommun. High Technol. Law **10**, 273–307 (2012)
17. Slavin, R., et al.: Toward a Framework for Detecting Privacy Policy Violations in Android Application Code. Association for Computing Machinery, New York (2016)
18. Wang, X., Qin, X., Hosseini, M.B., Slavin, R., Breaux, T.D., Niu, J.: GUILeak: tracing privacy policy claims on user input data for android applications. Association for Computing Machinery, New York (2018)
19. Reyes, I., et al.: Won't somebody think of the children? Examining COPPA compliance at scale. In: Proceedings on Privacy Enhancing Technologies (2018)

20. Okoyomon, E., et al.: On the ridiculousness of notice and consent: Contradictions in app privacy policies (2019)
21. Han, C., et al.: The price is (not) right: comparing privacy in free and paid apps. Proceedings on Privacy Enhancing Technologies **2020**(3), 222–242 (2020)
22. Zimmeck, S., et al.: MAPS: Scaling privacy compliance analysis to a million apps. In: 19th Privacy Enhancing Technologies Symposium (PETS 2019), July 2019, vol. 3, pp. 66–86. Sciendo, Stockholm (2019)
23. Andow, B., et al.: Actions speak louder than words: entity-sensitive privacy policy and data flow analysis with PoliCheck. In: USENIX Security Symposium (2020)
24. Google Play Unofficial Python API. https://github.com/NoMore201/googleplay-api. Accessed 15 Oct 2021
25. User Data—Privacy, Security, and Deception - Developer Policy Center. https://play.google.com/intl/en-US/about/privacy-security-deception/user-data. Accessed 15 Oct 2021
26. Internet Archive: Digital Library of Free & Borrowable Books, Movies, Music & Wayback Machine. http://archive.org. Accessed 15 Oct 2021
27. Hashmi, S.S., Ikram, M., Kaafar, M.A.: A longitudinal analysis of online ad-blocking blacklists. In: Proceedings of the IEEE 44th LCN Symposium on Emerging Topics in Networking, Osnabrück, Germany, pp. 158–165 (2019)
28. Help with the EU user consent policy - Company - Google (2018). https://www.google.com/about/company/user-consent-policy-help. Accessed 15 Oct 2021
29. Momento: Time Travel (2020). http://timetravel.mementoweb.org. Accessed 15 Oct 2021
30. Wilson, S., et al.: The creation and analysis of a website privacy policy corpus. In: Proceedings of the 54th Annual Meeting of the Association for Computational Linguistics (ACL). Association for Computational Linguistics, Berlin August 2016
31. Liu, F., Wilson, S., Story, P., Zimmeck, S., Sadeh, N.: Towards Automatic Classification of Privacy Policy Text. School of Computer Science Carnegie Mellon University, Pittsburgh, USA, Technical report. CMU-ISR-17-118R, June 2018
32. TF-IDF : A Single-Page Tutorial - Information Retrieval and Text Mining (2020). http://www.tfidf.com
33. Story, P., et al.: Natural language processing for mobile app privacy compliance. In: AAAI Spring Symposium on Privacy Enhancing AI and Language Technologies (PAL), March 2019
34. Beel, J., Gipp, B., Langer, S., Breitinger, C.: Research-paper recommender systems: a literature survey. Int. J. Digit. Libr. **17**(4), 305–338 (2015). https://doi.org/10.1007/s00799-015-0156-0
35. Chakraborty, G., Pagolu, M., Garla, S.: Text Mining and Analysis: Practical Methods, Examples, and Case Studies Using SAS. SAS Institute (2014)
36. Convert a collection of raw documents to a matrix of TF-IDF features. https://scikit-learn.org/stable/modules/generated/sklearn.feature_extraction.text.TfidfVectorizer.html. Accessed 15 Oct 2021
37. APP-350 Corpus (2019). https://usableprivacy.org/data. Accessed 15 Oct 2021
38. One-vs-the-rest (OvR) multiclass/multilabel strategy. https://scikit-learn.org/stable/modules/generated/sklearn.multiclass.OneVsRestClassifier.html. Accessed 15 Oct 2021
39. Naive Bayes classifier for multinomial models. https://scikit-learn.org/stable/modules/generated/sklearn.naive_bayes.MultinomialNB.html. Accessed 15-Oct 2021

40. Logistic Regression (aka logit, MaxEnt) classifier. https://scikit-learn.org/stable/modules/generated/sklearn.linear_model.LogisticRegression.html. Accessed 15 Oct 2021
41. Linear Support Vector Classification (SVC). https://scikit-learn.org/stable/modules/generated/sklearn.svm.LinearSVC.html. Accessed 15 Oct 2021
42. Apktool - A tool for reverse engineering Android apk files. https://ibotpeaches.github.io/Apktool/. Accessed 15 Oct 2021
43. Api reference—android developers. https://developer.android.com/reference. Accessed 15 Oct 2021
44. Java documentation: Naming a Package. https://docs.oracle.com/javase/tutorial/java/package/namingpkgs.html. Accessed 15 Oct 2021
45. Binns, R., Lyngs, U., Van Kleek, M., Zhao, J., Libert, T., Shadbolt, N.: Third Party Tracking in the Mobile Ecosystem Third Party Tracking in the Mobile Ecosystem. Association for Computing Machinery, New York (2018)
46. Lindorfer, M., Neugschwandtner, M., Weichselbaum, L., Fratantonio, Y., van der Veen, V., Platzer, C.: ANDRUBIS - 1,000,000 apps later: a view on current android malware behaviors. In: Proceedings - 3rd International Workshop on Building Analysis Datasets and Gathering Experience Returns for Security, BADGERS 2014, pp. 3–17 (2014)
47. Ren, J., Lindorfer, M., Dubois, D.J., Rao, A., Choffnes, D.R., Vallina-Rodriguez, N.: Bug fixes, improvements, ... and privacy leaks: a longitudinal study of PII leaks across android app versions. In: Proceedings of Network and Distributed System Security Symposium (2018)
48. GitHub - Eyasics/recon: Personal Information Exfiltration Detection Using Machine Learning (2016). https://github.com/Eyasics/recon. Accessed 15 Oct 2021
49. Ren, J., Rao, A., Lindorfer, M., Legout, A., Choffnes, D.: ReCon: revealing and controlling PII leaks in mobile network traffic. In: Proceedings of the 14th Annual International Conference on Mobile Systems, Applications, and Services, MobiSys 2016, pp. 361–374. Association for Computing Machinery, New York (2016)
50. ReCon - Controlled Experiments Code and Data (2016) https://recon.meddle.mobi/codeanddata.html. Accessed 15 Oct 2021
51. ReCon - Format validation and String manipulation (2016). https://github.com/Eyasics/recon/blob/master/code/src/meddle/RString.java. Accessed 15 Oct 2021
52. Android's UI/Application Excerciser Monkey. https://developer.android.com/studio/test/monkey. Accessed 15 Oct 2021
53. mitmproxy - an interactive HTTPS proxy. https://mitmproxy.org. Accessed 15 Oct 2021
54. Understanding Dual Stacking of IPv4 and IPv6 Unicast Addresses (2020). https://www.juniper.net/documentation/en_US/junos/topics/concept/ipv6-dual-stack-understanding.html
55. Zheng, H., et al.: Automated test input generation for android: towards getting there in an industrial case. IEEE Press (2017)
56. Gibler, C., Crussell, J., Erickson, J., Chen, H.: AndroidLeaks: automatically detecting potential privacy leaks in android applications on a large scale. In: Katzenbeisser, S., Weippl, E., Camp, L.J., Volkamer, M., Reiter, M., Zhang, X. (eds.) Trust 2012. LNCS, vol. 7344, pp. 291–307. Springer, Heidelberg (2012). https://doi.org/10.1007/978-3-642-30921-2_17
57. Viennot, N., Garcia, E., Nieh, J.: A Measurement Study of Google Play. Association for Computing Machinery, New York (2014)

58. Fitbit home-page on Google Play. https://play.google.com/store/apps/details?id=com.fitbit.FitbitMobile. Accessed 15 Oct 2021
59. Hashmi, S.S., Ikram, M., Smith, S.: On optimization of ad-blocking lists for mobile devices. In: Proceedings of the 16th EAI International Conference on Mobile and Ubiquitous Systems: Computing, Networking and Services, pp. 220–227 (2019)
60. Ikram, M., Beaume, P., Kâafar, M.A.: DaDiDroid: an obfuscation resilient tool for detecting android malware via weighted directed call graph modelling. In: Obaidat, M.S., Samarati, P. (eds.) Proceedings of the 16th International Joint Conference on e-Business and Telecommunications, ICETE 2019, SECRYPT, Prague, Czech Republic, 26–28 July 2019, vol. 2, pp. 211–219. SciTePress (2019)
61. Jo, S.-K., Ikram, M., Jung, I., Ryu, W., Kim, J.: Power efficient clustering for wireless multimedia sensor network. Int. J. Distrib. Sens. Netw. **10**(4), 148595 (2014)
62. Ikram., M., Kaafar, M.A.: A first look at mobile ad-blocking apps. In: 2017 IEEE 16th International Symposium on Network Computing and Applications (NCA), pp. 1–8 (2017)
63. Zhao, B.Z.H., Ikram, M., Asghar, H.J., Kaafar, M.A., Chaabane, A., Thilakarathna, K.: A decade of mal-activity reporting: a retrospective analysis of internet malicious activity blacklists. In: Proceedings of the 2019 ACM Asia Conference on Computer and Communications Security, pp. 193–205 (2019)
64. Libert, T.: An automated approach to auditing disclosure of third-party data collection in website privacy policies. In: Republic and Canton of Geneva, CHE: International World Wide Web Conferences Steering Committee (2018)

Design Validation of a Workplace Stress Management Mobile App for Healthcare Workers During COVID-19 and Beyond

Beenish Moalla Chaudhry$^{(\boxtimes)}$ ⓘ and Ashraful Islam ⓘ

School of Computing and Informatics, University of Louisiana at Lafayette, Lafayette, LA 70504, USA
{beenish.chaudhry,ashraful.islam1}@louisiana.edu

Abstract. There does not exist an appropriate mobile health (mHealth) app to address healthcare workers' (HCWs) stress management needs, even though mobile apps have shown efficacy in improving mental health of various populations. Inspired by our prior design requirements study, we designed a prototype mobile app to provide stress management support to HCWs in their workplaces during the COVID-19 pandemic. The app featured six components that aimed to provide social support, wellness monitoring, stress tracking, and health nudges. Twenty two HCWs validated the design of a proposed app by providing feedback on the prototypical implementation of each component. 54.6% participants rated the app as either useful or very useful and 59.1% were willing to use it. Most participants voted to include features related to social support and health nudges, modify features that supported wellness monitoring, and remove COVID-19 symptom checking and intelligent chatbot. The thematic analysis of the qualitative data helped uncover concerns, perceived benefits, and suggestions for improving these features. Based on these findings, we discuss implications for designing peer-to-peer support systems, health nudges, and intelligent chatbots aimed at providing stress management support to HCWs in their workplaces.

Keywords: COVID-19 · Health care worker · Mobile mental app · Stress

1 Introduction

The Healthcare workers (HCWs), such as physicians, nurses, community health workers, etc. experience a number of stressors that can have a negative impact on their mental well-being. This became apparent during the COVID-19 crisis when mental health challenges faced by the HCWs exacerbated as the pandemic

The original version of this chapter was revised: a link was added to reference number 7. The correction to this chapter is available at
https://doi.org/10.1007/978-3-030-94822-1_58

T. Hara and H. Yamaguchi (Eds.): MobiQuitous 2021, LNICST 419, pp. 306–321, 2022.
https://doi.org/10.1007/978-3-030-94822-1_17

became more widespread. Several studies reported high rates of clinically significant depression (23.2%), anxiety (22.8%), and insomnia (38.9%) among the HCWs in primary care and hospital settings [14,22,31]. Even though similar high rates of mental health issues have been reported during and following previous viral outbreaks and pandemics, e.g. Ebola, SARS, MARS, etc. [20,21], there remains a paucity of solutions that can address HCWs' mental health and well-being in workplaces.

The fear of stigma, time restrictions, and expectation of phlegm are factors that help explain why this issue tends to get ignored in the medical culture [9, 17]. Moreover, it is generally assumed that HCWs are already well-equipped to handle their mental health challenges by the virtue of their professional training. Therefore, appropriate measures to address HCWs' mental health needs are often not considered. This understanding needs to change because without adequate support to manage their mental health issues, HCWs are at the risk of developing a wide range of problems such as suicide ideation [16], depression [13], anxiety, obesity, etc. And, society is at the risk of losing an already limited trained workforce.

During the COVID-19 crisis, local and national organizations arranged mental well-being assistance for HCWs via telephone or Internet [19]. However, there was a limited attempt to address the mental health issues of HCWs in their work settings via mobile health apps (mHealth apps). Even before the pandemic, there was a limited investigation of mHealth solutions for stress management in HCWs. This is a missed opportunity because mobile apps have immense potential to improve mental health and well-being of individuals. For example, mobile apps can reinforce healthy habits and scaffold recovery processes [10]. They can provide digital self-help materials, which individuals prefer due to privacy and accessibility reasons [26].

The aforementioned reasoning motivated us to design a mobile app that could be used by HCWs to manage their mental health issues, particularly stress. We chose to target stress because many studies have shown that HCWs are at risk of experiencing acute stress in the work environment, especially during the pandemic [22]. Moreover, stress is the root cause of many illnesses and health issues [27]. Based on our prior findings [7], we designed a prototypical mobile app called `StressFree` with the goal of helping HCWs manage stress in their workplaces. We elicited feedback on the prototype from 22 HCWs on each designed feature. Based on the results, this work makes following contributions:

- Explores potential of various mobile app features in preserving HCWs' mental health.
- Discusses design considerations for a peer-to-peer system aimed at providing mental health support to HCWs.
- Suggests potential health nudges to preserve HCWs' mental health.

2   Literature Review

In recent years, mHealth apps have displayed potential to help individuals manage burnout and anxiety, and provide preventive and corrective health education.

Such mHealth apps aim at risk prevention and healthy behavior promotion in office settings, where workers are expected to sit for long hours. Specifically, these apps center on routine monitoring of behaviors such as sleep and nutrition to improve employees' mental resilience [18]. But limited evidence is available for the efficacy of these apps in workplaces and their feasibility for different types of workers (e.g. HCWs) [3,12,18].

Other stress management mHealth apps aim to promote engagement with self-help content such as relaxation training, music and cyber-interventions based on Stress Inoculation Training methodology that instructs people on how to cope with psychological stress [6,24]. But these apps have either limited empirical basis or use inadequate scientific evaluation methods [18]. Nonetheless, workers demonstrate greater commitment to use such apps when their content is sponsored and promoted by their employers [2,25]. Moreover, a critical factor in the success of any mHealth app depends on the app's ability to integrate with the workplace context and preserve user's privacy [18].

Since the peak of the COVID-19 pandemic, interest in developing mobile apps to help HCWs manage stress surged. The resultant apps [23,29] were designed to help HCWs assess their own mental health by answering survey questions and reviewing symptom reports. Another important component included in these apps were links to professional services, especially free and low-cost mental health counseling. Although currently no mobile app incorporates such resources, multimedia learning kits [4] that provide evidence-based advice, help, and signposting about psychological well-being were also developed. Such resources can be easily incorporated within a mobile app but it is yet to be attempted.

While the above-mentioned systems focus on providing self-management support resources to HCWs, the need to incorporate peer support was also recognized. Therefore, Cheng et al. [8] explored the efficacy of a peer-to-peer psychological support and crisis management infrastructure that was created within a popular social media mobile application, WeChat, available in China. Another direction for stress management was explored by Ibrahim et al. [15]. They investigated the value of smartphone-derived digital phenotypes in analyzing individuals' behaviors during COVID-19 and then proposing digital nudges based on that understanding of the user.

The interest in designing and evaluating stress management apps for HCWs surged only amidst the COVID-19 crisis, which signifies that this is an important area that requires further investigation. Moreover, the majority of the mobile apps [23,29] that surfaced during the pandemic did not consider the perspectives of the target users, i.e. HCWs in their conceptualization and development. Rather they were designed via input from other secondary and tertiary stakeholders, such as employers, i.e. hospital management. This research aims to address these gaps by seeking early feedback on a prototypical mobile app that was based on HCWs' needs identified in a prior study [7].

3   Design Process

3.1   Design Specifications

Our prior design specifications study [7] helped us identify stressors, existing strategies and challenges that were impacting HCWs' mental health during the pandemic, from HCWs perspectives. We used a mixed-methods approach to elicit stress management challenges and strategies from a group of HCWs. In particular, we conducted document analysis of HCWs' interviews published in newspaper articles and also surveyed 20 HCWs who were serving/had served COVID-19 patients during the pandemic. The collected data were analyzed using an open coding approach to uncover common and insightful issues that HCWs encountered in stressful situations during their frontline duties.

We found that to help HCWs manage stress, the target mobile app should be able to provide: (a) up-to-date information to enable HCWs to cope with the unknowns; (b) assurances to HCWs that they have not been infected; (c) accessible self-care resources to help HCWs self-manage their mental health issues; (d) self-monitoring tools to support HCWs in identification of their stress triggers; (e) light and fun distractions such as music, funny videos, imagery, calling a loved one to maintain upbeat mood; (f) connections to peers so HCWs can seek both work-related and emotional support; and (g) access to professional mental health services.

3.2   Prototyping

To address user needs identified from our design requirements study, we brainstormed various scenarios and settled on a few. After several iterations of screen sketches for these scenarios, we created an interactive mobile app prototype using a web-based wireframing tool called *MockPlus Cloud* [1]. The tool allows designers to create prototypes consisting of screen layouts and screen flows. Target users can then experience the proposed functionality via interactive means. Anyone can access and experience the prototype via a web link. StressFree's prototype is available at https://tinyurl.com/stressFreeDemo.

In real-life situation, StressFree will be password-protected and administered by hospital authorities, who will be able to create accounts for users (i.e., HCWs), update app content and monitor HCWs' activities recorded in the app. We conceptualized six components of the app that were organized under four main components to target user needs that were identified in the design requirements study: (a) AssignedTasks component was designed to support HCWs in self-monitoring; (b) MyNotifications component to address HCWs' informational needs; (c) GetHelp! component to connect HCWs to their peers and employers; and (d) WellnessCheck component to address HCWs' medical needs (e.g. symptom checking for infection possibility). We did not support HCWs' entertainment needs in this design, mainly because HCWs were already using other apps such as Headspace, YouTube, etc. for entertainment purposes according to the design requirement study.

3.3 Application Design

The assumption behind StressFree's deployment is that the HCWs are equipped with a smartphone connected to an external device such as a smartwatch, which can monitor HCWs' health indicators (e.g. stress level, blood pressure, body temperature, etc.) throughout the day. The HCWs can use StressFree as needed and receive notifications through wireless on their phones. The proposed components are described in more detail below:

AssignedTasks. This component allows the user to view a list of tasks assigned to them by their supervisors. These tasks are the same as the ones available in the patient electronic medical records. For each task, the user can self-report perceived stress levels and record task completion times. The user can also retrieve completed task details (i.e., date and time, status, and perceived stress levels) via the task history tab. The purpose of this component is give users the ability to keep a diary of stress levels to identify stress triggers later on. Figure 1(b) and (c) show screens from this component with pending and completed user tasks.

MyNotifications. This component provides health nudges by reminding the user of scheduled health activities e.g., sleep, physical exercise, meals, etc. and alerts the user beforehand. Furthermore, options are available to clear the notifications and to update notification settings. Users can adjust schedules of notifications according to their desires. The expectation is that the notifications and reminders will help the users become more engaged with self-care. Figure 2(a) shows an example notifications screen.

IChatBot. The Intelligent Chatbot (iChatBot) provides answers to HCWs' on-demand queries, particularly questions about patient care that are causing concerns, etc. The iChatBot is based on machine learning technology and is expected to improve its performance over time (Fig. 2(b)).

PeerChat. Whenever the iChatBot is unable to answer a query, the app automatically sends that query to the PeerChat component, where experienced peers can respond to the posted question. The user can directly access this component if the situation demands immediate communication with expert peers rather than the iChatBot. Knowing that they have direct access to knowledgeable peers should give HCWs peace of mind. Figure 2(c) demonstrates PeerChat in action.

SmartMonitor. This feature operates with the help of an external monitor such as a smartwatch or fitness tracker, which can capture vital physiological signs e.g., blood pressure, oxygen level, pulse, and body temperature, and wirelessly transmit the information to the app. Figure 3(a) and (b) show what the user will be able to see on the screen when they want to view their symptoms via SmartMonitor.

InfectionCheck. This component makes it easier for the user to manually perform symptom checking. The user interacts with a task-based chatbot by answering questions about the presence or absence of COVID-19 symptoms. Based on the user's responses, the chatbot helps the user decide whether they need further testing or not. The chatbot has the ability to connect the user to professional services for further guidance (e.g. making appointment for testing, etc.). Figure 3(c) shows the symptom checking chatbot in action.

Users can customize the `StressFree` app by entering relevant personal data, and specifying notification preferences. These features can be accessed via the hamburger icon available on every app screen.

Fig. 1. (a) `StressFree` homepage after successful log-in; (b) `AssignedTasks` component showing tasks currently assigned to the user (`PendingTasks` tab selected), and (c) `AssignedTasks` component showing completed tasks (`TaskHistory` tab selected)

4 Design Validation Study

The goal of this study was to validate the proposed design of a mobile application that provided stress management support to HCWs. The aim of a design validation is to provide evidence that the proposed design meets the design requirements and specifications. Our research questions were:

RQ1: Which features participants want to use for stress management?
RQ2: What is participants' feedback on the proposed features?
RQ3: How many participants are willing to use and accept the proposed app?

Fig. 2. (a) `MyNotifications` page showing various notifications. User can clear notifications, as well as jump to notification settings, (b) `iChatBot` allows HCWs obtain answers to queries and access required information e.g., updated protocols, new information about coronavirus symptoms, etc., and (c) Group Discussion supported by the `PeerChat` component can be accessed automatically when the chatbot is unable to response user's queries, or deliberately when the user demands it.

4.1   Methods

The study was approved by the ethical review board of our home institution. Participants were recruited via purposive and convenience sampling. Emails were sent to local medical services departments and HCWs mailing lists obtained through personal medical contacts. The email included a link to the survey from where participants could access the prototype. Recipients were asked to voluntarily complete the survey if they met the following criteria: (a) age of at least 18 years; (b) currently working or had worked with COVID-19 patients in a hospital or a primary care setting; (c) able to speak, write and understand English; (d) had familiarity with mobile applications. The survey took approximately 45–60 min. to complete.

4.2   Study Design

The survey consisted of four main parts. The first part was about explaining the purpose of the study and obtaining participants' consent. In the second part, we collected participants' demographics (i.e., gender, age-range, education level, occupation, employment status etc.). No identifying information such as name

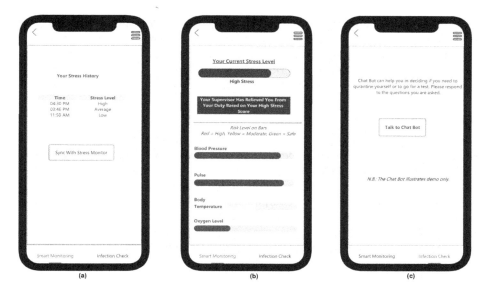

Fig. 3. Different tabs of `WellnessCheck` component. (a) `SmartMonitoring` provides the most recent stress history that can be synced with `StressMonitoring` component, (b) User's stress level showing the vital physiological measures in `StressMonitoring` component, and (c) `InfectionCheck` helps HCWs assess personal health.

or address, was collected. In the third part, a brief description of each component was provided, so participants could understand the purpose and underlying assumptions behind the design. The participants were then asked to interact with the proposed design via a link embedded within the survey, which opened up the prototype app in a separate window. Participants were asked to first analyze a component, and then answer the corresponding survey questions. The questions asked participants to explain anticipated benefits and perceived concerns about using the presented component. They were then asked to provide suggestions to improve the proposed design of the component. After exploring all the components, participants completed the fourth (and final) part of the survey, which consisted of three close-ended questions. The first question asked participants to give inclusion, modification or removal vote to each component Table 1. The final two questions collected (a) participants' assessment of app's usefulness, and (b) their willingness to use the app on 5-point Likert scales.

4.3 Participants

A total of 22 (female = 20) HCWs including 8 registered nurses (RNs), 2 nurse practitioners (NPs), 1 licensed practical nurse (LPN), 4 certified nurse assistants (CNAs), 2 physician assistants (PAs), 1 respiratory therapist (RT), and 2 physical therapists (PTs) from 15 different US states and the District of Columbia completed the survey. Participants' ages ranged from 18 years to 60 years ($mean = 34.98$ years, $SD = 8.55$ years). Except for one person who was on high-risk COVID-19 leave, all of the participants were employed at the time of the survey. Participants had a minimum of 1 year and a maximum of 35 years ($mean = 9.6$ years) of work experience. Two participants were students/intern nurses working in the emergency department.

4.4 Data Analysis

Thematic coding technique was used to identify insights from the qualitative data. Two researchers first independently read and re-read the survey responses and then coded them using inductive and deductive coding techniques. The researchers then met to compare their codes and resolve differences through a discussion process. For each component, the codes were synthesized into a paragraph that captured participants' appreciations, concerns and suggestions for improving its design. The quantitative data was obtained mainly from the final two questions and analyzed using simple descriptive statistics.

5 Findings

5.1 RQ1: Which Features Participants Want to Use for Stress Management?

Table 1. Participants' votes on individual components.

Component	Include as is	Include with modifications	Not include
AssignedTasks	9	9	4
iChatbot	5	7	10
PeerChat	10	7	5
InfectionCheck	9	2	11
StressMonitor	9	12	1
MyNotifications	11	9	2

Participants' voting of various app components are shown in Table 1. The most favored features were MyNotifications followed by PeerChat. AssignedTasks, InfectionCheck and StressMonitor were next and received the same number of votes. iChatBot received the lowest number of inclusion votes. In other words, all components except iChatBot were voted favorably by participants.

In terms of modifications, most participants thought that StressMonitor will benefit from a modified design. This was followed by AssignedTasks and MyNotifications. Participants gave the lowest number of modification votes to InfectionCheck. In sum, participants thought, with some modifications, all components except InfectionCheck, could help them manage stress.

iChatbot and InfectionCheck received the highest number of removal votes. Only one participant thought that StressMonitor should not be incorporated within the app.

The next subsection elucidates participants' reasoning behind their votes.

5.2   RQ2: What Is Participants' Feedback on the Proposed Features?

AssignedTasks. The majority of the participants thought that this feature should be modified or included as is in the final app. Four participants suggested removing this component because they thought it was time consuming to use this feature. Participants who favored including this feature thought that it would help them manage their tasks and time. Moreover, they thought that this feature would make them more productive. Participants did not agree that assigned tasks related to patient care should be included in this app. Participants who suggested removing this feature thought that it can compromise patients' privacy.

IChatbot. Approximately, the same number of participants wanted to include and remove this feature from the final version of the app. Participants thought that getting answers to their pressing questions from a iChatbot may help reduce stress, but they questioned the iChatbot's limits and capabilities in terms of serving their needs. They were concerned that the chatbot might not respond to their queries fast enough in the emergency room, or when a patient was requiring urgent care. They also thought that the feature would require considerable customization in order to be useful in their environments. A few participants suggested replacing this feature with a direct link to a healthcare professional who could help the user cope with stress.

PeerChat. Participants were very excited about this feature, as is evident by the high number ($n = 12$) of participants who voted for its inclusion. They thought that this feature will help them get in touch with expert peers and receive answers to their questions. Participants suggested that the usefulness of this feature will improve if respondent's identity was made known to group members. Participants thought that having the flexibility to post anonymous queries would encourage people to use this feature without fear or embarrassment. Participants believed that this feature should not be used for discussing patients' problems because that would compromise patients' privacy.

InfectionCheck. The number of participants who wanted to include this feature and those who wanted to remove it from the final version of the app was almost the same. Some participants believed that this feature would help them monitor their health, which, in turn, would lower their worries and stress. Those who were using a similar symptom checking app at work, thought that this feature would duplicate workload.

StressMonitor. Everyone except one participant favored this feature. Participants thought that the stress monitor could increase their awareness of their stress levels, which would encourage them to take better care of themselves. They appreciated the autonomous nature of this feature and its ability to minimize the data entry burden. However, participants were also concerned that this feature would give employers too much control over employees' health information, and may even encourage employers to use this information against the employees. In other words, participants perceived many privacy implications of this feature.

MyNotifications. Participants appreciated this feature and recognized that alerts and notifications could be very useful in healthcare settings. However, they were concerned that too many nudges may lead to alarm fatigue and, consequently, over-stimulation. While participants questioned the necessity of receiving notifications about daily behaviors such as eating and sleeping, they appreciated the flexibility of customizing notifications. They recommended centering the notifications around the following themes: (a) increasing awareness about health status; (b) promoting healthy behaviors, and (c) recommending coping strategies.

Overall. Participants agreed that the app could be a feasible and acceptable solution for stress management at work. That it would help them become more health conscious and increase their access to needed health content. However, they were concerned about the implementation and deployment of the app in their work settings. They were unsure whether their employers would be willing to deploy the app and allow its use in the workplace. They also thought that the app needed to provide assurances about safety and security of user's data. Participants also mentioned that the app's design had some ambiguity, specifically, they thought that it was unclear whether the app was for patient care or personal care. They requested focusing app's content on supporting HCWs' care, and removing all patient care related elements from the app.

5.3   RQ3: How Many Participants Are Willing to Use and Accept the Proposed App?

Usefulness. For measuring the usefulness, participants were asked to indicate their response to the following on a 5-point Likert Scale where 1 represented 'Not Useful' and 5 represented 'Very Useful': *"How usefulness do you think is StressFree?"*. 12 out of 22 participants or 54.6% rated StressFree as either useful or very useful overall. 7 out of 22 participants or 31.8% were neutral about StressFree's usefulness. However, 3 out of 22 participants or 13.6% thought that StressFree's usefulness was limited (Fig. 4(a)).

Willingness. Participants indicated their willingness to use StressFree by answering the following question on a 5-point Likert scale where 1 represented 'Very Unwilling' and 5 represented 'Very Willing': *"How willing are you to use StressFree at workplace?"*. 13 out of 22 participants or 59.1% indicated very high or high willingness to use StressFree. 4 out of 22 participants or 18.2% were neutral about their willingness to use the app. However, 5 out of 22 participants or 22.7% were either very unwilling or unwilling to use StressFree (Fig. 4(b)).

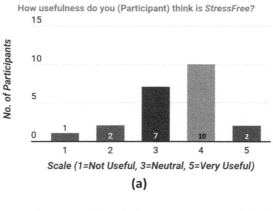

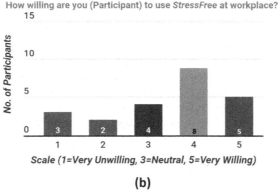

Fig. 4. Distribution of participants' ratings of the `StressFree` in terms of (a) its usefulness and (b) their willingness to use it in their workplaces.

6   Discussion

The majority of the removal votes went to `iChatbot` and `InfectionCheck`. Most participants voted to include all the remaining features while requesting modifications to the `StressMonitor`. The majority of the removal votes went to `iChatbot` and `InfectionCheck`. Participants highlighted concerns such as privacy, acceptability, and practicality of the proposed app in healthcare settings. But, they agreed that the app can help them manage stress by increasing their engagement in their own care. 54.6% thought that the app was useful and 59.1% were willing to use it. Some limitations of these findings are that they are based on the evaluation of a wireframe, which does not allow evaluation of the full function. Additional viewpoints could have strengthened the findings and provided deeper insight about concerns and benefits of the proposed system. Moreover, the quantitative analysis only evaluates the proposed system with no comparison with a baseline. Nonetheless, our study suggests that there are additional considerations for designing peer-to-peer support systems, digital health nudges, and intelligent chatbots when supporting stress management needs of HCWs in their workplaces. Below we discuss these considerations in more detail.

Researchers have built peer-to-peer psychological support and crisis management infrastructure using a popular Chinese social media smartphone app named WeChat [8]. The intention was to provide psychological support and intervention for the frontline HCWs serving in Wuhan, China during the COVID-19 outbreak with the help of HCWs working in the USA, Canada, and Australia. The infrastructure was successful in transitioning Chinese HCWs from anger and anxiety to hope and recovery. Other works have reported that HCWs commonly cite the need for ongoing social support and desire access to an in-app peer support community (i.e., social influence) [32]. In our study, we assessed participants' feedback on the use of a peer-to-peer support and crisis management social influence system for other issues such as seeking professional support, discussing patient problems, etc. We found that participants thought that such a system would be very useful, but they were hesitant to use it for the fear of being judged by their peers, receiving inaccurate responses, and compromising patients' privacy. Hence, our work contributes additional design considerations for peer-to-peer support and crisis management infrastructures for HCWs.

Published work recommends using digital nudges (or notifications) to help HCWs achieve the following during COVID-19: (a) establish social responsibility and increase connectivity, (b) maintain normal routine and ease anxiety, and (c) preserve mental health [15]. Our findings suggest that HCWs desire health nudges that: (a) increased their awareness of their health status, (b) promoted healthy behavior, and (c) recommended coping strategies (to manage stress). According to [5], digital nudges doing (a) are called signals (to merely indicate or remind of the behavior), digital nudges doing (b) are called sparks (to increase motivation for the pursuit of the behavior), and digital nudges doing (c) are called facilitators (to increase ability to pursue behaviors). It is important to understand how to design each type of digital nudge for HCWs, and therefore, more research is recommended in this area.

This work also makes important contributions in understanding the role of intelligent chatbots in healthcare settings. Earlier work focuses on understanding feasibility and acceptability of chatbots in patient populations [11,28,30]. Our work explores HCWs' thoughts about using intelligent chatbots in their workplaces. Specifically, we found that HCWs expected a high level of utility and efficiency from intelligent chatbots. Moreover, they believed that intelligent chatbots may not only pose privacy risk but also interfere with patient care. Yet, they believed that a source from where they can obtain answers to their questions can be very useful in relieving stress. Therefore, more work that can help us understand how to design intelligent chatbots to support HCWs in workplaces.

One question which this study indirectly answers is whether 'a specific app in one package?' is needed by HCWs, since many features proposed in StressFree have competitors, e.g. peer chat can be achieved via social networking apps and stress management could be achieved with the help of smartwatches. However, based on participants' feedback, it is apparent that participants envisioned several modifications to the existing solutions. For example, even though smart-watches monitor stress levels, they offer no or limited coping recommendations; social media apps such as WeChat either do not allow or do not make it easy for users to hide their identities (without being noticed by others in the same group). The symptom checking apps deployed during the pandemic require manual entry whereas HCWs prefer automated methods of stress detection. Therefore, `StressFree`'s features enhance the existing solutions and, with suggested modifications, it can be proposed as an independent app for HCWs.

7 Conclusion and Future Work

The goal of this study was to conduct design validation of a prototypical stress management application for HCWs. All features received inclusion votes, modification votes and removal votes by different participants. `PeerChat` received the highest number of inclusion votes while `iChatBot` received the lowest number; `StressMonitor` received the most modification votes while `InfectionCheck` received the least modification votes; and `InfectionCheck` received the highest number of removal votes while `StressMonitor` received the least number of removal votes. 54.6% (or 12 out of 22 participants) rated `StressFree` as either useful or very useful, and 59.1% (or 13 out of 22 participants) indicated willingness to use it. Based on participants' feedback, with appropriate modifications all proposed features have the potential to provide stress management support to HCWs. Specifically, HCWs think that health nudges can help them become aware of their own behaviors, motivate them to engage in healthy behaviors and facilitate execution of healthy behaviors. Moreover, they prefer a peer-to-peer support group that can help them obtain answers from credible sources while maintaining anonymity. Based on our study findings, `StressFree` has the potential to position itself as an independent stress management app for HCWs. We are in the process of developing a high fidelity version of `StressFree` that will be deployed for an in-situ evaluation with HCWs.

References

1. Mockplus. Online (2020). https://app.mockplus.com/
2. Ahtinen, A., et al.: Mobile mental wellness training for stress management: Feasibility and design implications based on a one-month field study. JMIR Mhealth Uhealth 1(2), e11 (2013). https://doi.org/10.2196/mhealth.2596. http://mhealth.jmir.org/2013/2/e11/
3. Balk-Møller, N.C., Poulsen, S.K., Larsen, T.M.: Effect of a nine-month web-and app-based workplace intervention to promote healthy lifestyle and weight loss for employees in the social welfare and health care sector: a randomized controlled trial. J. Med. Internet Res. 19(4), e108 (2017)
4. Blake, H., Bermingham, F., Johnson, G., Tabner, A.: Mitigating the psychological impact of COVID-19 on healthcare workers: a digital learning package. Int. J. Environ. Res. Public Health 17(9), 2997 (2020)

5. Caraban, A., Karapanos, E., Gonçalves, D., Campos, P.: 23 ways to nudge: a review of technology-mediated nudging in human-computer interaction. In: Proceedings of the 2019 CHI Conference on Human Factors in Computing Systems, pp. 1–15 (2019)
6. Carissoli, C., Villani, D., Riva, G.: Does a meditation protocol supported by a mobile application help people reduce stress? suggestions from a controlled pragmatic trial. Cyberpsychol. Behav. Soc. Netw. 18(1), 46–53 (2015)
7. Chaudhry, B.M., Islam, A., Matthieu, M.: Toward designs of workplace stress management mobile apps for frontline health workers during the COVID-19 pandemic and beyond: Mixed methods qualitative study. JMIR Formative Res. 6(1), e30640. https://pubmed.ncbi.nlm.nih.gov/34806985
8. Cheng, P., et al.: COVID-19 epidemic peer support and crisis intervention via social media. Community Ment. Health J. 56(5), 786–792 (2020)
9. Clough, B.A., March, S., Leane, S., Ireland, M.J.: What prevents doctors from seeking help for stress and burnout? A mixed-methods investigation among metropolitan and regional-based Australian doctors. J. Clin. Psychol. 75(3), 418–432 (2019)
10. Donker, T., Petrie, K., Proudfoot, J., Clarke, J., Birch, M.R., Christensen, H.: Smartphones for smarter delivery of mental health programs: a systematic review. J. Med. Internet Res. 15(11), e247 (2013)
11. Dworkin, M.S., et al.: Acceptability, feasibility, and preliminary efficacy of a theory-based relational embodied conversational agent mobile phone intervention to promote HIV medication adherence in young HIV-positive African American MSM. AIDS Educ. Prev. 31(1), 17–37 (2019)
12. Ebert, D.D., Lehr, D., Heber, E., Riper, H., Cuijpers, P., Berking, M.: Internet-and mobile-based stress management for employees with adherence-focused guidance: efficacy and mechanism of change. Scandinavian J. Work Environ. Health 382–394 (2016)
13. Hämmig, O.: Explaining burnout and the intention to leave the profession among health professionals-a cross-sectional study in a hospital setting in switzerland. BMC Health Serv. Res. 18(1), 1–11 (2018). https://doi.org/10.1186/s12913-018-3556-1
14. Hamouche, S.: COVID-19 and employees? mental health: stressors, moderators and agenda for organizational actions [version 1; peer review: 2 approved]. Emerald Open Res. 2(15) (2020). https://doi.org/10.35241/emeraldopenres.13550.1
15. Ibrahim, A., Zhang, H., Clinch, S., Poliakoff, E., Parsia, B., Harper, S., et al.: Digital phenotypes for understanding individuals' compliance with COVID-19 policies and personalized nudges: Longitudinal observational study. JMIR Form. Res. 5(5), e23461 (2021)
16. Ji, Y.D., Robertson, F.C., Patel, N.A., Peacock, Z.S., Resnick, C.M.: Assessment of risk factors for suicide among us health care professionals. JAMA Surg. 155(8), 713–721 (2020)
17. Jones, N., Whybrow, D., Coetzee, R.: UK military doctors; stigma, mental health and help-seeking: a comparative cohort study. BMJ Mili. Health 164(4), 259–266 (2018)
18. de Korte, E.M., Wiezer, N., Janssen, J.H., Vink, P., Kraaij, W.: Evaluating an mhealth app for health and well-being at work: mixed-method qualitative study. JMIR mhealth uhealth 6(3), e72 (2018). https://doi.org/10.2196/mhealth.6335. http://mhealth.jmir.org/2018/3/e72/
19. Lai, J., et al.: Factors associated with mental health outcomes among health care workers exposed to coronavirus disease 2019. JAMA Netw. Open 3(3), e203976–e203976 (2020)

20. Maunder, R.: The experience of the 2003 SARS outbreak as a traumatic stress among frontline healthcare workers in Toronto: lessons learned. Philos. Trans. R. Soc. Lond. Ser. B Biol. Sci. **359**(1447), 1117–1125 (2004)
21. McMahon, S.A., Ho, L.S., Brown, H., Miller, L., Ansumana, R., Kennedy, C.E.: Healthcare providers on the frontlines: a qualitative investigation of the social and emotional impact of delivering health services during sierra leone's ebola epidemic. Health Policy Plan. **31**(9), 1232–1239 (2016)
22. Mira, J.J., Acute stress of the healthcare workforce during the COVID-19 pandemic evolution: a cross-sectional study in Spain. BMJ Open 10(11) (2020). https://doi.org/10.1136/bmjopen-2020-042555, https://bmjopen.bmj.com/content/10/11/e042555
23. Mira, J.J., et al.: Preventing and addressing the stress reactions of health care workers caring for patients with COVID-19: Development of a digital platform (Be+ against COVID). JMIR mHealth and uHealth **8**(10), e21692 (2020)
24. Mistretta, E.G., Davis, M.C., Temkit, M., Lorenz, C., Darby, B., Stonnington, C.M., et al.: Resilience training for work-related stress among health care workers: results of a randomized clinical trial comparing in-person and smartphone-delivered interventions. J. Occup. Environ. Med. **60**(6), 559–568 (2018)
25. Motamed-Jahromi, M., Fereidouni, Z., Dehghan, A.: Effectiveness of positive thinking training program on nurses' quality of work life through smartphone applications. Int. Sch. Res. Not. **2017** (2017)
26. Proudfoot, J.G., Parker, G.B., Pavlovic, D.H., Manicavasagar, V., Adler, E., Whitton, A.E.: Community attitudes to the appropriation of mobile phones for monitoring and managing depression, anxiety, and stress. J. Med. Internet Res. **12**(5), e64 (2010)
27. Salleh, M.R.: Life event, stress and illness. Malays. J. Med. Sci. MJMS **15**(4), 9 (2008)
28. Thompson, D., et al.: Using relational agents to promote family communication around type 1 diabetes self-management in the diabetes family teamwork online intervention: longitudinal pilot study. J. Med. Internet Res. **21**(9), e15318 (2019)
29. UNC School of Medicine: Welcome to the heroes health initiative, a support tool for health workers (2020). https://heroeshealth.unc.edu/
30. Wang, C., et al.: Acceptability and feasibility of a virtual counselor (VICKY) to collect family health histories. Genet. Med. **17**(10), 822–830 (2015)
31. Yin, Q., et al.: Posttraumatic stress symptoms of health care workers during the corona virus disease 2019. Clin. Psychol. Psychother. **27**(3), 384–395 (2020). https://doi.org/10.1002/cpp.2477. https://onlinelibrary.wiley.com/doi/abs/10.1002/cpp.2477
32. Yoon, S., et al.: Perceptions of mobile health apps and features to support psychosocial well-being among frontline health care workers involved in the COVID-19 pandemic response: qualitative study. J Med Internet Res **23**(5), e26282 (2021). https://doi.org/10.2196/26282. https://www.jmir.org/2021/5/e26282

SEMEO: A Semantic Equivalence Analysis Framework for Obfuscated Android Applications

Zhen Hu[1], Bruno Vieira Resende E. Silva[1], Hamid Bagheri[1],
Witawas Srisa-an[1(✉)], Gregg Rothermel[2], and Jackson Dinh[1]

[1] School of Computing, University of Nebraska-Lincoln, Lincoln, NE 68588, USA
{bagheri,witawas}@unl.edu
[2] Department of Computer Science, North Carolina State University,
Raleigh, NC 27695, USA
gerother@ncsu.edu

Abstract. Software repackaging is a common approach for creating malware. Malware authors often use software repackaging to obfuscate code containing malicious payloads. This forces analysts to spend a large amount of time filtering out benign obfuscated methods in order to locate potentially malicious methods for further analysis. If an effective mechanism for filtering out benign obfuscated methods were available, the number of methods that analysts must consider could be reduced, allowing them to be more productive. In this paper, we present SEMEO, an obfuscation-resilient approach for semantic equivalence analysis of Android apps. SEMEO automatically and with high accuracy determines whether a repackaged and obfuscated version of a method is semantically equivalent to an original version thereof. SEMEO further handles widely-used and complicated types of obfuscations, as well as the scenarios where multiple obfuscation types are applied in tandem. Our empirical evaluation corroborates that SEMEO significantly outperforms the state-of-the-art, achieving 100% precision in identifying semantically equivalent methods across almost all apps under analysis. SEMEO consistently provides over 80% recall when one or two types of obfuscation are used and 73% recall when five different types of obfuscation are compositely applied.

Keywords: Malware · Android · Security

1 Introduction

Software repackaging is the leading approach employed to create Android malware [17], where cybercriminals modify a legitimate app by adding code that performs malicious behavior. To render malicious components more difficult to spot, malware developers typically obfuscate the entire codebase of a repackaged app [20]. From the malware author's perspective, they use obfuscation to

T. Hara and H. Yamaguchi (Eds.): MobiQuitous 2021, LNICST 419, pp. 322–346, 2022.
https://doi.org/10.1007/978-3-030-94822-1_18

permanently change the structure of a malicious app to avoid detection. However, these changes *must not be too drastic* such that they change the behaviors of the app. As such, malware authors utilize obfuscation techniques that maintain the semantic equivalence of the two programs. Because these two versions are semantically the same, the obfuscated version contains statically detectable semantic traces. Rastogi et al. refer to this type of obfuscation as *Detectable by Static Analysis* or DSA, and identify five classes of DSA obfuscation that can change the structure while preserving the original behaviors [37].

To further hide malevolent behavior, malware authors often apply these DSA obfuscation techniques in tandem. A study shows that only two layers of obfuscation are needed to defeat sophisticated, commercial malware scanners [37]. A recent study by Li et al. indicates that despite significant progress in the state-of-the-art in dealing with obfuscation, they still lose their effectiveness by as much as 75% when facing malware obfuscated with five layers [25].

From the security analyst's perspective, it is essential to analyze each detected malware to determine whether it is a true- or false-positive. If it is indeed malware, the analysts need to perform forensic to characterize attack patterns, attack surfaces, and threat models. To do so, they need to identify which components have been repackaged and further analyze the malicious code to develop knowledge-base, countermeasures, and detectors. Identifying which modified components to analyze is a challenging task, especially when malware authors obfuscate every component in the app [33].

Unfortunately, existing techniques to identify tampered components are not effective. These approaches often apply deobfuscation mechanisms to the obfuscated segments, followed by applying "differencing" techniques to compare the deobfuscated versions with the originals (e.g., [1,3,4,13,15,26]). Thus, increasingly sophisticated obfuscation types can hobble deobfuscators (Sect. 2 discusses this further). Even when deobfuscators can be applied, they do not necessarily retrieve code matching the original code; instead, they focus on re-engineering code into a format digestible by engineers. Thus, the differencing process may not produce accurate results.

This paper contributes a novel approach, called SEMEO, for automatically analyzing **sem**antic **e**quivalence of **o**bfuscated Android applications. Unlike all prior techniques that first require to apply deobfuscation mechanisms to the obfuscated segments, SEMEO has the potential to significantly expand the scope of semantic equivalence analysis by directly analyzing obfuscated methods in Android applications, without additional deobfuscation. This, in turn, enables reasoning about a broad range of sophisticated and widely-used obfuscation techniques, including those currently employed in practice by authors of Android malware in particular [20,29,32].

SEMEO first extracts an instruction summary of each method in the two apps and identify semantic traces, which are vital program traits that obfuscation cannot entirely mask. For example, because malware authors cannot apply obfuscation to Android API calls, one semantic trace is dataflow information into these calls. Using dataflow analysis, we can reconstruct such flows and compare them to similar flows in the unobfuscated app. Furthermore, SEMEO can identify data sources in the original app and look for similar sources in the unobfuscated app. The other vital semantic trace is information flows from these sources to data sinks. While the flows between the two apps may change, the source-sink information should generally remain the same. Once SEMEO automatically derives this information from each app, it conducts semantic equivalence analysis. For the forensic purpose, the analysis would identify and eliminate code portions in the obfuscated app that are semantically equivalent to those in the unmolested app. Scanty non-equivalent methods that remain can then be further analyzed to pinpoint possible malicious components, relieving the analysts of the error-prone and time-consuming task of scrutinizing the entire codebase.

We present the results of an empirical study assessing the efficiency and effectiveness of SEMEO, in which we applied it to 14 real-world Android apps of varying complexity. We also compare SEMEO's performance to that of FSQUADRA [42], a state-of-the-art approach for identifying repackaged apps. Our evaluation shows that SEMEO can achieve between 73% (when five obfuscation types are compositely applied) and 100% (when one or two types are applied) recall in identifying obfuscated methods. Given the worst-case recall of 73%, analysts need only consider the remaining 27% of the methods. SEMEO also achieved 100% precision (i.e., there was no misidentification of non-equivalent methods as equivalent) in 13 out of 14 cases. FSQUADRA, on the other hand, achieves between 20% and 99% recall, but it does not provide any information regarding its precision.

We also present the results of two additional case studies. In the first case study, we used ProGuard to apply a second layer of obfuscation to a subset of apps studied in our initial evaluation. Our results show that even under these conditions, SEMEO remains highly effective, while continuing to outperform FSQUADRA. In the second case study, we applied SEMEO to a repackaged, malicious version of *Pokémon Go*, and found SEMEO to be effective.

2   Background on Obfuscation Methods

Rastogi et al. [37] classify three categories of common obfuscation techniques: (1) trivial obfuscations, which can be easily detected by most antivirus tools; (2) DSA obfuscations, which theoretically can be detected by static analysis techniques; and (3) NSA obfuscations, which often apply encryption to the code. NSA obfuscations are, however, not permanent, as it requires the encrypted app to be decrypted prior to execution on a typical Android VM. A study has shown that the decrypted version can be copied from a device's memory just prior to execution [14].

This paper focuses on DSA obfuscations due to their ability to evade detection and preserve semantics. We focus further on five commonly found classes of DSA obfuscations [6,16,29,32]: junk code insertion, code reordering, method indirection, function inlining and function outlining [7,22,23,35,37,41].

Junk code insertion involves inserting unnecessary code such as a NOP operation (referred to hereafter as obfuscation type **T1**), a branch with predicates to ensure the branch can never be taken (**T2**), and dead code instructions (**T3**) into an app. The additional code does not affect program behavior [23,35,41].

Code reordering (T4) involves changing the execution order of statements or blocks of code. This obfuscation type can be difficult to detect and remove, and can render it difficult to determine whether obfuscated code is semantically equivalent to the original code. A reordered version, for example, can reverse the order of conditional tests.

Method indirection (T5) inserts additional calls into an app to manipulate call graphs. With this approach, a given method call (e.g., $m_0 \rightarrow m_1$) is converted to a call to a previously non-existing method (e.g., m_2) that then calls the originally called method; (e.g., yielding $m_0 \rightarrow m_2 \rightarrow m_1$). The technique is applicable to calls to framework libraries as well as calls to methods within an app [22].

Function inlining (T6) replaces method calls with the actual bodies of called methods. Normally used by compilers for optimization, this obfuscation type breaks abstraction boundaries created by the programmer [7].

Function outlining (T7) is the inverse of function inlining; it involves decomposing a function into multiple smaller functions. This process has been used (non-maliciously) to remove duplicate code in large programs [22]; in the context of obfuscation, its strength lies in requiring interprocedural analyses to perform deobfuscation.

3   SEMEO

We now present our approach for Semantic Equivalence Analysis of Obfuscated Code (SEMEO). Its key objective is *to provide an efficient technique for determining whether a method that has been obfuscated is semantically equivalent to the original version of the method.* Because a repackaged app typically includes only a small set of methods that have been semantically altered to enact malicious behavior, the majority of that app's obfuscated methods should be semantically equivalent to the original unmodified methods. Identifying a large percentage[1] of these semantically equivalent methods, enables security analysts to focus on the other methods that cannot be conclusively identified as semantically equivalent.

Figure 1 illustrates the workflow of SEMEO. It takes as input a pair of apps in the APK form: an app P and an obfuscated version P' of P that is suspected to have been repackaged. In *Step I*, SEMEO analyzes both P and P' to generate the necessary information including method call and instruction graphs. Once this information has been generated, SEMEO, in *Step II*, analyzes these graphs to produce interprocedural and intraprocedural control-flow and data-flow information. It then uses the information to perform semantic equivalence analysis.

---

[1] In general, the problem of determining the semantic equivalence of two programs is undecidable [18], so our approach is necessarily a heuristic.

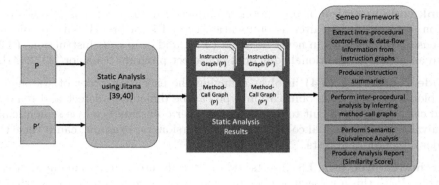

Fig. 1. Steps to perform semantic equivalence analysis in SEMEO

It then reports similarity score which reflects the percentage of methods determined to be semantically equivalent between P and P'.

Note that state-of-the-art approaches including REPDETECTOR (not publicly available) and FSQUADRA (used as our baseline system) also use pair-wise comparison [16,42]. Also note that app P can be previously obfuscated, and P' has one or more layers of obfuscation on top of P. SEMEO compares methods in P' (m'_j) to methods in P (m_i). The mapping of methods in P' to methods in P, however, may not be one-to-one as obfuscation techniques can merge methods, extract new ones, or obscure the mapping between obfuscated and original methods. SEMEO accounts for this.

For example, suppose that P contains three methods, (m_0, m_1, and m_2) and that P', an obfuscated, repackaged version of P, contains two methods, (m'_0 and m'_1), where m'_1 is the result of inlining m_1 and m_2. SEMEO begins by comparing m_0 to m'_0. If they are not found to be semantically equivalent, it then compares m_0 to m'_1, and so on. SEMEO uses the method-call graph of each app to help identify potential candidates based on the calling patterns. In case the methods m_0 and m'_0 *are* found to be semantically equivalent, they are marked as such. SEMEO does not need to visit m_0 again. It then compares m_1 with m'_1. In this case, the two modules are not semantically equivalent; m_1 calls m_2, so SEMEO considers both methods ($m_1 + m_2$) and evaluates whether the combined result is semantically equivalent to m'_1. Similarly, if outlining is used to split m_1 in P into m'_1 and m'_2 in P', they may together be semantically equivalent to m_1 in P. When SEMEO completes its analysis, it outputs a list of methods that have been determined to be semantically equivalent and not equivalent.

In the rest of this section, we describe each step of the process in turn.

3.1 Step I: Generating Basic Information

SEMEO compares a pair of apps at the method level. To support the necessary analysis, it first constructs the necessary analysis infrastructures such as instruction and method-call graphs. The static analysis step uses JITANA, a static

Table 1. Mutation instruction categories

Instruction category	Examples
Invoke	invoke static, invoke virtual
Read	iget, aget, sget
New	new array, new instance
Array	fill new array, fill array data
Write	iput, aput, sput
Move	move
Arithmetic op	binary, unary operation
Branch	if, go to, switch
Return	return
Comparison	if, ifz, cmp
Constant	const wide, const, const string
Exception	throw
No op	nop
Casting	check_cast, instance of

analysis framework for Android apps [39, 40]. This section describes the analysis process, with an emphasis on the important improvements on prior work.

SEMEO operates on Dex instructions by analyzing the instruction graph of each method. An instruction graph is a list of Dex instructions in a method. Thus, there is the same number of instruction graphs as that of the methods. In each instruction graph, JITANA embeds intra-procedural control-flow and data-flow information. Figure 2 illustrates an instruction graph of a method generated by JITANA. The intraprocedural control-flow graph appears as blue edges; and the intraprocedural data-flow graph appears as red edges. By traversing the instruction graphs, we can identify Dex instructions that can potentially change the structure of an app that uses them but preserve semantics. Table 1 shows categories and examples of such Dex instructions derived from the Android Specification [2].

As an example, applying junk code insertion may involve injecting a few **read** instructions such as **iget** and write instructions such as **iput** to perform field accesses and store the retrieved values into temporary registers (**move** can also be used in place of read/write). These operations, in effect, add more edges to the data-flow without changing the behavior. Branching type and return instructions can also be used for outlining. We refer to such instructions that can change the number of operations without changing the semantic of the program as "mutation instructions", forming the targets of our analysis. Other instruction categories, shown in bold in Table 1, can also change the structures of the app while preserving its semantic.

3.2 Step II: Performing Semantic Equivalence Analysis

In the first step, SEMEO selects the instruction graph (shown in Fig. 2) of each candidate method in the two apps. It then extracts the intra-procedural control-flow

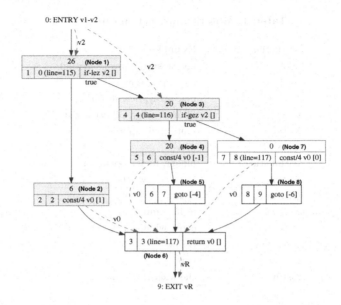

Fig. 2. Illustration of an instruction graph. (Color figure online)

(blue edges) and data-flow (red dotted edges) graphs from the instruction graph. It also infers interprocedural control-flow information from the method-call graph of each app. Algorithm 1 shows the procedure that is applied to a pair of methods m_0 and m_0'. In Line 2, the algorithm determines whether a method semantically equivalent to m_0 has been previously found. It does this using a bit map to represent the status for each method. If the mapping for m_0 is set, a semantically equivalent method in P' has already been found. The analysis continues if it is not set yet.

The algorithm uses the data-flow graph from the instruction graph for m_0 (Line 3). Each instruction consists of an opcode, registers and a constant value. Each node in the data-flow graph that is not the entry point (start of the program) has an incoming edge with registers based on the data-flow information. For example, *Nodes 1 and 3* have a shared incoming value from register *V2*.

Next, procedure `ExtractInstructionSummary` (called in Lines 4) traverses the extracted data-flow graph of each method using the DFS visitor in the *Boost graph library*, a graph processing library available on most computing platforms [38]. SEMEO traverses the data-flow graph one path at a time to check for mutation instructions. Each path summary includes instructions along these data-flow edges. The analysis constructs path summaries as an intermediate data structure so that it can inspect each path and filter out mutation instructions. When SEMEO visits the last node on each path, it combines the current path summary with the instruction summary, which is a collection of path summaries for a method. It then visits a new path and constructs a new path summary. For Fig. 2, the instruction summary of the method would have the following path summaries (PS): PS0 [Node 1], PS1 [Nodes 2 and 6], PS2 [Node 3], PS3 [Nodes 4 and 6], and PS4 [Nodes 7 and 6].

Algorithm 1. Equivalence Analysis

```
 1: procedure CHECKEQUIVALENCE:(Mi, Mj')
 2:     if (CheckMapBit(Mi) == false) then
 3:         Gi ← DataFlow(Mi)
 4:         Sum1 ← ExtractInstructionSummary(Gi)
 5:         if (CheckMapBit(Mj') == false) then
 6:             Gj ← DataFlow(Mj')
 7:             Sum2 ← ExtractInstructionSummary(Gj)
 8:             if SummariesMatch(Sum1, Sum2) then
 9:                 SetMappingFlag(Mi, Mj')
10:             end if
11:         end if
12:     end if
13: end procedure
```

In Line 5, the algorithm checks whether m_0' has already been determined to be semantically equivalent to an original method. Otherwise, the algorithm extracts its data-flow graph and produces associated instruction summary (Lines 7–8). Now, both summary sets are compared (Line 8) and if they are semantically equivalent, a map bit is set for (m_0, m_0').

In our example, method inlining is used to combine two original methods (m_1, m_2) in app P into one obfuscated method (m_1') in app P'. SEMEO first uses the method call graphs of P and P' to identify potential methods in P' that may be similar to m_1. In this example, it identifies m_1' as a candidate. It creates the instruction summaries for m_1 and m_1'. The analysis of an instruction summary of m_1 proceeds as described in Algorithm 2.

For each previously computed summary, whenever there is an **invoke** instruction (Line 3), the algorithm visits the callee methods (m_2) and retrieves its instruction graph. Next, it checks whether that method has been inlined with the caller's summary (Line 5). If it has, the analysis has already been done and the algorithm terminates. If it has not, the algorithm uses the DFS visitor method to compute an instruction summary for m_2 (Lines 5 to 8). Finally, it merges the result with the summary of m_1 (Line 9). Next, the algorithm removes the invoke instruction from the caller's summary (Line 10). This process also applies when a callee method calls other methods. It is repeated until there are no more invoke instructions in the caller's or callee's summaries. It then performs Equivalence Analysis on the two summaries.

Note that SEMEO can handle method outlining obfuscation by simply applying the same inlining analysis to the obfuscated method being compared instead of the original method. Inlining analysis can also be used to handle obfuscation through method indirection.

The comparison process applies several heuristics. Among others, by using the instruction summary, the algorithm can remove all inserted or removed code that does not change or only slightly change the data-flow information of the obfuscated program (e.g., junk code insertion). However, obfuscation approaches

---

Algorithm 2. Summary Inlining

```
 1: procedure INLINING(Sum, Inlined)
 2:     for each instruction Ins in Sum do
 3:         if Ins is "invoke" then
 4:             M ← GetCalleeMethod(Ins)
 5:             if NotInList(M,Inlined) then
 6:                 Inlined ← Inlined ∪ M
 7:                 G ← ExtractDataFlow(M)
 8:                 Sum_i ← ExtractInstructionSummary(G)
 9:                 Sum ← Sum ∪ Sum_i
10:                 Sum ← Sum − Ins
11:             end if
12:         end if
13:     end for
14: end procedure
```

---

such as those that change loop structures would also change data-flow patterns. To handle this, we also refer to common loop patterns (e.g., `for` loops and `while` loops) and look for cases where a pattern has been changed to another equivalent pattern. We then perform template matching to see if the obfuscation is simply changing the loop structure.

For code reordering obfuscation techniques, the purpose is to alter the execution flow of the program without changing its semantic meaning. SEMEO handles code reordering by deriving a canonical form of the summaries (Sum and Sum_i) by sorting them alphabetically in terms of their Dex instructions before conducting the comparison. Because each summary contains the relationship between a register and associated Dex instructions, after sorting, the order of appearance of instructions is no longer preserved. This helps remove effects caused by code reordering. In this case, the comparison between the two summaries would focus only on the register with its associated instructions.

After comparing instructions and data flow information, our approach analyzes constant values, which may provide additional insights because some constant values including strings may not change, since they provide specific information for the methods (e.g., URL strings, constant integers).

After visiting all of the methods in both apps, SEMEO examines the analysis result obtained for the obfuscated app and then calculates the *similarity score* based on the percentage of methods in the obfuscated app found to be semantically equivalent to those in the original app. If this number is less than 100%, SEMEO outputs the names of all methods in the obfuscated app that are not found to be semantically equivalent to methods in the original app. The complexity of the comparison process in Algorithm 1 is $O(n^2)$ in the worst case, and $O(n)$ in the best case, where n is the larger of the number of methods in P and P'.

4   Empirical Study

To evaluate SEMEO we conducted an empirical study, considering the following research questions.

- **RQ1.** What is the overall accuracy of SEMEO in detecting whether an app and a semantically equivalent obfuscated version of that app are in fact semantically equivalent compared to the state-of-the-art technique?
- **RQ2.** How effective is SEMEO in identifying repackaged methods in obfuscated apps compared to the state-of-the-art technique?
- **RQ3.** How efficient is SEMEO? What is the performance of SEMEO's semantic equivalence analysis?

4.1   Objects of Analysis

While SEMEO can operate directly on Dex code, for this study we needed to have source code so that we could apply the targeted obfuscation techniques (inlining and outlining) for which no automated tools could be found (an issue that is discussed further below). Finding malware samples that meet our requirements for objects of study in numbers that support quantitative analysis, however, is challenging. For example, commonly used malware samples for academic research are quite old and rarely have publicly available source code (i.e., they are distributed only as Dex code). Therefore, to answer RQ2, we also needed to create alternative versions of each original app by modifying some of their methods.

Ultimately, we selected 14 apps, nine apps that were created by DARPA to support their Automated Program Analysis for Cybersecurity (APAC) program [12] and five pairs of apps with known histories of revisions. To address RQ1, we applied various obfuscation techniques to create obfuscated versions. For the five pairs of revised apps, we used the original version of each pair of apps.

To address RQ2, we required repackaged apps. When considering malware, we are interested in methods into which malicious code has been injected, and to which obfuscations have then been applied. For the nine apps from DARPA, we asked an undergraduate student not familiar with this work to randomly select a number of methods for each app, prior to applying any obfuscation types, and manually modify their code. Target modifications involved relatively simple but provably semantics-affecting changes such as negating branch conditions, changing input parameters, removing method contents, and changing return types. This gave us the ability to use versions of methods that have been semantically modified in diverse manners, in numbers sufficient to support quantitative conclusions. For the remaining five pairs of revised apps, we simply obfuscated the revised version of each app and then compared the obfuscated versions with the original (i.e., unmodified and unobfuscated) app. This gives us the ability to evaluate apps that have been modified by real-world practitioners. Because these apps come with revision information including revised methods, we used these revised locations to help compute recall and precision.

Table 2. Objects of analysis

	App	Name	Methods	LoDC	Modified methods (RQ2)			
					G1–G5	G6	G7	G8
Apps from DARPA APAC program	App1	PicViewer	21	3888	2	2	2	2
	App2	CalcC	63	4593	6	6	6	6
	App3	DeviceAdmin2	161	9262	20	10	16	10
	App4	Orienteering	697	35263	20	20	20	20
	App5	SysMon	752	32549	18	10	10	10
	App6	Pond1	1573	58667	99	10	10	10
	App7	YARR	2027	48050	57	2	2	2
	App8	NewsCollator	2935	51806	19	2	2	2
	App9	TextSecure	7218	112804	243	10	10	10
Apps with known Rev.	App10	arxiv mobile	323	4684	8	5	5	10
	App11	KISS Launcher	811	11631	513	5	5	10
	App12	SolitaireCG	455	7260	12	5	5	10
	App13	Vanilla Music	1613	34103	23	5	5	10
	App14	WorkoutLog	748	1274	1	5	5	10

While the modifications and revisions we studied do not involve insertions of malicious code, we argue that malicious code would most likely be more complicated than these subtle modifications; thus, if SEMEO is able to correctly detect non-equivalent methods from among these, it is likely to be able to do so for methods involving actual malicious code. To verify this, we also conducted a case study to detected repackaged components using a malicious version of *Pokémon Go* (see Sect. 6.2).

Table 2 describes our objects. Column 1 provides identifiers that are used later to refer to the apps, Column 2 provides the app's actual names, Columns 3 and 4 list the numbers of methods and lines of Dex code (LoDC) in the apps. The numbers of modified methods created and used in our study are shown in Columns 5–8. As the table shows, the apps ranged in size from 21 to 7,218 methods, and from 1,274 to 112,804 lines of Dex code.

Next, we considered the seven DSA obfuscation types discussed in Sect. 2, where we assigned a "Type ID" (T1–T7) to each obfuscation type. For types T1–T5, we used ALAN [27], an Android malware obfuscation engine capable of applying one or more of these types to a given APK in any order. We chose ALAN because it is a state-of-the-art obfuscation tool; also, since SEMEO is not specifically designed to target ALAN obfuscations, this lets us avoid a potential threat to validity for the study.

ALAN can be configured to obfuscate an entire app or just a portion of an app. We chose to obfuscate entire apps to create a scenario similar to the one created by malware authors when they obfuscate repackaged apps. ALAN is able to apply obfuscation types T1–T5 individually or in any combinations, so we chose five methods for grouping obfuscation types (Table 3). Grouping G1 considers single obfuscation types; since there are five obfuscation types this yields cases in which just obfuscation type T1 is applied, just obfuscation type T2 is applied, and so

Table 3. Obfuscation type groupings

Grouping	Example grouping and sequence	Number
G1	T1, T2, T3, T4, T5	5
G2	T12, T23, T34, T45, T21	20
G3	T123, T345, T251, T231	60
G4	T1234, T1245, T4213	120
G5	T12345, T12453, T45213	120
G6	T6	1
G7	T7	1
G8	T6 + T7	1

forth. Grouping $G2$ considers all pairs of obfuscation types; for example, "T12" refers to the case in which obfuscation type T1 is applied followed by type T2.

The order in which obfuscations are applied also matters, so we considered all sequences of pairs (e.g., we also considered "T21"). In the case of Grouping $G2$, then, a total of 20 different sequences of obfuscations are applied. Similar reasoning applies to Groupings $G3$, $G4$, and $G5$, which involve all possible sequences of applications of all possible combinations of three, four, and five obfuscation types, respectively.

Unfortunately, as noted above, we were unable to find any tool support for the function inlining and outlining obfuscation types (T6 and T7), so for these we enlisted the help of two students who at that time had no knowledge of our approach for determining semantic equivalence. For inlining, we instructed the students to inline string operations and the contents of called methods. For outlining, we instructed the students to group branch condition bodies into other methods and to move some parts of functions into other small functions. The students applied these modifications to methods randomly selected from each of the apps. We applied function inlining and outlining singly and together; thus, there are three sequences of applications of these obfuscation types, which we refer to as G6, G7, and G8. We also sign these obfuscated apps with $SignAPK^2$ so that FSQUADRA (discussed next) can analyze them.

4.2   Variables and Measures

Independent Variables. Typically, when studying a new program analysis technique, we choose the technique itself as our primary independent variable, locating one or more other baseline techniques to compare against. For this study, we chose FSQUADRA as a baseline technique. FSQUADRA's ultimate goal is to detect repackaged apps while being insensitive to code changes. To do this, FSQUADRA analyzes the contents of the resource files instead of just analyzing code and reports how similar the two files are based on the Jaccard similarity

---

[2] Available from https://github.com/techexpertize/SignApk.

coefficient. Fundamentally, FSQUADRA's analysis attempts to identify similar resource files among all of the resource files used by the apps. To speed up the process, it uses hash of each file generated as part of app signing [42].

The main rationale behind FSQUADRA resides in an observation that a repackaged app attempts to change the app in a manner that maintains the app's look and feel. Therefore, the code may change but the resource files should remain the same [42]. As such, the results provided by FSQUADRA should be comparable to those provided by SEMEO in terms of their abilities to overcome the layer of analysis complexity induced by code obfuscation. While FSQUADRA would not be able to precisely locate methods that have been modified, we still expect that for RQ1 and RQ2, the similarity score produced by comparing the original app to an obfuscated version of the same app would be very high.

Because SEMEO may perform differently across obfuscation type groupings and we wish to assess such differences, we treat obfuscation type groupings as an independent variable. As noted earlier, our groupings consider each obfuscation type separately, while also considering all possible sequences of obfuscation types that are supported by ALAN.

Dependent Variables. As dependent variables, we chose metrics appropriate to our research questions, as follows.

Recall. For RQ1 and RQ2 we measure *recall*, which represents SEMEO's ability to identify semantically equivalent methods. We calculate recall using the following formula: $\frac{m_{seq}}{m_{total}-m_{mod}}$. Here, m_{total} represents the total number of methods, and m_{mod} represents the total number of modified methods. As such, the difference between them is the total number of semantically equivalent methods. m_{seq} *represents the number of semantically equivalent methods that have been correctly identified.* Note that for RQ1, the total number of modified methods for each app is 0 (i.e., $m_{mod} = 0$). For RQ2, recall is calculated using the same equation, but in this case each app has been modified so m_{mod} is non-zero.

Similarity. FSQUADRA reports similarity scores, each of which represents the ratio between the number resource files identified as similar (r_{sim}) and the total number of resource files (r_{total}) (i.e., $similarity = \frac{r_{sim}}{r_{total}}$). As such, for RQ1, our recall value is the same as FSQUADRA's similarity score; they both report the degree of similarity between the two apps. For RQ2, our recall value is different than FSQUADRA's similarity score. This is because when we calculate recall, the denominator of our formula represents only the number of unmodified methods. However, when FSQUADRA computes similarity, the denominator of FSQUADRA's Jaccard similarity coefficient represents the total number of resource files and not just the unmodified ones. Even though the two metrics differ, they both report the degree of similarity between the two apps. As such, we simply compare FSQUADRA's similarity scores with our recall values.

Precision. Precision represents SEMEO's ability to avoid incorrectly identifying methods that are not semantically equivalent as semantically equivalent.

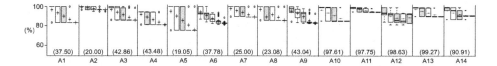

Fig. 3. Recall and similarity for obfuscation type groupings G1–G5 on RQ1 apps.

Modified methods mis-identified as semantically equivalent can be damaging to security analysis as they may be overlooked. For RQ1, where we do not have modified methods, the notion of precision does not apply. For RQ2, we calculate precision as $\frac{m_{seq}}{m_{neq}+m_{seq}}$, where m_{seq} again represents the number of methods in the app correctly identified as semantically equivalent (true positives), and m_{neq} represents the number of modified methods that have been mistakenly identified as semantically equivalent to original methods (false positives).

For example, suppose an app A has 100 methods (m_{total}), and five of these methods have been modified (m_{mod}). Suppose that SEMEO identifies 90 methods as semantically equivalent, with four methods incorrectly identified (m_{neq}) and 86 methods correctly identified (m_{seq}). In this case, recall is $\frac{86}{100-5}$ or 91% and precision is $\frac{86}{4+86}$ or 96%.

Efficiency. We calculate efficiency by measuring the time required by SEMEO to perform its analysis. We use seconds to report our results. The measurement is from the time SEMEO loads the two apps to when the analysis result is reported.

4.3   Study Operation

To address RQ1, we used SEMEO and FSQUADRA to compare the obfuscated apps with the original apps, and noted how many methods in the obfuscated apps were flagged as semantically equivalent to the original ones. To address RQ2 we applied the same process, but in this case we also noted how the results related to methods that were actually modified. To address RQ3 we followed the same process as for RQ1 and RQ2, and measured the amount of time needed to perform the analysis by each technique. To perform this study we used a MacBook Pro running OS X El Capitan version 10.11.2, with an 8 GB memory and a 2.5 GHz Intel Core i5. The performance times we gather are all recorded within this environment.

4.4   Threats to Validity

Where external validity is concerned, due to the time and effort required to apply Alan to the enormous numbers of combinations of obfuscations in grouping G1–G5, and the cost of manually applying obfuscation groupings G6–G8, we have studied only 14 apps, but they do represent an important sub-class of the apps that malware authors target, and they do vary in size and complexity. Furthermore, five of these apps contain modifications to the original apps so they represent real modifications made by developers. In addition, two of our obfuscation types, inlining and outlining, were applied by hand. We also do not consider actual malware, instead using semantic modifications made by software developers. One of the further studies we present in Sect. 6.2, however, helps address this threat by considering an application that does contain actual malware.

Where internal validity is concerned, errors in the tools we rely on could affect our results, but we have attempted to rigorously test them. Where construct validity is concerned, we measure precision, recall, and analysis time, but we do not collect any measures related to actual engineer effort.

4.5   Results for RQ1

RQ1 concerns the effectiveness of SEMEO and FSQUADRA at detecting whether an app and a semantically equivalent obfuscated version of that app are in fact semantically equivalent. Figure 3 presents boxplots showing the distribution of recall values achieved by SEMEO for obfuscation type groupings $G1$ through $G5$ (see Table 3 for grouping definitions) on all 14 apps. In the figure, the x-axis organizes the data per app. For each app, five boxes display the data for obfuscation type groupings $G1$ (leftmost box) through $G5$ (rightmost box), respectively. The y-axis reports recall percentages, computed using the equation provided in Sect. 4. The mean value within each grouping is denoted by a "+". We also include the reported similarity value for FSQUADRA in Fig. 3 just above the x-axis for each app (e.g., 37.50 for App1). We report only one value per app because FSQUADRA reports the same recall value for each app on obfuscation types $G1$–$G5$. Again, this is not surprising because FSQUADRA mainly analyzes resource files.

For each app, as obfuscation complexity increased, mean recall decreased. For obfuscation type grouping $G1$, in 12 of 14 cases there is little variance in results, and the mean recall values are between 93% (App12) and 100% (App2), indicating that with single obfuscations applied, SEMEO was highly effective at identifying semantically equivalent methods. Even in cases in which the most complex obfuscations were applied (obfuscation type grouping $G5$) the mean recall exceeds 80% on 13 of 14 apps. The lowest mean recall (76%) occurs on App5 for the most complex obfuscation type grouping $G5$. In nine of 14 cases $G2$ and $G3$ are the only obfuscation type groupings that display large degrees of variance. When only two or three types of obfuscations are applied they can interact in a wider variety of ways that impact SEMEO's performance more than when larger numbers are applied.

When we compare the performance of SEMEO to that of FSQUADRA, we see that SEMEO maintained a recall average of over 80% on 13 of 14 apps for $G1$–$G5$, whereas the similarity scores of FSQUADRA did not exceed 44% on the first nine apps (an average of 32.42%). FSQUADRA did perform substantially better, however, on the last five apps, containing real developer modifications. We discuss the main cause of this difference in performance in Sect. 5.

For function inlining and outlining (G6–G8), we compare the recall performance of SEMEO with the similarity score of FSQUADRA in Table 4. (Boxplots

Table 4. Recall and similarity for obfuscation type groupings G6–G8 on RQ1 apps

	G6		G7		G8	
	Sem.	FSq.	Sem.	FSq.	Sem.	FSq.
App1	90.48	69.23	91.3	69.23	82.61	69.23
App2	95.45	63.6	95.52	63.6	80.56	63.6
App3	94.41	95.74	90.96	95.74	91.72	95.74
App4	95.25	77.78	94.41	77.78	94.24	77.78
App5	100.00	92.31	99.61	92.31	99.61	92.31
App6	89.92	93.75	95.77	93.75	91.14	93.75
App7	100.00	76.47	99.86	76.47	99.95	76.47
App8	99.52	77.78	99.9	77.78	99.8	77.78
App9	83.33	38.12	83.72	38.12	83.22	38.12
App10	95.36	97.61	100.00	97.61	95.43	97.61
App11	95.85	97.75	100.00	97.75	95.89	97.75
App12	98.90	98.63	100.00	98.63	98.91	98.63
App13	98.76	99.27	99.32	99.27	98.15	99.27
App14	99.06	90.91	98.93	90.91	98.15	90.91
Average	95.44	83.50	96.38	83.50	93.53	83.50

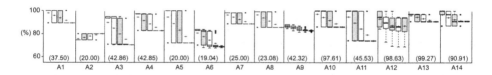

Fig. 4. Recall and similarity for obfuscation type groupings G1–G5 on RQ2 apps

are not appropriate in this instance, because we do not use multiple permutations of obfuscation technique orderings in this case, and thus do not have a distribution of data points). We find that SEMEO is more accurate than FSQUADRA on nine of the 14 apps. On average, SEMEO achieved average recalls of 95.44, 96.38, and 93.53 for G6, G7, and G8, respectively, whereas the average of the similarity scores for FSQUADRA is 83.50%. We discuss this further in Sect. 5.

4.6 Results for RQ2

RQ2 concerns the effectiveness of SEMEO at identifying repackaged methods in obfuscated apps. With respect to G1 and G5, Fig. 4 shows that SEMEO can achieve recall values ranging from 69% (App6, G5) to 100% (several apps). Also note that FSQUADRA's similarity scores did not exceed 45% on 10 of the 14 apps; in fact, its average similarity score across all 14 apps was only 45.30%. We also applied SEMEO to groupings G6, G7, and G8; Table 5 reports the average recall values and similarity scores. As shown, the greatest decrease in recall occurred on App2, which is a small app (recall levels decrease from 95.45%

Table 5. Recall and similarity for obfuscation type groupings G6–G8 on RQ2 apps

	G6		G7		G8	
	Sem.	FSq.	Sem.	FSq.	Sem.	FSq.
App1	84.21	69.23	72.73	69.23	72.73	69.23
App2	48.61	63.6	70.49	63.6	48.53	63.6
App3	88.98	95.74	77.24	95.74	80.56	95.74
App4	98.23	77.78	95.70	77.78	98.08	77.78
App5	99.18	92.31	97.08	92.31	97.61	92.31
App6	82.45	93.75	81.46	93.75	80.59	93.75
App7	81.64	76.47	80.84	76.47	80.84	76.47
App8	87.50	77.78	86.98	77.78	86.94	77.78
App9	90.69	21.8	90.69	21.8	90.69	21.8
App10	95.63	95.29	99.69	95.29	96.88	95.29
App11	57.39	45.53	57.83	45.53	57.76	45.53
App12	99.11	89.54	100.00	89.54	94.85	89.54
App13	95.83	99.27	95.78	99.27	95.65	99.27
App14	99.46	40.00	99.47	40.00	98.19	40.00
Average	86.35	74.15	86.14	74.15	84.28	74.15

for G6 and 80.56% for G8 in Table 4 to 48.61% and 48.53%, respectively, in Table 5). FSQuADRA, on the other hand, maintained nearly the same recall performance as achieved for the first nine apps in relation to RQ1, where it performed worse than SEMEO. On average, SEMEO still achieved an average recall of 86.35% while the average similarity score of FSQuADRA was 74.15%.

Turning to precision, SEMEO achieved 100% precision on 13 of 14 repackaged apps, for all obfuscation types and obfuscation type groupings. The only exception was App11, which has the largest number of modified method (513). For this app, the average precision achieved by SEMEO for G1 and G5 were 73% and 98%, respectively. (FSQuADRA, as noted earlier, does not report details at the method level; it reports only whether an app has been repackaged with respect to an original app through a comparison of resource usage – it analyzes certificate and manifest files. Thus, we cannot compare its precision to that of SEMEO.)

4.7 Results for RQ3

RQ3 concerns the efficiency of SEMEO. Our evaluation shows that the analysis overheads of apps measured while exploring RQ1 generally fell into four categories: (1) negligible overhead (a fraction of a second, App1–App3), (2) low overhead (less than 10 s, Apps4, App5, App10, App11, App12, App13, and App14), (3) moderate overhead (several hundred to 1000 seconds, App6 and App8), and (4) high overhead (several thousand seconds, App9). We also found that the runtime overhead of SEMEO increased as the obfuscation type grouping became more

Table 6. Performance of SEMEO and FSQUADRA on obfuscation type groupings G6–G8 on RQ1 apps (seconds)

	G6		G7		G8	
	Sem.	FSq.	Sem.	FSq.	Sem.	FSq.
App1	0.27	0.10	0.29	0.07	0.57	0.07
App2	0.31	0.09	0.29	0.10	0.40	0.09
App3	0.47	0.08	0.46	0.11	0.58	0.10
App4	2.14	0.10	2.33	0.09	2.47	0.12
App5	1.02	0.09	1.07	0.10	1.13	0.10
App6	125	0.11	55.88	0.14	117.99	0.11
App7	7.36	0.10	9.24	0.07	8.09	0.07
App8	26.95	0.12	27.24	0.10	21.21	0.10
App9	6808.98	0.15	7113.36	0.10	6056.00	0.09
App10	0.71	0.10	0.69	0.10	0.71	0.13
App11	1.74	0.14	1.78	0.14	1.75	0.13
App12	1.03	0.13	1.00	0.11	0.96	0.12
App13	2.61	0.13	2.46	0.12	2.45	0.12
App14	0.85	0.08	0.82	0.09	0.76	0.10

complex. The analysis overheads for FSQUADRA also increase across groupings, ranging from 10.54 ms to 30.42 ms. As previously reported, however, the recall performances for FSQUADRA are generally much lower than those for SEMEO.

Table 6 displays the performance values for SEMEO for the inlining, outlining, and hybrid obfuscation type groupings (G6–G8). As the data shows, SEMEO was quite efficient when the number of methods it analyzed was of small to moderate size. Only as the number of methods in an app exceeded 3000 (Apps 8 and 9) did SEMEO's worst case analysis time increase substantially, in those cases from 1267 s (21 min) to 12693.6 s (2.7 h). SEMEO was much faster when the original and obfuscated apps being analyzed were semantically identical. As previously reported in Table 4, the algorithm had nearly 100% recall for RQ1 on Apps7 and App8. In this case, the analysis times were also quite fast (less than 30 s as shown in Table 6) in spite of the presence of over 2000 methods. The analysis times for FSQUADRA, on the other hand, displayed a linear increase across all apps for grouping G6–G8 (70 ms to 170 ms). While FSQUADRA was more efficient than SEMEO, it was not as effective; its similarity scores were very low in many cases.

With respect to apps considered while exploring RQ2, the analysis overheads also fall into the same four categories, with the same set of apps for each category (e.g., App9 falls into the high overhead category). The analysis time for FSQUADRA continued to increase linearly across all groupings (from 10.13 ms to 46.36 ms) while yielding lower similarity scores for these groupings as previously reported in Fig. 4.

Table 7. Performance of SEMEO and FSQUADRA on groupings G6–G8 on RQ2 apps (seconds)

	G6		G7		G8	
	Sem.	FSq.	Sem.	FSq.	Sem.	FSq.
App1	0.31	0.07	0.38	0.07	0.34	0.07
App2	0.57	0.08	0.45	0.08	0.62	0.08
App3	1.05	0.08	0.90	0.08	1.29	0.08
App4	3.41	0.07	12.15	0.07	2.76	0.07
App5	2.71	0.07	3.62	0.08	3.84	0.07
App6	236.91	0.07	246.06	0.08	259.06	0.08
App7	403.91	0.07	419.63	0.07	414.03	0.07
App8	813.11	0.07	855.74	0.07	818.56	0.08
App9	6570.87	0.12	6738.51	0.12	6506.24	0.12
App10	0.68	0.08	0.73	0.07	0.72	0.07
App11	1.80	0.08	1.72	0.08	1.75	0.07
App12	1.01	0.09	0.97	0.08	0.96	0.07
App13	2.67	0.08	2.71	0.08	2.64	0.08
App14	0.78	0.06	0.81	0.07	0.69	0.07

Table 7 displays the performance values for SEMEO and FSQUADRA for the inlining, outlining, and hybrid obfuscation type groupings. The analysis times for RQ2 were generally consistent with those for RQ1, with the exception of the analysis times for App7 and App8. For these two apps, the analysis times increased from nine seconds to 404 s and from 27 s to 856 s, respectively. The performance overhead in these cases arises primarily due to the complexity of Algorithm 1 ($O(n^2)$). FSQUADRA, however, performs consistently across the three groupings; its analysis times ranged from 70 ms to 120 ms. Its similarity scores, however, were also quite low for eight of 14 apps as previously reported in Table 5.

5   Discussion

The main underlying hypothesis of FSQUADRA is that malware author would less likely to change the resource files as part of repackaging. However, our investigation shows that in apps that heavily use resources, certain types of obfuscation can have affect on these resources and thus, affecting FSQUADRA's ability to identify repackaged counterparts of an original app. We have seen similarity scores as low as 19.05% when it compares two apps; one has no modifications except for the various layers of obfuscation applied to it. This indicates that obfuscation can render FSQUADRA ineffective. SEMEO, on the other hand, due to its high recall performance can also be used to accurately identify repackaged counterparts of an app. Furthermore, by analyzing code instead of resource usage, it can also precisely report methods that have been modified, allowing analysts to directly analyzed those methods for malicious behaviors.

Our results show that some methods in obfuscated apps are incorrectly deemed by SEMEO to be non-equivalent to those in the original apps, for several reasons. First, SEMEO analyzes obfuscation grouping types $G1$ and $G2$ very accurately but this is less true for grouping types $G3$, $G4$, and $G5$, where three, four, and five layers of obfuscation have been applied. Such high degrees of composite obfuscation render analyzing apps for semantic equivalence more challenging.

As a second reason, we discovered that when we introduced modified methods that change application semantics, our recall degrades slightly because these modified methods can affect superclass and subclass relationships. Some modifications to global variables in modified methods can affect other methods that share these variables. These scenarios can cause SEMEO to identify some equivalent methods as non-equivalent. Still, the approach filters outs a large portion of equivalent methods, leaving only a small percentage of methods to be analyzed. The additional overhead is also very small, because the reported time for RQ2 is about the same as that for RQ1 on the same app.

For the apps that FSQUADRA returns high similarity scores, we noticed that obfuscation has very little effect on the size of the main class file (`classes.dex`). As an example, for App13, the size of `classes.dex` changes by 8% after obfuscation and the similarity score as reported in the study to answer RQ1 is 99.27%. However, for App14, the size of the class file increases by 54% after obfuscation and the similarity score decreases to only 90%. This shows indirect sensitivity to obfuscation. Furthermore, FSQUADRA does not report the locations of the code changes. Thus, analysts still need to identify such locations themselves. This can be quite challenging in heavily obfuscated apps.

In terms of analysis time, the analysis performed by FSQUADRA appears to take nearly constant time for both RQ1 and RQ2 in spite of the significant changes made to the code via various obfuscation sequences. This is because it focuses only on resource usage and not the code so obfuscation complexity applied to the code has no affect on its analysis time.

6   Additional Studies

We now report the results of two additional studies designed to evaluate the accuracy and performance of SEMEO in realistic settings. In the first study, we apply SEMEO to detect semantically equivalent methods when PROGUARD, a commonly used commercial obfuscation tool, is used in addition to our own obfuscation methods. In the second study, we use SEMEO to detect modified methods in a complex, real-world repackaged malware sample.

6.1   Applying SEMEO on Apps Obfuscated by PROGUARD

We assessed whether SEMEO can identify semantically equivalent methods in apps that have been obfuscated by PROGUARD. To perform our evaluation, we applied PROGUARD to the source code of apps that contain modifications and

Table 8. Recall and similarity (%) achieved by SEMEO and FSQUADRA when applying PROGUARD (groupings G1 and G5).

Apps	Modified methods	G1		G5	
		Sem.	FSq.	Sem.	FSq.
App1	3	73.34	37.50	55.56	37.50
App3	10	68.47	42.86	64.74	42.86
App7	11	94.36	25.00	84.11	25.00
App6	10	94.87	37.78	91.31	37.78
Average		82.76	35.79	73.93	35.79

were used to answer RQ2. We observed that once we applied PROGUARD to an app, the structure of the app can change due to optimizations such as dead code removal and code inlining. This can lead to different numbers of modified methods than those listed in Table 2. We then applied obfuscation type grouping G1 (individual obfuscation types) and obfuscation type grouping G5 (the largest composite obfuscation type grouping) to the apps. Due to space limitation, Table 8 only reports the results of apps from smallest (App1 and App3) to the largest (App7 and App6) based on LoDC, as previously reported in Table 2. The table lists the modified methods used and the recall and similarity values found, for SEMEO and FSQUADRA. Note that we could not apply PROGUARD to our largest app (App9).

As Table 8 shows, SEMEO is more effective than FSQUADRA at detecting semantically equivalent methods when we apply two or more layers of obfuscations (PROGUARD followed by our own additional obfuscation types). SEMEO achieved recall values ranging from 68.47% to 94.87% when two layers of obfuscation were applied, with an average recall value of 82.76%. When six layers of obfuscations were applied (i.e., PROGUARD and G5), SEMEO achieved recall values ranging from 55.56% to 91.31% with an average recall value of 73.93%. FSQUADRA, on the other hand, achieved similarity values ranging from 25% to 42.86% with an average of 35.79%. Further, as noted in Sect. 4.5, FSQUADRA was not sensitive to differences in obfuscation type groupings.

6.2 Applying SEMEO on Real-World Repackaged Malware

Popular apps attract the attention of cyber-criminals because they are highly downloaded, and thus, if repackaged, can infect a large number of devices quickly. For example, one version of *Pokémon Go* was repackaged with *DroidJack*, a *Remote Access Tool* or *RAT*. In this case, the malware author downloaded a legitimate version of *Pokémon Go* that had been obfuscated using PROGUARD. The malware author modified the app to contain a RAT tool called DROIDJACK, which allows cyber criminals to remotely take control of infected devices [8,11, 19,34]. The presence of this malicious version of the app was first detected three days after its official release.

In this case study, we investigated the effectiveness of SEMEO at identifying the repackaged components in the aforementioned repackaged release of *Pokémon Go*. The legitimate version contains 37,024 methods, whereas the repackaged version contains 38,878 methods. We used information from a security analysis result [19] to identify the methods that had been modified or added. In total, there were 1,854 such methods. We then used SEMEO to analyze both versions of the app. SEMEO found 95.23% of the methods in the two versions of the app to be equivalent. The remaining 4.77% of methods in fact include *all* of the modified methods that have previously been reported [19]. The analysis time required was approximately 2,300 s. We also used FSQUADRA to analyze these two versions of *Pokémon Go* and it produced the similarity score of 89.47%.

7   Related Work

REPDETECTOR [16], like FSQUADRA, performs semantic equivalence analysis by monitoring input and output states and employing an SMT solver to compute similarity scores between pair of apps. REPDETECTOR is efficient because it only focuses on core functions. This optimization may be reasonable for app-level comparisons but may be too coarse grained for method-level comparisons, which is the focus of our technique. Last, REPDETECTOR has not been publicly released.

In addition, there are de-obfuscation tools that can be used to indirectly help with the task SEMEO performs. In particular, a de-obfuscator can be applied to obfuscated modules, and then the de-obfuscated modules can be differenced against original unobfuscated modules. We considered using these in our empirical work but they all had drawbacks. ANDROSIM, which is a commonly used Android reverse engineering tool in the Androguard toolset [13], identifies similarities between two applications; however, it can handle only simple obfuscation types and it misclassifies many obfuscated methods in our apps as non-equivalent with respect to the original methods. Dex-oracle [3] looks only for specific patterns, and it cannot deobfuscate our programs. *Simplify* [4] is a deobfuscation-by-decryption tool so it does not function with the obfuscation techniques used in this work.

There has been work on detecting obfuscation types. Myles et al. [28] analyze binary code to look for similarities based on K-gram-based software birthmarks. However, their approach cannot handle junk code insertion or code reordering. SAFE, a malware detector, can handle only simple obfuscations (e.g., NOP insertions) [5]. Kruegel [24] uses static analysis on binaries to detect kernel-level rootkits. Apposcopy [15] is a semantics-based analysis tool that detects Android malware signatures. Dexteroid [21] is a tool that detects behavior-based malware based on the Android life cycle model. These tools cannot analyze obfuscated apps for semantic equivalence.

There are also tools such as ANDARWIN [10] and DNADROID [9] to detect cloned apps. As such, they are capable of working with some forms of obfuscation techniques. However, they are not publicly available. Symbolic semantic analysis tools can also be used to determine the semantic equivalence of two applications. However, they do not scale well for applications in large applications [30,31,36].

8   Conclusion and Future Work

We have presented SEMEO, a technique for directly identifying (without first deobfuscating) obfuscated methods in Android apps that are semantically equivalent to original non-obfuscated methods. Our comparison of SEMEO and FSQUADRA indicates that SEMEO is more accurate at identifying methods that have been modified. We also evaluated the capability of SEMEO to deal with PROGUARD and found that it can effectively handle obfuscation types that PROGUARD utilizes. Last, we used SEMEO and FSQUADRA to identify repackaged components of a version of *Pokémon Go* malware. SEMEO could detect all modified malicious methods while FSQUADRA mistakenly identified over 2000 benign methods as malicious.

In future work we intend to improve the scalability of our approach as discussed in Sect. 5. We will also consider methods for improving the approach's recall, particularly in cases where more complex composite obfuscations are used. Finally, we intend to conduct additional studies of the approach, including studies applying it to more repackaged malicious apps. We will publicly release SEMEO after the publication of this work.

References

1. Ponomarenko, A.: A tool for checking backward API/ABI compatibility of a Java library (2013). https://github.com/lvc/japi-compliance-checker
2. Android. Dalvik bytecode (2015). https://source.android.com/devices/tech/dalvik/dalvik-bytecode.html
3. Fenton, C.: A pattern based Dalvik deobfuscator which uses limited execution to improve semantic analysis (2015). https://github.com/CalebFenton/dex-oracle
4. Fenton, C.: Generic Android Deobfuscator (2015). https://github.com/CalebFenton/simplify
5. Christodorescu, M., Jha, S.: Static analysis of executables to detect malicious patterns. In: Proceedings of the 12th Conference on USENIX Security Symposium - Volume 12, SSYM'03, Washington, DC, pp. 12 (2003)
6. Collberg, C., Myles, G., Huntwork, A.: Sandmark-a tool for software protection research. IEEE Secur. Priv. 1(4), 40–49 (2003)
7. Collberg, C., Nagra, J.: Surreptitious Software: Obfuscation, Watermarking, and Tamperproofing for Software Protection, 1st edn. Addison-Wesley Professional, Boston (2009)
8. Contagio Mini Dump: Pokemon GO with Droidjack - Android sample (2016). http://contagiominidump.blogspot.com
9. Crussell, J., Gibler, C., Chen, H.: Attack of the clones: detecting cloned applications on android markets. In: Foresti, S., Yung, M., Martinelli, F. (eds.) ESORICS 2012. LNCS, vol. 7459, pp. 37–54. Springer, Heidelberg (2012). https://doi.org/10.1007/978-3-642-33167-1_3

10. Crussell, J., Gibler, C., Chen, H.: AnDarwin: scalable detection of semantically similar android applications. In: Crampton, J., Jajodia, S., Mayes, K. (eds.) ESORICS 2013. LNCS, vol. 8134, pp. 182–199. Springer, Heidelberg (2013). https://doi.org/10.1007/978-3-642-40203-6_11

11. Goodin, D.: Fake Pokémon Go app on Google Play infects phones with screenlocker (2016). http://arstechnica.com/security/2016/07/fake-pokemon-go-app-on-google-play-infects-phones-with-screenlocker/

12. DARPA: Automated Program Analysis for Cybersecurity (APAC) (2012). http://www.darpa.mil/program/automated-program-analysis-for-cybersecurity

13. Desnos, A.: AndroGuard, May 2013. http://androguard.blogspot.com/

14. Duan, Y., et al.: Things you may not know about android (un) packers: a systematic study based on whole-system emulation. In: 25th Annual Network and Distributed System Security Symposium, NDSS, San Diego, CA, pp. 18–21 (2018)

15. Feng, Y., Anand, S., Dillig, I., Aiken, A.: Apposcopy: semantics-based detection of android malware through static analysis. In: Proceedings of the 22nd ACM SIGSOFT International Symposium on Foundations of Software Engineering, FSE 2014, pp. 576–587. ACM, New York (2014)

16. Guan, Q., Huang, H., Luo, W., Zhu, S.: Semantics-based repackaging detection for mobile apps. In: Caballero, J., Bodden, E., Athanasopoulos, E. (eds.) ESSoS 2016. LNCS, vol. 9639, pp. 89–105. Springer, Cham (2016). https://doi.org/10.1007/978-3-319-30806-7_6

17. I. IDC Research: Smartphone OS Market Share, 2015 Q2. IDC Research Report (2015)

18. Jones, N.D.: Computability and Complexity: From a Programming Perspective. MIT Press, Cambridge (1997)

19. Sullivan, J.: Pokémon Go bundles with malicious remote administration tool DroidJack (2016). http://blog.trustlook.com/2016/09/02/pokemon-go-bundles-with-malicious-remote-administration-tool-droidjack/

20. Cannell, J.: Obfuscation: malware's best friend (2013). https://blog.malwarebytes.com/threat-analysis/2013/03/obfuscation-malwares-best-friend/

21. Junaid, M., Liu, D., Kung, D.C.: Dexteroid: detecting malicious behaviors in android apps using reverse-engineered life cycle models. CoRR arXiv:1506.05217 (2015)

22. Komondoor, R., Horwitz, S.: Semantics-preserving procedure extraction. In: Proceedings of the ACM Symposium on Principles of Programming Languages, pp. 155–169 (2000)

23. Konstantinou, E.: Metamorphic virus: analysis and detection. Technical Report RHUL-MA-2008-02, Royal Holloway, University of London, January 2008

24. Kruegel, C., Robertson, W., Vigna, G.: Detecting kernel-level rootkits through binary analysis. In: Proceedings of the 20th Annual Computer Security Applications Conference, ACSAC'04, Tucson, AZ, USA, pp. 91–100 (2004)

25. Li, Z., Sun, J., Yan, Q., Srisa-an, W., Tsutano, Y.: Obfusifier: obfuscation-resistant android malware detection system. In: Chen, S., Choo, K.-K.R., Fu, X., Lou, W., Mohaisen, A. (eds.) SecureComm 2019. LNICST, vol. 304, pp. 214–234. Springer, Cham (2019). https://doi.org/10.1007/978-3-030-37228-6_11

26. Linux Foundation: JavaAPI Compliance Checker (2015). http://ispras.linuxbase.org/index.php/Java_API_Compliance_Checker

27. Mr.Trojans. ALAN - Android Malware Evaluating Tools Released (2015). http://seclist.us/alan-android-malware-evaluating-tools-released.html

28. Myles, G., Collberg, C.: K-gram based software birthmarks. In: Proceedings of the 2005 ACM Symposium on Applied Computing, SAC'05, Santa Fe, New Mexico, pp. 314–318 (2005)
29. National Cyber Security Center (UK): Code Obfuscation (2014). https://www.ncsc.gov.uk/content/files/protected_files/guidance_files/Code-obfuscation.pdf
30. Partush, N., Yahav, E.: Abstract semantic differencing via speculative correlation. In: SIGPLAN Not., vol. 49, no. 10, pp. 811–828 (2014)
31. Person, S., Dwyer, M.B., Elbaum, S., Păsăreanu, C.S.: Differential symbolic execution. In: Proceedings of the 16th ACM SIGSOFT International Symposium on Foundations of Software Engineering, SIGSOFT'08/FSE-16, pp. 226–237. ACM, New York (2008)
32. Pomilia, M.: A study on obfuscation techniques for android malware. Technical Report, Sapienza University of Rome, March 2016. http://midlab.diag.uniroma1.it/articoli/matteo_pomilia_master_thesis.pdf
33. Preda, M.D., Maggi, F.: Testing android malware detectors against code obfuscation: a systematization of knowledge and unified methodology. J. Comput. Virol. Hacking Tech. **13**(3), 209–232 (2016). https://doi.org/10.1007/s11416-016-0282-2
34. Proofpoint Staff: DroidJack Uses Side-Load...It's Super Effective! Backdoored Pokemon GO Android App Found (2016). https://www.proofpoint.com/us/threat-insight/post/droidjack-uses-side-load-backdoored-pokemon-go-android-app
35. Rad, B.B., Masrom, M.: Metamorphic virus variants classification using opcode frequency histogram. In: Proceedings of the International Conference on Computers, pp. 147–155 (2010)
36. Ramos, D.A., Engler, D.R.: Practical, low-effort equivalence verification of real code. In: Gopalakrishnan, G., Qadeer, S. (eds.) CAV 2011. LNCS, vol. 6806, pp. 669–685. Springer, Heidelberg (2011). https://doi.org/10.1007/978-3-642-22110-1_55
37. Rastogi, V., Chen, Y., Jiang, X.: DroidChameleon: evaluating android anti-malware against transformation attacks. In: Proceedings of the ACM Symposium on Information, Computer and Communications Security, pp. 329–334 (2013)
38. Siek, J.G., Lee, L.-Q., Lumsdaine, A.: The Boost Graph Library: User Guide and Reference Manual. Addison-Wesley Longman Publishing Co., Inc., Boston (2002)
39. Tsutano, Y., Bachala, S., Srisa-an, W., Rothermel, G., Dinh, J.: An efficient, robust, and scalable approach for analyzing interacting android apps. In: Proceedings of the International Conference on Software Engineering, Buenos Aires, Argentina, May 2017
40. Tsutano, Y., Bachala, S., Srisa-an, W., Rothermel, G., Dinh, J.: JITANA: a modern hybrid program analysis framework for android platforms. J. Comput. Lang. **52**, 55–71 (2019)
41. Wong, W., Stamp, M.: Hunting for metamorphic engines. J. Comput. Virol. **2**(3), 211–229 (2006)
42. Zhauniarovich, Y., Gadyatskaya, O., Crispo, B., La Spina, F., Moser, E.: FSquaDRA: fast detection of repackaged applications. In: Atluri, V., Pernul, G. (eds.) DBSec 2014. LNCS, vol. 8566, pp. 130–145. Springer, Heidelberg (2014). https://doi.org/10.1007/978-3-662-43936-4_9

REHANA: An Efficient Program Analysis Framework to Uncover Reflective Code in Android

Shakthi Bachala[1], Yutaka Tsutano[1], Witawas Srisa-an[1(✉)], Gregg Rothermel[2], Jackson Dinh[1], and Yuanjiu Hu[1]

[1] School of Computing, University of Nebraska-Lincoln, Lincoln, NE 68588, USA
{sbachala,ytsutano,jdinh,yhu}@cse.unl.edu,
witawas@unl.edu
[2] Department of Computer Science, North Carolina State University, Raleigh, NC 27695, USA
gerother@ncsu.edu

Abstract. The recent adoption of dynamic features such as Java reflection and Android dynamic code downloading (RDCL) coupled with recent security attacks that can be detected only at runtime have led to higher usage of hybrid analysis to address dependability and security concerns. While effective, however, hybrid analysis can be inefficient due to a multi-step process involving static analysis, code instrumentation, and runtime information logging. As such, existing hybrid analysis techniques can work during code development and testing, but are too slow for production and security vetting.

In this paper, we introduce REHANA, a hybrid analysis framework for Android apps. We designed our framework to perform hybrid analysis efficiently through the use of a Virtual Class-Loader (VCL), which enables incremental program analysis. We then conducted a study to assess the program analysis performance of using VCL and found that it yields several benefits over the existing compiler-based program analysis approach. We also illustrated the hybrid analysis capability of REHANA by implementing a technique to detect and analyze dynamically loaded components based on reflection and dynamic code loading mechanisms in Android apps. We compared the performance of REHANA against that of STADYNA, a hybrid analysis approach that performs the same task. Our empirical evaluation shows that REHANA is as effective as STADYNA but also significantly more efficient and scalable.

Keywords: Program analysis · Android · Java reflection

1 Introduction

Researchers and practitioners have used static program analysis to enhance software quality, dependability, and security over the last few decades. The main idea

T. Hara and H. Yamaguchi (Eds.): MobiQuitous 2021, LNICST 419, pp. 347–374, 2022.
https://doi.org/10.1007/978-3-030-94822-1_19

of static program analysis is to analyze software (source code, intermediate representation code, or binary code) without executing programs [1,2,9,13,16,27,29]. The first step to perform static program analysis is loading a project. Existing static program analysis techniques take an approach similar to a compiler; that is, it first loads all code in the project to ensure completeness. It then analyzes the loaded code. This type of analysis often makes a "closed-world" assumption; that is, it analyzes the *complete* code to produce the results that *cannot change* [3]. Fundamentally, the goal is to analyze all relevant components in the project. However, achieving this goal is quite challenging in modern computing systems because the analysis requirements have changed to better address emerging security and dependability issues. Below, we highlight two existing challenges due to these changes.

Challenge 1. Modern programming languages and platforms provide rich library support. Therefore, loading just the application code alone may not be sufficient to ensure the dependability and security of an application. Recently, we have seen various instances of security vulnerabilities and software defects that affect a large number of computer systems worldwide [5,14,30]. In these examples, the root causes exist in the underlying systems or supporting libraries. *To detect these issues, we need to analyze the application code and the supporting libraries together. However, compiler-based analysis techniques can result in excessive memory consumption, making them infeasible to scale up to meet this requirement.*

Challenge 2. In addition to the high memory overhead, compiler-based analysis approaches also have issues dealing with the dynamism of modern programming languages. As an example, Android supports both Java Reflections and Dynamic Code Loading (collectively referred to in this work as RDCL). These mechanisms can load new classes at runtime, possibly from external sources [3,21,23,32]. Recently, we have seen RDCL used to deliver malicious payloads in highly elusive malware [8,10,11,18,22,31]. *When a compiler-based approach analyzes apps with RDCL, it cannot provide complete coverage because the application can add more classes to the existing code-base. These new classes make the initial static analysis results incomplete, creating the need to perform analysis on the entire code-base once again, even for a small code change* [3,32].

These challenges illustrate the inherent limitations of program analysis approaches that make the closed-world assumption. In this work, we address these two challenges by eliminating the "closed-world" assumption, and instead, rely on the "open-world" assumption achieved through the notion of "incrementality". Over the past two decades, there have been several advancements in *Java Virtual Machine (JVM)* and *Android Virtual Machine (AVM)* that make incremental static program analysis feasible.

The first advancement is the class-loader, a runtime system used in both Java and Android VMs to load only the necessary classes at runtime. A class-loader takes advantage of application structures that partition code into classes to naturally and incrementally load each needed class for execution. It also supports various forms of late binding to quickly resolve the ambiguity of finding which class to load through delegation. The second advancement is the Just-In-Time (JIT) compiler. A JIT compiler naturally performs program analysis in an *incremental* fashion; i.e., it only analyzes a small portion of the code at a time (e.g., a method or a trace [26]) and then performs optimization to generate the backend code. With a JIT compiler and a class-loader, it is possible to analyze each class right after it is loaded incrementally.

In this work, we propose ReHAna, a new incremental, hybrid program analysis framework, to address these two critical challenges. The key idea to support incremental analysis is by virtualizing the class-loading operations to load the program code on a per-class basis. We create a Virtual Class-Loader (VCL) to accomplish this task. Our *VCL* fully adheres to the published class-loader specification [20], but it operates as a stand-alone component in our framework; i.e., it does not operate as part of a language runtime system such as an Android Virtual Machine (AVM). The VCL uses reachability analysis to uncover classes that must be loaded and delegates to resolve all possible statically discoverable late binding targets. By employing VCL, we eliminate the need to load the entire project in one shot.

As our framework loads each class, it analyzes all the methods within that class to uncover more methods and classes to which these methods belong. This approach mimics a method-level JIT compiler that analyzes methods belonging to each loaded class. Our incremental analysis can generate class-loader, class, intraprocedural control-flow and data-flow, and method-call information as hierarchical graphs. It is important to note that our class-loading and analysis mechanisms do not distinguish between the application classes and the ADF classes so that it can include relevant classes in the ADF as part of an analysis effort. This capability addresses Challenge 1.

Because our VCL operates like an actual class-loader inside an AVM, it can also operate as a shadow class-loader to perform dynamic and hybrid analyses (i.e., an analysis approach that combines static and dynamic analysis results [4,21,24,28]). Through a connection with an AVM, ReHAna can observe relevant runtime events and generates essential program analysis information incrementally while the app is still running, allowing it to hide the analysis cost by interleaving it as part of the execution. This capability addresses Challenge 2.

We then investigate several research questions. First, we wish to identify and assess the performance differences between closed-world and open-world static analysis approaches. In this study, we compared the static analysis performance of ReHAna with that of Soot, a widely used program analysis framework for Java and Android. Next, we used ReHAna to analyze apps with RDCL and compare its effectiveness, efficiency, and scalability with those of StaDynA, a state-of-the-art approach in analyzing apps with RDCL. The results of our investigation reveal significant performance benefits of using ReHAna over Soot. Our results also indicate that ReHAna is as effective as StaDynA. However, it can cut down analysis time by as much as 50 times.

We organize the rest of this paper as follows. Section 2 provides the background information related to RDCL. Section 3 describes VCL and ReHAna.

Section 4 elaborates on our experimental designs. Section 5 reports the results of our investigation. Section 6 discusses our observations concerning the reported results. Section 7 highlights prior works that are closely related to ours. We conclude this paper in Sect. 8.

2 Background and Motivation

In this work, we use our proposed REHANA framework to create an efficient hybrid analysis approach to detect and analyze RDCL components. As such, we spend part of this section describing the underlying mechanism of RDCL. We also describe the mechanism by which hybrid analysis detects RDCL and discuss an existing state-of-the-art hybrid analysis technique for identifying RDCL components in Android applications. We then assess the cost of performing a closed-world analysis.

2.1 Reflection and Dynamic Code Loading (RDCL)

RDCL is commonly used to support several features in Android apps. These features include backward compatibility, dynamic updates, and component plugins. More recent usage of RDCL is to serve advertisements. Next, we describe how RDCL can be used to support these features.

An Android app is compiled to Dalvik Executable code (*dex code*) and then stored in the main dex file. The distinguishing feature of RDCL, where Android apps are concerned, is that the dynamically loaded classes are not part of the main dex file. There are at least two mechanisms for accessing classes in these external dex files at runtime. First, additional Dex files can already be inside the APK. Facebook uses this mechanism to overcome an Android limitation of having only a 16-bit integer to represent a method id, whereas Shedun uses this approach to hide malicious intents [22]. Another approach is to download additional dex files from remote servers. Software update features and serving advertisements are two examples that use this approach. We have also seen malware that uses this mechanism to deliver malicious components.

For example, through our analysis of downloaded viruses, we found particular adware that is a repackaged version of the *ispconfig* app, and that makes several attempts to download files from remote servers. One particular web-link (update.topapk.mobi) is reported to be malicious by virusshare.com. This particular downloaded file contains a custom class loader that can load more classes from downloaded dex files. They then use Java reflection to invoke methods to display advertisements that can link to a malicious website (when we tried to run the app, we found that the destination link was not active).

To further assess the extent to which Android apps use RDCL, we collected 60 apps from three major app categories (games, social network, and multimedia/miscellaneous) from Google Play in 2018. These apps included the top 20 games (e.g., NBA Live, Roblox), the top 20 social network apps (e.g., Facebook, Pinterest), and the top 20 miscellaneous apps (e.g., Pandora, Spotify). We performed a reflection analysis to statically determine whether each of these apps can dynamically load code by identifying the presence of RDCL call sites. Our analysis reveals that 34 out of 60 apps (57%) can use RDCL, which is a significant increase from an earlier reported result, wherein only 16% of the top 50 apps from 2013 used RDCL [21].

2.2 Hybrid Analysis Approaches for Detecting Dynamic Code Loading in Android Apps

The prevalence of RDCL motivates the need for a practical approach for efficiently and scalably detecting the use of RDCL and dynamically capturing downloaded components. In this work, we propose a framework to accomplish these goals. However, before we discuss our proposed framework, we point out some of the shortcomings of the current state of the art hybrid analysis approaches that help engineers and analysts effectively analyze Android apps that use RDCL.

As mentioned in Sect. 1, both TamiFlex and StaDynA use dynamic analysis to discover classes dynamically loaded via reflection and DCL, to increase the soundness of static analysis results. However, TamiFlex does not work on Android apps due to the lack of support for load-time instrumentation in the Android framework. As such, we turn our attention to StaDynA [32], a system that performs dynamic analysis (Phase 1) by modifying Dalvik, an Android VM, to extract the necessary runtime information. There are two major components in StaDynA: a client and a server.

Client. The client component is the modified Dalvik VM. Zhauniarovich et al. [32] modified the `libcore` component of the VM to capture events related to opening dex files. They also modified the invoke method to obtain class, method, and parameter information (e.g., paths with which to retrieve dynamically loaded classes and method names). Each invocation event is also accompanied by a stack trace so that an RDCL call site's information can be determined (e.g., which call site is responsible for the invocation). The logcat mechanism in Android sends information to the server component.

Server. The server component is responsible for constructing and annotating MCGs. According to Zhauniarovich et al. [32], the server component can support different program analysis engines. To date, Androguard[1] has been used as the analysis engine to construct MCGs. In the first step, Androguard analyzes an app to determine whether any RDCL call site exists within the app. If the app contains any RDCL call site (each call site is referred to in Reference [32] as a Method of Interest or MoI), it is installed onto a real device or an Android Virtual Device (AVD). The server component also statically generates the MCG of that app. Note that in this step, RDCL call sites appear as terminals in the initial MCG. Next, random event sequence generation tools such as Monkey are used to exercise the app.

---

[1] Available at https://github.com/androguard/androguard.

As previously mentioned, the client component monitors events related to class-loading and method invocations. This information is then sent to the server component by the client through the logcat mechanism. The server component selects only events related to MoIs and then copies the dynamically loaded classes from the client component and stores them for further processing. At the end of the run, it annotates the initial MCG with additional method calls. This step, in effect, concludes the dynamic analysis portion or Phase 1 of the RDCL analysis.

In Phase 2, the MCG built during Phase 1 is used by static analysis engines to perform more complex analyses (e.g., generating control flow, data flow, and points-to graphs). As noted earlier, the authors of Reference [32] did not conduct any evaluation of STADYNA concerning this phase. In the case of TAMIFLEX, however, SOOT was used to perform Phase 2 by statically analyzing previously-stored dynamically loaded classes and then transforming these class files to produce a program that replaces reflective method calls with standard Java method calls. It then performs further analyses of the transformed program to construct objects such as control flow and data flow graphs.

Note further that as TAMIFLEX transforms programs, it also uses instrumentation capabilities in SOOT to insert runtime checks to ensure that execution of any MoIs that have not been captured in the prior runs would provide warning messages to the user. These messages indicate that there are new MoIs that have not been previously exercised, and the user can conduct the Phase 1 analysis again to capture runtime information about these MoIs, and use this to further annotate the MCG. Any change to the MCG requires that Phase 2 analysis be reperformed to transform the newly captured methods and reconstruct various program analysis graphs.

In the preceding context, repeating Phase 2 is necessary because commonly used program analysis engines, including SOOT and ANDROGUARD, operate in a closed-world fashion. That is, before performing analysis, information that needs to be analyzed (e.g., code for all methods to be analyzed) must be available. For example, if an analysis chooses to ignore any RDCL call sites, all it needs to proceed further is statically discoverable methods. Later, if the same analysis is extended to include dynamically loaded classes, then a transformed program that includes dynamically discovered method calls would be needed. Any subsequent changes to the annotated MCG (e.g., an input sequence that exercised one or more previously uncovered MoIs or an RDCL target is replaced with a new version) would require the complete analysis to be repeated in order to account for these changes.

3   Approach

This section describes REHANA, our proposed VCL-based hybrid program analysis framework. We first describe the proposed VCL and then how we integrate it into REHANA. As a hybrid-analysis framework, REHANA can perform both static and dynamic analyses, and when applicable, it can integrate the analysis results. Next, we explain the essential operation of the Virtual Class-Loader (VCL), which is the critical component of REHANA.

3.1   Virtual Class-Loader

As previously mentioned, the runtime concepts such as class-loading and dynamic compilation and optimization inspire the creation of *VCL*. Naturally, class-loading supports incrementally loading of only the necessary classes. Each instance of `ClassLoader`, which is a Java class inherited from an abstract class `Ljava/lang/ClassLoader`, has a reference to a parent class-loader.

The class-loader specification [20] supports *Delegation Hierarchy Principle* that is used to discover and load classes through delegation [12]. When a class-loader cannot find a class, it delegates the task to its parent class-loader. A class can be located and loaded by one of the three class-loaders (i.e., Bootstrap, Extension, and Application). There are five supported methods: `loadClass`, `defineClass`, `findClass`, `findLoadedClass`, and `Class.forName`. These methods can be used to define a class or find a class, load it, and initialize it. The loaded classes are also unique.

VCL follows the Java classloading specification from Oracle [20]. It supports all essential methods to support various class-loading and defining activities. It also supports *Delegate Hierarchy Principle*, *Visibility Principle*, and *Uniqueness Property*. The *Delegate Hierarchy Principle* contains several rules to define how to find and load classes and ensure that the classloader does not load any duplicate classes. The principle also defines how delegation among the three classloaders should work.

As an example, if VCL needs to load a new class, it first delegates the request to *Application Classloader*, the request is further delegated to *Extension Classloader*, and finally, the last delegation is made to *Bootstrap Classloader*. Delegation creates the searching and loading hierarchy. *Bootstrap Classloader* first searches in the Bootstrap classpath to find the class. If it cannot find it in the Bootstrap classpath, *Extension Classloader* searches in the Extension classpath. If it cannot find it in the Extension classpath, *Application Classloader* searches in the Application classpath to find and load the class. If it is still not found, *VCL* generates an error.

During static analysis, VCL uses reachability analysis to identify classes that we need to load. The main idea is to analyze the methods in each class to identify any additional method calls within those methods to load classes to which these methods belong. For each class discovered through reachability, VCL applies the *Delegate Hierarchy Principle* to locate and load that class. This capability enables ReHAna to discover and analyze loaded classes incrementally.

In addition, VCL also preserves the *Visibility Principle*, which states that a class loaded by a parent class-loader (e.g., *Extension Classloader*) is visible to the child class-loader; i.e., the class is visible to *Extension* and *Application Classloaders* but not *Bootstrap Classloader*. It also ensures that each loaded class is unique (*Uniqueness Property*).

In dealing with dynamic polymorphism, *VCL* exploits an insight that at runtime, both a method or class name and the classloader information define a method or a class. Thus, it records class-loader information as part of an analysis, so that it can have information about the defining class-loader for a class. This information is similar to what being kept inside the JVM or AVM to resolve dynamic method dispatch. However, the information is not as precise, so all possible targets of a virtual interface are included. While this can add additional classes and methods that must be analyzed, it is still much smaller than loading the entire code-base. It is also a small tradeoff to ensure completeness.

Fig. 1. A method-call-graph of *Hello World* produced by SOOT.

To illustrate the operational difference between compiler-based and VCL-based analysis, we create a simple *HelloWorld* program that contains three classes: `HelloWorld`, `HelloWorldTwo`, and `HelloWorldThree`. `HelloWorld` invokes `helloClass2Method1`, which is a method in `HelloWorldTwo`. Method `helloClass2Method1` simply calls `println` with is a native method in `java.io` library. Note that the program does not invoke any method in class `HelloWorldThree`. Figure 1 illustrates the method call graph produced by SOOT, a compiler-based framework, and Fig. 2 illustrates the method call graph produced by our VCL-based approach. Also note that we use the same program for analysis but the one used by SOOT was compiled into Java bytecode and the one used by the VCL-based analyzer was compiled into Android Dex code.

As shown in Fig. 1, SOOT considers any calls to the underlying library (e.g., `java/lang/Object` and `java/io/PrintStream`) as terminals. That is, the analysis ends at these calls. The VCL-based approach, on the other hand, continues to load any of those system classes written in Dex. As such, its method call graph also includes system-level methods such as `finalize`, `hashCode`, and `wait`. The call appearing within the red circle in Fig. 2, represents the actual call from class `HelloWorld` to a method in class `HelloWorldTwo`.

The graph generated by the VCL-based approach also shows existing methods in a class even though they have not been invoked. (Note that each red arrow indicates a method invocation.) For example, methods such as `notifyAll`, `notify`, and `finalize` belong to class `java/lang/objects` but they are not invoked. Similarly, methods `helloWorldClass2Method2` and `helloWorldClass3Method1` belong to `hellowWorldClass2` and `hellowWorldClass3`, respectively. They are also not invoked but included because our approach analyzes all the Dex methods in every loaded class as part of the reachability analysis to ensure completeness.

Also note that our method call graph does not show `java/io/println`. Upon further inspection, because `java/io/PrintStream` is a native library, *VCL* cannot load it, and therefore, it is not analyzed. However, the call to `println` still appears as an instruction in the instruction graph (i.e., a list of instructions in a

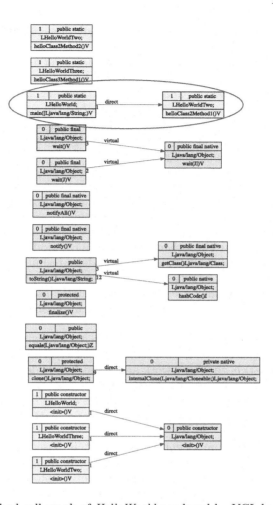

Fig. 2. A method-call-graph of *HelloWorld* produced by VCL-based analysis.

method) of `helloWorldClass2Method1`. Next, we describe how we utilize *VCL* to design ReHANA.

3.2   Introducing ReHANA

Imagine a scenario where an analyst is utilizing a compiler-based static program analysis as part of a hybrid analysis to detect and analyze RDCL components. The analysis process would involve performing the static analysis (STA_1) to create a method-call-graph (MCG) and identify methods that use RDCL functionality. The process continues with running the program using an existing input generator approach to perform dynamic analysis (DYN). If it needs more detailed analysis information after DYN, another round of static analysis

(STA_2) that also considers the code of the newly detected RDCL components is needed to generate the new MCG.

The goal of REHANA is to *reduce analysis overhead by removing the cost of performing the static analysis (STA_2) from the hybrid analysis process.* That is, our approach performs STA_1, and then DYN becomes a *continuous analysis* process wherein the cost of STA_2 is *proportional* to the size of the code change and is *hidden* as part of program execution time. As such, the process of generating detailed information should take as much time as the time needed to run the program during dynamic analysis.

To perform the continuous analysis, we exploit a general but essential characteristic of event-based apps, namely, that there are typically delays between events. These delays allow us to export information from an Android device to another workstation that performs the analysis. To accomplish this goal, we modified the Android VM to allow us to capture runtime events that occur as an app executes. At least two other techniques have modified the Android VM to help with RDCL analysis [21,32]. However, these techniques still log runtime events and perform static analysis in a separate off-line phase. This is because the analysis engines that they use to perform analysis, as previously mentioned, operate by using a closed-world approach. Our approach, on the other hand, performs analysis on-the-fly.

Figure 3 provides a conceptual view of REHANA when it is used to analyze an app that downloads classes from a remote server. Specifically, the figure shows how components within the framework are connected. It depicts an app running on an Android tablet with our modified Android VM. As it executes, dynamic information is generated (e.g., the app downloads a class from a remote server, a basic block is executed, or an app sends a request to another app) and processed by REHANA.

The static analysis component of REHANA is based on VCL, which has been designed to operate natively on Dex code. It produces various program analysis context data that includes a class-loader graph, class graph, method-call graph, and instruction graphs. The class-loader graph contains class-loader information that can be used to identify the defining class-loader for a class. The class graph contains all reachable classes that have been loaded for analysis. This includes both reachable application classes and ADF classes. The Method-call graph contains method-call relationships. Each instruction graph contains all instructions in a method. It also includes intraprocedural control-flow and data-flow information.

For REHANA to take runtime information from an Android VM, we created interfaces that would allow REHANA to receive information from the VM and send information to control the VM. To do this, we relied on the *Java Debug Wire Protocol (JDWP)* over *Android Debug Bridge (ADB)*. We then designed the data structures maintained by REHANA to match those maintained by the Android VM so that incoming information can be readily processed without the need to perform conversions. For example, both REHANA and the Android VM (Dalvik or ART) maintain the same data structures to record classes that have

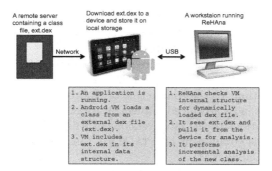

Fig. 3. Conceptual view of ReHAna.

already been loaded. As such, when a new class is loaded through reflection, for example, ReHAna specifically queries for information that includes the class name, method index, and class location to ensure precision.

We also discovered that in several instances, after a device downloads a class and the Android VM loads it, the original dex file for that class is deleted. This is a common practice when serving advertisements. This scheme can also be used to hide malicious content that has been dynamically downloaded. To prevent class files from being deleted, we cached dex files that have been downloaded as part of class loading; ReHAna then pulls any new class from the device so that it has an exact copy on the analysis workstation, which performs on-the-fly analysis to create the necessary information. The result is then added to the existing analysis graphs.

Note that ReHAna does not require that apps be instrumented. Runtime events are captured as they happen, so analysis can be performed without interruption. In all, we required about 500 lines of code to implement these features in both Dalvik and ART.

4   Evaluation

We want to assess the performance differences between the closed-world and open-world analysis. Thus, our evaluation compared the static analysis capability between Soot and ReHAna. We observed the number of methods analyzed by each approach. The amount of committed memory and analysis time during an analysis attempt. To investigate the effectiveness, efficiency, and scalability of ReHAna to perform hybrid analysis, we implemented a version of the framework to perform hybrid analysis of apps that utilize reflection and dynamic code loading (RDCL). To do this, we took the same approach as StaDynA, wherein our modified VM captures relevant events related to RDCL (e.g., construction of reflective classes and invocation of reflective methods). We then conducted a study comparing the static analysis results produced by the two systems. Next, we conducted dynamic analyses to assess ReHAna's effectiveness against that of STADYNA. We also compared the total hybrid analysis times of the two approaches. Last, we evaluated the scalability of REHANA by using real-world apps downloaded from the Play Store.

To conduct our investigations, we requested access to the source code from the authors of STADYNA, and they kindly granted it. We then successfully ported the modifications to the source tree of Android API 19 so that we could use the Dalvik VM's most advanced implementation. We, however, were not able to port the modifications to the later versions of Android. This issue was due to the dynamic analysis component of STADYNA that can only run on the older Android VM (i.e., Dalvik VM).

Next, we implemented the dynamic analysis component of REHANA on Android API 19 (KitKat), allowing us to evaluate STADYNA and REHANA on the same API platform, using the same set of apps. While API 19 is quite dated, apps developed for this API can run on 90% of existing devices. Further, as shown later, we were able to run all of the selected Play Store apps on this platform without any issues. For long term usability, we are porting our implementation to run on Android API 29 (the latest stable version).

In this section, we describe our methodology to investigate the following Research Questions (RQs):

RQ1: What are the performance differences between SOOT and REHANA?
RQ2: Is REHANA more effective than STADYNA?
RQ3: Is REHANA more efficient than STADYNA?
RQ4: Is REHANA more scalable than STADYNA?

4.1   Objects of Analysis

To answer all four RQs, we required apps that can run on REHANA, SOOT, and STADYNA. To compare the performances of SOOT and REHANA (RQ1), we randomly select a set of apps from Google's Play store. Our main criterion is to include apps of varying sizes that can run on the latest stable Android platform (Android 10). As part of this process, we collected 18 apps with APK sizes ranging from 18 KB to 80 MB.

To compare STADYNA with REHANA (RQ2 to RQ4), we focused on collecting apps that can run on Android API 19. We began by requesting access to the apps used to evaluate STADYNA. The authors of STADYNA kindly provided the 10 apps they had used; these included five benign apps and five malware samples. We also downloaded a set of apps from Play Store that can run on both systems. We selected 20 apps from each of the three categories (social media, games, and miscellaneous). We then attempted to determine how many apps used RDCL and found that 34 of them did. At the end of this step, we had 44 apps.

We also need to be able to automatically and repeatably exercise any apps that we wish to study. To do this we experimented with *Monkey*,[2] a random event sequence generator and *UI Automator*,[3] a UI testing framework, in an

---

[2] https://developer.android.com/studio/test/monkey.html.
[3] https://developer.android.com/training/testing/ui-automator.html.

Table 1. Basic characteristics of the Android apps (provided by the authors of STA-DYNA and downloaded from Play Store) used in our study.

App	APK size (MB)	# of methods	App	APK size (MB)	# of methods
Play Store Apps–API 29 (18)					
Snake	0.018	44	Battery Indicator	2	2337
BitClock	0.57	4743	AdBlockPlus	2.6	5656
Guitar Flash	45.2	10608	Calculator	4.3	10623
iFixit	3.3	10323	Slots Pharaohs Fire	45.1	17066
TypoLab	45.2	21735	Cute Animals	45.2	25647
Dolphin EMU	13.8	28648	BBC Weather	9.2	40105
Bike Citizens Bicycle GPS	45.2	43604	The Child of Slendrina	45.1	43611
Moto Rider	45.1	48812	Doodle Army	45.5	62957
BBC News	15.5	65677	Adobe Lightroom	80.4	101022
StaDynA Apps (8)					
Fakenotify	0.72	618	Anserverbot1	0.79	2961
Basebridge4	1.5	3148	ImageView	1.1	7563
FlappyBird	0.92	10880	Avast	9.2	30887
Symantec	5.4	41544	ViberVOIP	20	42200
Play Store Apps–API 19 (13)					
GeometryJumpLite	42	52176	ooVoo	53	52927
LedFlashLight	5	55213	SoundCloud	33	55894
Zedge	12	56085	Hulu Plus	31	56432
Pinterest	17	56438	slither	19	57858
SgiggleProduction	31	58080	RollingSky	33	58297
Waze	48	58833	duoLingo	12	59186
Mercari	24	59389			

attempt to exercise the apps. While neither approach was able to provide high code coverage, we found that *Monkey* could cover slightly more code than UI Automator, particularly in exercising events to reach known MoIs. (This observation confirms a prior finding by Choudhary et al. [7].) As such, we used *Monkey* to generate event sequences for use in dynamic analysis.[4]

We configured *Monkey* to generate 10,000 events, using five different seeds to generate five random but distinct sequences. For each app, we ran each of the five sequences; each run took between 275 and 400 s. We chose the seed that exercises the most significant number of RDCL call-sites, as shown by STADYNA. For example, in the case of *RollingSky*, we had a seed that exercised six RDCL call sites and another that exercised seven RDCL call sites, so we chose the last seed.

We were able to use Monkey to exercise only eight of the 10 apps provided by the authors of STADYNA. Two malware samples, *DroidKungfu* and *smsSend*, no longer operated and therefore were not included. We also found that Monkey could exercise RDCL call sites in 15 of the 34 Play Store apps. However, one of

---

[4] We are currently experimenting with a different, recently published technique [6] to see if it can exercise the 19 apps for which Monkey could not reach any RDCL call sites. If we are successful, we will include results on these in the next version of this paper.

these apps, (*Snapchat*), crashed after about two thousand events, so we removed it. We also used STADYNA to analyze these apps and found that it cannot analyze *colorSwitch*, so we also removed it. At the end of this step, 21 apps remained viable for use in the study (8 from STADYNA and 13 from Play Store). We used the apps provided by the authors of STADYNA to answer the dynamic analysis portions of RQ2 and RQ3 and the 13 Play Store apps to answer RQ4. Using the 13 Play Store apps allows us to examine whether both approaches can analyze them and whether one is more scalable than the other. Table 1 summarizes the basic characteristics of all 39 apps.

4.2 Variables and Measures

Independent Variables. Typically, when studying a new program analysis technique, we choose the technique itself as our primary independent variable, locating one or more other techniques to compare against or use as baselines. To answer RQ1, we use FLOWDROID as the baseline system. FLOWDROID is a program analysis framework based on SOOT that has been modified to support the analysis of Android apps. In its original form, SOOT performs analysis by assuming that the main method is the only entry point into the program. However, Android applications can have multiple entry points. FLOWDROID, an Android taint analysis tool built on top of SOOT, solved this issue by creating a custom main method that considers all possible combinations of outgoing methods.

Since we are interested in comparing the static analysis performance of SOOT and REHANA, we set up both tools to generate only the method call graph (MCG) of a single app at a time. We wrote a Java program to configure a SOOT instance with desired parameters, and then we instantiated FLOWDROID to use the existing SOOT instance to generate the method call graph without performing further analyses. In the remainder of this paper, we simply refer to FLOWDROID as SOOT.

To address RQ2 to RQ4, we performed the comparisons in a limited context. This is because STADYNA, the platform that works on Android apps, performs dynamic analysis (Phase 1) and then light-weight static analysis to construct the annotated MCG to include newly discovered components. It does not employ more complex static analyses to generate more analysis graphs. On the other hand, TAMIFLEX, the system that performs more complex static analysis after dynamic analysis, does not work for Android apps. We also considered HARVESTER but were not able to obtain it for this study. As such, the results reported for REHANA include the times spent on constructing analysis graphs, whereas the results reported for STADYNA do not.

Dependent Variables. As dependent variables, we consider metrics that track memory usage, efficiency, effectiveness, overhead, and slowdown factor.

Memory Usage. We first measure the memory usage of REHANA and FlowDroid by periodically monitoring the per-process memory usage reported in MB. We are particularly concerned with peak memory usage, as it is the most common limiting factor in performing very complicated analyses.

Next, we calculate memory efficiency (ME) using the following formula:

$$ME = \frac{\text{Number of Methods in the Callgraph}}{\text{the Peak Memory Consumption in MB}}$$

Note that a higher value of ME reflects a higher memory efficiency. This metric is used to answer RQ1. We repeat the experiments three times and measure the amount of memory required to perform the analysis of each app using the analysis techniques, each averaged over three attempts.

Efficiency. We calculate efficiency by measuring the time required by the techniques to perform their analyses (e.g., $time_{\text{SOOT}}$ and $time_{\text{ReHAna}}$). To do so, we measure the time in seconds required by each approach to perform analysis for each app in our collection with varying sizes. The measurement begins at the time we run an app and ends when the analysis result is reported. For RQ2 to RQ4, *the reported time does not include the cost of performing the initial static analysis used to identify MoIs.*

For StaDyna, the result reported for each app is the annotated MCG. For ReHAna, the results reported include various graphs generated during continuous analysis and the annotated MCG. Each reported result includes three overhead components, these being the time required to (i) execute an app, (ii) identify and capture dynamically loaded classes, and (iii) integrate these classes and produce the updated MCGs. We ran each measurement three times, and we report the average time in seconds.

Effectiveness. We assess effectiveness in two ways. First, we compare the results of using static analysis to determine MoIs using StaDyna and ReHAna. This is to determine whether our static analysis approach for identifying MoIs produces results similar to those of StaDyna. Second, we compare the number of RDCL targets that can be dynamically identified by ReHAna to the number dynamically identified by StaDyna.

To compare the detected RDCL targets, we begin by analyzing the report produced by StaDyna. The report lists the exercised RDCL method call sites (S_E), RDCL targets (S_T), and uncovered RDCL method call sites (S_U). Information in the report is at the method level. That is, if S_E contains more than one RDCL call statement, it is still treated as one method by StaDyna. ReHAna's report also lists the exercised RDCL method call sites (R_E) and detected targets (R_T). R_E, in this case, is reported at the statement level (i.e., each R_E is presented as a method and instruction index pair). However, we consider only method information, not instruction index information, to be consistent with StaDyna. Our analysis attempts to find cases in which $R_E \cap S_E$ and $R_E \cap S_U$. Together, these represent R_E sites from $S_U \cup S_T$ or MoIs targeted by StaDyna. We ran each analysis three times and reported the largest number of targets dynamically detected by each approach and the corresponding number of Monkey-generated events.

Overhead. We also calculate analysis overhead to help further explain the efficiency of each technique. We calculate overhead by comparing the time required by the techniques to perform their dynamic and static analyses (the same time used to calculate efficiency) to the time required to execute an app by itself using our input generator. The percent overhead of these two reported times is calculated using the equation $(\frac{time_{Analysis}}{time_{Monkey}} - 1) \times 100$, where $time_{Analysis}$ refers to the time taken by REHANA or STADYNA to complete its analysis.

Slowdown Factor. To assess the scalability of these two approaches (RQ3), we quantify the effect of hybrid analysis on the performance of each system in terms of the slowdown factor. We calculate the slowdown factor using the equation $\frac{time_{Analysis}}{time_{Monkey}}$. We then used the slowdown factor to report scalability.

4.3 Study Operation

To address RQ1, we compare the memory usage and efficiency of SOOT and REHANA. We report the number of methods analyzed by each technique and the time required to analyze each app. To address RQ2 to RQ4, we performed a head-to-head comparison between REHANA and STADYNA by observing the numbers of RDCL call sites or (MoIs) and targets identified by each approach (statically as *MoIs* and dynamically as *targets*) and measuring the time required for each approach to complete a similar analysis to generate the intended analysis result that also includes dynamically loaded code. For RQ3, we report the overhead of each approach and the speed-up of REHANA over STADYNA. For RQ4, we observe the analysis time in terms of the slowdown factor, as code size increases.

We conducted our experiments using several Nexus 7 tablets running the modified Android API 19 (Kitkat). Both REHANA and the server component of STADYNA ran on a laptop with Intel Core i7 and 16 GB of RAM running Apple OS X (Mojave). The communication between the tablets and the laptop was via USB-2. REHANA uses JDWP for communication, while STADYNA uses logcat to transport logging information.

4.4 Threats to Validity

Where external validity is concerned, we compared the performances of REHANA, SOOT, and STADYNA using only a subset of apps from Google Play store, together with a few others provided by the authors of STADYNA; however, the former subset of apps represent an important contingent of the most recent, commonly used apps that are available for Android devices. They also vary in size and complexity in terms of code size and reflection usage.

Where internal validity is concerned, errors in the tools we rely on could affect our results, but we have attempted to test them rigorously. As a first step, we created several micro-benchmark apps to test both implementations to ensure that they reported analysis correctly.

Where construct validity is concerned, we measured the times that ReHAna, Soot, and StaDyna need to perform analysis. We also compared each analysis time to the time required by each app to execute without any analysis as a method for calculating the overhead of each technique. We also compared their analysis results (both static and dynamic analyses) to evaluate their effectiveness. However, we do not collect any measures related to the actual engineer effort required to perform analyses in a company setting.

5 Results and Analysis

This section reports the results of our empirical investigations to answer the prior research questions.

RQ1: What are the performance differences between Soot and ReHAna?

We report the overall performance in Table 2. We report the number of analyzed methods in columns II and V for Soot and ReHAna, respectively. Note that ReHAna also analyzes methods in the ADF code, and therefore, it processes more methods than those processed by Soot. In columns III and VI, we report the amounts of memory (in MB) needed to support the analysis of each app by Soot and ReHAna. We report the analysis time of both systems in columns IV and VII.

Table 2. Comparing memory usage and analysis time between Soot and ReHAna.

App name [I]	Soot			ReHAna		
	Analyzed methods [II]	Utilized memory (MB) [III]	Analysis time (Seconds) [IV]	Analyzed methods [V]	Utilized memory (MB) [VI]	Analysis time (Seconds) [VII]
Snake	84	130	1	727	21	1
Battery Indicator	1,195	330	4	3,548	64	3
BitClock	57	175	1	4,631	57	2
AdBlockPlus	632	293	3	7,048	112	3
Guitar Flash	2,244	481	6	10,856	135	5
Calculator	2,850	737	8	12,898	180	5
iFixit	3,423	797	10	12,365	161	5
Slots Pharaohs Fire	3,148	787	12	18,421	218	6
TypoLab	4,242	834	13	22,782	252	8
Cute Animals	1,221	455	5	23,834	273	9
Dolphin EMU	2,867	786	12	28,290	390	12
BBC Weather	6,307	1,390	23	37,503	374	12
Bike Citizens Bicycle GPS	6,948	1,455	26	40,444	431	16
The Child of Slendrina	3,047	838	20	39,748	436	14
Moto Rider	4,880	1,369	28	44,279	460	14
Doodle Army	10,336	1,742	61	48,903	520	16
BBC News	9,461	1,727	67	49,139	570	16
Adobe Lightroom	n/a	1,408	n/a	47,304	503	21

Soot completed analysis for all but one Android app, *Adobe Lightroom*, presumably due to incompatibility from newer programming practices. In this situation, FlowDroid terminated with a runtime exception during the callgraph-construction phase. In all 18 apps, ReHAna analyzes significantly more methods than Soot. In the case of *BitClock*, the difference in the numbers of analyzed methods is about 81 times. In the case of *Battery Indicator*, the difference is about 3 times. On average, ReHAna analyzes 11.84 times more methods than Soot.

While ReHAna analyzes more methods than Soot in every application, it also requires less memory than Soot to complete the analysis for each application. In the case of *Snake*, our smallest app, Soot needs over 6 times more memory to analyze 8 times fewer methods. In the case of *Cute Animals*, Soot needs 1.67 times more memory to analyze 19 times fewer methods. On average, Soot needs 3.45 times more memory to analyze an app.

Next, we report memory efficiency (ME) in Table 3. As a reminder, ME is the ratio between the number of methods in a method call graph and peak memory usage. As the table shows, ME of ReHAna is significantly higher than that of Soot. In many cases, the efficiency gain is as high as 249 times. On average, the ME of Soot is 3.87 methods per one MB, while the ME of ReHAna is 79.98 methods per one MB. The average efficiency gain of ReHAna over Soot is 36.35 times.

Table 3. Comparing memory efficiency between Soot and ReHAna.

App	ME_{Soot}	ME_{ReHAna}	Gain ($\frac{ME_{\text{ReHAna}}}{ME_{\text{Soot}}}$)
Snake	0.65	34.62	53.57
Battery Indicator	3.62	55.44	15.31
BitClock	0.33	81.25	249.44
AdBlockPlus	2.16	62.93	29.17
Guitar Flash	4.67	80.42	17.24
Calculator	3.87	71.66	18.53
iFixit	4.29	76.80	17.88
Slots Pharaohs Fire	4.00	84.5	21.13
TypoLab	5.09	90.40	17.77
Cute Animals	2.68	87.30	32.53
Dolphin EMU	3.65	72.54	19.89
BBC Weather	4.54	100.28	22.10
Bike Citizens Bicycle GPS	4.78	93.84	19.65
The Child of Slendrina	3.64	91.17	25.07
Moto Rider	3.56	96.26	27.00
Doodle Army	5.93	94.04	15.85
BBC News	5.48	86.21	15.74
Average	3.70	79.98	36.35

In term of analysis time, Table 2 shows that for the small size apps (i.e., *Snake* to *Guitar Flash*), the analysis times of SOOT and ReHAna are comparable. However, as the apps become large, SOOT spends more time to analyze these apps. The two exceptions are *Cute Animals* and *Dolphin EMU*. These are small apps; however, they invoke a huge number of methods from the underlying framework. Small numbers of methods allow SOOT to perform analysis quickly. However, ReHAna ends up analyzing more than 19 times and 9 times more methods in these apps, respectively. ReHAna takes longer than SOOT to analyze *Cute Animals*, and it takes about the same time as SOOT to analyze *Dolphin EMU*. For very large apps such as DOODLE ARMY and *BBC News*, the analysis times of SOOT are 3.81 to 4.18 times higher than those of ReHAna.

While the peak memory consumption can provide the highest memory watermark for an analysis system, it does not provide the amount of memory the analysis system is using concerning time. For example, a system that occupies a large amount of memory for a short time may perform better than another system that uses less memory but for a much longer time. To observe memory usage over time, we recorded both ReHAna's and SOOT's memory usage throughout execution. We plot time (in seconds) on the x-axis and the memory consumption on the y-axis to form the memory-over-time graphs. Here we discuss the results of three apps that are most representative of the entire range of apps tested.

By the sizes of their Dex files, BBC News (4.3 MB), Dolphin EMU (2.0 MB), and Cute Animals Names and Sounds (1.3 MB) represent large, medium, and small Android apps. Again, when mentioning the size of Android apps, we are

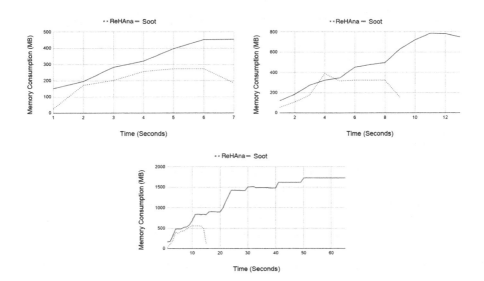

Fig. 4. Memory usage over time for analyzing a small app–cute animal sounds (top left), medium-sized app–Dolphin EMU (top right), and large app–BBC News (bottom).

Table 4. RDCL callsites statically identified by ReHAna and StaDynA and RDCL targets dynamically detected and captured by both systems. We used the eight apps provided by the authors of StaDynA.

App (I)	Uncovered RDCL callsites (MoIs)		ReHAna ∩ StaDynA (IV)	ReHAna \ StaDynA (V)	StaDynA \ ReHAna (VI)	Captured RDCL targets		ReHAna ∩ StaDynA (IX)	ReHAna \ StaDynA (X)	StaDynA \ ReHAna (XI)
	ReHAna (II)	StaDynA (III)				ReHAna (VII)	StaDynA (VII)			
Avast	24	5	4	21	1	21	4	4	17	0
Symantec	19	1	1	18	0	18	1	1	18	0
ViberVOIP	26	8	4	22	4	21	4	4	17	0
FlappyBird	19	3	1	18	2	18	1	1	17	0
ImageView	36	4	4	33	0	30	4	3	27	1
Anserverbot1	21	2	2	19	0	20	2	2	18	0
Basebridge4	54	2	2	52	0	40	2	2	38	0
Fakenotify	31	10	10	21	0	16	1	1	15	0

referencing the relative logical complexity, reflected by the size of Dex files. For example, *Cute Animals* has the largest APK size but the smallest DEX size, meaning that most of the files in its APK are not related to how the application works; instead, they are accessory files, such as media, used to support the application's functions.

We intend to analyze how Soot and ReHAna perform in analyzing real-world apps of varying complexities. For a small app shown in Fig. 4(top left), both systems achieve the same time of completion; however, the amount of memory needed by ReHAna reaches plateau much quicker. It also requires less peak memory. For a medium-sized app (Dolphin EMU) shown in Fig. 4(top right), ReHAna manages to use around 300 MB of memory during most of the analysis, while Soot's memory usage continued to increase to almost 800 MB.

The performance difference in memory usage becomes even more staggering when both systems analyze large apps. BBC News, whose APK has multiple DEX files, represents a reasonably complex Android app that an end-user would encounter in real life. As Fig. 4(bottom) shows, ReHAna outperforms Soot by a big margin, both in terms of speed and memory usage.

RQ2: Is ReHAna more effective than StaDynA?

We consider the effectiveness of each approach to perform hybrid analysis. As the first step, we evaluate the effectiveness of the static analysis portions of both systems. Table 4, columns II to VI report the number of uncovered RDCL call sites or MoIs within each program. For example, ReHAna uncovered 24 call sites while StaDynA only uncovered 5 call sites. We also report call sites uncovered by both approaches (column IV), ReHAna only (column V), and StaDynA only (column VI).

To identify why ReHAna uncovers more MoIs than Androguard (column V), we analyzed the log files generated by both systems. We found that the differences have to do with how ReHAna and Androguard operate. Androguard only analyzes application code. ReHAna, on the other hand, can also uncover additional call sites from within the framework and library code.

Table 5. Time required for ReHAna and StaDynA to analyze the eight apps provided by the authors of StaDynA.

App (I)	Monkey (sec.) (II)	Analysis time (sec.)		Overhead (%)		Speed-up (%) (VII)
		ReHAna (III)	StaDynA (IV)	ReHAna (V)	StaDynA (VI)	
Avast	321.55	368.17	744.30	14.50	131.47	102.16
Symantec	280.14	325.19	618.79	16.08	131.59	99.51
ViberVOIP	267.23	283.24	955.42	5.99	257.53	237.32
FlappyBird	295.09	311.28	332.01	5.49	12.51	6.66
ImageView	324.28	368.90	373.24	13.76	15.15	1.23
Anserverbot1	290.91	317.91	534.84	9.28	83.85	68.23
Basebridge4	288.52	320.23	454.58	11.02	57.55	41.91
Fakenotify	303.12	308.31	323.19	1.69	6.60	4.83

We also investigated why ANDROGUARD uncovers MoIs not uncovered by ReHAna (column VI). We found that the differences also have to do with how the two systems operate. For example, in Avast (Column VI), StaDynA identifies one additional MoI not detected by ReHAna. ReHAna analyzes only classes that can be loaded. For the analysis portion of ReHAna, any class that cannot be referenced is also not loaded (i.e., dead code in this case), and the static analysis engine does not analyze it. On the other hand, ANDROGUARD, as a compiler-based approach, analyzes all the code in an APK, including classes that would not have been loaded. As such, RDCL call sites in these classes are identified by ANDROGUARD but not by ReHAna.

Ultimately, the goal of both systems is to identify classes that have been loaded through RDCL so that both systems can include them when computing their initial static analysis results. We compare the numbers of dynamically loaded classes that both techniques can detect and capture (Table 4). As shown in Column IX, ReHAna can detect and capture the same target classes as StaDynA in seven out of eight apps. The only exception is *ImageView*. Also note that for all eight apps, Monkey succeeded in generating the requested 10,000 events for both systems, and it was able to exercise most of the MoIs so that the number of dynamically detected classes are very close to the uncovered MoIs. The two major exceptions are *Basebridge4* and *Fakenotify*, where Monkey failed to exercise at least 75% of MoIs.

To better understand why ReHAna is not able to capture a class in *ImageView*, we investigated reports generated by both systems. We discovered that even when we used the same seed to generate Monkey events, we could still experience execution non-determinism. This factor is quite profound in *ImageView*. We found that it received an RSS feed that Monkey would attempt to touch. When we ran StaDynA, Monkey was successful in instigating events on an RSS feed, so it called a method that belongs to a class that handles multi-touch gestures.[5] This scenario occurred only once in five execution attempts.

---

[5] The specific class name is `Ldk/nindroid/rss/ClickHandler$MultitouchHandler`.

When we ran ReHANA, however, the same method was not called. We conducted multiple runs to see if we could invoke the method, but none succeeded.

In summary, ReHANA was able to detect the same RDCL classes detected by StaDynA in all but one app, which was due to non-determinism. As such, we conclude that ReHANA is as effective at detecting RDCL targets as StaDynA.

RQ3: Is ReHANA more efficient than StaDynA?

Table 5 reports results related to RQ3. To evaluate overhead, we also needed to measure the time required to execute an app with 10,000 Monkey-generated events, but without any analysis overhead (Column II). We then measured the times for ReHANA and StaDynA to perform analysis based on the same 10,000 Monkey-generated events. We report the results in Table 5, Columns III, and IV. Columns V and VI in the table report the overhead of ReHANA and StaDynA, respectively. The overhead is the additional time needed by each system to perform an analysis of an app in terms of percentage. Note that the overheads of ReHANA range from 1.69% to 16.08%, whereas the overheads of StaDynA range from 6.60% to 257.53%.

Finally, Column VII reports the speed-ups of ReHANA over StaDynA, in the form of the ratio of StaDynA's analysis time (Column IV) to ReHANA's analysis time (Column III). As the data shows, the amount of time required by ReHANA to perform RDCL analysis for each app is consistently much less than the time required by StaDynA. The speed-up of ReHANA over StaDynA ranged from 1.23 % (for *ImageView*) to 237.32 % (for *ViberVOIP*, which is the largest app in terms of code size among the eight apps). As such, we conclude that ReHANA is more efficient than StaDynA.

Table 6. RDCL callsites statically identified by ReHANA and StaDynA and RDCL targets dynamically detected and captured by both systems. We used the 13 apps downloaded from Play store.

App (I)	Uncovered RDCL callsites (MoIs)		ReHANA ∩ StaDynA (IV)	ReHANA \ StaDynA (V)	StaDynA \ ReHANA (VI)	Captured RDCL targets		ReHANA ∩ StaDynA (IX)	ReHANA \ StaDynA (X)	StaDynA \ ReHANA (XI)
	ReHANA (II)	StaDynA (III)				ReHANA (VII)	StaDynA (VII)			
duoLingo	172	160	160	12	0	53	14	13	39	1
slither	101	99	99	2	0	23	1	1	22	0
HuluPlus	146	143	142	4	1	34	16	6	28	10
Mercari	97	93	93	4	0	38	9	9	29	0
ooVoo	87	86	82	5	4	21	5	5	16	0
Pinterest	98	96	96	2	0	8	6	2	6	4
GeometryJumpLite	105	102	102	3	0	27	5	5	22	0
SgiggleProduction	119	116	116	3	0	24	5	4	20	1
SoundCloud	100	99	97	3	2	10	5	4	6	1
LedFlashLight	146	140	140	6	0	27	14	8	19	6
RollingSky	152	143	143	9	0	13	7	0	13	7
Waze	106	103	103	3	0	22	3	3	19	0
Zedge	129	124	122	7	2	55	7	6	49	1

RQ4: Is ReHANA more scalable than StaDYNA?

For RQ4, we focus on the abilities of ReHANA and StaDyNA to analyze the 13 Play Store apps. As the first step, we collected the result of our static analysis investigation, as reported in Table 6, columns II to VI. The data in the table shows that ReHANA was able to identify the same MoIs in nine out of 13 apps. In the other four apps, the static analysis engine in StaDyNA was able to find between one and four MoIs not detectable by ReHANA. We also noticed that these large apps contain more MoIs than the eight used to answer RQ2 and RQ3.

Table 6, columns VII to XI compare the numbers of target classes that have been detected by both approaches. ReHANA can detect the same target classes as StaDyNA in 7 out of 13 apps. We also found several instances in which non-determinism is a factor that allows StaDyNA to detect one more class than ReHANA (as seen in *duoLingo*, *SgiggleProduction*, *SoundCloud*, and *Zedge*.) In apps with highly complex GUIs (*Hulu Plus* and *Pinterest*), we also found that information used to construct the GUIs is served dynamically. Thus, across different runs, the GUIs can differ substantially. This discrepancy can result in significant differences in the way these apps are exercised. For *LedFlashlight*, the difference is due to advertisements. For *RollingSky*, the game logic also deviates execution from run to run.

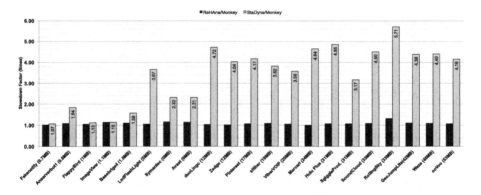

Fig. 5. Comparing the scalability of ReHANA and StaDyNA using all 21 apps (sorted from smallest to largest APK sizes); each exercised by 10,000 Monkey-generated events.

Figure 5 shows the scalability of each approach based on its ability to analyze all 21 apps. The x-axis is sorted based on the app's code size, from smallest to largest (we also report the code size after each app's name). As the figure shows, the slowdown factors of ReHANA remain below 1.32 (1.0 indicates no overhead). The smallest slowdown factor is 1.01 (or 1%) for *Mercari*. The largest slowdown factor is 1.32 (or 32%) for *RollingSky*. In contrast, StaDyNA incurs slowdown factors ranging from 1.07 (for *Fakenotify*, the smallest app) to 5.71 (for *RollingSky*), which is the same app that incurs the highest overhead with

REHANA. For the largest app, *ooVoo* (53 MB), STADYNA incurs a 4.16 slow-down while REHANA incurs a 1.07 slowdown.

Based on these results, we conclude that REHANA is more scalable then STADYNA. In addition, REHANA was able to analyze *colorSwitch* while STA-DYNA could not.

6   Discussion

Concerning RQ1, we further confirm that the primary reason for the differ-ence in the numbers of methods analyzed by SOOT and REHANAis due to the additional ADF methods. We explain this difference through an exam-ple. Figure 6(left) illustrates a snippet of the MCG generated by SOOT for the Snake app. As shown in this figure, SOOT does not analyze any ADF method and therefore, such API calls (i.e., requestFocus, setFocusable, and setFocusableInTouchMode) would be directed to runTimeException.init since those API methods are not in the project. On the other hand, when REHANA analyzes the same app, it also loads the class in the ADF to which these APIs belong. As shown in Fig. 6(right), it uncovers and analyzes more than 30 additional methods in these APIs.

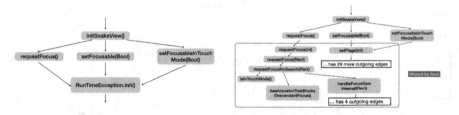

Fig. 6. Portions of method call graphs generated by SOOT *(left)* and REHANA *(right)*

For RQ2 to RQ4, REHANA also analyzes more methods than ANDROGUARD, the static analysis framework used in STADYNA. After performing a manual inspection of the generated results, we discovered that there are many RDCL call sites in these ADF classes. These RDCL call sites were not detectable by ANDROGUARD, because ANDROGUARD does not analyze these classes.

For Avast (Column VI), STADYNA identifies one additional MoI not detected by REHANA. Our further investigation shows that this difference stems from differences in the ways the two underlying static analysis frameworks operate. REHANA analyzes only classes that can be loaded. For the analysis portion of REHANA, any class that cannot be referenced is also not loaded (i.e., dead code in this case), and the static analysis engine does not analyze it. On the other hand, ANDROGUARD , as a compiler-based approach, analyzes all the code in an APK including classes that would not have been loaded. As such, RDCL call sites in these classes are identified by ANDROGUARD but not by REHANA.

In terms of performance, two major time components can dominate the cost of dynamic analysis: (1) the actual execution time of an app, and (2) the analysis time required by each approach. The analysis time includes the time required to perform initial static analysis to build the initial MCG for STADYNA or to build analysis context graphs such as CFGs, DFGs, and initial ICFGs for ReHAnA. This time component is highly dependent on the amount of code that must be statically analyzed. For example, *Mercari* has nearly 60,000 methods (Table 1); therefore, STADYNA incurs an analysis time of 737 s. It turns out that ReHAnA only needed about two seconds of wall-clock time to perform the same analysis. This is possible because ReHAnA can hide a significant portion of the static analysis cost within its dynamic analysis phase. STADYNA, on the other hand, cannot perform static analysis until the dynamic analysis is complete; this is because it needs to include dynamically loaded code components as part of its analysis context.

7   Related Work

Several research efforts attempt to improve the soundness of static analysis in the presence of dynamically loaded code through Java reflection. Livshits et al. [19] propose a static analysis algorithm that can approximate reflection targets using points-to information. Felt et al. [11] discuss the challenges of handling reflection in Android applications and then attempt to address them using STOWAWAY, a static analysis tool that is capable of identifying reflective calls and tracking reflection targets by performing flow-sensitive analysis. More recent static analysis approaches aim to improve precision. These approaches include DROIDRA [16], SPARTA [2], and SOLAR [17]. DROIDRA adapts TAMIFLEX to analyze Android apps for dynamically loaded code statically. Unlike TAMIFLEX, DROIDRA does not execute apps; instead, it uses a constraint solver to resolve reflection targets. It also uses its version of *Booster* to manipulate Jimple, an immediate representation used by SOOT directly. TAMIFLEX, on the other hand, manipulates Java bytecode. SPARTA implements annotations in the Checker framework to track information flow and a type inference system to trace reflective calls. SPARTA also operates at the source code level and not the bytecode or Dexcode level. However, these static analysis approaches can only work in cases where we can identify reflection targets from the source code. For the most up-to-date and comprehensive review of static analysis approaches for handling reflection, see Landman et al. [15].

Concerning dynamic analysis, Davis et al. [8] provide an app rewriting framework named RetroSkeleton that is capable of intercepting reflections at runtime; however, this approach does not work with custom classloaders. Sawin et al. [25] propose an approach that combines static string analysis with dynamic information to resolve dynamic class loading via Java reflection. This approach operates only on the standard Java library. EXECUTE THIS! [21] is a dynamic analysis approach that relies on an Android VM modification to detect reflection calls. It logs runtime events and performs static analysis off-line. Our approach, on the other hand, performs the continuous analysis.

8   Conclusion and Future Work

The ability to perform program analysis "at speed" is critical for enabling software engineers to quickly remove defects at production time and enable security analysts to evaluate deployed apps for vulnerabilities quickly. Currently, existing program analysis approaches, while useful, are too inefficient to provide such analysis capabilities. One primary reason for this inefficiency is that these approaches perform analyses in a closed-world fashion.

In this paper, we introduce REHANA, our proposed open-world analysis framework for Android. At the heart of REHANA is our proposed Virtual Class-Loader (VCL) that is capable of incrementally load and analyze classes. This capability is suitable for performing hybrid program analysis. We implemented an instance of REHANA to analyze apps for RDCL components and then used it to analyze a large corpus of apps. Our evaluation indicates that REHANA is as effective as STADYNA, an existing closed-world RDCL analysis approach, while significantly reducing analysis time.

In future work, we plan to create other instances of REHANA to support real-time code coverage visualizations and real-time policy enforcement. We plan to use the class-loading capability of REHANA to perform program decomposition that can make event sequence generation and verification of Android apps more tractable. We will make the source code of REHANA publicly available upon the acceptance of this paper.

Acknowledgments. We would like to thank Yury Zhauniarovich, Maqsood Ahmad, Olga Gadyatskaya, Bruno Crispo, and Fabio Massacci for sharing the source code of STADYNA and the applications used to evaluate STADYNA with us.

References

1. Abraham, J., Jones, P., Jetley, R.: A formal methods-based verification approach to medical device software analysis, February 2010. https://www.embedded.com/a-formal-methods-based-verification-approach-to-medical-device-software-analysis/
2. Barros, P., et al.: Static analysis of implicit control flow: resolving Java reflection and android intents (t). In: Proceedings of the 2015 30th IEEE/ACM International Conference on Automated Software Engineering (ASE), ASE 2015, pp. 669–679, Lincoln, NE, USA, November 2015
3. Bodden, E., Sewe, A., Sinschek, J., Oueslati, H., Mezini, M.: Taming reflection: aiding static analysis in the presence of reflection and custom class loaders. In: Proceedings of the International Conference on Software Engineering (ICSE), pp. 241–250, Honolulu, Hawaii, USA, May 2011
4. Bond, M.D., Coons, K.E., McKinley, K.S.: PACER: proportional detection of data races. In: Proceedings of the Conference on Programming Language Design and Implementation, pp. 255–268, Toronto, Ontario, Canada, June 2010
5. Chandra, B.: A technical view of the open SSL heartbleed vulnerability, May 2014. https://www.ibm.com/developerworks/community/files/form/anonymous/api/library/38218957-7195-4fe9-812a-10b7869e4a87/document/ab12b05b-9f07-4146-8514-18e22bd5408c/media

6. Chen, Y., et al.: Mass discovery of android traffic imprints through instantiated partial execution. In: Proceedings of CCS, pp. 815–828, Dallas, Texas, USA (2017)
7. Choudhary, S.R., Gorla, A., Orso, A.: Automated test input generation for android: are we there yet? In: Proceedings of the 2015 30th IEEE/ACM International Conference on Automated Software Engineering (ASE), ASE 2015, pp. 429–440 (2015)
8. Davis, B., Chen, H.: Retroskeleton: retrofitting android apps. In: Proceeding of the 11th Annual International Conference on Mobile Systems, Applications, and Services, MobiSys 2013, pp. 181–192, New York, NY, USA. ACM (2013)
9. Desnos, A.: Androguard: reverse engineering, malware and goodware analysis of android applications (2013). https://github.com/androguard/androguard
10. Duan, Y., et al.: Things you may not know about android (Un)packers: a systematic study based on whole-system emulation. In: Proceedings of Network and Distributed System Security Symposium, NDSS, San Diego, California, USA, February 2018
11. Felt, A.P., Chin, E., Hanna, S., Song, D., Wagner, D.: Android permissions demystified. In: Proceedings of the 18th ACM Conference on Computer and Communications Security, CCS 2011, pp. 627–638, New York, NY, USA. ACM (2011)
12. GeeksforGeeks. ClassLoader in Java, May 201r. https://www.geeksforgeeks.org/classloader-in-java/
13. Google. Lint (2019). http://tools.android.com/tips/lint
14. Jim, T.: Legacy C/C++ code is a nuclear waste nightmare that will make you WannaCry, June 2017. http://trevorjim.com
15. Landman, D., Serebrenik, A., Vinju, J.: Challenges for static analysis of java reflection - literature review and empirical study. In: Proceedings of the International Conference on Software Engineering, Buenos Aires, Argentina, May 2017
16. Li, L., Bissyandé, T.F., Octeau, D., Klein, J.: Droidra: taming reflection to support whole-program analysis of android apps. In: Proceedings of the 25th International Symposium on Software Testing and Analysis, ISSTA 2016, pp. 318–329, Saarbrücken, Germany (2016)
17. Li, Y., Tan, T., Xue, J.: Understanding and analyzing java reflection. ACM Trans. Softw. Eng. Methodol. **28**(2), 1–50 (2019)
18. Liang, S., Might, M., Horn, D.V.: Android: malware analysis of android with user-supplied predicates. CoRR, abs/1311.4198 (2013)
19. Livshits, V.B., Lam, M.S.: Finding security vulnerabilities in java applications with static analysis. In: Proceedings of the 14th Conference on USENIX Security Symposium, SSYM 2005, vol. 14 (2005)
20. Oracle Corp. Loading, linking, and initializing, November 2019. https://docs.oracle.com/javase/specs/jvms/se7/html/jvms-5.html
21. Poeplau, S., Fratantonio, Y., Bianchi, A., Kruegel, C., Vigna, G.: Execute this! analyzing unsafe and malicious dynamic code loading in android applications. In: Proceedings of NDSS, vol. 14, pp. 23–26, San Diego, CA (2014)
22. Ponomariov, P.: Shedun: adware/malware family threatening your Android device, September 2015. https://blog.avira.com/shedun/
23. Rasthofer, S., Arzt, S., Miltenberger, M., Bodden, E.: Harvesting runtime values in android applications that feature anti-analysis techniques. In: Proceedings of NDSS (2016)
24. Rus, S., Rauchwerger, L., Hoeflinger, J.: Hybrid analysis: static & dynamic memory reference analysis. Int. J. Parallel Program. **31**(4), 251–283 (2003)
25. Sawin, J., Rountev, A.: Improving static resolution of dynamic class loading in java using dynamically gathered environment information. Autom. Softw. Eng. **16**(2), 357–381 (2009)

26. Smith, J., Nair, R.: Virtual Machines: Versatile Platforms for Systems and Processes (The Morgan Kaufmann Series in Computer Architecture and Design). Morgan Kaufmann Publishers Inc., San Francisco (2005)
27. Späth, J., Lam, P.: Using Soot and TamiFlex to analyze DaCapo, August 2014. https://github.com/Sable/soot/wiki/Using-Soot-and-TamiFlex-to-analyze-DaCapo
28. Tikir, M., Hollingsworth, J.K.: Efficient instrumentation for code coverage testing. In: Proceedings of the 2002 ACM SIGSOFT International Symposium on Software Testing and Analysis, ISSTA 2002, pp. 86–96, Roma, Italy (2002)
29. Vallée-Rai, R.: Soot: a java bytecode optimization framework. Master's thesis, McGill University (2000)
30. Wu, D., Liu, X., Xu, J., Lo, D., Gao, D.: Measuring the declared SDK versions and their consistency with API calls in android apps. In: Ma, L., Khreishah, A., Zhang, Y., Yan, M. (eds.) Wireless Algorithms. Systems, and Applications, pp. 678–690. Springer, Cham (2017)
31. Xu, L.: Techniques and tools for analyzing and understanding android applications. PhD thesis, University of California, Davis (2013)
32. Zhauniarovich, Y., Ahmad, M., Gadyatskaya, O., Crispo, B., Massacci, F.: StaDynA: addressing the problem of dynamic code updates in the security analysis of android applications. In: Proceedings of the 5th ACM Conference on Data and Application Security and Privacy, CODASPY 2015, pp. 37–48, San Antonio, Texas, USA (2015)

A Route Guidance Method for Vehicles to Improve Driver's Experienced Delay Against Traffic Congestion

Yusuke Matsui[1] and Takuya Yoshihiro[2(✉)]

[1] Graduate School of Systems Engineering, Wakayama University, Wakayama, Japan
s216260@wakayama-u.ac.jp
[2] Faculty of Systems Engineering, Wakayama University, Wakayama, Japan
tac@wakayama-u.ac.jp

Abstract. The increase of the city population and the number of vehicles brought heavy traffic jam in many cities. To reduce traffic congestion is one of the important tasks in order to reduce economic loss as well as the environmental pollution. Several solutions to mitigate the traffic congestion has been proposed so far, but in most cases they try to optimize whole traffic in the area, and a few treats the route guidance methods when the traffic jam occurs. Once a traffic jam takes place, we hope to clear the jam immediately by means of changing paths of some vehicles. Several studies tackle this problem. However, they enforce vehicles located very close to the traffic jam to change their paths, which results in large delay due to inefficient detour paths. This not only fails to persuade the vehicle drivers to change their paths, but also causes another traffic jam on the detour paths. In this paper, based on the observation that some vehicles often have alternative paths to avoid congested road segments with similar taking time, we propose a new route guidance method that offers vehicles better alternative paths with which the time to reach their destinations would be minimized. Through evaluation, we demonstrated that the proposed method significantly reduces the traveling time of vehicles while clearing the traffic jam within the same time duration.

Keywords: Vehicular congestion avoidance · Intelligent transportation system · Dynamic Route Guidance System · SUMO

1 Introduction

In recent years, the increase of the city population and the number of vehicles causes traffic congestion in large cities, which is one of the serious social problems [1]. According to a study [3], the annual traffic congestion loss in Japan is about 3.81 billion person-hours, which corresponds to as much as 12 trillion JPY in the monetary value. Also, the traffic congestion causes environmental problems [2].

© ICST Institute for Computer Sciences, Social Informatics and Telecommunications Engineering 2022
Published by Springer Nature Switzerland AG 2022. All Rights Reserved
T. Hara and H. Yamaguchi (Eds.): MobiQuitous 2021, LNICST 419, pp. 375–389, 2022.
https://doi.org/10.1007/978-3-030-94822-1_20

For example, serious PM2.5 air pollution occurred in Beijing, China, in which PM2.5 particles caused by vehicle accounts for about 20% [4]. Reducing traffic congestions would reduce both the economical and environmental problems, and is strongly desired in many major cities in the world.

On the other hand, from the driver's point of view, delay in arrival time due to traffic congestion is the matter to be considered. If the traveling time of the vehicle is reduced by alleviating the traffic congestion, their time loss would be minimized. In minimizing economical loss due to traffic congestion, not only considering the total optimization, but also considering loss of individuals is important because people satisfaction would be one of the key evaluation items in reducing traffic congestion.

Currently, a method called DRGS (Dynamic Route Guidance System) [5] is attracting attention as a mean for reducing loss from traffic congestion. In DRGS, we can monitor traffic conditions with RSU (Road Side Unit), which is communication terminals installed on the side of the road, and when a traffic congestion occurs, the system adaptively guide a part of vehicles to change their routes to optimize traffic to reduce congestion.

Several DRGS studies proposed route guidance systems that change the route of vehicles running close to the congested road to reduce the traffic congestion [6–8]. However, in most cases, the invoked delay for vehicles in arrival time due to route guidance is significantly large because the offered routes are changed largely and are not good for the drivers of vehicles. Besides, in this case, even when the driver of each vehicle is advised to change the route by the system, they would not possibly change their route because they do not satisfy the offered routes. As a result, the DRGS systems may not work well as the system designer expected, the performance of the systems to reduce traffic congestion would be disappointed. Our idea for this problem is that, if the location of a vehicle is relatively far from the congested road, there will be an alternative route with smaller loss in time, i.e., with higher satisfaction, with higher probability. If we make route guidance that prioritizes the arrival delay, we would achieve both high performance in traffic congestion mitigation (i.e., minimizing time to mitigate congestion), and driver's satisfaction (i.e., minimizing the arrival time delay).

In this paper, we assume that RSU are installed on all the main roads and intersections in the target area so that the traffic conditions can be grasped completely. When a traffic congestion occurs, each RSU detects a congested road based on vehicle density and speed on the road, and the central server computes a feasible route guidance plan to eliminate the traffic congestion that cares for the arrival delay of each detouring vehicle. By controlling the traffic with this rerouting plan, the arrival delay of each vehicle is significantly reduced and the traffic congestion is eliminated by appropriately reducing vehicles injecting to the congested road. As a result of evaluating the proposed method with a well-known traffic flow simulator SUMO, the proposed method is proved to reduce traffic congestion with a smaller average arrival delay than existing methods.

The remainder of this paper is organized as follows. In Sect. 2, we describe the outline of DRGS, its related work, and its problems. In Sect. 3, we describe the proposed method. In Sect. 4, we evaluate the proposed method with traffic flow simulator SUMO. In Sect. 5, we describe the discussion about our method, and finally in Sect. 6 we conclude our study.

2   Related Work

DRGS is a system that obtains the traffic information on roads and provides advised routes to vehicles to achieve optimized traffic control. The main objective of DRGS systems is to reduce traffic congestion so that DRGS systems compute a traffic arrangement plan and guide a part of vehicles with the offered paths in order to mitigate traffic congestion in the minimum time delay.

There is a solid body of the literature in optimizing traffic conditions as vehicular routing problems. However, most of those does not catch up with the current situation where major vehicle movements can be measured as is done by companies such as Google [9] or TomTom [10]. Consequently, major vehicle routing problems treats optimal paths for a single or a small number of vehicles, or pre-planning of large number of vehicles to optimize the traffic conditions [11]. These kinds of studies are not practical in the current situation because they cannot treat dynamic occurrence of traffic congestions in the current transportation systems, nor controlling routes of vehicles to mitigate the congestions. However, recently, there are some practical studies that aims at local solution, i.e., they propose to detect traffic congestion and guide a part of vehicles to avoid it to mitigate the congestion.

Souza et al. [6] proposed a DRGS called CHIMERA (Congestion avoidance througH a trafflc classification MEchanism and a Re-routing Algorithm), which improves the overall spatial utilization of a road network and reduces the average vehicle traveling costs by avoiding vehicles from getting stuck in traffic congestion. It assumes that all vehicles provide their information (i.e., vehicleID, current position, planned route, and destination) to a central entity via mobile communication such as 4G and LTE. CHIMERA has two main phases; The first one is congestion detection and traffic classification, and the second one is route suggestion. In the first process, traffic congestion is detected from the classification results of traffic conditions using k-Nearest Neighbor (kNN) classifier. In the second process, CHIMERA computes alternative routes for all the target vehicles based on probabilistic k-Shortest Paths. By distributing vehicles to multiple routes according to the probabilistic distribution, the possibility of generating new traffic congestion is reduced.

Pan et al. [7] proposed a centralized system to obtain the vehicle speed and density in real time in order to detect traffic congestions. Once a congestion is detected, vehicles are rerouted based on rerouting strategies such as DSP (Dynamic Shortest Path), AR*(A* Shortest Path With Repulsion), RkSP (Random k-Shortest Path), EBkSP (Entropy Balanced k-Shortest Paths) and FBkSP (Flow Balanced k-Shortest Path). Here, DSP is a classical rerouting strategy, which computes the routes with the smallest travel time. However, there is a shortcoming that the new rerouting paths would cause a new congestion in another spot with high probability. AR* is a rerouting strategy, which takes into account the results of route guidance by other vehicles. By reflecting the results of other vehicles' route guidance when calculating the detour route for vehicles, it is difficult for vehicles to concentrate on a particular detour route. However, AR* cannot control traffic on detour routes with high accuracy because it dose not directly take the traffic capacity of the detour routes into account. RkSP randomly chooses a path among k-shortest paths to balance traffic. Although this strategy reduces the possibility of creating congestion in another spot, the traveling time of each vehicle is not much cared about and so far from optimal. EBkSP is the same as RkSP in that k-shortest paths are computed, but different in that the best paths in terms of entropy is selected among k paths. As a result, EBkSP provides more load-balanced traffic distribution than RkSP. FBkSP computes k-shortest paths and calculates the traffic volume of all road segments in the area. When providing a route to each vehicle, FBkSP chooses a path that leads to better balance in traffic volumes among roads. Different from EBkSP, which chooses paths based on entropy, FBkSP directly considers traffic load balancing so that more effective path selection is possible.

The above methods [6,7] would be the representative conventional methods to solve the problems we are targeting on, and have been chosen as comparison methods in many related papers. However, these do not directly take the arrival delay of each vehicle into account. Although the strategy that detouring vehicles located very close to the congested point may reduce the time to resolve the traffic congestion, it enforces individual vehicles to increase largely the traveling delay, and so reduces their satisfaction. Furthermore, because the vehicles close to the congested road is detoured, the traffic volume on the around roads would be easily raised due to detouring traffic, resulting in another congestion around there. In our strategy, it is possible to care for individual satisfaction of drivers while mitigating congestion within the same time scale. To the best of our knowledge, our method is the first route guidance method to mitigates traffic congestion that explicitly considers the time delay experienced by the detoured vehicles.

Shen et al. [8] proposed a DRGS system called NRR (Next Road Rerouting) that considers the feasibility of the system. It focuses on reducing computational cost and system implementation cost. NRR is assumed to be deployed as a software plug-in for SCATS [12], which has already been in use at more than 37,000 intersections in 27 countries. Extending an existing system would considerably reduce the introduction cost. When NRR detects a congested road, it guides the vehicles around it. Specifically, instead of calculating the detour paths to the destinations of vehicles, NRR just calculates the alternative road segment that each vehicle should follow next regardless of their destinations. After following the guidance, each vehicle travels to the destination based on its own VNS (Vehicular Navigation System) [13]. Since the functions of NRR in route guidance is limited, the calculation cost of the entire system can be reduced. However, this method has the similar problem to [6,7] because the vehicles at close to the congested road are detoured.

Our contributions are that proposed method can prevent secondary traffic congestion on detour routes and that it can plan detours considering the burden on drivers. The proposed method calculates how much allowable traffic for each road using the traffic information collected by RSUs. Using this information, it is possible to calculate the detour traffic volume with a certain degree of accuracy. In this way, we can systematically prevent secondary congestion on the detour routes and optimize traffic flow by maximizing the use of the detour routes. In the route planning, we minimize total travel time of all vehicles in target area using an original algorithm that prioritizes reducing the load on drivers during detours, i.e., the delay in destination arrival time due to route guidance. In the following section, we describe the proposed method in detail.

3   Proposed Method

Due to traffic congestion, the time for each vehicle to reach its destination is significantly increased. Our purpose is to mitigate traffic congestion while minimizing the arrival delay of all vehicles. In related work, route guidance is applied to vehicles located close to the congested road. Although the strategy detouring vehicles close to the congested point may reduce the time to mitigate the traffic congestion, it tends to increase the total traveling delay of vehicles. Our method estimates the arrival delay to reach the destination when a vehicle is guided to bypass a congested road at intersection. Then it guides the vehicle to the detour path with the smaller arrival delay. As a result, it is possible to mitigate the traffic congestion while minimizing the arrival delay of each vehicle to its destination. In our proposal, the traffic information necessary for detour plan is acquired by RSUs and aggregated in a central server. When the central server detects traffic congestion based on the aggregated information, it calculates the rerouting table for alleviating congestion and guides each vehicle along the routing plan. For example, it is assumed that the traffic jam occurs as shown in Fig. 1. Suppose that route guidance at point X of the delay in destination arrival time is 10 min, and route guidance at point Y of the delay in destination arrival time is 5 min. In this case, the total travel time of all vehicles can be reduced by guiding the route at point Y rather than at point X. Therefore, the proposed method eliminates traffic congestion by preferentially diverting vehicles that enter point Y.

The details of our method are described as follows. In Sect. 3.1, the notation used in our method is provided. In Sect. 3.2, we describe the method to construct the rerouting table. The rerouting table manages detour routes to guide vehicles, and enables us to judge which detour paths should be activated according to the magnitude of the occurring traffic congestion. In Sect. 3.3, we explains the algorithm to control vehicles based on the rerouting table.

3.1   Notation

A directed and weighted graph $G = (I, R)$ represents the road network, where I is the set of intersections, R is the set of road segments, $S \subset I$ is the set

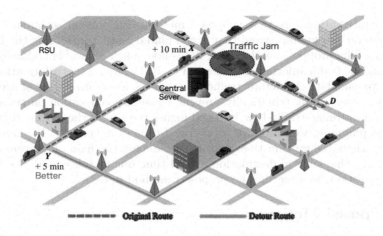

Fig. 1. Overview of Our Method

of sources and $D \subset I$ is the set of destinations of vehicles. $w(\cdot)$ is a function that represents the weight of the road segment. Specifically, $w(r)$ is a positive integer representing the weight for road segment $r \in R$. For a source $s \in S$ and a destination $d \in D$, $P_{(s,d)}$ represents the shortest path from s to d under the weight function $w(\cdot)$. $B_{(s,d)}$ represents the detour path from s to d defined as the shortest path under the weighting function $w(\cdot)$ in the road network $G' = (I, R - P_{(s,d)})$, where $P_{(s,d)}$ also represents the set of road segments included in $P_{(s,d)}$. Namely, $B_{(s,d)}$ is the shortest path from s to d in G that is edge-disjoint to $P_{(s,d)}$. For route P, $w(P)$ is the weight of P defined as the sum of the weights of all road segments included in P, i.e., $w(P) = \Sigma_{r \in P} w(r)$. $C_{(s,d)}^{diff}$ represents the difference in weight between the shortest path and the detour path from s to d, where $C_{(s,d)}^{diff} = w(B_{(s,d)}) - w(P_{(s,d)})$.

V is a set of vehicles existing in the road network. V_{len}^{avg} is the average vehicle length, and g_{min} is the minimum distance between two vehicles. For road segment r, len_r is the segment length and $lane_r$ is the number of lanes, and n_r^t is the number of vehicles on road r at time t. The vehicle density of r at time t is expressed as follows

$$K_r^t = \frac{n_r^t}{len_r}. \tag{1}$$

The maximum number of vehicles that can exist on r is $n_r^{max} = \frac{len_r}{V_{len}^{avg} + g_{min}} \times lane_r$. The maximum vehicle density of r is given as

$$K_r^{max} = \frac{n_r^{max}}{len_r}. \tag{2}$$

At time t, when the ratio of vehicle density to the maximum vehicle density of road r exceeds a predefined threshold δ, i.e., $\frac{K_r^t}{K_r^{max}} \geq \delta$, r is regarded as congested road.

The traffic volume on road r is defined as the number of vehicles passing r per unit time as follows

$$F_r^t = \nu_r^t \times K_r^t, \tag{3}$$

where ν_r^t represents the average speed of vehicles on road segment r at time t.

In this study, the state where no traffic congestion occurs is called the steady-state. ν_r^{std} represents the vehicle speed on the road segment r in the steady-state. The traffic capacity of road segment r is defined as

$$F_r^{cap} = \nu_r^{std} \times \delta K_r^{max}. \tag{4}$$

$F_r^{cap} - F_r^t$ is called the allowable traffic volume of r.

Assume that, at time t, the shortest path $P_{(s,d)}$ from intersection $s \in S$ to $d \in D$ passes through road segment r, and the congestion is detected at r. If we consider to guide vehicles that travels from s to d to bypass on $B_{(s,d)}$, the allowable traffic volume for $B_{(s,d)}$ is defined as

$$A_{(s,d)}^t = \min_{r \in B_{(s,d)}} (F_r^{cap} - F_r^t). \tag{5}$$

Therefore, we can guide the vehicles heading for the intersection d at the intersection s to the detour route $B_{(s,d)}$ up to the upper limit $A_{(s,d)}^t$.

3.2   Reroute Planning

Measuring Traffic Volume in Steady State. The digital road map of the target area is obtained in advance, i.e., we can obtain not only $G = (I, R)$ but also the road length len_r and the number of lanes $lane_r$ on each road $r \in R$. It is assumed that the traffic condition is always measured by RSUs installed beside the roads, i.e., RSUs can obtain the average vehicle speed ν_r^t, the number of vehicles n_t^r and traffic volume F_r^t on each road segment r at any time t. It is also assumed that each vehicle has original route given by its own VNS and the route is transmitted to the server through RSUs.

The steady state represents the state in which vehicles are traveling stably without congestion. Assuming that a certain time t is the steady state, the number of vehicles on each road n_{std}^r, travel speed v_{std}^r, and traffic volume F_{std}^r at that time can be measured by RSU. In this study, the steady state is used as the goal state to reduce the traffic volume on the road when it is congested, and to estimate the allowable additional traffic volume on each road in detour route. Surely, in reality, the road traffic condition differs depending on the time. However, under the condition that there is no traffic jam, it is recommended to obtain each value of the steady state by measuring the road traffic during the relatively congested of the day and the road traffic state updated at regular intervals.

Rerouting Table. The rerouting table essentially represents the priority of intersections to apply route guidance, and is calculated based on the steady-state

Table 1. Rerouting table

Priority $L_{(s,d)}$	Source intersection $s \in S$	Destination intersection $d \in D$	Arrival delay $C_{(s,d)}^{diff}[min]$	Traffic volume guided $E_{(s,d)}[/min]$	Cumulative $X_{(s,d)}[/min]$
1	s_1	d_1	3	26	26
2	s_2	d_2	3	28	54
3	s_1	d_2	6	25	79
4	s_3	d_1	8	21	100
5	s_1	d_3	8	34	134
6	s_4	d_2	9	31	165
7	s_3	d_4	11	14	179
:	:	:	:	:	:
:	:	:	:	:	:
j-1	s_7	d_{12}	31	$E_{(s_7,d_{12})}$	$X_{(s_7,d_{12})}$
j	s_{14}	d_5	33	$E_{(s_{14},d_5)}$	$X_{(s_{14},d_5)}$
:	:	:	:	:	:

traffic volume when traffic congestion on road segment r is detected. As shown in Table 1, rerouting table consists of priority $L_{(s,d)}$, source intersections $s \in S$, destination intersections $d \in D$, arrival delay $C_{(s,d)}^{diff}$, traffic volume to guide $E_{(s,d)}$, and $X_{(s,d)}$ where $X_{(s,d)}$ is the cumulative value of $E_{(s,d)}$. The priority $L_{(s,d)}$ is a positive integer sequentially assigned in the ascending order of $C_{(s,d)}^{diff}$. We also write $L_{(s,d)}$ as L_u where u is a pair of intersections $s \in S$ and $d \in D$. Similarly, we also write the traffic volume to guide as $E_u (= E_{(s,d)})$, and the cumulative value of E_u as $X_u (= X_{(s,d)})$. X_u is the sum of $E_{u'}$ for all intersection pairs u' whose priority is L_u or less.

When congestion on road segment r is detected at time t, we reduce the traffic volume injecting to road r to eliminate the traffic congestion on road r. The traffic volume required to reduce traffic congestion is expressed as follows

$$F_r^{exc} = F_r^{std} - F_r^t. \qquad (6)$$

Where F_r^{std} is the traffic volume on road r in steady-state, F_r^t is the traffic volume on road r at time t. We consider that the congestion will be resolved by guiding vehicles passing through the road r to the detour path by βF_r^{exc}, where β is the congestion expansion factor $\beta \geq 1$ introduced to take into consideration the expansion of congestion in near future.

In order to mitigate the congestion on road r, the pairs of intersections (s, d) to apply guidance are selected in the ascending order of priority in the rerouting table. The criteria to select the intersection pairs to apply in the rerouting table is as follows

$$\alpha X_u \geq \beta F_r^{exc}, \qquad (7)$$

where α is the probability of guided vehicles to follow route guidance. If the cumulative value of traffic that avoid r (i.e., αX_u) exceeds the traffic volume to be reduced (i.e., βF_r^{exc}), the congestion on road r will be eliminated before long. If the minimum value of the priority that fulfills Eq. (7) is j (remember that j determines X_u), route guidance with the priority less than or equal to j is applied to guide vehicles.

For instance, assume that $F_r^{exc} = 85$, $\alpha = 0.7$, $\beta = 1.3$. If route guidance is applied up to the sixth line in Table 1 (i.e., $j = 6$), $\alpha X_u = 115.5$ vehicles per unit time will change their paths to avoid the congested road r. Since the traffic volume that will avoid r exceeds $\beta F_r^{exc} = 110.5$, the congestion will be eliminated by the route guidance with these six intersection pairs.

Constructing Rerouting Table. The rerouting table is constructed by the following procedure, where U^{all} is the set of all the intersection pairs in the target area.

(1) The pair of intersections $u = (s, d) \in U^{all}$ is extracted in the ascending order of C_u^{diff}.
(2) If $r \notin P_u$, skip u and proceed to the next pair of intersections.
(3) If there is an intersection pair $u' = (x, d)$ in the rerouting table where $P_u \subset P_{u'}$, skip u and proceed to the next intersection pair.
(4) The allowable traffic volume A_u for the detour path in the steady state is set to the guiding traffic volume E_u (i.e., $E_u = A_u$), and add the corresponding entry to the rerouting table. (L is incremented by one every time an entry is added.)
(5) We update $A_{u'}$ for all $u' \in U$ with the values assuming that the traffic volume E_u is bypassed for u. If the detour traffic volume E_u is $E_u = 0$, proceed to the next pair of intersections without adding the entry for intersection pair u to the rerouting table.

In steps (1) and (2), all intersection pairs included in U^{all} are looped in the increasing order of C_u^{diff}.

Step (3) is a process to avoid guiding a single vehicle multiple times. Suppose two intersection pairs with the same destination $u_1 = (s_1, d)$ and $u_2 = (s_2, d)$. Then, assume P_{u_1} is included in P_{u_2} (i.e., $P_{u_1} \subset P_{u_2}$). (Here, note that P_{u_1} and P_{u_2} are the shortest paths between two intersections, so that they are either completely edge disjoint, or one is included in the other.) In this case, if $C_{u_2}^{diff} > C_{u_1}^{diff}$, the vehicle guided with u_2 at s_2 is again guided with u_1 at s_1. If planning the detour at intersection s_2, the traffic volume flowing into intersection s_1 will change. Then, the detour at intersection s_2 is contradictory the traffic volume flowing into intersection s_1. Therefore, in this case, route guidance for u_2 is not applied. As a result, the intersection pair u_2, which has the same destination as the intersection pairs u_1 with the smallest arrival delay (i.e., $C_{u_1}^{diff}$), is not included in the rerouting table.

In step (4), for each pair of intersections, the traffic volume to guide the detour path is determined based on the road capacity.

In step (5), since the traffic volume on each road changes as a result of route guidance, the allowable traffic volume for each intersection pair is updated. To update the allowable traffic volume in step (5), follow the procedure below.

(a) For each road segment $r' \in P_u$, subtract E_u from $F_{r'}^{std}$.
(b) For each road segment $r' \in B_u$, add E_u to $F_{r'}^{std}$.
(c) Update A_u^{std} for every intersection pair $u \in U^{all}$.

As shown in Step (5), our method does not provide route guidance when the traffic capacity of the detour route cannot be secured, in order to prevent congestion on the detour route. For severe congestion that cannot be solved only at the intersections where the traffic capacity of the detour route can be secured, the proposed method conducts the route guidance at them and allows the congestion to resolve naturally.

3.3   Rerouting Algorithm

This section describes the procedure for providing routes to vehicles based on the rerouting table created in Sect. 3.2. First, if congestion at road segment r is detected at time t, the current excessing traffic volume of road r is calculated, i.e., $F_r^{exc} = F_r^{std} - F_r^t$. Each vehicle has its own destination $d \in D$, and its own shortest path. The source intersection s and the destination intersection d are acquired from every vehicle v. At this time, it is assumed that the RSU can communicate with the vehicle at each intersection. After finding the intersection pair $u = (s, d)$ of each vehicle v, if the priority of u is equal to or less than j (j is the minimum value of the priority that fulfills Eq. (7)), the detour path B_u is provided to v for route guidance. The vehicles guided to the detour path are expected to change the route with probability α, and does not change with the probability $1 - \alpha$.

4   Evaluation

The purpose of the evaluation is to confirm that the proposed method can reduce the average travel time of the rerouted vehicles compared to conventional methods, and alleviate the traffic congestion. As a scenario, we regulate traffic on a road segment at a certain time t in the steady state to invoke traffic congestion. After that, using our method, we reduce the number of vehicles heading to the congested road by applying the route guidance and evaluate the efficiency in relieving the congestion. The performance of our method is compared with the case of no route guidance, and with the route guidance methods DSP, RkSP, EBkSP, FBkSP and AR* used in [7]. We believe these are the most representative methods in this field of study. The criteria for evaluation are the average travel time of the vehicles to which route guidance are applied, and the number of guided vehicles. The details of the evaluation are described as follows. We show the evaluation method in Sect. 4.1 and the evaluation results in Sect. 4.2.

4.1   Method

We use the well-known traffic flow simulator SUMO (Simulation for Urban MObility) [14] for evaluation. SUMO is a simulator widely used in the field of ITS

(Intelligent Transportation System). A mobility model that considers collisions with other vehicles and traffic signals is implemented, and realistic mobility can be generated. We obtained the road map of Osaka city from OpenStreetMap [15] for a real road network. From the map, small roads were removed to extract the main roads in order to avoid small or narrow roads to be used in route guidance.

As a result of the preprocessing, the road network has 66 intersections and 241 road segments connected to the intersections. Traffic signal is installed at every intersection and the time for one cycle of the signal is set to 120 s. Each vehicle has the departing point and the destination point as the edge of the road network. Vehicles are generated at regular time interval. The traffic volume is defined based on a official survey [16]. In [16], the traffic volume per 12 h for each road is described, and the traffic volume in the simulation is determined based on the values. The total number of vehicles generated within the simulation time was 21607. In addition, since the traffic volume for each destination is not described in [16], the traffic volume from the source to the destination is fairly defined as the following steps.

(1) For each source point $s \in S$, the traffic volume $T_d(d \in D)$ for all destination intersections and its total sum $\Sigma_{d \in D} T_d$ are calculated.
(2) The traffic volume ratio $p_{(s,d)}$ from each source point $s \in S$ to all destinations $d \in D$ is calculated from (1). Specifically, $p_{(s,d)} = \frac{T_d}{\Sigma T_d}$.
(3) The traffic volume to each destination $T_{(s,d)}$ is calculated by using the traffic volume at the intersection of source point $T_s(s \in S)$ and the ratio $p_{(s,d)}$. Specifically, $T_{(s,d)} = T_s \times p_{(s,d)}$.

In order to calculate the traffic volume in steady-state, we performed a preliminary simulation with SUMO using the above traffic volume. The simulation time for calculating the steady-state traffic volume was 10800 s. After calculating the traffic volume in the steady state, we set a cause of traffic congestion at a road segment to evaluate our method. The simulation time was 10800 s. The congested road is chosen from one of the most crowded roads in the steady state. To invoke congestion, we restricted 1 out of 3 lanes at the road. The time at which this traffic control was applied was 4200 s past from the beginning time of the simulation. To control the traffic, we use TraCI (Traffic Control Interface) [17]. TraCI allows traffic management in cooperation with SUMO in run-time during simulation. Moreover, it provides access and control simulation objects, and enables us to change their behavior. The time interval for detecting congestion is 300 s, the threshold δ for determining whether a road is congested or not is 0.7. The ratio of drivers following route guidance was set to $\alpha = 0.7$, and the traffic congestion expansion factor was set to $\beta = 1.3$. We summarize the simulation settings as shown in Table 2.

4.2   Result

First, we show the results of preliminary results in Fig. 2(a)(b). In this evaluation, we determine the parameters k and L of the conventional methods to apply in

Table 2. Simulation setting

Item	Description
Simulator	SUMO
Target area	Osaka city (only main roads)
Simulation time	10800 s
The time for one cycle of signal	120 s
Maximum speed of vehicle	60 km/h
Total number of vehicles	21607
Time interval for detecting congestion	300 s
Time to start traffic regulation	4200 s
δ	0.7
α	0.7
β	1.3

the main comparison, where k is the number of paths computed in k-shortest paths computation, and l is the maximum distance of vehicles from the congested road to apply route guidance. The distance between two road segments is defined as the number of road segments to reach, so distance between the neighboring roads are 1. Namely, if $L = 1$, only vehicles on the road neighboring the congested road are guided for the detour routes in the conventional methods. In Fig. 2(a), we show the results in which L is varied while k is fixed with 2. For all the conventional methods, $L = 3$ marks the best performance. This is because of the trade-off where small L would provide inefficient detour path whereas large L would invoke redundant detouring of vehicles. In Fig. 2(b), we show the results

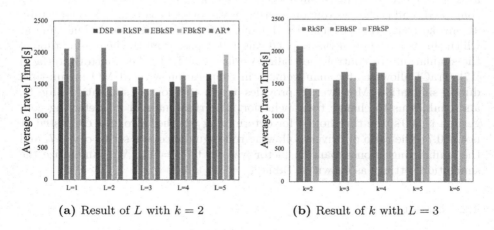

(a) Result of L with $k = 2$ (b) Result of k with $L = 3$

Fig. 2. Results of preliminary evaluation

with several values of k under $L = 3$, which shows that $k = 2$ is the best for conventional methods. Note that DSP and AR* do not appear here because DSP and AR* do not have parameter k. This is because too many paths enforce vehicles to use less quality paths. From the results, we set $k = 2$ and $L = 3$ for the conventional methods in the main evaluation.

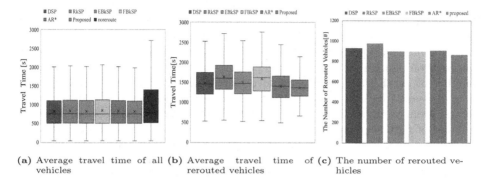

(a) Average travel time of all vehicles   (b) Average travel time of rerouted vehicles   (c) The number of rerouted vehicles

Fig. 3. Evaluation results

In Fig. 3(a) shows the travel time of all vehicles in the main simulation. Here, *noreroute* is the case where no route guidance methods are applied. We see that all guidance methods are far better than *noreroute* case, meaning that route guidance methods work effectively to mitigate traffic congestion. Next, in Fig. 3(b), we see the travel time of the rerouted vehicles only. We see that the average travel time of proposed method has the best performance among those four. Specifically, since the average travel time of steady-state results is about 800 s, the rerouted vehicle in the proposed method takes about 550 s in addition to the usual travel time in the steady state. In contrast, DSP, EBkSP and FBkSP takes additional 700–800 s, AR* takes additional 650 s, and RkSP takes additional 850 s. Furthermore, the variation of the travel time is the smallest in the proposed method. In Fig. 3(c), we see that the number of rerouted vehicles are almost the same among those four methods (rather, the proposed method is slightly smaller than the others). Note that 800 vehicles are about 4% of all vehicles appeared in the simulation. Consequently, we now see that the total traveling time of all rerouting vehicles are the smallest in the proposed method. From above, we conclude that the proposed method outperforms the conventional methods.

5 Discussion

The evaluation results show that the proposed method can reduce the travel time compared to the other methods. In the literature [7], which proposed a comparison method, the evaluation was also conducted from the viewpoint of computational complexity. However, we did not evaluate the computation time. The reason is that the assumptions of the proposed method and the comparison method are different, so the computation time cannot be compared. In addition, considering the practical aspect, we judged that the computation cost is not an issue. In [7], it is assumed that the calculation of routes is performed for each vehicle. On the other hand, in the proposed method, the detour is calculated not for each vehicle but for each intersection. In other words, the unit of calculation is different, so simple comparison is not possible. Our method assumes that the rerouting table is calculated on a central server in the cloud. In this way, When the computation is performed at the central server, the route calculation for each intersection pair can be performed in parallel, so it is considered that a sufficient number of parallel computers should be available for actual operation. For the map of Osaka City used in the evaluation, we performed route calculations for all intersection pairs using the Dijkstra algorithm 241 times, corresponding to the number of road segments connected to the intersection. Then the computation time was about 3 s on a desktop PC equipped with an 8th generation Intel i5.

From the evaluation, we showed that the proposed method can be applied to solve a single traffic jam. However, the proposed method cannot deal with multiple congestion occurring at the same time. Therefore, it is necessary to develop the method to solve multiple congestion problems simultaneously in the future. On the other hand, we believe that it is also important to deal with a single traffic jam. For example, our method can be applied to traffic jams caused by accidents. By expanding the target area, the possibility of accidents occurring simultaneously in multiple locations increases, but it is not very high. Also, if the number of vehicles traveling in a particular area increases, the possibility of multiple congestion occurring at the same time increases. However, if another traffic jam occurs as a result of vehicles in the surrounding area changing their routes in response to the first traffic jam, it is thought that solving the original traffic jam first will result in the gradual resolution of the traffic jams derived from it. In summary, while it is important to consider ways to solve multiple congestion problems at the same time, there are situations in which methods that address a single congestion problem can be effective.

6   Conclusion

In this paper, we proposed a route guidance method that are aware of the arrival delay to the destinations when vehicles bypass a congested road. Specifically, for each intersection, we care the difference in travel time between the shortest path and the detour path. The intersection pair with the smaller difference between the primary shortest path and the detour path is given the priority in applying route guidance. This enables us to reduce traffic congestion while suppressing the arrival delay to the destinations. In this study, we evaluated the efficiency of the proposed method to alleviate a congestion when it occurred in a part of the target area. We compared the proposed method with the no-reroute guidance case and the conventional methods. As a result, it was clarified that the proposed method reduces the average travel time of all vehicles that followed route guidance. Additionally, compared to the conventional methods whose parameters k and l should be optimally determined in advance, the proposed method does not need for this calibration to mark the best performance. From the above, we showed that our method is useful in the situation where a road is congested due to a sudden accident, and outperforms the conventional methods. Extensive evaluation in various scenarios would be one of the important future work.

References

1. Ministry of Land, Infrastructure, Transport and Tourism HP. https://www.mlit.go.jp/road/index.html. Accessed 1 June 2021
2. International Transport Forum: reducing transport greenhouse gas emissions: trends and data 2010, International Transport Forum (2010)
3. Schrank, D., Eisele, B., Lomax, T.: 2019 urban mobility report, Texas A&M Transportation Institute (2019)
4. Wang, J., Hu, M., Xu, C., Christakos, G., Zhao, Y.: Estimation of citywide air pollution in Beijing. PLoS One 8(1), e53400 (2013)
5. Sparmann, J.M.: Benefits of dynamic route guidance systems as part of a future oriented city traffic management system. In: Vehicle Navigation and Information Systems Conference (1991)
6. Souza, A.M.D., Yokoyama, R.S., Maia, G., Loureiro, A., Villas, L.: Real-time path planning to prevent traffic jam through an intelligent transportation system. In: IEEE Symposium on Computers and Communication, vol. 1, pp. 726–731 (2016)
7. Pan, J., Popa, I.S., Zeitouni, K., Borcea, C.: Proactive vehicular traffic re-routing for lower travel time. IEEE Trans. Veh. Technol. 62(8), 3551–3568 (2013)
8. Wang, S., Djahel, S., Zhang, Z., McManis, J.: Next Road Rerouting (NRR): a multi-agent system for mitigating unexpected urban traffic congestion. IEEE Trans. Intell. Transp. Syst. 17(10), 2888–2899 (2016)
9. http://www.google.com/mobile/
10. http://www.tomtom.com/en_gb/products/mobile-navigation/
11. Lin, C., Choy, K.L., Ho, G.T.S., Chung, S.H., Lam, H.Y.: Survey of green vehicle routing problem: past and future trends. Expert Syst. Appl. 41, 1118–1138 (2014)
12. Sims, A.G., Dobinson, K.W.: The Sydney coordinated adaptive traffic (SCAT) system philosophy and benefits. IEEE Trans. Veh. Technol. 29(2), 130–137 (1980)
13. Tsugawa, S., Aoki, M., Hosaka, A., Seki, K.: A survey of present IVHS activities in Japan. Control Eng. Pract. 5, 1591–1597 (1997)
14. Behrisch, M., Bieker, L., Erdmann, J., Krajzewicz, D.: SUMO-simulation of urban mobility an overview. In: International Conference on Advances in System Simulation, pp. 63–68 (2011)
15. OpenStreetMap. https://www.openstreetmap.org/. Accessed 1 June 2021
16. Survey of national road and street traffic situation (road traffic census) in 2015. https://www.mlit.go.jp/road/census/h27/. Accessed 1 June 2021
17. Wegener, A., Piorkowski, M., Raya, M., Hellbruck, H., Fischer, S., Hubaux, J.P.: TraCI: an interface for coupling road traffic and network simulators. In: Processing of the 11th Communications and Networking Simulation Symposium, pp. 155–163 (2008)

A Localization Method Using Reflected Luminance Distribution

Yoshihiro Yamashita[1(✉)], Shota Shimada[1], Hiromichi Hashizume[2],
Hiroki Watanabe[1], and Masanori Sugimoto[1]

[1] Hokkaido University, Sapporo, Japan
{yamash.lab,hiroki.watanabe,sugi}@ist.hokudai.ac.jp,
shimadas@frontier.hokudai.ac.jp
[2] National Institute of Informatics, Tokyo, Japan
has@nii.ac.jp

Abstract. Visible light positioning is expected to become an effective means of indoor localization, but most existing methods require the capture of direct light, which is a significant limitation. In this paper, we propose a novel localization method based on received signal strength, which does not need to use direct light signals but instead uses reflected light from the floor. Our method is based on two observations. First, assuming a flat floor, the reflected light from the light source decays according to a gradient model whose peak is just below the light source. Second, the decay can be estimated effectively even for a floor surface several meters away from the light source. Inspired by these observations, we propose a method for estimating the coordinates of the floor surface and the two-dimensional coordinates of the light receiver (a camera). The method uses pattern matching within the distribution of signal decay measurements obtained via photographs of an arbitrary floor surface. Although the proposed method is vulnerable to shadow effects such as those caused by the camera tripod used in our experiments, we achieved a 90th percentile of less than 32 cm in our offline experiments. After removing the tripod shadows from the captured video manually, the same technique achieved a 90th percentile of 22 cm. To investigate the efficiency of the pattern matching, we also conducted experiments on the relationship between pixel utilization and localization results. In this paper, we also discuss camera posture estimation and power consumption issues.

Keywords: Visible light positioning · Received signal strength (RSS) · Indoor positioning · Non-line of sight (NLoS)

1 Introduction

Indoor localization technology is exerting a major impact on human activities, in the same way that the Global Positioning System [8] revolutionized outdoor

© ICST Institute for Computer Sciences, Social Informatics and Telecommunications Engineering 2022
Published by Springer Nature Switzerland AG 2022. All Rights Reserved
T. Hara and H. Yamaguchi (Eds.): MobiQuitous 2021, LNICST 419, pp. 390–405, 2022.
https://doi.org/10.1007/978-3-030-94822-1_21

navigation. In 2020, indoor localization and indoor navigation technology generated \$12 million dollars in revenue in the United States (US) and is predicted to reach US\$35 million by 2026 [6]. However, even after decades of research, a simple and robust indoor localization solution is yet to be found [9,12,14,22]. Visible light positioning (VLP) [10,11] has recently been attracting attention because of the widespread use and low price of devices based on light-emitting diodes (LEDs). VLP systems have shown some promise for indoor positioning [7] but the unwieldy nature of cameras causes problems in realistic environments. There are three main challenges.

Limited Coverage of the System. Most methods require line-of-sight (LoS) signals from several LEDs simultaneously, requiring either dense or extremely dense arrangements of LEDs or coverage only in some places.

Difficulty of Capturing Multiple LED Signals. Even inside the coverage area of the system, the user will be forced to move the camera in unnatural ways, particularly if the ceiling is low.

Necessity of High-resolution Imaging. Most existing methods use a high-resolution image to detect light sources directly, which is both power hungry and computationally demanding. Note that this problem would remain an issue in implementing real-time positioning systems in the future.

In this paper, we propose an RSS-based method that does not require direct light, and instead captures reflected light from the floor surface to enable localization. The method identifies each of multiple LEDs installed on the ceiling by performing a discrete Fourier transform (DFT) on the reflected signal and using the modulation frequency as the LED's identity (ID). Normally, positioning using only reflected light would suffer from reduced accuracy because of the decrease in signal-to-noise ratio. Therefore, we aim to maintain high positioning accuracy by adopting pattern matching between the measured decay distribution of luminance values and an ideal distribution.

This paper also addresses the following two issues. First, we found experimentally that the positioning accuracy of our method is sensitive to shadows and that it is difficult to capture signals from the floor without shadows. As the percentage of shadowing in the field of view increases, the positioning accuracy decreases, with positioning becoming almost impossible if the shadows occupy more than half of the field of view. Moreover, if the photographer or camera moves, the shadows also move, making it difficult to remove the shadow from the field of view. Unfortunately, we could not eliminate the shadow effects in real time; instead, we removed the shadow manually offline and compared the accuracy with that before removal. Second, our method uses the entire screen and takes a long time to process, so positioning could not be done in real time. To address this, we investigated the relationship between positioning accuracy and the number of screen pixels used.

We implemented our proposed system and evaluated it in a 3.5-m square room with four LEDs on the ceiling. We estimated the position of each of 64 points (8×8 points) on the floor 100 times. The resulting accuracy was 0.32 m

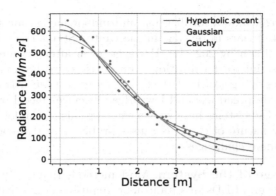

Fig. 1. Experimentally obtained values and distance decay models (Gaussian, hyperbolic secant, Cauchy).

at the 90th percentile, without compensating for shadow effects from the camera tripod. We then applied the offline manual shadow removal method to the same data, achieving an accuracy of 0.22 m at the 90th percentile. Next, we tested the effect of the method on positioning accuracy by reducing the number of pixels used for positioning at two locations with relatively low shadow effects and high positioning accuracy. At one location, we achieved 90th percentile positioning accuracies of 2.2 cm, 4.9 cm, and 48 cm using 1,228,800 pixels, 6,144 pixels, and 1,024 pixels, respectively. From the results of these experiments, we can assess the potential and limiting factors of the proposed method.

The contributions of this paper are summarized below.

- We have proposed a new positioning method using pattern matching and reflected light from the floor.
- We implemented a prototype of the proposed method, which achieved sub-meter positioning accuracy.
- We investigated the effects of shadows on the positioning accuracy and the trade-off between the number of pixels used and positioning accuracy.

2   Luminance Distribution Across the Floor

In this section, we describe the preliminary research we conducted prior to developing the proposed method. Our method is based on two observations.

The first is that, assuming a flat floor, the reflected light decays according to a gradient model whose peak is just below the LED. Shimada et al. [18] found that the decay of the reflected light on a Lambertian floor surface can be approximated by the hyperbolic secant distribution of the two-dimensional (2D) distance d_k between the floor surface and the kth LED. The RSS received by the camera from the kth LED is

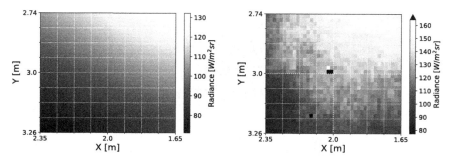

(a) Distribution of luminance from LED1 obtained by simulation.

(b) Distribution of luminance from LED1 obtained experimentally. Black blocks represent outliers.

Fig. 2. Comparison of experimental data and data obtained by simulation.

$$RSS_k = \frac{C_k}{e^{\frac{\pi}{2}\sigma_k d_k} + e^{-\frac{\pi}{2}\sigma_k d_k}},\tag{1}$$

where C_k and σ_k are parameters. Figure 1 shows the decay for the hyperbolic secant distribution, Gaussian distribution and Cauchy distribution obtained from the actual data using regression analysis. Note that the amplitude of the signal spectrum decreases as the 2D distance from the LED increases.

Second, the decay of the luminance of the reflected light on the floor can be observed even at a distance of several meters from the point directly under the LED. Figure 2a shows the heat map of the luminance values from LED1 at point $(1.0, 0.5)$, obtained via simulation using video data at 1280×980-pixel resolution with a lens height of 90 cm above the point $(2.0, 3.0)$. The data obtained in our laboratory with the same LED and camera configuration is shown in Fig. 2b. The actual data shows a luminance distribution close to the simulation, indicating that it is possible to estimate the camera coordinates using pattern matching.

Based on these two observations, we propose the new positioning method using floor reflection and pattern matching described in Sect. 3.3.

3   Proposed Method

In our method, signals are received from multiple LEDs installed on the ceiling as shown in Fig. 3. Normally, when multiple LEDs emit light at the same time, the signals overlap on the floor, making RSS detection impossible. To address this, each LED is modulated with a unique carrier frequency, and the RSS is detected by analysis in the frequency domain, using the carrier frequency as the location identity. The LEDs need to be modulated at a high enough frequency that the human eye does not experience flickering. We 100 Hz or higher (denoted F_{100}) as the carrier frequency, because ordinary fluorescent lamps oscillate at a frequency 100 Hz or higher [19]. Section 3.1 explains frequency aliasing and

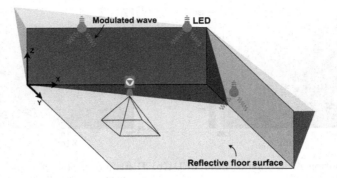

Fig. 3. Overview of the proposed method.

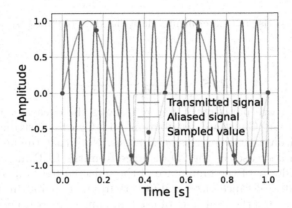

Fig. 4. The 2-Hz aliased signal obtained by sampling a 14-Hz signal 6 Hz.

gives the equation used to find the aliased frequency. In Sect. 3.2, we investigate the relationship between the RSS obtained by analyzing the carrier frequency and the distance from the LED. Section 3.3 estimates the 2D coordinates of an arbitrary point on the floor using pattern matching and the relational equation obtained in Sect. 3.2.

3.1   Frequency Aliasing

The VLP system uses signals modulated at F_{100} to enable identification of each transmitting LED. However, we know from the sampling theorem [16] that we cannot decode the signal accurately because we use a camera with a frequency 50 Hz in our experiment. If the modulated signal is sampled at a frequency below the Nyquist frequency, the aliased frequency obtained via DFT is given by

$$f_a = Min(f_o \bmod f_s, f_s - f_o \bmod f_s), \tag{2}$$

where f_a is the aliased frequency, f_o is the frequency of the transmitted signal, and f_s is the sampling frequency. For example, as shown in Fig. 4, if 14 Hz signal is sampled at a sampling frequency 6 Hz, the aliased frequency f_a is

$$f_a = Min(14 \bmod 6, 6 - 14 \bmod 6) = Min(2,4) = 2. \tag{3}$$

This shows that it is possible to identify $f_s/2 - 1$ LEDs, assuming that the aliased frequency of the carrier frequency assigned to each LED is known.

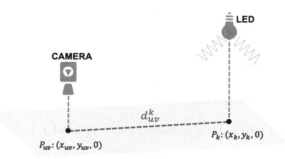

Fig. 5. Two-dimensional distance between camera and LED

3.2 Relationship Between Distance and RSS

Consider the 2D coordinates of the image sensor. Let (u, v) be a randomly selected image sensor, and let $P_{u,v}$ be the point on the floor corresponding to image sensor (u, v). Let P_k be the intersection point between the vertical line down from the kth LED and the floor surface, and let $d_{u,v}^k$ be the 2D distance between $P_{u,v}$ and P_k, as shown in Fig. 5. The $RSS_{u,v}$ value, which is obtained from the image sensor (u, v) using aliasing, decays according to the distance $d_{u,v}^k$. In this section, we develop the relationship between $RSS_{u,v}$ and $d_{u,v}^k$.

The signal emitted by the kth LED at time t can be expressed as follows.

$$b_k(t) = \sin(2\pi t f_k) + \alpha, \tag{4}$$

where α is the DC component keeping $b_k(t)$ always positive and f_k is the carrier frequency assigned to the kth LED. Assuming that the frame rate of the camera is f_c and the exposure time ratio is η, the shutter cycle is $T_c = 1/f_c$, the exposure time is ηT_c, and the time to start capturing the nth image is nT_c. The luminance value $I_{u,v}^n$ received by the image sensor (u, v) when capturing the nth image is

$$I_{u,v}^n = \sum_k \frac{2\pi X(d_{u,v}^k)}{T_c} \int_0^{\eta T_c} b_k(t + \delta T_c + nT_c)dt, \tag{5}$$

where δ denotes the delay in shutter timing relative to the signal and $X(d_{u,v}^k)$ is the decay function of the luminance value. Note that $X(d_{u,v}^k)$ is affected both by the distance $d_{u,v}^k$ and the transfer efficiency between the kth LED and the camera.

The camera captures N $(= f_c)$ images per second. The DFT of the video stream $\mathbf{I_{u,v}} = (I_{u,v}^0, I_{u,v}^1, ..., I_{u,v}^{N-1})$ at pixel (u, v) is

$$B_{u,v}^l = \frac{1}{N} \sum_{n=0}^{N-1} I_{u,v}^n e^{\frac{-j2\pi nl}{N}}. \tag{6}$$

Assuming that $\beta_{l,k}$ is obtained by the DFT of $b_k(t)$, $B_{u,v}^l$ is given by

$$B_{u,v}^l = \eta X(d_{u,v}^k) e^{j\pi f_k(2\delta+\eta)} \mathrm{sinc}\,(\pi f_k \eta)\, \beta_{l,k}. \tag{7}$$

By fixing the exposure time ratio to the intrinsic value $\eta = \eta_0$ and using the aliased frequency determined by

$$m_k = Min(f_k \bmod f_c, f_c - f_k \bmod f_c)., \tag{8}$$

we can focus on the decay of the amplitude at $l = m_k$. Under these conditions, the amplitude spectrum $|B_{u,v}^{m_k}|$ is affected only by the decay function $X(d_{u,v}^k)$. This amplitude spectrum (denoted by $RSS_{u,v,k}$) is then given by

$$\begin{aligned} RSS_{u,v,k} &= |B_{u,v}^{m_k}| \\ &= \eta_0 X(d_{u,v}^k)\mathrm{sinc}\,(\pi f_k \eta_0)\, |\beta_{m_k,k}|. \end{aligned} \tag{9}$$

It is difficult to specify an exact model of the luminance decay $X(d_{u,v}^k)$ because the floor is not an ideal Lambert surface [23]. Shimada et al. [18] have shown that $X(d_{u,v}^k)$ can be approximated using a hyperbolic secant distribution, as follows.

$$X(d_{u,v}^k) = \frac{C_k}{e^{\frac{\pi}{2}\sigma_k d_{u,v}^k} + e^{-\frac{\pi}{2}\sigma_k d_{u,v}^k}}, \tag{10}$$

where C_k and σ_k are parameters. Therefore, $RSS_{u,v,k}$ can be approximated as

$$RSS_{u,v,k} = \frac{C_k'}{e^{\frac{\pi}{2}\sigma_k d_{u,v}^k} + e^{-\frac{\pi}{2}\sigma_k d_{u,v}^k}}, \tag{11}$$

where $C_k' = \eta_0 C_k \mathrm{sinc}\,(\pi f_k \eta_0)\, |\beta_{m_k,k}|$.

3.3   Pattern Matching

In Sect. 3.2, it was found that the RSS corresponding to an arbitrary image sensor can be calculated as in (11). In this section, we describe a pattern matching process that uses the difference between the calculated RSS and the ideal distribution of luminance. Assuming that the image sensor located at the center of the screen $(0, 0)$ captures the corresponding floor surface (x, y), the floor-surface position corresponding to the image sensor (u, v) is $(x + W_x u, y + W_y v)$. W_x and W_y are the pixel pitches (i.e., distance between two points on the floor corresponding to a pair of adjacent pixels) in the horizontal and vertical directions, respectively. All pixel pitches can be approximated to the same value, with $W_x = W_y$ if the camera is assumed to be pointing downwards. If the coordinates of the kth LED are (x_k, y_k, z_k), the amplitude spectrum of the luminance of the floor corresponding to (u, v), calculated theoretically, is

$$RSS_{u,.v,k}^{theory} = \frac{C'}{e^{\frac{\pi}{2}\sigma d_{u,v}^k} + e^{-\frac{\pi}{2}\sigma d_{u,v}^k}}, \tag{12}$$

provided that

$$d_{u,v}^k = \sqrt{(x_k - x - W_x u)^2 + (y_k - y - W_y v)^2}. \tag{13}$$

Therefore, we can formulate the error function

$$e_{u,v,k} = RSS_{u,v,k}^{observed} - \frac{C'}{e^{\frac{\pi}{2}\sigma d_{u,v}^k} + e^{-\frac{\pi}{2}\sigma d_{u,v}^k}}, \tag{14}$$

where $RSS_{u,v,k}^{observed}$ is the RSS of the kth LED observed by the image sensor (u, v). Furthermore, we can formulate an equation J for the sum of squares of the error functions.

$$J = \sum_k \sum_{u,v} e_{u,v,k}^2. \tag{15}$$

If we consider J as an evaluation function, we can estimate the (x, y) position where J is minimized as the center of the screen. This problem can be thought of as an unconstrained nonlinear optimization problem, to which the Gauss–Newton method [13] can be applied.

4   Implementation Details

4.1   LED Transmitter

An overview of our experimental implementation is shown in Fig. 6. BXRE-50C4001-B-74-type LEDs from Bridgelux [1] were mounted on a heat sink and used as LED transmitters. Four LEDs were placed on the ceiling at a height of 2.6 m, and the coordinates of LED1, LED2, LED3, and LED4 were (1.0 m, 0.5 m, 2.6 m), (1.0 m, 3.0 m, 2.6 m), (3.2 m, 0.5 m, 2.6 m), and (3.2 m, 3.0 m, 2.6 m), respectively. This was the same arrangement as that of the fluorescent lamps originally installed in the building. Denoting f_k as the frequency of the signal emitted by LEDk, the respective frequencies for LED1, LED2, LED3, and LED4 101 Hz, 106 Hz, 113 Hz, 120 Hz, respectively. Because the frame rate f_c of the camera 50 Hz, the aliased frequencies were $m_k = (1\,\text{Hz}, 6\,\text{Hz}, 13\,\text{Hz}, 20\,\text{Hz})$,

Fig. 6. Overview of the implementation, including LEDs, function generator, and power supply

Fig. 7. Floor material in our conference room

respectively. Each LED emitted a sine wave generated by delta–sigma modulation of a pulse-width-modulated signal. A 5-V signal from a function generator (NF Corporation WF-1948) was amplified to 39.60 V using a power driver and power supply.

4.2   Camera Receiver

We used a Point Grey Flea3 FL3-U3-13S2C camera [4] as the receiver and used the software Flycapture SDK2 [2] to set the camera parameters. The shutter speed and ISO rating were set to avoid luminance saturation, and the frame rate f_c was set 50 Hz. Since the modulation frequency of fluorescent lamps in eastern Japan 100 Hz, this could be treated as a DC component.

4.3   Floor Material

We used the unmodified floor of our conference room, which was covered with 50-cm square nonfluorescent mats without gaps, as shown in Fig. 7. The mat

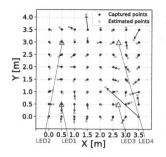 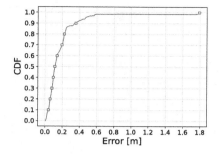

(a) Positioning-error map and LED place-ment. (b) Cumulative distribution function of positioning error.

Fig. 8. Map and cumulative distribution function of positioning error. (Color figure online)

surface texture had a linear grain, whose direction alternated between vertical and horizontal for adjacent mats. Because Shimada et al. [18] had shown that the color of the floor surface can affect the accuracy of positioning, we used gray mats, because gray is the color that was found to be the least affected by noise.

5   Experimental Evaluation

Our experiments to investigate the effectiveness of the proposed method were conducted in a 3.5×3.5-m room. For all experiments, the same 1280×960-pixel camera was used and the luminance values used were calculated from the average of 32×32 pixels. Because the parameters C_k and σ_k in (11) were different for each LED, calibration was performed for (x,y) = (1.0, 0.5), (1.0, 2.0), (2.0, 2.0), (3.0, 1.0), and (3.0, 3.0). During the experiments, it was found that shadows were having a significant impact on accuracy. We therefore repeated the calculations after removing shadows manually from the images, to confirm that the accuracy was improved. Finally, we examined the relationship between the number of pixels used and the positioning accuracy.

5.1   Estimation Using Captured Floor Signals

The images from the 1280×960-pixel image sensor were divided into 40×30 (=1200) blocks of 32×32 pixels, with a single luminance value being estimated as the average of the luminance values in each block. Because the distribution of luminance values can vary for each of the four LEDs, the Gauss–Newton method was applied to the total of $40 \times 30 \times 4 = 4,800$ blocks. The resulting solution was updated sequentially, until the solution converged to a point where the distance from the solution in the previous step was less than 0.001 (the "trough"). This was then considered the optimal solution. This process was performed at 64 points (8 points in the x-axis direction and 8 points in the y-axis direction),

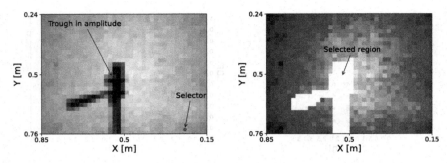

(a) Trough in amplitude and shadow selec-(b) Signal from removed part to be ignored
tor.   in estimation.

Fig. 9. An example of selecting trough in amplitude

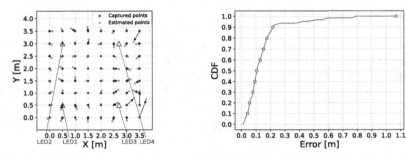

(a) Positioning error map after shadow re-(b) Cumulative distribution function of po-
moval and LED placement.   sitioning error after shadow removal.

Fig. 10. Map and cumulative distribution function of positioning error after shadow
removal.

with the error between the obtained optimal solution and the actual coordinates
being mapped in Fig. 8a. In this figure, the green triangles represent LEDs, the
blue circles represent the coordinates of the actual position, and the red circles
represent the average value of 100 positioning attempts.

In Fig. 8a, note that the central area, which is surrounded by LEDs, has
higher positioning accuracy than the outer areas. One reason for this is that
the positioning results are particularly susceptible to noise for the more remote
LEDs. We also found that shadows and other objects have a significant impact on
positioning accuracy. For example, the image at (1.5, 3.5) is about 30% covered
by shadows, and the image at (3.5, 0.0) is about 50% covered by a pillar, with
these two points having the worst overall positioning accuracy. The cumulative
distribution function (CDF) of the positioning error is shown in Fig. 8b. The
overall result of this experiment was to achieve a positioning error of 0.32 m at
the 90th percentile.

Table 1. Trade-off between the number of pixels used and the 90th percentile of positioning error.

	1200 blocks = 1,228,800	300 blocks = 307,200	48 blocks = 49,152	12 blocks = 12,288	6 blocks = 6,144	2 blocks = 2,048	1 blocks = 1,024
(**x, y**) = (1.5, 2.5)	0.026 [m]	0.028	0.027	0.04	0.049	0.084	0.655
(**x, y**) = (1.0, 2.0)	0.022 [m]	0.020	0.024	0.028	0.049	0.048	0.48

5.2 Estimation Using Captured Floor Signals After Shadow Removal

As mentioned above, shadows and objects greatly reduce the accuracy of positioning. Here, we describe reapplying the proposed method after manually removing the shadows and showing that the accuracy improved as a result.

When shadowing is present, some of the light from the LEDs is blocked and attenuated significantly, resulting in a trough in the amplitude of the luminance. Figure 9a shows the observed amplitude trough and the region selector used to exclude areas with troughs. The luminance values of the removed regions are masked as shown in Fig. 9b and are excluded when applying the Gauss–Newton method. The difference between the optimal solution and the actual coordinates obtained in this way is mapped in Fig. 10a. In this figure, note that the positioning results at the two points (1.5, 3.5) and (3.5, 0.0) were greatly improved. In addition, positioning in the neighborhood of an LED tended to improve the accuracy. This may be because positioning near the LED is more likely to be affected by the shadow of the camera tripod. The CDF of the positioning error is shown in Fig. 10b. As a result, a 90th percentile of 0.22 m was achieved, with the positioning accuracy being improved by nearly 0.1 m after shadow removal. This result confirms that the proposed method is sensitive to shadows and objects, but it also shows that the positioning accuracy can be improved substantially by shadow removal.

5.3 Effect of the Number of Blocks Used

Finally, we investigated the relationship between the number of pixels used and the positioning accuracy. In the previous experiments, the received image was divided into $30 \times 40 = 1200$ blocks. In this experiment, the number of blocks was reduced while maintaining the size of each block (32×32 pixels). The two locations, (1.5, 2.5) and (1.0, 2.0) were unaffected by shadows or objects and were selected for the experiment. Table 1 shows the 90th percentile of the positioning error when the number of pixels is reduced from 1,228,800 to 1,024. Although the positioning accuracy tends to decrease as the number of pixels used decreases, the 90th percentile of positioning error using two blocks remains within 10 cm. This shows that it is possible to implement a positioning system that can operate in real time by reducing the number of pixels used and the computational cost, if necessary.

6   Discussion

6.1   Estimation of Camera Posture

In our proposed method, we obtained the 2D coordinates of the camera without consideration of the camera posture. However, a theoretical analysis is possible for cases where the pitch angle of the camera is considered. In such cases, the camera's pitch angle θ can be varied freely while maintaining the level. The constraint in (13) is then

$$D_{u,v,\theta}^k = \sqrt{(x_k - X_{u,v}^\theta)^2 + (y_k - Y_{u,v}^\theta)^2}, \qquad (16)$$

where:

$$X_{u,v}^\theta = x + W_x u \cos\theta - W_y v \sin\theta \qquad (17)$$
$$Y_{u,v}^\theta = y + W_x u \sin\theta + W_y v \cos\theta. \qquad (18)$$

It should also be possible to include the roll and yaw angles in the calculation, but we would then not be able to use the approximation that all pitches have the same value and $W_x = W_y$. The specific mathematical formulas are omitted here because of the complexity of the calculations but, theoretically, it should be possible to estimate the camera's posture.

6.2   Power Consumption

The power consumption of the camera we used in our experiments was $3\,\mathrm{W}$. Although the full image-sensing capacity of the camera was used in the proposed method, sufficient positioning accuracy should be achieved even with a much smaller number of pixels, as described in Sect. 5.3. If only the necessary minimum of the image sensor capacity is activated and those signals are processed, the required power consumption can be reduced.

Table 2. Comparisons with proposed VLP method using LEDs

	RefRec	Luxapose	PIXEL	Rajagopal	STARLIT	Proposed
Accuracy	∼0.4 m	∼0.1 m	∼0.3 m	N/A	∼0.75 m	∼0.2 m
Reference	[17]	[10]	[21]	[15]	[20]	
Range [m]	4.0 × 4.0	1.0 × 1.0	2.4 × 1.8	3.9 × 8.0	7.0 × 10.0	3.5 × 3.5
Rolling shutter	No	Yes	No	Yes	Yes	No
Real time	Yes	No	Yes	No	Yes	No
LEDs	4	5	8	4	1	4
Resolution	32 × 32	7712 × 5360	120 × 160	1280 × 720	1080 × 1920	1280 × 960
LoS/NLoS	NLoS	LoS	LoS	NLoS	NLoS	NLoS

7   Related Work

Table 2 compares existing VLP methods with our proposed method. In this table, the term "Accuracy" refers to the 90th percentile of the positioning error. "Rolling shutter" refers to the rolling shutter effect in smartphones. (Customers often do not like the distortion of the image caused by the rolling shutter, which may disappear in the future [5].) "LoS/NLoS" (line of sight/non-line of sight) indicates whether the LED signals are assumed to be acquired directly (LoS) or indirectly (NLoS).

RefRec [17] also utilized floor-reflected light and uses only 32×32 pixels at the center of the screen. It is more sensitive to shadows and objects than our method, and less likely to be applied to camera posture estimation. RefRec achieved a 90th percentile error of 0.42 m in a 4.0×4.0-m conference room. We achieved better positioning accuracy since our method is more generalized. However, RefRec is able to perform real-time positioning.

Luxapose [10] can compute the position and posture of a smartphone by capturing ceiling light signals directly using a camera. The error is less than 10 cm and less than 3°. It uses 7712×5360 pixels in a WindowsPhone 8 smartphone camera as the receiver. The calculation requires a cloud server for high-quality image processing.

PIXEL [21] is a polarization-based localization method. Only 120×160 pixels are required. Measurements require several seconds, and the accuracy is 0.4 m. However, a polarizing filter must be attached to the camera, with the accompanying risk of impairing the original image.

Rajagopal's approach [15] uses light reflected from the floor. It is similar to our idea, but they focus on the rolling shutter distortion to receive the LED's ID from the reflected light. Carrier signals up to 8 kHz can be received with a channel separation 200 Hz. Tag information is transmitted by assigning ON and OFF bits to the different frequencies. The data rate is 10 bps, and up to 29 light sources can be uniquely separated. Positioning accuracy was not discussed in the paper because the research aimed at semantic positioning using differences in packet reception rates. Furthermore, because MATLAB [3] was used for calculation, processing was not in real time.

STARLIT [20] is a VLP system using floor reflections and utilizing RSS. To capture the ID tag from a single LED, the authors leverage the rolling shutter mechanism in a smartphone camera. STARLIT achieved an 80th percentile error of 55 cm in a 72-m^2 room and a response time of 0.87 s on average. They also noted that vertically spreading shadows can cause failures in positioning.

8   Conclusion and Future Work

VLP not only promises to play an active role in the future but is already expanding its use in a variety of fields. In this paper, we propose a new reflected-light-based positioning method using pattern matching across the entire image-capture screen. Using a prototype system, we achieved a 90th percentile error of 0.22 m after removing shadow effects, demonstrating the effectiveness of the method. We also investigated the trade-off between positioning accuracy and the number of pixels used. These investigations show that our proposed method can achieve high positioning accuracy in NLoS environments. Furthermore, we have shown that it has the potential to achieve positioning with less computational effort and power consumption. In future work, we aim to extend the proposed method to posture estimation and real-time positioning.

Acknowledgement. This research was supported by JSPS Kakenhi Grant Numbers 19H04222 and 20K21781.

References

1. Bridgelux led lighting v series v18b-gen8/v18c-gen 8. https://www.bridgelux.com/products/v-series#specifications. Accessed 19 July 2021
2. Flycapture sdk homepage. https://www.flir.com/products/flycapture-sdk/. Accessed 19 July 2021
3. Matlab homepage. https://www.mathworks.com. Accessed 19 July 2021
4. Point grey research flea3 fl3-u3-13s2c specifications. http://sine.ni.com/apps/utf8/nipc.specs?action=view_specs&asid=1102&pid=11401&tier=3. Accessed 19 July 2021
5. Sony Develops the Industry's First*1 3-Layer Stacked CMOS Image Sensor with DRAM for Smartphones. https://www.sony.net/SonyInfo/News/Press/201702/17-013E/. Accessed 19 July 2021
6. Indoor Location Based Services Market Research Report by Technology, by Industry, by Application - Global Forecast to 2026 - Cumulative Impact of COVID-19. https://www.researchandmarkets.com/reports/4896758/indoor-location-based-services-market-research (2021). Accessed 19 July 2021
7. De Lausnay, S., De Strycker, L., Goemaere, J.P., Nauwelaers, B., Stevens, N.: A survey on multiple access visible light positioning. In: 2016 IEEE International Conference on Emerging Technologies and Innovative Business Practices for the Transformation of Societies (EmergiTech), pp. 38–42 (2016). https://doi.org/10.1109/EmergiTech.2016.7737307
8. Groves, P.D.: Principles of GNSS, Inertial, and Multisensor Integrated Navigation Systems, 2nd edn. [book review]. IEEE Aerosp. Electron. Syst. Maga. **30**(2), 26–27 (2015). https://doi.org/10.1109/MAES.2014.14110
9. Hossain, A.M., Soh, W.S.: A survey of calibration-free indoor positioning systems. Comput. Commun. **66**, 1–13 (2015)
10. Kuo, Y.S., Pannuto, P., Hsiao, K.J., Dutta, P.: Luxapose: indoor positioning with mobile phones and visible light. In: Proceedings of the 20th Annual International Conference on Mobile Computing and Networking, pp. 447–458. Association for Computing Machinery, Maui (2014). https://doi.org/10.1145/2639108.2639109
11. Li, L., Hu, P., Peng, C., Shen, G., Zhao, F.: Epsilon: a visible light based positioning system. In: Proceedings of the 11th USENIX Symposium on Networked Systems Design and Implementation, NSDI 2014, pp. 331–343 (2014)
12. Lymberopoulos, D., Liu, J., Yang, X., Choudhury, R.R., Handziski, V., Sen, S.: A realistic evaluation and comparison of indoor location technologies: experiences and lessons learned. In: Proceedings of the 14th International Conference on Information Processing in Sensor Networks, pp. 178–189. Association for Computing Machinery, Seattle (2015). https://doi.org/10.1145/2737095.2737726

13. Marquardt, D.W.: An algorithm for least-squares estimation of nonlinear parameters. J. Soc. Ind. Appl. Math. **11**(2), 431–441 (1963)
14. Pavel, D., Robert, P.: A survey of selected indoor positioning methods for smartphones. IEEE Commun. Surv. Tutorials **19**(2), 1347–1370 (2016)
15. Rajagopal, N., Lazik, P., Rowe, A.: Visual light landmarks for mobile devices. In: IPSN-14 Proceedings of the 13th International Symposium on Information Processing in Sensor Networks, pp. 249–260 (2014). https://doi.org/10.1109/IPSN.2014.6846757
16. Shannon, C.E.: Communication in the presence of noise. Proc. IRE **37**(1), 10–21 (1949)
17. Shimada, S., Hashizume, H., Sugimoto, M.: RefRec: indoor positioning using a camera recording floor reflections of lights (2020)
18. Shimada, S., Hashizume, H., Sugimoto, M.: Indoor positioning using reflected light and a video camera. In: Proceedings 9th International Conference on Indoor Positioning and Indoor Navigation, Nantes, France, pp. 1–8 (2018)
19. Wilkins, A., Veitch, J., Lehman, B.: Led lighting flicker and potential health concerns: IEEE standard par1789 update. In: 2010 IEEE Energy Conversion Congress and Exposition, pp. 171–178 (2010). https://doi.org/10.1109/ECCE.2010.5618050
20. Yang, F., Li, S., Zhang, H., Niu, Y., Qian, C., Yang, Z.: Visible light positioning via floor reflections. IEEE Access **7**, 97390–97400 (2019). https://doi.org/10.1109/ACCESS.2019.2929160
21. Yang, Z., Wang, Z., Zhang, J., Huang, C., Zhang, Q.: Polarization-based visible light positioning. IEEE Trans. Mob. Comput. **18**(3), 715–727 (2019). https://doi.org/10.1109/TMC.2018.2838150
22. Zafari, F., Gkelias, A., Leung, K.K.: A survey of indoor localization systems and technologies. IEEE Commun. Surv. Tutorials **21**(3), 2568–2599 (2019). https://doi.org/10.1109/COMST.2019.2911558
23. Zhang, H., Yang, F.: Push the limit of light-to-camera communication. IEEE Access **8**, 55969–55979 (2020)

Is Adding More Modalities Better in a Multimodal Spatio-temporal Prediction Scenario? A Case Study on Japan Air Quality

Yutaro Mishima[1,2]([✉]), Guillaume Habault[1], and Shinya Wada[1]

[1] KDDI Research, Inc., 2-1-15, Ohara, Fujimino, Saitama Prefecture, Japan
yu-mishima@kddi-research.jp
[2] KDDI Corp., 3-10-10, Iidabashi, Chiyoda-ku, Tokyo, Japan

Abstract. Nowadays, several spatio-temporal datasets are made available for research purposes (e.g., location, traffic or meteorology dataset). These datasets are more and more utilized as multimodal inputs of neural networks in order to perform spatio-temporal predictions. However, there are few methods that include functions, which explicitly capture cross-modal relationships. This lack of information will be a serious problem when more complex modalities and dependencies among modalities will need to be taken into consideration. Considering that in the future more spatio-temporal datasets will be made available, it is of crucial importance to tackle this problem. In this paper, we conduct some preliminary experiments to confirm whether an existing multimodal spatio-temporal network performs better when another modality is added. These experiments compare air quality forecasting performance using a trimodal spatio-temporal dataset. This comparison is realized with several methods and especially one that has been modified to handle multiple modalities. Based on the obtained results, we confirm that prediction performance does not improve when another modality is simply added. Therefore, some methods are required to capture complex cross-modal relationships.

Keywords: Multimodal · Spatio-temporal · Air quality · Location · GPS

1 Introduction

With recent worldwide rise in economic activities, air pollution has grown to be a big issue. Forecasting air quality is decisive for preventing people from health damage caused by air pollution. Therefore, it is important to analyze the relation between air quality and human activities. Such outputs will help regulate air pollution. Meanwhile, people, organizations and governments have made recent efforts in order to share spatio-temporal datasets such as air quality but also others like meteorology or road traffic. This availability enables researchers to use these datasets in order to conduct various studies, such as the relationship between air pollution, natural phenomena (e.g., propagation by

© ICST Institute for Computer Sciences, Social Informatics and Telecommunications Engineering 2022
Published by Springer Nature Switzerland AG 2022. All Rights Reserved
T. Hara and H. Yamaguchi (Eds.): MobiQuitous 2021, LNICST 419, pp. 406–421, 2022.
https://doi.org/10.1007/978-3-030-94822-1_22

wind) and human activities. Many novel methods have been proposed that take not one (unimodal) but multiple inputs (multi-modal) – coming from different type of sources – in order to manage spatio-temporal datasets.

However, these methods are usually scenario-specific and few of them include functions or blocks designed to capture relationships between the different inputted modalities (cross-modal relationships). In other words, each modality is used independently and simply concatenated with the others in order to produce final outputs. However, such a technique is preventing neural networks from capturing any existing relation between the modalities. This associated loss of valuable information will prevent models in reaching more accurate performances. Especially, increasing the number and the variety of modalities will probably not allow models to capture more in-depth analysis and achieve significant improvements. For example, the performance in air quality prediction will not improve even though other modalities which would clearly affect air quality, such as human activity data, are added. This paper aims to investigate the aforementioned problem by tackling the following three questions:

1. Bui et al. said [2] that usual neural networks such as RNN do not work well when input data becomes multimodal. As a consequence, complex networks are necessary to handle multimodal datasets. Is this affirmation data-, scenario-specific or valid for any scenario?
2. Are complex architecture proposals scenario-, data-specific or are they generic enough to maintain outstanding performance with any scenario?
3. Do these complex architectures still perform well when more modalities are included? Or should they require dedicated functions or blocks to capture cross-modal relationships?

In Sect. 3, a multimodal dataset composed of air quality, meteorology and human dynamics data will be presented. This dataset is then used to answer our interrogations using different experiments (described in Sect. 4). Before concluding, Sect. 5 details the results and Sect. 6 further discusses how cross-modal relationships could be realized in order to improve future models.

Our main contributions in this paper are the following:

- We unveil a problem with recent spatio-temporal architectures. They lack significant improvement when dealing with more modalities, even though these new modalities have a clear relation with targeted data.
- We clarify the performance and robustness of one of the latest spatio-temporal proposals using a dataset with different spatial and temporal characteristics.

2   Related Research

In this section, we have selected four recent Machine Learning initiatives that deal with multimodal spatio-temporal scenario.

2.1 Multi-view Spatio-temporal Network for Taxi Demand Prediction

Yao et al. proposed a multi-view spatio-temporal network, called DMVST-Net [1], for taxi demand prediction. Their proposal method consists of 3 views, spatial-, temporal-, and semantic-view. Their architecture is composed of a local CNN to capture spatial relationships among regions; a LSTM layer to grasp temporal dependency; and embeddings in a weighted graph to encode similar taxi demand patterns among regions. Nodes of the graph represent regions, while weights represent functional similarity of demand patterns between two nodes. Each function respectively corresponds to one view (spatial, temporal, and semantic). For their experiment, they use a multimodal spatio-temporal dataset that includes taxi request and meteorological data. In addition, they consider some context information (presence of holiday, longitude and latitude of the region, etc.). However, each modality is inputted into the network independently and there is no function for modeling cross-modal relationships.

2.2 Multimodal Spatio-temporal Network Based on Encoder-Decoder Framework for Air Quality Prediction

Bui et al. proposed a multimodal spatio-temporal network, named STAR [2], targeting air quality prediction. They use a multimodal spatio-temporal dataset that includes air quality and meteorological data. As with DMVST-Net, it includes date information (presence of holiday, month, hour). Their architecture is based on an Encoder-Decoder framework. The encoder is a combination of CNN and LSTM, along with attention layers. Both air quality and meteorological data are transformed into heat-maps and fed into a CNN. Then, outputs are passed into a LSTM with weighted attention layer. Meanwhile, date information and meteorological data of the target area, along with date information, meteorological and air quality data from neighbor regions are concatenated and fed into other LSTM units. From there on, a fusion network determined best weights on hidden vectors, which are outputs of LSTMs. The decoder comprises a simple CNN-LSTM network associated with an up-sampling unit. This last unit generates a heat-map of future air quality as prediction. Similar to the method mentioned in Sect. 2.1, there is no function for explicitly modeling cross-modal relationships.

2.3 Deep Distributed Fusion Network for Air Quality Prediction

Yi et al. proposed a deep distributed fusion network, called DeepAir [3], aiming at predicting air quality. DeepAir operates in four steps. First, it performs a spatial transformation of air quality data. Then it determines embeddings of features, including meteorology and air quality data. Resulting outputs are then passed to multiple networks named FusionNet before going through a weighted merge function. Each FusionNet comprises 3 layers, a Residual Fully Connected layer that is sandwiched between 2 Fully Connected layers. Several combinations of features are fed into each FusionNet, and weighted merge function determines best weights on outputs of the FusionNet. This proposal mainly uses air quality and meteorological data, but do not explicitly focus on cross-modal relationships, even though they are concatenated and fed into FusionNet.

2.4 Encoding-Forecasting ConvLSTM Network for Air Quality Interpolation and Prediction

Le et al. applied Encoding-Forecasting ConvLSTM [4] to air quality interpolation and prediction tasks [5]. Encoding-Forecasting ConvLSTM was first proposed for precipitation nowcasting. It consists of 4 ConvLSTM layers. Both encoding and forecasting networks have 2 ConvLSTM layers. The last state of encoding network is copied as the initial states and outputs of the forecasting network. This work is very interesting in the sense that they use 4 types of spatio-temporal data: air quality, meteorological, traffic volume and driving speed. However, looking at the results, their proposal does not seem to be enough for capturing cross-modal relationships. In fact, the prediction performance with only air quality and meteorological data surpasses the performance when they use all data. Intuitively, traffic volume and driving speed data are useful for predicting air quality considering emissions of vehicles. Therefore, one would expect the performance to improve when these data are included if their proposed architecture would effectively capture associated relationships.

In summary, it is unclear if existing methods can handle many modalities properly. There is only one work which handles over 3 modalities and this work does not seem to draw the predictive power of multiples modalities.

3 Datasets

This section described the datasets used in the following experiments. Three types of spatio-temporal data have been used: air quality, meteorological and human dynamics. Air quality and meteorological comes from public Japanese datasets, while human dynamics is owned by a Japanese Mobile Network Operator (MNO).

Air Quality and Meteorological Data
Air Quality (AQ) and Meteorological (M) data from two urban areas in Japan, Tokyo prefecture and Kawasaki, have been collected from their government websites [6, 7]. As displayed in Fig. 1, the target areas cover most of Japan's central urban area and it accounts for about 12% of Japan's total population. This dataset is composed of records collected from October 1st 2017 to December 31st 2019 (2 years and 3 months) and originating from 51 monitoring stations. Every station records both hourly air quality and hourly meteorology information.

Regarding air quality, each station monitored a set of air pollutants among 12 different types, such as PM2.5, PM10, NO and NO2. PM2.5 is the only one available in all considered stations and with the least quantity of missing data. Therefore, our experiments will focus on determining the concentration of this pollutant in the air.

As for meteorological data, each station is monitoring four weather information: temperature, humidity, wind direction and wind speed. In our experiments, we use all available weather information. However, wind speed and wind direction are not used as-is. Indeed, wind information is transformed into horizontal (longitude) and vertical (latitude) components. These components are then multiplied with wind speed in order to obtain "horizontal wind speed" and "vertical wind speed". The reason behind this preprocessing is to avoid transposing wind direction as a linearly independent value by treating it as a categorical feature.

Finally, we applied a linear interpolation to fill-up missing information within both air quality and meteorological dataset. As a result, we end up with approximately 1 million records in the dataset.

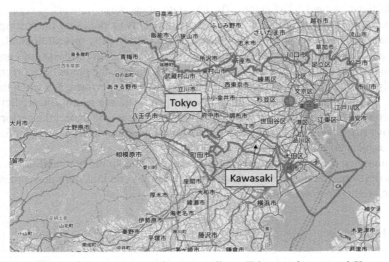

Fig. 1. Demarcation of the target areas by orange lines, Tokyo prefecture and Kawasaki city, (approximatively 2,300 km^2 area and 15 million people). © OpenStreetMap contributors

Human Dynamics Data

An MNO in Japan, named KDDI Corp., collects GPS logs of their users (several millions) who gave explicit permission to share their locations. This location information is then statistically processed in order to produce Human Dynamics (HD) data. It consists of estimating users' activity states - staying in a given location or moving - based on the spatial distribution of their locations. After that, numbers of both unique staying users and unique moving users are aggregated at each timestep and for each cell-grid defined by standards. The number of users who allow to hand out their locations represents only a subset of the total population. As a consequence, we normalized aggregated counts based on the ratio between the number of users and the total population in Japan in order to get the final data.

In this paper, we use Human Dynamics data from October 1st 2017 to December 31st 2019 (same period as previous datasets) for the target areas, Tokyo prefecture and Kawasaki. The size of a cell is 250 m by 250 m. Unique staying and moving users are counted on an hourly basis (same granularity that air quality and meteorology data).

Figure 2 illustrates profiles of Human Dynamics data. Top [resp. bottom] plot represents weekly trend of staying (Blue) and moving (Orange) users of a cell covering an office [resp. residential] area. These trends are calculated by averaging 4 weeks during the winter period. This figure shows two completely different trends. In the office area, the number of people rapidly increases in daytime and rapidly decreases in the evening – corresponding to usual working hours. Additionally, these numbers are less important during weekend compared to weekdays. On the other hand, in the residential area, the number of people moving and staying are significantly lower than in the office area. Besides, the number of staying people decreases in daytime and increases at night during weekdays. These plots show that Human Dynamics data accurately captures commonly known characteristics of these areas.

For sake of simplicity, in the rest of the paper, we will denote Air Quality data as "*AQ*" or "*AQ* data", Meteorological data as "*M*" or "*M* data" and Human Dynamics data as "*HD*" or "*HD* data".

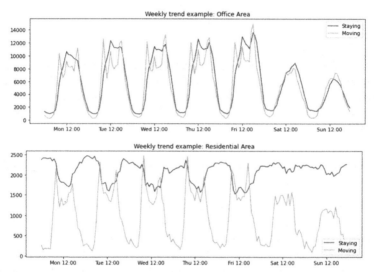

Fig. 2. Weekly trend plots of Human Dynamics data in two areas (office, top figure, and residential, bottom figure). X-axis represents the time while y-axis represents the normalized number of unique users in the area. (Color figure online)

4 Experiments

This section details the experiments that have been conducted in order to answer the three questions mentioned in Sect. 1. As most settings are the same among all experiments, we will first introduce them.

4.1 Settings

The problem setting of this study is to forecast future concentration of PM2.5 $[\mu g/m^3]$ for each station. These forecasts will be performed for different prediction horizons, i.e., 1, 3, 6 and 12 h after the latest measurements' timeslot. These predictions will all be made using the past 24 h of inputs data. For example, with a prediction horizon of

3 h, when features from 07/16/2019 15:00–16:00 to 07/17/2019 14:00–15:00 are used as inputs, the corresponding output will be the concentration of PM2.5 for 07/17/2019 at 17:00–18:00. Weights are learned for each timeslot to forecast.

All features are preprocessed and transformed to [0,1] using min-max normalization.

We use the data from 10/01/2017 to 09/30/2018 as training dataset, the data from 10/01/2018 to 06/30/2019 as validation dataset and the data from 07/01/2019 to 12/31/2019 as testing dataset. The ratio of training, validation and testing is 4:3:2.

Root Mean Squared Error (RMSE) is used to evaluate prediction performance of each model, which is defined as follows:

$$RMSE = \sqrt{\frac{1}{n} \sum_{i=1}^{n} (y_i - \hat{y_i})^2}$$

where y_i and $\hat{y_i}$ represent ground truth and prediction value respectively, and where n is the number of samples (predictions). Mean Squared Error (MSE) is selected as the loss function of all models because minimizing RMSE and minimizing MSE are mathematically equivalent. We evaluate predictions and ground truths of all stations with the same weight. Models' implementation has been realized with LightGBM [8] and Keras [9] frameworks.

4.2   Experiment 1: Prediction Using Usual Model with Either Unimodal or Multimodal Data

This first experiment aims at determining if usual neural networks such as GRU or LSTM work well with multimodal inputs data. As mentioned previously, according to study [2], in air quality prediction task, prediction errors of RNN and 1D-CNN increased when meteorological features were added to historical air quality features. This result shows that simple models are probably not good at handling multimodal spatio-temporal data. However, we cannot rule out the possibility that this result specifically depends on the data they used. Therefore, the experiment described below aims to confirm whether usual models have difficulty predicting data in a multimodal configuration.

For this goal, we compare the prediction performance of GRU and LSTM when (i) using only *AQ* data (unimodal) and (ii) using both *AQ* and *M* data (multimodal). The reason for choosing GRU and LSTM as usual models is that, even if they are more complex than RNN, they remain simpler compared to the most recent proposal such as the ones presented in Sect. 2. The parameters used for this experiment are listed in Table 1 below.

4.3   Experiment 2: Prediction with Multimodal Data Using Recent Spatio-temporal Proposal and Usual Models as Baselines

With this second experiment, we try to unveil if recent spatio-temporal architecture models are generic enough to provide good prediction accuracy with any dataset, while outperforming usual models. In this experiment, we choose DMVST-Net [1] as the recent method and historical average (HA), LightGBM, GRU as well as LSTM as simple models (also referred as baselines). Among all related researches presented in Sect. 2, DMVST-Net is the only method providing public source code. This access to the code ensures reproducibility of their results. As a result, DMVST-Net has been selected as the candidate for the recent spatio-temporal model. Although DMVST-Net originally focused on predicting taxi demand, its flexible structure makes it easy to apply it to air quality prediction. Moreover, this method was also adopted as a baseline in another study [3], which also targets air quality prediction.

Some additional preprocessing is necessary in order to apply this method to our dataset. In fact, DMVST-Net requires grid-like data as input to the Local-CNN. As air quality is available per station, we need to apply a spatial transformation in order to make it grid-like. First, we map every station to a 1 km × 1 km cell according to their latitude and longitude. Then, as inspired by the study [3], we interpolate data for cells that have no stations with Inverse Distance Weighting (IDW) [10] and we set the number of neighbor stations in IDW to 5. In our scenario, no cell contains multiple stations. As a consequence, the value of air quality of cells containing a station, solely corresponds to the value of the corresponding station. For predicting air quality of a specific station, the values of the 9 × 9 × 1 cell-grid centered on the station are fed into Local-CNN. As mentioned previously, we only use one pollution data (PM2.5), that is the reason why the channel of Local-CNN's input is 1. As for meteorological data, the processing is similar to the original study; they are fed into LSTM and then, these outputs are concatenated with the output of the Local-CNN. With regard to the embeddings of stations, we first calculate each station's weekly air quality pattern by averaging from their records over the training dataset. Then, we define a weighted graph, where stations are set as nodes and weights of edges are similarities between air quality patterns of two stations. As done in the original study [1], we define similarities between patterns with the formula below:

$$S_{ij} = \exp(-DTW(i,j))$$

where i, j represents nodes, and $DTW(i, j)$ is the distance of Dynamic Time Warping (DTW) between patterns. After that, we apply LINE [11] for generating embeddings of nodes. The dimension of embeddings is set to 32, same as in the original study.

However, contrary to the original study and because of GPU memory limitations, we have reduced by half some parameters in DMVST-Net (number of filters in the Local-CNN and hidden dimension of the LSTM layer). We use Adam optimizer and parameters beta_1, beta_2, epsilon and decay are set to the same values as the original study. The other parameters are summarized in Table 1.

We describe settings of baselines below:

Historical Average: Average of the last 24 h is used as prediction.

LightGBM: We use the latest values and some aggregated values in last 24 h of concentration of PM2.5, temperature, humidity, horizontal and vertical components of wind. As aggregated values, we calculate max/min/average values in the last 3/6/12/24 h. Thus, the number of features is of $5 + (5 * 3 * 4) = 65$. We do not normalize feature values and target values. After generating features, we search some hyperparameters for validation set by Bayesian Optimization. Target hyperparameters are 'num_leaves', 'feature_fraction', 'bagging_fraction', 'min_data_in_leaf' and 'min_sum_hessian_in_leaf'. We set 'init_points' to 5 and tuning iterations to 5. Iterations of LightGBM itself are set to 10000.

The parameters of LSTM and GRU used for this experiment are listed in Table 1.

4.4   Experiment 3: Prediction with Multimodal Data Using a Modified Version of Recent Spatio-temporal Proposal

This third experiment seeks to determine if recent spatio-temporal proposal can maintain good performances with more modalities. For this purpose, we extended DMVST-Net (referred as Ex-DMVST-Net) so that it can support one more modality. Then, we compare prediction performances between the original DMVST-Net that uses *AQ* and *M* data and Ex-DMVST-Net that uses *AQ*, *M* and *HD* data.

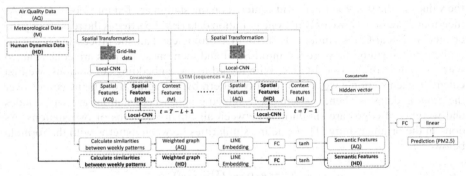

Fig. 3. The architecture of Ex-DMVST-Net. Blocks with bold-type letters and dashed border represent extended parts from original DMVST-Net.

The architecture of Ex-DMVST-Net, and changes made from the original DMVST-Net, is shown in the Fig. 3. In this figure, blocks that are drawn with bold-type letters and dashed border are our extensions for including *HD* as input from the original DMVST-Net. In Ex-DMVST, *HD* is treated like *AQ*. It is fed into a new Local-CNN block, then the output is concatenated with other features, i.e., the output of AQ Local-CNN and meteorological features generated from *M*. The resulting concatenation is then inputted into the LSTM layer. Meanwhile, *HD* is also used to generate a weighted graph of human dynamics by calculating similarities between HD patterns of two cells.

In the same manner as *AQ*, this weighted graph is fed into LINE and embeddings of cells are generated. These embeddings go through a fully-connected layer followed by a *tanh* activation and become Semantic Features of *HD*.

HD input is a cell-grid of shape $17 \times 17 \times 2$ and centered on the target station. As aforementioned, *HD* has 2 types of values, number of staying and moving people, therefore channel of *HD* input is 2. These inputs are then fed into a dedicated Local-CNN. Before generating the weighted graph, *HD* data is divided into 2×2 parts, staying/moving and weekday/holiday combinations. As shown in Fig. 2, weekdays patterns are very similar in most cells (and it is also the case for weekends patterns).

As a result, we first generate 4 daily patterns for each cell, then concatenate and treat them as a 96-dimensional vector (24 h × 4 patterns). We calculate daily patterns from the training set but exclude days with specific events or holidays (e.g., early May, mid-August and around New Year are holiday season in Japan). As a matter of fact, *HD* patterns during days with specific events/holidays differ completely from usual weeks. Contrary to AQ, in *HD*, Pearson correlation is used as the similarity method between patterns.

As Ex-DMVST-Net receives one more modality, a much larger size of GPU memory has to be allocated. As a consequence, the batch size is set to 8 * 51 and the learning rate is to 2.5e−5 in order to cope with our GPU limitations. All the other parameters are exactly the same as the original model, as summarized in Table 1.

Table 1. Models' parameters

Method	GRU		LSTM		DMVST-Net	Ex-DMVST-Net
Inputs	AQ	AQ + M	AQ	AQ + M	AQ + M	AQ + M + HD
Hidden dimension	128	128	128	128	LSTM 256 Local-CNN 16	LSTM 256 Local-CNN 16
Number of layers	1	1	1	1	1/3	1/3
Batch size	128 * 51	128 * 51	128 * 51	128 * 51	128 * 51	8 * 51
Learning rate	1.0e−2	5.0e−3	1.0e−2	1.0e−2	1.0e−4	2.5e−5
Optimizer	SGD	SGD	SGD	SGD	Adam	Adam
Momentum	0.9	0.9	0.9	0.9		
Beta_1, beta_2, epsilon, decay					0.9, 0.999, 1e−08, 1e−6	0.9, 0.999, 1e−08, 1e−6
Early stopping (patience)	Yes (10)	Yes (10)	Yes (10)	Yes (10)	Yes (10)	Yes (10)
Number of epochs	100	100	100	100	100	100
Batch normalization	No	No	No	No	No	No
Dropout	No	No	No	No	No	No

5   Results

This section presents the results of experiments introduced in Sect. 4.

5.1   Prediction Using Usual Model with Either Unimodal or Multimodal Input

As described in Sect. 4.2, performances of both GRU and LSTM have been tested when using AQ only (unimodal) and $AQ + M$ (multimodal). Table 2 lists the result of this experiment. As presented in Sect. 4.1, for each model AQ predictions will be computed at four different time horizons. Regarding GRU, adding one more modality is improving accuracy for two prediction horizons. On the contrary, an additional modality with LSTM is only improving RMSE for one out of four prediction horizons. These results confirmed the claims from previous study [2] that simple models are not good at handling multimodal spatio-temporal data.

Table 2. Prediction errors (RMSE) of GRU and LSTM with different inputs

Method	Inputs	+1 h	+3 h	+6 h	+12 h
GRU	AQ	3.265	**4.640**	5.807	**6.615**
GRU	$AQ + M$	**3.160**	5.003	**5.477**	7.348
LSTM	AQ	3.222	**4.689**	**5.774**	**6.621**
LSTM	$AQ + M$	**3.144**	4.890	6.895	7.178

5.2   Prediction with Multimodal Data Using Recent Spatio-temporal Proposal and Usual Models as Baselines

As mentioned in Sect. 4.3, prediction errors (RMSE) of DMVST-Net will be compared to various baselines, as presented in Table 3. $AQ + M$ is used as inputs for all methods. As shown in the table, DMVST-Net achieves better performance than historical average, GRU and LSTM. However, LightGBM surprisingly shows the best performance in 3 out of 4 predictions horizons. One probable reason for this interesting result is that only LightGBM uses aggregated features – min/max/average. They may capture general trends in target that help LightGBM better comprehend data. Therefore, DMVST-Net might achieve better performance for all prediction settings if aggregated features were fed into DMVST-Net, similar to LightGBM.

Table 3. Prediction errors (RMSE) of DMVST-Net and baselines with $AQ + M$ inputs

Method	+1 h	+3 h	+6 h	+12 h
HA	5.899	6.319	6.803	7.464
LightGBM	2.989	**4.398**	**5.387**	**6.282**
GRU	3.160	5.003	5.477	7.348
LSTM	3.144	4.890	6.895	7.178
DMVST-Net	**2.966**	4.521	5.756	6.645

5.3 Prediction with Multimodal Data Using a Modified Version of Recent Spatio-temporal Proposal

As shown in Table 4, this experiment compares prediction errors (RMSE) obtained with DMVST-Net and our extended version of DMVST-Net (Ex-DMVST-Net). Similar to Experiment 2, DMVST-Net is fed with $AQ + M$, while $AQ + M + HD$ datasets are fed into Ex-DMVST-Net. Prediction error increased in 3 out of 4 prediction settings when HD is added, and the improvement carried out in the last setting is not significant (~0.3%). This result indicates that Ex-DMVST-Net cannot utilize the potential of HD when predicting air quality.

Table 4. Prediction errors (RMSE) of DMVST-Net and Ex-DMVST-Net with different inputs

Method	Inputs	+1 h	+3 h	+6 h	+12 h
DMVST-Net	$AQ + M$	**2.966**	**4.521**	**5.756**	6.645
Ex-DMVST-Net	$AQ + M + HD$	3.210	4.684	5.779	**6.627**

6 Discussion

The previous experiments show that simply adding new modalities to prediction models does not guarantee an improvement in accuracy. The first experiment confirms that usual models are not handling properly multiple modalities. These results extend the study [2] and demonstrate that this phenomenon is model-specific and does not depend on the datasets. With more recent architectures, as shown by DMVST-Net in Experiment 2, it is possible to achieve better results when using multiple modalities. However, even if new architecture principles are extended to handle more modalities, it does not improve results, as shown in the third experiment. These experiments suggest that proposed models are not generic enough in order to handle any number of multiple modalities. As a consequence, there is a need for a generic mechanism that would enable a given architecture to achieve significant performance improvement using any number of modalities. We believe that this mechanism – referred in the rest of the paper as the *relationship mechanism* – would require to learn about both modality relationship with the target and cross-modal relationships.

Nevertheless, one could argue that performance may vary according to the modalities selected. In fact, in the case of the third experiment, there is no proof that HD data have the said potential to improve AQ predictions. Due to the relatively new availability of Human Dynamics data, no reference has been found to back-up this intuition.

We have conducted an additional study in order to investigate correlation between HD and AQ. Considering the strong relation of HD data with spatial position and time, it is difficult to determine a unique Pearson correlation value with AQ, which is defined per station. Indeed, correlation may vary with each cell. In addition, we assumed that HD values of cells directly surrounding a station will influence AQ measurements; but it is difficult to estimate the radius of surrounding cells as it might also depend on other parameters, such as wind or environment.

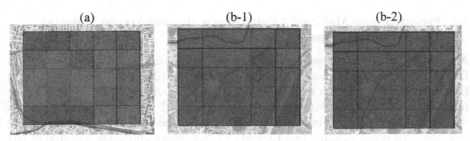

Fig. 4. Examples of correlation levels between the number of moving people and AQ for a 5 × 5 grid cells centered on different stations. (a) An example of correlation levels around a given station for any type of day and time. (b) Examples of correlation levels around another station on weekdays during (b-1) morning commuting period (5:00 to 11:00) and (b-2) late at night (1:00 to 5:00). (Color figure online)

Figure 4 shows examples of correlation levels between HD (the number of moving people) and AQ for grid-cell centered on two different monitoring stations. Red and blue shading represents the range of correlation from high to low respectively. As expected, and shown in Fig. 4a, depending on the location, correlations greatly vary. Nonetheless, sub-Figs. 4b unveil an interesting finding. In fact, HD correlation with air pollution of cells that cover main roads are greater than cells without. This result correlates with the fact that cars emit exhaust gas that directly impact air quality. Besides, Human Dynamics represents human behavior based on their position at regular time-intervals. Sub-Figs. 4b-1 and 4b-2 illustrate the correlation between HD and AQ for the same area, on weekdays, but for different time period (from 5 am to 11 am and 1 am to 5 am from respectively). These sub-figures clearly demonstrate that during commuting peak period (i.e., 5 am to 11 am) correlation with air pollution is higher for cells with main roads. On the other hand, late at night (i.e., 1 am to 5 am) correlations are almost the same for all considered cells of the grid. Same finding, but with different level of correlation, can be noticed for other stations. Time is playing an important role in this correlation study. And as mentioned previously, other parameters may influence correlation, such as the topography. These parameters could induce delays in the impact of HD on AQ, especially for cells that are relatively far from the station. Figure 5 plots distribution for all the considered stations of lagged Pearson correlation between HD and AQ. It shows that adding lag to the number of staying people has no impact on the studied correlation, while the number of moving people may have different delays with different stations. Indeed, the distribution spread more on the positive side (i.e., right) when adding a delay compared with no delay. Further analysis will be required to fully explain these results.

This investigation confirms that a correlation exists between AQ and both the number of moving and staying people. However, it is not straightforward as it depends on location, time and some delays. In addition, it appears that the definition of HD might be too generic. In fact, the number of moving people aggregates all the persons moving in a given cell. However, each transport mode will not have the same effect on AQ. Current HD data are mixing means of transportation that have no impact on AQ (e.g., walking, cycling, etc.) with those that have a negative impact on AQ (e.g., driving, etc.). It is therefore of crucial importance to have HD datasets that separate moving people based on their transport modes. Such new datasets associated with the *relationship mechanism* should help model better predict air pollution.

Finally, adding modalities to model is increasing the complexity for the model to find prediction patterns and thus does not guarantee better performance in terms of accuracy. In order to fully benefit from multiple modalities, it is important to have a specific mechanism to learn intra- and inter-relationships of inputs data. We are planning to further investigate this idea by adding a cross-modal attention block to the architecture. Indeed, adding spatial and temporal attention independently for each modality may not be sufficient. An additional block might be necessary to capture the cross-modal combination to determine how modalities affect each other.

In addition, meteorological data is unique compared to other datasets in our scenario. In fact, it may dynamically change relationships of other modalities. For example, the HD data of cells that may affect the PM2.5 concentration level of a given cell may completely vary according to the wind information. As proposed in a recent paper [12], modeling the propagation of PM2.5 could help models better predict air pollution. Unfortunately, this proposal does not support more than two modalities. To solve this problem, we propose to model propagation of PM2.5 in the atmosphere based on wind speed and direction and combine it with cross-modal effect of multiple modalities.

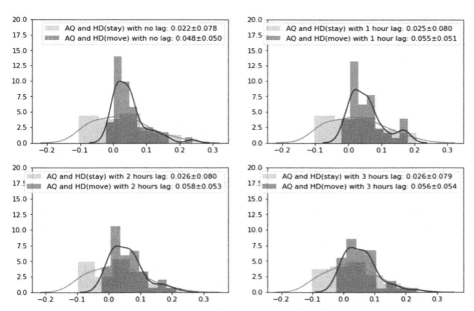

Fig. 5. Distributions for all the considered stations of lagged Pearson correlation between AQ and HD (people moving and staying). Lags are set from 0 to 3 h.

7 Conclusion

In this paper, we unveil a common and yet significant problem among studies which focus on handling multimodal spatio-temporal data. Indeed, adding more modalities does not guarantee an improvement in prediction accuracy, even though these additional modalities are related to the predicted data. We conduct some experiments in order to confirm that the problem exists with a recent spatio-temporal architecture proposal. The study shows that, even though efficient for Taxi Demand, the architecture DMVST-Net does not provide satisfying performance with Japan Air Quality dataset. And adding information on human activity, that correlates with air quality to some extent, is not improving the results. This study confirms the assumptions that recent Deep Learning architecture models might not be able to capture complex cross-modal relationships in any scenario.

For future work, we plan to propose a novel model architecture that can handle cross-modal relationships even though many modalities are inputted. In order to realize this, we advance to use specific attention layers to capture cross-modal relationships. And to further improve the knowledge of models in air pollution prediction scenario, we suggest to combine the former proposal with an explicit propagation model of air pollution in the atmosphere. Finally, for more practicality, we will consider providing a way to interpret these relationships, such as a visualization of attention weights.

Acknowledgments. This work was supported by KDDI Corporation in providing Human Dynamics Data.

References

1. Yao, H., et al.: Deep multi-view spatial-temporal network for taxi demand prediction. In: Proceedings of the AAAI Conference on Artificial Intelligence, vol. 32, no. 1 (2018)
2. Bui, T.-C., et al.: STAR: spatio-temporal prediction of air quality using a multimodal approach. In: Arai, K., Kapoor, S., Bhatia, R. (eds.) IntelliSys 2020. AISC, vol. 1251, pp. 389–406. Springer, Cham (2021). https://doi.org/10.1007/978-3-030-55187-2_31
3. Yi, X., Zhang, J., Wang, Z., Li, T., Zheng, Y.: Deep distributed fusion network for air quality prediction. In: Proceedings of the 24th ACM SIGKDD International Conference on Knowledge Discovery & Data Mining, pp. 965–973. Association for Computing Machinery, New York (2018)
4. Shi, X., Chen, Z., Wang, H., Yeung, D., Wong, W., Woo, W.: Convolutional LSTM network: a machine learning approach for precipitation nowcasting. In: Proceedings of the Advances in Neural Information Processing Systems, vol. 28 (2015)
5. Le, V., Bui, T., Cha, S.: Spatiotemporal deep learning model for citywide air pollution interpolation and prediction. In: 2020 IEEE International Conference on Big Data and Smart Computing, pp. 55–62 (2020)
6. Bureau of Environment, Tokyo Metropolitan Government. https://www.kankyo.metro.tokyo.lg.jp/air/air_pollution/torikumi/result_measurement.html. Accessed 17 June 2021
7. Kawasaki City Website. https://www.city.kawasaki.jp/kurashi/category/29-1-10-2-1-7-0-0-0-0.html. Accessed 17 June 2021
8. LightGBM. https://lightgbm.readthedocs.io/en/latest/. Accessed 18 June 2021

9. Keras. https://github.com/fchollet/keras. Accessed 18 June 2021
10. Lu, G.Y., Wong, D.W.: An adaptive inverse-distance weighting spatial interpolation technique. Comput. Geosci. **34**, 1044–1055 (2008)
11. Tang, J., Qu, M., Wang, M., Zhang, M., Yan, J., Mei, Q.: LINE: large-scale information network embedding. In: Proceedings of the 24th International Conference on World Wide Web, pp. 1067–1077. International World Wide Web Conferences Steering Committee, Republic and Canton of Geneva, CHE (2015)
12. Wang, S., Li, Y., Zhang, J., Meng, Q., Meng, L., Gao, F.: PM2.5-GNN: a domain knowledge enhanced graph neural network for PM2.5 forecasting. In: Proceedings of the 28th International Conference on Advances in Geographic Information Systems (SIGSPATIAL '20), pp.163–166. Association for Computing Machinery, New York (2020)

Expanding the Positioning Area for Acoustic Localization Using COTS Mobile Devices

Takumi Suzaki[1]([✉]), Masanari Nakamura[1], Hiroaki Murakami[2],
Hiroki Watanabe[1], Hiromichi Hashizume[3], and Masanori Sugimoto[1]

[1] Hokkaido University, Sapporo, Japan
{tsuzaki,masanari,hiroki.watanabe,sugi}@ist.hokudai.ac.jp
[2] The University of Tokyo, Tokyo, Japan
murakami@akg.t.u-tokyo.ac.jp
[3] National Institute of Informatics, Tokyo, Japan
has@nii.ac.jp

Abstract. In this paper, we propose a novel acoustic localization system using commercial off-the-shelf (COTS) mobile devices. Acoustic-based systems have advantages in terms of accuracy and cost. However, the measurable positioning area is limited because of the signal attenuation and the poor performance of microphones embedded in COTS mobile devices. Our system leverages a transmission scheme that combines time-division multiple-access (TDMA) and frequency-division multiple-access (FDMA) techniques to address the limitation. In the proposed approach, each speaker transmits different band chirps in a predefined sequence to mitigate multiple-access interference. A COTS device receives modulated signals via a built-in microphone. We exploit the received signals and estimate the position by calculating time difference of arrival (TDoA). We were able to reduce the error to a 90th-percentile error of 46.26 cm at a measurement point that could not be estimated by FDMA-based positioning. The experiment results show that our system is more accurate and has a larger area of positioning capability compared with FDMA-based positioning.

Keywords: Chirp · Acoustic indoor localization · TDoA · Smartphone · FDMA and TDMA · Sensing

1 Introduction

It has been reported [4] that people spend 88.9% of their days indoors on average and have many experiences that involve information about their indoor location. In addition, because of the COVID-19 pandemic, it is necessary to have a system that monitors whether sufficient social distancing is maintained. By 2025, the market value of indoor location information is expected to exceed 43 billion dollars [15], proving that there is a large demand for effective indoor localization

T. Hara and H. Yamaguchi (Eds.): MobiQuitous 2021, LNICST 419, pp. 422–437, 2022.
https://doi.org/10.1007/978-3-030-94822-1_23

technology. Unfortunately, it is difficult to use a global positioning system (GPS) indoors because the weak signals do not easily penetrate building walls [25]. Therefore, various indoor localization systems have been proposed, such as Wi-Fi [2], Bluetooth [7], and UWB [14]. However, a standard system for indoor localization systems has not yet been proposed because current systems need improvements regarding accuracy and implementation cost.

This paper describes an indoor localization system using acoustic signals. Acoustic signal-based localization technology leverages microphone sensors in mobile devices to capture acoustic signals transmitted by sound sources and to estimate user locations. Acoustic-based systems have been shown to achieve high localization accuracy. Furthermore, because microphones are embedded in COTS mobile devices and speakers are installed in an indoor environment, they can be used to estimate the positions without additional hardware.

Regarding positioning performance, the precision of positioning mainly depends on the transmitted signal. In general, the wider the bandwidth of the signal, the more precise TDoA estimation becomes. However, from the perspective of scalability, the bandwidth should be as narrow as possible. Similarly, the longer the length of the signal, the more precise TDoA estimation becomes due to signal-to-noise ratio (SNR). However, from the perspective of the positioning update rate, the length of the signal should be as short as possible. Given these facts, a signal with a narrow bandwidth and as short a length as possible is suitable for many environments.

However, a system with a narrow bandwidth and short signal length, as described, has a limited positioning area. This is because it is difficult to detect signals over a large area due to the low performance of the microphones embedded in COTS devices (described later).

In this paper, we propose a transmission scheme that combines TDMA and FDMA techniques to reduce the limitation of positioning area. Robust positioning is achieved by applying coherent averaging to the received signals.

To evaluate our proposed method, we experimented with three speakers performing two-dimensional positioning estimation using TDoA. To the best of our knowledge, the proposed method in this paper has not been reported in previous literature. Thus, this is the first attempt to show how it can effectively alleviate problems regarding acoustic positioning in practical situations.

The main contributions of this paper are as follows:

- We propose a transmission scheme that combines TDMA and FDMA techniques to expand the positioning area for COTS mobile devices.
- We utilize a coherent averaging for received signals to improve the range resolution.
- We investigate the delay that occurs when high-frequency signals are received by COTS devices.

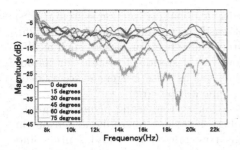

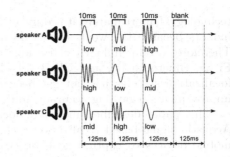

Fig. 1. Frequency response by arrival angle (Samsung Galaxy S10 plus)

Fig. 2. Outline of the transmission scheme

2   Proposed Method

2.1   Chirp Signals

We use a chirp signal, which is widely used in sonar and radar systems, as the transmission signal. It has a characteristic of the frequency increasing linearly with time (called up-chirp). A linear chirp can be expressed as:

$$s(t) = \sin\{2\pi(f_0 t + \frac{k}{2}t^2)\},\tag{1}$$

$$k = \frac{f_1 - f_0}{T},\tag{2}$$

where f_0 is the beginning frequency, f_1 is the end frequency, and T is the time to sweep from f_0 to f_1.

2.2   Transmission Scheme

We propose a novel transmission scheme to expand the measurable positioning area for acoustic localization. There are two main reasons why positioning cannot be performed over a wide area. First, in some scenarios, the range between a receiving device and the speaker required for positioning is quite long. It is commonly known that signal attenuation is proportional to the second power of distance. It is also known that the higher the frequency, the more it is affected by attenuation. For these reasons, these weak signals easily get contaminated by other signals and noise. Second, the receiver and speaker do not always face each other head-on. This indicates that the directivity of the speaker or the receiver or both will be poor in many environments. In particular, microphones embedded in COTS devices are greatly affected by their frequency responses because of the low performance of their electronic components.

We investigated the effect of various arrival angles on the frequency response between 7 kHz and 23 kHz using a COTS device. Figure 1 shows the frequency response of the Samsung Galaxy S10 Plus, which we use as the main device in this paper. The experiment was conducted every 15°, with 0° representing facing each other head-on. This result clearly shows the degradation effect of the arrival angle, especially around 20 kHz. Note that the distance was kept constant in each measurement, and the results would be worse if distance attenuation was added. For these reasons, it is difficult to receive the signals when the arrival angle is large.

We utilize a transmission scheme that combines TDMA and FDMA to address the limitation. TDMA-based positioning systems have the advantage of saving the frequency band, because they schedule transmission signals from speakers to avoid band collisions. On the flip side, the positioning update rate is slow because the device needs time to wait to receive signals for positioning. Only a signal from one node can be received in each time slot when the TDMA transmission scheme is adopted. This is a major disadvantage when positioning a moving target because the position where the signal is received is different each time.

FDMA-based positioning systems, on the other hand, have the advantage of positioning update rate, because they transmit different frequency band signals at the same time to prevent interference with each other. However, because different bands are transmitted at the same time, the total band inevitably becomes wide. Even though FDMA-based systems require a wide frequency band in total, they have been adopted for acoustic-based localization systems considering the benefit of positioning update rate.

In our proposed approach, we design each speaker to transmit predefined different band chirps in a predefined sequence, as shown in Fig. 2. For example, assuming there are three speakers and performing 2-D positioning, there are four time slots per cycle for each speaker. In this case, there are three bands of chirps: high, middle, and low, and the bands do not overlap. The first time slot indicates the beginning of transmission per cycle and all speakers do not send anything. In the last three time slots, each speaker transmits a chirp that does not interfere with other signals. Knowing the transmission schedule of the speakers, the receiving device can identify each speaker.

For large-area positioning, we leverage transmitting multiple frequency bands of chirps from each speaker to suppress the effects of frequency response. For example, in an environment where positioning is severe, it is difficult to receive signals during a single time slot because of either or both attenuation and frequency response. However, by occupying multiple time slots to transmit multiple frequency band chirps, we can suppress the cause of the positioning failure.

Another major benefit of our system is that the positioning update rate is faster than TDMA-based systems as long as the environment is capable of receiving signals. This is because the signal can be detected from speakers required for positioning during a single time slot, while TDMA-based systems require multiple time slots.

2.3   Received Signal

Matched filtering (MF) is a pulse compression technique widely used in radar systems for detecting signals. In MF, a received signal is convolved with the reference signal. Let s_a denotes analytic version of the transmitted signal expressed as follows.

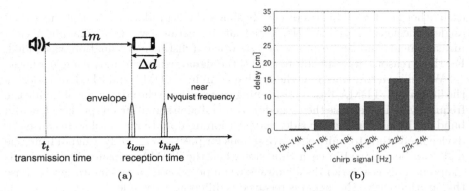

Fig. 3. (a) The reception time varies depending on the receiving frequency even though the distance is constant, (b) Ranging error caused by delay

$$s_a(t) = \exp\{j2\pi(f_0 t + \frac{k}{2}t^2)\}, \tag{3}$$

The MF output $R(\tau)$ is calculated as:

$$R(\tau) = \int_0^T s_a^*(t)r(t + \tau)dt, \tag{4}$$

where $r(\tau)$ is the received signal and $s_a^*(t)$ is the reference signal which is conjugated. We can also obtain an envelope $E(\tau)$ by calculating the magnitude of $R(\tau)$.

2.4   Group Delay

Because of the uniqueness of our transmission method, we noticed that the reception time varies depending on the frequency shown in Fig. 3a. For example, let t_t is the transmission time, t_{low} and t_{high} are the reception times of low and high frequency signals respectively, and Δd is the delay. Assuming the true distance between the speaker and the device is 1m, we can measure the range calculating $c \cdot (t_{low} - t_t)$ and $c \cdot (t_{high} - t_t)$ where c is the speed of sound. Even if the distance is the same, we observed that the reception time of the high frequency t_{high} is shifted, resulting in a longer estimated distance. Typically, anti-aliasing filter (AAF) is applied to limit near Nyquist frequency at the input of an analog-to-digital converter. This time delay is longer when recording with a COTS device that has an AAF with low performance. This time delay is called group delay [19]. The delay can be considered the propagation time delay of the envelope as it passes through a digital filter.

We conducted a preliminary experiment to investigate the delay. In the experiment, we first transmit 10–12 kHz up-chirp that is not affected by the AAF. Then, after the given time interval, we transmit a signal to be checked. A smartphone as a receiver is located 1 m away from the speaker. We compute MF to

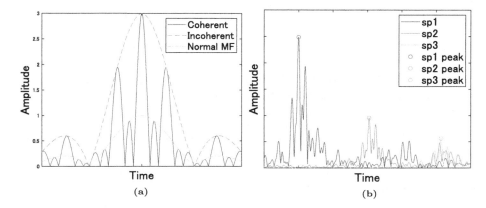

Fig. 4. (a) Simulation of the averaging techniques, (b) Envelope of actual received signal after coherent averaging

obtain the highest peak as the reception time. The time interval between the peak of the first transmitted signal and the peak of the signal being investigated should be the same as the given time interval if the group delay does not affect the signal. In this experiment, we used Samsung S10 plus, and 200 measurements were made for each signal. The results are shown in Fig. 3b. Note that the delay may vary depending on the COTS device. The results show that the delay increases as the frequency approaches the Nyquist rate. We also computed the variance of the delay, but they were all negligibly small. Therefore, the average value was used as the delay to be compensated in this paper.

2.5   Coherent Averaging

Because a speaker transmits multiple bands of signals in a single cycle (including multiple time slots), we take advantage of the combination of the received signals to improve the range resolution. In our approach, we use a technique of coherent averaging that improves SNR by collecting multiple signals and averaging them in time phase [19]. We first collect the signals in a single cycle. Second, MF is performed for each time slot using the reference signal in the same sequence as the signals transmitted by the speaker. Finally, MF outputs are added up and obtain the envelope. This implies that the smaller the phase difference between each MF output, the higher the peak will be. Near the mainlobe, the phase of the MF output is close to zero, and thus the magnitude is larger. By contrast, when the phases are not close to each other, they cancel each other out or weaken each other. Note that the envelope from other speakers can be created by changing the sequence of the reference signals.

We also compare the performance of coherent and incoherent averaging. The process of incoherent averaging averages in the envelope, while coherent averages before making the envelope. In the simulation Fig. 4a, the envelope of coherent averaging E_{pre} contains the highest and narrow mainlobe, and large sidelobes at both sides of the mainlobe. The narrower the mainlobe, the smaller the variance in reception time becomes due to the stabilization of the peak. In contrast, the variance of reception time for incoherent averaging is expected to be larger because the mainlobe is wider.

Figure 4b is an actual received envelope after coherent averaging. As shown in the simulation, large sidelobes appear on both sides of the mainlobe. It can suppress the sidelobes but requires a wider bandwidth. We set each chirp's bandwidth considering the trade-off in this paper.

Envelopes of coherent $E^i_{pre}[n]$ and incoherent averaging $E^i_{post}[n]$ from the i-th speaker are expressed as follows:

$$E^i_{pre}[n] = \| \sum_{l=2}^{M} R^i_l[N \cdot (l-1) + n - \Delta d^i_l] \| \quad 0 \le n \le N, \tag{5}$$

$$E^i_{post}[n] = \sum_{l=2}^{M} \| R^i_l[N \cdot (l-1) + n - \Delta d^i_l] \| \quad 0 \le n \le N, \tag{6}$$

where M is total number of time slots, R^i_l is the output of MF transmitted by speaker i in the l-th time slot, N is the total number of samples in a time slot, and Δd^i_l is the delay in samples for the calibration that depends on the transmitted signal (see Sect. 2.4). These equations show that the coherent averaging maintains the phase information after addition, while incoherent averaging loses it before. Near the mainlobe, the phase of each signal is aligned, resulting in high amplitudes, but when the phase is different, the amplitudes cancel each other out. The reception sample of speaker i is estimated as follows:

$$n^i_{pre} = \underset{n}{\mathrm{argmax}}\ E^i_{pre}[n], \tag{7}$$

$$n^i_{post} = \underset{n}{\mathrm{argmax}}\ E^i_{post}[n], \tag{8}$$

where the maximum peak is selected as the reception time transmitted from speaker i. The reception sample n is easily converted to the receiving time by considering the sampling rate and the speed of sound.

2.6   TDoA

To avoid requiring the mobile device to synchronize with the speaker, we use a TDoA technique to estimate the position. In TDoA, estimating the 2-D coordinates requires at least three speakers. Typically, N-dimensional position estimation requires at least N + 1 nodes. Assuming that the 2-D coordinates of each speaker are known, we can set up the following system of equations:

$$\sqrt{(x_1 - x)^2 + (y_1 - y)^2} - \sqrt{(x_2 - x)^2 + (y_2 - y)^2}$$
$$= c \cdot (\tau_1 - \tau_2), \tag{9}$$

$$\sqrt{(x_1 - x)^2 + (y_1 - y)^2} - \sqrt{(x_3 - x)^2 + (y_3 - y)^2}$$
$$= c \cdot (\tau_1 - \tau_3), \tag{10}$$

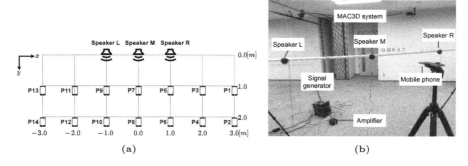

Fig. 5. Experimental environment: (a) speakers and measurement positions, (b) experiment scenario

where $(x_1, y_1), (x_2, y_2)$, and (x_3, y_3) denote x, y coordinate of each speaker, (x, y) is the estimated position of the device, and c is the speed of sound. τ_1, τ_2, and τ_3 are reception times from each speaker. With three speakers, we can construct the presented system of two equations with two unknowns (x and y). We use the following formula to compute the speed of sound c in this paper:

$$c = 331.3 + 0.606t, \tag{11}$$

where t is the air temperature in degrees Celsius.

3 Experimental Evaluation

3.1 Experimental Setup

To evaluate our proposed method, we experimented with three speakers performing two-dimensional positioning estimation using TDoA. We used a Fostex FT200D as the speaker, an NF WF1948 as the signal generator, and a Fostex AP20d as the amplifier. We located three speakers such that they were at the same height and conducted each positioning experiment at 14 positions shown in Fig. 5a. The experimental setup can be seen in Fig. 5b. We located each speaker and smartphone facing straight ahead horizontally. We used a Samsung Galaxy S10 Plus for a COTS device. The smartphone was held by a tripod, and the height was set to be the same as the speakers to estimate 2-D coordinates. We measured the position of the speakers and smartphone as the true value using the Cortex MAC3D system, an accurate motion capture system. The temperature in the room was 20.9°C. We recorded the audio data using a recording app and set 48 kHz as the sampling rate. In the experiments, we recorded the audio data via the built-in top microphone. The recorded experimental data were applied to our proposed method offline and evaluated. Received signals are upsampled by a factor of 16 to interpolate between samples.

When setting parameters, it is important to consider trade-offs such as bandwidth and signal length. In this paper, all signal lengths were set to 10 ms, and

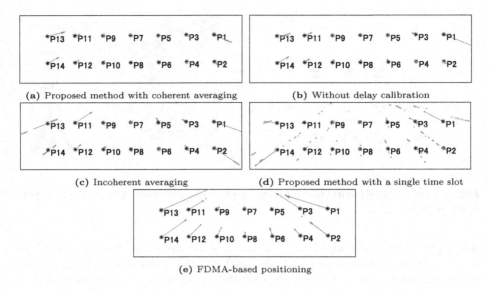

Fig. 6. 100 estimated positions (red points) and mean positions (blue arrows) for each method: (a) Proposed method with coherent averaging, (b) Without delay calibration, (c) Incoherent averaging, (d) Proposed method with a single time slot, (e) FDMA-based positioning

all signal bandwidths were set to 2 kHz. Aiming to avoid interference, our guard bandwidth between transmission signals was set to 2 kHz. In the experiment, we define 20–22 kHz up-chirp as high chirp, 16–18 kHz up-chirp as mid chirp, and 12–14 kHz up-chirp as low chirp. There are four time slots in total per cycle (500 ms) shown in Fig. 2, and the length of each time slot is set to 125 ms.

There were 100 measurements made in each position and evaluated. Figure 6 shows positions estimated by each experiment. Figure 7 shows the cumulative distribution function (CDF) for the measurements. Note that errors larger than 0.20 m were not included in the figure. We also defined that positioning is failed if the error was greater than 1 m or if TDoA had no real solution.

3.2 Our Proposed Approach

To investigate the positioning performance, experiments were conducted in which we applied our proposed transmission scheme. The first time slot indicates the beginning of transmission, and all speakers do not send anything. In the last three time slots, each speaker transmits a chirp that does not interfere with others. Each speaker transmitted the following predefined sequence per cycle:

– Speaker R: blank $\longrightarrow$ high $\longrightarrow$ mid $\longrightarrow$ low
– Speaker M: blank $\longrightarrow$ mid $\longrightarrow$ low $\longrightarrow$ high
– Speaker L: blank $\longrightarrow$ low $\longrightarrow$ high $\longrightarrow$ mid

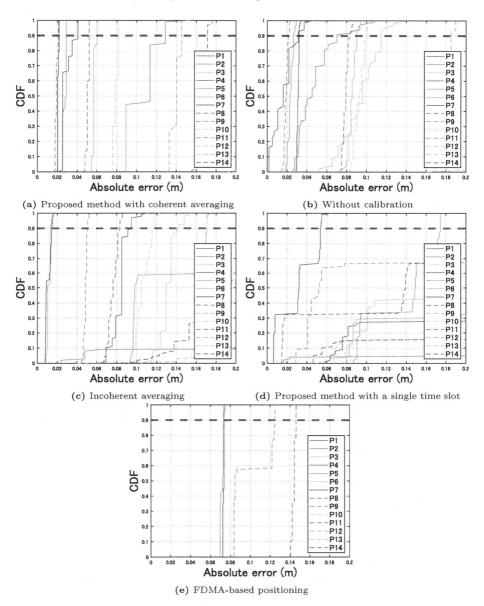

(a) Proposed method with coherent averaging

(b) Without calibration

(c) Incoherent averaging

(d) Proposed method with a single time slot

(e) FDMA-based positioning

Fig. 7. Cumulative error function for each positioning: (a) Proposed method with coherent averaging, (b) Without delay calibration, (c) Incoherent averaging, (d) Proposed method with a single time slot, (e) FDMA-based positioning

We applied coherent averaging to the received signals and found the maximum peaks to estimate the position per cycle. Figure 6a shows the result visually, and Fig. 7a represents the CDF for positioning. The maximum and minimum 90th-percentile errors were 46.26 cm at P13 and 0.65 cm at P5. The maximum and minimum standard deviations were 3.13 cm at P1 and 0.06 cm at P7.

3.3 Effect of Signal Delay

We also conducted some other experiments with the same data to compare the performance. First, we conducted coherent averaging without delay calibration to identify the effect of signal delay. Figure 6b shows the result visually, and Fig. 7b represents the CDF for positioning. The positioning did not succeed every time at P1. Excluding P1, the maximum and minimum 90th-percentile errors were 46.33 cm at P14 and 2.12 cm at P4, respectively. The maximum and minimum standard deviations were 6.47 cm at P1 and 0.09 cm at P7, respectively.

3.4 Incoherent vs. Coherent

We conducted incoherent averaging applying to the same data aiming to determine the variance. Figure 6c shows the result visually, and Fig. 7c represents the CDF for positioning. Similarly, excluding P1 and P13, the maximum and minimum 90th-percentile errors were 69.75 cm at P11 and 0.89 cm at P6, respectively. The maximum and minimum standard deviations were 12.81 cm at P1 and 0.19 cm at P6, respectively.

3.5 Single Time Slot vs. Three Time Slots

We experimented without any averaging techniques to estimate the position, that is, positioning during each time slot instead of three time slots. Figure 6d shows the result visually, and Fig. 7d represents the error for positioning. Similarly, excluding P1, P2, P3, P4, P11, P12, P13, and P14, the maximum and minimum 90th-percentile errors were 34.61 cm at P10 and 5.36 cm at P7, respectively. The maximum and minimum standard deviations were 12.33 cm at P9 and 1.93 cm at P7, respectively.

3.6 Comparison with FDMA-Based Positioning

To compare the performance with the conventional method, we experimented with an FDMA-based positioning system. In the experiment, Speaker R transmitted the high chirp, Speaker M transmitted the mid chirp, and Speaker L transmitted the low chirp continuously in a loop. To make the experiment fair, each speaker transmitted three times per cycle, and coherent averaging is applied to the received signals to estimate the position. Figure 6e shows the result visually, and Fig. 7e represents the CDF for positioning. We could not estimate the position at P1, P2, P3, P13, and P14. Excluding these positions, the maximum and minimum 90th-percentile errors were 58.21 cm at P12 and 6.65 cm at P7, respectively. The maximum and minimum standard deviations were 2.18 cm at P6 and 0.07 cm at P7, respectively.

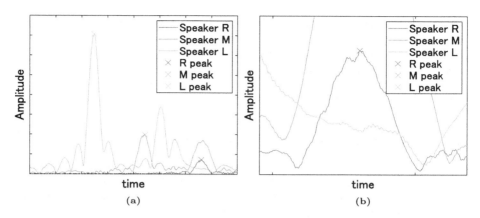

Fig. 8. (a) Envelope at P13 with FDMA positioning, (b) Enlarged view of the figure on the left

4 Discussion

Measurements at the edge positions such as P1, P2, P13, and P14 where the arrival angle from the speaker is severe make position estimation more difficult. Especially in the time slot where a high chirp is transmitted, it becomes even more difficult because of the frequency response shown in Fig. 1. However, our proposed method can mitigate the effect by using multiple frequency bands. Figure 8a is an envelope of the received signal at P13 performing FDMA-based positioning. We found that the signal from Speaker R, which is farthest from the device and with a severe arrival angle, is contaminated by the noise shown in Fig. 8b. This indicates that the peak is unstable and consequently estimates the wrong position. A similar waveform was also observed at P1, P2, P3, P13, and P14. For these reasons, the positioning error is large compared with our proposed approach.

We compared the performance without delay calibration. The results were nearly similar, but the variance is smaller for the proposed method. We believe the reason is that without delay correction, the signals do not add up properly near the mainlobe and become unstable.

We also compared the performance with positioning during a single time slot. Because positioning occurs during a single time slot, it is difficult to estimate the position over a large area. However, if the device is in an area where it can receive a sufficient signal, it is possible to estimate its position accurately. In the limited area, the positioning update rate is faster as long as the environment is conducive to signal reception. We can take advantage of TDMA and FDMA to estimate the accurate position using single time slot in the middle area where the error is little and using three time slots in the area where the positioning is difficult. However, the results show that the area is quite limited to the central area such as P5, P7, P8, and P9 where it is not easily affected by directivity.

It is difficult to estimate the position of a moving target because our proposed approach requires three time slots to perform averaging. In coherent averaging, signals are accumulated using phase information, but they are not added up properly if reception time varies in each time slot.

5   Related Work

5.1   Indoor Positioning Technologies for Smartphones

It is desirable for an indoor positioning system to be able to estimate a user's position using only a smartphone and without additional hardware. Therefore, many indoor positioning studies have been proposed for smartphones. We can summarize smartphone-based indoor positioning in terms of three categories: inertial-sensor-based tracking, radio-signal-based localization, and acoustic-signal-based positioning. The pedestrian dead reckoning (PDR) approach, which uses inertial sensors, is very useful because it is possible to estimate a relative position using only a smartphone [12]. However, it is necessary to combine it with other positioning methods because an initial smartphone position has to be acquired and positioning errors accumulate while walking [18]. In radio-signal-based localization, UWB based systems have proven to provide 10–20 cm accuracy [26], however, most of the current devices do not have UWB chip. For a smartphone system, an RSSI-based position-estimation method using Wi-Fi [2] or BLE [7] has become widely used. Furthermore, IEEE 802.11-2016 now includes a Wi-Fi Fine Time Measurement (FTM) protocol, and thus more robust approaches for Wi-Fi localization are proposed [24]. However, these methods have a positioning error of around 1 m and low accuracy. By contrast, an acoustic signal-based positioning method has a positioning accuracy as good as centimeter level. The acoustic signal enables high accuracy estimation because its propagation time is slower than a radio signal.

5.2   Acoustic Signal-Based Positioning Systems

Acoustic signals are suitable for device positioning in terms of accuracy, and many studies have been proposed.

Examples of such systems include Active Bats [10], Cricket [22], and DOLPHIN [8], which are ultrasonic 3-D positioning systems using the Time of Arrival (ToA). They can achieve highly accurate positioning. Moreover, Cricket [22] has been extended to Cricket Compass [23], which can measure the yaw angle of the target by Angle of Arrival (AoA).

It is also difficult for commercial mobile devices, including smartphones, to receive ultrasonic signals and provide high-speed and precise time synchronization between transceivers, as is required for ToA calculation. Only one example of such time synchronization has been proposed, which uses a smartphone, camera, and lighting [1]. Therefore, alternative TDoA-based methods, which do not require time synchronization, are more widely used rather than ToA-based systems. Examples of methods that use TDoA include ASSIST [11], ALPS [16], and Sonoloc [6].

FDMA-based transmission schemes are often used for basic acoustic-based positioning systems for improving the positioning update rate. In [17], the authors try to identify speakers by modulating chirp rate adaptation to save the frequency band. Similary in [13], the authors design optimal waveforms to mitigate the effect of multiple-access interference. A FDMA-plus-TDMA-based system is also used in [5]. They propose a unique transmission scheme that saves the frequency band and improves the update rate by shifting the transmission time slightly.

There are many other methods for acoustic-based positioning [3,9,20,21]. However, to the authors' knowledge, no previous works have been researched for expanding the positioning area.

6   Conclusion

In this paper, we propose a novel transmission scheme to expand the positioning area. In the transmission scheme, FDMA and TDMA techniques are combined to compensate for the disadvantages. Outputs of MF are then added up by applying the coherent averaging to improve the range resolution and SNR. Finally, the maximum peaks are selected as the reception times to compute TDoA. We also refer to the receiving delay that is affected by AAF. We conduct a preliminary experiment to calibrate the received signals in this paper. We installed three speakers in a room and conducted positioning experiments at 14 measurement positions. The result demonstrates high-accuracy positioning and small variance for all positions, confirming the robustness of our system and enabling larger-area positioning.

Acknowledgement. This research was supported by JSPS Kakenhi Grant Numbers 19H04222 and 20K21781.

References

1. Akiyama, T., Sugimoto, M., Hashizume, H.: Time-of-arrival-based indoor smartphone localization using light-synchronized acoustic waves. IEICE Trans. Fundam. Electron. Commun. Comput. Sci. **100**(9), 2001–2012 (2017)
2. Bahl, P., Padmanabhan, V.N.: Radar: an in-building RF-based user location and tracking system. In: Proceedings IEEE INFOCOM 2000. Conference on Computer Communications. Nineteenth Annual Joint Conference of the IEEE Computer and Communications Societies, vol. 2, pp. 775–784. IEEE (2000)
3. Cai, C., Zheng, R., Li, J., Zhu, L., Pu, H., Hu, M.: Asynchronous acoustic localization and tracking for mobile targets. IEEE Internet Things J. **7**(2), 830–845 (2019)
4. Carlyn, M., et al.: Effects of age, season, gender and urban-rural status on time-activity: Canadian human activity pattern survey 2 (chaps 2). Int. J. Environ. Res. Public Health **2**(11), 2108–2124 (2014)

5. Chen, X., Chen, Y., Cao, S., Zhang, L., Zhang, X., Chen, X.: Acoustic indoor localization system integrating TDMA+FDMA transmission scheme and positioning correction technique. Sensors **19**(10), 2353 (2019)
6. Erdélyi, V., Le, T.K., Bhattacharjee, B., Druschel, P., Ono, N.: Sonoloc: scalable positioning of commodity mobile devices. In: Proceedings of the 16th Annual International Conference on Mobile Systems, Applications, and Services, pp. 136–149 (2018)
7. Faragher, R., Harle, R.: Location fingerprinting with Bluetooth low energy beacons. IEEE J. Sel. Areas Commun. **33**(11), 2418–2428 (2015)
8. Fukuju, Y., Minami, M., Morikawa, H., Aoyama, T.: DOLPHIN: an autonomous indoor positioning system in ubiquitous computing environment. In: Proceedings IEEE Workshop on Software Technologies for Future Embedded Systems, WST-FES 2003, pp. 53–56. IEEE (2003)
9. Ge, L., Zhang, Q., Zhang, J., Huang, Q.: Acoustic strength-based motion tracking. Proce. ACM Interact. Mob. Wearable Ubiquit. Technol. **4**(4), 1–19 (2020)
10. Harter, A., Hopper, A., Steggles, P., Ward, A., Webster, P.: The anatomy of a context-aware application. Wireless Netw. **8**(2), 187–197 (2002)
11. Höflinger, F., et al.: Acoustic self-calibrating system for indoor smartphone tracking (assist). In: 2012 International Conference on Indoor Positioning and Indoor Navigation (IPIN), pp. 1–9. IEEE (2012)
12. Kang, W., Han, Y.: SmartPDR: smartphone-based pedestrian dead reckoning for indoor localization. IEEE Sens. J. **15**(5), 2906–2916 (2014)
13. Khyam, M.O., et al.: Simultaneous excitation systems for ultrasonic indoor positioning. IEEE Sens. J. **20**(22), 13716–13725 (2020)
14. Krishnan, S., Sharma, P., Guoping, Z., Woon, O.H.: A UWB based localization system for indoor robot navigation. In: 2007 IEEE International Conference on Ultra-Wideband, pp. 77–82. IEEE (2007)
15. Lanjudkar, P.: Indoor positioning and indoor navigation (IPIN) Market accessed May 23 2021 (2018). https://www.alliedmarketresearch.com/indoor-positioning-and-indoor-navigation-ipin-market
16. Lazik, P., Rajagopal, N., Shih, O., Sinopoli, B., Rowe, A.: ALPS: a Bluetooth and ultrasound platform for mapping and localization. In: Proceedings of the 13th ACM Conference on Embedded Networked Sensor Systems, pp. 73–84 (2015)
17. Lazik, P., Rowe, A.: Indoor pseudo-ranging of mobile devices using ultrasonic chirps. In: SenSys 2012 - Proceedings of the 10th ACM Conference on Embedded Networked Sensor Systems, pp. 391–392 (2012)
18. Liu, T., Niu, X., Kuang, J., Cao, S., Zhang, L., Chen, X.: Doppler shift mitigation in acoustic positioning based on pedestrian dead reckoning for smartphone. IEEE Trans. Instrum. Meas. **70**, 1–11 (2020)
19. Lyons, R.G.: Understanding Digital Signal Processing, 3rd edn. Prentice Hall, Upper Saddle River (2011)
20. Murakami, H., Suzaki, T., Nakamura, M., Hashizume, H., Sugimoto, M.: Five degrees-of-freedom pose-estimation method for smartphones using a single acoustic anchor. IEEE Sens. J. **21**, 8030–8044 (2020)
21. Nakamura, M., Hashizume, H., Sugimoto, M.: Simultaneous localization and communication methods using short-time and narrow-band acoustic signals. Sensor Device Technologies and Applications SENSORDEVICES 2020 (2020)
22. Priyantha, N.B., Chakraborty, A., Balakrishnan, H.: The cricket location-support system. In: Proceedings of the 6th Annual International Conference on Mobile Computing and Networking, pp. 32–43 (2000)

23. Priyantha, N.B., Miu, A.K., Balakrishnan, H., Teller, S.: The cricket compass for context-aware mobile applications. In: Proceedings of the 7th Annual International Conference on Mobile Computing and Networking, pp. 1–14 (2001)
24. Xu, S., Chen, R., Yu, Y., Guo, G., Huang, L.: Locating smartphones indoors using built-in sensors and Wi-Fi ranging with an enhanced particle filter. IEEE Access **7**, 95140–95153 (2019)
25. Zafari, F., Gkelias, A., Leung, K.K.: A survey of indoor localization systems and technologies. IEEE Commun. Surv. Tutorials **21**(3), 2568–2599 (2019)
26. Zafari, F., Papapanagiotou, I., Christidis, K.: Microlocation for internet-of-things-equipped smart buildings. IEEE Internet Things J. **3**(1), 96–112 (2015)

Body Part Detection from Neonatal Thermal Images Using Deep Learning

Fumika Beppu[1]([✉]), Hiroki Yoshikawa[1], Akira Uchiyama[1], Teruo Higashino[1],
Keisuke Hamada[2,3], and Eiji Hirakawa[4]

[1] Osaka University, Suita, Japan
f-beppu@ist.osaka-u.ac.jp
[2] Nagasaki Harbor Medical Center, Nagasaki, Japan
[3] Nagasaki University, Nagasaki, Japan
[4] Kagoshima City Hospital, Kagoshima, Japan

Abstract. Controlling thermal environment in incubators is essential for premature infants because of the immaturity of neonatal thermoregulation. Currently, medical staff manually adjust the temperature in the incubator based on the neonatal skin temperature measured by a probe. However, the measurement by the probe is unreliable because the probe easily peels off owing to immature skin of the premature infant. To solve this problem, recent advances in infrared sensing enables us to measure the skin temperature without discomfort or stress to the premature infant by using a thermal camera. The key challenge is how to extract skin temperatures of different body parts such as left/right arms, body, head, etc. from the thermal images. In this paper, we propose a method to detect the body parts from the neonatal thermal image by using deep learning. We train YOLOv5 to detect six body parts from thermal images. Since YOLOv5 does not consider relative positions of the body parts, we leverage the decision tree to check consistency among the detected body parts. For evaluation, we collected 4820 thermal images from 26 premature infants. The result shows that our method achieves precision and recall of 94.8% and 77.5%, respectively. Also, we found that the correlation coefficient between the extracted neck temperature and the esophagus temperature is 0.82, which is promising for non-invasive and reliable temperature monitoring for premature infants.

Keywords: Premature infant · Thermal image · Body part detection · Deep learning

1 Introduction

Premature infants require strict body temperature management because of the immaturity of neonatal thermoregulation to control their body temperature. Therefore, it is important to adjust the temperature in an incubator appropriately [3,5]. Currently, medical staff manually adjust the incubator temperature based on the skin temperature of a premature infant measured by a probe.

T. Hara and H. Yamaguchi (Eds.): MobiQuitous 2021, LNICST 419, pp. 438–450, 2022.
https://doi.org/10.1007/978-3-030-94822-1_24

However, the attachment of the probe to the neonatal skin is difficult owing to the premature neonatal skin, which often leads to inaccurate skin temperature measurement.

For non-invasive and reliable skin temperature measurement, thermal cameras attract attention recently. It enables measurement without giving premature infants discomfort or stress. However, medical staff need to manually specify regions in the thermal images to obtain the skin temperatures of body parts of interest such as face, neck and arms. This is a barrier to continuous measurement of neonatal skin temperature which enables appropriate control of incubator temperature.

Use of other non-invasive sensors such as a camera can help to detect body parts. However, we should avoid system complexity due to additional deployment and maintenance cost. Also, privacy issue may arise even for neonates. Therefore, we need a method to detect the body parts directly from thermal images. Although many methods such as OpenPose [1] for pose estimation have been proposed for visible cameras, thermal images are greatly different from visible images, which requires custom designs. Therefore, similarly to other research fields, deep learning has been applied for thermal images recently. Many face recognition methods for thermal images have been proposed for the purpose of nighttime surveillance [4]. Also, ThermalPose [2] achieves pose estimation for adults by re-training OpenPose for thermal images with ground truth obtained by a visible camera. However, the data collection of premature infants by both a thermal camera and a visible camera is difficult due to deployment cost and privacy concerns.

In this paper, we propose a method to detect six body parts from a thermal image of a premature infant in an incubator by using deep learning. We train YOLOv5 [6][1] to detect six body parts (i.e. head, torso, left/right arms, left/right legs) from thermal images. We choose the six body parts because they are key parts which enable further analysis for finding detailed parts. To enhance the accuracy, we apply the knowledge about the relative positions of the body parts. Since YOLOv5 does not consider relative positions of the body parts, we leverage the decision tree to check consistency among the detected body parts.

For evaluation, we collected 4820 thermal images from 26 premature infants in a hospital. The results show that our method achieves precision and recall of 94.8% and 77.5%, respectively. Also, to show the feasibility of the thermal images for the neonatal incubator control, we extract the skin temperature around the neck which is known to be close to the core body temperature. The neck region is defined based on the detected head and torso regions. The result demonstrates the correlation coefficient between the neck skin temperature and the esophageal temperature is 0.82, which is promising for non-invasive and reliable temperature monitoring for premature infants.

Our contributions are summarized below.

- To the best of the authors' knowledge, we are the first to propose body part detection from thermal images of premature infants using deep learning.

---

[1] https://github.com/ultralytics/yolov5.

Fig. 1. Data collection environment.

- Our method leverages the relative positions among the body parts to achieve accurate detection.
- We demonstrate the effectiveness of the skin temperature measurement by a thermal camera through the neck skin temperature extraction based on the detected body parts.

2   Data Collection

Figure 1 shows the data collection environment. A thermal camera is attached to the top of an incubator such that the whole body of a neonate fits within the thermal image. We captured an image every 20 min from the video taken for 72 h for each premature infant. In total, we obtained and labeled 4820 thermal images with various postures of 26 infants. The thermal image size is 320×256 pixels.

Some of the collected thermal images were recorded during intervention by medical staff. In addition, some others are not appropriate for temperature extraction since the target body parts are not visible, e.g., when a neonate lies on their side. Skin temperature extraction may be difficult and unreliable if we use such images. Therefore, we classify the input images into valid or invalid by using Convolutional Neural Network (CNN). For this purpose, we manually checked all the images and labeled them as valid if the neonate lies on their back without intervention and all of the six body parts are visible. Finally, 3868 images were labeled as invalid while the remaining 952 images were labeled as valid.

3   Proposed Method

3.1   Overview

Figure 2 illustrates the overview of the proposed method. First, we perform binary classification by CNN with thermal images as an input to remove invalid

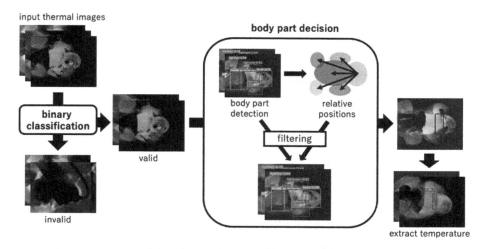

Fig. 2. Overview of the proposed method.

images as mentioned in Sect. 2. Second, we perform body part detection based on YOLOv5 trained by valid thermal images. Our target body parts are six, i.e. the head, torso, left/right arms, and left/right legs. Third, for the detected body parts, we extract features including relative positions to the detected head. The features of a detected body part are input to a decision tree model which classifies the input into one of the six body parts. If the classification result is consistent with the detection class by YOLOv5, we accept it. Otherwise, we reject the detection result as wrong detection. Finally, we extract the skin temperature of interest parts such as a neck based on the detected body parts. In this paper, we describe a method to extract the neck skin temperature based on the detected head and torso.

3.2 Classification of Valid Thermal Images

To filter the images which are not suitable for the body parts detection, we perform binary classification by CNN. The CNN architecture is shown in Fig. 3. We can distinguish between valid and invalid images by a simple model because there are clear differences in temperature distribution in addition to the shape and size. The effect of unnecessary parameters is also reduced by making the model smaller, which also avoids overfitting.

We used the LR range test [8] as a method to determine the initial learning rate. The LR range test gradually increases the learning rate over a certain range and adopts the learning rate of 0.00001 when the loss is the lowest. We built a model in which the convolution process by the 3×3 filter is performed 16 times in the first layer and 32 times in the second layer. We set the learning rate, the batch size, and the epoch to 0.00001, 16, and 100, respectively. The ReLU function is used as the activation function.

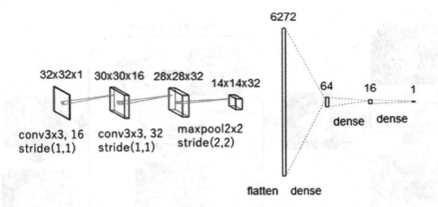

Fig. 3. CNN architecture for valid image classification.

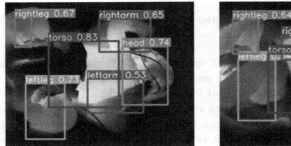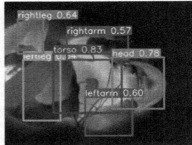

Fig. 4. Example of parts detection result.

3.3   Body Part Detection

We use the body part detection model learned by YOLOv5 [6]. The input is thermal images classified as valid by CNN. The output is the thermal images with the detected bounding boxes with their classes (i.e. body parts). We selected YOLOv5s model with 7 million parameters which is the smallest network among variations of YOLOv5. The batch size is set to 16 and the epoch is set to 1500 for learning.

In the proposed method, we only use at most one detection result with the highest confidence score for each body part because there is only one neonate in the incubator. The confidence score is given by YOLOv5 with the detection result. Figure 4 shows an example of the detection result.

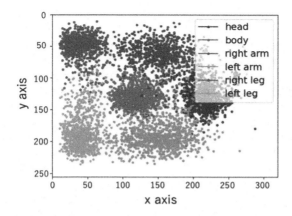

Fig. 5. Position distribution of each part.

Table 1. List of features.

Type	Features
Absolute position	x-coordinate, y-coordinate
Size	Bounding box area size
Relative position	Distance from head, x/y-component of directional vector from head

3.4   Filtering by Relative Positions

The input of the decision tree is the features calculated from the output of the body part detection model. The decision tree outputs one of the six body parts based on the input features.

We let B_p denote the bounding box of body part p output by the part detection model. We also let $D(B)$ be the output body part by the decision tree given the bounding box B as the input. We check the consistency between p and $D(B_p)$, and accept B_p if and only if $p = D(B_p)$. Otherwise, we reject B_p.

To design the features for the decision tree, we analyzed the distribution of the center coordinates of each part in the valid images as shown in Fig. 5. There are some trends in the relative positions among the parts. From this observation, we designed six features for the decision tree input as listed in Table 1. We note that the detected head is used as the reference of the relative positions. This is because the body part detection performance of the head detection is the highest, indicating stable and reliable results as shown in Sect. 4.3 later.

We discuss the effectiveness of each feature in Sect. 4.4. We use Decision-TreeClassifier implemented in scikit-learn.[2]

---

[2] https://scikit-learn.org/.

3.5   Extraction of Neck Temperature

To see the effectiveness of the skin temperature measurement by using the proposed method, we design a simple method to extract the neck skin temperature. Since the position of the thermal camera is fixed, the head of the neonate is always on the right side of the thermal images. Therefore, we assume that the neck area is between the head and the torso.

Specifically, we define the neck area as below. We let l_h and r_t denote the left side of the head bounding box and the right side of the torso bounding box, respectively. The neck area is a bounding box having the center coordinate which is the midpoint of the midpoints of l_h and r_t. The height and width of the bounding box are 60 and 20 pixels, respectively.

From the neck bounding box, we further extract the neck skin temperature. Since the bounding box may still contain other areas including backgrounds, we take the average of the top 25% in the temperature distribution of the neck bounding box. This process successfully extracts the neck skin temperature because it is known that the neck skin temperature is relatively high compared to other areas.

4   Evaluation

4.1   Evaluation Settings

For evaluation, we used the dataset collected as mentioned in Sect. 2. The dataset consists of 3868 invalid and 952 valid images. To avoid self-test, we randomly selected 762 invalid and 762 valid images for training of CNN. The same 762 valid images were also used for training of the body part detection model and decision tree. The remaining 3106 invalid and 190 valid images were used for the test. Since the ground truth of the body parts is labeled for the valid images, we used only the valid images for evaluation of the body part detection and decision tree. Meanwhile, we used the 3106 invalid and 190 valid images for evaluation of the extraction of the neck skin temperature.

Similarly to other classification problems, we use well-known metrics, i.e. precision and recall. Furthermore, object detection requires evaluation of the correctness of the detected area in addition to the classification. For this purpose, IoU (Intersection over Union) [7] is often used. IoU is defined as below.

$$\mathrm{IoU} = \frac{|B_p \cap \hat{B}|}{|B_p \cup \hat{B}|},$$

where B_p is the estimated bounding box labeled as body part p and $\hat{B}$ is the ground truth. The pair of the bounding boxes is chosen such that IoU is the highest. We note that IoU is regarded as zero if there is a mismatch in the class. In the following evaluation, we set the IoU threshold to 0.3 unless otherwise specified, i.e. a detected bounding box is regarded as correct if its IoU is 0.3 or more. We discuss the IoU threshold in Sect. 4.3.

Table 2. Confusion matrix of binary classification.

		Predicted class		
		Valid	Invalid	Recall(%)
	Valid	176	14	92.6
Actual class	Invalid	273	2833	91.2
	Precision(%)	39.2	99.5	

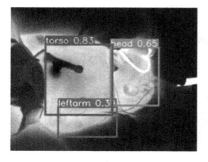 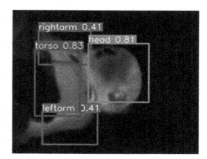

Fig. 6. An example of the body part detection for an invalid image classified as valid.

4.2   Binary Classification Performance

Table 2 shows the confusion matrix of the binary classification. The average precision and recall were 69.4% and 91.9%, respectively. Precision of the valid class is especially low because of the data imbalance between the classes (3106 vs. 190). Nevertheless, recall of both classes exceeds 91%.

We note that incorrect invalid classification means the loss of valid images while incorrect valid classification may lead to wrong body parts detection. Actually, we found that the images wrongly classified as valid were very similar to the valid images. The only difference was the lack of some body parts, e.g. both legs are out of the image. Even for such images, our method can still detects body parts that appear in the images. Figure 6 shows an example of the body part detection result for an invalid image classified as valid. Therefore, the performance of the binary classification is high enough to remove totally invalid images which lead to unreliable skin temperature extraction.

4.3   Body Part Detection Performance

To confirm the convergence in the training of the body part detection model, we show the mAP (mean Average Precision) over the epoch in Fig. 7. The result indicates that the training converges around 1000 epochs. We use this trained model for evaluation.

We evaluated precision and recall of the body part detection model. Figure 8 shows the results for the different IoU thresholds. We can see that decreasing

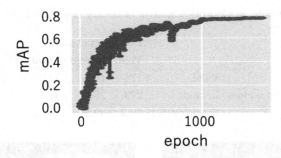

Fig. 7. mAP showing learning convergence of body part detection model.

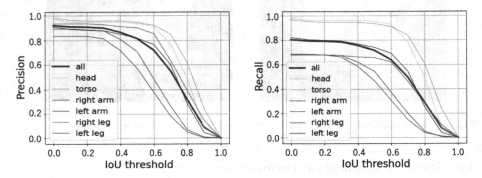

Fig. 8. Precision and recall for different body parts.

the IoU threshold improves both precision and recall. This is because, when the IoU threshold is low, the detected bounding box is regarded as a true positive even if the overlap with the ground truth is small. The IoU threshold less than 0.3 does not greatly improve the results. We also confirmed that the detected bounding boxes tend to be smaller than the ground truth.

However, if we successfully detect the rough positions of the body parts of interest, further processing based on the temperature distribution can extract the skin temperature of interest. Therefore, we set the IoU threshold to 0.3 in the following evaluation.

As for the difference between the body parts, the head and torso achieve high performance compared to the others (i.e. limbs). This is natural because the limbs are small and often appear in different positions owing to frequent movement.

4.4 Filtering Effect by Decision Tree

Figure 9 shows the decision tree model we trained. The results are also shown in Table 3. Precision and recall after filtering were 94.8% and 77.5%, respectively. Precision improved by 4.9% after filtering, which achieves approximately

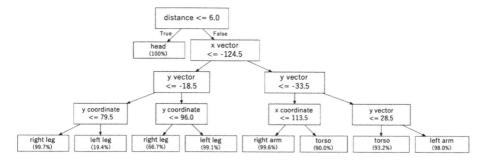

Fig. 9. Trained decision tree model.

Table 3. Part detection results before/after filtering.

	Precision	Precision (filtered)	Recall	Recall (filtered)
Head	94.8	94.8	96.4	96.4
Torso	95.8	**96.4**	94.7	94.7
Right arm	87.7	**94.9**	**67.5**	63.7
Left arm	81.2	**92.0**	**66.3**	65.9
Right leg	92.7	**95.8**	**67.5**	66.9
Left leg	87.6	**93.5**	**79.3**	77.4
Total	89.9	**94.8**	**78.6**	77.5

95% in the detection of the head and torso. In addition, precision of limbs also exceeded 90%. On the other hand, recall decreased by 1.1% after filtering. This result indicates some of the correct results were wrongly excluded due to filtering. Nevertheless, precision is the most important metric considering medical applications. Even if recall is low, we may be able to notify the fact that the target body parts are not detected. From the above results, we confirmed that filtering based on relative positions is effective to improve the precision while suppressing the decrease of recall.

Figure 10 shows the importance of each feature. We can see that the most important feature is the y-component (i.e. the vertical direction in the image) of the directional vector from the head position. We also see that the x-component of the directional vector and the distance from the head are equally important. These three features account for 98.2%, indicating the importance of the relative position from the head. This is because premature infants in incubators usually lie on their backs. This means the relative positions among the body parts are almost uniquely characterized by the direction and distance from the head.

4.5   Usefulness of Extracted Skin Temperature

Figure 11 shows examples of the extracted neck areas and neck skin temperature. We can see that most of the top 25% pixels are concentrated around the neck.

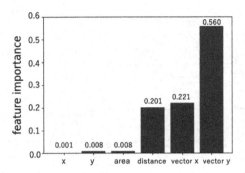

Fig. 10. Feature importance of the decision tree.

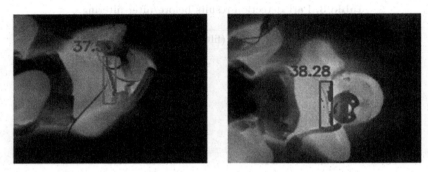

Fig. 11. Examples of extracted neck areas (blue boxes). The pink dots indicate the top 25% in the temperature distribution in the neck area. (Color figure online)

To see the usefulness of the extracted neck skin temperature, we see the correlation between the extracted neck skin temperature and the esophageal temperature measured by a probe. This is because the esophageal temperature is often used as the core body temperature, which is a key factor for medical care.

As we mentioned earlier, we used both invalid and valid images in this evaluation. This means the neck skin temperature may be extracted from some invalid images which are wrongly classified as valid. Even for invalid images, our method can extract the neck skin temperature as long as the head and torso are detected. Consequently, we extracted the neck skin temperature from 228 thermal images of which 170 are the valid images. Finally, we used 26 images to see the correlation between the esophageal temperature and the neck skin temperature since the esophageal temperature was measured for a part of the premature infants.

Figure 12 shows the correlation between the neck skin temperature and the esophageal temperature. The result shows that the correlation coefficient between the neck skin temperature and the esophageal temperature is 0.82, indicating strong correlation. Therefore, this result indicates the extracted skin temperature can be used as a reference to the core body temperature, highlighting the usefulness of our method.

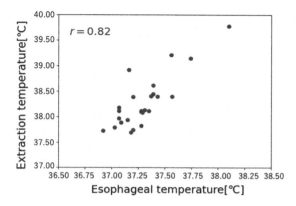

Fig. 12. Correlation between the esophageal temperature and the neck skin temperature extracted by the proposed method.

5   Conclusion

In this paper, we proposed body parts detection from neonatal thermal images using deep learning for the non-invasive skin temperature measurement. Our method combines CNN, YOLOv5, and the decision tree to improve the performance. The evaluation through 4820 thermal images collected from 26 premature infants shows that our method achieves precision and recall of 94.8% and 77.5%, respectively. Furthermore, we demonstrated that the neck skin temperature can be extracted based on the positions of the detected body parts. The correlation coefficient between the extracted neck temperature and the esophageal temperature was 0.82, which is promising for non-invasive and reliable temperature monitoring for premature infants.

For future work, we will further collect the data for analysis on the skin temperature and core body temperature. In addition, we will extract not only the neck temperature but also the temperature of other areas by using the detected body parts. Our future work also includes analysis on the appropriate temperature control of the neonatal incubators based on the extracted skin temperature.

References

1. Cao, Z., Hidalgo Martinez, G., Simon, T., Wei, S., Sheikh, Y.A.: OpenPose: realtime multi-person 2D pose estimation using part affinity fields. IEEE Trans. Pattern Anal. Mach. Intell. **43**(1), 172–186 (2019)
2. Chen, I.C., Wang, C.J., Wen, C.K., Tzou, S.J.: Multi-person pose estimation using thermal images. IEEE Access **8**, 174964–174971 (2020)
3. Knobel, R.B.: Thermal stability of the premature infant in neonatal intensive care. Newborn Infant Nurs. Rev. **14**(2), 72–76 (2014)
4. Krišto, M., Ivašić-Kos, M.: An overview of thermal face recognition methods. In: Proceedings of International Convention on Information and Communication Technology, Electronics and Microelectronics (MIPRO), pp. 1098–1103 (2018)

5. Ali, M., Abdelwahab, M., Awadekreim, S., Abdalla, S.: Development of a monitoring and control system of infant incubator. In: Proceedings of International Conference on Computer, Control, Electrical, and Electronics Engineering (ICCCEEE), pp. 1–4 (2018)
6. Redmon, J., Divvala, S., Girshick, R., Farhadi, A.: You only look once: unified, real-time object detection. In: Proceedings of IEEE Conference on Computer Vision and Pattern Recognition (CVPR), pp. 779–788 (2016)
7. Rezatofighi, H., Tsoi, N., Gwak, J., Sadeghian, A., Reid, I., Savarese, S.: Generalized intersection over union. In: Proceedings of IEEE Conference on Computer Vision and Pattern Recognition (CVPR), pp. 658–666 (2019)
8. Smith, L.N.: Cyclical learning rates for training neural networks. In: Proceedings of IEEE Winter Conference on Applications of Computer Vision (WACV), pp. 464–472 (2017)

The *MARBLE* Dataset: Multi-inhabitant Activities of Daily Living Combining Wearable and Environmental Sensors Data

Luca Arrotta, Claudio Bettini, and Gabriele Civitarese$^{(\boxtimes)}$

University of Milan, Milan, Italy
{luca.arrotta,claudio.bettini,gabriele.civitarese}@unimi.it

Abstract. While the sensor-based recognition of Activities of Daily Living (ADLs) is a well-established research area, few high-quality labeled datasets are available to compare the results of different approaches. This is especially true for multi-inhabitant settings, where multiple residents live in the same home performing both individual and collaborative ADLs. The reference multi-inhabitant datasets consider only environmental sensors data and two residents in the same home. In this paper, we present *MARBLE*: a novel multi-inhabitant ADLs dataset that combines both smart-watch and environmental sensors data. *MARBLE* includes sixteen hours of ADLs considering scripted but realistic scenarios where up to four subjects live in the same home environment. Twelve volunteers participated in data collection. We describe *MARBLE* also providing details on the design of data collection and tools. We also present initial benchmarks of ADLs recognition on *MARBLE*, obtained by applying state-of-the-art deep learning methods. Our goal is to share the result of a complex and time consuming data acquisition and annotation task, hoping that the challenge of improving the current baselines on *MARBLE* will contribute to the progress of the research in multi-inhabitant ADLs recognition.

Keywords: Activity recognition · Smart-home · Multi-inhabitant

1 Introduction

The recognition of Activities of Daily Living (ADLs) in smart-home environments is a well-known research area in pervasive computing enabling intelligent context-aware services [7]. Accurately recognizing ADLs is also crucial for complex health-care systems that continuously monitor the behavior of fragile elderly subjects in their homes. For instance, the sequence of ADLs performed by a subject and their execution modalities may reveal early symptoms of cognitive decline [19]. Among other methods, ADL recognition has been shown to be feasible through the intelligent analysis of data generated by unobtrusive sensors deployed in the home environment and/or sensors on wearable devices.

© ICST Institute for Computer Sciences, Social Informatics and Telecommunications Engineering 2022
Published by Springer Nature Switzerland AG 2022. All Rights Reserved
T. Hara and H. Yamaguchi (Eds.): MobiQuitous 2021, LNICST 419, pp. 451–468, 2022.
https://doi.org/10.1007/978-3-030-94822-1_25

Any new approach in this research area requires an empirical evaluation on labeled datasets, i.e., datasets in which the stream of timestamped sensor values has been annotated with the actual ADLs performed by a subject specifying the interval of time for each ADL. However, collecting these labeled datasets is costly, time consuming and intrusive [6]. Moreover, publishing a dataset is often constrained by privacy motivations [13]. Indeed, sensor and activity data can be considered sensitive, and sometimes can even be used to re-identify a subject even if explicit identifiers have been substituted by pseudonyms in the dataset. For these reasons, there are only a few high-quality and publicly available ADLs datasets. However, public datasets are necessary to make research more transparent through experiments reproducibility, to speed up new research contributions, and to provide reference benchmarks.

A limitation of most of the existing ADLs datasets is that they only include data from single-inhabitant settings, where only one subject is living in the home [13]. This scenario is actually realistic considering the large amount of elderly subjects living alone in their homes. However, multiple subjects may live in the same home (e.g., married couples of elderly subjects, an elderly and her caregiver, a whole family). In these settings it is often necessary to identify ADLs performed by specific residents as well as those performed collaboratively.

Multi-inhabitant ADLs recognition is still a poorly explored research area [4,13]. The main reference datasets are CASAS [8] and ARAS [2]. These datasets have been collected in real home environments inhabited by two subjects. However, only environmental sensors were considered for data collection.

Wearable sensors can provide important additional information to significantly improve ADLs recognition. By associating the physical movements of the subjects to environmental sensor events it is possible to accurately discriminate a larger number of activities (e.g., sitting at the kitchen table, eating at the kitchen table and drinking at the kitchen table). Moreover, wearable sensors can also monitor ADLs not captured only by environmental sensors. This is especially important considering that it can be too costly to deploy a significant amount of environmental sensors that can capture all the possible household items. Most importantly for multi-inhabitant settings, wearable sensors can be used to address the *data association* problem [4]: how to associate each environmental sensor event (e.g., the fridge has been opened) to the inhabitant that actually triggered it? In this context, a wearable, being a personal device, identifies the subject and can also reveal the proximity to the environmental sensor that was triggered. While constantly wearing devices may be considered unrealistic, smartwatches and wristbands nowadays are becoming quite common and they represent a non-intrusive technology that can be continuously worn in home environments.

Hence, in this paper we present *MARBLE*: a new publicly available dataset of ADLs performed in multi-inhabitant settings. Differently from existing datasets, *MARBLE* includes data from both wearable and environmental sensors. Moreover, *MARBLE* includes scenarios where up to four subjects perform activities in the same home environment. Overall, *MARBLE* includes data from 12 different subjects performing 13 types of ADLs. *MARBLE* contains around 16 h of labeled multi-inhabitant ADLs data.

We believe that *MARBLE* can be used by the activity recognition community to evaluate novel approaches both for single-inhabitant and multi-inhabitant ADLs recognition. Moreover, *MARBLE* can be used to investigate novel data association strategies.

The contributions of this paper are the following:

- We present a novel publicly available[1] dataset of multi-inhabitant ADLs that includes both environmental and wearable sensors data, where up to four subjects perform ADLs both jointly and independently.
- We describe in details how we designed the data acquisition/annotation tools and the collection of labeled data.
- We provide some benchmarks on the performance of state-of-the-art deep learning approaches on *MARBLE* that could be used as baselines for future work in this area.

2   Related Work

Single-inhabitant ADLs recognition has been extensively studied in the last decades [7]. Results have been validated on several public datasets collected in single-inhabitant settings, like the well-known OPPORTUNITY [14], CASAS [8], and Amsterdam [11] datasets.

On the contrary, the literature on the same problem in multi-inhabitant settings is less advanced. Only a few approaches have been proposed to tackle this problem (e.g., [1,3,20,22,24,25]). The lack of public datasets for multi-inhabitant ADLs recognition is indeed one of the major issues in this research area [13]. Some of the existing works validated their methods on datasets that are not publicly available. Some public datasets [10,12,17] have been acquired from video or audio streams, like the BEHAVE dataset [5]. However, those sensing approaches are often perceived as too intrusive for home environments (especially considering elderly subjects), even if data is processed locally to preserve residents' privacy.

The public CASAS dataset is actually a collection of datasets, including some that have been acquired in multi-resident settings [23]. For this reason, these datasets have often been considered as the reference benchmark datasets also for multi-resident ADLs recognition. The experimental setup in those datasets mainly includes simple environmental sensors, like PIR sensors, and magnetic sensors. Activities have been performed by the residents both individually and jointly. For instance, the Kyoto dataset ("WSU Smart Apartment ADL Multi-Resident Testbed") includes 15 different types of ADLs performed by two residents, including *reading a magazine*, *watering plants*, *playing a game of checkers*, and *setting dining room table*. Among the CASAS datasets, we also mention PUCK [9], that combines wearable and environmental sensors similarly to our dataset, but in a single-inhabitant setting.

Another public dataset that has been considered as a benchmark is ARAS [2], that was collected in two different home environments, each one inhabited by two

---

[1] The dataset can be downloaded here: tinyurl.com/marbledataset.

residents. Several environmental sensors have been used for data collection, including photocells, pressure mats, contact sensors, proximity sensors, float sensors, and infrared receivers. Overall, the dataset includes 27 different ADLs types, including *taking shower*, *brushing teeth*, *sleeping*, *having conversation*, and *watching tv*.

The major drawback of the two datasets described above is that they do not include wearable sensors data, which is very informative for the data association problem and to detect activities at a finer granularity, as described in the introduction. Moreover, those datasets are limited to two residents in the same home.

On the other hand, there are public datasets that only consider wearable sensors. For instance, the DyadHAR dataset [21] includes inertial sensor data from two subjects in an indoor environment wearing smart-phones on the belt and performing ADLs (e.g., participating in a meeting, coffee-break, work, lunch). The dataset also contains RSSI values from iBeacons in the environment.

The main advantage of *MARBLE* with respect to the described datasets is that it combines environmental and wearable sensors in a multi-inhabitant setting to capture a wide set of activities, and that it includes scenarios with up to four participants.

3   *MARBLE*: Data Collection Design and Tools

In this section, we describe in details the *MARBLE* dataset. We present our design choices, the experimental setup, the data collection process and tools, and the dataset format.

3.1   Dataset Design

The design of *MARBLE* was driven by the multi-inhabitant ADLs recognition problem, and in particular by *data association*. Indeed, during the design phase, we realized that monitoring ADLs with a combination of environmental sensors and wearable sensors is a promising but poorly explored direction [22]. Wearable devices have the potential of: a) collecting data about the physical movements of the subject, b) taking advantage of indoor positioning systems, and c) associating an identity to each subject. On the other hand, wearable sensors alone can not capture complex ADLs, while environmental sensors can provide precious information about the interaction of the residents with the home environment.

Hence, the *MARBLE* dataset includes both data from wearable devices and environmental sensors. We opted for smart-watches as wearables since they have low obtrusiveness, they are becoming very common, and they can capture hand gestures useful to reveal ADLs (e.g., washing dishes). Among environmental sensors we include magnetic sensors to detect open/close of drawers and doors, mat (pressure) sensors to detect when residents are sitting on chairs/sofa, plug sensors to detect the usage of home appliances. We also planned to deploy BLE beacons and WiFi APs to enable indoor positioning.

Due to privacy concerns, we were not able to acquire long term data from actual inhabitants in real homes. Nonetheless, based on our previous experience in real world deployments and in-the-lab data collections [18], we designed a new multi-inhabitant dataset acquisition campaign in a smart-home lab with significant efforts in making it realistic and diverse. Moreover, annotations are complete and very accurate.

Based on applications of interest for our lab, we planned the acquisition of the following activities: *Answering Phone, Clearing Table, Cooking, Eating, Entering Home, Leaving Home, Making Phone Call, Preparing Cold Meal, Setting Up Table, Taking Medicines, Using PC, Washing Dishes,* and *Watching TV.*

We carefully designed several single- and multi-inhabitant scenarios for data acquisition. Each scenario is a template that describes the type of activities that subjects should perform and their order. As we will explain later, each scenario has been performed several times by different subjects. We did not specify in details how each activity should be actually performed, allowing subjects to freely execute activities with the goal of introducing high variability in the dataset.

In the following, we represent the *MARBLE* scenarios through several tables. In these tables, the flow of time is represented vertically, from top to bottom. Except from Table 1 where each column describes a single-inhabitant scenario, each of the other tables describes a single scenario with a column for each resident. Horizontal dashed lines indicate transitions between subsequent activities. When residents collaboratively perform an activity the vertical line is suppressed. Each designed scenario is identified by a letter followed by the number of residents involved during the data acquisition for that scenario.

We designed four single-inhabitant scenarios graphically represented in Table 1.

Table 1. Single-inhabitant scripted scenarios

	A1	B1	C1	D1
morning		set table		
morning		cook		
morning	cook	eat	enter home	
morning	set table	clear table	watch tv	answer call
morning	eat	wash dishes	prepare meal	prepare meal
morning	clear table	watch tv	answer call	watch tv
morning	wash dishes	make call	make call	answer call
morning	use pc	watch tv	leave home	take meds
morning	answer call	take meds	enter home	leave home
afternoon	prepare meal	make call	take meds	enter home
afternoon	set table	cook	set table	wash dishes
afternoon	take meds	set table	prepare meal	use pc
afternoon	eat	eat	eat	make call
afternoon	make call	clear table	clear table	use pc
afternoon	clear table	leave home	wash dishes	cook
afternoon	use pc		watch tv	leave home
evening	leave home	enter home	cook	enter home
evening	enter home	prepare meal	eat	wash dishes
evening	eat	eat	take meds	watch tv
evening	watch tv	wash dishes	use pc	take meds
evening	make call	answer call	answer call	
evening	take meds	use pc	leave home	
evening		take meds		

We designed three different scenarios involving two subjects concurrently performing both independently and jointly the activities. These scenarios are shown in Table 3. Finally, we also designed four different scenarios of ADLs concurrently performed by four inhabitants, presented in Table 2.

Table 2. Multi-inhabitant scripted scenarios involving four subjects

A4

Subject 1	Subject 2	Subject 3	Subject 4
cook	set table	use pc	watch tv
eat			
wash dishes	watch tv	clear table	use pc

B4

Subject 1	Subject 2	Subject 3	Subject 4
watch tv	enter home		use pc
watch tv			
prepare meal	watch tv	eat	leave home

C4

Subject 1	Subject 2	Subject 3	Subject 4
set table	prepare meal	enter home	
eat		use pc	make call
watch tv			

D4

Subject 1	Subject 2	Subject 3	Subject 4
enter home			set table
eat			
clear table		watch tv	
wash dishes	cook	watch tv	answer call

Note that, despite scenarios describe the transition from an activity to another as instantaneous, this will not be the case for their executions since transitions will have a duration. Moreover, activities specified as concurrent for different subjects may begin and end at slightly different times with also different duration of transitions. For instance, Table 4 shows an execution of the scenario A4 that we acquired during data collection. Since subjects freely executed the ADLs, activities and transitions are not perfectly aligned as specified in A4.

3.2 Experimental Setup

Figure 1 illustrates how the smart-home lab is divided into six semantic areas, each representing a different room (hall, kitchen, dining room, medicine area, living room, and office).

Different environmental sensors were deployed to monitor the interaction of the subjects with their surrounding environment: five magnetic sensors, nine

Table 3. Scenarios involving two inhabitants

(a) A2 scenario

A2

	Subject 1	Subject 2
morning	set table	cook
	eat	eat
	clear table	wash dishes
	use pc	watch tv
	use pc	make call
	watch tv	watch tv
	answer call	take meds
afternoon	prepare meal	cook
	prepare meal	make call
	take meds	set table
	eat	eat
	use pc	clear table
	make call	clear table
	leave home	leave home
evening	enter home	enter home
	eat	eat
	eat	answer call
	take meds	use pc
	make call	take meds
	watch tv	watch tv

(b) B2 scenario

B2

	Subject 1	Subject 2
morning	set table	enter home
	cook	watch tv
	eat	watch tv
	watch tv	watch tv
	clear table	prepare meal
	wash dishes	make call
	watch tv	answer call
	make call	leave home
	take meds	enter home
	cook	take meds
afternoon	make call	prepare meal
	set table	prepare meal
	eat	eat
	wash dishes	clear table
	watch tv	watch tv
	leave home	watch tv
	enter home	enter home
	watch tv	watch tv
evening	prepare meal	cook
	eat	eat
	wash dishes	take meds
	answer call	use pc
	use pc	answer call
	take meds	leave home

(c) C2 scenario

C2

	Subject 1	Subject 2
morning	cook	enter home
	set table	watch tv
	eat	watch tv
	clear table	prepare meal
	wash dishes	answer call
	wash dishes	make call
	use pc	leave home
	answer call	enter home
afternoon	prepare meal	take meds
	set table	prepare meal
	take meds	set table
	eat	eat
	use pc	wash dishes
	make call	clear table
	watch tv	watch tv
	leave home	set table
	enter home	set table
	eat	eat
evening	eat	take meds
	watch tv	use pc
	take meds	watch tv
	make call	watch tv
	watch tv	watch tv
	watch tv	answer call
	watch tv	leave home

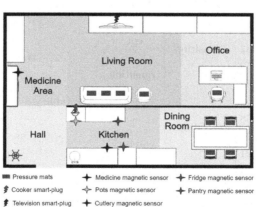

Fig. 1. The smart-home lab used in the dataset collection

pressure mats, and two smart-plugs. Figure 1 shows how these sensors were deployed in the environment. Magnetic sensors monitored the interactions with the pantry, the cutlery drawer, the pots drawer, the medicines cabinet, and the fridge. Pressure mats monitored the interactions with four dining room chairs, the office chair, and four different seats in the living room (i.e., a couch and an armchair). Smart-plugs monitored the interactions with the electric cooker and the television. The environmental sensors communicated their readings through the Z-Wave protocol to a Linux server in charge of storing data into a MongoDB database.

Table 4. One of the A4 multi-inhabitant scenario instances

A4 - Instance 1

Time	Subject 1	Subject 2	Subject 3	Subject 4
15:26:43				
15:26:55				
15:26:58		set table		
15:27:38				
15:28:37	cook		use pc	watch tv
15:29:34				
15:29:35		transition		
15:30:04			transition	
15:30:43				transition
15:30:46	transition		eat	
15:30:48		eat		
15:30:50			eat	
15:32:30		eat		
15:32:34		eat		
15:32:35		eat		
15:32:37	transition	eat		transition
15:32:52		transition		
15:32:53				
15:32:57			clear table	
15:32:58	wash dishes			
15:34:25		watch tv		use pc
15:35:21				
15:35:24				
15:35:35				

In order to acquire sensor data from wearables, we developed a WearOS application in charge of continuously transmitting the stream of inertial sensors data to our Linux server. As wearable devices, we used smart-watches running the WearOS operating system[2].

---

[2] We used Huawei Sport 2 and other brands with similar features.

Since we planned to monitor answering and receiving phone call activities, the subjects also carried an Android smartphone in their pockets. We developed an Android application in charge of communicating in real-time the phone events to our Linux server (i.e., start/end of receiving/making phone calls).

As we discussed in Sect. 3.1, we planned to take advantage of smart-watches also to collect data from indoor positioning systems to detect the semantic location of each subject. However, indoor localization is an orthogonal problem with respect to activity recognition. Hence, while we actually deployed a specific microlocalization infrastructure[3], *MARBLE* only includes the ground-truth about the semantic areas of the residents.

3.3 Data Collection

MARBLE includes data from 12 different volunteers that contributed to the data collection by performing several instances of the scenarios described in Sect. 3.1. The volunteers' age was 27 ± 5, and they had no connection with our research team. Ten volunteers contributed both to single- and multi-inhabitants scenarios, while the other two participated to single-inhabitant acquisitions only. Each volunteer contributed to multiple scenarios. Considering privacy concerns, each volunteer is only identified with a numeric pseudo-identifier in the dataset. Hence, *MARBLE* does not contain any explicit identifier and it is very unlikely that any re-identification can be performed based on sensor data. Before the acquisition, we showed the smart-home environment and tools to the volunteers, and we instructed them about the scenario they had to perform. As explained before, the volunteers were free to execute each ADL as they felt more appropriate. Since we had time restrictions for data collection (due to the availability of volunteers), we limited the execution time of each performed ADL to a duration that in some cases does not reflect the actual time a person would actually need, but long enough to obtain a significant amount of labeled data. For instance, considering *Eating* or *Cooking*, we asked our volunteers to perform the ADL only for a few minutes.

As we previously mentioned, each instance of a scenario was performed by different volunteers in order to guarantee sufficient variability and robustness. Overall, we acquired 12 single-inhabitant scenario instances (two instances for $D1$; three instances for $A1$ and $C1$; four instances for $B1$) and 20 multi-inhabitant scenarios instances (three instances for $A2$, $B2$, $B4$, and $D4$; two instances for $A4$, and $C4$; four instances for $C2$).

Table 5 shows, for each ADL type, the amount of recorded labeled data (in minutes), the average duration (in seconds), and the number of collected instances. Finally, Table 6 shows the overall amount of recorded labeled data (in minutes) and the average duration (in minutes) for single-, 2-, and 4-inhabitants scenarios.

---

[3] In our experimental setup, we used machine learning methods to analyse RSSI signal of BLE beacons and WiFi APs in order to classify the semantic location of each subject in real-time.

Table 5. Statistics on labeled activities

	Recorded minutes	Average duration (s)	Instances
ANSWERING PHONE	68.6	67.5	61
CLEARING TABLE	38.5	39.9	58
COOKING	80.5	81.9	59
EATING	150.2	28.2	320
ENTERING HOME	19.3	12.2	95
LEAVING HOME	13.7	16.1	51
MAKING PHONE CALL	63.6	53.8	71
PREPARING COLD MEAL	53.0	59.9	53
SETTING UP TABLE	53.9	39.4	82
TAKING MEDICINES	36.3	28.3	77
TRANSITION	276.1	12.9	1282
USING PC	94.1	86.9	65
WASHING DISHES	54.6	48.2	68
WATCHING TV	267.6	90.2	178

Table 6. Statistics on scripted scenarios

Type of scenarios	Recorded minutes	Average duration (min)
Single-inhabitant	307.5	25.6 ± 4.0
2-inhabitants	315.5	31.5 ± 7.7
4-inhabitants	84.0	8.4 ± 1.8

3.4   Data Annotation

In order to make data acquisition as realistic as possible, annotation was performed by a different team that was watching live video streams of what was happening in each area of the smart-home lab.

The members of this team used a dedicated software that we implemented to easily annotate in real-time: a) the ADL being performed by each subject, b) the semantic area in which the subject is performing the ADL, and c) the associations between environmental sensor events and the subjects that triggered them. The last type of annotation is particularly useful to evaluate the effectiveness of novel data association strategies. Moreover, it also can be used to isolate the environmental events triggered by each subject in order to evaluate single-inhabitant approaches. Clearly, sensor data collected from the smart-watches are automatically associated with the correct subject by the WearOS application. Since annotating multi-inhabitant scenarios turned out to be a very hard task, each member of the annotation team was in charge of annotating data for a single subject.

In order to obtain accurate annotations, both the environmental sensors and the annotation software communicated with the same gateway that was in charge of providing the timestamps both to data and annotations, before storing them in a MongoDB database. At the same time, the clocks of the smartwatches were synchronized with the one of the gateway.

4   Experimental Evaluation

In this section we provide some benchmarks on *MARBLE* that could be used as baselines for future work on multi-inhabitant ADL recognition methods. For the sake of this work, we assume that data association can be computed perfectly i.e., we assume that the association between each environmental sensor event and the resident that triggered it, is always correct.[4] We compare the performance of different deep learning solutions that we have adapted to be applied to *MARBLE* data.

4.1   Data Pre-processing

In order to provide sensor data as input for deep learning networks, we apply some simple pre-processing steps. Inertial sensors data are smoothed using a median filter to reduce the intrinsic noise of inertial sensors. Then, inertial and environmental sensors data are temporally aligned and segmented into windows of w seconds, with an ov overlap factor. The two types of data are provided as separate inputs to the networks.

For each window of inertial sensors data, we extract a matrix of shape $(9, L_w)$, where L_w is the average number of measurements collected by inertial sensors (according to the sampling rate) when the segmentation window size is equal to w seconds[5]. Each of the nine rows of the matrix encodes the measurements of one of the three axes of a specific inertial sensor.

Regarding environmental sensors, for each window we generate a binary matrix with shape $(25, w)$, where w is the window size. Each of the 25 rows represents a specific environmental sensor or a specific semantic location. Each column represents a specific second within the window (e.g., column 3 is the third second inside the window). The value of the matrix at row i and column j is 1 if sensor/location i was active at second j, 0 otherwise.

4.2   Considered Approaches

In the following, we describe the methods that we implemented as benchmarks. We warmly invite the researchers in this area to take advantage of this dataset to validate more sophisticated solutions and compare them with the provided baselines. We empirically determined the architecture of each network.

---

[4] We proposed in [3] a data association method evaluated on *MARBLE*. However, the dataset was not public yet and it was not described in detail.

[5] Since the number of measurements in a window may slightly differ from L_w, we interpolate missing values or downsample measurements when needed.

Fully Connected Deep Learning (DNN). The first method we evaluated is a simple fully connected Deep Neural Network (we will refer to this approach as DNN). We use DNN as a baseline to compare it with more advanced methods in the literature. The flow of inertial sensors data is composed of two Fully Connected (FC) layers of 64 neurons, two FC layers of 128 neurons, and four FC layers of 256 neurons interleaved by a Dropout layer (with 0.5 dropout rate). On the other hand, the flow of environmental sensors data is composed of four FC layers of 64, 32, 128, 32 layers, respectively. Within both the data flows, we flatten the output of the last layer with a Flatten layer. The two flows are then merged using a Concatenation layer. Then, the DNN has a FC layer with 64 neurons followed by a Softmax layer used for classification.

Convolutional Neural Network (CNN). This approach is quite popular in the literature, possibly due to its good performance, especially when multiple types of sensors are considered [15]. Inertial measurements are provided as input to a stack of two Convolutional layers, each one composed of 64 filters with a 2×2 kernel, followed by two Convolutional layers composed of 128 filters with a 2×2 kernel. Then, we flatten the output of the last convolutional layer with a Flatten layer. The flow continues with two FC layers (64 and 32 neurons, respectively) interleaved by a Dropout layer (0.5 as dropout rate). On the other hand, the flow of environmental sensors data is composed of a Convolutional layer of 16 filters with a 2×2 kernel, a Flatten layer, and two FC layers (128 and 32 neurons, respectively). The two flows are then merged using a Concatenation layer. Then, the CNN has a FC layer with 32 neurons. Finally, a Softmax layer is used for classification.

Convolutional and Recurrent Deep Learning (CNN-LSTM). Finally, we implemented an approach that combines convolutional and recurrent layers (we will refer to this approach as CNN-LSTM). In particular, we slightly adapted the method presented in [16] to include both inertial and environmental sensors. Inertial measurements are provided as input to two Convolutional layers composed of 64 filters with a 2×2 kernel, followed by two Convolutional layers composed of 128 filters with a 2×2 kernel. Hence, the output of the last Convolutional layer is flattened with a Flatten layer. The network continues with a LSTM layer of 256 units, followed by a Dropout layer with a 0.5 dropout rate and a 64 neurons FC layer. On the other hand, environmental sensor data are provided to a Convolutional layer of 8 filters with a 2×2 kernel, followed by a Flatten layer, a 128 units LSTM, a Dropout layer with a 0.5 dropout rate, and a FC layer with 32 neurons. Hence, the two flows are merged with a Concatenation layer. The network then continues with two FC layers with 64 and 32 neurons. Finally, a Softmax layer is used for classification.

4.3   Results

In the following, we show the performance on *MARBLE* of the approaches described above. For each approach, we trained the corresponding neural network with the data collected both in single- and multi-inhabitant scenarios. In this way, the evaluation is affected by the interactions between the subjects of multi-inhabitant scenarios. We chose the optimal segmentation parameters using a grid search approach. In particular the best parameters we found are $w = 6$, and $ov = 0.8$. Each approach was evaluated by considering an ideal perfect association between the environmental events and the subjects that triggered them.

We adopted three well-known evaluation methodologies and a new one that is particularly significant for a multi-inhabitant dataset. The first methodology simply consists of splitting the dataset in 70% for training, 10% for validation, and 20% for testing. The second one is a 10-fold cross validation. The third one is a *leave-one-subject-out* cross-validation: at each fold, one subject is used as test set and the remaining subjects as training set. The leave-one-subject-out is generally used to test the generalization capability of the classifier on subjects that did not contribute with labeled data. Finally, we propose a new evaluation methodology that we call *leave-one-scenario-out* cross-validation: at each fold, an instance of one of the *MARBLE* scenarios is used as test set, while the training set excludes both data from instances of the scenario considered in the test set as well as data related to subjects that contributed to the test set. This last methodology is the most restrictive one since it aims at assessing the generality of the classifier over unseen users and also over sequences of activities not included in the training set.

Figure 2 shows that the evaluation methodology has a significant impact on the measured F1 score. We observed that the 70/10/20 methodology overestimates the recognition rate. By using this evaluation methodology, it emerges that CNN-LSTM outperforms the other approaches. However, both the training and the test sets contain data samples related to the same subjects and scenarios, thus it is likely that this evaluation methodology suffers from overfitting problems.

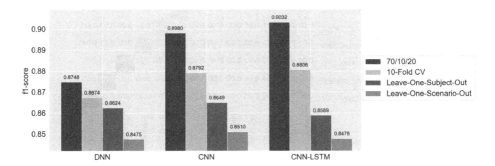

Fig. 2. Overall recognition rate based on the evaluation method

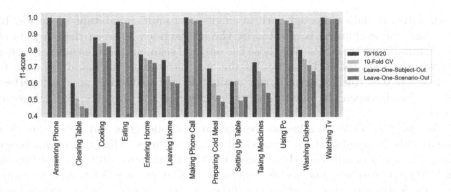

Fig. 3. Recognition rate of CNN-LSTM for each activity

The 10-fold cross-validation methodology is more robust and it provides a better estimate of the recognition rate. However, at each fold, training and test sets may still include data from the same subjects or scenarios. This type of evaluation confirms that CNN-LSTM reaches the highest recognition rates.

Leave-one-subject-out and leave-one-scenario-out methodologies provide a more robust assessment of the recognition rate than the other evaluation method-

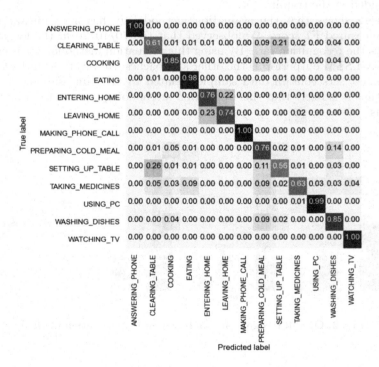

Fig. 4. Confusion matrix of CNN-LSTM (70/10/20)

ologies. By using these methodologies, we observed that all the considered approaches reach similar recognition rates. As expected, the leave-one-scenario-out methodology is the one that estimates the recognition rate with the lowest F1 score values. The lower recognition rates reached by these methodologies is due to the fact that our dataset includes activities that are particularly difficult to recognize on subjects/scenarios that were not observed during the training phase. Consider Fig. 3, that shows how the evaluation methodology affects the recognition rate of each activity.

We observed that activities like *Eating*, *Watching TV*, and *Using PC* reach high recognition rates independently from the evaluation methodology. This is due to the fact that these activities can be performed only in specific smart-home areas, triggering environmental sensors that are not involved in other activities. Some activities significantly decrease their recognition rate with more restrictive evaluation methodologies. This is also reflected by the confusion matrix in Fig. 4. For instance, *Clearing Table* and *Setting Up Table* are often confused between them since they share similar inertial signals and the same environmental sensors. *Preparing a Cold Meal* is sometimes confused with *Cooking* or *Washing Dishes* since all these actions are performed within the *Kitchen* semantic location.

It is important to note that the overall recognition rate reached by these baselines is relatively high. However, this is likely due to the fact that we considered an unrealistic perfect data association. Figure 5 shows a comparison between perfect data association (i.e., based on ground truth) and a naive data association strategy. In particular, we considered a naive method that associates each environmental sensors event with each subject in the home environment. In order to better highlight the impact of data association, we only considered environmental sensors and we discarded the activities that are not captured by those sensors in the dataset (i.e., *answering phone*, *entering home*, *leaving home*, *making phone call*, and *washing dishes*). We also grouped the activities *clearing table* and *setting up table* since it is not possible to discriminate them only by using environmental sensors in our dataset. A perfect data association of the environmental sensors events dramatically affects the recognition rate of some activities ($\approx +40\%$ in terms of F1 score), like *cooking* and *using pc*. On the other hand, the improvement is lower for those activities that are often performed at the same time by all the subjects of the scenario (e.g., *eating* and *watching tv*). We believe that researchers may use *MARBLE* to investigate novel data association strategies that outperform the recognition rate of the naive approach we presented as a baseline. At the same time, the recognition rate of the perfect data association can be considered as an upper bound while evaluating more realistic strategies.

Finally, since one of the contributions of our dataset is the combination of wearable and environmental sensors, we show in Fig. 6 the impact of the inertial sensors data provided by wearable sensors on the recognition rate of each activity. We observed that some activities like *clearing table*, *preparing a cold meal*, and *washing dishes* significantly benefit from wearable sensor data. Indeed, those activities include significant hand gestures that are typical for those activities. As expected, wearable sensor data do not have impact on those activities that are monitored by distinctive environmental sensors (e.g., *watching TV*).

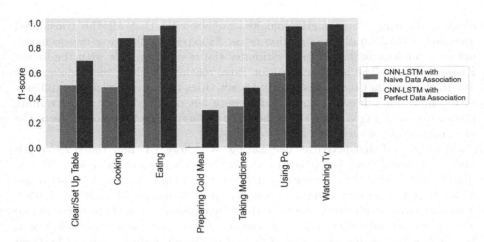

Fig. 5. Comparison between a naive data association strategy and a perfect data association with CNN-LSTM (70/10/20)

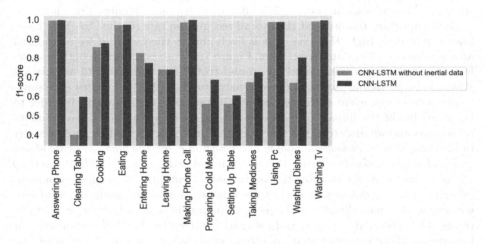

Fig. 6. Impact of inertial data on CNN-LSTM (70/10/20)

5   Conclusion

In this paper we address the need of more public multi-inhabitant ADLs datasets by the research community. We present *MARBLE*, a dataset that includes both wearable and environmental sensors data collected in scenarios where up to four residents concurrently and jointly perform activities in the same smart-home environment. The major limitation of *MARBLE* is that it has not been acquired by continuous monitoring of residents in real homes. Nonetheless, we dedicated a significant effort in designing realistic scenarios, in leaving freedom in activities execution, and in an accurate data acquisition, making the dataset as realistic as possible. We believe that *MARBLE* can be used in the future by several research groups to propose new approaches for single- and multi-inhabitant ADLs recognition. Moreover, *MARBLE* can be used to evaluate novel methods for data association, that is still one of the main open challenges of multi-inhabitant settings.

References

1. Alemdar, H., Ersoy, C.: Multi-resident activity tracking and recognition in smart environments. J. Ambient. Intell. Humaniz. Comput. **8**(4), 513–529 (2017). https://doi.org/10.1007/s12652-016-0440-x
2. Alemdar, H., Ertan, H., Incel, O.D., Ersoy, C.: ARAS human activity datasets in multiple homes with multiple residents. In: 2013 7th International Conference on Pervasive Computing Technologies for Healthcare and Workshops, pp. 232–235. IEEE (2013)
3. Arrotta, L., Bettini, C., Civitarese, G., Presotto, R.: Context-aware data association for multi-inhabitant sensor-based activity recognition. In: 2020 21st IEEE International Conference on Mobile Data Management (MDM), pp. 125–130. IEEE (2020)
4. Benmansour, A., Bouchachia, A., Feham, M.: Multioccupant activity recognition in pervasive smart home environments. ACM Comput. Surv. (CSUR) **48**(3), 34 (2016)
5. Blunsden, S., Fisher, R.: The behave video dataset: ground truthed video for multi-person behavior classification. Ann. BMVA **4**(1–12), 4 (2010)
6. Calatroni, A., Roggen, D., Tröster, G.: Collection and curation of a large reference dataset for activity recognition. In: 2011 IEEE International Conference on Systems, Man, and Cybernetics, pp. 30–35. IEEE (2011)
7. Chen, L., Hoey, J., Nugent, C.D., Cook, D.J., Yu, Z.: Sensor-based activity recognition. IEEE Trans. Syst. Man Cybern. Part C (Appl. Rev.) **42**(6), 790–808 (2012)
8. Cook, D.J., Crandall, A.S., Thomas, B.L., Krishnan, N.C.: CASAS: a smart home in a box. Computer **46**(7), 62–69 (2012)
9. Das, B., Cook, D.J., Schmitter-Edgecombe, M., Seelye, A.M.: Puck: an automated prompting system for smart environments: toward achieving automated prompting-challenges involved. Pers. Ubiquit. Comput. **16**(7), 859–873 (2012)
10. Das, S., et al.: Toyota smarthome: real-world activities of daily living. In: Proceedings of the IEEE/CVF International Conference on Computer Vision, pp. 833–842 (2019)
11. van Kasteren, T.L., Englebienne, G., Kröse, B.J.: Human activity recognition from wireless sensor network data: Benchmark and software. In: Chen, L., Nugent, C., Biswas, J., Hoey, J. (eds.) Activity Recognition in Pervasive Intelligent Environments. Atlantis Ambient and Pervasive Intelligence, vol. 4, pp. 165–186. Springer, Heidelberg (2011). https://doi.org/10.2991/978-94-91216-05-3_8
12. Kong, Q., Wu, Z., Deng, Z., Klinkigt, M., Tong, B., Murakami, T.: MMAct: a large-scale dataset for cross modal human action understanding. In: Proceedings of the IEEE/CVF International Conference on Computer Vision, pp. 8658–8667 (2019)
13. Li, Q., Gravina, R., Li, Y., Alsamhi, S.H., Sun, F., Fortino, G.: Multi-user activity recognition: challenges and opportunities. Information Fusion **63**, 121–135 (2020)

14. Lukowicz, P., et al.: Recording a complex, multi modal activity data set for context recognition. In: Proceedings of ARCS 2010 - 23th International Conference on Architecture of Computing Systems, pp. 161–166. VDE Verlag (2010)
15. Münzner, S., Schmidt, P., Reiss, A., Hanselmann, M., Stiefelhagen, R., Dürichen, R.: CNN-based sensor fusion techniques for multimodal human activity recognition. In: Proceedings of the 2017 ACM International Symposium on Wearable Computers, pp. 158–165 (2017)
16. Ordóñez, F., Roggen, D.: Deep convolutional and LSTM recurrent neural networks for multimodal wearable activity recognition. Sensors **16**(1), 115 (2016)
17. Rai, N., et al.: Home action genome: cooperative compositional action understanding. In: Proceedings of the IEEE/CVF Conference on Computer Vision and Pattern Recognition, pp. 11184–11193 (2021)
18. Riboni, D., Bettini, C., Civitarese, G., Janjua, Z.H., Bulgari, V.: From lab to life: fine-grained behavior monitoring in the elderly's home. In: 2015 IEEE International Conference on Pervasive Computing and Communication Workshops (PerCom Workshops), pp. 342–347. IEEE Computer Society, Washington, D.C. (2015)
19. Riboni, D., Bettini, C., Civitarese, G., Janjua, Z.H., Helaoui, R.: SmartFABER: recognizing fine-grained abnormal behaviors for early detection of mild cognitive impairment. Artif. Intell. Med. **67**, 57–74 (2016)
20. Riboni, D., Murru, F.: Unsupervised recognition of multi-resident activities in smart-homes. IEEE Access **8**, 201985–201994 (2020)
21. Rossi, S., Capasso, R., Acampora, G., Staffa, M.: A multimodal deep learning network for group activity recognition. In: 2018 International Joint Conference on Neural Networks (IJCNN), pp. 1–6. IEEE (2018)
22. Roy, N., Misra, A., Cook, D.: Ambient and smartphone sensor assisted ADL recognition in multi-inhabitant smart environments. J. Ambient. Intell. Humaniz. Comput. **7**(1), 1–19 (2016)
23. Singla, G., Cook, D.J., Schmitter-Edgecombe, M.: Recognizing independent and joint activities among multiple residents in smart environments. J. Ambient. Intell. Humaniz. Comput. **1**(1), 57–63 (2010)
24. Tran, S.N., et al.: On multi-resident activity recognition in ambient smart-homes. Artif. Intell. Rev. **53**(6), 3929–3945 (2019). https://doi.org/10.1007/s10462-019-09783-8
25. Wang, T., Cook, D.J.: Toward unsupervised multiresident tracking in ambient assisted living: methods and performance metrics. In: Assistive Technology for the Elderly, pp. 249–280. Elsevier (2020)

Comparative Analysis of High- and Low-Performing Factory Workers with Attention-Based Neural Networks

Qingxin Xia[1], Atsushi Wada[2], Takanori Yoshii[2], Yasuo Namioka[2], and Takuya Maekawa[1(✉)]

[1] Graduate School of Information Science and Technology, Osaka University, Osaka 5650871, Japan
{xia.qingxin,maekawa}@ist.osaka-u.ac.jp
[2] Corporate Manufacturing Engineering Center, Toshiba Corporation, Yokohama, Kanagawa 2350017, Japan
{atsushi3.wada,takanori.yoshii,yasuo.namioka}@toshiba.co.jp

Abstract. This study presents a new method that supports the comparative analysis of works performed by high- and low-performing factory workers. Our method, based on explainable deep learning, automatically detects a sensor data segment that potentially contains knowledge about the skill of works by analyzing acceleration sensor data from high- and low-performing workers. Our evaluation with industrial engineers using sensor data from actual factory workers revealed that 78% of sensor data segments detected by our method included knowledge about skill.

Keywords: Attention networks · Work performance · Wearable sensor · Factory work

1 Introduction

1.1 Background

The skill level of a factory worker of assembly work significantly influences the productivity of a production system in which the worker is involved. Assembly work is a common part of line production systems and typically involves factory workers performing a repetitive work process consisting of a sequence of operations, such as setting a board on a workbench and screwing parts onto the board. Mistakes and delays in each work period, that is, one iteration of the entire sequence of operations, are accumulated, significantly deteriorating the overall performance of the production system. Therefore, developing skills for low-performing workers is crucial to improve the efficiency of assembly work. For this purpose, industrial engineers have manually compared video recordings of works by a high-performing worker with those of a low-performing worker

T. Hara and H. Yamaguchi (Eds.): MobiQuitous 2021, LNICST 419, pp. 469–480, 2022.
https://doi.org/10.1007/978-3-030-94822-1_26

470   Q. Xia et al.

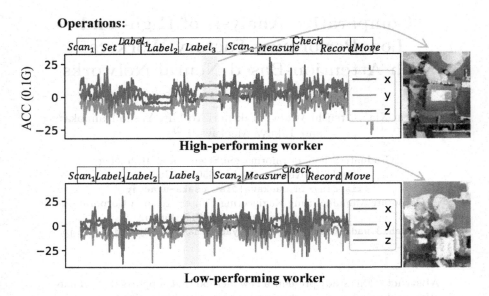

Fig. 1. Example time-series of acceleration data from two workers' right wrists. The yellow rectangles indicate segments that potentially contain knowledge about skill extracted by our method.

to extract hidden knowledge about skills [6], which is useful for training low-performing workers. However, because there are many workers in the factory, it incurs huge costs for industrial engineers to analyze the work manually.

1.2   Research Goal

Owing to the recent progress in sensing technologies, studies on work management and analysis using wearable sensors have been actively carried out [3,8,15,16]. Wearable sensors are a promising technology for achieving smart manufacturing because they enable the capture of fine-grained activities by workers that are difficult to capture by cameras in a factory where many obstacles exist. This study focuses on a line production system and attempts to help extract knowledge about skill from sensor data collected from high- and low-performing workers performing the same work process in order to support manual comparative analysis by industrial engineers. Specifically, we attempt to automatically detect a sensor data segment from a high-performing worker that potentially contains knowledge about skill, and then provide it to the industrial engineers with a video recording capturing that moment. Note that, because it is difficult for industrial engineers to understand the meaning of skill hidden in the data by watching only the data (or video), we also find a corresponding sensor data segment from the low-performing worker and present it to the industrial engineers with the segment from the high-performing worker. For example, when a segment corresponding to a screwing operation from a high-performing worker's data is detected, we also find a segment corresponding to the screwing operation from a low-performing worker's data. Comparing these segments (video recordings) permits the industrial engineer to understand the meaning of the skills hidden in the data.

Figure 1 shows example segments extracted by our proposed method (highlighted in yellow) described below. The segments (and video from a top-down view) reveal different postures between the high- and low-performing workers when attaching a label, where the high-performing worker kneels down to the level of the workbench by bending the knees to perform the work. In contrast, the low-performing worker largely bends the spine to perform the operation, and is more likely to suffer back pain. The industrial engineer can guide the low-performing worker based on the information.

1.3 Challenges and Approaches

This study has two technical challenges. The first challenge is to extract a candidate sensor data segment containing meaningful knowledge about skill by analyzing only the sensor data. In this study, we hypothesize that it is possible to extract meaningful knowledge about skills from candidate segments with the following two characteristics. (i) Sensor data from different periods by a worker are somewhat different. Segments containing a sensor data pattern (e.g., characteristic hand movement) that are found in all these periods are expected to be important and essential in the work process of interest [5]. (ii) When a sensor data pattern with the above characteristics is only available in data from the high-performing worker, the probability of the sensor data pattern relating to skill is high.

To find candidate segments with the above characteristics, we leverage explainable deep learning. Because deep learning does not require manual feature design, which is difficult for an industrial engineer for each work process, the engineer can obtain desired segments by simply feeding raw sensor data into a deep model. This is the advantage of the deep learning approach, and our experiment revealed that a simple signal matching-based approach did not work in our task. In this study, we first build a recurrent neural network that classifies time-series sensor data corresponding to a period into a high- or low-performing worker class. Because the network is trained to discriminate the sensor data of a high-performing worker from those of a low-performing worker with high accuracy, the network is expected to identify sensor data patterns containing the above two characteristics. This is because a sensor data pattern that is found in all the data from the high-performing worker but not in the low-performing worker data (and vice versa) is an important clue in the classification task. Therefore, we can leverage the trained network to automatically identify segments that potentially contain knowledge of skills. Our idea of revealing important sensor data patterns identified by the neural network, which is regarded as a black box, leverages attention mechanisms [14]. The attention mechanism provides information about importance (attention) for each data point in time series, enabling us to find a candidate segment with high attention that potentially contains knowledge about skill.

The above procedure extracts a candidate segment from the high-performing worker. We then extract a segment from the low-performing worker corresponding to the segment from the high-performing worker, which is the second challenge. Assume that a candidate segment corresponding to the screwing is detected from the high-performing worker data. This means that the screwing operation is different between the high- and low-performing workers; it is difficult to find a segment of screwing from the low-performing worker by using sensor data similarity. Our idea to address this issue is to introduce an autoencoder [10] into an attention-based network. The autoencoder extracts latent representations (compressed representations) of input data points while preserving the main components of the original data points, making it easier to find segments that are semantically similar to each other, that is, sensor data segments corresponding to the same operation.

1.4   Contributions

- This is the first study to analyze factory work using attention-based explainable deep learning.
- We extract a segment that potentially contains knowledge about skill using our network composed of an attention mechanism and an autoencoder.
- We performed qualitative and quantitative evaluations of our method using sensor data from actual factories with industrial engineers.

2   Related Work

Early studies on knowledge extraction related to factory work have relied on self-reporting [1,2], making it difficult to extract implicit knowledge about skills that can be included in an operation performed subconsciously. Recent studies have introduced activity data collected using electronic devices [4]. For example, Mirjafarl et al. [12] used mobile phones, wearables, and beacons to study differences in daily behavioral patterns (e.g., sleep) between higher and lower work performers in companies. Das Swain et al. [3] also leveraged sensors in commodity devices to investigate the relationship between work performance and the daily activities of workers. Many prior studies on analyzing work performance using sensor data collected during factory work build machine learning models that predict workers' work scores [7,13]. In contrast, our method tries to detect a data segment that potentially contains knowledge about skills using explainable deep learning.

Few recent studies leverage attention mechanisms to analyze time-series behavioral data. Zeng et al. [17] developed two attention models: temporal attention and sensor attention for detecting important sensor data segments and sensor modalities, respectively, which can be applied to identify the most important sensor data patterns and sensor modalities for detecting Parkinson's disease.

Maekawa et al. [9] also applied an attention-based neural network to animals' trajectories in order to detect segments in trajectories that are characteristic of one group, enabling biologists to focus on these specific segments and formulating new hypotheses. In contrast, this study proposes a network composed of an attention mechanism and autoencoder to enable a comparative analysis of factory works by industrial engineers.

3 Factory Work Analysis with Attention-Based Network

3.1 Preliminaries and Overview

In this study, we assume that high- and low-performing workers perform the same work process, with smartwatches worn on each worker's wrists recording three-axis accelerometer data. Multiple time-series data, with each time series corresponding to a period, from each worker are given.

Our method is composed of two steps. First, we train an attention-based neural network to automatically identify candidate segments that potentially contain knowledge about skills. Then, for each candidate, we detected the corresponding segments of the other worker.

3.2 Network for Comparative Analysis of Factory Work

Network Architecture. We designed an attention-based neural network to classify time series from high- and low-performing workers, as shown in Fig. 2. The autoencoder architecture, which is responsible for extracting feature representation f that preserves main components of an input, consists of three encoding blocks, including an 1-D convolutional layer (1D CNN), a batch-normalization layer (BatchNormalization) and a maxpooling layer (Maxpooling), and three decoding blocks, including an "1D CNN," a "BatchNormalization," and an upsampling layer (Upsampling). In addition, in the attention-based worker classifier architecture, four stacks of long short-term memory (LSTM) layers are connected to the encoder's output to extract long-term dependencies in the data used for high- and low-performer classification, enabling the extraction of candidate segments at various time scales. A block labeled "LSTM" includes LSTM and BatchNormalization layers. A block named "Atten" processes the output of "LSTM" using Eq. 1, which calculates the attention weight of the "LSTM" layer output. For each time-series input, a corresponding attention series is computed in each "Atten" layer, with the input series with a higher attention weight being more important over the entire input series for classification. A Block labeled "Mul" multiplies the attention and the outputs of "LSTM" to emphasize important timings for classification. Blocks "Concatenate" and "Softmax" refer to the concatenate and softmax layers, respectively. The equation of calculating attention at time t is denoted as follows:

$$\alpha_t = \exp(z_t) / \sum_{s=1}^{T} \exp(z_s) \qquad (1)$$

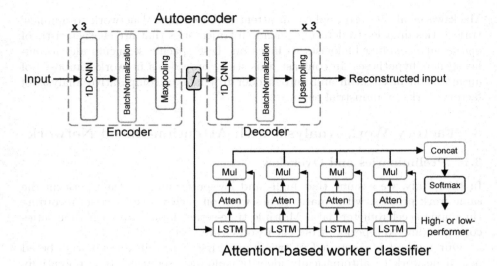

Fig. 2. Overview of proposed network.

$$z_t = \tanh(W h_t + b) \tag{2}$$

where T is the length of the latent representation f, z_t is a D-dimensional vector calculated by "Atten" at time t ($t \in \{1, ..., T\}$), and h_t is a hidden-state vector at time t output by "LSTM." W and b are the weight matrix and bias in "Atten," respectively.

Network Training. The loss of the network is composed of two components: reconstruction loss L_a (mean squared error between input and reconstructed input) and binary cross-entropy loss L_c. The reconstruction loss aims to learn latent representations using the autoencoder in an unsupervised manner while preserving the main components in the data. The binary cross-entropy loss is responsible for the binary classification (high- vs. low-performers). The overall loss function of the network is defined as $L = L_a + \lambda L_c$, where λ controls the trade-off between L_a and L_c.

Detecting Candidate Segments with Attention. Because the time-series data of different periods performed by a worker are different, we first find a representative input (period) for each worker that is most similar to all the remaining periods of the worker (i.e., the centroid of all instances). We use the dynamic time warping (DTW) algorithm to calculate the distance between each pair of time-series data, with the centroid instance giving the smallest overall distances.

After obtaining a centroid period for each worker, the corresponding attention values of the centroid from the trained network are used to extract the candidate segments. Because the attention values reveal the importance of each data point in the time series for predicting the skill level of performers, we extract segments with the top-k attention values as candidates for each layer (except the 1st layer), and then merge overlapping candidate segments.

3.3 Detecting Corresponding Segments

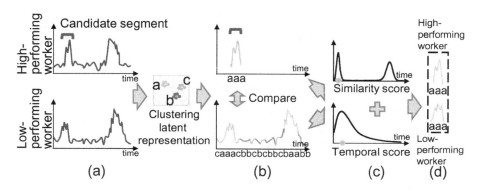

Fig. 3. Overview of the procedures to detect corresponding segments. (a) We start by clustering all data points using f to cluster similar activities. (b) We then symbolize the data points of high- and low-performers. (c) For each candidate of the high performer, we detect a corresponding segment of the low performer using a combination of similarity and temporal scores. (d) We present a pair of the candidate and corresponding segment to industrial engineers.

To support comparative analysis by industrial engineers, we then find the corresponding sensor data segment of each candidate segment. Figure 3 introduces the main idea of detecting a corresponding segment for a candidate, which is composed of four steps. First, we employed the k-means algorithm to cluster all data points using their latent representations f to group similar activities of the high- and low-performers into the same cluster, as latent representations of similar activities are supposed to be similar. Then, we symbolized each data point according to the clustering result. For each candidate, which was detected in the previous procedure, we identified a corresponding segment of a centroid period of the other worker by using a sliding time window across the entire data of the centroid period. For each time window, we calculated a combination of similarity and temporal scores, where the similarity score calculated the similarity between the symbolized candidate segment and symbol segments in the time window (inverse of Hamming distance), and the temporal score evaluates the temporal distance between the occurrence timings of the two segments in the periods because the occurrence times of the same operation in a period are expected to be similar between the high- and low-performing workers. Finally, we selected the segment with the highest score as the corresponding segment of the candidate segment.

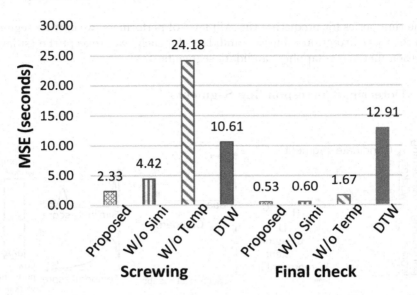

Fig. 4. Errors of the methods for detecting corresponding segments in two data sets.

4   Evaluation

4.1   Data Set

We used two acceleration data sets from four workers in a real factory using Sony SmartWatch3 SWR50 with a sampling rate 60 Hz. In the data set named "Screwing," workers were employed to install screws on the circuit boards. The number of periods for the high- and low-performers was 38 and 41, respectively, and the total duration of the data was 2337 and 2713 (s), respectively. In the data set named "Final check," workers were required to check the final products and record results; the number of periods for the high- and low-performers was 42 and 44, respectively, and the total duration was 2380 and 2797 (s), respectively.

4.2   Evaluation Methodology

We performed quantitative analysis to evaluate the performance of detecting corresponding segments. We prepared the following methods: (i) Proposed: The proposed method. (ii) W/o Simi: The proposed method without using the similarity score, (iii) W/o Temp: The proposed method without using the temporal score, and (iv) DTW: A method using raw sensor data and the DTW algorithm to find a corresponding segment. We calculated the mean squared error (MSE) between the estimated starting time of each corresponding segment by a method and the ground truth, which was manually identified.

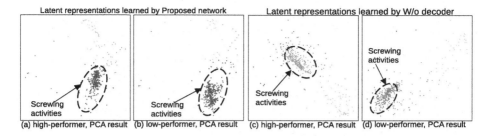

Fig. 5. Clustering result of latent representations for "Screwing" data set visualized by PCA. Different colors indicate different clusters.

We also performed a qualitative analysis to evaluate the ability of our attention-based network to detect knowledge about skills. The industrial engineers judged whether each candidate segment extracted by our method contained knowledge about the skill.

4.3 Results

Performance of Detecting Corresponding Segments. Figure 4 shows the MSE over all candidate segments in each data set. The proposed method achieved significantly small MSEs in the both data sets. In contrast, the DTW method had large MSEs on the datasets, indicating the difficulties in finding corresponding segments by only calculating raw sensor data similarity.

Figure 5 presents the clustering results of the latent representations corresponding to the two centroid instances of the "Screwing" data set visualized by principal component analysis (PCA). When we did not use the decoder block, the distributions of latent representations corresponding to the high- and low-performers are different. In contrast, our method generates similar distributions for high- and low-performers (e.g., distributions for screwing located at almost the same positions in Fig. 5). This result indicates that our idea of introducing the autoencoder enables the identification of corresponding segments (operations) of the other worker.

Analysis of Detected Segments by Attention. We qualitatively analyzed our method by asking industrial engineers to assess whether useful knowledge about skill exists in the detected segments, who followed the "principles of motion economy" strategy [11], which defines a set of rules to improve the manual work and reduce fatigue by manufacturing workers.

Table 1 shows knowledge about skill for each candidate segment detected in the two data sets, in which 7 out of 9 segments included knowledge of skill identified by the industrial engineers. The detected knowledge about skill was classified into three groups based on the principles of motion economy, which are (1) arrangement of the work place (No. 3 in "Final check"), (2) time conservation (No. 2 in "Screwing" and No. 5 in "Final check"), and (3) use of human body (No. 3, 4 in "Screwing" and No. 1, 2 in "Final check"). As mentioned above, we demonstrated that our method detected segments with knowledge of skill with high precision. In general, it takes a much longer time than the duration of the sensor data to analyze the data by an industrial engineer. We believe that our method will significantly reduce the efforts of engineers regarding the manual screening of long-term sensor data from many factory workers. While it is difficult to evaluate the recall of our method because the ground truth is unknown, the engineers noticed that our method could not detect one minute action of grabbing a tool that contains knowledge during the experiment. Improvement of our method to detect such minute actions is our important future work.

Table 1. Skill information for screwing and final check

No.	Detected operations in screwing	Knowledge
1	Set box and push button (4.23s)	-
2	Wait for next item (4.92s)	Quickly complete previous operations
3	Screwing (3.43s)	Use both hands simultaneously
4	Screwing (3.85s)	Use both hands simultaneously

No.	Detected operation in final check	Knowledge
1	Attach small label on box (4.63s)	Use left hand to guide labeling
2	Attach large label on box (4.10s)	Bend knees to reduce load
3	Stick large label on table (2.50s)	Put labels close to worker
4	Rotate box for final-check (3.03s)	-
5	Set box on table (4.63s)	Optimize the order of operations

5   Conclusion

In this study, we proposed an attention-based explainable neural network to extract sensor data segments that potentially contain knowledge about skill, which was applied to support industrial engineers to find knowledge about skill from workers. We employed the attention mechanism to emphasize important timings as candidate segments and clustered similar activities to detect corresponding segments. The results proved that industrial engineers can efficiently find knowledge about skill from the detected segments by using our method.

As part of our future work, we plan to increase the ability of our method to detect minute actions of workers with useful knowledge about skill.

Acknowledgements. This study is partially supported by JSPS JP16H06539 and JP21K19769.

References

1. Bakker, A.B., Tims, M., Derks, D.: Proactive personality and job performance: the role of job crafting and work engagement. Hum. Relat. **65**(10), 1359–1378 (2012)
2. Campbell, J.P., Mchenry, J.J., Wise, L.L.: Modeling job performance in a population of jobs. Pers. Psychol. **43**(2), 313–575 (1990)
3. Das Swain, V., et al.: A multisensor person-centered approach to understand the role of daily activities in job performance with organizational personas. Proc. ACM Interact. Mob. Wearable Ubiquit. Technol. **3**(4) (2019). https://doi.org/10.1145/3369828.
4. Hölzemann, A., Van Laerhoven, K.: Using Wrist-Worn activity recognition for basketball game analysis. In: Proceedings of the 5th International Workshop on Sensor-Based Activity Recognition and Interaction, iWOAR 2018. Association for Computing Machinery, New York (2018). https://doi.org/10.1145/3266157.3266217
5. Khan, A., et al.: Generalized and efficient skill assessment from IMU data with applications in gymnastics and medical training. ACM Trans. Comput. Healthc. **2**(1) (2021). https://doi.org/10.1145/3422168
6. Johnson, T.L., Fletcher, S., Baker, W., Charles, R.: How and why we need to capture tacit knowledge in manufacturing: case studies of visual inspection. Appl. Ergon. **74**, 1–9 (2019). https://doi.org/10.1016/j.apergo.2018.07.016. https://www.sciencedirect.com/science/article/pii/S0003687018302278
7. Lin, S., et al.: Sensing personality to predict job performance. In: Proceedings of the Extended Abstracts of the 2019 CHI Conference on Human Factors in Computing Systems, CHI EA 2019. Association for Computing Machinery, New York (2019)
8. Maekawa, T., Nakai, D., Ohara, K., Namioka, Y.: Toward practical factory activity recognition: unsupervised understanding of repetitive assembly work in a factory. In: Proceedings of the 2016 ACM International Joint Conference on Pervasive and Ubiquitous Computing, UbiComp 2016, pp. 1088–1099. Association for Computing Machinery, New York (2016). https://doi.org/10.1145/2971648.2971721
9. Maekawa, T., et al.: Deep learning-assisted comparative analysis of animal trajectories with DeepHL. Nat. Commun. **11**(1), 1–15 (2020)
10. Masci, J., Meier, U., Cireşan, D., Schmidhuber, J.: Stacked convolutional auto-encoders for hierarchical feature extraction. In: Honkela, T., Duch, W., Girolami, M., Kaski, S. (eds.) ICANN 2011. LNCS, vol. 6791, pp. 52–59. Springer, Heidelberg (2011). https://doi.org/10.1007/978-3-642-21735-7_7
11. Meyers, F.E., Stewart, J.R.: Motion and Time Study for Lean Manufacturing. Pearson College Division (2002)
12. Mirjafari, S., et al.: Differentiating higher and lower job performers in the workplace using mobile sensing. Proc. ACM Interact. Mob. Wearable Ubiquit. Technol. **3**(2) (2019). https://doi.org/10.1145/3328908
13. Ushada, M., Okayama, T., Suyantohadi, A., Khuriyati, N., Murase, H.: Kansei engineering-based artificial neural network model to evaluate worker performance in small-medium scale food production system. Int. J. Ind. Syst. Eng. **27**(1), 28–47 (2017)
14. Vaswani, A., et al.: Attention is all you need. In: Proceedings of the 31st International Conference on Neural Information Processing Systems, NIPS 2017, pp. 6000–6010. Curran Associates Inc., Red Hook (2017)
15. Xia, Q., Korpela, J., Namioka, Y., Maekawa, T.: Robust unsupervised factory activity recognition with Body-Worn accelerometer using temporal structure of multiple sensor data motifs. Proc. ACM Interact. Mob. Wearable Ubiquit. Technol. **4**(3) (2020). https://doi.org/10.1145/3411836

16. Xia, Q., Wada, A., Korpela, J., Maekawa, T., Namioka, Y.: Unsupervised factory activity recognition with wearable sensors using process instruction information. Proc. ACM Interact. Mob. Wearable Ubiquit. Technol. **3**(2) (2019). https://doi.org/10.1145/3328931
17. Zeng, M., et al.: Understanding and improving recurrent networks for human activity recognition by continuous attention. In: Proceedings of the 2018 ACM International Symposium on Wearable Computers, ISWC 2018, pp. 56–63. Association for Computing Machinery, New York (2018). https://doi.org/10.1145/3267242.3267286

Human Localization Using a Single Camera Towards Social Distance Monitoring During Sports

Ryosuke Hasegawa[1]([⊠]), Akira Uchiyama[1]iD, Fumio Okura[1]iD,
Daigo Muramatsu[2]iD, Issei Ogasawara[3]iD, Hiromi Takahata[3], Ken Nakata[3],
and Teruo Higashino[1]

[1] Graduate School of Information Science and Technology, Osaka University, Suita,
Osaka 565-0871, Japan
r-hasegawa@ist.osaka-u.ac.jp
[2] The Faculty of Science and Technology, Seikei University,
3-3-1 Kichijoji-Kitamachi, Musashino, Tokyo 180-8633, Japan
[3] Graduate School of Medicine, Osaka University,
2-2 Yamadaoka, Suita, Osaka 565-0871, Japan

Abstract. Coronavirus disease 2019 (COVID-19) is still prevalent in the world. Social distancing is more important during exercise because we may not be able to wear masks to avoid breathing problems, heatstroke, etc. For supporting management of social distancing, we are developing a human localization system using a single camera especially for sports schools and gyms. We rely on a single camera because of the deployment cost. The system recognizes people from a video and estimates the human positions for supporting management of social distancing. The challenge is the error owing to pose variation during sports. In order to solve the problem, we adjust the height of the waist according to the pose of the legs. For evaluation, we collected 80 images with 5 kinds of poses. The results show that we successfully reduce the absolute position error by 23 cm on average.

Keywords: Social distancing · Human detection · Localization

1 Introduction

COVID-19 is still prevalent in the world. Social distancing is more important during sports because we may not be able to wear masks to avoid breathing problems, heatstroke, etc. Because vision-based human detection and tracking has been actively investigated since before the pandemic, vision-based systems have been developed for supporting management of social distancing. These systems detect skeletons [1] or bounding boxes [4] of humans to estimate interpersonal distance. However, position error may become large during sports because human poses change frequently.

© ICST Institute for Computer Sciences, Social Informatics and Telecommunications Engineering 2022
Published by Springer Nature Switzerland AG 2022. All Rights Reserved
T. Hara and H. Yamaguchi (Eds.): MobiQuitous 2021, LNICST 419, pp. 481–486, 2022.
https://doi.org/10.1007/978-3-030-94822-1_27

In order to solve the problem, we propose human localization based on skeletons. Our system uses a single camera for low deployment cost and detects skeletons of people by using *OpenPose-STAF* [3]. We select the waist position estimated by *OpenPose-STAF* to represent the position of the person for its stability in human detection. To improve position error owing to pose variation, we adjust the height of the waist according to the pose of the legs.

For evaluation, we collected 80 images with 5 kinds of pose. The results show that we successfully improve the absolute position error by 23 cm on average. In particular, the error was improved by 60 cm on average when the target was sitting on the ground where the waist height changes significantly.

2   Method

2.1   Overview

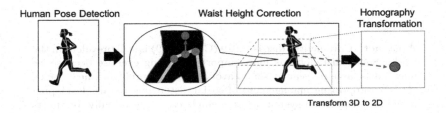

Fig. 1. Method overview

Figure 1 shows the overview of our method. We first detect persons by using the state-of-the-art skeleton detector called *OpenPose-STAF* [3]. We estimate the position of the detected person based on its skeleton and the coordinates of 4 points whose positions are given. We assume that a reference key point of the skeleton used for position estimation is at the same height as these four points. We choose the waist key point as the reference key point since *OpenPose-STAF* tends to detect the waist more reliable than the other body parts and the waist is close to the center of the body. However, the height of the waist changes depending on the pose. Therefore, we correct the height of the waist based on the key points of the legs.

2.2   Homography Transformation

For each frame, we estimate the position of the person whose skeleton is detected by using *OpenPose-STAF*. For localization, we use the homography [2], which is transformation that projects a plane to another plane, given the 4 point correspondences between the two planes. Therefore, a homography transformation matrix can transform pixel coordinates in an image into the actual positions, given the distance among 4 points in the real world. This means we need to measure the distance between these 4 points in advance.

When a coordinate in an image is (u, v)[pixel], the corresponding coordinate (x, y)[m] in the real world is obtained by the following equation.

$$(x, y) = H(u, v). \tag{1}$$

H is the homography transformation matrix represented by the following equation.

$$H = \begin{bmatrix} h_{00} & h_{01} & h_{02} \\ h_{10} & h_{11} & h_{12} \\ h_{20} & h_{21} & 1 \end{bmatrix}. \tag{2}$$

For each point with a given coordinate, we have two equations. Since H has 8 variables, we can solve H, given the actual positions of the 4 points in the image.

Our method uses the key point of the waist for the reference key point whose position is regarded as the position of the person. This is because the waist key point is stably detected even during movement compared with other key points such as legs. Therefore, the height of the 4 points for the homography transformation matrix is set to 0.9[m], which is the average waist height for adults.

2.3   Waist Height Correction

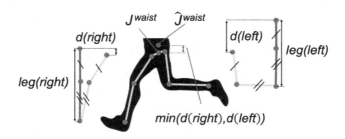

Fig. 2. Waist height correction

While walking and running, the height of the waist does not change largely. However, it can change greatly depending on poses such as sitting on a chair or the ground. Because the height error leads to the position error after the transformation, we mitigate the effect by mapping the position of the waist onto the plane with the height of 0.9[m]. The correction is performed before the homography transformation.

The overview of the correction is shown in Fig. 2. We let a coordinate of key point k be $J^k = [u^k, v^k]$. The length $l(p, q)$ between key points p and q is defined as:

$$l(p, q) = \sqrt{(u^p - u^q)^2 + (v^p - v^q)^2}. \tag{3}$$

For each leg, *OpenPose-STAF* outputs three key points which are the hip, the knee, and the ankle. The length $|leg|$ of the leg is obtained by combining the lengths between these joints as follows.

$$|leg| = l(hip, knee) + l(knee, ankle) \tag{4}$$

We call the difference between the ankle-to-hip height and $|leg|$ the *correction distance d*. The correction distance is defined as below.

$$d = |leg| - (v^{hip} - v^{ankle}). \tag{5}$$

If the leg angle against the ground becomes smaller, d becomes larger. This means the height of the reference key point (i.e. the waist) in the image is less than the assumed average waist height (i.e. 0.9[m]). Therefore, we correct the hip height by adding d to the original hip height. However, there are some cases where a leg is not on the ground because of jumping, balancing, etc. For the waist height correction, we need to use d of the grounded leg because d is calculated assuming the pose of the grounded leg lowers the waist height. If both legs are not on the ground, its duration is usually short. Therefore, we simply ignore such cases. On the other hand, when only one of the left and right legs is not on the ground, the vertical ankle-to-hip distance of the ungrounded leg becomes shorter than the grounded leg. In other words, d of the ungrounded leg is larger than the other since the lengths of the left and right legs should be almost the same. Therefore, we use either of the left or the right leg with the smaller correction distance. The coordinate of the waist $\hat{J}^{waist}$ after correction $\hat{v}^{waist}$ is given by:

$$\hat{v}^{waist} = v^{waist} + \min(d(left), d(right)). \tag{6}$$

We note that, if either of the legs is not detected, we do not perform the correction because we cannot determine detected leg is on the ground.

3   Evaluation

3.1   Evaluation Setting

For evaluation of human localization performance, we collected images from one subject. The subject was located at one of the lattice points in Fig. 3, and took 5 types of poses as shown in Fig. 4. The poses are standing, sitting (ground), sitting (chair), half-sitting, and crouching to evaluate the effect of the waist height correction. For each pose and position, we obtained images in which all key points of the lower body were detected.

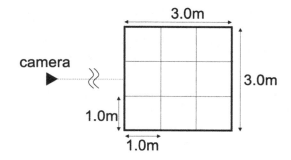

Fig. 3. Evaluation layout

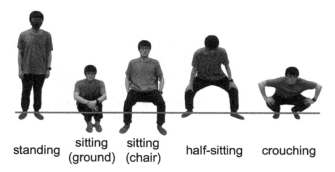

standing   sitting   sitting   half-sitting   crouching
            (ground)   (chair)

Fig. 4. Types of poses

3.2 Result

Table 1 shows the mean absolute error distance for each pose. From this result, we see that we can estimate the position of the standing person with low error. However, the error becomes larger as the waist height becomes closer to the ground. In addition, we succeeded to decrease the error by 23 cm on average by the waist height correction. However, we could not observe significant improvement for the pose of sitting on a chair. This is because the elevation angle of the camera and the angle of the leg are almost equal, which means the appearance of the leg length in the image is shorter than the actual length. In order to deal with this problem, we may need to obtain more accurate leg length by using a technique of estimating a 3D pose from a skeleton, for example.

Table 1. Mean absolute error for each pose [m]

Pose	Corrected	Original	Corrected - Original
Standing	0.056	0.064	−0.008
Sitting (ground)	0.729	1.338	−0.609
Sitting (chair)	0.716	0.779	−0.063
Half-sitting	0.370	0.641	−0.271
Crouching	0.712	0.915	−0.203
Average	0.517	0.747	−0.231

4   Conclusion

In this paper, we proposed human localization using a single camera during sports towards social distance monitoring. For evaluation, images with 5 poses were collected. As a result, we successfully reduced the absolute position error by 23 cm on average.

As our future work, we investigate a method using the upper body skeleton and/or the lower body skeleton in the previous frame for the waist height correction even when the lower body skeleton is not detected. Moreover, we are planning to use the proposed localization method for close-contact detection and tracking to quantify the risk of infection.

References

1. Aghaei, M., Bustreo, M., Wang, Y., Bailo, G., Morerio, P., Del Bue, A.: Single image human proxemics estimation for visual social distancing. In: Proceedings of the IEEE/CVF Winter Conference on Applications of Computer Vision (WACV), pp. 2785–2795, January 2021
2. Capel, D., Zisserman, A.: Computer vision applied to super resolution. IEEE Signal Process. Mag. **20**(3), 75–86 (2003). https://doi.org/10.1109/MSP.2003.1203211
3. Raaj, Y., Idrees, H., Hidalgo, G., Sheikh, Y.: Efficient online multi-person 2D pose tracking with recurrent spatio-temporal affinity fields. In: Proceedings of the IEEE Conference on Computer Vision and Pattern Recognition, pp. 4620–4628 (2019)
4. Rezaei, M., Azarmi, M.: Deepsocial: social distancing monitoring and infection risk assessment in COVID-19 pandemic. Appl. Sci. **10**(21), 7514 (2020)

Vehicle Routing for Incremental Collection of Disaster Information Along Streets

Yuga Maki$^{(\boxtimes)}$, Wenju Mu, Masahiro Shibata, and Masato Tsuru

Kyushu Institute of Technology, 680 Kawazu, Iizuka 820-8502, Japan
{maki.yuga692,wenju.mu142}@mail.kyutech.jp,
{shibata,tsuru}@csn.kyutech.ac.jp

Abstract. When a large-scale disaster occurs, it is necessary for an emergency response headquarters (HQ) to promptly collect disaster damage information. We consider monitoring such information along all streets in a town by a single vehicle equipping cameras, mics, and other sensors especially when high-speed communications infrastructures are unavailable. The vehicle starts from HQ, cruises through all streets, and finally backs to HQ to bring monitored information. Note that the vehicle can return to HQ on the way to drop a partial information monitored before. In this paper, a vehicle routing problem is posed for the information collecting vehicle by considering not only collection time of the entire information but also how much ratio and how long time the information is delayed in incremental collection to HQ for an early decision and a partial response. A grid map is used as a town's street network with three types of HQ location. Through an extensive search by leveraging Eulerian circles, we found good routes for incremental collection of disaster information. The experimental results suggest the importance of an appropriate number of returns to HQ with almost equally-sized intervals depending on the HQ location.

Keywords: Vehicle routing · Disaster information collection · Eulerian circle

1 Introduction

The increasing number of large-scale disasters such as earthquakes, typhoons and rainstorms in recent years has prompted an increasing concern and attention to the multifaceted impacts of large-scale natural disasters. An emergency response headquarters (HQ) is set up in or near the disaster area. It should collect the information on all areas and know the existence and extent of damage in a timely and accurate manner in order to make a better decision and response based on

Supported by NICT, Japan (No. 22007) and JSPS KAKENHI Grant Number 21K17706.

T. Hara and H. Yamaguchi (Eds.): MobiQuitous 2021, LNICST 419, pp. 487–492, 2022.
https://doi.org/10.1007/978-3-030-94822-1_28

the collected information. For information collection, it is often considered to use vehicles that equip cameras, mics, and other sensors and cruise through all streets in a town to monitor the disaster damage situation around each street.

In this paper, we assume that global and regional high-speed communications infrastructures are down or unavailable. In such conditions, the information collection vehicle should move not only to monitor the damage information along streets but also to bring that information to HQ by itself. As the simplest case, we use only a single information collection vehicle that starts from HQ and finally comes back to HQ. The vehicle should traverse every street at least once on the entire traveling route. On the other hand, it can return to HQ multiple times on the way of the route, drop the information monitored along the streets passed by that time, then depart from HQ again to cruise through the remaining streets. Multiple returns to drop the information for a part of all areas/streets to HQ is essential for making an early decision and a partial response.

We model the street map in a town as an undirected connected network graph. A HQ is located at a node of the network and is identically treated as that node. If the HQ has k links, the vehicle needs to return to HQ at least $\lceil k/2 \rceil$ times to cover those k links.

We focus on finding a good traveling route for an information collecting vehicle starting from and ending at HQ. This can be considered as a kind of Arc Routing Problem in Vehicle Routing Problem (VRP) [1]. However, in contrast to conventional VRPs where the shortest collection time is often pursued, we consider another evaluation criterion that represents how much ratio and how long time the disaster damage information is delayed in being brought to HQ by the vehicle. More precisely we use the following two criteria:

- Last information delay-time (LID):
  This is the time the vehicle finally comes back to HQ after traveling all links.
- Information delay-time product (IDP):
  Let $u(t)$ be the ratio of the information brought to HQ by the vehicle until time t, where t is the time spent from the vehicle's starting. The IDP is defined as $\int_0^{\text{LID}} (1 - u(t))dt$.

A small IDP can benefit an early decision and a partial response by HQ, which is expected to be realized by an appropriate number of multiple returns of the vehicle to HQ. To make "LID" small, the traveling route should be as short as possible. However, to make "IDP" small, it is not always true. Furthermore, even in the simplest case, i.e., as Eulerian m-balanced decomposition problem (a decomposition of an Euler graph to multiple balanced Euler graphs), finding a route is shown to be NP-complete [2].

Please note, for simplicity, the following two assumptions are adopted.

- The unit time is taken for the vehicle to pass through each link in one direction. In other words, the number of links passed by the vehicle is equal to the time taken for the vehicle's travel. Hence the LID is longer than or equal to the number of links of the graph.

– The amount of information monitored by the vehicle is proportional to the number of different links passed through by the vehicle. Hence, $u(t)$ is the ratio of the number of different links passed by the vehicle before returning to HQ by time t to the total number of links of the entire network.

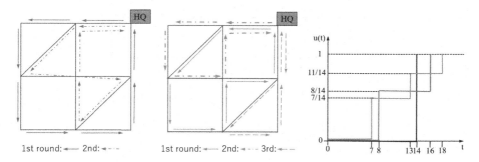

Fig. 1. A two-round route (left), a three-round route (center), and the time evolution of how much the information has been collected by HQ at t on each route (right).

2   Small Example

Suppose a street network consisting of 14 links shown in Fig. 1. There are a variety of Euler circles each of which is a shortest route to cover all links. On this example network, we fix the location of HQ where the HQ has only 2 links. Therefore, on any Euler circle route, the vehicle comes back to HQ exactly once at time 14 to bring all link information in the entire network at once.

We also consider multi-round routes although they cannot be Euler circles anymore. A round is a portion (of a route) starting and ending at HQ exactly once. On the left and center sides of Fig. 1, a two-round route and a three-round route are indicated by red and green, respectively. On the two-round route, the vehicle firstly returns to HQ at time 8 to drop a partial information and finally returns to HQ at time 16 to bring the remaining information. On the three-round route, the vehicle returns to HQ on the way at times 7, 13, and 18, to drop a partial information, respectively.

For any shortest single-round route, the above two-round route, and the above three-round route, the LIDs are 14, 16, and 18, respectively, that is in ascending order. On the other hand, computed by the blue, red, and green step functions on the right of Fig. 1, the IDPs of those routes are 14, $\frac{80}{7} \approx 11.43$, and $\frac{155}{14} \approx 11.07$, respectively, that is in descending order. This example suggests a partial drop of monitored information to HQ on the way can reduce the IDP even with a longer LID.

Note that it can be mathematically proven that 80/7 and 155/14 are the lower-bounds of IDP of any two-round route and any three-round route on this example (in terms of network and HQ location), respectively. For those good routes, we also see that the entire route is decomposed into well-balanced multiple rounds in length. Furthermore, the IDP of 155/14 is the minimum value among all possible any-round routes on this example.

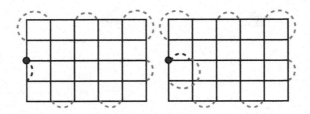

Fig. 2. Adding virtual links; two examples in case of $R = 2$ for HQ with 3 links. (Color figure online)

3   Searching a Good Route

Given an undirected connected network graph G with a HQ location (node) on it, we find good routes in terms of LID and IDP. For this purpose, we generate a variety of routes starting and ending at HQ and traversing all links on G.

Let k be the number of HQ's links. The number R of vehicle's returns to HQ is set as a parameter of routing. The return times R should be equal to or greater than $\lceil k/2 \rceil$. For a given R,

(1) add some $(2R - k)$ virtual links between HQ and its neighboring nodes on G as links used for each return of the vehicle. We can control the return times R of vehicle by adding appropriate virtual links connecting to HQ. The blue link in Fig. 2 shows such a virtual link in case of $R = 2$ for HQ with 3 ($k = 3$) links. There are choices of locations of such virtual links to add.

(2) Then add necessary virtual links to make the entire graph an Eulerian graph (i.e., to make the degree of each node even) by bridging a pair of odd-degree nodes. The red links in Fig. 2 show such a set of the virtual links. This is the same approach as Chinese Postman Problem [3]. We also have choices of the bridging pairs of odd-degree nodes and the virtual links to bridge them. Note that the number of necessary virtual links in (2) depends on the locations of links added in (1) as shown by two examples in Fig. 2.

The obtained Eulerian graph G' including virtual links is used to construct a vehicle's route that cover all (original) links, i.e., links on G, efficiently. On graph G', we can find an Eulerian circle on which the vehicle returns to HQ R times, i.e. a R-round route. There also are choices of such an Eulerian circle.

We change the above-mentioned choices to generate a variety of R-round routes for a given R; then select good candidates in terms of given evaluation criteria. Finally we repeat this process for different Rs to find good (best) routes.

4 Experimental Results

A 6×5 grid map is used as a town's street network for disaster information collection. There are 49 links and 30 nodes. Three types of HQ location are examined; the vertex (of the entire rectangle) with 2 links, the edge with 3 links, and the center with 4 links.

First, we consider the HQ location at the vertex with 2 links ($k = 2$) shown in Fig. 3 (top-left). The $u(t)$s of five exemplified routes on which the vehicle returns to HQ twice ($R = 2$) are shown in Fig. 3 (top-right). All routes have the same LID, while the IDPs are different by routes; case 3's IDP is the smallest. Figure 3 (bottom-left) illustrates the exact route of the best case 3. The $u(t)$s of five exemplified routes on which the vehicle returns to the HQ three times ($R = 3$) are also shown in Fig. 3 (bottom-right). For $R = 3$, the best route is also case 3 where the IDP is minimized and the LID is unchanged among the five. In those two good route examples for $R = 2$ and $R = 3$, we can see that the lengths of the rounds are well-balanced, i.e., the intervals between the succeeding returns to HQ are almost equalized.

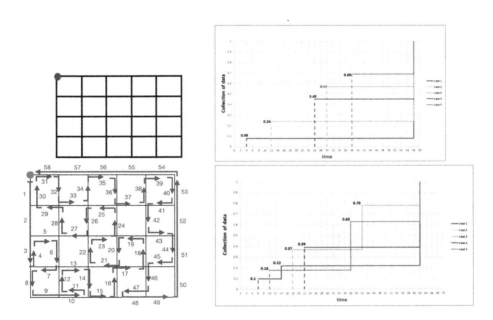

Fig. 3. HQ at a vertex (top-left); five cases of $u(t)$ for $R = 2$ (top-right); a best route for $R = 2$ (borrom-left); five cases of $u(t)$ for $R = 3$ (bottom-right).

Figure 4 compares the performance of ten good example routes for different Rs and in three types of HQ location. Regardless of the HQ location, we found that the LID is increased (at least not decreased) as the number R of the vehicle's returns to the HQ is increased. This is because the multiple returns increase duplicated traverses on the links connecting to HQ (blue links in Fig. 2 in Sec. 3) and at least it cannot decrease the number of duplicated traverses in total (blue and red links in Fig. 2). We also found that an appropriate number R of multiple returns to HQ can reduce the route's IDP. The best Rs in terms of IDP are 3, 3, and 5 when the HQ is located at the vertex, edge, and center, respectively. However, in case of HQ at the center, the IDPs of the best routes for $R = 3$ and $R = 5$ are almost the same while the LID of $R = 5$ is too large.

As a result, by considering the good balance between IDP and LID, $R = 2$, 3, and 3 are the good numbers of returns when the HQ is located at the vertex, edge, and center, respectively. Comparing the three types HQ location, we can adopt either the good case route for $R = 2$ with HQ at the vertex (LID is 58, the smallest; IDP is 42) or the good case route for $R = 3$ with HQ at the edge (LID is 60; IDP is 40.6, relatively small) as the best option of the HQ location and the number of returns.

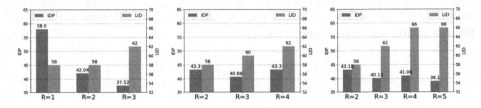

Fig. 4. IDP/LID of good cases for each R; HQ at vertex, edge, center (left to right).

5 Conclusion

A vehicle routing problem is considered in which a single information collection vehicle starts from an emergency response headquarters (HQ), cruises through all streets in a town to monitor the disaster damage situation, and finally backs to HQ to bring monitored information. On a grid map with different types of HQ location, traveling routes are investigated by considering a new criterion representing how much ratio and how long time the information is delayed in incremental collection. The experimental results suggest the importance of an appropriate number of returns to HQ with almost equally-sized intervals.

The future work could include (i) the use of multiple collaborating vehicles, (ii) the existence of uncertainty about street blocking, and (iii) the selection on a good HQ location in a deterministic or probabilistic sense.

References

1. Toth, P., Vigo, D. (eds.): The Vehicle Routing Problem. SIAM Discrete Mathematics and Applications (2002)
2. Ishii, S., et al.: The complexity of Eulerian k-balanced decomposition. In: Proceedings of the 74th JCEEE in Kyushu (2021). (in Japanese)
3. Grotschel, M., Yuan, Y.: Euler, Mei-Ko Kwan, Konigsberg, and a Chinese Postman. Documenta Mathematica: Optimization Stories, 43–50 (2012)

Smartwatch-Based Face-Touch Prediction Using Deep Representational Learning

Hamada Rizk[1,2], Tatsuya Amano[1(✉)], Hirozumi Yamaguchi[1],
and Moustafa Youssef[3]

[1] Osaka University, Suita, Japan
{hamada_rizk,t-amano,h-yamagu}@ist.osaka-u.ac.jp
[2] Tanta University, Tanta, Egypt
[3] Alexandria University, Alexandria, Egypt
moustafa@alexu.edu.eg

Abstract. World Health Organization (WHO) reported that viruses, including COVID-19, can be transmitted by touching the face with contaminated hands and advised people to avoid touching their face, especially the mouth, nose, and eyes. However, according to recent studies, people touch their faces unconsciously in their daily lives, and it is difficult to avoid such activities. Although many activity recognition methods have been proposed over the years, none of them target the prediction of face-touch (rather than detection) with other daily life activities. To address to problem, we propose *TouchAlert*: a system that automatically predict the occurrence of face-touch activity and warn the user before its occurrence. Specifically, *TouchAlert* utilizes commodity wearable devices' sensors to train a deep learning-based model for predicting the variable length face-touching of different users at an early stage of its occurrence. Our experimental results show high accuracy of F1-score of 0.98 and prediction accuracy of 97.9%.

Keywords: COVID-19 · Face touch · Activity recognition · Smartwatch

1 Introduction

The COVID-19 pandemic has impacted all spheres of our life. Infectious exposures of COVID-19 mainly occur in inhalation of virus-containing droplets into their lungs or deposition of the virus to exposed mucous membranes in the nose, mouth, or eyes. Experts said it is like any novel disease, but the critical threat lies in rapidly spreading infecting millions in a single week.

Touching the face with hands soiled is one of the primary ways of the deposition of exposed mucous membranes. Thus, World Health Organization (WHO) urges people to avoid touching their eyes, nose, and mouth to prevent infection not only from COVID-19 but also from other viral diseases such as seasonal

T. Hara and H. Yamaguchi (Eds.): MobiQuitous 2021, LNICST 419, pp. 493–499, 2022.
https://doi.org/10.1007/978-3-030-94822-1_29

influenza and Ebola virus. However, it was not possible for WHO representatives and specialists to avoid touching their faces.[1] The hand-to-face contact rate for normal people is as high as 10–26 times per hour [6]; this somehow justifies the exponential outbreak of the virus [19]. One study in Germany confirms that people are typically unaware that they are touching their faces, and they unconsciously perform this activity more frequently when they are stressed [4]. In this vein, face-touch is an instinctive activity and a hard habit to break. This motivates us to build a system for helping people **automatically detect and avoid the face-touch activity apriori** and thus reduce the possible infection transmission.

Deep learning has defined the state of-the-art performance in many application domains [1–3,9–17]. Specifically, Deep learning has enabled highly accurate human activity recognition (HAR) using inertial sensor data from widely used wearable devices. HAR is the problem of classifying sequences of multitudes of low-level sensor measurements (e.g., accelerometers and gyroscopes) into predefined movements. Current HAR techniques [8,18] involve walking, jogging, sitting, standing, etc. However, the patterns of these activities are different from the aimed face-touch one; therefore, the direct application of these techniques does set true for identifying face-touch.

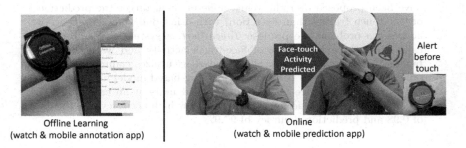

Offline Learning
(watch & mobile annotation app)

Online
(watch & mobile prediction app)

Fig. 1. Smartwatch-based face-touch prediction system

In this paper, we propose *TouchAlert*: a deep-learning-based *face-touch* prediction system to learn the non-linear relation between the sensor measurements captured by wearable devices and the activity in question (Fig. 1). To achieve highly accurate and robust activity detection, we leverage the LSTM autoencoder model to extract subject-invariant features and introduce model regularization techniques to avoid over-fitting. We evaluate the *TouchAlert* system using different smartwatches worn by *ten* different subjects practicing face-touch during pursuing different daily activities. The results show that *TouchAlert* can achieve accuracy and F1-score of 97.9% and 0.98, respectively. This is better than the state-of-the-art techniques in all scenarios.

---

[1] Even experts cannot avoid face touch activity: https://youtu.be/mA1wqjaeKj0.

2   Related Work

The system in [22] proposed a near-field communication (NFC)-based method for detecting the face-touch activity and warn users when the activity occurs. This method requires the user to wear an NFC reader and NFC tag in his/her wrist and ear, respectively. This design may not be convenient for all users as well as its success rate is not as high as the compared schemes. Few systems [7,21] have been proposed to detect the face-touch activity based on measurements captured by inertial sensors, including accelerometer and gyroscope. These systems either use hand-crafted features (e.g., mean and standard deviation) or neural network-based extracted features. Despite the simplicity of this technique, hand-crafted features cannot compete favorably in scenarios of overlapping activities as the overlapped activities (e.g., walking) will have a dominant sensory effect. Moreover, both techniques consider fixing length input leading to an inconsistent performance when tested with the variable-length activity of different subjects.

In contrast, TouchAlert, leverages a LSTM-autoencoder to automatically extract activity discriminative features from the variable length input stream. Therefore outperforming other schemes and boosts the feasibly and the required safety of this technology.

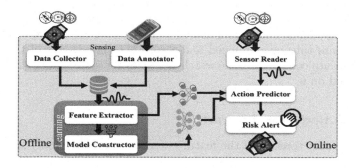

Fig. 2. *TouchAlert* system architecture.

3   System Overview

Figure 2 shows the overall system architecture. *TouchAlert* works in two stages: an offline training stage and an online sensing stage. *TouchAlert* initializes the offline stage by obtaining measurements of the smartwatch's on-board sensors, including both the accelerometer and gyroscope. These measurements represent 3-axial values from each sensor representing the acceleration and rotation along the accelerometer and gyroscope axis, respectively. This is accomplished by the Data Collector service running on the user's smartwatch. To facilitate ground-truth profiling, the Data Annotator app is installed on the connected mobile device. Next, the **Feature Extractor** module automatically learns to extract the main features from the low-level sensor measurements through the use of a deep model. These features are forwarded to the **Activity Detection Constructor** module to optimally build and train a deep model to identify the face touch activity. Finally, the trained models (i.e., *Feature Extraction* and *Activity Detection*) are stored for later use in the online phase.

During the online phase, the sensor measurements are forwarded to the online *Feature Extractor* module. And then, the **Action Predictor** module feeds these temporal features to the deep model constructed by *activity detection constructor* module to estimate the user is going to touch her face (and alert her) or not.

4   The *TouchAlert* System

This section describes the details of the *TouchAlert* system.

4.1   *TouchAlert* Sensing Part

Data is captured with two connected applications; the first is a Wear OS application running on the Android Watch and the other is an Android application installed on the user's smartphone. The watch application continuously collects 3-axis gyroscope and 3-axis accelerometer values from the IMU sensors. The smartphone application is leveraged to label the collected measurements. Both applications are time-synchronized and record the timestamps of the data collection. The data collected by the watch is sent to the smartphone via Bluetooth and processed on it.

4.2   *TouchAlert* Learning Part

The learning part consists of the feature extractor and the model constructor.

The Feature Extractor. The goal of this module is to obtain a fixed-length feature representation from a stream of sensor observations of variable length activities. Therefore, identifying the face-touch activity performed by different users and thus with different behaviors can be facilitated. Towards achieving this, *TouchAlert* has to learn the complex dynamics of input sequences as well as use internal memory to capture the temporal correlation across long and short input sequences. We employ a RNN version of autoencoder called LSTM Autoencoder [20], which is an implementation of an autoencoder for sequence data using stacked LSTM layers for feature extraction. This architecture has shown superior performance in many applications in other domains e.g., [11,12] which suggests leveraging it to automatically extract features of the face-touch activity.

The Classification Model Constructor. This module is responsible for leveraging the extracted features to train a classification model and find its optimal parameters. We construct a deep, fully connected neural network consisting of cascaded hidden layers of nonlinear processing neurons. The output layer consists of a single neuron corresponding to the activity of interest (face-touch). This network is trained to operate as a binary classifier (logistic regressor) by leveraging a Sigmoid activation function in the output layer. The model is trained using the Adaptive Moment Estimation (Adam optimizer [5]) to minimize the average cross-entropy between the estimated output probability distribution and the ground truth. The loss function is selected as binary cross-entropy.

The Online Action Predictor. This phase aims to predict the *face-touch* activity in real-time before the user's hand reaches her face. This can be done by processing the recorded sensor measurements and extracting the corresponding feature vector as described in Sect. 4.2. Thereafter, this vector is then fed to the trained *Activity Detection* model to get early recognition of either the activity is face-touch or not. The face-touch activity is detected if the output probability is higher than 0.5.

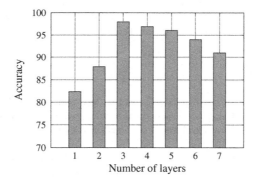

Fig. 3. Effect of number of layers

We evaluate the *TouchAlert* system using different smartwatches FOSSIL Carlyle HR or CASIO Protrek worn by *ten* different users practicing face-touch during pursuing different daily activities. The sampling rate of sensor data 100 Hz. Each face-touching activity lasted about 10–20 s and consisted of three steps: setting the hand away from the face, bringing the hand (watch) extremely close to the face, and returning the hand to its position. Users collected 20 face-touch samples for each of their arms and collected long-term watch sensor data in their daily lives, not including face touches. We used these data to evaluate the accuracy of face touch detection.

Figure 3 shows the effect of changing the number of layers on *TouchAlert* accuracy. The figure shows how increasing the number of layers of the location estimation network increases the location estimation accuracy until it reaches an optimal value at *three* layers. This can be justified as increasing the number of layers increases the model's computing power to avoid underfitting and thus better fit the function. However, the deeper the model, the more likely it is to overfit the training data, reducing its flexibility and accuracy when handling users from different providers. It's worth noting that applying the LSTM-autoencoder simplifies the classification problem in the latent encoded space. As a result, a three-layer network is sufficient for the classification of features.

5 Conclusion

This paper proposed a face touch detection system using acceleration and gyro sensor data from wearable devices. To extract robust features from time-series data of variable-length activity by different subjects, we employed an LSTM autoencoder. Our evaluation results show that the face-touch detection method can obtain 97.9% prediction accuracy with an F1-score of 0.98. These results highlight the feasibility of the proposed system for boosting public safety.

Acknowledgement. The work was supported by "Research and Development of Information and Communication Technologies that Contribute to Countermeasures against Infectious Diseases (222-C03)", the Commissioned Research of National Institute of Information and Communications Technology (NICT), JAPAN.

References

1. Abbas, M., Elhamshary, M., Rizk, H., Torki, M., Youssef, M.: WiDeep: WiFi-based accurate and robust indoor localization system using deep learning. In: Proceedings of the International Conference on Pervasive Computing and Communications (PerCom). IEEE (2019)
2. Alkiek, K., Othman, A., Rizk, H., Youssef, M.: Deep learning-based floor prediction using cell network information. In: Proceedings of the 28th International Conference on Advances in Geographic Information Systems, pp. 663–664 (2020)
3. Amano, T., Yamaguchi, H., Higashino, T.: Connected AR for combating COVID-19. IEEE Internet Things Mag. **3**(3), 46–51 (2020)
4. Grunwald, M., Weiss, T., Mueller, S., Rall, L.: EEG changes caused by spontaneous facial self-touch may represent emotion regulating processes and working memory maintenance. Brain Res. **1557**, 111–126 (2014)
5. Kingma, D.P., Ba, J.: Adam: a method for stochastic optimization. arXiv preprint arXiv:1412.6980 (2014)
6. Kwok, Y.L.A., Gralton, J., McLaws, M.L.: Face touching: a frequent habit that has implications for hand hygiene. Am. J. Infect. Control **43**(2), 112–114 (2015)
7. Michelin, A.M., et al.: FaceGuard: a wearable system to avoid face touching. Front. Robot. AI **8**, 47 (2021)
8. Radu, V., et al.: Multimodal deep learning for activity and context recognition. In: Proceedings of the ACM on Interactive, Mobile, Wearable and Ubiquitous Technologies, vol. 1, no. 4, pp. 1–27 (2018)

9. Rizk, H.: Device-invariant cellular-based indoor localization system using deep learning. In: The ACM MobiSys 2019 on Rising Stars Forum, pp. 19–23. ACM (2019)

10. Rizk, H.: SoloCell: efficient indoor localization based on limited cell network information and minimal fingerprinting. In: Proceedings of the 27th ACM SIGSPATIAL International Conference on Advances in Geographic Information Systems, pp. 604–605 (2019)

11. Rizk, H., Abbas, M., Youssef, M.: OmniCells: cross-device cellular-based indoor location tracking using deep neural networks. In: 2020 IEEE International Conference on Pervasive Computing and Communications (PerCom), pp. 1–10. IEEE (2020)

12. Rizk, H., Abbas, M., Youssef, M.: Device-independent cellular-based indoor location tracking using deep learning. Pervasive Mob. Comput. **75**, 101420 (2021)

13. Rizk, H., Shokry, A., Youssef, M.: Effectiveness of data augmentation in cellular-based localization using deep learning. In: Proceedings of the International Conference on Wireless Communications and Networking (WCNC). IEEE (2019)

14. Rizk, H., Torki, M., Youssef, M.: CellinDeep: robust and accurate cellular-based indoor localization via deep learning. IEEE Sens. J. **19**, 2305–2312 (2018)

15. Rizk, H., Yamaguchi, H., Higashino, T., Youssef, M.: A ubiquitous and accurate floor estimation system using deep representational learning. In: Proceedings of the 28th International Conference on Advances in Geographic Information Systems, pp. 540–549 (2020)

16. Rizk, H., Yamaguchi, H., Youssef, M., Higashino, T.: Gain without pain: enabling fingerprinting-based indoor localization using tracking scanners. In: Proceedings of the 28th International Conference on Advances in Geographic Information Systems, SIGSPATIAL'20, pp. 550–559. Association for Computing Machinery, New York (2020)

17. Rizk, H., Youssef, M.: MonoDCell: a ubiquitous and low-overhead deep learning-based indoor localization with limited cellular information. In: Proceedings of the 27th SIGSPATIAL International Conference on Advances in Geographic Information Systems. ACM (2019)

18. Ronao, C.A., Cho, S.B.: Human activity recognition with smartphone sensors using deep learning neural networks. Expert Syst. Appl. **59**, 235–244 (2016)

19. Shen, K., et al.: Diagnosis, treatment, and prevention of 2019 novel coronavirus infection in children: experts' consensus statement. World J. Pediatr. **16**(3), 223–231 (2020)

20. Srivastava, N., Mansimov, E., Salakhudinov, R.: Unsupervised learning of video representations using LSTMs. In: International Conference on Machine Learning, pp. 843–852. PMLR (2015)

21. Sudharsan, B., Sundaram, D., Breslin, J.G., Ali, M.I.: Avoid touching your face: a hand-to-face 3D motion dataset (COVID-away) and trained models for smartwatches. In: 10th International Conference on the Internet of Things Companion, pp. 1–9 (2020)

22. Zhang, J., Kumar, S.: NoFaceContact: stop touching your face with NFC. In: Proceedings of the 18th International Conference on Mobile Systems, Applications, and Services, pp. 468–469 (2020)

Radar-Based Gesture Recognition Towards Supporting Communication in Aphasia: The Bedroom Scenario

Luís Santana, Ana Patrícia Rocha$^{(\boxtimes)}$, Afonso Guimarães, Ilídio C. Oliveira,
José Maria Fernandes, Samuel Silva, and António Teixeira$^{(\boxtimes)}$

Department of Electronics, Telecommunications and Informatics,
Institute of Electronics and Informatics Engineering of Aveiro,
University of Aveiro, Aveiro, Portugal
{luis.santana,aprocha,afonso.guima,ico,jfernan,sss,ajst}@ua.pt

Abstract. Aphasia and other communication disorders affect a person's daily life, leading to isolation and lack of self-confidence, affecting independence, and hindering the ability to express themselves easily, including asking for help. Even though assistive technology for these disorders already exists, solutions rely mostly on a graphical output and touch, gaze, or brain-activated input modalities, which do not provide all the necessary features to cover all periods of the day (e.g., night-time). In the scope of the AAL APH-ALARM project, we aim at providing communication support to users with speech difficulties (mainly aphasics), while lying in bed. Towards this end, we propose a system based on gesture recognition using a radar deployed, for example, in a wall of the bedroom. A first prototype was implemented and used to evaluate gesture recognition, relying on radar data and transfer learning. The initial results are encouraging, indicating that using a radar can be a viable option to enhance the communication of people with speech difficulties, in the in-bed scenario.

Keywords: Smart environments · Communication · Gestures ·
FMCW radar · In-bed scenarios · Aphasia

1 Introduction

People suffering from communication impairments have much more difficulty expressing their needs in ways that other people can understand. These difficulties can lead to problems socialising and limit the person's independence, namely in asking for help when needed.

Existing assistive technology for augmenting or replacing speech includes devices providing a graphical interface and relying on non-verbal interaction modalities, such as touch, gaze, or brain-activated, together with speech-generation [2]. These solutions require interacting with a given device (e.g., tablet),

This work was supported by EU and national funds through the Portuguese Foundation for Science and Technology (FCT), in the context of the AAL APH-ALARM project (AAL/0006/2019), and funding to the research unit IEETA (UIDB/00127/2020).

T. Hara and H. Yamaguchi (Eds.): MobiQuitous 2021, LNICST 419, pp. 500–506, 2022.
https://doi.org/10.1007/978-3-030-94822-1_30

which may not be easily reached in some situations (e.g., lying in bed), rely on the use of cameras, which raises privacy concerns, and/or are too intrusive.

An alternative approach for assisting communication at a distance is the use of gestures. However, most contributions focus specifically on sign language [8]. Gesture recognition has also been explored in the context of human-computer interaction, relying on wearable sensors [5], vision-based sensors [7], or radars [1,3,4,9]. The latter have advantage of being the less intrusive and also preserving the user's privacy.

The ongoing project APH-ALARM – Comprehensive safety solution for people with Aphasia[1] – aims at allowing people suffering from aphasia (e.g., after a stroke) to communicate more easily with other people anywhere and anytime. In the scope of this project, our main objective is to enhance communication for people with speech difficulties, in the in-bed scenario (i.e., user lying in bed).

Towards this goal, we propose a system based on a Frequency Modulated Continuous Wave (FMCW) radar for supporting communication through gestures, in the considered scenario. A first prototype, where gesture recognition is performed by a model obtained through transfer learning and radar data, was developed to explore the viability of the technology. To the best of our knowledge, gesture interaction for the in-bed scenario, where some patients may spend a large part of their time, has not yet deserved much attention.

2   Radar-Based Gesture Recognition System

We propose the architecture of a system that aids communication when the user is alone in a bedroom, lying in bed, and may need to communicate with other people (e.g., caregiver, family member) to ask for help, for instance. As a first step towards a novel communication support system for patients with aphasia, we present a first prototype for radar-based gesture recognition.

2.1   General Architecture

An overview of the system is depicted in Fig. 1. A radar captures data from the detected targets, in this case the human body. These data are sent to a processing unit, where they are pre-processed by removing outliers. Features are then extracted and used to recognise the gesture being carried out. A final decision is made and sent to a smartphone.

2.2   First Prototype

As a proof-of-concept, we implemented a first prototype that relies on the setup shown on the left side of Fig. 1, which includes a bed and a radar. The radar is elevated 0.55 m from the ground, and placed at 1 m from the bed, on the left side of the subject, parallel to the longest side of the bed. The radar's 2D coordinate system is shown in Fig. 1.

---

[1] https://www.aph-alarm-project.com.

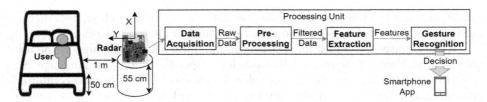

Fig. 1. Overview of the proposed system, including a possible setup for the bed and radar, as well as the pipeline for gesture recognition.

The radar is a Frequency Modulated Continuous-Wave (FMCW) radar from Texas Instruments, the AWR1642, with notable configurations entailing: frame rate (20 fps); resolution for range (4 cm) and radial velocity (0.22 m/s); maximum range (10.28 m) and radial velocity (3.47 m/s); for object detection, peak grouping in the Doppler (on) and range (off) directions, without clutter removal.

Data Acquisition: The data provided by the radar includes the X and Y coordinates, as well the Doppler index, for each detected moving target. In this first prototype, the data captured by the radar are saved to a computer.

Pre-processing: The acquired data are processed using a sliding window of 5 s without overlap. For each window, pre-processing consists of removing outliers corresponding to unwanted reflections or noise. A detected target is considered as an outlier if its Euclidean distance to the radar is outside the interval [0.5, 3] m or its absolute Doppler index is outside the interval [1e−5, 10]. All data samples with X and Y coordinates outside the intervals [−1.5, 1.5] m and [0, 2.25] m, respectively, were also discarded.

Feature Extraction: From the filtered data, three different maps are created, one for each data type versus the elapsed time (X-Time, Y-Time, and Doppler-Time). The beginning and ending of the window where no movement is detected are discarded. An example of the X-Time and Doppler-Time maps for a repetition of the third gesture described below ("Back and Forth") is presented in Fig. 2, where the colour represents the number of detected targets (bright yellow corresponds to the maximum value for each map, while dark blue corresponds to no detected target). The matrix associated to each map is used to obtain a normalised greyscale image. The three images are then combined into a single image (X-Time above Y-Time above Doppler-Time).

Gesture Recognition: The images resulting from feature extraction are fed into a model that performs gesture recognition. This model is previously trained using the transfer learning method, relying on a pre-trained deep neural network model for image classification, and a given dataset. For this prototype, the focus was on the recognition of the following three arm gestures, all starting with the arm parallel to the body and resting on the bed: (a) **Wave** – Move the arm and hand from left to right and back; (b) **Raise Arm** – Raise the arm until a 90° angle is formed with the body and then lower it back to initial position; (c)

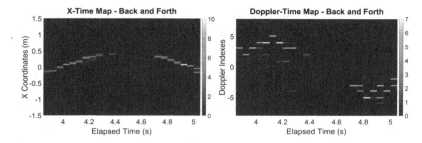

Fig. 2. Example of X-Time (left) and Doppler-Time (right) maps, for the "Back and Forth" gesture. (Color figure online)

Back and Forth – "Come to me" motion, where the forearm is moved towards the arm making an angle below 90°, and then returning to full extension.

These gestures were selected aiming at simplicity and based on initial feedback from therapists and carers on the gestures' suitability for aphasic patients lying in bed. Moreover, they can be used for generating simple messages (e.g., "I need help") and "Yes/No" answer.

3 Evaluation

An initial evaluation of the prototype was performed to explore the possibility of recognising the defined gesture set using radar data together with transfer learning, in the context of the in-bed scenario.

Subject and Experimental Protocol: Radar data were captured from a 23-year-old, right-handed male subject. The used setup is the one included in Fig. 1, where the subject was lying in bed on their back. Each considered gesture was executed 50 times. Even though the subject is right-handed, all gestures were performed with the left arm, due to the radar being on the left side of the bed. For each repetition, data recording was initiated before the gesture execution and stopped automatically after 5 s.

Datasets: The obtained dataset includes 150 images (50 per gesture). Since deep learning requires a large dataset to obtain reasonable results, we expanded the dataset relying on offline data augmentation, to obtain a better performance and avoid overfitting. For each image in the original dataset, 5 or 10 new images were created by adding noise to that image (resulting in two augmented datasets). The type of noise added to the image was randomly chosen and can be a combination of the following types: Gaussian, salt and pepper, and Poisson. For all except Poisson, the amount of noise was limited to a proportion of image pixels to replace of 0.002 (chosen empirically).

Gesture Recognition Models: To obtain a model that recognises the considered gestures, we used the transfer learning method. Since our aim is to run gesture recognition in a processing unit with limited memory and computing capability, from the pre-trained models directly available in Keras [6], we explored

three that achieved a top-5 accuracy equal or greater than 90% (ImageNet validation dataset) and have less than 10 million parameters: MobileNetV2, NASNet-
Mobile, DenseNet121. For each pre-trained model, the top layers were replaced
by a single fully connected layer with 256 neurons (ReLU as the activation function) and an output layer with 3 neurons (softmax activation function). The used
optimizer was ADAM (default parameters). Crossentropy was used as the loss
function, and accuracy as the evaluation metric during training and validation.

Evaluation Method: Each model was evaluated using the 10-fold cross-
validation approach, where 80% of the dataset is used for training, 10% for
validation, and 10% for testing, in each iteration. Training is stopped when the
validation loss has not decreased more than 0.1 for 5 epochs. The resulting model
is evaluated on the test data of the corresponding iteration.

4   First Results

Results were obtained for the three pre-trained models listed above and for three
different datasets: original (150 images); augmented 1 (750 images); augmented 2
(1500 images). The boxplots for the accuracy, F1 score, train time, and prediction
time per image, considering all 10 folds, are shown in Fig. 3.

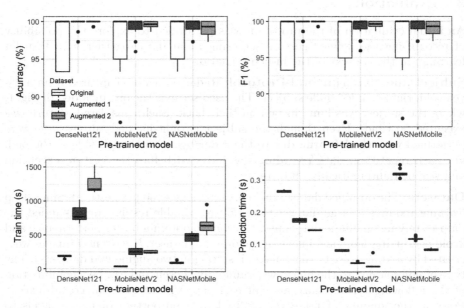

Fig. 3. Boxplots for the accuracy (left-top), F1 score (right-top), train time (left-
bottom), and prediction time (right-bottom), for each model and dataset.

We can see that augmenting the data has an overall positive effect when it
comes to the variability of accuracy and F1 score, for all three models. On the

other hand, the train time increases when the size of the dataset increases, as expected, but the prediction time per image decreases. For both train and prediction times, the difference among datasets is lower for the MobileNetV2 model, which also has the lowest median train and prediction times: 35 to 252 s and 0.03 to 0.08 s, respectively, versus 84 to 639 s and 0.08 to 0.32 s for NASNetMobile, and 185 to 1177 s and 0.14 to 0.27 s for DenseNet121. This was also expected, since MobileNetV2 is the smallest of the three pre-trained models ($\approx$3.5 M parameters), followed by NASNetMobile ($\approx$5.3 M parameters; DenseNet21 has $\approx$8.1 M). Despite its smaller size, MobileNetV2 still leads to a model with a median accuracy and F1 score similar to the other models ($\geq$99% for all datasets). Although these results are quite good, it can be because only three gestures were considered and all used data came from the same subject.

5 Conclusion and Future Work

Our long-term research goal is the implementation of gesture-based communication support system for people with speech difficulties, such as aphasics. This system would provide its users with a more assisted and independent life, including at night-time. Our initial results on gesture recognition are in line with those reported in other similar contributions using radars (in scenarios different from the in-bed setting) [3,4,9]. They show the feasibility of recognising a simple set of gestures, in the specific in-bed scenario, based on a radar, which is not invasive or intrusive and can be placed in the environment.

Our study has some limitations, such as a small dataset limited to one subject and three gestures. However, we intend to obtain a larger dataset including more gestures and data from a greater number of subjects. This dataset will allow us to investigate if a model trained with data from a given subject(s) can be used to recognise gestures performed by never seen subjects.

References

1. Ahmed, S., Kallu, K.D., Ahmed, S., Cho, S.H.: Hand gestures recognition using radar sensors for human-computer-interaction: a review. Remote Sens. **13**(3), 527 (2021)
2. Elsahar, Y., Hu, S., Bouazza-Marouf, K., Kerr, D., Mansor, A.: Augmentative and Alternative Communication (AAC) advances: a review of configurations for individuals with a speech disability. Sensors **19**(8), 1911 (2019)
3. Hazra, S., Santra, A.: Robust gesture recognition using millimetric-wave radar system. IEEE Sens. Lett. **2**(4), 1–4 (2018)
4. Ishak, K., Appenrodt, N., Dickmann, J., Waldschmidt, C.: Human gesture classification for autonomous driving applications using radars. In: IEEE MTT-S International Conference on Microwaves for Intelligent Mobility (ICMIM), pp. 1–4, November 2020
5. Jiang, S., Kang, P., Song, X., Lo, B., Shull, P.B.: Emerging wearable interfaces and algorithms for hand gesture recognition: a survey. In: IEEE Reviews in Biomedical Engineering, p. 1 (2021)

6. Keras: Keras applications. https://keras.io/api/applications/
7. Wang, T., et al.: A survey on vision-based hand gesture recognition. In: Basu, A., Berretti, S. (eds.) Smart Multimedia, pp. 219–231. Springer, Cham (2018)
8. Yasen, M., Jusoh, S.: A systematic review on hand gesture recognition techniques, challenges and applications. Peer J. Comput. Sci. **5**, e218 (2019)
9. Yu, M., Kim, N., Jung, Y., Lee, S.: A frame detection method for real-time hand gesture recognition systems using CW-radar. Sensors **20**(8), 2321 (2020)

Wi-Fi CSI-Based Activity Recognition with Adaptive Sampling Rate Selection

Yuka Tanno$^{(\boxtimes)}$, Takuya Maekawa, and Takahiro Hara

Osaka University, Suita, Japan
{tanno.yuka,maekawa,hara}@ist.osaka-u.ac.jp

Abstract. Activity recognition methods using Wi-Fi Channel State Information (CSI) have been actively studied in the mobile and ubiquitous computing community. Many prior studies on CSI-based context recognition systems employ CSI data collected at a high and constant sampling rate, resulting in always high computation costs for context recognition. In this study, we propose a CSI-based activity recognition method that adaptively adjusts the sampling rate using reinforcement learning. In the proposed method, the "action" in the reinforcement learning is defined as the selection of a sampling rate of CSI, and the "state" is defined as an intermediate output of a neural network for activity recognition in the environment, which is expected to include information describing the complexity of the current activity. Moreover, we design an activity recognition model that can accept CSI inputs collected at an arbitrary sampling rate in principle, and extract sampling-rate-independent intermediate representations in its intermediate layers, enabling the reinforcement learning agent to switch to an appropriate sampling rate regardless of the current sampling rate. We evaluated the proposed approach using data collected in real environments.

Keywords: Wi-Fi CSI · Activity recognition · Reinforcement learning

1 Introduction

With the development of sensing technology, research on recognizing human activity by analyzing real-world sensor data has been actively studied. Activity recognition is a technology that estimates an activity class of a target person based on real-world sensor data, and can be applied to building various real-world applications such as home automation and surveillance of elderly people living alone. In addition to conventional methods using video data from cameras and/or accelerometer data from wearable devices [5,6], activity recognition methods using Wi-Fi Channel State Information (CSI) have been attracting attention in recent years [8]. Wi-Fi CSI contains information about propagation paths of Wi-Fi obtained from the physical layer between the transmitter and receiver that perform wireless communication, and is composed of the amplitude and phase of the complex channel information for each subcarrier between

© ICST Institute for Computer Sciences, Social Informatics and Telecommunications Engineering 2022
Published by Springer Nature Switzerland AG 2022. All Rights Reserved
T. Hara and H. Yamaguchi (Eds.): MobiQuitous 2021, LNICST 419, pp. 507–512, 2022.
https://doi.org/10.1007/978-3-030-94822-1_31

each transmit-receive antenna pair. The methods using Wi-Fi have the following advantages over the conventional methods. (i) They do not suffer from privacy problems caused by methods using camera images. (ii) They can recognize a target's activity even when the target is at the camera's blind spot. (iii) No wearable device is required. (iv) Commercially available Wi-Fi access points can be used to construct a recognition system.

Because of the limited transmission range of Wi-Fi, multiple CSI-based activity recognition systems (i.e., transmitter and receiver pairs) are installed in an environment, e.g., office and house. When the system is installed for each room, for example, the amount of CSI data to process is proportional to the number of systems, requiring significant computation costs when we assume large-scale deployment of the systems. Because the computation costs of always-on monitoring systems are crucial for achieving green ICT, an energy-saving approach that maintains precise activity recognition is necessary. Our solution proposed in this study is to adaptively control the sampling rate of the CSI-based activity recognition system according to a state of an environment in which the recognition system is installed. Prior studies on CSI-based context recognition systems employ CSI data collected at a high and constant sampling rate [4,7]. However, when a person in an environment of interest is sleeping, for example, the high sampling rate CSI data is not required to recognize the simple activity.

Therefore, in this study, we propose a CSI-based activity recognition method that adaptively adjusts the sampling rate according to the current state of an environment of interest. The proposed method employs reinforcement learning to adjust the sampling rate of CSI sensing by the recognition system.

2   Proposed CSI-Based Activity Recognition Method

2.1   Overview

In this study, we assume an indoor environment where a transmitter and a receiver of Wi-Fi are installed. The transmitter transmits packets and the receiver receives them and obtains CSI for each packet. The frequency of the transmitter's packet transmission corresponds to the sampling rate of the CSI in this study. The proposed method estimates an activity class of a person in the environment for each time window of data, and at the same time the method determines the sampling rate to be used for the next time window. The sampling rate of the CSI is either one of three: HIGH, MIDDLE, and LOW, 25 Hz for HIGH, 5 Hz for MIDDLE, 1 Hz for LOW in our implementation.

The proposed method consists of an activity recognition model and a sampling rate selection module, as shown in Fig. 1.

2.2   Activity Recognition Model

Here we introduce the activity recognition model used in the proposed method shown in Fig. 1. The activity recognition model is a neural network trained to

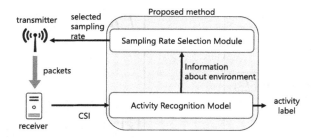

Fig. 1. Overview of proposed method

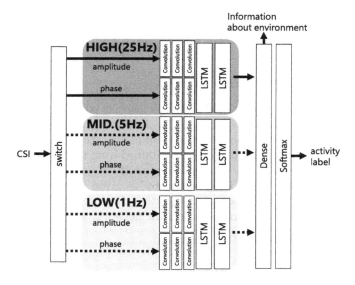

Fig. 2. Activity recognition model of proposed method

estimate an activity label of input CSI data. In the proposed method, the intermediate output of the activity recognition model is used as the input of the sampling rate selection module. The intermediate output of the activity recognition model can be regarded as features extracted from CSI data for activity recognition that contain information about the complexity of the current activity, and is useful for selecting the sampling rate. However, because the proposed method assumes CSI acquired at different sampling rates as an input, it is necessary to prepare a different activity recognition model for each sampling rate in general. Because the intermediate output of each model is considered to have different meanings, the intermediate outputs of the models cannot be simply used as an input of the sampling rate selection module. To address this issue, we design an activity recognition model that can process CSI data collected at different sampling rates as shown in Fig. 2.

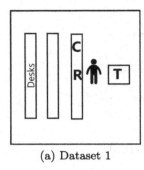

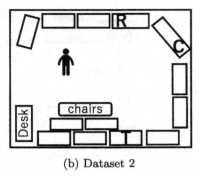

(a) Dataset 1   (b) Dataset 2

Fig. 3. Experimental environments. T is the transmitter, R is the receiver, and C is the camera for acquiring ground truth labels.

2.3 Sampling Rate Selection Module

The sampling rate selection module is implemented based on a reinforcement learning model, Deep Q Network (DQN) [3]. In this study, the "action" in reinforcement learning is selection of a CSI sampling rate (HIGH, MIDDLE, or LOW), and the "state" is the information obtained from the observed CSI (intermediate output of the activity recognition model). In order to achieve recognition at a low sampling rate, a higher "reward" is given when the reinforcement learning agent can correctly recognize an activity at a lower sampling rate.

Note that, to efficiently train the neural network, we modify the original DQN in several ways according to [2].

3 Evaluation Experiment

3.1 Dataset

The datasets for the evaluation experiment were collected in two different environments; Dataset 1 and Dataset 2. Dataset 1 consists of 12 sessions of labeled CSI data acquired in the environment depicted in Fig. 3(a). In each session, a participant performed a set of seven activities: walk, tooth brushing, using vacuum cleaner, abdominal exercises, squat, jumping rope, and side-to-side jumping, in a random order. Dataset 2 consists of 12 sessions of labeled CSI data acquired in the environment shown in Fig. 3(b). In each session, a participant performed a set of five activities; walk, sleeping on chairs, using a laptop, squat, and juggling with a ball, in a random order. The duration of each activity is about 20 s.

The transmitter and receiver were PCs equipped with Intel 5300 NIC Wi-Fi modules. We installed the CSI tool published by Halperin et al. [1] on each of them and used it to acquire CSI data. The transmitter has three antennas, the receiver has one antenna, and the number of subcarriers is 30.

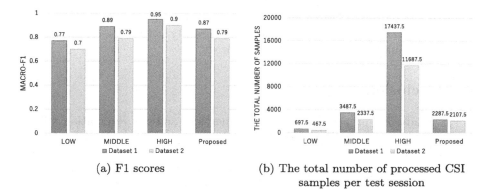

(a) F1 scores

(b) The total number of processed CSI samples per test session

Fig. 4. Results of the comparison methods and proposed method

3.2 Evaluation Method

To verify the effectiveness of the proposed method, we prepared the following comparison methods.

- HIGH: A method that constantly 25 Hz as the sampling rate
- MIDDLE: A method that constantly 5 Hz as the sampling rate
- LOW: A method that constantly 1 Hz as the sampling rate

In the experiment, we used 9-session data as training data for activity recognition, 1-session data as training data for reinforcement learning, and the remaining sessions as test data. For reinforcement learning, the 1-session training data was used by randomly changing the order of activities per episode.

Since the above methods output an activity estimate for each window, the macro-averaged F-measure (macro-f1 score) calculated with the estimates is used as an evaluation metric for recognition performance. In addition, the total number of CSI samples processed for recognition in the test data is used as a metric to evaluate the computational cost of recognition.

3.3 Results

Figure 4(a) shows the average F-measures of the comparison methods and the proposed method for Datasets 1 and 2. The F-measures of the proposed method were 0.87 for Dataset 1 and 0.79 for Dataset 2, which are almost identical to those of MIDDLE. The average numbers of total samples used in the processing of the comparison methods and the proposed method are shown in Fig. 4(b). The total numbers of samples of the proposed method were 2287.5 for Dataset 1 and 2107.5 for Dataset 2.

As shown the results of Dataset 1 in Fig. 4(a) and 4(b), the proposed method results in a reduction of the F-measure by only 2% compared to MIDDLE, while the number of samples processed was reduced by 35%. For dataset 2, the F-measure of the proposed method was identical to the F-measure of MIDDLE. In contrast, the number of samples processed was reduced by 10%. Therefore, we can say that the proposed method could significantly reduce the computational cost while maintaining the recognition accuracy.

4 Conclusion

In this study, we proposed a method to perform activity recognition with a lower sampling rate while maintaining high accuracy by adaptively adjusting the sampling rate according to the current state, and showed its effectiveness through evaluation experiments in real environments. As a part of our future study, we plan to construct a reinforcement learning agent that can work in any environments without the necessity of environment-dependent training.

Acknowledgement. This study is partially supported by JSPS JP16H06539 and JP21H03428.

References

1. Halperin, D., Hu, W., Sheth, A., Wetherall, D.: Tool release: gathering 802.11n traces with channel state information. Comput. Commun. Rev. **41**(1), 53 (2011). https://doi.org/10.1145/1925861.1925870
2. Hessel, M., et al.: Rainbow: combining improvements in deep reinforcement learning. CoRR abs/1710.02298 (2017). http://arxiv.org/abs/1710.02298
3. Mnih, V., et al.: Playing atari with deep reinforcement learning. Computing Research Repository, CoRR abs/1312.5602 (2013). http://arxiv.org/abs/1312.5602
4. Ohara, K., Maekawa, T., Matsushita, Y.: Detecting state changes of indoor everyday objects using wi-fi channel state information. In: Proceedings of the ACM on Interactive, Mobile, Wearable and Ubiquitous Technologies, IMWUT, vol. 1, no. 3, pp. 88:1–88:28 (2017)
5. Ravi, N., Dandekar, N., Mysore, P., Littman, M.L.: Activity recognition from accelerometer data. In: The Twentieth National Conference on Artificial Intelligence and the Seventeenth Innovative Applications of Artificial Intelligence Conference, pp. 1541–1546 (2005)
6. Ulutan, O., Rallapalli, S., Srivatsa, M., Manjunath, B.S.: Actor conditioned attention maps for video action detection. Computing Research Repository, CoRR abs/1812.11631 (2018). http://arxiv.org/abs/1812.11631
7. Wang, W., Liu, A.X., Shahzad, M., Ling, K., Lu, S.: Device-free human activity recognition using commercial WiFi devices. IEEE J. Sel. Areas Commun. **35**(5), 1118–1131 (2017). https://doi.org/10.1109/JSAC.2017.2679658
8. Wang, Y., Liu, J., Chen, Y., Gruteser, M., Yang, J., Liu, H.: E-eyes: device-free location-oriented activity identification using fine-grained WiFi signatures. In: The 20th Annual International Conference on Mobile Computing and Networking, MobiCom 2014, pp. 617–628 (2014). https://doi.org/10.1145/2639108.2639143

Air Handling Unit Explainability Using Contextual Importance and Utility

Avleen Malhi[1,2]($\boxtimes$), Manik Madhikermi[2,3]($\boxtimes$), Matti Huotari[2], and Kary Främling[2,3]

[1] Department of Computing and Informatics, Bournemouth University, Poole, UK
amalhi@bournemouth.ac.uk
[2] Department of Computer Science, Aalto University, Espoo, Finland
{avleen.malhi,manik.madhikermi,matti.huotari}@aalto.fi,
manik.madhikermi@protonmail.com
[3] Department of Computer Science, Umeå University, Umeå, Sweden
kary.framling@cs.umu.se

Abstract. Artificial intelligence has acted as an essential driver of emerging technologies by employing many sophisticated Machine Learning (ML) models, while lack of model transparency and results explanation limits its effectiveness in real decision-making. The eXplainable AI (XAI) has bridged this gap by providing the explanation of outcomes made by these complex ML model. In this paper, we classify the functioning of an air handling unit (AHU) using the neural network and utilise contextual importance and contextual utility (CIU) as an XAI module for explaining outcome of the neural Network. Here, we prove that CIU (XAI module) can generate transparent and human-understandable explanations, which the end-user can therefore utilize for making decisions proving the overall applicability of the method in a novel use-case. Visual and textual explanations for the causes of an individual prediction have been derived from the CIU that are numeric values calculated from the machine learning module results. We also have provided contrasting explanations against some causes that were not involved in the decision. We provide both in our proposed approach.

Keywords: Explainable artificial intelligence · Contextual importance · Contextual utility · Air handling unit

1 Introduction

The artificial intelligence (AI) has advanced increasingly from mature machine learning techniques in the last years. As an effect, a variety of use cases for these technologies has found their way into the everyday tlives of a multitude of users. The absence of transparency in AI decisions, might have an adverse impact on the system trustworthiness. This lack of trustworthiness can also decrease the overall user-experience [5, 11]. Even though the research on understandable and transparent AI systems is flourishing, but these explanations are mostly targeted for technical users and are ignored for the end-users in the realistic artificial intelligence

T. Hara and H. Yamaguchi (Eds.): MobiQuitous 2021, LNICST 419, pp. 513–519, 2022.
https://doi.org/10.1007/978-3-030-94822-1_32

systems. Overall, these concerns towards innovative technologies are considered as a critical matter for AI researchers to resolve [2,10]. Hence, the promotion of eXplainable Artificial Intelligence (XAI) is vital for enabling excellent exploitation and establishment of innovative machine learning algorithms in AI systems [1]. Many research studies recommend to model the explanations based on the relevant practical concepts which means providing complete and contrastive explanations to end-users for producing human understandable explanations [8]. Complete explanations provide the justification of an individual instance whereas contrastive explanations explains why a particular prediction was made contrary to other one.

In this paper, for our case-study we use a reference model that has a machine learning module for classifying the air handling unit and a module for making the explanation for the reasons of the classification made. The fact that detecting the failure cases from the normal behavior is a rather laborious task because of high number of dimensions and huge data. Further, because the reasons leading to a particular working state (e.g. fault situation) are often unknown and unique, the reasoning about the event-chain leading to a state is particularly burdensome; therefore Air Handling Unit (AHU) is a particularly good case-study for explainable artificial intelligence [7]. A proven AI method has been applied for the classifying module. For the explanation module we have used the Contextual Importance and Utility (CIU) method for explaining the classification results in more human understandable way [4]. CIU provides the explanations in the form of natural language and visual representations for explaining the test instances [3]. Our method provides both complete and contrastive explanations for the fault detection in air handling unit. The rest of the paper is organized as follows: Sect. 2 studies the related work in the explainable artificial intelligence, Sect. 2 presents the proposed approach based on contextual importance and utility (CIU) for an air handling unit. Section 3 discusses the results in the form of visual and textual explanations and, finally Sect. 4 concludes the paper.

2   Proposed Approach for Explaining the Events in an Air Handling Unit

Generally, it is a human tendency to ask for explanations for making a particular prediction instead of other which implies that what will be outcome if the input is changed. Hence, the explanations also play a major role in explaining the prediction results that something has happened instead of another. Complete explanations provide the justification of an individual instance [9]. The approach of contextual importance and utility can be used for both linear and non-linear models and it explains the predictions of the model for an individual test instance by calculating the contextual importance and utility for each feature. The contextual importance (CI) of an input has been defined by the current values of the inputs and the input range, and the contextual utility (CU) is defined by the output range and current output value. The contextual importance of an input on an output is then defined as the ratio:

$$CI(C, \{i\}, j) = \frac{Cmax(C, \{i\}, j) - Cmin(C, \{i\}, j)}{absmax_j - absmin_j} \tag{1}$$

where $absmax_j$ is the maximal possible value for output j, $absmin_j$ is the minimal possible value for output j, $Cmax(C, \{i\}, j)$ is the maximal value of output j observed when modifying the values on inputs $\{i\}$ and keeping the values of the other inputs at those specified by C. Correspondingly, $Cmin(C, \{i\}, j)$ is the minimal value of output j observed. The definition of CU is then

$$CU(C, \{i\}, j) = \frac{out_{C,j} - Cmin(C, \{i\}, j)}{Cmax(C, \{i\}, j) - Cmin(C, \{i\}, j)} \tag{2}$$

where $out_{C,j}$ is the value of the output j for the context C.

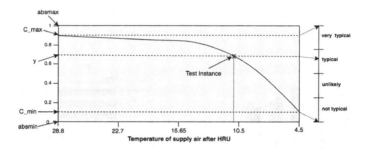

Fig. 1. Contextual importance and contextual utility illustration for case study of air handling unit

CI refers to the ratio of output range obtained by varying the input values for a certain feature x_1 through its whole range from minimum to maximum. The output range lies between the lowest possible output value (C_{min}) by varying feature values and the highest possible output value (C_{max}). CU refers to the position of the predicted output y_i for the selected test instance with context to the output range calculated by CI i.e. if the y_i is close to (C_{max}), it is having high utility and if it is close to (C_{min}), it is having low utility. This has been very clearly illustrated in the Fig. 1 which lists the C_{min}, C_{max}, CI and CU values for a particular test instance of air handling unit. The values are depicted for an input *feature temperature of supply air after HRU* which is an important feature in air handling unit. The results are explained for the normal functioning of air handling unit.

In this paper for our case-study we have used a method for decision making for a black-box model. We are explaining the results derived by neural network method (i.e. a continuous, non-linear method) [6,7]. The method takes into account the selection criteria and the importance of the criteria in a context for the air handling unit in question for making explanations. For our case-study of an air handling unit, the output is "working status" that has two values normal (0) and abnormal (1).

3   Performance Analysis

In this section we introduce the results of diagnosis of the air handling unit's working state (including but not solely faults), which are often onerous to detect based on individual input events of the AHU so that the end-user understands the rationale of the system. The result of explanations for a air handling unit are presented having two output classes, its normal and abnormal functioning. The dataset used in this example is real time data collected from *Enervent* company with 26700 instances consisting 18882 normal and 7818 abnormal instances. Normal state indicates the normal functioning of the air handling unit and Abnormal means there is no heat recovery. We calculated the CI and CU values for the normal and abnormal test instances based on which we provide the human understandable explanations in the form of visual and text based representation. The *absmin* and *absmax* are 0 and 1 respectively and value of C_{min} and C_{max} lies within the range of 0 and 1.

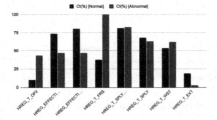

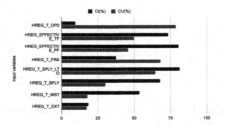

Fig. 2. The comparison of contextual importance values for normal and broken case of AHU

Fig. 3. The contextual importance and utility for all input variables in a normal AHU

The contextual importance and utility values are visually represented in Fig. 3 to depict the importance and utility for each input variable in a normal instance of air handling unit. It can be analyzed that current exhaust speed (EFFECTIVE_PF) and temperature of supply air after HRU (T_SPLY_LTO) are the most important features for the normal AHU working and the utility of T_SPLY_LTO is typical which means it is the considered feature in detection of normal functioning of AHU. The least considered characteristic is the temperature of the extracted air (T_EXT) which has the lowest utility. Again, the temperature of supply air (T_SPLY) which is an important feature is least considered for the normal state of AHU. The contextual importance (CI) is compared for the normal and abnormal instance of air handling unit as depicted in Fig. 2. When the feature's importance is compared for the normal and abnormal state of AHU, it is seen that the temperature of fresh incoming air (T_FRS) was most important feature in deciding abnormal state of AHU whereas current exhaust speed (EFFECTIVE_PF) and temperature of supply air after HRU (T_SPLY_LTO) were the most important ones for deciding normal AHU state. Considering the abnormal state, the most considered features with high utility values are temperature at operator panel (T_OP2) and current supply fan speed (EFFECTIVE_TF) and current exhaust fan speed (EFFECTIVE_PF). It implies that temperature of fresh incoming air (T_FRS) was most important feature which was considered and even though temperature at operator panel (T_OP2), current supply fan speed (EFFECTIVE_TF) were not very important feature but they were considered highly in deciding the abnormal functioning of air handling unit. Although temperature at operator panel (T_OP2) and temperature of fresh incoming air (T_FRS) are also most considered features with high utility in deciding abnormal functioning of AHU but their importance is less. The temperature of extracted air (T_EXT) is least important with less utility value. The temperature of fresh incoming air (T_FRS) is having least utility value explaining the abnormality of the system as shown in Table 1. In contrast, temperature of supply air after HRU (T_SPLY_LTO) is the most important considered feature for normal functioning of the AHU. The other important feature is current exhaust speed (EFFECTIVE_PF) but having comparatively less utility value. The other features which are most considered in deciding the normal functioning are temperature at operator panel (T_OP2), temperature of supply air (T_SPLY) which have high utility values but their feature importance is really less. The CI and CU values are compared for the normal and abnormal instances of air handling unit in Table 1.

Table 1. Comparison of CI and CU values for normal and abnormal case of AHU

		T_OP2	EFFECTIVE_TF	EFFECTIVE_PF	T_FRS	T_SPLY_LTO	T_SPLY	T_WST	T_EXT
Normal	CI (%)	9.81	73.46	80.63	37.46	81.22	67.98	53.65	18.59
	CU (%)	78.73	49.84	45.83	68.17	64.7	30.2	17.76	17.22
Abnormal	CI (%)	42.96	46.71	46.63	100	82.7	63.11	62.22	2.57
	CU (%)	97.45	89.63	89.79	41.86	50.63	66.34	67.28	49.68

The textual based explanations are shown in Fig. 4. It gives the complete and contrastive explanations for the normal and abnormal state of the air handling unit for justification of prediction of the particular class label (normal or abnormal). The contrastive explanations are also produced to discuss the possible contrasting explanations.

The model's prediction is 65% normal functioning of air handling unit, because:
The room temperature which is not important (CI=9.81%) feature, is very typical for its class (CU=78.71%).
The current supply fan speed which is very important (CI=73.45%) feature, is unlikely for its class (CU=49.84%).
The current exhaust fan speed, which is highly important (CI=80.64%) feature, is unlikely for its class (CU=45.83%).
The fresh air temp. which is important (CI=37.46%) feature, is typical for its class (CU=68.16%).
The fresh air temp. after HRU which is highly important (CI=81.22%) feature, is typical for its class (CU=64.69%).
The room supply air temperature after HRU which is very important (CI=67.99%) feature, is unlikely for its class (CU=30.21%).
The waste air temperature which is very important (CI=53.64%) feature, is not typical for its class (CU=17.75%).
The extracted room air temperature which is not important (CI=18.59%) feature, is not typical for its class (CU=17.22%).
 The most important features are fresh air temperature after HRU and exhaust fan speed.

The model's prediction is abnormal air handling unit because:
The room temperature which is important (CI=42.96%) feature, is very typical for its class (CU=97.45%).
The current supply fan speed which is important (CI=46.71%) feature, is very typical for its class (CU=89.63%).
The current exhaust fan speed, which is important (CI=46.63%) feature, is very typical for its class (CU=89.79%).
The fresh air temp. which is highly important (CI=100%) feature, is unlikely for its class (CU=41.86%).
The fresh air temp. after HRU which is highly important (CI=82.7%) feature, is typical for its class (CU=50.63%).
The room supply air temperature after HRU which is very important (CI=63.11%) feature, is typical for its class (CU=66.34%).
The waste air temperature which is very important (CI=62.22%) feature, is typical for its class (CU=67.28%).
The extracted room air temperature which is not important (CI=2.57%) feature, is unlikely for its class (CU=49.68%).

Fig. 4. The normal and abnormal states of AHU explainable by complete and contrastive explanations

4 Conclusion

The explanation method discussed provides adaptability for explaining any "black-box" model. The explanation method used in the study comprises the of getting the contextual importance and contextual utility for the individual instances to provide the complete visual and text-based explanations as well as contrastive explanations. We used case study of air handling unit to explain the fault detection scenarios. We provided the explanations for the normal as well abnormal working conditions of the air handling unit in the human-understandable manner. In the case-study, we used multiple criteria for decision making and transferred the results into understandable verbal format that including certain degree of uncertainty in the explanations as the events are not black-and-white classification situations. Future work includes testing of the approach for more complex building automation data comprising of multiple sensors and multi-class outputs.

References

1. (DARPA). Broad agency announcement, explainable artificial intelligence (XAI) (2016). https://www.darpa.mil/attachments/DARPA-BAA-16-53.pdf
2. Došilović, F.K., Brčić, M., Hlupić, N.: Explainable artificial intelligence: a survey. In: 2018 41st International Convention on Information and Communication Technology, Electronics and Microelectronics (MIPRO), pp. 0210–0215. IEEE (2018)
3. Främling, K.: Explaining results of neural networks by contextual importance and utility (1996)
4. Främling, K., Graillot, D.: Extracting explanations from neural networks. In: Proceedings of the ICANN, vol. 95, pp. 163–168. Citeseer (1995)
5. Linegang, M.P., et al.: Human-automation collaboration in dynamic mission planning: a challenge requiring an ecological approach. In: Proceedings of the human factors and ergonomics society annual meeting, vol. 50(23), pp. 2482–2486. SAGE Publications, Los Angeles (2006)

6. Madhikermi, M., Yousefnezhad, N., Främling, K.: Heat recovery unit failure detection in air handling unit. In: Moon, I., Lee, G.M., Park, J., Kiritsis, D., von Cieminski, G. (eds.) APMS 2018, Part II. IAICT, vol. 536, pp. 343–350. Springer, Cham (2018). https://doi.org/10.1007/978-3-319-99707-0_43

7. Madhikermi, M., Malhi, A.K., Främling, K.: Explainable artificial intelligence based heat recycler fault detection in air handling unit. In: Calvaresi, D., Najjar, A., Schumacher, M., Främling, K. (eds.) EXTRAAMAS 2019. LNCS (LNAI), vol. 11763, pp. 110–125. Springer, Cham (2019). https://doi.org/10.1007/978-3-030-30391-4_7

8. Miller, T.: Explanation in artificial intelligence: insights from the social sciences. Artif. Intell. **267**, 1–38 (2019)

9. Molnar, C.: Interpretable machine learning. a guide for making black box models explainable (2018)

10. Shahriari, K., Shahriari, M.: IEEE standard review-ethically aligned design: a vision for prioritizing human wellbeing with artificial intelligence and autonomous systems. In: 2017 IEEE Canada International Humanitarian Technology Conference (IHTC), pp. 197–201. IEEE (2017)

11. Stubbs, K., Hinds, P.J., Wettergreen, D.: Autonomy and common ground in human-robot interaction: a field study. IEEE Intell. Syst. **22**(2), 42–50 (2007)

Internet of Robot Things in a Dynamic Environment: Narrative-Based Knowledge Representation and Reasoning

Sabri Lyazid[1,2]([⊠]) [iD]

[1] LISSI, The Laboratory of Images, Signals and Intelligent Systems,
University Paris-Est, Champs-sur-Marne, France
[2] Computer Science Department, University of Mohamed El Bachir El Ibrahimi,
BBA, El Anceur, Algeria
sabri@lissi.fr, lyazid.sabri@univ-bba.dz

Abstract. Internet of Things (IoT) technologies interconnect increasing numbers of artifacts (e.g., robots, sensors) and individuals, allowing the setting up of Internet of Robotic Things (IoRT) systems in a dynamic environment (e.g., homes, hospitals). Semantic heterogeneity is among the main challenges that arise for developing those systems. Particularly to deal with the dynamic knowledge extraction from the heterogeneity of sensors and data that are spatially and temporally distributed, the sporadic occurrence of events, and also if there is a causality chain that explains an ordered occurrence of these events. Ontologies constitute de facto an ineluctable design to reduce this ambiguity by creating a semantic link between low-level digital data, allowing: i) dynamic knowledge management, and ii) enhancing environmental perception and anchoring functions.

This approach uses a model that overcomes the disadvantages of the semantic Web standards such as OWL/RDF-S. An IoRT system dedicated to monitoring and assisting the elderly in their everyday living is described and evaluated.

Keywords: Ontology · OWL · Narrative · Reasoning · Spatial-temporal representation · IoRT · IoT · Distributed systems

1 Introduction and Motivation

Joined into the Internet of Robot Things (IoRT) environment, robots are designed to ensure complex cognitive tasks such as assistance and monitoring dependent persons [5]. Fundamental requirements within such dynamic environments are dynamic knowledge management, handle the nontrivial aspects of spatial-temporal reasoning based on chronological and semantic analysis, about past and ongoing events. Robots endowed with formal ontological models and

T. Hara and H. Yamaguchi (Eds.): MobiQuitous 2021, LNICST 419, pp. 520–526, 2022.
https://doi.org/10.1007/978-3-030-94822-1_33

capabilities to i) deal with the dynamic knowledge extraction and processing from the heterogeneity of sensors spatially and temporally distributed, ii) perceiving and correlating events' semantic relationships (i.e., causal explanation and ordered occurrence) can accomplish tasks under different environmental conditions. To show the effectiveness of the proposed approach in an IoRT environment, let's start with the following motivating scenario that influenced the overall of our approach.

Consider an elderly named John, living alone. He has been using his laptop in the living room when someone rang. John moves towards the entrance to open the door. Using the sensor fixed on the door, the open-door event can be detected. John and his guest are heading towards the living room. A few minutes later, John goes to the kitchen and tries to prepare some coffee. At this moment, the presence sensor detects a motion in the living room. From the observations that can be perceived and correlated in this scenario, a reasoning system designed to control the habitat of John should be able to recognize particularly: John interrupts the activity (the use of a PC), and John is not alone. The latter knowledge is deduced since John cannot be present in two different spaces simultaneously. In this scenario, let us assume that John is wearing physiological sensors (e.g., the bracelet) that notify hospital staff if John feels bad or falls. After John's guest left, we suppose that John falls and does not push the emergency button. In this case, a robot has to localize and check John's status and evaluate his health state. Handling the semantic link between the real world abstraction and the knowledge bases through ontologies allows enhancing robot' environmental perception, interaction, actuation, control, and anchoring functions. Consequently, finding correlations between events over time is still an open issue and an important aspect that automatically builds up a causal explanation for an event/situation.

The best approach is to create a semantic link between low-level digital data derived from perception systems with high-level semantic representations of ontology to meet those requirements [3]. The aim here is to implement a process of grounding concepts defined in ontologies with the entities present in the real environment. The approach presented here enables the semantic description of heterogeneous entities that can change over time and interact with each other. The representation and reasoning about dynamics events/contexts use hierarchical structures of semantic predicates and functional roles of the Narrative Knowledge Representation Language (NKRL) [1]. NKRL overcomes the disadvantages of semantic Web ontological such as OWL/RDF-S by providing HTemp ontology. The latter uses n-ary hierarchical structures of predicates and n-ary semantic roles to represent dynamic events, spatial-temporal dependencies, and context knowledge.

1.1   NKRL Vs OWL-SWRL

Several ambient intelligence and robotics applications have been implemented using W3C approaches such as [4,6]. Even if these approaches offer a high level of expressiveness, their major disadvantages lie in generating a redundant description of temporal knowledge, the difficulty of defining predicates of any arity to represent the temporal dimension of properties, and rewriting most existing ontologies. Moreover, reasoning about the semantics of temporal relationships expressed with these ontologies can only be done with OWL-DL's reasoning engines [2]. Furthermore, standard OWL-like languages offer little support for building up rules. Indeed, the lack of the notion of variable in OWL makes it impossible to rely on this language in its native form to build real inference engines for rule processing and does not support rules and rule processing introduced in its specifications at the time of its conception.

Note that the argument often raised in a W3C context and stating that any n-ary representation can always be converted to one, making use only of binary relations without any loss of expressiveness is incorrect. A statement like: "the robot moves towards the place where John is localized and tries to check if he is conscious or not" requires being considered a single indivisible entity. So, it can be tough to describe this type of information in full, using the usual binary Semantic Web (SW) languages in the W3C style (RDF, OWL). Nevertheless, there are proposals for n-ary relations and n-ary datatypes; however, they are definitely excluded in OWL 2. Indeed, these proposals have unnecessarily increased the complexity of reasoning in different ontological layers. Therefore, it remains significant issues that are not handled by OWL 2 that make it unsuitable in terms of dynamic context/events recognition and spatial-temporal concept representation and thereby express a chronological ordering between events/context.

1.2 Spatio-Temporal Representation and Semantic Correlation Between Events

Based on time instant, NKRL uses two temporal attributes: date-1 and date-2, allowing annotating an event/context to reconstruct the logic of Allen interval. The temporal attribute, date-1, represents the event that begins to be true at the timestamp t1-the second date-2, which denotes the end of the same event at the timestamp t2. The time interval is organized into nine lists corresponding to three categories: precedence, coincidence, subsequence, see Fig. 1. The preceding category represents the events that appeared before the date indicated in the date-1 attribute. The subsequence category represents events that occurred after date-2. The coincidence category makes it possible to represent events using the obs(erve) modulator used to denote the beginning of an event. These three categories each consist of three lists. Each list is divided into three sections corresponding to period 1, period 2, and period 3. Finally, bound 1 and bound 2 delimit these periods.

Another possibility is that only an intermediate timestamp t3, between t1 and t2, is known. In all these cases, NKRL requires that we use only the first temporal attribute, date-1, i.e., the single timestamp available is systematically associated with date-1, the second attribute, date-2, being empty.

For example, the *home control system* observes that ENTITY_1 is sitting but does not give any information about the end of this event or its duration.

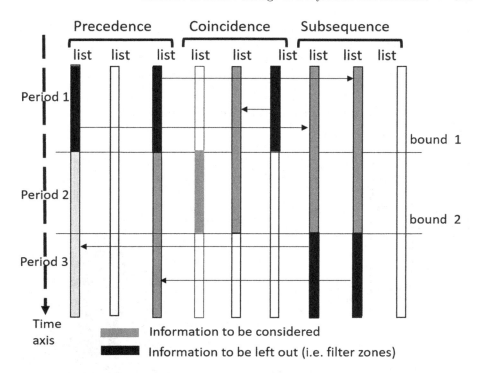

Fig. 1. The temporal index algorithm.

Such information is expressed in NKRL with the predicative occurrence *aal8.c29*. The *BEHAVE* predicate is used to express an event where an entity is performing a task (i.e., manifests a given behavior directly). The *ENTITY_1* instance as "filler" of the *SUBJ(ect)* role, the *sitting_position* property as filler of the *MODAL* role, finally *date−1* is the temporal attribute that marks the beginning of the event.

aal8.c29) PREDICATE: BEHAVE
          SUBJ: ENTITY_1: LIVING_ROOM_1
          MODAL: sitting_position
            { obs }
          date-1:24/06/2021:19:20:785
is instance of Behave:HumanProperty (1.1)

aal8.c28) PREDICATE: PRODUCE
          SUBJ: ROBOT_KOMPAI
          OBJ: detection_: LIVING_ROOM_1
          TOPIC: (SPECIF ENTITY_2(SPECIF different_from JOHN_))
          date-1:24/06/2021:19:42:556
is instance of Produce: Assessment/Trial

The predicative occurrence aal8.c28 allows specifying that ROBOT_KOMPAI observes an entity different to John present in the living room. Before inferring that John cannot be at two different locations, the system must first verify that the space where the person is detected is part of the habitat of John.

1.3   The Commonsense Reasoning and Evaluations

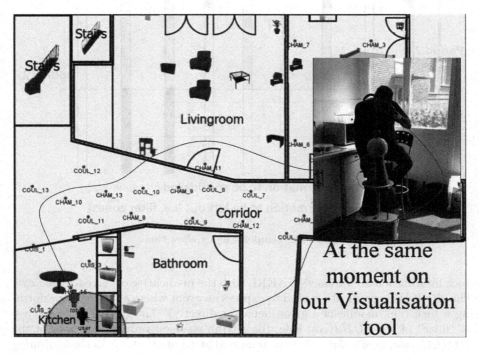

Fig. 2. Depending on the knowledge analysis, The robot accomplishes tasks under different environmental conditions and recognizes situations/contexts. Moreover, distributed IoT devices assist the robot in localizing John. In fact, a concept defined in an ontology becomes identifiable from the data provided by the sensors.

Ensuring the homogeneity of the knowledge base and classifying each entity according to its role allow easily aggregating spatial-temporal events. Indeed, the conceptual representation at the design time of events by predicative occurrences requires the definition of a generic model making semantic matching between the NKRL templates and an event observed in the environment. This matching model can be seen as a function that takes input a syntactic description of the event and objects (role, properties, appearance, etc.) and computes as output an NKRL template. Therefore, the interface communication ensures a coherent representation of the world situations by handling the link between the real world abstraction and the knowledge base, Fig. 2. The experiments were conducted at the laboratory. The environment includes the following components: 1) A robot named Kompai. It has various sensors (i.e., 2 RGB cameras, one microphone, 6 ultrasound sensors, and 16 laser sensors), actuators, and a processing unit with a touchscreen display. This robot provides several high-level services, such as managing the medical agendas and the medical treatment; it can recognize and synthesize voice, enable speech interaction, send emails, and navigate in unknown environments, 2) Sensors for measuring brightness, moisture, and temperature; and 3) A bracelet for detecting falls and measuring the pulse of a person. Regarding the temporal performance of the NKRL model, the response time required to recognize the context in the scenario presented at the beginning of this document is 3.7 s. This time is acceptable for ambient intelligence applications.

2   Conclusion

NKRL addresses the lack of expressiveness linked with the binary nature of the W3C languages prevents them from representing correctly high-level information. In NKRL, concepts are represented in the (usual) binary way. Nevertheless, elementary events/situations (and general classes of events/situations) are represented using n-ary predicate/roles. Moreover, special conceptual structures have been conceived to take the temporal phenomena into account. Therefore, we claim that NKRL can play an important role in the AmI domain and cognitive robots. The symbolic modeling and reasoning at a high semantic level about space and time are fundamental for recognizing situations and providing customized assistive services. Indeed, the narrative-based approach we explore allows semantic descriptions of entities, events, and relationships between events, uses an n-ary hierarchical structure of semantic predicates and functional roles.

References

1. Zarri, G.P.: NKRL, a knowledge representation language for narrative natural language processing. In: 16th International Conference on Computational Linguistics, Proceedings of the Conference, pp. 1032–1035, (1996)
2. Devi, R., Mehrotra, D., Zghal, H.B., Besbes, G.: SWRL reasoning on ontology-based clinical dengue knowledge base. Int. J. Metadata Semant. Ontol. **14**(1), 39–53 (2020)
3. Brunete, A., Gambao, E., Hernando, M., Cedazo, R.: Smart assistive architecture for the integration of IoT devices, robotic systems, and multimodal interfaces in healthcare environments. Sensors **21**, 2212 (2021)
4. Maamar, Z., Faci, N., Kajan, E., Asim, M., Qamar, A.: OWL-T for a semantic description of IoT. In: Darmont, J., Novikov, B., Wrembel, R. (eds.) ADBIS 2020. CCIS, vol. 1259, pp. 108–117. Springer, Cham (2020). https://doi.org/10.1007/978-3-030-54623-6_10

5. Sabri, L., Bouznad, S., Fiorini, S.R., Chibani, A., Prestes, E., Amirat, Y.: An integrated semantic framework for designing context-aware. internet of robotic things systems. Integr. Comput. Aided Eng. **25**(2), 137–156 (2018)
6. Byeong, J.M., Sonya, S.K., JongSuk, C.: Organizing the internet of robotic things: the effect of organization structure on users' evaluation and compliance toward IoRT service platform. In: IROS, pp. 6288–6295 (2020)

The First Workshop on Ubiquitous and Multi-domain User Modeling (UMUM2021)

An Empirical Study on News Recommendation in Multiple Domain Settings

Shuichiro Haruta$^{(\boxtimes)}$ and Mori Kurokawa

KDDI Research Inc., 2-1-15 Ohara, Fujimino-shi, Saitama 356-8502, Japan
{sh-haruta,mo-kurokawa}@kddi-research.jp
https://www.kddi-research.jp/english

Abstract. News recommendations using deep neural networks have been a hot research topic. However, most studies on news recommendations are based on the single domain setting. In this paper, we propose a news recommendation framework that uses freezing parameters and fine-tuning techniques for multiple domain settings. Since the model learned by data from multiple news platforms enables the representation of news articles to be much more robust, freezing the parameters of the news encoder effectively works in this setting. Moreover, the characteristics of domain-specific users are captured by fine-tuning the model on each domain data. Our empirical results with a real-world dataset demonstrate that using multiple domain data in the news recommendation results in a better performance. Despite its simplicity, the proposed framework works well, especially for domains where the number of data points is small. This framework has an AUC improvement of about 10% compared with the single domain setting.

Keywords: Recommender system · News recommendation · Deep learning

1 Introduction

Recently, an increasing number of news articles have been provided to us by various news platforms, such as Google news[1] and Gunosy.[2] Since it is impossible for users to read all of them, personalized news recommendation systems have become an important research topic [25]. On behalf of users, personalized news recommendation systems make recommendations by utilizing several pieces of information, such as users and news articles. Personally recommended articles help users save time and improves their user experience.

Although several news recommendation methods have been proposed, most recent research focuses on deep learning techniques [8,9,11,14,19–23] and aims

---

[1] https://news.google.com.
[2] https://gunosy.co.jp.

T. Hara and H. Yamaguchi (Eds.): MobiQuitous 2021, LNICST 419, pp. 529–540, 2022.
https://doi.org/10.1007/978-3-030-94822-1_34

to achieve higher performance by obtaining distributed representations of both users and articles. For example, in Ref. [14], the authors propose the mechanism that uses denoising autoencoder and triplet loss to represent news articles. The representations of users are based on their browsing history and sessions. NRMS [21] applies word2vec [13] to news titles. The obtained word embeddings are further fed into a multihead self-attention mechanism to capture word relationships. A pretrained language model such as BERT is also used in news recommendations [4,24].

However, to the best of our knowledge, recent research on news recommendations mentioned above deals with the single-domain setting, and there are not enough studies, especially on deep learning-based cross-domain news recommendations. In fact, there is a cross-domain situation where the data of multiple news platforms are available such that a news company deals with multiple news brands (e.g., Japanese news provider "Gunosy" has three brands named "Gunosy", "Newspass", and "Lucra"). In this setting, news articles might be more robustly represented compared with a single-domain setting, and users might show different characteristics in each domain. Therefore, we propose investigating the performance of deep learning-based methods under a cross-domain news recommendation setting.

In this paper, we propose pretraining the model by using all domains' data and freezing news-related model parameters for fine-tuning. It is expected that pretraining with all domains' data enables news embedding to be much more robust, and domain-specific user characteristics are expressed by fine-tuning. As a result of the experiments, the proposed framework worked well, especially in domains where the number of data points was small and increased improvement to 10 % compared with the single domain setting.

The contributions of this paper are as follows:

- To the best of our knowledge, this is the first study in the cross-domain news recommendation field.
- We find that using multiple domain data in the news recommendation brings better performance. Our results are useful for other researchers who would like to know the performance of deep models in this setting.

The remainder of this paper is constructed as follows: We describe the related works on news recommendation and state research questions in Sect. 2. The proposed framework to answer the research questions is described in Sect. 3. In Sect. 4, we evaluate the proposed framework. Finally, we conclude this paper and mention future works in Sect. 5.

2 Related Works

We can roughly classify the news recommendation methods into two approaches, "traditional methods" and "deep learning-based methods". We introduce the representative methods in this section.

2.1   Traditional Methods

In the early stage of research on news recommendations, traditional collaborative filtering methods [1,3,5,16] were representative. In those methods, the news that people with similar preferences liked (clicked) in the past is recommended to a user. However, since the user-user similarity and recommended items are defined based on articles' ID, it is intrinsically difficult to recommend novel news articles, which is also known as the "cold start problem". News recommendation is especially sensitive to this problem since news arrives continuously and users can easily change their preferences. To overcome the cold start problem, the features of news content have been proposed. For example, by using the TF-IDF (Term Frequency-Inverse Document Frequency)-like algorithm, some methods take the contents of news articles into consideration [2,6,7]. Since TF-IDF is a technique that can extract keywords from documents, it is utilized for creating a feature vector of news articles. Furthermore, popularity, categories, sentiment information, and news location are represented as features and incorporated into the model [10,12,15,18]. However, these types of handcrafted features are usually not optimal in representing the semantic information encoded in news texts [22].

2.2   Deep Learning-Based Methods

With the surge of deep learning techniques, almost all recent recommendation models adopt neural networks. In particular, the content of news articles is captured by a deep neural network-based NLP (Natural Language Processing) technique, and users are represented by their browsing history of news articles in many cases. In Ref. [14], the authors propose the mechanism that uses DAE (Denoising Auto Encoder) and triplet loss to represent news articles. The representations of users are based on their browsing history and sessions, which are also considered in other research [8,9]. To obtain a richer representation, CNNs (Convolutional Neural Networks) and attention mechanisms are applied to news content [19–21]. For example, in NRMS [21], it applies word2vec [13] to news titles. The obtained word embeddings are further fed into a multihead self-attention mechanism to capture word relationships. A pretrained language model such as BERT is also used in news recommendations [4,24]. In addition to using a deep NLP model, some works predict user behavior, such as "active-time" and "satisfaction" [11,23]. They learn the models in a multitask fashion and improve performance.

2.3   Question

To the best of our knowledge, recent research on news recommendations mentioned above addresses the single-domain setting, and there are not enough studies, especially on deep learning-based cross-domain news recommendations. Basically, the model should be learned by using a large amount of data with good quality in many machine learning scenarios. In this context, using multiple-domain data might compensate for the amount of data in a single domain. On the other hand, it is easy to assume that users' features are different in each news platform. We would like to find a good way to tune news articles and user embeddings in a cross-domain setting.

Our interests are summarized as follows;

1. Is news embedding much more robust if we use multiple domain data?
2. Should we consider the characteristics of domain-specific users?

We aim to answer these questions through the proposed framework.

3   Proposed Framework

To clarify the above questions, we propose pretraining the model by using all domain data and freezing news-related model parameters for fine-tuning. It is expected that pretraining with all of the domain data enables news embedding to be more robust, and domain-specific user characteristics to be expressed by fine-tuning.

We show the overview of the proposed framework in Sect. 3.1, and a detailed explanation of the proposed architecture is described in Sect. 3.2.

3.1   Overview

We consider the cross-domain situation where the data of all domains (platforms) are available such that a news company deals with multiple news brands. The data included in news domains is denoted as $\{T_i | 1 \leq i \leq N_{\text{domain}}\}$, where N_{domain} is the number of domains. T_i contains the information of user-news interactions, e.g., displayed news, clicked news, and timestamps. Please note that news is shared in each domain, but users are not shared in our assumption. Furthermore, T_i is divided into training, validation, and test sets. That is, $T_i = T_i^{\text{train}} \cup T_i^{\text{val}} \cup T_i^{\text{test}}$. Let S denote the data in which each T_i is combined. S^{train} is denoted as $S^{\text{train}} = \bigcup_i T_i^{\text{train}}$. The same holds on S^{val} and S^{test}. In our framework, the model is first learned by using S^{train} and S^{val}. Then, the model is fine-tuned by using T_i^{train} and T_i^{val} in each domain. Finally, test sets T_i^{test} and S^{test} are used for the evaluation. Figure 1 shows an example of data utilization flow.

3.2   Architecture and Procedure

We follow the recent models' architecture, which captures the contents of news articles by NLP, and users are represented by a set of browsed news embeddings. These types of methods are mentioned in Sect. 2. The following explanation accompanies Fig. 2. Let the user's browsed articles and the recommendation candidate article denote $\{D_i | 1 \leq i \leq H\}$ and D_{cand}, where H is the number of histories input to the model. Each of the browsed articles is input to news encoders whose projection is defined as f. The $\mathbf{e_i}$, i-th output of the news encoder, is formulated as

$$\mathbf{e_i} = f(D_i; \theta_{\text{news}}), \tag{1}$$

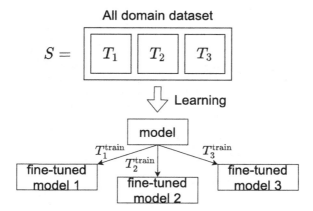

Fig. 1. Overview of the data flow. This is an example of the case where $N_{\text{domain}} = 3$. First, S is used for learning the recommendation model. The model is then fine-tuned in each domain using T_1, T_2, and T_3.

where θ_{news} is the trainable parameter. Let $\mathbf{u}$ denote an embedding of the user. $\mathbf{u}$ is expressed as

$$\mathbf{u} = g_1(E; \theta_1), \tag{2}$$

where g_1, E, and θ_1 are the aggregator & conversion function, set of $\mathbf{e_i}$, and trainable parameter, respectively. Similarly, the click prediction $\hat{p}$ is expressed as

$$\hat{p} = g_2(\mathbf{u}, \mathbf{e}_{\text{cand}}; \theta_2). \tag{3}$$

The model should output higher probability when D_{cand} is the article to be recommended, and vice versa. Since the number of news articles is generally too large, it is difficult to train the model by using all articles. To overcome that, most methods adopt a negative sampling strategy in the training phase. That is, $\mathbf{u}$, D^+ (clicked article), and $D_1^-, D_2^-, ..., D_K^-$, (K-sampled non-clicked articles) are used to train the model. Although the loss calculation depends on the base model, for example, it can be formulated as

$$\text{loss} = \sum_{i=0}^{K} \mathcal{L}(p_i, y_i), \tag{4}$$

where $y_0 = 1$, p_0 is the predicted click probability of the positive sample, $y_1, ..., y_k = 0$, $p_1, ..., p_K$ are those of the negative sample, and $\mathcal{L}$ is a loss function.

In the pretraining process, we use dataset S and train the above model parameters θ_{news}, θ_1, and θ_2 by minimizing loss using optimizers such as SGD (Stochastic Gradient Descent). In fine-tuning, T_i^{train} and T_i^{val} in each domain are used, and θ_{news} is frozen. Thus, we have i models that are dedicated to each domain.

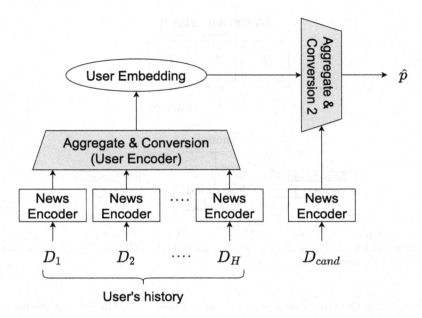

Fig. 2. Overview of the assumed model. Many works (e.g. [14, 19–21]) adopt this kind of architecture and we follow that. In this paper, we basically follow NRMS [21], architecture. Parameters in components of gray are fine-tuned in each domain, and other parameters are frozen.

4   Experiments

4.1   Base Model

In the following experiments, we select NRMS [21] as the base model and apply the proposed framework with the same hyper-parameter settings. This is because its architecture is simple and brings effective results. That model adopts an NLP-based news encoder, and user embeddings are based on their browsed history, which also suits our assumption. Please note that other models can also be used for our experiments.

4.2   Dataset

We use three datasets: "Gunosy", "Newspass", and "Lucra", which are the names of news platforms run by a single company. Table 1 shows the details of dataset. As shown in Table 1, the news articles are partly shared in each dataset, and users are not shared. Further, Lucra targets female users. Thus, its user characteristics are supposed to be different from other domains. Since each article is written in Japanese, we used Japanese word embeddings (GloVe) made by asahi.com [17]. We believe they are suitable for the news recommendation task because they are made from newspaper articles. Within the shown period, the data of 31st July 2020 are only used as the test set, and the others are the training and validation sets. For the training phase, we try two negative sampling strategies based on two sample sources: "All articles" and "Impression". When the source is "all articles", negative samples for a user are randomly chosen from all unread articles in the training set. These datasets include impression data, which is a set of news articles displayed in users' devices and also used as the negative sampling source by randomly choosing unread articles. The number of negative samples K is set to 4 by following NRMS.

Similarly, we make two types of evaluation data from test sets. In the first case, we randomly choose 200 negative samples from all articles in the test set for each user. In the second case, we use all negative samples in the impression data for each user. We denote "A" and "I" as negative sampling source ("All articles" and "Impression", which are mentioned above). For example, (A, I) indicates that train set contains negative samples picked from All articles and test set contains negative samples picked from Impression.

Table 1. The number of users and articles in each dataset. G, N, and L indicate Gunosy, Newspass, and Lucra, respectively. Shared users and articles are represented by X ∩ Y. We picked a maximum of 3,000 users who have a larger number of clicks from each domain and the articles they clicked were extracted.

Dataset	# User	# Article	Period
G	3000	28893	From 27th to 31st in July, 2020.
N	3000	26484	
L	817	10273	
G ∩ N	0	12942	
G ∩ L	0	2439	
N ∩ L	0	2058	
G ∩ N ∩ L	0	1455	

4.3   Metrics

Following NRSM, we evaluate AUC (area under the ROC curve), MRR (mean reciprocal rank), and nDCG@k (normalized discounted cumulative gain at k). All take values between 0.0 to 1.0. When the value is 1.0, it indicates that the model is perfect.

- **AUC:** AUC is a widely used metric and indicates overall performance. It takes a higher value when positive samples tend to rank higher than negative samples in the recommendation list.

- **MRR:** When positive samples tend to hit at the top of the recommendation list, MRR takes a higher value. In contrast, the value hardly improves when positive samples hit the bottom of the list.
- **nDCG@k:** For the top k news articles in the recommendation list, articles that should be highly recommended but appearing lower in a list are penalized. We evaluate the case of $k = 5$ and $k = 10$.

4.4 Performance

Overall Results. Table 2 shows the performance of the model in each dataset pair. As we can see from Table 2, learning with G+N+L and fine-tuning tend to achieve better results regardless of dataset and negative sampling sources. In many cases, the overall performance (AUC) and the quality of recommendation (MRR, nDCG) improved. This reflects the effectiveness of the proposed framework. Especially, AUC of Lucra is effectively improved compared with single domain setting. We consider this is because the number of articles in Lucra is relatively small and it targets female users. This is the just situation where the proposed framework seems to effectively work. Learning with G+N+L enables for news embeddings to be much more robust and the characteristics of users can be captured by domain-specific fine-tuning. On the other hand, the improvements in Gunosy and Newspass are relatively small. This is because Gunosy and Newspass share about 50% news articles and the user characteristics between them seem to be similar. In addition to that, the fact that Lucra's articles are targeting female users might be another reason. Even if the information of Lucra's article is reflected in the model, it does not impact on the recommendation results very much in those domains or works as noise in some cases.

Comparing negative sampling strategies, the models tested by "All articles" sampling (*, A) achieve better performance. In impression data, displayed news articles include the effect of recommendation system which have already been working. Thus, using impression data is more practical case and classification becomes more difficult. Although the results are better when training and testing adopt the same source, we cannot judge the superiority between training with All articles and training with Impression.

From the business perspective, this result implies that it is possible to transfer model trained by many articles to other platform dealing with similar news articles. Since it is unnecessary to share the user information in this framework, there is no privacy concern in providing the model. This is a useful merit and we consider there are many situation that the proposed framework can be applied in real setting.

Table 2. The performance on each dataset. G, N, and L are the same as Table 1. If the models are fine-tuned, the value on the column "FT" is True. NS indicates Negative Samples used in dataset. Test set results are shown. For fine-tuned models, the result of final epoch is shown. Bold values are the best results in the same NS-test pair.

Dataset			FT	AUC	MRR	nDCG	
NS	Train	Test	–	–	–	@5	@10
(A, A)	G	G	False	0.7310	0.0538	0.0996	0.1128
	G+N+L	G	False	0.7295	0.0577	0.1198	0.1283
	G+N+L	G	True	**0.7341**	**0.0612**	**0.1329**	**0.1351**
	N	N	False	0.7002	0.0631	0.1408	0.1395
	G+N+L	N	False	0.7035	0.0589	0.1409	0.1283
	G+N+L	N	True	**0.7136**	**0.0642**	**0.1628**	**0.1485**
	L	L	False	0.7173	0.0646	0.1879	0.1712
	G+N+L	L	False	0.7674	0.0952	**0.2877**	0.2272
	G+N+L	L	True	**0.7791**	**0.1013**	0.2873	**0.2428**
	G+N+L	G+N+L	False	0.7270	0.0581	0.1235	0.1293
(A, I)	G	G	False	0.6130	0.0441	0.0888	0.0867
	G+N+L	G	False	0.6269	0.0475	0.0978	0.1020
	G+N+L	G	True	**0.6276**	**0.0495**	**0.1048**	**0.1045**
	N	N	False	0.5646	0.0301	0.0486	0.0527
	G+N+L	N	False	0.5706	0.0298	**0.0544**	0.0457
	G+N+L	N	True	**0.5794**	**0.0327**	0.0492	**0.0532**
	L	L	False	0.5107	0.0290	**0.0509**	0.0409
	G+N+L	L	False	0.5584	**0.0297**	0.0345	**0.702**
	G+N+L	L	True	**0.5641**	0.0294	0.0476	0.0530
	G+N+L	G+N+L	False	0.6165	0.0444	0.0893	0.0934
(I, I)	G	G	False	0.6594	0.0605	0.1484	0.1367
	G+N+L	G	False	0.6467	0.0579	0.144	0.1294
	G+N+L	G	True	**0.6513**	**0.0628**	**0.1578**	**0.1422**
	N	N	False	0.5843	0.0394	0.0743	0.0716
	G+N+L	N	False	0.5945	**0.0415**	**0.0910**	0.0759
	G+N+L	N	True	**0.5976**	0.0406	0.0744	**0.0772**
	L	L	False	0.5472	0.0299	0.0616	0.0469
	G+N+L	L	False	0.5615	0.0314	0.0578	0.0733
	G+N+L	L	True	**0.5696**	**0.0377**	**0.0845**	**0.0962**
	G+N+L	G+N+L	False	0.6372	0.0544	0.1315	0.1181
(I, A)	G	G	False	0.724	0.0661	0.1562	0.1529
	G+N+L	G	False	0.7164	0.0643	0.1523	0.1453
	G+N+L	G	True	**0.7225**	**0.0688**	**0.1666**	**0.1580**
	N	N	False	0.6569	0.0562	0.1227	0.118
	G+N+L	N	False	0.6867	**0.0752**	0.2021	0.1729
	G+N+L	N	True	**0.6916**	0.0724	**0.2029**	**0.1732**
	L	L	False	0.6375	0.0723	0.1402	0.1621
	G+N+L	L	False	0.7236	0.0783	0.2291	0.1930
	G+N+L	L	True	**0.7317**	**0.0845**	**0.2788**	**0.2082**
	G+N+L	G+N+L	False	0.7134	0.0657	0.1587	0.1499

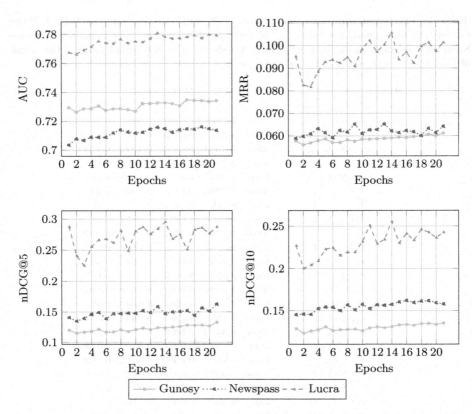

Fig. 3. The performance (AUC, MRR, nDCG@5, and nDCG@10) under fine-tuning. Gunosy(A, A), Newspass(A, A) and Lucra(A, A) are used as dataset.

Fine-Tuning Performance. Figure 3 shows the performance under fine-tuning. We only show the result of fine-tuning in Gunosy(A, A), Newspass(A, A), and Lucra(A, A) since the tendency is almost the same in other negative sampling pairs. In this experiment, although recommendation quality measures keep rising as epochs increases, we stop fine-tuning in epoch 20 since there is no large improvement.

As we can see from Fig. 3, the larger epochs become, the larger the metrics are. While the improvement is relatively large in Lucra, the results are saturated in other domains. This is the same reason mentioned in Sect. 4.4. We can say that domain-specific fine-tuning is effective in the domain whose user characteristics are different from pre-trained model and it is marginal in other domains. In practical use, domain-specific fine-tuning can be skipped in this kind of domains.

5   Conclusion

In this paper, we described a simple model for news recommendation tasks in multiple domain settings that uses freezing parameters and fine-tuning. Through experiments using the proposed framework on a real-world dataset, we found that a learning model using multiple domain data is effective for obtaining robust news embeddings. Moreover, our empirical results imply that the characteristics of domain-specific users can be captured from a multiple domain model by fine-tuning the domain. In particular, the proposed framework is effective in domains whose number of data points is small. As a future work, we would like to try additional experiments by changing the base model and clarify the effective type of models for cross-domain news recommendations.

Acknowledgements. The authors would like to thank Kojiro Iizuka (Gunosy) and Yoshifumi Seki (Gunosy) for their support and discussions. This research was partially supported by JST CREST Grant Number JPMJCR21F2, Japan.

References

1. Adomavicius, G., Tuzhilin, A.: Toward the next generation of recommender systems: a survey of the state-of-the-art and possible extensions. IEEE Trans. Knowl. Data Eng. **17**(6), 734–749 (2005)
2. Capelle, M., Frasincar, F., Moerland, M., Hogenboom, F.: Semantics-based news recommendation. In: Proceedings of the 2nd International Conference on Web Intelligence, Mining and Semantics, pp. 1–9 (2012)
3. Das, A.S., Datar, M., Garg, A., Rajaram, S.: Google news personalization: scalable online collaborative filtering. In: Proceedings of the 16th International Conference on World Wide Web, pp. 271–280 (2007)
4. Devlin, J., Chang, M.W., Lee, K., Toutanova, K.: BERT: pre-training of deep bidirectional transformers for language understanding. arXiv preprint arXiv:1810.04805 (2018)
5. Dwivedi, S.K., Arya, C.: A survey of news recommendation approaches. In: 2016 International Conference on ICT in Business Industry & Government (ICTBIG), pp. 1–6. IEEE (2016)
6. Gershman, A., Wolfe, T., Fink, E., Carbonell, J.G.: News personalization using support vector machines. Carnegie Mellon Univ. J. Contrib. (2011). https://www.semanticscholar.org/paper/News-Personalization-using-Support-Vector-Machines-Gershman-Wolfe/c665575cabc19aaba2cdf775602494cdd46c59fb
7. Goossen, F., IJntema, W., Frasincar, F., Hogenboom, F., Kaymak, U.: News personalization using the CF-IDF semantic recommender. In: Proceedings of the International Conference on Web Intelligence, Mining and Semantics, pp. 1–12 (2011)
8. Hidasi, B., Karatzoglou, A.: Recurrent neural networks with top-k gains for session-based recommendations. In: Proceedings of the 27th ACM International Conference on Information and Knowledge Management, pp. 843–852 (2018)
9. Hidasi, B., Karatzoglou, A., Baltrunas, L., Tikk, D.: Session-based recommendations with recurrent neural networks. arXiv preprint arXiv:1511.06939 (2015)
10. Lee, H.J., Park, S.J.: MONERS: a news recommender for the mobile web. Expert Syst. Appl. **32**(1), 143–150 (2007)

11. Liu, R., Peng, H., Chen, Y., Zhang, D.: HyperNews: simultaneous news recommendation and active-time prediction via a double-task deep neural network. In: IJCAI, pp. 3487–3493 (2020)
12. Liu, S., Dong, Y., Chai, J.: Research of personalized news recommendation system based on hybrid collaborative filtering algorithm. In: 2016 2nd IEEE International Conference on Computer and Communications (ICCC), pp. 865–869. IEEE (2016)
13. Mikolov, T., Sutskever, I., Chen, K., Corrado, G.S., Dean, J.: Distributed representations of words and phrases and their compositionality. In: Advances in Neural Information Processing Systems, pp. 3111–3119 (2013)
14. Okura, S., Tagami, Y., Ono, S., Tajima, A.: Embedding-based news recommendation for millions of users. In: Proceedings of the 23rd ACM SIGKDD International Conference on Knowledge Discovery and Data Mining, pp. 1933–1942 (2017)
15. Parizi, A.H., Kazemifard, M., Asghari, M.: EmoNews: an emotional news recommender system. J. Digit. Inf. Manag. **14**(6), 392–402 (2016). https://www.researchgate.net/profile/Mohammad-Kazemifard/publication/31357 4529_Emonews_An_emotional_news_recommender_system/links/5e3bcdb5299bf1cd b9116783/Emonews-An-emotional-news-recommender-system.pdf
16. Resnick, P., Iacovou, N., Suchak, M., Bergstrom, P., Riedl, J.: GroupLens: an open architecture for collaborative filtering of netnews. In: Proceedings of the 1994 ACM Conference on Computer Supported Cooperative Work, pp. 175–186 (1994)
17. Taguchi, Y., Tamori, H., Hitomi, Y., Nishitoba, J., Kikuta, K.: 同義語を考慮した日本語の単語分散表現の学習. IPSJ SIG Technical Report 2017-NL-233, no. 17, pp. 1–5 (2017)
18. Tavakolifard, M., Gulla, J.A., Almeroth, K.C., Ingvaldesn, J.E., Nygreen, G., Berg, E.: Tailored news in the palm of your hand: a multi-perspective transparent approach to news recommendation. In: Proceedings of the 22nd International Conference on World Wide Web, pp. 305–308 (2013)
19. Wang, H., Zhang, F., Xie, X., Guo, M.: DKN: deep knowledge-aware network for news recommendation. In: Proceedings of the 2018 World Wide Web Conference, pp. 1835–1844 (2018)
20. Wu, C., Wu, F., An, M., Huang, J., Huang, Y., Xie, X.: NPA: neural news recommendation with personalized attention. In: Proceedings of the 25th ACM SIGKDD International Conference on Knowledge Discovery & Data Mining, pp. 2576–2584 (2019)
21. Wu, C., Wu, F., Ge, S., Qi, T., Huang, Y., Xie, X.: Neural news recommendation with multi-head self-attention. In: Proceedings of the 2019 Conference on Empirical Methods in Natural Language Processing and the 9th International Joint Conference on Natural Language Processing (EMNLP-IJCNLP), pp. 6389–6394 (2019)
22. Wu, C., Wu, F., Huang, Y.: Personalized news recommendation: a survey. arXiv preprint arXiv:2106.08934 (2021)
23. Wu, C., Wu, F., Qi, T., Huang, Y.: User modeling with click preference and reading satisfaction for news recommendation. In: IJCAI, pp. 3023–3029 (2020)
24. Wu, C., Wu, F., Qi, T., Huang, Y.: Empowering news recommendation with pre-trained language models. arXiv preprint arXiv:2104.07413 (2021)
25. Zhong, E., Liu, N., Shi, Y., Rajan, S.: Building discriminative user profiles for large-scale content recommendation. In: Proceedings of the 21th ACM SIGKDD International Conference on Knowledge Discovery and Data Mining, pp. 2277–2286 (2015)

Concept Drift Detection with Denoising Autoencoder in Incomplete Data

Jun Murao[1], Kei Yonekawa[2], Mori Kurokawa[2], Daichi Amagata[1(✉)],
Takuya Maekawa[1], and Takahiro Hara[1]

[1] Osaka University, Osaka, Japan
jun88@sanken.osaka-u.ac.jp,
{amagata.daichi,maekawa,hara}@ist.osaka-u.ac.jp
[2] KDDI Research, Inc., Saitama, Japan
{ke-yonekawa,mo-kurokawa}@kddi-research.jp

Abstract. Recent e-commerce and location-based services provide personalized recommendations based on machine-learning models that take into account purchase and visiting histories. Because machine-learning models assume the same distributions between training and test data, they cannot catch up with concept drifts, i.e., changes of behavioral patterns over time. To keep recommendation accurate, it is important to detect concept drifts. Generally, to achieve this, we need complete data (i.e., data without missing values). In real-world datasets, however, there are many incomplete data, and existing concept drift detection techniques do not deal with incomplete data. To address this issue, we investigate how a deep learning technique (denoising autoencoder), which complements missing values, contributes to detecting concept drifts in incomplete data. We conduct experiments on synthetic and real datasets to evaluate the robustness of this technique, and our results show its advantages.

Keywords: Concept drift · Incomplete data · Denoising autoencoder

1 Introduction

Recent e-commerce and location-based services provide personalized recommendations based on machine-learning models that take into account purchase and visiting histories [14,25]. Highly accurate recommendations improve user satisfaction and profits [15], so taking purchase and visiting histories into account is important to train such recommendation models [18,26]. Generally, machine-learning models assume the same data distributions between training and test environments [19,20]. It is hence hard for such models to keep high recommendation accuracy if the distributions between these environments change over time. Such distributions changes are usual in real-world applications. For example, human behaviors changed after the COVID-19 pandemic, and models built before this pandemic may not be able to estimate current human behaviors, resulting in low accuracy performances.

T. Hara and H. Yamaguchi (Eds.): MobiQuitous 2021, LNICST 419, pp. 541–552, 2022.
https://doi.org/10.1007/978-3-030-94822-1_35

Such statistical change over time is called *concept drift* [22]. Existing works addressed the problem of concept drift detection, because this is important to maintain model accuracy [13]. For example:

EXAMPLE 1. *In recommendation applications, users are represented by dense vectors that are obtained from user behavior histories. (Throughout this paper, we use vectors and data interchangeably.) We often have user clusters in this model, where each cluster contains similar user vectors. Mass retailers have stores with diverse locations, and each store may have different customer segments and management policies. User cluster analysis is effective to deal with such diversity [5]. However, user clusters may change over time, so analysts have to judge when to rebuild user clusters. Detecting concept drifts helps with this judgement, and it enables us to keep tracking user preferences.*

Existing concept drift detection assumes complete data (i.e., data without missing values) [4,12], so they cannot detect concept drifts in incomplete data. In real-world applications, users' purchase and/or visiting histories are obtained by sensors (e.g., Wi-Fi signals), thus they may have some missing values (due to sensor errors) [24]. To detect concept drifts in incomplete data, missing values should be corrected. Some works have addressed this issue so far. MDL-FWF [11] does not run missing value complement but uses distance estimation to handle incomplete data. However, this approach has a drawback: to train the distance estimation model, it requires complete data. If a given dataset contains many missing values, its performance degrades.

To achieve high accuracy for concept drift detection in incomplete data, this paper investigates a deep learning approach that detects concept drifts in incomplete data by complementing missing values with a denoising autoencoder. Compared with existing models for missing value complement, denoising autoencoder models can complement missing values more accurately even if we have fewer complete data [9]. In addition, to be robust against datasets with many missing values, we apply a counter-intuitive approach that augments data by using incomplete data (with less missing values). Similarly to [11], we employ clustering, make histograms based on the clusters, and evaluate the dissimilarity between histograms by using Pearson's chi-square test to evaluate whether concept drift occurs or not. We conduct experiments to clarify the advantage of the deep learning approach on synthetic and real datasets.

Organization. The rest of this paper is organized as follows. Section 2 reviews related work. Section 3 presents the denoising autoencoder approach, and Sect. 4 reports our experimental results. Last, Sect. 5 concludes this paper.

2   Related Work

A qualitative definition of concept drift is that: "the statistical feature of a given domain changes over time" [21]. On one hand, its quantitative definition is as follows. Let $S_{o,t}$ be a set of samples obtained during a term $[0, t]$. Furthermore, let P_t be a probability distribution that $S_{o,t}$ follows. Then, concept drift occurs between $S_{o,t}$ and $S_{o,t+1}$ iff $P_t \neq P_{t+1}$. Concept drifts can occur for multiple reasons [17], but, in the context of unsupervised learning, concept drift detection is a task that detects a data distribution change. Hereinafter, we review existing techniques for concept drift detection in complete and incomplete data.

2.1 Concept Drift Detection in Complete Data

Concept drift detection techniques have some approaches that are based on error rates, data distributions, or multiple hypothesis testing [13]. (Multiple hypothesis testing is a hybrid of the other approaches.) Error-rates-based approaches [2, 23] detect concept drifts by monitoring classification errors. If the error rate significantly increases or decreases, it is assumed that concept drift occurs. This approach requires labeled datasets, thus its applications are limited: for example, applications that require unsupervised learning cannot employ this approach.

Data-distribution-based approaches [7,16] define dissimilarity between old and new datasets, and if the dissimilarity is significant, it is assumed that concept drift occurs. Generally, this approach fixes the base term (like landmark-based sliding window) and monitors the data distributions obtained from newer terms. In this approach, there are parametric and non-parametric methods. However, parametric methods, such as [10], assume a specific data distribution. Real-world datasets usually do not follow a specific data distribution, so the parametric method is not practical. We employ a non-parametric method in Sect. 3.

To quantify the dissimilarity between two datasets, histogram-based solutions are often utilized. Many works use a grid to build a histogram, the bin of which corresponds to a cell of the grid. However, the number of bins increases exponentially for datasets with large dimensions. To alleviate this issue, a tree-based bin is considered in QuantTree [4]. This method uses a kd-tree [3] to make a bin. EI-kMeans [12] leverages k-means clusters to make bins. We also use this clustering approach to make a histogram.

2.2 Concept Drift Detection in Incomplete Data

Missing values often appear in real-world datasets, but the above methods assume complete data (data without missing values). If missing values are complemented, these methods can still be available. However, note that the accuracy of complement may significantly affect the performance of concept drift detection.

Literature [11] proposed MDL-FWF to robustly detect concept drifts in incomplete data. MDL-FWF is a data-distribution-based non-parametric method and consists of MDL (Masked Distance Learning) and FWF (Fuzzy Weighted Frequency). MDL trains a gradient boosting decision tree model that estimates the distance between two samples by using complete data and synthetic incomplete data, the missing values of which are generated from complete data. FWF builds a histogram by taking the fuzziness of the estimated distance into account. Finally, MDL-FWF conducts a chi-square test to confirm concept drift. We use this method as a comparison in Sect. 4.

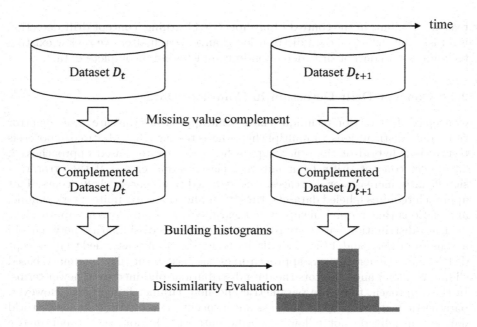

Fig. 1. Overview of concept drift detection between two incomplete datasets D_t and D_{t+1}. This method first complements missing values and obtains the complemented datasets D'_t and D'_{t+1}. Then, clustering is done on each dataset, and each cluster is used as a bin of a histogram. Last, the dissimilarity between the histograms (i.e., data distributions) is computed to detect concept drift.

3   Concept Drift Detection Based on Denoising Autoencoder

This section presents details of detecting concept drifts in incomplete data by using a denoising autoencoder.

3.1   Overview

Figure 1 illustrates an overview of concept drift detection on incomplete datasets. Similarly to [4,11,12], given two datasets D_t and D_{t+1} obtained at different times, we consider that they are two samples and concept drift detection between them is a task of statistical test. First, we complete the missing values in D_t and D_{t+1} and obtain the complemented datasets D'_t and D'_{t+1}. We next do clustering on D'_t and D'_{t+1} and then build histograms h_t and h_{t+1} from the clustering results. After that, we measure the dissimilarity between the two data distributions by using h_t and h_{t+1}.

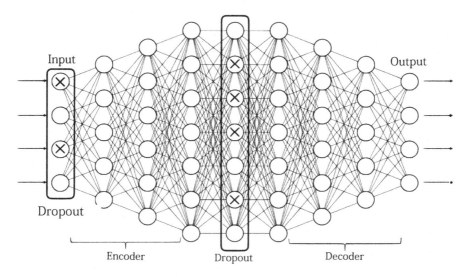

Fig. 2. Structure of the deep denoising autoencoder. The input and output are d-dimensions. A dropout layer (dropout rate is 0.5) is incorporated between encoder and decoder layers.

3.2 Complementing Missing Values via Denoising Autoencoder

As a missing value complement model, we employ a deep denoising autoencoder [9], which is shown in Fig. 2. Its input is a d-dimensional vector, and each layer in the encoder adds θ nodes while each layer in the decoder removes θ nodes. This model learns features so that it is robust against noise by decoding the original output. The loss function $f()$ is MSE (mean square error):

$$f(x, y) = \frac{1}{d} \sum_{i=1}^{d} (x_i - y_i)^2, \tag{1}$$

where x and y are respectively the input and output vectors, and x_i (y_i) is the i-th element of x (y). We add a dropout layer, the dropout rate of which is 0.5, between the encoder and decoder layers, to alleviate overfitting. In our implementation, we use LeakyReLU as the activation function, Adam as the optimization algorithm, 0.001 as learning rate, 128 as the batch size, and 500 as the number of epochs.

If we cannot obtain a sufficient number of complete data, we collect incomplete data with a small number of missing values. Let n be the cardinality of a given dataset. In our experiments, if the number of complete data in the dataset was less than $0.2n$, we did this data augmentation. For each dimension, we compute the average value and use it to complement the missing value in the corresponding dimension. These complemented data are employed as training data.

After training the above mode, we use it to complement the missing values in the incomplete data. Note that the input of the deep denoising autoencoder is a complete data, so when inputting incomplete data into the model, we replace the missing values with the average values of the corresponding dimensions.

3.3 Dissimilarity Test by Histograms

Building Histograms. To measure the dissimilarity between different data distributions, we build a histogram of each dataset by using the clustering result [11]. We employ k-means++ [1] to reasonably build it. Given two datasets, we first run k-means++ for one dataset, then run k-means++ for the other dataset by using the cluster centers of the first clustering to fix centroids. (In our experiments, we set $k = 20$.) After that, we make a histogram for each dataset, where each bin corresponds to a cluster and its frequency is the number of vectors belonging to the cluster.

Concept Drift Detection. We use Pearson's chi-square test [6] to evaluate the dissimilarity between the datasets. To enable it, we assume that the two datasets are i.i.d. We compute the p value from χ^2 and the degree of freedom (we set $\alpha = 0.05$), and if $p < \alpha$, we assume that no concept drift occurs between the two datasets.

4   Experiment

To evaluate the effectiveness of the deep denoising autoencoder-based approach, we conducted experiments on synthetic and real datasets. In Sects. 4.1 and 4.2, we respectively introduce the results from the synthetic and real data.

4.1   Experiment on Synthetic Data

Datasets. We generated UNI datasets where $d = 10$ and $n = 2000$. One of them (i.e., the original dataset) follows uniform distribution, and the others do the same but have noise in specific dimensions. (We followed [4] to make synthetic concept drifts.) Plus, we copied them and removed values of specific dimensions to generate incomplete datasets. The number of dimensions in which values were removed was 4, and $n \times \frac{m}{100}$ data have missing values, where $m \in [10, 90]$ [%].

Also, we generated GAU datasets where $d = 4$ and $n = 2000$. Its original dataset follows a Gaussian distribution, and the others have noises, as with UNI. Incomplete datasets were generated in the same way as for UNI.

Evaluation Criteria. Given a complete dataset, assume that it is difficult to detect concept drift in it. In this case, detecting concept drift in its incomplete version is also hard. We hence used Pearson's correlation to see the performance of missing value complement. Given x pairs $(a_1, b_1), (a_2, b_2), \cdots, (a_x, b_x)$, its Pearson's correlation is

$$r_{a,b} = \frac{\sum_{i=1}^{x}(a_i - \overline{a})(b_i - \overline{b})}{\sqrt{\sum_{i=1}^{x}(a_i - \overline{a})^2}\sqrt{\sum_{i=1}^{x}(b_i - \overline{b})^2}}, \tag{2}$$

where $\overline{a}$ and $\overline{b}$ are respectively the average of a_i and b_i ($i \in [1, d]$). In addition, we measured the concept drift detection rate r_{detect}, which is defined as:

$$r_{detect} = \frac{x_{reject}}{x_{test}},\qquad(3)$$

where x_{reject} and x_{test} are respectively the numbers of rejections and tests. This shows the rate of trials that judged it "concept detection occurs", so note that r_{detect} is not detection accuracy.

Evaluated Methods. We evaluated the following techniques.

- Full: a method that uses only original datasets (to measure Pearson's correlation).
- DDA: the method introduced in Sect. 3.
- Iterative Imputation: a variant of the method introduced in Sect. 3. Instead of using the denoising autoencoder, this method uses chain equations to complement missing values.
- MDL-FWF-Gau [11]: a state-of-the-art method for detecting concept drifts in incomplete data. This method uses a Gaussian distribution to estimate the distance between two samples.
- MDL-FWF-Tri [11]: a variant of the above method. This uses a triangle distribution to estimate the distance between two samples.

Result on UNI. Figure 3 shows our experimental results on UNI datasets (average of 50 tests). From Fig. 3(a), we see that each method generally keeps high correlation. In particular, Iterative Imputation shows high correlation even when m is large. MDL-FWF-Gau and MDL-FWF-Tri show high correlation when $m \leq 30$ but lowest when $m \geq 40$. This shows that, when the number of complete data is small, its distance estimation model cannot yield high accuracy. When $m \geq 80$, MDL-FWF could not detect concept drifts, thus we omit their results. DDA provides the second-highest correlation, implying that the robustness against missing values.

From Fig. 3(b), we see that each method is competitive when m is small. On the other hand, when m becomes larger, the performance difference becomes larger, as shown in Fig. 3(c). The performances of MDL-FWF-Gau and MDL-FWF-Tri particularly degrade. Figure 3(d) shows that, when m is very large, Iterative Imputation does not work well. Even when the noise scale is large (i.e., it is easy to detect concept drifts), its detection rate is less than 0.2. On the other hand, those of DDA and MDL-FWF-Gau are larger than 0.6.

Result on GAU. Figure 4 shows our experimental results on GAU datasets (average of 50 tests). From Fig. 4(a), it can be observed that, when $m \geq 50$, all methods have low correlation. (When the result of a given method is omitted, concept drifts were judged to have occurred in all tests.) As with the UNI case, each method shows competitive performance when m is small.

On the other hand, when $m = 40$, the methods for incomplete data could not reproduce the result of FULL. For example, even when the noise scale is

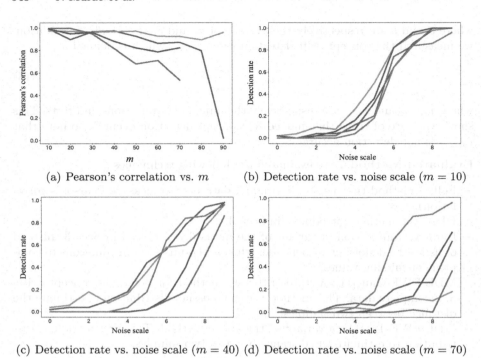

(a) Pearson's correlation vs. m (b) Detection rate vs. noise scale ($m = 10$)

(c) Detection rate vs. noise scale ($m = 40$) (d) Detection rate vs. noise scale ($m = 70$)

Fig. 3. Experimental results on UNI datasets. Purple, Full; blue, DDA; orange, Iterative Imputation; green, MDL-FWF-Gau; red, MDL-FWF-Tri. (Color figure online)

0 (i.e., no concept drifts), they wrongly detect concept drift with a probability of at least 0.2. This observation appears more clearly in Fig. 4(d). This performance degradation is perhaps due to the high rate of missing dimensions. In GAU, all dimensions can have missing values, so it is hard for machine-learning models to complement the missing values if m is large.

4.2   Experiment on Real Data

Dataset. We used a set of real visiting log data collected by free Wi-Fi services. Each log recorded the visiting user and location visited. Each user/location has a unique identifier. Moreover, each location has a categorical feature. Note that this is a private dataset, thus its source cannot be published (permissions to use this dataset have been obtained from all users involved in this dataset).

In our experiment, we made a user's visiting history from categorical features of the location visited by the user within 1 month. We defined a set of logs collected in 3/2020 (5/2020) as a data chunk C_a (C_b). They are 16-dimensional datasets and $n = 5000$.

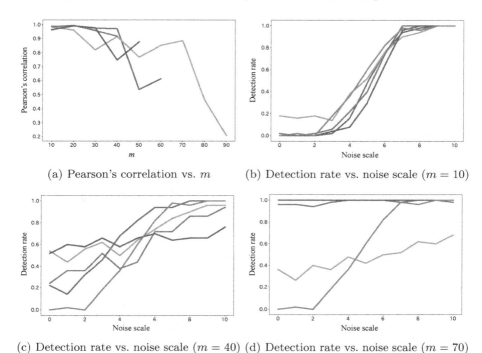

(a) Pearson's correlation vs. m (b) Detection rate vs. noise scale ($m = 10$)

(c) Detection rate vs. noise scale ($m = 40$) (d) Detection rate vs. noise scale ($m = 70$)

Fig. 4. Experimental results on GAU datasets. Purple, Full; blue, DDA; orange, Iterative Imputation; green, MDL-FWF-Gau; red, MDL-FWF-Tri. (Color figure online)

Evaluated Methods. We evaluated the following methods.

- QuantTree [4]: a state-of-the-art method of concept drift detection in complete datasets. We set 20 as its bin size and $B = 2000$, where B is a parameter for deciding on the test threshold.
- DDA.
- MDL-FWF-Gau.
- MDL-FWF-Tri.
- Wilcoxon-Mann-Whitney test (WMW) [8]: a non-parametric method that tests i.i.d. between two datasets.

Note that QuantTree and WMW assume complete data as their inputs. We therefore used Iterative Imputation to complement missing values for them.

Result. We randomly sampled 1000 complete data from C_a to generate a base dataset D_a. Then, we randomly sampled 1000 complete data from C_a and C_b to generate D_a^{test} and D_b^{test}, which are targets of concept drift from D_a. That is, we ran concept drift detection between (i) D_a and D_a^{test} and (ii) D_a and D_b^{test}. Also, we generated incomplete datasets by removing values in four dimensions and ran concept drift similarly. We performed this random sampling and concept drift detection 100 times.

Table 1. False-positive rate w.r.t. concept drift detection on real dataset

	$m = 20$		$m = 40$	
	Incomplete	Complete	Incomplete	Complete
QuantTree	1.00	1.00	1.00	1.00
DDA	0.00	0.10	0.02	0.10
MDL-FWF-Gau	0.01	0.10	0.22	0.10
MDL-FWF-Tri	0.76	0.10	0.00	0.10
WMW	0.00	0.00	0.00	0.00

Table 2. False-negative rate w.r.t. concept drift detection on real dataset

	$m = 20$		$m = 40$	
	Incomplete	Complete	Incomplete	Complete
QuantTree	0.00	0.00	0.00	0.00
DDA	0.00	0.07	0.00	0.07
MDL-FWF-Gau	0.00	0.07	0.00	0.07
MDL-FWF-Tri	0.29	0.07	0.55	0.07
WMW	1.00	1.00	1.00	1.00

Tables 1 and 2 respectively show the false-positive and false-negative rates w.r.t. concept drift detection. From these tables, we see that DDA provides high accuracy, both when $m = 20$ and $m = 40$. Real-world datasets usually have complex relationships between variables, and deep learning techniques can learn such relationships. We expect that DDA successfully learned a good model, so it functions well.

MDL-FWF-Gau shows a similar performance, but DDA is more robust. MDL-FWF-Tri is consistently worse than MDL-FWF-Gau. We found that QuantTree and WMW yield extreme results. This suggests that techniques for complete data are not appropriate for incomplete data, even if some complement is done.

5   Conclusion

Recent recommender systems employ well-personalized machine-learning models that are trained on personalized data obtained (implicitly) from sensors. To keep models fresh, it is important to detect concept drifts that can occur over time. This paper focused on incomplete data, which are usual in real-world datasets, and investigated how a deep denoising autoencoder that complements missing values contribute to concept drift detection in incomplete data. We conducted experiments on synthetic and real datasets to evaluate the missing value complement approach. The results show that this approach is more robust than existing techniques against missing values.

Acknowledgements. This research is supported by JST CREST Grant Number JPMJCR21F2.

References

1. Arthur, D., Vassilvitskii, S.: k-means++: the advantages of careful seeding. In: SODA, pp. 1027–1035 (2007)
2. Barros, R.S., Cabral, D.R., Gonçalves, P.M., Jr., Santos, S.G.: RDDM: reactive drift detection method. Expert Syst. Appl. **90**, 344–355 (2017)
3. Bentley, J.L.: Multidimensional binary search trees used for associative searching. Commun. ACM **18**(9), 509–517 (1975)
4. Boracchi, G., Carrera, D., Cervellera, C., Maccio, D.: Quanttree: histograms for change detection in multivariate data streams. In: ICML, pp. 639–648 (2018)
5. Boulanouar, S., Lamiche, C.: A new hybrid image segmentation method based on fuzzy c-mean and modified bat algorithm. Int. J. Comput. Digit. Syst. **9**(4), 677–687 (2020)
6. Box, G.E., Hunter, W.H., Hunter, S.: Statistics for Experimenters, vol. 664 (1978)
7. Dasu, T., Krishnan, S., Venkatasubramanian, S., Yi, K.: An information-theoretic approach to detecting changes in multi-dimensional data streams. In: Symposium on the Interface of Statistics, Computing Science, and Applications (2006)
8. Friedman, J.H., Rafsky, L.C.: Multivariate generalizations of the wald-wolfowitz and smirnov two-sample tests. Ann. Stat. **7**, 697–717 (1979)
9. Gondara, L., Wang, K.: MIDA: multiple imputation using denoising autoencoders. In: PAKDD, pp. 260–272 (2018)
10. Haug, J., Kasneci, G.: Learning parameter distributions to detect concept drift in data streams. arXiv preprint arXiv:2010.09388 (2020)
11. Liu, A., Lu, J., Zhang, G.: Concept drift detection: dealing with missing values via fuzzy distance estimations. IEEE Trans. Fuzzy Syst. **29**, 3219–3233 (2020)
12. Liu, A., Lu, J., Zhang, G.: Concept drift detection via equal intensity k-means space partitioning. IEEE Trans. Cybern. **51**, 3198–3211 (2020)
13. Lu, J., Liu, A., Dong, F., Gu, F., Gama, J., Zhang, G.: Learning under concept drift: a review. IEEE Trans. Knowl. Data Eng. **31**(12), 2346–2363 (2018)
14. Lyu, Y., et al.: Behavior matching between different domains based on canonical correlation analysis. In: ECNLP, pp. 361–366 (2019)
15. Nguyen, D., et al.: On the transferability of deep neural networks for recommender system. In: IAL, pp. 22–37 (2020)
16. Shao, J., Ahmadi, Z., Kramer, S.: Prototype-based learning on concept-drifting data streams. In: KDD, pp. 412–421 (2014)
17. Sun, Y., Tang, K., Minku, L.L., Wang, S., Yao, X.: Online ensemble learning of data streams with gradually evolved classes. IEEE Trans. Knowl. Data Eng. **28**(6), 1532–1545 (2016)
18. Sun, Z., Guo, Q., Yang, J., Fang, H., Guo, G., Zhang, J., Burke, R.: Research commentary on recommendations with side information: A survey and research directions. Electron. Commer. Res. Appl. **37**, 100879 (2019)
19. Wang, H., et al.: Preliminary investigation of alleviating user cold-start problem in e-commerce with deep cross-domain recommender system. In: ECNLP, pp. 398–403 (2019)
20. Wang, H., et al.: A DNN-based cross-domain recommender system for alleviating cold-start problem in e-commerce. IEEE Open J. Ind. Electron. Soc. **1**, 194–206 (2020)

21. Wang, S., Schlobach, S., Klein, M.: Concept drift and how to identify it. J. Web Semant. **9**(3), 247–265 (2011)
22. Widmer, G., Kubat, M.: Learning in the presence of concept drift and hidden contexts. Mach. Learn. **23**(1), 69–101 (1996)
23. Xu, S., Wang, J.: Dynamic extreme learning machine for data stream classification. Neurocomputing **238**, 433–449 (2017)
24. Yonekawa, K., et al.: Advertiser-assisted behavioral ad-targeting via denoised distribution induction. In: IEEE Big Data, pp. 5611–5619 (2019)
25. Yonekawa, K.,et al.: A heterogeneous domain adversarial neural network for trans-domain behavioral targeting. In: DLKT, pp. 274–285 (2019)
26. Zhang, Y., et al.: Personalized geographical influence modeling for poi recommendation. IEEE Intell. Syst. **35**(5), 18–27 (2020)

Synthetic People Flow: Privacy-Preserving Mobility Modeling from Large-Scale Location Data in Urban Areas

Naoki Tamura[1,2]($\boxtimes$) (iD), Kenta Urano[1] (iD), Shunsuke Aoki[1] (iD),
Takuro Yonezawa[1] (iD), and Nobuo Kawaguchi[1] (iD)

[1] Graduate School of Engineering, Nagoya University, Aichi, Japan
`tam@ucl.nuee.nagoya-u.ac.jp`
[2] National Institute of Informatics, Tokyo, Japan

Abstract. Recently, there has been an increasing demand for traffic simulation and congestion prediction for urban planning, especially for infection simulation due to the Covid-19 epidemic. On the other hand, the widespread use of wearable devices has made it possible to collect a large amount of user location history with high accuracy, and it is expected that this data will be used for simulation. However, it is difficult to collect location histories for the entire population of a city, and detailed data that can reproduce trajectories is expensive. In addition, such personal location histories contain private information such as addresses and workplaces, which restricts the use of raw data. This paper proposes Agent2Vec, a mobility modeling model based on unsupervised learning. Using this method, we generate synthetic human flow data without personal information.

Keywords: Spatio-temporal data analysis · Privacy preserving data mining · Unsupervised Learning

1 Introduction

Recently, there has been an increasing demand for traffic simulation and congestion prediction for urban planning, especially for infection simulation due to the Covid-19 epidemic. On the other hand, the widespread use of smartphones and wearable devices equipped with GPS (Global Positioning System) has made it possible to collect the location history of many users with high accuracy. Therefore, it is expected that the city-level human flow data, which shows how people move and stay in the urban environment, can be used for simulation. For example, large-scale data on location history has been used to analyze the effects of

Supported by AMED, JST-CREST, NICT.

T. Hara and H. Yamaguchi (Eds.): MobiQuitous 2021, LNICST 419, pp. 553–567, 2022.
https://doi.org/10.1007/978-3-030-94822-1_36

policies during a pandemic [1]. However, it is difficult to collect location histories for the entire population of a city, and detailed data that can reproduce trajectories is expensive. In addition, such personal location histories contain private information such as addresses and workplaces, which restricts the use of raw data. In this study, we generate synthetic people flow data which can reproduce the city-level people flow based on the real location history data. This data does not contain personal information because it does not correspond to the real user's location history and can be freely processed and visualized.

In order to generate a flow of agents, we need an activity model that defines how each agent moves and stays over time. Although many user activity modeling methods have been studied in the past, they mainly require a large amount of labeled data and detailed location histories. On the other hand, a method for modeling the usage of a region and the activity tendency of users using GPS data and unsupervised learning has been studied. This allows us to model user activities based on less frequent and unlabeled data than before. As the model is based on GPS data collected on a daily basis, it also has the advantage of being able to take into account changes in the environment over time, such as changes in social policy, pandemic outbreaks, and seasonal changes. This paper proposes Agent2Vec, a mobility modelling model based on unsupervised learning. This model abstracts the tendency of users to move and stay as a distributed representation. By clustering these distributed representations, we extract groups of users with similar tendencies. We can use each group of users as an activity model of synthetic agents, and generate synthetic people flow data. The main contribution of this work are given in the following:

- Agent2Vec: Unsupervised learning model that abstracts the tendency of users to move and stay as a distributed representation;
- Generating synthetic human flow data without personal information and with higher granularity(50 m mesh);
- Evaluation of synthetic data in terms of density of stay and amount of movement;

We have generated a synthetic dataset using a real GPS location dataset, and we have confirmed that the synthetic dataset reproduces real people flow by visualization and evaluation. However, we have also identified some challenges in terms of population distribution and distance traveled.

2   Related Work

In order to generate synthetic human flows, we need an activity model of how each agent moves and stays. There is a long history of attempts to model how people move and stay in their daily lives, based on person-trip surveys [2,3]. However, because of the high cost and low frequency of collection, person-trip surveys can only model typical patterns of activity and cannot model changes in people's activities as the environment changes.

On the other hand, with the recent proliferation of mobile devices, a large amount of CDR (Call Detail Record) and GPS location history has been obtained, and activity modeling using these data has become popular. For example, Song et al. [4] implemented an LSTM multi-task learning system for learning human mobility and traffic patterns and a city-level simulation system, mainly using GPS data. Yin et al. [5] uses the movement history from CDR to model the activity with hidden Markov model. Ouyang et al. [6] uses GPS trajectory data to model human mobility and synthetically generate movement trajectories. Borysov et al. [7] use deep learning-based methods to generate a large number of and more diverse user models and aim to generate unsampled models by combining their elements. Another example is the work on modeling the daily activity schedule of users under various and complex factors [8,9]. Other research exists that uses reinforcement learning-based activity modeling to generate more natural movement trajectories [10,11]. The challenge of these methods is that they require a large amount of detailed, labeled data and the setting of an appropriate reward function to train the model. However, labeling of movement trajectories is costly since the movement of an individual is generally high dimensional information based on various factors.

Research that has actually generated city-level synthetic-population flow data includes the use of GPS, CDR, as well as comprehensive datasets such as population distribution and traffic volume [12]. However, such data are generally expensive, and although the spatial granularity is around 250–500 m mesh, more granular human flow data are needed for congestion prediction and infection simulation. In this paper, we generate more granular human flows with a granularity of 50 m mesh from unlabeled GPS data.

3 Proposed Method

This method aim to generate synthetic human flow data that can reproduce real human flow from the original location history data. Input data is obtained as latitude, longitude, and timestamp of a real user with a terminal. The synthetic data is also generated as latitude, longitude, and timestamp of each agent. To generate synthetic data, we need an activity model of how each agent moves and stays respectively over time. This activity model is mainly modeled using unsupervised learning in this method.

Figure 1 shows an overview of the method. First, we generate a distributed representation of LU (Location Usage) for each mesh according to the tendency to stay and represent user's movement in the form of LU transitions. This LU is generated for each mesh by learning the tendency to stay at that mesh by Word2Vec. This allows the user's location information to be represented as information, including POIs (Points of Interest). Next, we extract travel and stay information from the location history of real users and abstract it in the form of a distributed representation for each user. Then, by clustering the distributed representation of each user, we classify users by their tendency to move and stay. The users in each cluster have a similar tendency to move and stay. For example,

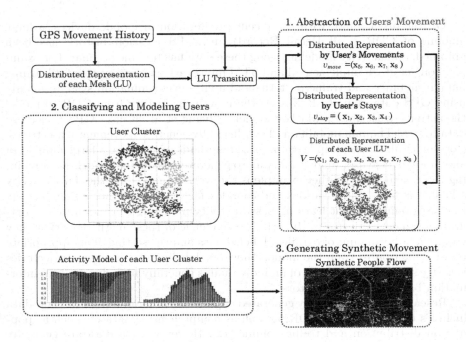

Fig. 1. Overview of the proposed method

users in the housewife cluster tend to spend most of their time at home, while users in the salaried worker cluster tend to go to work and leave work in the morning and evening. Finally, we model the activities of agents based on the movement and stay tendencies of the users in each cluster and generate synthetic human flow data. These methods are explained in detail in the following sections.

3.1 Abstraction of Real Users' Movement and Stay Tendency

In this section, to classify real users, we abstract the tendency of each user to move and stay as a distributed representation V. This section describes the procedure for calculating this V. First, we divide each user's location history into 30-min time slots and assign a mesh to stay in each slot. We then compute the LU, a distributed representation of the trend in usage over time for each mesh. It is possible to classify them according to their tendency to stay in the mesh by clustering them. In this paper, we refer to this cluster of meshes by LU as LU cluster. These LU clusters are, for example, residential clusters for long stays in the morning and evening, and office clusters for long stay in the daytime.

Then, we calculate the distributed representation reflecting the tendency of each user to stay and move, v_{stay} and v_{move}, independently in Agent2vec. Agent2Vec is an application of Word2Vec that generates a distributed representation of each user by learning the user's tendency to move and stay. Figure 2 illustrates the architecture of Agent2Vec. The input layer is a one-hot vector for each user, and the output layer is a one-hot vector with flagged dimensions for each movement or stays feature. The weights of the middle layer obtained by training the input vectors produce a distributed representation that reflects the tendency of each user to stay. The number of dimensions of this distributed representation for each user is equal to the one of the hidden layer N, In this case, the number of dimensions of both v_{stay} and v_{move} was set to $N = 4$. The stay features are learned by Agent2Vec using three pieces of information for each stay: a weekday or a holiday, the period of the stay, and the stay LU cluster. This makes it possible to compute a distributed representation v_{stay} based on the tendency of each user to stay in the mesh, i.e., when and what attributes they stayed in. The movement features are learned by Agent2Vec using four pieces of information for each travel: a weekday or a holiday, the period of the travel, the distance of the travel, and whether the travel is to the main mesh. This main meshes are the meshes in which each user has stayed for many days, such as home and office. In our method, we define the main mesh as the mesh where the user is observed to stay for more than half of the days in the data obtained for each user. This allows us to compute the distributed representation v_{move} based on the movement tendency, i.e., when, at what distance ,and to what mesh the user frequently visits. Finally, we combine v_{stay} and v_{move} to create V, a distributed representation of each user's tendency to move and stay.

3.2 Real User Classification

In this section, we classify users according to their tendency to move and stay by clustering their distributed representation V. We used Kmeans++ for clustering. Figures 3, 4 and 5 shows some examples from the actual clustering into 40 clusters. Figure 3 shows the percentage of LU clusters that stayed in each time slot on weekdays and holidays, while Figs. 4 and 5 show the number of moves, the percentage of distance traveled, and the percentage of moves to the main mesh in each time slot. The vertical axis in Figs. 4 and 5 is the percentage of moves in each period (every 30 min), normalized for the number of people in each user cluster, weekdays, and days off. From Fig. 3, clusters 1 and 2 tend to stay in the residential cluster during the evening hours and in the office cluster during the daytime, which is similar to that of a typical office worker. Cluster 3 stays in the residential area cluster except a few times during the daytime when it stays in the restaurant cluster, indicating that it tends to stay like a homemaker. On the other hand, cluster 2 has the peaks of travel between 7:00 and 9:00 in the morning and between 17:00 and 20:00, and the travel of 3 km to 5 km is conspicuous. In cluster 3, the amount of travel is lower than clusters 1 and 2, and the distance traveled is higher than 0.5 km. Figure 5 shows that clusters 1 and 2 have a high proportion of travels to the main mesh in the morning and evening, going to work and returning home. Cluster 3 has more travels to non-main meshes in the afternoon than clusters 1 and 2. These clusters are just examples, but by clustering, V in this way, we can classify not only the tendency of users to stay but also the tendency of users to move.

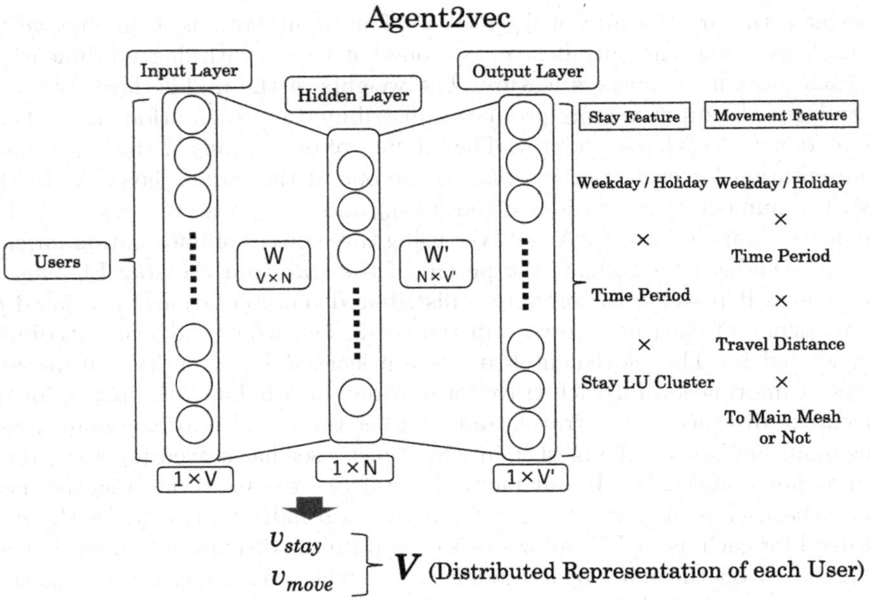

Agent2vec

Fig. 2. Architecture of Agent2Vec

3.3 Generating Synthetic Flow Data

In this section, we explain how to model the activity of agents from each classified user cluster and how to generate the location history of each agent. First, we decide which user cluster each agent will use as a model. The probability $P(u)$ that an agent uses the user cluster u as a model is defined as follows, using N_u that is the number of users belonging to the user cluster u(U is the number of user clusters).

$$P(u) = \frac{N_u}{\sum_{k=0}^{U} N_k} \tag{1}$$

That is, a typical cluster with many users is likely to be chosen as a model for agents.

Next, the location history of the agent is generated according to the selected user model. Specifically, for the mesh in which the agent is currently staying, we probabilistically select "1. whether to move or stay" and "2. to which mesh to move if to move" during each 30-min. time slot. The decision to move from the current stay mesh is made according to a Poisson distribution based on the average number of moves of real users λ. The probability P_{stay} that a agent does not move in a given time slot $t$is

$$P_{stay} = \frac{\lambda_t^0 exp(-\lambda_t)}{0!} = exp(-\lambda_t) \tag{2}$$

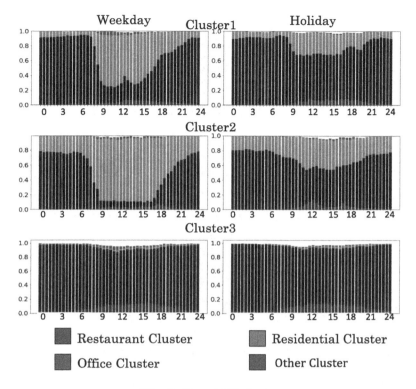

Fig. 3. Stayed LU cluster

At the same time, the probability that a agent moves is

$$P_{move} = 1 - exp(-\lambda_t) \tag{3}$$

This average number of travels λ is averaged for each time slot and for each LU cluster before the movement. This is based on the idea that the occurrence of travel is correlated not only with the time of day but also with the LU cluster before travel. For example, the probability that a user in the salaryman cluster moves to the residential cluster at 8:00 in the morning is considered to be different from that in the office cluster.

Finally, we explain the decision of which mesh to move to. This is mainly based on three factors: the density of stay in each time zone, the LU similarity, and the distance traveled.

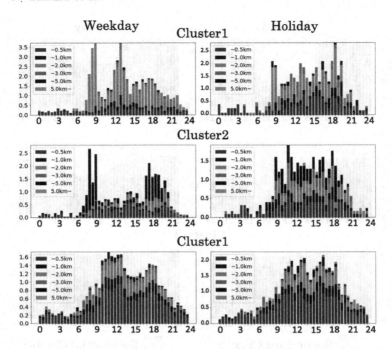

Fig. 4. Travel distance tendency

For the density of stay, the thickness of stay of actual users in each time zone is calculated in advance. The density of stay D_t in a given time slot t is calculated using the number of users $C(m)$ in the mesh m as follows(M is the number of meshes).

$$D_t(m) = \frac{C(m)}{\sum_{k=0}^{M} C(k)} \tag{4}$$

By considering this as the probability of migration, we can set a higher probability of migration to a mesh with more stays.

For LU similarity, we set the probability of moving to a mesh with LUs that have high resemblance to the destination LU cluster to generate a destination along with the user's POI. The destination LU cluster is determined according to the proportion of LU clusters (3) that stay in each time zone of the user cluster to which it belongs. To reduce the amount of computation, we take the average LU as a representative of each LU cluster and calculate the probability of moving based on the similarity of the average LU of each LU cluster.

As for the travel distance, we set the travel probability to the one with the appropriate travel distance to be high based on the trend of travel distance of real users (mean and variance of distance). Specifically, the probability of movement is assigned to each mesh according to a normal distribution based on the mean distance and variance.

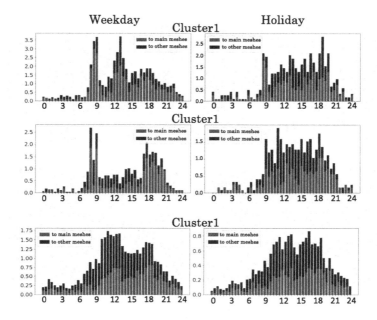

Fig. 5. Travel to main mesh tendency

In this way, the probability of moving to each mesh is calculated for each density of stay, LU similarity, and travel distance, the product of these probabilities generates a move to the mesh. Therefore, agents decide the destination mesh for each period based on the density of stay, POI, and distance from the source mesh. By generationg agent's travel probabilistically from each user model, we can generate synthetic people flow dataset for an arbitrary number of users.

4   Evaluation

To evaluate the proposed method, we generate synthetic human flow data using a GPS location history dataset provided by Blogwatcher. The target area was Nisshin City, Aichi Prefecture, and the period of the data was March 2020. We used the data of 2155 users whose location information was sufficiently available in the target area. The number of generated agents was 30000, the number of LU clusters was 4, and the number of user clusters was 40. Figure 6 shows a visualization of the generated data. The plots show the position of each agent, which moves over time according to the generative model. We can see that during the daytime hours there are more stays in the office area near the centre, while during the night there is a decrease in stays.

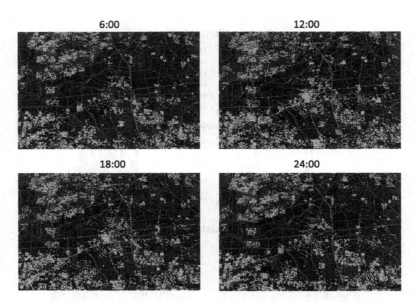

Fig. 6. Visualization of syntheic data

In the following, we evaluate the generated data regarding density of stay, amount of travel, and distance traveled. The evaluation method is based on the method used in [12]. As there is no correct data for urban flows, we basically compare the data with the original data, and for the density of stay, we compare the data with the population distribution dataset of mobile spatial statistics at each period.

4.1 Stay Density

We evaluated whether the generated data could reproduce the population distribution at each time. Figure 7 compares the density of stay of the generated data at 6:00, 12:00, and 18:00 with the respective data. From the top, the density of stay for Mobile Spatial Statistics (500 m mesh), Blogwatcher (500 m mesh), Blogwatcher (50 m mesh), and the density of stay for the generated data are plotted for each mesh. Since the population distribution data of Mobile Spatial Statistics is available only at the granularity of 500 m mesh, the comparison is made according to this mesh granularity. If the positive correlation between the density of stay in both data is high, the generated data will likely reproduce the actual population distribution. As for the plot with the Blogwatcher data, there is a positive correlation between 50 m and 500 m meshes. As for the plot with mobile spatial statistics, there are some meshes where the density of stay is high in the mobile spatial statistics data but low in the generated data.

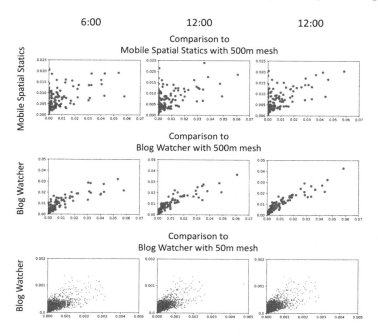

Fig. 7. Comparison of stay density

The Fig. 8 shows the correlation coefficients calculated for each period for each dataset. There is a strong correlation with the Blogwatcher data, especially at the 50 m mesh granularity (0.75–0.8), thus reproducing a highly granular population distribution. However, the correlation with mobile spatial statistics is low in all periods. This is because the sample size of the original Blogwatcher data is smaller than that of the mobile spatial statistics, and the stay history is biased. Figure 9 shows the difference in density of stay between the mobile spatial statistical data and the geographically drawn data, with the meshes with large discrepancies in the density of stay colored darker. The plots in the figure show Akaike and Nisshin stations, which are the main stations in the target area, and the meshes with a large difference in density of stay are located around the stations and at the periphery of the target area. The dataset from which the synthetic data is generated focuses on users in the area and whose positions are available for many hours during the period and excludes users who stay outside the area for many hours a day. This may be the reason for the dissociation between the density of stay in the synthetic data and the density of stay in the mobile spatial statistics around the station and the periphery of the area, and the red mesh in the figure is considered the area where users frequently enter and leave the area.

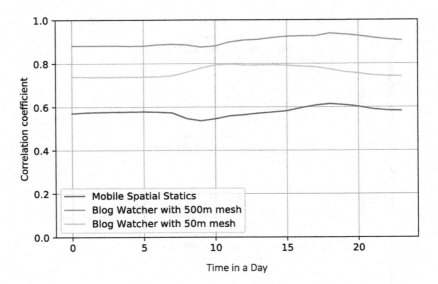

Fig. 8. Comparison of correlation

4.2 Amount of Travel

Figure 10 shows the comparison between the synthetic data and the original data, where the horizontal axis shows the hourly time, and the vertical axis shows the percentage of the travel. Compared with the original data, the generated data reproduces the peak hours, but the amount of travel during the midnight hours is lower than that of the original data.

Figure 11 shows the comparison of the travel distance between the synthetic data and the original data. We can see that the synthetic data tends to move longer distances than the original data, and especially the distance below 0.5 km is smaller. This may be because the density and LU similarity are too important when selecting the destination mesh. In addition, the distance traveled depends on the user's geographic location, such as the location of the user's home and workplace, this may be because these are not sufficiently modeled in the activity modeling of agents.

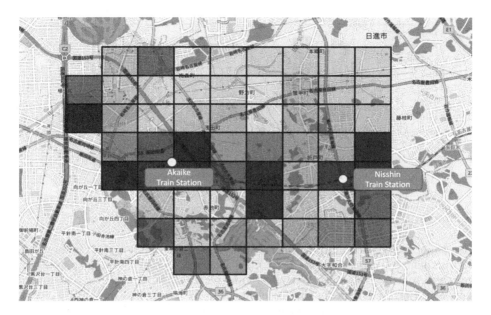

Fig. 9. Distribution of meshes with high RMSE

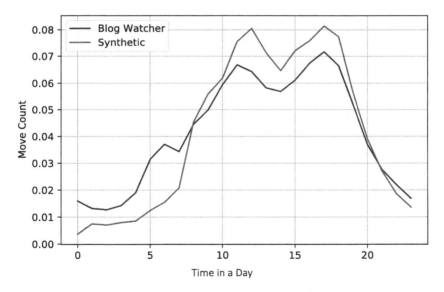

Fig. 10. Comparison of amount of travel

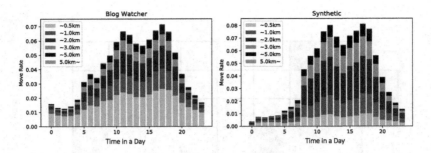

Fig. 11. Comparison of travel distance

5 Conclusion

This paper proposes a method to generate synthetic human flow data in an urban environment by utilizing large-scale GPS location history data. In particular, we realize unsupervised user activity modeling using Agent2Vec for distributed representation and Kmeans++ for clustering. By using this method, we were able to generate synthetic people flow data using only unlabeled data. This data reproduces the density of stay in the real world with finer granularity than the conventional data and models the agent's travel by LU transitions. Therefore, the synthetic traffic flow data can reproduce a more realistic flow by creating the travel along with the POI of real users. As for the prospects, we would like to generate more accurate human flow data for the distance traveled, which was not accurate in this evaluation. We are considering an approach that adds a geographical element to the user activity modeling. We also plan to evaluate our dataset by comparing it with various other datasets. In addition, we would like to improve our method to reproduce each agent's travel route, travel speed, and means of travel, as these are considered essential elements for reproducing urban human flows.

References

1. Yabe, T., Tsubouchi, K., Fujiwara, N., Wada, T., Sekimoto, S., Ukkusuri, S.: Non-compulsory measures sufficiently reduced human mobility in Tokyo during the COVID-19 epidemic. Sci. Rep. **10**, 18053 (2020)
2. Bhat, C.R. Frank, S.K.: Activity-based modeling of travel demand. In: Hall, R.W. (ed.) Handbook of transportation Science, International Series in Operations Research & Management Science, vol. 23, pp. 35–61. Springer, Boston (2003). https://doi.org/10.1007/978-1-4615-5203-1_3
3. Bowman, J.L., Moshe, E.B.: Activity-based disaggregate travel demand model system with activity schedules. Transp. Res. Part A: Policy Pract. **35**(1), 1–28 (2001)
4. Song, X., Hiroshi, K., Ryosuke, S.: DeepTransport: prediction and simulation of human mobility and transportation mode at a citywide level. In: IJCAI (2016), p. 16 (2016)

5. Yin, M., Sheehan, M., Feygin, S., Paiement, J.-F., Pozdnoukhov, A.: A generative model of urban activities from cellular data. IEEE Trans. Intell. Transp. Syst. **19**(6), 1682–1696 (2017)
6. Ouyang, K., Shokri, R., Rosenblum, D.S., Yang, W.: A non-parametric generative model for human trajectories. IJCA **I**(2018), 3812–3817 (2018)
7. Borysov, S.-S., Rich, J., Pereira, F.C.: How to generate micro-agents? A deep generative modeling approach to population synthesis. Transp. Res. Part C Emerg. Technol. **106**, 73–97 (2019)
8. Drchal, J., Čertický, M., Jakob, M.: Data-driven activity scheduler for agent-based mobility models. Transp. Res. Part C Emerg. Technol. **98**, 370–390 (2019)
9. Vecchio, P.D., Secundo, G., Maruccia, Y., Passiante, G.: A system dynamic approach for the smart mobility of people: implications in the age of big data. Technol. Forecast. Soc. Change. **149**, 119771 (2019)
10. Pang, Y., Tsubouchi, K., Yabe, T., Sekimoto, Y.: Development of people mass movement simulation framework based on reinforcement learning. Transp, Res. Part C Emerg. Technol. **117**, 102706(2020)
11. Pang, Y., Tsubouchi, K., Yabe, T., Sekimoto, Y.: Replicating urban dynamics by generating human-like agents from smartphone GPS data. In: Proceedings of the 26th ACM SIGSPATIAL International Conference on Advances in Geographic Information Systems, pp. 440–443 (2018)
12. Kashiyama, T., Pang, Y., Sekimoto, Y.: Open PFLOW: creation and evaluation of an open dataset for typical people mass movement in urban areas. Elsevier **85**, 249–267 (2017)

A Study on Metrics for Concept Drift Detection Based on Predictions and Parameters of Ensemble Model

Kei Yonekawa$^{(\boxtimes)}$, Shuichiro Haruta, Tatsuya Konishi, Kazuhiro Saito, Hideki Asoh,
and Mori Kurokawa

KDDI Research, Inc., Saitama, Japan
{ke-yonekawa,sh-haruta,tt-konishi,ku-saitou,hi-aso,
mo-kurokawa}@kddi-research.jp

Abstract. The performance of machine learning models deteriorates when the distribution of test data changes, which is called concept drift. One way to deal with concept drift is to continuously rebuild the model. If we want to minimize the frequency of rebuilding due to some constraints, however, it is important to detect concept drift as the timing when rebuilding is truly necessary. Taking advantage of ensemble models for concept drift detection may improve the detection accuracy. However, the behavior of ensemble model's predictions and parameters in the presence of concept drift has not been fully investigated. In this study, we investigated how the ensemble models constructed by two different methods behave in the presence of concept drift. In the experiments, we monitored some metrics including the metrics that can be calculated only by the ensemble model and the metrics based on the model parameters. As a result, we found that the metrics show some behaviors that seem to be influenced by concept drift, suggesting that the detection accuracy of concept drift may be improved by using these metrics.

Keywords: Concept drift detection · Neural networks · Ensemble learning

1 Introduction

Before a machine learning model can be integrated into a real service, the model alone or the machine learning pipeline[1] is built and verified in the development environment, and then deployed to the production environment [1]. The statistical properties of the data handled in a real service may differ in the distribution of the data between the time when the model is trained and the time when the model performs inference. For example, in a news service, user preferences change over time, so when recommending articles or products, a category with a high response rate in the past may have a low response rate in the recent past [2]. This phenomenon is called concept drift, and it is one of the causes in model performance degradation [2].

---

[1] A series of processes including preprocessing, model training, data and model validation, and inference using the model.

T. Hara and H. Yamaguchi (Eds.): MobiQuitous 2021, LNICST 419, pp. 568–581, 2022.
https://doi.org/10.1007/978-3-030-94822-1_37

There are two approaches to deal with concept drift: one is to retrain the model continuously, and the other is to retrain the model only when the statistical properties of the data change significantly [3]. In order to implement the former approach, the following conditions must be met: the labels necessary for training must be constantly available, and the possibility of production deployment of the retrained model must be automatically determined. On the other hand, in the latter approach, labels need to be obtained only when they are needed. Besides, in the latter approach, the retrained model can be manually audited, so that the validity of the inference basis can be verified in terms of fairness and causality before the decision to deploy is made. In this paper, we will deal with the latter case, assuming that the conditions for implementing the former are not met. In this case, it is important to detect concept drift as the timing when retraining is truly necessary.

One approach to concept drift detection is based on the change in model parameters when the model is updated with new data [13], which has potential for development in terms of explainability of concept drift and other aspects.

As a related field to concept drift detection, in the field of outlier detection, it has been proposed to increase the reliability of detection by using an ensemble of multiple methods [4]. As for ensembles of neural networks, it has been reported that predictions tend to be agreed upon among ensemble members depending on how the members are created [5]. Thus, it is possible that concept drift may be missed by simply monitoring the output of the model.

Taking advantage of ensemble models for concept drift detection may improve the detection accuracy. However, ensemble models may not be able to fully exploit the mutual agreement rate among ensemble members [12] or the uncertainty in the model output [20] because the predictions may be similar depending on how the members are composed [5]. Thus, it can be said that there are conflicting possibilities. On the other hand, model parameters retain sufficient diversity among members depending on how they are organized [5]. Thus, it can be said that ensemble models may be useful for concept drift detection if they are based on model parameters. In order to investigate these possibilities, this paper investigates how ensemble models constructed by two different methods behave in terms of predictions and model parameters in the presence of concept drift. To the best of our knowledge, this is the first work to monitor some metrics based on ensemble models under concept drift, such as cohesiveness of internal representations in the ensemble, cohesiveness of gradients in the ensemble, and so on.

2 Related Works

2.1 The Sources of Concept Drift

Let X be the input of the model and Y be the label. In the case of labeled data, the distribution of the data at a certain time t can be expressed by the joint probability $P_t(X, Y)$. This can be decomposed as $P_t(X, Y) = P_t(Y|X)P_t(X)$. Thus, there are three patterns in which the distribution of the data changes in comparison with time t and $t + 1$ as follows [6]. (1) When only the input distribution changes, i.e., $P_t(X) \neq P_{t+1}(X)$ but $P_t(Y|X) = P_{t+1}(Y|X)$. This is called a covariate shift or virtual drift. (2) When only the conditional distribution changes, i.e., $P_t(Y|X) \neq P_{t+1}(Y|X)$ but $P_t(X) = P_{t+1}(X)$.

This is called the actual drift or real drift. (3) When both the input distribution and the conditional distribution change, i.e., $P_t(X) \neq P_{t+1}(X)$ and at the same time $P_t(Y|X) \neq P_{t+1}(Y|X)$.

2.2 The Types of Concept Drift

The following four patterns of data distribution change over time have been pointed out [6]. (1) A case where the old data distribution is switched to a new one in a short period of time. This case is called *sudden drift*. (2) A case where the old data distribution is switched to the new data distribution over a period of time. Both distributions are mixed in a certain ratio in the middle of the switch, and the ratio of the new data distribution gradually becomes larger. This case is called *gradual drift*. (3) A case where the old data distribution is switched to the new data distribution over time passing through an intermediate distribution. In this case, the distribution itself change continuously during the switching process. This case is called *incremental drift*. (4) A case where the distribution switches from the old data distribution to the new data distribution and then switches back to the old data distribution after a certain period of time has elapsed. This case is called *reoccurring drift*.

2.3 Two Major Approaches to Deal with Concept Drift

There are two main ways to deal with the degradation of model performance due to concept drift [3]. The first approach is to adapt to changes in the data distribution by repeatedly retraining the model using the most recently obtained data. This is called continuous rebuild. The second approach is to retrain the model only when concept drift is detected based on some indicator. This is called triggered rebuild.

The advantage of continuous rebuild is that it adapts quickly to concept drift and does not require additional computation. The disadvantages are that labels are always needed, deployment frequency is high, data and model validation need to be automated, and computational resources are always consumed for retraining.

The advantages of triggered rebuild are that labels are obtained only when retraining is required, the number of deployments can be reduced, validation of data and models does not necessarily have to be automated, and computational resources for retraining can be reduced. The disadvantages are that the adaptation to concept drift is delayed by the detection delay, and that the detection algorithm requires additional computational burden in terms of memory and CPU power to run.

2.4 Concept Drift Detection Methods

The methods of concept drift detection can be classified into three categories according to the target to be monitored [7]. The first is a method that monitors the input of the model. There are methods based on the Hellinger distance between the feature distributions during training and inference [8], and methods based on principal component analysis [9]. While these methods do not require labels and are model-agnostic, they may react to changes that are unrelated to the degradation of model performance, and require a feature extractor when dealing with unstructured data. The second method is to monitor the output of the model. One method that requires labels is based on prediction error [10]. Methods that do not require labels include a method based on the number of cases that fall into the margin of the classifier [11], a method based on the mutual agreement rate among ensemble members [12], the method based on the distribution of the confidence in the model's output [3], and the method based on the uncertainty of the model's output [20]. While there is always a loss of accuracy or confidence in the model when these concept drift detection methods are reactive, labels are required or the model type is constrained. The third method is to monitor the parameters of the model. There are methods based on changes in the prior distribution of model parameters [13]. While the detection index is theoretically valid, it requires labels and is limited to models that can be handled by Bayesian learning.

2.5 Ensemble

In the field of outlier detection, it has been proposed to use multiple methods or ensembles of models, rather than relying on a single method or model, in order to reduce the possibility of missing outliers [4]. Compared to using a single model, uncertainty can be well quantified when using an ensemble of models [14]. Besides, the uncertainty measure calculated based on an ensemble of models can well reflect distributional shift [24]. Thus, it is expected that the accuracy of concept drift detection will be improved if we employ the uncertainty measure based on ensemble models.

For ensembles of neural networks, it has been reported that randomizing the initialization of model parameters is effective in improving performance [15]. On the other hand, there are cases where it is not practical to prepare multiple production models with different initializations of parameters to monitor the performance. In such cases, the subspace sampling technique can be applied to obtain multiple models that can be members of an ensemble from a single trained model. Subspace sampling is a method of obtaining multiple models with diversity by adding some noise to the models. The simplest method is to add random values to the model parameters. According to [5], random initialization has a larger performance gain than subspace sampling. It has also been reported that models obtained by subspace sampling tend to have similar predictions even if the weights are different [5].

3 Methods

Since we are interested in ensembles of neural networks, we use a multilayer perceptron as the base model. The number of units in each hidden layer was set to 7. For the activation function of the hidden layer, we used the Leaky ReLU [17], which has a slope of 0.01 when the input value is negative. For the activation function of the output layer, we used a sigmoid function. A bias term was provided for all units. All these choices are determined empirically.

Two methods for obtaining the ensemble members are investigated: random initialization and random subspace sampling [5]. In random initialization, the ensemble members are obtained by initializing the weights of the base model with random values and training it. In random subspace sampling, the ensemble member is obtained by adding random values to the learned main model. The random values to be added are calculated by multiplying a random unit vector by 10% or 20% of the L2 norm of the weights of the model. As the random unit vector, we obtained a random orthogonal matrix with the dimensionality of the model parameters as the number of rows and columns by the method of [18], and used its row vector. If the number of ensemble members to be created was larger than the number of dimensions of the model parameters, the random orthogonal matrix was obtained multiple times.

4 Experiments

4.1 Datasets

The dataset used in the experiment consists of five synthetic data using the scikit-multiflow package [21] and one real world data. The data used as synthetic data are MIXED, STAGGER, SINE, SEA, and AGRAWAL. In each data set, concept drift was introduced by changing the classification function (labeling rule). The number of classification functions varies depending on the dataset, but in all datasets, concept drift was introduced so that the number of classification functions cycled in ascending order (e.g., $0 \rightarrow 1 \rightarrow 2 \rightarrow 0$ in STAGGER). In terms of noise, two irrelevant features were introduced in SINE, the label flip rate was set to 10% in SEA, and the feature disturbance rate was set to 10% in AGRAWAL.

The data used as real-world data is Spambase [16]. The Spambase dataset is a dataset for a binary classification task. The target variable is the binary value of whether an e-mail is judged to be spam or not. The features include the percentage of occurrence of specific words (48 types), the percentage of occurrence of specific letters (6 types), and the mean, maximum, and sum of the lengths of consecutive capital letters. The number of samples is 4601.

Since Spambase is not stream data, concept drift needs to be artificially introduced. To artificially introduce sudden drift into Spambase, we refer to the procedure in [11]. Specifically, the features (continuous values) were normalized to the range [0, 1], and the absolute values of the correlation coefficients with the target variable (in [11], information gain was used instead) were calculated for each feature dimension and ranked. The samples are then arranged in a random order to simulate stream data. When a sudden concept drift is to be introduced, the order of the feature dimensions with the top 50% absolute values of the correlation coefficients is randomly reordered to simulate a sudden concept drift. This method makes it easier to observe the influence of concept drift on the prediction accuracy and the optimal solution of the model.

4.2 Evaluation

The evaluation was conducted in two phases: a warm-up phase and a prequential phase. The warm-up phase corresponds to a phase in which models were built in a development environment. The prequential phase corresponds to a phase in which the trained model is deployed in a production environment and trying to detect concept drift while performing inferences.

First, in the warm up phase, the training data and validation data are obtained from the data described above, and the trained main model is obtained by early stopping based on the monitoring of the validation loss. The number of samples for the training and validation data is 10000 and 2000 for the synthetic data, and 2760 and 460 for the real-world data. The base model has one hidden layer, the learning algorithm is Adam [19], the learning rate is 0.1, the batch size is 32, the number of steps per epoch is 10, the maximum number of epochs is 300, and the early stopping patience is 30 epochs.

Next, in the prequential phase, an ensemble is formed, and one batch of test data obtained from the data described above is acquired for each time step to perform prediction, performance evaluation, and model updating. During the process, a sudden concept drift was generated using the method described above. The number of samples for the test data is 25600 for the synthetic data and 1376 for the real-world data. The size of the batch to be acquired was set to 32. In the model update, the learning algorithm is Adam, and the learning rate is 0.1. The time steps when the concept drifts were introduced were 200, 400, and 600 for the synthetic data and 21 for the real-world data.

The following two methods were used to construct the ensemble: random initialization (RI) and random subspace sampling (RSS). When updating the model, all the ensemble members are updated. For the main model, two cases were investigated: updating (main model, MM) and not updating (Frozen). The number of members in an ensemble M is set to 10. Because of the randomness in the generation of data and the composition of the ensemble, the evaluation was performed 10 times using the same procedure.

4.3 Metrics

Several metrics were monitored in the prequential phase. To see how the performance changes with the concept drift introduced in each dataset, the batch-average of the loss and the accuracy per batch were calculated for each time step for Frozen, MM, RI, and RSS. These metrics were ensemble-averaged for RI and RSS (LOS and ACC, respectively).

To examine the diversity of the predictions in the ensemble, the ensemble standard deviation (SD) of the predictions was calculated and batch-averaged (YSD).

As predicted values are related to uncertainty of prediction, we also calculated the batch-average of the entropy of the ensemble-average of the predictions (ENT). Namely, $\text{ENT} = -\frac{1}{|\mathcal{B}|}\sum_{i\in\mathcal{B}}p_i\log p_i$, $p_i = \frac{1}{|\mathcal{M}|}\sum_{m\in\mathcal{M}}f_m(x_i; \theta_m)$. Here, $\mathcal{B}$ is a batch, $\mathcal{M}$ is the ensemble, and p_i is the ensemble-average of prediction by m-th model f_m in $\mathcal{M}$ parameterized by θ_m for i-th sample, whose feature is x_i.

To examine the diversity of model parameters in the ensemble, we calculated the dimension-average of the ensemble standard deviation of the model parameters (PSD). Namely, PSD $= \frac{1}{|\mathcal{D}|} \sum_{d \in \mathcal{D}} v_d$, $v_d = \sqrt{\frac{1}{|\mathcal{M}|} \sum_{m \in \mathcal{M}} (\theta_{md} - \overline{\theta_d})}$, $\overline{\theta_d} = \frac{1}{|\mathcal{M}|} \sum_{m \in \mathcal{M}} \theta_{md}$. Here, $\mathcal{D}$ is a set of dimensions in θ_m, v_d is the ensemble standard deviation of θ_{md}, which is d-th dimension of θ_m, and $\overline{\theta_d}$ is the ensemble-average of θ_{md}.

Since we suppose the diversity of model parameters is related to the internal representations, the ensemble-average of the centered kernel alignment (CKA) [23] between the internal representations of each ensemble member and those of the ensemble-average were also calculated (CKA). Namely, CKA $= \frac{1}{|\mathcal{M}|} \sum_{m \in \mathcal{M}} linear\_cka(z_{mB}, \overline{z_B})$, $\overline{z_B} = \frac{1}{|\mathcal{M}|} \sum_{m \in \mathcal{M}} z_{mB}$. Here, $linear\_cka$ is the CKA function with a linear kernel, z_{mB} is internal representations of the batch B obtained from model m, and $\overline{z_B}$ is the ensemble-average of z_{mB}. This metric indicates cohesiveness of internal representations in the ensemble. Here, CKA is considered to be a reasonable similarity measure for comparing the internal representations of neural networks [22].

We also focused on the dynamics of the model parameters. We calculated the ensemble-average of the cosine similarity between the gradient of each ensemble member and that of the ensemble-average (GCO). Namely, GCO $= \frac{1}{|\mathcal{M}|} \sum_{m \in \mathcal{M}} \cos(g_m, \overline{g})$, $\overline{g} = \frac{1}{|\mathcal{M}|} \sum_{m \in \mathcal{M}} g_m$. Here, g_m is the batch-average of gradient of for model m, and $\overline{g}$ is the ensemble-average of g_m. This metric indicates cohesiveness of gradients in the ensemble. We also calculated the ensemble-average of the L2 norm of the gradient (GNO). The above values were calculated for each evaluation trial, and then the mean and standard deviation were calculated for each time step.

5   Results

In the following figures, the solid line is the inter-trial mean of each metric for each time step, and the upper and lower bound of each error band are the inter-trial standard deviations. To make the graphs easier to read, the values are smoothed using moving averages. The window length of the moving average was set to 10 for the synthetic data and 3 for the real-world data.

5.1   Changes in Prediction Performance

We show how the performance changes with concept drift. Figure 1 shows LOS and Fig. 2 shows ACC. For all datasets except SEA, there is a significant increase in LOS and decrease in ACC at each time point of all drifts for Frozen, MM, RI, and RSS, indicating performance degradation due to concept drift. The exception is SEA, where the drift effects at t = 400 for Frozen and t = 200, 400 for the other models appear to be difficult to recognize.

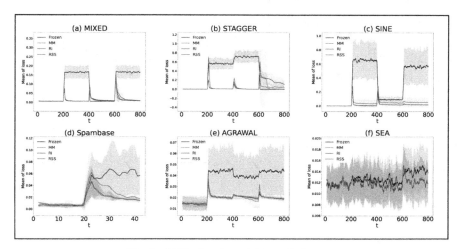

Fig. 1. LOS of each model in each dataset.

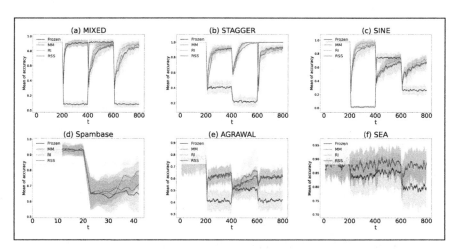

Fig. 2. ACC of each model in each dataset.

Table 1. Summary of changes of each metrics in each dataset in the case of RI.

	MIXED	STAGGER	Spambase	SINE	AGRAWAL	SEA
YSD	✓	✓	✓	✓	✓	
ENT	✓	✓	✓	✓		✗
PSD	✓	✓		✓		✗
CKA	✓	✓	✗			
GCO	✓		✓			✓
GNO	✓	✓	✓	✓	✓	

Table 2. Summary of changes of each metrics in each dataset in the case of RSS.

	MIXED	STAGGER	Spambase	SINE	AGRAWAL	SEA
YSD	✓	✓	✓	✓	✓	
ENT	✓	✓	✓	✓		✗
PSD	✓	✓	✗	✓		✗
CKA	✓	✓	✓			
GCO	✓		✓			
GNO	✓	✓	✓	✓	✓	

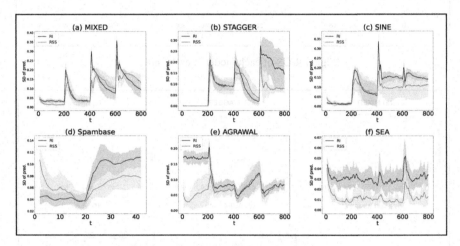

Fig. 3. YSD of each model in each dataset.

5.2 Changes in the Diversity of Predictions

We show how the concept drift changed the diversity of predictions in the ensemble. Table 1 for RI and Table 2 for RSS show how each metric changed at each drift point for each dataset. "✓"means that there was a significant change at all drift points, blank means that there was at least a minor change at some drift points, and "✗" means that the change was difficult to recognize at all drift points. The order of the datasets in the table is such that the dataset with the most ✓ is on the left. Figure 3 shows YSD. The value increases in most cases where the value changes at the drift point, indicating that the diversity of predictions has increased. The exception is AGRAWAL, which falls at t = 400, 600 for RI and RSS. In relation to the predictions, Fig. 4 shows ENT as an uncertainty measure. The value increases when the value changes at the drift time, indicating that the uncertainty of the prediction has increased.

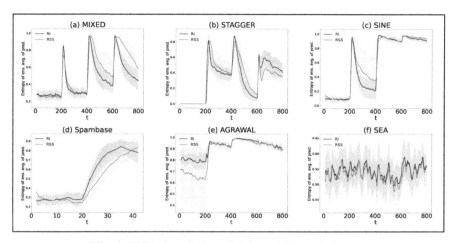

Fig. 4. ENT of prediction of each model in each dataset.

5.3   Changes in the Diversity of Model Parameters

We show how the concept drift changes the diversity of the model parameters in the ensemble. Figure 5 shows PSD. In most of the cases where the values change at the time of drift, they go down and then up, which can be interpreted as the model parameters becoming similar for a while and then diversifying. The exceptions are t = 200 for SINE, STAGGER, and MIXED, and Spambase, where the values rise without falling. In relation to the model parameters, Fig. 6 shows CKA. In most cases where the value changes at the drift point, it falls, which can be interpreted as a diversification of the internal representation. The exceptions are t = 200 for the RI of SINE and t = 600 for the RI and RSS of SEA, which show an increase. In relation to the dynamics of the model parameters, Fig. 7 shows GCO. When the values change at the drift point, there are almost the same number of upward and downward cases, and thus no consistency is observed. Figure 8 shows GNO. When the value changes at the point of drift, it is elevated and is considered to be linked to the increase in loss.

5.4   Comparisons

Prediction Error and the Other Metrics. One case where drift effects are difficult to recognize with prediction error-based metrics such as LOS and ACC is t = 400 for SEA. In this case, the metrics that show drift effects are YSD (RI), CKA (RSS), GCO (RI), and GNO (RI and RSS). It is suggested that the use of ensemble-specific and model-parameter-based metrics may improve the accuracy of concept drift detection based on prediction error.

Predictions and Model Parameters. The case where there is no significant change in the prediction-based metrics such as YSD and ENT is SEA t = 200. In this case, the metric that shows drift effects is GCO. It is desirable to clarify the mechanism of the behaviors of these metrics to create better metrics.

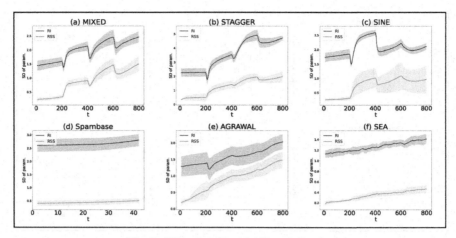

Fig. 5. PSD of each model in each dataset.

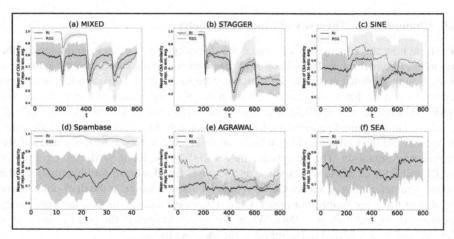

Fig. 6. CKA of each model in each dataset.

RI and RSS. RI may be more convenient because it has a higher diversity of ensemble members and shows more ensemble-specific characteristics, while RSS is more practical because its computational cost is lower than that of RI. In this paper, we discuss whether RSS can replace RI for each metric. The metrics based on predicted values are considered to be substitutable because the patterns in the Tables 1 and 2 are the same. The metrics based on model parameters are also considered to be substitutable because the overall pattern of the Tables 1 and 2 is similar. As an exception, in Spambase, it is difficult to recognize the effect of drift on PSD in RSS. On the other hand, it is difficult to recognize the effect of drift on CKA in RI. Besides, it was assumed that there would be a trade-off between the amount of computation and the prominence of the movement of the metrics. However, depending on the combination of data set and indicator, the movement of RSS

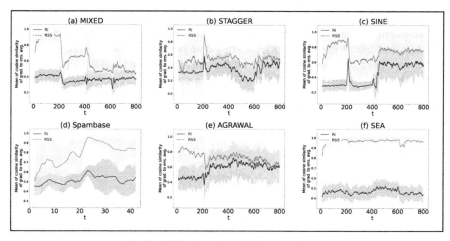

Fig. 7. GCO of each model in each dataset.

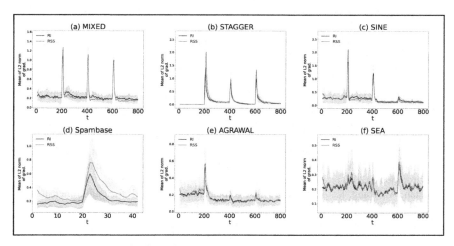

Fig. 8. GNO of each model in each dataset.

was larger than that of RI (e.g., CKA in AGRAWAL and SINE). This suggests that there may not necessarily be a trade-off. It is desirable that the mechanism of the behaviors of these metrics will be clarified to create better metrics.

6 Conclusion

In this study, we investigated the behavior of the predictions and parameters of ensemble models constructed by two different methods in the presence of concept drifts. The results showed that the metrics that can be calculated only by the ensemble model and the metrics based on the model parameters showed behaviors suggestive of concept drift.

Thus, it can be said that the detection accuracy of concept drift may be improved by using the parameters of the ensemble model. There were some metrics based on model parameters that complemented the metrics based on predicted values in terms of concept drift detection, and some indices behaved differently between RI and RSS. It is desirable to clarify the mechanism of the behaviors of these metrics to create better metrics.

Acknowledgments. This research is partially supported by JST CREST Grant Number JPMJCR21F2.

References

1. MLOps: Continuous delivery and automation pipelines in machine learning, https://cloud.google.com/architecture/mlops-continuous-delivery-and-automation-pipelines-in-machine-learning. Accessed 29 July 2021
2. Korycki, Ł., Krawczyk, B.: Class-incremental experience replay for continual learning under concept drift. In: CVPR Workshops (2021)
3. Lindstrom, P., Mac Namee, B., Delany, S.J.: Drift detection using uncertainty distribution divergence. In: ICDM Workshops (2011)
4. Zhao, Y., et al.: SUOD: accelerating large-scale unsupervised heterogeneous outlier detection. In: MLSys (2021)
5. Fort, S., Hu, H., Lakshminarayanan, B.: Deep ensembles: a loss landscape perspective. arXiv preprint arXiv:1912.02757v2 (2020)
6. Lu, J., Liu, A., Dong, F., Gu, F., Gama, J., Zhang, G.: Learning under concept drift: a review. IEEE Trans. Knowl. Data Eng. **31**(12), 2346–2363 (2020)
7. Lu, N., Zhang, G., Lu, J.: Concept drift detection via competence models. Artif. Intell. **209**, 11–28 (2014)
8. Ditzler, G., Polikar, R.: Hellinger distance based drift detection for nonstationary environments. In: IEEE Symposium on Computational Intelligence in Dynamic and Uncertain Environments (2011)
9. Qahtan, A., Wang, S.: A pca-based change detection framework for multidimensional data streams categories and subject descriptors. In: KDD (2015)
10. Gama, J., Medas, P., Castillo, G., Rodrigues, P.: Learning with drift detection. In: Bazzan, A.L.C., Labidi, S. (eds.) SBIA 2004. LNCS (LNAI), vol. 3171, pp. 286–295. Springer, Heidelberg (2004). https://doi.org/10.1007/978-3-540-28645-5_29
11. Sethi, T.S., Kantardzic, M.: On the reliable detection of concept drift from streaming unlabeled data. Expert Syst. Appl. **82**, 77–99 (2017)
12. Smutz, C., Stavrou, A.: When a tree falls: using diversity in ensemble classifiers to identify evasion in malware detectors. In: Proceedings 2016 Network and Distributed System Security (NDSS) Symposium, pp. 21–24. Internet Society, Reston (2016)
13. Haug, J., Kasneci, G.: Learning parameter distributions to detect concept drift in data streams. In: Proceedings of the 25th International Conference on Pattern Recognition (ICPR) (2020)
14. Tran, L., et al.: Hydra: preserving ensemble diversity for model distillation. In: ICML 2020 Workshop on Uncertainty and Robustness in Deep Learning (UDL) (2020)
15. Lakshminarayanan, B., Pritzel, A., Blundel, C.: Simple and scalable predictive uncertainty estimation using deep ensembles. In: NeurIPS (2017)
16. UCI Machine Learning Repository. http://archive.ics.uci.edu/ml. Accessed 29 July 2021
17. Maas, A.L., Hannun, A.Y., Ng, A.Y.: Rectifier nonlinearities improve neural network acoustic models. In: Proceedings of the International Conference on Machine Learning (ICML) (2013)

18. Stewart, G.W.: The efficient generation of random orthogonal matrices with an application to condition estimators. SIAM J. Numer. Anal. **17**, 403–409 (1980)
19. Kingma, D.P., Ba, J.: Adam: a method for stochastic optimization. In: Proceedings of the 3rd International Conference on Learning Representations (ICLR) (2015)
20. Baier, L., Schlör, T., Schöffer, J., Kühl, N.: Detecting concept drift with neural network model uncertainty. arXiv preprint arXiv:2107.01873 (2021)
21. Montiel, J., Read, J., Bifet, A., Abdessalem, T.: Scikit-multiflow: a multi-output streaming framework. J. Mach. Learn. Res. **19**(72), 1–5 (2018)
22. Kornblith, S., Norouzi, M., Lee, H., Hinton, G.: Similarity of neural network representations revisited. In: Proceedings of the 36th International Conference on Machine Learning (ICML) (2019)
23. Cortes, C., Mohri, M., Rostamizadeh, A.: Algorithms for learning kernels based on centered alignment. J. Mach. Learn. Res. **13**, 795–828 (2012)
24. Ovadia, Y., et al.: Can you trust your model's uncertainty? evaluating predictive uncertainty under dataset shift. In: NeurIPS (2019)

Event-Driven Interest Detection for Task-Oriented Mobile Apps

Fernando Kaway Carvalho Ota[(✉)] [iD], Farouk Damoun [iD], Sofiane Lagraa [iD],
Patricia Becerra-Sanchez [iD], Christophe Atten [iD], Jean Hilger [iD],
and Radu State [iD]

University of Luxembourg, 27 Avenue John F. Kennedy,
2167 Esch-sur-Alzette, Luxembourg
{fernando.carvalho,farouk.damoun,sofiane.lagraa,patricia.becerra,
radu.state}@uni.lu, jean.hilger@ext.uni.lu

Abstract. Mobile applications became the main interaction channel in several domains, such as banking. Consequently, understanding user behaviour on those apps has drawn attention in order to extract business-oriented outcomes. By combining Markov Chain and graph theory techniques, we successfully developed a process to model the app, to extract the click high utility events, to score the interest on those events and cluster the groups of interest. We tested our approach on an European bank dataset with over 3.5 millions of user's session. By implementing our approach, analysts can gain knowledge of user behaviour in terms of events that are important to the domain.

Keywords: Interest detection · Behaviour modelling · High utility events

1 Introduction

Nowadays, people depend on mobile applications, simply known as apps, to carry out daily activities including browsing the web, purchasing or checking bank accounts. These activities have attracted attention of different sectors, such as banking. Understanding the behavior of users when browsing mobile apps has increased interest in recent years to identify relevant products and make personalized offers [2]. This growing importance has driven focus of research on the analysis of task-oriented apps. This latter type of apps are defined to be when a user has a prior motivation in mind when starting a session [3], such as using the bank app to execute a wire transfer.

By analyzing navigation steps of the users' click events, we can identify the final user action, what we define as our High Utility Event (HUE). As instance, a user willing to check his bank balance has to navigate through the app until reaching the screen that presents his account. In this case, the HUE is the click event that contains the account balance. Click events consist of a series of ordered events triggered by user interactions when using the mobile app [4].

T. Hara and H. Yamaguchi (Eds.): MobiQuitous 2021, LNICST 419, pp. 582–598, 2022.
https://doi.org/10.1007/978-3-030-94822-1_38

In this sense, many researchers have proposed various techniques to mine HUEs focused on finding the right candidates to the high utility (importance) [5]. However, the main challenge of those investigations is to find the correct sequence of the user's navigation steps to obtain the target action.

In this paper, we propose a novel approach that combines Markov Chain and graph theory techniques to detect users' interest in HUEs a task-oriented mobile app. This approach mainly consists of mapping the whole mobile app by defining the source node based on the first event when the user starts the mobile app. The algorithm verifies all the possible routes, building a tree where the last nodes will be the events with high utility obtaining the target action or events of interest to the user. In the end, clusters are created to highlight the behavior of the users and the sessions by identifying the target action or the product of interest to the user, such as a purchase or a loan.

Problem Statement. Given an events' sequence of a mobile app, how to score the likelihood the user was to execute a certain target action in a session. As instance, a customer of a banking mobile app started to simulate a loan but did not submit a request. In this example, our goal is to identify how close the user was to finish the loan app.

For small apps, a list of target actions, namely HUEs, can be created by domain experts. However, more complex apps can have many candidates for target events, in other words, there can be several relevant actions that has to be filtered in order to provide real behavior knowledge. Additionally, complex apps from bigger enterprises are frequently changing, adding extra layer of manual mapping HUEs and its navigation paths. Usually, the search space is larger as the navigation events tend to appear in higher proportion than the targets.

Besides finding the right HUEs candidates, it is also necessary to detect the chain of events that lead to the execution of the target. By finding this sequence, it is possible to detect the intention of the user when he is navigating in the app in direction towards a certain action. Therefore, we are also investigating the sequential patterns of the app. By merging those research topics, we reach the term High Utility Event Mining.

2   Related Work

In this work, our goal is to find frequent sequential patterns in the session and identify the interesting ones for the business. In this sense, many researchers have focused on developing models for frequent sequential patterns. The research papers [6,7] used the Markov Chains model to identify users' navigation paths on websites. The model focused on analyzing the user's favorite web page without considering a more sophisticated analysis of user behavior. In [8], the researchers propose modeling user trails on the websites. The model obtained promising results in terms of accuracy and mean reciprocal rank, however, the model did not implement event timing modeling to help generate a non-stationary process in the analysis of random shipping lanes. In [9], they analyze the navigational click-stream data, but to social commerce platforms, which diverges from oriented-tasks app. In [10], they develop a user navigation behavior on a website model. This model focuses on visualizing web data without implementing user navigation path analysis. In [11], they present a framework for modeling the sequential data capturing pathways. In [12], they propose a model for discovering users' navigation. In both investigations, they implement a reduced sample size, affecting the analysis of user behavior and the model's scalability.

An unsupervised clustering method for analysing behavior based timed k-grams approach was proposed in [13]. Their k-grams construction is based on the event name interpolated with a category of a time interval. Then, their clusters are based on the frequencies of the k-grams in the user sessions. The approach was employed to clickstream datasets from Whisper and Renren social network apps, which contain 33 and 55 types of events, respectively. To those amount of event's types, this approach suits well, but it tends to become more computationally expensive as the k-grams construction exponentially increases when the app has a wider spectrum of events. As instance, the bank app we analysed had 311 events in the period we analysed, resulting in over a million 3-gram possibilities to count their frequencies per session, disregarded the time intervals categories. Therefore, this approach becomes unpractical to our use case in terms of processing and human comprehensible cluster visualisation.

One inspiration to our sequence discovery and subsequently graph modelling is found in [14]. In their effort to mine path in web sessions, they created the concept of a via-link to reduce the noise by removing the bigrams and 3-grams that does not reach a minimum occurrence count. To our use case, filtering off the bigrams or 3-grams that does not reach a probability threshold globally would result in removing also real events' transitions as some of them are likely to appear few times in the dataset. For example, some products that are not commonly purchased would disappear in the modelling with the global threshold proposed in this later paper.

The main contributions of this paper can be summarized as follows: First, a new technique is proposed for mapping the whole mobile app by defining the source node based on the user's first action. Second, a tree is built verifying all the possible routes without going through the same path determining the HUE. Finally, a cluster is created to group the behavior of the users in a behavioural perspective.

3   The Dataset

Our analysis was performed on a click event dataset from an European retail bank app. Each button of the app is uniquely named representing click events that are captured through a specific API HTTP call. This call is triggered at every click during user navigation to register the events with a timestamp and linked to an user and session identifiers.

The dataset contains approximately 3.8 million sessions from over 210 thousand different users in a data collection from 31 sequential days from 2021.

Those sessions have around 28 million events among 311 unique ones. Figure 1(a) shows how many sessions a single customer started in the period and (b) presents how many events a single session usually have. For the purpose of keeping the confidentiality agreement with the institution, we replaced the names of the real events by 'e' plus a number ranging from 0 to 311.

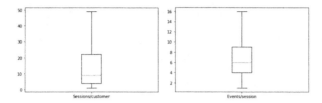

Fig. 1. (a) Boxplot of sessions per customer (b) Boxplot of events per session

3.1 Dataset Issues

An important part of the modelling is data cleansing to avoid analysis on noisy data caused by the occurrence of the following errors. The strategies for addressing those issues are presented in the next sections.

Late Event Registration Due to Disconnections. The user can lose the internet connection and continue using the mobile app. In the bank app we analysed, the strategy is sending the events when the user login again. In this case, the events from the previous session are registered under the current session id, resulting in a incorrect chain of events, as illustrated in Fig. 2.

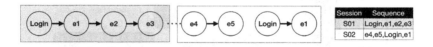

Fig. 2. Late event registration error

Lost Event Registration. There are some cases when the events are lost in the data pipeline. The reason for this varies from problems in the mobile app when sending the requests up to issues on the data flow from the servers to the bank mainframes. In any case, the dataset could contain samples of sequences with missing events as shown in Fig. 3.

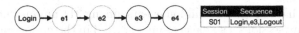

Fig. 3. Losing events error

Insufficient Samples for Modelling. In a fully data-driven approach as ours, all the events and its transitions are taken from samples on the dataset. Consequently, if some of the events are not hit or the transitions from one event to another does not have any sample, the model is under represented as in Fig. 4.

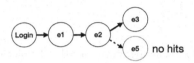

Fig. 4. Lack of event's hits for modelling

4 Methodology

By combining techniques from graph theory, Markov chains, high utility pattern mining, cumulative distribution function scoring and clustering, our approach below is capable of detecting users' interest in a certain event during their navigation in a task-oriented mobile app. Figure 5 depicts the whole processing pipeline of our approach described in the following subsections.

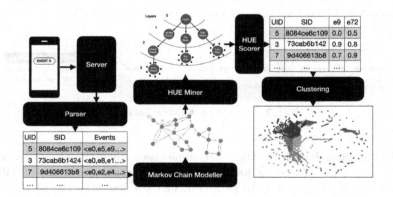

Fig. 5. Overview of the processing pipeline

4.1   Event Definitions

The events considered in this paper are the clicks on the bank app that are captured via API HTTP requests. We first give definitions and notations used throughout this paper, and then give more specific details about our events.

Definition 1. *An event e is a labeled click register generated during the navigation of a user in the app.*

Definition 2. *Let $E = \{e_1, e_2, \ldots, e_n\}$ be the set of events.*
$S((uid_i, sid_j), T_s, T_e)$ *denotes the click events sequence of the user uid_i in the session sid_j between the starting time T_s and the ending time T_e where $T_s < T_e$.*
$uid_i \in UID$ *where $UID = \{uid_1, uid_2, \ldots, uid_k\}$ is the set of users and k is the number of users.*
$sid_j \in SID$ *where $SID = \{(sid_1, T_{s_1}, T_{e_1}), (sid_2, T_{s_2}, T_{e_2}), \ldots, (sid_l, T_{s_l}, T_{e_l})\}$ is the set of sessions.*
The click events sequence $S = <(e_1, t_1), (e_2, t_2), \ldots, (e_n, t_n) >$, where $e_i \in E$, and $T_s \geq t_i \leq T_e$ such that $t_{i+1} > t_i$.

Table 1 provides an example of the dataset. In practice, the length click events sequences can be very long, and can reach up to a hundred of events per session. In order to mine and characterize causal relations between events, in the next step we introduce the notion of event graph model based on Markov chain as an intuitive graph representation for events.

4.2   Markov Chain Modeller

Our model is based on *n-gram* sequence. An *n-gram* is a contiguous sequence of n events from a given click event sequence. The intuition of the *n-gram* is that instead of computing the probability of an event given its entire history of events, we compute the transition probability of a n set of events occurring in sequence.

Thus, to calculate those transitions, we extract bigrams from the sequences to compute the conditional probability of original event e_o targeting the event e_t. In other words, we approximate it with the probability $P(e_o \rightarrow e_t)$.

Given the events sequence $S_{i,j} = <(e_{1_{i,j}}, t_{1_{i,j}}), (e_{2_{i,j}}, t_{2_{i,j}}), \ldots, (e_{ni,j}, t_{ni,j}) >$ of any user i in any session j, we compute the bigram of the sequence. To compute a particular bigram probability of an event given a previous events, we compute the count of the bigram $C(e_o e_t)$ and normalize it with the sum of all the bigrams that share the same first events:

Table 1. Click events dataset.

User ID	Session ID	Click events sequence
U01	S01	<e1, e2, e3, e5, e6>
U02	S02	<e1, e2, e5>
U02	S03	<e1, e3, e5, e7, e3, e5>

$$P(e_o \rightarrow e_t) = \frac{C(e_o e_t)}{\sum C(e_o)} \qquad (1)$$

Example 1. Let the following click events sequences of any user and any session from Table 1: $<e_1, e_2, e_3, e_5, e_6>$, $<e_1, e_2, e_5>$, $<e_1, e_3, e_5, e_7, e_3, e_5>$. Here are the calculations for some of the bigram probabilities from these sequences.
$P(e_1 \rightarrow e_2) = \frac{2}{3} = 0.66 | P(e_2 \rightarrow e_3) = \frac{1}{2} = 0.5 | P(e_3 \rightarrow e_5) = \frac{3}{3} = 1$

A Markov Chain is constructed from multiple successive events and their occurrence conditional probability. In other way, it is a directed graph that represents successive transitions between events click events sequences through the sessions and users.

Specifically, each vertex in the graph represents an event e_i and each edge (e_i, e_j) indicates that there is a continuous bigram between e_i and e_j. The Markov Chain over a set of type of events V is a weighted directed graph $G = (Vertex, Edge, \gamma)$:

- $Vertex$ is the set of events from E ($Vertex = E$).
- $Edge$ is a set of edges in G. Let e_u and e_v be be two events in $Vertex$. There is an edge $(e_u, e_v) \in Edge$ if and only if there exists a probability with a dependency rule: $e_u \xrightarrow{l_{e_u, e_v}} e_v$.
- γ is the function from Eq. 1 that assigns a probability for each edge (e_u, e_v).

The current transitions between events represent an order of the click events and the behavior of users when they use the app, but also represents the errors presented in Sect. 3.1. In order to reduce the potential noises caused by losing events registration presented in Fig. 3, some of the edges have to be removed. The first strategy for this removal is to exclude when they do not match a minimum transition probability.

Given the weighted directed graph $G = (Vertex, Edge, \gamma)$, and a minimum threshold $min\_support$, the filtered Markov Chain is a weighted directed graph $G_{Reduced} = (Vertex_{Reduced}, Edge_{Reduced}, \beta)$, where:

- $Vertex_{Reduced}$ is the subset of events from E ($Vertex_{Reduced} \subseteq Vertex$).
- $Edge_{Reduced}$ is the subset of edges in $G_{Reduced}$ where $Edge_{Reduced} \subseteq Edge$.
- β is a function that assigns for each edge $(e_u, e_v) \in Edge_{Reduced}$ the probability l'_{e_u, e_v} where $l'_{e_u, e_v} = l_{e_u, e_v} > min\_support$.

In Fig. 6, the minimum support threshold is set to 0.05 as an example. The transition probability from the Login to the event e7 is below this level, therefore, it is removed from the model.

4.3   High Utitily Event (HUE) Miner

Mining the high utility events can be complex in an app that has many events. Mostly because the definition of high utility varies depending on the desired outcomes, as instance, if it is business oriented, then product purchases would

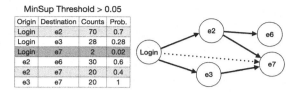

Fig. 6. Markov Chain noise reduction

be relevant, or in a cybersecurity perspective, a password exchange event draw more attention.

Notwithstanding task-oriented apps are likely to have navigation steps until reaching the event to execute the desired action. After executing this action, the user is usually taken back to the main menu or logout the app. If the app is designed in this fashion, consequently, it is possible to mine the HUE in a broad range by assuming the following:

Assumption. In a task-oriented app, HUEs are final states in unique sequences of events.

In this sense, by traversing the graph, the sequences of events can be outlined. However, finding the final states is challenging as it is hard to define the narrowing events of the sequence in an unsupervised way. Intuitively, we could assume that the events before a logout or a return to the main menu could be the candidates for our HUEs. Unfortunately, this assumption fails because the user can logout at any part of the app or return the steps in the sequence until returning to the main menu. Therefore, an algorithm based on this intuition would leave us with many imprecise HUEs candidates.

The solution is to search the graph from a source node, which is the first event when a user start the mobile app, and check on all the possible path are the nodes that can be reached without revisiting a node. Fortunately, the algorithms Depth-first search (DFS) [15] and Breadth-first search (BFS) [16] are techniques that can be employed to this end. Both algorithms traverses the graph and transform it into a tree containing the paths from the root node, the difference is that DFS tries to reach the deepest path while the BFS visit the node neighborhood before moving to the next depth level. To our use case, when a part of the app has multiple options, BFS tends to construct a layered tree where part of those leaves will not have descendants, consequently, outputting wrong candidates for HUEs. On the other hand, DFS group those options in the same level and constructs a tree where the leaves are the final states. By searching the filtered Markov Chain from the login event, DFS outputs a tree where the nodes with out degree equal 0 are our HUEs, as shown in Fig. 7.

DFS would output a perfect list of HUEs if the none of the events is lost during the collection. The cleaning process was done by the minimum support from the bigrams. However, a more frequent "dirty" transition would still persist in the database if their occurrence is above the threshold. Therefore, we adopted

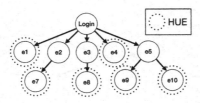

Fig. 7. DFS-based HUE mining

another strategy of creating a path traversal Markov Chain. The path traversal Markov Chain is built by designing a new model of transition analysis, which incrementally creates links (bigrams) and via-links (trigrams), where the edges are weighted according to the relationship between connected nodes. In other words, the co-occurrence of nodes in a session, through a sequence of a mobile app events where a subsequence of size 2 and 3 is considered a link and a via-link of a session, respectively. By setting an additional minimum support for the via-links, the Algorithm (1) will remove the misplaced transitions as double event loss occurrence is less likely to happen then a single loss. In Algorithm (1), we show the graph construction and cleaning as a preprocessing phase of the DFS algorithm in order to discover the data-driven HUEs.

4.4 HUE Scorer

For HUE scorer computation, we consider the Markov Chain as a weighted directed graph (G, w) where $G = (V, E)$ is a directed graph, V is the set of events in the Markov Chain, and E is a set of edges in G where the edge are the connections between events in the Markov Chain. $w : E \rightarrow \mathbb{R}_{\geq 0}$ is a non negative weight function. The weight represent the probability between two events in the Markov Chain.

The scoring method is derived from the definition of interest into a HUE. The more close the user is to hit a certain HUE in a session, the more interested he is into executing this action. To score the proximity, we used the Dijkstra algorithm [17] to calculate the distance of all the events to the HUEs in the Markov Chain.

This distance, weighted by the transition probability, represents the score of interest into an HUE. As the Dijkstra algorithm measures the distance to the target node, a lower score means a higher interest into the HUE.

Algorithm 2 represents the computation of the shortest distances of the events to the HUE. It is based on the Dijkstra algorithm on the weighted graph. The inputs are the HUEs and the weighed directed graph constructed from the Markov chain. The algorithm computes the shortest distances from each vertices to the HUE. The output is matrix of weighted distances to the HUEs.

To achieve a score of interest a session in relation to a certain HUE, every session has to be mapped from the event to its distance. The minimum value of this map represents the closest the session was to the HUE.

Algorithm 1. Path Traversal Markov Chain Construction

Input: A collection of app session traces S, η minimum support for links and κ minimum support for via-links

Output: Path Traversal Markov Chain

1: *unigram_dict* ← *dict()*
2: *link_dict* ← *dict()*
3: *via_link_dict* ← *dict()*
4: **for each** *s* in *S* **do**
5:     **if** *length(s) < 3* **then**
6:         **break;**
7:     **for** $i = 0; i < s.size() - 2; i + +$ **do**
8:         $v1 \leftarrow s[i]$ ▷ 1st vertex
9:         $v2 \leftarrow s[i + 1]$ ▷ 2nd vertex
10:        $v3 \leftarrow s[i + 2]$ ▷ 3rd vertex
11:        **if** $v1! = v2$ **then**
12:            *unigram_dict[v1]*+ = 1
13:            *link_dict[(v1,v2)]*+ = 1   ▷ create new key in dict or increase by 1
14:            **if** $v3! = v2$ **then**
15:                *via_link_dict[(v1,v2,v3)]*+ = 1
16: **for each** (v1,v2,v3) in *via_link_dict.keys()* **do**
17:     **if** *via_link_dict.get((v1,v2,v3)) / link_dict.get((v1,v2)) > κ* **then**
18:         **if** *link_dict.get((v1,v2)) / unigram_dict.get(v1) > η* **then**
19:         $G.setEdge(v1, v2)$
20:         **if** *link_dict.get((v2,v3)) / unigram_dict.get(v2) > η* **then**
21:         $G.setEdge(v2, v3)$
22: **while** $v = G.vertex()$ **do**
23:     **if** $!v.isConnected()$ **then**
24:         $G.removeVertex(v)$
25: **return** G

4.5 Clustering

Clustering the sessions or users based directly on the distances will output improper clusters as bigger the distance is, the lower is his interest to the HUE. Hence, an inversion step is required before running the clustering algorithms. The final score can be calculate in a simple way by applying MinMax function in $score = 1 - MinMax(dist(u))$.

To decide over the clustering algorithms, the size of the app has to be considered. If the app is too big with many HUEs, the amount of cluster tends to rocket as the possibilities are 2 to the HUEs power. Normally, the domain experts are not looking to extract groups of all the mixed HUEs, instead, they should select a group of correlated HUEs.

Algorithm 2. Distance of all events to the HUE.

Input: (G, w) and v. (G, w) an edge-weighted graph (G, w) where $G = (V, E)$ is a graph and $w : E \rightarrow \mathbb{R}_{\geq 0}$ is a non negative weight function. v is the the target vertex.

Output: $dist(u)$ the distance from u to v where v is the HUE.

1: $dist(v) \leftarrow 0$ and $dist(u) \leftarrow +\infty$ / $u \neq v$
2: Queue Q of all vertices in G using $dist$ as the key.
3: **while** $Q \neq \emptyset$ **do**
4:     $u \leftarrow min\{dist(x)|x \in Q\}$
5:     Remove $u \in Q$
6:     **for each** z adjacent to u and in Q **do**
7:         **if** $dist(u) + w((u, z)) < dist(z)$ **then**
8:             $dist(z) \leftarrow dist(u) + w(u, z)$
9:             update $z \in Q$
10: **return** dist

Considering this and the most common clustering algorithms K-Means and DBSCAN, for this type of data, DBSCAN seems to be better as it is not required to specify the numbe of clusters, but K-Means will perform better if the amount of HUEs to be clustered is larger [18].

5   Experiments

5.1   Environment

Our experiments were performed in a cluster with 4 nodes, 128 cores and 1 TB of RAM, running Spark 2.3.0. The parser and the n-grams extraction were implemented in Scala 2.11. The clustering, Algorithms 1 and 2 were coded in Python 3.

5.2   Parsing

The first effort of the work was parsing the API calls to extract the events and their timestamps. The calls persisting in HDFS RDDs consist of "user id, session id, call name, timestamp of the call and message" fields. UID and SID can be retrieved directly by querying the table. However, the message fields from the calls that register the events are the ones we are interested. By filtering those calls, we extract the messages' fields persisted in JSON files that are parsed to fetch the labels and click timestamp from the events, resulting in 2 new fields. Then, the resulting filtered dataset is grouped by the user and session ids. The events with the same user and session id are consolidated in a vector ordered by their timestamps. To fix the date issue 2 from the Sect. 3.1, we concatenate the first part of the events vector, trimmed at the login event, to the previous session in the call timestamp order. The resulting parsed dataset with the columns of Table 1.

5.3   Modelling the App

By iterating over the vectors of events per session to extract the bi-grams and calculating the transitions probabilities with the formula provided in Sect. 4.2, a "dirty" Markov Chain could be plotted. To clean the noisy transitions, we had to set a minimum support threshold based on their probabilities. However, as the threshold increases, we start to lose events and transitions, as seen in Fig. 8. This poses a challenge on how to calibrate the threshold without eliminating the real transitions. We expected that a visual indication would guide the estimation of the threshold.

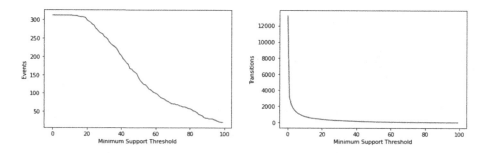

Fig. 8. Threshold distribution

At first glance on the events perspective, it is possible to see that 15% is a maximum threshold in order not to ban events from the model. But taking this 15% means that if the app has a menu with more than 10 possibilities, then at least one of this transitions would be less than 10%.

Another approach would be trying the elbow method for the transitions. Even though, there is an elbow in the right Fig. 8, the precise calibration is not yet straight forward. Actually, to determine this threshold, we had bank experts mapping the path for 7 HUEs, ranging from infrequent to frequent ones. By sliding the threshold in the range of the elbow, we stopped when we start to lose real transitions from the login to the HUE. The losing tendency is bigger to the events that are more infrequent as the transitions probabilities are lower until reaching those events. Finally, we reach a threshold of 2.75%, which seems to be the middle point of the elbow, and then the Markov Chain can be plotted, as the sample Fig. 9.

5.4   Mining the HUEs

The challenge of this task is again finding a minimum support threshold, but this time for the via-links required by Algorithm 1, besides the threshold already found. For this task, we mapped the via-links of the 7 expert HUEs. By identifying the undesired via-links and their probabilities on those HUEs, we reached the second threshold of 18.6% that is able to remove them. After running the algorithm and applying the output to DFS, 58 HUEs were discovered on top of the 312 events.

For the sake of fitting the output of the algorithm with the DFS in this paper, Fig. 10 illustrates only a subtree containing 42 navigation events leading to 22 HUEs, representing approximately one sixth of the whole tree. Notice that the navigation events are not ordered by their ocurrence when in the same edge, but, it means that those are the multiple clicking options at a certain screen, such as choosing a type of loan.

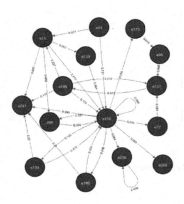

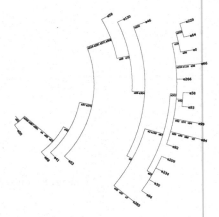

Fig. 9. Frequent Markov Chain   Fig. 10. Mined HUE subtree

5.5   Scoring HUEs

The HUEs are then submitted to the Algorithm 2, outputting a matrix with the weighted distance to all the events to the HUEs. In sequence, every column becomes a dictionary to translate the sessions events into the calculated distances. The minimum distance of each HUE for every session row becomes a new column, generating a frequency matrix for all the UIDs and SIDs.

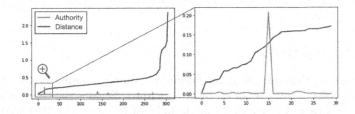

Fig. 11. HUE distances vs HUE authority

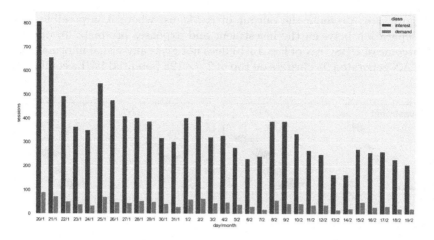

Fig. 12. Specific product interest and demand

This distance can be used a score to highlight the interest of a user in a HUE. To this end, the sessions that have distances below a certain level for a given HUE are the ones that shows interest and when this distance is 0, the user has actually demanded the HUE. In our experiments, we saw that the authority score from the hits algorithm [1] provides indication for determining the upper boundary for the HUE distance. In Fig. 11, it is possible to visualise the maximum distance for personal loan interest that can be set when the authority score raises drastically.

By setting this boundary, the session rows with distance above the level can be filtered off, resulting in a dataset that represents all the sessions interested in a certain HUE. Figure 12 illustrates the distribution of the interest and the actual demand for one of the products in the period we analysed.

5.6 Clustering by HUEs

Our clustering approach aims to identify the behavior of the customers for marketing purposes on the period analysed. To this task, we used the scores of the 7 previously selected HUEs. In order not to disclose any information about the bank's customers, we are not presenting the numbers or the HUEs of the clusters. Still, to ease readers understanding of the clusters, we divided those 7 HUEs in 2 groups: (1) investment (i.e. stock market operation) with 4 products and (2) expenses with 3 products (i.e. loan).

First, we grouped the sessions of the user keeping the maximum value of each HUE score. Second, Principal Component Analysis reduces the dimensionality of the matrix. In sequence, we applied K-Means with 7 HUEs to try to identify the products. The labels of K-Means are used by a Decision Tree Classifier to identify which HUEs are the most significant to each cluster. Finally, we runned DBSCAN to try to extract the total amount of clusters.

Figure 13(a) presents the output of K-Means, where it is possible to see a clear separation between the investment and expenses products. In opposition, the outcome of DBSCAN of Fig. 13(b) does not gives any visual information. Yet, DBSCAN generated 98 clusters on top of $2^7 = 128$ potential HUEs combinations.

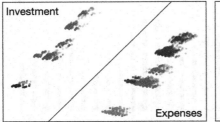 

Fig. 13. Clusters found by (a) K-Means and (b) DBSCAN

To our goal, K-Means is more human explainable, while, DBSCAN resulted in better product agglutination, allowing us to see the combination of products among the customers.

6   Limitations

The main bottleneck in our work is the scoring method with time complexity $O(|E| + |V|log|V|)$ [19]. The use of random or grid search does not scale well regarding our approach and the data size, while the influence of η and κ hyperparameters is undoubtedly important and we have no guarantee to explore the hyper-parameter space without putting human-in-the-loop, experts.

On the other hand, computing clustering accuracy is a limitation as to perform this computation we would need to have the bank experts labelling all the app events.

7   Conclusion and Future Work

The work presented here succeed in automatising the process of detecting interest in a HUE. Our approach can fully map task-oriented mobile apps in a data-driven fashion. The novel HUE mining approach can be extended to other mobile apps domains. Our clustering in combination with scoring techniques are capable of highlighting behavior of users and sessions.

In the future work, we intend to implement the whole process in real-time setup for scoring client sessions and handle the issues discussed in Sect. 3.1 in real-time.

References

1. Kleinberg, J.: Authoritative sources in a hyperlinked environment. J. ACM **46**(5), 604–32 (1999). https://doi.org/10.1145/324133.324140
2. Gan, W., Lin, J.C.W., Fournier-Viger, P., Chao, H.C., Tseng, V.S., Yu, P.S.: A survey of utility-oriented pattern mining. IEEE Trans. Knowl. Data Eng. **33**(4), 1306–1327 (2021). https://doi.org/10.1109/TKDE.2019.2942594
3. Raphaeli, O., Goldstein, A., Fink, L.: Analyzing online consumer behavior in mobile and PC devices: a novel web usage mining approach. Electron. Commer. Res. Apps **26**, 1–12 (2017)
4. Bucklin, R.E., Sismeiro, C.: Click here for internet insight: advances in clickstream data analysis in marketing. J. Interact. Mark. **23**(1), 35–48 (2009)
5. Truong-Chi, T., Fournier-Viger, P.: A survey of high utility sequential pattern mining. In: Fournier-Viger, P., Lin, J.C.W., Nkambou, R., Vo, B., Tseng, V.S. (eds.) High-Utility Pattern Mining. SBD, vol. 51, pp. 97–129. Springer, Cham (2019). https://doi.org/10.1007/978-3-030-04921-8_4
6. Schneider, F., Feldmann, A., Krishnamurthy, B., Willinger, W.: Understanding online social network usage from a network perspective. In: Proceedings of the 9th ACM SIGCOMM Conference on Internet Measurement, pp. 35–48 (2009)
7. Benevenuto, F., Rodrigues, T., Cha, M., Almeida, V.: Characterizing user behavior in online social networks. In: Proceedings of the 9th ACM SIGCOMM Conference on Internet Measurement, pp. 49–62 (2009)
8. Borisov A, Wardenaar M, Markov I, De Rijke M. A click sequence model for web search. In: 41st International ACM SIGIR Conference on Research & Development in Information Retrieval, SIGIR 2018, pp. 45–54 (2018). https://doi.org/10.1145/3209978.3210004
9. Kumar, A., Salo, J., Li, H.: Stages of user engagement on social commerce platforms: analysis with the navigational clickstream data. Int. J. Electron. Commer. **23**(2), 179–211 (2019)
10. Jindal, H., Sardana, N., Mehta, R.: Analysis and visualization of user navigations on web. In: Hemanth, J., Bhatia, M., Geman, O. (eds.) Data Visualization and Knowledge Engineering. LNDECT, vol. 32, pp. 195–221. Springer, Cham (2020). https://doi.org/10.1007/978-3-030-25797-2_9
11. Scholtes, I.: When is a network a network? Multi-order graphical model selection in pathways and temporal networks. In: Proceedings of the 23rd ACM SIGKDD International Conference on Knowledge Discovery and Data Mining, vol. F1296(i), pp. 1037–1046 (2017). https://doi.org/10.1145/3097983.3098145
12. Husin, H.S., Seid, N.: Discovering users navigation of online newspaper using Markov model. In: Proceedings of the 11th International Conference on Ubiquitous Information Management and Communication, pp. 1–4 (2017)
13. Wang, G., et al.: Unsupervised clickstream clustering for user behavior analysis. In: Proceedings of the 2016 CHI Conference on Human Factors in Computing Systems (2016)
14. Wang, Y.T., Lee, A.J.T.: Mining Web navigation patterns with a path traversal graph. Expert Syst. appl. **38**(6), 7112–7122 (2011)
15. Tarjan, R.: Depth-first search and linear graph algorithms. SIAM J.. Comput. **1**(2), 146–160 (1972)
16. Bundy, A., Wallen, L.: Breadth-first search, In: Bundy, A., Wallen, L. (eds.) Catalogue of Artificial Intelligence Tools. Symbolic Computation (Artificial Intelligence), pp. 13–13. Springer, Heidelberg (1984). https://doi.org/10.1007/978-3-642-96868-6_25

17. Barbehenn, M.: A note on the complexity of Dijkstra's algorithm for graphs with weighted vertices. IEEE Trans. Comput. **47**(2), 263 (1998)
18. Chakraborty, S., Nagwani, N.K., Dey, L.: Performance comparison of incremental k-means and incremental DBSCAN algorithms. arXiv preprint arXiv:1406.4751 (2014)
19. Barbehenn, M.: A note on the complexity of Dijkstra's algorithm for graphs with weighted vertices. IEEE Trans. Comput. **472**, 263 (1998). https://doi.org/10.1109/12.663776

The First International Workshop on Smart Society Technologies (IWSST2021)

Caring Without Sharing: A Federated Learning Crowdsensing Framework for Diversifying Representation of Cities

Michael Cho$^{(\boxtimes)}$ and Afra Mashhadi

Computing Software System, University of Washington, Bothell, WA, USA
{mikec87,mashhadi}@uw.edu

Abstract. Mobile Crowdsensing has become main stream paradigm for researchers to collect behavioural data from citizens in large scales. This valuable data can be leveraged to create centralized repositories that can be used to train advanced Artificial Intelligent (AI) models for various services that benefit society in all aspects. Although decades of research has explored the viability of Mobile Crowdsensing in terms of incentives and many attempts have been made to reduce the participation barriers, the overshadowing privacy concerns regarding sharing personal data still remain. Recently a new pathway has emerged to enable to shift MCS paradigm towards a more privacy-preserving collaborative learning, namely Federated Learning. In this paper, we posit a first of its kind framework for this emerging paradigm. We demonstrate the functionalities of our framework through a case study of diversifying two vision algorithms through to learn the representation of ordinary sidewalk obstacles as part of enhancing visually impaired navigation.

Keywords: Mobile crowd sensing · Federated learning · Privacy

1 Introduction

In the past decade the Mobile Crowdsensing paradigm (MCS) have leveraged power of crowds for a range of applications to help researchers and practitioners enhance their understanding of the cities and citizens. MCS allows users to participate in a campaign by providing passive or active data through their sensor enabled mobile devices. For instance, within the context of smart cities, MCS has enabled the optimization for various *passive sensing* applications, such as pollution, public transportation, traffic congestion, road conditions, etc. Active sensing applications have also helped to advance understanding of the cities through the active contribution of the crowds [34]. Such applications include FixMyStreet[1] where citizens actively report faults within their neighborhoods or others such as GeoNotify [18] where citizen report the sidewalk obstacles that could impact visually impaired navigation.

---

[1] https://www.fixmystreet.com.

© ICST Institute for Computer Sciences, Social Informatics and Telecommunications Engineering 2022
Published by Springer Nature Switzerland AG 2022. All Rights Reserved
T. Hara and H. Yamaguchi (Eds.): MobiQuitous 2021, LNICST 419, pp. 601–616, 2022.
https://doi.org/10.1007/978-3-030-94822-1_39

To this end, frameworks such as AWARE [10], Sensus [30], and SensingKit[17] have brought the feasibility of creating MCS tasks/campaigns to researchers and policy makers. For example AWARE framework allows users to design experiments and run data collection campaigns that tap into the smartphone sensors with a few lines of code. Indeed, common to all these frameworks is that they provide an easy interactive design for the scientific community to design the experiment through a web dashboard, and furthermore they offer storage and communication between the devices and the server.

However, there still remains privacy challenges that could act as participation barriers for MCS users [12]. These privacy concerns are in twofold: First, user's data could contain sensitive personal information. Secondly, personal information can be concluded by analyzing the data provided by the user and through continuous monitoring. For example, by collecting sensory data related to the user location on the device, the user's home location information can be obtained.

To overcome privacy concerns, the crowd-sensing community has recently started to explore alternatives and possibilities of a paradigm shift that would decouple the data collection and analysis from a centralized approach to a distributed setting. To this end, Federated Learning (FL) has emerged as a promising candidate for this paradigm shift [15]. In FL schema each participant's device holds on to their own data, and a FL server orchastrates a collaborative training by sending the shared model to the devices. In this way, the data always remains local to the client device.

Inspired by this trend, in this paper we present, FLOAT, a **F**ederated **L**earning framework for **A**ctive crowdsensing **T**asks. In the design of this framework we pay careful attention in the challenges and opportunities that incur in this paradigm shift. Our framework relies on Flower [6] to facilitate FL training on the device end and the orchestration on the server side. Our framework consists of an interactive dashboard allowing the researchers to setup their task and specify the training properties. On the device end, we design a range of functionalities to enable users to participate in a campaign. To demonstrate an application of our framework, we present algorithmic and system performance of an obstacle detection use case, where we train state-of-the-art vision models to enhance their representation of ordinary side walk objects. In summary, we make the following contributions:

- We propose, the first of its kind, an end-to-end framework for bringing FL into crowdsensing tasks. Our entire framework would be open-sourced and available under Apache 2.0 license for the crowdsensing community to use in their research.
- Using FLOAT as the underlying framework, we present experiments that explore both algorithmic and system-level aspects of federated mobile crowdsensing for an application of Obstacle Detection. We address important research questions as to: *How many users and how much data per user is required to learn representation of 5 ordinary sidewalk obstacles.*

– We propose a roadmap that we believe would empower the research community to address challenges that remain if we are to integrate FL into the MCS paradigm.

2 Background and Related Work

Federated Learning (FL) [1,16,19,23] has been proposed to provide a privacy-preserving mechanism to leverage de-centralized user data and computation resources to train machine learning models. Federated learning allows users to collaboratively train a shared model under the orchestration of a central server while keeping personal data on their devices. There are, in general, two steps in the FL training process (i) local model training on end devices and (ii) global aggregation of updated parameters in the FL server. The training process of such a FL system usually contains the following three steps as illustrated in Fig. 1:

1. The server initializes the global weights, specifies the global model hyper parameters and the training process, and sends the task to selected participants.
2. Participants locally compute training gradients and send the gradients or updated weights to the server.
3. The server performs aggregation and shares the new weights with participants. Steps 2–3 are repeated until the global loss function converges or a desirable training accuracy is achieved.

To this end, incorporating Federated Learning paradigm into Mobile Crowdsensing tasks can address some of the long existing challenges of MCS and create new opportunities [15]. In Mobile Crowdsensing the use of personal smart devices that have enough processing capabilities are a prime candidate to integrate with Federated Learning. The benefit of such methodology can be seen in two major aspects. First, Federated Learning helps to preserve the privacy of the user by never uploading the raw collected data. Secondly, it can be leveraged as a means to diversify the representation of the data and lead to more inclusive machine learning models.

It is worth noting that there also exists other great opportunities that arise from this paradigm shift and particularly from removing the burden of data collection and centralized training. For instance, in traditional MCS schemes the server must overlook the transmission, and the storage of data. The data is then pre-processed and used for a centralized training. These processes incur large overhead costs and maintenance and thus reducing those requirements by removing the need for centralized data repositories would lower the threshold for deployment campaigns. Moreover, MCS incurs large communication costs with the transfer of raw data into the server. This places a burden on the server itself to process this data and takes a large amount of bandwidth from the users as well. By bringing the model to the user and enabling local training, the need for resources in terms of bandwidth is greatly reduced. Finally, in terms of energy consumption, previous work has shown that federated learning

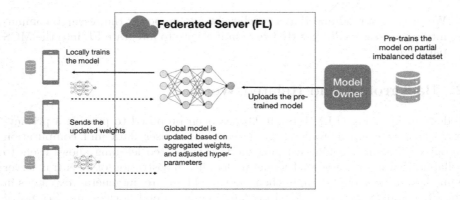

Fig. 1. The overview of the interactions between the model owner and the devices under orchestration of the FL server.

can play a large role in reducing CO_2 emission associated with training large AI models, by moving the training process into hand-held devices that do not require cooling [25, 27]. Furthermore, previous work has also shown that the energy and memory consumption that are required for on-device training for smart city applications is almost negligible [6, 22].

2.1   Applications of Federated Learning in MCS

To date, research in real-world applications of federated learning are still in infancy and limited to a handful examples. Smart security [3] is an emerging field that has seen most integration of federated learning in the context of smart cities. Based on machine learning, smart security can perform post event analysis and self-learning, constantly accumulating experience, and continuously improve pre-warning capabilities. Federated Learning offers a machine learning training scheme that allows the use of the large amounts of collected data in daily applications [24]. Outside of security applications Mashhadi et al. [22] proposed an application of federated learning for discovering urban communities. They showed that by using the GPS traces that are stored on each device, and collaboratively training a deep embedded clustering model, it is possible to detect meaningful urban communities without the need for location information to be shared.

3   Design Considerations

In this section we take a critical view of some of the design challenges that incur due to the suggested paradigm shift and decoupling the data from the centralized approaches. We address how we design for responding to these challenges in the proposed framework.

3.1 Challenges

In order to shift the MCS schema to a decentralized approach where the participants' data is only held on local devices, various challenges need to be addressed.

- **Challenge 1:** Perhaps most challenging aspect of a FL MCS proposed schema is that it reduces the *exploratory* scopes of MCS tasks. Indeed one of the benefits of MCS data collection, has always been on enabling researchers to collect a large volume of data first and then ask what type of research hypothesis could be addressed and which portion of the data is indeed needed to answer those question. In contrast, a federated schema, reduces the scope of this exploratory analysis and enforces researchers to not only have a very well defined research question and hypothesis, but most importantly a *model* prior to deployment.

  This property means that many phases of exploratory analysis needs to be shifted into a pre-training stage where the model is implemented and trained on a proxy dataset. Such proxy dataset may or may not be an accurate representation of the participant's data. Indeed, in this vein [22] showed that it is possible to *pre*-train an urban community detection model on an aggregated mobility dataset and then dispatch it to be re-trained under the FL setting on client's fine grain location data.

  Design Goal 1: In our framework we design for this functionality by enabling any pre-trained model and weights to be loaded to FLOAT. Figure 1 presents the proposed schema where the user (i.e., model owner) shares a pre-trained model with the framework which then gets pushed towards the client devices. Furthermore, we also cater for the applications of transfer learning. Transfer learning focuses on storing knowledge gained while solving one problem and applying it to a different but related problem. In many cases where the algorithms are pre-trained to learn a representation of a proxy dataset, it is possible to only retrain the final layer of the model to account for the specific task. Such approach also significantly reduces the convergence time and thus reduces the training at the local devices. In FLOAT, we provide an option to indicate whether the weights of the loaded model are to be fully re-trained or only fine tuned at the final layer.

- **Challenge 2:** A second challenge in designing for a federated MCS schema is the lack of *transparency*. That is because participants' data is unseen, it is difficult to assess the outcome of the training. Therefore, questions arise on "how much contribution did each participant make?" or "How many rounds of training would be needed for the model to converge?".

  Design Goal 2: To address this challenge, we design our framework with an interactive interface which enables the model owner to quantify the outcome of their model after each round. More specifically we provide two ways of validation:

  Server Validation: The model owner is able to specify a path to a centralized dataset that could be used to evaluate the accuracy of the updated model after each round of training.

Client Validation: The validation is entirely on the clients devices. For the cases that the model owner does not have a centralized validation dataset to validate the updated model against it, our framework enables client validation where a portion of participants are selected for validating the model.

3.2 Opportunities

There exists multiple great opportunities that arise from removing the burden of data collection and centralized training. For instance, in traditional MCS schemes the server must overlook the transmission and storage of data. The data is then pre-processed and used for a centralized training. These processes incur large overhead costs and maintenance. Reducing those requirements by removing the need for centralized data repositories would lower the threshold for deployment campaigns.

Moreover, MCS incurs large communication costs with the transfer of raw data into the server. This places a burden on the server itself to process this data and takes a large amount of bandwidth from the users as well. By bringing the model to the user and enabling local training, the need for resources in terms of bandwidth is greatly reduced.

Finally, in terms of energy consumption, previous work has shown that federated learning can play a large role in reducing CO_2 emission associated with training large AI models, by moving the training process into hand-held devices that do not require cooling [25,27]. Furthermore, previous work has also shown that the energy and memory consumption that are required for on-device training for smart city applications is almost negligible [22].

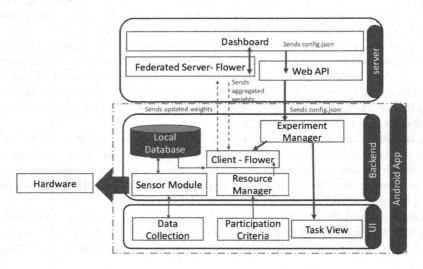

Fig. 2. Architecture of FLOAT depicting the server and the client part of the framework.

4   Overview of FLOAT Framework

Figure 2 presents the overall architecture design of our framework. As can be seen our framework consist of the server and the client end. Both these parts of the framework rely on Flower [6] as an underlying Federated Learning platform. We thus first describe Flower for the sake of clarity before moving on to describe each component of our framework and the interactions amongst them.

Flower. Our framework relies on Flower [6] as an agnostic and scale-able solution for federated learning. Flower offers a stable, language and ML framework-agnostic implementation of the core components of a federated learning system. In particular by using Flower as an underlying FL implementation, FLOAT is able to inherit the agnostic properties of Flower. That is our framework is able to support Machine Learning Models written in either Tensorflow or Pytorch.

Furthermore, Flower allows for rapid transition of existing ML training pipelines into a FL setup to evaluate their convergence properties and training time in a federated setting. This includes various strategies from aggregation methods (e.g., FedAvg [23], QffedAvg [20], and many others) and evaluation methods.

Most importantly, we chose Flower as it provides support for extending FL implementations to mobile and wireless clients, with heterogeneous compute, memory, and network resources (e.g., phone, tablet, embedded) and thus ideal for the smart city applications.

4.1   Server

The back-end server of our framework is responsible for taking the design of the experiment from the end user, communicating it with devices, and initiating the experiment.

Dashboard. To facilitate an easy interaction our framework has an interactive dashboard (Fig. 3) that enables researchers to load their own model and specify the training parameters such as the number of training devices (Design Goal 1), the number of data points per each participant, and the hyper-parameters of the experiment. We developed this dashabord in python-based Flask server [11] which enables us to build up the web-application and easily modify the components of the interface.

In addition to taking input from the user, FLOAT dashboard is designed to provide transparency into training (Design Goal 2) by integrating a live visualization dashboard implemented in TensorBoard [29]. Figure 4 presents this component of the dashboard. An alternative tab on the dashboard allows the users to switch to a debugging interface where the underlying Flower messages presenting INFO, DEBUG, and ERROR that are happening during the training round as observed by the RPC communication channel are displayed.

FL Server. To start an instance of the FL server, the information from the dashboard is directly communicated to the FL server python code. More specifically these are the following parameters: i) rounds of training; ii) aggregation

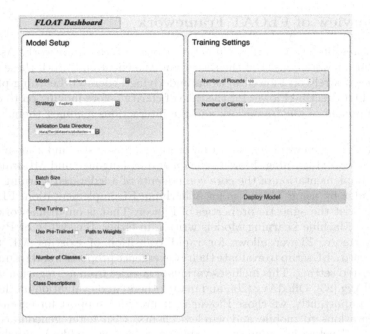

Fig. 3. Part of the FLOAT Dashboard that acts as an interface with the user to set up the task.

strategy, iii) evaluation strategy and path to a validation dataset (if applicable), and iv) number of clients. The FL (Flower) server configures the next round of FL by sending the required configurations to the clients via bi-directional gRPC channel, receives the resulting client updates (or failures) from the clients using the same gRPC, and aggregates the results using the strategy.

Web API Module. Additionally in order to communicate the experiment setting with the clients devices, the settings that are entered in the dashboard are saved as a *config.json* and sent directly to the clients device. This configuration file includes information regarding the hyper-parameters of the model and local training instructions: i) the model and the initialized weights (if applicable), ii) instructions on whether the model is to be fully retrained or fine-tuned, iii) number of data points per class, iv) finally number and description of classes.

4.2 Client

The client component of the FLOAT is currently designed to support Andriod devices. As depicted in Fig. 2, this component has two main parts: the Backend and the User Interface. We describe the interaction between each part next.

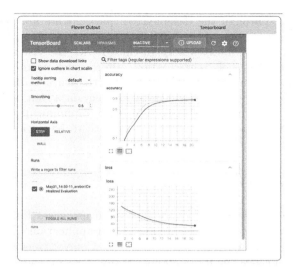

Fig. 4. The output component of the dashboard visualizing live results of the training.

Backend Modules. The modules in the backend part of the app are responsible to bridge between the FL server and the user interface. These are *Experiment Manager*, *FL Client*, *Resource Manager* and finally the *Sensor Module*.

Experiment Manager. As depicted in Fig. 2, this module is in charge of receiving the training instructions, parameters, and model from the server. It then communicates the information about the task to the participant through the Task View component of the UI. It is also responsible for setting up the FL client and initializing the training.

FL Client.   The FL client is responsible for training the shared model. As described earlier we use Flower as the underlying framework to support the on-device training. The flexibility of the flower architecture enables our framework to receive any models and weights and simply assemble a FL client code. Furthermore because Flower is designed for heterogeneous devices, the FL client module can be later integrated into different devices and platforms (e.g., iOS). As depicted in the Fig. 2, the FL client code also has direct access to user's local dataset. FL Client connects to the gRPC channel which is responsible for monitoring these connections and for sending and receiving Flower Protocol messages.

Resource Manager. The resource manager is responsible for monitoring the current device resources and communicating that with the flower client and server.

Sensor Module. This module is responsible for enable specific data to be used as part of the training tasks. This is done by direct communication with the Data Collection Module of the UI as we describe next.

User Interface. Through the designed UI, participants are able to view the information and description of the MCS task and provide consent in taking part in the campaign. Furthermore, we design the UI with the vision of enabling the participant to indicate their participation criteria such as minimum available resources or stable connectivity (WiFi). Finally the Data Collection module of the UI enables the participant to specifically collect data that is required for the active MCS task. This module therefore directly communicates with the sensor module of the client backend and has access both to hardware resources (e.g., camera, GPS etc.) and the on-device database.

5   Case Study: Obstacle Detection

In this section we present one of many possible use cases for our framework. The use case here is motivated by GeoNotify an application that was designed to assist visually impaired with navigation [18]. GeoNotify is a crowd-sourcing application that notifies the users about the obstacles on the sidewalks and re-routes them to avoid those obstacles using audio messages. To map the obstacles the system relies on crowdsourced information from the users by enabling them to take a photo of sidewalk obstacles and an audio description and submitting it to a centralized repository. The underlying back-end server learns: 1) the GPS location of the obstacle and uses this information to reroute other users; 2) the image representation of the obstacle. The focus of this section is on the latter component of the system which aims to retrain vision models to learn representation of everyday sidewalk obstacles.

5.1   Obstacle Detection Model

A large scale study by the Royal Institute of Blind People [26] interviewed 500 visually impaired participants for over three months. As part of this report the institute highlights that often the ordinary sidewalk obstacles are the most common causes of injury daily navigation of those with partial vision impairment. This report identifies five most common obstacles that impact visually impaired daily: cars parked on the pavement, advertising-boards, bins and recycling boxes on pavements, street furniture (such as chair and tables). Some of these classes (e.g., chair and table) are common objects that are labeled in image recognition datasets such as ImageNet [8] and thus are detectable using existing Convolutional Neural Network (CNN) models. However, the presentations of these common objects across the world can vary significantly. Others such as boards, sidewalk signs and potholes are specific to the context of this report and are not present as part of ImageNet. Indeed, earlier studies showed that the accuracy of the state-of-the-art models in detecting common sidewalk obstacles ranges between 10–40% [18].

  To enable vision models to learn a diverse representations of the sidewalk objects, we experiment with two state-of-the-art light weight models, namely MobileNet [13] and SqueezeNet [14]. Furthermore, as the system is designed to rely on the crowds' contribution to enhance these models, it is important to quantify the number of images that are required to train the models to learn the representation of the sidewalk objects. We thus seek to answer the following research questions:

- RQ1: How many participants are needed to collaboratively train each model?
- RQ2: How many photos per participant is required to enhance the model?
- RQ3: How much resources per client device is required to collaboratively train the model?

5.2   Experiment Setting

In order to answer the above research questions, we use FLOAT as underlying framework to simulate the described active crowdsensing task amongst devices. The details of our experiments are as follows:

Data. We used the manually curated dataset as published by [18]. We segmented the training portion of this dataset into equal and uniform distribution amongst the clients in an IID fashion. That is each client has an equal number of photos per class. Our dataset consists of 5 classes with a varying number of images, x, per class. We kept the validation part of this dataset, which includes 100 images per each class, as the validation dataset on the server.

Training. We experiment with pre-trained MobileNet and SqueezeNet models (weights of pretraining on ImageNet [8]) and study the impact of transfer learning of each model on algorithmic and system performance. To do so we freeze the learning on the earlier layers of the model where the weights are transferred from the pre-trained weights and then retrain the final layer of the network (i.e., the fully connected layer) to learn the representations of our domain specific images. We trained the each model for 20 rounds under the FL setting. During each of the 20 rounds, clients perform one epoch of SGD (batch size 32, momentum 0.9 and learning rate of 0.001) before sending the updated model parameters back to the server. The aggregation strategy was configured as FedAvg.

Platform. We ran an instance of the FLOAT framework on a local server with 4 GPU GeForce RTX 2080 Ti with CUDA 9. For answering the first two research questions we *simulated* the clients on the same server each with their own data private repositories. To answer the third research question and compute the system performance on the mobile devices, we ran an end-to-end instance of training on an Android device and measured the system usage of this device.

5.3   Experimental Results

In this section we present the algorithmic performance and system measurements of the described study.

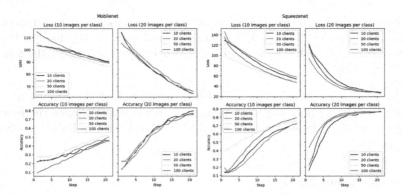

Fig. 5. Results of the algorithmic performance of MobileNet (left) and Squeezenet(right) for varying number of clients and images.

Algorithmic Performance. Figure 5 reports on the algorithmic performance of MobileNet and Squeezenet respectively for varying number of clients and varying data size. To answer the first research question on how many participants are needed to collaboratively contribute to the model, we can see that as little as 10 clients can improve the accuracy of the model to 0.4–0.8 for MobileNet and 0.6–0.8 for SqueezeNet. To answer the second research question on how many images (x) each participant requires to have, we can observe that the more images that users have (per class) the quicker the models converges. Particularly in the case of SqueezeNet we can see that the accuracy *exponentially* increases for $x = 20$, making the number of the participants not as important of a factor as when $x = 10$. For MobileNet we see that the model performes very poorly in learning the representation of the objects when participants images is $x = 10$ and after 20 rounds of training it leads to only 0.5 accuracy. SqueezeNet on the other hand reaches 0.8 accuracy with the larger number of clients ($n = 100$).

System Performance. Finally in terms of resources we measured memory, CPU, and energy consumption of the described experiments on a Samsung S21 Ultra, with 8GB RAM and 8 CPU cores. We experimented running each model with and without Transfer Learning (TF) on this device using a training dataset that is composed of 20 pictures per class. The client only performed the training and no validation was done on the client. Figure 6 illustrates the CPU and memory usage for MobileNet with and without TF respectively. We observe that the maximum memory usage during the entire training remains low. Indeed our comparison of the two models suggest that the memory usage is approximately between 300MB-700MB (3–7% of the total RAM) for Squeezenet and MobileNet respectively when the models are leveraging transfer learning. Table 1 shows the memory and training time for both models. In terms of energy consumption, one round of training (of MobileNet without TL) consumed 10.3 mAh on average that corresponds to less than 0.15% of the total available battery on a fully charged device.

Table 1. On device measurements of memory usage and training time for one round of local training.

Model	Time (per one round)	Max memory
MobileNet (TL)	180 s	728 MB
MobileNet (No TL)	340 s	2.8 GB
SqueezeNet (TL)	7 s	384 MB
SqueezeNet (No TL)	32 s	1.2 GB

Bringing these results together with the algorithmic performance we can see that our framework is a viable option for the described MCS task and can enhance the representation of the objects in as few as 10 rounds of training with very little participation burden (number of images and computational burden of the devices (time, energy, memory, and CPU).

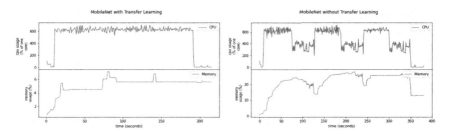

Fig. 6. CPU and Memory usage of one round of training of MobileNet on Samsung S21 Ultra with and without Transfer Learning.

6   Discussion

In this section we first describe some limitation and future extension to our work before putting forward a future road map on what we believe are the important challenges for the research community to tackle to ensure the adoption of the federated learning beyond theory and opportunities for integration in real-world studies.

6.1   Limitation

One limitation of the evaluation presented here is that the participation of users was simulated and we did not evaluate our framework on images *collected by* actual users who may present a more diverse representation of the objects across the world. Furthermore, as these images were collected from Internet, they might have a have higher quality and fail to represent the heterogeneity of the smart-phones devices, and the impact it might impose on the training.

Finally, although we designed our framework with paying particular attention to some of the design challenges, there are others that we have not addressed yet. One of such challenges is the impact of the *noisy labels*. That is where the participant intentionally (i.e., poison attacks) or unintentionally associate a wrong label with the input data. Noisy label detection is a hard task as they are ubiquitous in the real world and prominent in crowd-sourcing applications [31, 32]. Deep neural networks, including CNNs, have a high capacity to fit noisy labels [33]. That is, these models can memorize *easy* instances first and gradually adapt to hard instances as training epochs become large. When noisy labels frequently exist, deep learning models will eventually memorize these wrong labels, which leads to poor generalization performance. In our future work we plan to tackle this challenge by integrating a *TrustModule* in both the client side (in order to detect noisy labels) and on the server side (in order to select reputable participants).

6.2   Research Road Map

User Acceptance. We believe first and foremost important challenge with the proposed paradigm shift is to study and assess users' acceptance. Great amount of literature exists on user's privacy concerns in various platforms from Social Media [5, 28] to IoT [2, 21] and MCS [9, 12]. However, little is known on how users will perceive systems that rely on FL schema. Would such schema actually ease their privacy concerns? What type of awareness and education is needed for the users to understand the underlying benefits of such schema? We believe this is an urgent qualitative research question that the research community needs to answer if we are to see more real-world use cases and applications of federated MCS.

Participants Selection. The vast majority of federated methods are passive in the sense that they do not aim to influence which devices participate, or only select the participants based on the available resources (e.g., connected to WiFi and battery level). We believe that if we are to use a federated MCS in real-world use cases, it is important to account for the diversity not only at the point of aggregation but at the point of participant selection. We believe more research initiative is needed to enable participant selection based on alternative metrics, such as fairness criteria [4, 7], that could enable increasing fairness of the overall model.

Human Data Interaction. Finally we believe important conversations and debates are needed to take place if FL systems are to become more applicable in training ML models. For instance how to adapt policies such as *right to be forgotten* to federated schema. In other words, "how can a model forget users' contribution to it". We believe stepping away from centralized datasets, brings all new set of regulatory challenges and now is the crucial time for the research community to start on creating forums for these types of conversations.

7   Conclusion

In this paper we presented FLOAT, a federated learning framework for adapting active MCS tasks into a privacy-preserving FL schema. Through a use case, we demonstrated how FLOAT can be used to learn a diverse representation of sidewalk obstacles using as little as 10 images per object and 20 rounds of training. We also demonstrated the viability of our proposed framework through measuring resource consumption on an ordinary smart phone.

References

1. Aledhari, M., Razzak, R., Parizi, R.M., Saeed, F.: Federated learning: a survey on enabling technologies, protocols, and applications. IEEE Access **8**, 140699–140725 (2020)
2. Badii, C., Bellini, P., Difino, A., Nesi, P.: Smart city IoT platform respecting GDPR privacy and security aspects. IEEE Access **8**, 23601–23623 (2020)
3. Baig, Z.A., et al.: Future challenges for smart cities: cyber-security and digital forensics. Digi. Invest. **22**, 3–13 (2017)
4. Barocas, S., Hardt, M., Narayanan, A.: Fairness and Machine Learning. fairmlbook.org (2019). http://www.fairmlbook.org
5. Beigi, G., Liu, H.: A survey on privacy in social media: identification, mitigation, and applications. ACM Trans. Data Sci. **1**(1), 1–38 (2020)
6. Beutel, D.J., et al.: Flower: a friendly federated learning research framework. arXiv preprint arXiv:2007.14390 (2020)
7. Binns, R.: On the apparent conflict between individual and group fairness. In: Proceedings of the 2020 Conference on Fairness, Accountability, and Transparency, pp. 514–524 (2020)
8. Deng, J., Dong, W., Socher, R., Li, L.J., Li, K., Fei-Fei, L.: Imagenet: a large-scale hierarchical image database. In: 2009 IEEE Conference on Computer Vision and Pattern Recognition, pp. 248–255. IEEE (2009)
9. Diamantopoulou, V., Androutsopoulou, A., Gritzalis, S., Charalabidis, Y.: An assessment of privacy preservation in crowdsourcing approaches: towards GDPR compliance. In: 2018 12th International Conference on Research Challenges in Information Science (RCIS), pp. 1–9. IEEE (2018)
10. Ferreira, D., Kostakos, V.: Aware: open-source context instrumentation framework for everyone. https://awareframework.com/ (2018). Accessed 02 Sept 2020
11. Flask: flask project (2021). https://flask.palletsprojects.com/en/2.0.x/
12. Gustarini, M., Wac, K., Dey, A.K.: Anonymous smartphone data collection: factors influencing the users' acceptance in mobile crowd sensing. Pers. Ubiquit. Comput. **20**(1), 65–82 (2016)
13. Howard, A.G., et al.: Mobilenets: efficient convolutional neural networks for mobile vision applications. arXiv preprint arXiv:1704.04861 (2017)
14. Iandola, F.N., Han, S., Moskewicz, M.W., Ashraf, K., Dally, W.J., Keutzer, K.: Squeezenet: alexnet-level accuracy with 50x fewer parameters and < 0.5 mb model size. arXiv preprint arXiv:1602.07360 (2016)
15. Jiang, J.C., Kantarci, B., Oktug, S., Soyata, T.: Federated learning in smart city sensing: challenges and opportunities. Sensors **20**(21), 6230 (2020)
16. Kairouz, P., et al.: Advances and open problems in federated learning (2021)

17. Katevas, K., Haddadi, H., Tokarchuk, L.: Sensingkit: Evaluating the sensor power consumption in IOS devices. In: 2016 12th International Conference on Intelligent Environments (IE), pp. 222–225. IEEE (2016)
18. Kim, E., Sterner, J., Mashhadi, A.: A crowd-sourced obstacle detection and navigation app for visually impaired. In: Paiva, S., Lopes, S.I., Zitouni, R., Gupta, N., Lopes, S.F., Yonezawa, T. (eds.) SmartCity360° 2020. LNICST, vol. 372, pp. 571–579. Springer, Cham (2021). https://doi.org/10.1007/978-3-030-76063-2_38
19. Konečný, J., McMahan, H.B., Ramage, D., Richtárik, P.: Federated optimization: distributed machine learning for on-device intelligence. arXiv preprint arXiv:1610.02527 (2016)
20. Li, T., Sanjabi, M., Beirami, A., Smith, V.: Fair resource allocation in federated learning. arXiv preprint arXiv:1905.10497 (2019)
21. Liu, J., Shen, H., Narman, H.S., Chung, W., Lin, Z.: A survey of mobile crowdsensing techniques: a critical component for the internet of things. ACM Trans. Cyber-Phys. Syst. **2**(3), 1–26 (2018)
22. Mashhadi, A., Sterner, J., Murray, J.: Deep embedded clustering of urban communities using federated learning (2021)
23. McMahan, B., Moore, E., Ramage, D., Hampson, S., y Arcas, B.A.: Communication-efficient learning of deep networks from decentralized data. In: Artificial Intelligence and Statistics, pp. 1273–1282 (2017)
24. Preuveneers, D., Rimmer, V., Tsingenopoulos, I., Spooren, J., Joosen, W., Ilie-Zudor, E.: Chained anomaly detection models for federated learning: an intrusion detection case study. Appl. Sci. **8**(12), 2663 (2018)
25. Qiu, X., Parcollet, T., Beutel, D., Topal, T., Mathur, A., Lane, N.: Can federated learning save the planet? In: NeurIPS-Tackling Climate Change with Machine Learning (2020)
26. RIBP: the royal institute for blind people (2016)
27. Savazzi, S., Kianoush, S., Rampa, V., Bennis, M.: A framework for energy and carbon footprint analysis of distributed and federated edge learning. arXiv preprint arXiv:2103.10346 (2021)
28. Smith, M., Szongott, C., Henne, B., Von Voigt, G.: Big data privacy issues in public social media. In: 2012 6th IEEE International Conference on Digital Ecosystems and Technologies (DEST), pp. 1–6. IEEE (2012)
29. Tensorflow: tensorboard (2021). https://www.tensorflow.org/tensorboard
30. Xiong, H., Huang, Y., Barnes, L.E., Gerber, M.S.: Sensus: a cross-platform, general-purpose system for mobile crowdsensing in human-subject studies. In: Proceedings of the 2016 ACM International Joint Conference on Pervasive and Ubiquitous Computing, pp. 415–426 (2016)
31. Yan, Y., Rosales, R., Fung, G., Subramanian, R., Dy, J.: Learning from multiple annotators with varying expertise. Mach. Learning. **95**(3), 291–327 (2013). https://doi.org/10.1007/s10994-013-5412-1
32. Yu, X., Liu, T., Gong, M., Tao, D.: Learning with biased complementary labels. In: Proceedings of the European Conference on Computer Vision (ECCV), pp. 68–83 (2018)
33. Zhang, C., Bengio, S., Hardt, M., Recht, B., Vinyals, O.: Understanding deep learning requires rethinking generalization. arXiv preprint arXiv:1611.03530 (2016)
34. Zhong, Y., Kobayashi, M., Matsubara, M., Morishima, A.: A survey of visually impaired workers in Japanese and us crowdsourcing platforms. In Proceedings of HCOMP (2020)

AR-T: Temporal Relation Embedded Transformer for the Real World Activity Recognition

Hyunju Kim$^{(\boxtimes)}$ and Dongman

Korea Advanced Institute of Science and Technology, Daejeon, Korea
iplay93@kaist.ac.kr, dlee@kaist.ac.kr

Abstract. Activity recognition is a fundamental way to support context-aware services for users in smart spaces. Data sources such as video or wearable devices are used in many recognition approaches, but there are challenges in utilizing them in the real world. Recent approaches propose deep learning-based methods on IoT sensor data streams to overcome the issues. Since they only describe single user-based spaces, they are vulnerable to complex sequences of events triggered by multiple users. When multiple users exist in a space, various overlapping events occur with longer correlations than a single user situation. Additionally, ambient sensor-based events appear far more than actuator-based events, making it difficult to extract actuator-based events as important features. We propose a transformer-based approach to derive long-term event correlations and important events as elements of activity patterns. We also develop a duration incorporated embedding method to differentiate between the same type but different duration events and add a sequential manner to the transformer approach. In the experiments section, we prove that our approach outperforms the existing approaches based on real datasets.

Keywords: Activity recognition · Transformer · Temporal relation embedding · Multi-user smart spaces · Sensor data streams

1 Introduction

With the emergence of IoT (Internet of Things) technologies, smart objects around us generate their states with intelligence and turn our daily space into a smart space. One of key drivers for this is activity recognition that infers users' intentions to support their efficient and effective lives [3,25]. Various sources such as video or wearable devices are widely used to recognize activities [10,16] while they have limitations such as privacy issues or difficulties in collecting data reliably [2,9,24]. To avoid such issues, ambient sensing stream data such as user movement, sound or lighting from smart spaces is used.

Recent approaches [21–23,34,37,39] propose deep learning-based recognition models for inferring activities without hand-crafted feature engineering for each environment. In the activity recognition domain, major approaches are based

T. Hara and H. Yamaguchi (Eds.): MobiQuitous 2021, LNICST 419, pp. 617–633, 2022.
https://doi.org/10.1007/978-3-030-94822-1_40

on RNN-type structures that have abilities to find causal relations of context sequences in smart spaces. The *context* implies a value that abstractly expresses the situation that occurred over a certain period of time in the sensor stream data. Murad et al. [21] use LSTMs based model to capture long-term dependencies between contexts and Zhao et al. [39] leverage bidirectional LSTMs to tighten correlations overall context sequences by adding reverse temporal relations into the model. To extract major context sequence patterns of each activity in both spatial and temporal aspect, Ordóñez et al. [23] develop a hybrid deep learning model which combines both CNNs and LSTMs.

Despite of their outstanding outcomes, they have limitations in their application to a growing research field, a space where multiple users work together (e.g., smart seminar room or smart factory). In this paper, we define the space as a *Multi-user space*. The previous studies focus on single-user activities in which a user's actions occur sequentially. Multiple users perform multiple actions in the same time[4] without user identification [14] and it causes difficulty to define correlations among events in sequential manners as shown in Fig. 1. The issues pose three major challenges in recognizing activities in real-world, multi-user spaces.

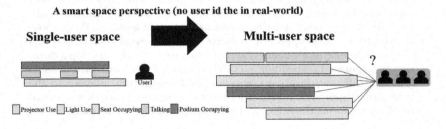

Fig. 1. Differences between single-user space and multi-user space in a smart space perspective

First, the existing models are sequence-based which lead to a gradient vanishing problem and has limitations in extracting long-term context relations. From a space perspective, the mix of events means that a significant amount of unrelated events occur consecutively between correlated events. It means that long-term correlated events may have more significant dependencies than events that occur immediately before or after relationships. In addition, multi-user activity generates relatively much longer context sequences than single-user activity, resulting in more long-term correlation events. Second, the existing studies are regarded all activities have the same importance. It makes infrequent but important events for recognizing certain activity (e.g. Stand in front of a podium in *Seminar*) are ignored when extracting activity patterns. Finally, previous research focus mainly on event types. Even if events of the same type are active in different duration, they are learned in the same contexts as they are the same event type.

In this paper, we propose a novel approach, AR-T (i.e. **A**ctivity **R**ecognition **T**ransformer), to complex contexts in multi-user spaces based on the transformer structure. AR-T employs the transformer [33] to discover long-term context correlations by computing attention scores between all context pairs. It also finds the importance weights of each context which makes infrequent but important contexts extracted as one of the activity patterns. To differentiate the same-type contexts with different duration, it embeds not only context type but also the duration and positional information as an input to the Transformer. We experiment with two datasets IoT sensor stream data which have been collected from multi-user based real-world testbeds, a seminar room testbed and a smart home testbed from CASAS group [31]. Compared to the existing approaches [17,21,39], experimental results show that AR-T improves the recognition accuracy by 12.57% in the seminar room testbed and 11.42% in the CASAS dataset.

The remaining of this paper is organized as follows. In Sect. 2, we introduce a related work of activity recognition methods focusing on deep learning and the previous studies based on the transformer. We describe key problems of the existing works in Sect. 3 and illustrates the key components of AR-T in Sect. 4 to solve those issues. In Sect. 5 and 6, we analyze the empirical evaluation results of AR-T and discuss them. We present the conclusion and future works in Sect. 7 .

2   Related Work

2.1   Existing Approaches for Activity Recognition in Smart Spaces

In order to recognize users' activities in a smart space, wearable sensors or video-based approaches are proposed [10,16]. However, those disciplines have privacy or accessibility issues to use in daily living, data streams generated by deployed smart objects (e.g. sound sensors, projectors, etc.) without user identification have been leveraged. Early approaches employ graphical models [6,35] or space-knowledge based models [5,28] that deriving semantic correlations among activities and events to represent the characteristics of complex activities, the schemes have difficulties in directly applying them to various spaces because they need to manually pre-define all sensors and probabilistic relations of activities.

Recent studies [21–23,37,39] use deep learning models for resolving the hand-crafted feature engineering problems [34]. The methods they use are classified into two categories: CNN and RNN. CNN-based approaches [22,23,37] compress complex patterns of activities to efficient representations using kernels and filters. Yang et al. [37] show that a CNN technology-based automated feature learning from raw sensor data has better performance than the traditional machine learning methods. In the activity recognition field, RNN based approaches [21,39] are mainstreams since RNN type models [7,13] are better to extract sequential patterns. Murad et al. [21] propose LSTM based recognition models for classifying activities from variable-length input sequences by capturing long dependencies between contexts. However, the LSTM model only contains forward information that loses event correlation information and Zhao et al. [39] use bidirectional LSTM to add reverse context information to overcome the issue. Ordóñez et al.

[23] propose a hybrid deep learning model which combines both CNN and LSTM layers. It is suitable for multimodal sensors in smart spaces since it trains patterns of sensor data in both spatial and temporal aspects and it outperforms the existing single models. However, these models still have limitations in extracting long-term correlations in a multi-user space and finding important but infrequent events of each activity.

2.2   Attention Mechanisms in Various Domains

In the NLP field, the seq2seq model called transformer [33] which consists of attention mechanisms becomes the mainstream, showing more effective performance for context understanding. Compared to the existing sequential deep learning models, it only utilizes attention mechanisms that reflect connections between all individual contexts in form of weights. Not only this enables finding important contexts but also results in greater parallelization. In addition, it is more appropriate for finding longer relations between contexts since it reduces the gradient vanishing problem compared to the previous techniques. Due to those advantages, many time series research domains try to recognize a specific context. Wu et al. [36] leverage the transformer for recognizing diseases like influenza and Yang et al. [38] propose a transformer-based approach for volatility recognition. A transformer is a promising method in the time-series domain, which means it is suitable for finding correlations in event streams in smart spaces, but only a small number of studies are conducted. Haresamudram et al. [12] introduce a pre-training method of the transformer to single-user smart spaces but focus less on how to deploy the transformer itself in a smart space. Ma et al. [17] utilize attention mechanisms with an RNN-type model (i.e. GRU [7]) and CNNs to capture correlations of multimodal sensor data from spatial and temporal perspectives. However, their approach is still difficult to long-term event correlations since it is RNN-based. Both approaches are single user-based environments that are vulnerable to real problems of multi-user spaces.

3   Problem Definition

This section describes issues of recognizing activities based solely on sensor streams in multi-user smart spaces.

3.1   Preliminaries

We represent a ith sensor value in timestamp t as s_t^i. Each sensor generates a raw data stream $(s_1^i, s_2^i, s_3^i, ...)$. In a preprocessing step, each sensor stream is converted to an event stream denoted by $(e_1^i, e_2^i, e_3^i, ...)$.

Definition 1. *An **event** is a value that converts raw sensor values into a human-understandable value to reduce fluctuations and noises in the real world. Changed event values are generated when user **actions** (i.e. user behavior such as 'sitting') changes. Each event has its value and duration as attributes. E.g. raw sound sensor value '76' is converted to event 'Sound_Level2' and raw projector value '1' is converted to event 'Projector ON'.*

All event streams are split appropriately through a window sliding step and transformed into a sequence of contexts $(c_{w1}, c_{w2}, c_{w3}, ...)$. wj indicates that it is the jth order window. The sequence becomes one of the patterns of a certain activity A^k. k means the type of activity.

Definition 2. *A **context** c_{wj} represents a set of events $\{e_{wj}^1, e_{wj}^2, ..., e_{wj}^i, ...\}$ in the jth window. It is an abstract value representing a specific situation. Similar to an event, it has a specific value and duration.*

Definition 3. *In this paper, an **activity** refers to a single user or multiple users performing a task in the same space. E.g. a 'seminar' is a task involving multiple users, but it is one activity as they perform it for the same one goal. An activity A^{k_1} consists of a sequence of contexts $(c_{w1}^{k_1}, c_{w2}^{k_1}, c_{w3}^{k_1}, ...)$.*

3.2   Problems

A multi-user activity has more complex activity patterns than a single-user activity since it involves interactions between users and various independent actions of each user [4]. In addition, in the real world, it is hard to collect and recognize identities of users, which raises problems of correlation between users and sensor data they generate [14]. In these aspects, we define four major problems that are not able to be solved by previous research.

Long-Term Correlations Between Contexts. In a multi-user environment, as shown in Fig. 1 which illustrates an activity *Seminar*, events are mixed from a space point of view since users perform actions at the same time or at overlapping times. It leads multiple, unrelated contexts to exist between pairs of related contexts, allowing them to have long-term relations. E.g. c_{w1} and c_{w10} are more relevant than c_{w1} and c_{w2}. Also, compared to a single-user activity, a multi-user activity creates a longer sequence of context. Not only does the duration of the activity increases, but changes in contexts also increase, resulting in a natural increase in a sequence length of contexts. However, the existing approaches assume that all events are performed sequentially in an activity and that a given context and its immediately preceding context are more relevant than the others. This hampers recognition performance of the existing approaches in multi-user spaces.

Unbalanced Frequencies Between Events. The number of occurrences between events in a space varies due to differences in the number of times users can change the state of smart objects. For example, when a *Seminar* activity occurs, users incur a *Light ON* event only once but make a *Sound Level2* event multiple times. The difference in the number of occurrences between events is even greater in a multi-user space . However, the existing approaches derive activity patterns based on frequency and give equal importance to all events. This makes it difficult to extract actuator-based events as elements of an pattern of specific activity, which is important for recognizing the activity.

Different Activities but Similar Context Sequences. The number of sensors installed and the number of events that can occur in one smart space is fixed. Thus, a context sequence consists of only a limited number of context types, resulting in many similar sequences are created between different activities. As the existing works do, methods only using the values of contexts are not able to distinguish them.

4   Proposed Approach: *Activity Recognition Transformer*

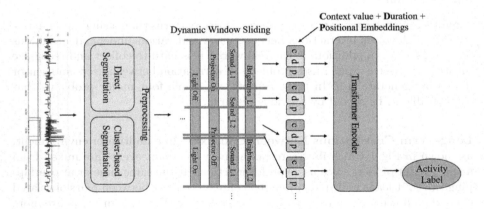

Fig. 2. Overall architecture and key components of AR-T

In this section, we details the key components of AR-T (i.e. **A**ctivity **R**ecognition **T**ransformer). Figure 2 illustrates the overall architecture of AR-T for recognizing activities solely using sensor streams generated in multi-user smart spaces. AR-T improves the recognition performance of activities through three steps: (1) AR-T transforms raw sensor values into events by direct and cluster-based segmentation. Then, AR-T obtains event streams of each sensor. (2) AR-T slides a window when any event changes in the entire event streams and converts the set of event values for each window into a single vectorized context embedding.

AR-T also constructs a duration embedding based on the actual duration length of each window and adds a positional embedding that represents the order of the window. (3) AR-T trains patterns of activities in smart spaces with the embeddings and transformer [33]. The transformer encoder of AR-T utilizes attention mechanisms to determine forward and reverse dependencies between contexts and calculate the importance weights of each context. Based on the trained attention values of each activity, AR-T infers the most probable activity in the recognition step.

4.1   Sensor Stream Preprocessing

In this step, AR-T transforms a raw sensor stream $(s_1^i, s_2^i, s_3^i, ...)$, s_t^i into an event stream $(e_1^i, e_2^i, e_3^i, ...)$. The result e_t^i consists of the duration and its event label. Sensor data generated in a smart space are classified into two types: Data from actuators (e.g. electronic lights or projectors) and data from ambient sensors (e.g. brightness or sound sensors).

Actuators are smart objects that users directly manipulate and they publish data when the state changes directly by users. Their values are discrete and AR-T translates them directly to event labels. The process of generating events based on the discrete sensor data type is called *Direct Segmentation*. On the other hand, ambient sensors publish constant observations of a space. They include a lot of noises (i.e. sensor data generated by some environmental factors rather than user action) and fluctuations that increase value changes of the sensors. AR-T reduces these problems by using a simple signal averaging [32] method. Then, it employs density-based clustering [15] to automatically find the optimal number of event levels for each ambient sensor and defines a range of sensor values for each cluster. Then, it gives each cluster a human-understandable level of event label and s_t^i that corresponds to a particular cluster is assigned the label of that cluster. This continuous sensor data type-based event generation method is called *Cluster-based Segmentation*.

When events with the same level occur consecutively, AR-T merges those events into one event. If an event with any other level appears, the merge process stops and that time point is considered the end time of the event. AR-T derives event streams from all types of sensors.

4.2   Temporal Relation Embedding

Multivariate event streams $\{(e_1^1, e_2^1, ...), ..., (e_1^i, e_2^i, ...), ...\}$ enter the embedding step as inputs. Compared to windows that are split into fixed sizes that the existing approaches do, AR-T slides a window according to changes in values of events. When e_{t-1}^i is changed to e_t^i, the point at which the event value changes, AR-T is regarded as the time when the window is split.

$\{e_{t-1}^1, e_{t-1}^2, ..., e_{t-1}^i, ...e_{t-1}^n\}$ is transformed into a single context embedding $c_{w(t-1)}$ by a popular word embedding method, Word2Vec[19]. The embedding is called *context embedding* as each embedding represents the entire contextual situation of a smart space. To differentiate situations even if types of context embeddings are the same, AR-T embeds temporal information using duration embedding and positional embedding methods. To generate a duration embedding $d_{w(t-1)}$, AR-T also employs the Word2Vec [19] method based on duration number of e_{t-1}^i. Since the transformer structure does not contain the sequential order information that LSTM [13] or GRU [7] have, AR-T incorporates a positional embedding $p_{w(t-1)}$ to represent the order of context embeddings $\{c_{w1}, c_{w2}, ..., c_{w(t-1)}, ...\}$. *sin* and *cos* functions are leveraged to calculate the position values of each context. Finally, AR-T creates an embedding output of each window E_{wj} by concatenating three embedding states c_{wj}, d_{wj} and p_{wj}.

4.3 Transformer [33] Based Activity Recognition

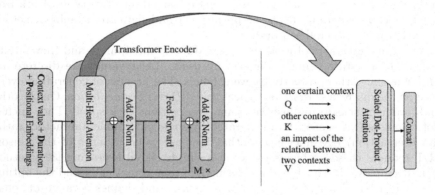

Fig. 3. Overall architecture of the transformer [33] and the detailed attention mechanism

When an embedding sequence $(E_{w1}, E_{w2}, E_{w3}, ...)$ comes in as an input, based on an attention mechanism, AR-T assigns importance weights to each context to preserve important contexts that appear in low frequency and extract long-term correlations between contexts. Figure 3 describes an overall architecture of the transformer [33] and the detailed attention mechanism.

Encoder Structure of AR-T. Each transformer encoder is composed of one multi-head attention element which calculates the importance weights of contexts and a feed-forward element as shown in the left one in Fig. 3. The attention element will be explained in the below section **Attention mechanism**. By connecting the M encoder, AR-T learns various aspects of context correlations and captures long-term dependencies better than the existing approaches. The result of a preceding encoder is input to the next encoder. The encoder utilizes a feed-forward element to avoid loss of temporal information between contexts by linear activation, expressed by the following formula:

$$FF(x) = Relu(0, xW_1 + b_1)W_2 + b_2 \qquad (1)$$

Using Add & Norm elements, AR-T maintains the same embedding shape between inputs and outputs of all encoders and normalizes the values.

Attention Mechanism. The attention mechanism computes the correlation weights between contexts and implicitly assigns the importance weights of each context. AR-T calculates the attention score representing correlation importance weights of a specific context using the following scaled dot product-based formula:

$$Attention(Q, K, V) = softmax(QK^T / \sqrt{d_k})V \qquad (2)$$

Referring to the right figure of Fig. 4, Q represents a specific context, K means other contexts and V stands for the importance of those correlations to recognize an activity. AR-T calculates attention scores for all events by the scaled dot product between Q and K and compresses them using a softmax method and dot product with V. For example, as shown in Fig. 4, if the context containing event *Podium Occupying* correlates with the context containing event *Projector Use*, their relations have a high attention score. As the name of multi-headed attention suggests, AR-T proceeds the attention process multiple times and allows covering context correlations in many aspects. AR-T concatenates outcomes from each attention process and the final result represents holistic context correlations that are important for recognizing activities.

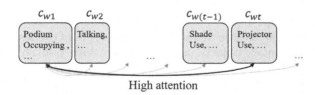

Fig. 4. An example of how to assign attention scores to correlated contexts

5   Experiments and Results

In this section, we explain comparison results between AR-T and the existing works [17,21,39] with accuracy, f1-score, recall and precision metrics. Unless otherwise specified, the representative of *recognition performance* mainly represents f1-score. Existing public datasets [27,29] for activity recognition approaches have several limitations. They are generated by controlled experiments in which well-defined instructions are given to experimental users. It implies that specific user and specific sensor values are coupled, which makes it unsuitable to verify recognition performance in real multi-user spaces. Second, they do not involve enough types of smart objects that covering various patterns of the real world smart spaces. We conduct experiments in a testbed in our university, a seminar room where we install various smart objects for capturing everyday usages. We also experiment with a public data set created by CASAS group [31] to evaluate applicability in various smart spaces.

5.1 Evaluation Description

We conduct our experiments on Intel Xeon Gold 5215 CPU (2.5GHz), 256GB RAM, and Ubuntu 18.04.5 LTS os. For recognition comparative experiments, we implement AR-T and the three existing approaches [17,21,39] in Python and Keras [11]. The comparison approaches are defined as follow:

LSTM-based (baseline): [21] A recognition approach with LSTMs
BiLSTM-based: [39] A recognition approach with bidirectional LSTMs
AttnSense: [17] A recognition approach with RNN type models and an attention mechanism
AR-T: A proposed temporal relation representable transformer-based approach

We obtain the final result as the average of the experimental results of 5 cross-validations. We apply the same values for parameters such as the number of hidden states, the dropout rate and the number of epochs for all approaches. To analyze the experimental results in detail, we use Matplotlib [18] to display confusion matrices of each approach. The code is publicly available to reproduce experimental results of AR-T[1].

5.2 Case 1: Real Seminar Room Dataset

Environment Setup. Figure 5 describes the installation configuration of smart objects in our testbed and the detailed generated types of events from them. We install twenty-one smart objects in our testbed which publish seven different types of events. They are developed by Raspberry Pi 3 and commercial sensor frameworks (e.g. Phidgets [26], Monnits [20] and DigiKeys [8]). The description of four major activities in our testbed is as follows:

Group Chatting: A pair of people sit down nearby and have a casual conversation
Seminar: One or more speakers make presentations, others discuss topics of the presentations
Technical Discussion: Using a projector to display discussion topics, many people discuss them
Group Study: Some people study together for a long time

We experiment with 111, 129, 52, and 40 examples of each activity. The maximum length of a context sequence for each activity is 31, 146, 141 and 106.

---

[1] We will release github later due to anonymity.

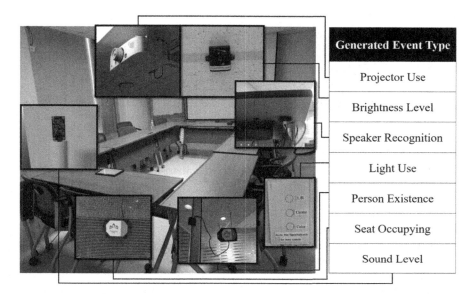

Fig. 5. Multi-user smart space testbed construction and deployed smart objects

Table 1. Recognition performance comparison in the seminar room testbed

Evaluation metrics	AR-T	AttSense	BiLSTM	LSTM(baseline)
Precision	**0.889** ± 0.044	**0.713** ± 0.164	**0.842** ± 0.059	**0.284** ± 0.228
Recall	**0.882** ± 0.038	**0.746** ± 0.105	**0.825** ± 0.060	**0.412** ± 0.068
F1-score	**0.879** ± 0.049	**0.717** ± 0.149	**0.828** ± 0.046	**0.274** ± 0.110
Accuracy	**0.882** ± 0.038	**0.746** ± 0.105	**0.825** ± 0.060	**0.412** ± 0.068

Recognition Performance Comparison. AR-T improves recognition performance by resolving the problems of previous approaches. As shown in Table 1, the AR-T performs better than the existing ones in terms of all performance metrics. The proposed scheme improves accuracy by 18.23%, 6.91%, and 114.08% compared to AttSense [17], BiLSTM-based approach [39], and baseline model [21], respectively. In addition, as expressed in Table 1, the performance values of AR-T are more stable than other approaches since AR-T discovers context correlation in various aspects. Figure 6 displays the confusion matrix of our testbed for detailed analysis at activity levels.

The multi-user space has a lot of long-term context correlations due to longer context sequences and complex events mixed by multiple users. Accordingly, the baseline model, which is the most vulnerable to the vanishing gradient problem, is difficult to capture these long-term relations and shows overwhelmingly low performance. As shown in Fig. 6, AR-T shows much better accuracy in *Group Study* (0.59) than the AttSense (0.16) and BiLSTM based approach (0.40). *Group Study* has many contexts that are relatively long-term related compared

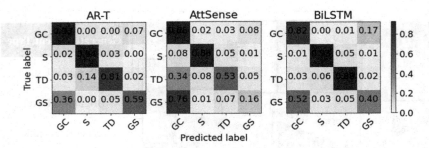

Fig. 6. Normalized confusion matrix comparison in the testbed

to other activities. It implies AR-T has better capability to capture long-term context correlations in longer sequences.

AR-T also aims to increase recognition performance by preserving important contexts which infrequently occur. According to *Seminar* in Fig. 6, AR-T shows the highest accuracy (0.94) since it assigns high importance scores to contexts containing important events such as *Projector On*. However, as a side effect, *Technical Discussion* is recognized as *Seminar* which also regarded *Projector On* as an important event.

The same type of contexts with different durations usually happen in the multi-user space. *Group Chatting* and *Group Study* have the same type of events as elements of activity patterns, however, their durations are very different. The context sequences generated by *Group Study* are much longer than by *Group Chatting* and duration embeddings assist to differentiate them. In this aspect, as represented in Fig. 6, AR-T recognizes *Group Chatting* (0.93) and *Group Study* (0.59) better than the existing approaches. The effects of incorporating durations in embeddings are described in Sect. 6.

5.3 Case 2: Multi-user CASAS Dataset

Dataset Description. To validate the applicability of AR-T to various environments, We conduct an additional experiment using the CASAS activity dataset [31] without using users' identification. It is a smart home testbed based on 51 motion sensors and 15 cabinet sensors and two users performed collaborative tasks together. The sensor configuration of this implies that the recognition approach should exploit context sequences representing users' movement paths for identifying activity patterns. The CASAS activity dataset contains 26 examples of four multi-user activities: *Move furniture*, *Play a game*, *Prepare for dinner* and *Pack a picnic*. The maximum length of a context sequence for each activity is 21, 46, 57 and 143.

Recognition Performance Comparison. As shown in Table 2 and Fig. 7, AR-T outperforms accuracy by 17.90%, 4.95%, and 179.24% compared to AttSense, BiLSTM-based approach, and baseline model, respectively. Since the

Table 2. Recognition comparison of the existing approaches and AR-T in the CASAS dataset [31]

Evaluation metrics	AR-T	AttLSTM	BiLSTM	LSTM(baseline)
Precision	**0.962** ± 0.029	**0.828** ± 0.168	**0.925** ± 0.058	**0.186** ± 0.147
Recall	**0.955** ± 0.033	**0.810** ± 0.162	**0.910** ± 0.065	**0.342** ± 0.210
F1-score	**0.954** ± 0.034	**0.794** ± 0.196	**0.909** ± 0.066	**0.208** ± 0.181
Accuracy	**0.955** ± 0.033	**0.810** ± 0.162	**0.910** ± 0.065	**0.342** ± 0.210

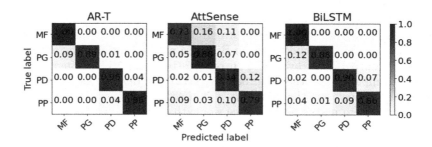

Fig. 7. Normalized confusion matrix comparison in the CASAS dataset

dataset consists of only two users' activities and the activities consist of simpler sequences of events, the overall recognition performance of all approaches are higher than those of the testbed. AR-T also shows reliable performance than others in this dataset as shown in Table 2.

In Fig. 7, ability of AR-T to correlate long-term relations of contexts makes recognizing *Prepare for dinner* (0.96) and *Pack a picnic* (0.96) better than others. Using the importance weights of contexts, AR-T supports the accuracy improvement of *Prepare for dinner* by leaving events that are important but infrequently occurring as elements of *Prepare for dinner* patterns. The duration embeddings in AR-T distinguish between *Prepare for dinner* and *Pack a picnic* sharing the same types of contexts as the elements of patterns of the activities.

6 Discussion

6.1 Effects of Embedding Types

In the embedding step of AR-T, we embed not only the context value but also the duration and positional information. We try to explore performance changes according to embedding methods. In our testbed, the duration incorporated embeddings-based method improves recognition performance by 5.65% for context only embeddings-based, and by 4.52% for context and positional embeddings-based. In the CASAS dataset, duration included embeddings-based method outperform by 4.26% compared to context only embeddings-based, and by 4.15% compared to context and positional embeddings-based. This means that the duration is a good distinction factor for distinguishing between activities composed of the same context types.

6.2 Recognition Performance of BiLSTMs with an Attention Mechanism

From the results shown in Table 1 and Table 2, one may guess that BiLSTMs with an attention mechanism (i.e. AttBiLSTM), which no approach has tried, could perform as good as the transformer. To figure out whether this assertion stands, we conduct an experiment on BiLSTM with attention. The result shows that AR-T outperforms by 9.06% in our testbed and 13.84% in the CASAS dataset. Compared to other approaches [17,21], it derives long-term context relations well, however, the fact that it is a sequential model with a gradient vanishing problem makes performance worse than AR-T.

6.3 Effects of Window Sliding Methods

We try to analyze how window size affects recognition performance. We compare a dynamic window sliding method of AR-T and a fixed window sliding. By the experiments, the dynamic window sliding method of AR-T improves recognition performance around 1%~2% than the fixed window sliding. We expect the dynamic window sliding approach to further improve recognition performance, but other sliding approaches are needed to find the optimal window size for a multi-user space.

7   Conclusion

In this paper, we propose AR-T, an accurate and applicability approach for activity recognition in multi-user smart spaces of the real world. The existing studies have difficulties in (1) correlating long-term relations between contexts, (2) finding important contexts that are infrequent, and (3) distinguishing activities that have the same types of contexts. AR-T utilizes the attention mechanism of the transformer [33] to find long-term context correlations. In addition, AR-T allows important but infrequent contexts to remain as elements of activity patterns, based on the importance weight of each context. AR-T uses duration embeddings to differentiate between the same type of context with different durations. This supports to differentiate between activities that share the same context sequences.

To recognize multiple activities in multi-user spaces, we plan to extend AR-T with multi-task learning [30]. We also plan to develop a sparse attention method [1] for sensor streams to build a more efficient and scalable structure in various spaces while retaining important contextual information.

Acknowledgement. This work was partly supported by Institute of Information & communications Technology Planning & Evaluation(IITP) grant funded by the Korea government(MSIT) (No.2019–0-01126, Self-learning based Autonomic IoT Edge Computing) and the ICT RD program of MSIT/IITP (No.2020–0-00857, Development of Cloud Robot Intelligence Augmentation, Sharing and Framework Technology to Integrate and Enhance the Intelligence of Multiple Robots).

References

1. Ainslie, J., Ontanon, S., Alberti, C., Cvicek, V., Fisher, Z., Pham, P., et al.: ETC: encoding long and structured inputs in transformers. In: Proceedings of the 2020 Conference on Empirical Methods in Natural Language Processing (EMNLP), pp. 268–284 (2020)
2. Al Ameen, M., Liu, J., Kwak, K.: Security and privacy issues in wireless sensor networks for healthcare applications. Journal of medical systems **36**(1), 93–101 (2012)
3. Benmansour, A., Bouchachia, A., Feham, M.: Multioccupant activity recognition in pervasive smart home environments. ACM Comput. Surv. (CSUR) **48**(3), 1–36 (2015)
4. Campion, M.A., Medsker, G.J., Higgs, A.C.: Relations between work group characteristics and effectiveness: implications for designing effective work groups. Personnel Psychol. **46**(4), 823–847 (1993)
5. Chen, L., Nugent, C.: Ontology-based activity recognition in intelligent pervasive environments. Int. J. Web Inf. Syst. (2009)
6. Chen, R., Tong, Y.: A two-stage method for solving multi-resident activity recognition in smart environments. Entropy **16**(4), 2184–2203 (2014)
7. Cho, K., Van Merriënboer, B., Gulcehre, C., Bahdanau, D., Bougares, F., Schwenk, H., Bengio, Y.: Learning phrase representations using RNN encoder-decoder for statistical machine translation. arXiv preprint arXiv:1406.1078 (2014)
8. DigiKey. www.digikey.com/. Accessed 31 Mar 2021
9. Foresti, G.L., Mähönen, P., Regazzoni, C.S. (eds.): Multimedia video-based surveillance systems: requirements, issues and solutions. Springer Science and Business Media, New York (2012)
10. Gavrilyuk, K., Sanford, R., Javan, M., Snoek, C.G.: Actor-transformers for group activity recognition. In: Proceedings of the IEEE/CVF Conference on Computer Vision and Pattern Recognition, pp. 839–848 (2020)
11. Gulli, A., Pal, S.: Deep learning with Keras. Packt Publishing Ltd (2017)
12. Haresamudram, H., Beedu, A., Agrawal, V., Grady, P.L., Essa, I., Hoffman, J., Plötz, T.: Masked reconstruction based self-supervision for human activity recognition. In: Proceedings of the 2020 International Symposium on Wearable Computers, pp. 45–49 (2020)
13. Hochreiter, S., Schmidhuber, J.: Long short-term memory. Neural Comput. **9**(8), 1735–1780 (1997)
14. Hsu, C. C., Wang, L. Z.: A smart home resource management system for multiple inhabitants by agent conceding negotiation. In: 2008 IEEE International Conference on Systems, Man and Cybernetics, pp. 607–612. IEEE (2008)
15. Kriegel, H.P., Kröger, P., Sander, J., Zimek, A.: Density-based clustering. Wiley Interdisciplinary Reviews: Data Mining and Knowledge Discovery **1**(3), 231–240 (2011)

16. Lara, O.D., Labrador, M.A.: A survey on human activity recognition using wearable sensors. IEEE communications surveys & tutorials 15(3), 1192–1209 (2012)
17. Ma, H., Li, W., Zhang, X., Gao, S., Lu, S.: AttnSense: multi-level attention mechanism for multimodal human activity recognition. In: IJCAI, pp. 3109–3115 (2019)
18. Matplotlib. matplotlib.org/. Accessed 31 Mar 2021
19. Mikolov, T., Chen, K., Corrado, G., Dean, J.: Efficient estimation of word representations in vector space. arXiv preprint arXiv:1301.3781 (2013)
20. Monnit. www.monnit.com/. Accessed 31 Mar 2021
21. Murad, A., Pyun, J.Y.: Deep recurrent neural networks for human activity recognition. Sensors 17(11), 2556 (2017)
22. Nweke, H.F., Teh, Y.W., Al-Garadi, M.A., Alo, U.R.: Deep learning algorithms for human activity recognition using mobile and wearable sensor networks: state of the art and research challenges. Expert Syst. Appl. 105, 233–261 (2018)
23. Ordóñez, F.J., Roggen, D.: Deep convolutional and lstm recurrent neural networks for multimodal wearable activity recognition. Sensors 16(1), 115 (2016)
24. Pantelopoulos, A., Bourbakis, N. G.: A survey on wearable sensor-based systems for health monitoring and prognosis. IEEE Trans. Syst. Man Cybern. Part C Appl. Revi. 40(1), 1–12 (2009)
25. Papagiannidis, S., Marikyan, D.: Smart offices: a productivity and well-being perspective. Int. J. Inf. Manage. 51, 102027 (2020)
26. Phidget. www.phidgets.com/ Accessed 31 Mar 2021
27. Reiss, A., Stricker, D.: Introducing a new benchmarked dataset for activity monitoring. In: 2012 16th International Symposium on Wearable Computers, pp. 108–109. IEEE (2012)
28. Riboni, D., Sztyler, T., Civitarese, G., Stuckenschmidt, H.: Unsupervised recognition of interleaved activities of daily living through ontological and probabilistic reasoning. In: Proceedings of the 2016 ACM International Joint Conference on Pervasive and Ubiquitous Computing, pp. 1–12 (2016)
29. Roggen, D., Calatroni, A., Rossi, M., Holleczek, T., Förster, K., et al.: Collecting complex activity datasets in highly rich networked sensor environments. In: 2010 Seventh International Conference on Networked Sensing Systems (INSS), pp. 233–240. IEEE (2010)
30. Ruder, S.: An overview of multi-task learning in deep neural networks. arXiv preprint arXiv:1706.05098(2017)
31. Singla, G., Cook, D.J., Schmitter-Edgecombe, M.: Recognizing independent and joint activities among multiple residents in smart environments. J. Ambient Intell. Human. Comput.1(1), 57–63 (2010)
32. Trimble, C.R.: What is signal averaging. Hewlett-Packard J.19(8), 2–7 (1968)
33. Vaswani, A., et al.: Attention is all you need. arXiv preprint arXiv:1706.03762 (2017)
34. Wang, J., Chen, Y., Hao, S., Peng, X., Hu, L.: Deep learning for sensor-based activity recognition: a survey. Pattern Recogn. Lett. 119, 3–11 (2019)
35. Wang, L., Gu, T., Tao, X., Chen, H., Lu, J.: Recognizing multi-user activities using wearable sensors in a smart home. Pervasive Mobile Comput. 7(3), 287–298 (2011)
36. Wu, N., Green, B., Ben, X., O'Banion, S.: Deep transformer models for time series forecasting: the influenza prevalence case. arXiv preprint arXiv:2001.08317 (2020)
37. Yang, J., Nguyen, M.N., San, P.P., Li, X., Krishnaswamy, S.: Deep convolutional neural networks on multichannel time series for human activity recognition. In: Ijcai, pp. 3995–4001 (2015)

38. Yang, L., Ng, T. L. J., Smyth, B., Dong, R.: Html: hierarchical transformer-based multi-task learning for volatility prediction. In: Proceedings of The Web Conference 2020, pp. 441–451 (2020)
39. Zhao, Y., Yang, R., Chevalier, G., Xu, X., Zhang, Z.: Deep residual bidir-LSTM for human activity recognition using wearable sensors. Math. Problems Eng. (2018)

Analysis of The Effects of Cognitive Stress on the Reliability of Participatory Sensing

Rio Yoshikawa[1]([✉]), Yuki Matsuda[1,2,3][iD], Kohei Oyama[1], Hirohiko Suwa[1,2][iD], and Keiichi Yasumoto[1,2][iD]

[1] Nara Institute of Science and Technology, Nara, Ikoma-shi 630–0192, Japan
{yoshikawa.rio.yo4,yukimat,oyama.kohei.ol8,h-suwa,yasumoto}@is.naist.jp
[2] RIKEN Center for Advanced Intelligence Project, Tokyo, Chuo-ku 103–0027, Japan
[3] JST Presto, Tokyo, Chiyoda-ku 102–0076, Japan

Abstract. As a result of the widespread of smart devices such as smartphones, participatory sensing, which is a method of sensing and sharing information about the surrounding environment using the user's own device, has been attracting increasing attention. However, the quality of the data relies on the attitudes of the users because they do not always give accurate and careful responses to participatory sensing tasks. In this study, we considered that the causes of the occurrence of careless responses in participatory sensing are not only the user's attitude toward the task, but also the cognitive stress conditions surrounding the user (e.g., time limits, ambient noise, walking). In this paper, we investigated whether the ratio of correct answers and the response status of a participatory sensing task differs under stressful and normal conditions. The results showed that the cognitive stresses of noise and walking significantly reduced the ratio of correct answers, whereas the cognitive stresses of walking and time limits increased and decreased the answering time, respectively. After the experiment, we conducted a subjective evaluation questionnaire regarding the effects of stress environment conditions on the participatory sensing task. The results showed that a combination of multiple stressful environmental conditions often hindered or affected task responses.

Keywords: Participatory sensing · Crowdsourcing · Response reliability · Satisficing · Cognitive stress

1 Introduction

Smart devices such as smartphones and wearable devices equipped with sensing, computing, and networking capabilities are rapidly growing in popularity. The widespread use of such devices has contributed to the realization of *participatory*

This study was supported R. Yoshikawa and Y. Matsuda are Co-first authors in part by JST PRESTO under Grant No. JPMJPR2039.

T. Hara and H. Yamaguchi (Eds.): MobiQuitous 2021, LNICST 419, pp. 634–649, 2022.
https://doi.org/10.1007/978-3-030-94822-1_41

sensing, a method of sensing and sharing information of surrounding environments using the user's own device [3]. Participatory sensing uses various sensors embedded in the devices of ordinary users, such as GPS, cameras, microphones, accelerometers, and gyroscopes. Therefore, it has the advantages of eliminating the need to install sensors and enabling data collection from a wide range of locations. However, the amount of data that can be obtained depends on the number of people who contribute to sensing tasks in the target area, and the quality of the data relies on the users' attitudes, since the user does not always give accurate and careful responses [1].

One of the risks to data quality in participatory sensing is careless responses, which is often explained in terms of *satisficing* (minimization of effort), where a person does not pay an appropriate cognitive cost for a given task [8]. The term *satisfice* is a composite of *satisfy* and *suffice*, and refers to a cognitive heuristic in which the finite nature of human cognitive resources leads to a tendency to minimize effort in response to demands, and to determine and pursue procedures that satisfy the minimum effort necessary to achieve an objective [22]. The attitude of users to a given task has been pointed out as one of the factors that cause satisficing [14]. Gogami *et al.* revealed the relationship between smartphone screen operation and satisficing, and as a result, built the careless response detection model [7].

In the real world, users typically use smartphones under various conditions that combine obstructive factors (e.g., noise, walking conditions) and mental factors (e.g., stress, mood). These factors affect smartphone operations, such as inducing a wrong operation [6,17,18,20].

From the above, we considered that the cause of a situation that a user gives a careless response is due to changes in not only the attitudes and behaviors of the user, but also obstructive factors surrounding the user (Fig. 1).

This study aimed to investigate the effects of obstructive factors on response reliability in a participatory sensing. In this paper, among the obstructive factors, we focused on "cognitive stress" and conducted an experiment to investigate its relationship with response reliability. In the experiment, we presented various cognitive stress conditions to participants while they were performing a specific participatory sensing task (questions about human flow). The correctness of the answer was used to assess the reliability of the users' responses. In addition, smartphone logs (embedded sensor data and touch panel operation) were used to analyze the effects of the cognitive stress condition in the users' responses. Based on these data, we analyzed whether the occurrence of careless responses or the smartphone logs differed under stressful and normal conditions. The results showed that the cognitive stresses of noise and walking significantly reduced the correct answer rate, and that the cognitive stresses of walking and time limits significantly reduced the answering time.

The organization of this paper is as follows. In Sect. 2, we outline existing studies related to the proposed method. Section 3 describes the analytical framework, Sect. 4 describes the setup of the survey experiment, Sect. 5 presents the experimental results and discussion, and Sect. 6 concludes the paper.

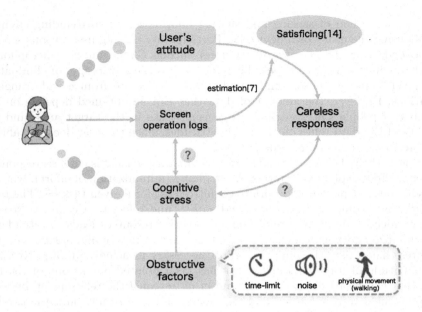

Fig. 1. Focus of this study

2   Related Work

Careless responses to questions in participatory sensing might introduce biases in the results of social surveys. Several studies have pointed out that there are many careless respondents, especially in online surveys [7,14,15]. Careless responses are thought to be caused by the attitude of trying to complete a questionnaire survey with the least amount of effort, which is referred to as *satisficing*, which several studies have attempted to detect. The details of these studies are described in Sect. 2.1.

In crowdsourcing, it has been shown that monetary incentives do not improve the quality of response data. We describe such a study in Sect. 2.2, which shows a method to inhibit careless responses to improve the quality of response data.

In addition, the influence of obstructive factors such as the stress surrounding the user on user behavior is also discussed in Sect. 2.3, as similar research has been conducted.

Based on these literature surveys, the position of this research is shown in Sect. 2.4.

2.1   Detection of Careless Responses

Several methods for detecting careless responses in questionnaire surveys have been proposed. Miura *et al.* [14] evaluated the efficiency and accuracy of the following methods for detecting careless responses: the Attentive Responding Scale (ARS) and the Directed Questions Scale (DQS) [10]. The ARS detects satisficing by scoring with two subscales: Inconsistency and Infrequency. Inconsistency is a measure of the difference in responses to questions that have similar meanings but different wordings. Infrequency is a measure of the difference in the choice that many people will select based on common sense and the choice actually selected. The DQS is a method in which some questions are inserted to instruct the user how to make a choice. If the user does not follow the instructions, he/she is considered to be satisficing. However, the predictive power of the various detection indices is generally not high; thus, it is more important to control the response environment or terminal depending on the survey content (e.g., instructing respondents to answer on a PC from home if the survey includes video stimuli). In addition, since these indices are similar to trick questions, they cause suspicion among the respondents, which increases their psychological burden and may result in careless responses.

Gogami *et al.* [7] developed a logger for smartphone screen operation and proposed a careless response detection method in online surveys based on features derived from obtained log data. As an example of these features, scrolling duration/speed/length, reverse scrolling, number of option changes, and text-deleting behavior have been newly employed. The results have revealed new features contributing to the improved accuracy of careless response detection in smartphone answer operation logs.

2.2   Suppression of Careless Responses

Crowdsourcing platforms such as Amazon Mechanical Turk have received increasing attention because of their ability to collect large amounts of data quickly and inexpensively [12]. Many studies have focused on how financial incentives in crowdsourcing affect the results of responses, and have shown that higher incentives for the same task increase the number of workers, but not the quality of the results [9,11,13]. On the other hand, volunteers have been shown not only to provide more reliable responses than crowdworkers who are given financial incentives, but also to have longer turnaround times and to be more likely not to complete the task. Therefore, volunteer crowdsourcing is inappropriate for time-limit tasks [2,5,16].

2.3   Effects of Stress on Behavior

In the fields of behavioral science and psychology, many studies have investigated the effects of stress on human daily life. Stress has been identified as a factor that is likely to have an impact on mobile interactions [19].

Sarsenbayeva *et al.* [18] used the Trier Social Stress Test to induce stress in participants and investigate the effects on performance in three common mobile interaction tasks: target acquisition, visual searches, and text entry. During stress induction, the access time and accuracy of the target in the target acquisition task and the completion time in the visual search task were significantly reduced compared with baseline.

Davide *et al.* [4] used a noninvasive approach to measure human stress levels by acquiring data from devices (e.g., touch operation, touch accuracy, touch intensity, touch duration, user movement, acceleration) and comparing the results during task execution in a stress-free environment versus a stress-affected environment (e.g., device vibration, loud and unpleasant sounds, unexpected device movement). The results showed that stress affected acceleration, the maximum and average touch intensity, user movement, and cognitive performance.

In addition, Schildbach *et al.* [21] focused on the background of the increasing number of people who use mobile phones while walking. They showed that walking, which can be an important environmental factor in mobile interactions, has a negative impact on tasks (e.g., target acquisition, text reading).

2.4 Study Position

Conventional research on careless responses has mainly focused on attitudes toward a given task, but has not considered the effects of cognitive stress from the outside world (i.e., obstructive factors). In participatory sensing, which is the subject of this study, we assume that the accuracy of responses is strongly influenced by not only human attitudes, but also obstructive factors. In this paper, we investigate the effects of obstructive factors on responses in participatory sensing by inducing cognitive stress in the user during the execution of a task.

3 Analytical Framework

3.1 Overview

To investigate the effects of obstructive factors on responses in participatory sensing, this experiment aimed to analyze how the quality of the responses and response behaviors change when users are subjected to the multiple cognitive stress conditions described below. The following participatory sensing scenarios were used. In this experiment, the user was asked to answer a question about people walking on the road, which could be confirmed visually while walking on the sidewalk. In the following sections, we describe the details of the analytical framework of the experiment.

3.2   Cognitive Stress Conditions

In this paper, we set up eight different cognitive stress conditions consisting of combinations of three different stress factors: answering under a time limit, answering in a noisy environment, and answering while walking. These stress environment conditions were set to simulate actual situations in participatory sensing, such as having a limited time to answer, being in a noisy environment such as a crowded urban area, and being in a situation in which a task is requested while moving. The details are shown below.

Cognitive Stress Due to Time Limits: In general, *time limits* are known to be stressful for the performance of any task. In the case of participatory sensing, time limits are considered to be severe because the user is required to observe and report within an ever-changing urban situation (e.g., information about people walking on the road in the scenario assumed in this paper) in a small amount of time, such as when waiting at a red light or at a meeting place. Therefore, time limit is included as the first stress factor.

Cognitive Stress Due to Environmental Noise: Environmental noise is perceived negatively by participants, with many commenting that it distracts them and negatively impacts their task performance [20]. In participatory sensing, it is assumed that the user is continuously exposed to the hustle and bustle of the city and other unpleasant noises while performing the task. Therefore, noise (in this case, urban noise) is included as the second stress factor.

Cognitive Stress Due to Body Movement (Walking): Walking negatively affects the performance of tasks (e.g., target acquisition, text reading) during interactions with mobile devices [21]. In the participatory sensing scenario assumed in this paper, the user is traveling on foot, and thus, is expected to move and perform the task at the same time. For this reason, we include walking as the third stress factor.

3.3   Investigation Metrics

As metrics that can be used in actual participatory sensing, we employ noninvasive data obtained from the device as follows.

Ratio of Correct Answers: In this experiment, we set a task in which the correct answer is uniquely determined; thus, the task answer rate is an index directly related to the reliability of the response. In this study, we hypothesized that the ratio of correct answers would change depending on the cognitive stress condition.

Answering Time: Stressed users rush through tasks, which results in lower task performance [18]. In this study, we hypothesized that the answering time would change depending on the given stress environment condition.

Table 1. Description of the devices used

Device	Main features
Smartphone (iPhone 11)	iOS 14.2
	6.1-in. touchscreen (1792×828 px)
	Accelerometer (100 Hz)
Large monitor	42-in.
Speaker (BOSE Companion 20)	30 W

Acceleration (User's Movement): Using data obtained from an accelerometer built into the device, we analyzed how and how much the user moves during the task in participatory sensing, as well as the effects of stressful environmental conditions on the user's movements. A related study [4] reported that stressed users tend to move more or suddenly, so we hypothesized that the user's movement would change depending on the given stress environment condition (e.g., variations in acceleration and angular acceleration data).

Screen Operation: We obtained smartphone screen operation logs (e.g., single-tap event, double-tap event, location on the screen touched) during task answering. Then, based on these logs, we analyzed the influence of stressful environmental conditions on screen operation. We hypothesized that the operation in the application would differ depending on the given stress environment condition.

4   Experiment

4.1   Experimental Outline

Based on the defined analytical framework, an experiment was conducted with 20 high school and graduate students (age range: 15–24 years, gender: 19 males, 1 female). This study was approved by the Ethical Review Committee for Research Involving Human Subjects at the Nara Institute of Science and Technology (Approval No.: 2020-I-16). Written informed consent was obtained from all participants before the study began.

In-the-wild experiments posed the following problems for this study: (1) it is difficult to align the experimental conditions in outdoor environments (e.g., the difficulty level of the task cannot be controlled), and (2) some cognitive stress environment conditions cannot be controlled (e.g., noise cannot be removed). Therefore, we decided to conduct the experiment by constructing an indoor virtual environment. We used a windowless laboratory ($21\,\mathrm{m}^2$) in a university as the experimental environment. A large monitor was used to display crowd images in a city, and virtual urban background noise was broadcast through several speakers. The details of the equipment used in the experiment are shown in Table 1. The experimental environment is shown in Fig. 2. For the crowd images used in the experiment, 24 photos were selected from the CityStreet dataset [23]. Figure 3 shows an example photo.

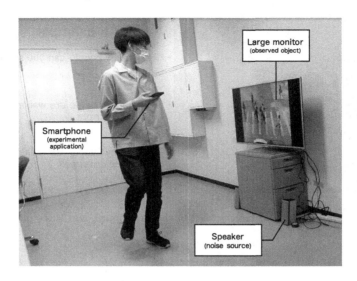

Fig. 2. Experimental environment

The specific task contents were set as follows according to the setting of the participatory sensing scenario in the analysis framework. These three questions are presented in a random order, and part of the question text (indicated by "⇔") is also presented randomly.

- How many people can you see in the photo?
- How many people are walking toward the "left" ⇔ "right"?
- How many people are walking "within" ⇔ "outside of" the crosswalk?

The cognitive stress conditions were presented as a set of $2^3 = 8$ patterns, as shown in Table 2. These are combinations of the presence and absence of three different stress items (i.e., time limit, noise, and walking) set in the analytical framework. The time limit was set at 10 s per question based on a preliminary survey of the time required to answer the above questions. We reproduced actual walking by marching in place in front of a large monitor so that it was always visible to the participants. To avoid order effects, these stress environment conditions were presented to the participants in random order.

4.2 Experimental Procedure

The experimental procedure is shown in Fig. 4 and below. The experiment, including the preceding explanations, took a total of about 30 min per participant.

Procedure 1) Preceding explanation to the participants

After entering the laboratory, the participants receive a briefing in advance. After explaining the outline and purpose of the study, the participants are

Fig. 3. Examples of crowd images used in the experiment and three questions [23]

Table 2. Obstructive factors

Pattern	Time limit	Noise	Walking
Pattern 0	✓	✓	✓
Pattern 1	✓	✓	–
Pattern 2	✓	–	✓
Pattern 3	✓	–	–
Pattern 4	–	✓	✓
Pattern 5	–	✓	–
Pattern 6	–	–	✓
Pattern 7	–	–	–

asked to fill out a consent form for participation in the study. Next, we explain the operation of the application to be used in the experiment (hereinafter referred to as the "experimental application"). Next, we explain the operation of the application used in the experiment (hereinafter referred to as the "experimental application") and ask the participants to try the task execution procedure once in the experimental application to become familiar with the operation. Finally, we explain the type of stress to be induced to the participants.

Procedure 2) Performing the task

The participant performs the participatory sensing task as instructed by the experimental application. The operation procedure in the experimental application is shown in Fig. 4 and below.

(A) Move to screen (B) by clicking the Pattern Display button. Resetting the order of the patterns and setting user IDs, which are for identifying each participant, are also done on this screen.

(B) The cognitive stress conditions for the trial are displayed. After confirming the cognitive stress conditions, the participant presses the Start button

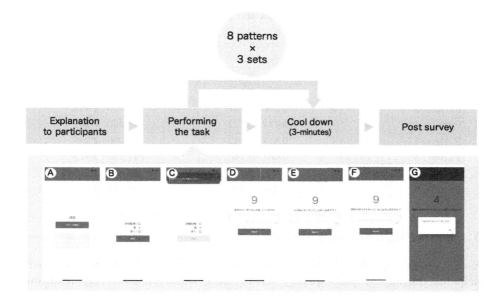

Fig. 4. Interface and operating procedure of the experimental application

to begin the experiment. Three seconds later, a notification from the experimental application is sent to the user's smartphone.

(C) Tap the notification message to go to screen (D).

(D–F) Task answer screen. When there is a time limit (time remaining), it is displayed as a red number. When the participant clicks the Submit button to submit his/her answer, the screen changes to the next. After answering the three tasks, the dialog shown in screen (G) is displayed.

(G) The Task Completion dialog box is displayed, and the experiment is completed. By clicking the OK button, the screen returns back to (A).

Procedure 3) Cool down

To prevent the effects of the previous stress conditions, a 3-minute rest period is provided after the completion of procedure 2).

Procedure 4) Repeat

Repeat procedures 2) and 3). In this experiment, three sets of eight patterns of cognitive stress conditions × were used, for a total of 24 trials.

Procedure 5) Post-survey

After all trials were completed, a post-survey was administered to the participants to provide a subjective assessment of the effects of the cognitive stress conditions on the participatory sensing task.

Table 3. Ratio of correct answers and answering time for each pattern

	Cognitive stress			Ratio of correct answers (%)		Answering time (s)	
	Time	Noise	Walking	Avg.	SD	Avg.	SD
Pattern 0	✓	✓	✓	0.667	0.149	17.767	2.575
Pattern 1	✓	✓	–	0.672	0.127	16.450	2.375
Pattern 2	✓	–	✓	0.656	0.101	17.150	2.443
Pattern 3	✓	–	–	0.711	0.122	16.400	2.205
Pattern 4	–	✓	✓	0.617	0.142	18.050	2.249
Pattern 5	–	✓	–	0.667	0.140	17.150	2.775
Pattern 6	–	–	✓	0.706	0.116	17.083	2.205
Pattern 7	–	–	–	0.706	0.136	17.417	2.189

5   Experimental Results

In this section, we present the results regarding the effects of stress on the participants during the participatory sensing task based on their responses and smartphone logs.

5.1   Analysis of Results

In this section, we present the results of the analysis of the evaluation indices. In this paper, only the results for the ratio of correct answers and answering time are discussed.

To examine the effects of the three types of stress items, a three-factor analysis of variance was conducted for each evaluation metric. To do so, we first averaged 480 data points (8 patterns × 20 people × 3 times) for each participant and obtained 160 data points (8 patterns × 20 people). A three-factor analysis of variance was then conducted based on the presence or absence of the three stress items (i.e., time limit, noise, walking). The mean values of the ratio of correct answers and answering time for each pattern are shown in Table 3.

The results of the analysis of variance confirmed that noise and walking stress showed a main effect (10% significance trend) on the ratio of correct answers. On the other hand, no interaction effect was found. These results indicate that the cognitive stresses of noise and walking cause differences in the ratio of correct answers. In other words, noise and walking stress degrade the ratio of correct answers.

Regarding answering time, we found main effects for walking (5% significance) and time limit (10% significance trend). In addition, we found an interaction (10% significance trend) of walking × noise. Therefore, we tested for a simple main effect of walking both with and without noise. We confirmed that, in the presence of noise stress, the presence of walking stress produces a significant difference (1% significance) in answering time.

These results indicate that walking and time-limit stresses lead to differences in answering time, i.e., walking and time-limit stresses lead to longer and shorter

Table 4. Post-experiment questionnaire results (Did these cognitive stress conditions hinder or affect your responses?)

	Cognitive stress			Choices				Average score
	Time	Noise	Walking	Never (1)	Not Very often (2)	Some of The time (3)	Most of The time (4)	
Pattern 0	✓	✓	✓	0 (0.0%)	1 (5.0%)	11 (55.0%)	8 (40.0%)	3.4
Pattern 1	✓	✓	–	1 (5.0%)	1 (5.0%)	15 (75.0%)	3 (15.0%)	3.0
Pattern 2	✓	–	✓	0 (0.0%)	4 (20.0%)	14 (70.0%)	2 (10.0%)	2.9
Pattern 3	✓	–	–	3 (15.0%)	8 (40.0%)	8 (40.0%)	1 (5.0%)	2.4
Pattern 4	–	✓	✓	3 (15.0%)	8 (40.0%)	8 (40.0%)	1 (5.0%)	2.4
Pattern 5	–	✓	–	9 (45.0%)	6 (30.0%)	5 (25.0%)	0 (0.0%)	1.8
Pattern 6	–	–	✓	6 (30.0%)	10 (50.0%)	3 (15.0%)	1 (5.0%)	2.0
Pattern 7	–	–	–	20 (100.0%)	0 (0.0%)	0 (0.0%)	0 (0.0%)	1.0

answering times, respectively. In addition, the results of a simple main effect test for walking × noise indicated that stress due to walking increases the answering time in the presence of stress due to noise.

We also analyzed the acceleration and screen operation logs in the same way, and found no correlations.

5.2   Analysis of Results of the Post-survey (Subjective Evaluation)

The results of the post-survey answered by the participants are shown in Table 4. The numbers below the column "Choices" indicate the number of respondents for each answer. In addition, the average of all respondents' answers is shown as "Average score" (1: no disturbance/effect – 4: great disturbance/effect). The higher the score, the more the cognitive stress conditions hindered or affected the responses.

As a result, we confirmed high scores of 3.4, 3.0, and 2.9 for Pattern 0 with all stresses, Pattern 1 with time-limit and noise stresses, and Pattern 2 with time-limit and walking stresses, respectively. In addition, we confirmed that the score decreased with the relaxation of the cognitive stress condition.

For each of the patterns 0 to 7, we asked the question *"Why did you think so?"*. Some of the collected answers are shown below.

- Pattern 0 (time limit, noise, walking)
  - The noise did not affect me much. Walking was a hindrance because of the increased eye movement. If the time limit were shorter, I might have been impatient.
  - I had to pay attention to the time limit, noise, and walking.
  - I felt a little distracted by the noise. It was a little difficult to count the number of people while walking because my vision was being shaken.
- Pattern 1 (time limit, noise, no walking)
  - I felt a sense of urgency because of the time limit and my concentration was hampered by the noise.
  - The time limit made me feel impatient. The noise was not a good feeling.
  - When counting a large number of people, the time limit made me panic. The noise did not bother me much.
- Pattern 2 (time limit, no noise, walking)
  - The eye movement takes a little time, so I thought it would have a slight effect.
  - When I counted a large number of people, I was in a hurry when there was a time limit. I was not bothered by the walking movements.
  - I feel impatient and the display was difficult to see.
- Pattern 3 (time limit, no noise, no walking)
  - Since there was no sound or walking, I was able to answer calmly despite the time limit.
  - There was relatively enough time to answer the questions, and it did not disturb my concentration.
  - I was not bothered when there were only a few people to count, but when there were many, I panicked.
- Pattern 4 (no time limit, noise, walking)
  - With noise and walking, I felt like I was using both my body and my brain.
  - Even if there were no time limit, I would not be able to tell how many people were counted in my head because of the noise. However, walking did not affect me much.
- Pattern 5 (no time limit, noise, no walking)
  - It was difficult to know how many people were counted when there was noise.
  - Because there was no time limit, I could count the number of people calmly. The noise did not bother me much.
- Pattern 6 (no time limit, no noise, walking)
  - I did not feel rushed because there were no restrictions other than moving.
  - Because there was no time limit, I could count the number of people calmly. I don't think the inclusion of walking movements had much of an impact.
- Pattern 7 (no time limit, no noise, no walking)
  - I was able to answer the questions carefully because there was nothing to interrupt me.

- Since there were no restrictions at all, I felt that it was most relaxing both mentally and physically.

As a whole, the respondents said that it was difficult for them to concentrate on answering when multiple cognitive stress conditions overlapped. When the number of people in the photo was small, the time limit did not bother them, but when the number of people in the photo was large, they felt rushed. As for the noise, the participants commented that it affected their answers because they felt it hindered their concentration. As for the cognitive stress caused by walking, the participants commented that it did not bother them as much as usual because it was an experimental environment and safety was taken into consideration. In future experiments, we would like to devise ways to present safe obstacles.

5.3   Discussion

The results of the present experiment and post-survey suggest that combinations of task types and obstructive factors cause different cognitive stresses. In this paper, we assumed that obstructive factors induce emotional effects such as impatience and restlessness. However, the results indicated that these factors also cause changes in task difficulty. For example, the task of crowd counting during walking requires paying more attention compared with a normal situation because the user needs to stabilize their gaze. The increase in cognitive costs for performing given tasks might result in careless responses. In future work, we will organize component elements of cognitive stress and investigate their relationships with obstructive factors.

6   Conclusion

This study aimed to investigate the effects of environmental factors on the response reliability of participatory sensing by inducing different cognitive stress conditions on the user during the execution of participatory sensing tasks.

In addition, we conducted a subjective evaluation of the effects of the cognitive stress conditions on the participatory sensing task after the experiment. The results revealed that the participants felt that combinations of multiple cognitive stress conditions hindered or affected their task responses.

The results of this experiment revealed that stress affects the ratio of correct answers and answering times, even in a safe indoor experimental environment, which suggests that users may feel more stress in actual participatory sensing. In the future, this hypothesis will be confirmed through experiments in scenarios similar to real environments.

References

1. Arakawa, Y., Matsuda, Y.: Gamification mechanism for enhancing a participatory urban sensing: survey and practical results. J. Inf. Process. **57**(1), 31–38 (2016). https://doi.org/10.2197/ipsjjip.24.31

2. Borromeo, R.M., Laurent, T., Toyama, M.: The influence of crowd type and task complexity on crowdsourced work quality. In: Proceedings of the 20th International Database Engineering and Applications Symposium, pp. 70–76 (2016)
3. Burke, J.A., et al.: Participatory sensing. Workshop on World-Sensor-Web (2006)
4. Carneiro, D., Castillo, J.C., Novais, P., Fernández-Caballero, A., Neves, J.: Multimodal behavioral analysis for non-invasive stress detection. Expert Syst. Appl. **39**(18), 13376–13389 (2012)
5. Gil, Y., Michel, F., Ratnakar, V., Hauder, M., Duffy, C., Dugan, H., Hanson, P.: A task-centered framework for computationally-grounded science collaborations. In: 2015 IEEE 11th International Conference on e-Science, pp. 352–361. IEEE (2015)
6. Goel, M., Findlater, L., Wobbrock, J.: Walktype: using accelerometer data to accomodate situational impairments in mobile touch screen text entry. In: Proceedings of the SIGCHI Conference on Human Factors in Computing Systems, pp. 2687–2696 (2012)
7. Gogami, M., Matsuda, Y., Arakawa, Y., Yasumoto, K.: Detection of careless responses in online surveys using answering behavior on smartphone. IEEE Access **9**, 53205–53218 (2021)
8. Krosnick, J.A.: Response strategies for coping with the cognitive demands of attitude measures in surveys. Appl. Cognit. Psychol. **5**(3), 213–236 (1991)
9. Li, Q., Ma, F., Gao, J., Su, L., Quinn, C.J.: Crowdsourcing high quality labels with a tight budget. In: Proceedings of the Ninth ACM International Conference on Web Search and Data Mining, pp. 237–246 (2016)
10. Maniaci, M.R., Rogge, R.D.: Caring about carelessness: participant inattention and its effects on research. J. Res. Personal. **48**, 61–83 (2014)
11. Mao, A., Kamar, E., Chen, Y., Horvitz, E., Schwamb, M.E., Lintott, C.J., Smith, A.M.: Volunteering versus work for pay: incentives and tradeoffs in crowdsourcing. In: First AAAI Conference on Human Computation and Crowdsourcing (2013)
12. Mason, W., Suri, S.: Conducting behavioral research on amazon's mechanical turk. Behav. Res. Methods **44**(1), 1–23 (2012)
13. Mason, W., Watts, D.J.: Financial incentives and the" performance of crowds". In: Proceedings of the ACM SIGKDD Workshop on Human Computation, pp. 77–85 (2009)
14. Miura, A., Kobayashi, T.: Exploring tips to detect "satisficing" in an online survey: a study using university student samples. Japanese J. Soc. Psychol. **32**(2), 123–132 (2016). 10.14966/jssp.0932. (in Japanese)
15. Miura, A., Kobayashi, T.: Influence of satisficing on online survey responses. Japanese J. Behav. **45**, 1–11 (2018). (in Japanese)
16. Rubya, S., Numainville, J., Yarosh, S.: Comparing generic and community-situated crowdsourcing for data validation in the context of recovery from substance use disorders. In: Proceedings of the 2021 CHI Conference on Human Factors in Computing Systems, pp. 1–17 (2021)
17. Sağbaş, E.A., Korukoglu, S., Balli, S.: Stress detection via keyboard typing behaviors by using smartphone sensors and machine learning techniques. J. Med. Syst. **44**(4), 1–12 (2020)
18. Sarsenbayeva, Z., et al.: Measuring the effects of stress on mobile interaction. Proceed. ACM Interactive Mobile Wearable Ubiquit. Technol. **3**(1), 1–18 (2019)
19. Sarsenbayeva, Z., van Berkel, N., Luo, C., Kostakos, V., Goncalves, J.: Challenges of situational impairments during interaction with mobile devices. In: Proceedings of the 29th Australian Conference on Computer-Human Interaction, pp. 477–481 (2017)

20. Sarsenbayeva, Z., van Berkel, N., Velloso, E., Kostakos, V., Goncalves, J.: Effect of distinct ambient noise types on mobile interaction. Proceed. ACM Interact. Mobile Wearable Ubiquit. Technol. **2**(2), 1–23 (2018)
21. Schildbach, B., Rukzio, E.: Investigating selection and reading performance on a mobile phone while walking. In: Proceedings of the 12th International Conference on Human Computer Interaction with Mobile Devices and Services, pp. 93–102 (2010)
22. Simon, H.A.: Rational choice and the structure of the environment. Psychol. Rev. **63**(2), 129 (1956)
23. Zhang, Q., Chan, A.B.: Wide-area crowd counting: multi-view fusion networks for counting in large scenes. arXiv preprint arXiv:2012.00946 (2020)

Design and Implementation of an Online and Cost-Effective Attendance Management System Using Smartphones and Cloud Services

M. Fahim Ferdous Khan$^{(\boxtimes)}$, Taisei Yamazaki, and Ken Sakamura

Faculty of Information Networking and Design (INIAD), Toyo University, Tokyo, Japan
{khan,ken}@sakamura-lab.org, s1f101701823@iniad.org

Abstract. Taking attendance in schools is an important daily activity which is directly related to students' academic performance. Traditional roll-call-based or signature-based approaches for attendance keeping are cumbersome, time consuming, and susceptible to manual errors and fraudulent maneuvers. With a view to digitalizing the process of taking and maintaining attendance record, in this paper, we present a distributed approach to attendance management using smartphones and cloud computing web services that offer high degree security and scalability. The main objective in developing the proposed attendance management system has been an implementation that does not rely on any dedicated infrastructure, and hence reduces cost as much as possible, enabling a wide range of organizations regardless of size and budgetary constraints to adopt such a system. It goes without saying that such cost reduction is inherently associated with some trade-offs which are also discussed in the paper.

Keywords: Attendance management system · Cloud services · Identity management · Application programming interface

1 Introduction

Grand initiatives like Industry 4.0 [19] and Society 5.0 [20] are proliferating at national, regional, or international levels. These endeavors aim at merging cyberspace and physical space by creating a super-smart and highly automated society. As we march toward making such visions a reality, different services that we experience on a day-to-day basis are going through rapid digital transformation. These services encompass all basic sectors of the society including administration, finance, health, and education. In the education sector, school attendance has traditionally been recorded by roll or name calls by instructors, or by having the students sign on a piece of paper that is passed around the class. Such manual and paper-based techniques are time consuming and prone to human errors. In large classrooms, there may also be problems of proxy attendance. Hence, significant amount of effort has been devoted to automating the process of taking attendance. In many affluent universities, students are provided with ID cards equipped with built-in integrated circuits. Such ID cards can be read by a card reader

T. Hara and H. Yamaguchi (Eds.): MobiQuitous 2021, LNICST 419, pp. 650–664, 2022.
https://doi.org/10.1007/978-3-030-94822-1_42

installed in classrooms, and hence students' attendance can be recorded. Unfortunately, many universities cannot afford such expensive systems. Therefore, there is a need for a cost-effective attendance management system which does not rely on a dedicated infrastructure. On this premise, in this paper, we present the design and implementation of a cost-effective attendance management system using smartphones and cloud service. The system is implemented using user (student) smartphones in combination with near-field communication (NFC) readable cards and Amazon Web Services (AWS). In order to make the system as cost-effective as possible, the focus has been on using already available components. Smartphones enjoy a high degree of penetration rate all over the world [21]. For the NFC readable cards, any general-purpose IC card or smartcard can be used, including the ones that are widely used for accessing public transportation in many parts of the world.

The rest of this paper is organized as follows. Section 2 discusses the major attendance management systems reported in the literature. Section 3 introduces our proposed attendance management system, and Sect. 4 explains its design and implementation. Section 5 evaluates our system and compares it merits and demerits to those of other systems. Finally, Sect. 6 concludes the paper.

2 Related Work

Different mechanisms have been proposed in order to automate the attendance management systems. Most of the approaches found in the literature can be categorized in one of the four approaches discussed below.

2.1 Smartphone-Based Attendance Management Systems

Noor et al. proposed an attendance management system for the purpose of contributing to paperless management, preventing data loss due to loss of paper records, and minimizing the cost of systemization [1]. This system scans and registers the student data in an online database which the class teacher can later download from a designated web server. Assuming that the teacher's smartphone is Android, no additional cost for hardware is required. It is necessary to install the apk file on the teacher's Android device. After launching the application with ID and password to log in, the app can scan student ID cards using the built-in camera of the smartphone. The fact that the faculty member can check the student ID card one by one using this system can be expected to be effective in preventing fraud, but it is also time-consuming and labor intensive. Smartcard is often used as an important component in many of the other system reported below.

2.2 RFID-Based Attendance Management Systems

A number of attendance management system for schools and workplaces using RFID technology have been proposed in the literature [2–5]. The basic idea is to have the students or employees carry some sort of RFID tag and read those by a reader installed in front of the entrance of classroom or event space. The read data is collected in a database from where administrators can access attendance record using web interfaces.

2.3 Bluetooth-Based Attendance Management Systems

Approaches based on Bluetooth communication have also been proposed [6, 7]. These approaches rely on the ability of an application installed on the instructor's mobile phone to query students' mobile phones to confirm their attendance. Such Bluetooth communication-based systems can also be used in combination with RFID [6].

2.4 Biometrics-Based Attendance Management Systems

As strong and definitive indicators of identity, biometrics have been incorporated in attendance management systems. Several biometrics-based systems are reported. Examples include fingerprint-based systems [8, 9], iris-recognition-based systems [10, 11], and face-recognition-based systems [12–14]. All of these rely on special hardware to read biometric data and analyze those using pattern recognition or deep-learning algorithms.

3   Overview of the Proposed Attendance Management System

The components of our proposed attendance management system are as follows. (1) FeliCa-based contactless smartcards that are commonly used for accessing public transport. For example, in Japan – where this research is based – Suica [24] or Pasmo [25] cards are widely used by commuters. In many other metropolitan areas of the world similar smartcards are used. Each FeliCa card has a unique 8-byte Manufature ID (IDm) [15] which is used as an important piece of information in our system. (2) Smartphone: iPhone is used in our implementation, but Android phones can also be used. (3) Amazon Web Services (AWS) [16] is used for storage and manipulation of attendance record.

The system sends an HTTP request to AWS together with JSON data using the POST method and records it in the database by program processing. This record serves as the attendance record of a student. The JSON data requires student ID, email address, name, operation code, and IDm. The iOS shortcuts app was used as a means to send HTTP requests. The AWS services that are used in the system are Lambda, DynamoDB, API Gateway, IAM, and S3. For the programming language of Lambda Python 3.8 was used.

It is necessary to read the FeliCa card with the reader application in advance to extract its IDm. In our implementation, we used an application called "Japan NFC Reader-Card Reader" [17] which can be downloaded from Apple App Store for free. Alternatively, a password and hash value can be used.

As discussed later in Sect. 4, this system has three functions: Register, Attend, and Check. Students can switch functions by using different operation codes.

Case-1: Using iPhone. We use the Shortcuts app provided by iOS 12.0 or higher [23]. This application has a *shortcut* function that allows one to freely customize a process by combining actions. A shortcut created this way can also be configured to be automatically triggered by an event; this phenomenon is called automation. Our implementation utilizes this automation function. When an IC card is touched on the upper-back side of an iPhone, the NFC reader reads the card and sends an HTTP request with JSON data to the set URL and receives a response. For multiple lessons, it is also necessary to have a screen that allows the user to select for which lesson to send the request to. Figure 1(a) shows

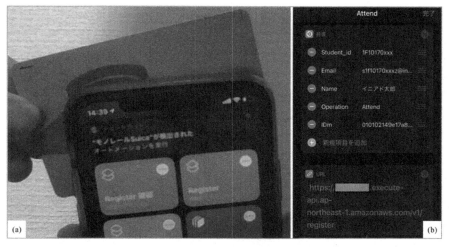

Fig. 1. (a) Touching Suica card on the iPhone's NFC reader and using the automation function of iOS Shortcuts app, (b) Information sent as attendance record includes student ID, e-mail, name, operation and IDm of the smartcard (in this example Suica) used

how IC card is touched on the iPhone and the shortcut is called using the automation function, and it is executed by tapping the banner at the top. Figure 1(b) shows what information is sent for the "Attend" operation.

Case-2: Using Android-Based Phone. Our system employs a method of sending HTTP requests to AWS from a student's personal device, assuming that the iOS Shortcuts app is used on the iPhone, but the same can be done on Android. An application called "HTTP Request Shortcuts" is available for free from the Google Play Store [18]. JSON data can be sent at the time of request and saved as a shortcut.

4 Design and Implementation

Now, referring to Fig. 2 and 3, we explain in detail how the different AWS components work together to realize the proposed attendance management system. We also explain how the attendance information can be handled by faculty members.

4.1 AWS API Gateway

The API Gateway issues a URL and connects an incoming HTTP request to another service. In this system, a URL for students to send is created as a REST API, and it functions as an API for operating Lambda, which will be described later in this section. This service uses resources, functions, deployment stages, and resource policies. A resource becomes a part of the URL, and if multiple resources are created, multiple services can be linked to one API simply by changing a part of the URL. To prevent complications in the proposed system, we created only "register" as a resource. Methods

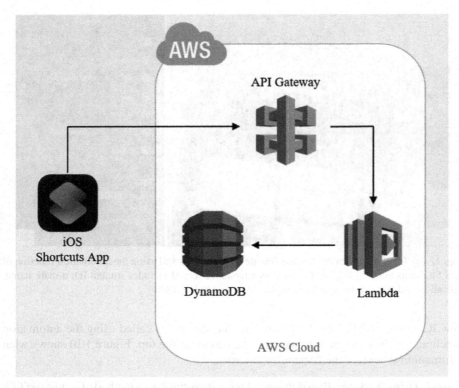

Fig. 2. The main AWS components utilized in the proposed attendance management system

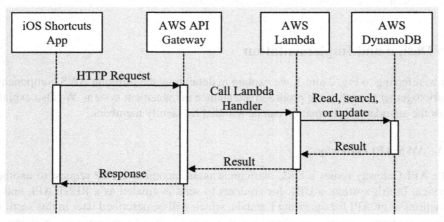

Fig. 3. Sequence diagram depicting the interaction between iOS Shortcuts app and major AWS components

can also be set for each resource, but only POST was created. Resource policy plays the most important role in this service. In attendance management systems via the Internet, in order to prevent fraud, it is necessary to limit from where students can send HTTP requests. The resource policy can control access to the API and is registered as JSON data. Since this system is premised on sending HTTP requests from the university, we adopted a whitelist type that accepts only the global IP address of the campus network where VPN blocking is enabled. Requests are rejected if the student is not connected to campus Wi-Fi.

4.2 AWS DynamoDB

DynamoDB is a NoSQL database on AWS. This system creates at least two tables: Student_info and Virtual_lecture. Assuming that the number of lessons is N, the number of tables needs to be N + 1 (i.e., N separate tables for N lectures). The rest of the explanation assumes that there is only one lecture, and hence two tables.

The Student_info table includes the following *attributes* (akin to *field* in relational database): Student_id (String, Partition key), Email (String, Sort key), Course (String), Grade (Number), Name (String), IDm (String). The Virtual_lecture table includes the following attributes: Student_id (String, Partition key), Email (String, Sort key), Class_id (String)Name (String), ClassData (Number). The combination of partition key and sort key is referred to as *composite primary key* in DynamoDB.

The attribute specified in the key is the information that Lambda needs to access the database. By specifying multiple attributes as keys, erroneous registration can be prevented if one is detected as incorrect.

```
Key = {
        'Student_id': student_id,
        'Email': email
}
```

There is also a function called Item Explorer that allows one to search for items in the table by entering the partition key or sort key. It is useful for large classes or when data need to be looked up immediately.

4.3 AWS IAM

IAM (Identity and Access Management) is a service that allows to create roles by attaching policies. Roles assign and authorize other services when they are created. In this system, Lambda needs permission to operate on DynamoDB, so "AmazonDynamoDB-FullAccess", and "AWSLambdaDynamoDBExecutionRole" are set so that Lambda has permission to fully access DynamoDB and update data. In addition, various policies are prepared depending on the application. For example, if read-only access is desired, the privilege level can be set to "AmazonDynamoDBReadOnlyAccess".

656   M. F. F. Khan et al.

4.4 AWS Lambda

The python program for the handler function is contained in AWS Lambda. The handler function is called after passing through the API Gateway whitelist type IP address filter. The transmitted JSON data is stored in the dictionary object event. The three functions are called according to the extracted operation code. The following example is a part of the program that refers to the operation code contained in event and acquires other data as well.

```
operation = event ['Operation']
```

The days and times when classes are held are stored in a data structure. For example, in the case of the class in the 3rd period on Friday, the combination of (day (str type), time (int type)) is ("Fri", 3). Requests are accepted only on the days of the week when classes are held.

There are four functions using which Lambda operates on DynamoDB: put_item, get_item, update_item, and delete_item. When executed, a response is returned with the HTTP status code, so a student can check whether the data operation was successful by referring to the status code and confirming that it is 200.

When DynamoDB operation is performed, metadata is returned, which is long and unnecessary for the students, and difficult to see on smartphones. Therefore, the response returned to students are formatted to include are HTTPStatusCode, Message, and other data for keeping the amount of information to a minimum.

Next, we discuss the three main functions provided by our attendance management system: Register, Attend and Check. These functions are defined in a file name lambda_function.py.

Register Function. Students must first register their information to the attendance management system, and the JSON data mentioned above must be saved in the Student_info table. For this initial registration, "Register" is specified in the operation code when sending an HTTP request. Only the grade is Number type, and the other attributes are String type, and these attributes saved using the put_item function. Among these, the student ID number is the partition key and the email address is the sort key. Data other than the operation code is updated for each execution. If the FeliCa card used is changed, the IDm is read again, and the database is updated using this function with the new IDm. The response includes the HTTP status code, message, and registered data. Definition of the Register function using put_item function is shown below as an example.

```
def operation_register(student_id, course, email, grade, name, idm):
    Response = student.put_item(
        Item = {
            'Student_id': student_id,
            'Course': course,
            'Email': email,
            'Grade': grade,
            'Name': name,
            'IDm': idm,
        }
    )
```

Attend Function. This function is used by students to register attendance information. The table that is updated is called Virtual_lecture, and information is saved on a class-by-class basis. Students specify "Attend" as the operation code. There are some conditions for this function to register attendance information in the database, and it is executed only when all of them are satisfied. Processing and determination of conditions are performed in the following order.

1) If the operation code is Attend, immediately save the date and time in the variable Datetime, and check that day of the week matches the day of the week when the class is held. If the day of the week is different, there will be no lessons and the request will be invalidated.
2) Execute the operation_attend function. Pass the student ID number, email address, name, request date and time, class time limit, and IDm as arguments.
3) Generate a key for registering in DynamoDB from the request date and time using the strftime function and save it in the variable Class_today. The format is "Class_yyyymmdd". For example, if the request date and time is December 23, 2020, then Class_today = Class_20201223.
4) Execute the timecmp function of the timetable.py module described later in this section. The lambda_function.py program imports this timetable.py module. Compare the time when the request was received with the reception start time, class start time, and the time when lateness is recognized for each class period (set to 20 min after the class start time in our implementation). A numerical attendance score is returned as follows. Normal attendance is 2, late arrival is 1, absenteeism is 0. However, if the request time is earlier than the acceptance start time, error code -1 is returned, the function is interrupted, and the request is invalidated.
5) Specify the student ID number and email address as keys from the Student_info table, and retrieve the data. If these two keys are correct, the data can be retrieved as an "Item" (akin to "row" in relational database). If there is an error, there is no corresponding data, so nothing is entered in the as attributes of "Item". In such cases, error code -2 is returned, and the request is invalidated.
6) Similarly, it is determined whether the IDm registered in the Student_info table and the IDm of the JSON data at the time of HTTP request match. If they are different, error code -3 is returned, and the request is invalidated.

7) Extract the data of the Virtual_lecture table. At the first execution, there is no student data in the Virtual_lecture table and the "Item" is None (i.e., empty table), so create a new "Item" using put_item method. The registered data refer to the JSON data when the HTTP request is sent. ClassData that records attendance information is initialized in a dictionary type object and recorded for each date and time corresponding to each class period. If the response is not 200, error code -4 is returned, the request is invalidated, and a message is returned to the user asking him to retry.

8) Try to register attendance information in the Virtual_lecture table using the try-except statement. If the ConditionExpression parameter is set in the update_item function that updates the database, the update will be executed according to the UpdateExpression parameter when the condition is matched. This condition specifies that "attendance information on the day of class does not exist in the database". Without this condition check, if multiple requests are sent, the last request will be overwritten. Since the attendance score is calculated at this point, there is a possibility that the score will decrease, such as the one with 2 recorded in normal attendance becoming 1 as late attendance. If this condition is not met, an exception occurs because attendance information has already been registered. Accordingly, the request is invalidated. The next two lines of code are a part of the program code that creates the ConditionExpression and UpdateExpression parameters.

```
condition_text = 'attribute_not_exists(ClassData.{})'.format(Class_today)
update_text = 'set ClassData.{}=:s'.format(Class_today)
```

(The ': s' part of update_text refers to the variable score.)

When the above conditions 1,4,5,6,7,8 are matched, it is saved as a dictionary object in ClassData of Virtual_lecture. The value of Class_today in step 3 is important. Based on this, the attendance score is calculated in step 4. As shown in Fig. 4(a), the response returns the HTTP status code, message, name, class name, and time accepted by AWS.

Check Function. After submitting attendance, students may want to check whether their attendance was properly recorded or not. The Check function serves this purpose. This function allows checking of the registration status of attendance information from the database for each class registered with the Attend function mentioned above. For IDm authentication, specify the student ID number and email address as keys from the Student_info table and retrieve them with get_item. If the two keys are different, error code − 2 is returned, and if the IDm is different, error code − 3 is returned to invalidate the request. If there is no error, the requested data are fetched from the Virtual_lecture table by the get_item function in the same way, and the database information, message, and HTTP status code are returned. Figure 4(b) shows the result of executing the Check function.

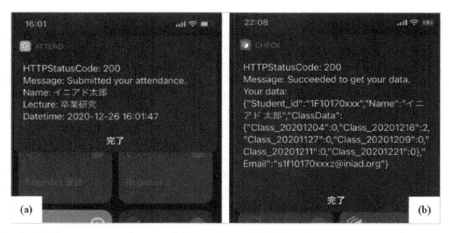

Fig. 4. (a) Screen output of successful attendance submission, (b) screen output of attendance check function

4.5 Time Comparison Method

The timetable.py module contains the class timetable and timecmp function. In the timetable, the reception start time of each time period, the class start time, and the time when lateness is recognized can be referred to in a dictionary type object. In our implementation, the reception start time is set to 30 min before the 1st and 3rd periods and 15 min before the 2nd, 4th, 5th and 6th periods. The timecmp function takes two parameters: the time when the request was received by AWS and the class period corresponding to the day of the week, and outputs a score by comparing it with the reception start time according to the timetable. If a request is received before the reception start time, -1 is returned and the request is invalidated. As mentioned before, normal attendance, late attendance and absenteeism are given a scores of 2, 1, and 0 respectively.

4.6 Handling of Attendance Data by Faculty Member

If faculty members want to organize attendance data at the end of the semester, DynamoDB data can be uploaded to Amazon S3 and downloaded locally. Amazon S3 is a cloud storage service where S3 means Simple Storage Service. In S3, one group is called a bucket, and it is created by giving it a name. A folder can be created in it. In our implementation, the bucket name is univ-attend, and a virtual_class folder is created in it. Folders for other classes can be created in the bucket in the same way. Next, the data from the DynamoDB Virtual_lecture table to the S3 virtual_class folder can be exported. The detailed procedure is as follows.

1) Select the Virtual_lecture table from the DynamoDB console and select Streams and Exports.
2) Select Export to S3 to browse or enter your destination S3 bucket. For example, "s3://univ-attend/virtual_class/".

3) Choose the S3 bucket owner. Make additional settings. Set export, file format, and encryption key type from a specific point in time or current time in the last 35 days. Select the current time, DynamoDB JSON, and Amazon S3 key, respectively, and select "Export" to export to S3.

4) Download the data locally from S3. A json.gz file is created in univ-attend/virtual_class/AWSDynamoDB /******/data, so select it, download it, and unzip it using the gunzip command. The ****** part is automatically assigned to a unique number when exported. The unzipped JSON file contains student attendance data.

Alternatively, any table can be directly downloaded as a csv file from DynamoDB console, but we have experienced formatting and encoding issues in files downloaded in this way especially if the table contains entries written in non-roman characters.

5 Evaluation

We tested the behavior of the proposed system in order to verify whether it can prevent unauthorized attendance and incorrect registration.

5.1 Testing

For verifying the correctness of operation of the system, the following six cases are considered.

Access from Off-Campus Network. The API Gateway resource policy described earlier rejects HTTP requests from locations other than the university. Figure 5(a) shows a request when the connection with Wi-Fi is disconnected. Access from the 4G network, for example (in the upper right of the image) is not allowed. VPN blocking is enabled.

Requests When There is no Class. Requests on days/times when there are no class are rejected. Figure 5(b) shows a request on a non-class day.

Incoming Requests Before the Reception Time. In our implementation, reception is 30 min (1st and 3rd period) or 15 min (2nd, 4th, 5th and 6th period) before the class start time. Any request before the reception time is rejected. Figure 5(c) shows a message informing a student that the reception time has not started yet.

Requests with Incorrect Key Specification. When searching or updating the DynamoDB database with Lambda, it cannot be accessed if the key specification is incorrect. In our system, the partition key is assigned to Student_id and the sort key is assigned to Email attribute. If either is incorrect, the desired item cannot be found. Figure 5(d) shows the message when the keys are incorrect.

Request with Incorrect IDm. The IDm is required when using the three functions, but if it is incorrect, the request is rejected. Figure 5(e) shows a message when the IDm is different from what is expected, prompting the student to confirm.

Multiple Requests. After the first successful request, subsequent requests are rejected in order to prevent the score from being overwritten (Fig. 5(f)).

Fig. 5. (a) Screen output for (a) request from off-campus network, (b) request for non-existent class, (c) request before class reception time, (d) request with incorrect key, (e) request with incorrect IDm, and (f) multiple request

5.2 Discussion

Our proposed attendance management system does not require any dedicated hardware or infrastructure. Smartphones are part and parcel of modern day-to-day life. FeliCa-based cards are also used widely by commuters in many cities. In the attendance management system, students can use the same FeliCa card they use for commuting. Services of AWS is not free, but it is not expensive either as long as requests are as simple as the ones used in our system. The cost incurred for AWS provides reliability, security and scalability as AWS services are fully managed by Amazon Inc. It can be argued that using cloud services is a better option rather than storing data in enterprise's own local servers considering management and maintenance issues.

One drawback of our system is that it cannot recognize the precise location of the student. It relies on requests coming from university network (with VPN blocking), so a student who may not be in the classroom can still be able to register attendance from somewhere else in the campus as long as he is connected to the campus Wi-Fi. Approaches that use GPS tracking also has the same problem as GPS measurement is not precise. This problem cannot be solved without introducing other components in the system, such as RFID or Bluetooth where physical proximity to the venue is required, for which additional hardware (reader, Bluetooth-enabled tag, or microcontroller as a separate token) and/or Bluetooth facility on mobile phones, is necessary. Other systems which are based on biometrics recognition are inherently expensive as dedicated hardware have to be purchased. These approaches are privacy-invasive as well. Moreover, the reader areas can get congested and may introduce a single point of failure in the system. On the other hand, our system takes a more distributed approach as students can register their attendance from anywhere in the class.

Preventing colluding students is also a challenge in our proposed system. A student may give his card to another student who can act as a proxy. To counter this, IMEI associated with each smartphone can be made a part of the request. Even with this addition, it is not completely secure, as – however unlikely it might be – a student can give his smartphone to his proxy. Therefore, in essence, the NFC readable card acts only as a week layer of security in the form of IDm check. To make it foolproof, smartcards based on asymmetric key cryptography approach would be necessary. For example, our eTRON architecture [22] can be used. This will incorporate a slight time lag in the processing of request, and an additional burden for managing cryptographic services. Such highly secure mechanisms are indeed necessary for critical operations, especially the ones involving financial transactions and sensitive private information, but we argue that they are not so important for a cost-effective attendance management system.

From a faculty member's perspective, the most important benefit of our system is that it can completely offload the burden of attendance management from him. He just has to download the attendance record from DynamoDB once or a few times in the semester. This will enable him to focus solely on planning and delivering lectures as attendance records are sent by students' own initiative. To summarize, the main contribution of this paper lies in implementing an attendance management system that uses devices and components that the user already owns, effectively eliminating any cost for additional infrastructure. Properties of the user-owned components are utilized in a systematic manner to manage attendance record leveraging fully managed and highly scalable AWS services.

6   Conclusion

In this paper, we have explained the design and implementation of an online attendance management system that utilizes students' smartphones, general-purpose FeliCa-based smartcards and cloud services. The system prevents fraudulent attendance by using techniques like identity management and IP address filtering. It can recognize three different levels of attendance, namely, in-time attendance, late attendance, and non-attendance. The system is cost-effective as it does not require any dedicated hardware or infrastructure to be implemented. It is also distributed in nature as students do not have to pass through any dedicated reader area which can often be congested. The trade-offs associated with our proposed system are also discussed in the paper. In short, we believe our system strikes a good balance between performance and cost-effectiveness.

References

1. Noor, S.A.M., Zaini, N., Latip, M.F.A., Hamzah, N.: Android-based attendance management system. In: IEEE Conference on Systems, Process and Control (ICSPC), pp. 118–122 (2015)
2. Koppikar, U., Hiremath, S., Shiralkar A., Rajoor, A., Baligar, V. P.: IoT based smart attendance monitoring system using RFID. In: 1st International Conference on Advances in Information Technology (ICAIT), pp. 193–197 (2019)
3. Nainan, S., Parekh, R., Shah, T.: RFID Technology Based Attendance Management System. Int. J. Comput. Sci. Iss. 10(1) (2013). https://arxiv.org/ftp/arxiv/papers/1306/1306.5381.pdf, Accessed 20 Jan 2022
4. Maramis, G.D.P., Rompas, P.T.D.: Radio frequency identification (RFID) based employee attendance management system. In: 2nd International Conference on Innovation in Engineering and Vocational Education (2017). https://iopscience.iop.org/article/10.1088/1757-899X/306/1/012045/pdf. Accessed 20 Jan 2022
5. Shengli, K., Jun, Z., Guang, S., Chunhong, W., Wenpei, Z., Tao, L.: the design and implementation of the attendance management system based on radio frequency identification technology. In: International Conference on Electronic Science and Automation Control, pp. 189–192 (2015)
6. Lodha, R., Gupta, S., Jain, H., Narula, H.: Bluetooth smart based attendance management system. In: International Conference on Advanced Computing Technologies and Applications (ICACTA), pp. 524–527 (2015)
7. Bhalla, V., Singla, T., Gahlot, A., Gupta, V.: Bluetooth based attendance management system. Int. J. Innov. Eng. Technol. (IJIET) 3(1), 227–233 (2013)
8. Mittal, Y., Varshney, A., Aggarwal, P., Matani, K., Mittal, V.K.: Fingerprint biometric based access control and classroom attendance management system. In: Annual IEEE India Conference (INDICON), pp. 1–6 (2015)
9. Adetiba, E., Iortim, O., Olajide, A.T., Awoseyin, R.: OBCAMS: an online biometrics-based class attendance management system. African J. Comput. ICT 6(3), 25–38 (2013)
10. Seifedine, K., Smaili, M.: Wireless attendance management system based on iris recognition. Sci. Res. Essays 5(12), 1428–1435 (2013)
11. Khatun, A., Haque, A.K.M.F., Ahmed, S., Rahman, M.M.: Design and implementation of iris recognition based attendance management system. In: International Conference on Electrical Engineering and Information Communication Technology (ICEEICT), pp. 1–6 (2015)
12. Arsenovic, M., Sladojevic, S., Anderla, A., Stefanovic, D.: FaceTime — Deep learning based face recognition attendance system. In: IEEE 15th International Symposium on Intelligent Systems and Informatics (SISY), pp. 53–58 (2017)
13. Varadharajan, E., Dharani, R., Jeevitha, S., Kavinmathi, B, Hemalatha, S.: Automatic attendance management system using face detection. In: Online International Conference on Green Engineering and Technologies (IC-GET), pp. 1–3 (2016)
14. Jayant, N.K., Borra, S.: Attendance management system using hybrid face recognition techniques. In: Conference on Advances in Signal Processing (CASP), pp. 412–417 (2016)

15. Sony Corporation – FeliCa Website. https://www.sony.net/Products/felica/. Accessed 20 Jan 2022
16. Amazon Web Services. https://aws.amazon.com/. Accessed 20 Jan 2022
17. Japan NFC Reader. https://japannfcreader.tret.jp/. Accessed 20 Jan 2022
18. HTTP Request Shortcuts – Apps on Google Play Store. https://play.google.com/store/apps/details?id=ch.rmy.android.http_shortcuts&hl=en&gl=US. Accessed 20 Jan 2022
19. Schwab, K.: The fourth industrial revolution: what it means, how to respond. World Economic Forum Homepage. https://www.weforum.org/agenda/2016/01/the-fourth-industrial-revolution-what-it-means-and-how-to-respond/. Accessed 20 Jan 2022
20. Hitachi-UTokyo Lab: Society 5.0: A people-centric super-smart society. Springer Nature Singapore Pte Ltd., Singapore (2020). https://doi.org/10.1007/978-981-15-2989-4
21. Smartphone penetration worldwide. https://www.statista.com/statistics/203734/global-smartphone-penetration-per-capita-since-2005/. Accessed 20 Jan 2022
22. Khan M.F.F., Sakamura, K.: Context-aware access control for clinical information systems. In: Proceeding of International Conference on Innovations in Information Technology (IIT), vol. 2012, pp. 123–128, IEEE (2012)
23. Shortcuts User Guide. https://support.apple.com/guide/shortcuts/welcome/ios. Accessed 20 Jan 2022
24. Suica Hompage. https://www.jreast.co.jp/e/pass/suica.html. Accessed 20 Jan 2022
25. PASMO Hompage. https://www.pasmo.co.jp/visitors/en/normalpasmo/. Accessed 20 Jan 2022

Daily Health Condition Estimation Using a Smart Toothbrush with Halitosis Sensor

Satoshi Yoshimura[1]([✉]), Teruhiro Mizumoto[1][iD], Yuki Matsuda[2][iD], Keita Ueda[3], and Akira Takeyama[3]

[1] Osaka University, Suita-shi, Osaka 565-0871, Japan
{s-yoshimura,mizumoto}@ist.osaka-u.ac.jp
[2] Nara Institute of Science and Technology, Ikoma-shi, Nara 630-0192, Japan
yukimat@is.naist.jp
[3] NOVENINE, Inc., Osaka-shi, Osaka 542-0081, Japan
{keita.ueda,akira.takeyama}@novenine.com

Abstract. The number of occupational injury claims and certifications for mental disorders increases every year. Therefore, the Ministry of Health, Labour and Welfare of Japan (MHLW) has mandated annual stress checks as a countermeasure. This gives rise to the having a daily health measurement using IoT devices. However, it has been found that managing multiple devices and active measurement behavior decreases users' motivation. This paper proposes a health measurement system that can be integrated with traditional brushing tools enabling a smooth gauging of health measures. This is done while people are performing their daily teeth brushing activity without any extra overhead. The proposed method estimates the recovery index for fatigue based on halitosis collecting by a smart toothbrush with a halitosis sensor. To evaluate the proposed method, we collected halitosis data and questionnaires about recovery index from 12 subjects every day for approximately two months and constructed a model to estimate each item of the questionnaires by Random Forest based on the halitosis data. As a result, we found a significant difference between the halitosis data and two measures of the recovery experience (MA and PD); furthermore, we achieved MA with an f-score of 0.60, PD with an F-score of 0.58 for three value classification, and sleep quality with an F-score of 0.71 with binary classification.

Keywords: Recovery estimation · Smart toothbrush · Measurement system

This research is partially supported by Initiative for Life Design Innovation (iLDi) Platform for Society 5.0.

T. Hara and H. Yamaguchi (Eds.): MobiQuitous 2021, LNICST 419, pp. 665–678, 2022.
https://doi.org/10.1007/978-3-030-94822-1_43

1   Introduction

The Ministry of Health, Labor and Welfare (MHLW) of Japan reports that the number of workers' compensation claims and certifications for mental disorders has been increasing every year in Japan [18]. In particular, the number of claims has increased tenfold in the past 20 years [16]. For a countermeasure, MHLW has obligated companies to offer annual stress checks [17] to employees in Japan. However, they can not observe minute changes in the mental status of workers and respond to mental health problems at the appropriate timing by the annual stress checks due to low frequency. For this reason, periodic and long-term observations are essential for keeping mental health and improving work performance.

On the other hand, IoT devices for measuring health conditions have become popular in recent years. These IoT devices can collect sensor data such as heart rate and sleep quality to measure health from various perspectives. However, if a user actively uses multiple IoT devices, he/she must understand how to use each device and manage applications for each device. In the use of multiple wearable devices, the users must periodically recharge each devices respectively. These periodically troublesome procedures reduce the motivation of users to continue health measurements; therefore, a way to continue using IoT devices in the long term is necessary [19].

This study proposes a system that estimates fatigue recovery while the user keeps motivation for health measurement in the long term. Recovery refers to the process of recovering from a stressed state [22]. It has been suggested that the process of recovery from work stress may be related to individual health and well-being and work performance [5]. Therefore, regular and long-term checks focusing on recovery are important for work. To keep the user's motivation for health measurement, we melt health measurement into the tooth brushing behavior that most people perform daily. Many people perform tooth brushing at waking up when the result of fatigue recovery appears prominently. Especially, halitosis is known as the link between stress [11]; therefore, we assume that the morning halitosis changes depending on the stress and recovery experience in the previous day. Therefore, the proposed system collects the halitosis data by a smart toothbrush with a gas sensor before the morning tooth brushing and then estimates the recovery based on the data. In the procedure, the users breathe to a toothbrush to measure recovery; there is no trouble for measurement.

We build a model that estimates recovery from halitosis data collected in tooth brushing. The estimation model is constructed by the Random-Forest algorithm with the halitosis data consisting of odor, temperature, humidity, pressure as input data and outputs the estimation of recovery index.

To evaluate the proposed method, we collected halitosis data and questionnaires about recovery index from 12 subjects every day for approximately two months and constructed a model to estimate each item of the questionnaires by Random Forest based on the halitosis data. In the experiment, each subject used a smart toothbrush (SMASH) with a gas sensor and collected halitosis data before brushing in the morning. In addition, as the ground truth of the training model, each subject answered the questionnaire about recovery used in research on industrial insurance [2, 6, 21, 22] in/after tooth brushing.

As a result, we found a significant difference in halitosis data among three degrees about the two measures of recovery experience (Mastery and Psychological detachment). Furthermore, we achieved Mastery with an f-score of 0.60, Psychological detachment with an F-score of 0.58 for three value classification, and sleep quality with an F-score of 0.71 with binary classification.

The contributions of this study is that We have realized less burdensome recovery measurement by incorporating sensing into daily tooth brushing behavior.

2   Related Works

2.1   Health Status Measurement Using IoT Devices

In recent years, a variety of health monitoring systems using IoT devices have been proposed [15]. Zhang et al. [23] develop a necklace-type IoT device monitoring human eating habits such as the number of feeding to detect eating disorders and real-time intervention. Leng et al. [13] propose a drowsiness detection system using a wristband type device. When the driver wears this device, it acquires sensor data and extracts features such as heart rate, pulse fluctuation, and respiratory rate based on the sensor data to detect drowsiness. Bui et al. [4] analyze whether it is possible to intervene in diabetic patients from IoT devices. Proposals for lifestyle improvement from IoT devices improve glycemic control by 0.8% on average in one year compared to conventional care for patients with type 2 diabetes. Inan et al. [8] provide remote monitoring of heart failure patients using wearable devices. By evaluating whether or not hospitalization is necessary for patients with heart failure using the lifelog of cardiac function collected from wearable terminals, it is possible to adjust the treatment specific to the patient and reduce the number of hospitalized patients.

Thus, using IoT devices, including wearable terminals, enables users to measure their health over a long period. However, more frequent management of IoT devices and more actions required for health measurements can have a negative impact on users.

Bonai [19] examines the possibility of diabetes treatment using IoT, and it is expected that long-term utilization of IoT affects improving blood glucose. However, without support, the IoT utilization rate will be low, more than 10% stop using it immediately after the introduction of IoT (within 2 weeks), and it is difficult to maintain motivation in about a year.

2.2   Relationship Between Oral Condition and Health

There are studies aimed at monitoring oral conditions. Shetty et al. [20] have developed a Remote Oral Behaviors Assessment System (ROBAS) using an electric toothbrush and a smartphone. It shows the possibility of accurately and reliably monitoring the brushing pattern in the home for a long time. Islam et al.

[10] have proposed a system for monitoring pH in the oral cavity. They mention the system can monitor a decrease in PH, an indicator of bacterial accumulation in the oral cavity, using a piezoelectric dental crown, while compensating for lost teeth.

On the other hands, Various studies were conducted on the relationship between oral condition and the psychological condition and quality of life.

A study investigating the relationship between depression, stress, self-esteem, and the short-form oral health impact profile (OHIP-14) in middle-aged women has reported that the lower the stress and the higher the self-esteem, the higher the oral health impact index [12]. A study of 452 university students investigating the relationship between stress and oral symptoms using a self-reported questionnaire has reported that stress has a profound effect on the symptoms of dry mouth, bad breath, and temporomandibular joint pain [14].

A study also investigates the relationship between oral health and general health and quality of life in elderly male cancer patients [9]. It concludes elderly male cancer patients who have problems with their mouth and teeth and have difficulty eating may have a lower quality of life, poorer mental health, and lower levels of physical function than those without these problems.

Based on these, it can be seen that the relationship between oral condition and stress is mentioned in a wide range of age groups. Understanding the oral condition is also important for improving one's mental and quality of life. In this study, we think that the relationship between bad breath and health conditions also occurs for recovery.

2.3   Positioning of This Study

Maintaining user motivation is an issue for continuous monitoring with IoT devices. Therefore, to eliminate the disadvantages of using IoT devices, we propose a health measurement method that is less burdensome for users in this study. By focusing on tooth brushing, users don't have to do new actions only for measuring health.

3   Smart Toothbrush System

3.1   System Overview

In this study, we propose a system that collects halitosis and estimates recovery by the flow of tooth brushing that many people perform every morning. Normally, a dedicated device is required to collect halitosis, but in proposed method, We use a smart toothbrush that integrates brushing teeth and collecting halitosis. Since toothbrushes are indispensable in daily life, users can reduce the trouble of managing and charging new equipment. All users have to do to collect halitosis is to press the button on the toothbrush and blow for 3-5 s. using halitosis collected from a smart toothbrush, users' recovery is estimated. It is known that there is a correlation between halitosis and poor lifestyle and stress [11], and we think that there is also a correlation between recovery and halitosis.

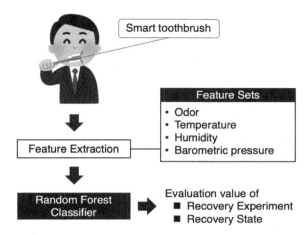

Fig. 1. overview of the recovery estimation model

3.2 Recovery Estimation Model

We describe the model that estimates recovery from collected halitosis data. The Fig. 1 shows the outline of the recovery estimation model.

Four types of features, odor, temperature, humidity, and barometric pressure, are extracted from the breath blown by the user. For temperature, humidity, and barometric pressure, extract their median values during a single measurement.

The output of this model is the evaluation value of recovery. In this study, the evaluation values are treated in two or three stages for each recovery measure. Therefore, a 3-class or 2-class classifier is used for each recovery measure. Random-Forest Classifier is used as the model for classifying recovery evaluation values. That is because we thought that it could be classified by clear numerical conditions according to each feature of halitosis. For the ground truth, we use the recovery questionnaire used in industrial insurance.

4 Questionnaire About Recovery

In this chapter, we describe the questionnaire used in the experiment. Recovery refers to the process of recovering from a stressed state [22]. It has been suggested that the process of recovery from work stress may be related to individual health and well-being and work performance [5]. There are two indicators for recovery: (1) recovery experience and (2) recovery state. Below, we explain the two indicators and describe the creation of the questionnaire based on them.

4.1 Recovery Experience

Recovery experience is an index of experience of recovering from stress such as work. Although the behavior for recovery varies from person to person, the underlying experience is divided into four distinct measures by Sonnentag et al. [22]. The four measures are Psychological detachment, Relaxation, Mastery, and Control. We describe these measures based on Sonnentag et al. [22].

Table 1. Recovery experience questionnaire

Q-1	I feel like I can decide for myself what to do	CO
Q-2	I learn new things	MA
Q-3	I forget about work	PD
Q-4	I decide my own schedule	CO
Q-5	I don't think about work at all	PD
Q-6	I kick back and relax	RE
Q-7	I seek out intellectual challenges	MA
Q-8	I do things that challenge me	MA
Q-9	I determine for myself how I will spend my time	CO
Q-10	I distance myself from my work	PD
Q-11	I do relaxing things	RE
Q-12	I use the time to relax	RE
Q-13	I take care of things the way that I want them done	CO
Q-14	I take time for leisure	PD
Q-15	I do something to broaden my horizons	MA
Q-16	I get a break from the demands of work	RE

PD = Psychological detachment, RE = Relaxation, MA = Mastery, CO = Control

Table 2. Recovery state questionnaire

Q-17	This morning I was able to physically refresh
Q-18	This morning, I was able to mentally refresh
Q-19	How do you rate your sleep quality as a whole?

Psychological detachment means not in a physical sense, such as leaving the workplace but keeping a distance from work in a psychological sense. You can recover from the effects of work stress by keeping a distance from work in a psychological sense. It is also known that psychological detachment affects the relationship between stress factors and the prevention of burnout [7].

Relaxation is a process related to leisure activities. It has been suggested that working for a long time in stressful work leads to illness caused by the work stress factors [3]. Therefore, relaxation is important to prevent such a situation. It is also known that the positive emotions obtained from the experience of relaxing play a role in reducing the influence of negative emotions [22].

Mastery refers to non-work activities other than work by providing rewarding experiences and learning opportunities outside of work. These activities are expected to affect recovery because it leads to the acquisition of new skills and qualifications and improving self-efficacy [1].

Control is the ability of a person to choose an action from two or more options. Here, it refers to the extent to which a person can decide what kind of activity he/she will perform in his or her leisure time and when and how he/she will perform the activity. This experience suggests that increasing feelings of self-efficacy and ability promotes well-being and enhances recovery.

In the questionnaire used in this study, we asked about how to spend time after the day's work to check the recovery experience of the subjects. We prepared a total of 16 questions, 4 for each of these 4 measures. The questions are shown in Table 1 and are quoted from reference [21,22]. All questions are rated on a scale of 5 from "1. Not applicable at all" to "5. Very well-applicable".

4.2 Recovery State

Recovery state refers to the state after recovery during the leisure period. There is a correlation between morning recovery and work performance for the day [2]. Therefore, checking the recovery status in the morning is important for workers to face their work.

In this study, we created a questionnaire quoting the mental and physical refreshment used in Reference [2] and the questions about sleep quality from Reference [6]. Reference [6] is widely used as an evaluation of sleep disorders.

Table 2 shows the actual questions and their order. There are two questions about refreshing mentally and physically: "This morning I was able to physically refresh" and "This morning, I was able to mentally refresh". These questions are rated on a scale of 5 from "1. Not applicable at all" to "5. Very well-applicable". The question about sleep quality is "How do you rate your sleep quality as a whole?". This question is rated on a four-point scale from "1. very bad" to "4. very good".

5   Experiment

In this section, we describe an experiment to evaluate a recovery estimation model based on halitosis data. The purpose of this experiment is to verify whether the recovery experience and recovery state can be estimated from the halitosis data when waking up. The period is two and a half months, and the number of subjects is 12. In the following sections, we describe the data collection, the evaluation method of the collected data, and the evaluation results.

5.1 Data Collection

In this section, we describe how to collect data for recovery estimation. To collect halitosis data, we used a smart toothbrush "SMASH" developed by NOVENINE Co., Ltd.[1], that can measure halitosis by a gas sensor (Fig. 2). The subjects blew on the smart toothbrush to measure halitosis data before tooth brushing in the morning. The subjects collected their halitosis data using SMASH as soon as getting up every morning. All the subjects have to do for measuring is press the button on SMASH and blow for about 5 s before tooth brushing. In addition, they answered the questionnaires shown in Sect. 4 by smartphone in/after tooth brushing. In the experiment period of approximately two and a half months, we collected valid data of 581 days.

Fig. 2. A smart toothbrush "SMASH" developed by NOVENINE Co., Ltd.

5.2 Analysis of Collected Data

We verified whether the recovery experience and recovery state evaluated by the questionnaire could be estimated from the halitosis data when waking up. The Kruskal-Wallis test was done to verify whether there was a significant difference between the questionnaire data and each feature. After that, for those with significant differences, multiple comparisons were performed using the Steel-Dwass Test.

First, because the subjects' answers were biased, especially few extreme answers, regarding the collected questionnaire data, those evaluated on a 5-grade evaluation were changed to a 3-class classification, and those evaluated on a 4-grade evaluation were changed to a 2-grade evaluation. On the 5-grade

---

[1] NOVENINE Co., Ltd. "SMASH": https://novenine.com/.

evaluation, 1 and 2 were regarded as 0, 3 was regarded as 1, and 4 and 5 were regarded as 2. On the 4-grade evaluation, 1 and 2 were regarded as 0, and 3 and 4 were regarded as 1.

Table 3. Kruskal-Wallis test on the questionnaire and each feature

Questionnaire	Measure	Class	Odor	Temperature	Humidity	Barometric pressure
Q-1	CO	3	-	$p < 0.05$	-	$p < 0.001$
Q-2	MA	3	$p < 0.05$	$p < 0.001$	-	$p < 0.001$
Q-3	PD	3	-	-	$p < 0.05$	$p < 0.001$
Q-4	CO	3	-	$p < 0.001$	-	$p < 0.05$
Q-5	PD	3	-	$p < 0.05$	$p < 0.05$	$p < 0.001$
Q-6	RE	3	$p < 0.05$	-	-	-
Q-7	MA	3	$p < 0.001$	$p < 0.001$	-	$p < 0.001$
Q-8	MA	3	$p < 0.001$	$p < 0.05$	-	$p < 0.05$
Q-9	CO	3	-	$p < 0.05$	-	$p < 0.05$
Q-10	PD	3	-	$p < 0.05$	$p < 0.001$	$p < 0.001$
Q-11	RE	3	-	-	-	$p < 0.05$
Q-12	RE	3	-	-	$p < 0.05$	-
Q-13	CO	3	-	$p < 0.05$	-	-
Q-14	PD	3	-	$p < 0.001$	-	-
Q-15	MA	3	$p < 0.001$	$p < 0.05$	$p < 0.05$	$p < 0.001$
Q-16	RE	3	-	$p < 0.05$	$p < 0.001$	$p < 0.001$
Q-17		3	-	$p < 0.05$	-	$p < 0.05$
Q-18		3	-	-	-	$p < 0.05$
Q-19		2	-	-	-	$p < 0.001$

"-" indicates that there is no significant difference in the feature among answers of the questionnaire ($p > 0.05$).

Next, the Kruskal-Wallis test was performed to verify whether there is a significant difference in each feature for each evaluation in the questionnaire. The results are shown in Table 3.

From this table, we describe the results for each measure of recovery. Regarding mastery, it was considered that there was a relatively significant difference between features other than humidity and question items. For each question item, multiple comparisons were performed using the Steel-Dwass Test. As a result, regarding Q-2, there was a significant difference in odor between 1 and 0 and between 1 and 2($p < 0.001$), and there was a significant difference in temperature and barometric pressure between 0 and 2($p < 0.001$). Regarding Q-7, there was a significant difference in odor between 1 and 0($p < 0.001$), and there was a significant difference in temperature and barometric pressure between 0 and 2($p < 0.001$). Regarding Q-8, there was a significant difference in odor and temperature between 2 and 0($p < 0.001$), and there was a significant difference in barometric pressure between 0 and 1($p < 0.01$). Regarding Q-15, there was a significant difference in odor and temperature between 0 and 1($p < 0.001$), and there was a significant difference in odor, temperature and barometric pressure between 0 and 2($p < 0.001$).

Regarding relaxation, there was not much significant difference in questions other than Q-16. In Q-16, as a result of multiple comparison using Steel-Dwass Test, there was a significant difference in temperature between 0 and 1($p < 0.01$), and there was a significant difference in temperature, humidity and barometric pressure between 0 and 2($p < 0.001$).

Regarding psychological detachment, there was a significant difference from each feature in Q-5 and Q-10. For these two questions, we performed multiple comparisons using the Steel-Dwass Test. As a result, regarding Q-5, there was a significant difference in odor, temperature, humidity between 1 and 0($p < 0.001$), and there was a significant difference in barometric pressure between 0 and 2($p < 0.001$). Regarding Q-10, there was a significant difference in temperature and humidity between 2 and 0($p < 0.01$), and also in barometric pressure between 2 and 0($p < 0.001$).

Regarding control, there was a significant difference between each question and temperature or barometric pressure, but there was no question that showed a significant difference as a whole.

Regarding the question about the recovery state, there was a significant difference between the evaluation value and the barometric pressure, but not so much from the other features.

Based on these, we thought that the answers of the questionnaire could be estimated by each features using numerical conditions, and constructed an estimation model using a random forest classifier.

Estimated questions are four questions for MA, Q-16 for RE, Q-5 and Q-10 for PD, and Q-4 for CO, which is the most influential question on this measure. Similarly, for the recovery state, we constructed a model that estimates the evaluation value of each questionnaire from halitosis data.

Table 4. Estimation score

Questionnaire	Measure	Class	Precision	Recall	f1-score
Q-2	MA	3	0.57	0.57	0.57
Q-4	CO	3	0.47	0.54	0.47
Q-5	PD	3	0.59	0.59	0.58
Q-7	MA	3	0.55	0.56	0.55
Q-8	MA	3	0.60	0.60	0.60
Q-10	PD	3	0.57	0.57	0.54
Q-15	MA	3	0.57	0.57	0.57
Q-16	RE	3	0.54	0.55	0.54
Q-17		3	0.51	0.54	0.50
Q-18		3	0.50	0.53	0.50
Q-19		2	0.71	0.74	0.71

5.3   Model Evaluation

We constructed a model to estimate the evaluation values of the questionnaire items described in the previous section from the collected halitosis data and verified by Leave-One-Person-Out Cross-Validation.

We evaluated the model using precision, recall, and f-score. Precision indicates the percentage of the results predicted by the model that were really correct. Recall indicates the percentage of the actual results that were predicted correctly. f-score is the harmonic mean of precision and recall.

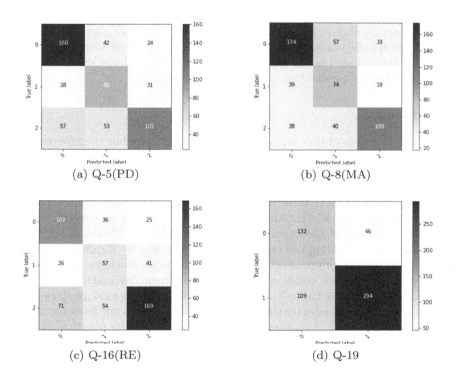

(a) Q-5(PD)   (b) Q-8(MA)

(c) Q-16(RE)   (d) Q-19

Fig. 3. Confusion matrix

The Table 4 shows the evaluation results.

For Q-4, which is a question about CO, we obtained an f-score of 0.47. We presumed that it was difficult to estimate because there was no significant difference in the features.

Q-8 had the highest score of the four questions about MA, with an f-score of 0.60. The Fig. 3(b) shows the confusion matrix of Q-8. This model rarely estimated that the true label of 0 is 2, and it can detect the state where MA is low.

Regarding the two questions regarding PD, Q-5 was a higher score, and its f-score is 0.58. The Fig. 3(a) shows the confusion matrix of Q-5. This model rarely estimated that the true label of 0 is 2, and it can detect the state where PD is low.

For Q-16, which is a question about RE, we obtained an f-score of 0.54. The Fig. 3(c) shows the confusion matrix of Q-16. It can be seen that the true label of 0 is hardly included in the prediction label of 2. If you do not have RE experience, you aren't presumed to have RE experience.

We describe the recovery state. For the mental and physical refreshing questions (Q-17, Q-18), an f-score of 0.50 was obtained. It is presumed that it was difficult to estimate because there was no significant difference in the features. For the question about sleep quality (Q-19), we obtained an f-score of 0.71. The Fig. 3(d) shows the confusion matrix of Q-19. It can be seen that the true label of 0 is hardly included in the prediction label of 1. If you have low sleep quality, this model doesn't predict your sleep quality is high.

5.4   Discussion

One of the purposes of this experiment was to verify whether the recovery experience and recovery state can be estimated from the halitosis data when waking up. We performed the Kruskal-Wallis test to verify whether there was a significant difference between the questionnaire data and each feature. As a result, we found that there was a relatively significant difference between halitosis features and MA. We also found that there was not much significant difference in CO. Some questions about the other two measures had a significant difference and others did not. Regarding the recovery state, there was no significant difference between mental and physical refreshment and halitosis features.

Based on these, we constructed an estimation model and validated it by Leave-One-Person-Out Cross-Validation to achieve the second purpose of this experiment that is to estimate the evaluation value of recovery from the halitosis data when waking up. As a result, our model detected the question of MA in the recovery experience with an f-score of 0.60, and the question of PD with an f-score of 0.58. Since This model rarely classifies inexperienced cases into experienced case, it is considered to be useful for detection when inexperienced case.

6   Conclusion

In this study, we focused on the tooth brushing that many people perform every morning and proposed a recovery estimation system from halitosis data collected by the natural flow of tooth brushing by the smart toothbrush. We extracted four features of odor, temperature, humidity, and barometric pressure from the breath blown by the user and constructed a model that outputs the evaluation value of recovery by Random Forest. To verify whether the halitosis data can be estimated for recovery and the proposed model, we experimented on 12 subjects.

In the experiment, we collected the halitosis from the prototype device of a smart toothbrush and the answers to the questionnaire about the recovery as the ground truth when the subjects woke up. As a result, we found a significant difference between the halitosis data and two measures of the recovery experience (MA and PD), and our three-value classification model detected MA with an f-score of 0.60, and PD with an f-score of 0.58. In addition, we considered that our model could firmly detect that the subjects have no recovery experience. From these results, a significant difference in halitosis for recovery was found. It was also shown that halitosis is useful for recovery estimation.

References

1. Bandura, A., Freeman, W., Lightsey, R.: Self-efficacy: the exercise of control. Br. J. Clin. Psychol. (1999)
2. Binnewies, C., Sonnentag, S., Mojza, E.J.: Daily performance at work: feeling recovered in the morning as a predictor of day-level job performance. J. Organ. Behav.: Int. J. Ind. Occup. Organ. Psychol. Behav. 30(1), 67–93 (2009)
3. Brosschot, J.F., Pieper, S., Thayer, J.F.: Expanding stress theory: prolonged activation and perseverative cognition. Psychoneuroendocrinology 30(10), 1043–1049 (2005)
4. Bui, A.L., Fonarow, G.C.: Home monitoring for heart failure management. J. Am. Coll. Cardiol. 59(2), 97–104 (2015). https://doi.org/10.1016/j.jacc.2011.09.044
5. De Croon, E.M., Sluiter, J.K., Blonk, R.W., Broersen, J.P., Frings-Dresen, M.H.: Stressful work, psychological job strain, and turnover: a 2-year prospective cohort study of truck drivers. J. Appl. Psychol. 89(3), 442 (2004)
6. Doi, Y., et al.: Psychometric assessment of subjective sleep quality using the Japanese version of the pittsburgh sleep quality index (PSQI-J) in psychiatric disordered and control subjects. J. Organ. Behav.: Int. J. Ind. Occup. Organ. Psychol. Behav. 97, 165–172 (2000)
7. Etzion, D., Eden, D., Lapidot, Y.: Relief from job stressors and burnout: reserve service as a respite. J. Appl. Psychol. 83(4), 577 (1998)
8. Inan, O.T., et al.: Novel wearable seismocardiography and machine learning algorithms can assess clinical status of heart failure patients. Circ. Heart Fail. 11(1), e004313 (2018). https://doi.org/10.1161/CIRCHEARTFAILURE.117.004313
9. Ingram, S.S., et al.: The association between oral health and general health and quality of life in older male cancer patients. J. Am. Geriatr. Soc. 53(9), 1504–1509 (2005)
10. Islam, S., Kim, A., Hwang, G., Song, S.H.: Smart tooth system for in-situ wireless PH monitoring. In: 2021 21st International Conference on Solid-State Sensors, Actuators and Microsystems (Transducers), pp. 755–758 (2021). https://doi.org/10.1109/Transducers50396.2021.9495706
11. Kim, S.Y., Sim, S., Kim, S.G., Park, B., Choi, H.G.: Prevalence and associated factors of subjective halitosis in Korean adolescents. PLoS ONE 10(10), 14–21 (2015)
12. Kwon, H.J., Yoon, M.S.: Relationship of depression, stress, and self-esteem with oral health-related quality of life of middle-aged women. J. Dent. Hyg. Sci. 15(6), 825–835 (2015)

13. Leng, L.B., Giin, L.B., Chung, W.Y.: Wearable driver drowsiness detection system based on biomedical and motion sensors. In: 2015 IEEE SENSORS, pp. 1–4 (2015). https://doi.org/10.1109/ICSENS.2015.7370355

14. Lim, H.R., Jeon, S.Y.: Relationship between stress, oral health, and quality of life in university students. J. Dent. Hyg. Sci. **16**(4), 310–316 (2016)

15. MarketsandMarkets Research Private Ltd: Wearable fitness technology market report. https://www.marketsandmarkets.com/Market-Reports/wearable-fitness-technology-market-139869705.html. Accessed 08 Sept 2021

16. Ministry of Health, Labour and Welfare: Compensation status for industrial accidents and public affairs accidents related to death from overwork. https://www.mhlw.go.jp/stf/newpage_04738.html. Accessed 08 June 2021

17. Ministry of Health, Labour and Welfare: Mental health measures and overwork measures in the workplace such as stress checks. https://www.mhlw.go.jp/bunya/roudoukijun/anzeneisei12/index.html. Accessed 08 Sept 2021

18. Ministry of Health, Labour and Welfare: Workmen's accident compensation status such as death from overwork. https://www.mhlw.go.jp/content/11402000/000796022.pdf. Accessed 08 Sept 2021

19. Ryotaro Bonai: Verification of blood glucose improvement effect through behavior change of IoT in type 2 diabetes: PRISM-J. https://www.amed.go.jp/content/000059276.pdf. Accessed 08 Sept 2021

20. Shetty, V., Morrison, D., Belin, T., Hnat, T., Kumar, S., et al.: A scalable system for passively monitoring oral health behaviors using electronic toothbrushes in the home setting: development and feasibility study. JMIR Mhealth Uhealth **8**(6), e17347 (2020)

21. Shimazu, A., Sonnentag, S., Kubota, K., Kawakami, N.: Validation of the Japanese version of the recovery experience questionnaire. J. Occup. Health **54**(3), 196–205 (2012)

22. Sonnentag, S., Fritz, C.: The recovery experience questionnaire: development and validation of a measure for assessing recuperation and unwinding from work. J. Occup. Health Psychol. **12**(3), 204 (2007)

23. Zhang, S., et al.: Necksense: a multi-sensor necklace for detecting eating activities in free-living conditions. CoRR abs/1911.07179 (2019). http://arxiv.org/abs/1911.07179

The Fourth International Workshop on Mobile Ubiquitous Systems, Infrastructures, Communications and AppLications (MUSICAL 2021 Fall)

Collision-Free Channel Assignment with Overlapped Channels in Multi-radio Multi-channel Wireless Mesh Networks

Yi Tian[1,2]($\boxtimes$)(iD) and Takuya Yoshihiro[3](iD)

[1] Graduate School of Systems Engineering, Wakayama University, Wakayama, Japan
denijapan@icloud.com
[2] Department of Information Management, Shangluo University, Shaannxi, China
[3] Faculty of Systems Engineering, Wakayama University, Wakayama, Japan
tac@sys.wakayama-u.ac.jp

Abstract. Multi-radio multi-channel (MRMC) technologies can greatly improve the performance of WMNs. In MRMC filed, using partially overlapped channel (POC) assignment is one of the most promising techniques, which can increase the network throughput by taking advantage of more simultaneous transmissions. In this study, we propose a joint routing and channel assignment scheme to achieve collision-free channel assignment with partially overlapped channels while considering traffic engineering. The idea in designing are as following: (1) We design a interference model with POCs. It is possible to enable all channels to be used, and more parallel transmissions result in higher peak throughput. (2) We jointly solve the channel assignment and routing problems using POCs, and we show that POCs are significantly effective to improve spatial reuse in WMNs. By systematically using all channels to avoid interference, we have achieved a higher number of simultaneous transmissions than using only three orthogonal channels.

Keywords: Routing · Collision freedom · Channel assignment · POCs

1 Introduction

Wireless Mesh Network (WMN) has become a widely accepted network topology owe to its advantages such as convenient implementation, low cost, and strong real-time scenarios. Interference from adjacent parallel transmissions caused capacity reduction is a main problem in WMNs. An efficient way to alleviate this problem is to use multiple interfaces configured on distinct channels per node, which is called multi-channel multi-radio (MCMR) technology. Commodity IEEE 802.11 devices are preferably used in multi-radio multi-channel wireless mesh networks (MCMR WMNs) because of easier deployment and lower cost.

Supported by organization x.

T. Hara and H. Yamaguchi (Eds.): MobiQuitous 2021, LNICST 419, pp. 681–692, 2022.
https://doi.org/10.1007/978-3-030-94822-1_44

It is known that 802.11 2.4 GHz provides 14 partially overlapped channels, and only the first 13 channels are permitted to use. In IEEE 802.11 2.4 GHz band, any two channels separated by more than 5 (channel number) are called non-overlapping channels or orthogonal channels (OCs), due to their signals do not overlap with each other. Otherwise, they are called partially overlapping channels (POCs). Interference occurs when the separation between the two channels in the radio spectrum is less than 5 and the physical position is close. Therefore, it is a very important issue to increase the number of simultaneous transmission in the network while avoiding signal interference among radios. There are a large number of studies have proved that channel assignment is one of the effective methods to solve this problem, which have been reported as surveys [1–5].

Since Mishra [6] and [7] proposed the opinion that POCs can dramatically improve the frequency utilization, in order to improve spectrum efficiency and network performance, the research of POC has attracted more and more attention. Liu et al. [8] and Zhao et al. [9] proposed different partially overlapped channel assignment algorithm to minimize total network interference. Wang et al. [10] and Yang et al. [11] proposed different partially overlapped channel assignment to avoid interference, which the routing paths are per-determined by AODV routing protocol. Wang et al. [12] designed a weighted conflict graph to model POCs interference in hybrid traffic scenario and proposed a heuristic scheme to solve the joint multicast routing and channel assignment problem. Simulation results show the scheme can reduce network interference. However, to best of our knowledge, using POCs and joint routing to achieve collision-free transmission has not been proposed.

In [13], we first proposed a joint routing and channel assignment scheme TACCA (Traffic-demand-Aware Collision-free Channel Assignment) which achieved collision-free transmission in 802.11-based MCMR WMN. However, the channel assignment in the OCs space result in a low channel spatial utilization, which wastes the radio spectrum usage and it is difficult to meet the rapid growth of IEEE 802.11 devices and wireless communication requirements. To extend TACCA to use all the available channels and achieve a higher number of simultaneous transmissions. In this paper, for using all available channels, we propose a new scheme. By systematically utilizing all channels to avoid interference between adjacent channels, we achieve better performance than using only three OCS. The following set of contributions are made:

(1) We design a interference model with POCs. By carefully allocating channels, the overall channel reuse is significantly improved, which lead to higher peak throughput and make all channels available to nodes for channel selection. (2) We jointly solve the channel assignment and routing problems using POCs, and we show that POCs are significantly effective to improve spatial reuse in WMNs. By systematically using all channels to avoid the interference among adjacent channels, we achieve a higher number of simultaneous transmissions. To best of our knowledge, our scheme is the first joint roting and channel assignment scheme using POCs to achieve collision-free transmission.

2 Related Work

One of the main problems in designing an efficient channel allocation scheme using POCs is adjacent channel interference, that is, the interference between two neighbors configured on adjacent (partially overlapping) channels. Interference model, which is defined as a technique for capturing radio interference belonging to nodes operating on partially overlapping channels in WMN. In [14], the authors classified the interference model into two criteria: (i) Interference factor model (I-factor); (ii) Interference matrix model (I-Matrix).

Yang et al. [11] used the I-Matrix model, and proposed a load-balance and interference-avoid partially overlapped channels assignment (LBIA-POCA) scheme. In LBIA-POCA, authors aimed to improve network throughput by the cooperative management of interfaces and channels. However, the assumed routing paths are pre-determined by AODV routing protocol. On the other hand, this scheme requires time-slot, however, commodity 802.11 NICs in MRMC WMNs do not support it. RAD et al. [15] used the I-factor model, and proposed a traffic-irrelevant channel assignment algorithm. They assigned channels to all links in the network, and took minimizing network interference as the optimization objective. However, they all assumed that routing paths are pre-determined. Currently there is no scheme that simultaneously optimizes routing and channel assignment in the context of POC studies.

On the other hand, regarding OCs, several advanced joint routing and channel assignment and schemes have been proposed. In particular, by introducing the CSMA-aware interference model, we proposed a joint routing and channel assignment scheme called TACCA [13], which achieves collision free transmission with 3–5 OCs in IEEE 802.11 2.4 GHz based MRMC WMNs. However, POCs are not directly applicable to TACCA in WMNs because of the difference in interference estimation between OCs and POCs Therefore, in this paper, we propose a new scheme, that introduces POCs to achieve collision-free transmission while considering traffic engineering.

3 Definition

3.1 Assumptions and Network Model

To model a MRMC WMN, we define a set of nodes N which connected by a set of directed links L, and let $G = (N, L)$ represent our network. For each node N, we assume there are N_v interface cards on it, and each interface card operates on a different channel $c \in C$, where C is a set of channels. We write a directed link as $l = (u, v, c) \in L$, which goes from node $u \in N$ to node $v \in N$ using channel c. Thus, there are potentially $2|C|$ available links for communications between each pair of neighboring nodes u and v in N. We assume the traffic demand matrix D is given, and $D(s, d)$ indicates the total traffic demand from node s to d, where $(s, d) \in N \times N$. Then, for each pair (s, d) and each link l, we define a variable $TF_l^{(s,d)} \in \{0, 1\}$ that represents whether the traffic flow for demand (s, d) goes through link l or not.

As known, in order to ensure communication, the same channel must be assigned to neighboring nodes. Then, if a link $l = (u, v, c)$ is used to transmit frames, we call the link used as a path of some flow the active link. We define a variable $A_l \in \{0, 1\}$, where $A_l = 0$ denotes that link l is inactive and $A_l = 1$ active. On the other hand, we define a variable $N_v^c \in \{0, 1\}$, which indicates whether an NIC on node v is assigned with a channel c or not. We define the variable U_{max} where $0 \leq U_{max} \leq 1$, which denotes the maximum link utilization among all links.

3.2   Pocs-CSMA-Aware Interference Model

The authors in [6] and [16] studied the interference between partially overlapping channels, and found that the interference between two links related to both their physical distance and channel separation. When the physical distance is fixed, their interference decreases as the physical distance increases. When two in-range transmitters operate on adjacent channels that partially overlap, they cause lesser degree of interference, which is called as adjacent channel interference. They let $\tau \in \{0, 1, 2, 3, 4, 5, 6, 7, 8, 9, 10, 11, 12\}$ indicate the channel separation (channel number) in IEEE 802.11 standard. For different channel separation, they define $R(\tau)$ to represent the interference range, it decrease with large of τ in channel separation. When $\tau = 0$, $R(\tau) = R(0)$, denotes the non-overlapping channel interference range. Only when the distance of any two nodes in large that their interference range or their channel separation is bigger than 5, the two nodes can be regarded as interference free, i.e., for two nodes $u, v \in N$, if $\tau < 5$ and $d(c_1, c_2) \leq R(\tau)$, the interference is existed between u and v.

In this paper, we assume a transmission on a given channels is interfered with the other transmission on the same channel within a certain range R, called the interference range, and same as CSMA-aware interference models this interference model built on top of the single disk model, in which both the communication range and the interference range are the same. Then, the interference range observed on adjacent channel is called the reduced interference range, can be obtained same as [10]. We let $I(c_1, c_2)$ as the reduced interference range ratio, which is normalized to a scale of $[0, 1]$ and is used to describe the reduction in interference range observed on adjacent channels c_1 and c_2. Thus, the interference range be defined as $I(c_1, c_2)R$ which between two transmission with channel c_1 and c_2, respectively.

As is known, carrier sense multiple access (CSMA) is a MAC protocol. CSMA requires each station to first check the state of the medium before initiating a transmission. This helps to avert potential collisions by listening to the broadcasting nodes and then informing devices to transmit when the channel is free. Therefore, in CSMA, multiple nodes would send and receive frames in turn on the same medium without collision unless hidden terminals exist. Therefore, same as [17], in this paper, we assume that the collision between links within carrier-sensing range are avoided due to CSMA, and assume that the two directed links interfere with each other only if they are located in the hidden-terminal position. Then, we introduce an Pocs-CSMA-aware interference model, see Fig. 1.

(a) Collision of two Data frame

(b) Collision of Data and Ack frame

Fig. 1. Interference model

Let $l_1 = (u_1, v_1, c_1)$ and $l_2 = (u_2, v_2, c_2)$ be a pair of two links in L. $d(u, v)$ is the Euclidean distance between u and v. Then, transmission on l_1 prevents l_2 owe to collision of the hidden terminal effect when the following conditions are met.

Case 1: Collision due to two Data frame.

(1) $d(u_1, v_2) \leq I(c_1, c_2)R$,
(2) $d(u_1, u_2) \geq I(c_1, c_2)R$,

Case 2: Collision due to Data and Ack frame.

(1) $d(v_1, v_2) \leq I(c_1, c_2)R$,
(2) $d(u_1, u_2) \geq I(c_1, c_2)R$.

Case 1 defines the conditions where the transmission of data frame on l_1 is interfered with the reception of data frames on l_2. See Fig. 1(a), node v_2 is within the transmission range R of both nodes u_1 and u_2, but nodes u_1 and u_2 are without the transmission range of each other. Then, collision may occur at node v_2 when nodes u_1 and u_2 simultaneously transmit frames to node v_1 and v_2, respectively. In Fig. 1(a), nodes v_1 and v_2 may be the same node. We called such links l_1 and l_2 as an interference link pair.

Figure 1(b) indicates the case 2, where the transmission of acknowledgment (ACK) frames on l_1 is interfered with the reception of data frames on l_2. As well known, ACK frames specify which data frames have successfully arrived at the receiving end of the link. However, this ACK frame may cause collision. See Fig. 1(b), node u_1 and u_2 can not sense each other. Therefore, the ACK frame from node v_1 and the data frame from node u_2 may collide at node v_2 if they simultaneously use the same channel to deliver frame to node v_1 and v_2, respectively. Also for this case, we called links l_1 and l_2 as an interference link pair.

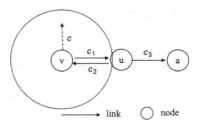

Fig. 2. Shared link capacity model

We assume that the interference is asymmetric, i.e., a transmission on link $l_1 \in L$ prevents communication of $l_2 \in L$ under this interference model. So that, we regard l_1 interferes l_2 and write as $l_1 \to l_2$. Thus, a set of interference link pairs are defined as follow,

$$I_G = \{(l_1, l_2) | l_1, l_2 \in L, l_1 \to \ell_2\}.$$

3.3   Shared Link Capacity Model with POCs

As the CSMA-aware interference model previously defined, links which using the same channel within the interference range and channels are assigned to same node which the channel separation distance less than 5 can sense each other. Therefore, those links are considered as shared the link capacity. In our scheme, we limit the amount of traffic loads through all these links to no more than ζ. Then, for each node v and each channel c, we give the our shared capacity links as follows,

$$S_v^c = \{(v, u, c_1) | (v, u, c_1) \in L, |c - c_1| < 5\} \cup \{(u, v, c_2) | (u, v, c_2) \in L,$$
$$d(v, u) \leq RI(c, c_2), c = c_2\} \cup \{(u, a, c_3) | (u, a, c_3) \in L,$$
$$d(v, u) \leq RI(c, c_3), c = c_3, a \neq v\}.$$

Figure 2 shows our shared link capacity model, where $u \in N$ is a node within the interference range of node $v \in N$, and $a \in N$ is without the interference range of v but within the interference range of u. Thus, if two different NICs on node v are assigned channels c and c_1, respectively, they share the link capacity when the channel separation distance less than 5, i.e., $|c - c_1| < 5$. On the other hand, if channel c is assigned to the links $(v, u, c_1), (u, v, c_2), (u, a, c_2)$, i.e., $c_1 = c_2 = c_3 = c$ they also share the link capacity ζ under CSMA. Note that, due to collides with (v, u, c), link such as (a, u, c) is not included in S_v^c.

4   Problem Formulation

In this part, our joint routing and channel assignment problem is formulated as a MILP which based on the definition and assumptions provided in Sect. 3.

Our optimization objective is to minimize the largest link utilization, therefore, we set (1) as the objective function.

$$min \quad U_{max} \tag{1}$$

To decrease interference, we allow the removal of some of the links from the topology. Therefore, the number of channels assigned to one node must be less than or equal to the number of the interface cards on each node. To represent this, we give the constraint (2).

$$\sum_{c \in C} N_v^c \leq N_v, \qquad \forall \ v \in N, \tag{2}$$

Next, we manage the relationship among assigned channel and active links. For each node v, we let $(v, u, c) \in L$ denote the output links, and $(u, v, c) \in L$ denote the input links, note that node u is the other node of links (v, u, c). Therefore, if channel c is assigned to an NIC on one node v, then $\sum_{(v,u,c) \in L} A_{(v,u,c)} + \sum_{(u,v,c) \in L} A_{(u,v,c)} \geq 1$ must be met. Constraint is given as (3).

$$N_v^c \leq \sum_{(v,u,c) \in L} A_{(v,u,c)} + \sum_{(u,v,c) \in L} A_{(u,v,c)}, \qquad \forall c \in C \ , \ \forall v \in N, \tag{3}$$

The other way round, as declared by (4), if channel c is assigned to none of the NICs on node v, then $A_{(u,v,c)} = 0$, i.e., link (u, v, c) must be inactive.

$$A_{(u,v,c)} \leq N_v^c, \ A_{(u,v,c)} \leq N_u^c, \ \forall \ (u, v, c) \in L, \tag{4}$$

We set (5) to ensure that the interfering links are not used for communication simultaneously.

$$A_{l_1} + A_{l_2} \leq 1, \qquad \forall \ (l_1, l_2) \in I_G, \tag{5}$$

(6) indicates the the traffic flows conservation conditions. $TF_{(u,v,c)}^{(s,d)}$ and $TF_{(v,w,c)}^{(s,d)}$ indicate if the links (u, v, c) and (v, w, c) have traffic demand (s, d) flow through them, where (u, v, c) is the input link and (v, w, c) is the output link. s and d are the source and destination nodes of traffic demand pair (s, d). In terms of flow conservation, the total volumes of flows sent by s must be equal to that received by d, and on each intermediate node the total input and output volume of flows must be equal. See (6), if node v is the source node, the value of (6) is equal to $-D(s, d)$. If node v is the destination node, the value of (6) is equal to $D(s, d)$. If not, it is an intermediate node, and the value of (6) is equal to 0.

$$\sum_{i:(i,j) \in L} TF_{(i,j)}^{(s,d)} - \sum_{z:(j,z) \in L} TF_{(j,z)}^{(s,d)} = \begin{cases} -D(s,d), \text{if } j = s, \\ D(s,d), \text{if } j = d, \quad i, j, s, d, z \in N, \\ 0, \text{otherwise.} \end{cases} \tag{6}$$

Constraint (7) means that, if there is one traffic flow goes through link l, then, $\sum_{(s,d) \in N \times N} TF_l^{(s,d)} \geq 1$, which means the link l must be activated, where M is a constant and is sufficiently large.

$$\sum_{(s,d)\in N\times V} TF_l^{(s,d)} \leq MA_l, \quad \forall\, l \in L, \tag{7}$$

In our scheme, the total traffic load on links in S_v^c must be within the link capacity ζ. Thus, if node v is assigned with channel c, then $\sum_{(s,d)\in N\times N, l\in S_v^c} D(s,d)P_l^{(s,d)} \leq \zeta$ must be satisfied for c and v. Otherwise, if node v is not assigned with channel c, there is no capacity constraint on these links. Constraint (8) covers both of the cases. Here, we put $U_{max}\zeta$ in place of ζ to minimize the largest link utilization U_{max} as the optimization function.

$$\sum_{(s,d)\in N\times N, l\in S_v^c} D(s,d)TF_l^{(s,d)} \leq U_{max}\zeta + (1 - N_v^c)\beta, \forall\, v \in N, \ \forall\, c \in C, \tag{8}$$

Our path length constraint is (9), where $\delta_{s\rightarrow d}$ represents the shortest path from s to d. $k(\geq 0)$ indicates the path stretch in integer, then $\delta_{s\rightarrow d}+k$ in (9) indicates the length of every path which is limited by the shortest path length plus k.

$$\sum_{l\in L} TF_l^{(s,d)} \leq \delta_{s\rightarrow d} + k, \quad \forall\, (s,d) \in N \times N, \tag{9}$$

With all the formulations, our scheme can generate a single path for every non-zero demand pair (s,d) in D using all the available channels, where all the constraints are fulfilled, and achieve our optimization objective.

5   Evaluation

5.1   Optimization Evaluation

In this part, we evaluate our scheme under the parameters of path stretch k and the number of NICs. The focus of our observation is whether the scheme achieve collision-free transmission and has better solution than TACCA.

Our MILP problem is solved with IBM CPLEX Optimizer [18]. Topology is designed as a 5×5 square grid, which the distance between each node is 400 m interval in both horizontal and vertical directions. We assume each NIC operates IEEE 802.11g and the link capacity is 6 Mbps. The traffic pattern is showed in Fig. 3(a) and (b) and 12 bi-directional flows are generate. Due to the CPLEX computation of this scheme would take for longer time than TACCA because of the large number of variables, in order to get the best possible solution, we set the evaluation time as 48 h, which all the scenarios of TACCA can get best solution within this time. Note that, in this test each of the traffic flow volume equal to 500 Kbps and each node is equipped with 2 NICs.

First, see Table 1, when $k = 0$, both TACCA and this scheme obtain no solution, which implies this scheme has no obvious advantage in such fixed node distance. When $k = 2$, this scheme obtains solution but TACCA cannot obtain solution which implies with more available channels this scheme more easily gets solution than TACCA under detouring path. When $k = 4$, we see this scheme

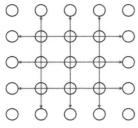
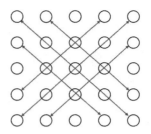

(a) Traffic Pattern 1 (Grid)   (b) Traffic Pattern 2 (Grid)

Fig. 3. Traffic pattern

Table 1. The U_{max} (Avg.) with k

k	TACCA	Proposed
0	–	–
2	–	0.5
4	0.5	0.3333
6	0.5	0.583

Table 2. The U_{max} (Avg.) with number of NICs

NIC	TACCA	Proposed
2	0.5	0.3333
3	0.5	0.3333
4	0.5	0.3333
5	0.5	0.3333

gets better solution than TACCA, which means that the proposed scheme balances the traffic load better than TACCA, and more available channels decreases the link utilization. Unfortunately, when $k = 6$, this scheme had not get better solution than TACCA within the limited time which because of computational complexity.

Table 2 shows the result of number of NICs with the maximum network link utility U_{max}, where each of the traffic flow volume equal to 500 Kbps. We set $k = 4$ for grid topology because of this is the minimize value of k which both TACCA and this scheme can obtain solutions. In the same way, we set $k = 2$ for random topology. From Table 2 we see that the number of NICs have no obvious effect on the solutions, which because for the same traffic pattern, the solution of a small number of NICs is included in the solution of a large number of NICs.

5.2 Communication Performance Evaluation

Scenargie version 2.1 [19] was used for simulation. The schedule computed with $k = 4$ are chose, and the per flow is 500 Kbps. The performance of this scheme are compared with TACCA. Recall that there is no such joint routing and POCs assignment scheme in MRMC WMNs. Therefore, in performance, most of the past schemes in the literature are not comparable. Since TACCA achieves a collision-free schedule but uses only OCs, the performance gain of this scheme coming from considering POCs can be seen. Thus, the TACCA schedule with the same parameters is used in the comparison.

Figure 4(a) shows the packet delivery ratio. We see that both TACCA and proposed scheme keep almost 100% delivery before the traffic volume reaches their network capacity. Because this scheme has more available channels to use in the same shared link capacity domain, which leads to reduce the maximum link utilization.

Figure 4(b) shows the aggregated throughput. We get that all the performs are good when the offered load are low both in TACCA and proposed scheme. However, due to the more available channels, this scheme provided more capacity space to support traffic which improve the network capacity and aggregate throughput.

Figure 4(c) shows the delivery delay. We see that the deliver delay rapidly increased when the network saturates in both TACCA and proposed scheme. However, more available channels enable proposed scheme to choose a shorter path, so it has less delay than TACCA.

Figure 4(d) shows the frame loss in MAC layer which due to collision or interference. In this figure, the number of loss frames are very small both in proposed scheme and TACCA. Therefore, our proposed scheme and TACCA have almost no frame loss owe to interference.

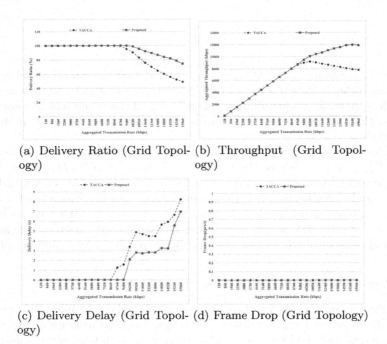

(a) Delivery Ratio (Grid Topology)

(b) Throughput (Grid Topology)

(c) Delivery Delay (Grid Topology)

(d) Frame Drop (Grid Topology)

Fig. 4. Communication performance evaluation

6   Conclusion

By designing a interference model with POCs, all IEEE 2.4Ghz band channels are used and achieve collision-free transmission among adjacent channels. Compared with TACCA, we achieve a higher number of simultaneous transmissions the restricting with the using of only orthogonal channels. This scheme also is the first collision-free transmission scheme which joint channel assignment and routing by using POCs. Simulation results show that efficient utilization of partially overlapped channels (POCs) allows significant improvement in parallel transmissions and overall network throughput.

References

1. Parvin, J.R.: An overview of wireless mesh networks. In: Wireless Mesh Networks-Security, Architectures and Protocols. IntechOpen (2019)
2. Zakaria, O.M., et al.: Joint channel assignment and routing in multiradio multi-channel wireless mesh networks: design considerations and approaches. J. Comput. Netw. Commun. 1–24 (2016)
3. Qu, Y., Ng, B., Seah, W.: A survey of routing and channel assignment in multi-channel multi-radio WMNs. J. Netw. Comput. Appl. **65**, 120–130 (2016)
4. Al Islam, A.A., Islam, M.J., Nurain, N., Raghunathan, V.: Channel assignment techniques for multi-radio wireless mesh networks: a survey. IEEE Commun. Surv. Tutor. **18**(2), 988–1017 (2015)
5. Musaddiq, A., Hashim, F., Ujang, C.A.B.C., Ali, B.M.: Survey of channel assignment algorithms for multi-radio multi-channel wireless mesh networks. IETE Tech. Rev. **32**(3), 164–182 (2015)
6. Mishra, A., Rozner, E., Banerjee, S., Arbaugh, W.: Exploiting partially overlapping channels in wireless networks: turning a peril into an advantage. In: Proceedings of the 5th ACM SIGCOMM Conference on Internet Measurement, pp. 29–29 (2005)
7. Mishra, A., Shrivastava, V., Banerjee, S., Arbaugh, W.: Partially overlapped channels not considered harmful. In: Proceedings of the Joint International Conference on Measurement and Modeling of Computer Systems, pp. 63–74, June 2006
8. Liu, K., Li, N., Liu, Y.: Min-interference and connectivity-oriented partially overlapped channel assignment for multi-radio multi-channel wireless mesh networks. In: 2017 3rd IEEE International Conference on Computer and Communications (ICCC), pp. 84–88. IEEE (2017)
9. Zhao, X., Li, L., Geng, S., Zhang, H., Ma, Y.: A link-based variable probability learning approach for partially overlapping channels assignment on multi-radio multi-channel wireless mesh information-centric IoT networks. IEEE Access **7**, 45137–45145 (2019)
10. Wang, J., Shi, W., Cui, K., Jin, F., Li, Y.: Partially overlapped channel assignment for multi-channel multi-radio wireless mesh networks. EURASIP J. Wirel. Commun. Netw. **2015**(1), 1–12 (2015). https://doi.org/10.1186/s13638-015-0259-8
11. Yang, L., et al.: Interference-avoid channel assignment for multi-radio multi-channel wireless mesh networks with hybrid traffic. IEEE Access **7**, 67167–67177 (2019)
12. Wang, J., Shi, W.: Joint multicast routing and channel assignment for multi-radio multi-channel wireless mesh networks with hybrid traffic. J. Netw. Comput. Appl. **80**, 90–108 (2017)

13. Tian, Y., Yoshihiro, T.: Traffic-demand-aware collision-free channel assignment for multi-channel multi-radio wireless mesh networks. IEEE Access **8**, 120712–120723 (2020)
14. http://dx.doi.org/10.5772/48476
15. Rad, A.H.M., Wong, V.W.S.: Partially overlapped channel assignment for multi-channel wireless mesh networks. In: IEEE International Conference on Communications, pp. 3770–3775 (2007)
16. Mishra, A., et al.: Partially overlapped channels not considered harmful. In: Proceedings of the Joint International Conference on Measurement and Modeling of Computer Systems, pp. 63–74 (2006)
17. Yoshihiro, T., Noi, T.: Collision-free channel assignment is possible in IEEE802.11-based wireless mesh networks. In: 2017 IEEE Wireless Communications and Networking Conference (WCNC), pp. 1558–2612, May 2017
18. IBM CPLEX Optimizer. https://www.ibm.com/analytics/cplex-optimizer. Accessed 10 Feb 2020
19. Scenargie VisualLab & Base Simulator-SPACE-TIME. https://www.spacetime-eng.com/en/. Accessed 1 Aug 2020

Evaluating Multiple-Access Protocols: Asynchronous Pulse Coding vs. Carrier-Sense with Collision Avoidance

Kenji Leibnitz[1]([⊠])[iD], Ferdinand Peper[1][iD], Konstantinos Theofilis[1][iD], Mikio Hasegawa[2][iD], and Naoki Wakamiya[3][iD]

[1] National Institute of Information and Communications Technology, Osaka, Japan
{leibnitz,peper,kostas}@nict.go.jp
[2] Tokyo University of Science, Tokyo, Japan
hasegawa@ee.kagu.tus.ac.jp
[3] Osaka University, Osaka, Japan
wakamiya@ist.osaka-u.ac.jp

Abstract. While the Internet of Things (IoT) is usually envisioned to support powerful functionality, like in self-driving cars, there is also increasing interest in simpler IoT applications that can be employed on massive scales at high densities, like in data gathering at meetings with large audiences. The latter vision requires low-cost devices consuming little energy, and it tends to come with a relaxed need for high-speed communication. Its realization necessitates the development of wireless protocols that are simple, yet that can effectively arbitrate multi-access to communication channels. *Carrier-Sense Multiple Access with Collision Avoidance (CSMA/CA)* is usually deployed in such contexts, but it tends to work less well when large numbers of nodes attempt to simultaneously access a wireless channel. *Asynchronous Pulse Code Multiple Access (APCMA)* has been developed with simultaneous asynchronous access to communication channels in mind by using a sparse representation of pulses to encode messages, but being relatively recent, its performance has never been systematically compared to CSMA/CA. This paper compares APCMA's performance with that of CSMA/CA in terms of the success probability (i.e., absence of errors) of message transmissions through the use of simulations and analytical models, under the assumption of equivalence in throughput. We find that APCMA with four pulses per code word performs worse than CSMA/CA, but the roles are reversed if five or six pulses are used.

Keywords: Internet of Things · Pulse-based encoding · Carrier-Sense Multiple Access

1 Introduction

Wireless sensor networks with cheap, small, and energy-efficient nodes will play a major role in the realization of ubiquitous environments and massive IoT applications. Various standards, like IEEE 802.15.4, have been developed that minimize the complexity

This research and development work is supported by MIC/SCOPE no. JP205007001.

T. Hara and H. Yamaguchi (Eds.): MobiQuitous 2021, LNICST 419, pp. 693–706, 2022.
https://doi.org/10.1007/978-3-030-94822-1_45

of nodes and their energy consumption, while allowing reasonable (but not necessarily high) data rates. Protocols in this standard typically require synchronization between senders and receivers, as well as contention resolution mechanisms to provide access to shared wireless channels in a fair way. Though various multiple access mechanisms have been developed, like *Code-Division Multiple Access (CDMA)*, in which multiple senders are able to transmit simultaneously on the same channel(s), they tend to require quite complex algorithms for encoding and decoding. Alternatively, contention resolution has been implemented based on *ALOHA* [6] and *Carrier-Sense Multiple Access with Collision Avoidance (CSMA/CA)* [3, 8]. ALOHA was among the first in this context, and it is easy to implement, but it tends to perform worse than CSMA/CA. However, CSMA/CA comes with its own disadvantages: fundamentally, it allows only a single sender to transmit on each band at a time, and it requires scheduling mechanisms to determine backoff times, clear channel assessment, and transmission initiation. Furthermore, it scales poorly: when the number of senders increases, the rate of successful transmissions drops significantly, even if many retrials are allowed.

These issues are addressed by a protocol that is proposed in [9], the so-called *Asynchronous Pulse Code Multiple Access (APCMA)*. In APCMA, information is encoded as the time intervals between successive pulses. It is based on the same principle as *Communication through Silence (CtS)* [17]. In CtS the intervals between pulses need to be silent, i.e., not interrupted by pulses from competing transmissions, and if this condition is not met, corruption of data occurs. In other words, CtS is not robust to collisions of messages from different nodes, which is the reason why it has been combined with multiple access mechanisms like CSMA/CA in [1, 2]. APCMA, on the other hand, is designed to cope with message collisions by adding redundant pulses to each code word such that the unique pattern of each code word can be picked up by a decoder at a receiver, even if the pulses in messages are interspersed by pulses from other messages. Collisions are much less of a problem in APCMA due to a number of factors: (1) Each code word contains only a small number of pulses, i.e., code words are sparse; (2) Collisions of pulses are no problem, because they do not disturb the underlying patterns of pulses in code words; (3) Even if a collision occurs, it can be successfully resolved with a high probability through the use of a pattern recognition algorithm that recognizes certain combinations of pulses as valid code words and rejects all others. In other words, APCMA allows multiple access, in which multiple messages can be transmitted by different senders at the same time on the same channel without there being a need to reschedule in case collisions occur. Another strong point of APCMA is that synchronization between senders and receivers is not required: any sender can initiate its transmission at any time without needing to check whether other transmissions are ongoing. In its current state, however, APCMA has a drawback in that it uses unary encoding. This makes code words quite long, thus increasing delay of messages. On the other hand, it also increases the sparsity of code words, which gives it the potential to allow thousands of devices to transmit at the same time [10, 11, 14, 15].

Since CSMA/CA is used in many protocols, it brings up the question of how it compares to APCMA. On one hand, packets in CSMA/CA-based protocols tend to be much shorter than packets in APCMA, but on the other hand there is a much higher chance of collisions in CSMA/CA if many senders are active at the same time. Errors in

CSMA/CA are defined differently than in APCMA: while in CSMA/CA an error is considered to have occurred either if a sender has failed to successfully transmit a message to a receiver after a certain limit on the number of retransmissions has been reached or if a transmission has collided with other transmissions rendering it unintelligible, in APCMA an error is considered to have occurred if a receiver has failed to decode a message unambiguously. While the nature of the errors is different for both protocols— in CSMA/CA the message has not been received at all, and in APCMA the message is hidden in a multitude of interpretations—in practice their outcomes are similar, i.e., a message will fail to reach its destination.

Comparing the throughput in both protocols is somewhat complicated. While in CSMA/CA throughput depends on the number of back-offs required to succeed in a transmission, as well as the average sleep interval between transmissions, in APCMA the throughput depends on the used pulse code, especially its sparsity, as well as on the average sleep interval between transmissions. In practice, however, there is little difference, since in the end it is about the number of bits per seconds that are transmitted by each node. A fair comparison between CSMA/CA and APCMA can be obtained when an equivalent throughput is assumed, after which the rates of successfully-received messages are measured.

This paper compares CSMA/CA with APCMA by computer simulations and analytical models. We use a model of CSMA/CA that is inspired by the IEEE 802.15.4 standard [5], but that is adjusted to make the comparison with APCMA easier. Parameters of the models are set such that throughput is similar, and based on these settings the rates at which transmitted messages successfully arrive at a receiver are investigated. The CSMA/CA model is investigated through simulation, as is the APCMA model for code words with four and five pulses each. Results for APCMA based on the analytical model in [10] are also added to the comparison, whereby four, five, and six pulses per code word are used. We investigate scenarios with numbers of nodes varying between one to up to 2500 transmitters, whereas all messages are received at one single receiver in a single-hop fashion. Three different scenarios corresponding to different throughputs are investigated, whereby the throughput in a scenario is reduced by increasing the sleeping periods between transmissions. In general, the success rate decreases with the increase in number of nodes for all models, as can be expected. When the sleep intervals between transmissions are increased in length, the success rate increases in all scenarios, which is also to be expected, since an increase in sleep will reduce the occupancy of a channel. In all scenarios the 4-pulse APCMA model performs worse than CSMA/CA in simulations. The 5-pulse and 6-pulse APCMA models, on the other hand, perform better than CSMA/CA in all scenarios where the success rate is high enough to be of practical value. The analytical APCMA model gives very similar performance as its simulated counterpart for four and five pulses, which suggests that the 6-pulse version of APCMA would follow its analytical model closely if it were to be simulated. All comparisons of performance are done with respect to the data link layer of the OSI model, and we assume perfect fidelity of the physical layer. Our justification is that only simple modulations of signals are used on which the physical layers are equally affected by noise for all models.

Fig. 1. (a) Length of the silent interval between two successive pulses (indicated by thick blue arrows) encodes the value x in the CtS scheme. (b) When there is an interspersed pulse from an unrelated message (indicated by the red arrow), then the interval is broken in two, giving two erroneous values x_1 and x_2. (Color figure online)

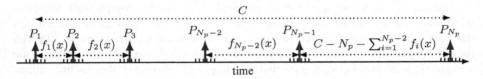

Fig. 2. Format of a code word in APCMA.

Comparison of CSMA/CA with APCMA is important for the realization of an Internet of Things (IoT) in which nodes are extremely simple and have low cost. Such nodes can be expected in ubiquitous environments, as well as in applications like asset tracking or monitoring of anomalous health signs (like high body temperature) at mass events [4,7].

This paper is organized as follows. Section 2 describes APCMA in more detail. Section 3 describes the particular form of CSMA/CA we use, whereas Sect. 4 describes the setup of the simulations in more detail and the simulation results. We finish this paper with a discussion and conclusions in Sect. 5.

2   Asynchronous Pulse Code Multiple Access Model

Our starting point is CtS, which encodes a value as the length of a silent time interval between successive pulses, like in Fig. 1(a). An integer x in the range $[0, V]$ is encoded as an interval of $x + 1$ empty time slots lying between two time slots each occupied by a pulse, whereby there is at least one empty time slot between two pulses transmitted from one and the same transmitter.

As can be seen from Fig. 1(b) this value becomes impossible to decode if the interval is interspersed by a pulse from another message. APCMA addresses this problem by adding redundant pulses such that the resulting code words differ as much as possible under all possible shift operations. The general format of a code word in APCMA contains N_p pulses, as illustrated in Fig. 2.

Hereby, the $N_p - 1$ intervals of successive lengths

$$f_1(x), \; f_2(x), \; \ldots, \; f_{N_p-2}(x), \; C - N_p - \sum_{i=1}^{N_p-2} f_i(x), \tag{1}$$

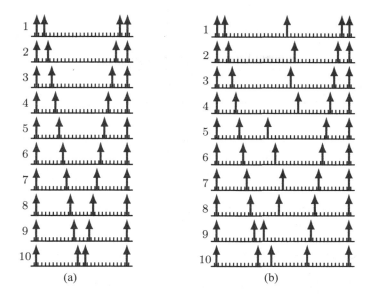

Fig. 3. (a) APCMA code with four pulses and ten code words, with encoding functions $f_1(x) = x + 1$ and $f_2(x) = C - 6 - 2x$ and code length $C = 25$. (b) APCMA code with five pulses and ten code words with code length $C = 36$.

encode the value x. The functions f_i, called the *encoding functions*, are one-to-one, and they are predetermined and shared among the transmitters and receivers, and C is the code length expressed as the number of time slots required for a code word. Examples of 4-pulse and 5-pulse APCMA codes, both with ten code words, are given in Fig. 3.

APCMA codes with five or more pulses tend to be less regular, but the APCMA codes in this paper have in common that their code books contain at most one pulse in each time slot (represented by a column in a code book), except for the first and last pulses, which are always present for all code words. Taking into account these conditions, we assume in this paper that the code length equals $C = (N_p - 2)N_c + N_p + 1$ time slots, whereby N_p is the number of pulses in each code word and N_c is the number of code words in the code.

We assume a single-hop network in which one node that is continuously listening receives the transmissions from the sender nodes. Sender nodes broadcast their messages according to the schedule in Fig. 4 that consists of cycles, each of which contains one broadcast and one sleep period. A broadcast lasts for C time slots, and it is followed by a sleep interval that is randomly distributed according to a uniform distribution over the interval $\left[S_{min}^{(a)}, S_{max}^{(a)} \right]$, whereby $S_{min}^{(a)}$ is the minimum sleep time and $S_{max}^{(a)}$ is the maximum sleep time, and the superscript is used to distinguish between APCMA (a) and CSMA/CA (c). $S_{min}^{(a)}$ is chosen to have value 1 in this paper, and $S_{max}^{(a)}$ has a value several times C, whereby the multiplier is determined such that a throughput is achieved that is equivalent to that of the CSMA/CA model.

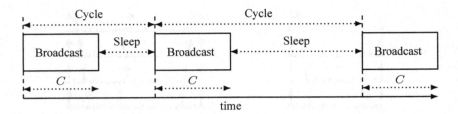

Fig. 4. Scheduling of a node. After each broadcast a node goes to sleep for a random time that is uniformly distributed. Each broadcast is conducted over C time slots, and it starts directly after its preceding sleep period.

It is important that there is sufficient spread in the lengths of the sleeping intervals in simulations of the model and in practical implementations, because this will allow the system to quickly reach a stationary state. Without this spread there will be a kind of phase locking in which waves of above-average numbers of nodes attempting to transmit messages are interspersed by less busy periods. This would significantly reduce the rate by which messages are successfully decoded at the receiver.

The average length of a cycle is now estimated as

$$K_{Cy} = C + \frac{S_{\min}^{(a)} + S_{\max}^{(a)}}{2}. \tag{2}$$

Since a unary code is used for APCMA, the number of bits transmitted in a single message is $\log_2 N_c$. In this paper we use $N_c = 1024$, which corresponds to 10 bits per message. Assuming a duration of a time slot in APCMA of $\Delta t^{(a)}$, we then arrive at a throughput of APCMA of approximately

$$\vartheta^{(a)} = \frac{\log_2 N_c}{K_{Cy} \Delta t^{(a)}} \quad \text{bits per second.} \tag{3}$$

This throughput is the raw bit rate that is transmitted by each node individually, without consideration of other nodes. It can be manipulated by varying the code length and the lengths of sleep intervals. Higher bit rates result in higher density of pulses, but they tend to cause decreased probabilities by which messages are successfully decoded at a receiver.

We consider a message to be decoded successfully when that message has been transmitted by a node and the decoder can unambiguously decode it. Using Eq. (8) in [10], we then arrive at a theoretical value of the success probability $p_s^{(a)}$ equaling

$$p_s^{(a)} = \left(1 - p^{N_p - 2}\right)^{N_c - 1}, \tag{4}$$

whereby p is the probability that a time slot is occupied by a pulse in case there are N_n transmitters in the network:

$$p = 1 - (1 - q)^{N_n} \tag{5}$$

Hereby the average density q of pulses over time is given by:

$$q = \frac{N_p}{K_{Cy}} \tag{6}$$

The analytical value for $p_s^{(a)}$ will be used in subsequent sections for comparison with the simulations of APCMA and simulations of CSMA/CA.

The success probability of APCMA in simulations is defined by

$$\widetilde{p}_s^{(a)} = \frac{1}{N_n} \sum_{k=1}^{N_n} \frac{U_k}{M_k}, \tag{7}$$

whereby U_k is the number of messages transmitted by node k that can be uniquely identified, i.e., without ambiguities, and M_k is the total number of messages transmitted by node k.

Decoding of messages at the receiver is conducted by pattern recognition algorithms that use either a type of finite automata operating on pulse sequences [9, 11] or a shift register that detects pulse sequences that are input at the left side of the register and that shift one cell to the right each time step [14, 15].

APCMA has been implemented on various hardware platforms, including the Arduino Mega 2560 microcontroller [11] and the Xilinx Spartan-3E FPGA [10, 14, 15]. APCMA has also been implemented and tested for the distribution of power packets in a small electric power network [16]. Such networks require routing of power to, for example, actuators in robots in a flexible way such that the amount of wiring stays limited. The simplicity of APCMA is a major advantage in applications like this. Currently under development are miniaturized nodes based on the Teensy 3.2 microcontroller (Fig. 5).

3 Carrier Sense Multiple Access Model

One of the most commonly found ways of providing multiple access over the wireless channel is by using *Carrier Sense Multiple Access/Collision Avoidance* (CSMA/CA) on the medium access control (MAC) sublayer of the data link layer. Slightly different variations of CSMA/CA exist in multi-access protocols, such as IEEE 802.11 [3] for wireless local area networks (WLAN) or IEEE 802.15.4 [5] for sensor networks and wireless personal area networks (WPAN) that take into account the characteristics of the connected devices and their available power limitations.

Several studies have investigated the dynamics of the backoff algorithm in IEEE 802.15.4 by simulation or theoretical analysis, e.g., [8, 12, 13]. For this paper, we consider a numerical simulation of CSMA/CA that roughly follows the mechanism in IEEE 802.15.4 to compare its performance with APCMA. In particular, we model the nodes in CSMA/CA to behave similarly as in APCMA by periodically transmitting their sensor data, followed by uniformly distributed sleep periods over the interval $\left[S_{\min}^{(c)}, S_{\max}^{(c)}\right]$. Our considered CSMA/CA model operates without an inactive period within the MAC layer superframe and does not use guaranteed time slots. Since the duration of a unit backoff period depends on the modulation type and frequency band, we make the assumption that a unit backoff period matches exactly the length of a single message ($L = 10$ bits) and the time for a unit backoff period is $\Delta t^{(c)} = 200\,\mu s$, where the superscript (c) stands for CSMA/CA. This corresponds to $20\,\mu s$ per bit when *Manchester coding* is used. Since the logical signal associated with Manchester coding is high or low each

Fig. 5. APCMA node under development, with a Japanese 500 Yen coin for size comparison.

half of the time, we use the time during which the bit has on average a logic high value as the pulse width to be used in the APCMA model, i.e., $\Delta t^{(a)} = 10\,\mu$s. This appears to be a fair way to match both models with each other, since the time slot next to a pulse in APCMA has always a logic low value.

In IEEE 802.15.4, each node first performs a random backoff within the interval of $[0, 2^{BE} - 1]$ before attempting to access the channel. The variable BE stands for the *backoff exponent* that is initialized as *minBE* $= 3$ and is doubled every time the channel is sensed to be busy during all transmission attempts of this packet. After the backoff timer expires, the node performs two *clear channel assessments* (CCA) in successive time slots to confirm that the channel is free. The attempting node will only begin its transmission if both CCAs are successful. When either one of the CCAs fails due to an ongoing transmission by another node, the attempting node will perform a new random backoff at an increased backoff window size and will try to access the channel again when this new backoff timer expires. This entire process continues until either the transmission attempt is successful or the maximum backoff limit *maxBO* is reached. We use for both values, i.e., the maximum backoff exponent *maxBE* and the maximum backoff limit *maxBO*, the default value of 5. A flowchart of the simulated CSMA/CA algorithm is shown in Fig. 6.

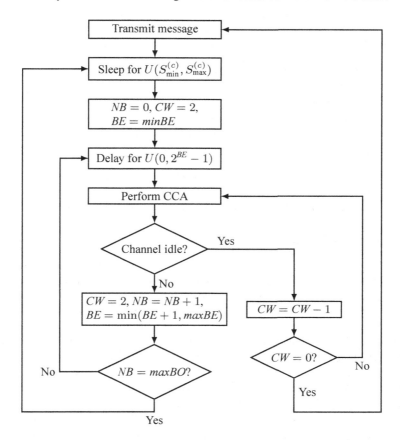

Fig. 6. Flowchart of CSMA/CA algorithm used in simulation

A node that is in a sleep state, will remain in that state for a uniformly distributed random number of unit backoff periods expressed as time slots of length $\Delta t^{(c)}$ in the interval $\left[S_{\min}^{(c)}, S_{\max}^{(c)} \right]$. In our simulations, we use $S_{\min}^{(c)} = 1$ and $S_{\max}^{(c)} = 118\ sf$, with the *sleep factor* sf having values $sf \in \{5, 10, 100\}$, and where the 118 reflects the worst possible number of unit backoff periods a node could be waiting before finally being able to transmit.

Let us assume that there are N_n nodes in the network, where each node k is operating with the same $S_{\min}^{(c)}$ and $S_{\max}^{(c)}$ values. At every time instant t when node k attempts to begin its transmission after two successful CCAs, we distinguish the two cases if node k is the only node beginning to transmit at t, or if there are possibly also other (multiple) nodes beside node k doing the same. We log both cases as A_{k1} and A_{km}, respectively. While from node k's viewpoint both cases would be regarded as successful transmissions, the A_{km} case could in fact lead to a garbled transmission that cannot be correctly decoded at the receiver. We define the success probability of CSMA/CA from a single simulation as

$$\widetilde{p}_s^{(c)} = \frac{1}{N_n} \sum_{k=1}^{N_n} \frac{A_{k1}}{A_{km}}. \tag{8}$$

In each simulation run we generate the same total number of $M = 100N_n$ messages over all nodes during T simulated backoff periods. We further know that each message has the same length of L bits, so we then obtain the throughput as follows in bits per seconds.

$$\vartheta^{(c)} = \frac{L\,M}{T\,\Delta t^{(c)}} \tag{9}$$

4   Comparative Evaluation of CSMA/CA and APCMA

4.1   Mapping the Parameters Between CSMA/CA and APCMA

Since APCMA and CSMA/CA are different protocols, we need to clarify how we set the parameters in each system to ensure a fair comparison. As our performance metric, we use the success probabilities as defined in Eqs. (4), (7), and (8) in both models. The basis for the comparison is a matching of the throughput of all models. Note that for CSMA/CA backoffs in themselves do not reduce its success probability according to Eq. (8), but they do reduce throughput, since the time intervals between successive transmissions will increase. In the comparison with APCMA when throughput of both models are matched, the success probability of CSMA/CA will then look relatively less favorable, so indirectly backoffs affect the relative performance of CSMA/CA.

For given values of N_n nodes and sleep parameters $S_{\min}^{(c)}$ and $S_{\max}^{(c)}$, we first perform 100 replications of the CSMA/CA simulations as described in the previous section to determine average values $\langle \widetilde{p}_s^{(c)} \rangle$ and $\langle \vartheta^{(c)} \rangle$ over all replications. Given that the APCMA code word length for N_p pulses is $C = (N_p - 2)N_c + N_p + 1$, we compute the maximum sleep limit $S_{\max}^{(a)}$ of the corresponding APCMA model that has the same average throughput as $\langle \vartheta^{(c)} \rangle$ from Eq. (10), where $\Delta t^{(a)}$ is the time for transmitting a single pulse in APCMA.

$$S_{\max}^{(a)} = \frac{2\,L}{\langle \vartheta^{(c)} \rangle \Delta t^{(a)}} - 2\,C - 1 \tag{10}$$

Using this value of $S_{\max}^{(a)}$, we can then determine the success probability of APCMA through simulation and analysis corresponding to the equivalent throughput achieved by CSMA/CA.

4.2   Numerical Results

We now describe the numerical results we obtained from the simulations and analysis described in the previous sections. We consider three different levels of system load having high, medium, and low values that are controlled by the sleep factor sf of the maximum sleep time $S_{\max}^{(c)}$ in the CSMA/CA simulation. Depending on the achieved throughput in the CSMA/CA simulation, we adjust the maximum sleep value $S_{\max}^{(a)}$

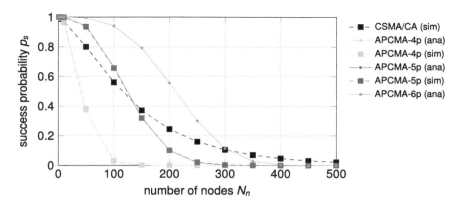

Fig. 7. Success probabilities of CSMA/CA with sleep factor $sf = 5$ and APCMA with corresponding throughput. Dashed lines show results from simulations and solid lines show analytical results. The results from simulation and analysis of APCMA show a near perfect match. The throughput varies between 164 bps for lower numbers of nodes to 129 bps for higher numbers of nodes.

of the APCMA simulation to reach the same throughput. Since the sleep time is randomly selected with a relatively large variance, stationarity of the simulations is almost instantly reached and we therefore don't need to consider an initial transient phase after which the simulation results must be extracted.

In Fig. 7, we show the results for the highly loaded case where we set $sf = 5$. Analytical values are shown for APCMA with solid lines, and simulated values for both models are shown as dashed lines. Each simulation is repeated 100 times with the same settings and since the confidence intervals are very small, we decided to leave them out from the figures for clarity.

We see in Fig. 7 that the success probability in CSMA/CA lies somewhere between that of the three variations of APCMA. The more pulses are used in APCMA, the better its success probability becomes. However, it can also be seen that already for 300 to 400 nodes all models show rather poor performance. Figures 7, 8 and 9 show that the analytical model of APCMA with four and five pulses matches very closely with the results of the simulations.

Figure 8 shows that when the CSMA/CA sleep factor is increased to $sf = 10$, all curves shift to the right and more nodes can be accommodated. The relative performance among all three APCMA models and the CSMA/CA model remains roughly the same.

Finally, Fig. 9 shows a significantly less loaded system with $sf = 100$. While the 4-pulse APCMA variant reaches 50% success probability for about 750 nodes, CSMA/CA and APCMA with five pulses can accommodate about 2500 nodes. At 2500 nodes, the APCMA variant with six pulses even remains above 85% success probability.

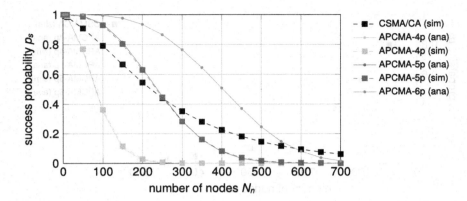

Fig. 8. Success probabilities of CSMA/CA with sleep factor $sf = 10$ and APCMA with corresponding throughput. Dashed lines show results from simulations and solid lines show analytical results. Again, the results from simulation and analysis of APCMA show a near perfect match. The throughput varies between 83 bps for lower numbers of nodes to 69 bps for higher numbers of nodes.

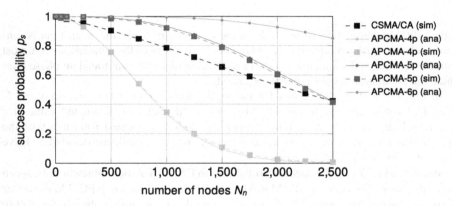

Fig. 9. Success probabilities of CSMA/CA with sleep factor $sf = 100$ and APCMA with corresponding throughput. Dashed lines show results from simulations and solid lines show analytical results. Again, the results from simulation of APCMA match the analysis very well. The throughput is around 8 bps for all numbers of nodes.

5   Discussion and Conclusions

We compared a CSMA/CA-like protocol with APCMA for four, five, and six pulses in terms of the probability that a transmission is successfully received/decoded at a receiver, whereby the parameters of all models are set such that they have similar throughput. Though no simulations were conducted for 6-pulse APCMA, they would likely show very similar performance as the analytical model, given that is the case for 4-pulse and 5-pulse APCMA. APCMA compares favorably to CSMA/CA when five or six pulses per APCMA code word are used, but not so in case of only four pulses, as our simulations and analytical models show. APCMA compares even more favorable to CSMA/CA when more than six pulses per code word are used according to the analytical model in [10].

CSMA/CA and APCMA are very different protocols, so there are points in which no match in operating conditions are possible. Notably, the employed CSMA/CA protocol is slotted, which means that all nodes are synchronized by a beacon signal. This requires that transmitter nodes need to have the functionality to receive beacon signals, even if they are only intended to be used as transmitters. Nodes working according to APCMA lack this requirement, and so all transmitters do not need receiver functionality. This significantly reduces hardware complexity and power consumption. Depending on the situation, this may also allow scenarios in which 4-pulse APCMA is preferable over CSMA/CA for small numbers (say tens) of nodes, even though 4-pulse APCMA shows a lower success probability.

The coding of CSMA/CA and APCMA also differ radically. Whereas CSMA/CA encodes its packets by binary coding, APCMA uses unary coding. This causes packets of APCMA to be much longer than those of CSMA/CA, but this does not pose problems, since APCMA is designed to be robust to overlaps in time of its transmissions. In fact, this robustness increases with the length of packet size, though it goes at the expense of throughput. The throughput for the fastest scenario investigated in this paper ranges from 129 to 164 bps, given a pulse width of $10\,\mu s$ in APCMA and an equivalent bit width of $20\,\mu s$ in CSMA/CA, but it decreases to around 8 bps for the slowest scenario. These bit rates are in line with the type of applications that are supported by the IEEE 802.15.4 standard, like wireless sensor networks.

In both CSMA/CA and APCMA no error correcting coding schemes were used, because we aimed to compare the raw performance of the models. We believe that especially APCMA will benefit from adding error correction, and we will report on this in more detail in future papers.

References

1. Chen, Y., Wang, D., Zhang, J.: Variable-base tacit communication: a new energy efficient communication scheme for sensor networks. In: Proceedings of the First International Conference on Integrated Internet Ad Hoc and Sensor Networks, InterSense'06. Association for Computing Machinery, New York (2006)
2. Feng, D., Das, S., Hajiaghajani, F., Shi, Y., Biswas, S.: Pulse Position Coded medium access in energy-starved networks. Comput. Commun. **148**, 62–73 (2019)
3. Bianchi, G.: Performance analysis of the IEEE 802.11 distributed coordination function. IEEE J. Sel. Areas Commun. **18**(3), 535–547 (2000)
4. Henning, K.: Overview of syndromic surveillance-what is syndromic surveillance? MMWR Morb. Mortal. Wkly. Rep. **53**(Suppl), 5–11 (2004)
5. IEEE STD 802.15.4-2020 (Revision of IEEE STD 802.15.4-2015): IEEE standard for low-rate wireless networks (2020)
6. Laya, A., Kalalas, C., Vazquez-Gallego, F., Alonso, L., Alonso-Zarate, J.: Goodbye, ALOHA! IEEE Access **4**, 2029–2044 (2016)
7. Memish, Z., et al.: Mass gatherings medicine: public health issues arising from mass gathering religious and sporting events. Lancet **393**(10185), 2073–2084 (2019)

8. Misic, J., Shafi, S., Misic, V.: The impact of MAC parameters on the performance of 802.15.4 PAN. Ad Hoc Netw. **3**(5), 509–528 (2005)
9. Peper, F., Leibnitz, K., Hasegawa, M., Wakamiya, N.: Spike-based communication networks with error correcting capability. Brain Neural Netw. **25**(4), 157–164 (2018)
10. Peper, F., et al.: High-density resource-restricted pulse-based IoT networks. IEEE Trans. Green Commun. Netw. **5**, 1856–1868 (2021)
11. Peper, F., et al.: On high-density resource-restricted pulse-based IoT networks. In: GLOBE-COM 2020–2020 IEEE Global Communications Conference, pp. 1–6 (2020)
12. Pollin, S., et al.: Performance analysis of slotted carrier sense IEEE 802.15.4 medium access layer. IEEE Trans. Wirel. Commun. **7**(9), 3359–3371 (2008)
13. Ramachandran, I., Das, A., Roy, S.: Analysis of the contention access period of IEEE 802.15.4 MAC. ACM Trans. Sensor Netw. **3**(1), 4-es (2007)
14. Tanaka, C., et al.: Performance evaluation of pulse-based multiplexing protocol implemented on massive IoT devices. Nonlinear Theory Appl. IEICE **12**(3), 1–12 (2021)
15. Tanaka, C., et al.: Implementation of pulse-based multiplexing protocol for massive IoT. In: Proceedings of the 2020 International Symposium on Nonlinear Theory and Its Applications (NOLTA), pp. 346–349 (2020)
16. Tanaka, C., Peper, F., Hasegawa, M.: Application of APCMA protocol to power packet networks for multiplexing power packet transmissions. Nonlinear Theory Appl. IEICE **11**(4), 433–445 (2020)
17. Zhu, Y., Sivakumar, R.: Challenges: communication through Silence in wireless sensor networks. In: Proceedings of the Annual International Conference on Mobile Computing and Networking, MOBICOM, pp. 140–147, August 2005

Rate Control for Multi-link and Multi-relay Wireless LANs Supporting Real-Time Mobile Data Transmissions

Kazuki Ikeda[1], Shohei Omoto[2], Hiroyuki Yomo[1,2(✉)], Yoshihisa Kondo[2], and Hiroyuki Yokoyama[2]

[1] Graduate School of Science and Engineering, Kansai University, Suita, Japan
yomo@kansai-u.ac.jp
[2] ATR Adaptive Communications Research Laboratories, Kyoto, Japan

Abstract. When a wireless LAN station (STA) installed on a mobile device, such as drone, communicates with an access point (AP) deployed over the ground, its link condition becomes unstable due to mobility and/or interference from surrounding equipment. In this paper, in order to realize reliable data transmissions in such a severe condition, we introduce a multi–link and multi–relay system integrated with broadcast transmissions employing packet–level forward error correction. As a proof–of–concept (PoC), we first conduct an experiment investigating the effectiveness and practicality of the considered multi–link and multi–relay system supporting data transmissions from a drone. Then, we enhance it by proposing rate control for STA to dynamically set its physical layer (PHY) rate based on its position and the link quality for surrounding relays. We also apply overhearing function to each relay to prevent redundant forwarding of the same packets by multiple relays. Our simulation results show an interesting observation that the multi–link and multi–relay system improves energy efficiency of relays when the proposed rate control and overhearing are jointly employed. Furthermore, we show that the multi–link and multi–relay system with link–level broadcast has superior performance to a common unicast based system.

Keywords: Wireless LAN · Drone · Robustness · Real–time data transmissions · Rate control · Relay

1 Introduction

Real–time transmissions of sensing and image/video data from a highly mobile terminal, such as drone, enable many applications such as disaster response,

This work includes results of the project entitled "R&D on Adaptive Media Access Control for Increasing the Capacity of Wireless IoT Devices in Factory Sites," which is supported by the Ministry of Internal Affairs and Communications as part of the research program "R&D for Expansion of Radio Wave Resources (JPJ000254)".

T. Hara and H. Yamaguchi (Eds.): MobiQuitous 2021, LNICST 419, pp. 707–723, 2022.
https://doi.org/10.1007/978-3-030-94822-1_46

environmental monitoring, infrastructure management, live event streaming, etc. [1,2]. In this paper, we focus on real–time data transmissions from a drone supported by wireless LAN (WLAN). The most common communication mode in WLAN is a *single–link unicast*: a station (STA) installed on a drone is associated/connected to a single access point (AP) deployed over the ground. However, data transmissions with a single AP are vulnerable to link disconnections due to interference and mobility of drone [3]. In order to overcome this problem, in our previous work, we advocated exploiting multiple reception points offered by multiple APs deployed over the ground [4]. Each data is transmitted by STA with link–level broadcast such that route diversity through multiple reception points is exploited while its reliability is enhanced by applying packet–level forward error correction. However, the deployment of multiple APs, which requires wired connections to a gateway (GW), increases its system cost, and also limits its flexibility to change the configuration of reception points. In order to solve this problem, in this paper, we introduce multiple relays into our system setting. The multiple reception points are realized by battery–operated, portable wireless relays, which can provide flexibility for their deployment. Furthermore, we also apply multi–link transmissions in order to enjoy channel diversity for WLAN transmissions. Since WLAN utilizes the unlicensed frequency band, an operating channel can suffer from severe interference caused by surrounding radio equipment. With multi–link transmissions over multiple operating channels, even if one channel is highly occupied by the interfering unlicensed devises, the other channel can be free of interference, which can enhance the robustness in highly–interfered scenarios.

An important parameter to be tuned in our system setting described above is physical layer (PHY) rate employed by STA. A smaller PHY rate increases the number of relays, to which STA can deliver data, thereby improving the spatial reliability. However, the duration of packet transmission is increased with the smaller PHY rate, which increases the airtime (i.e., channel occupancy period) and gives negative impact on the other radio equipment sharing the same channel. A common approach to PHY rate adaptation in WLAN is the rate control based on feedback (i.e., ACK) returned from a possible receiver. However, the system considered in this paper employs link–level broadcast by STA, which in general is difficult to employ ACK and retransmission mechanisms. Due to this difficulty, IEEE 802.11, which is employed for PHY and medium access control (MAC) protocol of WLAN in this paper, does not implement ACK for link–level broadcast. Therefore, we need to design rate control that does not count on feedback from receivers. Furthermore, high mobility of drone does not allow STA to spend sufficiently long time to decide its optimal PHY rate at each position. Therefore, it is necessary to design rate control that can promptly decide PHY rate to be employed at a given position of drone.

In this paper, as a proof–of–concept (PoC), we first conduct an experiment investigating the effectiveness and practicality of the considered multi–link and multi–relay system supporting data transmissions from a drone. Then, we enhance it by proposing a rate control for WLAN STA installed on drone, which promptly decides PHY rate to be employed at a given position based on its link conditions for surrounding relays without resorting to ACK. The proposed rate control introduces a calibration phase before system operations, during which the drone conducts test flight over the given communication area and preliminary observes the radio environment. Specifically, the drone transmits probing signals at different positions over the given area, with which each relay measures the received signal strength and forwards them to an AP. Based on the received/observed information, AP constructs a mapping table between different positions over the area and PHY rates to be employed, which is then set to STA. During the system operations, STA on drone decides its PHY rate based on its position and given mapping table. We also apply overhearing function to each relay in order to prevent redundant forwarding of the same packets by multiple relays. With computer simulations, we evaluate performance of multi–link and multi–relay transmissions with the proposed rate control in terms of packet delivery rate, delay, airtime, and energy consumption of wireless relays, and investigate the effectiveness of the proposed rate control as well as multi–link/multi–relay configurations.

Some existing work focus on the video streaming from drone to a ground station. For instance, video rate adaptation is investigated for adapting to variable air–to–ground channel in [1,2]. The PHY rate adaptation based on sensor state of unmanned aerial vehicle (UAV) is proposed in [3]. While these work focus on direct transmissions of video from drone to a ground station, the use of relay with routing protocols is also considered, e.g., in [5]. Unlike these work, our work introduces multi–link relaying combined with link–level broadcast and packet–level FEC into data transmissions from drone, for which PHY rate adaptation is proposed to take trade–off between reliability and efficiency.

2 System Model

The system model considered in this paper is shown in Fig. 1. A single AP, which is connected to a gateway (GW) through a wired connection, is deployed over a target communication area together with multiple relaying nodes (RNs). A drone flies over the communication area, and its onboard STA attempts to transmit data to GW through RNs and AP. We assume that GPS module is installed on the drone to identify its position. The STA is equipped with multiple WLAN IFs operating over different channels, which are used for multi–link data transfer. When multiple drones (i.e., STAs) are considered, the same set of channels can be allocated and shared by different STAs. Therefore, the number of required channels is not dependent on the number of considered drones. On the other hand, the number of WLAN IFs owned by each RN is assumed to be $N_{RN} = N_{STA} + N_F$, where N_{STA} is the number of IFs used by STA for multi–link transmissions and N_F is that employed by RN for data forwarding to AP. The number of IFs installed into AP, N_{AP}, is supposed to be sufficient to receive data transmitted by STA and/or RS over any channel. All the WLAN IFs are assumed to follow IEEE 802.11n protocols. The example in Fig. 1 shows the case with $N_{STA} = 2$, $N_F = 1$, and $N_{AP} = 4$, where different channels are assigned to separate IFs for data transmissions/forwarding by STA/RNs. This multi–link/multi–channel configuration allows us to exploit *channel diversity*: even if some channels are severely interfered by many unlicensed equipment, data transmitted by the other channels with less interference can be successfully delivered with high probability. Furthermore, in order to exploit multiple reception points realized by RNs, STA employs link–level broadcast combined with packet–level forward error correction (FEC). In this scheme, for a batch of K data packets to be transfered to GW, STA transmits $N = K + M$ packets at each IF, where M packets are redundant packets generated from K data packets by using random linear network coding (RLNC) [6]. At GW, if any set of K packets out of $N = K + N_{STA}M$ packets are successfully received, it can recover the original K data packets. This enables us to enjoy *route diversity*: GW can recover packets lost over a route between STA and GW from the other packets successfully received over the separate routes, thereby enhancing the reliability of mobile data transmissions.

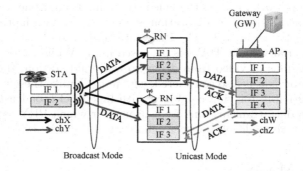

Fig. 1. Considered multi–link and multi–relay data transmission system.

On the other hand, we employ standard unicast transmissions for data forwarding from RNs to AP, considering that RNs and AP are static nodes. Each IF at RN for data forwarding is connected to an IF at AP, where retransmission mechanisms based on ACK exchange and dynamic rate control with automatic rate fallback (ARF) [7] are employed.

3   An Experiment on Multi–link and Multi–relay Transmissions from a Drone

As PoC of the multi–link and multi–relay system supporting data transmissions from a drone, we conducted an experiment to investigate its effectiveness and practicality. The experimental setting is shown in Fig. 2. The experiment was conducted at a test field set up by JUIDA [8]. The STA installed on a drone

(DJI phantom 4 [9]) and each RN are realized by Raspberry Pi 3 model B+ with commercial, off–the–shelf WLAN USB dongles. On the other hand, AP consists of a Raspberry Pi 3 model B+ and an off–the–shelf WLAN router. A laptop PC is used to aggregate data packets transmitted by STA through RNs. The drone with STA on board repeatedly flies over the test field with the height of 10m as shown in Fig. 2.

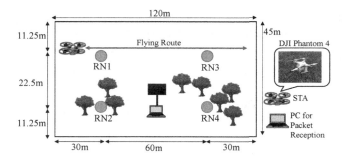

Fig. 2. Experimental settings of multi–link and multi–relay data transmissions from a drone.

Two WLAN USB dongles are inserted into the Raspberry Pi of STA, whose channels are set to different channels over 2.4 GHz band. For a regulatory reason, we employed 2.4 GHz for data transmissions from STA on drone. Similarly, two WLAN USB dongles set to operate over the corresponding 2.4 GHz channels are put into the Raspberry Pi of RN. Furthermore, an internal WLAN IF of the Raspberry Pi of RN is used to forward data packets to the WLAN router in AP, which uses a single channel over 5 GHz. The Raspberry Pi in AP also has two WLAN USB dongles to directly receive data from STA. That is, we have a configuration with $N_{STA} = 2$, $N_F = 1$, $N_{RN} = 3$, and $N_{AP} = 3$. For multi–link transmissions from STA, the same set of packets are transmitted with link–level broadcast over each IF, where its FEC rate is fixed to be $1/2$ ($K = 10$). The number of RNs is assumed to be 4 as shown in Fig. 2. These RNs are controlled to forward all packets successfully received from STA to AP with unicast mode, where PHY rate control implemented into the employed USB dongle by default is activated. The packets with their size of 1400 Bytes are transmitted with the interval of 10 ms, where the total number of data packets transmitted is fixed to be 6000.

In the experiment, we evaluated application–level packet delivery rate (PDR) (i.e., PDR after FEC decoding) and airtime per IF at STA for the transmissions employing multi–link and multi–relay broadcast explained in Sect. 2 (called ML–BC hereafter) and those activating only a single IF at STA, i.e., single–link and multi–relay broadcast (called SL–BC hereafter). Table 1 shows PDR and airtime per IF of ML–BC and SL–BC for different, fixed PHY rates set to STA. From this table, we can first see that PDR is improved by employing lower PHY rate. Specifically, by employing 14.4 Mbps as PHY rate at STA, PDR of 100% is achieved even for SL–BC. This is because smaller signal–to–noise ratio (SNR) is sufficient for packets transmitted with lower PHY rate to be received successfully at reception points, which however sacrifices airtime as observed in Table 1. In order to reduce airtime, it is preferred to employ higher PHY rate, however, SL–BC cannot offer PDR of 100% for PHY rate of 86.7 Mbps while it is possible with ML–BC. Furthermore, ML–BC largely improves PDR in comparison to SL–BC for PHY rate of 144 Mbps. This is thanks to channel diversity: even if a packet transmitted over one IF is lost due to low SNR or high interference, it can be delivered to a reception point successfully over the other IF. These experimental results and our implementation of multi–link and multi–relay system confirm its effectiveness and practicality.

Table 1. Experimental Results

	PDR [%]	Airtime per IF at STA [s]
SL–BC (14.4 Mbps)	100	10.25
SL–BC (86.7 Mbps)	98.37	2.12
SL–BC (144 Mbps)	63.77	1.48
ML–BC (14.4 Mbps)	100	10.25
ML–BC (86.7 Mbps)	100	2.12
ML–BC (144 Mbps)	83.33	1.48

4   Enhancements to Multi–link and Multi–relay System

In this work, we enhance the multi–link and multi–relay system supporting data transmissions from a drone by two mechanisms: PHY rate control and over-hearing. While overhearing is a well-known approach for wireless relaying [10] to select a best relay, there is no PHY rate control specific to multi–link and multi–relay system with link–level broadcast. Therefore, we newly propose a rate control mechanism explained below.

4.1   PHY Rate Control

In this paper, we propose a PHY rate control for WLAN STA on drone, which can cope with the rapid change of link qualities to surrounding RNs. We first divide the communication area into several grids, and STA decides its PHY rate to be employed according to its staying grid. The PHY rate to be employed in each grid is decided based on *test flight*, which is carried out just before its operations over the corresponding communication area. This kind of pre–measurement regarding connectivity/coverage is commonly employed for optimizing parameters at a given communication area, which is employed for PHY rate adaptation in this work. During test flight, the drone moves to the center of each grid and transmits control packets, which are then used by AP to decide the best rate at each grid. The decision on PHY rate consists of the following 2 steps:

Step 1: The objective of this step is to extract the average received signal strength indicators (RSSIs) between each IF at STA and surrounding RNs. The STA broadcasts packets including its GPS information (i.e., its location) from each IF at the center of each grid for a given period of time. Then, each RN forwards the received packets to AP, in which the information on RSSI observed when receiving each packet is added. During test flight, each RN is controlled to forward all received packets to AP. Based on the forwarded packets, AP calculates the average RSSIs between each IF at STA and its surrounding RNs for a given position of STA.

Step 2: In this step, PHY rate to be employed by each IF at STA at each grid is decided by using the information obtained in Step 1. Based on the average RSSIs between an IF and surrounding RNs, packet loss rate (PLR) for each PHY rate is first calculated for each link. To this end, we use Nist Error Rate Model [11]. Here, let us denote the available PHY rate as R_i ($1 \leq i \leq R_{max}$), where R_{max} is the number of available PHY rates. For each R_i, its PLR is calculated as PLR_i. Then, the number of RNs, to which STA is able to deliver its data with $PLR_i \leq PLR_{th}$, is calculated as N_i, where PLR_{th} is a given parameter to control the achieved reliability between each IF at STA and surrounding RNs. Then, PHY rate for a given grid j for an IF X at STA is decided as follows:

$$R_j^X = max\{R_i | N_i \geq N_{min}\}, \tag{1}$$

where N_{min} is the minimum number of RNs, to which STA should deliver data to achieve the required reliability. The basic idea of this decision process is that each STA should select as high rate as possible on condition that it can deliver its data to at least N_{min} RNs with high reliability.

Through the above 2 steps, a mapping table, which maps PHY rate to be employed into each grid ID, is constructed by AP for each IF at STA. This mapping table is notified to STA on drone before the main operations of data transfer over the communication area. During the main operations, STA on drone continuously checks its current position by using GPS information, and decides which grid it is belonging to. Then, by using the given mapping table, STA on drone extracts PHY rate to be employed in a given position, and transfers data with the selected rate. Note that the PHY rate is adapted based on *average* RSSI mainly affected by path loss, which is considered to be static over the operations of drone.

4.2   Overhearing

In addition to the proposed rate control, we employ overhearing (OH) mechanism in order to reduce the probability that the same packets are forwarded by different RNs. With OH mechanism, each RN stores each received packet for a given timer period, which is differently set for each RN. If the timer expires, RN forwards the stored packet to AP. On the other hand, if RN overhears the same packet as the stored one before the timer expires, it cancels the forwarding of the corresponding packet. This enables each RN to avoid redundantly forwarding the same packets to AP, which contributes to the reduction of data traffic as well as power consumption of each RN. The timer for the i-th RN, T_i is decided by AP as follows:

$$T_i = (DIFS + CW_{ave} \times t_s + \frac{B_p}{\gamma_{ave}}) \times \gamma_i. \tag{2}$$

Here, t_s is slot time, B_p is the packet size, and γ_{ave} is the average PHY rate to be employed by RN. Furthermore, CW_{ave} is given by

$$CW_{ave} = \frac{(minCW + 1) \times 2^{maxRN} - 1}{2}, \tag{3}$$

where $minCW$ is the minimum size of contention window and $maxRN$ is the maximum number of retransmissions. The basic idea of Eq. (2) is that each RN should set its timer to the average duration required for data forwarding multiplied by an coefficient γ_i decided based on the quality of link between RN_i and AP. Each RN notifies RSSIs observed over each IF for data forwarding to AP, based on which AP decides γ_i and notifies it to RN_i. For RN with the best link quality, this coefficient is set to 0 while it is increased by 1 for the following RNs with the decreasing order of link quality. With the above OH mechanism, we can increase the probability that each packet is forwarded by a RN with the better link quality to AP. Note that, in order to further reduce the congestion level between RNs and AP, each RN is controlled to forward at most K packets out of successfully received packets for each batch.

5   Numerical Results and Discussions

5.1   Simulation Model

The simulation model and parameters are respectively shown in Fig. 3 and Table 2. A drone installing STA is assumed to move inside the communication area based on Random Way Point model [14]. We assume that 2 IFs at STA operate over different 2.4 GHz channels (i.e., $N_{STA} = 2$) while a single IF at each RN to forward packets to AP employs a single channel over 5 GHz band (i.e., $N_F = 1$). The APs are supposed to have 5 IFs (i.e., $N_{AP} = 5$), 2 IFs with 2.4 GHz band to directly receive packets from STA if possible, and 3 IFs with 5 GHz band for receiving packets forwarded by each RN. Different channels over 5 GHz are allocated to 3 IFs at AP, and each operating channel at RN over 5 GHz is randomly selected. For the proposed rate control, we employ a grid size of 20 m × 20 m, $N_{min} = 2$, and $PLR_{th} = 1\%$. In this work, we consider that the target PDR is 99%. In order to take the impact of interference from surrounding unlicensed systems into account, we introduce a parameter of interference error rate (IER), which is defined as the probability for each packet to be lost due to interference. We fix IER over 5 GHz to be 5% while we vary IER over 2.4 GHz considering that more number of unlicensed devices exist over 2.4 GHz than 5 GHz, which can lead to highly interfered period. Specifically, for 2.4 GHz, we employ a model based on Gilbert-Eliot model shown in Fig. 4 [15]. We prepare two interference states, Good and Bad, which are transited with probability shown in Fig. 4. The transition of interference state is assumed to occur independently over different channels (i.e., interfaces), where $p = 1\%$ and $r = 10\%$. The IER over Good state is fixed to be 1% while we conduct simulations for different IER over Bad state, defined as IER_B, which is set to 10%, 50%, and 90%.

Table 2. Simulation parameters

Common parameters	Error model	Nist error model
	Tx. Power	20 mW
	Power Consumption in Tx. State	1.99 W [12]
	Power Consumption in Rx. State	1.27 W [12]
	PHY Rate (Mbps)	14.4, 28.9, 43.3, 57.8 86.7, 115.6, 130, 144.4
	Max. Num. Retransmissions	5
STA	Num. of IFs (N_{STA})	2
	Packet Size	1496 Bytes
	Packet Generation Period	0.03 s
	FEC Rate	1/3
	Mobility Model	Random Way Point
	Velocity	15 m/s
	Altitude	15 m
RN	Number of RNs	10
	Num. of IFs (N_{RN})	3
	Position	Random (Uniform)
AP	Num. of IFs (N_{AP})	5
	Position	Center of Area
Channel Model	Path Loss	Coefficient: 2.85 [13]
	Fading	Block Rayleigh (Block Length: 50 ms)

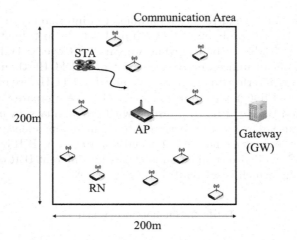

Fig. 3. Simulation model.

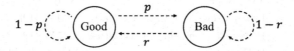

Fig. 4. The employed model for transiting interference states over 2.4 GHz.

We employ the following performance metrics in our evaluations:

– Packet Delivery Ratio (PDR)
  The ratio of number of packets transmitted by STA to that received at GW,
  all in application level.
– Average Delay
  The average time from packet generation at STA to its arrival at GW. Here,
  we take the reordering of packets into account, where AP is controlled to wait
  for the missing packets for at most 50 ms before its forwarding to GW. For
  simplicity, we neglect the delay for packet forwarding from AP to GW.
– Fractional Airtime of RN
  The ratio of total channel occupancy period of all RNs to total simulation
  period.
– Maximum RN Energy Consumption
  The maximum energy consumption of RN among all RNs.
– Fractional Airtime of STA
  The ratio of total channel occupancy period of STA to total simulation period.

As for reference schemes, we consider single–link broadcast (SL–BC), where
a single IF is employed for data transfer by STA (i.e., $N_{STA} = 1$), where FEC
rate of 1/3 is employed. Furthermore, we also consider multi–link unicast (ML–
UC), where multi–link transmissions with $N_{STA} = 2$ are employed by STA with
each IF connected to a reception point by using unicast mode. Each IF at STA

with ML–UC employs PHY rate adaptation based on ARF as well as handover control to switch its reception point. In the handover control, each IF at STA observes RSSIs of beacons transmitted by each reception point, which includes IFs at AP and all RNs, every 1 s, and calculates its averaged value. Then, if IF at STA detects better reception point, which offers higher average RSSI by 3 [dB] than its current link, it switches its reception point to the corresponding new point. On the other hand, we call the multi–link and multi–relay broadcast transmissions described in Sect. 2 as ML–BC. For FEC in ML–BC, different set of redundant packets are assumed to be transmitted by STA over each IF.

5.2   Simulation Results

First, in order to investigate the gain brought by multi–link and multi–relay transmissions, we compare performance of SL–BC and ML–BC, and those with and without RNs. Figures 5 and 6 respectively show PDR and average delay against different PHY rates employed by STA, where IER_B is set to 90%. Here, STA is supposed to employ a fixed rate depicted in horizontal axis in Figs. 5 and 6 for whole simulation period. First, from Fig. 5, we can see that the gain brought by introducing RNs is larger for higher PHY rates. With higher PHY rates, the communication range of STA becomes smaller, which results in higher proba-bility for STA to be located outside the communication range of AP. However, with the existence of RNs, STA can deliver data to AP through surrounding RNs even with higher PHY rates. That is why the benefit to utilize RN is larger for higher PHY rates. Next, Fig. 5 shows that ML–BC has better PDR than SL–BC. This is thanks to channel diversity, where packets lost over one interface due to interfer-ence can be received over the other interface with ML–BC. From Fig. 5, it can be seen that the target PDR of 99% can be achieved by ML–BC with RN when PHY rates equal to or less than 43.3 Mbps are employed by STA. The same tendency is observed for average delay as shown in Fig. 6, where smaller delay is achieved for higher PDR. For ML–BC with RN employing PHY rates equal to or less than 43.3 Mbps, PDR is sufficiently high, therefore, the average delay becomes smaller as PHY rate is increased. In summary, these two figures show the effectiveness of multi–link and multi–relay transmissions of ML–BC.

Next, we analyze the impact of OH and proposed rate control on achievable performance of ML–BC. Here, when we employ a fixed PHY rate for ML–BC (i.e., when we do not employ the proposed rate control), we adopt 43.3 Mbps based on the above results on PDR and average delay. Figures 7 and 8 respec-tively show fractional airtime of RN and maximum RN energy consumption against IER_B for ML–BC employing a fixed rate with and without OH, and ML–BC employing the proposed rate control with OH. In these evaluations, we confirmed that all three schemes achieve PDR higher than the target value of 99% for IER_B given in the figures. First, from Fig. 7, we can see that ML–BC with fixed rate can decrease fractional airtime of RN by introducing OH, which means that the suppression of redundant packets properly works at each RN. However, Fig. 8 shows that the introduction of OH into ML–BC with fixed rate does not provide gain in terms of RN energy consumption. This is because,

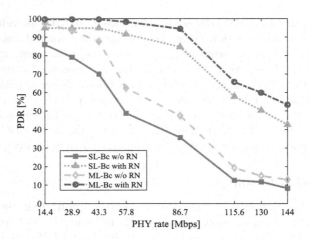

Fig. 5. PDR against different PHY rates employed by STA for SL–BC and ML–BC with and without RN ($IER_B = 90\%$).

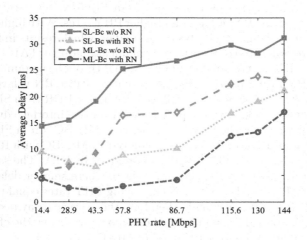

Fig. 6. Average Delay against different PHY rates employed by STA for SL–BC and ML–BC with and without RN ($IER_B = 90\%$).

while the energy consumed for transmissions of redundant packets is successfully reduced by OH, the additional energy is required with OH for each RN to observe any packet transmitted by the other RNs. However, we can see an interesting observation in these figures that we can achieve minimum airtime and energy consumption of RN by jointly applying OH and proposed rate control to ML–BC. The proposed rate control adjusts PHY rate of STA in such a way that minimum number of required RNs successfully decode packets transmitted by STA. This enables only RNs located closely to STA to successfully decode the transmitted packets, which contributes to limit the number of RNs involved into OH operations, and additionally, reduces the distance among RNs which attempts to mutually overhear the forwarded packets. This leads to the improvement of probability to successfully overhear each packet forwarded by a small number of RNs within the proximity of STA, thereby reducing the energy consumed by RN with ML–BC jointly employing OH and proposed rate control. From these results, we can confirm the effectiveness of our proposed rate control.

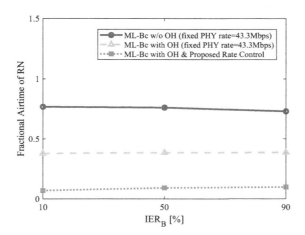

Fig. 7. Fractional airtime of RN against IER_B for ML–BC employing a fixed rate with and without OH and ML–BC employing the proposed rate control with OH.

Finally, we compare performance of ML–BC and ML–UC in order to clarify the benefit brought by broadcast mode employed at STA. Figure 9 shows PDR against IER_B while Figs. 10 and 11 respectively show fractional airtime of IF1 and IF2 at STA for ML–UC and ML–BC employing the proposed rate control and OH. Figure 9 shows that ML–BC realizes reliable data transmissions for any value of IER_B. On the other hand, ML–UC cannot offer PDR higher than the target value of 99% even for $IER_B = 10\%$, which degrades more for larger IER_B. This is due to the failure of handover and rate control for unicast mode, caused by high mobility of drone (i.e., STA). The switch of a reception point as well as employed rate cannot adapt to the rapid variation of link condition with ML–UC, which often causes continuous packet losses exceeding the maximum number of link–level retransmissions, thereby degrading PDR. Furthermore, the increased number of retransmissions of ML–UC results in larger fractional airtime as shown in Figs. 10 and 11, which deteriorates more as IER_B is increased. On the other hand, handover control is unnecessary for ML–BC, which enables STA to transmit data to surrounding reception points seamlessly. Furthermore, the proposed rate control allows STA to promptly change its PHY rate to a

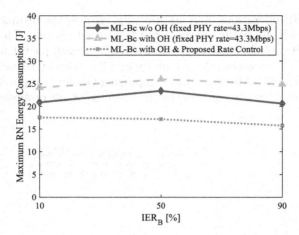

Fig. 8. Maximum RN energy consumption against IER_B for ML–BC employing a fixed rate with and without OH and ML–BC employing the proposed rate control with OH.

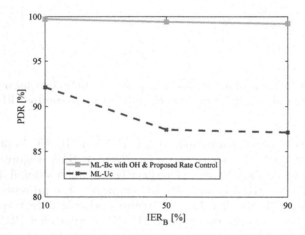

Fig. 9. PDR against IER_B for ML–BC employing the proposed rate control with OH and ML–UC.

proper value at a given location. Thanks to these advantages, ML–BC achieves higher PDR than ML–UC while achieving much smaller fractional airtime of STA than ML–UC. These results confirm the superiority of ML–BC to ML–UC.

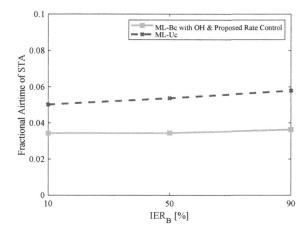

Fig. 10. Fractional Airtime of IF1 at STA against IER_B for ML–BC employing the proposed rate control with OH and ML–UC.

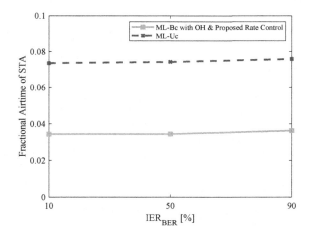

Fig. 11. Fractional Airtime of IF2 at STA against IER_B for ML–BC employing the proposed rate control with OH and ML–UC.

6   Conclusions

In this paper, we focused on real–time data transmissions from a drone supported by wireless LAN. In order to enhance the reliability, we introduced a multi–link and multi–relay system integrated with broadcast transmissions employing packet–level forward error correction. We first confirmed the effectiveness and practicality of the multi–link and multi–relay system supporting data transmissions from a drone by experiments. Then, we enhanced the multi–link and multi–relay system by proposing rate control for STA to dynamically set its physical layer (PHY) rate based on its position and the link quality for surrounding relays. We also applied overhearing function to each relay to prevent redundant forwarding of the same packets by multiple relays. With computer simulations, we extensively study packet delivery rate, delay, channel occupancy period, and energy consumption of each relay. Our simulation results showed that the multi–link and multi–relay system improves energy efficiency of relays when the proposed rate control and overhearing are jointly employed. Furthermore, we showed that the multi–link and multi–relay system with link–level broadcast enjoys channel and route diversity, and has superior performance to a common unicast based system.

Our future work includes experimental studies with the implementation of proposed rate control and overhearing functions into our testbed, considering the practical issues, such as GPS errors. Dynamic FEC control is also an interesting future work.

References

1. Wang, X., Chowdhery, A., Chiang, M.: SkyEyes: adaptive video streaming from UAVs. In: Proceedings of the 3rd Workshop on Hot Topics in Wireless, October 2016
2. Xiao, X., Wang, W., Chen, T., Cao, Y., Jiang, T., Zhang, Q.: Sensor-augmented neural adaptive bitrate video streaming on UAVs. IEEE Trans. Multimedia **22**, 1567–1576 (2019)
3. He, S., Wang, W., Yang, H., Cao, Y., Jiang, T., Zhang, Q.: State-aware rate adaptation for UAVs by incorporating on-board sensors. IEEE Trans. Veh. Technol. **69**(1), 488–496 (2020)
4. Ikeda, K., Imai, Y., Yomo, H., Kondo, Y., Yokoyama, H.: Data transmissions from a drone using multi-AP wireless LAN: a field trial. In: 2020 29th International Conference on Computer Communications and Networks (ICCCN) (2020)
5. Katila, C.J., Di Gianni, A., Buratti, C., Verdone, R.: Routing protocols for video surveillance drones in IEEE 802.11s wireless mesh networks. In: 2017 European Conference on Networks and Communications (EuCNC) (2017)
6. Matsuda, T., Noguchi, T., Takine, T.: Broadcasting with randomized network coding in dense wireless ad hoc networks. IEICE Trans. Commun. **E91-B**(10), 3216–3225, October 2008
7. Kamerman, A., Monteban, L.: WaveLAN-II: a high-performance wireless LAN for the unlicensed band. Bell Labs Tech. J. **2**, 118–133 (1997)
8. Japan UAS Industrial Development Association (JUIDA). https://uas-japan.org/en/
9. DJI phantom 4. http://www.dji.com/product/phantom-4
10. Song, W., Ju, P., Jin, A.L., Cheng, Y.: Distributed opportunistic two-hop relaying with backoff-based contention among spatially random relays. IEEE Trans. Veh. Technol. **64**(5), 2023–2036 (2015)
11. Pei, G., Henderson, T.R.: Validation of OFDM error rate model in NS-3. Boeing Research & Technology, Technical report (2010)
12. Halperin, D., Greenstein, B., Sheth, A., Wetherall, D.: Demystifying 802.11n power consumption. In: Proceedings of the 2010 International Conference on Power Aware Computing and Systems, HotPower 2010, p. 1. USENIX Association, USA (2010)

13. Zhou, T., Sharif, H., Hempel, M., Mahasukhon, P., Wang, W., Ma, T.: A deterministic approach to evaluate path loss exponents in large-scale outdoor 802.11 WLANs. In: 2009 IEEE 34th Conference on Local Computer Networks, pp. 348–351 (2009)
14. Saeed, A., Khan, L., Shah, N., Ali, H.: Performance comparison of two anycast based reactive routing protocols for mobile ad hoc networks. In: 2009 2nd International Conference on Computer, Control and Communication, pp. 1–6 (2009)
15. Bildea, A., Alphand, O., Rousseau, F., Duda, A.: Link quality estimation with the Gilbert-Elliot model for wireless sensor networks. In: 2015 IEEE 26th Annual International Symposium on Personal, Indoor, and Mobile Radio Communications (PIMRC), pp. 2049–2054 (2015)

Quality Analysis of Audio-Video Transmission in an OFDM-Based Communication System

Monika Zamlynska[1], Grzegorz Debita[1] (ID), and Przemyslaw Falkowski-Gilski[2(✉)] (ID)

[1] Faculty of Management, General Tadeusz Kosciuszko Military University of Land Forces, Czajkowskiego 109, 51-147 Wroclaw, Poland
grzegorz.debita@awl.edu.pl
[2] Faculty of Electronics, Telecommunications and Informatics, Gdansk University of Technology, Narutowicza 11/12, 80-233 Gdansk, Poland
przemyslaw.falkowski@eti.pg.edu.pl

Abstract. Application of a reliable audio-video communication system, brings many advantages. With the spoken word we can exchange ideas, provide descriptive information, as well as aid to another person. With the availability of visual information one can monitor the surrounding, working environment, etc. As the amount of available bandwidth continues to shrink, researchers focus on novel types of transmission. Currently, orthogonal frequency division multiplexing (OFDM) is widely utilized both in wired and wireless transmission. In this paper we investigate the quality of service (QoS) parameters of a simulated data transmission system, dedicated particularly to audio and video content distribution with orthogonal frequency division multiplexing. The audio research part involves a group of four language sets, namely: American English, British English, German, and Polish, processed using the Ogg Vorbis format. Whereas, in the video part we investigate a set of MPEG-4 video sequences coded at standard resolution of 480×270 pixels. Tests were performed under varying network and bandwidth conditions, including signal-to-noise ratio (SNR) and bit error rate (BER). Results of this study may aid parties interested in designing additional backup or supplementary services for portable devices and user terminals, including reliable means of contact, surveillance and monitoring for the Industry 4.0 and Internet of things (IoT) concept.

Keywords: IoT · Quality evaluation · Reliability · Video coding

1 Introduction

Designing and maintaining reliable communication services is a challenging task. With the outbreak of both desktop and mobile devices, followed by novel modulation and coding schemes, user expectations regarding the level of quality of a particular service continues to grow [1–4]. Currently, more and more solutions are based on orthogonal frequency division multiplexing (OFDM) [5, 6]. With fluctuating bandwidth conditions

T. Hara and H. Yamaguchi (Eds.): MobiQuitous 2021, LNICST 419, pp. 724–736, 2022.
https://doi.org/10.1007/978-3-030-94822-1_47

in heterogeneous networks, it is important to study how does it affect the quality of transmission.

Nowadays, its utilization in industrial networks seems to be of great interest, particularly in smart grids and the Industry 4.0 concept, including various signals, e.g. audio and video [7–10]. Considering the importance of the analyzed problem, we intended to determine the impact of several factors on the transmission of audio and video content. In our case, we utilize the orthogonal frequency division multiplexing technique. The study involved a set of speech samples as well as video sequences, coded and then processed in our custom-build OFDM telecommunication system, with respect to quality of service (QoS) requirements.

2 Audio Quality Evaluation

2.1 Audio Signal Processing

According to the 3rd Generation Partnership Project (3GPP) [11], when examining digital voice communication services, they can be divided into three groups. Table 1 describes principle voice (speech) services with their requirements, including delay and bit error rate (BER).

Table 1. Principle voice communication services with QoS requirements.

Heading level	Delay [ms]	BER
Conversational voice (real-time streaming)	100	10^{-2}
Non-conversational voice (buffered streaming)	300	10^{-6}
Interactive voice (live streaming)	100	10^{-3}

This particular study is focused on speech (voice) communication. According to Table 1, these services require a delay from less than 100 ms (conversational or interactive voice) to less than 300 ms (non-conversational voice). Whereas, when it comes to error rate, the accepted threshold ranges from 10^{-2} or 10^{-3} up to 10^{-6}, depending on the variant. This of course can affect the quality of transmitted speech samples.

2.2 Speech Signal Samples

The signal samples used during study were sourced from ITU-T P.501 [12], and consisted of sentences spoken by both female and male lectors in different languages. When examining the international profile of the broadcasting and streaming industry, we have selected 4 language sets: American English (AE), British English (EN), German (GE), and Polish (PL).

These samples were originally available in the WAV 16-bit PCM format. Next, each sample was coded using the Ogg Vorbis format [13, 14], the bitrate was set to 32 kbps, whereas the initial sampling frequency was changed to 44.1 kHz. Then all of them were transmitted via our communication system.

2.3 Simulated Communication System

In order to assess the quality of transmission in the modeled telecommunication system, we have utilized the Matlab/Simulink environment. The simulated model enabled to determine the BER for the transmission of audio files. The block diagram is shown in Fig. 1.

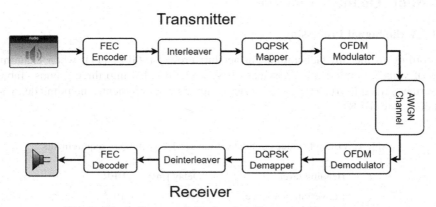

Fig. 1. Block diagram of simulated audio transmission system.

The modeled communication link was based on a well-known broadcasting chain utilized e.g. in digital audio broadcasting (DAB) [15–17]. The audio content used during the simulation was encoded using the Ogg Vorbis codec. It was transmitted over the channel in a single channel (mono) mode. Therefore, it did not require multiplexing during transmission. The coding itself was based on the DAB system.

2.4 Results

Not surprisingly, SNR has a profound impact on the overall error rate. Similar results may be observed regardless of the language set. An overall summary of the dependency of BER on SNR is shown in Fig. 2.

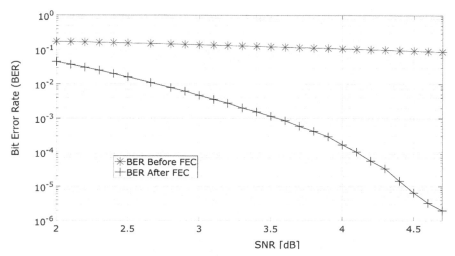

Fig. 2. Dependency of BER on SNR with and without the application of FEC for audio content.

2.5 Discussion

In this experiment, the Ogg Vorbis audio files, with a bitrate of 32 kbps and a sampling frequency of 44.1 kHz, were fed into the simulator. The input was composed of four language sets, namely: American English, British English, German, and Polish. Furthermore, in each case both female and male voices were distinguished.

All files were processed one by one, in a queue. The initial (input) as well as resulting (output) format remained unaltered. Additionally, the content processing chain did not cause change in either bitrate nor sampling frequency.

Overall, the test involved 24 audio files, with signal-to-noise ratio (SNR) ranging from 2.66 to 4.8 dB. The BER was monitored both before forward error correction (FEC) protection coding (so-called channel BER) and after FEC protection coding. Results of this experiment are described in Tables 2, 3, 4, and 5. Results for the American English (AE) language set are described in Table 2. Whereas, results for the following sets of speech samples, that is: British English (EN), German (GE), and Polish (PL), are described in Tables 3, 4, and 5, respectively.

Table 2. Results for transmitted speech samples in American English.

File name	SNR [dB]	BER after FEC	BER before FEC
AEfemale1	2.660	1.1088E−02	1.5166E−01
	3.530	1.0507E−03	1.2295E−01
	4.080	1.1567E−04	1.0594E−01
	4.450	1.0092E−05	9.4984E−02
	4.745	1.1755E−06	8.6652E−02

(continued)

Table 2. (*continued*)

File name	SNR [dB]	BER after FEC	BER before FEC
AEfemale2	2.660	1.0806E−02	1.5184E−01
	3.530	1.0295E−03	1.2319E−01
	4.080	1.0437E−04	1.0602E−01
	4.450	1.0999E−05	9.5014E−02
	4.745	1.2548E−06	8.6657E−02
AEmale1	2.660	1.0932E−02	1.5179E−01
	3.530	1.0671E−03	1.2311E−01
	4.080	1.2096E−04	1.0597E−01
	4.450	1.3148E−05	9.4996E−02
	4.745	1.0253E−06	8.6653E−02
AEmale2	2.660	1.1064E−02	1.5163E−01
	3.530	1.0716E−03	1.2297E−01
	4.080	1.1415E−04	1.0593E−01
	4.450	1.0590E−05	9.6452E−01
	4.745	1.0473E−06	8.6232E−02

According to obtained results, FEC has an enormous impact on the final error rate. The initial range of approx. 10^{-1} and 10^{-2} is shifted to a new range from 10^{-2} up to even 10^{-6}. What is worth mentioning, this increase is observable regardless of the audio sample.

Table 3. Results for transmitted speech samples in British English.

File name	SNR [dB]	BER after FEC	BER before FEC
ENfemale1	2.660	1.1316E−02	1.5173E−01
	3.530	1.0991E−03	1.2306E−01
	4.080	1.1305E−04	1.0589E−01
	4.450	1.1924E−05	9.4968E−02
	4.745	1.1621E−06	8.6317E−02
ENfemale2	2.660	1.1182E−02	1.5170E−01
	3.530	1.0625E−03	1.2297E−01
	4.080	1.2698E−04	1.0587E−01

(continued)

Table 3. (*continued*)

File name	SNR [dB]	BER after FEC	BER before FEC
	4.450	1.0897E−05	9.5876E−02
	4.745	1.0247E−06	8.6664E−02
ENmale1	2.660	1.0953E−02	1.5168E−01
	3.530	1.0119E−03	1.2299E−01
	4.080	1.1090E−04	1.0591E−01
	4.450	1.0980E−05	9.4998E−02
	4.745	1.3083E−06	8.5947E−02
ENmale2	2.660	1.1126E−02	1.5177E−01
	3.530	1.0424E−03	1.2314E−01
	4.080	1.2626E−04	1.0606E−01
	4.450	1.1053E−05	9.5845E−02
	4.745	1.1258E−06	8.6790E−02

The number of erroneous bits has been reduced by 10 times, in case of the lowest SNR value of 2.660 dB. Whereas, in case of the highest SNR value, that is 4.745 dB, the quality has been raised more than a thousand times.

Table 4. Results for transmitted speech samples in German.

File name	SNR [dB]	BER after FEC	BER before FEC
GEfemale1	2.660	1.1190E−02	1.5169E−01
	3.530	1.0604E−03	1.2308E−01
	4.080	1.0578E−04	1.0602E−01
	4.450	1.0543E−05	9.4999E−02
	4.745	1.0241E−06	8.6644E−02
GEfemale2	2.660	1.1114E−02	1.5177E−01
	3.530	1.0345E−03	1.2307E−01
	4.080	1.0335E−04	1.0594E−01
	4.450	1.1356E−05	9.6466E−02
	4.745	1.2803E−06	8.6679E−02
GEmale1	2.660	1.1301E−02	1.5172E−01
	3.530	1.0926E−03	1.2304E−01

(continued)

Table 4. (*continued*)

File name	SNR [dB]	BER after FEC	BER before FEC
	4.080	1.1373E−04	1.0592E−01
	4.450	1.1790E−05	9.5002E−02
	4.745	1.0334E−06	8.6656E−02
GEmale2	2.660	1.1299E−02	1.5181E−01
	3.530	1.0610E−03	1.2317E−01
	4.080	1.1319E−04	1.0613E−01
	4.450	1.0558E−05	9.5014E−02
	4.745	1.1809E−06	8.6596E−02

It can be seen that independently from the type of lector, that is either a female or male individual, obtained BER values are close in range. In case of both after and before FEC, obtained results most often differ only at the second or third decimal position.

Table 5. Results for transmitted speech samples in Polish.

File name	SNR [dB]	BER after FEC	BER before FEC
PLfemale1	2.660	1.0930E−02	1.5182E−01
	3.530	1.0603E−03	1.2309E−01
	4.080	1.0517E−04	1.0592E−01
	4.450	1.1673E−05	9.4971E−02
	4.745	1.0515E−06	8.6651E−02
PLfemale2	2.660	1.1021E−02	1.5179E−01
	3.530	1.0678E−03	1.2312E−01
	4.080	1.1854E−04	1.0560E−01
	4.450	1.0614E−05	9.4982E−02
	4.745	1.4726E−06	8.6631E−02
PLmale1	2.660	1.1245E−02	1.5172E−01
	3.530	1.0859E−03	1.2303E−01
	4.080	1.2338E−04	1.0588E−01
	4.450	1.1215E−05	9.5551E−02
	4.745	1.0268E−06	8.6481E−02

(*continued*)

Table 5. (*continued*)

File name	SNR [dB]	BER after FEC	BER before FEC
PLmale2	2.660	1.1096E−02	1.5177E−01
	3.530	1.0816E−03	1.2309E−01
	4.080	1.2623E−04	1.0597E−01
	4.450	1.1520E−05	9.5605E−02
	4.745	1.1515E−06	8.6650E−02

Not surprisingly, SNR has a profound impact on the overall error rate. Similar results may be observed regardless of the language set.

3 Video Quality Evaluation

3.1 Video Signal Processing

According to the 3rd Generation Partnership Project (3GPP) [11], video services can be divided into two main categories, depending on delay and bit error rate, as described in Table 6.

Table 6. Principle video transmission services with QoS requirements.

Heading level	Delay [ms]	BER
Conversational video (live streaming)	150	10^{-3}
Non-conversational video (buffered streaming)	300	10^{-6}

In this particular study we focused on BER ranging from 10^{-3} to 10^{-6}. In our case delay may be neglected.

3.2 Video Signal Samples

The processed video content, available in the MP4 format, coded with 8-bit resolution, was sourced from [18]. Each sample consisted of 5 sequences:

1. Walking man – static background with a single man walking along the street;
2. Windmill – static angle with numerous fast moving (rotating) windmills;
3. Traffic – static angle with cars passing along the road, at various speeds.
4. Toddler fountain – playful child walking around a fountain, with lots of movement in the background;

5. Toddler montage – similar material with a playful child recorded in slow-motion (much higher framerate);

   available in a number of bitrates (qualities), from standard definition (SD) up to Full-HD (1920 × 1080). For the purpose of this test, we have selected one video file, available in 480 × 270 resolution. We have chosen this resolution, the outcome of dividing 1920 × 1080 pixels by 4 in each axis, due to its scalability with the Full-HD format as well as popularity among many portable devices and user terminals, including media players and consoles [19].

3.3 Simulated Communication System

In order to assess the quality of transmission in the modeled telecommunication system, we have utilized the Matlab/Simulink environment. The simulated model enabled to determine the BER for the transmission of video files. The block diagram is shown in Fig. 3.

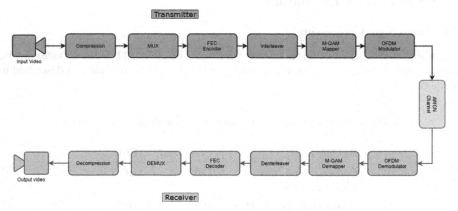

Fig. 3. Block diagram of simulated video transmission system.

The modeled communication link was based on a well-known broadcasting chain utilized e.g. in digital video broadcasting – terrestrial (DVB-T) [6, 20]. The video content was encoded using the MPEG-4 codec [21], undeniably on of the most popular formats for content processing and distribution, including a variety of consumer devices and streaming services [4]. It was transmitted over the channel in the red, green, blue (RGB) mode. The coding and multiplexing of particular streams was based on DVB [15]. Later on, data was interleaved with a random permutation, and then converted into 256-QAM symbols combined with OFDM [5, 22]. OFDM maintains the orthogonality of the sub-carriers, which reduces the risk of interference.

3.4 Results

During the experiment, the MPEG-4 video files, with a resolution of 480 × 270 pixels, were fed into the simulator. All files were processed one by one, in a queue. The original (input) as well as processed (output) format remained unaltered. Overall, the test involved varying SNR ranging from 24 to 29 dB, as well as monitored BER before and after forward error correction (FEC). Results of this analysis are shown in Fig. 4.

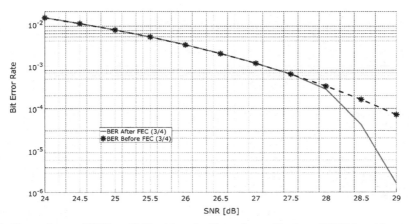

Fig. 4. Dependency of BER on SNR with and without the application of FEC for video content.

According to obtained results, FEC has a noticeable impact on the final error rate only from SNR equal to 27.5 dB and higher. The initial range of approx. 10^{-4} and 10^{-3} is shifted to a new range, in which the number of erroneous bits has been reduced by tens or even hundreds of times. However, the impact of both SNR and BER on quality of video content needs to be determined in a future subjective evaluation study.

3.5 Discussion

According to obtained results for lowest SNR equal to 24 dB (see first row of Fig. 5) was very poor. No details were visible, colors were distorted, whereas numerous elements did not have sharp edges. They looked grainy and/or blurred. Undeniably, stripes and checkered patterns were also noticeable, as a result of compression (coding) algorithms. This effect was clearly visible with a black and/or dark background. The walking man and cars were clearly noticeable, whereas the windmill presented something hard to determine. When it comes to the toddler, it was hard to determine whether it was water falling or just noise.

The second level of SNR equal to 24.4 dB (see second row of Fig. 5) provided similar observations. No significant changes were noticeable.

The third level of SNR equal to 27 dB (see third row of Fig. 5) was definitely better than the previous ones. The quality was still not acceptable, many pixel artefacts did occur. On the other hand, there was a visible decrease in the level of noise. The image was still noticeably divided into smaller segments (squares), but the colors were more precise and closer to reality. In this case, the windmill could be adequately labeled, so were the fountains.

In the fourth level of SNR equal to 28.3 dB (see fourth row of Fig. 5) there was a noticeable upgrade, however color mismatch and artefacts among many pixels were still present.

Fig. 5. Distorted frame of video sequence transmitted at different SNR.

Whereas the fifth level of SNR equal to 28.7 dB (see fifth row of Fig. 5) had only a little less noise, artefacts, and color distortions.

4 Conclusions

As shown, FEC correction coding can raise the quality of audio and video content processed and transmitted via a OFDM communication channel. Depending on the initial SNR value, this increase may be equal to ten times or even more than a thousand times. Furthermore, it has been proved that additional error correction mechanisms can raise the BER in case of all speech samples, regardless of the type of lector (female or male) or even spoken language (American English, British English, German, and Polish). As observed, similar results were obtained for all language sets. A small difference was only noticed on the second or third decimal point. When it comes to video coding, FEC had a noticeable impact on the final error rate only from SNR equal to 27.5 dB and higher.

This small difference in obtained BER, with and without FEC coding, when comparing each and every language set with one other, proved the correctness and accuracy of implementation of the transmission link. Moreover, it may be said that other language sets, more popular in various regions of the world, would perform similarly as the chosen and investigated portion of samples. Additionally, it would be also interesting to evaluate a different set of video content, including more static as well as dynamic sequences. This fact makes future studies, including various additional quality aspects, even more promising. One should keep in mind that, all in all, each system and service is designed to operate and interact with human end users. This implies many technical aspects, especially dependability and reliability [23].

Certainly, it would be interesting to determine the impact of SNR and BER, related with objective QoS, on the subjective judgements of the end user, referred to as quality of experience (QoE). Such an investigation would surely be valuable to both researchers and professionals active in the content creation and distribution link. They may include typical streaming or broadcasting services, as well as specific dedicated auxiliary solutions, e.g. utilizing portable mobile terminals. A good source of inspiration may be found in [24].

Further research should and will therefore focus on evaluating the set of both audio and video processed signal samples in a subjective listening test and video quality evaluation study. It would be interesting to directly link both SNR and BER parameters with a standard mean opinion score (MOS) judgement. Furthermore, it would be stimulating to broaden the range of content as well as research scenarios, followed by a subjective user evaluation. Future studies could be performed according to recommendations as well as best practices when it comes to crowdsourcing, which may be found in [25–28].

References

1. Hossfeld, T., et al.: Best practices for QoE crowdtesting: QoE assessment with crowdsourcing. IEEE Trans. Multim. **16**(2), 541–558 (2014)
2. Boz, E., Finley, B., Oulasvirta, A., Kilkki, K., Manner, J.: Mobile QoE prediction in the field. Pervas. Mobile Comput. **59**, 101039 (2019)
3. Kostek, B.: Music information retrieval – the impact of technology, crowdsourcing, big data, and the cloud in art. J. Acoust. Soc. Am. **146**(4), 2946 (2019)
4. Falkowski-Gilski, P., Uhl, T.: Current trends in consumption of multimedia content using online streaming platforms: a user-centric survey. Comput. Sci. Rev. **37**, 100268 (2020)
5. Cioni, S., Corazza, G.E., Neri, M., Vanelli-Coralli, A.: On the use of OFDM radio interface for satellite digital multimedia broadcasting systems. Int. J. Satell. Commun. Network. **24**(2), 153–167 (2006)
6. Aragón-Zavala, A., Angueira, P., Montalban, J., Vargas-Rosales, C.: Radio propagation in terrestrial broadcasting television systems: a comprehensive survey. IEEE Access **9**, 34789–34817 (2021)
7. Lazaropoulos, A.G., Cottis, P.G.: Transmission characteristics of overhead medium-voltage power-line communication channels. IEEE Trans. Power Deliv. **24**(3), 1164–1173 (2009)
8. Henry, P.S.: Interference characteristics of broadband power line communication systems using aerial medium voltage wires. IEEE Commun. Mag. **43**(4), 92–98 (2005)

9. Debita, G., Falkowski-Gilski, P., Habrych, M., Miedziński, B., Wandzio, J., Jedlikowski, P.: Quality evaluation of voice transmission using BPL communication system in MV mine cable network. Elektron. Elektrotech. **25**(5), 43–46 (2019)
10. Debita, G., et al.: BPL-PLC voice communication system for the oil and mining industry. Energies **13**(18), 4763 (2020)
11. 3GPP Technical Specification 23.203: Technical specification group services and system aspects; Policy and charging control architecture (2011)
12. ITU Recommendation P.501: Test signals for telecommunication systems (2017)
13. Kosaka, A., Yamaguchi, S., Okuhata, H., Onoye, T., Shirakawa, I.: VLSI implementation of Ogg Vorbis decoder for embedded applications. In: Proceedings of 15th Annual IEEE International ASIC/SOC Conference, pp. 20–24. IEEE, Rochester (2002)
14. Kosaka, A., Okuhata, H., Onoye, T., Shirakawa, I.: Design of Ogg Vorbis decoder system for embedded platform. IEICE Trans. Fundam. Electron. Commun. Comput. Sci. **88**(8), 2124–2130 (2005)
15. Harada, H., Prasad, R.: Simulation and Software Radio for Mobile Communications, 1st edn. Artech House, Norwood (2002)
16. Kim, G., Lee, Y.T., Park, S.R., Lee, Y.H.: Design and implementation of a novel emergency wake-up alert system within a conventional T-DMB service network. IEEE Trans. Consum. Electron. **60**(4), 574–579 (2014)
17. Zhang, H., Wang, H., Wang, G., Lu, M.: Design and implementation of the DAB/DMB transmitter identification information decoder. Int. J. Circuit. Syst. Signal Process. **11**, 59–64 (2017)
18. Netflix Open Content – Chimera Database. http://download.opencontent.netflix.com/?prefix= AV1/Chimera/Old/. Accessed 15 July 2021
19. Miranda, G., Macedo D.F., Marquez-Barja, J.M.: A QoE inference method for DASH video using ICMP probing. In: Proceedings of 16th International Conference on Network and Service Management, pp. 1–5. CNSM, Izmir (2020)
20. ETSI Standard EN 300 744: Digital video broadcasting (DVB); framing structure, channel coding and modulation for digital terrestrial television (2009)
21. Thibeault, J.: Streaming video fundamentals. SMPTE Motion Imaging J. **129**(3), 10–15 (2020)
22. Russell, M., Stüber, G.L.: Terrestrial digital video broadcasting for mobile reception using OFDM. Wirel. Pers. Commun. **2**, 45–66 (1995)
23. Zamojski, W., Mazurkiewicz, J., Sugier, J., Walkowiak, T., Kacprzyk, J. (eds.): Theory and Applications of Dependable Computer Systems: Proceedings of the Fifteenth International Conference on Dependability of Computer Systems DepCoS-RELCOMEX, June 29 – July 3, 2020, Brunów, Poland, 1st edn. Springer, Cham (2020)
24. Jeena Jacob, I., Kolandapalayam Shanmugam, S., Piramuthu, S., Falkowski-Gilski, P. (eds.): Data Intelligence and Cognitive Informatics: Proceedings of ICDICI 2020. Springer, Singapore (2021)
25. Korshunov, P., Shuting, C., Touradj, E.: Crowdsourcing Approach for Evaluation of Privacy Filters in Video Surveillance. In: Proceedings of ACM Workshop on Crowdsourcing for Multimedia, pp. 35–40. ACM, Nara (2012)
26. Figuerola Salas, Ó., Adzic, V., Shah, A., Kalva. H.: Assessing internet video quality using crowdsourcing. In: Proceedings of 2nd ACM International Workshop on Crowdsourcing for Multimedia, pp. 23–28. ACM, Barcelona (2013)
27. Anegekuh, L., Sun, L., Ifeachor, E.: A screening methodology for crowdsourcing video QoE evaluation. In: Proceedings of 2014 IEEE Global Communications Conference, pp. 1152–1157. IEEE, Austin (2014)
28. ITU Technical Report PSTR-CROWDS: Subjective evaluation of media quality using a crowdsourcing approach (2018)

Coordinated Multi-UAV Adaptive Exploration Under Recurrent Connectivity Constraints

Yaqianwen Su[1], Dianxi Shi[1,2(✉)], Chao Xue[2], Jiachi Xu[3], and Xionghui He[3]

[1] Artificial Intelligence Research Center, Defense Innovation Institute,
Beijing 100166, China
`dxshi@nudt.edu.cn`
[2] Tianjin Artificial Intelligence Innovation Center, Tianjing 300457, China
[3] College of Computer, National University of Defense Technology,
Changsha 410073, China

Abstract. In the field of multi-UAV collaborative exploration, communication is one of the most fundamental capabilities for effective target deployment and collaborative exploration during mission execution. In order to increase the quality and meet the real-time requirement in various real world situation, collaborate communication strategy has already been a research hotspot both in academia and industry. Recurrent connectivity is a representative strategy with which UAVs do not need to be connected to the base station all the time unless a specific event is triggered. However, in current researches based on the recurrent connectivity strategy, the condition threshold for triggering a new connection is set to be a fixed value during all mission process. This configuration lacks adaptability in real world mission with dynamic and various situations. This paper proposes a dynamic replanning mechanism, and establishes an adaptive multi-UAV collaborative exploration strategy based on recurrent connectivity. Extensive experiments in a well constructed simulation environment were done and the results show that the proposed strategy provides good situation awareness ability at the base station, while our strategy performs an efficient explanation in both complex and simple environments, it has a stronger ability to adapt to complex environments especially.

Keywords: Multi-UAV systems · Adaptive exploration · Communication constraints · Recurrent connectivity

This work was supported in part by the National Key Research and Development Program of China under Grant No. 2017YFB1001901.

T. Hara and H. Yamaguchi (Eds.): MobiQuitous 2021, LNICST 419, pp. 737–753, 2022.
https://doi.org/10.1007/978-3-030-94822-1_48

1   Introduction

Multi-UAV systems are widely used to perform missions such as exploration, map building [20], search and rescue [7,19]. Related researches show that collaborative exploration of Multi-UAV systems with communication restrictions is an important topic. Various exploration planning methods have been proposed in recent years, with some experiments presented [6,9,14,15]. UAVs not only need to complete the exploration mission efficiently but also need to exchange data with the base station at the appropriate time. Literatures propose multi-UAV exploration strategies that take into account different types of communication constraints [11,13,16,18]. Among them, recurrent connectivity is a method that can be applied to ensure situation awareness without excessively constraining the exploration mission. Recurrent connectivity means that the base station only ensures a global connection at the initial position of the UAVs, and reconnects with the UAVs every time when it needs to receive new data. As shown in Figs. 1, 2 and 3, they are schematic diagrams of recurrent connectivity.

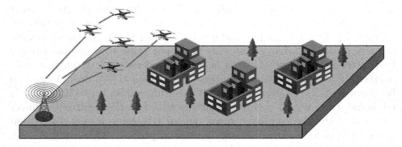

Fig. 1. The base station sends the goal's location to the UAVs.

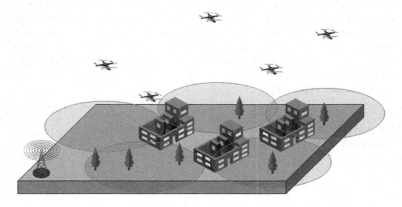

Fig. 2. The UAVs navigate to the goal's location and collects information.

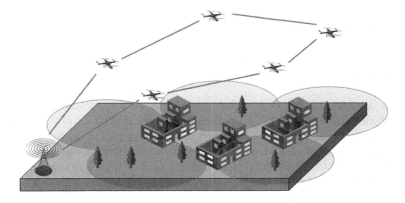

Fig. 3. UAVs transmit the collected information back to the base station and waits to receive the goal's location in the next stage.

However, in the existing exploration strategy under recurrent connectivity constraints, the specific event that triggers a new connection is usually a fixed replanning threshold. The fixed replanning threshold will bring about a series of problems, one is a UAV in the team fails, which makes it impossible to reach the preset threshold and the entire UAV system unable to replan, and the other is, when the threshold is small, frequent replanning will cause the planning to be time-consuming and affect the efficiency of exploration. In the exploration of the unknown environment, we need an exploration strategy that takes into account exploration efficiency and global situational awareness and consumes less energy.

Our work focuses on solving the problem of fixed and inflexible replanning threshold in existing exploration strategies under recurrent connectivity constraints. We propose an adaptive collaborative exploration strategy under recurrent connectivity constraints, construct an adaptive collaborative exploration framework, and designed an adaptive threshold planning algorithm.

In summary, the main contributions of this paper are as follows:

- An adaptive collaborative exploration strategy under recurrent connectivity constraints and an adaptive collaborative exploration framework, which takes into account exploration efficiency and global situational awareness.
- An adaptive threshold planning algorithm and a formal algorithm for Computing the adaptive replanning threshold, which calculates the replanning threshold adaptively according to the UAV's role and the communication path.
- Extensive simulation experiments that validate the proposed method both in complex and simple environments, and effectively reduces energy consumption.

The rest of the paper is organized as follows: Sect. 2 provides a short review of communication-constrained multi-UAV exploration. Section 3 first introduces the task scenario of this work and then proposes an adaptive collaborative exploration strategy under recurrent connectivity constraints. Section 4 presents our experimental results and Sect. 5 concludes the paper.

2   Related Work

Currently, exploration research under communication connectivity requirements is divided into three categories [1], namely exploration without any connectivity, exploration under continuous connectivity, and exploration under event-based connectivity. Since we aim to study the exploration under communication connectivity constraints, the exploration without any connection requirement will not be repeated.

Exploration under continuous connectivity is to maintain a continuous connection between all UAVs and the base station directly or in a multi-hop manner. Suitable scenarios of continuous connectivity include scenarios that require operators to have access to real-time image streams (such as search and rescue [10]) and scenarios that ensure a high degree of coordination between multi-UAV systems. When exploring under continuous connectivity, new plans are usually based on map knowledge shared by all the UAVs in the team. [13] developed a local search method to calculate the usefulness of team composition based on the distance from the nearest frontiers, configurations that did not meet continuous connectivity are severely penalized and are not selected by the algorithm. [12] proposed a distributed protocol to maintain the connectivity of the physical layer of mobile wireless networks. Obviously, ensuring continuous connectivity is associated with non-negligible costs of exploration performance.

Exploration under event-based connectivity refers to the UAV reconnecting with other UAVs and the base station based on a predetermined specific event trigger. The specific events include acquiring new information in the environment, passing a preset time interval, and so on. Exploration under event-based connectivity includes periodic connectivity and recurrent connectivity.

Periodic connectivity means that UAVs are allowed to autonomously explore unknown areas, but the perception data must be sent back to the base station regularly. Applicable scenarios of periodic connectivity include search and rescue in cities with many obstacles. Periodic connectivity is regarded as an asynchronous condition by some articles which is desirable but not enforced as a hard constraint. [21] includes a criterion that considers the probability of communication in the search strategy in order to prioritize places with a high probability of communication. [2] and [8] investigated stronger forms of asynchronous connectivity. The former focused on line-of-sight connectivity, and it proposed a behavior-based architecture and tested it in exploration scenarios of additional prior information about the environment. The latter did not explicitly consider a fixed BS, but it can fully explore the unknown environment in a decentralized way. The proposed architecture is based on actions and messages exchanged between the robot and the placed beacon.

Recurrent connectivity can be defined as ensuring a global connection only at the deployment location of the UAV and forcing the connection every time the

UAV collects new data. It not only has relatively loose requirements for communication connection but also can carry out timely global situational awareness. It is a trade-off between communication connection and the global situation and is widely used in search and rescue, reconnaissance scenarios.

[18] solved two problems, one is finding a deployment of relay nodes, which ensures global connectivity between each agent and the base station, this problem was reduced to the computation of a minimum Steiner tree with the agents' locations as a terminal set, and the other is given the current deployment and new locations agents should reach, finding the redeployment that minimizes UAVs' traveling time, this problem was solved by using a dynamic programming algorithm. [5] split the general optimization problem into sub-problems: Explorers placement, relays placement, and UAV path generation. In particular, given a set of candidate locations to be connected, relays placement is achieved by solving variations of the Steiner minimum tree problem with a minimum number of Steiner points and bounded edge length. [4] proposed a single-stage strategy based on Integer Linear Programming for selecting and assigning UAVs to locations. They design a two-stage strategy to improve computational efficiency, by separating the problem of locations' selection from that of UAV-location assignments. Extensive testing both in simulation and with real UAVs shows that the proposed strategies provide good situational awareness at the base station while efficiently exploring the environment.

3   Method

3.1   Scenario Description

In this paper, we consider using multiple UAVs to explore an initially-unknown, two-dimensional, continuous, and bounded environment, as shown in the Fig. 4. There are obstacles of different shapes in this environment. The base station(BS) as a supervising control center exists in a fixed, known location in the environment. There is a team of n UAVs to perform unknown environment exploration missions, and each UAV is equipped with finite-range sensors to detect the outer boundaries of obstacles and perceive the surrounding space. Whenever the UAV sends new information, the BS will update the map of the exploration area and is responsible for the planning of the UAV's goal location. The whole UAV team collaborates to explore until the exploration mission is completed, and the BS finally obtains a complete global map. Data exchange between UAV and UAV, UAV and the BS through an *ad hoc* network.

3.2   Adaptive Collaborative Exploration Strategy Under Recurrent Connectivity Constraints

Recurrent Connectivity means that the global connection is only maintained at the initial deployment position of the UAVs, and it can be disconnected for any length of time during the journey to the goal's location. A new connection

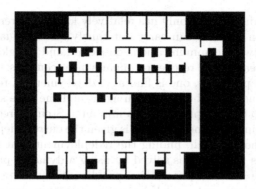

Fig. 4. Schematic figure of the scenario.

is triggered by a specific event (such as the completion of the transmission of information, a certain number of UAVs reach the ready state, etc.). In the current research work, this specific event that triggers a new connection is generally that a fixed number of UAVs reach the ready state (ready state refers to the UAV 1) reached its goal's location in this stage, 2) has transmitted its perceived data to the BS, 3) has no other UAVs still require it as a relay), that is, the time to trigger a new connection is when the replanning threshold reaches a preset fixed value.

Aiming at the initially unknown two-dimensional, continuous, and bounded environment exploration problem in Fig. 4, we propose an adaptive collaborative exploration strategy under recurrent connectivity constraints, and construct an adaptive collaborative exploration framework, as shown in Fig. 5.

This framework mainly describes the behavior of the BS and UAVs in the exploration process using the adaptive collaborative exploration strategy under recurrent connectivity constraints. The framework uses an adaptive collaborative exploration strategy under recurrent connectivity constraints to accomplish the exploration mission, which is usually divided into several stages. In each stage, the BS mainly performs global map update and preprocessing, UAV's state recognition and confirmation of whether replanning is required, and obtains the goal's position of each UAV and replanning threshold in the next stage through the adaptive threshold planning algorithm (ATP algorithm). The UAV mainly uses the sensing module to sense the communication environment, obstacles, and its own location, and exchange the perceived data with the BS. It receives the goal's location of the next stage sent by the BS and uses the navigation module to navigate to the goal's location autonomously, and updates the own map for the next stage of exploration. Figure 6 shows a snapshot of the exploration process.

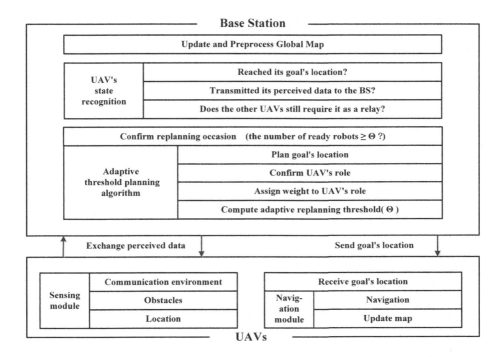

Fig. 5. Adaptive collaborative exploration framework.

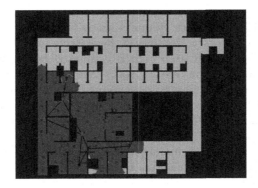

Fig. 6. Exploration snapshot. Blue and red - not ready and ready UAVs. Green squares - The BS. Green lines - current communication links. (Color figure online)

3.3   Adaptive Threshold Planning Algorithm (ATP Algorithm)

The adaptive threshold planning algorithm is divided into four parts, which are planning the goal's location, confirming UAV's role, assigning weight to UAV's role, and computing the adaptive replanning threshold. The overall flow ATP algorithm is shown in Fig. 7.

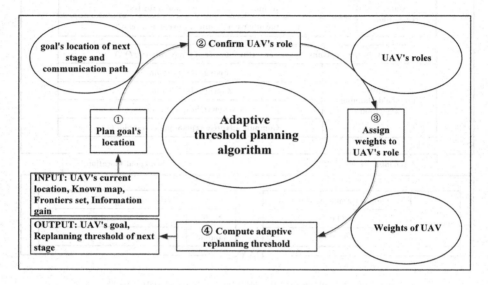

Fig. 7. The overall flow ATP algorithm.

The input of the algorithm is UAV's current location, known map, candidate frontiers set, and information gain. The candidate frontiers set and information gain are obtained by the discretization preprocessing of the map by the BS in this strategy. The candidate frontiers set is, based on the literature [22], clustered representation of the frontiers of the existing map, forming a candidate set of goal's location. Information gain is estimated by acquiring sensor data preprocessed map information (see [11, 16]). The first part of the algorithm is to plan the goal's location and obtain a communication path of the next stage. In the second part, the UAV's role is confirmed according to the degree of the node of the communication path tree and whether the location of the node belongs to the candidate frontiers set. The third part assigns weights to each UAV based on its contribution to the map update and information gain. The fourth part is to compute the replanning threshold of the next stage according to the adaptive replanning threshold formula. The output of the algorithm is the UAV's goal and the replanning threshold of the next stage.

Planning the Goal's Location. This part is to plan the goal's location and calculate the communication path based on the current location of the UAVs and the known map information. We work on a graph-based representation of the environment $G = (V, C)$ where vertices in V encode some discretization. Each vertex $v \in V$ is associated with a location, the edge set C encodes the availability of communication links between pairs of vertices. We select the goal's location from the candidate frontiers set according to the utility function [3], and arrange each UAV on the goal's location. Through the calculated goal's location information, the tree of the communication path of the next stage is obtained.

Confirming UAV's Role. Through the first part, we got the planned goal's location of each UAV in the next stage, and also got the tree of their communication path. Figure 8 is a snapshot of exploration. It can be seen that the communication link between the UAV and the BS forms a tree structure, and the root node of the tree is BS. We define UAVs as three types of roles based on their location and their contribution to updating the map, namely explorer, relay, and composite relay.

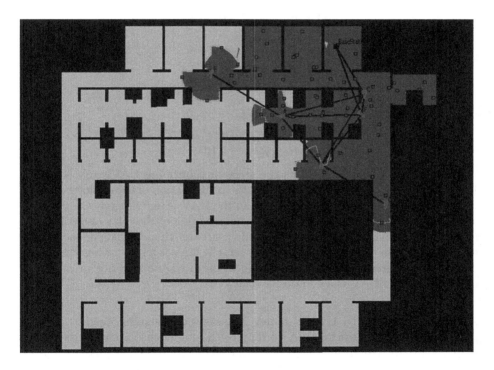

Fig. 8. A snapshot of exploration shows a tree structure.

- Explorer. The explorer is at the frontier of exploration during the exploration stage, and is only responsible for exploring unknown areas and updating the map, and does not undertake relay tasks. The formal definition is shown in Eq. (1), that is, the location of the UAV belongs to the candidate frontiers set, its information gain is greater than 0, and it has no relay function.

- Relay. The relay only undertakes the relay task and does not contribute to the map update during the exploration stage. The formal definition is shown in Eq. (2), that is, the location of the UAV does not belong to the candidate frontiers set, its information gain is 0, and it only has the relay function.
- Composite Relay. The composite relay is at the frontier of exploration, but also undertakes the relay task. The formal definition is shown in Eq. (3), that is, the location of the UAV belongs to the candidate frontiers set, its information gain is greater than 0, and it is also a relay.

According to the definition, UAVs E and D in Fig. 8 are explorers, UAVs C and F are relays, and UAVs A and B are composite relays.

$$\begin{cases} Info\_gain(Loc_{r_i}) > 0 \\ Loc_{r_i} \in Frontiers^t \\ IsRelay(r_i) = \text{FALSE} \end{cases} \tag{1}$$

$$\begin{cases} Info\_gain(Loc_{r_i}) = 0 \\ Loc_{r_i} \notin Frontiers^t \\ IsRelay(r_i) = \text{TRUE} \end{cases} \tag{2}$$

$$\begin{cases} Info\_gain(Loc_{r_i}) > 0 \\ Loc_{r_i} \in Frontiers^t \\ IsRelay(r_i) = \text{TRUE} \end{cases} \tag{3}$$

Algorithm 1 formally presents the steps of confirming UAV's role. On lines 1–3 of Algorithm 1, the algorithm shows the confirmation of the explorer, that is, when the degree of the node is equal to 0, the UAV is an explorer. On lines 4–9 of Algorithm 1, the algorithm shows the confirmation of the relay and composite relay, that is, when the degree of the node is greater than 0, and the location of the node is not in the candidate frontiers set, the UAV is a relay; when the degree of the node is greater than 0, and the location of the node is not in candidate frontiers set, the UAV is a composite relay.

Assigning Weight to UAV's Role. The steps of assigning weight to UAV's role are shown in Algorithm 2. According to the contribution of each role to the map update, we assign the weight of the three types of roles, the relay weight is 0 (Eq. (4)), the explorer weight is 1 (Eq. (5)), and the weight of the composite relay is assigned by the information gain of its location (Eq.(6)), where $r_i \in R_{cr}^{t+1}$.

$$\omega_r = 0 \tag{4}$$

$$\omega_e = 1 \tag{5}$$

Algorithm 1 Confirming UAV's role

Input: T^{t+1}, F^t
Output: $R_r^{t+1}, R_e^{t+1}, R_{cr}^{t+1}$
1: **for** each $r_i^{t+1} \in T^{t+1}$ **do**
2:      **if** $degree(r_i^{t+1}) = 0$ **then** $r_i^{t+1} \in R_e^{t+1}$
3:      **end if**
4:      **if** $degree(r_i^{t+1}) > 0$ **then**
5:          **if** $Loc_{r_i}^{t+1} \notin F^t$ **then** $r_i^{t+1} \in R_r^{t+1}$
6:          **end if**
7:          **if** $Loc_{r_i}^{t+1} \in F^t$ **then** $r_i^{t+1} \in R_{cr}^{t+1}$
8:          **end if**
9:      **end if**
10: **end for**
11: **return** $R_r^{t+1}, R_e^{t+1}, R_{cr}^{t+1}$

Algorithm 2 Giving weight to UAV's role

Input: $R_r^{t+1}, R_e^{t+1}, R_{cr}^{t+1}, Info\_gain(F^t)$
Output: W^{t+1}
1: **for** each $r_i^{t+1} \in R_r^{t+1}$ **do**
2:      $\omega_{r_i} = 0$
3: **end for**
4: **for** each $r_i^{t+1} \in R_e^{t+1}$ **do**
5:      $\omega_{r_i} = 1$
6: **end for**
7: **for** each $r_i^{t+1} \in R_{cr}^{t+1}$ **do**
8:      $\omega_{r_i} = Info\_gain(Loc_{r_i})$
9: **end for**
10: **return** W^{t+1}

$$\omega_{r_i} = Info\_gain(Loc_{r_i}) \tag{6}$$

Computing the Adaptive Replanning Threshold. We propose a formula (Eq. (7)) for Computing the adaptive replanning threshold, that is, the sum of the weights of all UAV roles is rounded down to get the replanning threshold for the next stage. Rounding down is due to our slack threshold strategy. According to the difference of three types of roles, our formula can be written in the form of Eq. (8). According to the weight assignment of different roles, the final form of the formula is Eq. (9).

$$\theta^{t+1} = \lfloor \sum_{r_i \in R^{t+1}} \omega_{r_i} \rfloor \tag{7}$$

$$\theta^{t+1} = \lfloor \sum_{r_i \in R_r^{t+1}} \omega_{r_i} + \sum_{r_j \in R_e^{t+1}} \omega_{r_j} + \sum_{r_k \in R_{cr}^{t+1}} \omega_{r_k} \rfloor \tag{8}$$

$$\theta^{t+1} = \lfloor n_r * 0 + n_e * 1 + \sum_{r_i \in R_{cr}^{t+1}} Info\_gain(Loc_{r_i}) \rfloor \qquad (9)$$

Through the above four parts, the final output of the adaptive threshold planning algorithm are obtained, that is, the UAV's goal and the replanning threshold of the next stage.

4   Experiments

4.1   Configuration of Experiments

The hardware and software configuration of our experiments is shown in Table 1. We choose the MRESim [17] simulator for its focus on communication and we select two environments of size 80 m × 60 m (represented by occupancy grids, whose cell edge length is 10 cm), shown in Fig. 9. Alabama and grass are from the MRESim repository (Alabama represents an environment with simple obstacles, and grass represents an environment with complex obstacles). We run simulations with teams of 6 UAVs moving at a constant speed of 0.7 m/s, and equipped with a depth camera with a maximum range of 5 m, a 60°FOV, and an angular resolution of 1°. For each experimental set, 5 runs of 90% explored area is executed for each environment, randomly varying the starting positions of the BS and UAVs. For the simulation experiments, we assume that the communication model UAVs are endowed with coinciding with the actual possibility of communicating in the simulated world while ensuring enough bandwidth.

Table 1. Configuration of experiments

Categories	Configuration	
Hardware	Processor	Intel Core i7-9700 3.0 GHz
	RAM	16G
Software	Operation System	Ubuntu 16.04 x64
	Language	Python,Java
	IDE	PyCharm,Apache NetBeans
	Simulator	MREsim v2.0

4.2   Simulation Experiments

Evaluation Metrics. For the evaluation and comparison of individual exploration algorithms, We use the following five metrics:

- Total time explored, the total time required for the UAV team to complete the exploration mission, reflects the efficiency of the exploration.

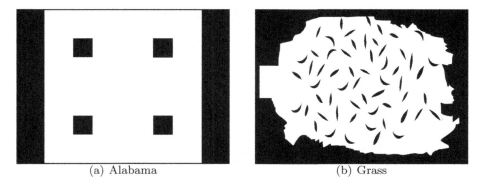

(a) Alabama   (b) Grass

Fig. 9. Simulation environments, approximate size 80 m × 60 m.

- Total time not in communication, the time the UAV team is in the "offline" state during the exploration process, reflects the situational awareness of the BS. The longer this time, the weaker the BS's overall situational awareness of the UAV team.
- Total distance traveled, the total distance traveled by the UAV team during the exploration process, reflects the energy consumption of the entire team.
- Total times replanned, the number of replanning by the UAV team during the exploration process, reflects the efficiency of the planning algorithm.
- Average time replanned, the average time for the BS to perform replanning, also reflects the efficiency of the planning algorithm.

We evaluated three methods separately, one is our adaptive threshold planning algorithm (ATP), one is the fixed threshold planning approximate algorithm(APX) [4], and the other is the Utility [16] method. Among them, the fixed threshold of the APX algorithm has six cases of 1–6.

Table 2. Comparison of APX and ATP

Environment	Algorithm	Total time explored [s]	Total times replanned	Average time replanned [s]
Alabama	**APX1**	481.6	65.4	1.303
	APX2	308.2	43.0	1.139
	APX3	387.5	34.2	1.138
	APX4	350.9	28.8	0.902
	APX5	305.7	28.8	0.861
	APX6	385.5	28.0	0.912
	ATP	**403.3**	**35.4**	1.194
Grass	**APX1**	658.2	83.8	2.185
	APX2	490.8	54.8	2.019
	APX3	341.8	42.0	1.579
	APX4	382.1	35.6	1.313
	APX5	576.1	36.8	1.639
	APX6	364.7	31.2	1.277
	ATP	**388.6**	**40.4**	1.780

Table 3. Comparison of APX, ATP, and Utility

Environment	Algorithm	Total time not in communication [ms]	Total distance traveled [px]
Alabama	APX1	247.2	12349.07
	APX2	380.8	12712.15
	APX3	550.1	15447.47
	APX4	523.3	15150.60
	APX5	659.8	15587.94
	APX6	592.6	14928.98
	ATP	**447.6**	**13689.92**
	Utility	2038.2	17747.25
Grass	APX1	312.8	13534.23
	APX2	420.4	14251.51
	APX3	363.6	16528.31
	APX4	413.4	16966.19
	APX5	545.1	17095.05
	APX6	429.1	15818.16
	ATP	**282.8**	**14201.22**
	Utility	2253.8	22692.65

Table 2 shows the comparison between APX and ATP in total time explored, total times replanned, and average time replanned in different environments. As shown in Table 2, from the perspective of the total exploration time, the ATP algorithm has a higher exploration efficiency than most APX algorithms, regardless of whether it is a simple environment or a complex environment. Judging from the total times replanned, the total times of the ATP algorithm are significantly reduced compared with the APX1 algorithm, the total times replanned have been reduced by 45.9% and 51.7%, respectively. From the perspective of the average time replanned, the ATP algorithm is at a medium level. It can be seen that the total replanning time of the ATP algorithm is greatly reduced, allowing the UAVs to have more time for exploration and improving the efficiency of exploration.

Table 3 shows the comparison between APX, ATP, and Utility in total time not in communication and total distance traveled in different environments. As shown in Table 3, from the perspective of total time not in communication, both the ATP algorithm and the APX algorithm have greater advantages than the Utility algorithm, and the time is reduced by 87.8% to 67.6%. This shows that both the ATP algorithm and the APX algorithm can allow the BS to maintain good situational awareness. In terms of the total distance traveled, the ATP algorithm also has a significant reduction compared with the Utility algorithm. This shows that the ATP algorithm consumes less energy. Regarding the above two indicators, we plot the experimental data as shown in Fig. 10, which can more intuitively see the excellent performance of our ATP algorithm.

In addition, we can see that the APX algorithm and Utility algorithm have a certain increase in total time explored, total time not in communication, and total times replanned in a complex environment. However, the above indicators of the ATP algorithm in a complex environment perform better than in a simple

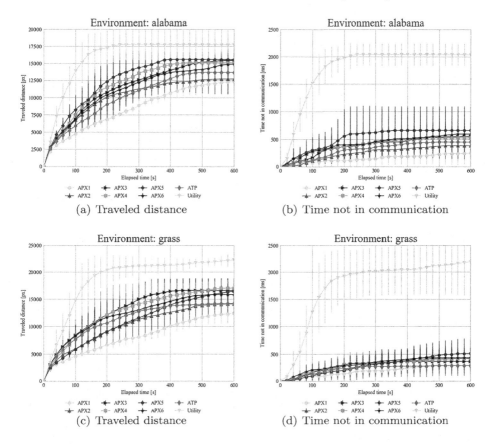

Fig. 10. Comparison of the planning approaches for 6 UAVs in the alabama and grass environments.

environment. This shows that our ATP algorithm has a stronger ability to adapt to complex environments.

5 Conclusion

In this work, we proposed an adaptive collaborative exploration strategy under recurrent connectivity constraints, construct an adaptive collaborative exploration framework, and designed an adaptive threshold planning algorithm. Our simulation results show that the ATP algorithm can greatly reduce the number of replanning and provide good situational awareness for the BS while ensuring a certain exploration efficiency in both complex and simple environments, and our ATP algorithm has a stronger ability to adapt to complex environments. Our future work will be as follows: One is to use deep neural networks to pre-categorize scene perception data for better adaptive cognition. The second is to model adaptive strategies as behaviors and use reinforcement learning methods of data-driven strategy adaptation and optimization.

References

1. Amigoni, F., Banfi, J., Basilico, N.: Multirobot exploration of communication-restricted environments: a survey. IEEE Intell. Syst. **32**(6), 48–57 (2017)
2. Arkin, R.C., Diaz, J.: Line-of-sight constrained exploration for reactive multi-agent robotic teams. In: 7th International Workshop on Advanced Motion Control. Proceedings (Cat. No. 02TH8623), pp. 455–461. IEEE (2002)
3. Banfi, J., Li, A.Q., Basilico, N., Rekleitis, I., Amigoni, F.: Asynchronous multirobot exploration under recurrent connectivity constraints. In: 2016 IEEE International Conference on Robotics and Automation (ICRA), pp. 5491–5498. IEEE (2016)
4. Banfi, J., Quattrini Li, A., Rekleitis, I., Amigoni, F., Basilico, N.: Strategies for coordinated multirobot exploration with recurrent connectivity constraints. Auton. Robot. **42**(4), 875–894 (2017). https://doi.org/10.1007/s10514-017-9652-y
5. Cheng, X., Du, D.Z., Wang, L., Xu, B.: Relay sensor placement in wireless sensor networks. Wireless Netw. **14**(3), 347–355 (2008)
6. Cieslewski, T., Kaufmann, E., Scaramuzza, D.: Rapid exploration with multi-rotors: a frontier selection method for high speed flight. In: 2017 IEEE/RSJ International Conference on Intelligent Robots and Systems (IROS), pp. 2135–2142. IEEE (2017)
7. Delmerico, J., et al.: The current state and future outlook of rescue robotics. J. Field Robot. **36**(7), 1171–1191 (2019)
8. Jensen, E.A., Lowmanstone, L., Gini, M.: Communication-restricted exploration for search teams. In: Groß, R., et al. (eds.) Distributed Autonomous Robotic Systems. SPAR, vol. 6, pp. 17–30. Springer, Cham (2018). https://doi.org/10.1007/978-3-319-73008-0_2
9. Meng, Z., et al.: A two-stage optimized next-view planning framework for 3-d unknown environment exploration, and structural reconstruction. IEEE Robot. Autom. Lett. **2**(3), 1680–1687 (2017)
10. Ochoa, S.F., Santos, R.: Human-centric wireless sensor networks to improve information availability during urban search and rescue activities. Inf. Fusion **22**, 71–84 (2015)
11. Pei, Y., Mutka, M.W., Xi, N.: Connectivity and bandwidth-aware real-time exploration in mobile robot networks. Wirel. Commun. Mob. Comput. **13**(9), 847–863 (2013)
12. Reich, J., Misra, V., Rubenstein, D., Zussman, G.: Connectivity maintenance in mobile wireless networks via constrained mobility. IEEE J. Sel. Areas Commun. **30**(5), 935–950 (2012)
13. Rooker, M.N., Birk, A.: Multi-robot exploration under the constraints of wireless networking. Control. Eng. Pract. **15**(4), 435–445 (2007)
14. Schmid, L., Pantic, M., Khanna, R., Ott, L., Siegwart, R., Nieto, J.: An efficient sampling-based method for online informative path planning in unknown environments. IEEE Robot. Autom. Lett. **5**(2), 1500–1507 (2020)
15. Selin, M., Tiger, M., Duberg, D., Heintz, F., Jensfelt, P.: Efficient autonomous exploration planning of large-scale 3-d environments. IEEE Robot. Autom. Lett. **4**(2), 1699–1706 (2019)

16. Spirin, V., Cameron, S., de Hoog, J.: Time preference for information in multi-agent exploration with limited communication. In: Natraj, A., Cameron, S., Melhuish, C., Witkowski, M. (eds.) TAROS 2013. LNCS (LNAI), vol. 8069, pp. 34–45. Springer, Heidelberg (2014). https://doi.org/10.1007/978-3-662-43645-5_5

17. Spirin, V., de Hoog, J., Visser, A., Cameron, S.: MRESim, a multi-robot exploration simulator for the rescue simulation league. In: Bianchi, R.A.C., Akin, H.L., Ramamoorthy, S., Sugiura, K. (eds.) RoboCup 2014. LNCS (LNAI), vol. 8992, pp. 106–117. Springer, Cham (2015). https://doi.org/10.1007/978-3-319-18615-3_9

18. Stump, E., Michael, N., Kumar, V., Isler, V.: Visibility-based deployment of robot formations for communication maintenance. In: 2011 IEEE International Conference on Robotics and Automation, pp. 4498–4505. IEEE (2011)

19. Tadokoro, S.: Rescue Robotics: DDT Project on Robots and Systems for Urban Search and Rescue. Springer, Heidelberg (2009). https://doi.org/10.1007/978-1-84882-474-4

20. Thrun, S., et al.: Robotic mapping: a survey (2002)

21. Visser, A., Slamet, B.A.: Including communication success in the estimation of information gain for multi-robot exploration. In: 2008 6th International Symposium on Modeling and Optimization in Mobile, Ad Hoc, and Wireless Networks and Workshops, pp. 680–687. IEEE (2008)

22. Yamauchi, B.: Frontier-based exploration using multiple robots. In: Proceedings of the Second International Conference on Autonomous Agents, pp. 47–53 (1998)

The Evaluation of the Angled Antenna Based Direction Estimation Scheme for RFID Tags

Kota Mizuno[1]([✉]), Katsuhiro Naito[1], and Masaki Ehara[2]

[1] Aichi Institute of Technology, Toyota, Aichi, Japan
{mizuno47,naito}@pluslab.org
[2] AIM Japan, Kumagaya, Saitama, Japan
masaki.ehara@aim-jp.org

Abstract. Radio Frequency Identification (RFID) has been used to improve services such as inventory management and behavior analysis in recent industries. Since these services require tracking the movement of objects where an RFID tag is attached, the direction estimation scheme for RFID tags has been attracting attention. Conventional estimation schemes require a large space for antenna installation or assume expensive small antennas, which poses a challenge for implementation in the field. This paper evaluates the performance of the proposed direction estimation scheme for several types of RFID tags because the authors have conducted the initial evaluation. Since the proposed scheme uses an angled single antenna, it should be a valuable scheme in practical service if the proposed scheme generally works for several types of RFID tags. The proposed scheme focuses on the features of change in Received Signal Strength Indicator (RSSI) and phase value caused by an angled antenna. The evaluation result shows that the proposed scheme can estimate the direction of movement accurately for multiple types of tags.

Keywords: RFID · Direction estimation · Single antenna

1 Introduction

The usage of Radio Frequency Identification (RFID) is expanding for several services. RFID is a short-range wireless communication technology between a reader and a tag for identification [1]. In particular, RFID-based systems have been introduced in the industry to improve work efficiency and reduce labor costs. RFID-Based systems include behavior analysis, inventory management, and security systems using anti-theft gates [2,3]. In behavior analysis, RFID tags are attached to products to obtain data such as combinations of products that customers purchased and how they are moving around in a store [4,5]. By analyzing the acquired data, it is possible to make more detailed sales plans [6,7].

© ICST Institute for Computer Sciences, Social Informatics and Telecommunications Engineering 2022
Published by Springer Nature Switzerland AG 2022. All Rights Reserved
T. Hara and H. Yamaguchi (Eds.): MobiQuitous 2021, LNICST 419, pp. 754–768, 2022.
https://doi.org/10.1007/978-3-030-94822-1_49

RFID-based inventory management differs from conventional barcode management in that it uses wireless communication. This makes it possible to read RFID tags attached to luggage even they cannot be visually recognized. In addition, the ability to read tags in batches can be used to improve work efficiency [10]. Since these services are operated by attaching tags to luggage and commodities, they can be combined with anti-theft gates in stores. Therefore, there is no need to attach security tags as in the past. It can improve operational efficiency and reduce costs.

These RFID systems mainly use passive RFID tags. They don't require batteries or other power sources and can be used semi-permanently because they are powered by electromagnetic energy from the reader [8]. In addition, because of their low cost, they are used on the premise of being disposable and are attached to products and luggage [9]. Since it is necessary to track the movement of objects attached to passive RFID tags in behavioral analysis, inventory management, and anti-theft gates, schemes for estimating the direction of movement of RFID tags have attracted much attention [11–13].

As existing direction estimation schemes, sensor-antenna, double antennas, and gated antenna schemes have been used [14]. In the sensor-antenna scheme, the antenna is installed, and electric light sensors are put on both sides of the antenna. The system identifies RFID tags by acquiring their data using the installed antenna and estimates the direction of movement by detecting the passage of RFID tags by sensors. The sensors can detect the passage of an object but cannot identify the RFID tags. Therefore, it isn't easy to detect which tag passed in which direction when several tags passed simultaneously from different directions. The double antennas scheme places two antennas side by side and measures the time difference of reading a tag between each antenna. It requires a large space for installation due to place two antennas, which limits the installation environment. The gated antenna scheme identifies tags passing through the gate that installing multiple antennas in the tunnel-like structure. Since it uses multiple antennas, it can estimate the direction accurately. However, the use of multiple antennas and the need for materials to install them in the tunnel structure result in high installation costs and large installation space. These problems prevent the installation of RFID services based on direction estimation technology.

We have proposed a single-antenna direction estimation scheme that uses only one inexpensive general-purpose antenna. The proposed scheme solves the problems of the installation environment and installation cost of the conventional scheme due to the use of only one inexpensive antenna. The fundamental evaluation with one type of RFID tag has shown that the proposed scheme works well to detect the movement direction [15]. On the contrary, typical RFID tags have various variations according to the combination of an RFID chip and an antenna. The difference in the combination causes the difference in communication performance. Therefore, we should evaluate the performance of the proposed scheme with various types of RFID tags released in the industry. In this paper, we evaluate the feasibility of the proposed scheme by comparing the performance of each RFID tag. We prepare ten types of RFID tags for the evaluations. The evaluation result shows that the proposed scheme can estimate the movement direction accurately for several types of tags.

2 Proposed System

2.1 Overview

We proposed a new direction estimation scheme using a single general-purpose antenna. Since the proposed scheme uses only one antenna, it is difficult to estimate the tag's movement direction by using the difference of reading times as in the conventional scheme. Therefore, we use the changes of RSSI and phase values acquired during tag reading. In the proposed scheme, the antenna is installed at an angle. The installation angle causes the feature to change the RSSI and phase values with the direction of movement. The proposed scheme can estimate the tag's movement direction due to analysis and detect the feature. RFID tags contain an Electronic Product Code (EPC), and the reader identifies the tag by reading the EPC [16]. The EPC is a unique code that the tag has and serves as an identifier. When multiple tags are read, the changes in RSSI and phase values of each identified tag are analyzed to estimate the direction. Therefore, the proposed scheme can estimate the direction of each tag even in the presence of multiple tags.

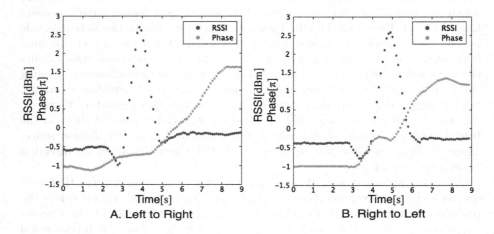

Fig. 1. Change process of RSSI and phase value in 0° antenna angle

2.2 The Installation Angle of Antenna

The conventional scheme places an antenna in parallel with the tag movement direction. Therefore, the characteristics of the RSSI and phase values are very similar when the tag passes to the right or the left. Figure 1 shows the change in RSSI and phase values when the tag moves in an arbitrary direction. The RSSI increases when the distance between the tag and the antenna gets closer. As a result, the RSSI increases and peaks in front of the antenna when the tag passes through. After reaching the peak, it decreases gradually.

Comparing the cases where the tag moves to the right and left, the process of RSSI and phase value is almost the same. Accordingly, it isn't easy to estimate the direction of the RFID tag when the antenna is installed parallel to the direction of movement. Therefore, we focus on the directivity of the antenna and install it with an angle. Figure 2 shows the change of RSSI and phase values when the antenna is installed with an angle.

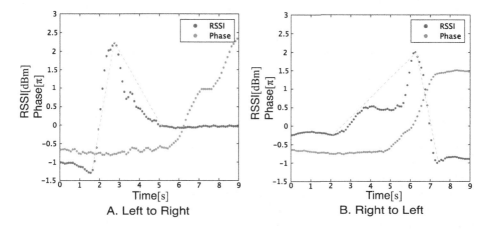

Fig. 2. Change process of RSSI and phase value in $45°$ antenna angle

When the antenna is angled to the right, and the tag is moved to the right direction, the RSSI increases rapidly until it reaches its peak and decreases slowly. On the contrary, the RSSI increases slowly until it reaches the peak and decreases rapidly when the tag moves to the left. In this way, the change process of RSSI before and after the peak differs according to the movement direction. The proposed scheme uses the features on the difference of change process of RSSI to estimate the direction of tag movement.

2.3 System Model

Figure 3 shows the proposed system model for the direction estimation system. Since it can control the RFID reader/writer, it requests a Query command to get the tag data from RFID tags. An RFID tag that received Query command backscatters its own data. The RFID reader/writer gets tag information such as EPC, RSSI, and phase value. The analysis module analyzes the tag information to estimate the direction of movement. Finally, the application obtains the estimation result.

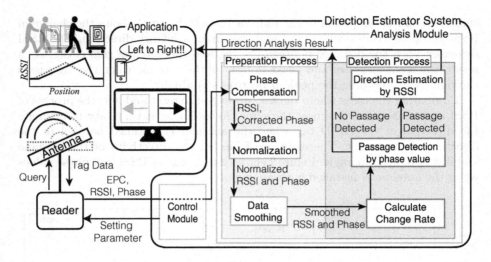

Fig. 3. System model

3   Analysis Module

3.1   Overview

The analysis module analyzes the RSSI and phase value calculated by the reader to estimate the direction of movement. The proposed algorithm for estimating the direction utilizes the features of RSSI and phase value change. The feature can be detected by using the change rate of RSSI and phase value. The processes phase compensation, data normalization, and data smoothing perform as preparation processes for feature detection. After the preparation processes, the analysis module calculates the change rate of RSSI and phase value. The change rate of phase value is used to detect tag passage. The result is sent to the application if the passage of the tag is not detected. When the tag passage is detected, the analysis module estimates the direction of tag movement and passes the result to the application.

3.2   Phase Compensation

The RFID reader/writer calculates RSSI and phase value when it receives tag information from the RFID tag. The calculated RSSI and phase value always contain some errors. In particular, the phase value often contains large errors. Figure 4 shows the phase value without and with the compensation.

Normally, the phase value will gradually increase to 1.0π, 1.1π, 1.2π, or decrease to 1.0π, 0.9π, 0.8π when the tag moves. However, the phase value calculated by the reader/writer is influenced by noise and reflected waves. The noise is caused by the thermal noise in the circuits of the reader/writer. A reflected wave occurs when a signal collides with an object or person, and it is reflected.

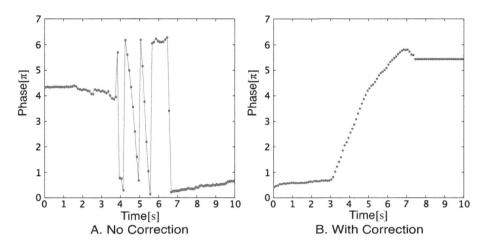

Fig. 4. Compare phase values without and with the compensation

The reflected wave travels a longer distance than the direct wave, which greatly affects the phase rotation of the high frequency. Because of these factors, the phase value may change drastically or even protrude from the previous one. Therefore, compensation processing is required to smoothing the phase value when the phase value changes dynamically.

In this paper, the phase value is corrected when the difference from the previous one is 0.5π or more. The first step in the correction process is to calculate the difference from the previous phase value. The corrected value is made by adding or subtracting the correction value to the original data. Table 1 shows the relationship between the difference from the previous phase value and the correction value.

Table 1. The difference between previous value

Difference of phase P $[\pi]$	compensation value$[\pi]$
$1.5 < P \leq 2.0$	$+1.5$
$1.0 < P \leq 1.5$	$+1.0$
$0.5 < P \leq 1.0$	$+0.5$
$-0.5 > P \geq -1.0$	-0.5
$-1.0 > P \geq -1.5$	-1.0
$-1.5 > P \geq -2.0$	-1.5

For example, the phase difference is 0.8π when the phase value fluctuates significantly, from 1.0π to 0.2π. Since the difference is greater than 0.5π and less than 1.0π, the analysis module corrects it to 0.7π by adding 0.5π to 0.2π. The correct phase value is shown in Fig. 4-B can be obtained with the compensation process.

3.3   Data Normalization

The scale of RSSI and phase value are different, and the amount of change in the values is significantly different. Therefore, the data should be normalized to facilitate the comparison of the data. With the original data as x, the mean as $\overline{x}$, and the standard deviation as s, the normalizes data x' is given in Eq. 1.

$$x' = \frac{x - \overline{x}}{s} \tag{1}$$

Figure 5 shows the data before and after normalization.

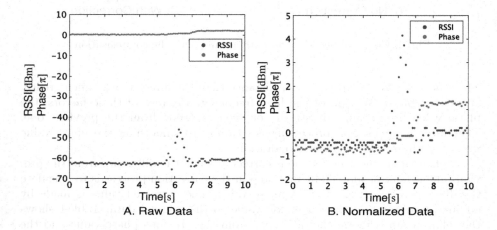

Fig. 5. The data before and after normalization

As shown in Fig. 5-A, the amount of change in the phase value before normalization is significantly different from that of RSSI. On the other hand, the data after normalization is based on the mean value, showing how far it is from that mean value. Therefore, the analysis module can compare the data with different units or when the amount of change in the original data is significantly different.

3.4   Data Smoothing

As shown in Fig. 5, there is variability in the data after normalization. The variability of the data makes it difficult to detect the feature of its change accurately. Therefore, a smoothing process is applied to facilitate feature detection. Figure 6 shows the normalized data and the smoothed data.

As shown in Fig. 6, the smoothed data is soother and with less change than the data before the smoothing process. The reduced variability of the data makes it easier to detect the characteristics of the change accurately.

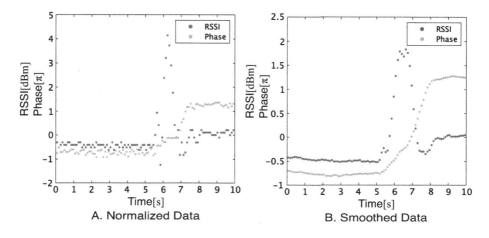

Fig. 6. The normalized data and smoothed data

3.5 Calculate the Rate of Change

The analysis module calculates the change rate of the data. The analysis module uses the change rate to detect the tag's passage and estimate the movement direction. The change rate CR_k between the kth data D_k and the j previous data D_{k-j} is given in Eq. 2.

$$CR_k = \frac{D_k - D_{k-j}}{j} \tag{2}$$

The change of data is milder when the rate of change is closer to 0. On the contrary, the data change is more rapid when the change rate is farther from 0.

3.6 Passage Detection by Phase

As shown in Fig. 6, the phase value changes when a tag passes in front of the antenna. In the proposed scheme, the change of phase value is used to detect the passage of the tag. In the case of the tag passing through, there is a difference between the value at the beginning and the end of the phase value change. In contrast, the value at the beginning and the end are almost equal when a tag doesn't pass. Therefore, it is possible to detect the passage of a tag by comparing the phase values at the beginning and end of the change.

3.7 Estimating the Direction of Movement by RSSI

Since the proposed system uses an angled antenna, RSSI dynamics' change rate differs depending on RFID tag movements' direction. Figure 7 shows the RSSI when the tag moves to the right and left. Figure 8 shows the rate of change when the tag moves in each direction. When the tag moves to the right, the

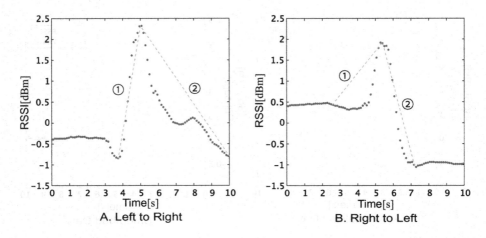

Fig. 7. The feature of change of RSSI

RSSI increases rapidly until the peak and decreases slowly. The rate of change is high when RSSI changes rapidly. On the other hand, the rate of change is low when RSSI changes slowly. In Fig. 7-A, the inclination of redline 1 is large, and that of redline 2 is small. Therefore, comparing the peaks of the rate of change in Fig. 8-A, it can be seen that the absolute value of the maximum is greater than that of the minimum (e.g., 0.35 for the maximum and 0.19 for the minimum). In contrast, when the tag moves to the left, the RSSI increases slowly until the peak decreases rapidly. Consequently, the absolute value of the minimum rate of change is greater than that of the maximum, as shown in Fig. 8-B. The proposed system focuses on the phenomenon to estimate the movement direction according to RSSI dynamics.

4   Implementation

We have implemented the prototype of the proposed system. The experiment uses an angled antenna called YAP-101CP from Yeon for Speedway Revolution R420 from Impinj as the RFID reader/writer. We also used the Impinj Octane SDK as the control module for the reader/writer and Visual Studio for Mac to implement the analysis module. The simple moving average method is used as the smoothing method in the analysis module. J in Eq. 2 was set to 1 for calculating the rate of change.

The phase value and the change rate after the compensation process are used to detect the passage of the RFID tag. It detects the passage of a tag by comparing the value at the start and end of the phase value change. Figure 9 shows the phase value and change rate of it.

The moment that the rate of change exceeds the threshold k is the starting point of change. The rate of change always has both positive and negative peaks. Therefore, if the negative peak is reached first when the value becomes less than

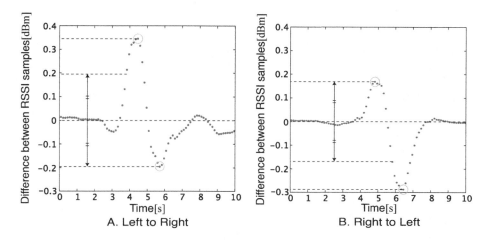

Fig. 8. The change rate of RSSI

zero for the first time after the positive peak is set as the endpoint. On the contrary, if the positive peak is reached first when the value becomes equal to or greater than zero for the first time after reaching the negative peak is set as the endpoint. The analysis module compares each phase value after detecting the start and endpoints. When the difference of the phase value is greater than or equal to the threshold L, the analysis module judges that the tag has passed. In this paper, we use $k = 0.03$, $L = 0.5$ for the evaluation.

The analysis module can estimate the direction of movement by comparing the absolute values of the maximum and minimum RSSI change rates. It detects the maximum and minimum values of the acquired RSSI data and calculates the absolute value. In this paper, since the antenna is angled to the right, the analysis module judges that the tag moved to the right when the absolute value of the maximum is larger. On the contrary, when the absolute value of the minimum value is larger, it is judged the tag moved to the left.

5   Evaluation

This paper evaluates the accuracy of the direction estimation according to the change of the installation angle, the moving speed of the RFID tag, and the type of tags. Figure 10 shows the RFID tags that we used. These tags are different in vendor, shape, and size. Different antenna shapes and sizes are expected to cause different features such as RSSI and phase value change. These differences are considered to affect the accuracy of direction estimation. Therefore, this evaluation clears the performance of the proposed system with different types of RFID tags.

The antenna angles changes from 10°, 20°, 30°, 45°, 60°, 70° and 80°. The RFID tag moves with a speed of 1 m/s or 2 m/s on a straight line of 0.5 m away

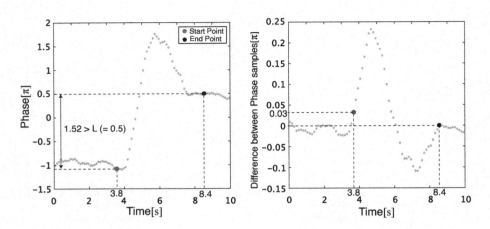

Fig. 9. Phase value and change rate

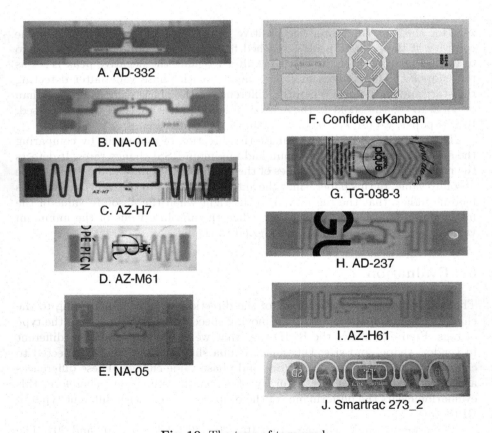

Fig. 10. The type of tags used

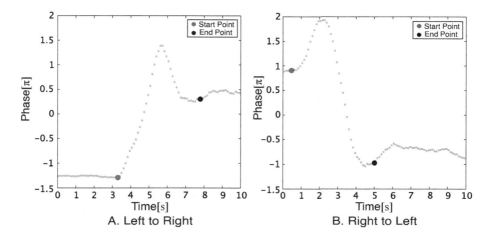

Fig. 11. The result of detecting the start and end point of phase change

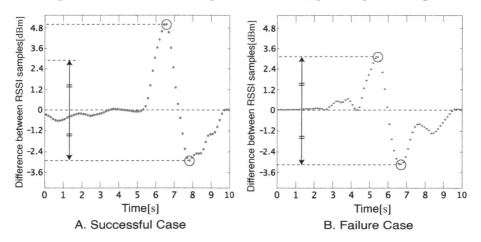

Fig. 12. Experimental successful and failure case

from the antenna and is the same height as the antenna's center. Under each condition, ten different tags are passed through 30 times.

Figure 11 shows the result of detecting the start and endpoints of the phase value change. From Fig. 11, we can see that the start and endpoints of change are detected almost accurately. Figure 12 shows the change rate of RSSI for successful and failure cases of direction estimation. In the success case, we can find that the maximum's absolute value is greater than the minimum. Therefore, the system estimated the accurate direction to the right. In the failure case, the absolute values of the maximum and the minimum are almost the same. As a result, the estimation process does not work well.

Table 2. The accuracy of direction estimation

A Angle / Speed	10°	20°	30°	45°	60°	70°	80°
1 m/s	83%	87%	93%	96%	90%	100%	100%
2 m/s	80%	90%	90%	97%	100%	100%	100%

B Angle / Speed	10°	20°	30°	45°	60°	70°	80°
1 m/s	80%	90%	90%	97%	100%	97%	100%
2 m/s	80%	90%	97%	90%	93%	100%	100%

C Angle / Speed	10°	20°	30°	45°	60°	70°	80°
1 m/s	83%	87%	90%	97%	97%	100%	100%
2 m/s	83%	83%	93%	97%	97%	97%	97%

D Angle / Speed	10°	20°	30°	45°	60°	70°	80°
1 m/s	80%	80%	87%	93%	100%	100%	97%
2 m/s	83%	80%	90%	100%	93%	100%	93%

E Angle / Speed	10°	20°	30°	45°	60°	70°	80°
1 m/s	83%	87%	87%	93%	93%	97%	93%
2 m/s	80%	87%	83%	90%	93%	90%	93%

F Angle / Speed	10°	20°	30°	45°	60°	70°	80°
1 m/s	87%	97%	90%	93%	100%	100%	97%
2 m/s	83%	97%	93%	87%	100%	100%	100%

G Angle / Speed	10°	20°	30°	45°	60°	70°	80°
1 m/s	83%	93%	90%	97%	93%	100%	100%
2 m/s	83%	87%	83%	90%	87%	100%	100%

H Angle / Speed	10°	20°	30°	45°	60°	70°	80°
1 m/s	97%	100%	100%	100%	100%	97%	100%
2 m/s	83%	90%	93%	100%	97%	100%	93%

I Angle / Speed	10°	20°	30°	45°	60°	70°	80°
1 m/s	90%	87%	90%	97%	97%	100%	97%
2 m/s	83%	90%	83%	93%	90%	90%	97%

J Angle / Speed	10°	20°	30°	45°	60°	70°	80°
1 m/s	93%	93%	93%	97%	100%	93%	100%
2 m/s	87%	90%	93%	93%	97%	93%	97%

Table 2 shows the estimation accuracy with a different installation angle of the antenna, difference speed, and different types of RFID tags. The result shows that the estimation accuracy is more than 80% in all tags. Additionally, the accuracy tends to be better when the angle is larger for most of the tags. This result is that detecting the feature is more difficult when the antenna angle is smaller.

When the installation angle is small, the difference between the absolute values of the maximum and the minimum of RSSI change rate is smaller than when the angle is large. Therefore, it is considered that false detection is more likely to occur. As the speed of RFID tags, the slower speed is better to estimate the direction accurately. The RSSI changes slowly before or after the peak when the tag passes in front of the antenna. If the change in RSSI is gradual, the change rate is low. The tag moves faster, the RSSI changes dynamically, and so the rate changes larger. Therefore, when the moving speed is high, the RSSI, which originally changes slowly, changes relatively rapidly. Since the change rate of the RSSI fluctuates greatly as the moving speed increases, the difference between the absolute values of the minimum and maximum becomes smaller. This makes it difficult to detect the characteristics of RSSI changes accurately, which is likely to lead to false detection of the direction of movement.

6   Conclusion

This paper has evaluated the accuracy of the proposed scheme. Since the RSSI and the phase value have special characteristics according to the movement directions, the proposed system can estimate the movement direction of RFID tags with an angled antenna. We have implemented the prototype of the proposed system and evaluated the accuracy of direction estimation. The evaluation result shows that the proposed system can estimate the direction with more than 80% accuracy for the ten types of tags.

Additionally, we can find the trend that the accuracy is higher when the antenna angle is larger. The result also shows that the estimation accuracy tends to be better when the speed of the RFID tag is slower. The future challenge is to improve the estimation accuracy by modifying the method of calculating the rate of change and making it possible to detect the changing features of RSSI and phase value more accurately. It is also necessary to evaluate how the accuracy changes when multiple tags are passed simultaneously.

References

1. Li, C., Lao, K., Tam, K.: A flooding warning system based on RFID tag array for energy facility. In: 2018 IEEE International Conference on RFID Technology Application (RFID-TA), pp. 1–4 (2018). https://doi.org/10.1109/RFID-TA.2018.8552767
2. Zhang, Y., Xie, L., Bu, Y., Wang, Y., Wu, J. and Lu, S.: 3-dimensional localization via RFID tag array. In: 2017 IEEE 14th International Conference on Mobile Ad Hoc and Sensor Systems (MASS), pp. 353–361 (2017). https://doi.org/10.1109/MASS.2017.22
3. Liu, Z., Wang, M., Qi, S., Yang, C.: Study on the anti-theft technology of museum cultural relics based on Internet of Things. IEEE Access 7, 111387–111395 (2019). https://doi.org/10.1109/ACCESS.2019.2933236
4. Han, J., et al.: CBID: a customer behavior identification system using passive tags. IEEE/ACM Trans. Netw. 24(5), 2885–2898 (2016). https://doi.org/10.1109/TNET.2015.2501103

5. Landmark, A.D., Sjøbakk, B.: Tracking customer behaviour in fashion retail using RFID—emerald insight. Int. J. Retail Distrib. Manage. **45**(7), 844–858 (2017). https://doi.org/10.1108/IJRDM-10-2016-0174
6. Pradel, B., et al.: A case study in a recommender system based on purchase data. In: Proceedings of the 17th ACM SIGKDD International Conference on Knowledge Discovery and Data Mining, KDD 2011, New York, NY, USA, pp. 377–385. Association for Computing Machinery (2011). https://doi.org/10.1145/2020408.2020470
7. Vijayakumar, V., Neelanarayanan, V. (eds.): Proceedings of the 3rd International Symposium on Big Data and Cloud Computing Challenges (ISBCC–2016). SIST, vol. 49. Springer, Cham (2016). https://doi.org/10.1007/978-3-319-30348-2
8. Finkenzeller, K.: RFID Handbook: Fundamentals and Applications in Contactless Smart Cards, Radio Frequency Identification and Near-Field Communication, 3rd edn. Wiley, New York (2010)
9. Inc., H.I.: Radio Frequency Identification (RFID) Frequently Asked Questions (2016)
10. Anssens, C., Rolland, N., Rolland, P.: A sensornetwork based on RFID inventory for retail application. In: 2011 IEEE International Conference on RFID-Technologies and Applications, pp. 64–67 (2011). https://doi.org/10.1109/RFID-TA.2011.6068617
11. Jie, W., Minghua, Z., Bo, X., Wei, H.: RFID based motion direction estimation in gate systems. In: 2018 IEEE 22nd International Conference on Computer Supported Cooperative Work in Design (CSCWD), pp. 588–593 (2018). https://doi.org/10.1109/CSCWD.2018.8465374
12. Buffi, A., D'Andrea, W., Lazzerini, B., Nepa, P.: UHF-RFID smart gate Tag action classifier by artificial neural networks. In: 2017 IEEE International Conference on RFID Technology Application (RFID-TA), pp. 45–50 (2017). https://doi.org/10.1109/RFID-TA.2017.8098900
13. Alvarez-Narciandi, G., Motroni, A., Pino, M.R., Buffi, A., Nepa, P.: A UHF-RFID gate control system based on a Convolutional Neural Network. In: 2019 IEEE International Conference on RFID Technology and Applications (RFID-TA), pp. 353–356 (2019). https://doi.org/10.1109/RFID-TA.2019.8892080
14. Oikawa, Y.: Tag movement direction estimation methods in an RFID gate system. In: 2009 6th International Symposium on Wireless Communication Systems, pp. 41–45 (2009). https://doi.org/10.1109/ISWCS.2009.5285228
15. Mizuno, K., Naito, K., Ehara, M.: Direction estimation scheme for RFID tag with an angled single antenna. In: IEEE International Conference on Radio Frequency Identification (RFID 2021), vol. 1(1), pp. 1–2 (2021)
16. Jechlitschek, C.: A survey paper on Radio Frequency Identification (RFID) trends (2010)

A Method for Expressing Intention for Suppressing Careless Responses in Participatory Sensing

Kohei Oyama[1]([✉]), Yuki Matsuda[1,2,3][iD], Rio Yoshikawa[1], Yugo Nakamura[4][iD], Hirohiko Suwa[1,2][iD], and Keiichi Yasumoto[1,2][iD]

[1] Nara Institute of Science and Technology, Ikoma-shi, Nara 630-0192, Japan
{oyama.kohei.ol8,yukimat,yoshikawa.rio.yo4,h-suwa,yasumoto}@is.naist.jp
[2] RIKEN Center for Advanced Intelligence Project, Chuo-ku, Tokyo 103-0027, Japan
[3] JST Presto, Chiyoda-ku, Tokyo 102-0076, Japan
[4] Kyushu University, Fukuoka-shi, Fukuoka 819-0395, Japan
y-nakamura@ait.kyushu-u.ac.jp

Abstract. In recent years, with the spread of mobile devices, "participatory sensing," in which users are asked to contribute information, such as their surrounding environment, via their smartphones, has attracted increasing attention. However, in active participatory sensing, which asks users to input text or upload photos, respondents often try to complete the request quickly and effortlessly, and consequently, not always accurately. In this study, we propose a method of _expressing intention to contribute_ (_EIC_) for suppressing careless responses in participatory sensing tasks. We implemented a prototype system that requests two types of EIC method (tap the button, shake the phone), and conducted the experiment over two weeks with 20 participants. Through the statistical tests, we found that proposed EIC methods significantly suppressed the number of careless responses compared with the normal situation.

Keywords: Participatory sensing · Mobile sensing · Response reliability · Satisficing · Answering behavior

1 Introduction

In recent years, with the increasingly widespread use of smartphones, participatory sensing [3] has been attracting attention as a means of collecting data regarding surrounding environments by requesting contributions from device users. Participatory sensing offers several advantages, such as enabling the acquisition of data from a wide area and not requiring the installation of sensors. In

This study was supported in part by JST PRESTO under Grant No. JPMJPR2039. K. Oyama and Y. Matsuda—Co-first authors.

particular, active participatory sensing, in which a mobile device user consciously provides information, makes it possible to acquire data based on human perceptions of environmental aspects such as congestion, noise, and scenery, which are difficult to calculate from values obtained from physical sensors [9].

A well-known issue with participatory sensing is that when asked to contribute to sensing tasks (e.g., uploading photos, inputting subjective feedback), respondents try to complete requests quickly and easily, often at the expense of accuracy. An approach that detects and excludes careless responses from collected response data is effective when there is a large amount of data, such as in crowdsourcing-type surveys. However, in participatory sensing, this approach might result in a lack of data. Some research has been conducted on paper-based and online questionnaires in an effort to suppress careless responses by asking users to express their intention to provide careful answers. These previous studies have been based on human psychological characteristics, such as once we make a decision or take a certain position, we tend to stick to that decision or position [11]. To the best of our knowledge, the effectiveness of methods for expressing an intention to help suppress careless responses has not yet been tested in the field of participatory sensing.

In this paper, we introduce a method for *expressing the intention of contributions (EIC)* to improve reliability in participatory sensing. In the prototype system, we implemented two types of simple motions for the EIC method: a tap screen and a gesture action. A tap screen involves pressing a button on a dialog with a finger, and a gesture action involves holding the smartphone and shaking it up and down. Using these motions in an experiment conducted under laboratory conditions over 2 weeks with 20 participants, we investigated whether our EIC method could significantly suppress careless responses. In addition, we analyzed the number of responses and response times, as well as the results of a post-survey, to assess the effects and challenges of the EIC method.

The structure of this paper is as follows. In Sect. 2, we describe related research and clarify the position of this study. In Sect. 3, we describe our proposed method and participatory sensing system. In Sect. 4, we describe the setup of an evaluation experiment using our system, and in Sect. 5, we present the experimental results and a related discussion. Finally, in Sect. 6, we conclude and discuss future prospects.

2   Related Work

Studies on questionnaire surveys have pointed out that the attitude of respondents who try to complete a task effortlessly and quickly, called *satisficing*, leads to a decrease in the reliability of the results. Miura *et al.* [10] reported that 51.2% and 83.8% of the responses to an online questionnaire survey conducted on 1,800 people by two different research companies were inappropriate. Careless responses caused by satisficing are undesirable as they make the survey results difficult to interpret.

2.1   Careless Response Detection

To address this problem, Maniaci *et al.* [6] devised the Attentive Responding Scale (ARS) and the Directed Question Scale (DQS) to detect satisficing. The ARS can be divided into two types: inconsistency and infrequency. Inconsistency focuses on differences between responses to questions with the same content but slightly different wording, while infrequency focuses on differences between expected and actual choices for a question with a choice expected to be chosen by everyone. For both scales, the higher the total difference score, the more likely it is to be satisficing. For the DQS, participants are instructed to choose a specific answer in a sentence, and if they do not follow the instruction, they are judged to be satisficing.

Gogami *et al.* [5] developed a satisficing detection system that records time-series data such as the amount of screen scrolling, response time per question, and changes in options when answering online surveys using a smartphone.

However, these methods are difficult to use in participatory sensing where a small number of questions is generally given and short response times can be assumed. Even if good and careless responses could be discriminated, excluding careless responses would result in a problematic lack of data.

2.2   Improving Motivation with Monetary/Non-monetary Incentives

To improve the quality of responses, methods for improving user motivation with monetary or non-monetary incentives have been proposed in the domains of crowdsourcing and participatory sensing.

Monetary incentives provide rewards (e.g., redeemable points) directly to responders. General crowdsourcing services such as Amazon Mechanical Turk[1] employ this scheme to motivate people to contribute to microtasks. However, several studies on crowdsourcing [2,7,12] have reported that monetary incentives do not improve the quality of responses.

Non-monetary incentives provide a type of experience (e.g., fun, fulfilling a desire) as a reward. In conventional participatory sensing, Arakawa *et al.* [1,14] attempted to increase the motivation of users to contribute by using gamification mechanisms. Gamification motivates users by adding gaming elements into sensing systems and tasks. However, many studies using gamification have reported that although it can increase the amount of data, cases in which it can even improve the quality of data are limited.

2.3   Careless Response Suppression

Ward *et al.* [15] examined the effects of the method which gives instructions and virtual presence when the quality of responses was low, for suppressing careless responses. Their results revealed a significant interaction effects between

---

[1] https://www.mturk.com/.

instructions and a virtual presence, although a virtual presence alone had no effect. However, it has also been pointed out that this method is not suitable for small screens such as smartphones.

Masuda *et al.* [8] introduced an opening pledge (a question that asks whether the respondent pledges to respond to an item seriously before answering) to prevent satisficing in PC-based online surveys. An opening pledge aims to take advantage of the fact that once a person declares a certain position, they feel natural psychological pressure to behave in a way consistent with that commitment [13]. Compared with the control group, the group that answered "I will answer seriously" to this question showed higher values in several indices of the quality of their answers. This finding suggested that such approaches can be useful for improving response behavior in participatory sensing. Hereinafter, we define these approaches as the *EIC* mechanism.

2.4   Study Position

Existing approaches for detecting careless responses are not suitable for participatory sensing, and methods for motivating respondents with monetary and non-monetary incentives have not been able to improve the quality of responses. In the present study, we aimed to establish a method for suppressing careless responses in participatory sensing by employing the EIC mechanism. In the following sections, we propose and verify the effectiveness of a new participatory sensing system utilizing the EIC mechanism.

3   Proposed Method

3.1   Expressing the Intention of Contributions (EIC) Method

In this section, we propose a new participatory sensing system utilizing an *EIC* mechanism to suppress careless responses.

As mentioned above, Masuda *et al.* [8] succeeded in placing psychological pressure on respondents to "answer seriously" by asking them to click a checkbox next to the sentence "I will answer seriously" before responding to an online questionnaire. To generate psychological pressure, the following two conditions must be satisfied:

1. The respondents read a statement saying, "I will respond seriously."
2. The respondents express their agreement with the statement.

To satisfy the above conditions in the participatory sensing system, the EIC method consists of the following two steps: (1) making the user read the sentence of agreement, and (2) eliciting the user to express their contribution intention.

Step (1) making the user read the sentence of agreement: In the study by Masuda *et al.* [8], agreement sentences and checkboxes were placed at the end of the questionnaire instructions. However, unlike web-based questionnaires, the tasks assumed in participatory sensing require only a short amount of time to answer each question (i.e., a question-and-answer format), so displaying a large amount of information on a single screen is considered a cause of skipping. In addition, since expressing consent generates psychological pressure, whether to read the consent statement is thought to be affected by the preceding action. Therefore, we propose a mechanism that makes it easier for the user to read the consent statement by changing the timing of the statement from "before reading the question" to "the moment the user taps the response field to respond to the question."

Step (2) eliciting the user to express their contribution intention: The study by Masuda *et al.* [8] have adopted a method involving having the user click a checkbox next to the agreement sentence. In the present study, we adopted a button-tapping method similar to the conventional method. We also propose a new method of expressing consent using gesture recognition based on the accelerometers in smartphones. This study adopts the gesture of "shaking the smartphone," which requires sufficiently large movements and is easy to imagine, since it is used by many standard smartphone applications.

The following section describes how to apply the express intention function in a participatory sensing application.

3.2   Implementation

To collect response data using the proposed method, we designed and implemented a smartphone application for participatory sensing, which we named *OathSurvey*. The system flow is shown in Fig. 1.

The respondent installs OathSurvey (hereafter "app") on their smartphone in advance. When the respondent receives a response request notification from the app and opens it, a question and text form for response input are displayed. Then, the respondent taps on the text form, which causes a dialog box asking the respondent to express their intention to appear on the screen. This dialog shows the agreement statement and the action to take in expressing one's intention when agreeing. By performing this action, the user is able to enter the answer input form. In this application, the user is presented with either "tap the button," which is the same as the conventional method, or "shake the smartphone," which is a newly proposed method in this paper. The screens displayed in each method are shown in Fig. 2 (a) and (b), respectively.

Moreover, to analyze the response behavior in this experiment, we implemented a function to record the timing of the following screen operation events: "notification published," "notification tapped," "text form tapped," "express intention dialog displayed," "express intention completed," "response data sent," "application goes to foreground," and "application goes to background." The response data are also stored in the database.

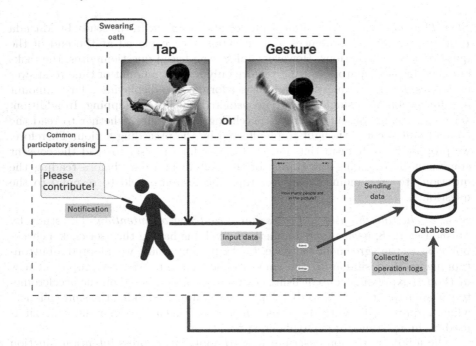

Fig. 1. System overview of "OathSurvey"

4   Evaluation Experiment

In this section, we describe an evaluation experiment to verify the effectiveness of the proposed method. This study was approved by the Nara Institute of Science and Technology Ethical Review Committee for Research Involving Human Subjects (Approval No.: 2020-I-16).

4.1   Experimental Settings

The purpose of the evaluation experiment was to clarify the effects of the EIC method on the suppression of careless responses in participatory sensing. For this purpose, to check whether the presence or absence of an EIC or differences in the EIC method affected the quality of responses (correct response rate) and response behavior (response time), we asked the participants in the experiment to use the application implemented in Sect. 3.2.

The participants in the experiment were 20 graduate students in their 20 s who belonged to our laboratory. The experimental period was 2 weeks, from April 13 to 27, 2021. The participants were briefed in advance and completed a consent form before participating in the experiment. In the preliminary explanation, we explained only that this was a survey on participatory sensing and did not explain careless response behavior because doing so in a survey on careless

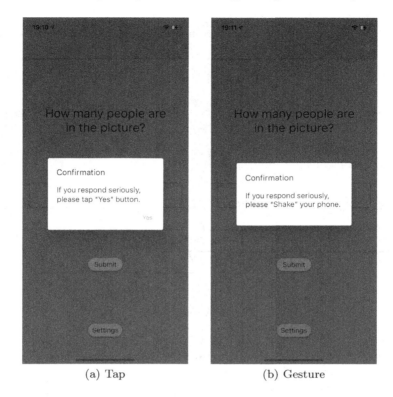

(a) Tap   (b) Gesture

Fig. 2. Screen examples requesting "EIC" (it is translated to English)

response behavior would affect the responses. After the experiment was finished, we explained that the experiment was about careless response behavior and confirmed the participants' consent to participate.

Before participating in the experiment, the participants installed the app on their Android or iOS device. The app requests the sensing tasks described in the next section. For each request, one of the following methods was selected and presented to the experiment participants: "no EIC (nothing)," "tap the button (tap)," and "shake the smartphone (gesture)." The participants followed the instructions for the presented EIC method and input their responses. The participants could also ignore the request.

4.2 Sensing Task Setting

The flow of the sensing task is shown in Fig. 3. The app scans an iBeacon signal placed in the hallway near the elevators and then sends a notification requesting the participants to perform the sensing task when they enter. After receiving the

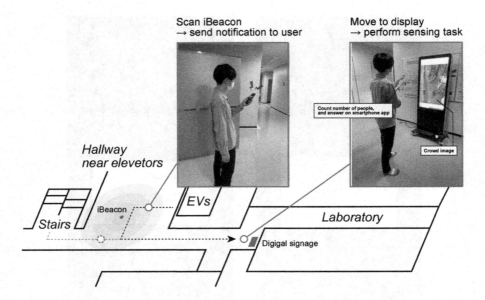

Fig. 3. Answer flow

notification, the participant moves toward the digital signage near the entrance of the laboratory, which displays the sensing target, and completes the requested task.

The sensing task is "counting the number of people in the crowd image," and the answer can be sent through the app. This task imitates a participatory sensing task that collects the level of congestion in the city (e.g., sightseeing attractions, bus stops, restaurants). This task is suitable for analyzing the quality of the response data because the correct answer value is uniquely determined. For the crowd images, we used the Beijing-BRT-dataset [4], the VisDrone2019-SOT dataset [17], and the CityStreet dataset [16]. An example of an image is shown in Fig. 4. The crowd image is updated at 0:00 (midnight) and 12:00 (noon) every day, and participants can answer up to twice a day.

4.3   Evaluation Method

To quantitatively clarify the effects of EIC on the quality of responses and response behavior in participatory sensing, we compared the correct response rate and response time for each EIC method. The correct response rate was calculated from the total numbers of responses and careless responses for each EIC method. The response time was collected separately as the EIC and response input times, and the sum of these is the total response time.

To confirm the impact of the EIC on the psychology of the respondents, a subjective evaluation was conducted by use of a post-survey. The following questions were asked using a four-point Likert scale: Q1) Did you find it troublesome

Beijing-BRT-dataset[4]   VisDrone2019-SOT[17]   CityStreet[16]

Fig. 4. Examples of crowd images used in this study

Table 1. Experimental results (summary of response data)

EIC method	All responses	Careless responses	Correct response rate [%]	EIC time[s]	Response time[s]	Total response time[s]	Dropout rate [%]
Nothing	99	7	92.9	–	8.6	8.1	7.5
Tap	113	3	97.3	1.2	9.1	10.3	14.4
Gesture	90	3	96.7	2.2	9.3	11.5	17.3

to declare your position by tapping?; Q2) Did you find it troublesome to declare your position by gesturing?; Q3) Did you think that the number of responses decreased because you were asked to declare your position?; and Q4) Did the declaration of your position make you feel that you should answer seriously? Additionally, to obtain feedback about the EIC method, we asked the participants to provide free-text comments (Q5: What did you think about being asked to state your position when answering?) and suggestions regarding the OathSurvey application (Q6: Do you have any suggestions for improving the OathSurvey application?).

5   Experimental Results

5.1   Quantitative Results

The results of the quantitative evaluation experiment are shown in Table 1. The quality of the responses and the differences in response behavior are described separately.

Analysis of Response Quality: As shown in Table 1, no significant difference was seen in the total number of responses for each EIC. The total number of responses for each EIC was 99, 113, and 90, with only 7, 3, and 3 incorrect responses, respectively. We assume that this was due to the fact that the participants in the experiment were students who belonged to the same laboratory as the authors.

The correct response rate when the EIC was not requested was lower than that when the EIC was requested. The results of a residual analysis of the cross-tabulation table showed that the adjusted standardized residual (one-sided P-value) for no EIC was significant at the 5% level, confirming that the actual frequency of careless responses was significantly larger than the expected frequency. This result indicates that the EIC had a positive impact on the awareness of the respondents.

In this experiment, we did not find any difference between the two types of EIC (button tap and gesture). This point needs to be clarified through future experiments with more participants.

Analysis of Response Behavior: As shown in Table 1, the total response time from the EIC to the completion of answer input increased by 1.2 s and 2.2 s with the addition of button tapping and smartphone shaking, respectively. However, even when only the response input actions were compared, the total response time increased by 0.5–0.7 s in the case of the EIC. We believe that this was due to the fact that the awareness of the respondents was affected by the EIC, and that they sought to complete the task more carefully than usual.

Analysis of the Dropout Rate: From the response data, we calculated the attrition rate (the percentage of respondents who stopped answering in the middle of the survey). Table 1 shows the average withdrawal rate for each statement method during the entire experiment. From the results, we could confirm that the withdrawal rate increased when an EIC was required. This may have been because requiring an expression of intention was stressful for the participants.

Analysis of Time-Series Changes: Daily trends in the number of careless responses during the experiment are shown in Fig. 5. From this graph, it could be confirmed that the defective responses were biased toward the latter half of the experiment. The reason for this reduction in the effect of suppressing careless responses may be that the respondents became accustomed to the response behavior or bored or stressed by the frequent EIC requests.

5.2   Subjective Evaluation

The results of the subjective evaluation through the post-survey are shown in Table 2.

The results show that the majority of the participants answered that they did not consider tapping the button to be troublesome at all, but they did find shaking the phone to be troublesome to some extent. We believe that this was partly due to the fact that the intensity required for shaking the phone was too high, as mentioned in the comments from the respondents shown below.

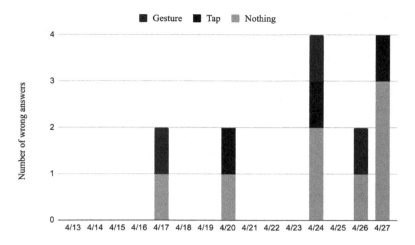

Fig. 5. Number of careless responses by day

Through the free-text comments on the EIC method (Q5), we gained several valuable insights. A summary of these comments is shown below.

- Positive comments
    - I am no longer inclined to respond in a random manner.
    - I think it was good to have the expressing intention because it made us aware that we should not answer carelessly.
- Negative comments
    - I thought it would be quite stressful to have to state a position several times before answering.
    - I had an uncomfortable feeling of not being trusted.
- Other comments
    - I didn't think much of it (I was trying to answer seriously from the beginning).
    - I didn't think anything of it.

The positive comments suggest that the EIC method exerted a certain effect in participatory sensing. The negative comments refer to the stress of repeatedly stating one's position. This point may be due to the negative effects of the characteristic of participatory sensing, in which a large task is divided into smaller tasks and solved by many people, as well as the psychological pressure exerted by such stance statements. To solve this problem, it will be necessary to investigate how long the effect lasts after declaring a position and to introduce a mechanism that does not require the declaration of a position every time.

Table 2. Post-survey questions and results of subjective evaluations

Question No.	Sentence
Q1	Did you feel it is troublesome? (Tap)
Q2	Did you feel it is troublesome? (Gesture)
Q3	Do you feel your answering frequency has decreased?
Q4	Did you feel the need to answer seriously?
Q5	What did you think about being asked to state your position when answering? (Free-text comments)
Q6	Do you have any suggestions for improving the OathSurvey application? (Free-text comments)

Question No.	Number of answers				Average score[a]
	Very much	A little	Not much	Not at all	
Q1	1 (5.0%)	2 (10.0%)	6 (30.0%)	11 (55.0%)	0.65
Q2	5 (25.0%)	9 (45.0%)	3 (15.0%)	3 (15.0%)	1.80
Q3	0 (0.0%)	0 (0.0%)	12 (60.0%)	8 (40.0%)	0.60
Q4	7 (35.0%)	11 (55.0%)	2 (10.0%)	0 (0.0%)	2.25

[a]This score was calculated with Very much = 3, A little = 2, and Not much = 1, Not at all = 0

Another possible solution is to estimate the number of people who need to express their intention (e.g., those who have answered inappropriately in the past) and to encourage them to express their intention at an appropriate time.

We also asked for suggestions to improve the OathSurvey application (Q6). A summary of these comments is shown below.

- I had to shake it very hard to get it to work.
- I felt that if I waved my phone in the street, I would worry about what the people around me were thinking.
- The text asking me to express my intention should be in red to convey a sense of urgency.
- I felt that more variety was needed for expressing my intention.

5.3 Limitations

This study had several limitations. As mentioned in Sect. 5.1, the overall quality of the data collected in this experiment was high. In this experiment, the respondents were students in the same laboratory, so they may have taken the task more seriously than normal respondents. In the future, it will be necessary to conduct experiments on people with a larger variety of attributes, as in ordinary participatory sensing.

In addition, the effect of suppressing careless responses progressively decreased in the latter half of the experiment. This may have been due to the fact that the respondents became bored, stressed, or accustomed to the high frequency of EIC every time they tried to answer. In the future, it will be necessary to develop a new way for requesting EIC that does not make the respondents feel bored or stressed, or allow them to become accustomed to it.

6   Conclusion and Future Prospects

In this paper, we have proposed a new participatory sensing system utilizing an EIC mechanism to suppress careless responses. At present, two types of EIC methods–button tap and gesture–have been implemented, and these can be applied regardless of the task content in participatory sensing. In the evaluation experiment, we investigated the effects of EIC on the quality of the response data and the response behavior. In the future, we plan to conduct a survey under conditions similar to those of actual participatory sensing to explore more effective methods of stating a position.

References

1. Arakawa, Y., Matsuda, Y.: Gamification mechanism for enhancing a participatory urban sensing: survey and practical results. J. Inf. Process. **57**(1), 31–38 (2016). https://doi.org/10.2197/ipsjjip.24.31
2. Borromeo, R.M., Toyama, M.: An investigation of unpaid crowdsourcing. Hum.-Centric Comput. Inf. Sci. **6**(1), 11 (2016). https://doi.org/10.1186/s13673-016-0068-z
3. Burke, J.A., et al.: Participatory sensing. In: Workshop on World-Sensor-Web (2006)
4. Ding, X., Lin, Z., He, F., Wang, Y., Huang, Y.: A deeply-recursive convolutional network for crowd counting. In: 2018 IEEE International Conference on Acoustics, Speech and Signal Processing (ICASSP), pp. 1942–1946 (2018). https://doi.org/10.1109/ICASSP.2018.8461772
5. Gogami, M., Matsuda, Y., Arakawa, Y., Yasumoto, K.: Detection of careless responses in online surveys using answering behavior on smartphone. IEEE Access **9**, 53205–53218 (2021). https://doi.org/10.1109/ACCESS.2021.3069049
6. Maniaci, M.R., Rogge, R.D.: Caring about carelessness: participant inattention and its effects on research. J. Res. Pers. **48**, 61–83 (2014)
7. Mao, A., et al.: Volunteering versus work for pay: incentives and tradeoffs in crowdsourcing. In: Hartman, B., Horvitz, E. (eds.) HCOMP. AAAI (2013). http://dblp.uni-trier.de/db/conf/hcomp/hcomp2013.html#MaoKCHSLS13
8. Masuda, S., Sakagami, T., Morii, M.: Comparison among methods for improving response quality of surveys. Japan. J. Psychol. **90**(5), 463–472 (2019). (in Japanese), https://doi.org/10.4992/jjpsy.90.18042
9. Matsuda, Y., Kawanaka, S., Suwa, H., Arakawa, Y., Yasumoto, K.: ParmoSense: a scenario-based participatory mobile urban sensing platform with user motivation engine. arXiv (2102.05586), pp. 1–24 (2021). https://arxiv.org/abs/2102.05586

10. Miura, A., Kobayashi, T.: Mechanical Japanese: survey satisficing of online panels in Japan. Jpn. J. Soc. Psychol. **31**(1), 1–12 (2015). (in Japanese), https://doi.org/10.14966/jssp.31.1_1
11. Robert, C.: Influence: Pearson New International Edition: Science and Practice. Pearson Education, London (2013)
12. Rubya, S., Numainville, J., Yarosh, S.: Comparing generic and community-situated crowdsourcing for data validation in the context of recovery from substance use disorders. In: CHI 2021: Proceedings of the 2021 CHI Conference on Human Factors in Computing Systems, New York, NY, USA. Association for Computing Machinery (2021). https://doi.org/10.1145/3411764.3445399
13. Staw, B.M.: The escalation of commitment to a course of action. Acad. Manag. Rev. **6**(4), 577–587 (1981)
14. Ueyama, Y., Tamai, M., Arakawa, Y., Yasumoto, K.: Gamification-based incentive mechanism for participatory sensing. In: 2014 IEEE International Conference on Pervasive Computing and Communication Workshops (PERCOM WORKSHOPS), pp. 98–103. IEEE (2014)
15. Ward, M., Pond, S.B.: Using virtual presence and survey instructions to minimize careless responding on internet-based surveys. Comput. Hum. Behav. **48**, 554–568 (2015). https://doi.org/10.1016/j.chb.2015.01.070
16. Zhang, Q., Chan, A.B.: Wide-area crowd counting: multi-view fusion networks for counting in large scenes. arXiv preprint arXiv:2012.00946 (2020). https://arxiv.org/abs/2012.00946
17. Zhu, P., Wen, L., Du, D., Bian, X., Hu, Q., Ling, H.: Vision meets drones: past, present and future. arXiv preprint arXiv:2001.06303 (2020)

A Privacy-Aware Browser Extension to Track User Search Behavior for Programming Course Supplement

Jihed Makhlouf[1,2]([✉]), Yutaka Arakawa[2], and Ko Watanabe[3]

[1] Osaka Prefecture University, Osaka, Japan
[2] Kyushu University, Fukuoka, Japan
jihed.makhlouf@m.ait.kyushu-u.ac.jp, arakawa@ait.kyushu-u.ac.jp
[3] University of Kaiserslautern and DFKI GmbH, Kaiserslautern, Germany
ko.watanabe@dfki.de

Abstract. There is an abundant and constantly growing amount of information that can be retrieved from online resources. Moreover, the access to such resources is becoming more and more convenient. Yet, finding the exact needed information is not easy, especially for programming search queries. In this paper, we present TrackThinkTS, a privacy-aware browser extension. It tracks users' behaviors when navigating the web. The extension logs various user actions related to tab management, search query, browsing, and clipboard management. The extension is built with a privacy-first mindset. In fact, the users have full control over the registered logs, they can manage, update and export the logs in a completely transparent way. The vision behind this work is twofold. On one hand, we aim to investigate the web search behavior of programming students and detect patterns of a successful search. On the other hand, the objective is to build a knowledge base that will serve as a course supplement for programming students. Therefore, the proposed extension in this paper is one of the building blocks of the whole system. Data collected from this extension will be also synchronized with log data coming from an online IDE used by programming students during the experiment phase.

Keywords: Web search · Browser extension · Programming learning · Course supplement

1 Introduction

In a digital world where an immense load of data is created every second, it became very important to know where and how to search for the right information in a timely manner. Terms such as "Information Overload" are frequently used to express the phenomena [11]. Moreover, individual web search behavior and abilities became topics of meticulous research [3,5,9,12].

T. Hara and H. Yamaguchi (Eds.): MobiQuitous 2021, LNICST 419, pp. 783–796, 2022.
https://doi.org/10.1007/978-3-030-94822-1_51

Additionally, the problem of finding the right information is amplified when searching for programming errors, examples, and code snippets [19]. In fact, traditional general-purpose search engines are not optimized for programming code search [24]. Instead, they are developed to handle natural text requests. Thus, sometimes they fail to recognize the context and semantics of the code search [18]. Several tools were created to address the code search problem like the Google Code Search [7], Source Graph [21], Searchcode [20] and many others. However, some of these tools were either discontinued or became obsolete [18].

Undoubtedly, web searching is an integral part of the software programmer's activities. The purpose of the web search can vary a lot depending on the context. But many studies found that web searching is one of the most frequent activities of software developers [8,19,24]. However, most of the studies about code search were conducted in a professional environment. The participants in these studies had different levels of expertise in programming. Less focus was given to investigate the web searching behavior of programming students.

In fact, during the process of learning programming, whether it is self-learning or in academic settings, students use the search engines for many various purposes. In addition, the recent events related to the COVID-19 pandemic made the situation even worse. Educational institutions had to shift to fully online learning. This reduced considerably the opportunities for students to communicate and collaborate with each other. Hence, they lost the chance to learn from each other. Moreover, the interactions with the professors and teachers lost the qualities of face-to-face communication. In the programming case, teachers used to monitor and help students more effectively. Industry and academia are trying to mitigate the negative effects of the lockdown. Nevertheless, students in general, and programming students in particular rely more than ever on online resources. It is crucial to help them acquire the skills that help them achieve fulfilling web searches. But, a few research works did focus on this sub-population of programming web search. Therefore, in this study, we introduce a tool that will be used to examine the web search behavior of students while they solve programming exercises.

In the current manuscript, we present a browser extension called Track-ThinkTS. This extension logs the browser usage while searching and surfing on the web. It was developed with a privacy-first mindset. Users have full access to view, edit and delete entries before exporting the data to CSV format. Along with their full consent, participants in the experiments using this extension have an aggregated view of the stored logs for an easier management.

This extension will serve as the building block for subsequent experiments and analysis that aim to investigate the following research questions:

- Is there any difference in web search skills between successful students and the others?
- To which extent this difference in web search skills influences the learning of the students?
- What are the common patterns of effective web search skills manifested through thought processes?

– What are the best ways of sharing these thought processes with the students through course supplements?

The rest of the paper is divided as follows: In Sect. 2, we will introduce the general context of our work by reviewing the related work about web search in general, and in the context of programming. Section 3 gives more details about the extension, its architecture, and the collected data. In Sect. 4, we will describe how we preserve users' privacy by giving them full control of the logs before exporting them by themselves. Section 5 is dedicated to discussing the vision and the possible use cases for the extension. We will also give an example of an experiment using the extension before concluding.

2   Related Work

2.1   User Web Search

The internet and the web became an integral part of our daily lives. It is a hub of rich content and various services. Searching on the web is one of the most common activities of internet users [9]. Therefore, understanding web search behavior is a necessary step to provide better services [11].

The approach used during information search on the web depends on several different factors. For example, the user's familiarity with computers, and the internet has a significant effect [9]. Researchers also found that knowledge-based factors, like domain knowledge, cognitive abilities, and even affective states can impact the effectiveness of the web search [9]. Other studies found that demographic elements, including age might also affect the effectiveness of the web search [9,12].

However, aside from these factors, there is a certain knowledge related to web search itself. In fact, there are different strategies that can be used for a successful web search. Studies found that reformulating the search query by removing words, stemming, word substitution or similar changes might lead to more interesting results for the user [10]. Moreover, the mainstream search engines have developed a set of rules using special characters that can alter the behavior of the search engine itself in the process of solving the search query. However, not all users are aware of the existence of such tricks to improve their search capabilities [23]. Therefore, the skills to properly use the search engines and formulate, also eventually reformulate, the search query is essential to maximizing the efficiency of the web search. The culmination of all these factors and skills is described as "Search Expertise" [3,23].

Hence, "Search Expertise" is a topic of interest to many researchers. Some of them investigated the aspects that differentiate between the "advanced" and "non-advanced" search engine users [23]. Other studies tried to find measures of search expertise [3]. Furthermore, a team of researchers from Microsoft explored some ways of transferring the search expertise between users [15].

The search expertise transfer is a very valuable concept that can have many different applications. In fact, it can be handy for the difficult topics of web search such as programming and code search. By nature, programming-related search queries carry an inherent complexity compared to traditional search engines [18]. Therefore, programming-related search queries constitute a particular sub-topic of research.

2.2 Programming Web Search

During the process of software development, developers usually rely on resources available on the web [18]. In fact, studies have found that developers spend 15% of their time on web search [24]. According to the same study, developers spend up to 35% of their time on web search if they are new to the organization or to the project [24]. However, the time spent on web search is not the only factor that influences the web search behavior. In fact, the authors also found that the number of queries varies a lot [24]. This suggests that many developers find the needed information by web navigation rather than web search, which is also a common behavior [5].

However, a high number of web search requests might indicate an ineffective strategy for searching. In addition, many studies pointed out that the traditional search engines are not well adapted for programming-related web searches [18, 19,24]. When they formulate properly their problems, developers can actually find decent results from their web search queries. This includes queries about debugging, documentation, etc. But, when they use the traditional search engines for code search such as code snippets, the search engines usually fail to deliver the appropriate results [18,19,22,24]. Some of the reasons behind that are the difficulties of search engines to deal with special characters that are heavily present in programming code.

Several tools and services tried to address the code search problems. However, they are still underused. Additionally, several researchers proposed to bring the web search closer to the developer for a seamless experience. They developed an extension for Eclipse IDE that launches a web search query related to the error and exceptions encountered [17]. Then, it fetches the relevant potential solutions to solve it. The whole process is done within the IDE, therefore the user does not have to switch his work environment [17].

While the proposed solutions are helpful and can be handy in many situations, they are more adapted to professionals that are looking quickly to solve the problem at hand. However, students and people who are starting to learn programming in general or a particular programming language do not benefit from these solutions. More adjustments need to be done to help them learn.

2.3 Programming Learning Web Search

In the study conducted by Xia et al. [24], they found that in general new recruits and new graduates spend more time engaging in web search and also formulate more search queries compared to more experimented colleagues. Such a behavior was also discussed in other studies conducted in a slightly different context. In fact, in another research work, the authors found that a clear different behavior for students learning a new programming language compared to professional developers [2].

It is clear that students need tools that provide them extra support during their learning phase of programming. In fact, one of the common ways of programming for newcomers is to look for existing code and change it according to their needs. This sort of behavior is called opportunistic programming [4]. Therefore, it is really important to help the students find the appropriate resources. The browser extension that we are presenting in this paper is a step toward achieving this goal.

3   The TrackThinkTS Extension

There were many tools that track the users' web search. However, most of them only capture the pages visited using the URL and provide some analytics and visualization based on that [1,6,14,25]. However, this approach does not grasp the whole web search behavior of the user. In addition, most modern browsers provide a complete API for a sophisticated access to the internal browser state and allow advanced manipulations.

The tool presented in this paper is the continuation of a previously discontinued proof-of-concept by the same name of TrackThink [16]. It was unfinished and suffered from a few problems. The main objective was to gather as much information as possible of the users' actions within the browser when they engage in web search to capture their "thought process". Compared to the previously mentioned tools, it did not rely solely on the history of the web pages and URLs. However, it was not published in the Chrome extension store and was used only by the developers. The UX needed a lot of improvements. Moreover, it was not optimally adjusted for user privacy nor for the user convenience.

Therefore, in the present update, we aim to transform the proof-of-concept into a fully working product and improve several critical aspects such as:

- Drastically improve the user privacy by giving full control to the user on the registered logs.
- Improve the UX and workflow for both the participants and the experiment organizers.
- Publish it in the Chrome store for easier distribution and installation in the students' machines.

Ultimately, TrackThinkTS inherits the name and some concepts of the original unfinished work, but it is fundamentally different in many aspects including the logs generation the storage, and the whole workflow and experiments.

3.1   Logs Generation

Many of the previous research works interested in user behavior when searching on the web used a limited set of information. They, gathered the history, represented mainly by URLs, of the web search. However, in our case, we would like to gather as much data as possible by exploiting the browser capabilities and API. Therefore, along with the visited pages URLs, TrackThinkTS captures several types of events within the browser. Particularly, the interest in gathering tabs management is driven by the nature of the use case. The users have to switch between tabs frequently. They use some tabs to search on the web, then get back to the online IDE where they continue working on the programming exercises. Therefore, tracking systems based on URLs only are not effective in our situation.

Tabs Management. There are 4 particular events related to tabs that Track-ThinkTS monitors: Tab creation, Tab activation, Tab update, and Tab delete. There are many advantages to using the browser extension Tab API. Tab creation in itself does not carry a lot of information, but can be useful to detect which is the default new tab page of the user and perhaps it can be used to detect advanced users. Tab activation is important to collect data about page switches. Tab update is triggered when a change happens to the page loaded in a tab. It can be a visit to a new page in the same tab, a refresh, or some new content being loaded on the page. This is particularly useful to capture events that do not require a full page reload (e.g. Javascript events). These events would be hard to detect if we rely only on the history and URLs. Finally, Tab delete is triggered when the user closes a Tab.

Window Operations. The extension also monitors users' specific actions, namely Scrolling and Clipboard usage. When the user scrolls on a page, we gather the corresponding coordinates and the visible content of the page. Additionally, we collect information about the viewport of the page. This way, we can easily recover which part of the information displayed on the web page was the most helpful. Additionally, if the user copies pieces of text, we detect it and save the copied text.

Every captured event is also appended to some additional information such as the timestamp, and user identifications. In fact, the user is attributed a randomly generated user id and we ask the participants to input their names as well.

3.2 Workflow

The development of the TrackThinkTS extension was achieved using the browser extension API. So far, TrackThinkTS supports officially the main chromium-based browsers like Google Chrome, Brave, and Vivaldi. Any other chromium-based browser might be able to use the extension, but we did not perform thorough testing.

Figure 1 shows the workflow of TrackThinkTS. There are two ways of storing the log data. The first method is to use a cloud-based database such as Firebase. This storage option is deactivated by default and only available when the experiment is conducted in a controlled environment (more details in Sect. 5). The second storage option is to save the log data in the browser local storage.

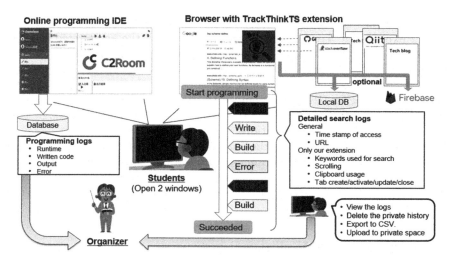

Fig. 1. TrackThinkTS workflow.

Later, the logs are aggregated and the user can manage the logs within an integrated dashboard of the extension. After checking the logs the user can export them into a CSV file and submit them to a submission location prepared by the experiment organizers. A proper manual was prepared for the users.[1]

The typical workflow will be as follows. Students will be solving programming problems and have the ability to search the web. They write their code in an IDE and when they are stuck or face an error they turn to the internet to find a solution. Meanwhile, the extension logs most of their actions within the browser.

On the other side, the researchers and experiment organizers can access the logs from 2 locations. If the experiment was conducted in a controlled environment with the cloud database upload activated, then they can access the dataset directly from there. Otherwise, the researchers have to prepare the appropriate structure to store the students' submissions before using them.

4 Logs Control

The TrackThinkTS extension logs almost all the users' actions in the browser. Therefore, there is a natural concern about the users' privacy. To address this issue we give the users full control over what they want to submit. There are two levels of control. The first level of control happens within the extension itself, the second level of control occurs when the user exports the logs into CSV and can manage the dataset as it is.

In fact, on the TrackThinkTS configuration page, we display the list of all actions aggregated by URL. That means each row represents a unique URL.

---

[1] https://ubi-naist.github.io/TrackThink/en/usage.

The row includes the number of actions that have been executed on that page. Figure 2 exposes the TrackThinkTS options page. All the aggregated data logs are displayed in an advanced datatable. Based on this aggregation the users can delete all the logs saved for a particular URL. However, the logs might be too long. So, the users can reorganize and order the entries or apply advanced filters to find specific URLs and remove the corresponding logs. In fact, URLs are unique, however they might share the exact same domain (e.g. google.com), so filtering is useful in such situations.

The options page also allows the participants to input their names, but more importantly, it allows the experiment organizers to apply advanced settings, which are the activation of the cloud upload of logs and the reset of the randomly generated user id. These settings are protected by a password and therefore users cannot tamper with them.

5   Use Cases and Vision

5.1   Experiments

It is worth noting that the TrackThinkTS browser extension is aimed to be a building block for several studies on web search behavior and course supplement. We will particularly focus on web search behavior in the case of programming learning and assignments. Two experiments have been recently performed using TrackThinkTS. The first experiment was conducted in a controlled environment where the participants have to use a dedicated computer in a reserved room. The computer had all the necessary tools installed, including TrackThinkTS. In this particularly controlled environment, the cloud-based database was used to gather the logs and the participants did have to export manually the logs. This was the setup before the TrackThinkTS extension was accepted for publishing in the Chrome extension store. The second experiment has been conducted on a larger scale after the extension was available in the store and participants could use their own computers. Therefore, the cloud-based logging using Firebase was disabled.

Both experiments consisted of a series of Functional Programming exercises. The participants used an online educational software called C2Room[2] that included an online IDE for programming. Within the C2Room software, they can access the exercises and start solving them using the built-in IDE. Each one of the experiments consisted of 10 exercises using the Scheme programming language with increasing difficulty. Participants were told that they are free to search for online resources when they needed.

5.2   Dataset Composition

As explained earlier, the TrackThinkTS browser extension logs different types of events related to the browser usage. Moreover, to solve the programming

---

[2] https://c2room.jp.

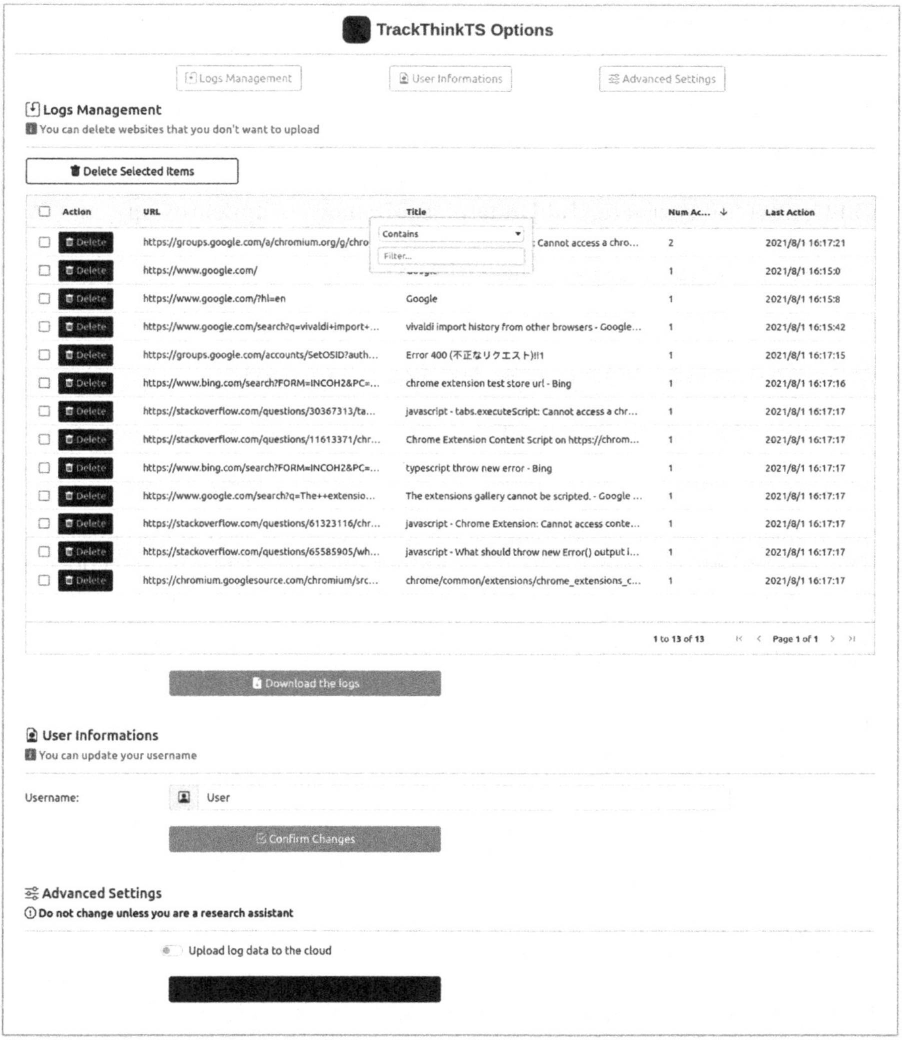

Fig. 2. TrackThinkTS options page.

exercises, the students used the C2Room educational software containing an online IDE. We could recover the students' usage logs from the C2Room software as well. Furthermore, we could gather additional information about the students participating in the experiments. Accordingly, the overall dataset is rich and diverse. Each recording in the dataset contains various information depending on the source. More details are provided as follows:

TrackThinkTS Information. Each row in the TrackThinkTS dataset represents an action done within the browser and is defined by this set of information:

Action related:

- UUID: A unique user ID generated for each user.
- User action: The type of the user action. It can be one of the following: TabCreate, TabActivate, TabUpdate, TabRemove, ClipboardCopy, and WindowScroll.
- Datetime: The timestamp of the action performed.

Tab related

- Title: The title of the page where the action happened.
- URL: The URL of the page where the action happened.
- BodyText: The whole content of the page where the action happened.

Contextual

- Scroll: Data is not filled here unless the User action is a WindowScroll event. The scroll data contain plenty of information related to the viewport, the scroll speed, the scroll rate, and the document width and height.
- Clipboard: Data is not filled here unless the User action is a ClipboardCopy event. The clipboard data basically contain the copied text.

C2Room Information. Each row in the C2Room dataset represents an action defined by this set of information:

Action related:

- UID: The user ID set up before the start of the experiment.
- ClassID: The ID of the class to which the user enrolled.
- TaskID: The ID of the task that the student is solving.
- Time: The timestamp of the action performed.
- OP: The operation type that the user has made. It can be one of the following: ConID, MoveTask, StartCompiling, EndCompiling, SubmitCode.

Data related to the compilation start:

- Code: It contains the programming code to be compiled.
- Lang: The environment that will handle the compilation of the code.
- stdin: The input to the compilation phase.

Data related to the end of the compilation:

- Response: It basically says if the compilation succeeded or failed. Therefore, its values are: success or error.
- Startime: The timestamp when the compilation started.
- stdout: The output of the code after compilation and execution.
- stderr: The error message if the compilation fails.

Students Information. The source of this dataset is diverse. Each entry in this dataset represents a student defined by this set of information:

- Personal Information: Such as the Name, Email address, Age, Gender, and the assigned userID
- Years of programming.
- Familiar Programming languages.
- Average number of days per week doing programming.
- Several questions about how they deal with programming errors.
- Feedback about the experiment and the exercises.
- Score: It is possible to recover the students' exam scores in the programming course.

5.3 Objectives

Using TrackThinkTS, we want to track the students' search behavior and thought process when they have to solve programming problems. Firstly, we want to investigate the difference in successful web searches between the high-performing students and the others. In fact, based on the diverse studies related to web search behavior [18,23,24], cognitive abilities and skills related to web search expertise have an influence on the success of the web search. Such meta-knowledge and search expertise can be shared and transferred [15]. Therefore, we aim at finding the patterns of search expertise expressed by successful students and transfer them to less successful students by means of course supplements to help them acquire the tools for an independent self-improvement. By using the exam score and the dataset from TrackThinkTS, we can compare the search behavior between successful students and the others. Moreover, in our case, measuring web search expertise is accomplished by finding the successful web searches in the context of programming errors. Accordingly, we also acquire the online resources used by the students to solve their programming errors. Thanks to the fine-grained data gathered by TrackThinkTS, we can store the exact information or code snippet that helped the students solve their errors. If we synchronize this type of data with the stack trace that we recover from the C2Room IDE, it is possible to provide timely help to future programming students.

5.4 Data Aggregation and Synchronization

So far, the research experiments were conducted using an online IDE. It is possible to recover the build status and executions states of the students and synchronize them with the web search logs. This allows to capture the successful build and recover accurately which text or page used was the most helpful to the students.

In addition, refined data aggregation using the scroll behavior and timestamp can lead to advanced metrics. Some of these metrics were used to study users browsing strategies [13]. We are interested in using them in students' web search behavior as well.

Bounce. A user's interaction is considered to be a bounce when the engagement time is relatively short and they leave (either switch tab or close it) quickly.

Shallow Engagement. This type of engagement refers to the user reading less than half of the page's content.

Deep Engagement. This engagement implies that the user did read more than half of the page's substance.

Complete Engagement. The strongest engagement is achieved when the user reads most of the content and decides to save it either as a bookmark, keep the tab open or save it somewhere else.

6 Conclusion

In this paper, we have introduced the TrackThinkTS browser extension. It aims at tracking the users' web search and browsing behavior while emphasizing on keeping the user's privacy. We achieve this by using the browser extension API that allows us to capture events related to tabs management, clipboard usage, and web pages meta-information. Having access to such data raises concerns about privacy. Therefore, we provide an aggregated view of the saved logs for easier management. In addition, users can export the logs, and before submitting them, they can access and manage the raw dataset.

Giving extensive control on the log data to the users might alter the viability of the dataset. To address this issue, we recommended the participants to install different browsers than the ones they usually use in their daily life, and use them to install TrackThinkTS and to proceed with the experiment.[3] In such a case, the users won't need to use the management functionality and remove personal websites and irrelevant URLs. However, even if the students follow this recommendation, there are still a few cases where they need to remove some logs. For example, if a user opens a media website to listen to music while working, he/she has the ability to remove the corresponding logs.

Recently, TrackThinkTS has been accepted in the Chrome extension store and has been used in experiments involving programming students. The objective is to build a system that provides course supplements to students who need support. The course supplement should provide timely suggestions to the students when they face build errors while solving programming problems. But also, the course supplement, eventually, supplies information and meta-knowledge of how to search for the appropriate solution.

Acknowledgment. This work was partially supported by JST CREST "Behavior change and harmonious collaboration by experiential supplements" (JPMJCR16E1).

---

[3] https://ubi-naist.github.io/TrackThink/en/.

References

1. Bae, J., Setlur, V., Watson, B.: GraphTiles: a visual interface supporting browsing and imprecise mobile search. In: Proceedings of the 17th International Conference on Human-Computer Interaction with Mobile Devices and Services, MobileHCI'15, pp. 63–70. Association for Computing Machinery, New York (2015). https://doi.org/10.1145/2785830.2785872
2. Bai, G.R., Kayani, J., Stolee, K.T.: How graduate computing students search when using an unfamiliar programming language. In: Proceedings of the 28th International Conference on Program Comprehension (2020)
3. Bailey, E., Kelly, D.: Developing a measure of search expertise. In: Proceedings of the 2016 ACM on Conference on Human Information Interaction and Retrieval, CHIIR'16, pp. 237–240. Association for Computing Machinery, New York (2016). https://doi.org/10.1145/2854946.2854983
4. Brandt, J., Guo, P.J., Lewenstein, J., Dontcheva, M., Klemmer, S.R.: Two studies of opportunistic programming: interleaving web foraging, learning, and writing code, pp. 1589–1598. Association for Computing Machinery, New York (2009). https://doi.org/10.1145/1518701.1518944
5. Dehghani, M., Jagfeld, G., Azarbonyad, H., Olieman, A., Kamps, J., Marx, M.: On search powered navigation. In: Proceedings of the ACM SIGIR International Conference on Theory of Information Retrieval, ICTIR'17, pp. 317–320. Association for Computing Machinery, New York (2017). https://doi.org/10.1145/3121050.3121105
6. ud Din, I., Khusro, S., Ullah, I., Rauf, A.: Semantic history: ontology-based modeling of users' web browsing behaviors for improved web page revisitation. In: Silhavy, R., Silhavy, P., Prokopova, Z. (eds.) CoMeSySo 2018. AISC, vol. 860, pp. 204–215. Springer, Cham (2019). https://doi.org/10.1007/978-3-030-00184-1_19
7. https://googleblog.blogspot.com/2011/10/fall-sweep.html . Accessed 26 Aug 2021
8. Hora, A.: Googling for software development: what developers search for and what they find. In: 2021 IEEE/ACM 18th International Conference on Mining Software Repositories (MSR), pp. 317–328 (2021). https://doi.org/10.1109/MSR52588.2021.00044
9. Hsieh-Yee, I.: Research on web search behavior. Libr. Inf. Sci. Res. **23**(2), 167–185 (2001)
10. Huang, J., Efthimiadis, E.N.: Analyzing and evaluating query reformulation strategies in web search logs. In: Proceedings of the 18th ACM Conference on Information and Knowledge Management, CIKM'09, pp. 77–86. Association for Computing Machinery, New York (2009). https://doi.org/10.1145/1645953.1645966
11. Hölscher, C., Strube, G.: Web search behavior of internet experts and newbies. Comput. Netw. **33**(1), 337–346 (2000)
12. Kim, J., McNally, B., Norooz, L., Druin, A.: Internet search roles of adults in their homes, pp. 4948–4959. Association for Computing Machinery, New York (2017). https://doi.org/10.1145/3025453.3025572
13. Liu, C., Liu, J., Wei, Y.: Scroll up or down?: using wheel activity as an indicator of browsing strategy across different contextual factors. In: Nordlie, R., Pharo, N., Freund, L., Larsen, B., Russel, D. (eds.) Proceedings of the 2017 Conference on Conference Human Information Interaction and Retrieval, CHIIR 2017, Oslo, Norway, 7–11 March 2017, pp. 333–336. ACM (2017). https://doi.org/10.1145/3020165.3022146

14. Morris, D., Ringel Morris, M., Venolia, G.: SearchBar: a search-centric web history for task resumption and information re-finding. In: Proceedings of the SIGCHI Conference on Human Factors in Computing Systems, CHI'08, pp. 1207–1216. Association for Computing Machinery, New York (2008). https://doi.org/10.1145/1357054.1357242

15. Morris, M.R., Moraveji, N., Morris, D.: Supporting the social transfer of web search expertise. In: CHI 2010 Workshop on the Next Generation of HCI and Education. ACM, April 2010. https://www.microsoft.com/en-us/research/publication/supporting-social-transfer-web-search-expertise/

16. Nagano, K., Arakawa, Y., Yasumoto, K.: TrackThink: a tool for tracking a thought process on web search. In: Proceedings of the 2017 ACM International Joint Conference on Pervasive and Ubiquitous Computing and Proceedings of the 2017 ACM International Symposium on Wearable Computers, UbiComp'17, pp. 681–687. Association for Computing Machinery, New York (2017). https://doi.org/10.1145/3123024.3129267

17. Rahman, M.M., Roy, C.: SurfClipse: context-aware meta-search in the IDE. In: 2014 IEEE International Conference on Software Maintenance and Evolution, pp. 617–620 (2014)

18. Rahman, M.M., et al.: Evaluating how developers use general-purpose web-search for code retrieval. In: Proceedings of the 15th International Conference on Mining Software Repositories, SR'18, pp. 465–475. Association for Computing Machinery, New York (2018). https://doi.org/10.1145/3196398.3196425

19. Sadowski, C., Stolee, K.T., Elbaum, S.: How developers search for code: a case study. In: Proceedings of the 2015 10th Joint Meeting on Foundations of Software Engineering, ESEC/FSE 2015, pp. 191–201. Association for Computing Machinery, New York (2015). https://doi.org/10.1145/2786805.2786855

20. https://searchcode.com/ . Accessed 26 Aug 2021

21. https://sourcegraph.com . Accessed 26 Aug 2021

22. Stolee, K.T., Elbaum, S., Dobos, D.: Solving the search for source code. ACM Trans. Softw. Eng. Methodol. 23(3), 1–45 (2014). https://doi.org/10.1145/2581377

23. White, R.W., Morris, D.: Investigating the querying and browsing behavior of advanced search engine users. In: Proceedings of the 30th Annual International ACM SIGIR Conference on Research and Development in Information Retrieval, SIGIR'07, pp. 255–262. Association for Computing Machinery, New York (2007). https://doi.org/10.1145/1277741.1277787

24. Xia, X., Bao, L., Lo, D., Kochhar, P.S., Hassan, A.E., Xing, Z.: What do developers search for on the web? Empir. Softw. Eng. 22(6), 3149–3185 (2017)

25. Xu, L., Fernando, Z.T., Zhou, X., Nejdl, W.: LogCanvas: visualizing search history using knowledge graphs, pp. 1289–1292. Association for Computing Machinery, New York (2018). https://doi.org/10.1145/3209978.3210169

Building a Crowdsensing Platform Based on Spatio-Temporal Fencing

Nobuhito Miyagawa[1]([✉]), Ryoga Tsuchimoto[2], Shota Suzaki[2], and Katsuhiko Kaji[1,2]

[1] Graduate School of Management Information Science, Aichi Institute of Technology, 1247 Yachigusa Yakusa, Toyota, Aichi 470-0356, Japan
b21731bb@aitech.ac.jp
[2] Faculty of Information Science, Aichi Institute of Technology, Toyota, Japan
https://www.ait.ac.jp

Abstract. In this research, we propose the concept of spatio-temporal fencing, which restricts the time and area of sensing, and construct crowdsensing platform based on this concept. We have focused on convenience and sense of security to address the issue of improving and maintaining collaborator motivation. For requesters who want to implement crowdsensing, defining the contents of a request is a time-consuming task with many items that must be defined. This platform simplifies the definition of the request and makes it easy to use, because the request can be basically defined only by setting the spatio-temporal fencing and the sensor to be used. Spatio-temporal fencing can make it clear to collaborators when and where sensing will take place, and provide sense of security by reducing privacy barriers caused by concerns about data provision and sensing. In this paper, we have designed, implemented, and verified the operation of this platform.

Keywords: Mobile computing · Ubiquitous computing · Sensing · Smartphone

1 Introduction

In recent years, the number of smartphones equipped with sophisticated sensors has been increasing, and a wide variety of sensors are becoming available. Therefore, there are a number of research that use smartphone sensors [1,2]. Crowdsensing is an attempt to utilize the sensing capability of smartphones [3–5]. Crowdsensing is currently being employed in research and surveys [6–8]. The implementation of crowdsensing requires the development of a dedicated system, which is expected to incur significant initial and running costs. In addition, in order to encourage many collaborators to cooperate in crowdsensing, there are issues such as reducing the time and effort required for collaborators and eliminating their anxiety. As for the time and effort required for collaborators, the burden of operating and communicating with smartphones can be mentioned.

© ICST Institute for Computer Sciences, Social Informatics and Telecommunications Engineering 2022
Published by Springer Nature Switzerland AG 2022. All Rights Reserved
T. Hara and H. Yamaguchi (Eds.): MobiQuitous 2021, LNICST 419, pp. 797–809, 2022.
https://doi.org/10.1007/978-3-030-94822-1_52

The concerns of the collaborators include worries about providing data due to privacy barriers of the collaborators and distrust of sensing. Furthermore, since crowdsensing handles a lot of sensitive data such as sensing-data, security and privacy protection measures are essential.

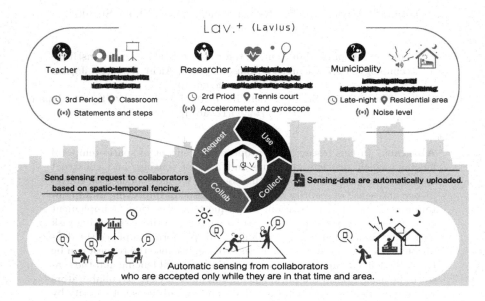

Fig. 1. Overview of this crowdsensing platform

In this research, we propose the concept of spatio-temporal fencing that limits the time and area of sensing, and build crowdsensing platform Lav.$^+$(Lavlus) in Figure 1 based on it. The purpose of this research is to realize a significant reduction of initial and running costs in research and surveys by simple use of crowdsensing and various data collection. As conventional research, crowdsensing platforms have been proposed to enable crowdsensing in various situations [9–14]. However, crowdsensing platform cannot realize diverse data collection without securing a larger number of collaborators. Therefore, it is necessary to improve and maintain the motivation of collaborators.

Therefore, Lavlus provides collaborators with convenience and sense of security to promote crowdsensing implementation and cooperation. For a requester who wants to implement crowdsensing, defining the contents of the request is time-consuming because there are so many items that need to be defined. However, Lavlus can basically define the request by only setting up the spatio-temporal fencing and the sensors to be used. Therefore, spatio-temporal fencing simplifies the definition of the request by the requester and makes it easier. For the collaborator, since it is clear when and where sensing will take place, it reduces privacy barriers due to concerns about data provision and sensing, and provides a sense of security. This makes it easier to cooperate with crowdsensing requests made through Lavlus, since they are all based on spatio-temporal fencing. In addition, to reduce the time and effort required for collaborators, sensing is performed automatically with minimal smartphone operation. This removes the sense of obligation for the collaborators to cooperate, and allows for continuous cooperation.

The contribution of this paper is the proposal, design and implementation of a system that aims to stimulate research and surveys using crowdsensing as a type of crowdsourcing. Although widely used smartphones are the best mobile devices for crowdsensing, their methods have not been generalized. This is because many conventional studies require the construction of a dedicated system. However, since the essence of these studies and investigations is the analysis and investigation of the collected sensing data, the construction of a dedicated system has a large initial cost and cannot be the essence of the studies and investigations. Even if a dedicated system is built, the next challenge is to get as many collaborators as possible.

2   Related Research

There are several research that use crowdsensing to collect data from a large number of people for estimation and analysis. For example, crowdsensing using mobile devices is used to collect and share ambient sounds to conduct noise surveys [6,7], and motion sensors such as accelerometers are used to collect data from car users to estimate road conditions such as icy and paved roads, and road geometry such as flat and hollow surfaces [8]. In these research, the development of a crowdsensing system is expected to incur significant costs. To implement crowdsensing, it is necessary to develop a sensing smartphone application exclusively for the collaborator and a server to manage the collected data.

Therefore, a crowdsensing platform would be very useful if the requester wishes to use crowdsensing to collect data. For the requester, it is no longer necessary to create and distribute a dedicated smartphone application for sensing for each research, thus eliminating the time and effort spent on these tasks. As for the collaborators, there is no need to install a separate smartphone application for each research, and there is no need to use separate applications for each research. In addition, the use of a common smartphone application can lead collaborators to other crowdsensing applications, which can lead to the acquisition of many collaborators.

Next, we discuss related research on crowdsensing platforms. There are already some that operate as simple platforms mainly for the purpose of reducing system development costs [9,10]. However, securing collaborators is very important for crowdsensing platforms. Related researches include those to improve and maintain the motivation of collaborators and to secure collaborators.

This includes research using monetary incentives [11] and research that uses gamification to provide non-monetary incentives [12]. There are also research that offer a flexible choice between monetary and non-monetary incentives. In this research, our approach is to remove disincentives for collaborators through spatio-temporal fencing, and we are considering introducing a mechanism that can provide incentives in the future.

3 Crowdsensing Platform Based on Spatio-Temporal Fencing

This chapter describes the details of Lav.$^+$(Lavlus), a crowdsensing platform based on spatio-temporal fencing. Each section is organized in the following order: Definition of spatio-temporal fencing, Implementation of Lavlus, and Verification of Lavlus operation.

3.1 Definition of Spatio-Temporal Fencing

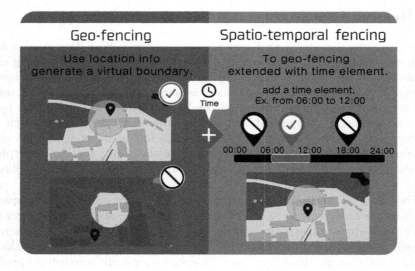

Fig. 2. Geofencing and spatio-temporal fencing

Spatio-temporal fencing is defined as a unique fencing method that extends geofencing by adding a time element in Fig. 2. In the figure, the pin marks are considered to be fencing targets. Geo-fencing is the process of creating a virtual boundary on a map, as shown by the circle in the figure, and using location estimation technologies such as GPS, Wi-Fi, and BLE beacons to provide specific services when a user enters or exits the boundary. In other words, spatio-temporal fencing is a fencing method that generates a virtual boundary by specifying the time and area. The specific service in Lavlus is sensing.

When the boundaries are delimited by time and area using spatio-temporal fencing, the requester can specify a variety of situations. For example, a park from 3:00 to 5:00 p.m., a specific classroom on a university campus during third period, or a cafeteria during the daytime. On the other hand, it is not suitable for data collection that does not depend on time or area. For example, such as sensing all day long or traveling by train. This is because such long-time sensing or sensing that is not certain when it will end places a heavy burden on the collaborator in terms of power consumption and anxiety about sensing. For this reason, Lavlus does not support all possible types of crowdsensing that a requester may expect.

Lavlus uses spatio-temporal fencing to make it easier for collaborators who have no contact with the requester to make decisions about cooperation. For example, when a collaborator who does not have any contact with the requester cooperates with the requester's crowdsensing, if the time of day or area where the sensing is to be performed is unclear, the collaborator will feel uneasy and will be less likely to cooperate. Therefore, we believe that time zone and area restrictions based on spatio-temporal fencing can provide a sense of security to collaborators and promote sensing cooperation.

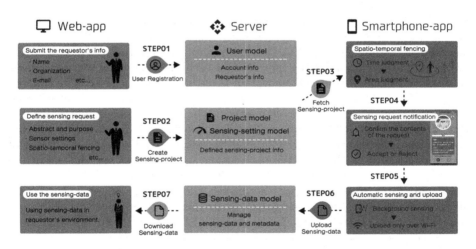

Fig. 3. Overall system flow of Lavlus

3.2   Implementation of Lavlus

Lavlus is composed of three components: server, web-app, and smartphone-app. In addition, the requester's crowdsensing requests are managed in units called projects (hereafter referred to as projects). The server is designed to manage projects and sensing-data, the web-app is a console for managing projects for the requester, and the smartphone-app is a sensing smartphone-app for the collaborator. In this section, we describe Overall system flow of Lavlus, Implementation of each component, and Security measures.

Overall System Flow of Lavlus. The overall system flow of Lavlus is shown in Fig. 3. We assume that the requester uses a PC and the collaborator uses a smartphone as the device used. In STEP01 of the figure, the user is asked to prepare in advance for using Lavlus. To use it as a requester, requestor registration through the web-app is required. To use it as a collaborator, installation of the smartphone-app is required.

As shown in STEP02, the requester first creates a project through a web application. The project defines time and area to be sensed, the purpose and outline of the sensing, the type of sensor to be used for sensing, and the sampling rate. This is the setting of the sensing and spatio-temporal fencing required for the smartphone-app, and also serves as the basis for presenting the project to collaborators and deciding whether or not to cooperate. The created project can be managed by the server.

Next, we ask the collaborators to cooperate with each project using the smartphone-app. As shown in STEP03, the smartphone-app first gets the project from the server. Then, for each acquired project, the operations are performed in the following order: spatio-temporal fencing, sensing request notification, sensing, and uploading. In STEP04, spatio-temporal fencing is performed to reference the spatio-temporal space specified for each project, and a sensing request notification is sent when the collaborator is in the spatio-temporal. The collaborator confirms the contents of the project from the sensing request notification, and decides whether to accept or reject it. The sensing request notification is sent as a heads-up notification, and the detailed screen is displayed by tapping the heads-up notification. In the detailed screen, you can check the contents of the project, such as the time period, sensing area, purpose and outline of the sensing, and the requester information. In STEP05, sensing is started only when the collaborator is satisfied with the project and is willing to cooperate. After sensing is completed, the sensing data is automatically uploaded to the server only when Wi-Fi is connected, as shown in STEP06.

The operation flow of the smartphone-app in the figure is the cooperation procedure of the collaborators. In order to minimize the amount of time and effort required, the only part of the cooperative procedure that requires the operation of the collaborator's smartphone is basically the acceptance or rejection of the sensing request notification. This is because all the processing in the spatio-temporal fencing, sensing, and uploading procedures is done in the background. Therefore, there are no operations such as opening the smartphone-app or having the collaborator start and stop sensing, which makes sensing cooperation easy. In addition, once a project is accepted, it is saved, and when the collaborator enters the same project's spatio-temporal again, sensing will start without sending a sensing request notification.

In STEP07, the requester uses the sensing data provided by the collaborator through a web application. The sensing-data can be downloaded in CSV or JSON format, which are provided in a uniform format. The requester downloads the sensing data from the web application and analyzes it using his or her own environment, and uses it for research and surveys. Currently, Lavlus needs to provide support to the requester, such as analysis and visualization of the sensing-data, but has not yet been able to implement such support. Therefore, we are investigating the filtering of bad data that may occur due to the nature of crowdsensing. Bad data is data that has been sensed contrary to the intent of the project. For example, in a project aimed at measuring locomotion, data sensed by a collaborator while the smartphone is placed on a table, or data sensed when the smartphone's sensor does not work properly, can be considered. In other words, we are considering implementing a function that filters out bad data and supports how reliable the sensing data is.

Implementation of Each Component. The server was designed as a JSON-based REST API that is highly compatible with both the web-app and the smartphone-app so that they can be linked smoothly. The web-app was implemented using a Single Page Application in Fig. 4. First, the requester registers as a requester using the web-app. The registered requester information is managed according to the User model defined on the server. At this time, the requester is asked to register real name, organization, e-mail address, and other requester information. This information is required because if the requester is anonymous or unclear, it may cause anxiety to the collaborators, making it difficult to obtain their cooperation. Although the requester information is personal data, the terms of use of Lavlus require the requester to disclose identity. The next step is to define the project based on the outline and purpose of the sensing request, sensor settings, spatio-temporal fencing, and other information. The defined project is managed according to the Project model and the SensingSetting model. The sensing-data provided by the collaborators is then managed according to the SensingData model, and the sensing data is acquired through a web-app.

The smartphone-app was implemented as an Android application. The smartphone-app works with the server to receive projects and upload sensing-data along with metadata. Projects are retrieved from the server as necessary and registered in the database in the smartphone-app. The smartphone-app searches for the nearest specified start time from the current time in the database, and sets the specified start time and specified end time to spatio-temporal fencing. Spatio-temporal fencing first determines the time in order to minimize location information acquisition, and then determines the area at the start time specified by the project.

The area determination determines whether the collaborator has entered or exited the sensing area defined in the project. However, if the collaborator is active near the boundary of the sensing area, the area judgment becomes unstable as it repeatedly makes entry/exit judgments. Therefore, we introduced the area margin in Fig. 5 to stabilize the area judgment determines. The area mar-

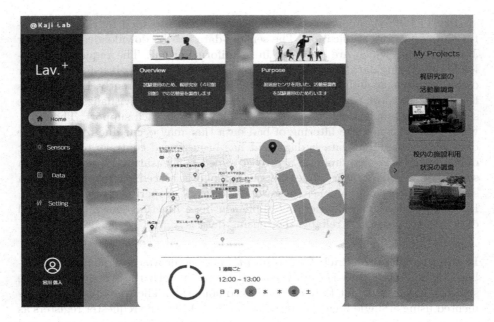

Fig. 4. Dashboard of the web-app

gin defines two types of areas, considering the inner and outer margins. The two areas are the inner area, which has been reduced in size relative to the sensing area, and the outer area, which has been expanded. As shown in the figure, when a collaborator stays in the inner area for a certain period of time, it is judged to have entered the sensing area, and when the collaborator who is judged to have entered stays outside the outer area for a certain period of time, it is judged to have left the sensing area. For this certain period of time, a value of 5 s has been set on a trial basis, but it is necessary to reset the optimal value through evaluation experiments. The introduction of an area margin also aims to deter the initiation of sensing when the collaborator stays only for a very short time, such as passing through the sensing area.

When a collaborator enters the sensing area during the time period specified in the project, a sensing request notification is sent. Tapping the heads-up notification and opening the application will display the detailed screen of the sensing request notification in Fig. 6. The detailed screen shows the current location and designated sensing area on a map, the time of day on a range slider, and the contents of the project in a box with a scroll bar. The map display of the requester location and the designated sensing area is a device to make it easier for the collaborator who has entered the space-time to understand the location of the current location.

After sensing is completed, the sensing-data is registered in the database with a file name and an un-uploaded flag. We only upload the data after verifying a Wi-Fi connection and then update the un-uploaded flag. The reason for this

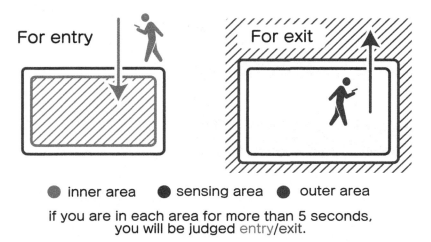

Fig. 5. Overview of area margin

is that uploading sensing-data while connected to a cellular connection would use the mobile communication volume of the collaborator, placing a burden on the collaborator. If there is no Wi-Fi connection, the upload is put on hold, and when the Wi-Fi connection is confirmed, the data is uploaded at once.

Security Measures. Since Lavlus is a platform that handles sensitive information such as sensing-data, we have implemented several security measures. First, the server uses JWT token authentication as a security measure. This prevents unauthorized access to each endpoint and prevents unintended access or falsification of information by third parties.

Next, due to the limitation of spatio-temporal fencing, which is the design basis, we do not perform sensing without specifying a time or sensing area. In addition, we do not perform sensing without the requester consent, even when the time and sensing area are specified. This minimizes the risk of privacy violations associated with the provision of unintended sensing-data by the collaborator.

Finally, the handling of sensing data will be strictly managed in accordance with the GDPR [15], which is the law governing the protection and handling of personal data in the EU. According to the definition of personal data in the GDPR (Article 4), each sensing-data itself provided by a collaborator is not classified as personal data. However, it may be classified as personal data if it is combined with information that accompanies the sensing-data. In addition to sensing data, Lavlus acquires metadata, which is terminal information such as the name of the terminal and the model number of the sensor, as environmental information about the sensing process. Therefore, metadata such as the IMEI, which is a device identification ID, will not be acquired when sensing-data is provided by the collaborator, as it is considered personal data. In addition to the IMEI, metadata that can be used to identify an individual by referencing sensing-

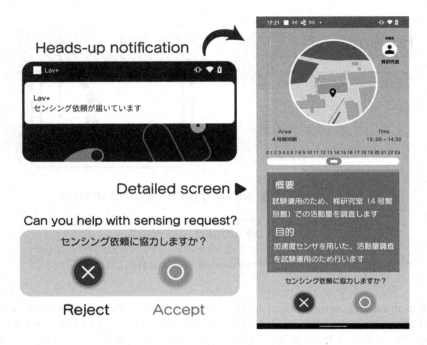

Fig. 6. Sensing request notification

data and metadata is also considered personal data, so only information that can identify the environment in which sensing was performed will be acquired.

3.3 Verification of Lavlus Operation

We set up a situation in which we investigate the amount of activity in the annex of Aichi Institute of Technology Building No. 4 from 13:00 to 14:00 using an acceleration sensor. Since this verification is in the initial stage of implementation, we do not assume complex situations such as exceptions to operations, but rather simple situations. As a preliminary preparation, the requester registered as a new requester with the web-app, and the collaborator installed a new the smartphone-app.

First, we verified that the server, the web-app, and the smartphone-app could requester and receive projects normally. After creating a project using the web-app, we checked the server and confirmed that it was created normally. After that, the smartphone-app received the project from the server. Since the project defined in the server was received without any problem, it is judged to be normal.

Next, based on the received project, the operation of the spatio-temporal fencing and sensing of the smartphone-app is verified. The sensing request notification was not sent even if the collaborator entered the operation verification sensing area before the specified start time, but was sent when the specified start time arrived. When the request was approved from the sensing request notification, sensing started normally. After leaving the sensing area, sensing was terminated, and after re-entering the area, sensing was started again. When the specified end time was reached while still in the sensing area, sensing was terminated. In the operation verification, since the sensing area was indoors, there was a location error in the area determination by GPS, but the operation was confirmed. As a result, we can conclude that the time judgment, area judgment, and sensing are normal.

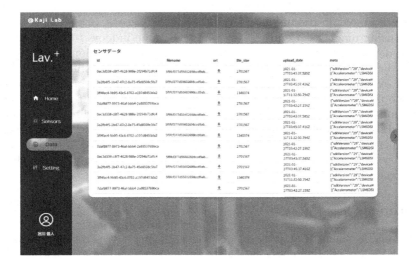

Fig. 7. Collected sensing-data confirmed using the web-app

Finally, we verified that the smartphone-app could upload sensing-data and the web-app could view sensing-data normally. Sensing was completed with no Wi-Fi connection. When we checked the server, we could not see any upload of sensing-data. After that, we reconnected to the Wi-Fi connection and checked the server again, and found that the sensing-data had been uploaded. In addition, when we checked the sensing-data using the web-app, the acceleration sensing-data was collected as per the situation in Fig. 7, so we consider the operation verification a success.

4   Conclusion

We aimed to build a platform that can be applied to various researches and surveys by collecting various data using crowdsensing. In conventional platforms, there are problems such as privacy violation concerns for collaborators and complicated definition of requests for requester. To solve this problem, we proposed the concept of spatio-temporal fencing and built a crowdsensing platform Lav.$^+$(Lavlus) based on it. Spatio-temporal fencing is a unique fencing method that extends geofencing by adding a time element and delimiting the boundaries by time and area. Spatio-temporal fencing reduces privacy barriers for collaborators by making it clear when and where sensing will take place, and simplifies the definition of requests for requester. We have implemented and verified Lavlus and verified that the system works properly.

Through operational verification, we found that GPS based area determination is not accurate enough in indoor areas where GPS information is unstable or in narrow spaces where GPS determination is difficult. Therefore, it is necessary to use radio wave positioning using Wi-Fi or BLE beacons, or geomagnetic positioning using magnetism emitted from a steel frame indoors to define the area in more detail. In addition, Lavlus is not yet ready for operation and evaluation. One of the issues for operation and evaluation is the establishment of terms of use. For example, in order to protect the privacy of collaborators, it is necessary to delete the provided sensing-data on the server upon their request. However, Lavlus method of providing sensing-data is through downloading. Therefore, we will establish terms of use that prohibit the retention of sensing-data beyond a certain period of time. In addition to solving the current issues, it is necessary to build a system that can be operated as a platform after conducting evaluation experiments using actual crowdsensing.

References

1. Suyama, A., Inoue, U.: Using geofencing for a disaster information system. In: 2016 IEEE/ACIS 15th International Conference on Computer and Information Science, pp. 1–5 (2016)
2. Daisuke, S., Takeshi, I., Michito, M.: A study about identification of pedestrian by using 3-axis accelerometer. In: 2011 IEEE 17th International Conference on Embedded and Real-Time Computing Systems and Applications, vol. 2, pp. 134–137 (2011)
3. Burke, J.A., et al.: Participatory sensing. In: Workshop on World-Sensor-Web: Mobile Device Centric Sensor Networks and Applications (2006)
4. Raghu, G., Fan, Y., Hui, L.: Mobile crowd sensing: current state and future challenges. IEEE Commun. Mag. **49**, 32–39 (2011)
5. Liu, J., Shen, H., Zhang, X.: A survey of mobile crowdsensing techniques: a critical component for the Internet of Things. In: 2016 25th International Conference on Computer Communication and Networks, pp. 1–6 (2016)
6. Eiman, K.: NoiseSPY: a real-time mobile phone platform for urban noise monitoring and mapping. MONET **15**, 562–574 (2010). https://doi.org/10.1007/s11036-009-0217-y
7. Nicolas, M., Matthias, S., Bartek, O.: Participatory noise pollution monitoring using mobile phones. Inf. Polity **15**, 51–71 (2010)
8. Bin, P., Kenro, A.: Detecting the road surface condition by using mobile crowdsensing with drive recorder. In: 2017 IEEE 20th International Conference on Intelligent Transportation Systems, pp. 1–8 (2017)
9. Tangmunarunkit, H., et al.: Ohmage: a general and extensible end-to-end participatory sensing platform. ACM Trans. Intell. Syst. Technol. **6**(3), 1–21 (2015)

10. Ferreira, D., Kostakos, V., Dey, A.K.: AWARE: mobile context instrumentation framework. Front. ICT **2**, 6 (2015)
11. Jayarajah, K., Balan, R.K., Radhakrishnan, M., Misra, A., Lee, Y.: LiveLabs: building in-situ mobile sensing & behavioural experimentation TestBeds. In: MobiSys 16: Proceedings of the 14th Annual International Conference on Mobile Systems, Applications, and Services, pp. 1–15 (2016)
12. Shogo, K., Yuki, M., Hirohiko, S., Manato, F., Yutaka, A., Keiichi, Y.: Gamified participatory sensing in tourism: an experimental study of the effects on tourist behavior and satisfaction. Smart Cities **3**(3), 736–757 (2020)
13. Yuki, M., Shogo, K., Hirohiko, S., Yutaka, A., Keiichi, Y.: ParmoSense: a scenario-based participatory mobile urban sensing platform with user motivation engine. arXiv (2021)
14. Mina, S., Takuro, Y., Tomotaka, I., Jin, N., Hideyuki, T.: MinaQn: web-based participatory sensing platform for citizen-centric urban development. In: ACM International Joint Conference on Pervasive and Ubiquitous Computing and the 2015 ACM International Symposium on Wearable Computers, UbiComp and ISWC 2015, pp. 1607–1614 (2015)
15. GDPR. https://eur-lex.europa.eu/eli/reg/2016/679/oj. Accessed 23 Jan 2021

Innovative Technologies
for the Healthcare Empowerment
(InnovTech4Health)

WatchID: Wearable Device Authentication via Reprogrammable Vibration

Jerry Q. Cheng[1(✉)], Zixiao Wang[1], Yan Wang[2], Tianming Zhao[2], Hao Wan[1], and Eric Xie[3]

[1] Department of Computer Science, New York Institute of Technology, New York, USA
jcheng18@nyit.edu
[2] Department of Computer and Information Sciences, Temple University, Philadelphia, USA
[3] Princeton High School, Princeton, NJ, USA

Abstract. Prevalent wearables (e.g., smartwatches and activity trackers) demand high secure measures to protect users' private information, such as personal contacts, bank accounts, etc. While existing two-factor authentication methods can enhance traditional user authentication, they are not convenient as they require participations from users. Recently, manufacturing imperfections in hardware devices (e.g., accelerometers and WiFi interface) have been utilized for low-effort two-factor authentications. However, these methods rely on fixed device credentials that would require users to replace their devices once the device credentials are stolen. In this work, we develop a novel device authentication system, *WatchID*, that can identify a user's wearable using its vibration-based device credentials. Our system exploits readily available vibration motors and accelerometers in wearables to establish a vibration communication channel to capture wearables' unique vibration characteristics. Compared to existing methods, our vibration-based device credentials are reprogrammable and easy to use. We develop a series of data processing methods to mitigate the impact of noises and body movements. A lightweight convolutional neural network is developed for feature extraction and device authentication. Extensive experimental results using five smartwatches show that WatchID can achieve an average precision and recall of 98% and 94% respectively in various attacking scenarios.

Keywords: Wearables · Device authentication · Vibration signals

1 Introduction

Due to ever-advancing communication, computing, and sensing technologies, wearables (e.g., smartwatches and activity trackers) have become increasingly ubiquitous for people to use in their daily lives. Many manufacturers produce such gadgets for activity tracking and vital signs monitoring in order to capitalize

© ICST Institute for Computer Sciences, Social Informatics and Telecommunications Engineering 2022
Published by Springer Nature Switzerland AG 2022. All Rights Reserved
T. Hara and H. Yamaguchi (Eds.): MobiQuitous 2021, LNICST 419, pp. 813–833, 2022.
https://doi.org/10.1007/978-3-030-94822-1_53

on the global rise in health and wellbeing awareness. More recently, building on their convenience in usage and popularity among customers, wearables expand their functionalities beyond health and activity monitoring into various applications in other fields, including mobile payment, smart home control, emailing and texting, etc. The growing usage of these applications in wearables provides more opportunities for attackers to compromise users' private information (e.g., email accounts, personal contact lists, etc.) and, more seriously, financial information (e.g., banking and credit card accounts). As a result, it is becoming increasingly vital to secure wearables to protect users' privacy and financial assets.

Existing authentication methods on wearable devices have very limited choices. Most wearables use passwords or PINs [17] to verify users' identities. Recently two-factor authentication has been adopted, using additional user inputs of text codes [2] or taking phone calls [14] for better protections. These methods require additional inputs from users and can only verify the identity of the user based on the knowledge of certain secret information (i.e., password, PIN, the content of additional messages and calls). These types of information are vulnerable to many attacks, such as shoulder surfing [22] and stolen attacks [36]. Once the user's credentials are compromised, the attacker can easily log into the user's accounts on the attacker's own device. Then the attacker can steal valuable personal information or abuse the user's account (e.g., making payment without users' permission, opening smart-door locks, etc.) inconspicuously.

Recently, researchers have discovered that computing devices can be identified based on their unique physical properties. For example, the frequency responses of smartphones' speakers are studied by Zhou *et al.* [41] to generate device identities using inaudible acoustic signals. The imperfections of radio frequency (RF) transmitter (e.g., the digital-to-analog converter (DAC) errors and the power amplifier (PA) non-linearity) are explored by Polak *et al.* [27] to identify wireless devices. The unique acceleration responses of motion sensors inside mobile devices (e.g., smartphones) are explored in Accelprint [11] to distinguish different mobile devices. These studies have shown that physical properties in hardware can be exploited to create unique device credentials as a second factor to enhance security in users' applications. However, most of the existing device authentication methods are rigid and suffer from stolen attacks because users cannot change their hardware-related device credentials. As a result, users will be forced to use a new device if their device credentials are stolen. In this work, we propose to utilize devices' vibration characteristics, as reprogrammable credentials, to enable practical device authentication in prevalent wearables.

Toward this end, we develop a device authentication system called *WatchID*, illustrated in Fig. 1, to identify a wearable device using vibration motions generated by its vibration motor and captured by its accelerometers. The key to this system is that the vibration motor and accelerometers of each individual wearable always have manufacture imperfections. As a result, the vibration signals will exhibit unique device-wise characteristic which we utilize for the purpose of device authentication. Compared to existing methods, WatchID is more flexible as it allows users to generate and reprogram various vibration patterns that are associated with different unique device credentials. Our system is also non-intrusive so users just need to wear their wearables without any active participations.

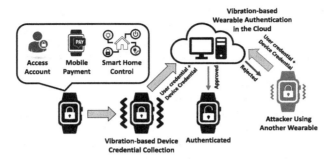

Fig. 1. Illustration of WatchID: the reprogrammable wearable authentication system using vibration-based device credentials.

In addition, it is low-cost and practical since it only uses the built-in vibration motors and accelerometers, which are readily available in wearables. In particular, when a user launches an sensitive application on his/her wearable (e.g., accessing a user account, using mobile payment, controlling smart home, etc.), our system uses the wearable's vibration motor to generate a predefined vibration pattern. Meanwhile, the wearable's accelerometers capture the unique vibration signals propagating through the device's body and send them with the user's credentials to a cloud server, where the user has pre-registered the device. Once the wearable's device credential and user credential are verified by the cloud server, the wearable receives the approval to proceed with the protected application.

In designing WatchID, we address several challenges to make it an accurate, fast, and robust device authentication system. First, the vibration characteristics that we use as device credentials should be unique enough to distinguish different wearables for the purpose of device authentication. Second, built-in vibration motors and accelerometers inside wearables are usually of low-quality with unstable vibration signals and low sampling rates. Third, many interfering factors such as wearable postures, body motions, and environmental noises can contaminate the device credentials. To address these challenges, we study the vibration motors and motion sensors in different models of wearables and develop vibration patterns that are suitable for device authentication. In addition, we apply vibration noise filtering methods to mitigate the impacts of motion artifacts and ambient noises to our system. With the denoised device credentials, our system applies a deep neural network designed to performance a robust device authentication process.

Through implementing WatchID, we have made several major contributions as follows:

- We extensively investigate the uniqueness of vibration motors and accelerometers in commodity wearables, analyze the vibration characteristics from different vibration patterns which are used for reprogrammable vibration-based device credentials.
- We develop a novel device authentication system with a light-weight deep neural network that can accurately and efficiently identify different wearables based on their vibration-based device credentials.

- We collect a large amount of experimental data using five commercial off-the-shelf (COTS) smartwatches in various scenarios and different days. Our results show that our device authentication system can achieve over 98% and 94% for precision and recall, respectively.

The rest of paper is organized as follows. Section 2 begins with an extensive review of related work in authentication methods for mobile devices and considers the uniqueness and advantage of our system that can bring into this research field. Section 3 provides attack models to WatchID. Section 4 describes feasibility studies which are used as the basis for our system. Section 5 introduces an overview of the design and process flow of our system. Section 6 explains our vibration noise filtering method and vibration-based device authentication method. Section 7 presents our experimental methodology and results of evaluating this system. Section 8 concludes this work with discussion.

2   Related Work

Traditional user authentication methods for mobile devices usually require user inputs such as usernames, passwords, graphic patterns, which are vulnerable to knowledge-based attacks (e.g., shoulder attacks and smudge attacks). Recently, researchers have proposed to use human biometrics for convenient mobile user authentication. These biometric-based methods can be classified into two types: behavioral-based and physiological-based approaches. The behavioral-based approaches [30, 34, 37] identify users based on users' activity patterns (e.g., keystroke entries, mouse movements, gaits in walking). Recently, Cong et al. [33] propose a behavior-based user authentication system using commodity WiFi, which is non-intrusive and low-cost. The physiological-based approaches are non-intrusive and usually exploit fingerprints [7, 29], iris patterns [31, 32], respiratory patterns [25, 26] and cardiac patterns [23, 24, 38, 40] to perform user authentication.

While the above mobile user authentication methods can effectively identify users, users' credentials can still bed be compromised by various attacks (e.g., fingerprint smudge attacks [39] and cardiac pattern attacks [13]). To solve these problems, researchers have exploited and utilized hardware imperfections as device credentials to verify whether certain sensitive operations originate from a legitimate device. According to the source of these credentials, we can classify the existing device credentials into three categories:

1. **Acoustic-based Device Credentials.** Variations in manufacturing processes, although usually small, can often introduce product imperfections off from pre-defined specifications. For example, microphones and speakers of the same brand and model will produce and receive sounds differently. Das et al. [9] exploit this observation to distinguish smartphones through playing and recording a pre-recorded audio sample. Daniel et al. [15] study statistical characterizations of frequency responses of microphones to identify different devices. Zhou et al. [41] exploit inaudible acoustic signals from microphones insides smartphones to generate unique device identity. All these acoustic-based approaches require access to microphones in recording and thus can create privacy concerns.

2. **RF-based Device Credentials.** Researchers also find that RF signals from mobile devices contain identifiable information related to the imperfections of the analog circuits inside these devices. For example, Danev *et al.* [8] compare several device identification systems using modulator circuitry, analog circuitry, and clock skew of WiFi transmitters to identify wireless devices. For the same purpose, Polak *et al.* [27, 28] exploit the digital-to-analog converter (DAC) errors and the power amplifier (PA) non-linearity of RF transmitter components. Brik *et al.* [6] leverage differentiating artifacts of individual wireless frames in the modulation domain caused by the minute imperfections of NICs. Among these RF-based approaches, the quality and speed of RF signal acquisition and processing are easily impacted by environmental factors so that the resulting device credential extraction is complex and difficult.

3. **Motion Sensor-based Device Credentials.** Motion sensors (i.e., accelerometers and gyroscopes) can also be used for fingerprinting as demonstrated in [5, 10, 11]: Bojinov *et al.* [5] exploit the unique linear bias of the accelerometer; Dey *et al.* [11] use vibration motors to stimulate accelerometers in mobile phones; Das *et al.* [10] use audio signals to trigger both accelerometers and gyroscopes in mobile phones with human motions. These research have shown that the motion sensor-based approach is a promising research field with further studies needed for utilizations of predefined vibration patterns, different frequencies and amplitudes. Currently existing studies mostly focus on mobile phones and tablets. And it remains unknown whether they can adapt to wearable devices since the contact surface of human wrists is very different from that of desks or human palms.

In this work, we develop a novel device authentication system for wearables to generate vibration-based device credentials by vibration motors and capture the credentials by accelerometers in wearables. Our work is close to [11] in exploring imperfections with vibration motors and accelerometers, but focusing on wearable devices. Furthermore, our system is reprogrammable in allowing users to change or customize the device credentials. By doing so, users can keep using their wearable devices even after the original device credentials are compromised by attackers.

3   Attack Model

Malicious users may attempt to attack WatchID in order to steal personal information or deny a legitimate user from using services on the device. To study the associated attack models, we assume that the attackers can not access the wearable device directly but may have the following capabilities: 1) the attacker has the capability of stealing the users' credentials, including user names and passwords for the target system; 2) the attacker may also have obtained the device credential that the user registers with the system. Specially, we consider the following attack strategies.

Random Attack/Blind Attacks. We assume that the attacker has obtained a user's credentials, but not the device credential, and the device is not in his possession. The attacker uses his device to generate some random vibration patterns to match the device credential and bypass WatchID.

Jamming Attacks. The goal of this attack is to make WatchID unable to authenticate legitimate devices. Researchers have found that motion sensors (i.e., accelerometers and gyroscopes) can capture the vibration signals caused by acoustic sounds (e.g., music and human speech) [35]. Based on this, attackers can launch a jamming attack by generating loud acoustic signals (e.g., loud music) with various frequencies near the wearable devices. As a result, vibration-based device credentials may be severely interfered by these loud sounds so that our system is not able to accurately verify the user's device identity.

Credential Stealing Attacks. In the case when attackers have obtained a user's credential as well as the device's credential, the attacker can impersonate the legitimate user using both types of credentials to fool the system. Once the attacker passes the authentication, he can steal the user's personal and financial information or even perform illicit acts. Attackers can launch such attacks by monitoring the communications between the device and the cloud part of WachID at the device registration phase or during normal operations.

4   Feasibility Study

In this section, we conduct feasibility studies of using the vibration characteristics to construct device credentials for the purpose of distinguishing different wearables.

4.1   Device Credential Based on Vibrations

The Background of Vibration Motors. Mobile devices and wearables usually have built-in vibration motors that can be programmed to vibrate in various patterns. Such vibrations are mostly used in mobile applications as an alternative notification mechanism for alarm clocks, incoming calls, text messages, etc. Based on their operating principles, vibration motors in mobile devices and wearables can be categorized into two types: eccentric rotating mass (ERM) vibration motors and linear resonant actuator (LRA) vibration motors. The vibrations of ERM motors are generated by the rotations of a non-symmetric mass, while the vibrations of LRA motors are generated by linear movements of a magnet mass interacting with a voice coil. Vibration motors of the both types in mobile devices and wearable are of miniature size with varying degrees in vibration strengths, stabilities, and frequency ranges due to the differences in their working principles and manufacturers.

Vibration-Based Device Credentials. In this work, we consider that a wearable's vibration motor, its device body, and accelerometers are working together as a one-way communication system. The vibration motor (a transmitter) generates a vibration wave that propagate through the device body (a channel) and are received by the accelerometers (receivers). During the propagation, the vibration wave experiences attenuation in its energy level along the transmitting path

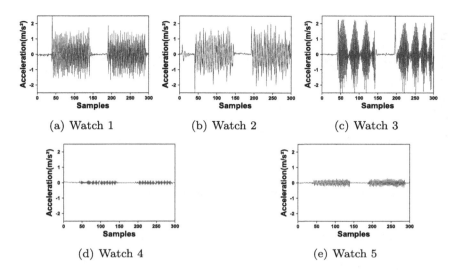

(a) Watch 1   (b) Watch 2   (c) Watch 3

(d) Watch 4   (e) Watch 5

Fig. 2. Z-axis accelerometer readings of 5 smartwatches when the watches have two repetitions of a vibration pattern (i.e., idle for 1 s and vibrating for 2 s with the vibration strength of 50). Watch 1 to Watch 3 are Fossil Gen 5, Watch 4 and Watch 5 are Moto 360 Gen 3.

as well as multipath interference when the wave hits two different media boundaries. Consequently, the received vibration signals (i.e., accelerometer readings) contain unique vibration characteristics as a result of manufacturing imperfections of the vibration motor and accelerometers, attenuations and the multipath interference from the device body. We contemplate that such vibration characteristics are unique for each wearable and can be utilized to identify wearables.

To demonstrate a proof of concept for utilizing such vibration characteristics for device authentication, we develop an app to generate vibrations and collect vibration data on five commodity smartwatches (Three Fossil Gen 5 watches and two Moto 360 Gen 3 watches). Specifically we use Google Wear OS (version 2.27) [16] on these smartwatches to change the vibration strength of the built-in vibration motors within a range of 0 to 255 and vibration durations. We place each watch on a wooden table with its face up and program the app to keep the watch still for 1 s and vibrating for 2 s with the vibration strength set to 50. Meanwhile, the app uses the watch's accelerometers to capture the vibration signals using their maximum sampling rate of 50 Hz. We repeat the same vibration pattern for comparison. Figure 2 shows two repetitions of the vibration waves (captured accelerations) along the vertical direction of the five smartwatches. We can observe that the acceleration patterns of all the watches are obviously different from each other in terms of their amplitudes and variations with some resemblance among watches of a same brand.

We repeat the same experiment 50 times for each watch and examine some summary quantities (e.g., mean, standard deviation, maximum, minimum of vibration

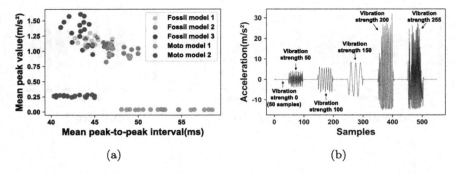

Fig. 3. Unique vibration characteristics of wearables: (a) a scatter plot of mean peak values and inter-peak duration of 50 vibration signals from five watches; (b) a sequence of z-axis accelerations captured when a smartwatch vibrates with five different vibration strengths, each segment contains 1 s of data.

amplitudes, frequency of the vibration signals, etc.) of the captured vibrations signals to quantitatively understand the distinguishable vibration patterns on wearables. Among these quantities, we pick the mean of peak values and inter-peak duration and make a two-dimensional scatter plot in Fig. 3 (a), from which we observe that the data points of the same watch are clustered together. We also find that the clusters of different watches are separable, especially for the watches of different brands (i.e., Fossil versus Moto). Moreover, we can see that the peak values of all Fossil watches are higher but more varied than the Moto watches. In contrast, the inter-peak duration of the Moto watches is more varied than that for all Fossil watches. These observations suggest that each wearable has its own unique vibration characteristics that can be utilized for device authentication.

4.2   Reprogrammable Vibration Patterns

Since existing device authentication methods use hardware manufacturing imperfections to generate rigid and unchangeable device credentials, users are forced to change their hardware to continue using their protected service in case when these device credentials are stolen by attackers. This is neither convenient nor economical. In contrast, WatchID uses the vibration characteristics as device credentials for authentication so that the credentials are configurable in terms of vibration amplitudes and durations. As a result, the corresponding vibration-based device credentials are not only unique, but also programmable (setting to patterns predefined by the manufacture or customized by users), thus making device authentication more convenient and flexible.

To illustrate the programmable vibration-based device credentials, we set the Fossil Gen 5 Watch 1 to vibrate at vibration strengths of 50, 100, 150, 200, and 255 for 1 s, respectively. Figure 3 (b) shows the z-axis accelerometer reading for this experiment. We can observe that the vibration characteristics of the same watch are significantly different when the vibration strength is set to different levels, even when the duration is the same. In addition, we combine vibration strengths and durations as our proposed device credentials for more accurate authentication.

5 System Overview

In this section, we first present several challenges in building a wearable device authentication system. Then we describe the system design of WatchID, which addresses those challenges.

5.1 Challenges

In order to build an effective, robust, and flexible wearable device authentication system using the vibrations generated and collected by wearable devices' vibration motors and accelerometers respectively, we need to address the following challenges for requiring:

- **Effective Credential Using Vibration Motors and Accelerometers in COTS Wearables**. Due to size and battery limitations, COTS wearables are usually equipped with vibration motors of lower quality and accelerometers with sample rates no more 50 Hz. As a result, it is difficult to obtain fine-grained measurements of the vibration signals from wearables in order to extract effective credentials for the devices.
- **Robust Vibration Signals for Practical Use**. In practice, a user might be moving or swinging his/her arms while the surrounding environment can be noisy and vibrant. Therefore the vibration signals captured by accelerometers from the user's watch are often mixed with noises. This will make it challenging to extract device credentials from the vibration signals for robust device identification.
- **Reprogrammable Device Credential**. Device credentials along with regular user login information are subject to various attacks from malicious users. When a particular set of device credential is compromised, the authentication system will disable the device and make it unusable for its protected services. In order to re-secure the device, the device authentication system should be able to provide a reprogrammable functionality for a new device credential thus to obsolete the stolen one.

5.2 System Design

To address the aforementioned challenges, we design WatchID as a reprogrammable device authentication system leveraging low-cost vibration motors and accelerometers in commodity wearables. The basic idea of the system is to identify wearables devices based on the unique vibration characteristics induced by the manufacture imperfection of wearables' vibration motors and accelerometers. When a wearable equipped with WatchID tries to perform a critical operation (e.g., mobile payment or online purchasing), it triggers WatchID to verify the authenticity of the operation by sending the user's user credentials and device credentials to a remote server. Figure 4 illustrates the overview of the our system design. WatchID first performs *Programmable Vibration Signal Generation* to generate a vibration signal that has been pre-registered with the

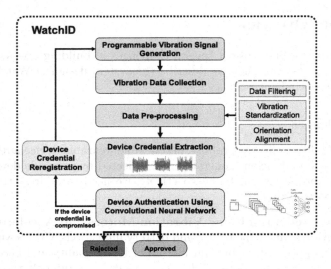

Fig. 4. Overview of the WatchID system.

remote server using the wearable's built-in vibration motor. Meanwhile, the system performs *Vibration Data Collection* to capture the vibration signals propagating from the vibration motor by the wearable's accelerometers. Then, the *Data Pre-processing* module performs on the vibration signals: removing high-frequency noises, standardizing sensing data, and aligning the signals' orientations to ensure the robustness of the system with different activities and poses in practice. Next, WatchID extracts the vibration-based device credential by examining the energy of the vibration signals in *Device Credential Extraction*. The device credentials will be transmitted to the remote server and perform *Device Authentication Using Convolutional Neural Network* to verify the identity of the wearable using an advanced deep neural network. In particular, we develop a lightweight convolutional neural network (CNN) to abstract a high-dimensional representation of the device credential and determine whether the representation is highly close to the device credential pre-registered with the server. If the answer is positive, WatchID verifies the identity of the user's device and approves the critical operation. Otherwise, WatchID will issue an rejection.

One significant advantage of WatchID is that WatchID allows the user to use the same device but change the vibration-based device credentials by reprogramming the vibration motor to induce new, unique vibration characteristics as device credentials. Compared to traditional device authentication methods that use unchangeable device credentials, WatchID is more practical and convenient if the device credentials are compromised. When WatchID rejects a device authentication, it sends the user's wearable device a warning message about the attempted unauthorized operation. The user then has the option to use a different vibration-based device credential by initiating *Device Credential Reregistration*. Here the user just needs to generate vibration signals of a new pattern on the wearable, preprocess the collected accelerometer data, extract the vibration-based device credentials, and send them to the server for registration through a secure channel. The user can define his/her own vibration pattern in terms of vibration strengths and duration or use factory-predefined patterns. After the registration, the user will be able to use the new device credential to perform the device authentication.

6 Watch Identification Using Vibration

6.1 Reprogrammable Vibration Signal Generation and Vibration Data Collection

The major advantage of WatchID is that the vibration-based device credentials are reprogrammable on the same device. Specifically, a vibration signal can be mainly determined by four independent parameters: *vibration strength*, *vibration duration*, *sleep duration* (i.e., idle time between two vibrations), and *vibration frequency*. Using different combinations of these four parameters, we can generate a large group of vibration patterns used for distinctive vibration-based device credentials.

In this work, we use Google WearOS (i.e., v2.27) [16] to configure the vibration strengths and vibration durations of the built-in vibration motors in commodity wearable via the *VibrationEffect* method. Here the vibration strength is an integer value between 0 to 255, and the vibration duration and sleep duration can be any length of time in seconds. We discover that the vibration strength values do not reflect the amplitude of the generated vibration signals. Moreover, the same vibration strength will produce different readings from different wearable's accelerometers (see, e.g., Fig. 2). This device-wise input-output relationship further validate our usages of vibration characteristics in wearables for the purpose of device authentication.

While there are many possible vibration patterns that can be generated as the vibration-based device credentials, not all of them are suitable for device authentication. The rule of thumb is that the vibration signals should be short in time (i.e., about 1s in our work) so that the device authentication process will have almost no impact to the user experience in using the device for normal applications. In addition, when reprogramming a vibration signal to replace the existing vibration-based device credential, it is important to choose a vibration signal that are much different from the previous one for better security. In this work, we use five vibration signals with different levels of the vibration strength as shown in Fig. 3 (b). We note users can also create their own vibration patterns.

6.2 Data Pre-processing

The accelerometers capture vibration signals carrying the unique vibrations characteristics of wearables as well as accelerations caused by human body movements and gravity. To ensure the system can extract the vibration-based device credentials accurately, we adopt the following methods to pre-process the vibration signals captured by the wearable's accelerometers.

Data Filtering. When collecting the vibration signals for device authentication on a wearable, the accelerometers also capture noises (e.g., ambient sound and thermal noise) and interferences (e.g., human body movements and background music). WatchID filters the accelerometer data using a band-pass filter with the passband centered at the vibration frequency of the generated vibration signals to mitigate these noises and interferences. Specifically, we first use the fast Fourier transform to discover that the range of all our wearables' vibration frequencies is between 11.3 Hz and 24.8 Hz. In addition, the frequency of most human activities is below 10 Hz [4]. Therefore we develop a Butterworth band-pass using the cutting-off frequencies of 10 Hz and 24.8 Hz to filter the vibration noises and interferences outside of this range.

Vibration Standardization. The vibration signals collected by a wearable's accelerometer are accelerations of three dimensions along x, y, and z axis. The range of values differ greatly among the three axes, even more among different device models. To ensure the comparability of data, the system applies the Z-score standardization method [21] to the accelerometer readings from each axis as follows:

$$a' = \frac{a - \mu}{\delta},$$

where a is a vibration acceleration value along a certain axis, μ and δ are the mean and standard deviation of the accelerations along the same axis respectively. After the standardization, the accelerometer data (a') is centered at 0 and scaled to have the standard deviation of 1. Thus, the data from different devices and dimensions are made to be comparable.

Orientation Alignment. Usually the orientation of a wearable keeps changing because its owner's wrist does not stay still for the most of the time. As a result, the directions of the three axes of the built-in accelerometers are varying accordingly. To ensure that our system can obtain the same device credentials regardless of the wearable's orientation, we need to subtract the gravitational acceleration (9.8 m/s^2) from the accelerometer readings projected in each of the three directions. In particular, we adopt a low-pass filter [3] for this purpose:

$$a''_i = (1 - \beta)(a_i - g_i), \qquad i = \{x, y, z\},$$

$$\beta = \frac{dT}{t + dT},$$

where g_i and a_i are the projection of the gravitational acceleration and raw acceleration captured by the accelerometer along the i-th axis respectively, β is a filter factor determined by filter's time constant t and event delivery rate dT. Here, a''_i will be used by the system as the aligned acceleration. In this work, we empirically choose β to be 0.2.

6.3 Device Credential Extraction

After pre-processing the accelerometer data, WatchID needs to extract the vibration-based device credential and send them to the remote server for device authentication. To ensure the robustness and accuracy of WatchID, we need to precisely determine the starting and ending points of the vibration signals used as the device credential. In particular, WatchID derives the short-time energy of the pre-processed accelerometer readings based on a sliding window:

$$E(t) = \sum_{n=t}^{t+w} a^2(n),$$

where $a(n)$ is the accelerometer reading at the time n and w is the size of the sliding window. The system examines $E(t)$ and determines the starting and ending points of the device credential depending on whether $E(t)$ is above or below the threshold, respectively. We empirically determine the threshold based on our study with three volunteers and five watches. We find that even if the volunteers' arms shake slightly, the short-time energy after Z-score standardization does not exceed the value of 0.4 for the Fossil watches and 0.01 for the Moto watches. Therefore, we set the threshold to 0.4 and 0.01 for the two types of watches respectively. In practice, this process can be done fairly easily and quickly. In addition, due to sampling variations in accelerometers, the number of samples of the same vibration duration may be slightly different. To solve this problem, we employ the cubic spline interpolation [12] to ensure the extracted device credentials have the same number of samples every time. Specifically, we interpolate each device credential to 200 samples, which can well preserve the details of a device credential captured by the maximum sampling rate (i.e., 50 Hz) of wearables' accelerometers within 4 s.

6.4 Device Authentication Using Convolutional Neural Network

While the vibration-based device credentials are observed to be unique for different wearables, modeling based analyses can quantitatively answer the question whether the set of device credentials of a particular device is a legitimate one. Toward this end, we propose to train a 1-dimensional convolutional neural network (1D CNN) on the fine-grained representations of device credentials and perform the device authentication on the remote server. With this approach, there is no need for the feature extraction process, which is required for traditional machine learning methods. Instead we can directly utilize the device credentials after pre-processing without loss of any information.

1D CNN has been used for signal processing and acceleration data analysis [1, 18,20]. In this work, we design a 1D CNN with 4 convolutional layers, 2 max pooling layers, 1 flatten layer, 1 dropout layer and 1 fully connected layer. The parameters of our 1D CNN are specified in Fig. 5. In the first two convolutional layers, we define 64 kernels with a kernel size of 2. Max pooling layer is introduced to reduce the complexity of the output of previous layer. In the third and fourth convolutional layers, 256 kernels with a kernel size of 2 are designed to learn more advanced features. A dropout layer is added to avoid overfitting and improve the generalization of the CNN model. In the fully connected layer, a softmax activation function is used to reduce the features to a vector of 2. We use the

Fig. 5. Architecture of the 1D CNN used in WatchID.

binary cross entropy as the loss function. An Adam optimizer [19] with a learning rate of 0.001 is used to optimize the neural network. The output of the softmax activation function contains the probabilities of two labels (i.e., 1 for legitimate device and 0 otherwise). Upon receiving a device credential, WatchID transforms the device credential into a 4×200 vector and feeds the vector into the 1D CNN to determine whether the received device credential matches the pre-registered device credential of the legitimate wearable.

7   Evaluation

7.1   Experimental Hardware and Scenarios

We use three Fossil Gen 5 and two Moto 360 Gen 3 smartwatches to evaluate the performance of WatchID. An app is developed to collect the vibration-based device credentials on these smartwatches using Google Wear OS (version 2.27) [16]. The collected device credentials are downloaded to a desktop to perform the model training and device authentication.

We evaluate the system under two scenarios: *on desk* and *on wrist* for practical usage situations. In the first scenario, we collect the vibration-based device credentials of each smartwatch when it is fixed on the desk, while in the second, we carry the operation when the watch is worn on a human wrist.

7.2   Data Collection

In the *on desk* scenario, we focus on studying the efficacy of the vibration-based device credentials. For each smartwatch, we collect 120 device credentials. In the *on wrist* scenario, we collect device credentials with different settings on the smartwatches to evaluate the efficacy and robustness of the system. In particular, we conduct experiments with 5 different vibration patterns, and 3 jamming attacks under different sound noises. In total, we have two participants collecting around 600 device credentials in the *on desk* scenario and 1680 device credentials in the *on wrist* scenario across over 4 weeks.

Unless stated otherwise, we use the vibration strength of 50 with 1 s vibration duration and 1 s sleep duration to generate vibrations. We use the maximum sampling rate of the smartwatches' accelerometers (i.e., 50 Hz) to collect data. We randomly select 30 device credentials from a legitimate device and 30 device credentials from the other four watches (as attackers) to construct a training dataset. The rest of the data (i.e., 90 device credentials from the legitimate user and 90 device credentials from the attacker) is used for testing. We repeat the training and testing five times and use the average results to evaluate our system's performance.

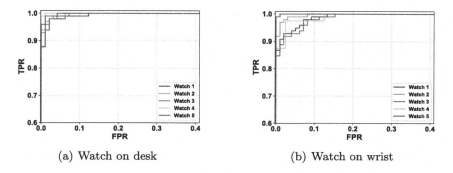

(a) Watch on desk   (b) Watch on wrist

Fig. 6. Overall performance of WatchID with different smartwatches in different scenarios.

7.3   Evaluation Metrics

Precision. Precision is the ratio between the number of device credentials correctly predicted as from the legitimate user (i.e., true positive) to the overall number of the device credentials predicted as from the legitimate user (i.e., true positive + false positive). We want to have a high precision to avoid mistakenly identifying the attacker's device credentials as an legitimate one.

Recall. Recall is the ratio between the number of device credentials correctly predicted as the legitimate (i.e., true positive) to the overall number of legitimate device credentials (i.e., true positive + false negative). A low recall means a sizable amount of legitimate user's device credentials are mistakenly identified as the illegitimate ones. This is not desirable for user experience.

Rejection Rate. We define the rejection rate as the ratio between the number of the attacker's device credentials successfully identified as the illegitimate ones (i.e., true negative) to all the stolen device credentials (i.e., true negative + false positive). We want to achieve a high rejection rate since none of the attacker's device credentials should pass the device authentication.

ROC Curve. ROC curve plots true positive rate (TPR) against false positive rate (FPR). The TPR denotes the rate of the legitimate user's device credentials passing the system, while FPR denotes the rate of the attackers' device credentials passing the system. Through varying prediction thresholds, we can get a series of TPR and FPR and draw ROC curves to evaluate the system performance. The closer to the point $(0, 1)$ the ROC curve, the better the performance. Thus, we choose the TPR and FPR at the point closest to $(0, 1)$ on the ROC curve as our system's optimal performance.

7.4   Overall Performance

We first evaluate the performance of our system with the watch on human wrist or on the desk. For the *on desk* scenario, a watch is horizontally laying on the

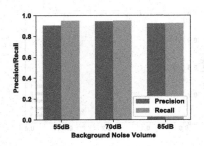

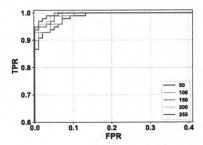

(a) Under jamming attacks.

(b) Watch 1 under five different vibration strengths.

Fig. 7. Performance under jamming attacks and different vibration strengths.

surface of a desk with its face up and its belt taped the desk by sticky tapes. This is quite an ideal case with few impacting factors to disturb the data collection process. For the *on wrist* case, the watch is worn on a person's wrist with his forearm horizontally laying on the desk and the watch facing up. Specifically, 5 smartwatches are used to collect the vibration data. We alternatively select one watch as a legitimate device and the other four watches as attackers. Figure 6 (a) shows the ROC curve of the *on desk* scenario, and we can observe that our system can achieve an average optimal TPR of 98% and FPR of 2% among 5 smartwatches.

For the *on wrist* situation, our system can still achieve an average optimal TPR of 95% and FPR of 5% as shown in Fig. 6 (b). From these two figures, we find that human wrist slightly impacts the performance in our authentication system. Moreover, the two Moto watches (i.e., Watch 4 and 5) have slightly better performance than the three Fossil watches (i.e., Watch 1, 2, and 3). This observation is in line with our observations from Fig. 3 where the two Moto watches have more distinguishable features from the Fossil watches. Overall, those results demonstrate that our system have good authentication performances no matter whether a watch is put on a desk or worn on human wrists. Therefore vibration signals from wearables can indeed serve as a reliable and consistent device credential.

7.5   Effectiveness Under Different Attacks

Against Random Attacks. We first explore the robustness of our system against random attacks. Specifically, we alternatively select two watches out of the five with one as a legitimate watch and the other as an illegitimate watch. Then, we train our system using the device credentials from those two selected watches and use the other three unselected watches to mimick random attacks. Our experimental results show that the three random attackers are always classified as the illegitimate watches by our system with a 100% rejection rate. Therefore our system is robust against random attacks.

Table 1. Performance under jamming attacks.

Noise(dB)	Precision (%)	Recall (%)
55	90.57	95.31
70	94.68	95.31
85	92.51	92.8

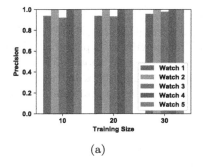
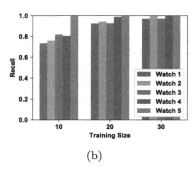

(a)   (b)

Fig. 8. Performance under different training sizes.

Against Jamming Attacks. We next test our system under jamming attacks by playing different volumes (i.e., 55 dB, 70 dB, 85 dB) of background sound noises. These volumes are selected to correspond to various real-life environmental noises. For instance, the average decibel level of human speech is near 55 dB. Living room music, radio or TV-audio, and sound of vacuum cleaner are close to 70 dB. Power mowers, motorcycles, diesel trucks can produce noises about 85 dB. As shown in Fig. 7 (a) and Table 1, our system can achieve an average precision and recall around 92% and 94% under the jamming attacks at various typical audio volumes. This result indicates that our system can still perform well under realistic jamming attacks.

Against Credential Stealing Attacks. Here we assume an attacker has gained access to a legitimate user's device credential and our system has informed the user to reset his/her device credential. Specifically, we select one watch as the legitimate device and reset its credential by using a new vibration strength (i.e., 100) from the original strength (i.e., 50 by default). The other four watches are treated as illegitimate ones with their original device credentials.

After the legitimate user's device credential is reset, we retrain a new 1D CNN model after the same data collection and preprocessing steps. To simulate the credential stealing attacks, the attacker will still try to use the previous legitimate user's device credential to bypass the system. Our experimental result show that this type of requests are denied by our system using the newly trained 1D CNN model with a 100% rejection rate. This demonstrates that reprogrammable WatchID can successfully defend against credential stealing attacks.

7.6 Robustness Under Different Vibration Patterns

Device credential reconfiguration plays an important role in the our system. Hence, we study the robustness of our system under different vibration patterns to generate the device credentials. We know that different vibration strengths of a smartwatch can generate different device credentials as shown in Fig. 3(b). In this study, we test 5 different device credentials of a legitimate user's watch (i.e., Watch 1) by setting 5 different vibration strengths (i.e., 50, 100, 150, 200, 255). And the device credentials of the other four watches (i.e., illegitimate ones) are generated using the same vibration strength (i.e., 50). Figure 7 (b) shows the ROC curves of our system under different vibration patterns. We find that our system has a similar optimal performance (i.e., about 95% in TPR and 5% in FPR) under different vibration patterns. Therefore our system has achieved good authentication results under different levels vibration strengths or associated vibration patterns.

Table 2. Performance under different training sizes (P: Precision (%); R: Recall (%)).

Training size	Watch 1		Watch 2		Watch 3		Watch 4		Watch 5	
	P	R	P	R	P	R	P	R	P	R
10	93.54	72.91	100	75.42	91.82	81.25	100	79.94	100	100
20	93.42	92.17	100	93.88	92.85	92.34	100	98.51	100	100
30	95.54	96.8	100	99.2	97.54	96.85	100	100	100	100

It is also worth noting that a larger vibration strength (e.g., 255) can generate a slightly better performance. However, since a lower vibration strength generates more stable patterns as demonstrated in Sect. 4, we adopt the value of 50 as the default vibration strength in WatchID.

7.7 Impact of Training Size

Amount of data required by an authentication system is an importance parameter in order to ensure and maintain a high level of performance. To study the impact of different data sizes to our system, we generate 10, 20, 30 sets of device credentials for each of the five watches. For a specific size (i.e., 10), we pick one watch (i.e., Watch 1) as a legitimate device and use all the 10 sets of its credentials with the label of 1 as a part of the training data, and pick another 10 sets randomly from the other four watches with the labels of 0 as the other part of the training data. Then WatchID performs the device authentication process for this set of data. Our experimental results are presented in Fig. 8 and Table 2.

We observe that our system can achieve an average precision of 97% using only 10 device credentials for a legitimate device (20 in total). As the size of the training data grows, the system performance improves accordingly. More specifically, the average precision and recall reach 98% and 99% respectively when 20 or more device credentials for a legitimate device are used. These results indicate our system can achieve good performance with only a limited number of device credentials. As a result, our system is fast and efficient in training of authentication models with a high level of performance.

8   Conclusion

In this paper, we devise WatchID, a vibration-based device authentication system for wearables. The system can provide an extra layer of security to the traditional user authentication methods without requiring a user's participation. WatchID utilizes the manufacturing imperfections of a wearable's vibration motor, device body, and accelerometers to create unique vibration characteristics, using them as device credentials to determine the wearable's identity. Our system is more practical and convenient than existing methods as the vibration-based device credentials are reprogrammable by changing the vibration patterns on wearables. We extensively study the vibration characteristics of different wearables and develop data pre-processing methods to ensure the system's robustness. We also develop a lightweight CNN model to capture the unique vibration characteristics and predict the wearable's identity under various practical scenarios. Over 2500 vibration-based device credentials are collected in the experiments with five commodity smartwatches across 4 weeks. We demonstrate that our system can achieve an average precision and recall of 98% and 94% under various scenarios of vibration patterns and training sizes. We also show that our system can achieve a 100% rejection rate under different types of attacks.

Acknowledgement. This work was partially supported by the NSF Grants CCF19 09963, CCF2000480, CCF2028858, CCF2028873, CNS1954959, CNS2120276, and CNS 2120350.

References

1. Abdoli, S., Cardinal, P., Koerich, A.L.: End-to-end environmental sound classification using a 1D convolutional neural network. Expert Syst. Appl. **136**, 252–263 (2019)
2. Aloul, F., Zahidi, S., El-Hajj, W.: Two factor authentication using mobile phones. In: 2009 IEEE/ACS International Conference on Computer Systems and Applications, pp. 641–644. IEEE (2009)
3. AndroidDeveloper: Work with raw data, use the accelerometer. https://developer. android.com/guide/topics/sensors/sensors_motion#sensors-motion-accel
4. Antonsson, E.K., Mann, R.W.: The frequency content of gait. J. Biomech. **18**(1), 39–47 (1985)
5. Bojinov, H., Michalevsky, Y., Nakibly, G., Boneh, D.: Mobile device identification via sensor fingerprinting. arXiv preprint arXiv:1408.1416 (2014)
6. Brik, V., Banerjee, S., Gruteser, M., Oh, S.: Wireless device identification with radiometric signatures. In: Proceedings of the 14th ACM International Conference on Mobile Computing and Networking, pp. 116–127 (2008)

7. Clancy, T.C., Kiyavash, N., Lin, D.J.: Secure smartcardbased fingerprint authentication. In: Proceedings of the 2003 ACM SIGMM Workshop on Biometrics Methods and Applications, pp. 45–52 (2003)
8. Danev, B., Zanetti, D., Capkun, S.: On physical-layer identification of wireless devices. ACM Comput. Surv. (CSUR) **45**(1), 1–29 (2012)
9. Das, A., Borisov, N., Caesar, M.: Do you hear what i hear? Fingerprinting smart devices through embedded acoustic components. In: Proceedings of the 2014 ACM SIGSAC Conference on Computer and Communications Security, pp. 441–452 (2014)
10. Das, A., Borisov, N., Caesar, M.: Tracking mobile web users through motion sensors: attacks and defenses. In: NDSS (2016)
11. Dey, S., Roy, N., Xu, W., Choudhury, R.R., Nelakuditi, S.: AccelPrint: imperfections of accelerometers make smartphones trackable. In: NDSS (2014)
12. Dukkipati, R.V.: Numerical methods (2010)
13. Eberz, S., Paoletti, N., Roeschlin, M., Kwiatkowska, M., Martinovic, I., Patané, A.: Broken hearted: how to attack ECG biometrics (2017)
14. Fujii, H., Shigematsu, N., Kurokawa, H., Nakagawa, T.: Telelogin: a two-factor two-path authentication technique using caller id. NTT Tech. Rev. **6**(8), 1–6 (2008)
15. Garcia-Romero, D., Espy-Wilson, C.Y.: Automatic acquisition device identification from speech recordings. In: 2010 IEEE International Conference on Acoustics, Speech and Signal Processing. pp. 1806–1809. IEEE (2010)
16. Google: Wear OS. https://wearos.google.com/
17. Jøsang, A., Sanderud, G.: Security in mobile communications: challenges and opportunities. In: Proceedings of the Australasian Information Security Workshop Conference on ACSW Frontiers 2003-Volume 21, pp. 43–48. Citeseer (2003)
18. Kim, J.W., et al.: A study on fault classification of machining center using acceleration data based on 1D CNN algorithm. J. Korean Soc. Manufact. Process Eng. **18**(9), 29–35 (2019)
19. Kingma, D.P., Ba, J.: Adam: a method for stochastic optimization. arXiv preprint arXiv:1412.6980 (2014)
20. Kiranyaz, S., Avci, O., Abdeljaber, O., Ince, T., Gabbouj, M., Inman, D.J.: 1D convolutional neural networks and applications: a survey. Mech. Syst. Signal Process. **151**, 107398 (2021)
21. Kreyszig, E.: Advanced Engineering Mathematics 10th Edition (2009)
22. Lashkari, A.H., Farmand, S., Zakaria, D., Bin, O., Saleh, D., et al.: Shoulder surfing attack in graphical password authentication. arXiv preprint arXiv:0912.0951 (2009)
23. Li, H., et al.: VocalPrint: a MM wave-based unmediated vocal sensing system for secure authentication. IEEE Trans. Mob. Comput. (2021)
24. Lin, F., Song, C., Zhuang, Y., Xu, W., Li, C., Ren, K.: Cardiac scan: a non-contact and continuous heart-based user authentication system. In: Proceedings of the 23rd Annual International Conference on Mobile Computing and Networking, pp. 315–328 (2017)
25. Liu, J., Chen, Y., Dong, Y., Wang, Y., Zhao, T., Yao, Y.D.: Continuous user verification via respiratory biometrics. In: IEEE INFOCOM 2020-IEEE Conference on Computer Communications, pp. 1–10. IEEE (2020)
26. Liu, J., Wang, Y., Chen, Y., Yang, J., Chen, X., Cheng, J.: Tracking vital signs during sleep leveraging off-the-shelf WiFi. In: Proceedings of the 16th ACM International Symposium on Mobile Ad Hoc Networking and Computing, pp. 267–276 (2015)
27. Polak, A.C., Dolatshahi, S., Goeckel, D.L.: Identifying wireless users via transmitter imperfections. IEEE J. Sel. Areas Commun. **29**(7), 1469–1479 (2011)

28. Polak, A.C., Goeckel, D.L.: RF fingerprinting of users who actively mask their identities with artificial distortion. In: 2011 Conference Record of the Forty Fifth Asilomar Conference on Signals, Systems and Computers (ASILOMAR), pp. 270–274. IEEE (2011)
29. Ratha, N.K., Bolle, R.M., Pandit, V.D., Vaish, V.: Robust fingerprint authentication using local structural similarity. In: Proceedings Fifth IEEE Workshop on Applications of Computer Vision, pp. 29–34. IEEE (2000)
30. Ren, Y., Chen, Y., Chuah, M.C., Yang, J.: Smartphone based user verification leveraging gait recognition for mobile healthcare systems. In: 2013 IEEE International Conference on Sensing, Communications and Networking (SECON), pp. 149–157. IEEE (2013)
31. Revenkar, P., Anjum, A., Gandhare, W.: Secure iris authentication using visual cryptography. arXiv preprint arXiv:1004.1748 (2010)
32. Sanchez-Reillo, R., Sanchez-Avila, C.: Iris recognition with low template size. In: Bigun, J., Smeraldi, F. (eds.) AVBPA 2001. LNCS, vol. 2091, pp. 324–329. Springer, Heidelberg (2001). https://doi.org/10.1007/3-540-45344-X_47
33. Shi, C., Liu, J., Borodinov, N., Leao, B., Chen, Y.: Towards environment-independent behavior-based user authentication using WiFi. In: 2020 IEEE 17th International Conference on Mobile Ad Hoc and Sensor Systems (MASS), pp. 666–674. IEEE (2020)
34. Sun, L., Wang, Y., Cao, B., Yu, P.S., Srisa-an, W., Leow, A.D.: Sequential keystroke behavioral biometrics for mobile user identification via multi-view deep learning. In: Altun, Y., et al. (eds.) ECML PKDD 2017. LNCS (LNAI), vol. 10536, pp. 228–240. Springer, Cham (2017). https://doi.org/10.1007/978-3-319-71273-4_19
35. Trippel, T., Weisse, O., Xu, W., Honeyman, P., Fu, K.: WALNUT: waging doubt on the integrity of mems accelerometers with acoustic injection attacks. In: 2017 IEEE European Symposium on Security and Privacy (EuroS&P), pp. 3–18. IEEE (2017)
36. Wazid, M., Zeadally, S., Das, A.K.: Mobile banking: evolution and threats: malware threats and security solutions. IEEE Consum. Electron. Mag. 8(2), 56–60 (2019)
37. Zeng, Y., Pande, A., Zhu, J., Mohapatra, P.: WearIA: wearable device implicit authentication based on activity information. In: 2017 IEEE 18th International Symposium on A World of Wireless, Mobile and Multimedia Networks (WoWMoM), pp. 1–9. IEEE (2017)
38. Zhang, Q., Zhou, D., Zeng, X.: HeartID: a multiresolution convolutional neural network for ECG-based biometric human identification in smart health applications. IEEE Access 5, 11805–11816 (2017)
39. Zhang, Y., Xia, P., Luo, J., Ling, Z., Liu, B., Fu, X.: Fingerprint attack against touch-enabled devices. In: Proceedings of the Second ACM Workshop on Security and Privacy in Smartphones and Mobile Devices, pp. 57–68 (2012)
40. Zhao, T., Wang, Y., Liu, J., Chen, Y., Cheng, J., Yu, J.: TrueHeart: continuous authentication on wrist-worn wearables using ppg-based biometrics. In: IEEE INFOCOM 2020-IEEE Conference on Computer Communications, pp. 30–39. IEEE (2020)
41. Zhou, Z., Diao, W., Liu, X., Zhang, K.: Acoustic fingerprinting revisited: generate stable device id stealthily with inaudible sound. In: Proceedings of the 2014 ACM SIGSAC Conference on Computer and Communications Security, pp. 429–440 (2014)

Premises Based Smart Door Chains System Using IoT Cloud

Abdul Hannan[1] , Faisal Hussain[2]([✉]) , Sehrish Munawar Cheema[1],
and Ivan Miguel Pires[3]

[1] University of Management and Technology, Sialkot, Pakistan
abdul.hannan@skt.umt.edu.pk
[2] Al-Khwarizmi Institute of Computer Science, University of Engineering & Technology,
Lahore 54890, Pakistan
faisal.hussain.engr@gmail.com
[3] Instituto de Telecomunicações, Universidade da Beira Interior, 6200-001 Covilhã, Portugal
impires@it.ubi.pt

Abstract. Internet of 'things (IoT) allows people and objects to be connected anytime, anywhere, in any way/shape and function that can build a dynamic network. IoT is a critical enabling technology for smart home facilities like smart locks, automatic light control, smoke detection, temperature monitoring, etc. With the adoption of these systems, security and privacy have come up as the primary concerns. Due to the security threats, developing such a system that can smartly identify and restrict the people coming within the house premises is needed. Although these systems exist in the modern world where the intruder's entry is based on authentication, these systems provide security until the intruder enters the house's premises. We propose a framework for a smart door chain system (SDCS) to ensure the home's security even after the visitor enters the house to overcome this security issue. The proposed framework provides access to visitor's categories that are family, friend, and unknown. The SDCS has a synchronized chain of doors that are unlocked accordingly after the authentication of a visitor. By implementing the proposed framework, it is determined that the security of the house increases compared to the security provided by the previous automated systems. The proposed SDCS framework is beneficial, especially for old ages, disabled and working people if any nasty situation is raised at home in their absence.

Keywords: Internet of Things · IoT · Home automation · Smart door · Smart home security · Smart home · Smart systems

1 Introduction

A home is where you dream or want to live in a long day of sorrow. People on return to home used to turn ON the lights, close the doors, play their favorite music, and many other things by using mobile app interface operate with virtual switches and sliders to monitor

T. Hara and H. Yamaguchi (Eds.): MobiQuitous 2021, LNICST 419, pp. 834–846, 2022.
https://doi.org/10.1007/978-3-030-94822-1_54

and control appliances. The IoT or Internet of Things is a system in which computing devices, physical objects, and various machines are interlinked via the Internet forming wired or unwired network infrastructure [1]. The term IoT was first coined in 1999 by Kevin Ashton [2]. In today's era, smart devices are commonly used to collect and control data and share information between them. Moreover, with the advancement in nanotechnology, microprocessors and small chips are used to convert simple physical devices into IoT devices. IoT joins the physical devices through the Internet and performs sensing, collecting, storing, and processing information or data [3].

Fig. 1. Home automation system

The smart city is a tremendous application of IoT incorporating vast fields such as automating street lighting, managing transportation, video surveillance system, auto management of parking, municipal Wi-Fi, fire monitoring, weather forecast, measuring air quality, and managing electricity and waste and water [4, 5]. IoT enables chat-based, text, audio, and video-based commands fitted with natural language processing to control home devices and make the earth feel better [6]. In current circumstances, nearly 71% of the total use of IoT is in industry, and the rest of 29% use is under consumer [7]. Home atomization is emerging day by day, and it has gained a lot of attention in both research and the commercial field. As shown in Fig. 1, automated systems via different mediums have made it possible to reduce energy consumption [8]. Although wired networks were in demand at the early stages of the home automation systems, nowadays, wired networks are replaced with wireless communication to avoid the complex setup.

Furthermore, the advanced wireless systems are more extensible and flexible than the previous ones [9]. A wireless smart home is getting popular nowadays because of its portability, flexibility, and lower installation cost. It reduces the effort of human beings to manage devices at home remotely and is especially beneficial for working people [10]. Low-cost sensing devices and Wi-Fi-enabled smart devices are commonly used to communicate with people or systems [11].

Traditionally, physical keys, security cards, passwords, or patterns are used to lock or unlock the doors. So, carrying out a bundle of keys, Cards for different locks is clumsy. It also increases the chance of losing or misplacing, causing identity fraud and robbery. Moreover, it is very hectic for a household to enter a passcode every time enters the house. To overcome this problem, we propose a framework for a smart door chain system (SDCS) to ensure the home's security even after the visitor enters the house. The proposed SDCS framework requires no physical keys to lock or unlock the doors. Moreover, it also enhances the security and privacy of the home as security is one of the most critical elements in everyone's life, which cannot be compromised at any cost. So, to keep the house safe from unknowns or strangers, the proposed SDCS framework restricts the entry of every visitor unless or until the system has recognized them.

The proposed SDCS framework is an IoT-based efficient system that provides an optimal solution for breach of privacy by giving access to the home premises only to the authorized visitors. Moreover, for ease of people, the system is fully automated. The main aim of this framework is to make the home secure so that the people feel safer and more protected in their premises. The critical contribution of this work can be summarized as follows:

- The incoming visitors' identification is based on three defined categories (Family, Friend, and Unknown) to keep the house safe from unknowns or strangers.
- We synchronized the smart doors of the building in the form of the chain according to the respective building blueprint by establishing a connection among the smart doors chain and the cloud server to authenticate the incoming person.
- We proposed a hybrid computing architecture, i.e., edge and cloud processing, for decentralized computing tasks to minimize computational delay and increase response time.
- We notify the insiders of the house about visitors' arrival by sending text and speech notifications.

The rest of the paper is organized as follows: Sect. 2 discusses the literature review. Section 3 explains the proposed SDCS framework. The workflow of the proposed system is presented in Sect. 4. Experimental Analysis with results & discussion is described in Sect. 5. Finally, Sect. 6 concludes the work.

2 Literature Review

IoT envisioned a global network of devices and machines to interact with each other [1]. As a result, IoT has been recognized as a future technology paradigm and achieving vast attention in many domains due to its features like connectivity, safety, sensing, intelligence, dynamic nature, scalability, less energy consumption [12–15].

Almost everything is getting digitalized and automatic, so the concept of home automation is implementing day by day [16, 17]. With the implementation of home automation, home security has become one of the most concerning issues [18–23].

As the house doors are the essential means of accessing the premises of the specific house, to make the homes safer, we need to make the house doors secure considering all the privacy and security aspects. For this purpose, Smart locks used in traditional doors are already introduced and named smart doors. Therefore, using smart doors instead of conventional doors ultimately opens the door to a new set of security and privacy issues, such as by taking control of surveillance devices or activating false alarms, user's private data can be accessed. Therefore, people are reluctant to adopt smart home technologies due to different security attacks [20].

Research conducted by Refni Wahyuni et al. developed a system for home security by using WEMOS D1, Buzzer, and HC-SR501 sensors for telegram notification when a theft or unknown person enters the house [24]. WEMOS D1 processes the pear sensor for motion detection and buzzer for putting an alarm in case of theft [24]. Balakrishna Gokaraju et al. implemented home security by comparing the design and implementation of ARM microprocessor ATmega microprocessor [25]. In a study conducted by G. M. Sultan Muhmud Rana et al., cost-saving and flexible home security systems were designed and implemented [26].

A study presented a motion detection technique for home security systems using IoT. Two low-cost motion detectors named pyroelectric infrared radial (PIR) and microwave sensors implemented this technique. Raspberry Pi acts as the leading platform to receive signals from sensors and notify a user when an intruder is detected [27]. The deep learning-based face recognition technique was proposed by A. R. Syafeeza1 et al. Raspberry Pi acts as the main controller to process face detection, locking, and youth systems. A camera captures the image of an intruder and enables the user to access the door control via IoT [28].

An architecture for a cost-effective door sensor was presented with its implementation. The system informs the user about door open events of a house or an office environment through the android application. The proposed architecture experimented with an Arduino compatible Elegoo Mega 2560 Microcontroller and Raspberry Pi to communicate with a web server that implements a RESTful API [29]. An IoT-based structure and model was proposed by E.Shirisha et al. for an automated earth system that supports a variety of earth tools, for example, an energy management system. The system uses a Raspberry Pi and a Wi-Fi module to control the devices via a mobile app using Google assistant. It also customized their project to a home protection system using ESP32 camera Node MCU module to notify the house owners of intruders' entry [30].

An efficient critical generation method named Triangle Based Security (TBSA) was proposed by Pirbhulal et al. Low power Wi-Fi was integrated with WSNs to develop an innovative IoT-based smart home for secure data transmission between sensor nodes over sensor nodes extended coverage of the network. The proposed TBSA algorithm observed relatively low energy consumption [31]. A smart wireless home security system was built to notify the house owner of trespass or raise the alarm as an option. The authors ensured that the same experimental setup could also be used for home automation. The system used a TI-CC3200 Launchpad board embedded with a micro-controller and an onboard Wi-Fi shield to control and manage electrical appliances in the home [32]. Two IoT frameworks NETPI and BLYNK hardware agnostic with cloud, websites, security systems, deep learning, smartphones, and data mining. A system using NETPI was proposed to manage various NODEMCU controllers within a single framework and to monitor home appliances remotely [33]. In [34], Pirbhulal et al. discussed a resource allocation model named 'MMSA' for implementing energy, security, drain and cost factors in IoT-based systems. Experimental analysis of MMSA demonstrates its outperformance incorporating security and mobility factors with optimal resources allocation. The aforementioned related studies discussed the security challenges in home automation systems and proposed solutions, but these solutions are either costly or inappropriate or consume more energy.

3   Proposed Framework

The proposed framework for a smart door chain system (SDCS) consists of five stages. These stages include data collection, face recognition, user authentication, owner access, and action triggering, as shown in Fig. 2. The detailed description of each stage is shown below:

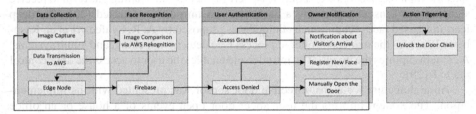

Fig. 2. Block diagram of the proposed framework

3.1   Data Collection

In this stage, the incoming visitor or intruder's face image is captured and sent to the Edge Node for the face detection process. The detected face image is sent to the Amazon Web Service (AWS) cloud server for recognition. The Raspberry pi (microprocessor) acts as an Edge Node, which has a camera mounted on it, to capture the picture of a visitor at run time. The edge node sent data to AWS S3 bucket storage and AWS Rekognition module. AWS S3 bucket storage is used to store the dataset of categories, namely friends, family, and unknown. Each category class starts with a unique ID such as Family = Famxx, Friends = Frxx. The dataset contains the images of the persons belonging to the friends and family categories. The dataset includes 20 images; 10 belong to the family category, and ten are from the friend category. Every image has a unique face Id. The face ids corresponding to all images are shown below in Table 1 and Table 2:

Table 1. Family dataset

Image Name	Face Id
Fam01	'a4405fe3-797b-4235-9c07-12b3250549f6'
Fam02	'83c3875d-8ad9-4d48-a91f-7c1a25275e87'
Fam03	'99d832d4-a251-497f-ba7b-824b75ebd672'
Fam04	'3364a3c3-0c52-4ade-b843-1356c6b3b605'
Fam05	'4a6e01f6-4c48-4422-ae18-dbbd41549cca'
Fam06	'11074d02-6bc7-441e-aae6-3afa3093ef03'
Fam07	'58dee87f-aff2-4842-8370-2472d148f1d9'
Fam08	'fbd3ea99-3ac7-4f5b-a175-41bd6df5eebf''
Fam09	'eff90b32-c8d5-4bfb-81ee-7000aa2f034d'
Fam10	'c3702087-e99f-4a10-8f38-04f565f257fa'

Table 2. Friends' dataset

Image Name	Face Id
Fr01	'e5a4c8fa-66d0-46cd-a0a2-d28638690cf1'
Fr02	'be1bd738-6b4b-486a-a727-becd4c5a7a9f'
Fr03	'3f119329-5090-4a31-acdb-439cad3488b4'
Fr04	'63562c5f-0bcb-4b2d-9cf0-fec82eb185cc'
Fr05	'fa7bb870-39b2-4c36-9d4f-a9da2d4ba1f6'
Fr06	'91fbc9dd-c286-4488-a348-82d22415c79a'
Fr07	'f9a17d59-3f4f-42c9-829d-3c47821ca4e0'
Fr08	'e3d52ed3-3d1d-4f7e-be62-e74876ed302d'
Fr09	97362a21-71cb-4d1b-a33e-34fa0718baa7'
Fr10	'8be3abe2-ba82-464c-a5a2-523e828a01f4'

3.2 Face Recognition on AWS

In this stage, the captured face detected image is sent to the AWS Face Rekognition module for recognition with the already defined categorized face images dataset. After face comparison with the AWS S3 bucket dataset, the face recognition result is sent back to the edge node to triggering the smart door chain pattern. Moreover, the connection of the edge node is also established with the firebase cloud database to send the categorized face comparison data. It is ultimately sent to all smart doors based on the action triggering module.

3.3   User Authentication

In this stage, the user is authenticated based on the comparison result received from the firebase. However, if the incoming visitor's picture is matched with more than 75% confidence index with any one of the face pictures placed in AWS categorized dataset, then they are declared as an authorized person, and the user "Access Granted" is enabled to get the access of the in-house premises according to the class category smart door pattern rule. On the other hand, if the visitor's face is not recognized after the comparison process, they have declared a person, and the user "Access Granted" module is in disable state.

3.4   Owner Notification

This stage provides an owner android-based interface to perform multiple actions such as register new faces, switching smart doors chain mode, and getting voice notifications about the incoming visitor. Moreover, if an unknown person arrives, the owner has an option in the application to register a new face, and user "Access Denied" is granted. However, the owner still wants to give access to in-house premises to the incoming visitor, and then it is done by using the "Switch Mode" to manual for smart doors chain pattern.

3.5   Action Triggering

This stage is liable for ongoing activities such as unlocking the door chain for a specific time interval according to the category. Moreover, the incoming visitor is recognized as an authorized person. Then, the chain of doors is opened for that visitor according to the respective category to whom the incoming intruder belongs.

4   Workflow of the System

Figure 3 represents the hierarchy of the proposed system. The proposed mechanism requires that whenever an intruder arrives, they have to stand in front of a camera in a particular line of the frame for at least 30 s so that the runtime picture of the visitor is captured more precisely. We have used the Amazon web services to store the dataset of two categories, namely friends and family, to the AWS collection. First, the intruder captured image is sent to the edge node module. Then, the face is detected on the edge node to reduce the computation delay on the AWS cloud service. Once the face is detected, the image is directed to the AWS face recognition module for face recognition, respective to the predefined stored categories of the incoming visitor. It matches the intruder face image with the Aws data collection category. The action triggering module is enabled once the user is authenticated. The comparison result is received on the edge node, which is ultimately passed to the real-time database (firebase). After that, the edge node unlocks the respective door chain according to the category for a specific time interval. The doors are closed automatically after that time interval.

In contrast, if the incoming visitor is declared an unauthorized person after the comparison, then the SDCS considered that person in the unknown category. In this class, house residents can switch the door lock mode from "automatic" to "manual" to give them access to the house premises. You have to register that face by using the android application as per the criteria mentioned above.

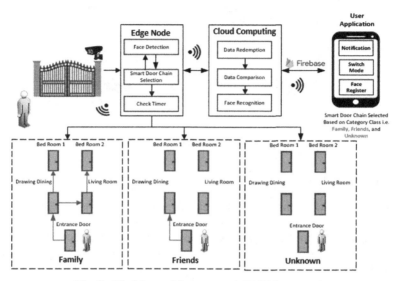

Fig. 3. Workflow of the proposed SDCS framework

5   Experimental Analysis

5.1   Experimental Setup

Figure 4 shows the proposed system architecture. Initially, the incoming visitor's picture is captured by the pi camera mounted on the microcontroller. Then the captured image is passed to AWS for comparison (face recognition). Microcontroller received that comparison result and further passed that result to firebase real-time database. After that, the Arduinos are placed on the doors received from firebase and then unlock the door chain according to the category. An Android application's connection is also established with firebase, and it is developed for performing the following tasks; "Notification about visitor's arrival", "Manually open the doors" (whenever required), and "Register new face" (if an unknown arrives).

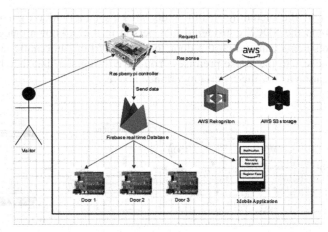

Fig. 4. System architecture of the SDCS

5.2 Performance Evaluation

The proposed smart door chain scheme is evaluated based on two performance metrics, i.e., accuracy and error rate. The parameters as defined as:

Accuracy: It is defined as the ability of the system to correctly classify the image of family and friend as family and friend respectively and other persons as an "unknown". It describes the ratio of correct predictions concerning all samples. mathematically, it is expressed in Eq. (1):

$$Accuracy = \frac{TP + TN}{TP + TN + FP + FN} \tag{1}$$

Error Rate: The inaccuracy of predicted output values is termed the error of the method. It is also defined the proportion of cases where the prediction is wrong. Mathematically, it is expressed Eq. (2):

$$ErrorRate = \frac{|\text{Approximate Value} - \text{Exact Value}|}{|\text{Exact Value}|} \tag{2}$$

The performance of the proposed SDCS framework is successfully tested. Two face recognition techniques are compared to get the one with the highest efficiency and accuracy between HAAR and SDCS. We compared a typical face recognition algorithm (HAAR) and the proposed mechanism (SDCS) in terms of percentage similarity index. Our proposed face recognition mechanism (SDCS) employs hybrid computing architecture, i.e., edge and computational cloud nodes. Thus, SDCS is more effective for face recognition than the traditional HAAR algorithm. However, the percentage similarity index of the proposed system didn't drastically affect the system efficiency, as shown in Fig. 5.

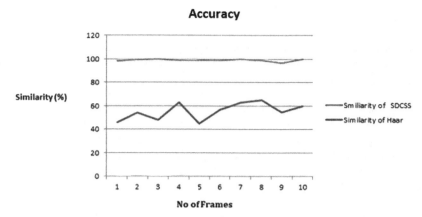

Fig. 5. Accuracy comparison of the proposed SDCS with HAAR algorithm

The error rate of the SDCS is computed by fixing a threshold at >60%. If the confidence value lies between 61–100%, the system recognizes the intruder and identifies them according to its predefined category. As the distance from the camera view focus increases, the confidence value starts to decrease. For example, Fig. 6 depicts, as the intruder goes beyond the camera's view, i.e., the distance greater than 29 cm, the mounted camera on the edge node will not capture the face image, increasing the error rate of the proposed system.

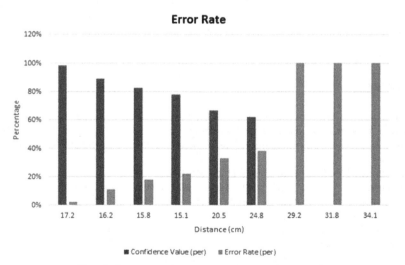

Fig. 6. Error rate of the proposed SDCS framework

6 Conclusion

The proposed framework for a smart door chain system (SDCS) is a real-time system that follows the IoT infrastructure. The SDCS framework used digital information such as face recognition through the Raspberry Pi camera for authentication instead of the legacy key system. It uses cloud services to verify the visitor's identity. Data processing and storage activities were done using the cloud server, far better and more efficient than the conventional file storage system. As there is a large amount of information to be stored for the recognition of the visitor, so we used a database. Three categories are specified based on which the visitor is identified, i.e., Family, Friends, and Unknown. In case of any familiar visitor whose data is not already been updated on the cloud server and falls in the third category, an action triggering module is enabled to switch the system mode from "automatic" to "manual" to give them access inside the home premises. The house doors are synchronized in the form of a chain and are unlocked according to each visitor category. SDCS is a source of pleasure and satisfaction for the people worrying about the security of their significance and small assets. Moreover, the proposed system helps the incoming intruder who experienced long-lasting wait due to the household patients, in-house privacy, and efficiently indulging in daily routine tasks.

Acknowledgments. This work is funded by FCT/MEC through national funds and co- funded by FEDER—PT2020 partnership agreement under the project UIDB/50008/2020 (Este trabalho é financiado pela FCT/MEC através de fundos nacionais e cofinanciado pelo FEDER, no âmbito do Acordo de Parceria PT2020 no âmbito do projeto UIDB/50008/2020).

This article is based upon work from COST Action IC1303–AAPELE–Architectures, Algorithms and Protocols for Enhanced Living Environments and COST Action CA16226–SHELD-ON–Indoor living space improvement: Smart Habitat for the Elderly, supported by COST (European Cooperation in Science and Technology). More information in www.cost.eu.

References

1. Ghazanfar, S., Hussain, F., Rehman, A.U., Fayyaz, U.U., Shahzad, F. and Shah, G.A.: March. IoT-flock: An open-source framework for IoT traffic generation. In: 2020 International Conference on Emerging Trends in Smart Technologies (ICETST), pp. 1–6. IEEE (2020)
2. Ashton, K.: That Internet of Things Thing. RFID J. (2009)
3. Mehmood, Y., Ahmad, F., Yaqoob, I., Adnane, A., Imran, M., Guizani, S.: Internet-of-Things-based smart cities: recent advances and challenges. IEEE Commun. Mag. **55**(9), 16–24 (2017). https://doi.org/10.1109/MCOM.2017.1600514
4. Pires, I.M., Hussain, F., Garcia, N.M., Zdravevski, E.: Improving human activity monitoring by imputation of missing sensory data: experimental study. Future Internet **12**(9), 155 (2020)
5. Talal, M., et al.: Smart home-based IoT for real-time and secure remote health monitoring of triage and priority system using body sensors: Multi-driven systematic review. J. Med. Syst. **43**(3), 42 (2019)
6. Hamdan, O., Shanableh, H., Zaki, I., Al-Ali, A.R., Shanableh, T.: IoT-based interactive dual-mode smart home automation. In: 2019 IEEE International Conference on Consumer Electronics (ICCE), pp. 1–2. IEEE (2019)

7. Ray, A. K., Bagwari, A.: IoT based Smart home: security aspects and security architecture. In: 2020 IEEE 9th International Conference on Communication Systems and Network Technologies (CSNT), pp. 218–222. IEEE (2020)

8. Marikyan, D., Papagiannidis, S., Alamanos, E.: A systematic review of the smart home literature: a user perspective. Technol. Forecast. Soc. Change **138**, 139–154 (2019)

9. Sivapriyan, R., Rao, K. M., Harijyothi, M.: Literature review of IoT-based home automation system. In 2020 Fourth International Conference on Inventive Systems and Control (ICISC), pp. 101–105. IEEE (2020)

10. Vaidya, V.D., Vishwakarma, P.: A comparative analysis on the smart home system to control, monitor, and secure home, based on technologies like gsm, IoT, Bluetooth, and pic microcontroller with Zigbee modulation. In: 2018 International Conference on Smart City and Emerging Technology (ICSCET), pp. 1–4. IEEE (2018)

11. Gyrard, A., Zimmermann, A., Sheth, A.: Building IoT-based applications for smart cities: how can ontology catalogs help? IEEE IoT J. **5**(5), 3978–3990 (2018). https://doi.org/10.1109/JIOT.2018.2854278

12. Pires, I.M., Hussain, F., Marques, G., Garcia, N.M.: Comparison of machine learning techniques for the identification of human activities from inertial sensors available in a mobile device after the application of data imputation techniques. Comput. Biol. Med. **135**, 104638 (2021)

13. Ashraf, M.U., Hannan, A., Cheema, S.M., Ali, Z., Alofi, A.: Detection and tracking contagion using IoT-edge technologies: confronting COVID-19 pandemic. In: 2020 International Conference on Electrical, Communication, and Computer Engineering (ICECCE), pp. 1–6. IEEE (2020)

14. Hussain, F., et al.: A framework for malicious traffic detection in IoT healthcare environment. Sensors **21**(9), 3025 (2021)

15. Munir, M.S., Bajwa, I.S., Cheema, S.M.: An intelligent and secure smart watering system using fuzzy logic and blockchain. Comput. Electr. Eng. **77**, 109–119 (2019)

16. Stolojescu-Crisan, C., Crisan, C., Butunoi, B.P.: An IoT-based smart home automation system. Sensors **21**(11), 3784 (2021)

17. Sheikh, J.A., Cheema, S.M., Ali, M., Amjad, Z., Tariq, J.Z., Naz, A.: IoT and AI in precision agriculture: designing smart system to support illiterate farmers. In: Ahram, T. (ed.) Advances in Artificial Intelligence, Software and Systems Engineering: Proceedings of the AHFE 2020 Virtual Conferences on Software and Systems Engineering, and Artificial Intelligence and Social Computing, July 16-20, 2020, USA, pp. 490–496. Springer International Publishing, Cham (2021). https://doi.org/10.1007/978-3-030-51328-3_67

18. Geneiatakis, D., Kounelis, I., Neisse, R., Nai-Fovino, I., Steri, G., Baldini, G.: Security and privacy issues for an IoT-based smart home. In: 2017 40th International Convention on Information and Communication Technology, Electronics and Microelectronics (MIPRO), pp. 1292–1297. IEEE (2017)

19. Hassija, V., Chamola, V., Saxena, V., Jain, D., Goyal, P., Sikdar, B.: A survey on IoT security: application areas, security threats, and solution architectures. IEEE Access **7**, 82721–82743 (2019)

20. Touqeer, H., Zaman, S., Amin, R., Hussain, M., Al-Turjman, F., Bilal, M.: Smart home security: challenges, issues and solutions at different IoT layers. J. Supercomput. **77**(12), 14053–14089 (2021)

21. Ali, W., Dustgeer, G., Awais, M., Shah, M.A.: IoT-based smart home: Security challenges, security requirements, and solutions. In: 2017 23rd International Conference on Automation and Computing (ICAC), pp. 1–6. IEEE (2017)

22. Yu, Z., Song, L., Jiang, L., Sharafi, O.K.: Systematic literature review on the security challenges of blockchain in IoT-based smart cities. Kybernetes **51**(1), 323–347 (2022)

23. Ray, A.K., Bagwari, A.: IoT based Smart home: Security Aspects and security architecture. In: 2020 IEEE 9th International Conference on Communication Systems and Network Technologies (CSNT), pp. 218–222. IEEE (2020)

24. Wahyuni, R., Rickyta, A., Rahmalisa, U., Irawan, Y.: Home security alarm using Wemos D1 and HC-SR501 sensor-based telegram notification. J. Robot. Control (JRC) **2**(3), 200–204 (2021)

25. Gokaraju, B., Yessick, D., Steel, J., Doss, D.A., Turlapaty, A.C.: Integration of intrusion detection and web service alarm for home automation system using 'ARM' microprocessor. In: SoutheastCon 2016, Norfolk, VA, pp. 1–2 (2016) https://doi.org/10.1109/SECON.2016.7506717

26. Mahmud Rana, G.M.S., Mamun Khan, A.A., Hoque, M.N., Mitul, A.F.: Design and implementation of a GSM-based remote home security and appliance control system. In: 2013 2nd International Conference on Advances in Electrical Engineering (ICAEE), Dhaka, pp. 291–295 (2013). https://doi.org/10.1109/ICAEE.2013.6750350

27. Tiong, P.K., Ahmad, N.S., Goh, P.: Motion detection with IoT-based home security system. In: Arai, K., Bhatia, R., Kapoor, S. (eds.) Intelligent Computing: Proceedings of the 2019 Computing Conference, Volume 2, pp. 1217–1229. Springer International Publishing, Cham (2019). https://doi.org/10.1007/978-3-030-22868-2_85

28. Radzi, S.A., Alif, M.M.F., Athirah, Y.N., Jaafar, A.S., Norihan, A.H., Saleha, M.S.: IoT-based facial recognition door access control home security system using raspberry pi. Int. J. Power Electron. Drive Syst. **11**(1), 417 (2020)

29. Hoque, M.A., Davidson, C.: Design and implementation of an IoT-based smart home security system. Int. J. Netw. Distrib. Comput. **7**(2), 85–92 (2019)

30. Shirisha, E.: IoT based home security and automation using google assistant. Turkish J. Comput. Math. Educ. (TURCOMAT) **12**(6), 117–122 (2021)

31. Pirbhulal, S., et al.: A novel secure IoT-based smart home automation system using a wireless sensor network. Sensors **17**(1), 69 (2017)

32. Kodali, R.K., Jain, V., Bose, S., Boppana, L.: IoT-based smart security and home automation system. In: 2016 International Conference on Computing, Communication, and Automation (ICCCA), pp. 1286–1289. IEEE (2016)

33. Alani, S., Mahmood, S.N., Attaallah, S.Z., Mhmood, H.S., Khudhur, Z.A., Dhannoon, A.A.: IoT based implemented comparison analysis of two well-known network platforms for smart home automation. Int. J. Elect. Comput. Eng. (IJECE) **11**(1), 442 (2021). https://doi.org/10.11591/ijece.v11i1.pp442-450

34. Pirbhulal, S., Wu, W., Muhammad, K., Mehmood, I., Li, G., de Albuquerque, V.H.C.: Mobility enabled security for optimizing IoT-based intelligent applications. IEEE Netw. **34**(2), 72–77 (2020)

A Multimodal Approach to Synthetic Personal Data Generation with Mixed Modelling: Bayesian Networks, GAN's and Classification Models

Irina Deeva[✉], Andrey Mossyayev, and Anna V. Kalyuzhnaya

ITMO University, Saint-Petersburg, Russia

Abstract. Personal data is multimodal, as it is represented by various types of data - tabular data, images, text data. In this regard, the generation of synthetic personal data requires a large number of interconnected datasets, but it is often very difficult to collect tabular data, images or texts for the same people. The problem of having interconnected datasets can be solved by separating the models to generate each type of data and combining them into a single model pipeline. This paper presents a multimodal approach to generating synthetic personal data of a social network user, which allows generating socio-demographic information in the user's profile (tabular data), an image of the user's avatar and content images that correlates with the user's interests. The multimodal approach is based on the combined use of Bayesian networks, generative adversarial networks and discriminative model. This approach, due to the independent training of models, allows us to solve the problem of the presence of interconnected data sets (info + photos) and can also be used for example to anonymize medical data. A quantitative assessment shows that the obtained synthetic profiles are quite plausible.

Keywords: Synthetic personal data · Bayesian networks · Generative adversarial networks · Multimodal approach · Classification models

1 Introduction

Dataset availability is a critical factor in the development of artificial intelligence and machine learning projects. More broadly, data is needed to train and test machine learning models and evaluate already developed applications. The McKinsey Global Institute points out that data access is one of the main challenges hindering the ubiquity of machine learning projects [6]. Deloitte's analysis showed that data access problems are among the top three problems that companies face when implementing artificial intelligence projects [13]. If we are talking about personal data, then the main reason for the inaccessibility of such data is the presence of confidentiality restrictions.

© ICST Institute for Computer Sciences, Social Informatics and Telecommunications Engineering 2022
Published by Springer Nature Switzerland AG 2022. All Rights Reserved
T. Hara and H. Yamaguchi (Eds.): MobiQuitous 2021, LNICST 419, pp. 847–859, 2022.
https://doi.org/10.1007/978-3-030-94822-1_55

For example, medical data also contains personal information. In this case, we are talking about the need to anonymise data. Many companies facing these challenges prefer to use open-source datasets. However, the main drawback of such datasets is the lack of diversity and the specificity of the composition, which is associated with the task for which the dataset was collected. Data synthesis can solve the problems listed above and enable analysts to work with diverse and realistic data. Synthetic data is not personal data, which means that privacy restrictions do not apply to them.

Since personal data often contain different types of data, such as tabular data and images, it is multimodal (Fig. 1). And in this case, to train the generation model, you need interconnected data, which is rather difficult to collect. This article presents an approach that combines multiple models to generate each data type. The main advantage of this approach is that each model is trained separately on its own set of data, and their combination allows, as a result, to obtain synthetic multimodal data. In the article, all experiments were carried out on the example of generating a user profile of a social network, however, this approach can be extended to any area.

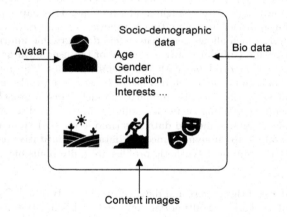

Fig. 1. Personal profile as a multimodal object for generation.

2   Related Work

This section presents existing approaches for modelling and generating synthetic quantitative and categorical variables and synthetic images.

Personal data generation and further analysis of its properties have long been used in many industries, such as modelling the dynamics of transmission of infectious diseases in American Samoa [28], modelling demographics of households [10], building and testing information discovery systems [17], modelling the behaviour of social media users [23], etc. However, to create synthetic profiles of people, it is required to generate not only socio-demographic data but also graphic data (an image of a person, pictures of interest).

Various algorithms and methods have been proposed over the past 20 years to generate synthetic population. Standard techniques for synthetic data generation methods can be divided into two categories, corresponding to two different approaches: the first, called Synthetic Reconstruction (SR), aims to create a vector of traits for each entity [27]. The second method, called Combinatorial Optimization (CO), consists of duplicating known real individual data records [26]. Also, there are other proposed methods as Copula-Based Population Generation, which used to understand the dependency structures among different distributions [14]. Bayesian networks are also one of the methods for generating synthetic data and are used to generate synthetic personal data [8]. However, all of the above approaches generate only distributions of numerical data.

Synthetic images generation is one of the most rapidly developing areas. Depending on the architecture, auxiliary image data, there are different kinds of generators. Additional information for generation may serve noise, conditional data (such as classes), text or another image. Bright representative of image generator from noise is Generative Adversarial Network (GAN) [11]. It consists of two competitive networks, Generator and Discriminator, where Generator objective is to output realistic images trying to fool Discriminator. Incorporating side information into the process of generation, researchers came up with Conditional GAN (CGAN) [18]. Depending on the scheme of how additional information fed into models, the architectures like ACGAN [20], cGANs with Projection Discriminator [19] were proposed. The class of models for Image-to-Image generation, which could be used for a generation and Variational Autoencoders (VAE) [16]. VAEs work differently because their objective is to generate such images which distributed as close as possible to the distribution of real images. Indeed, pure generative models still suffering from different kinds of artefacts and occlusions and sometimes cannot deal with complex conditions. For that case, discriminative models have to be used. The new generation of ones utilizes an unsupervised approach for the task, called zero-shot classification. An example of such a model is CLIP [21], where there is an opportunity to map images and texts into the same dimensions, resulting from the probability distribution of the image's caption being described by the text.

The difficulty is the generation of cross-modal profiles, in which data with different nature are aggregated (for example, posts and photos on social networks, demographic data). In [15], approaches based on autoencoders for the simultaneous generation of text and images, or the restoration of missing parts, are proposed. However, such an approach requires many associated tagged data, which is not always available, especially if we try to generate faces and socio-demographic information. Our approach, based on combining Bayesian networks for generating socio-demographic information, GANs for generating a portrait and a zero-shot classification model for getting the content images, allows us to train each model on each dataset separately. Also, such a separation will enable you to get rid of a significant bias in the data when, for example, a portrait of a black person is not generated for the characteristics of a person with higher education. The segregated training that we offer is free from such mistakes. And as you know, the tolerance of artificial intelligence is a big problem [29,30].

3 Method

The multimodal method for generating synthetic personal data consists of the sequential use of three models: Bayesian network, InterFaceGAN and classifier model.

3.1 Tabular Data Generation Model

A Bayesian network is used to generate socio-demographic data. Bayesian network is an oriented probabilistic model that allows you to reduce the size of the original multidimensional data due to the rule of conditional independence. Thus, having a set of real data, you can train a Bayesian network on them and generate synthetic data by sampling from the trained network. The simplest algorithm for learning the structure of a network is the greedy Hill-Climbing algorithm, the essence of which is to find a structure that maximizes the scoring function [5,9]. The likelihood or, for example, the K2 function [7] can be chosen as a score function. For learning the parameters of distributions at network nodes in the presence of both continuous data and discrete data, it is common practice to discretize continuous data, but this leads to information loss. In our previous studies [4], we investigated a way to learn distribution parameters in nodes on mixed data without discretization by using conditional Gaussian distributions. Therefore, it does not result in a loss of quality and will be used in this study. Forward sampling from the Bayesian network is used to generate synthetic data [12].

3.2 Faces Images Generation Model

To generate a synthetic personality portrait, it was necessary to take into account the fact that the appearance of a synthetic personality must be combined with the generated biographical data. Therefore generation strategy was taken from InterFaceGAN [24], i.e. images were generated in an unconditional manner from noise, then passed to auxiliary classifiers (Fig. 2). In our case, the classification of portraits by gender, age and ethnicity was chosen, since it is these characteristics that most clearly define a person's appearance. These classifiers were trained with Logistic Regression on top of the embeddings. Embeddings retrieved using Dlib [2] package on UTKFace dataset [3]. The dataset consists of 20k face images in the wild with all needed parameters labelled.

3.3   Content Images Generation Model

Except for the portrait images, it is natural for users to post ones of nature, pets, cars etc. Indeed, the distribution of topics of such images is complex and described by various social environments and circumstances. For simplicity, we decided to condition content images entirely on topics of user's interest. That is shown in Fig. 3, where keywords taken from the top 3 most probable topics of user interest, then mentioned keywords have to be pre-processed, following recommendations from [21] and added one placeholder class whose aim is to spread the probabilities and make filtering more granular. Coupling with source images from [1], they passed to CLIP [21] model, resulting in "conjugate" matrix, where elements correspond to probability image having concrete text description. This approach rather filtering and discriminative than generative. Nevertheless, it works in an unsupervised manner and grants flexibility and trustworthiness; in this case, some of the topics' keywords might change. We recalculate text embeddings and get a new resulting matrix.

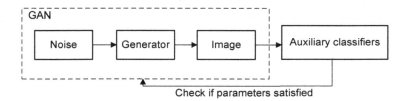

Fig. 2. Conditional image generation pipeline.

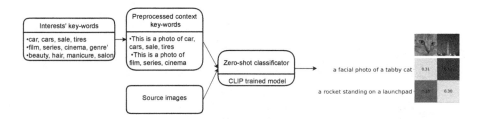

Fig. 3. Profile content images generation pipeline.

3.4   Multimodal Data Generation approach

The proposed multimodal method consists of sequentially running the following steps:

1. A user sets the criteria for a synthetic personality (age and gender). If the criteria are not set, then random personality will be generated;
2. The function of sampling from the Bayesian network is started with the parameters set at the first step;
3. The name (ethnicity) is randomly assigned to the generated personal data;
4. The generated synthetic personal data is fed to the GAN input, which generates a portrait for each synthetic personality;
5. A textual description of the first most likely interests of a person is fed to the input of the classifier model, and three pictures are selected for the synthetic profile;
6. The result is displayed as an example of synthetic profiles.

The main advantage of this approach is that each pipeline model can be trained separately on its own data, which does not require the presence of an associated dataset (information + images). Also, the peculiarity of the method is that information about the user is generated separately, and in this generation, there is no link to nationality since the node with the ethnicity is not connected with the rest of the nodes of the Bayesian network. This was done so that the resulting profiles were more diverse; for example, there was a sufficient number of black people with higher education. In this way, we try to reproduce rare combinations of characteristics in sufficient numbers to increase diversity. The model for generating faces is also trained on its face database. Such independent learning allows us to generate a portrait of a synthetic person that is not subject to bias that occurs in interconnected datasets (for example, where only white people have profiles of people with higher education). Figure 4 illustrates the general scheme of the developed service for generating synthetic personal data, which implements the described method.

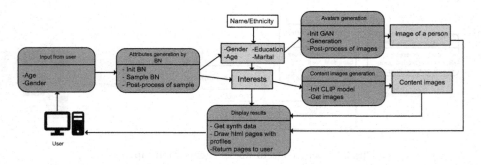

Fig. 4. Pipeline of the service for generating multimodal synthetic personal data.

4   Experiments Results

4.1   Generating Common Datasets

A Bayesian network was first learned on data from a social network. The dataset has 30000 users. Such fields as name, gender, age, higher education, marital status and vector of interests were allocated for experiments. User interests were obtained using the Additive regularization model for topic modelling process (ARTM), and its program implementation BigARTM for Python programming language, running on user subscriptions (groups) [22,25]. In total, 26 different interests were identified, which are described by keywords (5–10 words for each interest). It should be noted that now the interests are highlighted and generated in their raw form, that is, in the form of keywords that describe them. This is necessary for the further development of the profile since the generation of media content of a synthetic user will be added, which will rely on the vector of interests that is now obtained.

Figure 5 shows the structure of the resulting Bayesian network, which was used for tabular data generation. Figure 6, Fig. 7 and Fig. 8 illustrate the results of generating synthetic data in comparison with real data.

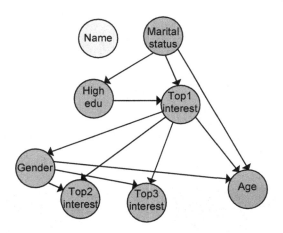

Fig. 5. Bayesian network structure.

The quality of the obtained synthetic data was assessed through the accuracy of the classifier model. A logistic regression model was trained on data where half was real data (labelled "1"), and a half was synthetic data (labelled "0"). Then the accuracy was checked on a test sample and showed the value of the ROC-AUC metric equal to 0.49. This suggests that the classifier does not distinguish between real and synthetic data, which means they are quite similar.

Then, three fields from the synthetic dataset (age, gender, name) are passed to the face generator's input. The accuracy of face generation by input characteristics has been measured. Table 1 shows the quality of persons' generation

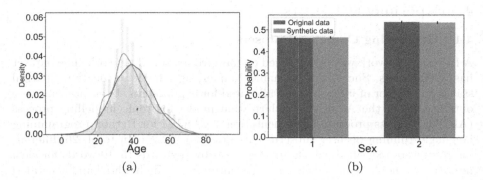

Fig. 6. Comparison of marginal distributions of the original data and synthetic data for age and sex.

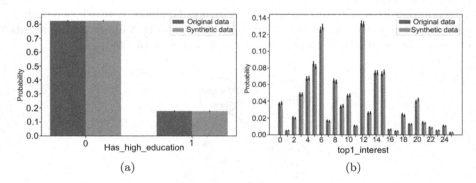

Fig. 7. Comparison of marginal distributions of the original data and synthetic data for education and top1 interests.

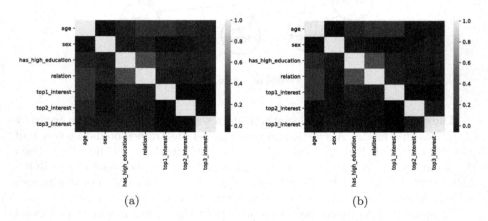

Fig. 8. Correlation matrices based on real data (a) and synthetic data (b).

according to the given characteristics of ethnicity (determined by name), age and gender. Also, a textual description of the first three most likely interests was submitted to the input of the discriminator model, and three pictures suitable for the topic were selected.

Table 1. Accuracy score for faces generation task.

Attribute	Precision	Recall	F1-score
Generation by ethnicity			
White	0.86	0.92	0.89
Black	0.89	0.9	0.89
Asian	0.91	0.95	0.93
Indian	0.74	0.8	0.77
Generation by age			
Teen (15–20)	0.9	0.83	0.87
Adult (21–45)	0.85	0.91	0.88
Old (46–90)	0.84	0.77	0.8
Generation by gender			
Male	0.93	0.93	0.93
Female	0.93	0.93	0.93

Examples of the obtained synthetic profiles are shown in Fig. 9, Fig. 10 and Fig. 11. The profile displays a synthetic portrait, socio-demographic information, interests and content images.

To assess the credibility of the resulting profiles, we surveyed 80 random people. People were given ten synthetic profiles and estimated whether they believe that this profile belongs to a real person. As a result, 70% of people believed in the reality of the shown synthetic profiles.

(a)   (b)

Fig. 9. Examples of synthetic profiles of people with different characteristics (women).

4.2   Generation of Specific Populations

To test the possibility of generating by our service not only common datasets but also populations of people, combined according to a number of characteristics, the following experiments were carried out. At first, users were identified by marital status. From the entire dataset, people with the marital status "married" were selected, then the distribution of the "top 1 interest" for this group of people was built. To generate synthetic data for people with this marital status, the "relation" node was initialized to "married" and sampled. Figure 12a shows the distribution of the "top 1 interest" field for real data and sampling. It can be seen that for this group of people, the most likely interest is interest with code 18 - 'school, education, question, topic', which is also reproduced in the synthetic dataset.

An experiment was also conducted to generate data for a specific gender group. All women were selected from the dataset, and the distribution of the "top 3 interest" parameter was built for them. Then, on the network, the gender node was initialized to "female", and sampling was performed. The figure shows a comparison of the resulting interests. It can be seen in Fig. 12b that in real data

(a)   (b)

Fig. 10. Examples of synthetic profiles of people with different characteristics (men).

(a)   (b)

Fig. 11. Examples of synthetic profiles of people with different ethnitics.

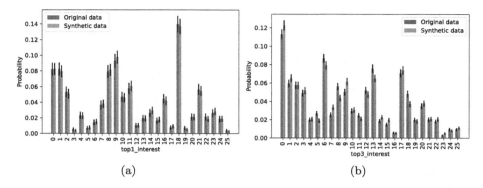

(a)   (b)

Fig. 12. Distribution of real and synthetic data for two social groups. a - distribution for top1 interest for married people. b - distribution for top3 interest for women.

for the gender group "women", the most probable value of the "top 3 interest" field is the interest with the code 0 - 'beauty, hair, manicure, salon', which is reproduced in the synthetic data.

5   Conclusion

This paper presented a multimodal approach for generating synthetic personal data. The method based on the joint use of Bayesian networks, GANs and classification model allows independent training of models, which solves the problems of the presence of associated marked datasets (for example, biographical data + photos), and also increases the variety of the resulting profiles, since the incoherence of the datasets on which the models are trained is deprived bias and can generate a variety of profiles. Accuracy measurements have shown that the resulting profiles are quite believable. Experiments also show that such an approach can be used to model data from certain social groups. In the future, it is planned to add additional fields characterizing a person to the synthetic profile and add synthetic text messages. This addition will be based on the vector of interests, which is now being generated in the form of keywords describing the interest. This form will be convenient to use for generating posts. It would also be interesting to consider the possibility of generating rare combinations of characteristics of people as a task of modelling distribution tails to increase the diversity of existing social datasets.

Acknowledgement. The reported study was funded by RFBR, project number 20-37-90117.

References

1. Flickr8k dataset (2020). https://www.kaggle.com/adityajn105/flickr8k
2. Library for embeddings (2020). http://dlib.net/
3. Dataset of faces (2021). https://susanqq.github.io/UTKFace/
4. Bubnova, A.V., Deeva, I., Kalyuzhnaya, A.V.: MIxBN: library for learning Bayesian networks from mixed data. arXiv preprint arXiv:2106.13194 (2021)
5. Chickering, D.M.: Optimal structure identification with greedy search. J. Mach. Learn. Res. **3**(Nov), 507–554 (2002)
6. Chui, M.: Artificial intelligence the next digital frontier, vol. 47, pp. 3–6. McKinsey and Company Global Institute (2017)
7. Cooper, G.F., Herskovits, E.: A Bayesian method for the induction of probabilistic networks from data. Mach. Learn. **9**(4), 309–347 (1992)
8. Deeva, I., Andriushchenko, P.D., Kalyuzhnaya, A.V., Boukhanovsky, A.V.: Bayesian networks-based personal data synthesis. In: Proceedings of the 6th EAI International Conference on Smart Objects and Technologies for Social Good, pp. 6–11 (2020)
9. Gámez, J.A., Mateo, J.L., Puerta, J.M.: Learning Bayesian networks by hill climbing: efficient methods based on progressive restriction of the neighborhood. Data Min. Knowl. Disc. **22**(1), 106–148 (2011)
10. Geard, N., McCaw, J.M., Dorin, A., Korb, K.B., McVernon, J.: Synthetic population dynamics: a model of household demography. J. Artif. Soc. Soc. Simul. **16**(1), 8 (2013)
11. Goodfellow, I.J., et al.: Generative adversarial networks. arXiv:1406.2661 (2014)
12. Guo, H., Hsu, W.: A survey of algorithms for real-time Bayesian network inference. In: Join Workshop on Real Time Decision Support and Diagnosis Systems (2002)
13. Insights, D.: State of AI in the enterprise (2018)
14. Jeong, B., Lee, W., Kim, D.S., Shin, H.: Copula-based approach to synthetic population generation. PLoS ONE **11**(8), e0159496 (2016)
15. Karpathy, A., Fei-Fei, L.: Deep visual-semantic alignments for generating image descriptions. In: Proceedings of the IEEE Conference on Computer Vision and Pattern Recognition, pp. 3128–3137 (2015)
16. Kingma, D.P., Welling, M.: Auto-encoding variational Bayes. CoRR arXiv:1312.6114 (2014)
17. Lin, P.J., et al.: Development of a synthetic data set generator for building and testing information discovery systems. In: Third International Conference on Information Technology: New Generations (ITNG'06), pp. 707–712. IEEE (2006)
18. Mirza, M., Osindero, S.: Conditional generative adversarial nets. arXiv:1411.1784 (2014)
19. Miyato, T., Koyama, M.: cGANs with projection discriminator. arXiv:1802.05637 (2018)
20. Odena, A., Olah, C., Shlens, J.: Conditional image synthesis with auxiliary classifier GANs. In: ICML (2017)
21. Radford, A., et al.: Learning transferable visual models from natural language supervision. arXiv:2103.00020 (2021)
22. Rehurek, R., Sojka, P.: Software framework for topic modelling with large corpora. In: Proceedings of the LREC 2010 Workshop on New Challenges for NLP Frameworks. Citeseer (2010)
23. Sagduyu, Y.E., Grushin, A., Shi, Y.: Synthetic social media data generation. IEEE Trans. Comput. Soc. Syst. **5**(3), 605–620 (2018)

24. Shen, Y., Gu, J., Tang, X., Zhou, B.: Interpreting the latent space of GANs for semantic face editing. In: 2020 IEEE/CVF Conference on Computer Vision and Pattern Recognition (CVPR), pp. 9240–9249 (2020)
25. Uteuov, A.: Topic model for online communities' interests prediction. Procedia Comput. Sci. **156**, 204–213 (2019)
26. Williamson, P., Birkin, M., Rees, P.H.: The estimation of population microdata by using data from small area statistics and samples of anonymised records. Environ. Plann. A **30**(5), 785–816 (1998)
27. Wilson, A.G., Pownall, C.E.: A new representation of the urban system for modelling and for the study of micro-level interdependence. Area **8**, 246–254 (1976)
28. Xu, Z., Glass, K., Lau, C.L., Geard, N., Graves, P., Clements, A.: A synthetic population for modelling the dynamics of infectious disease transmission in American Samoa. Sci. Rep. **7**(1), 1–9 (2017)
29. Zuiderveen Borgesius, F., et al.: Discrimination, artificial intelligence, and algorithmic decision-making (2018)
30. Zuiderveen Borgesius, F.J.: Strengthening legal protection against discrimination by algorithms and artificial intelligence. Int. J. Hum. Rights **24**(10), 1572–1593 (2020)

MeAct: A Non-obstructive Persuasive End-to-End Platform for Active and Healthy Ageing Support

John Gialelis[1]([✉]), Vassilis Tsakanikas[2], Nikos Tsafas[1], Kostas Stergiou[3], and Vassilis Triantafyllou[2]

[1] University of Patras and Industrial Systems Institute/RC ATHENA, 26500 Patras, Greece
gialelis@isi.gr
[2] University of Peloponnese, 26500 Patras, Greece
[3] Ergologic S.A., 26442 Patras, Greece

Abstract. The essence of active ageing is embracing a healthy lifestyle, a choice that reflects on many aspects of a citizen's everyday life and routine, namely consumption and nutrition patterns, physical activity and stress management. Such a choice would effectuate a decrease in the risk of obesity, diabetes, dementia and other non-communicable diseases. Cardiovascular diseases and cancer are the dominant causes of avoidable deaths for people under 70 years old in Europe. Promoting and upkeeping health by integrating preventive practices in the daily lives of citizens is deemed a priority if not an urgency by policy makers. Modern technology and ICT tools are most valuable allies in this battle providing effective low-cost solutions. MeAct facilitates personalized and non-invasive guidance and encouragement in the direction of a healthier lifestyle. The approach introduced is a service-oriented, low-cost and easy-to-use integrated system, which, on the one hand, empowers and motivates citizens towards healthy and active living, while on the other hand, delineates the profile of their lives in terms of quality.

Keywords: Active ageing · Healthy lifestyles · wearable device · Service-oriented cloud services

1 Introduction

As ageing population has become a salient feature of western civilization societies into 21st century, most countries strive to enforce economically sustainable policies that would establish a high standard of quality living for ageing residents. Responding to this requisite, World Health Organisation (WHO) released the active ageing policy framework in 2002, to lead countries into the development of strategies and guidelines advocating a life of quality for senior population [1]. The concept of active ageing addresses the matter of prolonging life expectancy with a multitude of aspects [2, 3]. Attempting to cultivate healthy behaviors in all age ranges, WHO's global strategy and action plan from 2016 to 2020 endorsed healthy diet eating habits, physical activity and avoidance

T. Hara and H. Yamaguchi (Eds.): MobiQuitous 2021, LNICST 419, pp. 860–871, 2022.
https://doi.org/10.1007/978-3-030-94822-1_56

of tobacco and alcohol consumption, as means of preventing and impeding the development of chronic diseases. However, the limitations confiding health systems attending to the needs of low and middle-income citizens had to be taken into account [4]. Industry stepped up, capitalising on its expertise and developed new products or adapted existing ones to meet the needs of the users. The positive outcomes of this initiative are reduction of hospitalization days and degrees of surgery and abetment of self-care at home [5].

From a technological point of view sensors, wearable devices, communication protocols, networks and cloud computing are increasing in number and are becoming more personalized [6]. This allows for the development of tailored technological solutions promoting health. In this setting, a European Innovation Partnership on Active and Healthy Ageing (EIP on AHA) was launched during 2011 by the European Commission, aiming at improving the quality of life of ageing people and its vision is to sustain healthy living of European citizens [7]. The EIP on AHA can be considered a milestone in the EU Information and Communication Technologies (ICT) and ageing policy. While initially focused on active ageing at work, after 2007 the scope of the policy widened to support independent living at home, at work and in the community (e-inclusion). The inevitable next step was to include health in the EU's ageing and technology policy with 2012 EIP on AHA. The link between health and ageing is clearly stated in its ambitious goal, *"adding two years of healthy living to the average life expectancy of European citizens"*. In addition, the partnership emphasizes the role of national, regional and local stakeholders, to best demonstrate the benefits of ICT for active and healthy ageing. The goal of ICT solutions is to focus on the well-being of the ageing population by collecting data regarding the daily routine of the elderly in order to produce information about lifestyle and assess how their choices affect their ageing. The impact and relevance of these solutions on the well-being of the elderly is very substantial, as they monitor and provide feedback on physical activity, sleep patterns, eating habits, social interaction, emotional state, cognitive state, etc. Nevertheless, they do not yet provide a holistic solution for the issues they are addressing, while in the same time avoiding to further stigmatize this already sensitive target population.

What is presented in this paper is a service oriented end-to-end platform based on an architecture aiming to promote a healthy and active way of living by continuously monitoring the users' activities, the quality of their ambient environment, the quality of their sleep, their psychological stress levels and their health status, recommending appropriate activities and supporting them to improve their everyday life quality. The proposed scalable architecture has been used to develop an m-health application for Android smartphones that fosters active ageing for elderly people. This mobile application allows users to perform different types of activities depending on their health and psychological status as well and makes sure the environmental quality conditions are the appropriate ones. The system employs off-the-shelf unobtrusive low-cost sensors efficiently mounted on a wearable embedded device based on state-of-the art microcontroller utilizing contemporary communications and exhibiting long autonomy.

The rest of this paper is structured in sections according to its content. Section 2 outlines the related work, Sect. 3 depicts the architecture of MeAct platform and the detailed description of its constituents, while in Sect. 4 the findings as well the validation steps are being discussed. Section 5 outlines the conclusion and reveals the next steps to be taken.

2 Related Work

This section examines existing work that is related to the proposed integrated platform by lining up various systems' architectures which support active and healthy ageing and presenting different solutions regarding their constituents, such as the portable sensing device, the mobile platform application, the dashboard and the services. Our goal is to present solutions aiming towards active and healthy ageing and how MeAct stands out in the case of user – centric approach. During recent years, numerous technologies and ICT frameworks have been proposed, mostly from the academia and lately from the industry, aiming at promoting active and healthy ageing. In relation to the increasingly ageing population, there is an increase in the use of ICT by the corresponding age group. In fact, older adults now represent the fastest growing population adopting Internet and ICT technology, so there is a clear evidence of adapting initiatives such as telemedicine, telecare, telepresence and the challenge of active ageing [8]. In this context, it is possible to analyse the users' individualities and collect data to guide the technological development in order to improve the human-machine interaction achieved. A considerable number of ICT-type solutions regarding interventions towards active and healthy ageing are presented below:

- applications on management and coordination of e-health interventions to promote physical activity [9]
- platforms to promote active and healthy ageing [10, 11]
- applications on personalized coaching of elderly persons to support active ageing [12, 13]
- cognitive training applications [14]
- telehealth applications to support self-management [15–17]
- telemedicine systems for direct intervention of the clinicians [12, 18, 19]
- applications targeting rehabilitation [20]
- systems targeting social inclusion and participation [21]

However, most systems are not user-centric yet and consequently the adoption and application of these technologies to real life conditions, especially those based on intrusive sensing devices is still limited. The main barriers to their partial success mainly involve:

- low acceptance and low system usability by the final users, and
- lack of interoperability with new and potentially advanced external devices, which implies a limited product and service suite to be offered to the users.

The first issue is directly connected to the system design that is highly technology-oriented instead of user-oriented. Indeed, systems are usually defined starting from the analysis of available technologies and not from the users' needs. Consequently, those systems are conceived by skilled and healthy people that are not deeply involved and fully aware how frail people live and think.

The second issue mainly derives from the adoption of the existing standards of communication (i.e. BLE, Bluetooth, WiFi, etc.), which can guarantee a set of compliant devices able to get into the network and exchange information. The result is a blinded system where personalization is hard to realize and evolution is limited to the development of a specific standard.

In this paper, we propose MeAct, an integrated end-to-end ICT platform, which aims to tackle the aforementioned deficiencies by proposing a rich set of cloud services from which the end user can benefit from, under the objective of essentially mproving the quality of life by utilizing a minimal intrusive state-of-the-art wrist wearable device able to collect the photoplethysmogram (PPG), the linear acceleration in 3-Axes (ACC), the ambient environment parameters (AEN) and the air quality parameters (AQU), along with a GPS equipped mobile device having access to weather data.

3   The Proposed MeAct Platform

The platform's architecture proposed to develop an end-to-end integrated system aiming to improve and increase the activity levels of elders is depicted in Fig. 1. MeAct's contribution to the latest technology can be summarized in the following critical features:

- User centric design characteristics
- Fusion of data from various sources
- Personalized services based on incremental learning models
- Involvement of healthcare professionals and medical experts

The proposed platform comprises three main layers: the edge layer, the fog layer, and the cloud layer. Different modules comprise each layer as following: (a) the edge layer comprises the sensors (PPG, ACC, AEN, AQU), the wearable embedded device (ESP32 - based) and the firmware, (b) the fog layer comprises the smart mobile device (GPS, Weather Data) and the app, (c) the cloud layer comprises the back end, the front end, and the cloud services. Each of the modules has the capacity to collect data and perform computations at a different scale. As presented in Table 1, each module is responsible for acquiring different kind of data which are either processed locally or forwarded to the upper level. The design of the MeAct platform is based on the cloud offloading strategy, meaning that the data from the three processing layers are forwarded for processing to the next level, only if they need to be fused with other data sources. In any other case, the data generator module handles the processing locally, thus providing a stable, fault tolerant platform.

This section is divided into three subsections. The first subsection presents the constituents both hardware and firmware as well as the computations of the Edge layer, the second subsection reveals the characteristics of the application residing in the Fog layer and the third subsection reveals the details of the services residing in the Cloud layer.

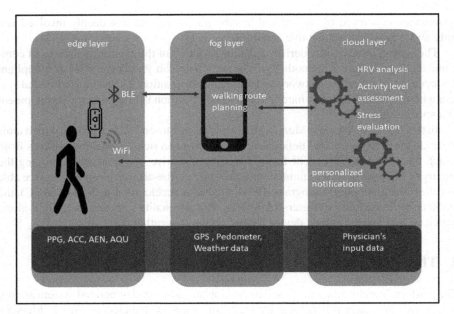

Fig. 1. MeAct platform architecture.

Table 1. Modules, collected data, computations.

Module	Collected data	Computations
Wrist Wearable Device	PPG, ACC, AEN, AQU	Heart Rate (HR), Activity Level, Environment Quality
Mobile Device	GPS, Weather Data	Suggestions about Time and Place to perform activities
Cloud Services	Physician's Data	Alerts/Notifications about: Training Schedule Heart Rate Variability (HR-V) Psychological Stress Sleep Quality Health Status

3.1 Edge Layer Components

• Wearable Embedded device

The wrist wearable embedded device is designed and developed in house based on ESP-WROOM-02 board which is a low power 32-bit MCU Wi-Fi/BLE module using the ESP32 chip which incorporates TCP/IP network stacks, 10-bit ADC and HSPI/UART/PWM/I2C/I2S interfaces. The ESP-WROOM-02 uses a 2 MB SPI flash connected to HSPI, which acts as an SDIO/SPI slave, with SPI speeds of up to 8 Mbps. The device is powered through a Li-Po 1600 mAh 3.7V battery, thus providing great autonomy. An external switch has been added to the board to easily turn on and off the device. The housing of the device is designed in Autodesk Fusion 360 and implemented in a 3D printer from PLA material.

- Sensors and corresponding adapters

The photoplethysmography (PPG) sensor used is Maxim's MAX3010x, which can deliver an accurate reading of the user's pulse and be processed to extract the analog signal's metrics [22]. Analog Device's ADX1362 accelerometer provides the linear acceleration in 3-Axes, which is used to derive the movement status in form of rest, sleep, mild and intense activity as well as determine the reliability of the system's measurement as sensors readings are affected by sudden movement [23]. Bosch's BME280 MEMS sensor with high accuracy is used to aggregate ambient air temperature, air humidity and atmospheric pressure [24]. ScioSense's CCS811 sensor is used to aggregate the percentage of Organic Compounds in the air as well as the eCO2 (equivalent calculated carbon-dioxide) concentration [25]. AMS's TSL2591 is used for measuring indoors luminosity while SiSonic's SPW2430 is used for the ambient noise [26, 27].

- Processing/Computations

As the wearable device transmits its measured data either via WiFi or BLE, it is important to execute certain preprocessing techniques to reduce the number of total transmissions that greatly affect energy consumption thus battery life expectancy. Sensor fusion techniques undertake the transforming of sampling values into average measurements as well as extracting conclusions (i.e. movement status from acceleration data points, altitude from barometric pressure etc.). Signal processing techniques to filter the inputs of the analog sensors are also present, offering stable readings and noise artifacts removal, such as low pass filtering of the PPG signal and peak detection algorithms to calculate the HR. Kalman filtering acts as a smoother for time series measurements of the 3-axis accelerometer. Based on the calculation of the three-dimensional acceleration vector's magnitude and setting of the thresholds of the corresponding motion state to rest, mild or intense, the type of activity is eventually classified as idle, walk or run. The technique utilized for the classification is a neural network specially designed and deployed for microcontroller use from the edge impulse platform [28].The network model is tested online showing 1 ms inference time and 99.3% accuracy as depicted in Fig. 2.

3.2 Fog Layer

- Application Characteristics

The mobile app is designed under the basic principles of the Human-Machine interaction, while the User Interface is designed using a minimal color pallet. The mobile app acts as the communication interface between the end user and the collection of services. Thus, it hosts POST and GET endpoints, in order to interact both with the wearable device and the cloud infrastructure. Finally, the mobile application is used for everyday message exchange between the physician and the end user.

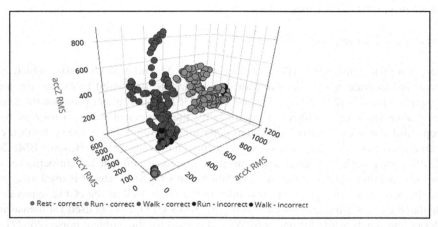

Fig. 2. Acceleration Vector Accuracy.

- Processing/Computations

The main service offered by the mobile app is the suggestions about the most preferable time of a day that the user can exercise outdoors, as well as the place-route where to perform the activities as depicted in Fig. 3. The suggestions are based on an incremental machine learning model which uses as input the weather data, the past actions of the user and the suggestions implied by the physician.

3.3 Cloud Layer

- Services Characteristics

The method of interacting with the central platform in the Fog layer, in any case, is HTTP POST as POST is a reliable and efficient HTTP-supported method used by the World Wide Web. This method, which is commonly used to carry small loads of data, allows them to be sent as a packet in a separate communication which means that data sent via the POST method is not visible to the URL as parameters are not sent with the URL. These HTTP POST specifications make it ideal for interconnecting low-power and low-resources devices with the Internet, especially when there is an immediate need to send data to a trusted server. The cloud services residing at the server are responsible for performing complex computations in order to acquire useful analytics. As the system collects a lot of data whose volume changes as the recording time is extended, the heterogeneity of the data, as it arises from the nature of the different sensors, makes

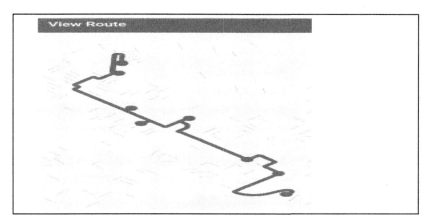

Fig. 3. Exercise Route Suggestion.

it necessary to come in a common format for the system to manage. Therefore, the requirement for homogeneity of data and their description by clearly defined models should be addressed. To this end, MeAct stipulates that all data that is handled and processed is described by the FIWARE Data Models which are based on the NGSIv2 standard and is part of a set of technologies and architectures proposed through the EC FIWARE project [29].

- Processing/Computations

A cloud service performs a meta-analysis of the HR by calculating a set of significant metrics related to the HR as the ones presented in Table 2. All these metrics are selected at rest timeslots and reported back to the physician in order to acquire useful insights about the user.

As a metanalysis streamline service, a psychological stress model is implemented assessing the user's corresponding levels and informing the physician accordingly, as proposed in [30]. The aforementioned model is based on a binary classification tree, which explores metrics such as lf and pNN50 to classify an HR window as stress or non-stress [31].

Additionally, fusing the above metrics with the user's activation levels and the guidelines of the physician, the "personal trainer" service is triggered to provide personalized suggestions about the amount of exercise a user should perform.

Another cloud service is responsible for issuing alerts about critical circumstances, as tachycardia, and informing the physician. While at this point the models for issuing the aforementioned alerts are knowledge based, machine learning models are planned to be incorporated after the collection of the appropriate datasets.

4   Discussion – Evaluation

MeAct is a modular platform which can utilize "as many data as it can collect", process them either locally or on the cloud and produce tailor made activity suggestions.

Table 2. HR metrics

	HR metric	Description
Time domain	bpm	Beats per minute
	ibi	Inter beat interval
	sdnn	Standard deviation if intervals between adjacent beats
	sdsd	Standard deviation of successive differences between adjacent R-R intervals
	rmssd	Root mean square of successive RR interval differences
	pnn20	Percentage of successive RR intervals that differ by more than 20 ms
	pnn50	Percentage of successive RR intervals that differ by more than 50 ms
	hr_mad	Median absolute deviation of RR intervals
	sd1/sd2	Length of the transverse/longitudinal line of the Poincare analysis
Frequency domain	br	Breathing rate
	vlf	Absolute power of the very-low-frequency band (0.0033–0.04 Hz)
	lf	Absolute power of the low-frequency band (0.04–0.15 Hz)
	hf	Absolute power of the high-frequency band (0.15–0.4 Hz)
	lf_nu	Normalized power of the low-frequency band (0.04–0.15 Hz)
	hf_nu	Normalized power of the high-frequency band (0.15–0.4 Hz)

As the wearable wrist device offers both WiFi and BLE communication interfaces, it can communicate directly with the mobile app and/or the cloud services. This system design feature enables the assessment of both indoor and outdoor activity levels, allowing the MeAct platform to support the end users in both settings. While reducing the indoor time is one of the objectives of MeAct, assessing the activity levels during the time an end user spends at home is crucial. By incorporating edge computing applications, the wearable device can infer the intervals the user performs no activity and according to user's profile, to produce a recommendation. For supporting the outdoor activities, the utilization of the sensing and computation capacity of the mobile device is necessary, in order to acquire more accurate readings of the user's activity levels, mostly based on the pedometer sensor of the mobile device.

MeAct platform has undergone preliminary laboratory testing phase with respect to usability and system performance. The evaluations of the various components of the platform regarding the usability, the quality and the easiness of the interactions, are ongoing and performed mainly by experts depicting their subjective findings in questionnaires and interviews based on the System Usability Scale (SUS) [32]. System performance evaluations include functionality tests of the system components such as dependability measures, task execution robustness and timeliness, wearable devices performance and autonomy, transmission reliability and performance, and services responsiveness.

This preliminary phase provided the opportunity to listen to the feedback from care-givers/experts comprising a critical users' group. This users' group noticed the need related to the fusion of HR metrics with the user's activation levels, entailing to the implementation of the "personal trainer" functionality making the system personalized and engaging the users to goals setting. Regarding system performance, the wearable device exhibited remarkable findings since there was no observation of system halts or hesitations and its autonomy ranged between 36–40 h depending on the various internal operations modes applied. The performance of the backed end system and the corresponding services kept very stable regardless the number of virtual users, thus providing us with confidence about its robustness.

5 Conclusion

This work is about presenting the architecture and the constituent components of the MeAct platform, which provides services promoting active ageing to all citizens. The overall solution consists of two subsystems that are integrated via well-defined interfaces, but each one performs autonomous functions in an opaque manner. Those two are: i) the subsystem of bio and environmental parameters collection - recording and ii) the back-end subsystem of storage, data processing and services. This platform continuously monitors physiological parameters and activities, performs health and psychology status assessment, and provides personalized feedback to improve well-being. The novelty of the proposed platform predominantly lies on the minimal design of the wearable sensing devices, allowing a least disturbing interaction with the end user. The role of the wearable is to collect biosignals, facilitating the creation of the user's profile based on calculations of a set of metrics and analytics. Having established that profile, a persuasive coaching agent uses it as a base, in order to encourage the end user towards a more active way of living with improved physical activity. Furthermore, in comparison with similar solutions, MeAct platform has the advantage of functioning without the aid of a paired smartphone for collecting and delivering the biosignals to the back-end system, thus enhancing its user-friendly attribute for users with low digital literacy.

Albeit MeAct platform is a novel well-thought design, there is still room for future improvements. The independence of the wrist device, meaning it will be working "smart-phoneless" especially during outdoor activities, can be achieved by including a GPS sensor and a 5G GSM communication module instead of the existing WiFi & BLE. Moreover, the robust estimation of the respiratory rate will render possible by implementing additional health-oriented algorithms. Adding the gamification process to the solution with enhanced capabilities, should further motivate the user by setting a game like environment with scores and highlighting the optimal way to reach the set goal.

Acknowledgment. This research has been co-financed by the European Union and Greek national funds, the Regional Operational Program "Western Greece 2014–2020", under the Call "Financial Strengthening research development and innovation projects in the priority area of RIS3 –ICT" (project: 5038641 entitled "Integrated ICT" - based Active Living Support System "MeACT").

References

1. World Health Organization (WHO). Active Ageing: A Policy Framework. WHO, Geneva (2002). https://www.who.int/ageing/publications/active_ageing/en/
2. Lionis, C., Midlov, P.: Prevention in the elderly: a necessary priority for general practitioners. Eur. J. Gen. Pract. **23**(1), 203–208 (2017)
3. Robbins, T.D., Lim Choi Keung, S.N., Arvanitis, T.N.: E-health for active ageing. A systematic review. Maturitas, **114**, 34–40 (2018)
4. World Health Organization (WHO). The global network for age-friendly cities and communities. https://www.who.int/ageing/gnafcc-report-2018.pdf?ua=1
5. Llewellyn, J., Chaix-Viros, C.: The Business of Ageing: Older Workers, Older Consumers: Big Implications for Companies, London. http://www.nomuraholdings.com/csr/news/data/news30.pdf
6. Hood, L., Flores, M.: A personal view on systems medicine and the emergence of proactive P4 medicine: predictive, preventive, personalized and participatory. New Biotechnol. **29**(6), 613–624 (2013)
7. EIP on AHA, Action Plan on 'Innovation for Age-Friendly Buildings, Cities & Environments.' https://ec.europa.eu/research/innovation-union/pdf/active-healthy-ageing/d4_act ion_plan.pdf
8. Chiu, C., Liu, C.: Understanding older adult's technology adoption and withdrawal for elderly care and education: Mixed method analysis from national survey. Eur. J. Gen. Pract. **19**(11), 374 (2017)
9. Muellmann, S., Forberger, S., Mollers, T., Zeeb, H., Pischke, C.: Effectiveness of ehealth interventions for the promotion of physical activity in older adults: a systematic review. Syst. Rev. **108**, 93–110 (2018)
10. Madureira, P., et al.: My-AHA: software platform to promote active and healthy ageing, MDPI. Information **11**(9), 438 (2020)
11. Vercelli, A., et al.: My-active and healthy ageing (My-AHA): an ICT platform to detect frailty risk and propose intervention. In: SoftCOM, pp. 1–4 (2017)
12. Jongstra, S., et al.: Development and validation of an interactive internet platform for older people: the healthy ageing through internet counselling in the elderly study. Telemed. J. E Health **23**(2), 96–104 (2017)
13. Orte, S., et al.: A decision support system for personalised coaching to support active ageing, Workshop on Artificial Intelligence for Ambient Assisted Living 2018, pp. 16–36
14. Reijnders, J., Geusgens, C., Ponds, R., van Boxtel, M.: Keep your brain fit! Effectiveness of a psychoeducational intervention on cognitive functioning in healthy adults: a randomised controlled trial. Neuropsychol. Rehabilit. **27**(4), 455–471 (2017)
15. Lee, E., Han, S., Jo, S.: Consumer choice of on-demand mHealth app services: context and contents values using structural equation modeling. Int. J. Med. Inf. **97**, 229–238 (2015)
16. Tiedemann, A., et al.: Health coaching and pedometers to enhance physical activity and prevent falls in community-dwelling people aged 60 years and over: study protocol for the Coaching for Healthy AGEing (CHAnGE) cluster randomised controlled trial. BMJ Open **6**(5), 1–8 (2016)
17. Dalgaard, L., Gronvall, E., Verdezoto, N.: Mediframe: a tablet application to plan, inform, remind and sustain older adults' medication intake. In: ICHI '2013, pp. 36–45 (2013)
18. Henriquez-Camacho, C., Losa, J., Miranda, J., Cheyne, N.: Addressing healthy ageing populations in developing countries: unlocking the opportunity of eHealth and mHealth. Emerg. Themes Epidemiol. **11**(1), 136 (2014)
19. Keijser, W., et al.: DG connect funded projects on information and communication technologies (ICT) for old age people: Beyond Silos, CareWell and SmartCare. J. Nutr. Health Aging **20**(10), 1024–1033 (2016). https://doi.org/10.1007/s12603-016-0804-0

20. Kaufman, H.: From where we sit: augmented reality for an active ageing European society. J. Cyberther. Rehabil. **5**(21), 35–37 (2012)
21. Ferreira, S., Sayago, S., Blat, J.: Older people's production and appropriation of digital videos: an ethnographic study. Behav. Inf. Technol. **6**(6), 557–574 (2017)
22. MAX30101. https://www.maximintegrated.com/en/products/interface/sensor-interface/MAX30101.html
23. ADXl362. https://www.analog.com/media/en/technical-documentation/data-sheets/ADXL362.pdf
24. BME280 MEMS. https://www.hellasdigital.gr/electronics/sensors/temperature-sensors/gravity-i2c-bme280-environmental-sensor-temperature-humidity-barometer-sen0236/?sl=en
25. CCS811. https://www.sciosense.com/products/environmental-sensors/ccs811-gas-sensor-solution/
26. TSL2591. https://ams.com/tsl25911
27. SPW2430. https://www.evelta.com/silicon-mems-microphone-breakout-spw2430/
28. Edge Impulse. https://docs.edgeimpulse.com/docs/continuous-motion-recognition
29. FIWARE. https://www.fiware.org/developers/data-models/
30. Richman, J.S., Moorman, J.R.: Physiological time-series analysis using approximate entropy and sample entropy. Am. J. Physiol. Heart Circ. Physiol. **278**, H2039–H2049 (2000)
31. Melillo, P., Formisano, C., Bracale, U., Pecchia, L., Classification tree for real-life stress detection using linear heart rate variability analysis. Case study: students under stress due to university examination. In: IFMBE World Congress on Medical Physics and Biomedical Engineering, pp. 477–480 (2012)
32. SUS. https://www.usability.gov/how-to-and-tools/methods/system-usability-scale.html

Brain Activity Analysis of Stressed and Control Groups in Response to High Arousal Images

Wardah Batool$^{(\boxtimes)}$, Sanay Muhammad Umar Saeed, and Muhammad Majid

Department of Computer Engineering, University of Engineering and Technology, Taxila, Pakistan
wardah.batool@students.uettaxila.edu.pk, {sanay.muhammad, m.majid}@uettaxila.edu.pk

Abstract. Stress is known as a state in which an individual tussles with psychological or social demands. It can be detected in response to high arousal images, but the existing dataset of such images might not be effective to induce stress for the population of financially and politically unstable countries. This study examines the effects of stress-inducing high arousal images selected from the Geneva Affective Picture Database (GAPED) on the brain activity of stressed and control groups. Twenty-seven healthy participants of the same educational background and ethnicity took part in this study voluntarily. The electroencephalography (EEG) data signals are recorded using a single-channel headset and all participants are advised to close their eyes for one minute and avoid thinking about anything. Negative images with high arousal values are presented to the participants for one minute. EEG data signals are recorded again with closed eye condition for one minute. The t-test is applied to check the effects of high arousal images on brain activities of all participants, stressed participants, and participants in the control condition. The results of this study reveal that there are no statistically significant changes observed in all EEG bands after the presentation of the high arousal images. This study is the first step that points to the need for a new image dataset for high arousal images to induce stress for the population of developing countries.

Keywords: Electroencephalography · Brain activity · Statistical analysis · Human stress · High arousal images

1 Introduction

Stress is a condition in which a particular individual feels overwhelmed due to mental or psychological demands. These demands can be tied to work, family matters, and financial affairs [1]. Stress can overcome the immune system and could be a reason for functional disability while performing routine tasks [2]. It is a cause of various physical and mental diseases, for example, it enhances the chances of cardiac arrest, depression, coronary artery disease, and gastroesophageal reflux disease [3]. Therefore, it is important to measure and manage stress effectively.

T. Hara and H. Yamaguchi (Eds.): MobiQuitous 2021, LNICST 419, pp. 872–883, 2022.
https://doi.org/10.1007/978-3-030-94822-1_57

Stress can be assessed using psychological, physical, and physiological measures. Psychological questionnaires are based on an individual's rating of items on different scales [4–6]. Physical features like blink rate, facial expressions [7], pupil dilation, voice, and eye gaze are sensitive to stress. Physiologically, hormones are released relatively in a greater amount when a person is feeling stressed. The effect of these stress hormones can be measured through invasive (e.g., acquisition of blood, saliva, and urine samples) and non-invasive methods [8]. The stressful situations often lead to changes in the autonomous nervous system (ANS) [9]. ANS and the physical response of humans in stress are directly connected [10, 11]. ANS is organized into the sympathetic and parasympathetic nervous systems [12]. They both help in controlling heart rate variability (HRV), skin conductance, blood pressure, respiration, and brain waves [8–13].

Stress has a significant effect on the brain activity of an individual [14]. Electroencephalography (EEG), functional magnetic resonance imaging (fMRI), and positron emission tomography (PET) are used to analyze functional changes in the brain's activity [15]. EEG helps to measure brain disorders, which are associated with the electrical activity of the brain [16]. Therefore, EEG is regarded as an effective and non-invasive form of neuroimaging to obtain the cortical response to stress [17]. Moreover, EEG has been correlated directly with other stress response measures such as HRV [18].

EEG can be used to classify stress levels as it reflects the electrical activity of the brain [19]. Four rhythms of EEG tend to change with the changing level of stress [20]. For stress measurement, EEG recordings have been conventionally performed using 128, 64 and, 32 channel headsets but these headsets are not easy to wear [21]. Fourteen channel headsets are relatively easy to wear but it becomes difficult to wear in circumstances where frequent data acquisition is required. Therefore, we use a single-channel dry-sensor EEG headset to measure mental stress, which has an electrode at the frontal side of the head. Neuro-chemical changes due to stress response have a significant impact on the frontal part of the brain [22]. Therefore, this headset is preferred to be used in the experiment.

Several methods exist for stimulating subjects such as images can be displayed to the participant, they can watch movies, hear sounds, and can play games [23]. Stress can be assessed by measuring physiological signals in response to high arousal images and interviews [12]. Multimedia stimuli can induce emotions and these emotions are translated from the body response [24]. Geneva Affective PicturE Database (GAPED) is a relatively large, and effective dataset used to invoke specific emotions [25, 26]. The images of the dataset were rated based on valence and arousal scores [25]. Valence illustrates positive or negative affectivity; arousal deals with the extent of the calming or relaxing ability of the material. Negative images with high arousal values such as violence against humans and animals induce stress, which is indicated by heart rate variability, physiological stress parameters, EEG, and subjective rating [27, 28].

In this study, we intend to analyze the brain activity of stressed and control groups in response to high arousal images using a single-channel dry sensor headset. To evaluate the stress of 27 participants, PSS is used as a stress questionnairere. The reliability and validity of PSS-10 for perceived stress is found in many researches such as [29, 30]. Based on the PSS score, participants are divided into stressed and control groups. Immediately after filling the questionnaire by the participants, EEG signals are recorded using a single-channel NeuroSky's headset. After this, GAPED dataset is used to induce psychological stress in the participants. Participants are presented with twenty selected high arousal images of the first four categories such as snakes, spiders, emotion concerning, and animal mistreatment. The reason behind this is that they physiologically awake the humans and capture their attention [31]. Each picture was presented to the participants on a screen. After displaying selected GAPED images to participants, EEG signals of participants are recorded again. For statistical analysis, a paired t-test is applied on frequency bands of EEG signals. These EEG signals are acquired before and after the presentation of images to the participants.

The rest of the paper is organized as follows. The detailed methodology is explained in Sect. 2. Section 3 explains the results of the experiment such as data labeling and statistical results. This section also includes a discussion of brain activity analysis when high arousal images are presented as a stimulus. The conclusion is presented in Sect. 4.

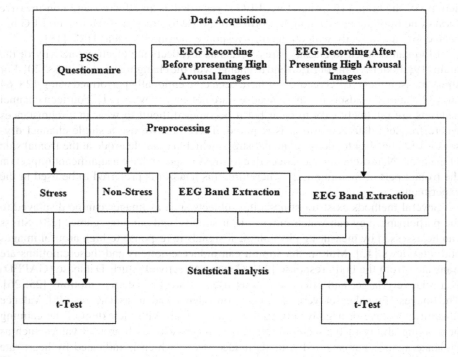

Fig. 1. Block diagram of the methodology employed for the brain activity analysis of the stressed and control groups.

2 Methodology

A block diagram to show the methodology adopted in this study is presented in Fig. 1. Initially, participants are asked to fill the PSS-10 questionnaire. The scores of the PSS questionnaire are recorded. After this, EEG data is recorded using NeuroSky's Mindwave headset. Recorded EEG data is then transformed into the frequency domain to extract various EEG bands such as theta, low gamma, mid gamma, low alpha, high alpha, low beta, high beta, and delta. These frequency bands are categorized based on their frequency ranges as shown in Table 1.

Table 1. Frequency ranges of EEG bands used in the study.

Sr. No	Band	Frequency Range (Hz)
1	Delta	1–3
2	Theta	4–7
3	Low-alpha	8–9
4	High-alpha	10–12
5	Low-beta	13–17
6	High-beta	18–30
7	Low-gamma	31–40
8	Mid-gamma	41–50

2.1 Participants

In this study, 27 healthy participants (67% male and 33% female) participated within the age range of 22–33 years, with a mean value of 27.5 years. Participants of this study belong to the same ethnicity i.e., Asia Pacific, and with almost the same educational background. Participants involved in this study belong to the field of education i.e., faculty, and students.

The PSS questionnaire is designed to be used by participants with at least a junior high school education, whereby the questions are easy to comprehend and make the responses simpler. The participants selected for this study fulfill all the basic requirements for PSS. The study is approved by the Board of Post Graduate Studies of the. Computer Engineering Department, UET Taxila.

PSS-10 questionnaire is used in this study to divide the participants into two groups i.e., stressed, and control group. PSS-10 comprises 10 questions that ask about the frequency of stressful incidents. These stressful incidents may have occurred in the span of last month or earlier. The participants are asked to rate each question on a scale of 0 to 4. PSS score is then used to categorize participants as stressed or control. EEG data was recorded using NeuroSky's Mindwave headset, which was easy to wear EEG device with a single electrode positioned at FP1. It was configured as a single channel with a sampling frequency of 512 Hz. EEG signals for each participant were recorded in the same environment. The experiment was conducted in a quiet environment to avoid acoustic noise. Every participant was asked to sign an informed consent and could leave the experiment of his/her will. To avoid any disturbance during the experiment lights were adjusted according to the comfort level of the participants. It was also ensured that no syncing error occurred during EEG signal recording.

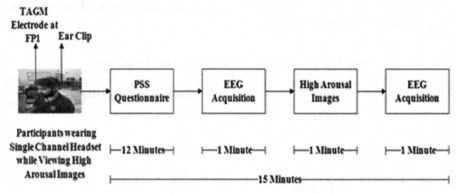

Fig. 2. Time flow diagram of the experiment.

All participants were advised to wear the EEG device. They were instructed to close their eyes for one minute and empty their minds from all thoughts. EEG of each participant was recorded for 1 min in an eye-closed condition. Images with high arousal values were presented to the participants for 1 min and after displaying of images participants were advised to close their eyes for 1 min and EEG data was recorded again. The t-test is then applied to frequency bands of the EEG data, recorded before the presentation of GAPED images to the participants and after displaying high arousal images. The time flow diagram of the experiment is shown in Fig. 2.

2.2 Stimuli

For this study, twenty GAPED dataset images are selected as a stimulus and are presented to the participants to induce mental stress. The images having a mean rating value for arousal, ranging from 51.829 to 91.290 points are selected. The mean rating value for arousal is in the range of 0.779 to 45.437. These images are projected on a full screen of 55 inches display, at three meters away from the participant. Twenty high arousal images are displayed for 1 min. Each image was displayed for a duration of five seconds. Figure 3 shows a grid of selected images from GAPED dataset based on high arousal values.

2.3 T-test

Statistical tests have great importance in the field of biomedical research. Various factors play an important role in the selection of appropriate t-Test as their inaccurate use may lead the research in the wrong direction and hence provide inaccurate results.

Fig. 3. 20 selected high arousal images from GAPED image dataset used as stimulus in this study.

The student's t-test is mostly used for statistical analysis; the William Gossett test that is known as the t-Test. The t-test determines the significant difference between the means of two groups, which are related to each other. The selection is dependent on data and the type of analysis required under specific criteria. The results obtained are termed as statistically significant if the p-value is less than 0.05. Unpaired t-test is used to determine the significant difference between the means of two independent variables. Paired t-test determines the significant difference between the means of two dependent variables. It is also appropriate for the data in which pair consists of before and after the measurements on a single group of subjects or two measurements on the same subjects are paired. In our case, paired t-test is applied over the frequency bands of the participants before and after the stimulus to check the difference between their means.

3 Experimental Analysis

The statistical analysis for overall (all participants), control, and stressed groups is presented in this section. Data labeling for stressed and control groups is described in the following subsection.

3.1 Data Labeling

The participants involved in the study are grouped into a stressed or control group using their PSS score. Figure 4 shows the PSS score of each participant. The overall mean (μ) and standard deviation (σ) of the total responses of PSS scores collected from participants were 17 and 4, respectively. For the stressed participants, the threshold value is calculated from the PSS scores using a formula such as [$\mu + \sigma/2$]. This value comes out to be 19 in our case. So, the participants having a value equal to or greater than threshold values are considered to be stressed. Similarly, for the control group, the threshold value is calculated from PSS scores using the formula [$\mu - \sigma/2$] which is 15. So, the participants having PSS scores below or equal to this threshold are considered the control group. The eight participants having PSS scores in the range (16 to 18) are ignored. Being ignored does not show a complete absence of one or other condition. 9 out of 27 participants were labeled as stressed while the rest of the participants are labeled as a member of control group.

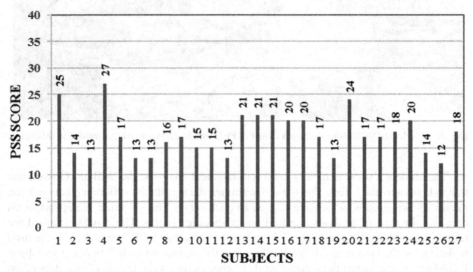

Fig. 4. Distribution of PSS Score of subjects participated in this study

3.2 Statistical Results

To analyze both groups two-sample (stressed and control group) paired t-test is applied to the frequency bands before displaying images (EC1) and after displaying images (EC2). The test decision is based on groups. The t-test results for EEG frequency bands before and after the presentation of the stimulus for overall, control, and stressed participants are shown in Table 2. It is evident from the results that none of the EEG frequency bands is significantly different before and after displaying high arousal images to all the participants except high alpha and high beta bands and participants belong to stressed and control groups.

The distributional characteristics of each band for all participants are presented using box plots, and these box plots represent an overall response of each frequency band. Whiskers represent 25% of the data values of the bottom and top, whereas interquartile ranges represent 50% of data values. A straight horizontal line marks the median of the data. Box plot of the EEG oscillations was captured using a single-channel headset before and after the presentation of GAPED images.

Here frequency band values before the presentation of images are denoted by EC1 and frequency band values after displaying images are denoted by EC2. Figure 5 shows the box plots of different EEG bands before and after displaying high arousal images for the overall group. It is evident from the presented results that no significant difference exists in any of the EEG frequency bands before and after displaying high arousal images. Figure 6 presents the box plots of different EEG bands before and after the presentation of GAPED high arousal images for the control group. A slight variation is observed in the means and standard deviation of EEG frequency bands. Thus, it shows that a minimal difference exists before and after displaying GAPED high arousal images Fig. 7 shows the Whisker box plot results for the stressed group.

Table 2. p-values of different EEG frequency bands before and after displaying high arousal images for overall, control, and stressed groups.

Sr. No	Frequency bands	p-value (p) (Overall)	p-value (p) (Control)	p-value (p) (Stressed)
1	Delta	0.33	0.88	0.81
2	Theta	0.79	0.34	0.17
3	Low alpha	0.22	0.36	0.79
4	High alpha	0.09	0.14	0.50
5	Low beta	0.16	0.24	0.58
6	High beta	0.09	0.46	0.66
7	Low gamma	0.29	0.68	0.33
8	Middle gamma	0.19	0.33	0.81

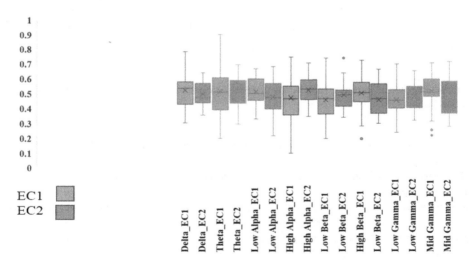

Fig. 5. Boxplot of different EEG bands of all the participants before and after presentation of high arousal images

From the results, it is noticed that no significant difference is present in any of the EEG frequency bands before and after displaying high arousal images i.e., EC1 and EC2. However, a slight variation is observed in the means and standard deviation of EEG frequency bands. Thus, it shows that there is a minimal difference before and after the presentation of GAPED high arousal images. The p-values obtained from paired T-test in EEG frequency bands show increased activity of high alpha and high beta bands as compared to other frequency bands. The p-value of high alpha in overall (Control and stressed group) show that there is only 91% confidence level that there is a significant difference. Also, the control and stressed group depicts 86% and 50% confidence level respectively that there is a significant difference, which indicates that the high alpha band was highly active during the presentation of high arousal images.

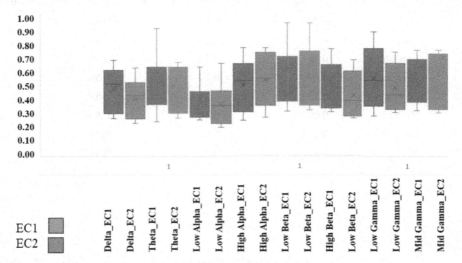

Fig. 6. Boxplot of different EEG bands of control group before and after presentation of high arousal images.

The p-value of the high beta band shows the confidence level of 91%, 54%, and 34% for overall (control and stressed group), control and stressed group respectively that there is a significant difference. Thus, from all the above discussion it is concluded that high alpha and high beta bands were relatively active to the high arousal images as available in the literature [32, 33]. But at a 95% confidence level, none of the frequency bands are significantly different. Table 2 shows the result of p-values of different EEG bands before and after of the high arousal images for the overall, control, and stressed groups. The limitation of the study is a smaller number of GAPED images presented to the participants. Thus, due to the lesser number of participants and data further investigation is required. If the number of GAPED images and the participants is increased, we may obtain a significant value for alpha and beta bands.

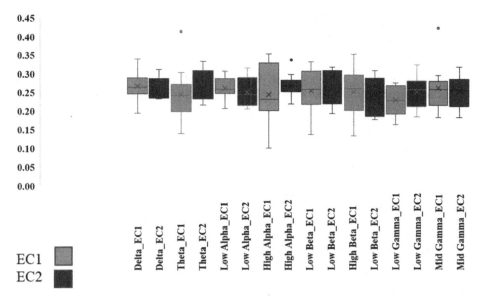

Fig. 7. Boxplot of different EEG bands of Stressed group before and after presentation of high arousal images.

4 Conclusion

The T-test is applied on frequency bands of all the participants, stressed, and control groups, before and after displaying high arousal images. It has been observed that there is no statistically significant difference in the frequency bands before and after the stimulus of high arousal images except the high alpha and high beta bands which show the relatively increased activity. These high arousal images were taken from GAPED dataset, which was made considering the population of developed countries. We can say from this preliminary study that there is a need to develop a new image dataset keeping in view the population of financially and politically unstable countries as these images might not affect their brain activities. A limited number of images are selected in this preliminary study for experiment according to mentioned criteria. In the future, we intend to acquire more data to validate these findings.

References

1. Li, H., Zhao, S.: Study on the psychological stress and its mediator factors: An empirical study of high school students. In: 2010 2nd Int. Conf. Commun. Syst. Networks Appl. ICCSNA 2010, vol. 1, pp. 143–146 (2010)
2. Pruessner, J.C., Rietschel, M., Deuschle, M., Meyer-lindenberg, A.: City Living and Urban Upbringing Affect Neural Social Stress Processing in Humans, pp. 5–8 (2011)
3. Subhani, A.R., Mumtaz, W., Saad, M.N.B.M., Kamel, N., Malik, A.S.: Machine learning framework for the detection of mental stress at multiple levels. IEEE Access **5**, 13545–13556 (2017)

4. A.E.U. Berbano, Pengson, H.N.V., Razon, C.G.V., Tungcul, K.C.G., Prado, S.V.: Classifi-cation of stress into emotional, mental, physical and no stress using electroencephalogram signal analysis. In: Proc. 2017 IEEE Int. Conf. Signal Image Process. Appl. ICSIPA 2017, pp. 11–14 (2017)
5. Pakarinen, T., Pietila, J., Nieminen, H.: Prediction of self-perceived stress and arousal based on electrodermal activity. In: Proc. Annu. Int. Conf. IEEE Eng. Med. Biol. Soc. EMBS, pp. 2191–2195 (2019)
6. Vaishali, B., Amalan, S., Preejith, S.P., Joseph, J., Sivaprakasam, M.: HRV based stress assessment of individuals in a work environment. In: IEEE Med. Meas. Appl. MeMeA 2020 - Conf. Proc. (2020)
7. Alimuradov, A.K., Tychkov, A.Y., Churakov, P.P.: EMD-based voiced speech processing method for intelligent recognition systems of stressed states in humans. In: Proc. - 2020 Int. Russ. Autom. Conf. RusAutoCon 2020, pp. 541–546 (2020)
8. Setiawan, F., Khowaja, A.G., Prabono, Yahya, B.N., Lee, S.L.: A framework for real time emotion recognition based on human ANS using pervasive device. In: Proc. - Int. Comput. Softw. Appl. Conf., vol. 1, pp. 805–806 (2018)
9. Zhang, J., Wen, W., Huang, F., Liu, G.: Recognition of real-scene stress in examination with heart rate features. In: Proc. - 9th Int. Conf. Intell. Human-Machine Syst. Cybern. IHMSC 2017, vol. 1, pp. 26–29 (2017)
10. Dieleman, G.C., et al.: Alterations in HPA-axis and autonomic nervous system functioning in childhood anxiety disorders point to a chronic stress hypothesis. Psychoneuroendocrinology **51**, 135–150 (2015)
11. Suganthi, L., Devi, M.S.S., Ilakkiya, M., Tamizharasi, G.: Effect of physical stress on human electro dermal activity. In: 2017 Int. Conf. Energy, Commun. Data Anal. Soft Comput. ICECDS 2017, pp. 2505–2508 (2018)
12. Arsalan, A., Majid, M., Butt, A.R., Anwar, S.M.: Classification of perceived mental stress using a commercially available EEG headband. IEEE J. Biomed. Heal. Inf. **23**(6), 2257–2264 (2019)
13. Subahni, A.R., Xia, L., Malik, A.S.: Association of mental stress with video games. In: ICIAS 2012 - 2012 4th Int. Conf. Intell. Adv. Syst. A Conf. World Eng. Sci. Technol. Congr. - Conf. Proc., vol. 1, pp. 82–85 (2012)
14. Sabouni, A., Khamechi, M., Honrath, M.: Stress effects in the brain during transcranial magnetic stimulation. IEEE Magn. Lett. **10**, 1–4 (2019)
15. Dubois, J., Adolphs, R.: Building a science of individual differences from fMRI. Trends Cogn. Sci. **20**(6), 425–443 (2016)
16. Donmez, H., Ozkurt, N.: Emotion Classification from EEG Signals in Convolutional Neural Networks. In: Proc. - 2019 Innov. Intell. Syst. Appl. Conf. ASYU 2019 (2019)
17. Ugarte, D.E., Linares, D., Kemper, G., Almenara, C.A.: An algorithm to measure the stress level from EEG, EMG and HRV signals. In: Proc. - 2019 Int. Conf. Inf. Syst. Comput. Sci. INCISCOS 2019, pp. 346–353 (2019)
18. Subhani, A.R., Xia, L., Malik, A.S., Othman, Z.: Quantification of physiological disparities and task performance in stress and control conditions. In: Proc. Ann. Int. Conf. IEEE Eng. Med. Biol. Soc. EMBS, pp. 2060–2063 (2013)
19. Sulaiman, N.: Offline LabVIEW-based EEG Signals Analysis for Human Stress Monitoring, no. August, pp. 3–4, 2018
20. Craig, A., Tran, Y., Wijesuriya, N., Nguyen, H.: Regional brain wave activity changes associated with fatigue. Psychophysiology **49**(4), 574–582 (2012)
21. Zhao, J., Pan, P., Fu, W., Ma, C.: Research on mental fatigue detection based on portable EEG acquisition equipment. In: Proc. World Congr. Intell. Control Autom., vol. 2015-March, no. March, pp. 5143–5146 (2015)

22. McEwen, B.S., Morrison, J.H.: The brain on stress: vulnerability and plasticity of the prefrontal cortex over the life course. Neuron **79**(1), 16–29 (2013)
23. Hosseini, S.A.: Emotional Stress Recognition System Using EEG and.pdf (2010)
24. Koelstra, S., et al.: DEAP: a database for emotion analysis: using physiological signals. IEEE Trans. Affect. Comput. **3**(1), 18–31 (2012)
25. Dan-Glauser, E.S., Scherer, K.R.: The Geneva affective picture database (GAPED): a new 730-picture database focusing on valence and normative significance. Behav. Res. Methods **43**(2), 468–477 (2011)
26. Horvat, M., Duvnjak, D., Jug, D.: GWAT: The Geneva Affective Picture Database WordNet Annotation Tool, p. 5 (2015)
27. Qin, S., Hermans, E.J., van Marle, H.J.F., Luo, J., Fernández, G.: Acute psychological stress reduces working memory-related activity in the dorsolateral prefrontal cortex. Biol. Psychia. **66**(1), 25–32 (2009)
28. Hermans, E.J. et al.: Stress-related noradrenergic activity prompts large-scale neural network reconfiguration. Science (80) **334**(6059), 1151–1153 (2011)
29. Baik, S.H., et al.: Reliability and validity of the perceived stress scale-10 in hispanic americans with English or Spanish language preference. J. Health Psychol. **24**(5), 628–639 (2019)
30. Lee, B., Jeong, H.I.: Construct validity of the perceived stress scale (PSS-10) in a sample of early childhood teacher candidates. Psychiatry Clin. Psychopharmacol. **29**(1), 76–82 (2019)
31. Kensinger, E.A., Schacter, D.L., College, B., Hill, C.: Processing emotional pictures and words: effects of valence and arousal avocado. Cogn. Affect Behav. Neurosci. **6**(2), 110–126 (2006)
32. Moraes, H., et al.: Beta and alpha electroencephalographic activity changes after acute exercise. Arq. Neuropsiquiatr. **65**(3a), 637–641 (2007)
33. Schaefer, R.S., Vlek, R.J., Desain, P.: Music perception and imagery in EEG: alpha band effects of task and stimulus. Int. J. Psychophysiol. **82**(3), 254–259 (2011)

Correction to: Mobile and Ubiquitous Systems: Computing, Networking and Services

Takahiro Hara and Hirozumi Yamaguchi

Correction to:
T. Hara and H. Yamaguchi (Eds.): *Mobile and Ubiquitous*
Systems: Computing, Networking and Services,
LNICST 419, https://doi.org/10.1007/978-3-030-94822-1

In an older version of Chapter 4, a DOI was missing from reference number 15. In addition, the name of Beenish Chaudhry was spelt incorrectly in Sect. 2.2. Both of these errors have been corrected.

In an older version of Chapter 17, a link was missing from reference number 7. This has been corrected.

The updated version of these chapters can be found at
https://doi.org/10.1007/978-3-030-94822-1_4
https://doi.org/10.1007/978-3-030-94822-1_17

Short Papers

Short Papers

A Method for Estimating Actual Swimming Distance Using an Accelerometer and Gyroscope

Daisuke Watanabe$^{(\boxtimes)}$ and Kazuya Murao

Ritsumeikan University, Kyoto, Japan
daisuke.watanabe@iis.ise.ritsumei.ac.jp, murao@cs.ritsumei.ac.jp

Abstract. In this paper, we propose a system for estimating the actual swimming distance of a meandering swimmer using accelerometers and angular rate sensors. In this paper, we propose a system for estimating the actual swimming distance of a meandering swimmer using accelerometer and angular rate sensor. Although wristwatch and goggle devices are available to assist swimming practice, these devices cannot measure the distance of a meandering swimmer. Existing researches include position estimation methods using Wi-Fi signal strength, but there are environments where these methods cannot be used. In the proposed method, the actual swimming distance is obtained by correcting the obtained data. In the experiment, we fixed the sensor to a flutter board and walked a predetermined route, and we fixed the sensor to a subject and swam the same route. From the estimation results, it was found that the distance traveled could be estimated correctly with this method, and that it was most accurate when the sensor was attached to the subject's waist.

Keywords: Swimming · Accelerometer · Gyroscope · Distance estimation

1 Proposed Method

Devices that can check swimming performance and time have been released[1][2]. Though some swimmers may unconsciously meander, these devices cannot detect it. Distance estimation method using Wi-Fi signal strength [1] shows large error (a few meters). In this paper we propose a method that estimates the actual distance swam even when meandering with an accelerometer and a gyroscope.

Theoretically, the distance traveled by the sensor device can be calculated by double-integrating the acceleration, however simply integrating the sensor data results in a large error. Therefore, the proposed method corrects the integration result of the accelerometer data with the angle obtained from the angular velocity data, assuming that the length of the pool lane is known. Our method calculates

---

[1] Garmin Swim2, https://www.garmin.co.jp/products/intosports/swim-2-slate/.

[2] Form Smart Swim Googles, https://www.formswim.com/.

© ICST Institute for Computer Sciences, Social Informatics and Telecommunications Engineering 2022
Published by Springer Nature Switzerland AG 2022. All Rights Reserved
T. Hara and H. Yamaguchi (Eds.): MobiQuitous 2021, LNICST 419, pp. 887–889, 2022.
https://doi.org/10.1007/978-3-030-94822-1

the swimming distance in the direction parallel to the lane, and find a correction factor so that the calculated distance is equal to the length of the pool lane (25 m in a 25 m pool). Then, the actual swimming distance is estimated by correcting the distance swum at an angle with the coefficient.

2   Evaluation

The experiment was conducted in a pool 18 m wide and 25 m long under two conditions: a straight route from the center of the short side of the pool to the opposite side without turning for 25 m and a curving route in which the participant swam straight through the center of the pool until 12.5 m, then quickly changed direction and swam toward the corner of the pool. In the curving route, the swimmer changed the direction of travel by 35.75°C to the right side forward at 12.5 m, and then proceeded straight toward the corner of the pool, which resulted in 27.90 m. In the first experiment, a waterproof sensor was mounted on a flutter board to remove the sensor value from the swimming motion, and one of the authors swim straight and curved routes. In the second experiment, a waterproof sensor was attached to the four participants, and the participants were asked to swim along the straight and curved routes. The sensor used was TSND151 manufactured by ATR-Promotions, and the sampling rate was 1,000 Hz. Table 1 shows the estimated results of an experiment with a sensor was mounted on a flutter

Table 1. Estimation results when a sensor was mounted on the flutter board.

Trial	Straight route	Curved route
1	25.03 m	31.98 m
2	25.01 m	29.65 m
3	25.01 m	29.09 m
4	25.01 m	28.96 m

Table 2. Estimated results when a sensor was attached to the participants.

		Back of the body		Back of the head		Waist	
Subject	Trial	Straight	Curved	Straight	Curved	Straight	Curved
1	1	25.19 m	30.20 m	25.15 m	33.37 m	25.07 m	28.63 m
	2	25.61 m	28.37 m	25.17 m	26.43 m	25.22 m	27.58 m
2	1	25.97 m	26.97 m	25.55 m	29.69 m	25.04 m	30.25 m
	2	25.70 m	26.41 m	25.36 m	28.22 m	25.23 m	30.05 m
3	1	25.44 m	31.48 m	26.35 m	31.68 m	25.06 m	30.21 m
	2	25.70 m	26.41 m	28.90 m	33.49 m	25.06 m	28.75 m
4	1	26.03 m	29.26 m	25.81 m	27.90 m	25.03 m	29.16 m
	2	26.16 m	36.69 m	26.22 m	27.31 m	25.06 m	29.45 m

board. Table 2 shows the estimated results of an experiment with a sensor was attached to the participants.

Reference

1. Sunkyu, W., et al.: Application of WiFi-based indoor positioning system for labor tracking at construction sites: a case study in Guangzhou MTR. Autom. Constr. **20**(1), 3–13 (2011)

Design and Implementation of a Finger Sack with an Electrode Array to Generate Multi-touch

Marina Okamoto[✉] and Kazuya Murao

Ritsumeikan University, Kyoto, Japan
marina.okamoto@iis.ise.ritsumei.ac.jp, murao@cs.ritsumei.ac.jp

Abstract. With the widespread of devices equipped with capacitive touch panels, such as smartphones and laptops, users can directly input data by touching the screen with a finger or a stylus. There are two input methods for touch panels such as smartphones: single-touch and multi-touch. Multi-touch requires the use of two fingers. In this paper, we develop a device that generates multi-touch by using only a thumb, even when the user is holding a smartphone with one hand. The proposed device consists of an Arduino Uno, a circuit consisting of a mechanical relay, an electrode array, a pressure sensor, and a power supply. When the relay is on, the corresponding electrode is connected to GND. Multi-touch is generated by continuously grounding multiple electrodes and moving the center of the capacitance change. A prototype device was created, and after preliminary experiments to determine the appropriate electrode spacing for generating touch interaction, the device was implemented.

Keywords: Smartphones · Multi-touch input · Electrode array

1 Introduction

Devices equipped with capacitive touch panels, such as smart phones and laptops, have become widespread. There are two types of touch panel input methods: single touch and multi-touch. The multi-touch methods include pinch-in, pinch-out, press-and-touch, and rotation. In this paper, we propose a finger sack that enables users to perform multi-touch operations with only their thumbs even when holding a smartphone with one hand.

2 Proposed Device

In this paper, we construct a device that generates multi-touch by sewing an electrode array using conductive thread on a finger sack that can be worn on the thumb. The proposed device consists of an Arduino Uno, a circuit consisting of mechanical relays, an electrode array, a pressure sensor, and a power supply.

© ICST Institute for Computer Sciences, Social Informatics and Telecommunications Engineering 2022
Published by Springer Nature Switzerland AG 2022. All Rights Reserved
T. Hara and H. Yamaguchi (Eds.): MobiQuitous 2021, LNICST 419, pp. 890–892, 2022.
https://doi.org/10.1007/978-3-030-94822-1

The electrode array on the finger sack is made by sewing nine regular hexagonal electrodes into a honeycomb structure with a sewing machine using conductive thread on a fabric in the shape of a finger sack. Each electrode is connected to an individual relay, and when the relay is turned on, the corresponding electrode is connected to GND. When the electrode array touches the touch panel, it is recognized as if a finger touches the touch panel, and a touch is generated. The proposed device generates multi-touch by continuously switching multiple electrodes to ground and shifting the center of the capacitance change.

3   Evaluation

In the experiment, we measured the success rate of generating touch interactions for six touch interactions: single touch, swipe, pinch-in, pinch-out, press-and-touch, and rotation, by changing the time to ground the electrode and the time to unground the electrode. Single touch, swipe, press-and-touch and rotation was generated 100 times. Pinch-in and pinch-out were generated 50 times. Expect for the single touch, an interval of 1000 ms was set between the end of the touch interaction and the start of the next touch interaction. The touch panel used was Lenovo ThinkPad X1 Yoga.

4   Result

The results of the evaluation experiments show that the proposed device can generate touch interactions other than rotation with high accuracy. Single touch, swipe, pinch-in, and pinch-out can be generated with a success rate of 100% by keeping the electrode grounding time and the electrode ungrounding time above a certain length, and press-and-touch can be generated with a success rate of 80%. However, the success rate of rotation was only achieved up to 42%.

5   Conclusion

In this paper, we proposed a finger sack that generates multi-touch on a smartphone touch panel using only one thumb. We evaluated the success rates of six types of touch interaction generation. The proposed device generates single touch, swipe, pinch-in, and pinch-out with a success rate of 100%, and press-and-touch with a success rate of 80%. However, the success rate for rotation was only achieved up to 42%.

References

1. Okamoto, M., Murao, K.: Multi-touch interaction generation device by spatiotemporally switching electrodes. MDPI Electron. **10**(12), 1475 (2021)
2. Rekimoto, J.: SmartSkin: an infrastructure for freehand manipulation on interactive surfaces. In: Proceedings of the 20th Annual ACM Conference on Human Factors in Computing Systems (CHI 2002), pp. 113–120 (2002)

3. Kato, K., Miyashita, H.: Extensionsticker: a proposal for a striped pattern sticker to extend touch interfaces and its assessment. In: Proceedings of the 33rd Annual CHI Conference on Human Factors in Computing Systems (CHI2015), pp. 1851–1854 (2015)

A Method for Identifying Individuals Entering a Bathtub Using a Water Pressure Sensor

Naoki Kurata[✉] and Kazuya Murao

Ritsumeikan University, Kyoto, Shiga, Japan
naoki.kurata@iis.ise.ritsumei.ac.jp, murao@cs.ritsumei.ac.jp

Abstract. It is reported that the number of fatal accidents is particularly high in the bathtub in the housing environment. Therefore, it is useful to sense the bio-information during bathing and to manage it by linking it to individuals. In this study, we proposed a method to identify a person entering water by obtaining the change of water level at the time of entering water using a water pressure sensor in the pouring and overflow situations. The proposed method calculates the DTW distance between the entering water waveform of an unknown person in each situation and the entering water waveform in the normal situation, which is registered in advance with the individual, and outputs the individual in the registered data obtained by the k-nearest neighbor method as the identification result. In the evaluation experiment, the average F-value of the identification result was 0.792 in the pouring situation and 0.592 in the overflow situation.

Keywords: First keyword · Second keyword · Another keyword

1 Introduction

The authors have proposed a method to identify bathers by using change of water level during bathing from a water pressure sensor installed at the bottom of the bathtub so as not to burden bathers [1]. However, this method only covers the situation where the amount of water in the bathtub is constant. In this paper, we propose a method to identify persons entering water while pouring hot water in the bathtub and overflowing water from the bathtub by entering water.

2 Proposed Method

To segment the waveform when entering water in the acquired data, the deviation value between the obtained water pressure value $p(t)$ and the moving average $p_a(t) = \frac{1}{m}\sum_{m=0}^{m-1} p(t-m)$ is calculated by $p_d(t) = |p_a(t) - p(t)|$, where m is the window size of the moving average set to $m = 200$. The start time of entering water t_s is set to the time when $p_d(t)$ exceeds the threshold h_1 ($h_1 = 7.0$) for 50

T. Hara and H. Yamaguchi (Eds.): MobiQuitous 2021, LNICST 419, pp. 893–895, 2022.
https://doi.org/10.1007/978-3-030-94822-1

consecutive samples, and the end time of entering water t_e is set to the time when the deviation value falls below the threshold h_2 ($h_2 = 3.0$) for 100 consecutive samples after the start time. The water pressure data $p_{in}(t) = [p_f(t_s), \ldots, p_f(t_e)]$ is used as the entering-water waveform. Then the situation of water in the bathtub is recognized. To determine the situations: normal, pouring, and overflow, $p_d(t - i)$ ($i = 0, \ldots, 99$) of immediate past 100 samples at t_s is calculated, and if they all satisfy $h_L < p_d(t - i) < h_H$ ($h_L = 0.5$, $h_H = 3.0$), the situation is pouring. If not satisfied, $p(t - i)$ ($i = 0, \ldots, 9$) of immediate past 10 samples at t_s is calculated, and if they all satisfy $p_f(t-i) > h_M$ ($h_M = 427.5$), the situation is overflow. If neither of the situation is satisfied, the situation is normal.

When the situation is pouring, the entering-water waveform differs depending on the amount of water poured. Therefore, pouring water amount $p_p(t)$ is estimated by first-order approximation using the least-squares method, and entering-water waveform $p_e(t)$ without the effect of pouring is obtained. For identification in the pouring situation, training data is the entering water waveform in the normal situation, and test data is $p_e(t)$, and calculate the DTW distance [2] between all test data and training data. The recognition result is determined by majority vote. For identification in the overflow situation, training data is in the normal situation, and test data is in the overflow situation $p_{in}(t)$. However, the initial water level is different between the situations. Therefore, SPRING [3], which is a DTW-based method for extracting subsequences similar to the query sequence from the data stream, is used to find the subsequence with the smallest DTW distance to test data among all training data, and use the label of the training data as the result.

3   Evaluation

Four male participants in their 20's (A~D) joined the experiment. The F-values of subjects A and D in the pouring situation are 0.946 and 1.000, while subjects B and C are 0.571 and 0.600. The F-values of subjects A and D in the overflow situation are 0.909 and 0.888, while subjects B and C are 0.571 and 0.000. Subjects B and C are similar in physical stature compared to the other subjects, therefore they were misidentified with each other.

4   Conclusion

We proposed a method to identify individuals entering water by using a water pressure sensor installed at the bottom of the bathtub in the pouring and overflow situations. The evaluation experiment showed that the average F-values of four subjects were 0.792 and 0.592 in the pouring and overflow situations, respectively.

References

1. Murao, K., Nakayama, S., Mochizuki, M., Nishio, N.: User identification method in a bathtub with a water pressure sensor. In: Proceedings of MoMM2018, pp. 133–139 (2018)

2. Li, G., Wang, Y., Li, M., Wu, Z.: Similarity match in time series streams under dynamic time warping distance. In: Proceedings of CSSE 2008, pp. 399–402 (2008)
3. Sakurai, Y., Faloutsos, C., Yamamuro, M.: Stream monitoring under the time warping distance. In: Proceedings of ICDE2007, pp. 1046–1055 (2007)

Designing a Smartphone-Based Assistance System for Blind People to Recognize Intersections and Obstacles in Indoor Corridors

Masaki Kuribayashi[1]([✉]), Seita Kayukawa[1], Jayakorn Vongkulbhisal[2], Chieko Asakawa[3], Daisuke Sato[4], Hironobu Takagi[2], and Shigeo Morishima[5]

[1] Waseda University, Tokyo, Japan
[2] IBM Research - Tokyo, Tokyo, Japan
[3] IBM Research, New York, USA
[4] Carnegie Mellon University, Pittsburgh, USA
[5] Waseda Research Institute for Science and Engineering, Tokyo, Japan

1 Introduction

People with visual impairment face significant difficulties when navigating in indoor corridors. As an indoor corridor may contain obstacles (*e.g.*, boxes and chairs), blind people need to be aware of them to avoid accidents. In addition, they also face another challenge when they have to turn at an intersection. Detecting an intersection may be challenging for blind people, as they may not notice its existence even if they are in it. For example, when an obstacle is in front of an intersection, blind people may walk past the intersection without noticing as they cannot walk along the wall. In this work, we propose a system for navigating blind people safely in an indoor corridor by assisting them to avoid obstacles and detect intersections using only one smartphone.

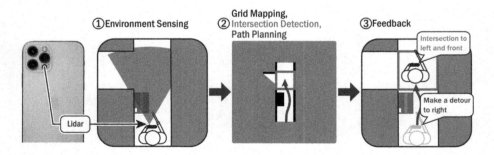

Fig. 1. The overview of our system.

Supported by JST-Mirai Program (JPMJMI19B2) and JSPS KAKENHI (JP20J23018).

T. Hara and H. Yamaguchi (Eds.): MobiQuitous 2021, LNICST 419, pp. 896–898, 2022.
https://doi.org/10.1007/978-3-030-94822-1

To detect intersections in indoor corridors, Garcia *et al.* proposed to use a quadcopter to capture RGB images and perform the detection using a convolution neural network [1]. However, this method may not be able to robustly detect intersections when applied to people with visual impairment as photos taken by blind people may contain motion blur [11]. Therefore, we present a robust method to detect upcoming intersections for blind people. As for obstacle avoidance, previous research proposed to use wearable devices [2, 5] and robots [7, 8]. Since such systems require blind people to carry heavy devices [3, 4] and have expensive operation cost [3, 4. 6], smartphones, which are widely used by blind people [9], can be considered as an alternative solution. This paper aims to utilize a single iPhone 12 Pro to assist blind people with these two tasks.

2 System Overview

We propose a smartphone-based navigation system for assisting blind people to detect intersections and avoid obstacles in an indoor corridor. The system first utilizes the Lidar sensor to acquire a point cloud of the surrounding environment, which contains the 3D-position and the normal vector for each point. Based on each point's position and normal vector, the system distinguishes each point between floor and obstacle, constructs a grid map of the environment. Figure 1–2 illustrates an example of the grid map. Each cell in the grid map is classified as either obstacle (black cells), floor (white cells), or not occupied (gray cells). The classification of the cells is used to determine the shape of the corridor, detect intersections, and plan an obstacle-avoiding path for safe navigation.

Intersection Detection. The system detects an intersection using the YOLOv3 [10] detector. To avoid motion blur of RGB images, we instead use the image of the grid map as the input of the detector. For training, we constructed a data set by gathering the images of the grid maps and annotating them. When the intersection ahead is detected, the system will vibrate to notify the existence of it. Once the user enters the intersection, the system will convey which way it leads to by audio feedback (*e.g.*, *"Intersection to left and front."* Fig. 1–3).

Obstacle Avoidance. The system performs path planning to assist the user to safely move forward in indoor corridors. First, the system sets the path planning destination to a point in the middle of the corridor 3.5 m away. Then the system plans an obstacle-avoiding path using the A* path planning algorithm [12]. When the user is following the generated path, the system will remain silent. The system will provide spatialized audio feedback via a bone-conducting headset when the user is veering off the path. The user is required to point the smartphone to the orientation in which it does not give any feedback. Also, when the system detects an obstacle, the system will tell the user to make a detour to a specific side to avoid collision (*e.g.*, *"Make a detour to the right"* Fig. 1–3) then guide the user to circumnavigate the obstacle.

3 Conclusion and Future Work

In this paper, we present a system to assist blind people to detect intersections while avoiding obstacles using only one smartphone. For future work, we plan to conduct a user study to evaluate the validity of the system.

References

1. Garcia, A., Mittal, S., Kiewra, E., Ghose, K.: A convolutional neural network vision system approach to indoor autonomous quadrotor navigation. In: 2019 International Conference on Unmanned Aircraft Systems (2019). https://doi.org/10.1109/ICUAS.2019.8798183
2. Pradeep, V., Medioni, G., Weiland, J.: Robot vision for the visually impaired. In: 2010 IEEE Computer Society Conference on Computer Vision and Pattern Recognition - Workshops (2010). https://doi.org/10.1109/CVPRW.2010.5543579
3. Fallah, N., Apostolopoulos, I., Bekris, K., Folmer, E.: The user as a sensor. In: Proceedings of the SIGCHI Conference on Human Factors in Computing Systems (2012). https://doi.org/10.1145/2207676.2207735
4. Jain, D.: Path-guided indoor navigation for the visually impaired using minimal building retrofitting. In: Proceedings of the 16th International ACM SIGACCESS Conference on Computers & Accessibility - ASSETS 2014 (2014). https://doi.org/10.1145/2661334.2661359
5. Lee, Y.H., Medioni, G.: Wearable RGBD indoor navigation system for the blind. In: Agapito, L., Bronstein, M.M., Rother, C. (eds.) ECCV 2014. LNCS, vol. 8927, pp. 493–508. Springer, Cham (2015). https://doi.org/10.1007/978-3-319-16199-0_35
6. Ran, L., Helal, S., Moore, S.: Drishti: an integrated indoor/outdoor blind navigation system and service. In: Proceedings of the Second IEEE Annual Conference on Pervasive Computing and Communications 2004 (2004). https://doi.org/10.1109/PERCOM.2004.1276842
7. Guerreiro, J., Sato, D., Asakawa, S., Dong, H., Kitani, K., Asakawa, C.: CaBot: designing and evaluating an autonomous navigation robot for blind people. In: The 21st International ACM SIGACCESS Conference on Computers and Accessibility (2019). https://doi.org/10.1145/3308561.3353771
8. Kayukawa, S., Ishihara, T., Takagi, H., Morishima, S., Asakawa, C.: Guiding blind pedestrians in public spaces by understanding walking behavior of nearby pedestrians. In: Proceedings of the ACM on Interactive, Mobile, Wearable and Ubiquitous Technologies, vol. 4, pp. 1–22 (2020). https://doi.org/10.1145/3411825
9. Morris, J., Mueller, J.: Blind and deaf consumer preferences for android and iOS smartphones. In: Langdon, P.M., Lazar, J., Heylighen, A., Dong, H. (eds.) Inclusive Designing, pp. 69–79. Springer, Cham (2014). https://doi.org/10.1007/978-3-319-05095-9_7
10. Redmon, J., Farhadi, A.: YOLOv3: an incremental improvement. https://arxiv.org/abs/1804.02767
11. Sanketi, P., Coughlan, J.: Anti-blur feedback for visually impaired users of smartphone cameras. In: Proceedings of the 12th International ACM SIGACCESS Conference on Computers and Accessibility - ASSETS 2010 (2010). https://doi.org/10.1145/1878803.1878847
12. Hart, P., Nilsson, N., Raphael, B.: A formal basis for the heuristic determination of minimum cost paths. IEEE Trans. Syst. Sci. Cybern. 4, 100–107 (1968). https://doi.org/10.1109/TSSC.1968.300136

Author Index

Printed in the United States
by Baker & Taylor Publisher Services